Wildlife Disease Ecology

Linking Theory to Data and Application

Just like humans, animals and plants suffer from infectious diseases, which can critically threaten biodiversity. This book describes key studies that have driven our understanding of the ecology and evolution of wildlife diseases. Each chapter introduces the host and disease, and explains how that system has aided our general understanding of the evolution and spread of wildlife diseases, through the development and testing of important epidemiological and evolutionary theories.

Questions addressed include: How do hosts and parasites coevolve? What determines how fast a disease spreads through a population? How do coinfecting parasites interact? Why do hosts vary in parasite burden? Which factors determine parasite virulence and host resistance? How do parasites influence the spread of invasive species? How do we control infectious diseases in wildlife? This book will provide a valuable introduction to students new to the topic, and novel insights to researchers, professionals, and policymakers working in the field.

KENNETH WILSON is Professor of Evolutionary Ecology at Lancaster University, UK. With more than 25 years' experience in studying wildlife disease ecology, he has published more than 130 peer reviewed articles and chapters, and is Senior Editor of *Journal of Animal Ecology*.

ANDY FENTON is Professor of Theoretical Ecology at the University of Liverpool, UK. He is on the Editorial Boards of *Journal of Animal Ecology* and *Parasitology*.

DAN TOMPKINS is Project Manager Science Strategy at Predator Free 2050 Ltd, Auckland, and Honorary Professor in the Department of Zoology, University of Otago, New Zealand.

Ecological Reviews

Ecological Reviews publishes books at the cutting edge of modern ecology, providing a forum for volumes that discuss topics that are focal points of current activity and likely long-term importance to the progress of the field. The series is an invaluable source of ideas and inspiration for ecologists at all levels from graduate students to more-established researchers and professionals. The series has been developed jointly by the British Ecological Society and Cambridge University Press and encompasses the Society's Symposia as appropriate.

Biotic Interactions in the Tropics: Their Role in the Maintenance of Species Diversity
Edited by David F. R. P. Burslem, Michelle A. Pinard and Sue E. Hartley

Biological Diversity and Function in Soils
Edited by Richard Bardgett, Michael Usher and David Hopkins

Island Colonization: The Origin and Development of Island Communities
By Ian Thornton
Edited by Tim New

Scaling Biodiversity
Edited by David Storch, Pablo Margnet and James Brown

Body Size: The Structure and Function of Aquatic Ecosystems
Edited by Alan G. Hildrew, David G. Raffaelli and Ronni Edmonds-Brown

Speciation and Patterns of Diversity
Edited by Roger Butlin, Jon Bridle and Dolph Schluter

Ecology of Industrial Pollution
Edited by Lesley C. Batty and Kevin B. Hallberg

Ecosystem Ecology: A New Synthesis
Edited by David G. Raffaelli and Christopher L. J. Frid

Urban Ecology
Edited by Kevin J. Gaston

Wildlife Disease Ecology

Linking Theory to Data and Application

Edited by

KENNETH WILSON
Lancaster University

ANDY FENTON
University of Liverpool

DAN TOMPKINS
Predator Free 2050 Ltd

CAMBRIDGE
UNIVERSITY PRESS

CAMBRIDGE
UNIVERSITY PRESS

University Printing House, Cambridge CB2 8BS, United Kingdom

One Liberty Plaza, 20th Floor, New York, NY 10006, USA

477 Williamstown Road, Port Melbourne, VIC 3207, Australia

314–321, 3rd Floor, Plot 3, Splendor Forum, Jasola District Centre,
New Delhi – 110025, India

79 Anson Road, #06–04/06, Singapore 079906

Cambridge University Press is part of the University of Cambridge.

It furthers the University's mission by disseminating knowledge in the pursuit of
education, learning, and research at the highest international levels of excellence.

www.cambridge.org
Information on this title: www.cambridge.org/9781107136564
DOI: 10.1017/9781316479964

First published 2019

Printed in the United Kingdom by TJ International Ltd, Padstow Cornwall

A catalogue record for this publication is available from the British Library.

Library of Congress Cataloging-in-Publication Data
Names: Wilson, Kenneth, 1963– editor.
Title: Wildlife disease ecology : linking theory to data and application / edited by Kenneth
Wilson, Lancaster University, Andy Fenton, University of Liverpool, Dan Tompkins,
Predator Free 2050 Ltd.
Description: Cambridge, United Kingdom ; New York, NY : Cambridge University Press,
2019. | Series: Ecological reviews | Includes bibliographical references and index.
Identifiers: LCCN 2019012298 | ISBN 9781107136564 (alk. paper)
Subjects: LCSH: Communicable diseases.
Classification: LCC RC112 .W54 2019 | DDC 616.9–dc23
LC record available at https://lccn.loc.gov/2019012298

ISBN 978-1-107-13656-4 Hardback
ISBN 978-1-316-50190-0 Paperback

Additional resources for this publication at www.cambridge.org/9781107136564.

Contents

Colour plates can be found between pages 316 and 317.

Contributors

STEVE D. ALBON
Ecological Sciences
The James Hutton Institute
Aberdeen
UK
steve.albon@hutton.ac.uk

EMILY S. ALMBERG
Montana Fish, Wildlife and Parks
Bozeman
MT
USA
ealmberg@mt.gov

SONIA ALTIZER
Odum School of Ecology
University of Georgia
Athens
GA
USA
saltizer@uga.edu

BEN ASHBY
Mathematical Sciences
University of Bath
Bath
UK
b.n.ashby@bath.ac.uk

ANDREW W. BATEMAN
Department of Geography
University of Victoria
Victoria

Canada
andrew.w.bateman@uvic.ca

BRIANNA R. BEECHLER
College of Veterinary Medicine
Oregon State University
Corvallis
OR
USA
brianna.beechler@oregonstate.edu

MIKE BEGON
Department of Evolution, Ecology
and Behaviour
University of Liverpool
Liverpool
UK
mbegon@liv.ac.uk

THOMAS E. BESSER
Veterinary Microbiology and
Pathology
Washington State University
Pullman
WA
USA
tbesser@vetmed.wsu.edu

BRIAN BOAG
The James Hutton Institute
Invergowrie
UK
Brian.Boag@hutton.ac.uk

JAMIE BOJKO
School of Biology
University of Leeds
Leeds
UK
jamie.bojko@ufl.edu

CHERYL J. BRIGGS
Ecology, Evolution and Marine
Biology
University of California, Santa
Barbara
Santa Barbara
CA
USA
cherie.briggs@lifesci.ucsb.edu

EMILY BRUNS
Department of Biology
University of Maryland
College Park
MD
USA
ebruns@umd.edu

SARAH A. BUDISCHAK
Keck Science Department
Claremont McKenna, Pitzer, and
Scripps Colleges
Claremont
CA
USA
sbudischak@kecksci.claremont.edu

CARLA E. CÁCERES
Department of Animal Biology
University of Illinois
Urbana
IL
USA
caceres@life.illinois.edu

ANJA M. CARLSSON

Department of Environmental
Research and Monitoring
Swedish Museum of Natural History
Stockholm
Sweden
anja.carlsson@nrm.se

ISABELLA M. CATTADORI
Center for Infectious Disease
Dynamics
The Pennsylvania State University
University Park
PA
USA
imc3@psu.edu

DYLAN Z. CHILDS
Department of Animal and Plant
Sciences
University of Sheffield
Sheffield
UK
d.childs@sheffield.ac.uk

BRENDAN CONNORS
Fisheries and Oceans Canada
Sidney
Canada
brendan.connors@dfo-mpo.gc.ca

STEPHEN DAVIS
School of Mathematical and
Geospatial Sciences
RMIT University
Melbourne
Australia
stephen.davis@rmit.edu.au

RICHARD J. DELAHAY
National Wildlife Management
Centre
Animal and Plant Health Agency
Woodchester Park

Nympsfield
UK
Dez.Delahay@apha.gov.uk

MARIE-LAURE DESPREZ-LOUSTAU
UMR Biogeco
INRA, Université Bordeaux
Pierroton
France
marie-laure.desprez-loustau@inra.fr

ANDRÉ A. DHONDT
Laboratory of Ornithology
Cornell University
Ithaca
NY
USA
aad4@cornell.edu

JAIMIE T.A. DICK
School of Biological Sciences
Queen's University, Belfast
Belfast
UK
j.dick@qub.ac.uk

ANDREW P. DOBSON
Department of Biology and
Evolutionary Ecology
Princeton University
Princeton
NJ
USA
dobber@princeton.edu

MEGHAN A. DUFFY
Department of Ecology and
Evolutionary Biology
University of Michigan
Ann Arbor
MI
USA
duffymeg@umich.edu

ALISON M. DUNN

School of Biology & water@leeds
University of Leeds
Leeds
UK
a.dunn@leeds.ac.uk

GREG DWYER
Department of Ecology and
Evolution
University of Chicago
Chicago
IL
USA
gdwyer@uchicago.edu

BRET D. ELDERD
Department of Biological Sciences
Louisiana State University
Baton Rouge
LA
USA
elderd@lsu.edu

VANESSA O. EZENWA
Odum School of Ecology and
Department of Infectious Diseases
University of Georgia
Athens
GA
USA
vezenwa@uga.edu

ANDY FENTON
Institute of Integrative Biology
University of Liverpool
Biosciences Building
Liverpool
UK
a.fenton@liverpool.ac.uk

ROMAIN GARNIER
Department of Veterinary Medicine
University of Cambridge
Cambridge

UK
rg535@cam.ac.uk

AMANDA K. GIBSON
Biology Department
University of Virginia
Charlottesville
VA
USA
akg5nq@virginia.edu

SEAN GODWIN
Department of Biological Sciences
Simon Fraser University
Burnaby
Canada
sgodwin@sfu.ca

ERIN E. GORSICH
School of Life Sciences & the Zeeman
Institute
University of Warwick
Coventry
UK
erin.gorsich@warwick.ac.uk

ANDREA L. GRAHAM
Department of Ecology and
Evolutionary Biology
Princeton University
NJ
USA
algraham@princeton.edu

BRYAN T. GRENFELL
Department of Ecology and
Evolutionary Biology
Princeton University
Princeton
NJ
USA
grenfell@princeton.edu

SPENCER R. HALL
Department of Biology

Indiana University
Bloomington
IN
USA
sprhall@indiana.edu

ODD HALVORSEN
Natural History Museum
University of Oslo
Oslo
Norway
odd.halvorsen@nhm.uio.no

RODRIGO HAMEDE
School of Natural Sciences
University of Tasmania
Hobart
Australia
rodrigo.hamedeross@utas.edu.au

FRÉDÉRIC M. HAMELIN
IGEPP
Agrocampus Ouest
INRA
Université de Rennes 1, Université
Bretagne-Loire
Rennes
France
Frederic.hamelin@agrocampus-
ouest.fr

MELANIE J. HATCHER
School of Biology
University of Leeds
Leeds
UK
m.j.hatcher@btinternet.com

ADAM D. HAYWARD
Moredun Research Institute
Penicuik
Midlothian
UK
adam.hayward@moredun.ac.uk

WESLEY M. HOCHACHKA
Laboratory of Ornithology
Cornell University
Ithaca
NY
USA
wmh6@cornell.edu

PAUL HOHENLOHE
Department of Biological Sciences
University of Idaho
Moscow
ID
USA
hohenlohe@uidaho.edu

PETER J. HUDSON
Center for Infectious Disease
Dynamics
Pennsylvania State University
University Park
PA
USA
pjh18@psu.edu

MARK D. HUNTER
Department of Ecology and
Evolutionary Biology
University of Michigan
Ann Arbor
MI
USA
mdhunter@umich.edu

GREGORY D.D. HURST
Institute of Integrative Biology
University of Liverpool
Liverpool
UK
G.Hurst@liverpool.ac.uk

R. JUSTIN IRVINE
Ecological Sciences
James Hutton Institute
Aberdeen

UK
justin.irvine@hutton.ac.uk

PIETER T.J. JOHNSON
Ecology and Evolutionary Biology
University of Colorado
Boulder
CO
USA
pieter.johnson@colorado.edu

ANNA E. JOLLES
College of Veterinary Medicine and
Department of Integrative Biology
Oregon State University
Corvallis
OR
USA
jollesa@science.oregonstate.edu

JORDAN E. JONES
Institute of Integrative Biology
University of Liverpool
Liverpool
UK
jordan.jones@liverpool.ac.uk

MENNA E. JONES
School of Natural Sciences
University of Tasmania
Hobart
Australia
Menna.Jones@utas.edu.au

PAULINE L. KAMATH
School of Food and Agriculture
University of Maine
Orono
ME
USA
pauline.kamath@maine.edu

ROBERT J. KNELL
School of Biological and Chemical
Sciences

Queen Mary University of London
London
UK
r.knell@qmul.ac.uk

MARTIN KRKOŠEK
Department of Ecology and
Evolutionary Biology
University of Toronto
Toronto
Canada
martin.Krkošek@utoronto.ca

ANNE LAUDISOIT
Department of Biology
University of Antwerp
Antwerp
Belgium
anne.laudisoit@uantwerpen.be

HERWIG LEIRS
Department of Biology
University of Antwerp
Antwerp
Belgium
herwig.leirs@uantwerpen.be

MARK A. LEWIS
Department of Biological Sciences
University of Alberta
Edmonton
Canada
mark.lewis@ualberta.ca

CURTIS M. LIVELY
Department of Biology
Indiana University
Bloomington
IN
USA
clively@indiana.edu

KEZIA MANLOVE
Department of Woodland Resources
and Ecology Center

Utah State University
Logan
UT
USA
kezia.manlove@usu.edu

BENOIT MARÇAIS
UMR IAM
INRA, Université de Lorraine
Seichamps
France
benoit.marcais@inra.fr

JESÚS MARTÍNEZ-PADILLA
Department of Biodiversity,
Conservation and Ecosystem
Restoration
Biodiversity Conservation Group
Pyrenean Institute of Ecology (CSIC)
Jaca
Spain
jmartinezpadilla12@gmail.com

HAMISH MCCALLUM
Griffith School of the Environment
Griffith University
Brisbane
Australia
h.mccallum@griffith.edu.au

JENNI L. MCDONALD
Centre for Ecology and Conservation
University of Exeter
Penryn
UK
jennifer.mcdonald@cats.org.uk

ROBBIE A. MCDONALD
Environment and Sustainability
Institute
University of Exeter
Penryn
UK
r.mcdonald@exeter.ac.uk

FRANÇOIS MOUGEOT
Department of Ecology
Institute for Game and Wildlife
Research
Ciudad Real
Castilla-La Mancha
Spain
Francois.Mougeot@uclm.es

ELIZABETH P. MURCHISON
Department of Veterinary Medicine
University of Cambridge
Cambridge
UK
epm27@cam.ac.uk

ASHUTOSH PATHAK
Department of Infectious Diseases
The University of Georgia
Athens
GA
USA
ash1@uga.edu

STEPHANIE J. PEACOCK
Department of Biological Sciences
University of Calgary
Calgary
Canada
stephaniepeacock@ucalgary.ca

AMY B. PEDERSEN
Institute of Evolutionary Biology
School of Biological Sciences
University of Edinburgh
Edinburgh
UK
amy.pedersen@ed.ac.uk

JOSEPHINE M. PEMBERTON
Institute of Evolutionary Biology,
University of Edinburgh
Edinburgh
UK

j.pemberton@ed.ac.uk

LORENZO PÉREZ-
RODRÍGUEZ
Department of Ecology
Institute for Game and Wildlife
Research
Ciudad Real
Castilla-La Mancha
Spain
lorenzo.perez@uclm.es

STUART PIERTNEY
School of Biological Sciences
University of Aberdeen
Aberdeen
UK
s.piertney@abdn.ac.uk

JILL G. PILKINGTON
Institute of Evolutionary Biology
University of Edinburgh
Edinburgh
UK
j.pilkington@ed.ac.uk

RAINA K. PLOWRIGHT
Department of Microbiology and
Immunology
Montana State University
Bozeman
MT
USA
raina.plowright@montana.edu

STEPHEN M. REDPATH
School of Biological Sciences
University of Aberdeen
Aberdeen
UK
s.redpath@abdn.ac.uk

JONAS REIJNIERS
Department of Biology
University of Antwerp

Antwerp
Belgium
jonas.reijniers@uantwerpen.be

JACOBUS C. DE ROODE
Department of Biology
Emory University
Atlanta
GA
USA
jderood@emory.edu

PAUL SCHMID-HEMPEL
Institute of Integrative Biology (IBZ)
ETH Zürich
Zürich
Switzerland
psh@env.ethz.ch

REGULA SCHMID-HEMPEL
Institute of Integrative Biology (IBZ)
ETH Zürich
Zürich
Switzerland
rsh@env.ethz.ch

PAUL STEBBING
Centre for Environment Fisheries
and Aquaculture Science
Weymouth
UK
paul.stebbing@cefas.co.uk

AUDUN STEIN
Department for Arctic Ecology
Norwegian Institute for Nature
Research
Tromsø
Norway
audun.stien@nina.no

GRANT D. STENTIFORD
Centre for Environment, Fisheries
and Aquaculture Science
Weymouth
UK
grant.stentiford@cefas.co.uk

ANDREW STORFER
School of Biological Sciences
Washington State University
Pullman
WA
USA
astorfer@wsu.edu

DAN TOMPKINS
Predator Free 2050
New Zealand
daut@pf2050.co.nz

KATHRYN A. WATT
Institute of Evolutionary Biology &
Centre for Immunity, Infection and
Evolution
University of Edinburgh
Edinburgh
UK
Kathryn.watt@ed.ac.uk

MARIUS WENZEL
School of Biological Sciences
University of Aberdeen
Aberdeen
UK
marius.wenzel@abdn.ac.uk

MARK Q. WILBER
Ecology, Evolution and Marine
Biology
University of California, Santa
Barbara

Santa Barbara
CA
USA
mark.wilber@lifesci.ucsb.edu

LENA WILFERT
Institute of Evolutionary Ecology and
Conservation Genomics
University of Ulm
Ulm

Germany
lena.wilfert@uni.ulm.de

KENNETH WILSON
Lancaster Environment Centre
Lancaster University
Lancaster
UK
ken.wilson@lancaster.ac.uk

Preface: Wildlife Disease Ecology

KENNETH WILSON, ANDY FENTON & DAN
TOMPKINS

Introduction

Infectious diseases are ubiquitous and account for some of the most dramatic
impacts in human history. These include The Black Death, caused by the
bacterium *Yersinia pestis*, which killed at least 25 million people across
Eurasia between 1347 and 1352 (Cohn, 2002); the Spanish Flu pandemic of
1918, caused by a highly virulent form of the influenza virus, which caused the
deaths of 25–50 million people (Taubenberger, 2006); and, more recently, the
global AIDS epidemic, caused by the human immunodeficiency virus (HIV),
which is responsible for the mortality of an estimated 35 million people
worldwide since its emergence in the early 1980s (Fajardo-Ortiz et al., 2017).
In many instances, microparasites like influenza mutate and evolve over time
into new lethal forms, re-emerging as new epidemics or global pandemics
(Nichols, 2006).

However, infectious diseases are not exclusive to humans; wildlife, both
animals and plants, experience potentially huge burdens of disease. Indeed,
many of the most devastating infectious diseases of humans, including all
those mentioned above, had a wildlife (zoonotic) origin. Infectious diseases are
a significant driver of global biodiversity loss, illustrated by the amphibian
species extinctions and population declines globally caused by the fungal
disease chytridiomycosis (Fisher et al., 2009), and more localised impacts
such as the loss of much of the native Hawaiian avifauna due to avian malaria
and pox (Atkinson & LaPointe, 2009). With ongoing wildlife disease emergence, arising primarily from increasing human-driven global connectivity
(Tompkins et al., 2015), the understanding for management that wildlife
disease ecology gives has never been more important.

Not all parasites, though, cause high levels of mortality, but instead cause
significant morbidity in terms of reduced growth rate and fertility. This is
particularly true of macroparasites, such as gut helminths and ectoparasites,
where morbidity increases as a function of parasite load (Wilson et al., 2002).
Even when not resulting in extinctions or declines, wildlife diseases can have

profound ecological and evolutionary impacts on their wildlife hosts, causing the evolution of costly resistance mechanisms, potentially driving sexual selection for exaggerated traits, altering host population dynamics, and shaping the structure of ecological communities. There has thus been a considerable effort to understand and address disease across a wide range of wildlife systems in which management is important for both conservation and public health reasons. Many of the most influential studies of infectious diseases in wildlife systems have achieved their status by coupling intensive observational and experimental studies together with a strong connection to mathematical models of infectious disease dynamics. In recent decades this has allowed the amendment, advancement and refining of earlier theories and ideas.

Mathematical models have played a key part in our understanding of human infectious diseases and their control since the first epidemiological models developed over a century ago by people such as Ronald Ross and George Macdonald (Smith et al., 2012). In the late 1970s and early-mid 1980s, Roy Anderson and Robert May applied the same basic principles to the diseases of wildlife (Heesterbeek & Roberts, 2015). Those models allowed simple exploration of key aspects of host–parasite ecology; for example, by laying bare the potential for parasites to regulate host populations, or to drive cycles in host population dynamics. Since then, a burgeoning array of mathematical models have been developed for wildlife diseases, parameterised with empirical data collected during meticulous field and laboratory studies. The aim of this book is to present a core group of those studies, some of which are now decades old, highlighting the connection of these studies to general epidemiological and evolutionary theory, and emphasising the contribution they have made, and continue to make, in advancing our understanding of the spread and impact of infectious diseases more generally.

This book is aimed at researchers working in the field but we specifically asked authors to write their chapters in an engaging style that would also appeal to non-experts such as advanced undergraduates. To help the novice reader, we have included a Glossary of Terms (page xvi) and provide both technical Abstracts and non-technical Lay Summaries (available online at www.cambridge.org/9781107136564).

Book structure

The book is loosely divided into three parts depending on the scale of the interactions that are the main focus of each chapter. Perhaps inevitably, given the inherent multi-scale nature of disease ecology (Johnson et al 2015), no chapter is limited in scope to their 'assigned' part, but this grouping was chosen as an attempt to bring together chapters that deal with similar concepts, and is perhaps preferable to (or at least no less arbitrary than) one based on taxonomy or geography.

Part I deals with our understanding of within-host processes, such as interactions between different parasite strains and species within individual hosts, the evolution of parasite virulence, host resistance and the immune system, and host–parasite coevolution. Part II explores our understanding of between-host processes, such as the roles that parasites play in regulating and driving host population dynamics, the factors influencing parasite transmission between individuals, and herd immunity. Part III expands out to interactions at the host community and landscape scale, including the effects of climate and seasonality, trophic interactions, host migration, and spatial and multi-host dynamics.

Case studies were selected for inclusion based on their contributions to the field of wildlife disease ecology, and to cover the comprehensive range of theoretical concepts in disease epidemiology, evolution, and ecology. To illustrate the ubiquity of wildlife diseases, we chose a broad variety of host taxa (including plants, insects, gastropods, crustacea, fish, amphibia, birds, and mammals) and geographical regions (Europe, Americas, Australasia, Asia, and Africa). We wanted authors to focus on their particularly well-understood study systems but also to place their work in the broader context of other wildlife disease ecology studies; we also asked them to reflect on why their studies had been so successful, to discuss the history and natural history of the system and, where appropriate, to highlight its applied relevance.

Although all the case studies are guided by theoretical considerations, the extent of the system-specific mathematical modelling varies. We asked authors to reflect on the reasons for this, and to identify areas for future empirical and modelling work, particularly where this might benefit from advances in methods and theory (such as novel molecular or statistical approaches, new remote sensing and biologging technology, and enhanced computational capacity).

Some concluding remarks

Several common themes emerge from this book. First, our understanding of wildlife disease ecology is greatly enhanced by studies that: (i) collect long-term observational field data, providing time series and accumulated knowledge of the system (i.e. most of the chapters in this book); (ii) combine observational data with well-designed field and laboratory experiments, especially those that include experimental perturbations such as short-term parasite removals/additions (e.g. Chapters 3, 4, 5, 8, 10, 12, 14, 21); (iii) have a strong theoretical component and integrate empirical data with statistical, simulation and/or mathematical models (again, most of the chapters in this book); (iv) take advantage of new and developing technologies, such as modern molecular approaches to characterise host/parasite genetic variation (e.g. Chapters 1, 2, 4, 10, 13, 15, 18), or sophisticated statistical approaches, particularly allowing the rigorous fitting of models to data (e.g. Chapter 8).

A second theme to emerge is that the types of questions that can be addressed, and their success, are often determined by the specific natural history of the system and the logistical constraints they present. For example, the ladybird system provides an ideal opportunity for studying sexually transmitted infections (STIs) in the field because mating contacts and the STI (an ectoparasitic mite) are both easily scored visually (Chapter 7). Likewise, the fact that the snail *Potamopyrgus antipodarum* has both sexual and asexual (parthenogenic) females, often in the same lake, makes it an ideal system for studying the interaction between mode of reproduction and parasite resistance (Chapter 2). Isolated populations, such as the Soay sheep on St Kilda (Chapter 4) and the reindeer on Svalbard (Chapter 14), provide relatively simple ecological systems in which to study wildlife diseases in the absence of significant pressure from predators or competitors (although the logistics of getting there can often add an extra layer of complexity!). Most ecological systems, however, are not this simple and some, such as the three aquatic systems in this book (Chapters 9, 16 and 19), as well as the monarch butterfly system (Chapter 17), seem to lend themselves particularly well to studying these multi-trophic interactions.

A third theme to emerge is the key role that variation and heterogeneity play in determining wildlife disease dynamics at all scales. The theory of host–parasite interactions initially developed in a 'mean field' manner, such that accompanying mathematical models frequently contained simplifying assumptions and parameter values expressed as population or subpopulation averages. This was not solely due to the developmental stage of the field of study, but also to the data requirements to accurately parameterise more complex models. Many of the long-term studies presented here show that when sufficient data are amassed, allowing more complex models to be employed, our understanding of wildlife disease dynamics is improved through the realisation of how variation alters previous mean field predictions. In turn, this allows more accurate projections, and more effective management, of wildlife disease impacts.

This consideration of management illustrates a final theme to emerge from this book – while some systems are ideally placed to ask interesting and fundamental questions about wildlife disease ecology and evolution, others have the added attribute that they also have significant applied relevance. For example, a number of the study systems in this book focus on emerging diseases that have conservation and policy relevance (e.g. Chapters 5, 9, 11, 13, 15, 17, 18, 20) or impact on the management of harvested stocks (e.g. Chapters 8 and 19).

With increased international movements and global change (climate, land use, population growth, etc.), we are likely to see continued emergence of infectious diseases in humans, livestock and wildlife, and further exchange of infectious diseases between them. Based on the work presented in this book, it seems to us that the ongoing development and application of new tools and approaches makes the field of wildlife disease ecology better placed than ever to understand and overcome these challenges.

Acknowledgements

We would like to thank all our authors for their hard work and patience during the long process of pulling this book together. We would also like to thank Mike Boots for his input during the early stages of book development and the many reviewers who helped to improve the chapters. During the editing of this book, KW was in receipt of funding from Innovate UK and the UK's Biotechnology and Biological Sciences Research Council (BB/P023444/1, BB/P004970/1, TS/P000436/1, BB/L026821/1) and AF received funding from the UK's Natural Environment Research Council (NE/N009800/1).

References

Atkinson, C.T. & LaPointe, D.A. (2009) Ecology and pathogenicity of avian malaria and pox. In: Pratt, T.K., Atkinson, C.T., Banko, P.C., Jacobi, J.D. & Woodworth, B.L. (eds.), *Conservation Biology of Hawaiian Forest Birds*. New Haven, CT: Yale University Press.

Cohn, S.K. (2002) *The Black Death Transformed: Disease and Culture in Early Renaissance Europe*. London: Arnold.

Fajardo-Ortiz, D., Lopez-Cervantes, M., Duran, L., et al. (2017) The emergence and evolution of the research fronts in HIV/AIDS research. *PLoS ONE*, **12**(5), e0178293. https://doi.org/10.1371/journal.pone.0178293

Fisher, M.C., Garner, T.W.J. & Walker, S.F. (2009) Global emergence of *Batrachochytrium dendrobatidis* and amphibian chytridiomycosis in space, time, and host. *Annual Review of Microbiology*, 63, 291–310.

Heesterbeek, J.A.P. & Roberts, M.G. (2015) How mathematical epidemiology became a field of biology: a commentary on Anderson and May (1981) 'The population dynamics of microparasites and their invertebrate hosts'. *Philosophical Transactions of the Royal Society*, **370**, 20140307. http://dx.doi.org/10.1098/rstb.2014.0307

Johnson, P.T.J., de Roode, J.C., & Andy Fenton, A. (2015) Why infectious disease research needs community ecology. *Science*, **349** (6252), 1259504. DOI:10.1126/science.1259504

Nichols, H. (2006).Pandemic influenza: the inside story. *PLoS Biology*, **4**(2), e50.

Smith, D.L., Battle, K.E., Hay, S.I., et al. (2012) Ross, Macdonald, and a theory for the dynamics and control of mosquito-transmitted pathogens. *PLoS Pathogens*, **8**(4), e1002588. https://doi.org/10.1371/journal.ppat.1002588

Taubenberger, J.K. (2006).The origin and virulence of the 1918 "Spanish" Influenza Virus. *Proceedings of the Americal Philosophical Society*, **150**(1), 86–112.

Tompkins, D.M., Carver, S., Jones, M.E., Krkosek, M. & Skerratt, L.F. (2015). Current emerging infectious diseases of wildlife: a critical perspective. *Trends in Parasitology*, **31**(4), 149–159.

Wilson, K., Bjørnstad, O.N., Dobson, A.P., et al. (2002) Heterogeneities in macroparasite infections: patterns and processes. In: Hudson, P.J., Rizzoli, A., Grenfell, B.T., Heesterbeek, J.A.P. & Dobson, A.P. (eds.), *The Ecology of Wildlife Diseases* (pp. 6–44). Oxford: Oxford University Press.

Glossary of Terms

ANDY FENTON, DAN TOMPKINS AND KENNETH WILSON

Term Definition

Acquired immunity	*Antigen*-specific immunity gained from prior exposure to that *antigen*.
Adaptive immunity	The components of the vertebrate *immune system* involved in developing *acquired immunity*.
Aetiology/aetiological agent	The cause/causative agent of a *disease*.
Agent-based (or individual-based) models (ABMs or IBMs)	Computational simulation models in which individuals or groups of individuals ('agents') are explicitly modelled, for example to consider how variation in states, actions or experiences between those individuals combine to affect population-level dynamics.
Aggregated parasite distribution	The often-observed highly skewed distribution of *macroparasite* burdens among *hosts*, characterised by high variance: mean ratios, such that typically most hosts are observed to have relatively light (or zero) burdens, but some hosts have very high burdens. The observed distribution is often described statistically by a *negative binomial distribution*.
Akaike Information Criteria (AIC), Watanabe–Akaike Information Criteria (WAIC), Bayesian Information Criteria (BIC), etc.	Measures of the statistical fit of a model to data that take into account the goodness of fit (often related to the likelihood of the data given the model parameters) and model complexity (penalising in some way models with higher numbers of parameters).

Allee effect	Demographic and behavioural changes that cause fitness to increase with population density (positive density dependence) at low population density.
Antibody	Large protein, specific to a given **antigen**, used as part of the vertebrate **immune system** to fight certain parasites containing that antigen.
Antigen	A foreign substance which stimulates an immune response.
Antimicrobial peptides (AMPs)	Peptides produced by all classes of **hosts** (vertebrates, invertebrates and plants) as part of their innate immune system, to combat bacteria, viruses and fungi.
Apex predator	The predator species at the top of a food chain.
Apparent competition	A negative interaction occurring between two or more **host** species, mediated by a shared natural enemy
Arrested development	A life-cycle stage of some helminth **parasites** in which infecting worms undergo a temporary cessation of development or dormancy inside the host.
Assortative contact	The tendency to make contact with individuals of the same type as self. Contrast with **disassortative contact**.
Basic reproductive number/ratio/rate (R_0)	A measure of the **parasite's** maximum potential to spread through a **host** population. Defined differently for **microparasites** (the number of secondary infections produced by a single primary infection in an otherwise wholly **susceptible** host population) and **macroparasites** (the number of mature parasite offspring produced by a single mature parasite in a wholly **susceptible** host population)
Capture–Mark(–Release)–Recapture (CMR or CMRR)	The recapturing of previously marked individuals to allow estimation of (for example) population sizes, and (state-dependent) survival, state transition and recapture probabilities.

Coefficient of variation	A measure of relative variability, defined as the standard deviation of a trait divided by its mean, producing a scalable measure of variation.
Coinfection (or co-infection or polyparasitism)	Simultaneous infection of an individual *host* by multiple *parasite* genotypes (intraspecific coinfection) or species (interspecific coinfection).
Community assembly	The order in which the species in an ecological community (e.g. a parasite *infracommunity*) assemble, and the underlying processes determining that order.
Compartmental model	Mathematical model of *host–parasite* population dynamics, in which the abundances of *hosts* and/or *parasites* are represented as 'compartments', with flows of individuals into and out of compartments being determined by epidemiologically important processes (births, deaths, *transmission*, recovery). See *SIR, SEIR, SIS, etc. models*.
Competitive release	The expansion or increase in abundance of a competitively inferior species due to suppression or removal of a dominant competitor.
Contact network	Who contacts whom at an individual level, defined in terms of nodes (the individuals on network) and edges or links (the contacts between nodes); often used within a *network-based model*.
Covert infections	Non-lethal *infections* that may be hard to detect, but which can contribute to overall *transmission* and persistence of the *parasite* in the *host* population.
Cytokine	Small signalling molecules secreted by cells of the *immune system*.
Density-dependent prophylaxis	A phenomenon where *hosts* invest more in defence at high densities.
Density-dependent transmission	*Transmission* in which the *per-capita* rate of acquisition of new infections increases

	with **host** density. Contrast with **frequency-dependent transmission**.
Deterministic	A system or modelling framework which does not incorporate any random components. Contrast with **stochastic**.
Dilution effect	The phenomenon by which low competence **host** species reduce infection risk for other potential host species, through the removal of **parasite** infective stages.
Directly transmitted parasites	**Parasites** which transmit from one **host** to another, possibly via an environmental stage, but without involvement of an alternative, intermediate, or vector host species.
Disassortative contact	The tendency to make contact with dissimilar individuals, those of the opposite type to self. Contrast with **assortative contact**.
Disease	The pathological, detrimental impact of parasitic infection on **host** health.
Disease triangle	A concept that recognises that the occurrence and outcome of **infection** depends on the interaction between the **parasite,** the **host** and the environment they occur in.
Effective partner acquisition rate	A measure of partner acquisition for a **sexually transmitted infection (STI)**, measured from the perspective of the infection, rather than **hosts** generally, which includes both mean and variation in partner acquisition.
Emerging infectious disease (EID)	An **infectious disease** which has recently emerged in a novel **host** species or population.
Endemic (infection)	An **infectious disease** regularly found infecting a population of **hosts**.
Enemy release hypothesis	The hypothesis that **invasive alien species** perform better in their introduced habitat because they have been introduced without natural enemies (predators and **parasites**) from their native range.

Enzootic	An *infectious disease* regularly found infecting a population of wild animal *hosts*. Contrast with *epizootic*.
Epidemic	A rapid increase in the occurrence of an *infectious disease* in a population.
Epizootic	An *infectious disease* that suddenly increases in frequency in a wild animal population. Contrast with *enzootic*.
Extirpation	The local extinction of a species from a given location.
Faecal egg count (FEC)	The number of eggs of a gastrointestinal *parasite* counted from a faecal sample of the *host*, often used as an indirect measure of the *infection intensity* of the host.
Force of infection	The *per-capita* rate at which *susceptible* individuals become infected.
Frequency-dependent transmission	*Transmission* in which the *per-capita* rate of acquisition of new infections is independent of *host* density, but increases with the frequency of infection in the host population. Contrast with *density-dependent transmission*.
Functional response	The relationship between resource availability and consumer ingestion rate.
Gene-for-gene model of host–parasite compatibility	Genetic model of *host–parasite* compatibility in which there is a universally infective *parasite* genotype that experiences high infection rates across all *host* genotypes. Contrast with *inverse gene-for-gene, matching alleles* and *inverse matching alleles models of host–parasite compatibility*.
Handicap principle	The hypothesis that the honesty of extravagant sexual signals of quality relies on costs (possibly mediated by parasitic infection) involved in their production or maintenance. See also *Immunocompetence Handicap Hypothesis (ICHH)*.
Healthy herds hypothesis	The hypothesis that predators selectively remove *diseased* individuals, thereby

	raising the overall health of the remaining prey population.
Heterogeneity (e.g. in contacts, susceptibility, etc.)	The occurrence of differences among individuals or groups of individuals that result in *transmission* deviating from assumptions of *mass action*.
Horizontal transmission	*Transmission* occurring between host individuals that does not involve direct mother-to-offspring (*vertical*) transmission.
Host	An organism infected by a *parasite*.
Immune priming	The reduction in *host* susceptibility to infection due to prior exposure to the same *parasite*.
Immune system	The collection of cells and molecules that a *host* uses to fight infection.
Immunocompetence Handicap Hypothesis (ICHH)	An extension of the *handicap principle* of the evolution of extravagant sexual signals, which argues that androgens (e.g. testosterone) mediate a trade-off between enhanced sexual behaviours or signals and ability to resist *parasites* via *immunosuppression*.
Immunomodulation/ immunosuppression	The alteration of a host's immune response by an infecting *parasite*. If immune function is in some way impaired, this is termed immunosuppression.
Immunoparasitology	The study of the interaction between parasitic infection and the immune response of the *host*.
Immunosenescence	The loss in *immune* function as the individual ages.
Infection	The presence of a *parasite* within a *host*.
Infection intensity	Number of *parasites* in an infected *host*.
Infectious disease	*Disease* (pathology) caused by a *parasite*, capable of being transmitted between *hosts*.
Infracommunity	The collection of parasites *coinfecting* an individual *host*.
Innate immunity	The non-specific (or less specific) immune response. Contrast with *adaptive immunity*.

Integral projection (or population) models (IPMs)	A population dynamic modelling approach which links demographic rates across individuals to population dynamics.
Interactionist parasite communities	Within-*host parasite* communities which are structured by interactions between *coinfecting* parasites. Contrast with *isolationist parasite communities*.
Intraguild predation (IGP)	Predation among competitors within a trophic level.
Invasive alien species (IAS)	Species that have been introduced and established outside their native range.
Inverse gene-for-gene model of host–parasite compatibility	Genetic model of *host–parasite* compatibility in which there is a universally *resistant* host genotype that experiences reduced *infection* rates for all parasite genotypes. Contrast with *gene-for-gene, matching alleles* and *inverse matching alleles models of host–parasite compatibility*.
Inverse matching alleles model of host–parasite compatibility	Genetic model of *host–parasite* compatibility by which a host must genetically match its parasite at relevant loci in order to *resist infection*. Contrast with *gene-for-gene, inverse gene-for-gene* and *matching alleles models of host–parasite compatibility*.
Isolationist parasite communities	Within-*host parasite* communities in which interactions between *coinfecting parasites* are rare, there are many vacant niches, and species infect largely independently of each other. Contrast with *interactionist parasite communities*.
Iteroparous	An organism which reproduces multiple times in its life. Contrast with *semelparous*.
Koch's postulates	Criteria established by Robert Koch to identify the causative (*aetiological*) agent of a *disease*.
Latent period	The time between an individual becoming infected with a *parasite*, and it becoming infectious to other individuals.

Macroparasite	*Parasites* which do not multiply inside individual *hosts* (e.g. helminths, ectoparasites); typically the *parasite* is the unit of study (e.g. the number of infecting worms). Contrast with *microparasite*.
Major Histocompatibility Complex (MHC)	A cluster of genes that code for cell-surface proteins, which are used by the *adaptive immune response* to recognise specific *antigens*.
Mass action transmission	The assumption that susceptible and infectious individuals contact each other, and therefore transmit infections, randomly.
Matching alleles model of host–parasite compatibility	Genetic model of *host–parasite* compatibility by which a *parasite* must genetically match its *host* at relevant loci in order to infect. Contrast with *gene-for-gene, inverse gene-for-gene* and *inverse matching alleles models of host–parasite compatibility*.
Mean field approximation	The approximation of a large number of individual effects by a single averaged effect. This approximation is commonly used in *compartmental models* of disease spread (see *SIR*, etc.).
Metapopulation	A collection of discrete populations in isolated patches, connected by occasional dispersal events.
Microbiota	The community of microorganisms associated with individual *hosts*.
Microparasite	*Parasites* which multiply inside individual *hosts* (e.g. viruses, bacteria, protozoa); typically the *host* is the unit of study (e.g. the number or proportion of infected *hosts*). Contrast with *macroparasite*.
Migratory allopatry	The spatial separation of adults and juveniles after breeding, which can reduce infection risk from adults to vulnerable juveniles.

Migratory culling	Mortality of infected **hosts** during long-distance movement events.
Migratory escape	Migration of **hosts** from **parasite**-contaminated areas, thereby lowering their risk of **infection**.
Mixing matrix	Mathematical matrix that defines the contact patterns of individuals from one population group with individuals of another group.
Muller's ratchet	The accumulation of deleterious mutations in clonal (asexual) lineages.
Negative binomial distribution	Discrete statistical distribution often used to describe the typically observed **aggregated** distribution of **macroparasite** burdens across the **host** population.
Network-based models	Models that include explicit contact network structure between individuals (see **contact network**).
Ordinary infectious disease (OID)	A **parasite** where the majority of transmission infection occurs infectiously outside of mating contact. Contrast with **sexually transmitted infection (STI)**.
Oxidation Handicap Hypothesis (OHH)	An extension of the **Immunocompetence Handicap Hypothesis** of sexual signalling, which argues that the main cost of elevated testosterone is increased oxidative stress.
Pair approximation	**Deterministic** model approximating the dynamics of pairs of individuals in a network (see **contact network**), rather than the dynamics of individuals themselves.
Pandemic	An **epidemic** of **infectious disease** that has spread across a large region, such as multiple continents or globally.
Parasite	An organism that lives in (**endoparasite**) or on (ectoparasite) another organism (the **host**), and obtains resources from it.
Pathogen	**Parasites** that typically cause acute, highly pathogenic **infections**, often used as a synonym for **microparasite**.

Pathosystem	Part of an ecosystem that involves **parasitism**.
Phenology	The pattern and timing of life-history events such as of birth, maturation, reproduction, and death through the year.
Phyllosphere	The above-ground elements of plants, particularly in terms of the microbes associated with it.
Polygyny/polyandry	Where a single male mates with more than one female, and where a single female mates with more than one male, respectively.
Population Viability Analysis (PVA)	An analytical tool that seeks to predict the viability and extinction risk of a population.
Prevalence	The proportion of infected individuals in the **host** population.
Regulation (of host population dynamics)	The limitation of (**host**) population size through density-dependent feedback processes.
Reservoir (environmental)	The persistence of **parasite** infective stages in the abiotic environment, acting as a potential source of new **infections**.
Reservoir (host)	A **host** species, or collection of species, that maintains a **parasite** and acts as a source of infection to another **host** species.
Resistance	The ability of **hosts** to prevent an **infection** from establishing or to limit its growth rate. Contrast with **tolerance**.
Semelparous	An organism that reproduces once in its life. Contrast with **iteroparous**.
Sexually transmitted infection (STI)	A **parasite** transmitted during its **host**'s mating activity. Contrast with **ordinary infectious disease (OID)**.
SIR, SEIR, SIS, etc. models	**Compartmental models** of **microparasite** dynamics, structured according to assumptions about the flow of **host** individuals between compartments defined by their **infection** status (***S=susceptible*** (uninfected), *I*=infected (and infectious), *E*=exposed (infected but

	not infectious), R=recovered (and immune from reinfection)).
Social immunity	Collective **host** behaviours that reduce the likelihood of **infection** in social or communal species.
Spillover	The process by which **parasites** from one host species (typically a **reservoir host**) cross over to infect a different **host** species.
Stochastic	A system or modelling framework which incorporates some element of random variation. Contrast with **deterministic**.
Subclinical infections	Infections which result in no obvious signs of **disease** in the **host**.
Supershedder	Individuals that are highly infectious through high levels of release of **parasite** infective stages. See also **superspreader**.
Superspreader	An individual **host** that contributes disproportionately highly to parasite transmission (e.g. due to their high number of contacts with other individuals). See also **supershedder**.
Susceptible [host]	A **host** that can be infected by a specific **parasite**.
Th1/Th2 immune response	Characterisation of the immune response into the 'T-helper 1' (Th1) and 'T-helper 2' (Th2) arms, based on the different **cytokines** and **antibodies** produced, typically in response to intracellular (~**microparasitic**) or extracellular (~**macroparasitic**) infections, respectively. Often these arms of the **immune response** are assumed to trade-off against each other, such that investment in one response limits the ability of the **host** to invest in the other.
Threshold population size/critical community size	The minimum **host** population size required for a **parasite** to persist.
Tolerance	The ability of **hosts** to reduce the detrimental impact of a given **infection**. Contrast with **resistance**.

Trait-mediated effects (of parasitism)	*Infection* alters **host** traits such as appearance or behaviour, which affects vulnerability to predation, potentially affecting population, community, or ecosystem dynamics.
Trait-mediated indirect effects (TMIE) (predator-mediated)	Indirect effects on a **host–parasite** interaction, mediated by another member of the community. May be predator-mediated (e.g. non-lethal effects of natural enemies on **hosts**, which alter traits such as **host** behaviour, rather than survival) or resource plant) mediated (e.g. plant traits affect the interaction between herbivores and their natural enemies).
Transmission	The process by which a **susceptible** (uninfected) **host** acquires a new **infection**.
Trickle infection	Experimentally infecting **hosts** with low, repeated doses of **parasites**, to mimic the natural rate of acquisition of **infections**.
Trophic cascade	Changes in the structure of a community occurring when predators reduce the density of their prey, which has knock-on effects at lower trophic levels.
Trophic transmission	The **transmission** of **parasites** between trophic levels through the ingestion of infected prey by predators, which then become infected.
Vertical transmission	**Transmission** directly from parent to offspring, for example trans-placental (in mammals) or via eggs (e.g. in insects). Contrast with **horizontal transmission**.
Virulence	The impact of a **parasite** on its **host's** fitness (i.e. through reduction in individual **host** survival or reproduction). See also **virulence (density-dependent)**.
Virulence (density-dependent)	**Host** fitness cost of **infection** (**virulence**) increases as host density increases.
Zoonosis	An **infectious disease** that is maintained in a wild **reservoir**, but which may cause **infection** in humans.

PART I

Understanding within-host processes

CHAPTER ONE

Pollinator diseases: the *Bombus–Crithidia* system

PAUL SCHMID-HEMPEL, LENA WILFERT
AND REGULA SCHMID-HEMPEL

1.1 Introduction

Bee pollinators are critically important for ecosystem functioning and food security, and bumblebees are the most important large pollinators in temperate and alpine habitats, as well as for many crops (Goulson, 2003b; Velthuis & van Doorn, 2006). Today, some species are expanding their range (Inoue et al., 2010; Schmid-Hempel et al., 2013), but most are declining in range and abundance (Biesmeijer et al., 2006; Goulson et al., 2008; Cameron et al., 2011). Declines can be attributed to various reasons (Fitzpatrick et al., 2007), but parasites seem to play a role in many cases (Cameron et al., 2011). Hence, the study of host–parasite interactions in bumblebees is, on one hand, of importance for the monitoring and possible management of pollinators. On the other hand, the *Bombus–Crithidia* system (Figure 1.1) has proven an excellent test ground to scrutinise basic scientific questions surrounding host–parasite interactions.

Until the early 1980s, parasites had been the almost exclusive domain of traditional parasitologists. By then, behavioural ecologists started to realise that the selective pressures exerted by parasites affect a wide range of seemingly unconnected phenomena. Examples include sexual selection and the meaning of conspicuous male ornaments (Hamilton & Zuk, 1982), the maintenance of genotypic diversity in populations (Hamilton, 1980), or the manipulation of host behaviour to increase transmission success (Ewald, 1980; Moore, 1984). At the same time, students of evolutionary population biology started to wonder not only whether parasites could regulate their host populations (Anderson & May, 1978), but also why – beyond the obviously different mechanisms that are involved – some parasites have evolved to be very damaging to the host, whereas others only cause mild symptoms. A new approach was therefore taken, asking what might be the selective advantage for the parasite when harming its host (Anderson & May, 1982; Ewald, 1983). The question of what virulence towards its host a parasite should 'choose' to

Figure 1.1 (a) Worker of *Bombus terrestris* visiting flowers of *Ajuga reptans* (photo: P. Schmid-Hempel). (b) SEM micrograph of *Crithidia bombi*. The length is around 10 μm (photo: Boris Baer, ETH Zürich). (A black and white version of this figure will appear in some formats. For the colour version, please refer to the plate section.)

maximise its fitness illustrates, in a nutshell, the concepts and ramifications of this approach, but also the difficulties and the kind of research needed to make progress. The *Bombus–Crithidia* system is a good example that shows what can and what cannot be asked and how natural host–parasite systems can be scrutinised to add to the theoretical concepts. Because the bumblebee hosts are social insects, a 'host' can either be the individual – where infection and immune defence unfold – or the colony as a whole, which is the tightly knit reproductive community. Colony members only gain fitness by raising close kin to become reproductives (daughter queens and sons, the drones) that go on to found the next generation. Colony success can also be understood as the founding female's (the queen's) success, which she achieves by building up a colony that ensures her reproductive success. Here, we generally focus on the individual host that is embedded in this background, but as far as the consequences of infection and defence go, these – evolutionarily speaking – accumulate at the colony level.

1.2 Natural history of the study system

Worldwide, some 250 species of bumblebees exist (genus *Bombus* Latreille 1802, Apidae). They inhabit temperate areas of the Holarctic, Neotropics, and South East Asia (Williams et al., 2008); four species were introduced to New Zealand and one to Tasmania. Bumblebees are social insects with an annual cycle. The queen on her own starts the colony at the beginning of the season (Figure 1.2). Once the first workers, the non-reproducing daughters, have hatched, the queen remains egg-laying in the nest as the colony grows in worker numbers.

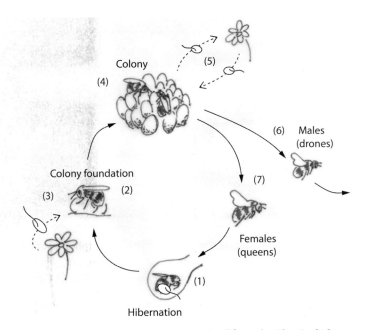

Figure 1.2 Sketch of host and parasite life cycle. The *Crithidia* parasites are directly transmitted, infect via ingestion of infective cells, and after passage through the bee, infective cells are shed with faeces. In bumblebees, (1) the queen hibernates alone and in soil. At this stage, some queens harbour an infection, which is the parasite's only way of passage through the hibernation period. (2) In spring, queens found their own colony. At this stage, they either have already carried an infection through hibernation, or may have acquired a new infection when foraging for food (3). When the colony has grown (4), the queen stays in the nest and an existing infection is passed on to other colony members inside the nest. As workers forage for food outside, they may carry a new infection back via contact on flowers (5). At the end of the colony cycle, sexual offspring are produced; both sexes can become infected inside the nest. (6) Males leave to mate and eventually perish, and do not pass on the infection. (7) Females (daughter queens) carry the infection into hibernation. They can also contract a new infection when foraging before going into hibernation.

Towards the end of the colony cycle, sexual offspring are produced – drones (males) and daughter queens (females, the reproductive daughters) which leave the colony and mate. Now, the colony's social fabric decays, no new worker brood is produced, and the colony's queen and her remaining workers perish. The males also die before the onset of winter, either having successfully mated or having unsuccessfully searched for females. Therefore, only the mated daughters enter hibernation (or other forms of a seasonal diapause), typically remaining buried in the soil. They emerge the next season as queens that attempt to found their own colonies (Goulson, 2003a).

Bumblebees have a number of parasites, such as viruses (McMahon et al., 2015; Manley et al., 2017), microsporidia (Li et al., 2012), neogregarines (Maharramov et al., 2013), and trypanosomes (Schmid-Hempel, 2001). Here, we illustrate the interaction between the host *Bombus terrestris* L. and its infectious gut parasite *Crithidia bombi* Lipa & Triggiani 1988 (Trypanosomatidae) (cf. Figure 1.1), which has been studied since 1985 and has effectively become a model system of host–parasite evolutionary ecology. The biology of two newly discovered species, *C. expoeki* (Schmid-Hempel & Tognazzo, 2010) and *C. mexicana* (Gallot-Lavallée et al., 2016), as well as other host *Bombus* species that are infected worldwide by these trypanosomes, are likely to be similar.

Taxonomically, *Crithidia* is a poorly defined paraphyletic genus. The taxa of *Crithidia* infecting bumblebees are closely related to *Leishmania* and *Leptomonas* (Schmid-Hempel & Tognazzo, 2010; Flegontov et al., 2015; Ravoet et al., 2015; Schwarz et al., 2015; Ishemgulova et al., 2017). The bumblebee-infecting *Crithidia* have no known vector or intermediate hosts; they are therefore classified as monoxenous (having only one host) (cf. Figure 1.2).

The life cycle of the parasite within the host starts with a primary infection of a host individual *per os* (i.e. the ingestion of infective cells via the mouth). The parasite cells pass through the digestive tract and eventually accumulate in the hind gut (the rectum). There, the cells attach to the gut wall, absorb amino acids from the gut lumen (Schaub, 1992), divide and eventually multiply to high numbers with infection intensities in the millions of cells. No evidence exists that *Crithidia* ever crosses the gut wall and spreads inside the host's body. As the parasite multiplies and the parasite population grows, infective cells are shed via the host's faeces as soon as 3–4 days post-infection. Peak intensity and peak shedding is typically reached around 10–12 days, where intensities often start to decline (Schmid-Hempel & Schmid-Hempel, 1993). Transmission from colony to colony is via flower visits (Durrer & Schmid-Hempel, 1994; Graystock et al., 2015) (Figure 1.2). Infected workers transfer the parasite's cells to either flower nectar or, more likely, the flower surface (Cisarovsky & Schmid-Hempel, 2014a), such that a bee visiting the same flower subsequently can become infected. The likelihood of transmission depends on the architecture of the inflorescence (complex ones lead to less transmission) and the bee species involved (Durrer & Schmid-Hempel, 1994; McArt et al., 2014). Within the nest, transmission occurs via contaminated surfaces or, for instance, via the nectar stores or infected larvae (Folly et al., 2017). In social insects with overlapping generations, such as bumblebees, vertical transmission between generations is equivalent to direct transmission within the nest (Imhoof & Schmid-Hempel, 1999), because bee-infecting *Crithidia* cannot be transmitted via eggs, in contrast to those in solitary insects (Dias et al., 2014). Bee-infecting *Crithidia* also have no durable stages that can persist outside their living host for the hibernation period

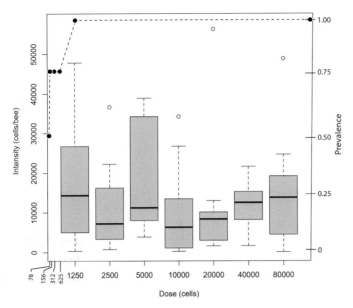

Figure 1.3 Dose–response curve. Box plots are shown of the resulting infection intensities (parasite cells per bee) when the inoculum (dose) varies from 78 to 80,000 cells (a logarithmic scale). The broken line is prevalence of infection (percentage infected individuals) as a function of dose. Each dose was applied to $n = 8$ bees. Data for doses below 1250 cells from Schmid-Hempel et al. (1999).

(Schmid-Hempel et al., 1999). Hence, during the winter months all infections are contained in the overwintering bumblebee queens.

From a conceptual stance, the infective dose, i.e. how many parasite cells are needed to start an infection, has recently been linked to the absence or presence of cooperation among infecting cells; without cooperation between the infecting cells, each cell can infect individually, with a low infectious dose being sufficient for infection, whereas cooperating cells necessitate a high infectious dose (Schmid-Hempel & Frank, 2007; Leggett et al., 2012). For cocktails of mixed *C. bombi* genotypes (which we also call 'strains'), experimental infections suggested that already with doses of around 1000 cells, infection is certain (i.e. prevalence – the fraction of hosts infected – among test bees is 100%) (Figure 1.3). However, doses as low as a few dozen cells seem sufficient to infect at least half of the exposed hosts (Schmid-Hempel et al., 1999); yet, regardless of dose, the resulting infection intensity (parasite cells/bee) also varies among colonies (Yourth, 2004). Unfortunately, little is known about quantitative differences in infective doses among different genotypes of the parasite, but it is clear that some strains do not infect well even at very high doses. Therefore, following the theoretical considerations outlined above, *C. bombi* does not seem to use cooperation tactics when infecting a host.

Likely, factors selecting against such cooperation are the suspected very low number of cells that can be transmitted via flowers (Durrer & Schmid-Hempel, 1994) and the small chance to encounter a suitable host genotype in the first place, as discussed below.

By definition, parasites gain fitness at the expense of their host's survival and reproductive success ('virulence' in the widest sense). Obviously, these effects vary with host condition, parasite type, and environmental conditions, among others. More generally, there are long-standing debates, for example, about how much virulence is necessary for host populations to evolve and maintain sex and recombination in defence (Hamilton et al., 1990). Against this background, *C. bombi* infections in workers of *B. terrestris* – disappointingly at first sight – cause only benign effects. Yet, effects appear when workers are stressed – for example, by food deprivation, where mortality increases 1.5-fold (Brown et al., 2000). Even more interestingly, infection reduces the ovary size of workers, likely by the sequestering of amino acids from the host's gut (Schaub, 1992). In addition, reproduction in the colony as a whole is delayed (Shykoff & Schmid-Hempel, 1991). Partial castration matters in particular when, instead of workers, spring queens (i.e. the emerging overwintered daughters that now start their own colony) become infected. Infected queens have poor chances to establish a successful colony, and lose roughly half of their average fitness (Brown et al., 2003b). This amounts to a considerable virulence effect, albeit only during a defined period of the host life cycle. However, contrary to the now 'classical theory' of virulence evolution (Frank & Schmid-Hempel, 2008), infection intensity, i.e. the number of potential propagules in the host, seems not to relate to survival (a virulence component) (Brown et al., 2000; Yourth, 2004). This raises the question whether bees have evolved the capacity to reduce the effects of infection – termed 'tolerance' (Råberg et al., 2007) – rather than preventing an infection in the first place ('resistance'). If anything, this would complement the underlying genotypic variation in 'resistance' as discussed below.

Beyond the immediately visible virulence effects, such as castration or increased mortality, *Crithidia* infection (as well as infestation by parasitic flies: Schmid-Hempel & Stauffer, 1998; Gillespie et al., 2015) also subtly changes the foraging behaviour of bumblebee workers. For example, steadiness – the tendency to visit the same species of flowering plant – decreases (Otterstatter et al., 2005; Gegear et al., 2006; Gillespie & Adler, 2013), with obvious consequences for pollination efficiency (Richardson et al., 2016) and pathogen dispersal in the environment. Infection does not seem to change behaviour within the nest though, nor do nest mates recognise infected workers (P. Schmid-Hempel, M. Brown & P. Korner, unpublished data), although the amount (but not the composition) of secretion from the Dufour's gland, which is used in nest mate recognition, is significantly increased in experimentally infected workers (P. Schmid-Hempel, D. Morgan, & G. Jones, unpublished data).

1.3 Parasite prevalence in space and time

The patterns of how host–parasite interactions unfold in space and time shape the coevolution of, generally speaking, host defence and parasite virulence, as modelled for example in Gandon and Michalakis (2002) and Howard and Lively (2002) (see also Chapter 2). Hence, an important piece of natural history is to know how common parasites actually are in space and time. As far as *Crithidia* is concerned, infections are widespread in field populations but vary in prevalence (i.e. the fraction of infected bees) among localities, years, and host species. This situation is illustrated by a study in the Swiss Jura mountains (Durrer & Schmid-Hempel, 1995; Durrer, 1996). In this region, local communities of bumblebee species were surveyed in detail at 12 localities for two consecutive years. On average, 11.7% of all bees (n = 3481 bees checked) were infected with *Crithidia*, but prevalence varied on a rather small spatial scale and from one year to the next. Prevalence remained different among host species in both years, yet showed no consistent patterns (Figure 1.4). The *B. terrestris*-complex (*B. terrestris, B. lucorum*, and potentially two other cryptic species; Williams et al., 2012) may represent an exception, as these species show consistently elevated infection levels. In fact, *B. terrestris* is quite an opportunistic species, i.e. it feeds on a wide range of plant species and can be highly invasive (Schmid-Hempel et al., 2013). Host species might therefore simply accumulate infections depending on their ecology. In fact, the patterns of flower visitations that dominate a particular ecological community affects the genetic fabric of *Crithidia* genotypes present across the different host species (Salathé & Schmid-Hempel, 2011; Ruiz-Gonzalez et al., 2012). Together with the observation that infection is transmitted via flowers (Durrer & Schmid-Hempel, 1994; Graystock et al., 2015), niche overlap in flower usage among different host species seems to be a driver of the spread of *Crithidia* within bumblebee communities and ecological guilds – a pattern that may be of general relevance in pollinator populations (Fürst et al., 2014).

Similarly, taking spring queens of the most common host, *B. terrestris*, as an indicator shows that over a period of 15 years, infection prevalence is around 8–9%. The two sites differ somewhat and fluctuations between years occur (Figure 1.5). Moreover, prevalence is somewhat lower among spring queens than among the workers sampled in summer (cf. Figure 1.4). Indeed, also in experimental tests, queens are generally more refractory to becoming infected by *C. bombi* than either workers or males. As the season progresses, infections that were carried through the hibernation period by the spring queens rapidly spread in the local population (Imhoof & Schmid-Hempel, 1999). No infection

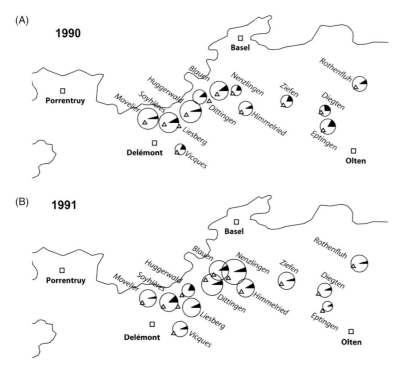

Figure 1.4 Prevalence of *C. bombi* infections in 12 study populations and in all host species. (A) Prevalence in 1990; $n = 2000$ bees checked (15 species). (B) Prevalence in 1991; $n = 1481$ bees checked (13 species). There is no correlation of prevalence in a site between the two years ($r = -0.11$, $p = 0.74$, $n = 12$ sites), but infection prevalence varies among host species in both years (for 1990: $x^2 = 89.8$, $df = 14$, $p < 0.0001$; for 1991: $x^2 = 230.8$ $df = 11$, $p < 0.0001$). Size of circles proportional to sample size; prevalence is black sector. Based on Durrer (1996).

was discovered in 2011 and 2013 at site Neunforn. Either the infection must have been at a very low level, and/or it was introduced by immigration of queens into this area somewhat later as the season progressed. The first possibility can be assessed by checking the likelihood that an infected queen was missed; in this case, with sample sizes around 150–200 bees, the population prevalence could be only a few percent with any confidence. On the other hand, the study of an ongoing invasion event, where *B. terrestris* was introduced in South America and keeps spreading by some 200 km per year, suggests that queens habitually disperse widely from their natal site every year (Schmid-Hempel et al., 2013). This is also suggested by occasional observations of long-distance migration of bumblebee queens in spring (Mikkola, 1984). Furthermore, the genetic structure of populations of *B. terrestris* in Central Europe suggests pan-mixis, with only some offshore islands being more isolated (Estoup et al., 1996; Widmer et al., 1998; Widmer & Schmid-Hempel, 1999).

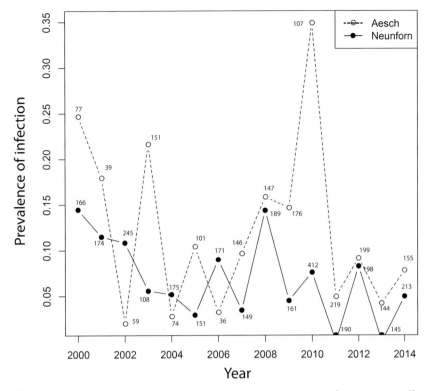

Figure 1.5 Prevalence of *C. bombi* infections in spring queens of *B. terrestris*, collected at two locations (Aesch, Neunforn) in Northern Switzerland over 15 consecutive years. Small numbers are sample sizes (number of queens examined). A total of *n* = 4677 spring queens were checked. The average prevalence for Aesch was 11.7% and for Neunforn 6.5% (overall 8.5%).

1.4 Parasite genetics

From a theoretical perspective, one of the most important elements of host–parasite coevolution is the genetic basis of the interaction. The exact nature of the genotype–genotype effects, such as additive or epistatic variance, are relevant, for example, in the context of the evolution and maintenance of sex and recombination (Hamilton et al., 1990; Peters & Lively, 1999; Salathé et al., 2008). A number of explicit genetic models for host and parasite traits, respectively, had been postulated, such as gene-for-gene (Sasaki, 2000), inverse gene-for-gene (Fenton et al., 2009), or quantitative inheritance (Frank, 1994). In fact, the interaction may not necessarily be based on complex genetics, and can be dominated by a single step of the infection process, with a relatively simple genetic basis (Routtu & Ebert, 2015; Ebert et al., 2016). But how does this compare to the situation in the *Bombus–Crithidia* system?

Trypanosomatids have a complex genetic system with variation in chromosome numbers, polyploidy, and a special structure, called the kinetoplast, that contains its own genetic material (Tait et al., 2011). Trypanosomatids also have unique gene expression systems with polycistronic transcription and trans-splicing mechanisms (Martinez-Calvillo et al., 2010). As many trypanosomes seem to follow a standard Mendelian segregation scheme (MacLeod et al., 2005), the analysis can, at least in principle (de Meeus et al., 2006), be based on the standard tools of population genetics. This is the case for *C. bombi*. Its genome is around 34 Mb in size and can be analysed as a diploid using a number of polymorphic microsatellites (Schmid-Hempel & Reber Funk, 2004). A small number of loci already captures a vast range of different strains (i.e. multi-locus genotypes). *Crithidia* infections reside in the hind gut and infective cells are constantly shed. Thus, raw infections (i.e. the multi-locus allelic pattern for the pooled infection in a host) can be genotyped either from the faeces in the live animal, or by extracting and dissecting the gut. Typically, in a population, the number of different alleles at any one locus is limited; yet, the number of multi-locus genotypes that are found is very large. In fact, regardless of how many infections have already been typed in a population of hosts, there are always new genotypes discovered. For example, even with sample sizes approaching 200 typed infections, the number of new genotypes discovered does not saturate, with the ratio of new genotypes to sample size remaining close to one (Schmid-Hempel & Reber Funk, 2004; Salathé & Schmid-Hempel, 2011). This high ratio suggests (but is not a proof, as misleadingly claimed by Erler et al., 2012) that at least occasional sexual exchange, rather than a purely clonal reproductive mode, is the rule for *C. bombi*. Furthermore, pooled infections of individual hosts often contain more than two alleles at a given locus (Schmid-Hempel et al., 1999, 2013;Schmid-Hempel & Reber Funk, 2004; Tognazzo et al., 2012). Because the parasite is diploid, and heterozygotes have two alleles at a locus, this suggests mixed-genotype infections. This has been confirmed directly by separating the raw infections into single-cell clonal lines prior to genotyping (Salathé & Schmid-Hempel, 2012). Using this approach, mixed-genotype infections are found in roughly half of the host individuals (Schmid-Hempel & Reber Funk, 2004; Tognazzo et al., 2012).

Frequent multiple infections of the same host individual set the stage for possible sexual reproduction of the parasite. For *C. bombi* this was confirmed experimentally. After individual bees were infected by two 'parental' genotypes, the resulting infection, i.e. the parasite population, was sampled one week later. This population now contained not only parental but also novel genotypes. These were either standard Mendelian recombinants of the parental types (i.e. having the same alleles, but in new multi-locus combinations), or genotypes with novel alleles, i.e. containing alleles that were not already present in the parents (Schmid-Hempel et al., 2011). In numbers, in the infections from 15 of 91 bees, at least one non-parental genotype had emerged. At the same time, among a total of $n = 2083$ clones extracted and genotyped from the set of all infected bees, only 3% were non-parental (Schmid-Hempel et al., 2011). This percentage may seem small, but given frequent coinfections and the many thousands of workers in a local population, the number of non-parental genotypes that are generated in the field must, overall, be enormous. Such emergent diversity of parasite genotypes fits the observation of a large number of genotypes circulating in a host population in the first place (Salathé & Schmid-Hempel, 2011). These findings relate to the subject of a major debate: that is, whether protozoan parasites, such as trypanosomes, are strictly clonal or whether recombination is frequent enough to break the process of clonal evolution ('clonal theory'; Tibayrenc & Ayala, 2002, 2013). For *C. bombi*, it is as yet unclear whether the patterns of linkage disequilibria are sufficient to reject the clonal theory.

Strikingly, though, *C. bombi* has unusually high rates of sexual exchange (Schmid-Hempel et al., 2011) compared to other trypanosomes (Gaunt et al., 2003; MacLeod et al., 2005; Akopyants et al., 2009). We therefore speculate that *C. bombi* may rely on short generation times (estimated at 10–16 h; Salathé et al., 2012) and escape the host's defences by generating variable offspring, instead of persisting and changing surface as is the case in the African trypanosomes (Barry & McCulloch, 2001). For *C. bombi*, such diversification may be particularly important, as successful infection depends very much on a 'compatible' matching of parasite and host genotypes, and even sister workers differ in their susceptibility towards the same parasites (Schmid-Hempel et al., 1999; Baer & Schmid-Hempel, 2003; and discussed below). New offspring types could continue to reside in the current host, the host colony, or be capable of infecting new hosts. Furthermore, being a parasite of a socially living host allows leaving the current host early and to quickly transmit to another one nearby (Schmid-Hempel & Schmid-Hempel, 1993). Indeed, insects such as *B. terrestris* show specific immune responses, and have also been shown to establish immune priming, both when secondarily exposed to the same pathogen as well as in offspring of previously exposed mothers (see below; Sadd et al., 2005; Sadd & Schmid-Hempel, 2006) – capacities that would make infection by the same parasite generally more difficult the next time. However, because novel genotypes are produced at a low rate (Schmid-Hempel et al., 2011), the parasite's strategy will only be successful if offspring genotypes can infect the next host at a low dose, which is actually observed (Figure 1.3). This offspring diversification strategy is at least consistent with the observation that different parasite genotypes in an infection do not necessarily compete with each other, but rather seem to occupy different 'niches'. This is suggested by the observation that infection intensity (i.e. number of parasitic cells/bee) correlates positively with the number of parasite genotypes in the infection (Schmid-Hempel et al., 1999;

Ulrich et al., 2011; Ulrich & Schmid-Hempel, 2015). Furthermore, experimental coinfection of founding queens at the start of the season with two *C. bombi* genotypes each (five genotypes in 10 combinations) shows that several hundreds of non-parental genotypes can be retrieved from infected bees until the time when males and daughter queens appear in the colony (R. Schmid-Hempel et al., unpublished data). Therefore, in *C. bombi*, genetic exchange during coinfections is a powerful process that diversifies parasite offspring and generates large numbers of novel genotypes in the subsequently transmitted parasite population.

Specificity in the interaction between host and parasite is an essential element and, in theory, crucially affects the coevolutionary process (e.g. Carius et al., 2001; Luijckx et al., 2013). In fact, only certain strains of the parasite, *C. bombi*, are able to infect a given colony of the host, *B. terrestris*. Likewise, a given host colony can be infected only by some but not by all strains of the parasite. Colonies represent a tight genotypic background, as workers are closely related (Schmid-Hempel & Schmid-Hempel, 2000), but experiments with multiply inseminated queens show that susceptibility towards strains of *C. bombi* varies among the worker patrilines (Baer & Schmid-Hempel, 2003). Hence, there is a direct genetic component to resistance because hymenopteran males are haploid and sperm a clonal copy of the father, whereas at the same time, patrilines share the same environment and differ only by the sperm used to sire them. Quantitative trait loci (QTL) analyses have additionally demonstrated the presence of genomic regions significantly associated with resistance to *Crithidia* infection (Wilfert et al., 2007). The specific interaction of *C. bombi* with *B. terrestris* is 'asymmetric' in the sense that parasite strains vary in the range of host colonies they are able to infect – some strains infect almost all colonies, others can only infect a few. Similarly, the resistance of colonies varies primarily in the range of parasite strains able to infect. We therefore have varying 'bandwidths' of infectiousness by the parasites, and varying 'bandwidths' of resistance by the hosts. This amounts to a genotype-versus-genotype interaction based on 'bandwidths of compatibility'. The underlying reasons for the difference in bandwidths of either hosts or parasites are not clear. One factor might be the variation in dose necessary to establish an infection. Hence, strains that, on average, infect with a lower dose may be able to infect a wider range of host colonies than those needing higher doses, and host colonies resisting higher infective doses of *C. bombi* could be able to exclude many more strains from the infectious set. Variation in infection success could also depend on how successful the attachment of the parasite to the gut wall of the host is (just as with bacteria infecting *Daphnia*; Routtu & Ebert, 2015). In this case, variation in parasite surface proteins for attachment or defensive host proteases might be decisive. For the time being this must remain speculative, but is open to testing.

Box 1.1: Sketch of the dynamics of *Crithidia* infections

From the available data, the dynamics of *Crithidia* infections can be sketched as follows (cf. Figure 1.2). During the winter period, the only host individuals present are the overwintering queens. They harbour all infections of *Crithidia* present in the area and represent a collection of parasite genotypes circulating and being produced in the previous season. At least in laboratory tests, infection itself seems not to seriously reduce the chances of queens surviving the winter, given the hibernation period is not too long (4–6 months). However, with natural hibernation periods of 6–7 months, typical for Central Europe, and adverse conditions when preparing for diapause or before breaking it, this may differ. Regardless, as spring arrives the queens emerge from their winter quarters and start to feed. As a result, the infection is spread to other foraging queens and, if already present, to the early workers of other colonies (Durrer & Schmid-Hempel, 1994). However, spring queens that had been infected at emergence have a reduced chance of successfully founding their own colony (Brown et al., 2003b). Therefore, we must assume that most infections that are spread at this stage will be transferred to as yet uninfected queens and colonies. We currently lack information on the quantitative aspects of this process. Furthermore, we have no information on how many queens will immigrate into an area and carry their own infections with them, and how successfully the infection is subsequently spread to others in the local population. Queens seem to disperse over large distances (Mikkola, 1984; Schmid-Hempel et al., 2013). Also, continental European populations of *B. terrestris* are genetically quite homogeneous (Estoup et al., 1996). Hence, the exchange of queens among populations is likely to be common and, as a consequence, infections will also be spread over larger distances. The scenario is supported by the differentiated population structure of *C. bombi* in South America, which largely corresponds to the geographical pattern of invasion of its host, *B. terrestris*, in the region (Schmid-Hempel et al., 2013) and where a steady state of mutual exchange among populations presumably has not yet been reached.

As the colonies grow, workers are produced and go outside to forage. In the process, the infection is spread further. Observations have shown that the force of infection in the field can be very high, such that healthy colonies become infected within days of being transferred to the field (Imhoof & Schmid-Hempel, 1999). As the season progresses, infections by *C. bombi* accumulate in the colony and continue spreading among the workers within; larvae can thereby act as a reservoir (Folly et al., 2017). While the infection resides in a colony, the parasite population changes. On

Box 1.1: (cont.)

one hand, it starts to adapt to its current colony environment and loses infectiousness towards other colonies (Yourth & Schmid-Hempel, 2006). In the process, the infecting mixture of strains (parasite genotypes) becomes sorted according to the colony background, that is, some strains are not successful and get lost, either over a complete cycle of transmission-infection from one colony to another (Schmid-Hempel et al., 1999), or as a filtering process within the same colony (Ulrich et al., 2011; Ulrich & Schmid-Hempel, 2012). In addition, the parasites themselves seem to change too, as can be demonstrated by the experimental evolution of single strains (genotypes) of *C. bombi* (Marxer et al., 2016a). When a rich mixture of parasite genotypes is circulating within the colony, there is also a high degree of multiplicity within a single host individual, i.e. several genotypes coinfecting a single colony worker (Tognazzo et al., 2012). This leads to genetic exchange among strains and to the formation of novel genotypes (Schmid-Hempel et al., 2011). Moreover, only a few colonies grow large and eventually manage to produce daughter queens at the end of the season (Müller & Schmid-Hempel, 1993; Imhoof & Schmid-Hempel, 1999). These large colonies have many workers and thus harbour a large infecting population and many parasite strains. The combined effect is that only a small fraction of all colonies in the population – the large ones – not only produce the majority of new parasite genotypes by genetic exchange, but also the bulk of all parasites in the first place that are, on one hand, spread by its many colony workers to the local population (Cisarovsky & Schmid-Hempel, 2014b; Ulrich & Schmid-Hempel, 2015). On the other hand, large colonies more likely have daughter queens to which the infection is passed on (Ulrich & Schmid-Hempel, 2015) – infections residing in other colony members are eliminated each year, because workers perish as the colony decays, and as far as is known, there is no transmission from males to females during mating. Hence, the few large colonies dominate the ecology and direction of host–parasite coevolution and the system is characterised by the parasite and host population undergoing a substantial bottleneck every year, driven by the distribution of colony sizes.

1.5 Host defences

Host defence against parasites can happen at various levels. This includes avoidance of an infection in the first place, hygienic behaviour, or having body surfaces that are hard to penetrate. Bumblebees acquire infections by foraging on flowers. They seem capable of sensing previous visits to flowers by other bees (Stout & Goulson, 2001), and to discriminate against flowers that previously were associated with dangers (Abbott, 2006). Possibly, they also avoid flowers when they are contaminated with cells of *C. bombi* (Fouks & Lattorff, 2011). In addition, bumblebees may be able to control or reduce infections with secondary metabolites collected on flowers and, hence, could choose those flowers that provide nectar containing such metabolites (Richardson et al., 2015). Genotypically diversifying the workers also mitigates against the negative effects of infections at the colony level (Baer & Schmid-Hempel, 1999). This seems an effective strategy against a hyper-variable parasite such as *C. bombi*. However, most bumblebee species do not take advantage of this effect, as most queens are singly mated (Schmid-Hempel & Schmid-Hempel, 2000), due to a mating plug transferred by the male that prevents further mating (Sauter et al., 2001). Among other things, resistance to parasites also reflects on sexual antagonism, where selection drives males and females into different directions, with males often investing less into defences than females (Zuk & Stoehr, 2002).

When infection has become unavoidable, defence relies on the activation of the immune system or on withholding crucial resources from the parasites, for example by sequestering iron in the case of bacterial infections (Schmid-Hempel, 2011). As in other insects, immune defence by bumblebees is based on innate mechanisms, involving the canonical Toll-, Imd-, and JAK/stat-pathways. With the release of the bumblebee genome (Sadd et al., 2015), it also became clear that bumblebees, just like other bees, have fewer genes in several immune gene families than other insect genera (Barribeau et al., 2015). Nevertheless, their defence against *Crithidia* and other parasites is efficient. Upon infection, the immune defence is recruited rapidly, within hours, and then lasts for days (Korner & Schmid-Hempel, 2004). Gene expression studies show that when exposed to *C. bombi*, some genes such as *peroxidase* respond early and the antimicrobial peptides (AMPs) *defensin, abaecin*, and *hymenoptaecin* are recruited within 12 h (Riddell et al., 2011); their presence is no longer visible after a week or two (Brown et al., 2003a). The bumblebee genome possesses four kinds of AMPs (*abaecin, apidaecin, defensin*, and *hymenoptaecin*) (Barribeau *et al.*, 2015), and knock-down studies suggest that AMPs are necessary for defence against *Crithidia* (Deshwal & Mallon, 2014).

Gene expression studies also provide a window into how the host defence system responds to different infections by *C. bombi*, as the response varies according to population, colony, infecting parasite genotype (Barribeau & Schmid-Hempel, 2013; Brunner et al., 2013) and with colony strain interaction (Barribeau et al., 2014). Remarkably, the expressed genes that add much to this interaction are two of the AMPs (*apidaecin, abaecin*) (Barribeau et al., 2014). AMPs differ in many ways, and functionally they are not equivalent (Zasloff, 2013). Some AMPs are specialised proteins that are able to open the parasite's cell membrane; others can enter the parasite cell itself. This is also the case in

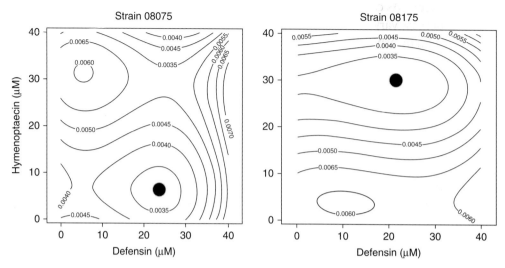

Figure 1.6 Synergistic action of antimicrobial peptides (AMPs) against *C. bombi* in experimental cultures. The contours represent maximal growth rates of two different *C. bombi* strains (nos. 08075, 08175) when treated with varying combinations of dose (in M) of the AMPs *defensin* and *hymenoptaecin*. Contours reflect a least-square polynomial of third-order to fit the estimated maximal growth rate for each observed combination of AMP. Circles denote the dose combination of best effect, i.e. lowest maximum growth rate for the strain. Each landscape represents the mean of three replicates for each strain. Reprinted from Marxer et al. (2016b), with permission from The Royal Society.

bumblebees. For example, *abaecin* is not effective against Gram-negative bacteria (*Escherichia coli*) when deployed alone, but takes effect when combined with *hymenoptaecin* (Rahnamaeian et al., 2015). The same is found when AMPs are used against *C. bombi*, where they act together to impede the growth of *C. bombi*. In addition, the best combined effect is not necessarily achieved with maximum doses of each (Marxer et al., 2016b) (Figure 1.6).

The theoretical debate on specific host defences and host–parasite coevolution has also focused on whether mounting an immune response is costly to the host (Schmid-Hempel, 2003; Cotter et al., 2004; Van Boven & Weissing, 2004). If so, costs would explain why responses are specific or why responses are sometimes moderated rather than unleashed at full scale. The *Bombus–Crithidia* system has been one of the early examples where such costs, in the sense of evolutionary ecology, were demonstrated (König & Schmid-Hempel, 1995). Yet, costs (increased worker mortality) are explicit only under adverse conditions, as set by energy constraints (Moret & Schmid-Hempel, 2000). Hosts seem to keep the infection in check when conditions are good, such that the extra costs can be compensated by increased food intake. Only when conditions turn bad will the negative consequences of *C. bombi* infections become visible. As costs depend on the environmental conditions, the coevolutionary process varies with the environment, e.g. Blanford et al. (2003).

Many aspects of the immune defence of bumblebees against parasites such as *Crithidia* are still unclear. Because bee-infecting *Crithidia* are parasites that reside in the gut, the mechanisms of gut immunity (Lemaitre, 2012) assume an important role. Little is known for bees, but infections in the gut elicit a local as well as a complex, systemic response. For instance, in the honeybee, oxidative stress and the recruitment of AMPs are responses against microsporidian and *Crithidia* infections (Dussaubat et al., 2012; Schwarz & Evans, 2013) and immune suppression is also reported in Antúnez et al. (2009). Based on the transcriptomic studies, a similar situation is likely for bumblebees infected by *C. bombi* (Riddell et al., 2009, 2011, 2014; Schlüns et al., 2010; Barribeau & Schmid-Hempel, 2013; Brunner et al., 2013; Barribeau et al., 2014).

In social insects, genetically and otherwise similar host individuals stay close together and interact frequently with one another. These are not only favourable physical conditions for the spread of any parasite, but make it additionally likely that the same parasite that has successfully infected a nest mate can also infect the next worker nearby (Schmid-Hempel, 1998). In aggregating locusts, for example, density-dependent prophylaxis, which relies on stepping up the expression of the melanisation–encapsulation pathways, is a defence strategy that pre-emptively reduces the cost of social grouping (Wilson et al., 2002). For social insects, it would also be an advantage to prepare for an infection that is already circulating in a colony, or that was infecting the founding queen.

Because workers of a colony of social insects cooperate and gain fitness through the production of kin, defences against parasites not only include individual responses, such as activating the immune system, but also a repertoire of other processes, such as allogrooming among nest mates to remove infective spores, compartmentalisation of the division of labour in the nest, and the exclusion of sick individuals, for example. These responses have been collectively termed 'social immunity' (Cremer et al., 2007) and offer a powerful toolbox not available to solitary host species. Bumblebees show none of the mentioned behaviours. On the other hand, immune 'priming' (Little & Kraaijeveld, 2004), known from other insects (e.g. Rheins & Karp, 1986), also exists in bumblebees. Indeed, workers previously challenged by a bacterial infection are less susceptible to a subsequent infection by the same as compared to another bacterial challenge (Sadd & Schmid-Hempel, 2006; Figure 1.7). Queen mothers also protect offspring – workers from mothers exposed to a given bacterial infection are better protected towards the same challenge, as compared to worker offspring from unchallenged mothers or mothers exposed to a different bacterium (Sadd et al., 2005; Sadd & Schmid-Hempel, 2007). Transcriptional studies suggest that this protection is

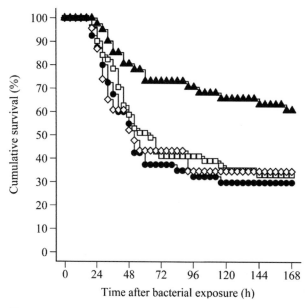

Figure 1.7 Immune priming ('memory') in bumblebees. Workers of *B. terrestris* that had already been exposed 22 days earlier to a non-lethal dose of the bacterium survived better upon secondary exposure to the same bacterium (homologous infection, triangle, $n = 51$) as compared to workers having been exposed to another bacterium (heterologous, squares, $n = 51$ bees), or a related one (congeneric infection, diamonds, $n = 23$). Cox regression (heterologous vs. homologous): $b = 0.77 \pm 0.30$, *Wald* $= 6.46$, $df = 1$, $P = 0.01$; odds $= 2.16$. Reprinted from Sadd and Schmid-Hempel (2006), with permission from Elsevier.

associated with a gene expression profile that mimics a small infection in the descendant workers (Barribeau et al., 2016). Such priming actually carries a cost, that is, workers primed against bacteria become more susceptible towards infections by *C. bombi* (Sadd & Schmid-Hempel, 2009). So far, however, there is no evidence for direct priming against *Crithidia*.

1.6 Social insects and their microbiota

Recently, the subtle role of the microbiota – particularly, the symbiotic bacteria inhabiting the gut (Engel & Moran, 2013b) – for defence against parasites has become clearer, especially for the resistance of bumblebee workers against infection by *Crithidia* (Koch & Schmid-Hempel, 2011b). The microbiota of bees is relatively simple, compared to what is known from vertebrates (Ley et al., 2008), but also distinct among and diversified within each host individual (Koch & Schmid-Hempel, 2011a; Martinson et al., 2011; Engel et al., 2012; Engel & Moran, 2013a). In social insects, the microbiota is transmitted maternally, from mother to offspring, and within the nest, i.e. socially within the colony (Koch & Schmid-Hempel, 2011b). Hence, the composition of the microbiota varies among colonies, and among individuals within colonies (Moran et al., 2012). Some of its constituent parts are more closely allied to their host species, whereas others may be horizontally acquired from elsewhere (Koch et al., 2013; Cariveau et al., 2014; Kwong et al., 2014). Colony differences can also be shown experimentally. Exposure of bumblebees to microbiota reveals an effect of host identity, i.e. the colony background, on the composition of the microbiota that eventually manages to establish (Näpflin & Schmid-Hempel, 2018).

The microbiota has differential effects, depending on its constituent parts. For example, the presence of bee-specific *Gilliamella apicola* (Orbaceae) and *Lactobacillus* (Bifidobacteriaceae) is associated with higher resistance to infection by *Crithidia* (Cariveau et al., 2014). These bacterial taxa usually occur at high abundance. In addition to the effect of single taxa, the overall composition of the microbiota is also predictive. In particular, a more diverse microbiota in terms of the OTUs (operational taxonomic units, or 'species') that are present, counter-intuitively, does not protect more but actually less against infections by *C. bombi* (Figure 1.8a). More generally, it is likely that bees with a skewed microbiota consisting of few highly abundant OTUs, typically summarised as the core microbiota (Moran et al., 2012), and many rare species are more resistant against infection.

The microbiota not only provides a general protection against infections by *C. bombi* (Koch & Schmid-Hempel, 2011b) but – as indicated by the various observations mentioned above – the protection depends on the particular isolate (or transplant in an experiment) that is present in a bee. In particular, microbiota that originate from different colonies vary in their protection level against *C. bombi*, and this level additionally differs for different strains of the parasite (Figure 1.8b). In other words, at least a part of the variation in resistance against different strains is not due to the actual host genotype (e.g. Baer & Schmid-Hempel, 2003) but results from differences in the microbiota, which in turn seem to result from differences in its composition (Cariveau et al., 2014; Näpflin & Schmid-Hempel, 2018). Because different microbes each have their own biochemistry and physiology, diverse mixtures of taxa that make up different microbiota could rather easily show variation in their overall response towards infection. Such differences in microbial systems would thus allow more specific responses or responses that can adapt more quickly to different parasites than is possible with the 'hard-wired' responses of the canonical immune pathways. Yet, the relationship of host background, especially host genotype, and its associated microbiota will be a crucial determinant of such plasticity. In *B. terrestris*, the host genotype still seems to matter, because the composition of the microbiota that eventually establishes varies with host background (Mikaelyan et al., 2015; Näpflin & Schmid-Hempel,

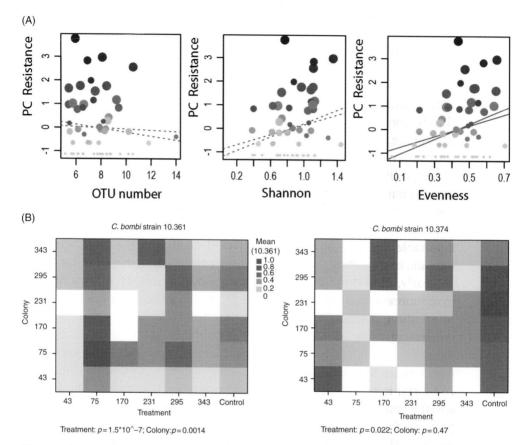

Figure 1.8 (A) Microbiota alpha-diversity prior to parasite exposure explains infection outcome. The panels show the relationship between variation in infection outcome (*y*-axis: a PC1-score combining infection intensity with diversity of parasite strains residing in the host; explaining 80.5 % of variance) with alpha-diversity measures (based on operational taxonomic units, OTUs) prior to parasite exposure (*x*-axis: OTU number in microbiota; Shannon = Shannon–Wiener Index of OTU diversity; Evenness of OTUs). Lines are fitted linear regression lines (general linear mixed model accounting for colony identity as a random factor). Solid lines represent statistically significant relationships ($p < 0.05$). Circle size is proportional to infection intensity, and darker fill colour indicates a higher number of resident parasite strains. Reprinted from Näpflin and Schmid-Hempel (2018). (B) Specific protection by microbiota. The heat maps for the average infection load (*C. bombi* cells in host faeces after 7 days; cells/μl faeces, see scale) are shown as a function of host background (*y*-axis, 'Colony') and the origin of the microbiota (*x*-axis, 'Treatment') that was transplanted into sterile workers from a given background. 'Controls' are bees with no transplants. The two panels refer to infection by different strains of *C. bombi*. Per panel, total $n = 356$ individuals tested (on average, 8.5 individuals per square). Reprinted from Koch and Schmid-Hempel (2012), with permission from Elsevier. (A black and white version of this figure will appear in some formats. For the colour version, please refer to the plate section.)

2018). The association is not very strong, though, and potentially leaves much leeway for the established microbiota. Regardless, such findings expand the earlier view that host–parasite interactions are based only on genotype–genotype matches in that the host genotype seems to set the stage for a third important player, the symbionts in the form of microbiota, rather than being a 'hard-wired' effect. In some sense, the microbiota can thus be considered a kind of 'extended phenotype' (Dawkins, 1982). For the time being, the actual mechanisms through which the microbiota provides protection are not known. The possibilities range from a direct effect, such as the production of effector molecules against microbial infections, to the recruitment of the host's immune response against an invading competitor. Last but not least, the protective effect could also simply be physical competition for space in the gut, especially access to the gut wall, where a suitable microbiota might close any gaps that would otherwise allow *Crithidia* to attach.

Clearly, over the last 25 years this research was a success story, but many more questions and challenges remain. The *Bombus–Crithidia* system offers the opportunity to better understand the underlying processes of defence against parasites, such as the role and ecology of the microbiota, the dynamics of coinfection and the structure of genotype × genotype interactions. Similarly, it can add to the study of how social organisms like the social insects deal with parasitism and how in turn parasitism shapes social evolution (Schmid-Hempel, 2017). The system holds especially great promise for the study of disease epidemics and its effect on pollination biology. Sites of parasite transmission (i.e. flowers; Durrer & Schmid-Hempel, 1994) are easily identified and manipulated, the genetic characterisation of host and parasite strains at large scales is now possible, and the background ecological knowledge for both parties is extensive. Hence, in another 25 years, the *Bombus–Crithidia* system may have also proven its worth for translating laboratory insights back into the field, and for establishing a field of experimental epidemiology with its necessary aspects of genetics, behaviour, ecology, and, eventually, its relevance for solving practical problems.

1.7 Conclusions

The *Bombus–Crithidia* host-parasite system uses large and important pollinators of the temperate zones, which can be easily bred and kept in artificial nests, and rapidly multiplying protozoa that can be cloned, maintained in culture, and cryopreserved for years. Hence, the system can easily be manipulated and studied in both the laboratory and the field. Both the host (Barribeau et al., 2015; Sadd et al., 2015) and the parasite (Schmid-Hempel et al., 2018) genomes are now available and characterised.

Furthermore, there is extensive additional knowledge available, for bumblebees have been intensively studied with respect to their ecology, behaviour, evolution, physiology (Goulson, 2003a), and immune defences (Schmid-Hempel, 2005), while the trypanosomatids to which *Crithidia* belong have similarly been intensively investigated with respect to genetics, genomics, physiology, and epidemiology (Gibson & Stevens, 1999; Simpson et al., 2006; Tait et al., 2011). Hence, the *Bombus–Crithidia* system offers many advantages that make it a prime system to study general as well as system-specific questions surrounding host–parasite interactions. Not the least, topics such as pollinator health and food security have recently gained much prominence, and the *Bombus–Crithidia* system is one of the best investigated cases among wild pollinators that helps to study these problems.

1.8 Acknowledgements

We thank the many collaborators that have added to the knowledge of this system as the studies unfolded over many years. Special thanks to our technicians, Christine Reber Funk and Roland Loosli, and to the Genetic Diversity Centre (GDC) at ETH. The studies were primarily supported by the Swiss National Science Foundation (SNF), the European Research Council (ERC), and intra-mural funds.

References

Abbott, K.R. (2006) Bumblebees avoid flowers containing evidence of past predation events. *Canadian Journal of Zoology*, **84**, 1240–1247.

Akopyants, N.S., Kimbllin, N., Secundino, N., et al. (2009) Demonstration of genetic exchange during cyclical development of *Leishmania* in the sand fly vector. *Science*, **324**, 265–268.

Anderson, R.M. & May, R.M. (1978) Regulation and stability of host–parasite population interactions. I. Regulatory processes. *Journal of Animal Ecology*, **47**, 219–247.

Anderson, R.M. & May, R.M. (1982) Coevolution of hosts and parasites. *Parasitology*, **85**, 411–426.

Antúnez, K., Martín-Hernández, R., Prieto, L., et al. (2009) Immune suppression in the honey bee (*Apis mellifera*) following infection by *Nosema ceranae* (Microsporidia). *Environmental Microbiology*, **11**, 2284–2290.

Baer, B. & Schmid-Hempel, P. (1999) Experimental variation in polyandry affects parasite loads and fitness in a bumble-bee. *Nature*, **397**, 151–154.

Baer, B. & Schmid-Hempel, P. (2003) Bumblebee workers from different sire groups vary in susceptibility to parasite infection. *Ecology Letters*, **6**, 106–110.

Barribeau, S.M., Sadd, B., du Plessis, L., et al. (2015) A depauperate immune repertoire precedes evolution of sociality in bees. *Genome Biology*, **16**, 83.

Barribeau, S.M., Sadd, B.M., du Plessis, L. & Schmid-Hempel, P. (2014) Gene expression differences underlying genotype-by-genotype specificity in a host–parasite system. *Proceedings of the National Academy of Sciences of the United States of America*, **111**, 3496–3501.

Barribeau, S.M. & Schmid-Hempel, P. (2013) Qualitatively different immune response of the bumblebee host, *Bombus terrestris*, to infection by different genotypes of the trypanosome gut parasite, *Crithidia bombi*. *Infection, Genetics and Evolution*, **20**, 249–256.

Barribeau, S.M., Schmid-Hempel, P. & Sadd, B. M. (2016) Royal decree: gene expression in transgenerationally immune primed bumblebee workers mimics a primary immune response. *PLoS ONE*, **11**, e0159635.

Barry, J.D. & McCulloch, R. (2001) Antigenic variation in trypanosomes: enhanced phenotypic variation in a eukaryotic parasite. *Advances in Parasitology*, **49**, 1–70.

Biesmeijer, J.C., Roberts, S.P.M., Reemer, M., et al. (2006) Parallel declines on pollinators and insect-pollinated plants in Britain and the Netherlands. *Science*, **313**, 351–354.

Blanford, S., Thomas, M.B., Pugh, C. & Pell, J.K. (2003) Temperature checks the Red Queen? Resistance and virulence in a fluctuating environment. *Ecology Letters*, **6**, 2–5.

Brown, M.J.F., Loosli, R. & Schmid-Hempel, P. (2000) Condition-dependent expression of virulence in a trypanosome infecting bumblebees. *Oikos*, **91**, 421–427.

Brown, M.J.F., Moret, Y. & Schmid-Hempel, P. (2003a) Activation of host constitutive immune defence by an intestinal trypanosome parasite of bumble bees. *Parasitology*, **126**, 253–260.

Brown, M.J.F., Schmid-Hempel, R. & Schmid-Hempel, P. (2003b) Strong context-dependent virulence in a host–parasite system: reconciling genetic evidence with theory. *Journal of Animal Ecology*, **72**, 994–1002.

Brunner, F.S., Schmid-Hempel, P. & Barribeau, S. M. (2013) Immune gene expression in *Bombus terrestris*: signatures of infection despite strong variation among populations, colonies, and sister workers. *PLoS ONE*, **8**, e68181.

Cameron, S.A., Lozier, J.D., Strange, J.P., et al. (2011) Patterns of widespread decline in North American bumble bees. *Proceedings of the National Academy of Sciences of the United States of America*, **108**, 662–667.

Carius, H.J., Little, T.J. & Ebert, D. (2001) Genetic variation in a host–parasite association: potential for coevolution and frequency-dependent selection. *Evolution*, **55**, 1136–1145.

Cariveau, D.P., Powell, J.E., Koch, H., Winfree, R. & Moran, N.A. (2014) Variation in gut microbial communities and its association with pathogen infection in wild bumble bees (*Bombus*). *The ISME Journal*, **8**, 2369–2379.

Cisarovsky, G. & Schmid-Hempel, P. (2014a) Combining laboratory and field approaches to investigate the importance of flower nectar in the horizontal transmission of a bumblebee parasite. *Entomologia Experimentalis et Applicata*, **1–7**, 1–7.

Cisarovsky, G. & Schmid-Hempel, P. (2014b) Few colonies of the host *Bombus terrestris* disproportionately affect the genetic diversity of its parasite, *Crithidia bombi*. *Infection, Genetics and Evolution*, **21**, 192–197.

Cotter, S.C., Kruuk, L.E.B. & Wilson, K. (2004) Costs of resistance: genetic correlations and potential trade-offs in an insect immune system. *Journal of Evolutionary Biology*, **17**, 421–429.

Cremer, S., Armitage, S.A.O. & Schmid-Hempel, P. (2007) Social immunity. *Current Biology*, **17**, R693–R702.

Dawkins, R. (1982) *The Extended Phenotype*. Oxford: W.H. Freeman.

de Meeus, T., McCoy, K.D., Prugnolle, F., et al. (2006) Population genetics and molecular ecology or how to "debusquer la bête". *Infection, Genetics and Evolution*, **7**, 308–332.

Deshwal, S. & Mallon, E.B. (2014) Antimicrobial peptides play a functional role in bumblebee anti-trypanosome defense. *Developmental & Comparative Immunology*, **42**, 240–243.

Dias, F.d.A., Vasconcellos, L.R.d.C., Romeiro, A., et al. (2014) Transovum transmission of trypanosomatid cysts in the milkweed bug, *Oncopeltus fasciatus*. *PLoS ONE*, **9**, e108746.

Durrer, S. (1996) Parasite load and assemblages of bumblebee species. PhD thesis. Department of Environmental Sciences, ETH Zurich, Zürich: Verlag Studentenschaft.

Durrer, S. & Schmid-Hempel, P. (1994) Shared use of flowers leads to horizontal pathogen transmission. *Proceedings of the Royal Society of London B*, **258**, 299–302.

Durrer, S. & Schmid-Hempel, P. (1995) Parasites and the regional distribution of bumble bee species. *Ecography*, **18**, 114–122.

Dussaubat, C., Brunet, J.-L., Higes, M., et al. (2012) Gut pathology and responses to the microsporidium *Nosema ceranae* in the honey bee, *Apis mellifera*. *PLoS ONE*, **7**, e37017.

Ebert, D., Duneau, D., Hall, M.D., et al. (2016) A population biology perspective on the stepwise infection process of the bacterial pathogen *Pasteuria ramosa* in *Daphnia*. *Advances in Parasitology*, **91**, 265–310.

Engel, P., Martinson, V.G. & Moran, N.A. (2012) Functional diversity within the simple gut microbiota of the honey bee. *Proceedings of the National Academy of Sciences of the United States of America*, **109**, 11,002–11,007.

Engel, P. & Moran, N.A. (2013a) Functional and evolutionary insights into the simple yet specific gut microbiota of the honey bee from metagenomic analysis. *Gut Microbes*, **4**, 60–65.

Engel, P. & Moran, N.A. (2013b) The gut microbiota of insects – diversity in structure and function. *FEMS Microbiological Reviews*, **37**, 699–735.

Erler, S., Popp, M., Wolf, S. & Lattorff, H.M.G. (2012) Sex, horizontal transmission, and multiple hosts prevent local adaptation of *Crithidia bombi*, a parasite of bumblebees (*Bombus* spp.). *Ecology and Evolution*, **2**, 930–940.

Estoup, A., Solignac, M., Cornuet, J.M., Goudet, J. & Scholl, A. (1996) Genetic differentiation of continental and island populations of *Bombus terrestris* (Hymenoptera: Apidae) in Europe. *Molecular Ecology*, **5**, 19–31.

Ewald, P.W. (1980) Evolutionary biology and the treatment of signs and symptoms of infectious disease. *Journal of Theoretical Biology*, **86**, 169–176.

Ewald, P.W. (1983) Host–parasite relations, vectors, and the evolution of disease severity. *Annual Review of Ecology and Systematics*, **14**, 465–485.

Fenton, A., Antonovics, J. & Brockhurst, M.A. (2009) Inverse gene-for-gene infection genetics and coevolutionary dynamics. *The American Naturalist*, **174**, E230–E242.

Fitzpatrick, U., Murray, T.E., Paxton, R.J., *et al.* (2007) Rarity and decline in bumblebees – a test of causes and correlates in the Irish fauna. *Biological Conservation*, **136**, 185–194.

Flegontov, P., Butenko, A., Firsov, S., et al. (2015). Genome of *Leptomonas pyrrhocoris*: a high-quality reference for monoxenous trypanosomatids and new insights into evolution of *Leishmania*. *Scientific Reports*, **6**, 23704.

Folly, A.J., Koch, H., Stevenson, P.C. & Brown, M.J.F. (2017) Larvae act as a transient transmission hub for the prevalent bumblebee parasite *Crithidia bombi*. *Journal of Invertebrate Pathology*, **148**, 81–85.

Fouks, B. & Lattorff, H.M.G. (2011) Recognition and avoidance of contaminated flowers by foraging bumblebees (*Bombus terrestris*). *PLoS ONE*, **6**, e26328.

Frank, S.A. (1994) Coevolutionary genetics of hosts and parasites with quantitative inheritance. *Evolutionary Ecology*, **8**, 74–94.

Frank, S.A. & Schmid-Hempel, P. (2008) Mechanisms of pathogenesis and the evolution of parasite virulence. *Journal of Evolutionary Biology*, **21**, 396–404.

Fürst, M.A., McMahon, D.P., Osborne, J.L., Paxton, R.J. & Brown, M.J.F. (2014) Disease associations between honeybees and bumblebees as a threat to wild pollinators. *Nature*, **506**, 364–366.

Gallot-Lavallée, M., Schmid-Hempel, R., Vandamme, R., Vergara, C.H. & Schmid-Hempel, P. (2016) Large scale patterns of abundance and distribution of parasites in Mexican bumblebees. *Journal of Invertebrate Pathology*, **133**, 73–83.

Gandon, S. & Michalakis, Y. (2002) Local adaptation, evolutionary potential and host–parasite coevolution: interactions between migration, mutation, population size and generation time. *Journal of Evolutionary Biology*, **15**, 451–462.

Gaunt, M.W., Yeo, M., Frame, I.A., et al. (2003) Mechanism of genetic exchange in American trypanosomes. *Nature*, **421**, 936–939.

Gegear, R.J., Otterstatter, M.C. & Thomson, J.D. (2006) Bumble-bee foragers infected by a gut parasite have an impaired ability to utilize floral information. *Proceedings of the Royal Society of London B*, **273**, 1073–1078.

Gibson, W. & Stevens, J. (1999) Genetic exchange in the Trypanosomatidae. *Advances in Parasitology*, **43**, 1–46.

Gillespie, S.D. & Adler, L.S. (2013) Indirect effects on mutualisms: parasitism of bumble bees and pollination service to plants. *Ecology*, **94**, 454–464.

Gillespie, S.D., Carrero, K. & Adler, L.S. (2015) Relationships between parasitism, bumblebee foraging behaviour, and pollination service to *Trifolium pratense* flowers. *Ecological Entomology*, **40**, 650–653.

Goulson, D. (2003a) *Bumblebees – Their Behaviour and Ecology*. New York, NY: Oxford University Press.

Goulson, D. (2003b) Conserving wild bees for crop pollination. *Food, Agriculture & Environment*, **1**, 142–144.

Goulson, D., Lye, G.C. & Darvill, B. (2008) Decline and conservation of bumble bees. *Annual Review of Ecology and Systematics*, **53**, 191–208.

Graystock, P., Goulson, D. & Hughes, W.O.H. (2015) Parasites in bloom: flowers aid dispersal and transmission of pollinator parasites within and between bee species. *Proceedings of the Royal Society of London B*, **282**.

Hamilton, W.D. (1980) Sex versus non-sex versus parasite. *Oikos*, **35**, 282–290.

Hamilton, W.D., Axelrod, A. & Tanese, R. (1990) Sexual reproduction as an adaptation to resist parasites (a review). *Proceedings of the National Academy of Sciences of the United States of America*, **87**, 3566–3573.

Hamilton, W.D. & Zuk, M. (1982) Heritable true fitness and bright birds: a role for parasites? *Science*, **218**, 384–387.

Howard, R.S. & Lively, C.M. (2002) The Ratchet and the Red Queen: the maintenance of sex in parasites. *Journal of Evolutionary Biology*, **15**, 648–656.

Imhoof, B. & Schmid-Hempel, P. (1999) Colony success of the bumble bee, *Bombus terrestris*, in relation to infections by two protozoan parasites, *Crithidia bombi* and *Nosema bombi*. *Insectes Sociaux*, **46**, 233–238.

Inoue, M.N., Yokoyama, J. & Tsuchida, K. (2010) Colony growth and reproductive ability of feral nests of the introduced bumblebee *Bombus terrestris* in northern Japan. *Insectes Sociaux*, **57**, 29–38.

Ishemgulova, A., Butenko, A., Kortisiova, L., *et al.* (2017) Molecular mechanisms of thermal resistance of the insect trypanosomatid *Crithidia thermophila*. *PLoS ONE*, **12**, e0174165.

Koch, H., Abrol, D.P., Li, J. & Schmid-Hempel, P. (2013) Diversity and possible evolutionary patterns of bacterial gut associates of corbiculate bees. *Molecular Ecology*, **22**, 2028–2044.

Koch, H. & Schmid-Hempel, P. (2011a) Bacterial communities in Central European bumblebees: low diversity and high specificity. *Microbial Ecology*, **62**, 121–133.

Koch, H. & Schmid-Hempel, P. (2011b) Socially transmitted gut microbiota protect bumble bees against an intestinal parasite. *Proceedings of the National Academy of Sciences of the United States of America*, **108**, 19,288–19,292.

Koch, H. & Schmid-Hempel, P. (2012) Gut microbiota instead of host genotype drive the specificity in the interaction of a natural host–parasite system. *Ecology Letters*, **15**, 1095–1103.

König, C. & Schmid-Hempel, P. (1995) Foraging activity and immunocompetence in workers of the bumble bee, *Bombus terrestris* L. *Proceedings of the Royal Society of London B*, **260**, 225–227.

Korner, P. & Schmid-Hempel, P. (2004) In vivo dynamics of an immune response in the bumble bee *Bombus terrestris*. *Journal of Invertebrate Pathology*, **87**, 59–66.

Kwong, W.K., Engel, P., Koch, H. & Moran, N.A. (2014) Genomics and host specialization of honey bee and bumble bee gut symbionts. *Proceedings of the National Academy of Sciences of the United States of America*, **111**, 11,509–11,514.

Leggett, H.C., Cornwallis, C.K. & West, S.A. (2012) Mechanisms of pathogenesis, infective dose and virulence in human parasites. *PLoS Pathogens*, **8**, e1002512.

Lemaitre, B. (2012) The drosophila gut: a new paradigm for epithelial immune response. *Cytokine*, **59**, 494.

Ley, R.E., Lozupone, C.A., Hamady, M., Knight, R. & Gordon, J.I. (2008) Worlds within worlds: evolution of the vertebrate gut microbiota. *Nature Reviews Microbiology*, **6**, 776–788.

Li, J., Chen, W., Wu, J., et al. (2012) Diversity of *Nosema* associated with bumblebees (*Bombus* spp.) from China. *International Journal of Parasitology*, **42**, 49–61.

Little, T.J. & Kraaijeveld, A.R. (2004) Ecological and evolutionary implications of immunological priming in invertebrates. *Trends in Ecology and Evolution*, **19**, 58–60.

Luijckx, P., Fienberg, H., Duneau, D. & Ebert, D. (2013) A matching-allele model explains host resistance to parasites. *Current Biology*, **23**, 1–4.

MacLeod, A., Tweedie, A., McLellan, S., et al. (2005) Allelic segregation and independent assortment in *Trypanosoma brucei* crosses: proof that the genetic system is Mendelian and involves meiosis. *Molecular and Biochemical Parasitology*, **143**, 12–19.

Maharramov, J., Meeus, I., Maebe, K., et al. (2013) Genetic variability of the Neogregarine *Apicystis bombi*, an etiological agent of an emergent bumblebee disease. *PLoS ONE*, **8**, e81475.

Manley, R., Boots, M. & Bayer-Wilfert, L. (2017) Condition-dependent virulence of Slow Bee Paralysis Virus in *Bombus terrestris*: are the impacts of honeybee viruses in wild pollinators underestimated? *Oecologia*, **184**, 305–315.

Martinez-Calvillo, S., Vizuet-de-Rueda, J.C., Florencio-Martinez, L.E., Manning-Cela, R. G. & Figuera-Angulo, E.E. (2010) Gene expression in trypanosomatid parasites. *Journal of Biomedicine and Biotechnology*, **2010**, 525241.

Martinson, V.G., Danforth, B.N., Minckley, R.L., et al. (2011) A simple and distinctive microbiota associated with honey bees and bumble bees. *Molecular Ecology*, **20**, 619–628.

Marxer, M., Barribeau, S.M. & Schmid-Hempel, P. (2016a) Experimental evolution of a trypanosome parasite of bumblebees and its implications for infection success and host immune response. *Evolutionary Biology*, **43**, 160–170.

Marxer, M., Vollenweider, V. & Schmid-Hempel, P. (2016b) Insect antimicrobial

peptides act synergistically to inhibit a trypanosome parasite. *Philosophical Transactions of the Royal Society B*, **371**, 20150302.

McArt, S.H., Koch, H., Irwin, R.E. & Adler, L.S. (2014) Arranging the bouquet of disease: floral traits and the transmission of plant and animal pathogens. *Ecology Letters*, **17**, 624–636.

McMahon, D., Fürst, M., Caspar, J., et al. (2015) A sting in the spit: widespread cross-infection of multiple RNA viruses across wild and managed bees. *Journal of Animal Ecology*, **84**, 615–624.

Mikaelyan, A., Thompson, C.L., Hofer, M.J. & Brune, A. (2015) Deterministic assembly of complex bacterial communities in guts of germ-free cockroaches. *Applied and Environmental Microbiology*, **82**, 1256–1263.

Mikkola, K. (1984) Migration of wasp and bumble bee queens across the Gulf of Finland (Hymenoptera: Vespidae and Apidae). *Notulae Entomologica*, **64**, 125–128.

Moore, J. (1984) Parasites and altered host behavior. *Scientific American*, **250**, 108–115.

Moran, N.A., Hansen, A.K., Powell, J.E. & Sabree, Z.L. (2012) Distinctive gut microbiota of honey bees assessed using deep sampling from individual worker bees. *PLoS ONE*, **7**, e36393.

Moret, Y. & Schmid-Hempel, P. (2000) Survival for immunity: the price of immune system activation for bumblebee workers. *Science*, **290**, 1166–1168.

Müller, C.B. & Schmid-Hempel, P. (1993) Correlates of reproductive success among field colonies of *Bombus lucorum* L.: the importance of growth and parasites. *Ecological Entomology*, **17**, 343–353.

Näpflin, K. & Schmid-Hempel, P. (2018) Host effects on microbiota community assembly. *Journal of Animal Ecology*, **87**, 331–340.

Näpflin, K. & Schmid-Hempel, P. (2018) High gut microbiota diversity provides lower resistance against infection by an intestinal parasite. *American Naturalist*, **192**, 131–141.

Otterstatter, M.C., Gegear, R.J., Colla, S. & Thomson, J.D. (2005) Effects of parasitic mites and protozoa on the flower constancy and foraging rate of bumble bees. *Behavioural Ecology and Scoiobiology*, **58**, 383–389.

Peters, A.D. & Lively, C.M. (1999) The Red Queen and fluctuating epistasis: a population genetic analysis of antagonistic coevolution. *The American Naturalist*, **154**, 393–405.

Råberg, L., Sim, D. & Read, A.F. (2007) Disentangling genetic variation for resistance and tolerance to infectious diseases in animals. *Science*, **318**, 812–814.

Rahnamaeian, M., Cytryńska, M., Zdybicka-Barabas, A., et al. (2015) Insect antimicrobial peptides show potentiating functional interactions against Gram-negative bacteria. *Proceedings of the Royal Society of London B*, **282**, 20150293.

Ravoet, J., Schwarz, R.S., Descamps, T., et al. (2015) Differential diagnosis of the honey bee trypanosomatids *Crithidia mellificae* and *Lotmaria passim*. *Journal of Invertebrate Pathology*, **130**, 21–27.

Rheins, L.A. & Karp, R.D. (1986) Effect of gender on the inducible humoral immune response to honeybee venom in the American cockroach (*Periplaneta americana*). *Developmental and Comparative Immunology*, **9**, 41–49.

Richardson, L.L., Adler, L.S., Leonard, A.S., et al. (2015) Secondary metabolites in floral nectar reduce parasite infections in bumblebees. *Proceedings of the Royal Society of London B*, **282**, 20142471.

Richardson, L.L., Bowers, M.D. & Irwin, R.E. (2016) Nectar chemistry mediates the behavior of parasitized bees: consequences for plant fitness. *Ecology*, **97**, 325–337.

Riddell, C., Adams, S., Schmid-Hempel, P., Mallon, E.B. & Rankin, D.J. (2009). Differential expression of immune defences is associated with specific host–parasite interactions in insects. *PLoS ONE*, **4**, e7621.

Riddell, C.E., Lobaton Garces, J.D., Adams, S., et al. (2014) Differential gene expression and alternative splicing in insect immune specificity. *BMC Genomics*, **15**, 1031.

Riddell, C.E., Sumner, S., Adams, S. & Mallon, E. B. (2011) Pathways to immunity: temporal dynamics of the bumblebee (*Bombus terrestris*) immune response against a trypanosome gut parasite. *Insect Molecular Biology*, **20**, 529–540.

Routtu, J. & Ebert, D. (2015) Genetic architecture of resistance in *Daphnia* hosts against two species of host-specific parasites. *Heredity*, **114**, 241–248.

Ruiz-Gonzalez, M.X., Bryden, J., Moret, Y., et al. (2012) Dynamic transmission, host quality and population structure in a multi-host parasite of bumble bees. *Evolution*, **66**, 3052–3066.

Sadd, B., Kleinlogel, Y., Schmid-Hempel, R. & Schmid-Hempel, P. (2005) Trans-generational immune priming in a social insect. *Biology Letters*, **1**, 386–388.

Sadd, B. & Schmid-Hempel, P. (2006) Insect immunity shows specificity in protection upon secondary pathogen exposure. *Current Biology*, **16**, 1206–1210.

Sadd, B. & Schmid-Hempel, P. (2007) Facultative but persistent trans-generational immunity via the mother's eggs in bumblebees. *Current Biology*, **17**, R1046–R1047.

Sadd, B. & Schmid-Hempel, P. (2009) A distinct infection cost associated with trans-generational immune priming of antibacterial immunity in bumble-bees. *Biology Letters*, **5**, 798–801.

Sadd, B.M., Barribeau, S.M., Bloch, G., et al. (2015) The genomes of two key bumblebee species with primitive eusocial organization. *Genome Biology*, **16**, 76.

Salathé, M., Kouyos, R.D. & Bonhoeffer, S. (2008) The state of affairs in the kingdom of the Red Queen. *Trends in Ecology and Evolution*, **23**, 439–445.

Salathé, R. & Schmid-Hempel, P. (2011) Genotypic structure of a multi-host bumblebee parasite suggests a major role for ecological niche overlap. *PLoS ONE*, **6**, e22054.

Salathé, R. & Schmid-Hempel, P. (2012) Probing mixed-genotype infections I: extraction and cloning of infections from hosts of the trypanosomatid *Crithidia bombi*. *PLoS ONE*, **7**, e49046.

Sasaki, A. (2000) Host–parasite coevolution in a multilocus gene-for-gene system.

Proceedings of the Royal Society of London B, **267**, 2183–2188.

Sauter, A., Brown, M.J.F., Baer, B. & Schmid-Hempel, P. (2001) Males of social insects can prevent queens from multiple mating. *Proceedings of the Royal Society of London B*, **268**, 1449–1454.

Schaub, G.A. (1992) The effects of trypanosomatids on insects. *Advances in Parasitology*, **31**, 255–319.

Schlüns, H., Sadd, B.M., Schmid-Hempel, P. & Crozier, R.H. (2010). Infection with the trypanosome *Crithidia bombi* and expression of immune-related genes in the bumblebee *Bombus terrestris*. *Developmental and Comparative Immunology*, **34**, 705–709.

Schmid-Hempel, P. (1998) *Parasites in Social Insects*. Princeton, NJ: Princeton University Press.

Schmid-Hempel, P. (2001) On the evolutionary ecology of host–parasite interactions – addressing the questions with bumblebees and their parasites. *Naturwissenschaften*, **88**, 147–158.

Schmid-Hempel, P. (2003) Variation in immune defence as a question of evolutionary ecology. *Proceedings of the Royal Society of London B*, **270**, 357–366.

Schmid-Hempel, P. (2005) Natural insect host–parasite systems show immune priming and specificity – puzzles to be solved. *BioEssays*, **27**, 1026–1034.

Schmid-Hempel, P. (2011) *Evolutionary Parasitology – The Integrated Study of Infections, Immunology, Ecology, and Genetics*. Oxford: Oxford University Press.

Schmid-Hempel, P. (2017) Parasites and their social hosts. *Trends in Parasitology*, **33**, 453–462.

Schmid-Hempel, P., Aebi, M., Barribeau, S., et al. (2018) The genomes of *Crithidia bombi* and *C. expoeki*, common parasites of bumblebees. *PLoS ONE*, **13**(1), e0189738.

Schmid-Hempel, P. & Frank, S.A. (2007) Pathogenesis, virulence, and infective dose. *PLoS Pathogens*, **3**, 1372–1373.

Schmid-Hempel, P., Puhr, K., Kruger, N., Reber, C. & Schmid-Hempel, R. (1999) Dynamic and genetic consequences of variation in horizontal transmission for a microparasitic infection. *Evolution*, **53**, 426–434.

Schmid-Hempel, P. & Reber Funk, C. (2004) The distribution of genotypes of the trypanosome parasite, *Crithidia bombi*, in populations of its host, *Bombus terrestris*. *Parasitology*, **129**, 147–158.

Schmid-Hempel, P. & Schmid-Hempel, R. (1993) Transmission of a pathogen in *Bombus terrestris*, with a note on division of labour in social insects. *Behavioural Ecology and Sociobiology*, **33**, 319–327.

Schmid-Hempel, P. & Stauffer, H.P. (1998). Parasites and flower choice of bumblebees. *Animal Behaviour*, **55**, 819–825.

Schmid-Hempel, R., Eckhardt, M., Goulson, D., et al. (2013) The invasion of southern South America by imported bumblebees and associated parasites. *Journal of Animal Ecology*, **83**, 823–837.

Schmid-Hempel, R. & Schmid-Hempel, P. (2000) Female mating frequencies in social insects: *Bombus* spp. from Central Europe. *Insectes Sociaux*, **47**, 36–41.

Schmid-Hempel, R. & Tognazzo, M. (2010) Molecular divergence defines two distinct lineages of *Crithidia bombi* (Trypanosomatidae), parasites of bumblebees. *Journal of Eukaryotic Microbiology*, **57**, 337–345.

Schmid-Hempel, R., Tognazzo, M., Salathé, R. & Schmid-Hempel, P. (2011) Genetic exchange and emergence of novel strains in directly transmitted trypanosomatids. *Infection, Genetics, and Evolution*, **11**, 564–571.

Schwarz, R.S., Bauchan, G., Murphy, C., et al. (2015) Characterization of two species of Trypanosomatidae from the honey bee *Apis mellifera*: *Crithidia mellificae* Langridge and McGhee, 1967 and *Lotmaria passim* n. gen., n. sp. *Journal of Eukaryotic Microbiology*, **62**, 567–583.

Schwarz, R.S. & Evans, J.D. (2013) Single and mixed-species trypanosome and microsporidia infections elicit distinct, ephemeral cellular and humoral immune responses in honey bees. *Developmental & Comparative Immunology*, **40**, 300–310.

Shykoff, J.A. & Schmid-Hempel, P. (1991) Parasites delay worker reproduction in bumblebees: consequences for eusociality. *Behavioral Ecology*, **2**, 242–248.

Simpson, A., Stevens, J. & Lukes, J. (2006) The evolution and diversity of kinetoplastid flagellates. *Trends in Parasitology*, **22**, 168–174.

Stout, J.C. & Goulson, D. (2001) The use of conspecific and interspecific scent marks by foraging bumblebees and honeybees. *Animal Behaviour*, **62**, 183–189.

Tait, A., Morrison, L.J., Duffy, C.W., et al. (2011). Trypanosome genetics: populations, phenotypes and diversity. *Veterinary Parasitology*, **181**, 61–68.

Tibayrenc, M. & Ayala, F.J. (2002) The clonal theory of parasitic protozoa: 12 years on. *Trends in Parasitology*, **18**, 405–410.

Tibayrenc, M. & Ayala, F.J. (2013) How clonal are *Trypanosoma* and *Leishmania*? *Trends in Parasitology*, **29**, 264–269.

Tognazzo, M., Schmid-Hempel, R. & Schmid-Hempel, P. (2012) Probing mixed-genotype infections II: high multiplicity in natural infections of the trypanosomatid, *Crithidia bombi*, in its host, *Bombus* spp. *PLoS ONE*, **7**, e49137.

Ulrich, Y., Sadd, B. & Schmid-Hempel, P. (2011) Strain filtering and transmission of a mixed infection in a social insect. *Journal of Evolutionary Biology*, **24**, 354–362.

Ulrich, Y. & Schmid-Hempel, P. (2012) Host modulation of parasite competition in multiple infections. *Proceedings of the Royal Society of London B*, **279**, 2982–2989.

Ulrich, Y. & Schmid-Hempel, P. (2015) The distribution of parasite strains among hosts affects disease spread in a social insect. *Infection, Genetics, Evolution*, **32**, 348–353.

Van Boven, M. & Weissing, F.J. (2004) The evolutionary economics of immunity. *The American Naturalist*, **163**, 277–294.

Velthuis, H.H.W. & van Doorn, A. (2006) A century of advances in bumblebee domestication and the economic and environmental aspects of its commercialization for pollination. *Apidologie*, **37**, 421–451.

Widmer, A. & Schmid-Hempel, P. (1999) The population genetic structure of a large temperate pollinator species, *Bombus pascuorum* (Scopoli) (Hymenoptera, Apidae). *Molecular Ecology*, **8**, 387–398.

Widmer, A., Schmid-Hempel, P., Estoup, A. & Scholl, A. (1998) Population genetic structure and colonization history of *Bombus terrestris* s.l. (Hymenoptera: Apidae) from the Canary Islands and Madeira. *Heredity*, **81**, 563–572.

Wilfert, L., Gadau, J., Baer, B. & Schmid-Hempel, P. (2007) Natural variation in the genetic architecture of a host–parasite interaction in the bumblebee, *Bombus terrestris*. *Molecular Ecology*, **16**, 1327–1339.

Williams, P.H., Brown, M.J.F., Carolan, J.C., et al. (2012) Assessing cryptic species of the bumblebee subgenus *Bombus* s. str. world-wide with COI barcodes (Hymenoptera: Apidae). *Systematics and Biodiversity*, **10**, 21–56.

Williams, P.H., Cameron, S.A., Hines, H.M., Cederbergc, B. & Rasmont, P. (2008) A simplified subgeneric classification of the bumblebees (genus *Bombus*). *Apidologie*, **39**, 1–29.

Wilson, K., Thomas, M.B., Blanford, S., et al. (2002) Coping with crowds: density-dependent disease resistance in desert locusts. *Proceedings of the National Academy of Sciences of the United States of America*, **99**, 5471–5475.

Yourth, C.P. (2004) Virulence and transmission of *Crithidia bombi* in bumble bees. PhD thesis, ETH Zurich. Zurich: ETH Zurich.

Yourth, C.P. & Schmid-Hempel, P. (2006) Serial passage of the parasite *Crithidia bombi* within a colony of its host, *Bombus terrestris*, reduces success in unrelated hosts. *Proceedings of the Royal Society of London B*, **273**, 655–659.

Zasloff, M. (2013) *Antimicrobial Peptides*. New York, NY: John Wiley & Son.

Zuk, M.& Stoehr, A.M. (2002) Immune defence and host life history. *American Naturalist*, **160**, S9–S22.

CHAPTER TWO

Genetic diversity and disease spread: epidemiological models and empirical studies of a snail–trematode system

AMANDA K. GIBSON AND CURTIS M. LIVELY

2.1 Introduction

Questions in disease ecology/evolution often concern the relationship between genetic diversity and disease spread: does host genetic diversity reduce the spread of infection through a population? Is sex favoured as a strategy to diversify offspring in the face of coevolving parasites?

In the present chapter, we address these questions with theory, combined with field and experimental data. In the first section, we review recent work that brings some ecological and epidemiological realism into population genetic models of host–parasite coevolution. Relaxing a few simplifying assumptions allows for feedbacks between ecology, epidemiology, and evolution. With this combination of genetics and ecology, we explore the effect of genetic diversity and coevolution on disease spread in an epidemiological model.

In the second section, we review recent empirical work on a snail–trematode interaction. We discuss evidence for the assumptions and predictions of theoretical models in this natural host–parasite interaction. Long-term field studies suggest that genetic variation in the snail *Potamopyrgus antipodarum* may suppress the spread of the castrating parasite *Microphallus*. Experimental work and biogeographic surveys also support the prediction that coevolution can increase the spread of disease and select for sexual reproduction. Throughout the chapter, we endeavour to show the positive synergism between theory and data.

2.2 Coevolutionary models of sex and disease spread

In the past decade, we've attempted to infuse the population genetic models of host–parasite coevolution with more epidemiological and ecology reality (following May & Anderson, 1983). The early models of host–parasite coevolution, including ours, made several simplifying assumptions. One such assumption was that each host comes into contact with exactly one parasite propagule.

This is a useful simplifying assumption, because the probability of infection for each host genotype then depends only on the frequency of parasites that can infect that genotype. However, in nature, it seems much more likely that hosts come into contact with a variable number of parasites, and that this number changes in time and space. The question is: would it matter? Is the simplifying assumption of population genetic models robust to epidemiological details? The problem can also be turned on its head: epidemiological models typically assume that all hosts are equally susceptible to infection. Are the conclusions of epidemiological models robust to the inclusion of genetic variation for resistance among host genotypes? In other words, does genetic variation affect disease spread?

2.2.1 Genetic diversity and disease spread

Combining genetic variation with epidemiology complicates the model, but it allows for the possibility of generation-by-generation feedbacks between ecology and evolution. In an analytical model of disease spread, we introduced genetic variation by including multiple host and parasite genotypes. We assumed that parasites must genetically match their hosts to infect, which mirrors the self–non-self recognition system of invertebrates. This is known as the matching alleles model (see Box 2.1). Importantly, we relaxed the assumption that all hosts are exposed to a single parasite propagule. We instead assumed that the number of exposures per host depends on the number of infected hosts in the previous time step (Lively, 2010c).

R_0 is the standard measure of a parasite's potential for disease spread. It gives the number of secondary infections produced by an infected host in a susceptible population. In Lively's (2010b) model, R_0 turns out to be density-dependent, as in standard epidemiological models. It also turns out to be dependent on the frequencies of the different host genotypes. However, the effects of density are asymptotic on host abundance, such that increasing host density has very minor effects on R_0 in host populations greater than several hundred individuals (King & Lively, 2012). Taking the limit as host density increases to infinity, density drops out of the expression for R_0, which simplifies to:

$$R_0 = B/H, \tag{2.1}$$

where H is the number of host genotypes and B is the number of parasite propagules produced by each infection that makes contact with hosts. Thus, the variable, B, can be seen as a maximum for parasite fitness. It is easy to see from Equation 2.1 that R_0 is inversely proportional to the number of matching host genotypes in the population (Figure 2.1). This result gives weight to the conventional wisdom that increasing genetic diversity reduces the risk of disease spread (King & Lively, 2012).

Box 2.1: Simple models of infection genetics

The outcomes of coevolutionary models depend upon how we choose to model the genetic interaction of a host and parasite. This box gives a basic introduction to classic models of infection genetics. Typically, in these models, a parasite genotype is able to infect some host genotypes and not others, and a host genotype is able to resist some parasite genotypes and not others.

Matching alleles
Parasites 'match' to infect. This model reflects a self–non-self recognition system of host defence, modelled after the invertebrate immune system. Parasites are under selection to match the host's 'self' markers to avoid being identified as 'non-self'. The host's immune system destroys anything marked as 'non-self' (Grosberg & Hart, 2000). Because parasites must genetically match a host to infect, a parasite can only infect one, or a subset, of host genotypes (Frank, 1993, 1996) (infection only on diagonals – Figure B2.1.1A). Matching alleles interactions can favour local adaptation of the parasite: if we assume that hosts kill parasites that fail to match, parasites are under strong selection to match local hosts. Coevolutionary models that use a matching alleles interaction tend to support the idea that antagonistic coevolution can maintain genetic variation and sexual reproduction. The reason is that there is an advantage to being a rare genotype in matching alleles systems: parasite genotypes that can match rare host genotypes are themselves likely rare. Accordingly, Equation 2.1 shows that adding genotypes, or diversity, to host populations decreases the frequency of hosts that a parasite can infect, thereby suppressing disease spread (Lively, 2010, 2016; King & Lively, 2012).

Inverse-matching alleles
Hosts match to resist. This model is the reverse of the matching alleles model. For this model, we can imagine that hosts are under selection to identify (match) specific markers on or produced by a parasite, much like the MHC recognition system of vertebrates. Identification triggers an immune response, and the host successfully resists the matched parasite (Frank, 1993, 1994). From the parasite perspective, inverse-matching interactions mean that parasites can infect all but the host or subset of hosts with which it has a genetic match (infection on off-diagonals – Figure B2.1.1B). This system does not favour local adaptation of the parasite: inverse-matching places stronger selection on the host to match local parasites. We can see that the inverse-matching system will not favour rare host genotypes: common parasite genotypes will probably be able to infect rare host genotypes, which have not been selected for specific resistance against the circulating parasite genotypes. Similarly, genetic diversity increases disease spread under the inverse-matching system, because

Box 2.1: (cont.)

adding host genotypes increases the frequency of hosts that a parasite can infect (Lively, 2016).

Gene-for-gene

This model is much like the inverse-matching alleles model, with the addition of a universally infective parasite genotype. The gene-for-gene model arose from the study of plant–parasite interactions, notably those of crop plants (Flor, 1956). In its simplest form, a parasite produces an elicitor (like the parasite markers in inverse-matching, above). The host either lacks the receptor for this elicitor, in which case infection results, or has the receptor, in which case the host resists (e.g. Figure B2.1.1C: host 2 has a receptor that recognises an elicitor from parasite 2, but not parasite 3). The key difference from inverse-matching alleles is that a parasite genotype may theoretically lack an elicitor altogether, in which case it can infect all host genotypes (parasite genotype 1 in Figure B2.1.1C; universal infectivity, also known as virulence in the plant literature). As for inverse-matching alleles, there is no advantage to rare genotypes in this system. However, by adding costs for host resistance and parasite infectivity, a gene-for-gene interaction could theoretically maintain genetic variation (reviewed in Frank, 1992).

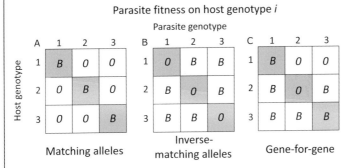

Figure B2.1.1 Infection matrixes for three models of infection genetics: (A) matching alleles, (B) inverse-matching alleles, and (C) gene-for-gene. Each matrix shows the outcomes of the interaction between three host genotypes (rows) and three parasite genotypes (columns). Diagonals are shaded grey and off-diagonals white. The value in the box gives the fitness of the parasite. '0' means the infection fails and the parasite makes zero offspring, i.e. transmissible propagules. The host experiences no fitness cost of parasitism. 'B' means the parasite successfully infects the host and makes B transmissible propagules (see Equation 2.1). The host experiences a corresponding fitness loss.

One might, of course, wonder how well these simple models reflect the infection genetics underlying natural host–parasite interactions. Real-world interactions may blend multiple infection models (as in Agrawal &

Box 2.1: (cont.)

Lively, 2002; Engelstädter & Bonhoeffer, 2009) or have multiple steps for infection, each with unique genetics (as in Agrawal & Lively, 2003; Fenton et al., 2012). Interestingly, the results of coevolutionary models are often robust to these complexities. For example, Engelstädter and Bonhoeffer (2009) tested if recombination was favoured under a wide range of non-standard infection matrixes. Selection for recombination is thought to require the strict specificity characteristic of the matching alleles model. However, they commonly observed selection for recombination in these non-standard matrixes. The key was not strict matching but a negative covariance between host and parasite fitness. Agrawal and Lively (2002) modelled a two-step infection process, in which hosts first detected parasites under a matching alleles interaction and then attacked them under a gene-for-gene interaction. The resulting dynamics tended to resemble those characteristics of a single interaction model, with pure matching alleles or pure gene-for-gene patterns depending upon the parameters.

References

Agrawal, A. & Lively, C.M. (2002) Infection genetics: gene-for-gene versus matching-alleles models and all points in between. *Evolution Ecology Research*, **4**, 79–90.

Agrawal, A. & Lively, C.M. (2003) Modelling infection as a two-step process combining gene-for-gene and matching-allele genetics. *Proceedings of the Royal Society of London B: Biological Sciences*, **270**, 323–334.

Engelstädter, J. & Bonhoeffer, S. (2009) Red Queen dynamics with non-standard fitness interactions. *PLoS Computational Biology*, **5**, e1000469.

Fenton, A., Antonovics, J. & Brockhurst, M.A. (2012) Two-step infection processes can lead to coevolution between functionally independent infection and resistance pathways. *Evolution*, **66**, 2030–2041.

Flor, H.H. (1956) The complementary genetic system in flax and flax rust. *Advances in Genetics*, **8**, 29–54.

Frank, S.A. (1992) Models of plant–pathogen coevolution. *Trends in Genetics*, **8**, 213–219.

Frank, S.A. (1993) Specificity versus detectable polymorphism in host–parasite genetics. *Proceedings of the Royal Society of London B*, **254**, 191–197.

Frank, S.A. (1994) Recognition and polymorphism in host–parasite genetics. *Philosophical Transactions of the Royal Society of London B*, **346**, 283–293.

Frank, S.A. (1996) Statistical properties of polymorphism in host–parasite genetics. *Evolutionary Ecology*, **10**, 307–317.

Grosberg, R. & Hart, M. (2000) Mate selection and the evolution of highly polymorphic self/nonself recognition genes. *Science*, **289**, 2111–2114.

King, K. & Lively, C. (2012) Does genetic diversity limit disease spread in natural host populations? *Heredity*, **109**, 199–203.

Lively, C.M. (2010) The effect of host genetic diversity on disease spread. *American Naturalist*, **175**, E149–E152.

Lively, C.M. (2016) Coevolutionary epidemiology: disease spread, local adaptation, and sex. *American Naturalist*, **187**, E77–E82.

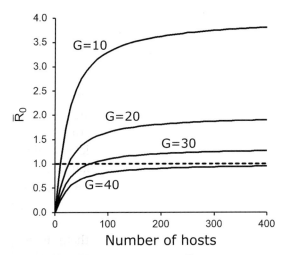

Figure 2.1 Mean parasite fitness, $\bar{R}_0$, as a function of the number of hosts in the population and the number of host genotypes (G) in the population. The dotted line gives the minimum value of $\bar{R}_0$ for the spread of infection. Redrawn from Lively (2010b).

2.2.2 Covariance and disease spread

The analytical model described above made a further simplifying assumption. It assumed that the parasite genotypes introduced into the host population are essentially random with respect to the frequencies of matching host genotypes. In other words, the model did not allow for the host and parasite populations to coevolve with each other. If coevolving parasites track common host genotypes, coevolution could lead to non-random distributions of genotypes. The frequencies of matching host and parasite genotypes would thus covary. Covariance here refers to the degree to which two variables vary together. A positive covariance means that a host genotype and its matching parasite genotype tend to both be common or both be rare. A negative covariance means that a host genotype tends to be common while its matching parasite genotype is rare, and vice versa. The question then becomes, what is the effect of covariance on disease spread (R_0)? And does the covariance change over time?

It turns out to be relatively simple to reformulate the solution for the average value of R_0 ($\bar{R}_0$) in a way that allows for a covariance between matching host–parasite genotypes (Lively, 2016). The solution becomes:

$$\bar{R}_0 = B[\text{Pcov}(p, h) + 1/H],\tag{2.2}$$

where $\text{cov}(p,h)$ is the covariance between matching parasite and host genotypes. The parameter P is the number of parasite genotypes and H is the number of host genotypes. We assume that $P = H$. The covariance term captures the coevolution between host and parasite. It can increase or decrease $\bar{R}_0$ depending on its sign. We expect a positive covariance between parasite genotype frequencies and their matching host genotype frequencies when the parasite population is adapted to infect the common genotypes circulating in the host population. This positive covariance increases disease spread. It is easy to see that if the covariance is equal to zero, then the solution simplifies to the previous model: $\bar{R}_0 = B/H$.

A numerical simulation showed that the covariance does differ from zero in most generations (Lively, 2016). More specifically, the covariance oscillates from positive to negative. However, the covariance was positive on average, especially when virulence (the fitness cost of infection) was high. In other words, matching host and parasite genotypes tended to both be common or both be rare. The exact reason for why the mean covariance is positive is not clear. It may stem from the model's assumption that a host kills any non-matching parasites. This assumption means that selection is stronger on the parasite, leading to a more rapid response to selection relative to the host population. Increasing parasite virulence increases the amplitude of the coevolutionary oscillations, which contributes to an increase in the magnitude of the covariance term.

This model can be used as a guide to understand adaptation by parasites to their local (sympatric) host populations. Assuming weak migration, the covariance between host and parasite genotypes in allopatric combinations should be near zero, as there is no coevolution between allopatric host and parasite populations, which are foreign to one another. In this case, R_0 is given by Equation 2.2 for sympatric pairings and Equation 2.1 for allopatric pairings. The fold-increase in R_0 for sympatric versus allopatric parasites is then:

$$L = 1 + PHcov(p,h). \tag{2.3}$$

Hence, intuitively, the strength of local adaptation depends on the covariance between host and parasite genotype frequencies in the sympatric populations (Lively, 2016). A more general result (which does not assume weak migration) was first derived by Gandon and Nuismer (2009). Note that the strength of local adaptation also depends on the number of host (H) and parasite (P) genotypes. However, the covariance term is unlikely to be independent of P and H. It may, in fact, be negatively correlated with these terms if the probability of a matching interaction declines as the number of host and parasite genotypes increases. In this case, increasing genetic diversity would reduce disease spread, even for a coevolving parasite.

All of the results mentioned above rely on the assumption that parasites must match their hosts to infect. What happens if the assumption is flipped, and hosts must match parasites to resist? This is the idea behind the inverse-matching alleles model of infection genetics (Box 2.1). The answer seems to be that (1) parasites would not be locally adapted, (2) they would not drive strong oscillatory dynamics in host genotype frequencies, and (3) they would not select for sexual reproduction in host populations (Lively, 2016). Hence, it would seem that some kind of self–non-self recognition system is critical to the conclusions drawn above. Fortunately for the model, evidence for self–non-self recognition systems is accumulating, at least in animal systems (Dybdahl et al., 2008; Luijckx et al., 2013; Bento et al., 2017).

2.2.3 Disease spread, coevolution, and sex

One of the major problems in evolutionary biology is the persistence of sexual reproduction in natural populations. This problem lies at the heart of our work on host–parasite coevolution. In a nutshell, the problem stems from the fact that males in sexual populations do not produce offspring. Thus, there is a reduction in the per-capita birth rate of the sexual population. This makes a sexual population subject to invasion and replacement by clonal lineages that produce only females (Maynard Smith, 1971). Using a strong-inference approach, early empirical work suggested that the presence of parasites was the best ecological predictor of the biogeographic distribution of sexual reproduction in a freshwater snail (Lively, 1987, 1992), which we introduce below. Experimental studies also showed strong local adaption by the most common parasite, a highly virulent trematode (Lively, 1989; Lively et al., 2004; King et al., 2009).

Early simulation models of host–parasite coevolution showed that parasites could indeed prevent the fixation of clonal lineages in otherwise sexual populations (Hamilton, 1980; Hamilton et al., 1990). Further models showed that host–parasite coevolution could fuel the accumulation of mutations in clonal lineages (Muller's ratchet), leading to their elimination (Howard & Lively, 1994, 1998). There is, however, one apparent weakness to the hypothesis that antagonistic coevolution maintains sex: parasite virulence and the risk of infection need to be very high to overcome the twofold cost of producing males in the short term (Howard & Lively, 1994; Otto & Nuismer, 2004). In what follows, we review two ecological considerations that could enhance the selective force of parasites in natural populations: epidemiological feedbacks and density-dependent virulence.

2.2.3.1 *Epidemiological feedbacks*

As pointed out above, most simulation models assume that each host makes contact with a single parasite propagule. Under the matching alleles model, this useful assumption means that the probability of infection depends only on the frequency of the different parasite genotypes. In a simulation model (Lively, 2010c), we relaxed this assumption, such that the probability of infection depended on both the frequency of matching parasite genotypes and the total number of host exposures to parasites. We then evaluated the spread of a clone into a sexual population.

In this model (Lively, 2010c), the clone produced the same total number of offspring as the average female in the sexual population. However, all the offspring of clonal females were themselves clonal females, whereas only half of the offspring produced by sexual females were female. This leads to a twofold increase in the per-capita birth rate of the clones, because the males in the sexual population do not directly produce offspring (Maynard Smith, 1971). Hence, Maynard Smith (1971) named the reduction in offspring production by sexual females the 'twofold cost of males'. In the absence of a countervailing force, clones rapidly replace sexuals due to the cost of males, at least in simulation models (Lively, 2009, 2010a, 2010c). Parasites could present a countervailing force, especially if parasite evolution leads to a positive covariance of host and parasite genotype frequencies. In other words, as the clonal genotype becomes common, an evolving parasite population becomes dominated by the parasite genotypes that can infect the common clone, leading to a positive covariance and thus parasite-mediated selection against the clone.

This predicted result turns out to be the case in computer simulations (Lively, 2016). There is also evidence for this effect in natural populations (Lively & Dybdahl, 2000; Jokela et al., 2009; Koskella & Lively, 2009). Interestingly, in simulations, the combination of epidemiology and genetics can increase the strength of parasite-mediated selection against common clones: as the host clone becomes increasingly common, the overall frequency of infection in the population increases. This leads to a greater number of exposures to parasite propagules in the next generation (Figure 2.2). Hence, there is a positive feedback between parasite evolution and the force of infection, which can increase the overall strength of selection against common host genotypes. Thus, selection is stronger against common clones and for sexual reproduction (Lively, 2010c). Such an effect would be missed in standard population genetic models, because they generally assume that all hosts are exposed to exactly one parasite in every generation. The effect would be equally missed in a genetics-free epidemiological model.

2.2.3.2 *Density-dependent virulence*

A complementary feedback between ecology and evolution has been observed in another model. In this model, the standard assumption of fixed virulence was relaxed so as to make virulence dependent on host density. This is known as density-dependent virulence. The idea here is simply that the fitness cost of infection for the host becomes more severe as host density increases. We can imagine multiple reasons that this might happen, such as starvation or stress leading to decreased body condition. There is also empirical evidence for

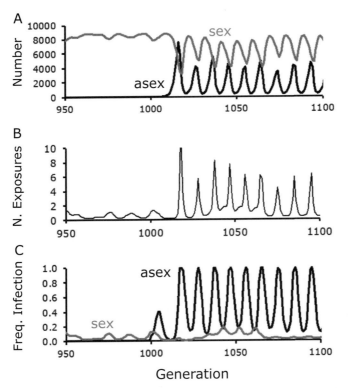

Figure 2.2 Computer simulation results showing (A) the number of sexual (sex) and asexual (asex) individuals over time; (B) the number of exposures per host over time; and (C) the frequency of infection in sexual and asexual individuals over time. The results show an unpublished but representative run of the simulation from Lively (2010c). The parameter values used in the simulations are as given in figure 4D–F of Lively (2010c). A single asexual clone was introduced at generation 1000. Note that the number of exposures tracks the frequency of asexual individuals with a slight lag. The rise and fall in the number of exposures signifies epidemiological feedbacks driven by fluctuations in the frequency of the clonal host.

density-dependent virulence (Augspurger & Kelly, 1984; Lively et al., 1995; Tseng, 2004; Bell et al., 2006).

Our model assumed that the host's carrying capacity (*K*) was not fixed, but rather dependent on the mean birth rate of the host population, as modelled by Pielou (1969). Under this assumption, the spread of a clone into a sexual population increases *K*, because the mean birth rate of the population increases as the clone becomes common. Accordingly, host density, and hence parasite virulence, increases as the clone becomes common. This increases the strength of parasite selection against the clone and leads to stronger selection for sexual reproduction (Lively, 2009).

2.3 Empirical parallels

The models described above are rooted in biological reality. They were partially inspired by the freshwater snail *Potamopyrgus antipodarum* and its sterilising trematode parasites, in particular the virulent *Microphallus*. Below, we will discuss the field and experimental data that support the assumptions and conclusions of these coevolutionary epidemiological models.

2.3.1 Natural history

2.3.1.1 *The host*

Potamopyrgus antipodarum (Gray) is a prosobranch snail of the family Hydrobiidae. It is a dominant member of invertebrate communities of sub-alpine lakes in its native New Zealand (Forsyth & McCallum, 1981; Biggs & Malthus, 1982; Talbot & Ward, 1987; Collier et al., 1997). Reproductively mature female snails range from 1.5 to 8.9 mm in shell length, with a median of 4.8 mm. Males are smaller, ranging from 1.6 to 7.1 mm, with a median of 3.8 mm (unpublished data). In the laboratory, females can take over six months to reach reproductive maturity (Winterbourn, 1970). They are ovoviviparous, retaining offspring in a brood sac until they are mobile. *Potamopyrgus* can live for multiple years in the laboratory (Wallace, 1992), but it is unknown at present whether they can live this long in the field.

This snail has been used as a model for testing major hypotheses for the costs and benefits of sexual versus asexual reproduction. In the native range of *P. antipodarum*, sexual and asexual females coexist, allowing comparison of reproductive modes within a single population. Sexual lineages are dioecious (male/female) and obligately outcrossing. Asexual lineages are mitotic parthenogens (Wallace, 1992). Sexual subpopulations have half the per-capita birth rate of asexual subpopulations (Gibson et al., 2017), consistent with the two-fold cost of males (Maynard Smith, 1971). Sexual individuals may dominate a population (90–100%) or be entirely absent (0%) (Winterbourn, 1970; Lively, 1987; Dybdahl & Lively, 1995). For those lakes with coexisting sexual and asexual individuals, genetic analyses indicate that the clonal genotypes are the result of repeated, independent mutations of the local sexual genotypes (Dybdahl & Lively, 1995; Neiman et al., 2005). The clonal population itself is immensely diverse: Jokela et al. (2003) detected 27 different clonal genotypes per 100 individuals at Lake Alexandrina, a commonly studied lake. Clearly, there is ample potential for spatial and temporal variation in genetic diversity. This system is thus useful for examining the relationship between genetic diversity and disease spread.

2.3.1.2 *The parasite*

In its native range, at least 20 species of trematode parasites infect *P. antipodarum* (Hechinger, 2012). These trematodes impose a major fitness

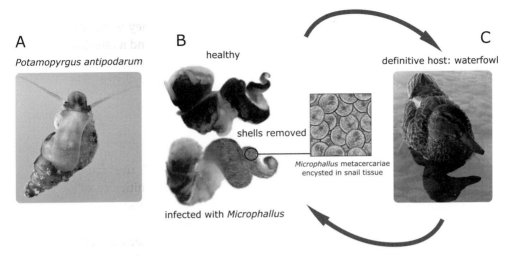

Figure 2.3 Life cycle of *Microphallus*. (A) The snail *Potamopyrgus antipodarum* dominates invertebrate communities of sub-alpine lakes of New Zealand, where it is native. Image courtesy of Bart Zijlstra, © Bart Zijlstra, www.bartzijlstra.com. (B) At least 20 species of trematode parasite infect *P. antipodarum*. The trematode species *Microphallus* is particularly prevalent in some lake populations of *P. antipodarum*. Here, two snails are shown without their shells. The upper snail is healthy. The lower snail is infected with *Microphallus* and hence sterilised: host tissues have been replaced by metacercarial cysts, magnified to the right. Image courtesy of Gabriel Harp, used under Creative Commons BY-SA 4.0. Modified from originals: images combined, line and text elements added. (C) *Microphallus* is transmitted from snail to snail by waterfowl, including this dabbling duck of the genus *Anas*. Photo taken by A.K. Gibson. (A black and white version of this figure will appear in some formats. For the colour version, please refer to the plate section.)

cost: sterilisation. They have complex life cycles that include a vertebrate definitive host (e.g. birds, eels) and, for some species, a second intermediate host (e.g. fish, crustaceans). For all taxa, *P. antipodarum* is the first intermediate host and, in some cases, may serve as the second intermediate host (Hechinger, 2012).

We primarily focus upon *Microphallus*, a particularly prevalent trematode species that is trophically transmitted (Figure 2.3). *Microphallus* matures and reproduces in the digestive tracts of waterfowl, including dabbling ducks (introduced mallards, native grey ducks, and their hybrids of genus *Anas*). Parasite eggs are then shed in duck faeces and *P. antipodarum* ingests these parasite eggs while foraging. After successfully establishing in a snail, *Microphallus* proliferates asexually, replacing the snail's digestive tract and gonads with germinal balls. Over the course of ~90 days, these larvae develop into metacercariae, which are infective to waterfowl. Waterfowl contract *Microphallus* by inadvertently consuming infected snails while foraging (Hechinger, 2012).

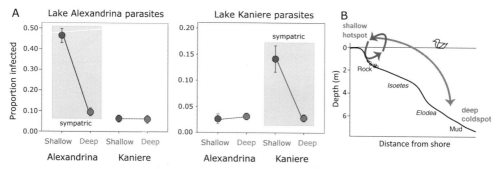

Figure 2.4 Geographic mosaic of coevolution. (A) Data from King et al. (2009). *Microphallus* trematodes are adapted to infect local (sympatric) snail hosts: Lake Alexandrina parasites are far more successful at infecting sympatric hosts, collected from the shallows of Lake Alexandrina, than they are at infecting allopatric hosts, from the shallows of Lake Kaniere (left panel). The same pattern is repeated in the right panel, showing adaptation of Lake Kaniere parasites to specifically infect local, shallow-water Lake Kaniere hosts. The y-axes reflect susceptibility, the proportion of hosts infected following controlled exposures to parasites. We also see that parasites are unsuccessful at infecting deep-water hosts from their local lakes; in fact, the parasites are no better at infecting deep-water hosts from their local lake than they are at infecting hosts from allopatric lakes. These results are consistent with the idea that host and parasite genotype frequencies covary in sympatric, shallow habitats. They also suggest that the covariance falls to zero in allopatric combinations, including in the deep. (B) These findings suggest that coevolution of hosts and parasites is restricted to the shallow margins of lakes. This hypothetical cross-section of a lake shows the proposed decline in coevolution, and the covariance of host and parasite genotype frequencies, with depth. The definitive hosts of *Microphallus*, ducks, forage in the shallow rocks and roots zone. Therefore, parasites infecting hosts here contribute offspring to the next generation, allowing them to adapt to infect common host genotypes in the shallow-water habitat. Ducks do not dive to forage in the deeper regions (e.g. *Elodea*). This behaviour reduces the potential for coevolution of parasites infecting hosts in the deep water, and deep-water hosts are accordingly less susceptible to the local parasite population (King et al., 2009). (A black and white version of this figure will appear in some formats. For the colour version, please refer to the plate section.)

Microphallus populations are locally adapted to their sympatric *P. antipodarum* populations (Lively, 1989; Lively et al., 2004). In controlled cross-inoculations, the interaction of *P. antipodarum* and *Microphallus* populations (G×G) explains the majority of variation in infection rate (i.e. susceptibility) (Lively et al., 2004). More specifically, infection rates are higher in sympatric combinations of host and parasite populations than in allopatric combinations (Lively, 1989; Lively & Dybdahl, 2000; Jokela et al., 2009; King et al., 2009, 2011) (Figure 2.4A). Local adaptation indicates that host and parasite populations diverge in the identity and/or frequency of alleles linked to infection. The success of parasites on local hosts points to reciprocal adaptation in driving this divergence

(Parker, 1985; Lively, 1989, 2016; Gandon, 2002). Migration of the parasite between populations (Dybdahl & Lively, 1996) may in fact fuel this divergence by providing the genetic variation necessary for adaptation to local hosts (Gandon et al., 1996; Lively, 1999; Gandon & Michalakis, 2002). Given the strong evidence for parasite local adaptation, we can make inferences about the genetic and coevolutionary basis of the *Potamopyrgus–Microphallus* interaction.

2.3.2 Genetic diversity and disease spread in *Potamopyrgus–Microphallus*

Equations 2.1 and 2.2 show that host genetic diversity can reduce disease spread. This result requires a matching alleles model for host–parasite compatibility (Box 2.1). Strong local adaptation of *Microphallus* supports the matching alleles model over alternative infection models. Parasite local adaptation tells us that parasite genotypes are compatible with only a subset of host genotypes, as in the matching alleles model. Strong local adaptation does not support the inverse-matching alleles model, which predicts parasite local maladaptation: hosts are resistant to their local parasite genotypes because they are under selection to identify (match) and resist them (Lively, 2016). Those same parasites will be more infective to foreign hosts that are poorly adapted to identify them. We also see time-lagged adaptation of *Microphallus* to infect common host genotypes (Dybdahl & Lively, 1998; Koskella & Lively, 2007, 2009; Jokela et al., 2009). We would expect such a pattern when parasites are under strong selection to 'match' the dominant genotypes in the local host population.

More fundamentally, a link between genetic diversity and disease spread requires a genetic basis for infection. In addition to the local adaptation findings, many experimental data point to a strong genetic basis for infection in *Potamopyrgus–Microphallus*. Koskella et al. (2011) reported rapid evolution of host resistance to *Microphallus* under experimental selection. The strong response to selection requires significant additive genetic variation for resistance. Variation in host condition does not affect the relative resistance of host genotypes (Dybdahl & Krist, 2004), nor does the upregulation of plastic immune responses (Osnas & Lively, 2005, 2006). These results indicate a robust contribution of genetic variation to resistance. In controlled exposures, infection rate rapidly approaches an asymptote with increasing parasite dose, with the height of the asymptote a function of host–parasite combination (Osnas & Lively, 2004; King et al., 2011). These results argue for a simple genetic basis for infection, rooted in the interaction of host and parasite genotype. In Dybdahl et al. (2008), interpopulation hybrid parasites showed marked outbreeding depression (reduced infectivity) on sympatric, but not allopatric, hosts. This result again indicates a specific genetic basis to infection, with non-additive interactions between two or more loci.

Empirical data from *Potamopyrgus–Microphallus* support the assumptions of Equations 2.1 and 2.2: there is a genetic basis for infection that fits the predictions of the matching alleles model. We would therefore predict that host diversity would reduce the spread of *Microphallus*. Host diversity is, theoretically, higher in sexual relative to asexual subpopulations. Sex can continually recreate lost or rare genotypes, thereby maintaining genetic diversity. In contrast, selection and drift may readily purge genotypes from asexual subpopulations, reducing genetic diversity and evenness of genotype frequencies (Hamilton et al., 1990). Although there are exceptions to this idea (Fontcuberta Garcia-Cuenca et al., 2016), it very likely applies to lake populations of *P. antipodarum*: asexual genotypes are derived from the local sexual subpopulation and subsample the genetic diversity circulating in sexual lineages (Dybdahl & Lively, 1995; Neiman et al., 2005). Hence, we would predict that *Microphallus* should spread more readily through an asexual subpopulation relative to its coexisting sexual subpopulation.

Vergara et al. (2014) provide a test of this prediction. This study reported the proportion of sexual and clonal females infected with *Microphallus* at four sites at Lake Alexandrina, where sexual and clonal females coexist. Based upon weighted means across sites, infection prevalence was 1.5–1.9-fold greater in clones relative to sexual females in four of five years (2001–2004). In the fifth year (2005), prevalence in clones plummeted, and sexual females were twice as infected as clones. Averaging across all years, clonal females were 1.4-fold more infected than sexual females, consistent with the prediction that reduced genetic variation promotes disease spread.

In recent years (2012–2016), however, we find the opposite result: clones are on average less infected than sexual females at these same sites (Gibson et al., unpublished data). One hypothesis to explain this contrasting field pattern is that clones have become relatively infrequent in more recent years and thus evade adaptation by coevolving parasites. This hypothesis stems from Equation 2.2, in which disease spread is a function of both genetic diversity and parasite adaptation to common host genotypes. We discuss this idea further at the end of Section 2.3.3.

2.3.3 Covariance and disease spread in *Potamopyrgus–Microphallus*

Equation 2.2 shows that disease spread increases as a function of the covariance of matching host and parasite genotype frequencies (Lively, 2016). King et al. (2009, 2011) gave life to this covariance term. Snails from a lake's shallow-water habitat were found to be highly susceptible to the local *Microphallus* population. By susceptibility, we mean the infection rate of hosts following controlled exposure to a fixed dose of parasites. High susceptibility suggests a positive covariance of host and parasite allele frequencies. In contrast, snails from the same lake's deep-water habitat were not susceptible to the local *Microphallus* population. In fact, deep-water hosts were no more susceptible to their sympatric *Microphallus* population than were allopatric hosts from geographically distant lakes. Low susceptibility (high resistance) suggests that the covariance of host and parasite allele frequencies is zero or low (Figure 2.5A).

Why is there such divergence within a single lake? The covariance of allele frequencies should be strongly positive where the parasite can coevolve and thus 'track' common host genotypes. The definitive hosts of *Microphallus* (dabbling ducks) typically forage no deeper than 0.5 m. Therefore, only parasites that establish infection in shallow-water snails have the chance to continue their life cycle and contribute to the next generation of parasites. Parasites that establish infections in deep-water hosts fail to reproduce. Hence, coevolution is more likely in the shallow-water habitat. A lake's parasite population is unable to track deep-water host genotypes, resulting in low or no covariance of parasite allele frequencies with deep-water host allele frequencies (Figure 2.4B) (see also Vergara et al., 2013).

It is important to note that, in these particular studies (King et al., 2009, 2011), we cannot discern the relative contributions of covariance and divergence in allele identity to variation in susceptibility. For the snail host, allelic identity diverges substantially between populations: significant population structure suggests very little gene flow between lake populations of *P. antipodarum* (Dybdahl & Lively, 1996). Even within a lake, distinct clones reside in the shallow, mid-water, and deep habitats (Fox et al., 1996; Paczesniak et al., 2014). Hence, at the among-habitat and among-lake scale, variation in the compatibility (i.e. host susceptibility) of different combinations of host and parasite populations may reflect both divergence in the identity and frequency of alleles.

Recent work points more specifically to the significance of covariance in allele frequencies in explaining variation in susceptibility. We uncovered dramatic variation in susceptibility to local parasites in the shallow-water habitat of Lake Alexandrina (Gibson, Jokela & Lively, 2016). For the host, there is no genetic structure at neutral loci between the shallow-water sites at this lake (Fox et al., 1996; Paczesniak et al., 2014). Variation in susceptibility may therefore reflect variation in the frequency, but not necessarily identity, of host alleles between sites. At highly susceptible sites, we predict high frequencies of the host alleles that match the most common alleles in the local parasite population (high covariance). As in the shallow–deep work (Figure 2.4), we hypothesise that these 'coevolutionary hotspots' are sites where ducks forage preferentially. Susceptibility was highest along the eastern shore, suggesting that ducks may prefer to forage along the shallow, relatively protected banks there. Data on duck

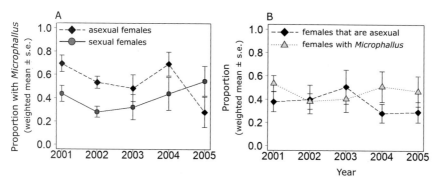

Figure 2.5 Sex and disease spread. Vergara et al. (2014) presented a survey of infection in asexual and sexual snails at four sites from 2001 to 2005. (A) Clonal females (diamonds) had a higher mean prevalence of *Microphallus* than sexual females (circles) in four of five years. (B) Frequency of females identified as asexuals (diamonds) and the overall prevalence of *Microphallus* in all female snails (grey triangles). Points show weighted means and standard errors across the sampled sites. Peaks in infection prevalence (all females and clonal females) follow a peak in the frequency of clones. Panels redrawn from data presented in Vergara et al. (2014), © 2014 by the University of Chicago.

distribution and foraging behaviour at Lake Alexandrina are needed to test this hypothesis.

We have argued that the susceptibility of *P. antipodarum* to *Microphallus* reflects the covariance term in Equation 2.2, particularly for within-habitat studies where it is predominantly the frequency, rather than the identity, of alleles that varies. Hence, within a habitat, disease spread should increase with host susceptibility to local parasites. Gibson et al. (2016) supported this prediction. Within the shallow-water habitat of Lake Alexandrina, we observed dramatic variation in the prevalence of *Microphallus* between 13 sites over the course of 10 years (as well as in the prior decade: Jokela et al., 2009) (Figure 2.6A,B). For example, in one year, we found that over 50% of females were sterilised by *Microphallus* at one site, while, at a nearby site, we found almost no infected females. Mean infection prevalence at a site was positively correlated with susceptibility of hosts to local parasites, with mean susceptibility over three years explaining 36% of the variation in mean prevalence between sites (Figure 2.6C). This finding is consistent with the prediction that infection prevalence increases with increasing covariance of host and parasite alleles.

The covariance term can also help us to understand the finding of Vergara et al. (2014). This study showed that clones at Lake Alexandrina were, on average, more infected than sexual females from 2001 to 2005 (Figure 2.5A). Lively (2016) showed that sexual reproduction depresses the covariance term, limiting disease spread. In contrast, coevolving parasites may more easily

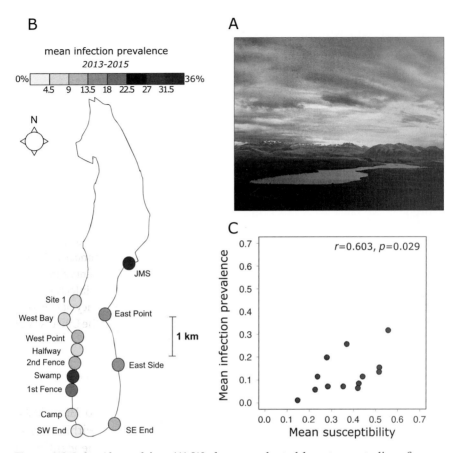

Figure 2.6 Lake Alexandrina. (A) We have conducted long-term studies of *P. antipodarum* and *Microphallus* at the 13 shallow-water sites at Lake Alexandrina, which is located in the Mackenzie Basin of New Zealand's South Island (Jokela et al., 2009; Gibson et al., 2016). (B) In spite of the proximity of these sites, snails from different sites differ significantly in prevalence of *Microphallus*. Shown here is the mean prevalence of *Microphallus* in female snails from 2013 to 2015 at the 13 sites (2014 and 2015 for Halfway). The values depicted are length-corrected estimates of mean prevalence derived from a generalised linear model, as reported in Gibson et al. (2016). (C) At sites around Lake Alexandrina, mean infection prevalence is positively correlated with mean susceptibility of hosts to Lake Alexandrina parasites. Each point represents one of 13 sites around Lake Alexandrina. Here, susceptibility is given by the mean infection rate of snails in controlled exposures in 2013, 2014, and 2015. High susceptibility may reflect a high covariance of the allele frequencies of the hosts at that site with allele frequencies of the parasite population at Lake Alexandrina. This positive correlation therefore suggests that infection prevalence increases with increasing covariance of host and parasite alleles. Data given for female snails only. Photo taken by A.K. Gibson. Panels (B) and (C) modified from Gibson et al. (2016),© 2016 by the University of Chicago.

track common asexual genotypes, increasing the covariance and thus disease spread. Consistent with these theoretical predictions, we see from Vergara et al. (2014) that the mean infection prevalence of clonal females across sites reached a maximum of 69% in both 2001 and 2004, meaning that over two-thirds of clonal individuals were sterilised in two separate years. We might expect such an elevated infection prevalence when the parasite population adapts to infect a common clone in the asexual subpopulation, inflating the covariance term. Such extreme infection/sterilisation rates were not seen in the sexual subpopulation (yearly mean ≤ 55%) (Figure 2.5A). This is consistent with a relative suppression of disease spread because sex depresses the covariance term.

Moreover, we saw earlier (Section 2.2.3) that adding epidemiology to coevolutionary models revealed a positive feedback in which the spread of a common clone increases the risk of exposure to parasites for the entire host population (Lively, 2010c). Consistent with this idea, the peak in the mean frequency of clones in 2003 (51% of the population) (Figure 2.5B) was followed by a peak in mean infection prevalence of clones (69%) (Figure 2.5A) and of the snail population as a whole (51%) in 2004 (Vergara et al., 2014) (Figure 2.5B). We might tentatively interpret these dynamics as an increase in the covariance and force of infection under rapid reciprocal adaptation by *Microphallus*. Parasite evolution should therefore select against asexual reproduction. Indeed, clonal frequency declined substantially after 2003. The variation around these yearly estimates is large; however, additional field data are needed to test the strength and generality of these findings.

More recently, clones have become rare in the shallow-water habitats at Lake Alexandrina: they were entirely absent from three of six sites in 2012. We found clones to be relatively less infected than sexual females during this period of rarity (2012–2016). As we might expect, the average rate of *Microphallus* infection across the population as a whole was lower in 2012–2016 than in 2001–2005 (Gibson et al., 2018). These findings suggests that the covariance of host and parasite alleles and the force of infection is depressed when asexuals are rare and common clones are likely absent. Similarly, we find that asexuals are relatively rare at sites (Gibson, Xu & Lively, 2016; McKone et al., 2016), habitats (King et al., 2009, 2011; Vergara et al., 2013), and lakes (Lively, 1987; Lively & Jokela, 2002) where we think parasites are able to rapidly adapt to local hosts or, in other words, where the potential is highest for parasite evolution to inflate the host–parasite covariance.

2.4 Generalisations to other systems

Are the patterns we outline here more general? Most importantly, does genetic diversity broadly limit the spread of disease? The clearest pattern arises from agricultural systems: infection rates are greater in monoculture relative to polyculture, in which multiple crop genotypes or species are mixed (Jensen, 1952; Pilet et al., 2006) (reviewed in Browning & Frey, 1969; Wolfe, 1985; Garrett & Mundt, 1999; Mundt, 2002). In a particularly striking example, the rate of rice blast disease on susceptible rice varieties fell from 20% in monoculture to 1% in polyculture, and yield increased by 86% in polyculture (Zhu et al., 2000). Common crop genotypes also tend to suffer dramatic epidemics as pathogens adapt to infect them (e.g. the Irish Potato Famine) (reviewed in Adams et al., 1971).

Data from natural populations are scarcer (reviewed in King & Lively, 2012). Analogous to agricultural systems, Schmid (1994) reported higher rates of powdery mildew over time in experimental plots of goldenrod (*Solidago altissima*) with low diversity relative to plots with high diversity. In a review of multiple plant systems, Laine et al. (2011) found a positive relationship between the diversity of resistance phenotypes of a population and the mean resistance to infection. We would then predict a negative relationship between the diversity of resistance phenotypes in a population and the prevalence of infection. Thrall and Burdon (2000) and Thrall et al. (2001) provide tentative support for this prediction in the wild flax *Linum marginale* and its rust fungus *Melampsora lini*. Specifically, they report weak negative relationships between infection prevalence and diversity of resistance phenotypes. King and Lively (2012) provide an additional review of this literature (see also Meagher, 1999).

Many of the patterns we've uncovered in *Potamopyrgus–Microphallus* are powerfully corroborated by studies of *Daphnia magna* and its parasites. Infection by the bacterium *Pasteuria ramosa* shows remarkable genetic specificity. Host genotypes are either entirely resistant (~0% infected) or entirely susceptible (~100% infected) to individual parasite clones (Luijckx et al., 2011). Parasite success hinges upon its ability to attach to receptors in the host's oesophagus (Duneau et al., 2011). This compatibility has a simple genetic basis: if a host is resistant to parasite A and susceptible to B, a single allelic change can result in susceptibility to A and resistance to B (Luijckx et al., 2012, 2013; Metzger et al., 2016). Importantly, there is no universal infectivity; parasite genotypes are restricted to infecting a subset of host genotypes (Carius et al., 2001). All of these findings provide strong support for the matching alleles model of infection. A field-based study additionally points to adaptation of *P. ramosa* to infect contemporary *D. magna* clones (Decaestecker et al., 2007). This is a system in which we would predict disease spread to decline with the addition of host genotypes to a population. Although that prediction has not been tested in the *D. magna–P. ramosa* system, results from other *Daphnia*-parasite systems support it. Altermatt and Ebert (2008) and Ganz and Ebert (2010) found that augmenting genetic diversity slowed the rate of spread and reduced the prevalence, respectively, of the microsporidian *Octosporea bayeri* in experimental populations of *D. magna*. In addition, theoretical work suggested that genetic diversity in the susceptibility of *D. dentifera* to the fungal pathogen *Metschnikowia* reduces the size and duration of epidemics in field populations (Duffy & Sivars-Becker, 2007).

The *Potamopyrgus–Microphallus* system also shares many characteristics with the interaction of human *Schistosoma* trematodes and their various snail hosts. There is a clear genetic basis to infection in snail–*Schistosoma* systems. Success depends upon the interaction of host and parasite genotype. Parasites are relatively unsuccessful on allopatric snail populations, suggestive of a matching alleles interaction (Newton, 1953; Richards & Merritt, 1972; Richards, 1975; Webster & Woolhouse, 1998; Webster & Davies, 2001; Webster et al., 2004, 2007). We would then predict that the addition of allopatric snail genotypes would reduce the prevalence of infection in the local snail population for a period of time. The downstream effect of this manipulation should be to reduce the rate at which the local human community contacts infective stages and subsequently acquires schistosomiasis. Although this vision is largely hypothetical at this point, it shows that there is much to be gained by fusing genetics and epidemiology.

2.5 Conclusion

We began this chapter by reviewing recent models that combine epidemiological reality with traditional population genetic models of host–parasite co-evolution. These models make three important predictions. First, adding genetic diversity to a host population will reduce disease spread (R_0) if parasites must genetically match their hosts to infect (Lively, 2010b, 2016; King & Lively, 2012). Second, coevolution can increase disease spread by increasing the covariance of host and parasite genotype frequencies (Lively, 2016). Third, epidemiological and evolutionary feedbacks can increase parasite selection against common clonal genotypes, thereby favouring sexual reproduction (Lively, 2009, 2010c, 2016). We then discuss how these models apply to a natural system, the snail *P. antipodarum* and its parasite *Microphallus*. Empirical data are consistent with the assumption that *Microphallus* genotypes must match to infect (Lively, 1989; Lively et al., 2004). There is also tentative support for the first prediction: the infection rate of an asexual population was higher on average than that of their coexisting sexual population during a period when asexuals were common (Vergara et al., 2014). The second prediction is supported by a positive relationship between the prevalence of *Microphallus* and the susceptibility of snails to their local parasites, our measure of covariance (Gibson, Xu & Lively, 2016). We find substantial support for the third prediction as well: a population's overall infection prevalence was elevated when asexuals were common (Gibson et al., unpublished data), common clones declined in frequency after they became overinfected (Dybdahl & Lively, 1998; Jokela et al., 2009; Koskella & Lively, 2009), and clones are relatively rare in areas where parasites rapidly evolve to infect local hosts (Lively, 1987; Lively & Jokela, 2002; King et al., 2009, 2011; Vergara et al., 2013; Gibson, Xu & Lively, 2016; McKone et al., 2016). In fusing epidemiology with genetic variation, the simple models we have outlined can serve as powerful conceptual tools to untangle the relationship between disease spread, genetic variation, and coevolution in natural systems.

2.6 Acknowledgements
We are grateful to Ken Wilson, Andy Fenton, and Dan Tompkins for organising this volume and for providing valuable guidance. AKG was supported by a US NIH training grant (IU's T32 Common Themes in Reproductive Diversity Traineeship) and the NIH IRACDA programme Fellowships in Research and Science Teaching (FIRST) at Emory University (K12GM000680). Much of the research presented here was funded by US National Science Foundation LTREB grants to CML and Jukka Jokela (DEB-9904840 and DEB-0640639).

References

Adams, M.W., Ellingboe, A.H. & Rossman, E.C. (1971) Biological uniformity and disease epidemics. *BioScience*, **21**, 1067–1070.

Altermatt, F. & Ebert, D. (2008) Genetic diversity of *Daphnia magna* populations enhances resistance to parasites. *Ecology Letters*, **11**, 918–928.

Augspurger, C.K. & Kelly, C.K. (1984) Pathogen mortality of tropical tree seedlings: experimental studies of the effects of dispersal distance, seedling density, and light conditions. *Oecologia*, **61**, 211–217.

Bell, T., Freckleton, R.P. & Lewis, O.T. (2006) Plant pathogens drive density-dependent seedling mortality in a tropical tree. *Ecology Letters*, **9**, 569–574.

Bento, G., Routtu, J., Fields, P.D., et al. (2017) The genetic basis of resistance and matching-allele interactions of a host–parasite system: the *Daphnia magna–Pasteuria ramosa* model. *PLoS Genetics*, **13**, e1006596.

Biggs, B. & Malthus, T. (1982) Macroinvertebrates associated with various aquatic macrophytes in the backwaters and lakes of the upper Clutha

Valley, New Zealand. *New Zealand Journal of Marine and Freshwater Research*, **16**, 81–88.

Browning, J.A. & Frey, K.J. (1969) Multiline cultivars as a means of disease control. *Annual Review of Phytopathology*, **7**, 355–382.

Carius, H.J., Little, T.J. & Ebert, D. (2001) Genetic variation in a host–parasite association: potential for coevolution and frequency-dependent selection. *Evolution*, **55**, 1136–1145.

Collier, K., Ilcock, R. & Meredith, A. (1997) Influence of substrate type and physico-chemical conditions on macroinvertebrate faunas and biotic indices of some lowland Waikato, New Zealand, streams. *New Zealand Journal of Marine and Freshwater Research*, **32**, 1–19.

Decaestecker, E., Gaba, S., Raeymaekers, J.A.M., et al. (2007) Host–parasite 'Red Queen' dynamics archived in pond sediment. *Nature*, **450**, 870–873.

Duffy, M.A. & Sivars-Becker, L. (2007) Rapid evolution and ecological host–parasite dynamics. *Ecology Letters*, **10**, 44–53.

Duneau, D., Luijckx, P., Ben-Ami, F., Laforsch, C. & Ebert, D. (2011) Resolving the infection process reveals striking differences in the contribution of environment, genetics and phylogeny to host–parasite interactions. *BMC Biology*, **9**, 11.

Dybdahl, M.F., Jokela, J., Delph, L.F., Koskella, B. & Lively, C.M. (2008) Hybrid fitness in a locally adapted parasite. *American Naturalist*, **172**, 772–782.

Dybdahl, M.F. & Krist, A.C. (2004) Genotypic vs. condition effects on parasite-driven rare advantage. *Journal of Evolutionary Biology*, **17**, 967–973.

Dybdahl, M.F. & Lively, C.M. (1995) Diverse endemic and polyphyletic clones in mixed populations of the freshwater snail, *Potamopyrgus antipodarum. Journal of Evolutionary Biology*, **8**, 385–398.

Dybdahl, M.F. & Lively, C.M. (1996) The geography of coevolution: comparative population structures for a snail and its trematode parasite. *Evolution*, **50**, 2264–2275.

Dybdahl, M.F. & Lively, C.M. (1998) Host-parasite coevolution: evidence for rare advantage and time-lagged selection in a natural population. *Evolution*, **52**, 1057–1066.

Fontcuberta Garcia-Cuenca, A., Dumas, Z. & Schwander, T. (2016) Extreme genetic diversity in asexual grass thrips populations. *Journal of Evolutionary Biology*, **29**, 887–899.

Forsyth, D. & McCallum, I. (1981) Benthic macroinvertebrates of Lake Taupo. *New Zealand Journal of Marine and Freshwater Research*, **15**, 41–46.

Fox, J., Dybdahl, M.F., Jokela, J. & Lively, C.M. (1996) Genetic structure of coexisting sexual and clonal subpopulations in a freshwater snail (*Potamopyrgus antipodarum*). *Evolution*, **50**, 1541–1548.

Gandon, S. (2002) Local adaptation and the geometry of host–parasite coevolution. *Ecology Letters*, **5**, 246–256.

Gandon, S., Capowiez, Y., Dubois, Y., Michalakis, Y. & Olivieri, I. (1996) Local adaptation and gene-for-gene coevolution in a metapopulation model. *Proceedings of the Royal Society of London B*, **263**, 1003–1009.

Gandon, S. & Michalakis, Y. (2002) Local adaptation, evolutionary potential and host–parasite coevolution: interactions between migration, mutation, population size and generation time. *Journal of Evolutionary Biology*, **15**, 451–462.

Gandon, S. & Nuismer, S.L. (2009) Interactions between genetic drift, gene flow, and selection mosaics drive parasite local adaptation. *American Naturalist*, **173**, 212–224.

Ganz, H.H. & Ebert, D. (2010) Benefits of host genetic diversity for resistance to infection depend on parasite diversity. *Ecology*, **91**, 1263–1268.

Garrett, K.A. & Mundt, C.C. (1999) Epidemiology in mixed host populations. *Phytopathology*, **89**, 984–990.

Gibson, A.K., Jokela, J. & Lively, C.M. (2016) Fine-scale spatial covariation between infection prevalence and susceptibility in a natural population. *American Naturalist*, **188**, 1–14.

Gibson, A.K., Xu, J.Y. & Lively, C.M. (2016) Within-population covariation between sexual reproduction and susceptibility to local parasites. *Evolution*, **70**, 2049–2060.

Gibson, A.K., Delph, L.F. & Lively, C.M. (2017) The two-fold cost of sex: experimental evidence from a natural system. *Evolution Letters*, **1**, 6–15.

Gibson, A.K., Vergara, D., Delph, L.F. & Lively, C.M. (2018) Periodic parasite-mediated selection for and against sex. *American Naturalist*, **192**, 537–551.

Hamilton, W.D. (1980) Sex versus non-sex versus parasite. *Oikos*, **35**, 282–290.

Hamilton, W.D., Axelrod, R. & Tanese, R. (1990) Sexual reproduction as an adaptation to resist parasites (a review). *Proceedings of the National Academy of Sciences of the United States of America*, **87**, 3566–3573.

Hechinger, R.F. (2012) Faunal survey and identification key for the trematodes (Platyhelminthes: Digenea) infecting *Potamopyrgus antipodarum* (Gastropoda: Hydrobiidae) as first intermediate host. *Zootaxa*, **3418**, 1–27.

Howard, R.S. & Lively, C.M. (1994) Parasitism, mutation accumulation and the maintenance of sex. *Nature*, **367**, 554–557.

Howard, R.S. & Lively, C.M. (1998) The maintenance of sex by parasitism and mutation accumulation under epistatic fitness functions. *Evolution*, **52**, 604–610.

Jensen, N.F. (1952) Intra-varietal diversification in oat breeding. *Agronomy Journal*, **44**, 30–34.

Jokela, J., Dybdahl, M.F. & Lively, C.M. (2009) The maintenance of sex, clonal dynamics, and host–parasite coevolution in a mixed population of sexual and asexual snails. *American Naturalist*, **174**, S43–S53.

Jokela, J., Lively, C.M., Dybdahl, M.F. & Fox, J. (2003) Genetic variation in sexual and clonal lineages of a freshwater snail. *Biological Journal of the Linnean Society*, **79**, 165–181.

King, K.C., Delph, L.F., Jokela, J. & Lively, C.M. (2009) The geographic mosaic of sex and the Red Queen. *Current Biology*, **19**, 1438–1441.

King, K.C., Delph, L.F., Jokela, J. & Lively, C.M. (2011) Coevolutionary hotspots and coldspots for host sex and parasite local adaptation in a snail–trematode interaction. *Oikos*, **120**, 1335–1340.

King, K.C. & Lively, C.M. (2012) Does genetic diversity limit disease spread in natural host populations? *Heredity*, **109**, 199–203.

Koskella, B. & Lively, C.M. (2007) Advice of the rose: experimental coevolution of a trematode parasite and its snail host. *Evolution*, **61**, 152–159.

Koskella, B. & Lively, C.M. (2009) Evidence for negative frequency-dependent selection during experimental coevolution of a freshwater snail and a sterilizing trematode. *Evolution*, **63**, 2213–2221.

Koskella, B., Vergara, D. & Lively, C.M. (2011) Experimental evolution of sexual host populations in response to sterilizing parasites. *Evolutionary Ecology Research*, **13**, 315–322.

Laine, A.L., Burdon, J.J., Dodds, P.N. & Thrall, P. H. (2011) Spatial variation in disease resistance: from molecules to metapopulations. *Journal of Ecology*, **99**, 96–112.

Lively, C.M. (1987) Evidence from a New Zealand snail for the maintenance of sex by parasitism. *Nature*, **328**, 519–521.

Lively, C.M. (1989) Adaptation by a parasitic trematode to local populations of its snail host. *Evolution*, **43**, 1663–1671.

Lively, C.M. (1992) Parthenogenesis in a freshwater snail: reproductive assurance versus parasitic release. *Evolution*, **46**, 907–913.

Lively, C.M. (1999) Migration, virulence, and the geographic mosaic of adaptation by parasites. *American Naturalist*, **153**, S34–S47.

Lively, C.M. (2009) The maintenance of sex: host–parasite coevolution with density-dependent virulence. *Journal of Evolutionary Biology*, **22**, 2086–2093.

Lively, C.M. (2010a) Antagonistic coevolution and sex. *Evolution: Education and Outreach*, **3**, 19–25.

Lively, C.M. (2010b) The effect of host genetic diversity on disease spread. *American Naturalist*, **175**, E149–E152.

Lively, C.M. (2010c) An epidemiological model of host–parasite coevolution and sex. *Journal of Evolutionary Biology*, **23**, 1490–1497.

Lively, C.M. (2016) Coevolutionary epidemiology: disease spread, local adaptation, and sex. *American Naturalist*, **187**, E77–E82.

Lively, C.M. & Dybdahl, M.F. (2000) Parasite adaptation to locally common host genotypes. *Nature*, **405**, 679–681.

Lively, C.M., Dybdahl, M.F., Jokela, J., Osnas, E.E. & Delph, L.F. (2004) Host sex and local adaptation by parasites in a snail–trematode interaction. *American Naturalist*, **164**, S6–S18.

Lively, C.M., Johnson, S.G., Delph, L.F. & Clay, K. (1995) Thinning reduces the effect of rust infection on jewelweed (Impatiens capensis). *Ecology*, **76**, 1859–1862.

Lively, C.M. & Jokela, J. (2002) Temporal and spatial distributions of parasites and sex in a freshwater snail. *Evolutionary Ecology Research*, **4**, 219–226.

Luijckx, P., Ben-Ami, F., Mouton, L., Du Pasquier, L. & Ebert, D. (2011) Cloning of the unculturable parasite *Pasteuria ramosa* and its *Daphnia* host reveals extreme genotype–genotype interactions. *Ecology Letters*, **14**, 125–131.

Luijckx, P., Fienberg, H., Duneau, D. & Ebert, D. (2012) Resistance to a bacterial parasite in the crustacean *Daphnia magna* shows Mendelian segregation with dominance. *Heredity*, **108**, 547-551.

Luijckx, P., Fienberg, H., Duneau, D. & Ebert, D. (2013) A matching-allele model explains host resistance to parasites. *Current Biology*, **23**, 1085-1088.

May, R.M. & Anderson, R.M. (1983) Epidemiology and genetics in the coevolution of parasites and hosts. *Proceedings of the Royal Society of London B*, **219**, 281-313.

Maynard Smith, J. (1971) The origin and maintenance of sex. In: Williams, G.C. (ed.), *Group Selection* (pp. 163-175). Chicago, IL: Aldine Atherton.

McKone, M., Gibson, A.K., Cook, D., et al. (2016) Fine-scale association between parasites and sex in *Potamopyrgus antipodarum* within a New Zealand lake. *New Zealand Journal of Ecology*, **40**, 1.

Meagher, S. (1999) Genetic diversity and *Capillaria hepatica* (Nematoda) prevalence in Michigan deer mouse populations. *Evolution*, **53**, 1318-1324.

Metzger, C.M.J.A., Luijckx, P., Bento, G., Mariadassou, M. & Ebert, D. (2016) The Red Queen lives: epistasis between linked resistance loci. *Evolution*, **70**, 480-487.

Mundt, C. (2002) Use of multiline cultivars and cultivar mixtures for disease management. *Annual Review of Phytopathology*, **40**, 381-410.

Neiman, M., Jokela, J. & Lively, C.M. (2005) Variation in asexual lineage age in *Potamopyrgus antipodarum*, a New Zealand snail. *Evolution*, **59**, 1945-1952.

Newton, W.L. (1953) The inheritance of susceptibility to infection with *Schistosoma mansoni* in *Australorbis glabratus*. *Experimental Parasitology*, **2**, 242-257.

Osnas, E.E. & Lively, C.M. (2004) Parasite dose, prevalence of infection and local adaptation in a host-parasite system. *Parasitology*, **128**, 223-228.

Osnas, E.E. & Lively, C.M. (2005) Immune response to sympatric and allopatric parasites in a snail-trematode interaction. *Frontiers in Zoology*, **2**, 8.

Osnas, E.E. & Lively, C.M. (2006) Host ploidy, parasitism and immune defence in a coevolutionary snail-trematode system. *Journal of Evolutionary Biology*, **19**, 42-48.

Otto, S.P. & Nuismer, S.L. (2004) Species interactions and the evolution of sex. *Science*, **304**, 1018-1020.

Paczesniak, D., Adolfsson, S., Liljeroos, K., et al. (2014) Faster clonal turnover in high-infection habitats provides evidence for parasite-mediated selection. *Journal of Evolutionary Biology*, **27**, 417-428.

Parker, M.A. (1985) Local population differentiation for compatibility in an annual legume and its host-specific fungal pathogen. *Evolution*, **39**, 713-723.

Pielou, E.C. (1969) *An Introduction to Mathematical Ecology*. New York, NY: John Wiley & Sons.

Pilet, F., Chacon, G., Forbes, G.A. & Andrivon, D. (2006) Protection of susceptible potato cultivars against late blight in mixtures increases with decreasing disease pressure. *Phytopathology*, **96**, 777-783.

Richards, C.S. (1975) Genetic factors in susceptibility of *Biomphalaria glabrata* for different strains of *Schistosoma mansoni*. *Parasitology*, **70**, 231-241.

Richards, C.S. & Merritt, J.W. (1972) Genetic factors in the susceptibility of juvenile *Biomphalaria glabrata* to *Schistosoma mansoni* infection. *American Journal of Tropical Medicine and Hygiene*, **21**, 425-434.

Schmid, B. (1994) Effects of genetic diversity in experimental stands of *Solidago altissima*: evidence for the potential role of pathogens as selective agents in plant populations. *Journal of Ecology*, **82**, 165-175.

Talbot, J. & Ward, J. (1987) Macroinvertebrates associated with aquatic macrophyties in Lake Alexandrina, New Zealand. *New Zealand Journal of Marine and Freshwater Research*, **21**, 199-213.

Thrall, P.H. & Burdon, J.J. (2000) Effect of resistance variation in a natural plant host-pathogen metapopulation on disease dynamics. *Plant Pathology*, **49**, 767-773.

Thrall, P.H., Burdon, J.J. & Young, A. (2001) Variation in resistance and virulence among demes of a plant host-pathogen metapopulation. *Journal of Ecology*, **89**, 736-748.

Tseng, M. (2004) Sex-specific response of a mosquito to parasites and crowding. *Proceedings of the Royal Society of London B*, **271**, S186–S188.

Vergara, D., Jokela, J. & Lively, C.M. (2014) Infection dynamics in coexisting sexual and asexual host populations: support for the Red Queen Hypothesis. *American Naturalist*, **184**, S22–S30.

Vergara, D., Lively, C.M., King, K.C. & Jokela, J. (2013) The geographic mosaic of sex and infection in lake populations of a New Zealand snail at multiple spatial scales. *American Naturalist*, **182**, 484–493.

Wallace, C. (1992) Parthenogenesis, sex and chromosomes in *Potamopyrgus antipodarum*. *Journal of Molluscan Studies*, **58**, 93–107.

Webster, J., Shrivastava, J., Johnson, P. & Blair, L. (2007) Is host-schistosome coevolution going anywhere? *BMC Evolutionary Biology*, **7**, 91.

Webster, J. & Woolhouse, M. (1998) Selection and strain specificity of compatibility between snail intermediate hosts and their parasitic schistosomes. *Evolution*, **52**, 1627–1634.

Webster, J.P. & Davies, C.M. (2001) Coevolution and compatibility in the snail-schistosome system. *Parasitology*, **123**, 41–56.

Webster, J.P., Gower, C.M. & Blair, L. (2004) Do hosts and parasites coevolve? Empirical support from the *Schistosoma* system. *American Naturalist*, **164**, S33–S51.

Winterbourn, M. (1970) Population studies on the New Zealand freshwater gastropod, *Potamopyrgus antipodarum*. *Proceedings of the Malacological Society of London*, **39**, 139–149.

Wolfe, M. (1985) The current status and prospects of multiline cultivars and variety mixtures for disease resistance. *Annual Review of Phytopathology*, **23**, 251–273.

Zhu, Y., Chen, H., Fan, J., et al. (2000) Genetic diversity and disease control in rice. *Nature*, **406**, 718–722.

CHAPTER THREE

Wild rodents as a natural model to study within-host parasite interactions

AMY B. PEDERSEN AND ANDY FENTON

3.1 Introduction

Parasites are thought to make up over half of the world's biodiversity. It is perhaps not surprising, then, that coinfection – the simultaneous infection of an individual host by multiple parasite species – appears to be the norm in nature. Surveys of natural populations typically show that most individuals harbour multiple species, and some can carry a diverse array of parasite taxa including both macroparasites, encompassing endoparasites (e.g. helminths) and ectoparasites (e.g. ticks, fleas, biting flies), and microparasites (i.e. pathogens) such as viruses, bacteria, fungi, and protozoa (Petney & Andrews, 1998; Cox, 2001; Lello et al., 2004). One of the early questions concerning parasite coinfection in wild systems was to identify to what extent these within-host parasite communities are structured by interactions between species ('interactionist'), or whether they are largely random assemblages of species from the wider community ('isolationist') (Price, 1980). This distinction is important because if coinfecting parasites really do interact with each other within a host individual, then the presence of one species may alter (positively or negatively) that host's susceptibility to infection by another species, the success (or not) of targeted treatment or vaccination, and the rate and severity of disease progression, potentially affecting the likelihood of host mortality (Pedersen & Fenton, 2007; Griffiths et al., 2011). As such, identifying the occurrence, strength, and mechanisms of interspecific interactions among coinfecting parasites is a major research focus for both public health and wildlife disease ecology.

Many laboratory rodent studies show very strong potential for coinfecting parasites to interact, either directly (e.g. via competition for infection sites) or indirectly (e.g. via resource competition or the host's immune response; see Box 3.1 for an overview). Given the high number of parasite species that may be coinfecting a single host, and the potential for a diverse array of interactions between them, it seems reasonable to consider the within-host

Box 3.1: Coinfection studies in laboratory rodents

Much of our current understanding of within-host coinfection dynamics comes from controlled-infection studies involving laboratory mice (Holmes, 1961, 1962; Cox, 2001). These studies typically involve infecting mice with controlled doses of two or more parasite species, either simultaneously or sequentially, and measuring the response, in terms of the growth and reproduction of each parasite species, and/or the host's immunological response to single versus coinfection. Laboratory coinfection studies in rodents have been instrumental in demonstrating the potential for parasites to interact within a host, frequently finding strong effects of prior or concurrent infection by one species on the infectivity, growth, and fecundity of the other species (e.g. Holmes, 1961, 1962; Cox, 2001; Graham, 2008). Many studies have also found strong host responses under coinfection, with both specific and general immune responses being either exacerbated or reduced under coinfection (Maizels et al., 2004). By conducting a meta-analysis on helminth–microparasites coinfection studies in laboratory mice, Graham (2008) found strong evidence for both (i) a top-down interaction between parasites whereby immunomodulatory helminths reduced the levels of IFN-γ, a specific microparasite inhibitor, and this resulted in a subsequent increase in microparasite density (Figure B3.1.1A), and (ii) a bottom-up interaction: when helminths and microparasites both consume red blood cells, microparasite density was significantly reduced in helminth coinfected mice (Figure B3.1.1B).

While laboratory studies benefit from being highly controlled, and allow frequent, detailed examination of parasitological and host responses, they are, however, highly artificial. Typically, laboratory coinfection studies use high doses to ensure infection success, are conducted on genotypically identical hosts (e.g. inbred mouse strains) who are fed ad-lib in controlled environments, and often use unnatural host–parasite combinations (i.e. infecting with parasite species that do not infect mice in nature, thus lacking a coevolutionary history). As such, it is hard to know how to extrapolate from these findings based on laboratory mice to understand more broadly the occurrence and consequences of coinfection in natural systems. What is needed is natural wildlife systems, which are amenable to intensive study of individual infection dynamics, ideally allowing experimentation (see below), and potentially enabling the use of the sophisticated immunological toolbox that has been developed primarily on laboratory mice (Pedersen & Babayan, 2011), to infer host responses and mechanisms of parasite interaction under coinfection. Arguably, by these criteria, wild rodents provide the ideal taxonomic group to bridge from those laboratory studies to the natural environment (Behnke et al., 2001).

Box 3.1: (cont.)

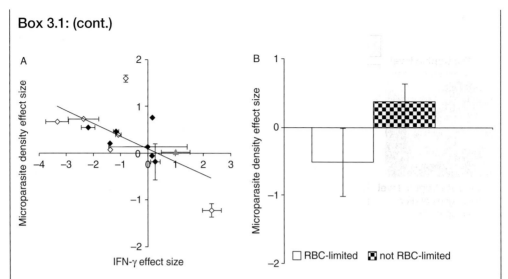

Figure B3.1.1 (A) Using data from 54 coinfection studies, Graham (2008) found that in helminth-coinfected mice, levels of IFN-γ, an immune molecule which targets microparasites, were negatively correlated with microparasite density. (B) Graham (2008) also found support for an indirect interaction between coinfecting parasites through shared resource use. Specifically, when the helminths and microparasites both consumed red blood cells, microparasite density was significantly reduced, compared to coinfected mice where the helminths did not consume red blood cells. From Graham (2008).

environment of each individual host as a discrete ecosystem (Rynkiewicz et al., 2015). This within-host ecosystem comprises the community of parasitic and commensal taxa existing within the internal host's environment, in addition to the resources on which the parasites feed (e.g. blood, gastrointestinal tract) and the immune response which, in vertebrate hosts, elicits a range of specific and general mechanisms to eliminate or control parasites (Figure 3.1; Pedersen & Fenton, 2007; Rynkiewicz et al., 2015). Recognising the similarities between within-host parasite communities and 'free-living' communities allows the application of both theoretical concepts and empirical tools from community ecology which will enable a better understanding of the processes driving the structure, assembly, and dynamics of within-host communities (Johnson et al., 2015).

In this chapter, we assess the role that wild rodent studies have played in understanding the occurrence and consequences of parasite coinfection. We first summarise the existing body of general theory on coinfection, before exploring how studies of wild rodent parasite communities have investigated within-host interactions. In particular, we assess the various empirical techniques used to study coinfection, and show how these studies connect with general theory to provide guidelines on how to infer the presence of

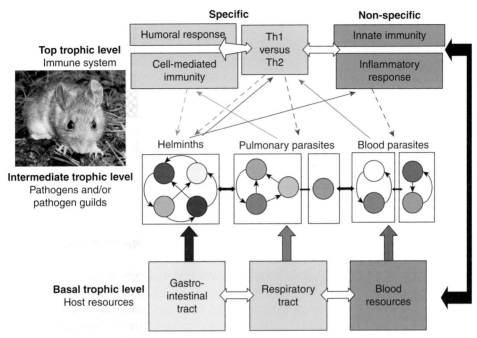

Figure 3.1 Analogous to trophic connections that define free-living communities, here we show the parallel concept for a within-host parasite community of a vertebrate host. The basal trophic level is made up of the host resources, while the intermediate trophic level consists of the macro- and microparasites that consume components of the host in order to develop, reproduce, and transmit. Finally, the top trophic level is the immune system, which acts similarly to a top predator in that it can destroy and/or control the abundance of infecting parasites. Within-host parasite interactions can be positive or negative, and can occur either directly between two coinfecting species (indicated by arrows) or indirectly through a top-down interaction (via a shared immune response) or a bottom-up interaction (via a shared host resource). We note that parasites that share the same niche within the host (here demonstrated as consuming the same host resource and being attacked by the same components of the immune system) are most likely to interact directly. Lastly, we highlight that unlike free-living communities, here the basal and top trophic levels are part of the same host and changes in either will affect host fitness. From Pedersen and Fenton (2007).

interspecific parasite interactions. Throughout, we assess these studies in their ability to address three key questions: (1) do coinfecting parasites interact within a host or are they simply a loose assembly of species, infecting the host independently of each other; (2) how can we detect or measure these interactions in natural populations; and (3) how do within-host interactions scale up to affect dynamics at the host population level? Lastly, we end with outstanding questions and approaches for future investigation, particularly relating to the implications of coinfection interactions for disease control, and emphasise the advances that could be made by a closer pairing of field and laboratory studies with general theory, using rodents as a natural bridge between these research areas.

3.2 General concepts and theory of within-host coinfection interactions

3.2.1 Do coinfecting parasites interact? Early ecological concepts relating to parasite community structure

Among the first attempts to apply 'free-living' community ecology concepts to within-host parasite communities was to understand the extent to which parasite communities are 'interactive', where communities are saturated and species interact strongly with each other, or 'isolationist', where there are many vacant parasite niches and infection by one parasite is largely independent of other coinfecting parasites (Price, 1980; Bush & Holmes, 1986; Holmes & Price, 1986; Kennedy, 2006). Many field studies across a range of host taxa suggested that although typically highly species-rich, many parasite communities are not saturated in terms of the available niches within a host, and may lie closely to the isolationist end of the spectrum (Price, 1980; Bush & Holmes, 1986; Stock & Holmes, 1988; Poulin, 1996, 1997). As such, despite laboratory studies showing very strong potential for coinfecting parasites to interact (Box 3.1), the strict niche specificity of many parasites suggested that interactions between them may be rare in natural systems (Dobson, 1985). An important point to make is that parasite ecologists had typically defined a parasite's niche just in terms of its spatial location within a host, likely due to the focus on parasitic helminths, which often exhibit strong infection site fidelity, in many of these early studies (Poulin, 2007). Hence, the focus was primarily on potential 'bottom-up' control of parasite community structure (Figure 3.1). However, this limited focus on the spatial dimension of parasite niches, while gaining support via a recent meta-analysis (Griffiths et al., 2014; discussed further below), largely ignores the potential for parasites infecting distant locations to interact indirectly, for example via the host's immune response (i.e. top-down regulation; Figure 3.1). Overall, then, to address our key question 1 (do coinfecting parasites interact?), these early attempts to define parasite communities suggested largely that they tend more towards being isolationist assemblages than highly interactive communities.

While the idea of isolationist versus interactive communities was largely conceptual, questions about the dynamical consequences of within-host parasite interactions require a more formal theoretical basis. As such, a body of research using mathematical modelling has arisen to understand and predict these often non-linear, density-dependent processes, and their consequences at both the individual and population scale. Many of the original models of coinfection dynamics focused on interactions among multiple coinfecting strains of the same parasite species (intraspecific coinfection), with the intention of understanding the processes driving strain polymorphism and/or the evolution of parasite virulence, and therefore incorporated processes such as recombination between strains and kin selection (e.g. Gupta et al., 1994, 1996; May & Nowak, 1995; van Baalen & Sabelis, 1995). Here, though, our primary interest is in coinfection dynamics among different parasite species (interspecific coinfection), so we restrict our consideration to those models. We emphasise that this overview of coinfection theory is not intended to be exhaustive. Rather, we describe a subset of studies, grouped by the types of parasites and parasite interactions considered, to illustrate key points that emerge from the broader literature on interspecific coinfection interactions, and will likely provide the best links to empirical coinfection studies.

3.2.2 Helminth–helminth coinfection models

Perhaps the first concerted attempt to explicitly model interspecific coinfection dynamics was in helminth–helminth coinfection models (Dobson, 1988; Roberts & Dobson, 1995; see also Gatto & De Leo, 1998). These primarily epidemiological models, based on the original single-helminth epidemiological models of Anderson and May (1978), were extended to incorporate multiple helminth species. They focused on the factors that lead to parasite species coexistence or exclusion at the host population level (i.e. where the number of available hosts is the limiting resource that the parasites are competing over). In particular, these models considered two competitive scenarios. The first was 'exploitation' competition, where the parasite species are distributed across the host population independently of each other, and only compete by affecting the number of hosts available to the other species. This model provides a nice example of how parasites that do not interact directly within individual hosts can still affect each other at the host population scale through their demographic impact on host population size. The second scenario, 'interference' competition, is a phenomenological way to account for potential within-host interactions (e.g. physical, chemical or immunological interactions) or correlations in exposure (e.g. via shared intermediate hosts), whereby the joint distribution function of the parasite species was modified to account for positive/ negative covariance in their distributions at the host population level. Although adopting a host–macroparasite framework, these models showed that the conditions for species coexistence were qualitatively the same as those for species coexistence in the standard Lotka-Volterra interspecific competition model (Lotka, 1932; Gause, 1934): parasite coexistence is favoured (at the host population level) if the parasite species are highly aggregated in their distributions (which increases intraspecific regulation) and if the distributions of the species covary negatively with respect to each other (e.g. via interspecific competition within the host for resources, or cross-immunity; Dobson, 1985). Certainly the former is true for most host–helminth systems (Shaw & Dobson, 1995; Shaw et al., 1998), and may go some way to explain why many host populations harbour highly species-rich parasite communities.

Since those early epidemiological models, other models of helminth–helminth coinfection dynamics have been developed to further explore the population dynamic (epidemiological) consequences of a wider range of within-host interspecific parasite interactions (e.g. Bottomley et al., 2005, 2007; Fenton et al., 2010; Yakob et al., 2013). As an example, Fenton et al. (2010) developed an individual-based model (IBM) to investigate whether it was possible to infer the direction and magnitude of within-host helminth–helminth interactions using only population-level parasite association data (which is what is typically available from wildlife studies). This IBM framework explicitly modelled the dynamics of infection by two different parasite species within each individual host in the population through time (Figure 3.2). This meant that it was possible for the coinfection dynamics to play out independently within each individual host, based on each of their specific helminth burdens (number of worms), rather than being restricted to only modelling aggregate measures such as mean helminth burdens, as was the case for many other approaches. Using this framework, Fenton et al. (2010) explored a range of within-host interaction scenarios (i.e. allowing the coinfecting helminth species to affect each other's establishment, survival, and/or fecundity according to specified burden-dependent interaction functions), and asked whether it is possible to infer the existence, direction, and magnitude of those interactions from patterns of parasite association across the host population (Figure 3.2), thereby addressing our key question 2 (can we detect parasite interactions from patterns of parasite occurrence?). They showed that, frequently, the signal of any within-host interaction can easily be lost at the host population level, particularly if those interactions are antagonistic (negative). Furthermore, even if those interactions could be detected based on the statistical association between parasite species, the strength of those statistical associations (as measured by the effect size) was often weak, suggesting those interactions may be dismissed as being biologically insignificant, even if they were actually having a large effect on parasite fitness or dynamics (Figure 3.2). We discuss the practical implications of these results below (see Section 3.4), but broadly they imply, specifically to key question 3 (how do within-host interactions affect dynamics at the host population level?), that the scaling relationships between within-host coinfection interactions and between-host patterns of association are not straightforward, potentially making it very hard to infer the occurrence or direction of within-host interactions from population-level data. It is likely that these patterns

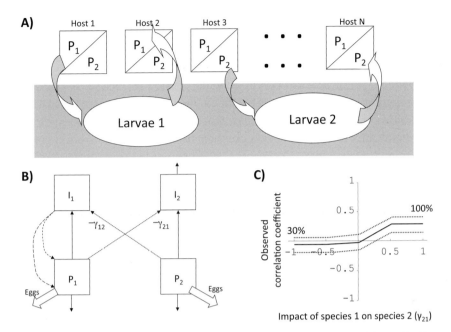

Figure 3.2 Overview of the macroparasite–macroparasite IBM model used by Fenton et al. (2010) to explore the relationship between the strength and direction of within-host interactions between two coinfecting macroparasite (helminth) species, and the resulting patterns of parasite association across the host population. (A) Schematic diagram of the host population (epidemiological) component; the population comprises N host individuals, and keeps track of the adult helminth burden of each parasite species (P_1 and P_2) within each of those hosts. The parasites produce eggs, which pass into the environment where they form pools of infective stages, which get picked up at random by hosts (drawn from a specified 'exposure' distribution to generate overdispersed parasite distributions) to complete the life cycle. (B) Schematic diagram of the within-host component of the model, showing how the helminth burden of each parasite species (P_1 and P_2) stimulates, and is countered by, the species-specific immune response (I_1 and I_2) in each host. In addition, each parasite species may stimulate or suppress the immune response towards the other, coinfecting parasite species at rate γ_{ij}, to generate alternative forms of within-host interspecific interaction. (C) Results from the analysis of Fenton et al. (2010) showing Spearman rank correlation coefficients in infection intensity between the two parasite species across the host population (mean ± 95% CI of 1000 simulation runs) for different values of γ_{21}, the strength of within-host interaction of parasite species 1 on species 2. The percentage labels show the percentage of the 1000 runs in which a statistically significant correlation in parasite intensities was found, either for a maximally positive compared to negative interaction ($\gamma_{21} = 1$: ~100% success, compared to $\gamma_{21} = -1$: ~30% success). These results show that positive within-host interactions were far more likely to be correctly inferred from between-host patterns in parasite association than negative interactions; however, even when correctly inferred, the resulting correlation coefficients tended to be rather weak.

extend beyond just helminth interactions and are common across a range of parasite types.

3.2.3 Helminth–microparasite coinfection models

One area where coinfection interactions are increasingly recognised as being of applied importance is in the management of important microparasite (pathogen) infections of humans. In particular, due to the well-known potential for parasitic helminths to immunomodulate their hosts, there have been increasing calls to incorporate mass deworming programmes to assist in the control and treatment of diseases such as malaria, TB, and HIV (Bentwich et al., 1999; Harms & Feldmeier, 2002; Druilhe et al., 2005; Harris et al., 2009). As such, models which allow exploration of how within-host helminth interactions affect individual-level health, population-level pathogen transmission, and the consequences of deworming for both, are becoming increasingly necessary.

To assess how within-host interactions between helminth and coinfecting microparasites may affect the epidemiology of each species, Fenton (2008) developed a hybrid coinfection model which combined the standard macroparasite (helminth) and microparasite (pathogen) models originally developed by Anderson and May (Anderson & May, 1978, 1981, 1992). This model used the established *SI* or *SIR* pathogen frameworks, but also kept track of the dynamics of the mean helminth burden within each of the *S, I* and *R* compartments (see Box 3.2 for details). This framework allowed exploration of how host and parasite life-history traits affect microparasite–macroparasite coexistence and stability, and the abundance or prevalence of each parasite species, under a variety of within-host interaction scenarios. In the absence of any direct within-host interaction between the parasite species, the model showed that the presence of one parasite tends to reduce the basic reproduction number (R_0) of the other parasite, by the demographic impact of reducing the pool of susceptible hosts available to the other species, through parasite-induced host mortality (Fenton, 2008), equivalent to the 'exploitation' model of Dobson (1985). However, parasite coexistence (at the population level) was possible, particularly if neither parasite species was too infectious or too virulent, or if the host species was long-lived. Furthermore, this framework showed how within-host coinfection interactions could favour invasion and persistence of each parasite species at the host population scale, for example by helminths increasing host susceptibility to pathogen infection. Conversely, though, coinfection interactions may reduce the likelihood of parasite species persistence, for example if hosts suffer increased mortality due to coinfection. Hence, to address our third key question, the strength and direction of any within-host interaction could have significant consequences for disease dynamics (invasion or persistence) at the host population scale.

Box 3.2: A primer on the theory of macroparasite–microparasite interactions

Fenton (2008, 2013) developed a hybrid microparasite–macroparasite model, based on the classic *SIR* microparasite framework, but which also keeps track of the mean helminth burden within each of those microparasite-infection classes (Figure B3.2.1A). This framework enables exploration of the population dynamic consequences of a range of potential coinfection interactions, via modifications of key parameters (susceptibility, survival, and infectiousness).

Figure B3.2.1B,C (modified from Fenton, 2008) show the baseline effect of coinfection on the basic reproductive number (R_0) of the microparasite ($R_{0,VW}$) and the macroparasite ($R_{0,WV}$), respectively, in the absence of any direct interaction between the parasites. In both cases, coinfection reduces R_0 due to the demographic impact of one parasite species reducing host population size through the negative effects of infection, and therefore the potential number of individuals available for infection by the other parasite species. Together these effects suggest that at the host population level, both parasite species can only coexist within a relatively narrow range of parameter space, as illustrated by Figure B3.2.1D; if, as in this example, the transmission rate of either species is sufficiently high (where β_V denotes transmission rate of the microparasite ('virus') and β_w denotes transmission rate of the macroparasite ('worm')) then it has the potential to drive the host population to sufficiently low levels such that R_0 of the other species falls below 1, and that species is unable to persist. However, within-host interactions may alter this condition, as shown by the dashed line in Figure B3.2.1D. Here the macroparasite is assumed to increase host susceptibility to the microparasite (for example, via immune-suppression or -modulation). Now the macroparasite facilitates microparasite transmission, allowing it to persist at the host population scale when it would otherwise not be able to.

Finally, this framework has allowed exploration of how coinfection and in particular how varying helminth burdens in microparasite-coinfected individuals affect host longevity (Figure B3.2.1E, modified from Fenton, 2013). In the absence of any direct interaction between the helminth and the microparasite (black line), increasing worm burdens tend to decrease host lifespan due to the assumed cumulative negative effect of helminths on host survival. This effect can be exacerbated if helminths reduce the ability of the host to clear ongoing microparasite infections (light grey solid line), or if they increase the pathogenic impact of the microparasite under coinfection (dark grey dashed line). However, if the helminth either increases the ability of the host to clear the microparasite infection (light grey dashed line) or

Box 3.2: (cont.)

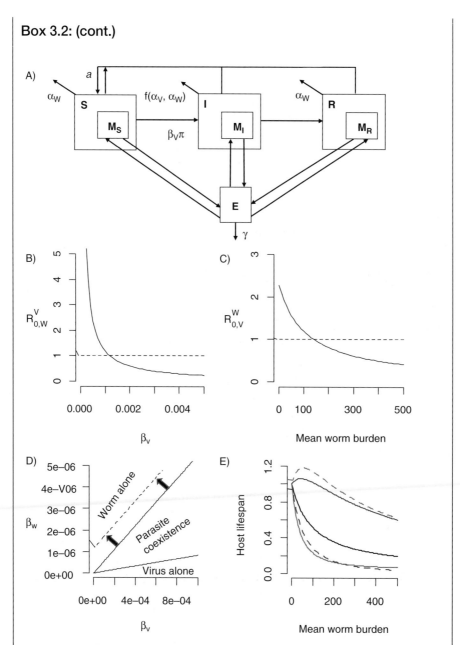

Figure B3.2.1 (A) Schematic diagram of the hybrid microparasite–macroparasite model (modified from Fenton, 2008, 2013). (B,C) The effect of coinfection on the basic reproductive number (R_0) of the microparasite ($R_{0,V}^W$) and the macroparasite ($R_{0,W}^V$), respectively, in the absence of any direct interaction between the parasites. (D) Parameter space showing combinations of microparasite and macroparasite transmission rates (β_V and β_w, respectively) that result in either the microparasite ('virus', V) or macroparasite ('worm', W) persisting alone, or in coexistence of both.

Box 3.2: (cont.)

Caption for Figure B3.2.1   (cont.)

The arrows and dashed line denote how the boundary between the regions of coexistence and macroparasite-only persistence changes in the presence of a coinfection interaction whereby the macroparasite increases host susceptibility to the microparasite. (E) The effect of mean worm burden on host lifespan under alternative interactions with a coinfecting microparasite: black line = no direct interaction; light grey solid line = worms reduce the ability of the host to clear ongoing microparasite infections; dark grey dashed line = worms increase the pathogenic impact of the microparasite; light grey dashed line = worms increase the ability of the host to clear the microparasite infection; dark grey solid line = worms reduce the pathogenicity of the microparasite. Modified from Fenton (2013).

reduces the pathogenicity of the microparasite (dark grey solid line) then coinfection can have opposite effects on host survival, depending on mean helminth burden; low burdens are beneficial to the host (either increasing the likelihood of clearing the microparasite, or reducing the damage it causes), whereas high helminth burdens are harmful due to their direct, detrimental effect on the host. As such, this theory shows that understanding whether helminth–microparasite coinfection is harmful to the host and, therefore, whether deworming is likely to be beneficial requires an understanding not just of the mechanism and qualitative direction of any coinfection interactions that are occurring, but also how these interactions vary quantitatively with helminth burden.

Variations of this hybrid macroparasite–microparasite model have subsequently been developed. For example, Ezenwa and colleagues developed a modified version, in which helminth infection levels were assumed to be static, tailored to model helminth-TB coinfection in Cape buffalo (Ezenwa et al., 2010; see also Ezenwa et al., this volume, Chapter 5) – a rare example where coinfection theory has been closely integrated with a specific empirical system. As in Fenton (2008), their model predicted that within-host immunosuppression by helminths could facilitate population-level invasion by TB (i.e. raise its $R_0 > 1$) due to increased host susceptibility to infection under coinfection. However, in a follow-up paper, Ezenwa and Jolles (2015) showed that the demographic impact of increased mortality of coinfected hosts may limit TB spread (matching the generic predictions of Fenton 2008); hence, deworming hosts may actually facilitate TB spread at the population level by allowing TB (co)infected hosts to survive long enough to transmit to other hosts. In addition, Fenton (2013) used a modified version of the original microparasite–

macroparasite hybrid model to explore the extent to which the individual- and population-level impacts of coinfection depend on helminth burden. This model showed, first, at the individual host level, that increasing helminth burdens tend to reduce host life expectancy, and this can be exacerbated under coinfection. However, if there is a negative interaction on a coinfecting pathogen, increasing helminth burdens (at least up to intermediate levels) may actually benefit the host, by protecting it from the often more harmful pathogen infection. Second, at the host population level, increasing helminth burdens may often reduce the pathogen's R_0 but, under some coinfection interaction scenarios (e.g. if coinfected hosts are more susceptible to pathogen infection), increasing burdens (at least up to intermediate levels) may facilitate pathogen invasion and spread (i.e. increase the pathogen's R_0; Fenton, 2013), in a similar manner to that shown by Ezenwa and colleagues (Ezenwa et al., 2010). However, even in this scenario, if helminth burdens become too high, or if the helminths themselves are highly pathogenic, then their negative impact on host survival outweighs any benefit to the pathogen of increased host susceptibility, resulting in a net negative effect on the pathogen's R_0 (Fenton, 2013).

Overall then, various parasite coinfection models have been developed, exploring a range of scales, from within-host (e.g. Fenton & Perkins, 2010), between-host (e.g. Dobson, 1985) to explicitly scaling from within-to-between hosts (e.g. Fenton, 2013; Ezenwa & Jolles, 2015) and interactions between different parasite types. To date, though, there have been few attempts to connect much of this theory to data (but see Ezenwa & Jolles, 2015, and Ezenwa et al., this volume, Chapter 5). There is then a clear need to move beyond laboratory studies and develop wild animal systems where this theory can be tested. In what follows we explore how wild rodents are proving themselves to be a highly suitable system to bridge these laboratory–field–theory divides.

3.3 Wild rodent studies of within-host coinfection dynamics
3.3.1 Overview of parasite communities studies in wild rodents
Wild rodents are typically highly abundant in their native habitat, are reasonably easy to catch using standard mark–recapture methods, and in many cases, their parasite communities have been well studied. As such, they have been at the forefront of research into within-host coinfection dynamics. Many of these studies, particularly in Europe, have focused on mice in the genus *Apodemus*, for example wood mice (*A. sylvaticus*) and yellow-necked mice (*A. flavicolis*). These studies have tended to focus on coinfection interactions among the gastrointestinal (GI) helminths, ectoparasites, or between GI helminths and ectoparasites or other pathogens (e.g. Elton et al., 1931; Montgomery & Montgomery, 1990; Muller-Graf et al., 1999; Abu-Madi et al., 2000; Behnke et al., 2001; Stanko et al., 2002; de Bellocq et al., 2003; Ferrari

et al., 2009; Krasnov et al., 2010; Knowles et al., 2013). However, a number of coinfection studies have also been conducted on voles (e.g. bank voles (*Myodes glareolus*), field voles (*Microtus agrestis*)), and these investigations have often focused on microparasite–microparasite or microparasite–macroparasite interactions (e.g. Telfer et al., 2010; Salvador et al., 2011). In the USA, coinfection research has focused primarily on mice of the genus *Peromyscus*, again with an emphasis on GI parasite interactions (Pedersen & Antonovics, 2013). That said, there have been coinfection studies of other rodent species including gerbils (Gutiérrez et al., 2014), squirrels (e.g. Nieto et al., 2010), and rats (e.g. Costa et al., 2014). However, as well as working on a variety of different taxa, these studies have also adopted a diverse array of approaches to explore specific aspects of within-host parasite interactions, making it difficult at times to compare across studies and obtain general insight into the occurrence and importance of within-host parasite interactions in structuring parasite communities. Here we review some papers of parasite coinfection in wild rodent hosts, and use them to provide an overview of the approaches used and whether any general patterns emerge.

3.3.2 Early studies of parasite coinfection in wild rodents

Much early work in this area, dating back to the original studies of Charles Elton and colleagues (e.g. Elton et al., 1931), tended to compile lists of parasites (typically GI helminth species) found in wild rodents. These studies focused more on whether extrinsic (environmental) factors such as season or site and/or intrinsic (host individual) factors such as age or sex influenced the occurrence or abundance of each parasite species in turn (e.g. Rausch & Kuns, 1950; Rausch, 1952; Thomas, 1953; Sharpe, 1964; Lewis, 1968a, 1968b; Montgomery & Montgomery, 1988; Abu-Madi et al., 1998, 2000), rather than considering the role of interspecific parasite interactions in driving the dynamics of each parasite species or in structuring the parasite community as a whole. However, from the late 1980s onwards, possibly inspired by the increased application of evolutionary theory and concepts from community ecology to parasite community ecology (e.g. community assembly rules, species packing and niche theory; Bush & Holmes, 1986; Holmes & Price, 1986), 'wild' studies began to ask what role, if any, interspecific parasite interactions played in structuring within-host ('infracommunity') parasite communities. Studies on rodent parasite communities (along with fish parasite communities) arguably led the field in this direction.

3.3.3 Attempts to infer interspecific parasite interactions from observational data

3.3.3.1 *Helminth–helminth coinfection*

One of the first studies that explicitly sought to apply community ecology techniques and theories to understand the role of interspecific interactions in structuring wild rodent parasite communities was that of Montgomery and Montgomery (1990). The authors characterised the stability of helminth parasite communities of wood mice (*A. sylvaticus*) through time using two diversity indices from 'free-living' community ecology, the Jaccard index and Sale's similarity index. Importantly, this study was facilitated by the ability to collect a very large data set (> 4000 mice), which is a recurring feature of many rodent studies, enabling sufficient power to conduct the analyses while controlling for potential confounding factors. Montgomery and Montgomery (1990) found that parasite communities were more similar between successive monthly samples than between samples separated by longer time intervals (i.e. community similarity decayed with time). However, those similarity indices did not differ significantly from the values predicted by null models where relative occurrences were assigned randomly from observed prevalence data. Furthermore, analysis of pairwise species associations of co-occurrence data found few significant associations, and when they did occur they tended to be weak or inconsistent (Montgomery & Montgomery, 1990).

Following on from this, a similar analysis using alternative null models to infer the extent to which interspecific parasite interactions shape parasite communities was conducted on helminth data from shrew populations in Finland (Haukisalmi & Henttonen, 1998). Their study was the first to 'ground-truth' the various null models using simulated data, where the degree of association between species (positive and negative) could be controlled. They found that all of the null models had low Type 1 error rates (i.e. they would rarely reject true null hypotheses), and were far more successful at detecting positive associations than negative ones. Interestingly, similar results have also been found in other simulation-based assessments of such methods at inferring the existence of interspecific interactions, both in free-living communities (Hastings, 1987) and in parasite communities (Fenton et al., 2010), suggesting that negative interactions may be particularly difficult to detect from ecological data taken at the population scale. When applying those null models to the shrew–parasite community data, Haukisalmi and Henttonen (1998) found that the patterns of association were variable between data sets and, perhaps more worryingly, across null models (i.e. the conclusion of whether there were biologically significant interspecific associations depended on the specific association metric used).

In a parallel set of papers, the same authors (Haukisalmi & Henttonen, 1993a, 1993b) examined whether coinfecting GI parasites of bank voles (*Clethrionomys* (=*Myodes*) *glareolus*) showed evidence of interspecific interactions by first examining whether the physical distribution of the different parasite species were shifted by the presence of other coinfecting parasites (a phenomenon seen in laboratory coinfection studies; Holmes, 1961, 1962). Largely, there were few instances of shifts in distribution under coinfection, although any shifts that were found tended to be between pairs of species with a large overlap in distribution, but not in feeding mode (Haukisalmi & Henttonen, 1993b). Hence, any competition that was occurring would appear to be driven more by interference competition (i.e. physical competition for space) than by exploitation competition for resources. Next they tested for associations in both co-occurrence (presence/absence) and helminth burden between all observed pairs of infecting parasite species. However, they rarely detected significant pairwise associations (seven of 22 pairs), and several of these associations were not consistent across sites or subsets of the host population, which suggested that the vole GI parasite community is more isolationist than interactive (Haukisalmi & Henttonen, 1993a).

Behnke et al. (2005) describe arguably the most extensive series of statistical analyses applied to observational data of rodent helminth communities; comprising > 500 wood mice with helminth burdens for up to 10 different parasite species (e.g. nematodes, cestodes, and digeneans) collected across different sites, months, years, and different studies. Using a wide range of statistical tools, they assessed pairwise interactions between infection status (presence/absence or burden) while controlling for potential intrinsic and extrinsic factors. Importantly, the authors were able to test specific hypotheses concerning whether infection with the nematode *Heligmosomoides polygyrus* facilitated subsequent infection with other helminths, in contrast to analysing all possible pairwise interactions. *H. polygyrus* is closely related to *H. polygyrus bakeri*, one of the best-studied laboratory models of GI nematodes due to its strong immunomodulatory properties (Maizels et al., 2004; Behnke & Harris, 2010), and so may be expected to facilitate infection by other parasites. The authors found an excess of positive associations compared against a random, null expectation, corresponding with the findings of Haukisalmi and Henttonen (1998). Furthermore, many of the species-pairs that occurred more often than expected involved the immunomodulatory species *H. polygyrus*. Importantly, however, these strong patterns often disappeared when the models controlled for potential confounding intrinsic and extrinsic cofactors, suggesting that those apparent interactions were driven simply by demographic or environmental heterogeneities and not interactions between species (Behnke et al., 2005). Overall, and of relevance to our first key question above, these various studies provided little compelling evidence that interspecific parasite interactions played a major role in structuring the parasite communities in these systems.

3.3.4 Coinfection studies involving microparasites
Studies of helminth–microparasite or microparasite–microparasite interactions in wild rodents have been historically less common that those of

helminth–helminth interactions. However, in a study of how coinfection impacts the important zoonotic pathogen Puumala hantavirus, Salvador et al. (2011) used a cross-sectional design to show that bank voles infected with the nematode *Heligmosomoides mixtum* were more likely to have Puumala hantavirus antibodies, and bank voles infected with the nematode *Aonchotheca* (=*Capillaria*) *muris-sylvatica* were more likely to have a high viral titre. It was hypothesised that these nematodes facilitated Puumala hantavirus infection through a trade-off from the more microparasite-focused Th1 immune response to the more macroparasite-focused Th-2 immune response (Salvador et al., 2011). In contrast, Luong et al. (2010) tested whether micro-parasites could impact helminth infection dynamics in wild yellow-necked mice (*A. flavicolis*). However, they found no evidence that any of the five microparasites investigated had a significant effect on the nematode *Heligmosomoides polygyrus* and, instead, host intrinsic factors, such as reproductive condition and sex, were the best predictors of nematode fecundity.

While many studies have sought evidence for coinfection interactions among diverse parasite taxa, others have examined interactions and associations among closely related species. In these within-host parasite communities of phylogenetically related species (i.e. within the same family or genus) we may expect high degrees of both immune cross-reactivity and resource competition, potentially resulting in an excess of negative interactions (see Box 3.1). For example, Gutiérrez et al. (2014) sought evidence of coinfection interactions among lineages of the bacterial genus *Bartonella* both in their mammalian host (wild gerbils; *Gerbillus andersoni*) and their flea vectors. They found that 89% of *Bartonella* infections carried by mammalian hosts and fleas were coinfected with both phylogenetically distant and closely related *Bartonella* species, which challenged the previous suggestion that most infections were with a single genotype. On average, infected wild gerbils were found to have 18 different *Bartonella* operational taxonomic units (OTUs), while infected fleas had an average of 17 OTUs, suggesting a very high rate of coinfection. Overall, Gutiérrez et al. (2014) found evidence for a strong negative relationship between *Bartonella* lineages, suggesting that these closely related lineages (all belonging to the same genus) may indeed compete with each other.

All the studies described so far have used cross-sectional surveys to seek evidence for interactions among coinfecting parasite species. In contrast, relatively few wild rodent coinfection studies have taken a longitudinal approach, where individuals are marked and then followed over time using recapture methods. In perhaps the largest study of its kind, Telfer et al. (2010) used an unprecedented longitudinal data set on wild field voles (*Microtus agrestis*), in which they had over 14,000 captures for nearly 6000 individual voles sampled monthly over the course of their lives, to seek evidence of interspecific interactions among four different microparasite species. The authors found a dense network of interactions between the microparasites, including both negative and positive associations, due to both current infection (comparable to the observational cross-sectional data described above) and previous infection. For example, the authors found that infection with the protozoan *Babesia microti* was more than five times more likely if the vole also became infected with the bacterium *Anaplasma phagocytophilum* over the same time interval, whereas voles were 50% less likely to become infected with *B. microti* if they had been infected with *A. phagocytophilum* in the previous month. The results of this longitudinal coinfection study challenged the conventional wisdom that most within-host parasite interactions are rare and weak, and instead suggested that they may be more important predictors of infection risk than both intrinsic and extrinsic factors (Telfer et al., 2010).

3.3.5 Experimental approaches to quantifying interspecific parasite interactions

The studies detailed above used observational data to infer the existence or importance of within-host parasite interactions, either by testing for significant pairwise associations between parasite species or departures of observed infection frequency distributions from null models. However, it is well known from free-living community ecology that it can be very hard to detect interspecific interactions from observational data alone (Schluter, 1984). As such, there is increasing interest in using experimental approaches to more directly quantify parasite interactions (Pedersen & Fenton, 2015). These studies typically follow a classic perturbation approach, using anti-parasite treatments to remove a target parasite species (or group of species) and then measuring the response in other, non-drug–target coinfecting parasite species. If the non-target species increase or decrease in the likelihood of infection or in burden/abundance post-treatment then this provides the clearest demonstration that the target parasite species either suppresses or facilitates infection by non-target species.

In a well-studied population of wild yellow-necked mice (*A. flavicolis*) in northern Italy, Ferrari et al. (2009) used both a cross-sectional and experimental approach to test whether the dominant nematode, *H. polygyrus*, interacted with the tick, *Ixodes ricinus*. Their cross-sectional study found, in addition to a very strong effect of habitat variation, that tick intensity was negatively correlated with *H. polygyrus* burdens, but this relationship was stronger in mice that were not in breeding condition compared to those that were breeding. They then tested this with a field experiment, and found that mice treated with a standard anthelmintic to reduce nematode burdens subsequently had higher tick intensities compared to control mice. Their results ran counter to the predictions from laboratory studies (Maizels et al., 2004), which suggest that the immunosuppressive effects of the closely related nematode *H. polygyrus bakeri* facilitate tick infections and so, in theory, removing *H. polygyrus* through drug treatment should reduce tick burdens. The authors were not able to identify the mechanism underlying this interaction, although they did rule out resource competition (i.e. bottom-up control; Figure 3.1), and suggested it is more likely due either to an immune-mediated interaction or the release of toxic products (i.e. top-down effects; Figure 3.1). In terms of divergence from the results from the laboratory model, the authors speculated that the laboratory species (*H. polygyrus bakeri*) may have been selected to be more immunosuppressive than the natural species (*H. polygyrus polygyrus*) (Ferrari et al., 2009), but this has not been explicitly tested.

In possibly the most comprehensive experimental assessment of parasite coinfection interactions in a wild system, Knowles (2013) treated wild wood mice (*A. sylvaticus*) with the common anthelmintic, Ivermectin, to suppress nematode infection, and then followed animals over both short (1–3 weeks) and longer (>4 weeks) time periods to quantify the response of several non-drug–target parasite species. They showed that Ivermectin successfully reduced the target nematodes (dominated by *H. polygyrus*, which accounted for ~80% of all nematode infections), lowering prevalence among treated animals by ~70% within 3 weeks of treatment (Knowles et al., 2013; Figure 3.3A). However, this suppressive effect was very short-lived; Ivermectin only reduced egg shedding for up to 3 weeks, after which there was a dramatic increase back to pre-treatment levels (Knowles et al., 2013). Very similar patterns of parasite suppression and reinfection are also seen in human populations following treatment (e.g. Basáñez et al., 2012), suggesting that wild rodent–parasite systems may be a potentially valuable model for assessing the success and efficacy of mass drug administration programmes.

In terms of coinfection, most of the non-target parasites (including bacteria, cestodes, and protozoa) showed no response to drug treatment, which suggests that the parasite community may be reasonably stable to perturbations, at least over the timescale measured, and that interspecific interactions are rare. This result was surprising because *H. polygyrus*, like many nematodes, is thought to be a strong immunomodulator (Maizels et al., 2004) and, as such, it was hypothesised that reducing *H. polygyrus* infection should result in an increase in prevalence and/or burden of coinfecting parasites. However, the authors did find evidence of one very strong interaction: the gastrointestinal coccidial protozoan, *Eimeria hungaryensis,* increased 15-fold in burden (as measured by faecal oocyst count) 1–3 weeks after anthelmintic treatment (Figure 3.3B; Knowles et al., 2013). Furthermore, by 4 weeks post-treatment, when nematode infection was back to pre-treatment levels, *E. hungaryensis* burdens also returned to pre-treatment

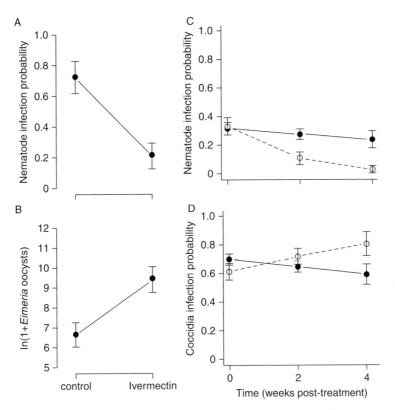

Figure 3.3 Evidence of interspecific interactions among coinfecting parasites in wild rodent systems, as obtained through targeted drug treatment using the anthelmintic Ivermectin to remove nematodes: (A) and (B) from Knowles et al. (2013), and (C) and (D) from Pedersen and Antonovics (2013). (A) and (C) show reduction in the target parasite group (nematodes) post-treatment: (A) comparing nematode prevalence in untreated vs. treated mice 1–3 weeks post-treatment; (C) nematode prevalence in untreated (solid line) vs. treated (dashed line) mice up to 4 weeks post-treatment. (B) and (D) show increase in non-target parasites following treatment: (B) log oocyst production by *Eimeria hungaryensis* 1–3 weeks post-treatment; (D) coccidia prevalence in untreated (solid line) vs. treated (dashed line) mice up to 4 weeks post-treatment.

levels. Overall, these findings suggest a very strong negative within-host interaction, such that nematodes (most likely driven by *H. polygyrus*) naturally suppress *E. hungaryensis* burdens, but when the nematodes are removed by drug treatment, *E. hungaryensis* burdens (or at least oocyst production) can dramatically increase.

Notably, similar experimental evidence of a negative interaction between nematodes and coccidia have also been found in a taxonomically different, but ecologically similar, system: nematodes and *Eimeria* spp. coinfecting wild

Peromyscus maniculatus and *P. leucopus* (deer mice and white-footed mice) in the USA (Pedersen & Antonovics, 2013). Here the same anthelmintic treatment (Ivermectin) reduced nematode infections in treated mice (Figure 3.3C), and resulted in a significant increase in the probability of coccidia infection over the same short timescale (Figure 3.3D). Furthermore, there was a significant increase in the probability of treated animals becoming infected with cestodes over the same time period. Although these two experiments were conducted on different continents with different host and parasite species, their correspondence suggests there may be some generality to these nematode–coccidia interactions (Knowles et al., 2013; Pedersen & Antonovics, 2013). Intriguingly, in a study on humans (Blackwell et al., 2013), individuals given the anthelmintic drug Mebendazole were found to have increased risk of infection with *Giardia lamblia* which, like *Eimeria*, is a protozoal parasite that infects the host's gut mucosa. It is therefore possible that the phenomenon of nematodes suppressing gut-dwelling protozoa may be more common than realised, and that rodents may be ideal models for their study. Importantly, there is a steady increase in the use of drug treatments in wildlife, and while the goal of many of these studies is to either minimise or measure the negative consequences of parasitism in the wild, these experimental perturbations have great potential application to the study of within-host parasite interactions and coinfection (Pedersen & Fenton, 2015).

At the moment, the mechanism(s) of these interactions are unknown. However, in the Knowles et al. (2013) study, the coinfecting parasite species (*E. hungaryensis*) lives and reproduces within the epithelium cells in the same part of the gut (upper duodenum) as *H. polygyrus* (Nowell & Higgs, 1989). Furthermore, *H. polygyrus* feeds by grazing on the gut villi, and it is therefore possible that this negative interaction is due to either resource competition or physical interference while *H. polygyrus* feeds (bottom-up or intraguild interactions; Figure 3.1). Alternatively, the interaction may be immune-mediated (top-down interaction; Figure 3.1), in which case it would have to be a highly localised immune response, as a related *Eimeria* species (*E. apionodes*) which resides further down the gastrointestinal tract did not significantly increase post-treatment (Knowles et al., 2013). The idea that most interactions are highly localised was also found in a recent systematic review of reported human coinfection studies, which showed that most reported interactions occurred between locally infecting parasite species, clustering around organs and locations within the human body (Griffiths et al., 2014). The emerging evidence for localised interactions are in agreement with the earlier studies of parasite communities (Montgomery & Montgomery, 1990; Haukisalmi & Henttonen, 1998; Behnke et al., 2001), which suggested that interspecific interactions between parasites may be relatively rare, and that rodent parasite communities may be more 'isolationist' than 'interactive', with species tending to occupy fairly strict, isolated niches from each other. Wild rodent systems, with their amenability to experimentation and possible links to immunological analyses developed on laboratory mice (see Box. 3.1), will continue to be an appropriate and tractable system to further address these issues.

3.4 What have wild rodent studies told us about how to detect interspecific parasite interactions from field data?

The above studies suggest that interspecific interactions can certainly occur within wild rodent (and presumably other) systems. However, there seems to be great variability across studies in the extent to which they conclude such interactions occur and are important. Some studies (e.g. Montgomery & Montgomery, 1990; Haukisalmi & Henttonen, 1993a; Behnke et al., 2005) suggest that interspecific interactions are not important in structuring within-host parasite communities, whereas other studies (e.g. Lello et al., 2004; Telfer et al., 2010) find dense networks of significant interactions. Certainly, it may be that coinfection interactions are context-dependent, but there is also a question of how best to detect or quantify parasite interactions in wild systems (our second key question from the Introduction). Because different studies often use different methodologies, it may be that variation in the methods underlies the variation in the inferred presence or absence of within-host parasite interactions. Theoretically, several studies have shown non-linear, or even opposite, relationships between the direction of interaction at the within-host scale and the pattern of association between parasites at the host population scale (Bottomley et al., 2005; Fenton et al., 2010; see Section 3.2; Fenton, 2013). Furthermore, some empirical studies that have compared different analytical methods on the same data set have found variable results (e.g. Haukisalmi & Henttonen, 1998) and, therefore, studies that use different approaches to infer the presence or direction of an interspecific parasite interaction may produce conflicting results.

Wild rodents have provided perhaps the clearest test of this hypothesis, and of the model predictions (Fenton et al., 2010; Fenton, 2013). In particular, the negative within-host interaction between nematodes and coinfecting coccidia in wild mice described above (Knowles et al., 2013; Pedersen & Antonovics, 2013) provides an ideal test case to assess how successful analytical approaches are at quantifying within-host parasite interactions. Fenton et al. (2014) applied a range of statistical tests to parasite co-occurrence data from untreated, observational mice (wood mice in the UK and *Peromyscus* spp. from the USA) from the data of Knowles et al. (2013) and Pedersen and Antonovics (2013) to test their ability to detect the underlying negative interaction apparent from the experimental manipulations. In many ways the results were depressing; very few analyses revealed associations in the

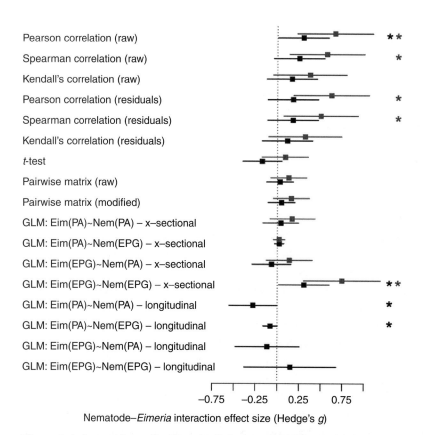

Nematode–*Eimeria* interaction effect size (Hedge's *g*)

Figure 3.4 Comparison of various statistical analyses in their ability to detect the experimentally determined negative interaction between nematodes and *Eimeria*, based on associations between the two parasites among observational (untreated) mice (from Fenton et al., 2014). Data points show mean (±95% confidence intervals) effect sizes (Hedge's *g*) of the relationship between nematode and *Eimeria* infections for each analytical approach examined for the *Apodemus sylvaticus* (black; using data from Knowles et al., 2013) and *Peromyscus* spp. (grey; using data from Pedersen & Antonovics, 2013) studies. Negative values of Hedge's *g* are in the same direction as the underlying interspecific interaction, and asterisks indicate statistical approaches where the relevant 95% CI of effect size does not overlap with zero.

direction as the demonstrated interaction (negative), and even fewer were statistically significant (Figure 3.4; Fenton et al., 2014). The best-performing approaches used longitudinal data, in which nematode infection status at one time point was used to predict coccidia infection at the following time point, thereby better capturing the cause-and-effect direction of the interaction. Cross-sectional approaches that relied on concurrent snapshot data performed particularly poorly, often leading to the inference of a positive underlying interaction. In addition, including intrinsic and extrinsic cofactors (e.g. host age, sex, site, month) which are typically used to control for potential confounding effects (i.e. possible correlated exposure between parasites, or other population substructuring which may cause spurious associations, or mask genuine ones) had very little effect on the ability to correctly infer the direction of the underlying interaction (Fenton et al., 2014).

Overall, this analysis, together with previous theory (Bottomley et al., 2005; Fenton et al., 2010; Fenton, 2013), demonstrates that conclusions about the occurrence or importance of interspecific parasite interactions based purely on observational, cross-sectional data are likely to be inaccurate. This is likely due to the fact that the observed levels of parasite infection across individuals are influenced by the interaction of multiple factors which vary between hosts (e.g. individual level rates of (co-)exposure, past infection history, immune stimulation and effect, etc.; all of which may covary with host age, nutrition, behaviour, etc.). Thus, snapshot observations of contemporary parasite co-occurrence provide little ability to disentangle the effects of interspecific parasite interactions from the various other factors that may drive positive or negative associations in co-occurrence (Fenton et al., 2010). This is one of the major issues associated with moving from the within-host scale to the host population scale (our third key question), resulting in the underlying within-host interactions having non-linear effects on patterns of parasite co-occurrence at the population scale (Fenton, 2008, 2013; Ezenwa & Jolles, 2015). Longitudinal studies can be more reliable as they allow insight into the cause-and-effect directionality of the underlying interaction; however, this is only the case if the time between samples is appropriate to reflect the timescale over which the interaction happens (Fenton et al., 2014). This is often very difficult to know a priori, as well as practically difficult to achieve for logistical reasons (e.g. collecting samples at the correct times for wild individuals). Where possible, we advocate an experimental approach, like the classic perturbation experiments in ecology, where the response of one species (or more) is measured following the experimental removal of another species (e.g. Ferrari et al., 2009; Ezenwa et al., 2010; Knowles et al., 2013; Pedersen & Antonovics, 2013; see also Ezenwa et al., this volume, Chapter 5). Of particular relevance to this chapter, wild rodent systems, due to their typically high population densities, amenability to repeated capture, and baseline data on drug toxicity levels in laboratory rodents, make good model systems for testing and developing these approaches further.

3.5 Outstanding issues, and how to move forward

Moving forward we can identify several key issues that will be important for addressing the questions raised at the start of this chapter. Perhaps the biggest issue is why so many field studies do not find strong support for coinfection interactions when so many laboratory studies do. This discrepancy could be due to the difference in approach: fine dose-controlled coinfection experiments vs. field experiments, which are often limited to using relatively coarse drug-treatment (but see Forbes et al., 2015). Or it is possible that the 'real-world' situation in the field is simply too complex, comprising a multitude of factors (e.g. high levels of heterogeneity, trickle infections, poor nutrition, stress from predation and competition, other parasite infection, etc.) which make it difficult to find a statistical association or interaction between two specific parasite species.

Related to this point, it is quite possible that within-host interactions may be present in the field setting but highly context-dependent, such that two parasites may interact strongly but only in hosts of a specific age, sex, condition, environment, etc. These types of context dependency have been found when researchers have investigated both the efficacy and consequences for host health when using anti-parasite treatments in wildlife (Pedersen & Fenton, 2015). Following the possibility that interactions are only detectable in a specific host type, it is also possible that interactions are parasite-burden-dependent, only occurring, becoming important, or detectable when burdens reach a certain threshold. This possibility has been shown theoretically (Fenton, 2013), but has been considered much less frequently in empirical studies (but see Behnke et al., 2001). Lastly, there is evidence to suggest that at least some field-detectable parasite interactions are localised rather than systemic (Knowles et al., 2013; Griffiths et al., 2014); however, it remains important to ask whether this is truly the case, and how general this phenomenon may be.

It is becoming increasingly clear that wild rodents and their diverse parasite communities make ideal systems to investigate the causes and consequences of coinfection. Given the close taxonomic relatedness of wild rodent systems to standard laboratory mouse models of infection and coinfection, we advocate a strong connection between these 'wild' and 'laboratory' models in the future. The laboratory can provide a controlled setting in order to understand mechanisms of interaction, especially the immunological response (Graham, 2008; Pedersen & Babayan, 2011), but the 'wild' (even in semi-natural enclosures) can test the importance and consistency of these within-host interactions in real-world settings, while measuring their implications for host fitness (e.g. Quinnell, 1992; Forbes et al., 2015). Importantly, testing the dynamics of coinfection in a laboratory setting, but with hosts that are naturally infected with those parasites species (i.e. sharing a common coevolutionary history), will be an important step in understanding how 'real-world' parasites interact. These types of controlled settings could be achieved by either bringing formerly wild mice into a controlled laboratory setting, or, in turn, bringing former laboratory mice into a more wild environment (e.g. a semi-natural mesocosm). Another key area to investigate will be how the host microbiome, especially the gut microbiome, may influence either the likelihood or outcome of within-host parasite interactions. A recent laboratory mouse study found that the nematode *Trichuris muris* failed to hatch when not exposed to a specific commensal bacterium commonly found in the mouse GI tract (Hayes et al., 2010). While there are an increasing number of studies which investigate the gut microbiome in wild rodents (Kreisinger et al., 2015; Maurice et al., 2015), understanding the interactions between the microbiome and coinfecting parasites will be an important next step.

At present, most of empirical work on wild rodents has focused on the ecological issues of coinfection; however, the applied issue of whether those interactions affect host health or alter the success or impact of disease control strategies has received very little empirical attention. Coinfection theory has made some attempt to address these issues in a general sense (e.g. showing how interspecific parasite interactions can alter host longevity (Fenton, 2013), or the level of treatment coverage required to control a coinfecting parasite (Fenton, 2008)). However, to date, there has been little empirical work in these areas (although Bordes and colleagues have made progress relating polyparasitism rates to host immune metrics and fecundity; Bordes & Morand, 2009; Bordes et al., 2011), and little attempt to bring this theory closer to the empirical systems (but see Ezenwa et al., 2010; Ezenwa & Jolles, 2015). Given the amenability of wild rodent systems for investigating coinfection, there is clear potential to conduct alternative, well-replicated parasite control scenarios that are not possible with human populations. Such studies would thereby provide valuable empirical data from a natural vertebrate model system to parameterise and validate current general theory on the impact and implications of disease control programmes.

3.6 Conclusions

Within-host parasite communities likely fit somewhere between a pure isolationist community, with few within-host parasite interactions, and a pure interactionist community, where all parasites interact strongly with each other. In real-world systems, it is very likely that the network of within-host interactions has 'small-world' properties like many ecological (and other) networks (Watts & Strogatz, 1998; Sole & Montoya, 2001; Strogatz, 2001; Montoya & Sole, 2002), which would suggest that most coinfection interactions are both rare and weak, although some parasites interact strongly. Such network structure can convey stability to perturbation (Sole & Montoya, 2001), which would fit with the findings of Knowles et al. (2013), where only one significant interaction was

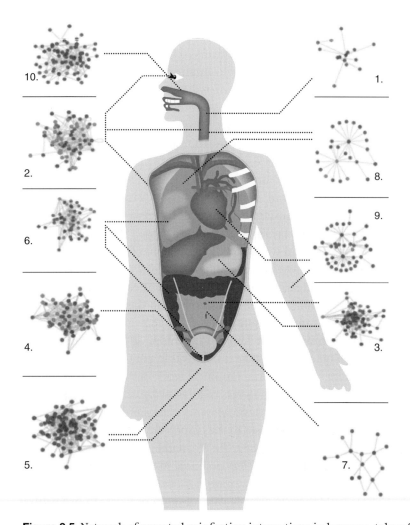

Figure 3.5 Network of reported coinfection interactions in humans, taken from a survey of 316 published articles (from Griffiths et al., 2014). The coinfection network comprises parasite (blue), immune (green), and resource (pink) nodes, forming 10 distinct modules, eight of which are associated with particular bodily sites (1, throat; 2, mixed; 3, GI; 4, genitals; 5, urinary tract or skin; 6, other mucosa; 7, bowel; 8, lower respiratory tract; 9, blood; 10, mouth). (A black and white version of this figure will appear in some formats. For the colour version, please refer to the plate section.)

observed post-treatment, and the community rapidly returned to its pre-perturbation state shortly afterwards. A recent meta-analysis of human coinfection data clearly demonstrates similar patterns, finding that most within-human parasite interactions were highly clustered, primarily centred around shared locations in the body (Figure 3.5; Griffiths et al., 2011).

However, it is important to ask whether within-host parasite interactions in wild systems are indeed rare, or whether the tools that we use to measure them simply do not have sufficient resolution or power. It may be that because we can only collect samples at specific time points in the field, we may miss the timescale over which many interspecific interactions can be detected. Also, as opposed to laboratory settings, field studies can't control the timing of infection and coinfection, and thus we have to seek a signal from a mixture of infection and coinfection histories (e.g. which parasite infects first, time points between infection, doses, etc.), all of which can be hard to measure accurately in the field. While experimental field studies may not be able to overcome all of these challenges, we suggest that they are the best way to measure responses across a broad parasite community, ideally linked to laboratory studies using the same (or at least closely related) host and parasite species. Rodent systems appear well placed to allow this, and closer integration of studies in the laboratory, field, and theory has the potential to improve our understanding of the occurrence and consequences of coinfection interactions more broadly.

3.7 Acknowledgements

We would like to thank all the people who have helped us while working on coinfection biology in wild rodents – in particular Sarah Knowles, Godefroy Devevey, Melanie Clerc, Susan Withenshaw, Simon Babayan, Owen Petchey, and all the technicians and field assistants, without whom we would have no data to talk about. We also thank the 'EGLIDE' group (Amy Sweeny, Saudamini Venkatesan, Dishon Muloi, Alexandra Morris, Lisa Gecchele, Dave Daversa, Shaun Keegan, and Kayleigh Gallagher) for their very helpful comments on an earlier draft. This work was funded by grants from NERC (NE/G006830/1, NE/G007349/1, NE/I024038/1 and NE/I026367/1) to ABP and AF, and a Wellcome Trust CIIE Advanced Fellowship (095831) and University of Edinburgh Chancellors Fellowship to ABP.

References

Abu-Madi, M.A., Behnke, J.M., Lewis, J.W. & Gilbert, F.S. (1998) Descriptive epidemiology of *Heligmosomoides polygyrus* in *Apodemus sylvaticus* from three contrasting habitats in southeast England. *Journal of Helminthology*, **72**, 93–100.

Abu-Madi, M.A., Behnke, J.M., Lewis, J.W. & Gilbert, F.S. (2000) Seasonal and site specific variation in the component community structure of intestinal helminths in *Apodemus sylvaticus* from three contrasting habitats in south-east England. *Journal of Helminthology*, **74**, 7–15.

Anderson, R.M. & May, R.M. (1978) Regulation and stability of host–parasite population interactions. I. Regulatory processes. *Journal of Animal Ecology*, **47**, 219–247.

Anderson, R.M. & May, R.M. (1981) The population dynamics of microparasites and their invertebrate hosts. *Philosophical Transactions of the Royal Society of London B*, **291**, 451–524.

Anderson, R.M. & May, R.M. (1992) *Infectious Diseases of Humans: Dynamics and Control.* Oxford: Oxford University Press.

Basáñez, M.-G., French, M.D., Walker, M. & Churcher, T.S. (2012) Paradigm lost: how parasite control may alter pattern and process in human helminthiases. *Trends in Parasitology*, **28**, 161–171.

Behnke, J. & Harris, P.D. (2010) *Heligmosomoides bakeri*: a new name for an old worm? *Trends in Parasitology*, **26**, 524–529.

Behnke, J.M., Bajer, A., Sinski, E. & Wakelin, D. (2001) Interactions involving intestinal nematodes of rodents: experimental and field studies. *Parasitology*, **122**, S39–S49.

Behnke, J.M., Gilbert, F.S., Abu-Madi, M.A. & Lewis, J.W. (2005) Do the helminth parasites of wood mice interact? *Journal of Animal Ecology*, **74**, 982–993.

Bentwich, Z., Kalinkovich, A., Weisman, Z., et al. (1999) Can eradication of helminthic infections change the face of AIDS and tuberculosis? *Immunology Today*, **20**, 485–487.

Blackwell, A.D., Martin, M., Kaplan, H. & Gurven, M. (2013) Antagonism between two intestinal parasites in humans: the importance of co-infection for infection risk and recovery dynamics. *Proceedings of The Royal Society of London B*, **280**, 20131671.

Bordes, F., Guegan, J.F. & Morand, S. (2011) Microparasite species richness in rodents is higher at lower latitudes and is associated with reduced litter size. *Oikos*, **120**, 1889–1896.

Bordes, F. & Morand, S. (2009) Coevolution between multiple helminth infestations and basal immune investment in mammals: cumulative effects of polyparasitism? *Parasitology Research*, **106**, 33–37.

Bottomley, C., Isham, V. & Basanez, M.G. (2005) Population biology of multispecies helminth infection: interspecific interactions and parasite distribution. *Parasitology*, **131**, 417–433.

Bottomley, C., Isham, V. & Basanez, M.G. (2007) Population biology of multispecies helminth infection: competition and coexistence. *Journal of Theoretical Biology*, **244**, 81–95.

Bush, A.O. & Holmes, J.C. (1986) Intestinal helminths of lesser scaup ducks: an interactive community. *Canadian Journal of Zoology – Revue Canadienne de Zoologie*, **64**, 142–152.

Costa, F., Porter, F.H., Rodrigues, G., et al. (2014) Infections by Leptospira interrogans, Seoul Virus, and Bartonella spp. among Norway rats (*Rattus norvegicus*) from the urban slum environment in Brazil. *Vector-borne and Zoonotic Diseases*, **14**(1), 33–40. DOI:10.1089/vbz.2013.1378.

Cox, F.E.G. (2001) Concomitant infections, parasites and immune responses. *Parasitology*, **122**, S23–S38.

de Bellocq, J.G., Sara, M., Casanova, J.C., Feliu, C. & Morand, S. (2003) A comparison of the structure of helminth communities in the woodmouse, *Apodemus sylvaticus*, on islands of the western Mediterranean and continental Europe. *Parasitology Research*, **90**, 64–70.

Dobson, A.P. (1985) The population dynamics of competition between parasites. *Parasitology*, **91**, 317–347.

Dobson, A.P. (1988) The population biology of parasite-induced changes in host behavior. *Quarterly Review of Biology*, **63**, 139–165.

Druilhe, P., Tall, A. & Sokhna, C. (2005) Worms can worsen malaria: towards a new means to roll back malaria? *Trends in Parasitology*, **21**, 359–362.

Elton, C., Ford, E.B. & Baker, J.R. (1931) The health and parasites of a wild mouse population. *Proceedings of the Royal Society of London B*, **101**, 657–721.

Ezenwa, V.O., Etienne, R.S., Luikart, G., Beja-Pereira, A. & Jolles, A.E. (2010) Hidden consequences of living in a wormy world: nematode-induced immune suppression facilitates tuberculosis invasion in African buffalo. *American Naturalist*, **176**, 613–624.

Ezenwa, V.O. & Jolles, A.E. (2015) Opposite effects of anthelmintic treatment on microbial infection at individual versus population scales. *Science*, **347**, 175–177.

Fenton, A. (2008) Worms and germs: the population dynamic consequences of microparasite–macroparasite co-infection. *Parasitology*, **135**, 1545–1560.

Fenton, A. (2013) Dances with worms: the ecological and evolutionary impacts of deworming on coinfecting pathogens. *Parasitology*, **140**, 1119–1132.

Fenton, A., Knowles, S.C.L., Petchey, O.L. & Pedersen, A.B. (2014) The reliability of observational approaches for detecting interspecific parasite interactions: comparison with experimental results. *International Journal for Parasitology*, **44**, 437–445.

Fenton, A. & Perkins, S.E. (2010) Applying predator–prey theory to modelling immune-mediated, within-host interspecific parasite interactions. *Parasitology*, **137**, 1027–1038.

Fenton, A., Viney, M.E. & Lello, J. (2010) Detecting interspecific macroparasite interactions from ecological data: patterns and process. *Ecology Letters*, **13**, 606–615.

Ferrari, N., Cattadori, I.M., Rizzoli, A. & Hudson, P.J. (2009) *Heligmosomoides polygyrus* reduces infestation of *Ixodes ricinus* in free-living yellow-necked mice, *Apodemus flavicollis*. *Parasitology*, **136**, 305–316.

Forbes, K.M., Henttonen, H., Hirvela-Koski, V., et al. (2015) Food provisioning alters infection dynamics in populations of a wild rodent. *Proceedings of the Royal Society of London B*, **282**, 20151939.

Gatto, M. & De Leo, G.A. (1998) Interspecific competition among macroparasites in a density-dependent host population. *Journal of Mathematical Biology*, **37**, 467–490.

Gause, G.E. (1934) *The Struggle for Existence*. Baltimore, MD: Williams & Wilkins.

Graham, A.L. (2008) Ecological rules governing helminth–microparasite coinfection. *Proceedings of the National Academy of Sciences of the United States of America*, **105**, 566–570.

Griffiths, E.C., Pedersen, A.B., Fenton, A. & Petchey, O.L. (2011) The nature and consequences of coinfection in humans. *Journal of Infection*, **63**, 200–206.

Griffiths, E.C., Pedersen, A.B., Fenton, A. & Petchey, O.L. (2014) Analysis of a summary network of co-infection in humans reveals that parasites interact most via shared resources. *Proceedings of the Royal Society of London B*, **281**, 20132286.

Gupta, S., Maiden, M.C.J., Feavers, I.M., et al. (1996) The maintenance of strain structure in populations of recombining infectious agents. *Nature Medicine*, **2**, 437–442.

Gupta, S., Swinton, J. & Anderson, R.M. (1994) Theoretical studies of the effects of heterogeneity in the parasite population on the transmission dynamics of malaria. *Proceedings of the Royal Society of London B*, **256**, 231–238.

Gutiérrez, R., Morick, D., Cohen, C., Hawlena, H. & Harrus, S. (2014) The effect of ecological and temporal factors on the composition of *Bartonella* infection in rodents and their fleas. *ISME Journal*, **8**, 1598–1608.

Harms, G. & Feldmeier, H. (2002) HIV infection and tropical parasitic diseases – deleterious interactions in both directions? *Tropical Medicine and International Health*, **7**, 479–488.

Harris, J.B., Podolsky, M.J., Bhuiyan, T.R., et al. (2009) Immunologic responses to *Vibrio cholerae* in patients co-infected with intestinal parasites in Bangladesh. *PLoS Neglected Tropical Diseases*, **3**, e403.

Hastings, A. (1987) Can competition be detected using species co-occurrrence data? *Ecology*, **68**, 117–123.

Haukisalmi, V. & Henttonen, H. (1993a) Coexistence in helminths of the bank vole *Clethrionomys glareolus*. 1. Patterns of co-occurrence. *Journal of Animal Ecology*, **62**, 221–229.

Haukisalmi, V. & Henttonen, H. (1993b) Coexistence in helminths of the bank vole *Clethrionomys glareolus*. 2. Intestinal distribution and interspecific interactions. *Journal of Animal Ecology*, **62**, 230–238.

Haukisalmi, V. & Henttonen, H. (1998) Analysing interspecific associations in parasites: alternative methods and effects of sampling heterogeneity. *Oecologia*, **116**, 565–574.

Hayes, K.S., Bancroft, A.J., Goldrick, M., et al. (2010) Exploitation of the intestinal microflora by the parasitic nematode *Trichuris muris*. *Science*, **328**, 1391–1394.

Holmes, J.C. (1961) Effects of concurrent infections on *Hymenolepis diminuta* (Cestoda) and *Moniliformis dubius* (Acanthocephala). 1. General effects and comparison with crowding. *Journal of Parasitology*, **47**, 209–216.

Holmes, J.C. (1962) Effects of concurrent infections on *Hymenolepis diminuta* (Cestoda) and *Moniliformis dubius* (Acanthocephala). Effects on growth. *Journal of Parasitology*, **48**, 87–96.

Holmes, J.C. & Price, P.W. (1986) Communities of parasites. In: Kikkawa, J. & Anderson, D. J. (eds.), *Community Ecology: Patterns and Processes* (pp. 187–213).Oxford: Blackwell Scientific Publishers.

Johnson, P.T.J., De Roode, J.C. & Fenton, A. (2015) Why infectious disease research needs community ecology. *Science*, **349**.

Kennedy, C.R. (2006) *Ecology of the Acathocephala*. Cambridge: Cambridge University Press.

Knowles, S.C.L., Fenton, A., Petchey, O.L., et al. (2013) Stability of within-host parasite communities in a wild mammal system. *Proceedings of the Royal Society of London B*, **280**, 20130598.

Krasnov, B.R., Matthee, S., Lareschi, M., Korallo-Vinarskaya, N.P. & Vinarski, M.V. (2010) Co-occurrence of ectoparasites on rodent hosts: null model analyses of data from three continents. *Oikos*, **119**, 120–128.

Kreisinger, J., Bastien, G., Hauffe, H.C., Marchesi, J. & Perkins, S.E. (2015) Interactions between multiple helminths and the gut microbiota in wild rodents. *Philosophical Transactions of the Royal Society of London B – Biological Sciences*, **370**, 20150295.

Lello, J., Boag, B., Fenton, A., Stevenson, I.R. & Hudson, P.J. (2004) Competition and mutualism among the gut helminths of a mammalian host. *Nature*, **428**, 840–844.

Lewis, J.W. (1968a) Studies on the helminth parasites of the long-tailed field mouse, *Apodemus sylvaticus sylvaticus* from Wales. *Journal of Zoology*, **154**, 287–312.

Lewis, J.W. (1968b) Studies on the helminth parasites of voles and shrews from Wales. *Journal of Zoology*, **154**, 313–331.

Lotka, A.J. (1932) The growth of mixed populations: two species competing for a common food supply. *Journal of the Washington Academy of Science*, **22**, 461–469.

Luong, L.T., Perkins, S.E., Grear, D.A., Rizzoli, A. & Hudson, P.J. (2010) The relative importance of host characteristics and co-infection in generating variation in *Heligmosomoides polygyrus* fecundity. *Parasitology*, **137**, 1003–1012.

Maizels, R.M., Balic, A., Gomez-Escobar, N., et al. (2004) Helminth parasites – masters of regulation. *Immunological Reviews*, **201**, 89–116.

Maurice, C.F., Knowles, S.C.L., Ladau, J., et al. (2015) Marked seasonal variation in the wild mouse gut microbiota. *ISME Journal*, **9**, 2423–2434.

May, R.M. & Nowak, M.A. (1995) Coinfection and the evolution of parasite virulence. *Proceedings of the Royal Society of London B*, **261**, 209–215.

Montgomery, S.S.J. & Montgomery, W.I. (1988) Cyclic and non-cyclic dynamics in populations of the helminth parasites of wood mice, *Apodemus sylvaticus*. *Journal of Helminthology*, **62**, 78–90.

Montgomery, S.S.J. & Montgomery, W.I. (1990) Structure, stability and species interactions in helminth communities of wood mice, *Apodemus sylvaticus*. *International Journal for Parasitology*, **20**, 225–242.

Montoya, J.M. & Sole, R.V. (2002) Small world patterns in food webs. *Journal of Theoretical Biology*, **214**, 405–412.

Muller-Graf, C.D.M., Durand, P., Feliu, C., et al. (1999) Epidemiology and genetic variability of two species of nematodes (*Heligmosomoides polygyrus* and *Syphacia stroma*) of *Apodemus* spp. *Parasitology*, **118**, 425–432.

Nieto, N.C., Leonhard, S., Foley, J.E. & Lane, R.S. (2010) Coinfection of western gray squirrel (*Sciurus griseus*) and other sciurid rodents with *Borrelia burgdorferi* sensu stricto and *Anaplasma phagocytophilum* in California. *Journal of Wildlife Diseases*, **46**(1), 291&296. http://dx.doi.org/10.7589/0090-3558-46 .1.291.

Nowell, F. & Higgs, S. (1989) *Eimeria* species infecting wood mice (genus *Apodemus*) and the transfer of two species to *Mus musculus*. *Parasitology*, **98**, 329–336.

Pedersen, A.B. & Antonovics, J. (2013) Anthelmintic treatment alters the parasite community in a wild mouse host. *Biology Letters*, **9**, 20130205.

Pedersen, A.B. & Babayan, S.A. (2011) Wild immunology. *Molecular Ecology*, **20**, 872–880.

Pedersen, A.B. & Fenton, A. (2007) Emphasising the ecology in parasite community ecology. *Trends in Ecology & Evolution*, **22**, 133–139.

Pedersen, A.B. & Fenton, A. (2015) The role of antiparasite treatment experiments in assessing the impact of parasites on wildlife. *Trends in Parasitology*, **31**, 200–211.

Petney, T.N. & Andrews, R.H. (1998) Multiparasite communities in animals and humans: frequency, structure and pathogenic significance. *International Journal for Parasitology*, **28**, 377–393.

Poulin, R. (1996) Richness, nestedness, and randomness in parasite infracommunity structure. *Oecologia*, **105**, 545–551.

Poulin, R. (1997) Species richness of parasite assemblages: evolution and patterns. *Annual Review of Ecology and Systematics*, **28**, 341–358.

Poulin, R. (2007) *Evolutionary Ecology of Parasites*, 2nd edition. Princeton, NJ: Princeton University Press.

Price, P.W. (1980) *Evolutionary Biology of Parasites*. Princeton, NJ: Princeton University Press.

Quinnell, R.J. (1992) The population dynamics of *Heligmosomoides polygyrus* in an enclosure population of wood mice. *Journal of Animal Ecology*, **61**, 669–679.

Rausch, R. (1952) Studies on the helminth fauna of Alaska. 11. Helminth parasites of microtine rodents – taxonomic considerations. *Journal of Parasitology*, **38**, 415–444.

Rausch, R. & Kuns, M.L. (1950) Studies on some North American shrew cestodes. *Journal of Parasitology*, **36**, 433–438.

Roberts, M.G. & Dobson, A.P. (1995) The population dynamics of communities of parasitic helminths. *Mathematical Biosciences*, **126**, 191–214.

Rynkiewicz, E.C., Pedersen, A.B. & Fenton, A. (2015) An ecosystem approach to understanding and managing within-host parasite community dynamics. *Trends in Parasitology*, **31**, 212–221.

Salvador, A.R., Guivier, E., Xuereb, A., et al. (2011) Concomitant influence of helminth infection and landscape on the distribution of Puumala hantavirus in its reservoir, *Myodes glareolus*. *BMC Microbiology*, **11**, 30.

Schluter, D. (1984) A variance test for detecting species associations, with some example applications. *Ecology*, **65**, 998–1005.

Sharpe, G.I. (1964) The helminth parasites of some small mammal communities. I. The parasites and their hosts. *Parasitology*, **54**, 145–154.

Shaw, D.J. & Dobson, A.P. (1995) Patterns of macroparasite abundance and aggregation in wildlife populations: a quantitative review. *Parasitology*, **111**, S111–133.

Shaw, D.J., Grenfell, B.T. & Dobson, A.P. (1998) Patterns of macroparasite aggregation in wildlife host populations. *Parasitology*, **117**, 597–610.

Sole, R.V. & Montoya, J.M. (2001) Complexity and fragility in ecological networks. *Proceedings of the Royal Society of London B*, **268**, 2039–2045.

Stanko, M., Miklisova, D., de Bellocq, J.G. & Morand, S. (2002) Mammal density and patterns of ectoparasite species richness and abundance. *Oecologia*, **131**, 289–295.

Stock, T.M. & Holmes, J.C. (1988) Functional relationships and microhabitat distributions of enteric helminths of grebes (Podicipedidae): the evidence for interactive communities. *Journal of Parasitology*, **74**, 214–227.

Strogatz, S.H. (2001) Exploring complex networks. *Nature*, **410**, 268–276.

Telfer, S., Lambin, X., Birtles, R., et al. (2010) Species interactions in a parasite community drive infection risk in a wildlife population. *Science*, **330**, 243–246.

Thomas, R.J. (1953) On the nematode and trematode parasites of some small mammals from the Inner Hebrides. *Journal of Helminthology*, **27**, 143–168.

van Baalen, M. & Sabelis, M.W. (1995) The dynamics of multiple infection and the evolution of virulence. *American Naturalist*, **146**, 881–910.

Watts, D.J. & Strogatz, S.H. (1998) Collective dynamics of 'small-world' networks. *Nature*, **393**, 440–442.

Yakob, L., Williams, G.M., Gray, D.J., et al. (2013) Slaving and release in co-infection control. *Parasites & Vectors*, **6**, 157.

CHAPTER FOUR

From population to individual host scale and back again: testing theories of infection and defence in the Soay sheep of St Kilda

ADAM D. HAYWARD, ROMAIN GARNIER,
DYLAN Z. CHILDS, BRYAN T. GRENFELL,
KATHRYN A. WATT, JILL G. PILKINGTON,
JOSEPHINE M. PEMBERTON AND ANDREA
L. GRAHAM

4.1 Introduction

Forty years have passed since Roy Anderson and Robert May proposed a comprehensive framework to explain ecological and coevolutionary dynamics of host–parasite interactions (Anderson & May, 1979, 1982; May & Anderson, 1979), generating an array of predictions about the causes of variation in disease dynamics and parasite burden. Theoretical predictions have, however, often outpaced empirical research in disease ecology. The lag in testing disease ecology theories has arguably arisen because their dynamical predictions pose huge empirical demands, particularly in natural systems. For example, in nature, it is difficult to quantify both the exposure and defence heterogeneities that are predicted to explain observed variation among hosts in the burden of macroparasites such as gastrointestinal helminths (Anderson & May, 1979; Shaw et al., 1998; Wilson et al., 2002). Likewise, quantification of both the costs and benefits of immune defence is challenging, yet necessary to test the expectation that they combine to explain defence heterogeneity (Sheldon & Verhulst, 1996; Cressler et al., 2015). The empirical data required to test theory include a battery of host and parasite phenotypes as well as evolutionary fitness metrics (e.g. survival, fecundity, transmission success). Such requirements necessitate longitudinal monitoring of populations and, often, of individual hosts.

The challenge of collecting such data is now being met, as evidenced throughout this book. However, one of the greatest challenges is to link within- and between-host processes. Indeed, a 'holy grail' in disease ecology has been to quantify rigorously the predicted feedbacks between within-host and population-level processes (Grenfell et al., 1995; Wilson et al., 2002; Borer et al., 2011; Day et al., 2011; Mideo et al., 2011; Penczykowski et al., 2015). For example, selection pressures that shape parasite dynamics and diversity can only be quantified via analysis of within-host selection in relation to transmission probabilities (Day et al., 2011; Mideo et al., 2011). Likewise, testing predicted cycles of negative frequency-dependence for disease resistance (Bowers et al., 1994; Thrall & Antonovics, 1994; Boots et al., 2009) requires dynamical data on exposure, and benefits and costs of defence on relevant timescales.

We suggest that testing and improving theoretical models in disease ecology, outside of tightly controlled experimental mesocosms (e.g. Westra et al., 2015), will first be possible in exceptionally well-monitored wild populations. In this chapter, we argue that the Soay sheep population of St Kilda represents such a system. Building towards cross-scale tests of disease ecology theory requires foundational data at the population and individual scales themselves. Below, we characterise the Soay sheep population and outline how data on this system have led to insights at each scale, before returning to consider cross-scale dynamics.

4.2 The Soay sheep of St Kilda

4.2.1 Population history

The St Kilda archipelago lies 70 km west of the Outer Hebrides, Scotland, 57° 49′N8°35′W (Figure 4.1). The largest island, Hirta (638 ha), was home to a human population from the Bronze Age until 1930, when the remaining permanent inhabitants were evacuated at their own request (Steele, 1979). Meanwhile, a small population of sheep (*Ovis aries*), descendants of early Northern European domesticated sheep (Chessa et al., 2009), was abandoned on the adjacent island of Soay (99 ha) several thousand years ago. During the human occupation of Hirta, improved sheep breeds were brought to the islands, and genetic evidence supports a historical report of admixture via introduction of a few males of the now-extinct 'Dunface' breed on Soay (Feulner et al., 2013). The Soay sheep lived unmanaged until 1932, when 107 individuals were moved from Soay onto Hirta (Clutton-Brock et al., 2004). These sheep have therefore lived free of predators, interspecific competition, and management by humans for thousands of years, their only natural ene-mies being the parasites (many of which likely accompanied them from the mainland) and the great skuas (*Stercorarius skua*) which occasionally take weak lambs. Their frequent production of twins suggests a domesticated past, but small size, agility, shedding of wool, and behaviour suggest a long history independent of artificial breeding and management (Figure 4.2). The Hirta population was first counted in 1952, with regular population counts from 1955 to the present day using the same method. In the 1960s and 1970s, newborn lambs were tagged, enabling ground-breaking demographic studies including the demonstration of contrasting survival curves of males and females (Jewell et al., 1974), and providing an initial marked sample of sheep

(A)

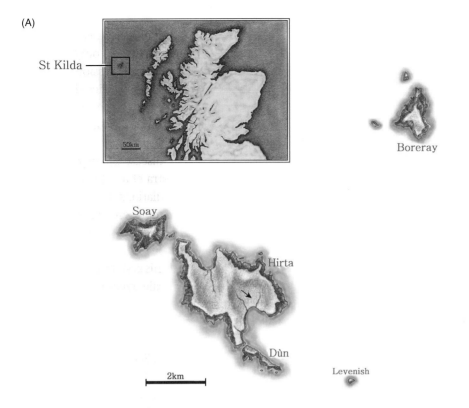

Becky Holland

(B)

Figure 4.1 The location of the isolated St Kilda archipelago and the layout of the islands (A), with the photograph of the Village Bay study area (B) taken from the approximate location and direction indicated by the black arrow. Map drawn by Becky Lister-Kaye, originally used in Graham et al. (2016) and reprinted with permission; photograph by Alexandra Sparks and used with permission. (A black and white version of this figure will appear in some formats. For the colour version, please refer to the plate section.)

Figure 4.2 An illustration of some of the genetically determined variations in horn type and coat colour in St Kilda Soay sheep. Clockwise from top left: normal-horned light wild ewe with dark wild twins (photo by Kara Dicks); normal-horned dark wild ram (photograph by Arpat Ozgul); dark self ewe; scurred dark wild female with dark self lamb (both by Kara Dicks). All photos are used with permission. (A black and white version of this figure will appear in some formats. For the colour version, please refer to the plate section.)

for the present study, which began in 1985. Since 1985, the sheep inhabiting the Village Bay area of Hirta have been the subject of a much more intensive individual-based study (Clutton-Brock & Pemberton, 2004).

4.2.2 The sheep year and longitudinal study design

Lambs are born in spring, as singletons or twins (~12% of litters 1985–2016; annual range, 2–21%) and >95% are captured within a week of birth. Each lamb is given unique identifying ear tags and is weighed, blood-sampled, and tissue-sampled for genetic analysis. Most maternal identities are known from behavioural interactions and both maternal and paternal identities are inferred using 315 unlinked single nucleotide polymorphisms (SNPs), enabling construction of a comprehensive genetic pedigree (Bérénos et al., 2014). Each August, a team erects a series of corral traps to recapture as many tagged individuals as possible. On average, 50% (or ~240 animals) of the Village Bay population is captured each year, with a range of 35–75% (~150–350 animals), apart from in two very low-density years in 1986 and 1989 in which capture rates were < 20%. Captured individuals are weighed and checked for ectopar-asites, various skeletal measurements are taken, and blood and faecal samples are collected. During the November rut, males search for and defend oestrous females, with the heaviest males with the largest horns and testes gaining greatest access to females and the majority of paternities (Preston et al., 2003; Johnston et al., 2013). Soay sheep are highly precocious (young-of-the-year of both sexes, aged around 7 months, may participate in the rut) and promiscu-ous (males and females mate multiply). Immigrants from outside Village Bay are opportunistically captured, tagged, and tissue-sampled for genetic ana-lyses. Immigration rates are relatively low: females in particular are strongly-philopatric (Coltman et al., 2003) and the Village Bay population is well-defined. As of January 2017, the population database contained information on 10,989 individuals; the earliest-known individuals are two ewes born in 1975.

Ten population censuses are conducted in each of the three field seasons each year, and a whole-island population count is performed each August, providing accurate estimates of population size. Most mortality occurs at the end of winter, just before lambing commences. During late winter, daily searches of Village Bay mean that the majority of tagged individuals are found when newly dead, providing accurate estimates of death date and life-span, and enabling timely necropsies. The Village Bay population is therefore a demographically well-defined population with low (im)migration rates, strong philopatry, accurate information on birth and death rates, and inten-sive longitudinal monitoring of individual phenotypes.

4.2.3 Suitability as a study population in disease ecology

The St Kilda Soay sheep present a number of strengths in the quest to link population- and individual-level processes in host–parasite evolutionary ecology. First, intensive, longitudinal monitoring of individual phenotype and fitness enables studies of natural selection (Clutton-Brock & Sheldon, 2010). Second, the extended population time series enables study of link-ages between population dynamics and individual phenotypes. Third, parasite transmission potential can be quantified by both the shedding of infective stages from individual hosts and the distribution of parasites in the environment. Fourth, because sheep are an important domesticated animal, resources for genotyping and phenotyping individuals are readily available. The Ovine SNP50 Beadchip (Illumina) has allowed genotyping of all individuals at ~37,000 SNPs, providing an accurate genetic pedigree and enabling identification of loci linked to traits of interest (Johnston et al., 2011, 2016; Bérénos et al., 2014, 2015). Additionally, the most prevalent and virulent parasites on St Kilda are the same species of gastrointestinal strongyle nematodes which infect domesticated sheep (Wilson et al., 2004). Key aspects of the immune response to strongyles have been revealed over decades of experiments on domesticated sheep (e.g. Smith et al., 1985; Stear et al., 1995; Houdijk et al., 2005; Halliday et al., 2007), which has recently enabled a suite of techniques and reagents for measuring immunological and physiological traits to be applied in the Soay sheep. The types of data collected have expanded as the Soay sheep collaboration has grown and as technical advancements have permitted new areas of investigation in the Soays and other wild populations (Garnier & Graham, 2014). Whenever possible, new assays have been applied to banked samples to retrospectively generate an extended time series (Graham et al., 2010; Hayward et al., 2014a; Nussey et al., 2014). Recent investigations, however, have required alternatives to the default method of processing and storage at −20°C: samples have also been stored at −80°C for analysis of oxidative stress (Christensen et al., 2015) and preserved in fixative for analysis of T-cell phenotype (Nussey et al., 2012; Watson et al., 2016). Some of the time series discussed below are therefore relatively short compared to the 30+ years of data on demography, size, fitness, and parasite burdens in the Soay sheep, but nonetheless remain rare in their longitudinal nature at the individual scale.

Although the St Kilda Soay sheep system has many strengths, it inevitably falls short of the 'ideal' disease ecology system. Parasite burden can only be estimated from faecal egg counts, rather than measured directly in vivo; blood and faecal sampling of individuals, although intensive in August and often spring, is infrequent or absent through the rest of the year; although many individuals are sampled every year, some individuals, particularly those living on the periphery of the study area, are not. Despite these shortcomings, the Soay sheep study combines intensive monitoring of fitness, annual parasite burdens and defences of individuals of known genotype and relatedness, all in the context of wider population-scale monitoring. These attributes make the St Kilda Soay sheep a promising system for answering disease ecology questions at both the population and individual scales, and for quantifying mutual feedbacks between within-individual and population-level processes.

Lastly, while the Soay sheep study has benefitted from technologies in veterinary immunoparasitology, we also see great potential for reciprocal benefits: the St Kilda Soay sheep experience the varying food supply, wild weather, and parasite heterogeneity which sheep on pasture experience, but which experimental domestic animals do not. Therefore, quantification and explanation of individual heterogeneity among Soay sheep has the potential to greatly expand understanding of domesticated sheep as well, particularly if quantifiable variation in host defence arises from population-level processes such as parasite transmission on pasture. A synergy of understanding between

St Kilda Soay sheep and domesticated animals is a theme which we will return to throughout the chapter.

Intensive study of host–parasite interactions in the Soay sheep began in 1988, when collection of faecal egg count data began in earnest. Progress of the first 15 years of research has been reviewed previously (Wilson et al., 2004), particularly regarding drivers of variation in prevalence and intensity of infection and the effects of infection on sheep health and dynamics. Throughout this chapter, rather than picking up where the previous work left off, we will review how work over the full history of the study to date has enabled us to provide a more complete understanding of disease ecology at, and across, the population and individual scales.

4.3 Population-scale disease ecology in the Soay sheep system

Over 30 years of monitoring of Soay sheep and their parasites has revealed much about the population-scale disease ecology of both hosts and parasites. The data have addressed concepts such as predictors of host and parasite diversity, the extent to which parasites regulate host abundance, and temporal patterns in parasite transmission potential.

4.3.1 Diversity and dynamics of hosts

St Kilda Soay sheep exhibit 'boom–bust' population dynamics, characterised by increases in population size across several years, followed by high-mortality winters, or 'crashes' (Grenfell et al., 1992, 1998; Coulson et al., 2001) (Figure 4.3A). Post-mortem gross pathological analyses suggest that mortality is largely due to starvation, exacerbated by the effects of parasitic infection (Gulland, 1992), which were posited as joint drivers of host population dynamics in the seminal work of Anderson and May (Anderson & May, 1978; May & Anderson, 1978). This 'negative spiral' (Koski & Scott, 2001) between malnutrition and parasites may be exacerbated in Soay sheep by wet and windy weather impacting energy budgets and feeding behaviour (Coulson et al., 2001). The net result is that, like grouse on the moors (Hudson et al., 1998; Chapter 1, this volume), mice in the mountains (Pedersen & Greives, 2008; Chapter 8), reindeer on the tundra (Albon et al., 2002; Chapter 10) or indeed vertebrates in general (Watson, 2013), parasites may play a role in regulating the Soay sheep population.

During the history of the Soay sheep project, a handful of experiments have used anthelmintic boluses to remove helminth parasites (see below) for a period of up to 10 weeks at a time (Gulland, 1992). Such experiments are currently more difficult to obtain permission for, due to the conservation status of St Kilda, but they have helped to reveal the effects of parasites on sheep dynamics. Anthelmintic treatment delayed but did not prevent mortality in the high-mortality winter of 1989–1990 (Gulland, 1992), but did reduce

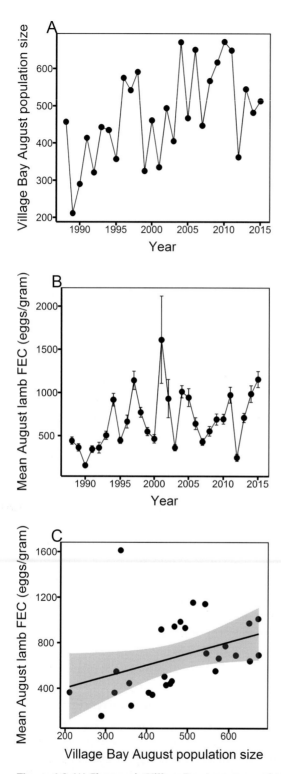

Figure 4.3 (A) Changes in Village Bay August population size, 1988–2015; (B) changes in mean lamb strongyle faecal egg count (FEC) at capture in August, 1988–2015. Points and lines show change in mean FEC, from a total of 2355 samples, while error bars show ±1 standard error (SE); (C) the positive correlation between August population size and mean lamb FEC across 1988–2015 ($R^2 = 0.38$, $P = 0.049$). Points show data, line and shaded area show linear regression and SE, respectively.

mortality risk in female lambs and male yearlings in the high-mortality winter of 1992–1993 (Gulland et al., 1993). A later experiment, treating animals with anthelmintics before the high-mortality winter of 2001–2002, showed no effect of treatment on the overwinter survival of two-year-old sheep of either sex, although strongyle worm counts in treated sheep were lower at death (Craig et al., 2009). In domesticated sheep, heavy parasite infection is known to induce anorexia, but the 2001–2002 experiment suggested that treatment did not influence bite rate, feeding time, or feed intake rate: hence, there was no evidence that helminth infections induced anorexia in Soay sheep (Jones et al., 2006). Finally, an anthelmintic treatment of adult females across the low-mortality winter of 2003–2004 revealed no influence of treatment on fecundity or lamb traits (birth weight, survival, growth rate), but that weight loss between years was lower in treated females (Tempest, 2005). Taken together, along with the fact that the Soays are able to develop effective acquired immune responses to strongyle nematodes (see below), these results suggest that parasites likely influence the amplitude of populations cycles, but not their initiation (Wilson et al., 2004). Another result of these dynamics is that ecological conditions vary considerably between years, particularly with respect to competition for food, parasite transmission, and population demography. Such variation is likely to influence individual health and performance and the strength of natural selection, as discussed below.

The fact that the Hirta population was founded by just 107 individuals from an already small and isolated source population might lead to the expectation of low genetic diversity (Pemberton et al., 2004). Indeed, among sheep breeds, the Soay population does have somewhat depressed levels of genetic variation at most molecular markers including microsatellites (Lawson Handley et al., 2007) and SNPs (Kijas et al., 2012) and the estimated effective population size for the population, 194, is low (Kijas et al., 2012). On the other hand, the population exhibits relatively high genetic diversity at protein loci in comparison to other mammals (Bancroft et al., 1995), harbours a number of striking phenotypic polymorphisms (Gratten et al., 2007, 2010; Johnston et al., 2011; Figure 4.2), and shows substantial heritability and inbreeding depression for a variety of quantitative traits (Bérénos et al., 2014, 2016), indicating that the population nevertheless harbours substantial expressed genetic variation. It is possible that additive genetic variation may be partly maintained by variation in selection across environmental conditions in time and space (Milner, Elston & Albon, 1999; Wilson et al., 2006; Robinson et al., 2008; Hayward et al., 2018). Three spatial subpopulations of sheep (or 'hefts') exist in Village Bay, inhabiting distinct areas, differing in demographic rates, and exhibiting differences in microsatellite allele frequencies (Coulson et al., 1999; Coltman et al., 2003). Spatially structured genetic diversity and forage quality may thus influence parasite transmission in different areas (Wilson et al., 2004).

4.3.2 Diversity and dynamics of parasites

The most significant parasites infecting the Soay sheep, in terms of prevalence, intensity of infection, and effects on health and fitness, are the gastrointestinal strongyle nematodes *Teladorsagia circumcincta* and *Trichostrongylus* spp. (Gulland, 1992; Gulland & Fox, 1992; Wilson et al., 2004; Craig et al., 2006). These directly transmitted parasites (Figure 4.4) are found in the abomasum ('true stomach') and small intestine, where adults copulate and release eggs that are expelled with faeces. The eggs hatch on the pasture at a rate depending upon abiotic conditions (Albrecht, 1909; Nielsen et al., 2007) and undergo two moults to reach the infective L3 larval stage. Ingested larvae undergo two further moults to reach adulthood and begin producing eggs, which are first seen in faeces 17 or 18 days post-ingestion (Denham, 1969). The prevalence of adult worms in the gut at post-mortem varies among strongyle species, with *T. circumcincta* and *Trichostrongylus* spp. found with almost 100% prevalence, other strongyles at < 50% and *Nematodirus* spp. at 30–90% (Gulland, 1992; Craig et al., 2006). As well as

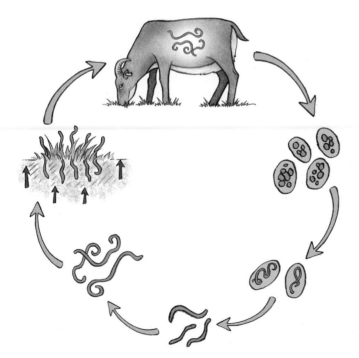

Figure 4.4 Life cycle of parasitic strongyle nematodes, such as *T. circumcincta*. Drawing by Becky Lister-Kaye, used with permission.

species diversity, there is considerable genetic variation within *T. circumcincta*: mitochondrial ND4 sequence variation in the parasite is greater within hosts than between hosts (Braisher et al., 2004). Other prevalent, directly transmitted GI parasites include coccidia, with five *Cryptosporidium* spp. at > 50% prevalence (Connelly et al., 2013) and 11 *Eimeria* spp. at 10–30% prevalence (Craig et al., 2007).

Strongyles and coccidia are also prevalent in domesticated sheep on the Scottish mainland, which increases the potential for synergistic research on St Kilda and in domesticated populations. There are, however, some differences in the parasite fauna of St Kilda Soay sheep and domesticated sheep. The abomasal nematode *Haemonchus contortus* is absent on Hirta, potentially because the ancestors of Soay sheep were removed from mainland Europe before *Haemonchus* arrived (Wilson et al., 2004). Other helminth parasites which are present in mainland systems (Abbott et al., 2012) but absent or rare on Hirta include *Capillaria* spp. and *Oesophagostomum* spp. (Chambers et al., unpublished).

Likewise, bacterial and viral pathogens that are prevalent in mainland sheep are rare on Hirta (Graham et al., 2016). An acute Paramyxovirus, Parainfluenza-3, which induces 96% annual seroprevalence in flocks on the Scottish mainland (Clark & Bruelisauer, 2008), was undetectable across 14 years on St Kilda, whereas 6.5% of the sheep were seropositive for chronic, non-immunising *Leptospira* bacteria (Graham et al., 2016). These findings accord with the theoretical expectation that acute immunising infections are unlikely to persist in small, isolated populations (Lloyd-Smith et al., 2005).

In contrast, several species which are rare on the mainland (Abbott et al., 2012) are more abundant on Hirta, including the strongyle nematodes *Bunostomum trigonocephalum* and *Chabertia ovina* (Wilson et al., 2004; Craig et al., 2006; Chambers et al., unpublished). Both of these species are highly susceptible to anthelmintic drugs and the very limited use of anthelmintics on Hirta (restricted to the handful of experiment studies described above) has likely allowed these species to persist. Although not rare on the mainland, the cestode *Taenia hydatigena* is unexpected on Hirta because of the lack of definitive (dog) hosts, but it occurs at increasing prevalence with age in Soay sheep and it is likely that cysts are transported from the mainland by birds (Torgerson et al., 1995). Furthermore, the Soay sheep are exposed to trypanosomes transmitted by ectoparasitic keds (*Melophagus ovinus*) (Gibson et al., 2010), the latter having been largely eliminated from domestic sheep. The Soay sheep therefore harbour a suite of infectious diseases that reflect their phylogeny, isolation, small population size, seabird neighbours, and long-term freedom from management.

Long-term monitoring has focused upon dynamics of the strongyle nematodes. Parasite burden has been estimated with faecal egg counts (FEC) using a modified version of the McMaster egg-counting technique since the late 1980s (Craig, 2005). The proportion of sheep with non-zero FEC exceeds 50% across years and age classes (Gulland & Fox, 1992; Craig et al., 2006). Lambs and males are most likely to have non-zero FEC and higher intensity of infection, compared to adult sheep, which have presumably acquired varying degrees of immunity to infection, and females (Wilson et al., 2004; Craig et al., 2006). As 4-month-old lambs sampled in August have yet to acquire immunity to strongyles, they may be considered sentinels for exposure to nematodes, and longitudinal monitoring of lambs shows interannual variation in the force of infection (Figure 4.3B). Years of higher population size are associated with higher force of strongyle infection in terms of L3 larval densities on pasture (Wilson et al., 2004) as well as intensity of infection in lambs (Wilson et al., 2004; Hayward et al., 2014a; Figure 4.3C). This suggests density-dependence of transmission, as formalised in theory (Liu et al., 2007), although host density-dependence in Soay sheep–nematode dynamics has yet to be tested formally.

4.4 Individual-scale disease ecology in the Soay sheep system

Longitudinal data on strongyle FEC, immune phenotypes, morphometrics, survival, and reproductive success (and, increasingly, genomic data) on individual Soay sheep have enabled us to best realise the potential of this system at the individual host scale. The data enable quantification of variation in nematode burden and immune defence, as well as exploration of the costs and benefits of different strategies for defence: resistance, which is the ability of the host to limit parasite growth and survival; and tolerance, the ability of the host to maintain health or fitness in the face of increasing parasite burden (Simms, 2000).

4.4.1 Predictors and consequences of heterogeneity in nematode burden

Macroparasites such as nematodes do not replicate within the host and therefore each exposure (e.g. to an L3 larva) leads to, at most, one reproductive adult (Cornell, 2010). In addition, pathology and mortality risk increase with increasing macroparasite burden, and burden is notoriously heterogeneous among hosts (Shaw & Dobson, 1995; Shaw et al., 1998). Causes and consequences of heterogeneity in macroparasite burden are thus essential to understand, yet challenging to disentangle. For example, what are the relative contributions of exposure variation, defence variation, and differential survival of individuals to the observed distribution of parasites among hosts? A phenomenological approximation – the negative binomial distribution – captures aggregation of macroparasites among hosts (Anderson & May, 1978,

1979; Pacala & Dobson, 1988) with few exceptions (Shaw et al., 1998). If aggregation decreases with host age, a parasite density-dependent effect, such as acquired immunity or parasite-induced host mortality, is inferred (Pacala & Dobson, 1988; Cattadori et al., 2005, 2007). However, data on heterogeneities in exposure, immunity, and mortality risk are required to aid inference from such distributions.

The Soay sheep system is beginning to enable such insights. Post-mortem examination of animals dying over winter reveals heavy strongyle burdens (Craig et al., 2006) and associated pathology and gut wall damage (Gulland, 1992), just as in domestic sheep (Simpson, 2000). A causal role of strongyles in Soay sheep mortality has been demonstrated by anthelmintic treatments as described above (Gulland, 1992; Gulland et al., 1993), but restrictions on experimental treatments on St Kilda Soay sheep mean that much of the work on individual variation in strongyle infection intensity has been conducted observationally using strongyle FEC. The available evidence suggests that FEC is linearly associated with worm burden in Soay sheep both on St Kilda (Gulland, 1992; Grenfell et al., 1995) and in a population on the island of Lundy (introduced in 1942; Boyd, 1999; Wilson et al., 2004), unlike in domesticated animals where density-dependent competition within hosts limits worm fecundity (Bishop & Stear, 2000). A drawback of FEC as a measure of strongyle burden is that it is impossible to distinguish the eggs of six strongyle species by eye, and so 'strongyle FEC' comprises multiple species (Wilson et al., 2004). If the species have markedly different pathological effects, two individuals with equal FEC may therefore experience different consequences of infection. Despite these concerns, the various strongyle species have a similar mode of living, cause similar pathologies, and immune responses to the different species appear to be cross-reactive (Watt et al., unpublished). Future work using meta-barcoding techniques (Chambers et al., unpublished) may help determine how between-individual variation in parasite species composition impacts upon pathology.

Studies using FEC suggest that the Soay sheep, like so many other animals (Shaw et al., 1998), vary in worm burden according to the negative binomial distribution (Grenfell et al., 1995; Figure 4.5A,B). The data also support the prediction that heavy nematode burdens harm and kill sheep. Lambs are most vulnerable to parasite-induced mortality over winter: August strongyle FEC is associated with reduced winter survival of lambs, but not adults (Hayward et al., 2011). Higher strongyle FEC is also associated with lower body weight (Coltman et al., 1999, 2001a; Robinson et al., 2009), which itself is associated with both reduced survival (Milner et al., 1999; Jones et al., 2005) and fecundity (Clutton-Brock et al., 1996; Preston et al., 2003) in adults. Furthermore, adults with higher strongyle FEC have higher coccidian faecal oocyst counts and the

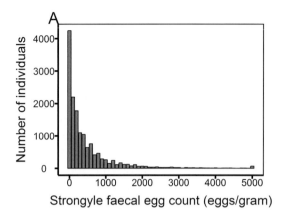

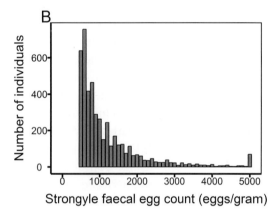

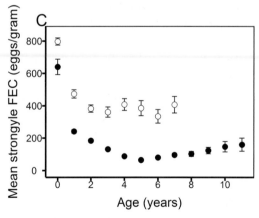

Figure 4.5 (A) The distribution of 14,991 strongyle nematode faecal egg counts, collected 1988–2016 from 3476 individuals. Sixty-nine counts of $\geq$ 5000 eggs/g have been binned and are represented by the column at 5000 eggs/g. (B) The same data, focusing on the 4631 counts of $\geq$ 500 eggs/g in order to better display variation at high counts. (C) Mean $\pm$ 1SE August counts for females (closed points) and males (open points) across this time period. Counts for males aged $\geq$ 7 and females aged $\geq$ 11 have been combined in the oldest age categories.

two types of parasite are independently associated with lower adult body weight (Craig et al., 2008). A wealth of evidence therefore suggests that strongyle nematodes influence health and exert a powerful selective force in this population.

Exposure variation is likely to drive some of the variation in nematode burden. Indeed, interannual variation in the force of infection (Figure 4.3B) means that population density is predictive of the FEC of individuals within years (Wilson et al., 2004; Hayward et al., 2014a) (Figure 4.3C). Nonetheless, we expect transmission intensity and exposure to be higher and more consistent than in other systems, as pasture counts of nematode larvae are typically high throughout the year (Wilson et al., 2004). Individual variation in exposure is presently challenging to quantify in the Soay sheep system, but is an important area for future work.

Predictors of strongyle FEC include demographic and genetic factors which are consistent with an important role for defence heterogeneity. Between-individual variation in FEC (Figure 4.5C) is linked to sex, with males generally exhibiting higher counts than females (Gulland & Fox, 1992), and age, with lambs experiencing very high counts (Craig et al., 2006) and adults showing generally decreasing counts with age (Wilson et al., 1996; Hayward et al., 2009). These findings are consistent with patterns of lower burden of infection in females (Zuk & McKean, 1996; Moore & Wilson, 2002; Morales-Montor et al., 2004) and with age (Anderson, 1986) in other species. Quantitative genetic 'animal models' (Henderson, 1950; Kruuk, 2004; Wilson et al., 2010) have been used to estimate the additive genetic basis of FEC. Heritability estimates have ranged from 0 to 0.39, depending on host sex, age, season, and pedigree depth (Coltman et al., 2001a; Beraldi et al., 2007; Robinson et al., 2009; Brown et al., 2013; Hayward et al., 2018), well within the range of estimates from domesticated sheep and previous estimates from the Soay sheep gained from the superseded method of parent–offspring regression (Smith et al., 1999). Searches for individual loci associated with resistance in the Soays have revealed weak evidence for associations (Coltman et al., 2001b; Beraldi et al., 2007; Brown et al., 2013). First, the OLADRB MHCII locus is associated with both strongyle FEC and survival in lambs (Paterson et al., 1998). Second, the 126 bp allele at the o(IFN)-γ (interferon-gamma) microsatellite marker is associated with reduced FEC and increased production of *T. circumcincta*-specific immunoglobulin (Ig)A antibodies (Coltman et al., 2001b), which appears especially significant given the role of the cytokine IFN-γ in suppressing immune responses to nematodes. Neither of these studies, however, controlled for familial relationships between subjects, and so require revisiting. Studies in domesticated sheep have reached no consensus regarding the loci underlying variation in resistance, which is perhaps to be expected given the polygenic nature of resistance, although common genetic pathways do exist (Sayre & Harris, 2012). A broad conclusion is that the contribution of additive genetic effects to variation in FEC is relatively low. Given that variation in FEC is underpinned by sex, age, and sheep genetics, a major vein of enquiry in recent years has been to determine the role of immune responses in regulating strongyle FEC, and to identify the demographic and genetic drivers of variation in immune responses among individuals.

4.4.2 Immune defence mechanisms and associations among markers

The importance of strongyle infections in domesticated sheep (Nieuwhof & Bishop, 2005) means that the sheep immune response to strongyle infection has been exceptionally well-studied. Resistant sheep regulate strongyles with a T-helper cell 2 (Th2)-type response, key effectors of which include parasite-specific antibodies of isotypes IgG, IgA, IgE, and IgM (Smith et al., 1985; Stear et al., 1995; Martinez-Valldares et al., 2005; Pernthaner et al., 2006; McRae et al., 2015) which kill larvae and reduce the length and fecundity of adult nematodes. In the Soay sheep, pairwise correlations between plasma antibodies of different specificities and isotypes are generally positive (Nussey et al., 2014) and correlations among faecal and plasma antibodies of the same and different isotypes are also positive (Watt et al., 2016). This suggests among-individual variation in potency of antibody responses, although only a subset of antibodies are predictive of parasite burden and sheep fitness (see below). Quantitative genetic studies of plasma antibody concentrations have consistently found substantial between-individual variation and moderate additive genetic effects, with heritability estimates ranging from 0.07 to 0.45 (Graham et al., 2010; Brown et al., 2013; Hayward et al., 2014a). More recent work has undertaken the serious challenge of cell phenotyping. Key findings include complex associations among antibody responses, T-cell populations, and white blood cell counts (Watson et al., 2016), and age- and sex-specific variation in lymphocyte telomere length (Fairlie et al., 2016; Watson et al., 2017). In due course, these may help explain observed variation in nematode resistance among sheep, or within sheep with age.

  These results show that individuals vary widely in immune phenotype and that measuring one marker is insufficient to capture all the variation in function in the immune system. Some markers, however, provide more ecologically relevant information than others: markers that are associated with reduced parasite load and increased fitness may reasonably be described as indicators of resistance (Graham et al., 2011). In order to identify the evolutionary origins and consequences of variation in immune function, it is essential to estimate associations between immune measures, parasite burden and fitness (Bradley & Jackson, 2008; Graham et al., 2011). A series of recent studies on the Soay sheep have achieved this by quantifying links between strongyle FEC, immune function, survival and reproductive success.

4.4.3 Associations between defence and fitness

The idea that stronger immune responses (e.g. higher antibody titres) necessarily indicate greater fitness is called into question by likely costs of induced defence, a foundational concept in ecoimmunology (Sheldon & Verhulst, 1996; Schmid-Hempel, 2003). These include resource costs, such as using proteins which could be channelled into other functions; immunopathology costs, such as self-damage induced by inflammation; and multiple fronts costs between different arms of the immune system (Lochmiller & Deerenberg, 2000; Graham et al., 2005; Colditz, 2008). An optimal defence strategy, including the rate at which hosts ought to purge parasites, is expected to maximise the benefit:cost ratio (Behnke et al., 1992; Cressler et al., 2015). These economics of defence can provide insight into the varied immune defences that shape variation in parasite burden and host survival, as demonstrated by our recent work on the Soay sheep system.

The first study investigating links between immune function and fitness in the Soay sheep focused on anti-nuclear antibodies (ANA) (Graham et al., 2010). ANA concentrations are positively associated with overwinter survival, but negatively associated with prior reproductive success. Crucially, ANA are not associated with lifetime fitness, suggesting that genetic variation in ANA is maintained by a trade-off between survival benefits and reproductive costs (Graham et al., 2010). ANA concentrations do not, however, meet the criteria for a marker of nematode resistance, as they are not associated with FEC; they are, however, positively associated with nematode-specific antibody titres (Graham et al., 2010).

More recent studies have found that concentrations of strongyle-specific antibodies represent an effective marker of resistance against the strongyles. For example, concentrations of strongyle-specific antibody in plasma (Hayward et al., 2014a; Figure 4.6A) and faeces (IgA and IgG; Watt et al., 2016; Figure 4.6B) are negatively associated with FEC and positively associated with age. Importantly, sheep with higher concentrations of strongyle-specific IgG in summer have higher winter survival probability (Nussey et al., 2014; Watson et al., 2016; Figure 4.6C). These results are consistent with the notion that strongyle-specific antibodies reduce transmission and promote host fitness by enhancing survival. There is, however, evidence that these antibody responses are also costly: for example, males with high antibody concentrations in August are less likely to sire a lamb during the subsequent rut (Hayward et al., 2014a; Figure 4.6D).

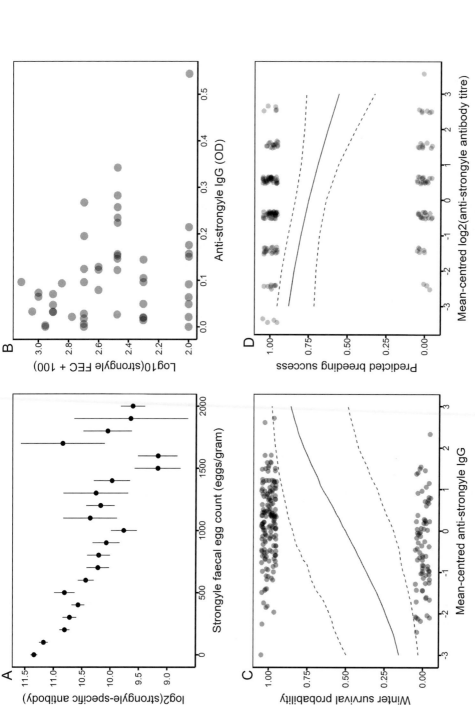

Figure 4.6 Associations between *T. circumcincta*-specific antibody responses, strongyle FEC, and fitness in Soay sheep. (A) Higher levels of pan-isotypic *T. circumcincta*-specific antibody are associated with lower strongyle FEC. Points show mean antibody titre for each category of FEC ± 1 SE. (B) Higher concentrations of *T. circumcincta*-specific IgG measured in faecal samples are negatively associated with strongyle FEC, with points showing raw data. (C) Higher levels of *T. circumcincta*-specific IgG are associated with higher subsequent winter survival. Points show individual data; lines show fit from binomial generalised linear mixed-effects model ± 1 SE. (D) Higher levels of *T. circumcincta*-specific pan-isotypic antibody are associated with lower subsequent breeding success in males. Points show individual data; lines show fit from binomial generalised linear mixed-effects model ± 1 SE. Figures are redrawn from Hayward et al. (2014a) (A and D; © 2014 by The University of Chicago); Watt et al. (2016) (B); and Nussey et al. (2014) (C). All figures are used with permission.

An alternative mode of defence, distinct from immune-mediated resistance, is tolerance of infection, which involves attenuation of the damage caused by infection (Simms, 2000; Schneider & Ayres, 2008; Råberg et al., 2009; Medzhitov et al., 2012). While a more resistant host minimises parasite burden and transmission, a more tolerant host loses health or fitness at a slower rate as parasite burden increases. Work on laboratory animals has shown that tolerance can vary among genotypes and covary with resistance (Råberg et al., 2007), but work in the Soay sheep has been among the first to explore variation in individual-scale tolerance and links with resistance and fitness in the wild (also see Blanchet et al., 2010; Jackson et al., 2014; Mazé-Guilmo et al., 2014). Using a random regression statistical framework developed for studying tolerance in domestic animals (Kause, 2011; Doeschl-Wilson et al., 2012; Kause et al., 2012), we estimated tolerance as the slope of body weight on strongyle FEC and found that individuals vary in how quickly they lose weight with increasing FEC (Hayward et al., 2014b; Figure 4.7A,B). Tolerance is positively associated with lifetime fitness (Figure 4.7C): the most tolerant sheep have more offspring (Hayward et al., 2014b). Intriguingly, and consistent with theory (see below), there is no evidence that variation in tolerance has an additive genetic basis. Other individual factors, such as previous experience of infection or habitat quality, may be responsible for tolerance variation. Finally, there is no evidence of a trade-off between tolerance and resistance: indeed, there is a trend for sheep with higher strongyle-specific antibody concentrations to have higher tolerance (Hayward et al., 2014a).

4.4.4 Roles of malnutrition in heterogeneous mortality risk and varied defences

Host nutritional plane likely influences all of the foregoing patterns, as it does in domestic sheep (Houdijk et al., 2005). Malnutrition is expected to impact disease susceptibility by setting up vicious circles of poor condition, immunosuppression, and escalating susceptibility to infection (Koski & Scott, 2001; Beldomenico et al., 2008). Indeed, theory posits a central role for resource availability and assimilation in the efficacy of host defences (e.g. Tate & Graham, 2015). Gut pathologies at necropsy of Soay sheep dying over winter are consistent with dual contributions of malnutrition and parasites to mortality (Gulland, 1992). Quantitative histopathology of Soay sheep liver tissue (Caudron et al., 2017) confirms that malnutrition-induced, infection-induced, and inflammatory processes likely all contribute to mortality. Thus, pathological data in individuals support the population-level inference that parasites combine with intraspecific competition to contribute to population regulation.

Recent work has deployed physiological metrics widely used on domesticated sheep to explore how intraspecific competition for food translates to

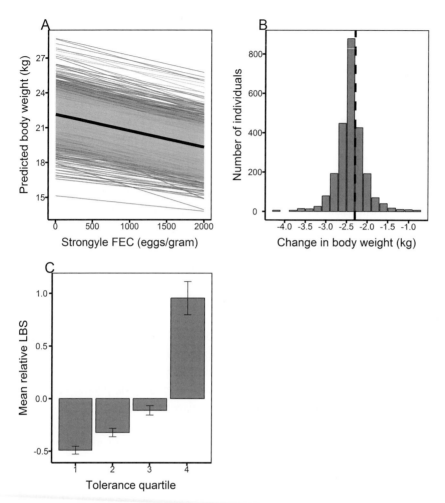

Figure 4.7 (A) Estimated tolerance slopes for 2438 individuals, where each grey line represents an individual and the thick black line represents the population average; (B) a histogram of weight loss between FEC = 0 and FEC = 2000 (analogous to variation in the slopes in A), where the dashed black line again shows average weight loss; (C) individuals in higher tolerance quartiles (which lost less weight across increasing FEC) had higher lifetime breeding success (LBS) than individuals with lower tolerance. Figures redrawn from Hayward et al. (2014b), with permission.

variation in nutritional plane and allocation to defence. The abomasum is the main site of protein digestion in ruminants and nematodes disrupt this process by inhibiting acid secretion; as pH increases, protein goes undigested (Simpson, 2000). Next, as the nematodes damage the intestinal mucosa, the dominant serum protein, albumin, leaches out of the blood into the intestine, potentially disrupting homeostasis (Sand et al., 2015). Finally, catabolism of body muscle begins (Sahoo et al., 2009), which may result in wasting (Murray et al., 2006). In the Soay sheep, albumin stores of individuals decrease with increasing population density in adults of both sexes (Garnier et al., 2017a). Such physiological effects of competition are exacerbated by nematode-induced inappetence and poorer grazing available in winter (Crawley et al., 2004).

Because the fitness effects of infection may be mediated through nutritional status, elucidating the role of nutrition in defence may provide new insight into the mechanisms underpinning resistance and tolerance. We recently began determining the role of nutrition in defence with a study of ANA and strongyle-specific IgG as immune markers, and albumin and total protein as nutritional markers (Garnier et al., 2017b). Together, nutritional plane and antibody responses (arguably joint indicators of host 'condition') are associated with winter survival independently of body weight (Garnier et al., 2017b), which is itself a strong predictor of winter survival (Clutton-Brock et al., 1997). Taking varied condition into account, an age-dependent resource trade-off became apparent, with surviving prime-aged females favouring antibodies and senescent females favouring nutrition (Garnier et al., 2017b). This suggests a change of strategy with age, such as a switch towards nutrition-dependent tolerance due to effects of immunosenescence on antibody production (Nussey et al., 2012; Watson et al., 2016). We have only begun to scratch the surface of the relations between nutritional status, immunity, and fitness, let alone any role for selective grazing (Hutchings et al., 2002). However, the long time series of samples available and the capacity to measure new phenotypes in stored and new samples makes the Soay sheep an excellent system for further progress in disentangling these associations.

4.4.5 Outlook at the individual scale

The foregoing sections show that we have best realised the potential of this system at the individual host scale (Figure 4.8). Our research in this area both benefits from, and provides insight for, studies of defence against infection in domestic animals. There is increasing interest in breeding domestic animals for tolerance rather than resistance (Bishop, 2012; Doeschl-Wilson & Kyriazakis, 2012; Doeschl-Wilson, Villanueva & Kyriazakis, 2012), because sheep bred for resistance often lose productivity (Colditz, 2008); vaccines remain desirable but elusive (Nisbet et al., 2013); and anthelmintic drugs are expensive and increasingly ineffective (Nieuwhof & Bishop, 2005). While our initial analyses do not provide evidence for heritable variation for tolerance (Hayward et al., 2014b), the positive individual-level association between resistance and tolerance in Soay sheep (Hayward et al., 2014a) suggests a potential role for nutrition or other environmental factors. Explanations for the non-genetic drivers of between-individual variation may include early-life developmental effects or individual experience of habitat quality,

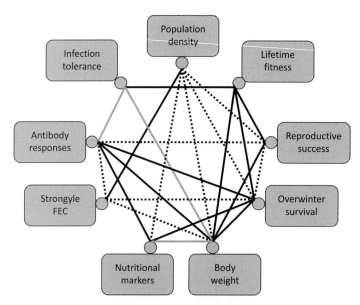

Figure 4.8 Over two decades of research on St Kilda Soay sheep has demonstrated associations among immune function, infection intensity, and host fitness. Positive pairwise associations are shown with solid black lines, negative associations with broken black lines, and null associations in grey. The figure is intended to demonstrate pairwise associations only: not all of these associations are straightforward and may, for example, vary in strength depending on host age and sex and environmental conditions, as detailed in the text. The figure is not intended to represent a path diagram: many of the variables are measured simultaneously (e.g. at capture in August) and as such the directionality and directness of associations cannot be known with certainty.

food availability or infection. The known role of nutrition in health and defence in domestic sheep, coupled with known temporal and spatial variation in grazing quality across the Village Bay area, make the Soay sheep a potentially tractable system for identifying the factors underpinning tolerance variation.

Several other areas of research on individual-scale processes in the Soay sheep are either in the early stages of investigation or have yet to begin. Our focus has been host-centric, but parasite genetic variation in virulence, fecundity, longevity, and/or immunomodulation will also influence associations between infection, immunity, and fitness. While macroparasites have been the major focus of studies on the Soay sheep, the epidemiology of microparasites, defence against such infections, and their influence on host health and fitness have rarely been addressed (Craig et al., 2007; Graham et al., 2016). The ability to repeatedly collect faecal samples at will from known individuals and the fact that faecal antibody concentrations likely reflect secretion of antibodies at the site of infection mean that faecal antibodies offer a powerful new tool for longitudinal monitoring of immune responses. Faecal sampling will also be key to studying gut inflammation and gut microbiota diversity, which play important roles in links between nutrition, infection, and health in laboratory populations, but which have rarely been studied in wild populations. The next-generation sequencing technologies that microbial work would require will also make the Soay sheep an attractive system for studies of within-parasite species genetic structure and diversity (Chambers et al., unpublished). Research on the St Kilda population on all of these subjects could benefit from parallel experimental studies in domesticated animals. While research in the Soay sheep can reveal patterns of (co)variation and selection, concurrent experimental work in domestic animals, with manipulated host or parasite genotypes, inoculating dose, nutrition, reproductive state, and/or hormone concentrations, can reveal molecular mechanisms of the sheep–nematode interaction.

4.5 Prospects for bridging scales

A unified framework bringing together population- and individual-level processes represents a key goal for the evolutionary ecology of disease (Grenfell & Dobson, 1995; Wilson et al., 2002; Boots et al., 2009; Day et al., 2011; Mideo et al., 2011). Sections 4.3 and 4.4 review our progress in (1) describing sheep and parasite diversity and dynamics at the population level, and (2) determining the factors affecting individual-level variation in parasite burden and defence strategies and how selection acts upon such variation. We now turn to the challenge of determining how processes at one scale affect processes at the other.

Our progress in elucidating cross-scale dynamics in the Soay sheep system has been limited thus far, and as such this section largely describes current work, ambitions for the near future, and more distant possibilities. Despite this, our within-scale progress lays crucial foundations for cross-scale work. Thus, while other host–parasite systems, particularly those amenable to experimental anthelmintic treatments, offer greater potential for testing the role of parasites in regulating host populations (Hudson et al., 1998; Albon et al., 2002; Pedersen & Greives, 2008; Chapters 1, 8, and 10 of this volume) or how coinfections influence host defence and parasite transmission (Lello et al., 2004; Cattadori et al., 2007; Jolles et al., 2008; Ezenwa et al., 2010; Pathak et al., 2012; Murphy et al., 2013; Ezenwa & Jolles, 2015; Henrichs et al., 2016; Chapters 16 and 21 of this volume), the Soay sheep excel as a system for assessing how host heterogeneity and macroparasite transmission interact to drive system dynamics. Initially accessible questions concern immune priming and feedbacks between exposure and defence.

4.5.1 Immune priming: how parasites on pasture translate to acquired immunity

A crucial cross-scale process is the acquisition of parasite-specific immunity in individuals who are exposed to infection, and whose excretion of parasite eggs depends on immune status. Indeed, mammalian adaptive immunity (including parasite-specific antibody responses) depends upon the rate of encounter between lymphocytes and parasite antigens. The dose-dependence of immune response induction by nematodes (Lippens et al., 2016) and of the dynamics of nematode expulsion (Paterson et al., 2008) can be investigated in laboratory experiments, although natural transmission rates may be more important than dose per se (Scott, 1991, 2006). The exposure that translates to immune system readiness to defend is generally termed 'priming' and theory predicts substantial impacts on subsequent disease dynamics in host populations (Tate & Rudolf, 2012; Tidbury et al., 2012).

We recently began exploring tests of these predictions with a mathematical model (Garnier et al., 2016) which updates an earlier framework (Grenfell et al., 1995) to account for improved biological understanding of antibody-mediated host resistance (McNeilly et al., 2009). Data from *T. circumcincta* 'trickle infection' experiments on domestic sheep using varying doses (Hong et al., 1987; Nisbet et al., 2013) were used to parameterise model terms for effects of immunity on killing larvae, slowing their maturity, and reducing egg excretion by adults (Figure 4.9). This model was able to closely capture the dose-dependent priming of resistance and subsequent egg excretion rates in control animals from infection trials (Hong et al., 1987; Nisbet et al., 2013), providing a vital bridge between experiments and field infection dynamics.

To translate this model for use on the Soay sheep, we must explicitly incorporate age- as well as dose-dependence of priming, and then draw upon our extensive empirical data set. In a natural setting, each host ingests a random number of parasites, drawn from the empirical distribution of infectious L3 larvae, per unit time (Wilson et al., 2004). Age-specific acquisition of immunity under these exposure conditions can then be modelled (Grenfell et al., 1995) and built into our updated dose-dependent 'priming' model (Garnier et al., 2016). This would enable us to quantify how exposure determines strongyle FEC as immunity accrues via infection experience, using data on FEC and antibodies across ages, sexes, and years. To analyse the effects of quantitative variation in these parameters, we could now use the empirical distribution of resistance (Figure 4.9B) to parameterise the immunity of individuals (I_A) and better estimate $\mu_{L/D/E}$ (Figure 4.9A), and the empirical distribution of tolerance (Figure 4.7B) to parameterise the per-parasite death rate of hosts. This would in turn enable us to generate testable predictions about nematode disease dynamics – e.g. interannual variation in FEC and antibody distributions – among Soay sheep. This pathway to empirically grounded

(A)

(B)

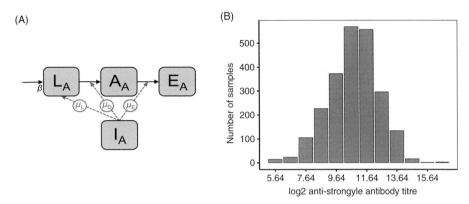

Figure 4.9 (A) Schematic diagram of the epidemiological model describing the infection of sheep by *Teladorsagia circumcincta* and the production of eggs by the nematodes. Modified from Garnier et al. (2016) and used with permission. Such models can be parameterised by data collected from the Soay sheep (see text), with the number of larval parasites, adult parasites and eggs L_A, A_A, E_A dependent upon the infection rate β and the influence of immunity I_A upon larval killing (μ_L), slowing of development to adults (μ_D), and egg excretion (μ_E). (B) Histogram of $\log_2$-transformed plasma titres of strongyle-specific antibody (reported in Hayward et al., 2014a) that could be used to estimate the empirical distribution of resistance among hosts.

theory on cross-scale dynamics of macroparasites bodes well for the Soay sheep as a model system for feedbacks between host immune systems and parasites.

4.5.2 Reciprocal feedbacks between parasite exposure and economics of defence

A second example of cross-scale feedbacks explicitly considers natural selection on induced defences. Population-scale ecological feedbacks are expected to affect host–parasite coevolution, because variation in host defence will affect the abundance of parasites in the environment and the relative costs of infection and defence to hosts. For example, resistance and tolerance are predicted to have divergent effects on parasite transmission that feed back to alter selection on defence (Boots et al., 2009). Resistance of individual hosts reduces prevalence and intensities of parasite infections and decreases parasite transmission, until transmission reaches such a low level that costs of resistance (Beisel, 1977; Klasing, 2004) outweigh the risk of parasitism. Resistance is then selected against; parasites can once again invade; eventually, parasite transmission is high enough to once more impose selection for resistance (Thrall & Antonovics, 1994; Roy & Kirchner, 2000; Miller et al., 2005). Thus, host resistance is a negative frequency-dependent trait and promotes heterogeneity. Tolerance, by contrast, is expected to increase parasite prevalence, infection intensity and faecal egg counts, generating positive frequency-dependence: tolerance maintains host fitness without reducing parasite abundance, which enhances transmission, sustaining selection for greater tolerance, enhancing transmission, and so on until tolerance alleles become fixed (Roy & Kirchner, 2000; Miller et al., 2005). However, theory predicts that tolerance variation may also be maintained under certain conditions: if a trade-off between resistance and tolerance operates at the individual level (Fineblum & Rausher, 1995; Restif & Koella, 2003; Miller et al., 2006); if tolerance promotes host fecundity rather than survival (Best et al., 2008); or if resistance and tolerance differ in efficacy or cost (Behnke et al., 1992; Restif & Koella, 2004; Carval & Ferriere, 2010).

We have yet to begin work in this area, but one potential way to begin testing such ideas would be to undertake reciprocal demographic modelling, using empirical data from the Soay sheep. Matrix population models (MPMs) enable tracking of the dynamics of discrete characters (Caswell, 2001), and their application to the Soay sheep system underpins our understanding of their population dynamics (Coulson et al., 2001). Integral projection models (IPMs) are analogous to MPMs, but allow the dynamics of continuous phenotypic characters to be modelled (Easterling et al., 2000). IPMs can be readily extended to allow the modelling of a mixture of discrete and continuous characters (Rees & Ellner, 2009), and can incorporate density-dependence and unmeasured sources of individual and environmental heterogeneity (Coulson et al., 2010; Coulson, 2012). IPMs of the Soay sheep population already illustrate the power of the technique (Childs et al., 2011; Coulson, 2012; Rees et al., 2014). However, despite enormous power and flexibility, IPMs have rarely been used in disease ecology and epidemiology (Metcalf et al., 2016). To our knowledge, the only exceptions are a successful model of the dynamics of an aspergillosis epidemic in corals (Bruno et al., 2011) and more recent models developed to investigate chytrid infections of amphibians (Wilber et al., 2016, 2017; Chapter 12, this volume).

In the Soay sheep system, a first step would be to integrate the individual-level details of resistance and tolerance (and other relationships depicted in Figure 4.8) into a framework to ask how they impact reciprocal host–parasite interactions. IPMs could track parasite burden (FEC) quantitatively, thus incorporating the key features of macroparasite epidemiology: that each individual parasite is acquired via transmission and contributes to host state and mortality risk (Cornell, 2010). IPMs could also allow us to understand how antibody titre variation varies with the environment, and how titre changes subsequently impact infection, host vital rates, and population dynamics. For example, IPMs would enable estimation of how fecundity influences the distribution of antibody responses in the population (Figure 4.9B): we may expect years of high sheep fecundity to be associated with low mean antibody titres. IPMs could also allow us to separate the direct (e.g. increased mortality) and indirect trait-mediated (e.g. body-weight–mediated) effects of infection on host demography (Ozgul et al., 2010, 2012). Importantly, body-weight-mediated effects of infection status on demography are synonymous with our framework for estimating tolerance (Hayward et al., 2014b). Pursuing these analyses once the full time series of immunological metrics (1988–present) become available would facilitate cross-scale disease ecology modelling.

Current IPMs could also examine the role of environmental variation: for example, warming temperatures may alter strongyle dynamics and exacerbate effects of infection on productivity in domestic sheep (Kenyon et al., 2009; Morgan & van Dijk, 2012). An IPM approach could thus inform management issues by elucidating individual- to population-scale resistance and tolerance across environmental variation. IPM approaches could also provide valuable cross-scale information for domestic populations, for example by predicting the transmission consequences of breeding for resistance or tolerance (Bishop, 2012). For example, a more resistant flock might be predicted to result in reduced parasite transmission but reduced sheep fecundity and productivity, while a tolerant flock might be predicted to reduce parasite-associated damage but increase transmission rates, with dire consequences for less-tolerant populations in the vicinity (Miller et al., 2005, 2006). IPMs have also been used to make inferences about the role of evolution in phenotypic change (Ozgul et al., 2010; Traill et al., 2014). Concerns have recently been raised about their suitability for making evolutionary inferences, due to the way the development (growth) and parent–offspring covariance functions are typically formulated (Chevin, 2015; Janeiro et al., 2017). IPMs can only predict phenotypic change arising from evolutionary processes when they incorporate an explicit model of genetic inheritance, a process which has already begun (Childs et al., 2016; Rees & Ellner, 2016; Coulson et al., 2017). If appropriately analysed this way, IPMs could be used to predict the (evolutionarily) stable value of resistance vs. tolerance.

4.6 Conclusions

Theoretical work in disease ecology explains how patterns of variation in parasite transmission, prevalence, abundance, and defence can develop in host populations. This includes models of population-level processes, such as how parasites can regulate host dynamics, and individual-level processes, such as how selection acts upon variation in defence. Empirical tests of many of these predictions have been rare, because of the difficulty of collecting relevant longitudinal data in natural host–parasite systems. The Soay sheep population of St Kilda has been intensively studied for over 30 years and is an excellent system for disease ecology research, due to comprehensive data on population dynamics, parasite burden, parasite-specific immune responses, and fitness. Research on the Soay sheep has largely focused on individual-level processes: we have identified factors governing variation in parasite burden and parasite-specific immunity; determined how parasite-specific immunity and tolerance are associated with fitness; and begun to elucidate the role of nutrition in mediating links between immunity and fitness. Our next aim is to bridge these scales. We hope that research on the Soay sheep will soon enable rigorous empirical tests of how population- and individual-level processes interact through mutual feedbacks.

4.7 Acknowledgements

We thank the National Trust for Scotland for permission to work on St Kilda and QinetiQ and Elior for logistics and other support on the island. We are grateful to all project members and many volunteers who have helped with field work on the island and all those who have contributed to keeping the project going over many years, including T. Clutton-Brock, M. Crawley, S. Albon, T. Coulson, L. Kruuk, J. Slate, and D. Nussey. We also thank D. Nussey and T. McNeilly for huge contributions to the immunoparasitological work reviewed here. We thank S. Albon, M. Festa-Bianchet, and K. Wilson for highly constructive reviews of all aspects of this chapter, and N. Sargison and A. Chambers for insightful comments, particularly regarding their knowledge of the comparative parasite fauna of St Kilda and domesticated sheep. We thank the Wellcome Trust Clinical Research Facility Genetics Core in Edinburgh for SNP genotyping. The long-term project on St Kilda, including field assistant JGP, has been largely funded by the UK Natural Environment Research Council, and much of the recent immunoparasitology has been funded by the UK Biotechnology and Biological Sciences Research Council, while the SNP genotyping was supported by the European Research Council. ADH is funded by a University of Stirling Impact Research Fellowship. ALG thanks members of the Research Coordination Network on *Infectious Disease Evolution Across Scales*, funded by the US National Science Foundation, for inspiring dialogue that helped to develop the ideas presented here.

References

Abbott, K.A., Taylor, M.A. & Stubbings, L.A. (2012) *Sustainable Worm Control Strategies For Sheep: A Technical Manual For Veterinary Surgeons and Advisers.* Malvern: UK SCOPS (Sustainable Control of Parasites in Sheep), National Sheep Association.

Albon, S.D., Stien, A., Irvine, R.J., et al. (2002) The role of parasites in the dynamics of a reindeer population. *Proceedings of the Royal Society of London B*, **269**, 1625–1632.

Albrecht, A. (1909) Zur Kenntnis der Entwicklung der Sklerostomen beim Pferde. *Zeitschrift fur Veterinarkunde*, **21**, 161–181.

Anderson, R.M. (1986) The population dynamics and epidemiology of intestinal nematode infections. *Transactions of the Royal Society of Tropical Medicine and Hygiene*, **80**, 686–696.

Anderson, R.M. & May, R.M. (1978) Regulation and stability of host–parasite population interactions. I. Regulatory processes. *Journal of Animal Ecology*, **47**, 219–247.

Anderson, R.M. & May, R.M. (1979) Population biology of infectious diseases: Part I. *Nature*, **280**, 361–367.

Anderson, R.M. & May, R.M. (1982) Coevolution of hosts and parasites. *Parasitology*, **85**, 411–426.

Bancroft, D.R., Pemberton, J.M. & King, P. (1995) Extensive protein and microsatellite variability in an isolated, cyclic ungulate population. *Heredity*, **74**, 326–336.

Behnke, J.M., Barnard, C.J. & Wakelin, D. (1992) Understanding chronic nematode infections: evolutionary considerations, current hypotheses and the way forward. *International Journal for Parasitology*, **22**, 861–907.

Beisel, W.R. (1977) Magnitude of the host nutritional responses to infection. *The American Journal of Clinical Nutrition*, **30**, 1236–1247.

Beldomenico, P.M., Telfer, S., Gebert, S., et al. (2008) Poor condition and infection: a vicious circle in natural populations. *Proceedings of the Royal Society of London B*, **275**, 1753–1759.

Beraldi, D., McRae, A.F., Gratten, J., et al. (2007) Quantitative trait loci (QTL) mapping of resistance to strongyles and coccidea in the free-living Soay sheep (*Ovis aries*). *International Journal for Parasitology*, **37**, 121–129.

Bérénos, C., Ellis, P.A., Pilkington, J.G., et al. (2015) Heterogeneity of genetic architecture of body size traits in a free-living population. *Molecular Ecology*, **24**, 1810–1830.

Bérénos, C., Ellis, P.A., Pilkington, J.G. & Pemberton, J.M. (2014) Estimating quantitative genetic parameters in wild populations: a comparison of pedigree and genomic approaches. *Molecular Ecology*, **23**, 3434–3451.

Bérénos, C., Ellis, P.A., Pilkington, J.G. & Pemberton, J.M. (2016) Genomic analysis reveals depression due to both individual and maternal inbreeding in a free-living

mammal population. *Molecular Ecology*, **25**, 3152–3168.

Best, A., White, A. & Boots, M. (2008) Maintenance of host variation in tolerance to pathogens and parasites. *Proceedings of the National Academy of Sciences of the United States of America*, **105**, 20,786–20,791.

Bishop, S. (2012) A consideration of resistance and tolerance for ruminant nematode infections. *Frontiers in Genetics*, **3**, 168.

Bishop, S.C. & Stear, M.J. (2000) The use of a gamma-type function to assess the relationship between the number of adult *Teladorsagia circumcincta* and total egg output. *Parasitology*, **121**, 435–440.

Blanchet, S., Rey, O. & Loot, G. (2010) Evidence for host variation in parasite tolerance in a wild fish population. *Evolutionary Ecology*, **24**, 1129–1139.

Boots, M., Best, A., Miller, M.R. & White, A. (2009) The role of ecological feedbacks in the evolution of host defence: what does theory tell us? *Philosophical Transactions of the Royal Society of London B: Biological Sciences*, **364**, 27–36.

Borer, E., Antonovics, J., Kinkel, L., et al. (2011) Bridging taxonomic and disciplinary divides in infectious disease. *EcoHealth*, **8**, 261–267.

Bowers, R.G., Boots, M. & Begon, M. (1994) Life-history trade-offs and the evolution of pathogen resistance: competition between host strains. *Proceedings of the Royal Society of London B*, **257**, 247–253.

Boyd, H.E.G. (1999) The early development of parasitism in Soay sheep on St Kilda. Thesis, University of Cambridge.

Bradley, J.E. & Jackson, J.A. (2008) Measuring immune system variation to help understand host–pathogen community dynamics. *Parasitology*, **135**, 807–823.

Braisher, T.L., Gemmell, N.J., Grenfell, B.T. & Amos, W. (2004) Host isolation and patterns of genetic variability in three populations of *Teladorsagia* from sheep. *International Journal for Parasitology*, **34**, 1197–1204.

Brown, E.A., Pilkington, J.G., Nussey, D.H., et al. (2013) Detecting genes for variation in parasite burden and immunological traits in a wild population: testing the candidate gene approach. *Molecular Ecology*, **22**, 757–773.

Bruno, J.F., Ellner, S.P., Vu, I., Kim, K. & Harvell, C.D. (2011) Impacts of aspergillosis on sea fan coral demography: modeling a moving target. *Ecological Monographs*, **81**, 123–139.

Carval, D. & Ferriere, R. (2010) A unified model for the coevolution of resistance, tolerance and virulence. *Evolution*, **64**, 2988–3009.

Caswell, H. (2001) *Matrix Population Models*, 2nd edition. Sunderland, MA: Sinauer Associates.

Cattadori, I.M., Albert, R. & Boag, B. (2007) Variation in host susceptibility and infectiousness generated by co-infection: the myxoma–*Trichostrongylus retortaeformis* case in wild rabbits. *Journal of The Royal Society Interface*, **4**, 831–840.

Cattadori, I.M., Boag, B., Bjørnstad, O.N., Cornell, S.J. & Hudson, P.J. (2005) Peak shift and epidemiology in a seasonal host–nematode system. *Proceedings of the Royal Society of London B*, **272**, 1163–1169.

Caudron, Q., Garnier, R., Pilkington, J.G., et al. (2017) Robust extraction of quantitative structural information from high-variance histological images of livers from necropsied Soay sheep. *Royal Society Open Science*, **4**, 170111.

Chessa, B., Pereira, F., Arnaud, F., et al. (2009) Revealing the history of sheep domestication using retrovirus integrations. *Science*, **324**, 532–536.

Chevin, L.-M. (2015) Evolution of adult size depends on genetic variance in growth trajectories: a comment on analyses of evolutionary dynamics using integral projection models. *Methods in Ecology and Evolution*, **6**, 981–986.

Childs, D.Z., Coulson, T.N., Pemberton, J.M., Clutton-Brock, T.H. & Rees, M. (2011) Predicting trait values and measuring selection in complex life histories: reproductive allocation decisions in Soay sheep. *Ecology Letters*, **14**, 985–992.

Childs, D.Z., Sheldon, B.C. & Rees, M. (2016) The evolution of labile traits in sex- and age-structured populations. *Journal of Animal Ecology*, **85**, 329–342.

Christensen, L.L., Selman, C., Blount, J.D., et al. (2015) Plasma markers of oxidative stress are uncorrelated in a wild mammal. *Ecology and Evolution*, **5**, 5096–5108.

Clark, D. & Bruelisauer, F. (2008) *Mapping the Prevalence of JSRV and Other Endemic Infections*. Inverness: Scottish Government.

Clutton-Brock, T.H., Illius, A.W., Wilson, K., et al. (1997) Stability and instability in ungulate populations: an empirical analysis. *American Naturalist*, **149**, 195–219.

Clutton-Brock, T.H. & Pemberton, J.M. (2004) Individuals and populations. In: Clutton-Brock,T.H. & Pemberton, J.M. (eds.), *Soay Sheep: Dynamics and Selection in an Island Population* (pp. 1–13). Cambridge: Cambridge University Press.

Clutton-Brock, T.H., Pemberton, J.M., Coulson, T., Stevenson, I.R. & MacColl, A.D.C. (2004) The sheep of St Kilda. In: Clutton-Brock,T.H. & Pemberton, J.M. (eds.), *Soay Sheep: Dynamics and Selection in an Island Population* (pp. 17–51). Cambridge: Cambridge University Press.

Clutton-Brock, T. & Sheldon, B.C. (2010) Individuals and populations: the role of long-term, individual-based studies of animals in ecology and evolutionary biology. *Trends in Ecology & Evolution*, **25**, 562–573.

Clutton-Brock, T.H., Stevenson, I.R., Marrow, P., et al. (1996) Population fluctuations, reproductive costs and life-history tactics in female Soay sheep. *Journal of Animal Ecology*, **65**, 675–689.

Colditz, I.G. (2008) Six costs of immunity to gastrointestinal nematode infections. *Parasite Immunology*, **30**, 63–70.

Coltman, D.W., Pilkington, J.G., Kruuk, L.E.B., Wilson, K. & Pemberton, J.M. (2001a) Positive genetic correlation between parasite resistance and body size in a free-living ungulate population. *Evolution*, **55**, 2116–2125.

Coltman, D.W., Pilkington, J.G. & Pemberton, J.M. (2003) Fine-scale genetic structure in a free-living ungulate population. *Molecular Ecology*, **12**, 733–742.

Coltman, D.W., Pilkington, J.G., Smith, J.A. & Pemberton, J.M. (1999) Parasite-mediated selection against inbred Soay sheep in a free-living, island population. *Evolution*, **53**, 1259–1267.

Coltman, D.W., Wilson, K., Pilkington, J.G., Stear, M.J. & Pemberton, J.M. (2001b) A microsatellite polymorphism in the gamma interferon gene is associated with resistance to gastrointestinal nematodes in a naturally parasitized population of Soay sheep. *Parasitology*, **122**, 571–582.

Connelly, L., Craig, B.H., Jones, B. & Alexander, C.L. (2013) Genetic diversity of *Cryptosporidium* spp. within a remote population of Soay Sheep on St. Kilda Islands, Scotland. *Applied and Environmental Microbiology*, **79**, 2240–2246.

Cornell, S.J. (2010) Modelling stochastic transmission processes in helminth infections. In: Michael,E. & Spear, R.C. (eds.), *Modelling Parasite Transmission & Control* (pp. 66–78). New York, NY: Springer.

Coulson, T. (2012) Integral projections models, their construction and use in posing hypotheses in ecology. *Oikos*, **121**, 1337–1350.

Coulson, T., Albon, S., Pilkington, J.G. & Clutton-Brock, T.H. (1999) Small-scale spatial dynamics in a fluctuating ungulate population. *Journal of Animal Ecology*, **68**, 658–671.

Coulson, T., Catchpole, E.A., Albon, S.D., et al. (2001) Age, sex, density, winter weather, and population crashes in Soay sheep. *Science*, **292**, 1528–1531.

Coulson, T., Kendall, B.E., Barthold, J., et al. (2017) Modeling adaptive and nonadaptive responses of populations to environmental change. *The American Naturalist*, **190**, 313–336.

Coulson, T., Tuljapurkar, S. & Childs, D.Z. (2010) Using evolutionary demography to link life history theory, quantitative genetics and population ecology. *Journal of Animal Ecology*, **79**, 1226–1240.

Craig, B.H. (2005) Parasite diversity in a free-living host population. Thesis, University of Edinburgh.

Craig, B.H., Jones, O.R., Pilkington, J.G. & Pemberton, J.M. (2009) Re-establishment of nematode infra-community and host survivorship in wild Soay sheep following anthelmintic treatment. *Veterinary Parasitology*, **161**, 47–52.

Craig, B.H., Pilkington, J.G., Kruuk, L.E.B. & Pemberton, J.M. (2007) Epidemiology of parasite protozoan infections in Soay sheep (*Ovis aries* L.) on St Kilda. *Parasitology*, **134**, 9–21.

Craig, B.H., Pilkington, J.G. & Pemberton, J.M. (2006) Gastrointestinal nematode species burdens and host mortality in a feral sheep population. *Parasitology*, **133**, 485–496.

Craig, B.H., Tempest, L.J., Pilkington, J.G. & Pemberton, J.M. (2008) Metazoan–protozoan parasite co-infections and host body weight in St Kilda Soay sheep. *Parasitology*, **135**, 433–441.

Crawley, M., Albon, S., Bazely, D., et al. (2004) Vegetation and sheep population dynamics. In: Clutton-Brock,T.H. & Pemberton, J.M. (eds.), *Soay Sheep: Dynamics and Selection in an Island Population* (pp. 89–112). Cambridge: Cambridge University Press.

Cressler, C.E., Graham, A.L. & Day, T. (2015) Evolution of hosts paying manifold costs of defence. *Proceedings of the Royal Society of London B*, **282**, 20150065.

Day, T., Alizon, S. & Mideo, N. (2011) Bridging scales in the evolution of infectious disease life-histories: theory. *Evolution*, **65**, 3448–3461.

Denham, D.A. (1969) The development of *Ostertagia circumcincta* in lambs. *Journal of Helminthology*, **43**, 299–310.

Doeschl-Wilson, A.B., Bishop, S., Kyriazakis, I. & Villanueva, B. (2012) Novel methods for quantifying individual host response to infectious pathogens for genetic analyses. *Frontiers in Genetics*, **3**, 266.

Doeschl-Wilson, A.B. & Kyriazakis, I. (2012) Should we aim for genetic improvement in host resistance or tolerance to infectious pathogens? *Frontiers in Genetics*, **3**, 272.

Doeschl-Wilson, A.B., Villanueva, B. & Kyriazakis, I. (2012) The first step towards genetic selection for host tolerance to infectious pathogens: obtaining the tolerance phenotype through group estimates. *Frontiers in Genetics*, **3**, 265.

Easterling, M.R., Ellner, S.P. & Dixon, P.M. (2000) Size-specific sensitivity: applying a new structured population model. *Ecology*, **81**, 694–708.

Ezenwa, V.O., Etienne, R.S., Gordon, L., Beja-Pereira, A. & Jolles, A.E. (2010) Hidden consequences of living in a wormy world: nematode-induced immune suppression facilitates tuberculosis invasion in African buffalo. *The American Naturalist*, **176**, 613–624.

Ezenwa, V.O. & Jolles, A.E. (2015) Opposite effects of anthelmintic treatment on microbial infection at individual versus population scales. *Science*, **347**, 175–177.

Fairlie, J., Holland, R., Pilkington, J.G., et al. (2016) Lifelong leukocyte telomere dynamics and survival in a free-living mammal. *Aging Cell*, **15**, 140–148.

Feulner, P.G.D., Gratten, J., Kijas, J.W., et al. (2013) Introgression and the fate of domesticated genes in a wild mammal population. *Molecular Ecology*, **22**, 4210–4221.

Fineblum, W.L. & Rausher, M.D. (1995) Tradeoff between resistance and tolerance to herbivore damage in a morning glory. *Nature*, **377**, 517–520.

Garnier, R., Bento, A.I., Hansen, C., et al. (2017a) Physiological proteins in resource-limited herbivores experiencing a population die-off. *The Science of Nature*, **104**, 68.

Garnier, R., Cheung, C.K., Watt, K.A., et al. (2017b) Joint associations of blood plasma proteins with overwinter survival of a large mammal. *Ecology Letters*, **20**, 175–183.

Garnier, R. & Graham, A.L. (2014) Insights from parasite-specific serological tools in eco-immunology. *Integrative and Comparative Biology*, **54**, 363–376.

Garnier, R., Grenfell, B.T., Nisbet, A.J., Matthews, J.B. & Graham, A.L. (2016) Integrating immune mechanisms to model nematode worm burden: an example in sheep. *Parasitology*, **143**, 894–904.

Gibson, W., Pilkington, J.G. & Pemberton, J.M. (2010) *Trypanosoma melophagium* from the sheep ked *Melophagus ovinus* on the island of St Kilda. *Parasitology*, **137**, 1799–1804.

Graham, A.L., Allen, J.E. & Read, A.F. (2005) Evolutionary causes and consequences of immunopathology. *Annual Review of Ecology, Evolution, and Systematics*, **36**, 373–397.

Graham, A.L., Hayward, A.D., Watt, K.A., et al. (2010) Fitness correlates of heritable variation in antibody responsiveness in a wild mammal. *Science*, **330**, 662–665.

Graham, A.L., Nussey, D.H., Lloyd-Smith, J.O., et al. (2016) Exposure to viral and bacterial pathogens among Soay sheep (*Ovis aries*) of the St Kilda archipelago. *Epidemiology and Infection*, **144**, 1–10.

Graham, A.L., Shuker, D.M., Pollitt, L.C., et al. (2011) Fitness consequences of immune responses: strengthening the empirical framework for ecoimmunology. *Functional Ecology*, **25**, 5–17.

Gratten, J., Beraldi, D., Lowder, B.V., et al. (2007) Compelling evidence that a single nucleotide substitution in TYRP1 is responsible for coat-colour polymorphism in a free-living population of Soay sheep. *Proceedings of the Royal Society of London B*, **274**, 619–626.

Gratten, J., Pilkington, J.G., Brown, E.A., et al. (2010) The genetic basis of recessive self-colour pattern in a wild sheep population. *Heredity*, **104**, 206–214.

Grenfell, B. & Dobson, A. (1995) *Ecology of Infectious Diseases in Natural Populations*. Cambridge: Cambridge University Press.

Grenfell, B.H., Price, O.F., Albon, S.D. & Clutton-Brock, T.H. (1992) Overcompensation and population cycles in an ungulate. *Nature*, **355**, 823–826.

Grenfell, B.T., Wilson, K., Finkelstadt, B.F., et al. (1998) Noise and determinism in synchronized sheep dynamics. *Nature*, **394**, 674–677.

Grenfell, B.T., Wilson, K., Isham, V.S., Boyd, H.E.G. & Dietz, K. (1995) Modelling patterns of parasite aggregation in natural populations: trichostrongylid nematode-ruminant interactions as a case study. *Parasitology*, **111**, S135–S151.

Gulland, F.M.D. (1992) The role of nematode parasites in Soay sheep (*Ovis aries* L.) mortality during a population crash. *Parasitology*, **105**, 493–503.

Gulland, F.M.D., Albon, S.D., Pemberton, J.M., Moorcroft, P.R. & Clutton-Brock, T.H. (1993) Parasite-associated polymorphism in a cyclic ungulate population. *Proceedings of the Royal Society of London B*, **254**, 7–13.

Gulland, F.M.D. & Fox, M. (1992) Epidemiology of nematode infections of Soay sheep (*Ovis aries* L.) on St Kilda. *Parasitology*, **105**, 481–492.

Halliday, A.M., Routledge, C.M., Smith, S.K., Matthews, J.B. & Smith, W.D. (2007) Parasite loss and inhibited development of *Teladorsagia circumcincta* in relation to the kinetics of the local IgA response in sheep. *Parasite Immunology*, **29**, 425–434.

Hayward, A.D., Garnier, R., Watt, K.A., et al. (2014a) Heritable, heterogeneous, and costly resistance of sheep against nematodes and potential feedbacks to epidemiological dynamics. *The American Naturalist*, **184**, S58–S76.

Hayward, A.D., Nussey, D.H., Wilson, A.J., et al. (2014b) Natural selection on individual variation in tolerance of gastrointestinal nematode infection. *PLoS Biology*, **12**, e1001917.

Hayward, A.D., Pemberton, J.M., Bérénos, C., et al. (2018) Evidence for selection-by-environment but not genotype-by-environment interactions for fitness-related traits in a wild mammal population. *Genetics*, **208**, 349–364.

Hayward, A.D., Wilson, A.J., Pilkington, J.G., et al. (2011) Natural selection on a measure of parasite resistance varies across ages and environmental conditions in a wild mammal. *Journal of Evolutionary Biology*, **24**, 1664–1676.

Hayward, A.D., Wilson, A.J., Pilkington, J.G., Pemberton, J.M. & Kruuk, L.E.B. (2009) Ageing in a variable habitat: environmental stress affects senescence in parasite resistance in St Kilda Soay sheep. *Proceedings of the Royal Society of London B*, **276**, 3477–3485.

Henderson, C.R. (1950) Estimation of genetic parameters. *Annals of Mathematical Statistics*, **21**, 309–310.

Henrichs, B., Oosthuizen, M.C., Troskie, M., et al. (2016) Within guild co-infections influence parasite community membership: a longitudinal study in African Buffalo. *Journal of Animal Ecology*, **85**, 1025–1034.

Hong, C., Michel, J.F. & Lancaster, M.B. (1987) Observations on the dynamics of worm burdens in lambs infected daily with *Ostertagia circumcincta*. *International Journal for Parasitology*, **17**, 951–956.

Houdijk, J.G.M., Kyriazakis, I., Jackson, F., Huntley, J.F. & Coop, R.L. (2005) Effects of protein supply and reproductive status on local and systemic immune responses to *Teladorsagia circumcincta* in sheep. *Veterinary Parasitology*, **129**, 105–117.

Hudson, P.J., Dobson, A.P. & Newborn, D. (1998) Prevention of population cycles by parasite removal. *Science*, **282**, 2256–2258.

Hutchings, M.R., Milner, J.M., Gordon, I.J., Kyriazakis, I. & Jackson, F. (2002) Grazing decisions of Soay sheep, *Ovis aries*, on St Kilda: a consequence of parasite distribution? *Oikos*, **96**, 235–244.

Jackson, J.A., Hall, A.J., Friberg, I.M., et al. (2014) An immunological marker of tolerance to infection in wild rodents. *PLoS Biology*, **12**, e1001901.

Janeiro, M.J., Coltman, D.W., Festa-Bianchet, M., Pelletier, F. & Morrissey, M.B. (2017) Towards robust evolutionary inference with integral projection models. *Journal of Evolutionary Biology*, **30**, 270–288.

Jewell, P.A., Milner, C. & Boyd, J.M. (1974) *Island Survivors: The Ecology of the Soay Sheep of St Kilda*. London: Athlone Press.

Johnston, S.E., Bérénos, C., Slate, J. & Pemberton, J.M. (2016) Conserved genetic architecture underlying individual recombination rate variation in a wild population of Soay sheep (*Ovis aries*). *Genetics*, **203**, 583–598.

Johnston, S.E., Gratten, J., Berenos, C., et al. (2013) Life history trade-offs at a single locus maintain sexually selected genetic variation. *Nature*, **502**, 93–95.

Johnston, S.E., McEwan, J.C., Pickering, N.K., et al. (2011) Genome-wide association mapping identifies the genetic basis of discrete and quantitative variation in sexual weaponry in a wild sheep population. *Molecular Ecology*, **20**, 2555–2566.

Jolles, A.E., Ezenwa, V.O., Etienne, R.S., Turner, W.C. & Olff, H. (2008) Interactions between macroparasites and microparasites drive infection patterns in free-ranging African buffalo. *Ecology*, **89**, 2239–2250.

Jones, O.R., Anderson, R.M. & Pilkington, J.G. (2006) Parasite-induced anorexia in a free-ranging mammalian herbivore: an experimental test using Soay sheep. *Canadian Journal of Zoology*, **84**, 685–692.

Jones, O.R., Crawley, M.J., Pilkington, J.G. & Pemberton, J.M. (2005) Predictors of early survival in Soay sheep: cohort-, maternal-, and individual-level variation. *Proceedings of the Royal Society of London B*, **272**, 2619–2625.

Kause, A. (2011) Genetic analysis of tolerance to infections using random regressions: a simulation study. *Genetics Research*, **93**, 291–302.

Kause, A., van Dalen, S. & Bovenhuis, H. (2012) Genetics of ascites resistance and tolerance in chicken: a random regression approach. *G3: Genes|Genomes|Genetics*, **2**, 527–535.

Kenyon, F., Sargison, N.D., Skuce, P.J. & Jackson, F. (2009) Sheep helminth parasitic disease in south eastern Scotland arising as a possible consequence of climate change. *Veterinary Parasitology*, **163**, 293–297.

Kijas, J.W., Lenstra, J.A., Hayes, B., et al. (2012) Genome-wide analysis of the world's sheep breeds reveals high levels of historic mixture and strong recent selection. *PLoS Biology*, **10**, e1001258.

Klasing, K.C. (2004) The costs of immunity. *Acta Zoologica Sinica*, **50**, 961–969.

Koski, K.G. & Scott, M.E. (2001) Gastrointestinal nematodes, nutrition and immunity: breaking the negative spiral. *Annual Review of Nutrition*, **21**, 297–321.

Kruuk, L.E.B. (2004) Estimating genetic parameters in natural populations using the 'animal model'. *Philosophical Transactions of the Royal Society of London. Series B: Biological Sciences*, **359**, 873–890.

Lawson Handley, L.-J., Byrne, K., Santucci, F., et al. (2007) Genetic structure of European sheep breeds. *Heredity*, **99**, 620–631.

Lello, J., Boag, B., Fenton, A., Stevenson, I.R. & Hudson, P.J. (2004) Competition and mutualism among the gut helminths of a mammalian host. *Nature*, **428**, 840–844.

Lippens, C., Guivier, E., Faivre, B. & Sorci, G. (2016) Reaction norms of host immunity, host fitness and parasite performance in a mouse–intestinal nematode interaction. *International Journal for Parasitology*, **46**, 133–140.

Liu, W.-C., Bonsall, M.B. & Godfray, H.C.J. (2007) The form of host density-dependence and the likelihood of host–pathogen cycles in forest-insect systems. *Theoretical Population Biology*, **72**, 86–95.

Lloyd-Smith, J.O., Schreiber, S.J., Kopp, P.E. & Getz, W.M. (2005) Superspreading and the effect of individual variation on disease emergence. *Nature*, **438**, 355–359.

Lochmiller, R.L. & Deerenberg, C. (2000) Tradeoffs in evolutionary immunology: just what is the cost of immunity? *Oikos*, **88**, 87–98.

Martinez-Valldares, M., Vara-Del Rio, M.P., Cruz-Rojo, M.A. & Rojo-Vazquez, F.A. (2005) Genetic resistance to *Teladorsagia circumcincta*: IgA and parameters at slaughter in Churra sheep. *Parasite Immunology*, **27**, 213–218.

May, R.M. & Anderson, R.M. (1978) Regulation and stability of host-parasite population interactions: II. Destabilizing processes. *Journal of Animal Ecology*, **47**, 249–267.

May, R.M. & Anderson, R.M. (1979) Population biology of infectious diseases: Part II. *Nature*, **280**, 455–461.

Mazé-Guilmo, E., Loot, G., Páez, D.J., Lefèvre, T. & Blanchet, S. (2014) Heritable variation in host tolerance and resistance inferred from a wild host–parasite system. *Proceedings of the Royal Society of London B*, **281**, 20132567.

McNeilly, T.N., Devaney, E. & Matthews, J.B. (2009) *Teladorsagia circumcincta* in the sheep abomasum: defining the role of dendritic cells in T cell regulation and protective immunity. *Parasite Immunology*, **31**, 347–356.

McRae, K.M., Stear, M.J., Good, B. & Keane, O.M. (2015) The host immune response to gastrointestinal nematode infection in sheep. *Parasite Immunology*, **37**, 605–613.

Medzhitov, R., Schneider, D.S. & Soares, M.P. (2012) Disease tolerance as a defense strategy. *Science*, **335**, 936–941.

Metcalf, C.J.E., Graham, A.L., Martinez-Bakker, M. & Childs, D.Z. (2016) Opportunities and challenges of Integral Projection Models for modelling host–parasite dynamics. *Journal of Animal Ecology*, **85**, 343–355.

Mideo, N., Nelson, W.A., Reece, S.E., et al. (2011) Bridging scales in the evolution of infectious disease life histories: application. *Evolution*, **65**, 3298–3310.

Miller, M.R., White, A. & Boots, M. (2005) The evolution of host resistance: tolerance and control as distinct strategies. *Journal of Theoretical Biology*, **236**, 198–207.

Miller, M.R., White, A. & Boots, M. (2006) The evolution of parasites in response to tolerance in their hosts: the good, the bad, and apparent commensalism. *Evolution*, **60**, 945–956.

Milner, J.M., Albon, S.D., Illius, A.W., Pemberton, J.M. & Clutton-Brock, T.H. (1999) Repeated selection of morphometric traits in the Soay sheep on St Kilda. *Journal of Animal Ecology*, **68**, 472–488.

Milner, J.M., Elston, D.A. & Albon, S.D. (1999) Estimating the contributions of population density and climatic fluctuations to interannual variation in survival of Soay sheep. *Journal of Animal Ecology*, **68**, 1235–1247.

Moore, S.L. & Wilson, K. (2002) Parasites as a viability cost of sexual selection in natural populations of mammals. *Science*, **297**, 2015–2018.

Morales-Montor, J., Chavarria, A., De León, M.A., et al. (2004) Host gender in parasitic infections of mammals: an evaluation of the female host supremacy paradigm. *Journal of Parasitology*, **90**, 531–546.

Morgan, E.R. & van Dijk, J. (2012) Climate and the epidemiology of gastrointestinal nematode infections of sheep in Europe. *Veterinary Parasitology*, **189**, 8–14.

Murphy, L., Pathak, A.K. & Cattadori, I.M. (2013) A co-infection with two gastrointestinal nematodes alters host immune responses and only partially parasite dynamics. *Parasite Immunology*, **35**, 421–432.

Murray, D.L., Cox, E.W., Ballard, W.B., et al. (2006) Pathogens, nutritional deficiency, and climate influences on a declining moose population. *Wildlife Monographs*, **166**, 1–30.

Nielsen, M.K., Kaplan, R.M., Thamsborg, S.M., Monrad, J. & Olsen, S.N. (2007) Climatic influences on development and survival of free-living stages of equine strongyles: implications for worm control strategies and managing anthelmintic resistance. *The Veterinary Journal*, **174**, 23–32.

Nieuwhof, G.J. & Bishop, S.C. (2005) Costs of the major endemic diseases of sheep in Great Britain and the potential benefits of reduction in disease impact. *Animal Science*, **81**, 23–29.

Nisbet, A.J., McNeilly, T.N., Wildblood, L.A., et al. (2013) Successful immunization against a parasitic nematode by vaccination with recombinant proteins. *Vaccine*, **31**, 4017–4023.

Nussey, D.H., Watt, K., Pilkington, J.G., Zamoyska, R. & McNeilly, T.N. (2012) Age-related variation in immunity in a wild mammal population. *Aging Cell*, **11**, 178–180.

Nussey, D.H., Watt, K.A., Clark, A., et al. (2014) Multivariate immune defences and fitness in the wild: complex but ecologically important associations among plasma antibodies, health and survival. *Proceedings of the Royal Society of London B*, **281**, 20132931.

Ozgul, A., Childs, D.Z., Oli, M.K., et al. (2010) Coupled dynamics of body mass and population growth in response to environmental change. *Nature*, **466**, 482–485.

Ozgul, A., Coulson, T., Reynolds, A., Cameron, T.C. & Benton, T.G. (2012) Population responses to perturbations: the importance of trait-based analysis illustrated through a microcosm experiment. *The American Naturalist*, **179**, 582–594.

Pacala, S.W. & Dobson, A.P. (1988) The relation between the number of parasites/host and host age: population dynamic causes and maximum likelihood estimation. *Parasitology*, **96**, 197–210.

Paterson, S., Wilkes, C., Bleay, C. & Viney, M.E. (2008) Immunological responses elicited by different infection regimes with *Strongyloides ratti*. *PLoS ONE*, **3**, e2509.

Paterson, S., Wilson, K. & Pemberton, J.M. (1998) Major histocompatibility complex variation associated with juvenile survival and parasite resistance in a large unmanaged ungulate population (*Ovis aries* L.). *Proceedings of the National Academy of Sciences of the United States of America*, **95**, 3714–3719.

Pathak, A.K., Pelensky, C., Boag, B. & Cattadori, I.M. (2012) Immuno-epidemiology of chronic bacterial and helminth co-infections: observations from the field and evidence from the laboratory. *International Journal for Parasitology*, **42**, 647–655.

Pedersen, A.B. & Greives, T.J. (2008) The interaction of parasites and resources cause crashes in a wild mouse population. *Journal of Animal Ecology*, **77**, 370–377.

Pemberton, J.M., Coltman, D.W., Bancroft, D.R., Smith, J.A. & Paterson, S. (2004) Molecular genetic variation and selection on phenotype. In: Clutton-Brock, T.H. & Pemberton, J.M. (eds.), *Soay Sheep: Dynamics and Selection in an Island Population* (pp. 217–242). Cambridge: Cambridge University Press.

Penczykowski, R.M., Walker, E., Soubeyrand, S. & Laine, A.-L. (2015) Linking winter conditions to regional disease dynamics in a wild plant-pathogen metapopulation. *New Phytologist*, **205**, 1142–1152.

Pernthaner, A., Cole, S.-A., Morrison, L., et al. (2006) Cytokine and antibody subclass responses in the intestinal lymph of sheep during repeated experimental infections with the nematode parasite *Trichostrongylus colubriformis*. *Veterinary Immunology and Immunopathology*, **114**, 135–148.

Preston, B.T., Stevenson, I.R., Pemberton, J.M., Coltman, D.W. & Wilson, K. (2003) Overt and covert competition in a promiscuous mammal: the importance of weaponry and testes size to male reproductive success. *Proceedings of the Royal Society of London B*, **270**, 633–640.

Råberg, L., Graham, A.L. & Read, A.F. (2009) Decomposing health: tolerance and resistance to parasites in animals. *Philosophical Transactions of the Royal Society of London B*, **364**, 37–49.

Råberg, L., Sim, D. & Read, A.F. (2007) Disentangling genetic variation for resistance and tolerance to infectious diseases in animals. *Science*, **318**, 812–814.

Rees, M., Childs, D.Z. & Ellner, S.P. (2014) Building integral projection models: a user's guide. *Journal of Animal Ecology*, **83**, 528–545.

Rees, M. & Ellner, S.P. (2009) Integral projection models for populations in temporally varying environments. *Ecological Monographs*, **79**, 575–594.

Rees, M. & Ellner, S.P. (2016) Evolving integral projection models: evolutionary demography meets eco-evolutionary dynamics. *Methods in Ecology and Evolution*, **7**, 157–170.

Restif, O. & Koella, J.C. (2003) Shared control of epidemiological traits in a coevolutionary model of host–parasite interactions. *The American Naturalist*, **161**, 827–836.

Restif, O. & Koella, J.C. (2004) Concurrent evolution of resistance and tolerance to pathogens. *The American Naturalist*, **164**, E90–E102.

Robinson, M.R., Pilkington, J.G., Clutton-Brock, T.H., Pemberton, J.M. & Kruuk, L.E.B. (2008) Environmental heterogeneity generates fluctuating selection on a secondary sexual trait. *Current Biology*, **18**, 751–757.

Robinson, M.R., Wilson, A.J., Pilkington, J.G., et al. (2009) The impact of environmental heterogeneity on genetic architecture in a wild population of Soay sheep. *Genetics*, **181**, 1639–1648.

Roy, B.A. & Kirchner, J.W. (2000) Evolutionary dynamics of pathogen resistance and tolerance. *Evolution*, **54**, 51–63.

Sahoo, A., Pattanaik, A.K. & Goswami, T.K. (2009) Immunobiochemical status of sheep exposed to periods of experimental protein deficit and realimentation. *Journal of Animal Science*, **87**, 2664–2673.

Sand, K.M.K., Bern, M., Nilsen, J., et al. (2015) Unraveling the interaction between FcRn and albumin: opportunities for design of albumin-based therapeutics. *Frontiers in Immunology*, **5**, 682.

Sayre, B.L. & Harris, G.C. (2012) Systems genetics approach reveals candidate genes for parasite resistance from quantitative trait loci studies in agricultural species. *Animal Genetics*, **43**, 190–198.

Schmid-Hempel, P. (2003) Variation in immune defence as a question of evolutionary ecology. *Proceedings of the Royal Society of London B*, **270**, 357–366.

Schneider, D.S. & Ayres, J.S. (2008) Two ways to survive infection: what resistance and tolerance can teach us about treating infectious disease. *Nature Reviews Immunology*, **8**, 889–895.

Scott, M.E. (1991) *Heligmosomoides polygyrus* (Nematoda): susceptible and resistant strains of mice are indistinguishable following natural infection. *Parasitology*, **103**, 429–438.

Scott, M.E. (2006) High transmission rates restore expression of genetically determined susceptibility of mice to nematode infections. *Parasitology*, **132**, 669–679.

Shaw, D.J. & Dobson, A.P. (1995) Patterns of macroparasite abundance and aggregation in wildlife populations: a quantitative review. *Parasitology*, **111**, S111–S133.

Shaw, D.J., Grenfell, B.T. & Dobson, A.P. (1998) Patterns of macroparasite aggregation in wildlife host populations. *Parasitology*, **117**, 597–610.

Sheldon, B.C. & Verhulst, S. (1996) Ecological immunity: costly parasite defences and tradeoffs in evolutionary ecology. *Trends in Ecology and Evolution*, **11**, 317–321.

Simms, E. (2000) Defining tolerance as a norm of reaction. *Evolutionary Ecology*, **14**, 563–570.

Simpson, H.V. (2000) Pathophysiology of abomasal parasitism: is the host or parasite responsible? *The Veterinary Journal*, **160**, 177–191.

Smith, J.A., Wilson, K., Pilkington, J.G. & Pemberton, J.M. (1999) Heritable variation in resistance to gastrointestinal nematodes in an unmanaged mammal population. *Proceedings of the Royal Society of London B*, **266**, 1283–1290.

Smith, W.D., Jackson, F., Jackson, E. & Williams, J. (1985) Age immunity to *Ostertagia circumcincta*: comparison of the local immune responses of 4 1/2- and 10-month-old lambs. *Journal of Comparative Pathology*, **95**, 235–245.

Sparks, A.M., Watt, K., Sinclair, R., et al. (2019) The genetic architecture of helminth-specific immune responses in a wild population of Soay sheep (*Ovis aries*). bioRxiv 02871.

Stear, M.J., Bishop, S.C., Doligalska, M., et al. (1995) Regulation of egg production, worm burden, worm length and worm fecundity by host responses in sheep infected with *Ostertagia circumcincta*. *Parasite Immunology*, **17**, 643–652.

Steele, T. (1979) *The Life and Death of St Kilda*. Glasgow: Fontana/Collins.

Tate, A.T. & Graham, A.L. (2015) Dynamic patterns of parasitism and immunity across host development influence optimal strategies of resource allocation. *The American Naturalist*, **186**, 495–512.

Tate, A.T. & Rudolf, V.H.W. (2012) Impact of life stage specific immune priming on invertebrate disease dynamics. *Oikos*, **121**, 1083–1092.

Tempest, L.J. (2005) Parasites and the cost of reproduction in Soay sheep. PhD thesis, University of Stirling.

Thrall, P. & Antonovics, J. (1994) The cost of resistance and the maintenance of genetic polymorphisms in host–pathogen systems. *Proceedings of the Royal Society of London B*, **257**, 105–110.

Tidbury, H.J., Best, A. & Boots, M. (2012) The epidemiological consequences of immune priming. *Proceedings of the Royal Society of London B*, **279**, 4505–4512.

Torgerson, P.R., Pilkington, J., Gulland, F.M.D. & Gemmell, M.A. (1995) Further evidence for the long distance dispersal of taeniid eggs. *International Journal for Parasitology*, **25**, 265–267.

Traill, L.W., Schindler, S. & Coulson, T. (2014) Demography, not inheritance, drives phenotypic change in hunted bighorn sheep. *Proceedings of the National Academy of Sciences of the United States of America*, **111**, 13,223–13,228.

Watson, M.J. (2013) What drives population-level effects of parasites? Meta-analysis meets life-history. *International Journal for Parasitology: Parasites and Wildlife*, **2**, 190–196.

Watson, R.L., Bird, E.J., Underwood, S., et al. (2017) Sex differences in leucocyte telomere length in a free-living mammal. *Molecular Ecology*, **26**, 3230–3240.

Watson, R.L., McNeilly, T.N., Watt, K.A., et al. (2016) Cellular and humoral immunity in a wild mammal: variation with age & sex and association with overwinter survival. *Ecology and Evolution*, **6**, 8695–8705.

Watt, K.A., Nussey, D.H., Maclellan, R., Pilkington, J.G. & McNeilly, T.N. (2016) Fecal antibody levels as a noninvasive method for measuring immunity to gastrointestinal nematodes in ecological studies. *Ecology and Evolution*, **6**, 56–67.

Westra, E.R., van Houte, S., Oyesiku-Blakemore, S., et al. (2015) Parasite exposure drives selective evolution of constitutive versus inducible defense. *Current Biology*, **25**, 1043–1049.

Wilber, M.Q., Knapp, R.A., Toothman, M. & Briggs, C.J. (2017) Resistance, tolerance and environmental transmission dynamics determine host extinction risk in a load-dependent amphibian disease. *Ecology Letters*, **20**, 1169–1181.

Wilber, M.Q., Langwig, K.E., Kilpatrick, A.M., McCallum, H.I. & Briggs, C.J. (2016) Integral projection models for host–parasite systems with an application to amphibian chytrid fungus. *Methods in Ecology and Evolution*, **7**, 1182–1194.

Wilson, A.J., Pemberton, J.M., Pilkington, J.G., et al. (2006) Environmental coupling of selection and heritability limits evolution. *PLoS Biology*, **4**, 1270–1275.

Wilson, A.J., Réale, D., Clements, M.N., et al. (2010) An ecologist's guide to the animal model. *Journal of Animal Ecology*, **79**, 13–26.

Wilson, K., Bjornstad, O.N., Dobson, A.P., et al. (2002) Heterogeneities in macroparasite infections: patterns and processes. In: Hudson, P.J., Rizzoli, A., Grenfell, B.T., Heesterbeek,H. & Dobson, A.P. (eds.), *The Ecology of Wildlife Diseases* (pp. 6–44). Oxford: Oxford University Press.

Wilson, K., Grenfell, B.T., Pilkington, J.G., Boyd, H.E.G. & Gulland, F.M.D. (2004) Parasites and their impact. In: Clutton-Brock, T.H. & Pemberton, J.M. (eds.), *Soay Sheep: Dynamics and Selection in an Island Population* (pp. 113–165). Cambridge: Cambridge University Press.

Wilson, K., Grenfell, B.T. & Shaw, D.J. (1996) Analysis of aggregated parasite distributions: a comparison of methods. *Functional Ecology*, **10**, 592–601.

Zuk, M. & McKean, K.A. (1996) Sex differences in parasite infections: patterns and processes. *International Journal for Parasitology*, **26**, 1009–1024.

CHAPTER FIVE

The causes and consequences of parasite interactions: African buffalo as a case study

VANESSA O. EZENWA, ANNA E. JOLLES,
BRIANNA R. BEECHLER, SARAH A.
BUDISCHAK AND ERIN E. GORSICH

5.1 Introduction

Most hosts are infected by more than one type of parasite simultaneously, thus the typical parasite lives in a multi-species community (Petney & Andrews, 1998; Cox, 2001). This biological reality has helped fuel a new and emerging perspective on studying infectious diseases – one that focuses on understanding the interactions that occur among parasite species. Ecologists are particularly well-suited to tackling questions about parasite interactions given a long history of similar work in free-living species communities (Bender et al., 1984; Callaway & Walker, 1997; Brown et al., 2001). Indeed, like most free-living species, parasites can interact directly and indirectly, positively and negatively (reviewed in Pedersen & Fenton, 2007). For example, parasites that share the same physical location within a host might compete directly for space, exerting negative effects on one another (Stock & Holmes, 1987, 1988), or one parasite might facilitate another by modifying the habitat in a way that positively affects the growth or replication of the second species (Xu et al., 2012). Even more intriguing, parasites often interact indirectly via the host's response to infection (reviewed in Pedersen & Fenton, 2007). For instance, the effect some parasites have on the host immune system can facilitate the establishment and replication of other species, as exemplified by interactions between HIV and tuberculosis in humans (Pawlowski et al., 2012). In contrast, one parasite can also thwart the success of another if the immune response it triggers in the host is cross-protective against other parasites (Romano et al., 2015). Although there is strong evidence, mainly from laboratory and human studies, that support a variety of hypotheses about how different parasites *should* interact within a host, the extent to which these interactions occur in free-living animals, the relative strength of such interactions, and their real-world consequences for individual, population, and broader-scale processes are only just beginning to be understood.

It is in the past two decades that an increasing number of wildlife studies have begun to tackle questions related to the causes and consequences of parasite interactions (Lello et al., 2004; Telfer et al., 2010; Knowles et al., 2013). This pattern has paralleled a surge in biomedical understanding of vertebrate immunology and physiology and how these processes impact and are impacted by parasites (Allen & Maizels, 2011; Beura et al., 2016; Reese et al., 2016). An important advantage of this parallel trajectory is that questions about parasite interactions in wildlife benefit in tandem from ecological approaches for identifying species interactions and describing disease dynamics, and from immunological and physiological concepts and tools that help probe the mechanistic basis of these interactions. This chapter focuses on insights gleaned from a body of work on wild African buffalo (*Syncerus caffer*) and their parasites. In this study system, approaches from ecology, epidemiology, parasitology, and immunology have been combined to identify the types of interactions occurring between parasites, understand the mechanisms accounting for these interactions, and explore the potential consequences for disease dynamics, host health, and fitness.

5.2 African buffalo as a wild model for studying parasite interactions

African buffalo are gregarious, large-bodied mammals that live in herds ranging in size from tens to thousands of individuals (Figure 5.1). With over 800,000 buffalo distributed throughout southern, eastern, and western Africa, this species is simultaneously an icon of conservation and a villain of disease-eradication programmes (Michel & Bengis, 2012). The latter role stems from the buffalo's status as an important reservoir for several infectious

Figure 5.1 Images of a single adult African buffalo and a group of buffalo at a watering hole. (A black and white version of this figure will appear in some formats. For the colour version, please refer to the plate section.)

diseases of economic concern on the African continent (e.g. bovine tuberculosis, foot-and-mouth disease, theileriosis). Indeed, buffalo are host to a broad diversity of microparasites and macroparasites. The extreme social behaviour of the species might help explain the buffalo's ability to support such a diverse parasite fauna (Schmid-Hempel, 2017); for example, increasing herd size has been linked to the prevalence of certain parasites in buffalo (Ezenwa, 2004). Other behavioural and life-history traits of this species (e.g. body size, lifespan) may also help account for the diversity of parasites which they harbour (Ezenwa et al., 2006).

The endoparasites infecting buffalo span from bacteria and viruses to protozoa and helminths (Table 5.1). Common bacterial infections of buffalo include tick-borne pathogens such as *Anaplasma* spp. and *Ehrlichia* spp., as well as the causative agents of bovine tuberculosis (*Mycobacterium bovis*) and brucellosis (*Brucella abortus*). At least 12 viral pathogens have been described in buffalo, including zoonotic vector-borne pathogens such as Rift Valley Fever virus and the highly contagious foot-and-mouth disease virus, considered to be among the most economically important diseases of livestock worldwide. Protozoan infections of buffalo include tick-borne parasites like *Babesia* spp. and *Theileria* spp., and faecal–oral transmitted parasites such as *Cryptosporidium* spp. Finally, key helminth parasites identified in buffalo include nematodes such as *Cooperia* spp., *Haemonchus* spp., and *Trichostrongylus* spp., and trematodes such as *Schistosoma* spp. Importantly, a significant fraction of the parasites described in African buffalo are also known to infect livestock (Table 5.1), and the role of buffalo in the maintenance and transmission of parasites that infect livestock has garnered significant attention for decades (Gomo et al., 2012; Michel & Bengis, 2012; Miguel et al., 2013). As a consequence, buffalo are relatively unique among African ungulates in terms of the breadth and depth of research that has focused on infectious diseases. This history, coupled with a rich knowledge base on buffalo behaviour, ecology and population biology (Sinclair, 1977; Prins, 1996), and the close phylogenetic relationship between buffalo and domestic cattle, has set the stage for African buffalo to serve as a valuable model for addressing ecological questions about infectious diseases in natural populations.

5.3 Pairwise interactions between parasites in buffalo

Building on the strong foundation of information on buffalo biology and infectious diseases, Ezenwa, Jolles, and colleagues have studied interactions occurring between some of the most common and economically important parasites of this species. The studies focused on African buffalo populations in two high-profile parks in South Africa, Kruger National Park (KNP) and Hluhluwe-iMfolozi Park (HIP). Early work in HIP took advantage of the park's bovine tuberculosis control programme to perform cross-sectional and short-

Table 5.1 *List of key parasite species reported in buffalo by taxon. The proportion of species reported in livestock was estimated as the percent of the species listed that also occur in livestock as reported in either the Merck Veterinary Manual or primary literature. Asterisks indicate parasites species that are unique to buffalo.*

Parasite	Species reported	% in livestock	Examples of economically important diseases	Representative references
Bacteria	*Anaplasma marginale* subsp. *centrale*; *Anaplasma marginale* *Brucella abortus* *Chlamydia abortus*; *Chlamydia pneumonia** *Ehrlichia ondirii*; *Ehrlichia ruminantum*; *Leptospira* sp. *Mycobacterium bovis*	89%	Anaplasmosis (*Anaplasma marginale*) Brucellosis (*Brucella abortus*) Bovine tuberculosis (*Mycobacterium bovis*) Heartwater (*Ehrlichia ruminantum*)	Rodwell et al., 2001 Pospischil et al., 2012 Eygelaar et al., 2015 Atherstone et al., 2014 Gradwell et al., 1977
Helminths	*Africanastrongylus giganticus**; *Africanastrongylus buceros** *Cooperia fuelleborni**; *Cooperia hungi** *Haemonchus contortus*, *Haemonchus placei* *Moniezia* sp. *Nematodirus* sp. *Oesophagostomum* sp. *Parabronema* sp. *Schistosoma mattheei* *Trichostrongylus defexus** *Trichuris* sp.	38%	Haemonchosis (*Haemonchus contortus*) Schistosomiasis (*Schistosoma mattheei*)	Pitchford, 1976 Hoberg et al. 2008, 2010 Taylor et al., 2013 Budischak et al., 2015 Roug et al, 2016

Protozoa	*Babesia bovis; Babesia occultans* *Cryptosporidium bovis; Cryptosporidium* *ubiquitum* *Theileria buffeli; Theileria mutans;* *Theileria parva; Theileria velifera*	100%	Babesiosis (*Babesia bovis*) East Coast Fever or Corridor disease (*Theileria parva*)	Abu Samra et al., 2013 Chaisi et al., 2013 Eygelaar et al., 2015
Viruses	Alcelaphine herpesvirus type 2; Bovine herpesvirus 1; Bovine herpesvirus 4; Ovine herpesvirus type 2 Bluetongue virus Bovine ephemeral fever virus Bovine viral diarrhoea Foot-and-mouth disease virus Lumpy skin disease virus Parainfluenza 3 virus Rift Valley Fever virus	100%	Infectious bovine rhinotracheitis (Bovine herpesvirus 1) Malignant Catarrhal Fever (Alcelaphine herpesvirus type 2, Ovine herpesvirus type 2) Rift Valley fever (Rift Valley Fever virus)	Anderson & Rowe, 1998 Ayebazibwe et al., 2012 Fagbo et al., 2014 Hamblin et al., 1980, 1990

term experimental studies. More recent work in KNP combined longitudinal and experimental approaches by capturing and tracking a cohort of free-ranging animals over time (Box 5.1). To date, three key pairwise interactions between parasites have been examined in some detail. First, interactions between a common group of macroparasites (intestinal helminths) and a microparasite (*Mycobacterium bovis*, causative agent of bovine tuberculosis (TB)) were investigated using an experimental manipulation of host worm burdens, analyses of cross-sectional data and mathematical models. Second, the relatively recent introduction of TB into the system set the stage for an examination of interactions between an invasive microparasite and a long established one (Rift Valley Fever virus). Last, patterns of helminth reassembly after experimental manipulation were leveraged to explore interactions occurring between macroparasites. Importantly, these studies place an emphasis on parameterising models with data in order to translate within-host processes to population-level outcomes.

Box 5.1: An experimental approach to studying parasite interactions in the wild

The African buffalo study in Kruger National Park, South Africa was designed with the core goal of understanding the outcome of interactions between gastrointestinal helminths and bovine tuberculosis. The study design involved following a cohort of ~216 free-ranging female buffalo over four years. At initial capture, animals were tested for TB infection and only TB-free individuals were recruited into the study. To evaluate the effects of worms on TB, worm burdens were artificially reduced using a long-acting anthelmintic drug (Panacur bolus, Intervet UK). Half of the study animals were randomly assigned to the treated group at initial capture, while the other half served as untreated controls (Figure B5.1.1). Any individuals that were lost due to death or emigration during the course of the study were replaced, and replacement animals were assigned the treatment status of the original animal. Each individual was fitted with a radio-collar to facilitate resampling. Recaptures occurred at six-monthly intervals so that treated animals could be re-dosed with the anthelmintic drug and key information on infection status (worm intensity, TB status), immune function (e.g. cytokine profiles), physiology (e.g. condition, nutritional status, stress) and demography (e.g. survival, reproduction) could be gathered (Figure B5.1.1). Faecal and blood samples were used to quantify parasites and to perform host immune and physiological assays. Along with core data on GI worms and TB, the study design enabled the collection of information on a suite of other pathogens. For example, animals were tested for other key diseases such as brucellosis and Rift Valley fever; the community

Box 5.1: (cont.)

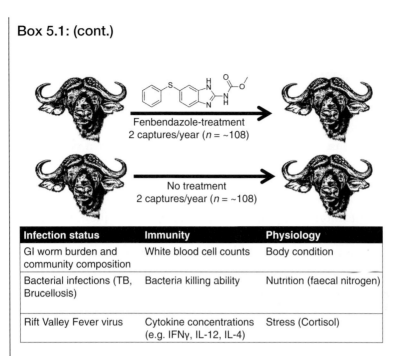

Infection status	Immunity	Physiology
GI worm burden and community composition	White blood cell counts	Body condition
Bacterial infections (TB, Brucellosis)	Bacteria killing ability	Nutrition (faecal nitrogen)
Rift Valley Fever virus	Cytokine concentrations (e.g. IFNγ, IL-12, IL-4)	Stress (Cortisol)

Figure B5.1.1 Schematic of the design of the African buffalo parasite interaction study including examples of key parasite, immunological and physiological variables collected at six-monthly intervals.

composition of GI parasites was evaluated; and ticks and tick-borne pathogens were routinely quantified. By coupling these parasite data with immunological, physiological and demographic information, this single powerful study design has and continues to yield interesting insights into the causes and consequences of parasite interactions in the wild.

5.3.1 Macroparasite–microparasite interactions: gastrointestinal worms and bovine tuberculosis

Interactions between macroparasites (particularly the helminths or 'worms') and microparasites have received increasing attention from both biomedical researchers and disease ecologists in recent years. This is, in part, due to the commonness of worm infections in human and animal hosts combined with the strong effects these parasites are known to have on the mammalian immune system. For example, helminths can affect the outcome of microparasitic infections in individual hosts via two key immune mechanisms. First, helminths typically trigger a T-helper cell 2 (Th2)-type immune response in the host, which is characterised by the production of cytokines such as interleukin-4 (IL-4), IL-5 and IL-13. These cytokines orchestrate a range of anti-parasite responses that promote worm clearance (Else & Finkelman, 1998), but simultaneously downregulate Th1-type cytokines (e.g. interferon gamma (IFNγ), IL-12) which are involved in defence against microparasites (Mosmann & Sad, 1996). Second, some helminths induce the proliferation of regulatory T cells (Tregs), which suppress both Th1 and Th2 cytokine responses (McSorley & Maizels, 2012; Taylor et al., 2012). Because these two effects can compromise the immune response of hosts to microparasites, there is great potential for worms to influence both the course of microparasite infections within individuals and their transmission between individuals. A number of studies have found evidence that helminths can influence the trajectory of individual microparasite infections across a range of host–helminth–microparasite systems in the laboratory (Su et al., 2005; Chenine et al., 2008; Osborne et al., 2014), but less is known about whether similar effects arise in a natural context and if these effects have population-level implications for hosts or parasites.

African buffalo are the major reservoir for bovine tuberculosis in Southern Africa (Fitzgerald & Kaneene, 2013), and they also host a healthy community of gastrointestinal nematode parasites. The first evidence that these two parasites interact in buffalo came from work based in HIP. A cross-sectional study by Jolles et al. (2008) documented a consistent negative correlation between strongyle nematodes and TB at the population, group, and individual levels (Box 5.2). In an initial attempt to understand the mechanistic basis of this pattern, the study documented correlational evidence of a trade-off between Th1 and Th2 immune defences in buffalo and used a modified susceptible–infected (SI) model to evaluate the relative importance of immune-mediated interactions in explaining observed empirical associations between worms and TB (Box 5.2). The hypothesis that worm-induced immune responses downregulate Th1 immunity was then supported experimentally in a follow-up study which showed that short-term artificial reduction of worm burdens in buffalo using anthelmintic drugs increased levels of the Th1 cytokine, IFNγ, in the blood (Ezenwa et al., 2010). Because IFNγ has been linked to the control of *M. bovis* and *M. tuberculosis* infection in livestock and people, respectively (Flynn & Chan, 2001; Welsh et al., 2005), this result provided initial support for an immune-mediated interaction between worms and TB. Crucially, this experiment showed that worm infections can suppress Th1 immune defences in wild mammals in the same manner as had been described in humans, livestock, and laboratory rodents. Together, this combination of observational studies, experimental studies, and models helped shape the hypothesis that worms, via their immune effects on buffalo, are capable of influencing the population dynamics and distribution of TB.

Box 5.2: Do gastrointestinal helminths drive patterns of TB infection in African buffalo? Field observations and disease dynamic models

At Hluhluwe-iMfolozi Park, South Africa, TB was first detected in buffalo in 1986, presumably due to spillover from cattle (Jolles et al., 2017). In the late 1990s, an active surveillance and control programme for TB was initiated, with the aim of limiting disease prevalence in buffalo and curbing spread to vulnerable species including lions and rhinoceros. The disease control programme operates by capturing buffalo each year, targeting different areas within the park on a rotational basis. Buffalo are tested for TB, positives are culled and TB-negatives released back into the park. The test-and-cull programme provided a unique opportunity for studying disease patterns across most of HIP's buffalo population (3000–5000 animals). Field data from HIP showed striking negative correlations between TB and gastrointestinal worms when comparing age–prevalence patterns (Figure B5.2.1A), prevalence across buffalo herds (Figure B5.2.1B), and individual infection patterns (Figure B5.2.1B, inset).

These patterns raise the question of whether worm infections play a role in determining individual- and population-level patterns of TB infection in buffalo. Interactions between GI worms and *Mycobacterium bovis* could occur via at least two mechanisms. First, coinfected animals may have poor survival, which could result in decreased TB transmission in herds harbouring heavy worm burdens. Consistent with this idea, coinfected animals at HIP were in poorer body condition than uninfected or singly infected buffalo; and no TB-positive buffalo supported extremely high worm burdens. Second, animals that are actively resisting infection by worms may be less able to mount effective immune responses against TB infection at the same time, leading to enhanced susceptibility to TB in worm-free animals. In support, buffalo with strong Th2-type immune responses (quantified in this study in terms of the concentration of eosinophils) had comparatively weak Th1 responses (measured as concentrations of IFNγ).

To discover whether these putative interaction mechanisms could plausibly account for the observed individual- and population-level infection patterns, a disease dynamic model including both infections was constructed. The modified SI model (Figure B5.2.1C) partitioned buffalo into susceptible (S), TB-infected (I_{TB}), worm-infected (I_W), and coinfected animals (I_{CO}). Separate mortality parameters were defined for susceptible animals (b), and each infected group ($b + \alpha_W$, $b + \alpha_{TB}$, $b + \alpha_{CO}$), so that the effect of elevated mortality in coinfected buffalo on disease patterns could be tested. In addition, distinct TB-transmission rates for animals with and without worms ($\beta_{TB}^S, \beta_{TB}^W$) reflected the hypothesis that worms may alter the

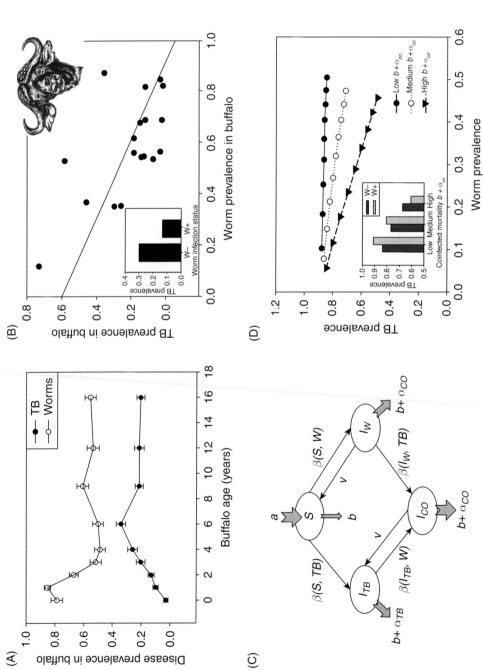

Figure B5.2.1 Field data show striking negative correlations between TB infection and gastrointestinal helminths when comparing age–prevalence patterns (A), prevalence across 18 herds of buffalo (B), and individual infection patterns (B, inset). A modified SI model (C), which partitioned buffalo into susceptible (S), TB-infected (I_{TB}), worm-infected (I_W), and coinfected animals (I_{CO}), reproduced observed patterns (D), when: (i) coinfected mortality ($b + \alpha_{CO}$) was assumed to exceed the mortality rates of TB-infected ($b + \alpha_{TB}$), susceptible (b) and worm-infected ($b + \alpha_W$) animals, and (ii) animals that resisted worm infection were assumed to be more susceptible to TB than wormy buffalo (i.e. $\beta_{TB}^S > ; \beta_{TB}^W$), because worm-resistant animals mount a stronger Th2 immune response, resulting in low or undetectable worm burdens.

Box 5.2: (cont.)

susceptibility of buffalo to TB. The transmission rate for worms (β_W) was independent of TB status in this model, and recovery from worms was included (v), whereas TB infection was assumed to be lifelong. These assumptions result in the following model equations, where H reflects buffalo herd size, and the parameter ω defines the strength of density dependence in the population as described in Jolles et al., 2006 (where the corresponding parameter is named alpha):

$$\frac{dS}{dt} = a(S + I_W) + a_{TB}(I_{TB} + I_{CO}) + vI_W - \beta_{TB}^S S(I_{TB} + I_{CO}) - \beta_W S - bS(1 + \omega H)$$
(5.1)

$$\frac{dI_{TB}}{dt} = \beta_{TB}^S S(I_{TB} + I_{CO}) + vI_{CO} - \beta_W I_{TB} - (b + \alpha_{TB})I_{TB}(1 + \omega H)$$
(5.2)

$$\frac{dI_W}{dt} = \beta_W S - vI_W - \beta_{TB}^W I_W(I_{TB} + I_{CO}) - (b + \alpha_W)I_W(1 + \omega H)$$
(5.3)

$$\frac{dI_{CO}}{dt} = \beta_{TB}^W I_W(I_{TB} + I_{CO}) + \beta_W I_{TB} - vI_{CO} - (b + \alpha_{CO})I_{CO}(1 + \omega H)$$
(5.4)

High mortality among coinfected animals resulted in a negative association between TB and worm infection in modelled populations (Figure B5.2.1D); however, the observed individual-level pattern of a low likelihood of TB infection in wormy animals was only reproduced by models that also included heterogeneity in TB transmission according to worm infection status (i.e. $\beta_{TB}^S > \beta_{TB}^W$) (Figure B5.2.1D, inset). Both hypothesised mechanisms were thus necessary to reproduce the disease patterns that were observed in HIP buffalo herds.

It is important to note that heterogeneity in TB transmission rates might be constitutive, i.e. due to variation among hosts in immune genotype, or inducible reflecting ecological interactions among the parasites, mediated by the host's immune responses. These possibilities have contrasting implications for TB management. If genetic heterogeneity underlies infection patterns, then selection for resistance to TB could imply selection for susceptibility to worms. On the other hand, if ecological interactions among parasites cause the observed patterns of infection, then anthelmintic treatment might be an option for reducing TB transmission. Subsequent experimental work in Kruger National Park helped to evaluate the latter hypothesis (see Box 5.1; Figure B5.2.1).

In general, for the immune effects of worms to have population-level consequences for a microparasite, one key condition must be met – the host's immune response to worm infection must alter the magnitude of key parameters that determine the microparasite's population dynamics. Furthermore, because multiple parameters combine to determine a microparasite's population growth rate (i.e. its basic reproduction number, R_0), predicting the effect of worms on microparasite dynamics requires that all of the relevant disease parameters be considered together (Box 5.3). For TB, which is a chronic disease from which infected animals are not known to recover, population dynamics depend solely on transmission and mortality rates. As such, one way to begin understanding the potential impact of worm coinfection on TB dynamics is to quantify the effects of worms on: (i) the rate at which susceptible hosts become infected with TB, and (ii) the rate at which infected individuals die of the disease. Ezenwa and Jolles (2015) did this in buffalo by using data from a longitudinal anthelmintic treatment experiment based in KNP (Box 5.1) to quantify differences in TB infection risk and TB-related mortality between naturally worm-infected individuals and those cleared of their worm infections. As was previously seen in the buffalo population in HIP, anthelmintic-treated animals had consistently stronger IFNγ responses than control animals, speaking to the generality of the phenomenon of worm-induced immune suppression in buffalo. Intriguingly, though, this increase in anti-TB immunity was not associated with reduced incidence of TB disease – treated animals were as likely to acquire TB over the course of the study as were control individuals (Figure 5.2A). However, treated animals were approximately seven times less likely to die of TB disease (Figure 5.2B), suggesting that worm-induced immune suppression translates into much stronger effects on TB-induced mortality than on TB susceptibility.

This experimental study allowed for an unprecedented estimation of the effect of worms on TB infection probability and mortality risk in a natural population, and the results were rather surprising. Indeed, previous models of worm–TB coinfection in buffalo had assumed that concurrent worm infection would affect both TB transmission and mortality, predicting that in the absence of worms TB would have an $R_0 < 1$, failing to invade a buffalo population (Ezenwa et al., 2010). However, R_0 estimates based on parameters derived from the experimental study were 15 in a worm-free buffalo population compared to only 2 in a worm-infected population (Figure 5.2C). Thus, TB may actually spread more rapidly in the absence of worms. This occurs because worm presence accelerates TB-induced mortality, reducing the duration of infectiousness in TB-positive individuals and slowing disease spread, whereas, when worms are removed from the system (e.g. via anthelmintic treatment), TB-infected individuals survive longer, contributing more to disease spread. An important caveat of this result is that the study did not quantify infectiousness,

Box 5.3: Predicting the effect of helminths on the population dynamics of microparasites

Disease dynamic models can be used as a tool to bridge the gap between individual- and population-level processes in infectious disease studies. In the context of helminth–microparasite interactions, these models enhance our ability to predict when immune-mediated interactions between parasites might translate into changes in parasite population dynamics. For example, a susceptible–infected–recovered (SIR) model framework can be used to conceptualise the consequences of helminth coinfection for microparasite population dynamics. An easy-to-interpret measure of microparasite dynamics that can be derived from an SIR model is R_0, which is defined as the number of secondary infections a single index case is expected to generate in a naïve host population. The parameters determining R_0 are the parasite transmission rate (β), the parasite disease-induced host mortality rate (α), and the recovery rate (v). The invasion of a microparasite into a host population is only possible when its transmission rate exceeds its duration of infectiousness, reflected by the rate of parasite loss through host death or recovery from infection:

$$R_0 = \frac{\beta}{\alpha + v + b} > 1 \quad (\text{b is the background host mortality rate}) \quad (5.5)$$

Parasite spread is generally more rapid with increasing R_0 (Anderson & May, 1991); thus, helminth coinfection could influence the rate of spread of a given microparasite by affecting the magnitude of any of the three disease-related parameters that determine R_0 (β, α, or v). Theoretically, helminths can do this through their effects on host immune function. For example, helminth coinfection may increase the microparasite transmission rate by enhancing the susceptibility of naïve hosts to infection or by increasing the infectiousness of infected hosts. Likewise, the disease-induced host mortality and recovery rates may be affected if helminths dampen the efficiency of microparasite clearance. It is also important to note that these effects can occur in concert.

Biomedical studies performed across a range of host–helminth–microparasite systems support the idea that helminths can modulate parameters relevant to microparasite dynamics (e.g. Su et al., 2005; Chenine et al., 2008; Graham, 2008; Osborne et al., 2014). Moreover, in cases where effects of helminths on these parameters have been detected, patterns of modulation tend to be fairly consistent within a given parameter (reviewed in Ezenwa & Jolles, 2011). Both the microparasite transmission rate and disease-induced host mortality rate tend to increase in response to helminth coinfection,

Box 5.3: (cont.)

whereas the recovery rate tends to decrease. Crucially, each change has distinct consequences for R_0. All else being equal, transmission effects will tend to *increase* R_0, host mortality effects will tend to *decrease* R_0, and recovery effects will tend to *increase* R_0. One observation that emerges from these trends in the literature is that the effects of helminths on the numerator of R_0 should typically *enhance* microparasite spread, whereas effects on the denominator (i.e. the infectious period) can either *enhance* or *dampen* spread depending on whether disease-induced host mortality or recovery is differentially affected (Ezenwa & Jolles, 2011). Therefore, when multiple effects occur simultaneously, which may be common, the relative magnitude of these effects on different parameters is crucial. What this means is that the population dynamic outcome of helminth–microparasite interactions might often depend on the net effect of helminth-induced immunological shifts on all relevant disease parameters. This observation underscores the need for studies that attempt to quantify how coinfection translates into changes in the relative magnitude of multiple disease parameters under natural conditions.

which is a key component of transmission. If treated animals were less infectious, perhaps as a result of increased Th1 immunity, then this would serve to reduce the TB transmission rate, dampening the effect of reduced disease-induced mortality on R_0. However, estimates of the potential impact of such an effect suggest that it would take an almost 90% reduction in TB infectiousness in worm-treated animals to overcome the positive effect of mortality reduction on R_0 (Figure 5.2D). Such a massive reduction in infectiousness seems unlikely.

This work highlights the importance of ground-truthing key assumptions about how processes occurring at the within-host level as a result of coinfection (e.g. immune responses) translate into real-world changes in relevant disease parameters. Indeed, the strong asymmetrical effect of worm removal on TB infection risk versus TB mortality observed in the buffalo study raises intriguing new questions. For instance, are there host or parasite traits that can help explain when the effect of worms on microparasite transmission should exceed effects on disease-induced mortality or vice versa? The fact that treated buffalo survived TB infection better than untreated individuals contributed directly to the estimated increase in the population growth rate of TB, so is this tension between hierarchical scales a general phenomenon in multi-parasite systems? When should we expect individual- and population-level outcomes to coincide versus conflict? From an applied perspective,

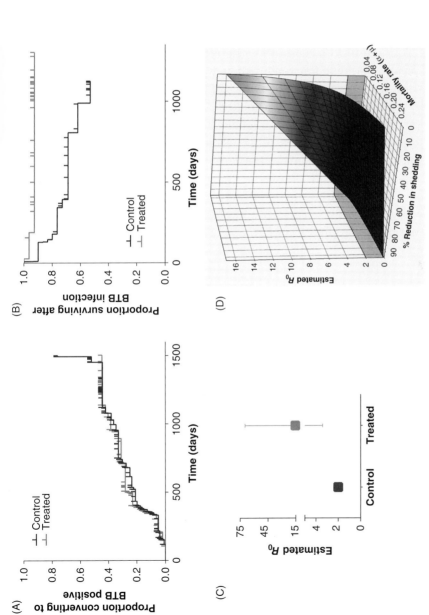

Figure 5.2 (A) Survival curves showing the proportion of treated and control buffalo converting to TB-positive as a function of time measured in days. Control and treated individuals had approximately equal probabilities of acquiring bovine TB (BTB). (B) Survival curves showing the proportion of TB-infected buffalo that survived as a function of time in days. The probability of death given infection was significantly higher for control compared with treated individuals. For both curves, vertical lines indicate individuals that were right censored from the data set because they were removed from the study (e.g. due to emigration from the study area). (C) The estimated reproductive number (R_0) of TB for control and treated subsets of the buffalo population. R_0 is approximately eight times higher for treated individuals (2 vs. 15.5), with upper and lower estimates of 3.4 and 69.8, respectively (confidence intervals were not calculated for controls). (D) Estimated R_0 of TB across the range of mortality rates observed for treated buffalo and control buffalo (approx. 0.03–0.24), accounting for possible reductions in bacteria shedding (i.e. TB infectiousness) due to treatment (range: 0% to 90%). The area shaded in gray shows the baseline R_0 for control buffalo ($R_0 = 2$). At a mortality rate of ~0.03, as observed for treated buffalo, a reduction in shedding of at least 90% is needed to decrease R_0 to baseline levels.

answering these types of questions will have profound implications for designing disease prevention and control strategies.

5.3.2 Microparasite–microparasite interactions: bovine tuberculosis and Rift Valley Fever virus

Helminths influence the dynamics of TB through their effects on host immunity, but they are not the only parasites that can have profound effects on the host immune system. *Mycobacterium bovis*, the causative agent of TB, is itself known to be a potent regulator of host immunity. Once infected with TB, buffalo do not recover (Cousins et al., 2004; Renwick et al., 2007), and *M. bovis* infection in ruminants can dynamically alter the host immune system in ways that facilitate pathogen survival and replication (Pollock et al., 2006; Waters et al., 2011). Thus, similar to helminths, the effects of TB on host immunity make it a prime candidate for studying how within-host immune responses to one pathogen might alter the dynamics of another. For example, animals initially mount a strong inflammatory immune response to *M. bovis* infection (Thacker et al., 2007; Pirson et al., 2012; Maggioli et al., 2015), that may be cross-protective against other intracellular microparasites, but later in infection *M. bovis* may suppress Th1 type immune responses, facilitating microparasite invasion (Pirson et al., 2012). Because *M. bovis* is an invasive pathogen in sub-Saharan Africa that was introduced into the ecosystem by European cattle, exploring how this pathogen might impact other pathogens in the system represents what will likely be an increasingly important topic in disease ecology, i.e. understanding how invasive pathogens modify the dynamics and health outcomes of previously established ('native') infections. Indeed, what we know about the interactions and consequences of invasive species in free-living communities (Lowry et al., 2013; Walsh et al., 2016; Mollot et al., 2017) highlights both the basic and applied relevance of this research theme. Interestingly, although some attention has been paid to how native infections may alter the success or spread of invasive pathogens (Telfer & Bown, 2012), the reverse effect has received less attention even though the lack of coevolutionary history between hosts and invasive pathogens might drive more extreme host responses, with greater repercussions for host-mediated interactions between native and invasive pathogens. In support, studies in the African buffalo system focused on interactions between TB and Rift Valley Fever virus (RVFV) reveal that invasive pathogens have real potential to modify both the dynamics and impact of native pathogens.

RVFV is an intracellular, mosquito-borne Phlebovirus that causes outbreaks in domestic livestock, wildlife, and humans mainly during wet periods (Pienaar & Thompson, 2013; Nanyingi et al., 2015). In KNP, buffalo serve as an important host for RVFV during interepidemic periods (Beechler et al.,

2015a; Manore & Beechler, 2015). Effective protection against RVFV infection requires that the host mount a strong innate immune response (Biron et al., 1999; Flick & Bouloy, 2005; Pepin et al., 2010), but two independent observations suggest that chronic TB infection can impair this protective response, making buffalo more susceptible to RVFV infection. First, during a 2008 outbreak of RVFV at a buffalo breeding facility near KNP, animals with TB were twice as likely to acquire RVFV as their TB-free counterparts (Beechler et al., 2015b). Second, TB-positive buffalo that were part of the longitudinal KNP study (described in Box 5.1) were twice as likely to test positive for RVFV antibodies six months after an RVFV outbreak occurred (Beechler et al., 2015b). In support of this latter observation, TB-infected individuals in the KNP study also had lower innate immune responses, as measured by the *Escherichia coli*–killing ability of whole blood (Beechler et al., 2015b), suggesting that a reduced innate immune response in TB-positive animals might explain the enhanced susceptibility to RVFV.

Changes in host immunity resulting from TB infection are not only relevant in terms of the likelihood of a buffalo becoming infected with RVFV, but also in terms of the health outcomes of infection. RVFV typically causes a transient illness in buffalo characterised by a strong inflammatory response and abortion in pregnant females (Swanepoel & Coetzer, 2004). An analysis of abortion patterns in the buffalo breeding facility adjacent to KNP showed that TB-positive animals were six times more likely to abort their pregnancies due to RVFV infection than TB-negative animals (Beechler et al., 2015b), indicating that the fitness impact of RVFV is more severe for TB-coinfected individuals. Abortion due to RVFV can result from direct infection of the foetus by RVFV, or from the pathological side effects of the proinflammatory immune response mounted after infection has occurred (Entrican, 2002; Regidor-Cerillo et al., 2014). However, the observation that TB-positive buffalo in the field study had elevated levels of IL-12, a proinflammatory cytokine important in the regulation of RVFV, supports the hypothesis that enhanced proinflammatory responses acted as a cause of abortion during RVFV–TB coinfection (Beechler et al., 2015b). Additional work is needed to fully understand the role that proinflammatory skew plays in driving the elevated abortion rate during coinfection. Nevertheless, these data strongly suggest that immune-mediated consequences of TB coinfection impact both host susceptibility to RVFV infection and the fitness costs of the disease. Overall, this suggests that the consequences of invasive pathogens for hosts are not only limited to direct effects on fitness, but may also include indirect effects driven by interactions with native pathogens. Importantly, the ability of TB to alter host susceptibility to RVFV could have further implications for RVFV dynamics.

To explore whether the observed increase in RVFV infection among TB-positive buffalo has relevance for RVFV epidemics, Beechler and colleagues (2015b) modified a mathematical model of RVFV transmission in buffalo to account for TB coinfection (Figure 5.3A; Manore & Beechler, 2015). Key insights of the model, derived by varying two core parameters – the overall prevalence of TB in herds and the added transmission of RVFV from mosquitoes to TB-positive buffalo – were that both RVFV outbreak size and RVFV prevalence in TB-negative individuals increased with TB prevalence within a herd (Figure 5.3B,C; Beechler et al., 2015b). The implication of this result is that TB may exacerbate the within-herd spread of RVFV in buffalo. Given the role of buffalo as a reservoir for RVFV during interepidemic periods and RVFV's status as a zoonotic pathogen, any positive effect of TB coinfection on RVFV dynamics in buffalo has serious implications in terms of potential spillover events to livestock and humans. More generally, the changes in the host immune response due to TB infection may also lead to altered dynamics for other zoonotic and economically important microparasites of buffalo (see Table 5.1). In this way, TB could potentially act as a cryptic within-host ecosystem engineer. An outstanding and fascinating question remains whether the interactions observed between TB and RVFV in buffalo reflect a more general pattern of particularly intense interactions between invasive and native pathogens or whether they are simply a function of the strong immuno-modulatory effects of TB.

5.3.3 Macroparasite–macroparasite interactions: gastrointestinal worms

Unlike gastrointestinal worms and TB or TB and RVFV, parasites that share the same microhabitat within the host have the opportunity to interact both directly with one another and via their effects on the host. For example, buffalo harbour at least seven different species of nematodes in their intestinal tract (Budischak et al., 2015), but if and to what degree these parasites interact with one another is unknown. In community ecology, species interactions can be examined by studying the process by which communities assemble. In general, community assembly can be deterministic – shaped by environmental (i.e. host) traits or species interactions, or stochastic – shaped by chance dispersal events or priority effects. When compared to free-living species, the processes shaping the assembly of parasite communities are poorly understood; however, existing data suggest that these communities range from highly variable stochastic assemblages to strongly deterministic ones (Poulin, 1996; Krasnov et al., 2014). To date, most studies of parasite community assembly have used cross-sectional data sets to infer assembly processes (Poulin, 1996; Krasnov et al., 2014, but see Kuris, 1990 for a notable exception). This is in contrast to studies of free-living species

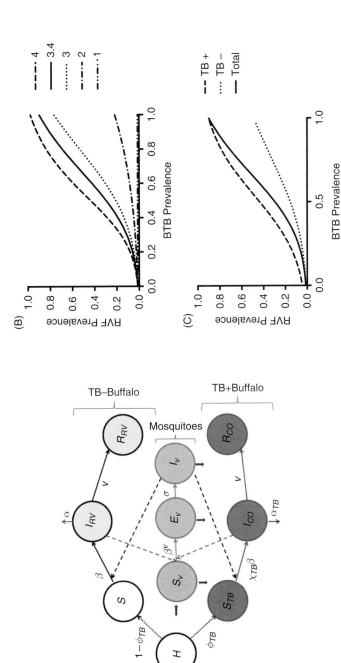

Figure 5.3 (A) Disease dynamic model used to evaluate how TB affects RVFV epidemic size. The model linked mosquitoes and buffalo to accurately represent infection patterns; infected mosquitoes could infect susceptible buffalo and infected buffalo could infect susceptible mosquitoes. Two subpopulations of buffalo were tracked: those with TB, and those without. The force of infection for TB positive buffalo was set between 1 and 4 times higher than that for buffalo without TB to represent an increased risk of transmission in TB-positive individuals, and the prevalence of TB was varied between 0 and 100%, with prevalence in the study area ranging between 30% and 50%. (B) The model shows that as TB prevalence increases, so does the total RVFV outbreak size, but the extent of the increase depends on the factor by which transmission is increased (each line is a different transmission factor increase) due to TB. (C) When the transmission factor for TB-positive buffalo is fixed at 3.4 times the rate in TB-negative buffalo (based on the best fit from empirical data), increasing TB prevalence results in increased RVFV prevalence for both TB-negative and -positive buffalo.

where experimental perturbations are frequently used as the gold standard for deriving insights about community assembly (Segre et al., 2014; Dini-Andreote et al., 2015; Fayle et al., 2015). The longitudinal anthelmintic treatment experiment in KNP buffalo (described in Box 5.1) therefore provided a unique opportunity to study the assembly of gastrointestinal worms after perturbation in a long-lived host. Among other things, this work evaluated the extent to which interactions between these parasites might be occurring, and explored the role of deterministic versus stochastic processes in shaping the worm community of buffalo.

The gastrointestinal worm community of buffalo is dominated by strongyle nematodes. In the basic life cycle of these parasites, adults reproduce sexually in the intestinal tract of their hosts, and parasite eggs pass out into the external environment in host faeces. The eggs develop in the faeces and hatch into infective larvae which disperse onto surrounding vegetation, where they get ingested by new hosts. The three most common strongyle species infecting buffalo in KNP are *Cooperia fuelleborni*, *Haemonchus contortus* and *H. placei*. *C. fuelleborni* (*Cf*) resides primarily in the small intestine and seems to pose minimal fitness cost on individuals, whereas the two *Haemonchus* (*H*) species reside in the abomasum and their bloodsucking habits are associated with anaemia and reduced condition in buffalo (Budischak et al., 2012, 2018).

To explore whether these two dominant parasites interact with one another Budischak and colleagues (2016) examined patterns of parasite reassembly in anthelmintic-treated buffalo. Adult nematodes were collected from the intestinal tract of sacrificed animals and identified to species morphologically (Budischak et al., 2015). Two main approaches were then used to draw inferences about community assembly. First, the temporal dynamics of community assembly were evaluated by analysing the relationship between reassembly period (i.e. time since most recent anthelmintic treatment and parasite sampling) and parasite community structure and by comparing the structure of reassembling communities and unperturbed communities. Second, different assembly processes that might generate the observed reassembly patterns were tested for by examining the effects of environmental parasite availability (stochastic: dispersal), host traits (deterministic: habitat filtering), and coinfection (deterministic: species interactions) on longitudinal and cross-sectional patterns of infection.

The first set of analyses revealed that reassembly period, which spanned 3–11 months, was strongly associated with both total worm abundance and Simpson's diversity. The overall number of worms increased over time and the worm community decreased in diversity (Figure 5.4A,B). Reassembled communities became less diverse over time because *Cf* grew to dominate the community, reaching 10-fold higher abundance than any other species late in the reassembly process (Figure 5.4C,D), and on average, reassembled communities were less diverse and even than were unperturbed communities. The second set of analyses painted a complex picture where different processes accounted for patterns of community assembly at different times. During the early stages of community reassembly, environmental parasite availability failed to explain differences in the proportional abundance of *Cf* versus *H* within communities (Figure 5.4E,F), suggesting that stochastic dispersal could not account for early community structure. Later in the reassembly process, the parasite community within hosts began to better resemble patterns of environmental parasite availability indicating that stochastic dispersal does play a role in shaping community structure at later stages of reassembly (Figure 5.4E,F). Finally, in untreated, control animals, host traits such as age and herd membership were significantly associated with community structure, suggesting that deterministic processes related to habitat filtering play a role over longer timescales (Budischak et al., 2016). Therefore, in sum, early stages of reassembly appeared to be non-stochastic, while later stages could be explained by stochastic dispersal, but eventually host traits seemed to play a deterministic, filtering role on worm community composition.

Evidence for a role of deterministic species interactions in shaping parasite community structure in buffalo was more equivocal. The observation that buffalo disproportionately accumulated *H* (a rarer species) early in reassembly, followed by an increase in *Cf* over time and relative stagnation in *H* seems to be a classic hallmark of interspecific competition (Budischak et al., 2016). Competition–colonisation theory predicts that dominant competitors eventually outcompete subordinate species erasing early differences in composition that arise due to asymmetries in colonisation ability (Tilman, 1994). In this scenario, *H* could be a superior coloniser but inferior competitor compared to *Cf*. However, nothing that is currently known about the life cycle or development time of *H* and *Cf* suggests key differences in colonisation ability between the two genera, although it is important to note that this information is based on studies of domestic ungulates and the specific biology of these parasites in buffalo is not well-described. Therefore, to better understand whether competition–colonisation dynamics are occurring for these two parasites in buffalo (and in similar contexts for other host species) infection experiments that allow for both colonisation and competition to be studied simultaneously will be required. Moreover, the key interaction occurring between *Cf* and *H*, if they do interact, may not be competition. In fact, an analysis of longitudinal patterns of infection showed that coinfection with *Cf* and *H* occurred more frequently than expected by chance (Budischak et al., 2016). If the two parasites were competing, the expectation would be that they would co-occur less often than expected, not more often. In contrast, the observation of positive co-occurrence suggests that the two worms potentially facilitate one another's

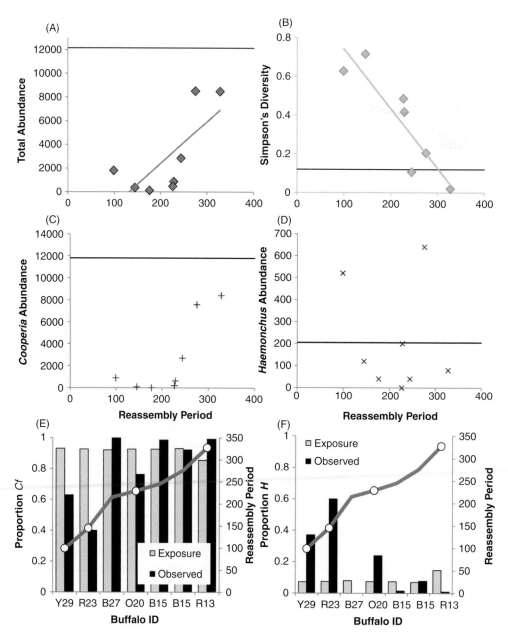

Figure 5.4 The relationship between the reassembly period and (A) total abundance of adult nematodes, (B) Simpson's diversity index and species-specific abundances of (C) *Cooperia fuelleborni* and (D) *Haemonchus* spp. in treated host individuals. Horizontal black lines (panels A–D) indicate mean values for control individuals. Panels E and F compare adult worm community composition with estimates of the environmental availability of nematode larvae during each individual's recolonisation period. The grey line indicates the reassembly period and white dots indicate significant differences between observed and expected relative abundance estimates for a buffalo.

presence, for example via a mechanism such as host immune suppression (Maizels et al., 2012). However, if hosts have a tendency to be coexposed to both parasites, then coexposure could be an alternative explanation for the positive co-occurrence pattern, further emphasising the need for an experimental approach.

Overall, patterns of worm community reassembly observed in buffalo highlight that understanding the speed and resilience of parasite community reassembly can be vital for managing and predicting host and parasite dynamics. For example, when the drivers of parasite assembly are dynamic as in buffalo, the best strategy for managing parasite communities may need to fluctuate over time. To better understand parasite community assembly in wildlife, the ideal approach would entail infecting individuals with different initial parasite types and then manipulating exposure to subsequent infections. Unfortunately, this study design requires removing hosts from their natural environments and exposure processes and in many situations quickly becomes intractable when dose effects or multiple parasite species must be considered. However, an expanded version of the longitudinal field experiment used in buffalo could be extremely informative. For example, experimentally removing parasites from different cohorts of individuals at different times of year (to correct for temporal variation in exposure versus time since clearance), then following community reassembly and host physiology over time could provide strong insight into species interactions and the dynamic processes shaping parasite community assembly. Importantly, this approach is sensitive to temporal variation in species interactions, a factor which community ecology studies (Tilman, 1994) and the buffalo–worm case study (Budischak et al., 2016), both suggest is critical.

5.4 Embracing complexity: multi-parasite interactions

Because most hosts are infected with more than one parasite species most of the time, host–parasite interactions inevitably occur within the context of taxonomically and functionally diverse, temporally and spatially variable communities. Given this, the interactions occurring within these communities are likely best described in terms of networks, rather than as a series of pairwise interactions. However, understanding disease dynamics in terms of the dynamics of parasite infracommunities, while a compelling idea, is enormously challenging. In addition to the obvious logistical and diagnostic challenges associated with identifying and quantifying multiple parasite infections in natural host populations, it is not clear, a priori, which parasites are essential to the system's behaviour and must be included in empirical and theoretical studies. Moreover, parasites may interact via several mechanisms simultaneously; thus, it is difficult to predict which mechanisms dominate the system's behaviour and should form the basis of predictive disease dynamic frameworks. Given these complexities, it is not surprising that even studies that assess multiple infections tend to focus their analyses on pairwise interactions (e.g. Telfer et al., 2010).

The multi-parasite interaction question is only beginning to be addressed in the African buffalo system. Henrichs et al. (2016) used the system to investigate the extent to which infection by three tick-borne bacteria (*Anaplasma centrale, A. marginale*, and *A.* sp. 'Omatjenne') was mediated by other tick-borne infections (*Theileria* spp.), gastrointestinal macro- and microparasites (worms and coccidia), and chronic bacterial infections (bovine tuberculosis and brucellosis). This work took advantage of the longitudinal study based in KNP (described in Box 5.1) to screen the same animals for the focal range of pathogens repeatedly over time. Due to the observational approach to data collection, inferences about parasite interactions were drawn in part by comparing the magnitude of coinfection effects with that of host (age, reproductive status, body condition) and environmental effects (season, herd) on infection patterns. Results indicate that season and age were important drivers of infection patterns for all parasites studied, but coinfection by other parasites using the same location within the host (i.e. blood) was by far the strongest predictor of infection patterns (Figure 5.5A,B). In contrast, these parasites were rarely affected by pathogens that localise in other host tissues (Figure 5.5A). This result is consistent with findings from an analysis of human pathogens, which suggested that interactions were strongest between parasites occupying the same physical location within the host (Griffiths et al., 2014), and with a study of wild rodent parasites which found that the gastrointestinal worms interacted most strongly with coccidia that shared a common infection location in the intestinal tract (Knowles et al., 2013). Taken together, these similarities among studies are encouraging, because they suggest that, despite the complexity of multi-parasite–host associations, general patterns that hold true across different parasite communities and host populations may be discoverable.

Despite this encouraging news, observational studies of parasite interactions have some significant limitations, which point to several directions for future empirical and analytical work. First, the microparasite diagnostic techniques used in the buffalo study were qualitative: only the presence or absence of infection was measured and information on the parasite burden that the animals experienced was lacking. This issue is problematic for persistent infections where parasite burdens can be highly variable among individuals and over time, determining the outcome of the infection for the host. Tick-borne *Theileria* species infections serve as a case in point: five different *Theileria* species were present at very high prevalence in buffalo, reaching nearly 100% during some sampling periods (Henrichs et al., 2016). This lack of variability in parasite occurrence

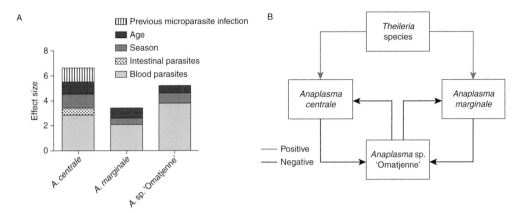

Figure 5.5 (A) Results of logistic regression analyses comparing the relative importance of parasite, seasonal, and demographic predictors of infection. Predictor variables were standardised to allow comparison among covariates. The height of each bar represents the standardised regression coefficients. (B) Within-guild haemoparasite interactions between *Anaplasma centrale, Anaplasma marginale, Anaplasma* sp. 'Omatjenne', and *Theileria parva*. Grey arrows indicate positive interactions; black arrows indicate negative interactions.

complicates analyses based on presence. However, it is likely that the intensity of these *Theileria* infections varied among hosts and over time, so future work focused on these types of parasites requires the use of quantitative assays. With the rise of next-generation sequencing methods, such an approach is now more feasible and cost-effective for a range of microparasites (Fischer et al., 2015; Levitt et al., 2017).

A second limitation of the buffalo multi-parasite interaction study is that the analytical approaches used did not capture the full complexity of the system. Independent generalised linear mixed models were used to evaluate the effects of multiple parasites on each focal infection. Given the longitudinal study design, this approach allowed for the reconstruction of which infections tended to follow one another or co-occur (Fenton et al., 2014), expressing the relative likelihood of sequential and simultaneous coinfections. However, the power of inference from these linear models can be limited if the actual structure of the system is non-linear, resembling a web of direct and indirect interactions. In such case, statistical approaches such as structural equation modelling, network analysis, and ordination techniques, all of which have been used to analyse the structure of ecological communities, could help pave the way forward. Indeed, approaches such as network analysis are increasingly being applied to questions related to multi-host and multi-parasite interactions (Griffiths et al., 2014; Pilosof et al., 2015). Likewise, ordination methods and random forest models are widely used in microbiome research and have recently been used to study interactions between microbial symbionts and parasites (Kreisinger et al., 2015; Morton et al., 2015; Newbold et al., 2017). Applying these tools to longitudinal data sets is more challenging, but could transform our understanding of parasite community dynamics.

Finally, experiments are ultimately needed to robustly test for parasite interactions (Fenton et al., 2014). It is well-documented that all parasites within the same taxonomic group do not necessarily trigger identical host responses (e.g. Walson et al., 2008; Hoverman et al., 2013; Budischak et al., 2018); as such, species identity can matter profoundly for the outcome of parasite interactions. However, anti-parasitic drugs, which are increasingly used in wildlife disease studies (reviewed in Pedersen & Fenton, 2015), are often only available for broad groups of parasites, such as nematodes, ectoparasites, or bacteria, rather than for individual species. By contrast, vaccines are often very specific, and thus could provide promising tools for targeted manipulation of parasite communities (Pedersen & Fenton, 2015). Importantly, the ability to manipulate individual parasite species with vaccines would help eliminate non-target effects, allowing for more fine-tuned detection of species interactions. Vaccinations would also help overcome several challenges associated with studying microparasites, few of which are amenable to manipulation with drugs. For instance, vaccine-based experimental studies could help with distinguishing coexposure or cotransmission from true interactions. Such studies could also allow the effects of microparasites on macroparasites to be quantified more rigorously than is currently possible in most natural populations. While the availability of effective vaccines is often limited for wildlife species, vaccines developed for closely related domestic animals might be transferable in many cases where the focal wildlife species has a close domestic relative. Combining field studies with laboratory-based work, where infection status can be manipulated through experimental infections, is another promising approach for studying multi-parasite interactions, at least for host species that are amenable to captive or semi-captive conditions. More generally, because parasite burdens, and the interactions between parasites, are dynamic over time, longer-term experimental studies will also be key for unravelling how and when parasites interact and the consequences of these interactions.

5.5 Conclusions

A wealth of information on the biology of African buffalo and their many parasites set the stage for this species to become a unique model for studying interactions between different taxonomic groups of parasites. Studies in this system have yielded important insights into both the causes and consequences of parasite interactions by using a multi-pronged study design spanning from cross-sectional studies to longitudinal experiments and an integrated toolkit involving   ecological,   parasitological,   immunological,   and   modelling approaches. This body of work shows that when parasites interact, changes in multiple population-relevant parameters can be triggered simultaneously. Moreover, because the consequences for disease dynamics depend on combinatorial effects, an important frontier in coinfection research is to understand when key parameters might respond in the same way versus in very different ways. Intriguingly, the type and strength of the interactions occurring between parasites can also change over time as communities assemble and reassemble. This is particularly relevant as old parasites invade new communities and new parasites emerge into existing communities, because interactions between invasive and native parasites may be particularly intense. Finally, given that most hosts, including buffalo, are infected with multiple parasite species simultaneously, another key research frontier involves blending experimental, longitudinal, and quantitative approaches in a way that facilitates the study of parasite interactions from a whole-community perspective.

5.6 Acknowledgements

The work described in this chapter was made possible by support from KwaZulu-Natal (KZN) Wildlife, KZN State Veterinary Service, South African National Parks (SANParks), and SANParks Veterinary Wildlife Services. In particular, we thank D. Cooper, P. Buss, and M. Hofmeyr. We also thank an amazing group of students and technicians for assistance in the field and laboratory. This work was supported by grants from the US National Science Foundation (DEB-0541762/DEB-0541981 and EF-0723918/EF-0723928/DEB-1102493).

References

Abu Samra, N., Jori, F., Xiao, L.H., Rikhotso, O. & Thompson, P.N. (2013) Molecular characterization of *Cryptosporidium* species at the wildlife/livestock interface of the Kruger National Park, South Africa. *Comparative Immunology, Microbiology and Infectious Diseases*, **36**, 295–302.

Allen, J.E. & Maizels, R.M. (2011) Diversity and dialogue in immunity to helminths. *Nature Reviews Immunology*, **11**, 375–388.

Anderson, E.C. & Rowe, L.W. (1998) The prevalence of antibody to the viruses of bovine virus diarrhoea, bovine herpes virus 1, rift valley fever, ephemeral fever and bluetongue and to *Leptospira* sp. in free-ranging wildlife in Zimbabwe. *Epidemiology and Infection*, **121**, 441–449.

Anderson, R.M. & May, R.M. (1991) *Infectious Diseases of Humans:Dynamics and Control*. Oxford: Oxford University Press.

Atherstone, C., Picozzi, K. & Kalema-Zikusoka, G. (2014) Short Report: Seroprevalence of *Leptospira* Hardjo in cattle and African buffalos in Southwestern Uganda. *American Journal of Tropical Medicine and Hygiene*, **90**, 288–290.

Ayebazibwe, C., Mwiine, F.N., Balinda, S.N., Tjornehoj, K. & Alexandersen, S. (2012) Application of the Ceditest (R) FMDV type O and FMDV-NS enzyme-linked immunosorbent assays for detection of antibodies against foot-and-mouth disease virus in selected livestock and wildlife species in Uganda. *Journal of Veterinary Diagnostic Investigation*, **24**, 270–276.

Beechler, B.R., Bengis, R., Swanepoel, R., et al. (2015a) Rift Valley Fever in Kruger National Park: do buffalo play a role in the inter-epidemic circulation of virus? *Transboundary and Emerging Diseases*, **62**, 24–32.

Beechler, B.R., Manore, C.A., Reininghaus, B., et al. (2015b) Enemies and turncoats: bovine tuberculosis exposes pathogenic potential of Rift Valley fever virus in a common host, African buffalo (*Syncerus caffer*). *Proceedings of the Royal Society of London B*, **282**, 20142942.

Bender, E.A., Case, T.J. & Gilpin, M.E. (1984) Perturbation experiments in community ecology: theory and practice. *Ecology*, **65**, 1–13.

Beura, L.K., Hamilton, S.E., Bi, K., et al. (2016) Normalizing the environment recapitulates adult human immune traits in laboratory mice. *Nature*, **532**, 512–516.

Biron, C.A., Nguyen, K.B., Pien, G.C., Cousens, L.P. & Salazar-Mather, T.P. (1999) Natural killer cells in antiviral defense: function and regulation by innate cytokines. *Annual Review of Immunology*, **17**, 189–220.

Brown, J.H., Whitham, T.G., Morgan Ernest, S.K. & Gehring, C.A. (2001) Complex species interactions and the dynamics of ecological systems: long-term experiments. *Science*, **293**, 643.

Budischak, S.A., Hoberg, E.P., Abrams, A., Jolles, A.E. & Ezenwa, V.O. (2015) A combined parasitological molecular approach for noninvasive characterization of parasitic nematode communities in wild hosts. *Molecular Ecology Resources*, **15**, 1112–1119.

Budischak, S.A., Hoberg, E.P., Abrams, A., Jolles, A.E. & Ezenwa, V.O. (2016) Experimental insight into the process of parasite community assembly. *Journal of Animal Ecology*, **85**, 1222–1233.

Budischak, S.A., Jolles, A.E. & Ezenwa, V.O. (2012) Direct and indirect costs of co-infection in the wild: linking gastrointestinal parasite communities, host hematology, and immune function. *International Journal for Parasitology: Parasites and Wildlife*, **1**, 2–12.

Budischak, S.A., O'Neal, D., Jolles, A.E. & Ezenwa, V.O. (2018) Differential host responses to parasitism shape divergent fitness costs of infection. *Functional Ecology*, **32**, 324–333.

Callaway, R.M. & Walker, L.R. (1997) Competition and facilitation: a synthetic approach to interactions in plant communities. *Ecology*, **78**, 1958–1965.

Chaisi, M.E., Sibeko, K.P., Collins, N.E., Potgieter, F.T. & Oosthuizen, M.C. (2011) Identification of *Theileria parva* and *Theileria* sp. (buffalo) 18S rRNA gene sequence variants in the African Buffalo (*Syncerus caffer*) in southern Africa. *Veterinary Parasitology*, **182**, 150–162.

Chenine, A.L., Shai-Kobiler, E., Steele, L.N., et al. (2008) Acute *Schistosoma mansoni* infection increases susceptibility to systemic SHIV clade C infection in rhesus macaques after mucosal virus exposure. *PLoS Neglected Tropical Diseases*, **2**, e265.

Cousins, D.V., Huchzermeyer, H., Griffin, J., Van Rensburg, I.B.J.B.G. & Kriek, N. (2004) Tuberculosis. In: Coetzer, J. & Tustin, R.C. (eds.), *Infectious Diseases of Livestock.* (pp. 1973–1991). Oxford: Oxford University Press.

Cox, F.E.G. (2001) Concomitant infections, parasites and immune responses. *Parasitology*, **122**, S23–S38.

Dini-Andreote, F., Stegen, J.C., van Elsas, J.D. & Salles, J.F. (2015) Disentangling mechanisms that mediate the balance between stochastic and deterministic processes in microbial succession. *Proceedings of the National Academy of Sciences of the United States of America*, **112**, E1326–E1332.

Else, K.J. & Finkelman, F.D. (1998) Intestinal nematode parasites, cytokines and effector mechanisms. *International Journal for Parasitology*, **28**, 1145–1158.

Entrican, G. (2002) Immune regulation during pregnancy and host–pathogen interactions in infectious abortion. *Journal of Comparative Pathology*, **126**, 79–94.

Eygelaar, D., Jori, F., Mokopasetso, M., et al. (2015) Tick-borne haemoparasites in African buffalo (*Syncerus caffer*) from two wildlife areas in Northern Botswana. *Parasites & Vectors*, **8**, 26.

Ezenwa, V.O. (2004) Host social behavior and parasitic infection: a multifactorial approach. *Behavioral Ecology*, **15**, 446–454.

Ezenwa, V.O., Etienne, R.S., Luikart, G., Beja-Pereira, A. & Jolles, A.E. (2010) Hidden consequences of living in a wormy world: nematode-induced immune suppression facilitates tuberculosis invasion. *American Naturalist*, **176**, 613–624.

Ezenwa, V.O. & Jolles, A.E. (2015) Opposite effects of anthelmintic treatment on microbial infection at individual versus population scales. *Science*, **347**, 175–177.

Ezenwa, V.O., Price, S.A., Altizer, S., Vitone, N.D. & Cook, K.C. (2006) Host traits and parasite species richness in even and odd-toed hoofed mammals, Artiodactyla and Perissodactyla. *Oikos*, **115**, 526–536.

Fagbo, S., Coetzer, J.A.W. & Venter, E.H. (2014) Seroprevalence of Rift Valley fever and lumpy skin disease in African buffalo (*Syncerus caffer*) in the Kruger National Park and Hluhluwe-iMfolozi Park, South Africa. *Journal of the South African Veterinary Association*, **85**, e1–e7.

Fayle, T.M., Eggleton, P., Manica, A., Yusah, K. M. & Foster, W.A. (2015) Experimentally testing and assessing the predictive power of species assembly rules for tropical canopy ants. *Ecology Letters*, **18**, 254–262.

Fenton, A., Knowles, S.C.L., Petchey, O.L. & Pedersen, A.B. (2014) The reliability of observational approaches for detecting interspecific parasite interactions: comparison with experimental results. *International Journal for Parasitology*, **44**, 437–445.

Fischer, N., Indenbirken, D., Meyer, T., et al. (2015) Evaluation of unbiased next-generation sequencing of RNA (RNA-seq) as a diagnostic method in influenza virus-positive respiratory samples. *Journal of Clinical Microbiology*, **53**, 2238–2250.

Fitzgerald, S.D. & Kaneene, J.B. (2013) Wildlife reservoirs of bovine tuberculosis worldwide: hosts, pathology, surveillance, and control. *Veterinary Pathology*, **50**, 488–499.

Flick, R. & Bouloy, M. (2005) Rift Valley fever virus. *Current Molecular Medicine*, **5**, 827–834.

Flynn, J.L. & Chan, J. (2001) Immunology of tuberculosis. *Annual Review of Immunology*, **19**, 93–129.

Gomo, C., de Garine-Wichatitsky, M., Caron, A. & Pfukenyi, D.M. (2012) Survey of brucellosis at the wildlife–livestock interface on the Zimbabwean side of the Great Limpopo Transfrontier Conservation Area. *Tropical Animal Health and Production*, **44**, 77–85.

Gradwell, D.V., Schutte, A.P., Vanniekerk, C. A. & Roux, D.J. (1977) Isolation of Brucella abortus biotype 1 from African buffalo in Kruger National Park. *Journal of the South African Veterinary Association*, **48**, 41–43.

Graham, A.L. (2008) Ecological rules governing helminth–microparasite coinfection. *Proceedings of the National Academy of Sciences of the United States of America*, **105**, 566–570.

Griffiths, E.C., Pedersen, A.B., Fenton, A. & Petchey, O.L. (2014) Analysis of a summary network of co-infection in humans reveals that parasites interact most via shared resources. *Proceedings of the Royal Society of London B*, **281**, 20132286.

Hamblin, C., Anderson, E.C., Jago, M., Mlengeya, T. & Hipji, K. (1990) Antibodies to some pathogenic agents in free-living wild species in Tanzania. *Epidemiology and Infection*, **105**, 585–594.

Hamblin, C., Hedger, R.S. & Condy, J.B. (1980) The isolation of parainfluenza 3 virus from free-living African buffalo (*Syncerus caffer*). *Veterinary Record*, **107**, 18.

Henrichs, B., Oosthuizen, M.C., Troskie, M., et al. (2016) Within guild co-infections influence parasite community membership: a longitudinal study in African Buffalo. *Journal of Animal Ecology*, **85**, 1025–1034.

Hoberg, E.P., Abrams, A. & Ezenwa, V.O. (2008) An exploration of diversity among the Ostertagiinae (Nematoda: Trichostrongyloidea) in ungulates from sub-Saharan Africa with a proposal for a new genus. *Journal of Parasitology*, **94**, 230–251.

Hoberg, E.P., Abrams, A. & Pilitt, P.A. (2010) A new species of trichostrongyloid in African buffalo (*Syncerus caffer*). *The Journal of Parasitology*, **96**, 129–136.

Hoverman, J.T., Hoye, B.J. & Johnson, P.T.J. (2013) Does timing matter? How priority effects influence the outcome of parasite interactions within hosts. *Oecologia*, **173**, 1471–1480.

Jolles, A.E., Etienne, R.S. & Olff, H. (2006) Independent and competing disease risks: implications for host populations in variable environments. *American Naturalist*, **167**, 745–757.

Jolles, A.E., Ezenwa, V.O., Etienne, R.S., Turner, W.C. & Olff, H. (2008) Interactions between macroparasites and microparasites drive infection patterns in free-ranging African buffalo. *Ecology*, **89**, 2239–2250.

Jolles, A.E., Le Roex, N.I.C.K.I., Flacke, G., et al. (2017) Wildlife disease dynamics in carnivore and herbivore hosts in the Hluhluwe-iMfolozi Park. In: Cromsigt, J. P., Archibald, S. & Owen-Smith, N. (eds.), *Conserving Africa's Mega-Diversity in the Anthropocene: The Hluhluwe-iMfolozi Park Story*. Cambridge: Cambridge University Press.

Knowles, S.C., Fenton, A., Petchey, O.L., et al. (2013) Stability of within-host–parasite communities in a wild mammal system. *Proceedings of the Royal Society of London B*, **280**, 20130598.

Krasnov, B.R., Pilosof, S., Stanko, M., et al. (2014) Co-occurrence and phylogenetic distance in communities of mammalian ectoparasites: limiting similarity versus environmental filtering. *Oikos*, **123**, 63–70.

Kreisinger, J., Bastien, G., Hauffe, H.C., Marchesi, J. & Perkins, S.E. (2015) Interactions between multiple helminths and the gut microbiota in wild rodents. *Philosophical Transactions of the Royal Society of London B:Biological Sciences*, **370**, 20140295.

Kuris, A.M. (1990) Guild structure of larval trematodes in molluscan hosts: Prevalence, dominance, and significance of competition. In: Esch, G.W., Bush,A.O. & Aho,J.M. (eds.), *Parasite Communities: Patterns and Processes* (pp. 69–100). London: Chapman and Hall.

Lello, J., Boag, B., Fenton, A., Stevenson, I.R. & Hudson, P.J. (2004) Competition and mutualism among the gut helminths of a mammalian host. *Nature*, **428**, 840–844.

Levitt, B., Obala, A., Langdon, S., et al. (2017) Overlap extension barcoding for the next generation sequencing and genotyping of *Plasmodium falciparum* in individual patients in Western Kenya. *Scientific Reports*, **7**, 41108.

Lowry, E., Rollinson, E.J., Laybourn, A.J., et al. (2013) Biological invasions: a field synopsis, systematic review, and database of the literature. *Ecology & Evolution*, **3**, 182–196.

Maggioli, M.F., Palmer, M.V., Thacker, T.C., Vordermeier, H.M. & Waters, W.R. (2015) Characterization of effector and memory T cell subsets in the immune response to bovine tuberculosis in cattle. *PLoS ONE*, **10**, e0122571.

Maizels, R.M., Hewitson, J.P., Murray, J., et al. (2012) Immune modulation and modulators in *Heligmosomoides polygyrus* infection. *Experimental Parasitology*, **132**, 76–89.

Manore, C.A. & Beechler, B.R. (2015) Inter-epidemic and between-season persistence of rift valley fever: vertical transmission or cryptic cycling? *Transboundary Emerging Diseases*, **62**, 13–23.

McSorley, H.J. & Maizels, R.M. (2012) Helminth infections and host immune regulation. *Clinical Microbiology Reviews*, **25**, 585–608.

Michel, A.L. & Bengis, R.G. (2012) The African buffalo: a villain for inter-species spread of infectious diseases in southern Africa. *Onderstepoort Journal of Veterinary Research*, **79**(2).

Miguel, E., Grosbois, V., Caron, A., et al. (2013) Contacts and foot and mouth disease transmission from wild to domestic bovines in Africa. *Ecosphere*, **4**, art51.

Mollot, G., Pantel, J.H. & Romanuk, T.N. (2017) The effects of invasive species on the decline in species richness: a global meta-analysis. In: Bohan, D.A., Dumbrell, A.J. & Massol, F. (eds.), *Advances in Ecological Research* (pp. 61–83). New York, NY: Academic Press.

Morton, E.R., Lynch, J., Froment, A., et al. (2015) Variation in rural African gut microbiota is strongly correlated with colonization by *Entamoeba* and subsistence. *PLOS Genetics*, **11**, e1005658.

Mosmann, T.R. & Sad, S. (1996) The expanding universe of T-cell subsets: Th1, Th2 and more. *Immunology Today*, **17**, 138–146.

Nanyingi, M.O., Munyua, P., Kiama, S.G., et al. (2015) A systematic review of Rift Valley Fever epidemiology 1931–2014. *Infection Ecology & Epidemiology*, **5**, 28024.

Newbold, L.K., Burthe, S.J., Oliver, A.E., et al. (2017) Helminth burden and ecological factors associated with alterations in wild host gastrointestinal microbiota. *ISME Journal*, **11**, 663–675.

Osborne, L.C., Monticelli, L.A., Nice, T.J., et al. (2014) Virus–helminth coinfection reveals a microbiota-independent mechanism of immunomodulation. *Science*, **345**, 578.

Pawlowski, A., Jansson, M., Sköld, M., Rottenberg, M.E. & Källenius, G. (2012) Tuberculosis and HIV co-infection. *PLOS Pathogens*, **8**, e1002464.

Pedersen, A.B. & Fenton, A. (2007) Emphasizing the ecology in parasite community ecology. *Trends in Ecology & Evolution*, **22**, 133–139.

Pedersen, A.B. & Fenton, A. (2015) The role of antiparasite treatment experiments in assessing the impact of parasites on wildlife. *Trends in Parasitology*, **31**, 200–211.

Pepin, M., Bouloy, M., Bird, B.H., Kemp, A. & Paweska, J. (2010) Rift Valley fever virus (Bunyaviridae: Phlebovirus): an update on pathogenesis, molecular epidemiology, vectors, diagnostics and prevention. *Veterinary Research*, **41**, 61.

Petney, T.N. & Andrews, R.H. (1998) Multiparasite communities in animals and humans: frequency, structure and pathogenic significance. *International Journal for Parasitology*, **28**, 377–393.

Pienaar, N.J. & Thompson, P.N. (2013) Temporal and spatial history of Rift Valley fever in South Africa: 1950 to 2011. *Onderstepoort Journal of Veterinary Research*, **80**(1).

Pilosof, S., Morand, S., Krasnov, B.R. & Nunn, C.L. (2015) Potential parasite transmission in multi-host networks based on parasite sharing. *PLoS ONE*, **10**, e0117909.

Pirson, C., Jones, G.J., Steinbach, S., Besra, G.S. & Vordermeier, H.M. (2012) Differential effects of *Mycobacterium bovis*-derived polar and apolar lipid fractions on bovine innate immune cells. *Veterinary Research*, **43**, 54.

Pitchford, R.J. (1976) Preliminary observations on the distribution, definitive hosts and possible relation with other schistosomes, of *Schistosoma margrebowiei*, Le Roux, 1933 and *Schistosoma leiperi*, Le Roux, 1955. *Journal of Helminthology*, **50**, 111–123.

Pollock, J.M., Rodgers, J.D., Welsh, M.D. & McNair, J. (2006) Pathogenesis of bovine tuberculosis: experimental models of infection. *Veterinary Microbiology*, **112**, 141–150.

Pospischil, A., Kaiser, C., Hofmann-Lehmann, R., et al. (2012) Evidence for *Chlamydia* in wild mammals of the Serengeti. *Journal of Wildlife Diseases*, **48**, 1074–1078.

Poulin, R. (1996) Richness, nestedness, and randomness in parasite infracommunity structure. *Oecologia*, **105**, 545–551.

Prins, H.H.T. (1996) *Ecology and Behaviour of the African Buffalo: Social Inequality and Decision Making*. London: Chapman and Hall.

Reese, T.A., Bi, K., Kambal, A., et al. (2016) Sequential infection with common pathogens promotes human-like immune gene expression and altered vaccine response. *Cell Host & Microbe*, **19**, 713–719.

Regidor-Cerrillo, J., Arranz-Solís, D., Benavides, J., et al. (2014) *Neospora caninum* infection during early pregnancy in cattle: how the isolate influences infection dynamics, clinical outcome and peripheral and local immune responses. *Veterinary Research*, **45**, 10.

Renwick, A.R., White, P.C.L. & Bengis, R.G. (2007) Bovine tuberculosis in southern African wildlife: a multi-species host–pathogen system. *Epidemiology and Infection*, **135**, 529–540.

Rodwell, T.C., Kriek, N.P., Bengis, R.G., et al. (2001) Prevalence of bovine tuberculosis in African buffalo at Kruger National Park. *Journal of Wildlife Diseases*, **37**, 258–264.

Romano, A., Doria, N.A., Mendez, J., Sacks, D.L. & Peters, N.C. (2015) Cutaneous infection with *Leishmania major* mediates heterologous protection against visceral infection with *Leishmania infantum*. *The Journal of Immunology*, **195**, 3816.

Roug, A., Muse, E.A., Smith, W.A., et al. (2016) Demographics and parasites of African buffalo (*Syncerus caffer* Sparrman, 1779) in Ruaha National Park, Tanzania. *African Journal of Ecology*, **54**, 146–153.

Schmid-Hempel, P. (2017) Parasites and their social hosts. *Trends in Parasitology*, **33**, 453–462.

Segre, H., Ron, R., De Malach, N., et al. (2014) Competitive exclusion, beta diversity, and deterministic vs. stochastic drivers of community assembly. *Ecology Letters*, **17**, 1400–1408.

Sinclair, A.R.E. (1977) *The African Buffalo, A Study of Resource Limitation of Populations*. Chicago, IL: Chicago University Press.

Stock, T. & Holmes, J.C. (1987) *Dioecocestus asper* (Cestoda: Dioecocestidae): an interference competitor in an enteric helminth community. *The Journal of Parasitology*, **73**, 1116–1123.

Stock, T. & Holmes, J.C. (1988) Functional relationships and microhabitat distributions of enteric helminths of grebes (Podicipedidae): the evidence for interactive communities. *The Journal of Parasitology*, **74**, 214–227.

Su, Z., Segura, M., Morgan, K., Loredo-Osti, J.C. & Stevenson, M.M. (2005) Impairment of protective immunity to blood-stage malaria by concurrent nematode infection. *Infection and Immunity*, **73**, 3531–3539.

Swanepoel, R. & Coetzer, J. (2004) Rift valley fever. *Infectious Diseases of Livestock*, **2**, 1037–1070.

Taylor, M.D., van der Werf, N. & Maizels, R.M. (2012) T cells in helminth infection: the regulators and the regulated. *Trends in Immunology*, **33**, 181–189.

Taylor, W.A., Skinner, J.D. & Boomker, J. (2013) Nematodes of the small intestine of African buffaloes, *Syncerus caffer*, in the Kruger National Park, South Africa. *Onderstepoort Journal of Veterinary Research*, **80**, 1–4.

Telfer, S. & Bown, K. (2012) The effects of invasion on parasite dynamics and communities. *Functional Ecology*, **26**, 1288–1299.

Telfer, S., Lambin, X., Birtles, R., et al. (2010) Species interactions in a parasite community drive infection risk in a wildlife population. *Science (New York, N. Y.)*, **330**, 243–246.

Thacker, T.C., Palmer, M.V. & Waters, W.R. (2007) Associations between cytokine gene expression and pathology in *Mycobacterium bovis* infected cattle. *Veterinary Immunology and Immunopathology*, **119**, 204–213.

Tilman, D. (1994) Competition and biodiversity in spatially structured habitats. *Ecology*, **75**, 2–16.

Walsh, J.R., Carpenter, S.R. & Vander Zanden, M. J. (2016) Invasive species triggers a massive loss of ecosystem services through a trophic cascade. *Proceedings of the National Academy of Sciences of the United States of America*, **113**, 4081–4085.

Walson, J.L., Otieno, P.A., Mbuchi, M., et al. (2008) Albendazole treatment of HIV-1 and helminth co-infection: a randomized, double blind, placebo-controlled trial. *AIDS (London, England)*, **22**, 1601–1609.

Waters, W.R., Palmer, M.V., Thacker, T.C., et al. (2011) Tuberculosis immunity: opportunities from studies with cattle. *Clinical Developmental Immunology*, **2011**, 768542.

Welsh, M.D., Cunningham, R.T., Corbett, D.M., et al. (2005) Influence of pathological progression on the balance between cellular and humoral immune responses in bovine tuberculosis. *Immunology*, **114**, 101–111.

Xu, D.-H., Pridgeon, J.W., Klesius, P.H. & Shoemaker, C.A. (2012) Parasitism by protozoan *Ichthyophthirius multifiliis* enhanced invasion of *Aeromonas hydrophila* in tissues of channel catfish. *Veterinary Parasitology*, **184**, 101–107.

CHAPTER SIX

Effects of host lifespan on the evolution of age-specific resistance: a case study of anther-smut disease on wild carnations

EMILY BRUNS

6.1 Introduction

Periodic epidemics of 'childhood diseases' such as measles, chickenpox, and smallpox have long been an important component of human ecology (McNeill, 1976; Diamond, 1997). The term 'childhood disease' refers to pathogens whose transmission and persistence is dependent on a susceptible juvenile age class. Childhood diseases are also common in wildlife populations. For example, Altizer et al. (2004) showed that prevalence of a bacterial eye disease (*Mycoplasma galliseptiucum*) in house finches peaked in the autumn, and that infection rates were higher among juvenile birds. Periodic outbreaks of Phocine distemper virus in seals have also been associated with seasonal breeding aggregations and the concentration of immunologically naïve susceptible pups (Härkönen et al., 2007). Such juvenile-dependent epidemics are not confined to vertebrate hosts with adaptive immune systems. Several plant diseases also specialise on juvenile stages; for example, 'damping-off' diseases caused by soil-borne oomycetes such as *Pythium* target young seedlings (Hendrix & Campbell, 1973; Packer & Clay, 2000).

Childhood diseases are successful because they take advantage of higher levels of susceptibility in juveniles. In humans and other vertebrates, juveniles are born immunologically naïve and build immunity through encounters. While direct assessment of susceptibility is not always possible in mammals, correlative studies in primates and rabbits have found higher levels of parasitism in juveniles, consistent with increased susceptibility to disease at this stage (Müller-Graf et al., 1997; Oppelt et al., 2010). In invertebrates, where susceptibility has been directly assessed through infection studies, there is strong evidence that disease resistance increases with age (Sait et al., 1994; Rosengaus & Traniello, 2001; Kubi et al., 2006; Garbutt et al., 2014). Additionally, in plants, disease resistance has been shown to increase with age in nearly every major crop species (reviewed in Panter & Jones, 2002).

From an evolutionary perspective, the persistence of juvenile susceptibility across a wide variety of taxa is puzzling. Classic life-history theory predicts that traits that improve survival at early life stages should be under stronger selection than traits that affect survival at later life stages (Charlesworth, 1980), so why do we observe higher levels of disease resistance in adults than in juveniles? One freely invoked possibility is that juvenile resistance is physiologically or developmentally constrained, in that there has not been time or energy to build up defence mechanisms at the juvenile stage. For example, in humans, growth rate is fastest and most energetically expensive during infancy, and it has been argued that this intense growth comes at the cost of immune function (McDade, 2003). In plants, it has also been argued that limited resources at the seedling stage constrain the development of resistance, at least towards herbivores (Boege & Marquis, 2005). However, genetic variation in seedling resistance has been observed in a variety of natural plant populations (Burdon et al., 1983; Parker, 1988; Jarosz & Burdon, 1990; Chung et al., 2012), indicating that populations have the capacity to respond to selection. Additionally, in agriculture, crop breeding has successfully led to marked improvements in seedling resistance (Line & Chen, 1995).

Here I argue that evolutionary explanations for the observed patterns of juvenile susceptibility have not been fully explored, especially how resistance evolves when the costs and benefits of resistance are age-specific, and when there are trade-offs in resistance at juvenile and adult stages. Lifespan is likely to be a particularly important host trait affecting the evolution of resistance. In longer-lived hosts, adult stages are more likely to encounter infectious disease during their lifetimes, and perhaps there is therefore stronger selection for investment in resistance and immunity in adult stages (Miller et al., 2007; Boots et al., 2013, Bruns et al., 2015). However, it is unknown whether increased selection for resistance in longer-lived hosts is correlated with resistance in the juvenile phase.

My interest in age-specific resistance arose from demographic studies of a fungal disease in a natural plant population. Plant populations have the advantage that when patterns of disease incidence are found in the field, it is possible to carry out follow-up studies involving inoculation experiments, something more difficult in many animal populations. I begin by describing two interesting patterns about host age and disease resistance that have emerged from demographic studies of anther-smut disease on natural plant populations, namely (1) a negative relationship between host lifespan and disease transmission rates, and (2) the higher susceptibility of juvenile stages vs. adult stages in a long-lived carnation host. I then explore theoretically the question of how host lifespan affects the evolution of age-specific disease resistance, considering not just the costs and benefits of such resistance, but also the numerical feedbacks that are likely to be critical in natural wildlife systems.

6.2 Age-specific resistance in anther-smut disease

Anther-smut (Box 6.1) has become a model system for studying the disease dynamics in natural populations (Bernasconi et al., 2009), because the 'smutty' anthers provide an easy visual system of disease detection in the field, and experimental inoculation protocols are well established. Moreover, because the pathogen is not agriculturally important, its dynamics and evolution have never been affected by disease control measures. The system is highly amenable to demographic study: individual plants can be easily marked and followed to determine transmission rates. Comparative studies are also possible because multiple species within the carnation family are infected with phylogenetically distinct anther-smut pathogens (le Gac et al., 2007; Petit et al., 2017). Below I focus on two observed patterns of resistance and host life history that have arisen from demographic studies of anther-smut disease in natural plant populations.

6.2.1 Observation 1: Negative relationship between host lifespan and transmission rate

Marr and Delph (2005) were the first to note a negative correlation between host lifespan and anther-smut transmission in the field. Their comparison was motivated by an eight-year study of anther-smut disease on the exceptionally long-lived alpine tundra species, *Silene acaulis* (estimated lifespan 100–300 years; Morris & Doak 1998). They found that even in populations with relatively high disease prevalence (18–26%), fewer than 1% of marked healthy plants became infected per year, resulting in an average frequency-dependent transmission rate of $\beta = 0.109$. The pattern of decreasing transmission rate in longer-lived hosts continues to hold when subsequent

---

Box 6.1: Anther-smut disease in natural populations

Pathogen life cycle: Anther-smut disease is caused by fungi in the genus *Microbotryum* (Basidiomycota). The disease gets its name from the brown 'smutty' teliospores that are produced on the anthers of infected plants in place of pollen (Figure B6.1.1). Transmission is facilitated by insect pollinators that transport spores from diseased to healthy flowers, a transmission process with close analogies to vector and/or sexual transmission in animals (Antonovics, 2005). Spores germinate and penetrate the plant epidermis, establishing a systemic intercellular infection (Schäfer et al., 2010)

Box 6.1: (cont.)

such that every flower on an infected plant typically produces spore-bearing anthers. In many host species, there is a one-year delay between infection and the production of smutted flowers. For this reason, the disease can only be maintained on perennial species (Thrall et al., 1993; Antonovics et al., 2003; Hood et al., 2010).

Transmission: Although pollinators deposit spores on flowers, infection is not restricted to floral tissue and can occur through vegetative tissue of non-flowering plants. In the field, transmission to vegetative plants can occur through passive aerial spore dispersal from nearby infected plants (Alexander, 1990; Bruns et al., 2017), and field studies have shown that aerial transmission often plays a critical role in disease dynamics in natural populations. Alexander and Antonovics (1988) showed that disease persistence in a roadside metapopulation of *Silene latifolia* was not possible without accounting for vegetative transmission. Carlsson-Granér (2006) showed that transmission to vegetative plants was necessary to explain the disease prevalence in *S. rupestris* but not in *Lychnis alpina*. More recently, we showed that the prevalence and persistence of anther-smut in a large populaliton of alpine carnations, *Dianthus pavonius*, is strongly dependent on transmission to the vegetative stage (Bruns et al., 2017).

Virulence: The disease does not affect host mortality but infected flowers are sterilised because the fungus converts the anthers to spore production and the ovary fails to mature. In *Dianthus pavonius*, infection results in complete sterilisation of all flowers on a plant (Figure B6.1.1C) and recovery is rare (<5%; Bruns et al., 2017). Incomplete sterilisation and higher rates of recovery (up to 64% overwinter) have been noted in *Silene latifolia* (Biere & Antonovics, 1996; Buono et al., 2014).

Disease resistance: Genetic variation in resistance to anther-smut has been found in several host species including *Silene latifolia* (Alexander, 1989; Alexander et al., 1993; Alexander & Antonovics, 1995), *S. dioica* (Carlsson-Granér, 1997), *S. vulgaris* (Cafuir et al., 2007), and *S. maritima* (Chung et al., 2012). Genetic variation in pathogen infectivity appears more limited; Kaltz et al. (1999) found variation in pathogen infectivity among but not within populations of *S. latifolia*. Moreover, they found that pathogen strains tended to have lower infectivity on their local host population than on allopatric populations, suggesting that hosts are able to evolve resistance more rapidly than pathogens in this system. At present, the genetic and molecular mechanism underlying resistance are not known, but they do not appear to follow the classic gene-for-gene model (Flor, 1956) common to many plant–pathogen interactions in agriculture.

Figure B6.1.1 Anther-smut disease on *Dianthus pavonius*. (A) Healthy flower (note light-coloured pollen) and (B) diseased flower with dark, smutty spores. (C) A large infected individual where every flower is diseased. (D) Surveying population size and disease prevalence along a 100-m transect in the *Parco Naturale del Marguareis* in the Western Italian Alps. (A black and white version of this figure will appear in some formats. For the colour version, please refer to the plate section.)

studies of anther-smut on other host species are included (Figure 6.1; Bruns et al., 2015).

One explanation for the negative relationship between host lifespan and disease transmission rate is that longer-lived hosts have evolved higher levels of disease resistance than shorter-lived hosts. Indeed, in the *S. acaulis* example, transmission appears to be limited by high levels of host physiological resistance to infection, rather than low pollinator visitation rates, as anther-smut spores were found on healthy flowers within several metres of diseased plants (Marr & Delph, 2005). Similarly, in our studies of anther-smut on *Dianthus pavonius*, a moderately long-lived species (6–10 years), we have found anther-smut spores on 80% of healthy flowers in the field, but have observed very few successful transmissions (<4% of plants became infected during an eight-year study; Bruns et al., 2017). In addition, in greenhouse inoculation experiments where spores were applied to the flowers or axillary meristems of adult *D. pavonius* plants, less than 4% of individuals became infected. In contrast, demographic studies of the shorter-lived host *Silene latifolia* found much higher infection rates in the field (30–83%, Alexander & Antonovics, 1988), and correspondingly higher infection rates in controlled inoculation tests (18–42%; Alexander et al., 1993; Kaltz & Shykoff, 2001). In Section 6.3, I use an analytical model to explore the effect of lifespan on the evolution of disease resistance.

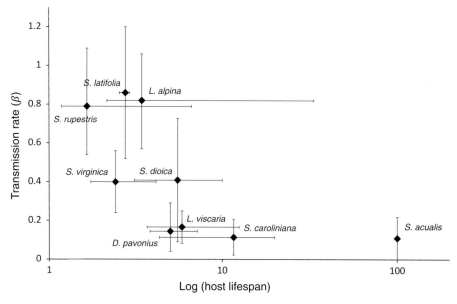

Figure 6.1 Relationship between host lifespan (years) and transmission rates for different species of Caryophyllaceae infected by *Microbotryum* causing anther-smut disease. Lifespan is the reciprocal of *b*, the average per-year mortality rate. Transmission rate (*β*) was calculated as the proportion of healthy plants that become diseased over a one-year period, divided by the disease prevalence. Error bars represent the range of values reported for transmission rate and mortality. For *S. rupestris* and *L. alpinum*, *β* values are from Carlsson-Granér (2006) and were estimated by linear regression. Data sources: *S. latifolia* (Alexander & Antonovics, 1988); *S. virginica* (Antonovics et al., 1996); *S. caroliniana* and *D. pavonius* (Bruns et al., 2015); *S. acaulis* (Marr & Delph, 2005), all others (Carlsson-Granér & Thrall, 2006). Figure reproduced from Bruns et al. (2015).

6.2.2 Observation 2: Increased susceptibility to disease at juvenile stage

Anther-smut has been held up as a model plant system for sexually transmitted disease (Antonovics, 2005) because transmission occurs between reproducing adults: pollinators pick up spores from diseased flowering plants and transport them to healthy flowering plants. However, it has long been known that infection can occur during earlier host life stages if spores fall on vegetative non-flowering plants, as can happen if seeds germinate and grow in close proximity to diseased adult plants (Alexander, 1990; Box 6.1). Indeed, epidemiological models have shown that this type of pre-floral transmission is important for the maintenance of anther-smut disease in *S. latifolia* (Alexander & Antonovics, 1988) and *S. rupestris* (Carlsson-Granér, 2006).

Our group has been studying a diseased population of *Dianthus pavonius* (Figure B6.1.1) in the Maritime Alps region of Italy for the past 10 years, and we have discovered that here, too, transmission to this susceptible seedling stage plays a critical role in disease dynamics (Bruns et al., 2017). The disease has maintained a steady prevalence of ca. 40% within this population since 2007, while the population size has declined markedly by over 50%. However, the transmission rate to adult flowering plants is surprisingly low: over an eight-year period, only 4% of healthy, flowering plants became infected, despite high levels of spore deposition on flowers. Greenhouse inoculation experiments have shown that susceptibility to anther-smut is age-dependent: adult plants are extremely resistant to infection, but young seedlings are highly susceptible (Figure 6.2A). Epidemiological models based solely on pollinator-mediated transmission to flowering plants strongly underpredict disease prevalence, unless the transmission model is expanded to allow transmission to both adults and juveniles. In the field, young seedlings likely come into contact with anther-smut spores if they germinate near a diseased plant: we have found high spore deposition on sticky traps within 30 cm of diseased plants.

The evolution of juvenile resistance is physiologically possible in this system: progeny from 18 field-collected maternal families inoculated as 10-day old seedlings varied significantly in infection rate ($\chi^2 = 46.9$, df = 17, $p = 0.0001$). While the majority of maternal families were highly susceptible (>80% infected) a few families had significantly lower infection rates (ca. 50%, Figure 6.2B). In addition, I have been able to increase levels of seedling resistance (<30% infection) after three generations of selection (Figure 6.2C). In contrast, adult resistance, measured as the infection rate of 25 different cloned genotypes from the field, revealed overall high levels of resistance (Figure 6.3D) and little genetic variation ($\chi^2 = 2.18$, df = 24, $p = 0.999$).

From an evolutionary perspective, the high observed level of juvenile susceptibility in our studied population is surprising, because disease prevalence and plant density (often > 10 plants/m^2) are high, and have been for at least 14 years, so strong selection for seedling resistance would have been expected. In Section 6.4, I develop an age-specific model to explore the evolution of adult vs. juvenile resistance.

6.3 The evolution of resistance in non-age-structured populations

Understanding the evolution of resistance is not straightforward. The issue goes beyond simply estimating the particular costs and benefits of resistance because the evolution of resistance feeds back to both lower disease prevalence and changes in population size. As I show below (see also Bruns et al., 2015), this can lead to very counter-intuitive effects. Because of this complexity, it is essential to understand the results of the simplest scenario, where

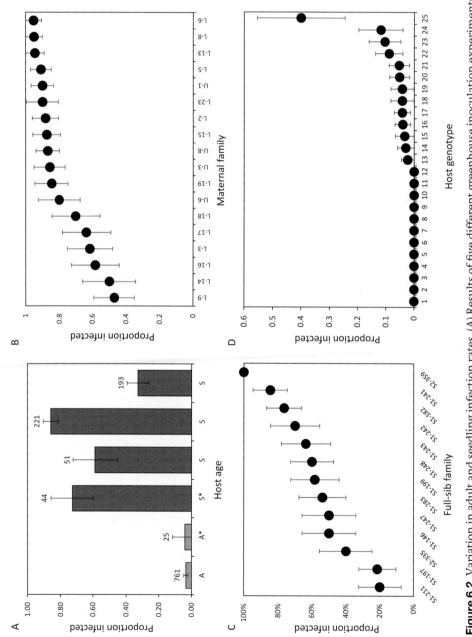

Figure 6.2 Variation in adult and seedling infection rates. (A) Results of five different greenhouse inoculation experiments conducted on either adult plants (light bars) or seedlings (dark bars). Asterisks indicate the results from the experiment carried out for this study. Numbers indicate

resistance is constitutive and is constant throughout the host's lifespan, and the pathogen is genetically uniform (Antonovics & Thrall, 1994). For simplicity, I assume a haploid host where resistance is controlled by a single locus with two alleles (S, susceptible; R, resistant). The model is loosely based on the anther-smut system, where transmission is frequency-dependent (Antonovics & Alexander, 1992), the disease sterilises but does not kill its host (Alexander, 1989), and there is no recovery. However, the outcomes are qualitatively similar for density-dependent transmission, and where disease causes mortality rather than sterility (Bruns et al., 2015).

6.3.1 The basic model

The rate of change in the numerical abundance of healthy susceptible (S), resistant (R) and infected hosts (I) can be described by the following equations:

$$\frac{dS}{dt} = S\left(a - b - kH - \beta_S \frac{I}{H}\right) \tag{6.1}$$

$$\frac{dR}{dt} = R\left(a - c - b - kH - \beta_R \frac{I}{H}\right) \tag{6.2}$$

$$\frac{dI}{dt} = S\beta_S \frac{I}{H} + R\beta_R \frac{I}{H} - bI \tag{6.3}$$

where a is the birth rate, b is the disease-independent death rate, and β_S and β_R are the frequency-dependent transmission rates. Getz and Pickering (1983) showed that diseases with frequency-dependent transmission cannot regulate host population size. The model therefore includes disease-independent population regulation in the form of kH, where k is a constant describing the strength of density-dependent population regulation on new recruits and H is the total

---

Caption for Figure 6.2   (cont.)

sample size, error bars are ± 1 SE. All experiments used seeds and inoculum originating near the main study site. (Figure reprinted from Bruns et al., 2017). (B) Variation in seedling infection rate for 18 field-collected maternal families. (C) Variation in seedling infection rate for 13 full-sib families after three generations of selection for resistance. For each generation all seedlings were inoculated with a standard mixture of five *Microbotryum* strains originally collected from the main field site. Plants that survived and remained healthy were randomly crossed in a full-sib design, and the procedure was repeated for three generations. For both B and C only families where 10 or more plants survived and flowered are shown. (D) Variation in infection rate among 25 cloned adults (2 years old). Each host genotype was split into 50 clones, and inoculated on the apical meristem with one of two strains of field-collected *Microbotryum*. There was no difference in infection rate among the two fungal strains.

population size (S + R + I). While the model has a superficial appearance to a classic SIR model, it should be noted that resistance is a constitutive genetic trait, and not acquired following exposure as in classical SIR models for animals. It is also assumed that resistance is quantitative, in that the 'resistant' genotype has a lower transmission rate than the 'susceptible' genotype ($\beta_R < \beta_S$). Resistance is therefore not absolute but relative to the susceptible host genotype. A cost of resistance, c, is incorporated in the form of reduced fertility in Equation 6.2.

Antonovics and Thrall (1994) showed that the evolutionarily stable state of Equations 6.1–6.3 depends on the level of resistance (e.g. the difference between β_S and β_S) and the fertility cost of resistance, c, but the outcome is complicated and can be best represented by the phase plane shown in Figure 6.3A. As expected, the resistance gene will become fixed in the population if it provides a moderate level of resistance and the cost is low (grey area, Figure 6.3). However, at higher levels of resistance ($\beta_R \ll \beta_S$), there are several important counter-intuitive outcomes. First, numerical changes in disease prevalence make it possible to maintain stable polymorphisms for resistance (dashed area, Figure 6.3A). Such polymorphisms cannot be maintained in purely genetic models that do not account for numerical changes in disease, even at high costs (Jayakar, 1970). Second, genes that confer higher levels of disease resistance are less likely to evolve to fixation than genes that only confer small to moderate levels of resistance. Third, the costs required to maintain resistance polymorphism can be quite small.

I used the same equations to show that host lifespan (formally equivalent to the reciprocal of mortality) affects the evolution of resistance (Bruns et al., 2015). Figure 6.3B shows that resistance evolves to fixation across a greater range of conditions in a longer-lived host. The effect of lifespan on the rate of resistance evolution can be illustrated by introducing a resistance gene at low frequency (0.01) into a diseased population of susceptible individuals at stable equilibrium and determining the number of time steps required for fixation. If β_S is held constant, longer-lived hosts evolve resistance more rapidly than shorter-lived hosts (Figure 6.3C). This happens because the strength of selection for resistance increases with lifespan. Longer-lived hosts are more likely to encounter the disease at some point during their lifetime, and they also support higher levels of disease prevalence (Figure 6.3C, dashed lines), because infected individuals remain in the population and continue to transmit disease.

Results from this general model show that longer-lived hosts can actually evolve resistance more rapidly than shorter-lived hosts, a prediction that is consistent with the observed pattern of lower transmission rates in longer-lived hosts in the anther-smut system (Figure 6.3). However, the model does not explain why resistance levels vary across host developmental stages.

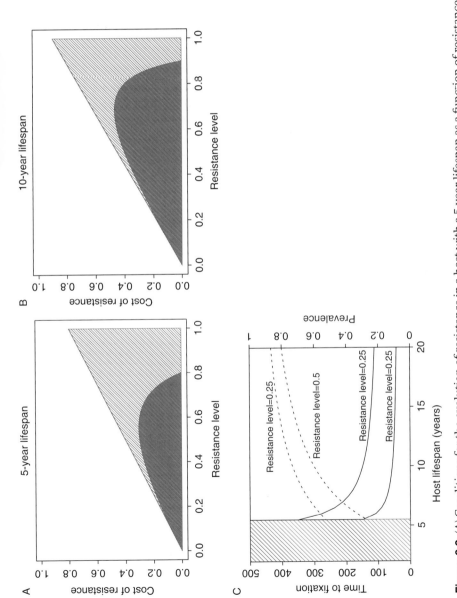

Figure 6.3 (A) Conditions for the evolution of resistance in a host with a 5-year lifespan as a function of resistance level $(\beta_S - \beta_R)/\beta_S$, and cost of resistance, c, derived from Equations 6.1–6.3. Resistance is fixed in the dark-shaded parameter space, but lost in the white space. Polymorphism is maintained in the striped parameter space. (B) Conditions for resistance evolution in a host with a 10-year lifespan. (C) Disease prevalence at equilibrium (dashed lines) and time to resistance fixation (solid black lines) as a function of host lifespan. Two different resistance levels are shown. Other parameters: $\beta_S = 0.5$, $a = 1$, $c = 0.05$, $k = 0.001$. The shaded area represents lifespans where the resistant genotype does not sweep to fixation. Adapted from Bruns et al. (2015).

6.4 The evolution of resistance in age-structured populations

To address the general question of how disease affects selection for resistance at adult and juvenile stages, I expanded the previous model to account for age structure. Here, I do not address the more complex issue of trade-offs between juvenile and adult traits, but address the following quite fundamental and simple questions. (1) What is the relative benefit of extending resistance to the juvenile stage, and how does this benefit change with host lifespan? (2) What level of resistance and cost will favour the evolution of a juvenile resistance gene over a gene that only provides resistance at adult stages?

6.4.1 The age-structured model

The transmission coefficient, β, used in the previous model is a complex parameter describing both the likelihood of contact given a particular disease prevalence, p (e.g. encounter rate), and the probability of infection given contact, δ (e.g. level of physiological resistance). Because my interest here is in the evolution of physiological resistance, I decomposed the transmission function into:

$$F = S * \left[1 - (1-\delta)^{p\frac{I}{H}}\right] \tag{6.4}$$

where F is the force of infection, S is the density of susceptible hosts, I is the density of infected hosts, and H is the total host population density.

I used a life table approach to vary physiological resistance (δ), and its fertility costs (c) at different age classes. For simplicity, I define the first age class as the juvenile class and assume that juveniles do not reproduce. All other ages are categorised as adults, with $a > 0$. I assume that the mortality (b) and disease encounter rate (p) do not differ across age classes.

There are three different alleles that affect the onset of resistance. I refer to these as: 'susceptible' (S), 'adult-onset resistance' (R_A), and 'juvenile-onset resistance' (R_J). The life table for the susceptible genotype is given as:

Susceptible (S)

Age	Prob. of infection	Fecundity
1	δ_S	0
2	δ_S	a
3	δ_S	a
.	.	.
.	.	.
x	δ_S	a

The adult-onset resistant genotype (R_A) has increased physiological resistance, i.e. a lower probability of infection per contact (δ_R), where $\delta_R <$

δ_S, at all adult age classes, but maintains susceptibility in the first age class. The juvenile-onset resistant genotype (R_J) has increased resistance at all age classes compared to the susceptible genotype. The lifetables are given below.

Juvenile-onset (R_J)

Age	Prob. of infect	Fecundity
1	δ_R	0
2	δ_R	$a(1-c)$
3	δ_R	$a(1-c)$
.	.	.
.	.	.
x	δ_R	$a(1-c)$

Adult-onset (R_A)

Age	Prob. of infect.	Fecundity
1	$\delta_S > \delta_R$	0
2	δ_R	a
3	δ_R	$a(1-c)$
..	..	..
x	δ_R	$a(1-c)$

As in the previous model, I assumed a fertility cost, c, associated with resistance. I assumed that fertility costs would occur only after the onset of resistance, as would happen if the expression of resistance slowed host growth and reproduction. For the adult-onset genotype (R_A), the birth rate in the second year was identical to the susceptible genotype (S), but was negatively affected by the cost in all subsequent years. For the juvenile-onset (R_J) genotype, the birth rate was reduced by c at all reproductive ages.

6.4.2 Invasion of adult and juvenile resistance genes

I first present the results in the absence of costs, in order to illustrate how the relative benefit of additional juvenile resistance varies with host lifespan. For each genotype, I calculated the probability of surviving and remaining healthy (uninfected) to each age class, Lx, as:

$$Lx = (1-b)^x * (1 - F_{ix=1}) * \ldots \ldots (1 - F_{ix=x}) \tag{6.5}$$

where F is the force of infection at age x on host genotype i. The expected lifetime reproductive output of each genotype W_i can then be expressed as:

Table 6.1 *Transmission and birth rates of the susceptible S genotype required to maintain a population size of 2250 and 40% disease prevalence at equilibrium.*

Lifespan	b	a	δ_S	Ave. age at infection
3.3	0.3	6.6	0.3895	1.89
4.0	0.25	4.025	0.297	2.3
5.0	0.2	2.46	0.219	2.9
6.7	0.15	1.455	0.1525	3.9
10.0	0.1	0.785	0.095	5.89
20.0	0.05	0.3285	0.0445	11.87

$$W_i = \sum L_{ix} * a_{ix}. \tag{6.6}$$

To illustrate the relative fitness of adult and juvenile resistance onset when disease prevalence is constant, I adjusted the birth rate (a_i) and physiological resistance (δ_R) for each lifespan so that the population size was ca. 2200 at equilibrium and disease prevalence was 40%, i.e. the approximate population size and prevalence observed in our natural population of *D. pavonius*. I then calculated the period of the life expected to be disease-free (or expected age at first infection) as the reciprocal of the probability of not remaining healthy or alive:

$$\text{Average age at first infection} = \frac{1}{1 - \left[(1-b)(1-\delta)^{p_H^I}\right]}. \tag{6.7}$$

I chose to keep the ecological conditions (prevalence, population size) constant rather than the individual life-history parameters (birth rate, transmission rate) because a constant transmission rate means that equilibrium disease prevalence will be much higher in longer-lived populations (Antonovics & Thrall, 1994). From a modelling perspective, transmission rates that result in 40% prevalence in shorter-lived hosts cannot be sustained in populations with longer-lived hosts because they either lead to disease-driven extinction (which is feasible for diseases with frequency-dependent transmission) or lead to large oscillation cycles in prevalence. Moreover, studies in the anther-smut system have not revealed any positive correlation between host lifespan and average disease prevalence.

Table 6.1 shows that when prevalence and contact rate, p, are held constant, the expected age at first infection increases as a function of lifespan. This means that long-lived individuals are less likely to become infected at younger ages. In the absence of costs the juvenile-onset R_J

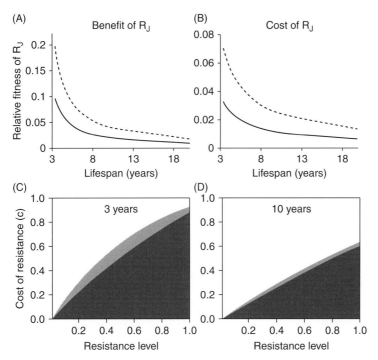

Figure 6.4 (A) Relative fitness of the R_J resistance genotype relative to the R_A genotype (calculated as $(W_J - W_A)/W_A$) when disease prevalence is 40% and there are no costs of resistance. Solid line: $\delta_R = 0.75 * \delta_S$, dashed line: $\delta_R = 0.50 * \delta_S$, where δ is the probability of becoming infected given contact. (B) Fitness cost of the R_J genotype relative to R_A in the absence of disease. Solid line: $c = 0.1$, dashed line: $c = 0.2$, where c is the cost of resistance. (C,D) Relative fitness across a range of resistance levels (calculated as of $(\delta_S - \delta_R/\delta_S)$ and costs when disease prevalence is 40%. Shading indicates the genotype with the highest relative fitness: white (S), light grey (R_A), dark grey (R_J). (C) Lifespan = 3.3 years, (D) Lifespan = 10 years.

genotype always has higher fitness than the adult-onset R_A genotype; however, the relative benefit declines with host lifespan (Figure 6.4A). The cumulative costs of resistance also scale with lifespan. In the absence of disease, the cost of the juvenile-onset genotype R_J relative to the adult-onset R_A genotype decreases in longer-lived hosts (Figure 6.4B). Thus, while the relative benefits of a juvenile-onset of resistance decline with host longevity, so does the cost.

To determine how the costs and benefits of resistance could affect the ability of these two different resistance genes to invade a susceptible population, I used Equation 6.6 to calculate expected fitness of each host genotype across the range of fertility costs and levels of resistance investigated above. Results show that the R_J genotype has higher fitness than the R_A genotype across a wide range of costs (Figure 6.4C). However, the range of conditions favourable to either type of resistance gene decreased in longer-lived hosts (Figure 6.4D).

6.4.3 Numerical dynamics of adult and juvenile resistance genes

The above illustrations have made the implicit assumption that disease prevalence is static. I now include the fitness estimates in a dynamic model that allows the possibility of epidemiological feedbacks:

$$S_{ix=1(t+1)} = \sum {}_{x=2}^{x=x} S_{ix(t)}(1-b)\left(1 - F_{ix(t)}\right)a_{ix}\frac{1}{1+kH_{(t)}} \tag{6.8}$$

$$S_{ix(t+1)} = S_{ix(t)}(1-b)\left(1 - F_{Six(t)}\right) \tag{6.9}$$

$$I_{(t+1)} = \left[\sum {}_{S=1}^{S=i} H_{x(t)}(1-b)F_{Six(t)}\right] + I(1-b)\theta \tag{6.10}$$

where $S_{ix(t)}$ is the number of healthy hosts of genotype i at age x at time t.

In Equation 6.8 the number of new juveniles is determined by multiplying the number of healthy, surviving individuals in each age class by their age-specific fertility rates. As in the previous model, juvenile establishment is assumed to be density-dependent, where k is a constant describing the strength of density-dependent regulation and $H_{(t)}$ is the total number of hosts at time t. Juveniles and adults thus all contribute equally to density effects. In Equation 6.9 the number of healthy individuals in each adult age class is determined by the probability of surviving to the next age class and not becoming infected. In Equation 6.10 the number of diseased individuals in the population is the sum of all newly infected hosts plus any surviving diseased individuals. All infected ages are assumed to contribute equally to transmission.

I ran simulations using Equations 6.8–6.10 where R_A and R_J genotypes were introduced at low frequency (0.01) into a resident population of susceptible genotypes at a stable age distribution. Each simulation was run for 5000 time steps and the evolutionary outcome was categorised as either fixation of a single genotype, dimorphism between two genotypes, or three-way polymorphism. Again, for comparison with field expectations, I assumed 40% disease prevalence and compared the outcomes for host lifespans of three and 10 years, as this spanned the expected life cycle of *Dianthus pavonius*.

As expected, the results of the single invasions mirrored those seen in non-age-structured models; both the adult-onset and juvenile-onset resistance genes were more likely to become fixed if they provided only moderate resistance at low cost (Figure 6.5A,B). Higher levels of resistance led to stable polymorphism with the susceptible gene. The less costly R_A gene was fixed under a greater range of parameter values than the R_J gene.

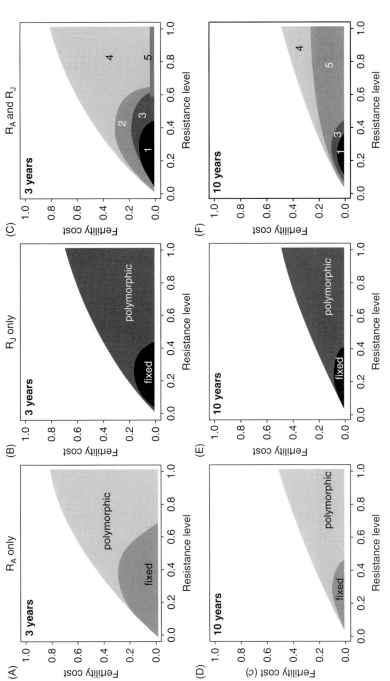

Figure 6.5 Evolutionary outcomes of introducing either (A,D) adult-only resistance or (B,E) juvenile-plus-adult resistance or (C,F) both adult and juvenile-plus-adult resistance into a susceptible population at 40% prevalence. Resistance is maintained in the shaded areas: 1, fixation of R_J; 2, fixation of R_A; 3, stable polymorphism between R_A and R_J; 4, stable polymorphism between R_A and S; 5, transient three-way polymorphism. Top row shows the outcomes when the host lifespan is 3.3 years, the bottom row shows the outcomes when the host lifespan is 10 years.

However, if both resistance genes were introduced together, the R_J gene could only persist in the narrow parameter space where both the level of resistance and cost were low (regions 1 and 3 in Figure 6.5C). If the level of resistance was high, then the R_J gene was lost and the population evolved a stable dimorphism between the S and R_A genes (region 4, Figure 6.5C). Thus, under a large proportion of the parameter space, the population retained polymorphisms for resistance at the adult stage but all individuals were susceptible as juveniles.

High levels of resistance (>50%) and very low costs (<10%) led to three-way polymorphism between S, R_A, and R_J (region 5, Figure 6.5C); however, further investigation showed that this was not a stable state. Running the simulation out beyond 5000 time steps led to the eventual loss of the lifetime R_J resistance gene, leaving a stable dimorphism between the S and R_A genes that could not be invaded. Interestingly, fixation of the adult-onset R_A gene was rare, because the majority of the parameter space that would have led to its fixation in single-invasion simulations (Figure 6.5A) was more favourable to the juvenile-onset R_J gene.

Numerical feedbacks are critical to understanding why the evolutionary outcomes predicted by the simulations differ from a simple fitness analysis. In the initial stages of invasion, both resistance genes increase rapidly in frequency, with the more beneficial R_J gene increasing first (Figure 6.6). If the level of resistance conferred by these genes is high ($\delta_R > \delta_S$), their increase drives a substantial decrease in disease prevalence (Figure 6.6, dotted line). As disease prevalence declines, the average age of first infection increases, reducing the relative benefit of juvenile-onset resistance. Selection then favours the less-costly adult-onset gene, and this drives a decline and eventual loss in the juvenile-onset gene. If the fitness cost of R_J relative to R_A is small, the decline in R_A occurs slowly and can result in a long-lasting transient three-way polymorphism.

Juvenile onset of resistance was even less likely to evolve in longer-lived hosts (Figure 6.5C–F). The reason for this is that the transmission rate required to maintain a high prevalence decreased with lifespan, resulting in an increased in average age of first infection (Table 6.1). Consequently, the probability of becoming infected as a juvenile decreased with lifespan, thereby decreasing the benefit of higher resistance during this life stage.

6.4.4 Implications for the evolution of age-specific resistance

The naïve prediction that infectious disease should always favour resistance at the juvenile stage than at later stages is not tenable if less-costly genes that result in a later onset of resistance are also present. The model shows that if there is genetic variation for the onset of resistance, an early juvenile onset

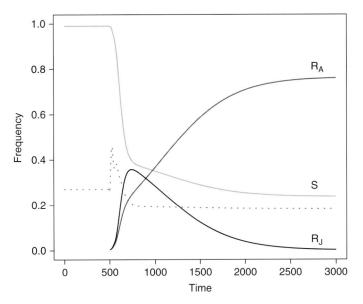

Figure 6.6 Dynamics of resistance evolution when resistance level (δ_R) is 50%, the cost of resistance is 20%, and lifespan is 5 years. Solid lines indicate genotypes S (susceptible), R_A (adult-onset resistance) and R_J (juvenile-onset resistance). Both R_A and R_J increase rapidly in frequency, during the initial phase. The increase in resistance results in a decrease in disease prevalence (dotted line). At lower prevalence, the more costly juvenile resistance gene is lost and the outcome is a stable dimorphism between the susceptible S and adult-resistance R_A genes.

will only evolve under a narrow set of conditions; namely, at low resistance levels and at a low cost, and then largely in short-lived hosts. In contrast, adult-onset resistance (and the maintenance of susceptibility at the juvenile stage) is predicted under a broader range of conditions. The model presented here thus provides an alternative explanation for the predominance of juvenile suscept-ibility observed in nature that does not invoke developmental or physiological constraints.

An important take home is that numerical feedbacks are likely to play a critical role in the evolution of age-specific resistance. The initial evolution of resistance can drive declines in disease prevalence that in turn, change the average age of first infection and reduce the strength of selection for resistance in juveniles. In several cases, the genotype with the highest relative fitness at the beginning of the invasion was eventually lost from the population, following a decline in prevalence. Feedbacks have previously been shown to be critical for the maintenance of resistance polymorphism (Antonovics & Thrall, 1994; Donnelly et al., 2015) as well as the evolution of innate versus acquired resistance (Miller et al., 2007).

Table 6.2 *Effect of age-specific variation in encounter rate, p, on the evolution of juvenile-onset resistance. Columns 2–4 show the proportion of parameter space where resistance evolves when the encounter rate is lower for juveniles than adults ($p_J = 1$, $p_A = 2$), equal ($p_J = 2$, $p_A = 2$), or higher for juveniles than adults ($p_J = 3$, $p_A = 2$). Other parameters are the same as the top row in Figure 6.5.*

Encounter rate	R_A and/or R_J maintained	R_J gene maintained	R_J gene fixed
$p_J < p_A$	0.361	0.010	0.001
equal	0.485	0.067	0.028
$p_J > p_A$	0.618	0.225	0.078

I developed this model largely for heuristic reasons, and in any real-world system many of the assumptions are likely to be violated. In particular, encounter rates are unlikely to be constant across life stages. In the *Dianthus* example, at low density adult flowering plants are much more likely to encounter disease than juveniles because diseased plants do not produce seed, and their spores can only come into contact with healthy plants largely via pollinators. Likewise in primates, disease encounter rates are hypothesised to be greater among adults, which have higher contact rates through mating and territorial disputes (Nunn & Altizer, 2006). In such cases, juvenile resistance should evolve under an even narrower set of conditions than if encounter rates are constant. However, if juveniles have higher disease encounter rates than adults, as may occur in animals that breed seasonally in large dense groups but are otherwise solitary (such as sea turtles on beaches or frogs in ponds), juvenile resistance should evolve under a wider range of conditions. Indeed, varying the contact rate, *p*, in the model confirms these predictions (Table 6.2)

The genetics of resistance are also likely to be much more complex in real-world systems. In crop plants, juvenile resistance is indeed typically associated with single genes of major effect (termed 'qualitative resistance'; Panter et al., 2002), and in some cases similar genes have been found that confer resistance only at the adult stage (Develey-Rivière & Galiana, 2007; Chen, 2013). However, adult plant resistance is also typically associated with an increase in polygenic resistance, involving multiple traits such as the development of thicker leaf epidermis and secondary chemicals (Poland et al., 2009), which I did not account for. Real-world systems are also likely to involve trait correlations, something our group is currently investigating in the *Dianthus* system. For example, in *Drosophila*, Fellous and Lazzaro (2011) showed that there was a strong positive correlation between larval and adult expression of the constitutive immune gene *diptericin*.

I assumed that costs of resistance only affected host fertility and did so in an age-dependent manner. However, costs of age-specific resistance could be modelled (and may be instantiated) in many other ways. While there is now a large body of evidence demonstrating that resistance is indeed costly (Bergelson & Purrington, 1996; Lochmiller & Deerenberg, 2000; Armitage et al., 2003; Susi & Laine, 2015), we have almost no information on the relative costs of adult and juvenile forms of resistance. In the anther-smut system, Biere and Antonovics (1996) found a strikingly high fitness cost of adult resistance: families that had low rates of adult infection in the field also produced fewer flowers in a disease-free common garden. However, even in this well-studied system, we still do not know if there are costs associated with seedling resistance and how these reflect later-life fitness components. On the one hand, limited resource availability and growth requirements at the juvenile stage could make investment in resistance more costly at the juvenile stage (McDade, 2003; Boege & Marquis, 2005). On the other hand, new forms of resistance may also be present at the adult stage that carry additional costs. For example, in vertebrates, the adaptive immune system is better developed in adults, but there can be significant costs associated with mounting an immune response (Raberg et al., 2000; Hanssen et al., 2004). Similarly, plants develop additional constitutive defensive traits such as thicker cell walls and an arsenal of secondary chemicals as they grow, which could be more costly (Barton & Koricheva, 2010). Maternal effects could also impact costs of resistance by transferring the cost of juvenile resistance from the offspring to the parent. For example, in humans and other mammals, antibodies present in the mother's milk can help protect against disease (Brambell, 1970; Kallio et al., 2010; Garnier et al., 2014). Studies that measure costs of resistance across different host developmental stages would provide valuable insight into evolution of age-specific resistance.

The model was developed to understand the evolution of innate resistance to systemic diseases, but I have not yet explored whether the same evolutionary principles developed in the model will apply to foliar plant pathogens (that only live as long as individual leaves), or to hosts with acquired immunity (the dominant immune system in many vertebrates). While acquired resistance on its own can drive a pattern of increasing resistance with age (hosts build antibodies in response to pathogen encounters), it cannot fully explain the widespread pattern of high juvenile susceptibility. For example, Baird (1998) found that adult Javenese migrants to a malaria-endemic region of Indonesia acquired resistance much more rapidly than their children. Because both adults and children in the study experienced the same period of exposure, the results indicate that there is a strong age-specific component to acquired malaria resistance. More recently, Kurtis et al. (2001) found that acquired resistance to malaria increases following puberty. Expanding the model presented here to allow for differing degrees of acquired immunity could provide a first step towards understanding the complex evolutionary processes underlying age-specific resistance in humans and wildlife.

6.5 Future directions

The models developed here predict that longer-lived hosts will be more likely to maintain susceptibility at the juvenile stage than shorter-lived hosts. At this point, our knowledge of age-specific resistance among anther-smut hosts is limited to just two species: the short-lived *S. latifolia*, where we see similar levels of juvenile and adult resistance, and the longer-lived *D. pavonius*, where juveniles are significantly less resistant than adults. Additional estimates of juvenile and adult resistance in other anther-smut host species that vary in lifespan would provide a test of the model predictions.

The finding that selection may favour the evolution of resistance at the adult but not the juvenile stage raises new questions about coevolution and mode of transmission. Will the strength of antagonistic coevolution be lowered if pathogens evolve to take further advantage of the susceptible juvenile stage? In the *Dianthus* system, the strong difference in resistance between adult and juvenile stages means that aerial dispersal of spores onto seedlings now accounts for a larger proportion of the total transmissions than pollinator-vectored transmission routes. Our group is currently investigating the effect of age-specific resistance on the evolution of pathogen transmission mode.

6.6 Conclusions

Juvenile susceptibility is a widespread and important pattern in nature, providing an opportunity for rapid pathogen transmission, and leading to the classic periodic and seasonal dynamics seen in childhood diseases of humans and wildlife. However, the evolutionary origins of this high juvenile susceptibility remain an important open question. Here I have shown that juvenile resistance will only evolve under a relatively narrow set of conditions, which further narrows with increasing host lifespan. The model assumes no absence of genetic variation at the juvenile stage, or that the costs exceed the direct fitness benefits when considered outside a population context. Instead, it shows that the dynamics within the system make even small costs sufficient to prevent the evolution of resistance at the juvenile stage.

It is also my hope that the chapter has convinced you that demographic studies of disease transmission in wild plant populations can generate new insight into disease ecology in animal systems, where sometimes the difficulty of doing experiments such as artificial inoculations precludes thinking about issues that such experiments may reveal. Our empirical studies of anther-smut on *Dianthus pavonius*, where we found evidence that disease dynamics are dependent on a susceptible, juvenile class, has resulted directly in the development of the theory presented here on the evolution of juvenile disease resistance and the role of host lifespan in this process.

6.7 Acknowledgements

The referenced empirical field studies on *Dianthus pavonius* were carried out in collaboration with Janis Antonovics and Michael Hood. Extensive field support was provided by Valentina Carasso and Ivan Pace at the Parco Naturale del Marguareis. Wendy Cranage helped with greenhouse management for the inoculation studies. I am very grateful to Janis Antonovics, Andy Fenton, and two anonymous reviewers who provided feedback on this chapter.

References

Alexander, H.M. (1989) An experimental field study of anther-smut disease of *Silene alba* caused by *Ustilago violacea*: genotypic variation and disease incidence. *Evolution*, **43**, 835–847.

Alexander, H.M. (1990) Epidemiology of anther-smut infection of *Silene alba* caused by *Ustilago violacea*: patterns of spore deposition and disease incidence. *Journal of Ecology*, **78**, 166–179.

Alexander, H.M. & Antonovics, J. (1988) Disease spread and population dynamics of anther-smut infection of *Silene alba* caused by the fungus *Ustilago violacea*. *Journal of Ecology*, **76**, 91–104.

Alexander, H.M. & Antonovics, J. (1995) Spread of anther-smut disease (*Ustilago violacea*) and character correlations in a genetically variable experimental population of *Silene alba*. *Journal of Ecology*, **83**, 783–794.

Alexander, H.M., Antonovics, J. & Kelly, A.W. (1993) Genotypic variation in plant disease resistance–physiological resistance in relation to field disease transmission. *Journal of Ecology*, **81**, 325–333.

Altizer, S., Davis, A.K., Cook, K.C. & Cherry, J.J. (2004) Age, sex, and season affect the risk of mycoplasmal conjunctivitis in a southeastern house finch population. *Canadian Journal of Zoology*, **82**, 755–763.

Antonovics, A.J., Stratton, D., Thrall, P.H. & Jarosz, A.M. (1996) An anther-smut disease (*Ustilago violacea*) of Fire-pink (*Silene virginica*):
its biology and relationship to the anther-smut disease of white campion (*Silene alba*). *American Midland Naturalist*, **135**, 130–143.

Antonovics, J. (2004) Long-term study of a plant-pathogen metapopulation. In: *Ecology, Genetics, and Evolution of Metapopulations* (pp. 471–488). Amsterdam: Elsevier.

Antonovics, J. & Alexander, H.M. (1992) Epidemiology of anther-smut infection of *Silene alba* (= *S. latifolia*) caused by *Ustilago violacea*: patterns of spore deposition in experimental populations. *Proceedings of the Royal Society of London B*, **250**, 157–163.

Antonovics, J., Hood, M.E., Thrall, P.H., Abrams, J.Y. & Duthie, G.M. (2003) Herbarium studies on the distribution of anther-smut fungus (*Microbotryum violaceum*) and *Silene* species (Caryophyllaceae) in the eastern United States. *American Journal of Botany*, **90**, 1522–1531.

Antonovics, J. & Thrall, P.H. (1994) The cost of resistance and maintenance of genetic polymorphism in host–pathogen systems. *Proceedings of the Royal Society of London B*, **257**, 105–110.

Armitage, S.A.O., Thompson, J.J.W., Rolff, J. & Siva-Jothy, M.T. (2003) Examining costs of induced and constitutive immune investment in *Tenebrio molitor*. *Journal of Evolutionary Biology*, **16**, 1038–1044.

Baird, J.K. (1998) Age-dependent characteristics of protection v. susceptibility to

Plasmodium falciparum. *Annals of Tropical Medicine and Parasitology*, **92**, 367–390.

Barton, K.E. & Koricheva, J. (2010) The ontogeny of plant defense and herbivory: characterizing general patterns using meta-analysis. *The American Naturalist*, **175**, 481–493.

Bergelson, J. & Purrington, C.B. (1996) Surveying patterns in the cost of resistance in plants. *The American Naturalist*, **148**, 536–558.

Bernasconi, G., Antonovics, J., Biere, A., et al. (2009) *Silene* as a model system in ecology and evolution. *Heredity*, **103**, 5–14.

Biere, A. & Antonovics, J. (1996) Sex-specific costs of resistance to the fungal pathogen *Ustilago violacea* (*Microbotryum violaceum*) in *Silene alba*. *Evolution*, **50**, 1098–1110.

Boege, K. & Marquis, R.J. (2005) Facing herbivory as you grow up: the ontogeny of resistance in plants. *Trends in Ecology and Evolution*, **20**, 441–448.

Boots, M., Donnelly, R. & White, A. (2013) Optimal immune defence in the light of variation in lifespan. *Parasite Immunology*, **35**, 331–338.

Brambell, F.W.R. (1970) *The Transmission of Passive Immunity from Mother to Young*. Amsterdam: North Holland.

Bruns, E., Hood, M.E. & Antonovics, J. (2015) Rate of resistance evolution and polymorphism in long- and short-lived hosts. *Evolution*, **69**, 551–560.

Bruns, E.L., Antonovics, J., Carasso, V. & Hood, M. (2017) Transmission and temporal dynamics of anther-smut disease (*Microbotryum*) on alpine carnation (*Dianthus pavonius*). *Journal of Ecology*, **105**, 1413–1424.

Buono, L., López-Villavicencio, M., Shykoff, J.A., Snirc, A. & Giraud, T. (2014) Influence of multiple infection and relatedness on virulence: disease dynamics in an experimental plant population and its castrating parasite. *PLoS ONE*, **9**, e98526.

Burdon, J.J., Oates, J.D. & Marshall, D.R. (1983) Interactions between *Avena* and *Puccinia* species. I. The wild hosts: *Avena barbata* Pott Ex Link, *A. fatua* L. and *A. ludoviciana* Durieu. *Journal of Applied Ecology*, **20**, 571–584.

Cafuir, L., Antonovics, J. & Hood, M.E. (2007) Tissue culture and quantification of individual-level resistance to anther-smut

disease in Silene vulgaris.*International Journal of Plant Sciences*, **168**, 415–419.

Carlsson-Granér, U. (1997) Anther-smut disease in *Silene dioica*: variation in susceptibility among genotypes and populations, and patterns of disease within populations. *Evolution*, **51**, 1416–1426.

Carlsson-Granér, U. (2006) Disease dynamics, host specificity and pathogen persistence in isolated host populations. *Oikos*, **112**, 174–184.

Carlsson-Granér, U. & Thrall, P.H. (2006) The impact of host longevity on disease transmission: host–pathogen dynamics and the evolution of resistance. *Evolutionary Ecology Research*, **8**, 659–675.

Charlesworth, B. (1980) *Evolution in Age-structured Populations*. Cambridge: Cambridge University Press.

Chen, X. (2013) High-temperature adult-plant resistance, key for sustainable control of stripe rust. *American Journal of Plant Science and Biotechnology*, **4**, 608–627.

Chung, E., Petit, E., Antonovics, J., Pedersen, A. B. & Hood, M.E. (2012) Variation in resistance to multiple pathogen species: anther smuts of *Silene uniflora*. *Ecology and Evolution*, **2**, 2304–2314.

Develey-Rivière, M.P. & Galiana, E. (2007) Resistance to pathogens and host developmental stage: a multifaceted relationship within the plant kingdom. *New Phytologist*, **175**, 405–416.

Diamond, J. (1997) *Guns, Germs and Steel: The Fates of Human Societies*. New York, NY: Norton.

Donnelly, R., White, A. & Boots, M. (2015) The epidemiological feedbacks critical to the evolution of host immunity. *Journal of Evolutionary Biology*, **28**, 2042–2053.

Fellous, S. & Lazzaro, B.P. (2011) Potential for evolutionary coupling and decoupling of larval and adult immune gene expression. *Molecular Ecology*, **20**, 1558–1567.

Flor, H.H. (1956) The complementary genic systems in flax and flax rust. *Advances in Genetics*, **8**, 29–54.

Garbutt, J.S., O'Donoghue, A.J.P., McTaggart, S. J., Wilson, P.J. & Little, T.J. (2014) The development of pathogen resistance in *Daphnia magna*: implications for disease spread in age-structured populations. *The*

Journal of Experimental Biology, **217**, 3929–3934.

Garnier, R., Gandon, S., Harding, K.C. & Boulinier, T. (2014) Length of intervals between epidemics: evaluating the influence of maternal transfer of immunity. *Ecology and Evolution*, **4**, 568–575.

Getz, W.M. & Pickering, J. (1983) Epidemic models: thresholds and population regulation. *The American Naturalist*, **121**, 892–898.

Hanssen, S.A., Hasselquist, D., Folstad, I. & Erikstad, K.E. (2004) Costs of immunity: immune responsiveness reduces survival in a vertebrate. *Proceedings of the Royal Society of London B*, **271**, 925–930.

Härkönen, T., Harding, K., Rasmussen, T.D., Teilmann, J. & Dietz, R. (2007) Age- and sex-specific mortality patterns in an emerging wildlife epidemic: the phocine distemper in European harbour seals. *PLoS ONE*, **2**, e887.

Hendrix, F.F. & Campbell, W. (1973) *Pythiums* as plant pathogens. *Annual Review of Phytopathology*, **11**, 77–98.

Hood, M.E., Mena-Alí, J.I., Gibson, A.K., et al. (2010). Distribution of the anther-smut pathogen *Microbotryum* on species of the Caryophyllaceae. *The New Phytologist*, **187**, 217–229.

Jarosz, A.M. & Burdon, J.J. (1990) Predominance of a single major gene for resistance to *Phakopsora pachyrhizi* in a population of *Glycine argyrea*. *Heredity*, **64**, 347–353.

Jayakar, S.D. (1970) A mathematical model for interaction of gene frequencies in a parasite and its host. *Theoretical Population Biology*, **1**, 140–164.

Kallio, E.R., Begon, M., Henttonen, H., et al. (2010) Hantavirus infections in fluctuating host populations: the role of maternal antibodies. *Proceedings of the Royal Society of London B*, **277**, 3783–3791.

Kaltz, O., Gandon, S., Michalakis, Y. & Shykoff, J. A. (1999) Local maladaptation in the anther-smut fungus *Microbotryum violaceum* to its host plant *Silene latifolia*: evidence from a cross-inoculation experiment. *Evolution*, **53**, 395–407.

Kaltz, O. & Shykoff, J.A. (2001) Male and female *Silene latifolia* plants differ in per-contact risk of infection by a sexually transmitted disease. *Journal of Ecology*, **89**, 99–109.

Kubi, C., Van Den Abbeele, J., De Deken, R., et al. (2006) The effect of starvation on the susceptibility of teneral and non-teneral tsetse flies to trypanosome infection. *Medical and Veterinary Entomology*, **20**, 388–392.

Kurtis, J.D., Onyango, F.K. & Duffy, P.E. (2001) Human resistance to *Plasmodium falciparum* increases during puberty and is predicted by dehyroepiandrosterone sulfate levels. *Infection and Immunity*, **69**, 123–128.

le Gac, M., Hood, M.E., Fournier, E. & Giraud, T. (2007) Phylogenetic evidence of host-specific cryptic species in the anther smut fungus. *Evolution*, **61**, 15–26.

Line, R.F. & Chen, X. (1995) Successes in breeding for and managing durable resistance to wheat rusts. *Plant Breeding*, **79**, 1254–1255.

Lochmiller, R.L. & Deerenberg, C. (2000) Trade-offs in evolutionary immunology: just what is the cost of immunity? *Oikos*, **88**, 87–98.

Marr, D.L. & Delph, L.F. (2005) Spatial and temporal pattern of a pollinator-transmitted pathogen in a long-lived perennial, *Silene acaulis*. *Evolutionary Ecology Research*, **7**, 335–352.

McDade, T.W. (2003) Life history theory and the immune system: steps toward a human ecological immunology. *American Journal of Physical Anthropology*, **122**(Suppl. 46), 100–125.

McNeill, W.H. (1976) *Plagues and Peoples*. New York, NY: Anchor Books.

Miller, M.R., White, A. & Boots, M. (2007) Host life span and the evolution of resistance characteristics. *Evolution*, **61**, 2–14.

Morris, W. & Doak, D. (1998) Life history of the long-lived gynodioecious cushion plant *Silene acaulis* (Caryophyllaceae), inferred from size-based population projection matrices. *American Journal of Botany*, **85**, 784–793.

Müller-Graf, C., Collins, D., Packer, C. & Woolhouse, M. (1997) *Schistosoma mansoni* infection in a natural population of olive baboons (*Papio cynocephalus anubis*) in Gombe Stream National Park, Tanzania. *Parasitology*, **115**, 621–627.

Nunn, C. & Altizer, S. (2006) *Infectious Diseases in Primates*. Oxford: Oxford University Press.

Oppelt, C., Starkloff, A., Rausch, P., Von Holst, D. & Rodel, H. (2010) Major histocompatibility complex variation and age-specific endoparasite load in subadult European rabbits.*Molecular Ecology*, **19**, 4155–4167.

Packer, A. & Clay, K. (2000) Soil pathogens and spatial patterns of seedling mortality in a temperate tree. *Nature*, **404**, 278–281.

Panter, S. & Jones, D.A. (2002) Age-related resistance to plant pathogens. *Advances in Botanical Research*, **38**, 251–280.

Parker, M.A. (1988) Polymorphism for disease resistance in the annual legume *Amphicarpaea bracteata*. *Heredity*, **60**, 27–31.

Petit, E., Silver, C., Cornille, A., et al. (2017) Co-occurrence and hybridization of anther-smut pathogens specialized on *Dianthus* hosts. *Molecular Ecology*, **26**, 1877–1890.

Poland, J.A., Balint-Kurti, P.J., Wisser, R.J., Pratt, R.C. & Nelson, R.J. (2009) Shades of gray: the world of quantitative disease resistance. *Trends in Plant Science*, **14**, 21–29.

Raberg, L., Nilsson, J.A., Ilmonen, P., Stjernman, M. & Hasselquist, D. (2000) The cost of an immune response: vaccination reduces parental effort. *Ecology Letters*, **3**, 382–386.

Rosengaus, R.B. & Traniello, J.F.A. (2001) Disease susceptibility and the adaptive nature of colony demography in the dampwood termite *Zootermopsis angusticollis*. *Behavioral Ecology and Sociobiology*, **50**, 546–556.

Sait, S., Begon, M. & Thompson, D.J. (1994) The influence of larval age on the response of *Plodia interpunctella* to a granulosis virus. *Journal of Invertebrate Pathology*, **63**, 107–110.

Schäfer, A.M., Kemler, M., Bauer, R. & Begerow, D. (2010) The illustrated life cycle of *Microbotryum* on the host plant *Silene latifolia*. *Botany*, **88**, 875–885.

Susi, H. & Laine, A.-L. (2015) The effectiveness and costs of pathogen resistance strategies in a perennial plant. *Journal of Ecology*, **103**, 303–315.

Thrall, P.H., Biere, A. & Antonovics, J. (1993) Plant life-history and disease susceptibility – the occurrence of *Ustilago violacea* on different species within the Caryophyllaceae. *Journal of Ecology*, **81**, 489–498.

CHAPTER SEVEN

Sexually transmitted infections in natural populations: what have we learnt from beetles and beyond?

BEN ASHBY, JORDAN E. JONES, ROBERT J. KNELL AND GREGORY D.D. HURST

7.1 Introduction

Parasites and pathogens have diverse means of transmission, such that it appears every feasible means of moving from one host to another is used by at least one parasite. A subset of parasites and pathogens, the sexually transmitted infections or STIs, have evolved to use mating contact between hosts as their primary means for transmission. This set of parasites is thus epidemiologically distinct in that the mating biology of the host is linked to the infection process, which is then affected by variables such as partner number and choice. This transmission process means that STI dynamics are driven by the well-characterized biology of mating, presenting opportunities for direct observation and study of transmission-relevant contacts. Furthermore, these diseases may feed back into the evolution of mating behaviour.

STIs can be defined in epidemiological terms as infections whose transmission opportunities are affected by the patterns of sexual contact between hosts. This definition allows us to consider a broad range of epidemiologically similar infections that are nevertheless biologically diverse (Table 7.1). In addition to infections of the reproductive tract that are classically considered STIs, a variety of ectoparasites transmit during mating, and for some the prolonged contact of copulation provides the most important transmission route. There are also cases of respiratory disease where close encounter is necessary for transmission, and these too can behave epidemiologically as STIs when the species is solitary and encounters associated with mating represent the predominant opportunity for transmission. Possum TB, for instance, is an infection which in many biological senses is a classic respiratory tract infection, but for which transmission during sexual contact likely represents an important infection route (Ji et al., 2005). Finally, diseases of plants transmitted by pollinators can also be regarded as STIs (see Chapter 6).

The characterisation of STIs in epidemiological terms distinguishes them from other types of infections transmitted during reproduction. In particular,

Table 7.1 *Examples of sexually transmitted infections in animals and plants.*

Host	Infection	Site of infection	Impact on host	References
Silene alba (white campion)	Anther-smut fungus, *Ustilago violacea*	Flowers	Sterilizing	Alexander and Maltby, 1990
Coccinellid beetles	*Hesperomyces virescences* (Laboulbeniales fungi)	Cuticular	Reduces longevity	Welch et al., 2001
	Coccipolipus mites	Sub elytral	Sterilizing on females, reduced overwinter survival for males	Hurst et al., 1995; Webberley and Hurst, 2002
Spodoptera frudiperda moths	*Noctuidonema guyanese* nematode	Ectoparasite	Field-collected females have lower longevity and fecundity with the STI	Simmons and Rogers, 1990, 1994
Gryllodes sigillatus crickets	*Mehdinema alii* nematode	Gut, genitals	Female host not invaded; gut infection develops in male hosts	Luong et al., 2000
Orycetes monoceros beetle	*Orycionema genitalis* nematode	Genitals	Some pathology, but not measurable impact on fertility	Poinar, 1970
Helix aspersa snail	*Nemhelix bakeri* nematode	Genitals	Reduced fecundity	Morand and Faliex, 1994
Koala	*Chlamydia pecorum*	Venereal, ocular, systemic	Conjunctivitis; soggy bottom disease	Cockram and Jackson, 1974; Handasyde, 1986

Horses	*Trypanosoma equiperdum* (protozoa)	Venereal, systemic	Disease of Dourine – weight loss, poor coordination	Hagos et al., 2010; Suganuma et al., 2016
	Taylorella equigenitalis; *Taylorella asinigenitalis* (beta proteobacteria)	Venereal	Contagious equine metritis: temporary fertility loss in females	Sugimoto et al., 1983; Baverud et al., 2006
Various primates	Simian Immunodeficiency Viruses (SIV)	Venereal, systemic	Vary from asymptomatic to immunodeficiency illness, depending on host species	Chahroudi et al., 2014

the definition excludes infections solely transmitted vertically from parent to offspring, processes that have been conflated into the single term 'STI' in some recent treatments (Smith & Mueller, 2015). The confluence of terms arises partly from pathogens that show both transmission between partners during mating and vertical transmission, such that reproductive activity in all forms is associated with transmission (see paragraph below for discussion of these infections). However, it is important to recognise that vertical transmission differs epidemiologically from sexual transmission because on the one hand, maternal and paternal transmission rates (mother–offspring and father–offspring) are insensitive to patterns of mating contact, and on the other hand, infections that are acquired during copulation do not require reproduction per se for transmission (and indeed are often sterilising). Understanding disease dynamics for true STIs versus agents solely showing vertical transmission therefore requires very different treatments, and thus we here deal with the narrow (and perhaps more common) usage of STIs, as infections where transmission occurs between adult hosts and is associated with mating activity.

Within this diversity of transmission routes (venereal, mating contact, mating proximity), there is also variation in the degree to which sexual transmission drives pathogen/parasite dynamics. At one end of the continuum are STIs where sexual transmission is sufficient to understand parasite/pathogen dynamics. The spring/summer epidemics of the sexually transmitted mite *Coccipolipus hippodamiae* on its two-spot ladybird host (Figure 7.1), for example, are well described in models that solely include transmission during host copulation (Hurst et al., 1995; Webberley et al., 2006a). There are then cases where sexual transmission is required for parasite/pathogen maintenance, but is not sufficient because it occurs alongside other necessary transmission modes. For instance, agents associated with the reproductive tract that are sexually transmitted are also commonly vertically transmitted (the presence in the reproductive tract makes mother–offspring transmission likely), and this vertical transmission is in some cases an important component of disease epidemiology. As an example, vertical transmission of *Chlamydia* in koalas establishes a class of infection in non-sexually mature individuals (Jackson et al., 1999), which may then seed epidemics when the individuals become reproductively active. Moving along the continuum, there are infections where sexual transmission occurs, but is probably not necessary for pathogen maintenance, one example being deformed wing virus in *Apis mellifera* honey bees. This is known to transfer from male to female during copulation (Amiri et al., 2016), but the predominant infection route is through *Varroa* mites (which represents the only means of infection into drone males). Finally, there are infections where sexual transmission either does not occur, or occurs so rarely it has hardly any importance in infection dynamics.

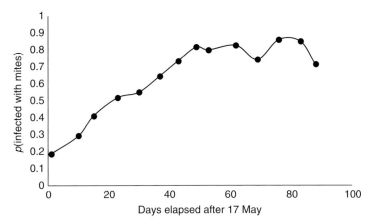

Figure 7.1 Spring epidemic of *C. hippodamiae* through the cohort of *A. bipunctata* following emergence from diapause in Stockholm suburb populations in 2010. Time elapsed since 17 May is given on the *x*-axis, and the proportion of adult beetles samples that carried *C. hippodamiae* infection on the *y*-axis (*N* = 40–120 beetles per sample point). Following emergence and a brief period of feeding, adult beetles begin mating, with each beetle mating with a different partner every 2–5 days in May and early June (depending on temperature and food supply). This mating activity results in an epidemic of the mite, which goes on to infect nearly all adult beetles within seven weeks. Original data in Ryder et al. (2014).

Infections like these are sometimes contrastingly termed 'OIDs' (ordinary infectious diseases) in the STI literature (Lockhart et al., 1996).

While STIs are defined by transmission biology, these infections share two other characteristics that make them dynamically distinct. First, STIs are commonly persistent infections, not cleared by immune system activity. For instance, infection with *Neisseria gonorrhoeae*, the causative agent of gonorrhoea, commonly persists over six months in the absence of treatment (Handsfield et al., 1974). Likewise, *C. hippodamiae* mite infection of ladybirds is usually retained until host death. Thus, natural populations of hosts are typically characterised by susceptible and infected individuals, with little recovery and a small/absent immune class (but see Grassly et al., 2005).

The second distinctive feature of STIs is that they commonly have a low impact on host mortality and a strong tendency to induce host sterility (Lockhart et al., 1996; Knell & Webberley, 2004). This unusual feature is explicable in terms of STI adaptation to maximise transmission. Infection transmission requires a healthy, mating host, and thus STIs are selected to not reduce the mating rate. Thus, they are selected to not make the host less vital or attractive. Extracting energy from reproduction rather than maintenance represents one means of achieving this fitness 'goal'. Further, in species where pregnancy/parental care leads to mating cessation, sterilisation of females has been hypothesised to lead to repeated ovulatory cycles and maintenance of host mating activity. This would be adaptive for the STI where the female then mates with new male partners. That sterility represents an adaptation rather than a by-product of infection that affects the reproductive tract has been argued on the basis of mechanistic complexity underlying the sterility phenotype for internal infections (Apari et al., 2014). The adaptive nature of sterility is also evidenced by the induction of sterility by ectoparasitic STIs, in which there is no plausible by-product mechanism for the infertility phenotype (Hurst et al., 1995).

In this chapter, we first outline theory developed with respect to STI dynamics; this relates mating system biology to transmission to predict disease epidemiology, and has largely been developed to understand the dynamics of STIs in human populations. We then examine the extent to which this theory is reflected in data from natural populations, and outline areas of future research with respect to the epidemiology of these infections in natural populations.

7.2 STI dynamics: a theoretical perspective

The epidemiology of STIs typically differs from that of other directly transmitted pathogens in a number of important ways.

(1) The number of sexual contacts is generally much lower than the number of social contacts because individuals tend to mate with relatively few partners during their lifetime compared to the total population size. Thus, opportunities for sexual transmission are usually less common than for other transmission routes. However, the intimate and protracted nature of the interaction may result in high transmission efficiency per contact.

(2) The sexual contact rate (and in turn the rate of new infections) is unlikely to vary strongly with population density; thus, transmission is likely to be *frequency-dependent* rather than *density-dependent*. As a consequence, STIs may not have a threshold population size for disease to spread and are less likely to regulate population density (Getz & Pickering, 1983). Indeed, pathogens with frequency-dependent transmission that cause demographic loss may drive their host to extinction, as low density does not reduce their transmission.

(3) High degrees of heterogeneity in sexual contact both within sexes (reproductive skew) and between the sexes (polygyny vs. polyandry) can have a profound impact on disease spread and dynamics (Ashby & Gupta, 2013).

(4) Many STIs are asymptomatic, can be chronic persistent infections, and confer little or no protective immunity to reinfection. Further, they are generally more likely to cause sterility and less likely to cause mortality than other infectious diseases (Lockhart et al., 1996).

Together, these key differences suggest that the epidemiological dynamics of STIs should be treated separately from other infectious diseases.

Heterogeneity in sexual contact rates has a particularly large impact on epidemiological dynamics and as such was the primary focus of early theoretical studies of human diseases such as HIV/AIDS and gonorrhoea (Yorke et al., 1978, May & Anderson, 1979, 1987; Hethcote & Yorke, 1984; Gupta et al., 1989). A key result from this early body of work was that heterogeneity in sexual contact number always increases the *basic reproductive ratio* or R_0 for the infection – a measure of transmissibility defined as the average number of secondary infections produced by a single individual in an otherwise susceptible population – which indicates if an epidemic will occur ($R_0 > 1$) and how quickly the disease will initially spread (Box 7.1). While this work was primarily motivated by epidemics of human STIs and the impact of a core group of so-called 'super spreaders' (e.g. sex workers), the key results are equally applicable to animal populations, which often exhibit high levels of heterogeneity in sexual contact number (e.g. due to dominance hierarchies).

7.2.1 Modelling heterogeneity in sexual contact
In a homogeneous and randomly mixed population where each individual has n sexual contacts, the basic reproductive ratio of an STI with transmission rate β and average infectious period D is $R_0 = \beta Dn$ (Box 7.1). However, if there is variation in the number of sexual contacts with mean m and variance σ^2 then

$$R_0 = \beta Dc \tag{7.1}$$

Box 7.1: Modelling the epidemiological dynamics of STIs

STIs typically conform to the *SIS* model of infectious disease, whereby susceptible individuals (S) may become infected through sexual contact with infectious individuals (I), and may recover from infection without protective immunity, becoming susceptible to reinfection. In the simplest case where hosts are homogeneous and mate randomly, the dynamics are given by the following differential equations:

$$\frac{dS}{dt} = a(N) - (\lambda + b)S + \nu I \tag{B7.1}$$

$$\frac{dI}{dt} = \lambda S - (\alpha + \nu + b)I \tag{B7.2}$$

where $a(N)$ is the birth rate, α and b are the disease-associated and natural mortality rates, ν is the rate of recovery, and λ is the force of infection. If we assume that sexual activity does not increase with population density

Box 7.1: (cont.)

(i.e. transmission is *frequency-dependent*), then the force of infection is the product of the number of sexual contacts, n, the transmission rate per sexual contact, β, and the frequency of infectious individuals, I/N (i.e. $\lambda = \beta n I/N$, with $N = S + I$). From these equations we can derive a key epidemiological quantity known as the *basic reproductive* ratio or R_0, which gives the average number of secondary infections in an otherwise susceptible population:

$$R_0 = \frac{\beta n}{\alpha + \nu + b} = \beta D n \tag{B7.3}$$

where $D = 1/(\alpha + \nu + b)$ is the average infectious period. Hence, if $R_0 < 1$ the disease will die out (on average each infectious case leads to less than one new infection), but if $R_0 > 1$ then an epidemic may occur (on average each infectious case leads to more than one new infection). If there is heterogeneity in the number of sexual contacts per individual, we can group individuals by their number of sexual contacts, giving an effective contact number of

$$n = \frac{\sum_i i^2 N_i}{\sum_i i N_i} = m + \frac{\sigma^2}{m} \tag{B7.4}$$

where N_i is the frequency of individuals with i sexual contacts, m is the mean contact number and σ^2 is the variance. This gives

$$R_0 = \beta D m (1 + V^2) \tag{B7.5}$$

where $V = \sigma/m$ is the *coefficient of variation*. It is clear that even a small increase in heterogeneity can lead to relatively large increase in R_0 (Figure B7.1.1) (May & Anderson, 1987).

When individuals are split into g risk groups (e.g. according to sexual contact number), the dynamics for group i are given by

$$\frac{dS_i}{dt} = a_i(N) - \left(\frac{1}{N}\sum_{j=1}^{g}\beta_{ij}p_{ij}I_j + b\right)S_i + \nu I_i \tag{B7.6}$$

$$\frac{dI_i}{dt} = \frac{S_i}{N}\sum_{j=1}^{g}\beta_{ij}p_{ij}I_j - (\alpha + \nu + b)I_i \tag{B7.7}$$

where p_{ij} is the number of sexual contacts between individuals in groups i and j given by a *mixing matrix* (Equation 7.4). The mixing matrix can capture both random and preferential mating patterns, the nature of which can drastically change the epidemiological dynamics (Figure B7.1.2).

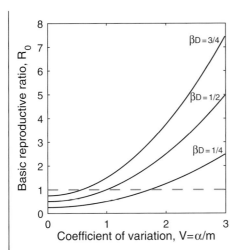

Figure B7.1.1 Heterogeneity in the number of sexual contacts (as measured by the coefficient of variation, V) always increases the basic reproductive ratio, R_0. The dashed horizontal line is the epidemic threshold, $R_0 = 1$.

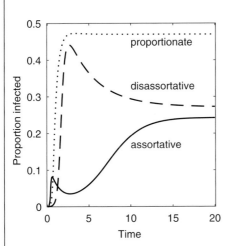

Figure B7.1.2 Different mating patterns affect the epidemiological dynamics of STIs. Mating patterns are *assortative* (solid curve) when individuals mostly mate with similar members of the population, are *disassortative* (dashed curve) when mating tends to be between groups, and are *proportionate* (dotted curve) when mating occurs randomly. Here, the population is split into two groups, where 10% of the population have 10 sexual partners and the remaining 90% have a single sexual partner. The dynamics were generated using the group model described in this box, with a constant host population size and ratio of individuals in the two groups. The mixing matrices are given in Equations 7.7 (proportionate) and 7.8 (assortative, $\delta = 0.97$; disassortative: $\delta = 0$).

where $c = m(1 + V^2)$. The quantity c is then the *effective partner acquisition rate* and $V = \sigma/m$ is the *coefficient of variation*. Any variation in the number of sexual partners per individual therefore increases R_0 and hence both the likelihood that an epidemic will occur and its initial growth rate (Figure B7.1.1).

The above formulation of R_0 assumes that the probability of transmission from males to females (β_m) is equal to the probability of transmission from females to males $\left(\beta_f\right)$ and that the mean and variance in mating success is the same for both sexes $\left(c_m = c_f\right)$. However, if there is greater variance in mating success in one sex – in polygynous or polyandrous species, for instance (Ashby & Gupta, 2013) – or if there is a bias in the risk of transmission towards one sex, then we have to adjust R_0 accordingly to account for these additional heterogeneities, giving

$$R_0 = D\sqrt{\beta_m \beta_f c_m c_f}. \tag{7.2}$$

It can be shown that during the early stages of an epidemic, the ratio of cases in males (C_m) to females (C_f) is then given by

$$\frac{C_m}{C_f} = \sqrt{\frac{\beta_f c_f}{\beta_m c_m}} \tag{7.3}$$

(Anderson & May, 1991; May et al., 2001).

Splitting the population into groups according to their risk of transmission is a natural way to capture important heterogeneities in disease transmission. One of the most straightforward ways to capture heterogeneity in sexual contact is by grouping individuals according to their number of sexual partners and using a *mixing matrix* to determine how often individuals from group i mate with individuals from group j, p_{ij} (Gupta et al., 1989):

$$p = \begin{pmatrix} p_{11} & \cdots & p_{1n} \\ \vdots & \ddots & \vdots \\ p_{n1} & \cdots & p_{nn} \end{pmatrix}. \tag{7.4}$$

The transmission rate – a scalar quantity for homogeneous populations – is then given by the entrywise product of p and β, where β is an $n \times n$ matrix describing transmission rates per contact for each group by group pairing. If individuals mate randomly then the number of sexual contacts between individuals in groups with n_i and n_j sexual contacts is determined proportionately:

$$p_{ij} = \frac{n_i n_j}{\sum_k n_k N_k} \tag{7.5}$$

where N_k is the frequency of individuals in group k. If there are two types of individual in a randomly mixing population where a proportion ρ of individuals have n_1 sexual partners and the remainder have n_2 sexual partners, then the mixing matrix is

$$p = \frac{1}{n_1\rho + n_2(1-\rho)} \begin{pmatrix} n_1^2 & n_1 n_2 \\ n_1 n_2 & n_2^2 \end{pmatrix}. \tag{7.6}$$

For example, if 10% of individuals have 10 sexual partners and the remaining 90% have one sexual partner, then

$$p = \frac{10}{19} \begin{pmatrix} 100 & 10 \\ 10 & 1 \end{pmatrix}. \tag{7.7}$$

In this example the mean number of sexual partners is $m = 1.9$ and the variance is $\sigma^2 = 8.1$, giving a coefficient of variation of $V \approx 1.5$. Accounting for heterogeneity in sexual contact number therefore more than triples R_0 (since $1 + V^2 = 3.25$) compared to a homogeneous population with the same mean number of contacts.

Mixing matrices can also be used to capture preferential (non-random) contact patterns when individuals tend to mate more frequently with certain members of the population. If mating occurs more frequently between similar individuals then mixing is *assortative* and conversely is *disassortative* when most mating is between dissimilar individuals. Assortative and disassortative mating can apply in the context of both physiological and behavioural traits, with individuals mating more (or less) frequently with others that are of similar size, colouration, choosiness, social rank, health, or other trait. When the population consists of two groups, as in the example above, we can capture preferential mating by adjusting the mixing matrix to be

$$p = \begin{pmatrix} \delta n_1^2 & (1-\delta)n_1 n_2 \\ \frac{(1-\delta)n_1^2 N_1}{N_2} & n_2^2 - \frac{(1-\delta)n_1 n_2 N_1}{N_2} \end{pmatrix} \tag{7.8}$$

where $n_1 \geq n_2$ and $0 \leq \delta \leq 1$ controls the extent to which mating occurs between individuals within the same group. When $\delta \approx 1$ mating is highly assortative (mating primarily occurs within groups) and when $\delta \approx 0$ mating is highly disassortative (mating primarily occurs between groups, where possible). More generally, we can measure the degree of assortativity, Q (Gupta et al., 1989), in a population with g activity or risk groups as

$$Q = \frac{1}{g-1}\left(\sum_{i=1}^{g} \lambda_i - 1\right) \tag{7.9}$$

where λ_i are the eigenvalues of the normalised mixing matrix defined by

$$\hat{p}_{ij} = \frac{N_i p_{ij}}{\sum_{k=1}^{g} N_i p_{ik}}. \qquad\qquad (7.10)$$

This matrix gives the proportion (rather than total number) of sexual contacts for individuals in group i that occur with individuals from group j. The degree of assortativity is 0 for random mating, tends towards 1 as mating within groups becomes more frequent (i.e. as p becomes dominated by terms on the main diagonal), and tends towards $-1/(g-1)$ as mixing becomes more disassortative. Assortative mating concentrates early disease spread among high-risk individuals, leading to faster initial growth compared to random or disassortative mating and, for highly assortative mating, successive waves as the epidemic passes from group to group (Figure B7.1.2).

Splitting the population into classes according to sexual activity can capture important heterogeneity in the risk of infection for different groups, but the dynamics are still based on a *mean-field approximation* whereby all individual interactions are replaced with an average interaction over each group. A more realistic approach is to construct a *sexual contact network* to capture precisely who mates with whom at an individual level. A sexual contact network consists of *nodes* (individuals) and *edges* or *links* between nodes, which represent sexual contact (and potential routes of transmission) between individuals. This approach is especially advantageous when sexual contacts are relatively stable (e.g. serial monogamy) or when individuals only mate with a small subset of the population. This approach is comparable to placing OID dynamics on a social network framework (e.g. Rushmore et al., 2013, 2014).

Crucially, the epidemiological and evolutionary dynamics of STIs on one network can be very different to the dynamics on another or as predicted by mean-field models. This difference is because networks produce local correlations in the spread of disease (i.e. if an individual is infected, his or her sexual partners are more likely to be infected than a randomly chosen individual). Understanding disease spread in the context of sexual contact networks can therefore provide important insights into the epidemiology and evolution of STIs. For example, the risk of disease extinction during the early stages of an epidemic is generally lower in network-based models, and disease spread tends to be much slower in spatially structured networks than in random networks (Keeling, 2005). However, while sexual contact networks have the advantage of introducing greater realism by allowing one to model disease spread at the level of individual interactions, the system is usually much more complex to analyse than group-based approaches. Obtaining accurate parameter estimates, and model overfitting are also potential issues with these more refined models; in addition, strong sexual network data are only available for a limited number of systems.

7.2.2 Network approximations

Network-based models can be analysed using agent-based simulations, where disease spreads stochastically between connected individuals. However, agent-based simulations can be numerically intensive and so deterministic approaches have been developed that attempt to capture network structure while retaining analytic tractability or improving computational efficiency. One such method is *pair approximation*, which focuses not on the number of individuals in each state, but rather the number of individuals in one state who are connected to individuals in another state (Keeling, 1999; Eames & Keeling, 2002). Hence, rather than track the number of susceptible (*S*) and infectious (*I*) individuals separately, the aim is to track sexual contacts between pairs of susceptible and infectious individuals, [*SI*], along with all other combinations. The major advantage of this method is that it captures local correlations in infection that are neglected in traditional *mean-field approaches* (as in Box 7.1). Ignoring births and deaths, a pair approximation of the single-class mean-field *SIS* model from Box 7.1 is

$$\frac{d[SS]}{dt} = -\beta[SSI] + \nu[SI] \tag{7.11}$$

$$\frac{d[SI]}{dt} = \beta([SSI] - [SI] - [ISI]) + \nu([II] - [SI]) \tag{7.12}$$

$$\frac{d[II]}{dt} = \beta([SI] + [ISI]) - \nu[II]. \tag{7.13}$$

Note that the dynamics of each pair depends on higher-order correlations (triples) in the network (e.g. how many [*SS*] pairs are connected to an infectious individual, [*SSI*]). In turn, the dynamics of the triples depend on even higher-order correlations (e.g. [*SSSI*]), and so on. The system can be closed by approximating the number of triples of a given type by the number of pairs within each triple. Specifically, in a network where each individual has n sexual contacts, the triple [*ABC*] can be approximated by

$$[ABC] \approx \left(\frac{n-1}{n}\right) \frac{[AB][BC]}{B} \left(1 - \phi + \frac{\phi N}{n} \frac{[AC]}{AC}\right) \tag{7.14}$$

where ϕ is the ratio between triangles (the special case when A, B, and C are all connected to each other) and triples (Keeling, 1999). If all sexual contact is between individuals of opposite sexes, then $\phi = 0$ and the triple approximation reduces to

$$[ABC] \approx \left(\frac{n-1}{n}\right) \frac{[AB][BC]}{B}. \tag{7.15}$$

These approximations can also be extended to capture variation in the number of sexual contacts between individuals in the population (Eames & Keeling, 2002).

Deterministic pair approximations generally match the epidemiological and evolutionary dynamics of stochastic agent-based simulations despite a considerable reduction in the complexity of the system (Keeling, 1999; Eames & Keeling, 2002). The reduction in complexity facilitates rapid simulation of the dynamics, along with the derivation of robust analytic predictions for epidemic thresholds and the strength of selection in different sexual contact networks, and improved parameter estimation from observational data. Pair approximations therefore represent a powerful method for studying host–STI interactions.

7.2.3 Summary of STI theory

The epidemiology of STIs is fundamentally different to other infectious diseases. Early theory of STI dynamics – primarily driven by interest in human STIs but equally applicable to wildlife diseases – revealed that heterogeneity in sexual contact plays a crucial role in disease spread. Heterogeneity can occur for many reasons, including variation in mating success (e.g. through dominance hierarchies) and non-random mating patterns (e.g. assortative/disassortative mating, inbreeding avoidance). The simplest way to model heterogeneity is to split the population into risk groups and use a mixing matrix to capture interactions between individuals in each group. A more realistic (but computationally intensive) approach is to use a sexual contact network to stochastically simulate disease spread at an individual level. Deterministic pair approximations of sexual contact networks offer many advantages, as they capture local correlations that arise during epidemics while being computationally efficient and analytically tractable.

The theory related above presumes sexual transmission as the only epidemiologically significant form of transmission. As noted previously, sexual transmission can combine with vertical transmission (density-independent, but seeding the next cohort with infection) or social transmission (potentially density-dependent). These have been approached both in terms of general frameworks (e.g. sexual vs. social transmission: Ryder et al., 2007) and also specific case studies (e.g. sexual and vertical transmission of *Chlamydia* in koala: Augustine, 1998). These analyses predict that the risk of parasite-driven extinction may be reduced with increasing importance of social transmission, and that vertical transmission aids persistence and spread of infections that also have sexual transmission.

7.3 Reconciling theory to STI epidemiology in natural populations

Despite the presence of STIs in many sexual species, the vast majority of detailed longitudinal studies of STI dynamics derive from contemporary human populations, rather than wildlife. Detailed accounts of STI epidemiology with targeted longitudinal sampling are available for the ladybird–*Coccipolipus* mite system (Webberley et al., 2006a; Ryder et al., 2014), for the eucalypt beetle–*Parobia* interaction (Seeman & Nahrung, 2004; Nahrung & Clarke, 2007) (see Box 7.2), and the anther-smut–*Silene* interaction (see Chapter 6).

We use these (and selected other case studies) to examine the degree to which predictions from theory are observed in natural populations, and extend this to determine if current theory needs enriching. We ask the following questions.

(1) Does promiscuity lead to high prevalence of STIs as predicted by theory? Here we examine evidence from studies of STI dynamics in nature, and argue the core expected link is present, both from longitudinal studies in invertebrates and from comparisons of the prevalence of infection in promiscuous versus non-promiscuous individuals in birds.

(2) Do all promiscuous species have STIs, or are there other barriers to STI transmission? We argue that promiscuity is not sufficient for STI maintenance, and that heterogeneities in mating contact – particularly seasonality – may place a hard barrier on STI persistence generally not considered in human-focused models.

(3) Does variation in mating system and patterns of sexual selection affect STI epidemiology in the manner predicted by theory? We particularly examine whether patterns of sex-biased prevalence – predicted where males have higher variance in mating rate than females – are observed in nature.

(4) Are there host sex biases in transmission in STIs of wildlife? As noted in Section 7.2.1, sex biases in prevalence may additionally be created by differences in the likelihood of male to female versus female to male transmission. We examine the patterns of transmission for STIs in wildlife.

(5) Are there host behaviours that reduce the risk of infection and would therefore alter STI dynamics in natural populations? The models outlined above presume mating systems and behaviours are static. However, STIs are costly, and thus there may be selection on the host to avoid infection, and in some circumstances, transmitting infection onward. We ask if there is evidence for host evolution to avoid acquiring an STI that would then interrupt transmission.

(6) What factors prevent STIs driving their host extinct? Frequency-dependent transmission makes STIs liable to increase to very high prevalence that might damage populations, but nevertheless STIs do persist in natural

---

Box 7.2 Podapolipid mite–beetle interactions as a model system for STI dynamics

The Podapolipidae are a family of mites that have adapted to an obligate haematophagous lifestyle on arthropods. The adult stage is sessile and blood feeding, with female mites producing eggs on the host which then hatch into larvae (Figure 7.4). These larvae are a non-feeding dispersal stage. Because the dispersal stage is non-feeding and can survive for less than a day away from the host, these parasites have commonly become adapted to transmission following direct host–host contact. In many cases, they have become specialised to transmission during sexual contact, and are STIs. In the two best described systems – *Coccipolipus* on coccinellid (ladybird) beetles, and *Parobia* on eucalypt (chrysomelid) beetles – the larval mites accumulate at the tip of the elytra. Here they remain until the host mates, and then they move to the other host individual during copulation.

The primary driver making these a model system for STI dynamics is the ease of scoring infection. Beetles can be taken from the field, placed upside down by gentle force against Blu-Tak, and the underside of their elytra revealed by gently pushing away from the body with an entomological pin. Having revealed the underside of the elyta, mite presence/absence and stage/intensity of infection can be scored easily. The beetle host can then be returned to the field unharmed. This ease of access and ability to score infection without invasive procedures makes these systems an extraordinarily rich source of epidemiological information. Regular sampling through the season can establish the dynamics of infection. Further to this, host sex and, in seasonal climates, host cohort can be easily scored at the same time as mite infection, such that any sex biases in prevalence can easily be noted. In addition to being able to document the dynamics of infection, the systems also lend themselves to measurement of transmission producing contacts. Many beetles, and most ladybirds, have long copulations, such that mating rate – the primary transmission route – can be estimated in the field with reasonable accuracy.

The accessibility of the systems to field observation is mirrored in the systems being good 'lab rats'. Laboratory study can be used to estimate specific aspects of infection and transmission biology accurately and under a range of scenarios. For instance, the per mating transmission rate, latent period of infection and incubation period can be measured accurately and non-invasively under a variety of environmental and social environments. Further, laboratory populations may be maintained under a variety of conditions and with good replication, which allows testing of specific

Box 7.2 (cont.)

epidemiological hypotheses – for instance, that transmission rate is independent of density (a classic STI prediction).

Finally, the impact of infection on the host can be measured easily in the laboratory environment. Importantly, the main 'general' demographic impact of STIs – induction of host sterility – is observed in *Coccipolipus*–ladybird interactions. Female hosts become sterile within 10 days of infection in the laboratory, and field-caught females carrying adult mites are also sterile. Impacts on male hosts are less profound, but include raised overwinter mortality.

The systems thus allow a beautiful marriage of detailed data from field dynamics, laboratory estimation of transmission parameters and replicated experimental test of hypotheses at a population level. These then allow the development of finely tuned models that allow the impact of variation in conditions to be explored in detail, and then tested in the laboratory. The one limitation of these study systems is that contact and social structure are much less heterogeneous than observed in vertebrates. Ladybirds are promiscuous – which is important for STI maintenance – but do not show any partner fidelity or social bonds, dominance hierarchies or other complex contact structures found in mammals. Eucalypt beetles, for instance, show simple scramble competition based on encounters of males with females, followed by acceptance/rejection of mating by the female, and this pattern also represents ladybird mating systems. Altogether, reproductive skew is much lower in these insect systems than found in mammal and bird systems, such that a major aspect of STI dynamics cannot be easily investigated.

A last benefit of the system is that ladybirds in particular are both charismatic and a well-appreciated species, such that the systems also allow many opportunities for wider dissemination of broadly relevant epidemiological findings. The juxtaposition of a beetle named after the Virgin Mary and a species with high promiscuity and carrying highly prevalence STIs is also rather amusing.

populations, and show repeatable patterns (stable dynamics). What are the factors stabilising these interactions?

(7) What is the importance of non-sexual transmission for wildlife STIs? Most STI models for animals are based on sexual transmission alone. However, mixed modes of transmission are common for many infections. We examine whether this elaboration is needed for wildlife STIs.

(8) Is a single host–single infection model sufficient for understanding the dynamics of wildlife STIs? Studies of many wildlife infections have led to the conclusion that the dynamics of any particular infection cannot be understood in isolation for other circulating diseases (Ezenwa et al., 2010; Telfer et al., 2010). Other circulating infections may affect host demography, affecting transmission, and/or alter immune function, altering infection outcome. We examine whether a community infection framework is needed for STIs in wildlife.

7.3.1 Does promiscuity lead to high prevalence of STIs as predicted by theory?

The *Adalia*–mite and eucalypt beetle–mite interactions both show profound, repeated seasonal epidemics. For *Adalia* in the northern hemisphere, adult beetles emerge from diapause in spring. Early summer reproduction in May and June is associated with epidemics of the mite in which nearly all of the overwintered adult individuals become infected in a six-week period (Figure 7.1) (Webberley et al., 2006a); similar seasonal epidemics are observed for *Parobia* mites on eucalypt beetles in the southern hemisphere, with prevalence rising to 80% of adult individuals infected by November/December (Seeman & Nahrung, 2004; Nahrung & Clarke, 2007). STI prevalence is only diluted on recruitment of the new generation of adult beetles.

A key prediction for an STI is that high mean mating rate is associated with more profound STI epidemics. This prediction has been validated in the *Adalia*/*Coccipolipus* mite interaction. In this system, microsatellite analysis of paternity reveals the host is highly promiscuous (Haddrill et al., 2008, 2013). Laboratory study further reveals host mating rate is in part determined by food supply, with females more willing to mate when well fed (Perry et al., 2009). Experimental study indicates food supply determines the rate of spread of the STI in microcosms (Ryder et al., 2013b). Significantly, observations of epidemics in natural populations indicate STI spread occurs much more slowly where ladybirds reside on trees with a low density of aphid food than on adjacent bushes with high aphid density. These local differences in food supply are reflected in profound differences in mating rate, with 18.3% of beetles sampled on the high food supply bushes being observed mating at any one point in time, compared to 1.3% of beetles on the neighbouring low food supply trees (Ryder et al., 2013). Comparative analysis across four host ladybird species also supports the prediction that high host mating rate results in larger STI epidemics (Webberley et al., 2004).

There is also evidence that increased mate diversity affects microbiota diversity in lizards and birds. Studies of female *Zootoca vivipara* common lizards revealed polyandrous females had more diverse cloacal bacterial assemblages, and that microbial diversity increases with female age, a further product of mate diversity (White et al., 2011). Likewise, in a study of four passerine bird species, likely sexually transmitted microbes (*Chlamydia*, *Candida*, *Salmonella*) were more commonly recorded in individuals from polyandrous and promiscuous species than in monogamous comparators (Poiani & Wilks, 2000). Thus, there is good evidence for an impact of mating partner diversity on microbiota, and also on particular infections that are likely to represent STIs.

7.3.2 Do all promiscuous species have STIs, or are there other barriers to STI transmission?

There are many promiscuous species for which there is no record of an STI. Lack of a record may, in some cases, simply reflect absence of focused study, and it is likely that there are many promiscuous species that have unrecorded STIs. Nevertheless, there are promiscuous species and populations where intense study of natural enemies has not led to any 'pure' STIs being identified. Social insects, for instance, have a notable paucity of records of infections that rely exclusively on sexual transmission (Schmid-Hempel, 1998), indicating that STIs are not ubiquitous in promiscuous species. Further, interpopulation variation in STI presence in natural populations exists in species that are promiscuous across their range. The *A. bipunctata*–*Coccipolipus* interaction, for instance, shows geographical variation in STI incidence, with some populations consistently free from the STI (Webberley et al., 2006b). Individuals in populations without the STI are not less promiscuous than individuals from STI present populations (Jones et al., 2015). Thus, promiscuity is not sufficient for STI maintenance.

Understanding patterns of presence/absence within a species provides insight into the factors determining the presence/absence of STIs in promiscuous species more widely. In European *A. bipunctata*, the sexually transmitted mite is absent from northern and western populations. This is best documented in Sweden, where patterns of presence/absence have been consistent over a 10-year period, with presence in lowland southern populations, but absence in southern populations at altitude and in the north of the country (Webberley et al., 2006b; Pastok et al., 2016). The presence/absence divide is associated with presence/absence of reproductive contact between the generations. In the far north, the overwintered cohort starts reproducing later in the year, and dies off earlier, such that the new cohort of adult beetles emerges after the death of the parental generation, preventing infection transfer (Pastok et al., 2016) (Figure 7.2). Seeman and Narung (2004) and Knell and Webberley (2004) both note STIs in temperate regions will be restricted to host species that diapause as adults unless alternate transmission routes exist. Pastok et al. (2016) extended this to suggest that within species that diapause as adults,

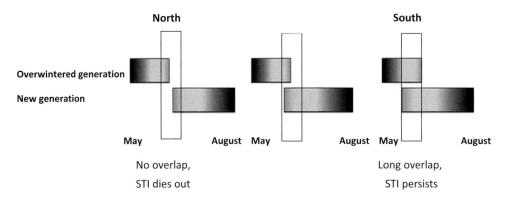

Figure 7.2 Pictorial representation of the phenology of *A. bipunctata* in Sweden. For each location (left, north > 61°N, centre boundary 61–59°N, right south < 59°N), the presence of mature adult *A. bipunctata* is given through a season, with the overwintered generation presented on the top bar, and the adult progeny of the next cohort below. Dark shading represents larger population size.

STIs will occur more commonly further from the poles, as this creates the context for intercohort transmission. Conceptually, cohort separation is an extreme form of temporal heterogeneity in contact, in which infected and uninfected classes do not mix at one time of year, leading to loss of infection.

The impact of seasonal breeding has not been examined in other taxa. Morand (1993) notes the importance of iteroparity in the maintenance of sexually transmitted nematodes in snails. Elsewhere, there has been little consideration of the impact of short, defined breeding seasons on STI dynamics in long-lived vertebrates. We would conjecture that brief mating seasons may interfere with STI maintenance if there is a latent period which would limit transmission within a breeding season, and interseason transmission would require the infection to be long-lived. This pattern of mating may represent a barrier for an infection evolving sexual transmission.

7.3.3 Do mating system and patterns of sexual selection affect STI epidemiology in the manner predicted by theory?

Theory, as discussed above, has focused on the impact of variance in the mating rate on STI dynamics, with the sex with greater variance in reproductive success predicted to have lower prevalence of infection. Raised prevalence in female hosts compared to male was noted for SIV and STLV infection in primates, likely associated with high variance in reproductive success of males compared to females (Nunn & Altizer, 2004). However, comparative analysis across primate/STI interactions more widely did not support the presence of sex-biased prevalence of STI (Nunn et al., 2014). More consistently, higher prevalence of STI *Parobia* mites on female (compared to male) eucalypt beetles was observed in three field seasons (Seeman & Nahrung, 2004; Nahrung & Clarke, 2007). This species has a mating system described as scramble competition whereby males actively search, with varying success, for females. This increased variation in male mating success is associated with a reduced prevalence of mites on male hosts (Nahrung & Clarke, 2007).

While there has been little defined epidemiological study in birds, the core requirement for 'super spreader' males is supported. In an intraspecific study, male rufous-collared sparrows *Zonotrichia capensis* with high testosterone titre (which typically mate more frequently than low-testosterone individuals) carry a higher microbial diversity in their cloaca, and in particular a higher prevalence of *Chlamydia*, probably a sexually transmitted pathogen (Escallón et al., 2017). Thus, these males will disproportionately drive *Chlamydia* R_0, and prevalence of *Chlamydia* is expected to be biased towards females as a result. These results for STIs contrast with the pattern for other infectiously transmitted agents in largely polygynous mammals, where male hosts are more commonly infected, associated with reduced immune activity (Moore & Wilson, 2002).

7.3.4 Are there sex biases in transmission of STIs in wildlife?

Differences in the efficacy of male to female versus female to male transmission of STIs represent important additional drivers of sex biases in prevalence, and also modulators of STI epidemiology more widely. Sex biases in STI transmission have been tested for experimentally in the ectoparasite STI/insect interactions, and not observed: male host to female transmission rates are similar to those observed from female host to male (e.g. Nahrung & Clarke, 2007; Ryder et al., 2014). This is not perhaps surprising given that in these cases, the parasite moves itself (rather than being passively transmitted), and commonly infects the same tissues in males and females (wing cases).

In contrast, the study of birds does reveal asymmetry in transmission rate. Experimental infection of zebra finch with *Bacillus licheniformis* PWD1 revealed transmission from male host to female host was over four times more efficient than female host to male (Kulkarni & Heeb, 2007). It is likely that the combination of differences in infection sites between the sexes, and the passive transmission of the microbes (compared to the active movement of ectoparasites) will commonly create asymmetries in transmission risk for microbial STIs, with male to female passage, along with flow of ejaculate, being commonly more efficient than female to male.

7.3.5 Are there host behaviours that reduce the risk of infection and would therefore alter STI dynamics?

Carrying an STI is commonly harmful, and thus the presence of an STI may select on the host for behaviours that prevent infection. Avoidance may occur directly through mate choice or post-copulatory grooming behaviour, or indirectly through selection for reduced mating rate. These behaviours would then impact on STI transmission and dynamics.

The most obvious route to reduce the risk of infection is to choose uninfected mates (Hamilton, 1990; Loehle, 1995). However, studies across several STI systems have failed to find any evidence that hosts are able to discriminate between infected and uninfected individuals (Abbot & Dill, 2001; Webberley et al., 2002; Nahrung & Allen, 2004). Further, the hypothesis that pre-copulatory genital inspection rituals in primates are driven by the benefit of STI avoidance was not upheld, with these behaviours occurring equally in promiscuous and non-promiscuous species (Nunn, 2003).

The failure to find evidence for mate choice against infected individuals may in part be due to the strong selection pressure on STIs to be cryptic. If an STI causes detectable damage to their hosts, and hosts are able to discriminate between uninfected and infected individuals, then it would be unlikely that the STI will persist in the system. To allow persistence, STIs should therefore evolve to be undetectable, particularly if they exist in a mating system with strong female choice (Knell, 1999). In the eucalypt beetle, no detectable impact of infection with the sexually transmitted mite upon host longevity, fecundity, or fertility was observed (Nahrung & Clarke, 2007), supporting the idea that STIs are under strong selection to be cryptic through low virulence (Knell, 1999). For the ladybird STI, viability impacts are typically detected only under stress, such as during diapause (Webberley & Hurst, 2002). Strong selection for undetectable, low-virulence STIs will in turn reduce the benefit of mate choice among hosts, which is predicted to lead to a reduction in mate choice and a potential resurgence in STI virulence (Ashby & Boots, 2015).

A second avenue for selection is on host mating rate. This has been considered originally as driving mating system evolution in wildlife (Kokko et al., 2002), with the theory applied more recently to the evolution of human social systems (Bauch & McElreath, 2016). Theoretical models more subtly indicate that promiscuity can persist in a system in the presence of an STI if there is any fitness benefit to multiple mating (Boots & Knell, 2002). As the proportion of individuals who mate less often increases, the prevalence of the STI will decrease, allowing individuals who mate more often to 'take advantage' of risky behaviour. Rather than selecting for a reduced mating rate in all individuals, therefore, the presence of an STI may instead lead to the coexistence of high and low mating rate strategies within a population. The impact of STI presence on the evolution of mating rate has to date been examined only in the ladybird–*Coccipolipus* mite system. Here, no evidence was found to suggest that individuals in populations with high STI presence have reduced mating rate compared to non-STI present comparators (Jones et al., 2015). However, this study was not broad enough to exclude the evolution of the predicted risky/low-risk polymorphism in the presence of the STI.

The theory regarding mating rate and STIs that exists currently does not include male- and female-specific fitness effects. For instance, many STIs have stronger sterilising influence on female than male hosts. In contrast, each extra mating may have greater positive impact on male fitness than female (the Bateman gradient: Bateman, 1948). Thus, mating rate in the presence of an STI may be subject to intense sexual conflict, with strong selection on females to reduce mating but no selection on males. The outcome of selection thus depends on which sex has power in determining mating rate.

The above treatment emphasises the avoidance of contacts as a means of preventing infection. Alternate adaptations to prevent STI acquisition may arise from post-copulatory 'flushing out' behaviours in males. For instance, post-copulatory grooming and urination may be adaptations to prevent acquisition of an STI (Hart et al., 1987). Waterman (2010) views the intense post-copulatory masturbation observed in male Cape ground squirrels in the same frame. While the presence of an STI has not been established in this system, the promiscuity of individuals during oestrous (a female will have up to 10 partners in three days) and the timing of masturbation *after* copulation led to STI avoidance being proposed as the most parsimonious explanation for the data.

Finally, there may additionally be adaptations to avoid transmitting infection to the partner. Ejaculates commonly possess antimicrobial activity (Samakovlis et al., 1991; Otti et al., 2013), and this can act to prevent pathogen transmission. For instance, *Nosema apis* can be transmitted from male to female honey bees (*Apis mellifera*) during copulation, with this sexual transmission complementing other transmission routes. The presence of *N. apis* induces an immune response in seminal fluid that kills *N. apis* spores or makes them sporulate prematurely, and thus reduces transmission (Peng et al., 2016; Grassl et al., 2017). In the case of bees and *N. apis*, there are good reasons to believe the responses are an adaptation to prevent onward STI transmission. However, in other cases antimicrobial properties of seminal fluid may simply be an adaptation to preserve sperm and ejaculates that also (as a by-product) prevents or reduces STI transmission.

The above account views host adaptation on mating biology to reduce the chance of STI acquisition. However, the STI is of course selected to increase host mating rate. As noted earlier, the sterilising effect of STIs in species with pregnancy is considered as one means of achieving this, preventing the mating cessation usually associated with pregnancy and lactation. More widely, it is thought that sexually transmitted viruses in crickets may actively increase male desire to mate (Adamo et al., 2014). Thus, the expectation from theory based on host adaptation may be subject to countervailing selection on the parasite.

7.3.6 What factors stabilise STI–host dynamics?

The regulatory role of host density in the dynamics of other infectious diseases has been long recognised. When transmission is density-dependent, any infection that reduces host population size reduces its own transmission, providing a limit to the impact of the infection on the host population, and tending to stabilise infection prevalence around an endemic equilibrium. Density-dependent regulator processes are commonly considered to be less likely for STIs, as the contact relevant to transmission (mating) may be relatively insensitive to host density (see Section 7.2). Thus, STIs that sterilise or are virulent may maintain high transmission rates even if they drive the host population to low density, potentially causing local or even global host extinction. In contrast, stabilisation would be provided either by density dependence of transmission, or heterogeneities in contact which protect a subset of individuals, or limits to demographic losses.

Declines in mating rate with density are the most commonly considered mechanisms to stabilise STI–host dynamics. The biological drivers of mating rate are a topic of intense research in the field of behavioural ecology, and have also attracted attention from conservation biologists interested in whether failure to find mates leads to Allee effects. From these two schools, it has now been recognised that mating rate is in part a property of host density (Kokko & Rankin, 2006; Gascoigne et al., 2009; Fauvergue, 2013). While the relationship between density and mating rate will vary between species, it is likely that very low density is accompanied by reduced mating rates in all species, as mate search capacity limits mating rate. Indeed, STI transmission in ladybirds in microcosms was observed to be density-dependent across the range of encounter rates tested (Ryder et al., 2005), which would be strongly stabilising.

It is also the case that mating rate is likely to saturate as density increases: females of most species will refuse mating opportunities when these become common (although occasionally the reverse occurs, and mating rate increases to avoid harassment, e.g. Rowe, 1992). Thus, the characterisation of STI transmission as purely frequency-dependent is rarely likely to be accurate – biologically, it is likely to transition from being density-dependent at low host densities to frequency-dependent at high density. This more complex relationship would provide weaker regulation than pure density-dependent transmission but wider conditions for maintenance of virulent/sterilising STIs than pure frequency dependence (Figure 7.3). Clearly, focused study of the density

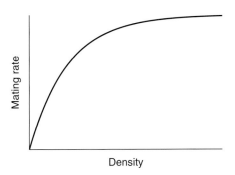

Figure 7.3 Potential dependence of mating rate on density in insects under scramble competition. At low density, mating rate is limited by individuals failing to find each other, whereas at high density encounters become saturated through female reluctance to mate above a certain rate. The point at which this transition occurs is expected to be related to both the biology of mate finding and of female willingness to re-mate. For instance, use of pheromones or other cues for mate location will reduce the effect of low density on mating rate, and selection on females for reluctance to mate/male use of anti-aphrodisiacs to prevent female re-mating will cause mating rate to plateau at lower density.

dependence of mating rate and transmission in field populations is needed if we wish better to understand STI dynamics.

While less studied, limits to demographic loss associated with an STI (combined with the presence of other, stronger density-dependent factors influencing survival) may commonly be key to stabilising dynamics in natural populations. Not all STIs have profound impacts on survival and fertility: Morand (1993) concluded that the low impact of the sexually transmitted nematode *Nemhelix bakeri* on individual *Helix aspersa* snail host survival and fertility was key in permitting stable maintenance of the STI/host interaction. Furthermore, the study considers that morbidity/mortality losses can be compensated for by declines in the intensity of other causes of morbidity/mortality.

A limited impact of infection is also seen in the koala–*Chlamydia* system. In this interaction the severity of disease symptoms, and thus the impact of infection on the host, depends on environmental conditions. Although the full extent of disease caused by the infection has not yet been fully investigated, it is known to be responsible for keratoconjunctivitis (Cockram & Jackson, 1974), urinary tract disease (Brown & Grice, 1984) and genital tract infection (Brown & Grice, 1984), the latter of which is associated with infertility and reproductive decline in koala populations (McColl et al., 1984). Although high infection prevalences have been reported, outward clinical signs of the disease are usually low. In a population of free-ranging koalas in south-eastern Queensland, 46 of 65 (71%) koalas were infected with *Chlamydia*, yet only six (13%) of these showed clinical signs of the disease (Weigler et al., 1988). These observations suggest that additional stress factors appear to be responsible for clinical signs of chlamydial infection. This inference is further supported by a study investigating the effect of climate change on koala populations in north-west New South Wales, which found clinical chlamydio-sis to increase over a two-year period following stressful periods of drought and extreme hot temperatures (Lunney et al., 2012). With increased *Chlamydia*-induced mortality, this would ultimately result in a loss of *Chlamydia* from the population. However, the dynamic is stable when infections are asymptomatic or only weakly deleterious.

Limits to demographic loss are also likely to be important in maintaining the *Adalia–Coccipolipus* interaction. Here, the impact of the STI on the infected individual is strong – mite infection sterilises female hosts within 10 days. The STI also reaches very high prevalence, with nearly all ladybirds collected in June being infected with the mite. Thus, the system fulfils the two conditions for an STI to drive host extinction. Nevertheless, the host–parasite dynamic is stable. Each year is characterised by a seasonal epidemic (Figure 7.1), which takes the mite from 10% to 20% frequency at the start of the season to infect nearly all adult beetles by mid-June. The ladybird population remains viable despite these recurrent epidemics. The epidemic's impact on host population size is limited because the majority of oviposition occurs early in the repro-ductive season before the mite epidemic reaches high frequency and impacts on host fertility. Indeed, eggs laid late in the season are heavily predated and cannibalised by earlier hatching individuals. Density-dependent mortality of eggs and larvae laid late in the season may remove any net demographic impact of the mite.

The host ladybird population thus remains viable because prevalence is low on emergence from overwintering. The question that follows is what factors make prevalence low at the start of the spring/summer mating season? The answer here lies in the phenology of the ladybird host, which produces heterogeneity in contact (Pastok et al., 2016). The ladybird eggs laid in May/June take around 30 days to develop into adults, and these adults take a further minimum 10 days to be reproductively active (Figure 7.4). The emergence of the new cohort of hosts occurs at a time when the previous cohort (by now nearly all infected with the mite) is dying out, and is associated with a massive decline in mite prevalence. The force of infection drops as only sporadic mating occurs between rare old cohort beetles and the large new cohort. Thus, the mite frequency is predictably reduced to low prevalence in the pre-diapause period, during which mating rate is also very low and emergence of uninfected adults is maintained. In addition to the drop in prevalence associated with recruitment, the mite increases overwinter (diapause) mortal-ity of the host (Webberley & Hurst, 2002), further reducing prevalence on

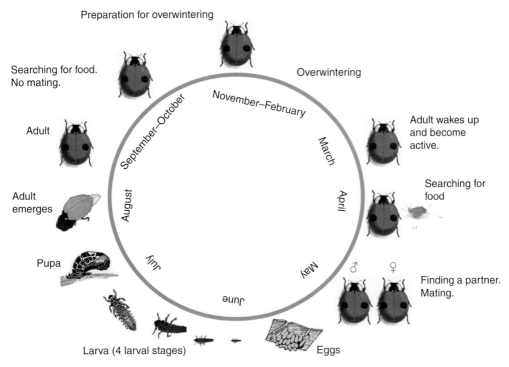

Figure 7.4 The *A. bipunctata* annual cycle in northern temperature regions, as typified in Stockholm, Sweden. Timings are approximate and vary between years, with new generation ladybirds emerging in July–August. Created by Dr D Pastok, with permission. (A black and white version of this figure will appear in some formats. For the colour version, please refer to the plate section.)

emergence from overwintering. Thus, dynamical stability is created by the importance of early reproduction for ladybird population size (limits to demographic loss) and the limited capacity for the overwintered cohort to infect the subsequent generation with the mite, reducing parasite prevalence at the point of entry into the crucial spring reproductive season (mating contact heterogeneity).

7.3.7 What is the importance of non-sexual transmission for wildlife STIs?

Longitudinal studies of STI dynamics in natural populations have focused on STIs where sexual transmission is necessary and sufficient for maintenance. A variety of infections combine vertical and sexual transmission. This is likely to be particularly common for microbial infections in viviparous species, as infection of the genital tract (common for STIs) is associated with transmission during birth as well as copulation.

The best studied of these are *Chlamydia* that infect koala. In addition to sexual transmission, chlamydiae can also be transmitted from mother to joey, either during birth or through pap feeding while still in the mother's pouch. A study on the *Chlamydia* infections of a free-range koala population in Mutdapilly, Queensland found 58% of sexually immature koalas to be infected with *C. pecorum* (Jackson et al., 1999). This study demonstrates the significance of mother to joey transmission in natural populations and highlights the importance of it in the dynamics of the *Chlamydia*–koala system. The combined dynamics of frequency-dependent sexual and vertical transmission will ultimately increase infection prevalence within a population, and explains why such high infection prevalence has been observed in wild populations (McColl et al., 1984; Mitchell et al., 1988; Weigler et al., 1988; White & Timms, 1994). Indeed, stochastic population modelling of the *Chlamydia*–koala system predicted that eliminating vertical transmission would reduce prevalence by up to 34.6%, demonstrating its importance in the system (Augustine, 1998).

In contrast to many other STIs, seasonality is less significant for the persistence of chlamydial infection in the koala. As vertical transmission represents such a major transmission route, the infection does not require sexual contact between cohorts. In each new generation, a certain percentage of new individuals will be infected directly from their mothers, and mating between these and other non-infected individuals is required for the continued spread of the infection throughout the newly emerged population. This can be contrasted with the mite/beetle case studies above where mating between the two generations is required for the disease to persist and spread throughout the population (Seeman & Nahrung, 2004).

Many viral infections of insects combine sexual and vector transmission, through either mammalian or plant hosts (see Knell & Webberley, 2004). Both these transmission processes commonly show strong elements of frequency-dependent transmission, such that infection is expected to reach high prevalence. Both transmission routes also select for infections to be relatively benign in their insect host, as transmission requires the host to find individuals with which to mate and on which to feed. Thus, selection favours infections that have very low mortality/vitality burdens, which stabilises dynamics.

7.3.8 Is a single host–single infection model sufficient for understanding the dynamics of wildlife STIs?

The presence of other circulating infections may alter STI dynamics through either altering transmission rate or infection outcome. Both of these may occur at a within-individual level, where the presence of one infection alters the chance of acquiring a second, or of the outcome of infection. There may also be effects at the population level, where the demographic effect of one infection changes contact patterns or host condition that then impact on transmission and infection outcome. For a particular STI, it is of course relevant to discuss their interaction with other co-circulating STIs, but it is also more widely relevant to account for interaction with other infections.

The co-occurrence of STIs in humans is more common than expected by chance. In part, this is a result of multiple infections being acquired by individuals with high-risk behaviour, leading to clustering of infection. However, the effect may be exacerbated by the presence of one STI increasing the per-contact likelihood of both transmitting a second one onward, or of acquiring a second infection, for instance through lesions facilitating invasion (Cohen, 1998). In either case, the dynamics of the infections become linked, as mortality/sterility effects are compounded in the former case, and transmission enhanced in the latter case.

A variety of wildlife species carry more than one STI, and of course coinfections occur (e.g. Riddick, 2010). There is also evidence from wildlife systems for co-occurrence of infection in excess of that expected from chance. For instance, in koalas, *Chlamydia* infection is strongly associated with the presence of herpesvirus infections, with *Chlamydia*-infected individuals 60 times more likely to carry herpesvirus than *Chlamydia*-uninfected conspecifics (Stalder et al., 2015). The cause(s) of this association are, however, unclear: potentially one or more of joint exposure, increased transmission, or increased susceptibility.

In contrast to this, there are also some cases where one sexually transmitted infection inhibits the action of another. GB virus C is sexually transmitted in humans, and inhibits both HIV virulence and HIV vertical transmission (Xiang et al., 2001). It has, indeed, been hypothesised that extra-pair copulation in birds may be driven by selection to acquire 'good bacteria' to prevent infection with bad (Lombardo et al., 1999). Tree swallow ejaculates, for instance, can carry both lactobacilli (probably beneficial) and *Salmonella* or *E. coli* (probably harmful). This type of thinking has led to promiscuity being hypothesised to be a mechanism by which females 'shop for' beneficial microbiota to prevent establishment of pathogens (Smith & Mueller, 2015). This hypothesis contrasts with the 'STIs drive lower mating rate' model described in Section 7.3.5.

There may also be interactions between STIs and infections transmitted without sexual contact. In humans, of course, the effects of HIV infection on host immune function potentiates the spread of other parasites and pathogens, and this reciprocally impacts upon the survival of HIV-positive people, and thus HIV transmission. However, the connections between STIs and other circulating parasites/pathogens in wildlife systems have not been well established in general.

One exception to this are studies of the impact of male-killing bacterial symbionts on STI epidemiology in ladybirds (Ryder et al., 2014). As well as STIs, female *A. bipunctata* ladybirds may also be infected with maternally inherited male-killing bacteria (*Wolbachia*, *Rickettsia*, or *Spiroplasma*) (Werren et al., 1994; Hurst et al., 1999a, 1999b). The frequency with which females are infected with male-killers varies between locations. In Torun, Poland, for instance, 5–10% of females carry a male-killing *Spiroplasma*, and the sex ratio of ladybirds on emergence as adults is close to one female per male. These data result in mean male mating rate being close to mean female mating rate. Compatible with this, the seasonal STI epidemic in Poland shows no heterogeneity by sex, with coincident epidemics of the STI on male and female beetles. In Stockholm, Sweden, by contrast, nearly 75% of female beetles carry a male-killer, such that populations have in excess of four female ladybirds per male. Thus, mean male mating rate is fourfold that of females, and male exposure to the STI is thus raised. This asymmetry is reflected in the observation that the spread of the mite on male ladybirds during the spring/summer epidemic is accelerated compared to that observed on female ladybirds. In this case study, the impact of the male-killing symbiont occurs exclusively through its influence on host demography and contact rates–symbiont infection does not change susceptibility (Ryder et al., 2014).

7.4 Conclusions and future directions

The exploration of STI epidemiology and evolutionary ecology is well developed in terms of predictive mathematical models. These studies direct us to particular aspects of wildlife mating systems that are likely to determine STI epidemiology in natural populations. The mean and variance in partner number, asymmetries in transmission between host sexes, and patterns of social contact are likely to be major drivers of STI dynamics. A weak dependence of mating rate on density has led to these infections commonly being considered as having unstable dynamics, such that virulent or sterilising STIs have the potential to produce host extinction. Evolutionary modelling predicts an impact on mating system evolution, including mate choice against infected individuals, and selection for reduced mating rate.

To date, the study of wildlife animal host/STI systems has been developed through a few model systems, notably the *A. bipunctata–Coccipolipus* mite association. Here, detailed longitudinal studies of STI dynamics have been completed alongside laboratory measurement of transmission parameters, testing of mate choices, and laboratory emulation of dynamics. While these studies confirm basic tenets of theory (promiscuity drives epidemics; sex ratio bias alters dynamics), they perhaps unsurprisingly point to many complexities not considered in models. The major heterogeneity that prevents STI takeover is phenology – ladybirds of one cohort becoming heavily infected, but then only transmitting infection on to the new cohort in a narrow window. Further, it is phenological variation (rather than variation in promiscuity or mating system) that explains spatial variation in STI incidence.

Study of these systems also challenges the assumptions and predictions of STI models. The assumption that sexual transmission is completely density-independent is not supported in this system, and it is likely that mating rate will show some degree of sensitivity to density in all species with the details of this relationship probably depending on the intricacy of the mating system. Further, there is no support in the ladybird/mite system for the predictions that STIs drive the evolution of mate choice or changes in promiscuity. The capacity for selection to drive changes in host mating biology may well depend on the degree to which infection differentially affects males and females, and the level of 'power' of each sex to determine the outcome of male–female encounters. This latter factor is widely variable between species, and it is possible that STIs predominate in species like ladybirds where female hosts are in general more affected by STIs and have weaker control of mating decisions.

Studies of ladybird STI interactions have thus provided a rich insight into the complexities of 'real-world' disease dynamics. The beetle–mite interactions represent STIs circulating in a species with scramble competition for mates. This pattern of mate acquisition is a very simple mating system. It is clear that directed study of mammalian and bird STIs is required, as here there are complex social contact and dispersal networks which are predicted to have a great influence over STI dynamics. To date, the study of mammalian and bird systems is in its infancy; with the exception of the koala–*Chlamydia* interaction, there is very little detailed study in the field, and commonly sexually transmitted infections are poorly characterised even in terms of transmission and impact on the host. Even for the koala system, the nature of the host species and infection means there are limited longitudinal data available. Detailed study of vertebrate systems is both scientifically and logistically challenging and important.

7.5 Acknowledgements

We wish to thank the NERC for funding (fellowship to BA, grant to GH and RK) and three reviewers for helpful and constructive feedback. We are grateful to Dr Daria Pastok for drawing Figure 7.4.

References

Abbot, P. & Dill, L.M. (2001) Sexually transmitted parasites and sexual selection in the milkweed leaf beetle, *Labidomera clivicollis*. *Oikos*, **92**, 91–100.

Adamo, S.A., Kovalko, I., Easy, R.H. & Stoltz, D. (2014) A viral aphrodisiac in the cricket *Gryllus texensis*. *Journal of Experimental Biology*, **217**, 1970–1976.

Alexander, H.M. & Maltby, A. (1990) Anther-smut infection of *Silene alba* caused by *Ustilago violacea*: factors determining fungal reproduction. *Oecologia*, **84**, 249–253.

Amiri, E., Meixner, M.D. & Kryger, P. (2016) Deformed wing virus can be transmitted during natural mating in honey bees and infect the queens. *Scientific Reports*, **6**, 33065.

Anderson, R.M. & May, R.M. (1991) *Infectious Diseases of Humans: Dynamics and Control*. Oxford: Oxford University Press.

Apari, P., De Sousa, J.D. & Müller, V. (2014) Why sexually transmitted infections tend to cause infertility: an evolutionary hypothesis. *PLoS Pathogens*, **10**, e1004111.

Ashby, B. & Boots, M. (2015) Coevolution of parasite virulence and host mating strategies. *Proceedings of the National Academy of Sciences of the United States of America*, **112**, 13,290–13,295.

Ashby, B. & Gupta, S. (2013) Sexually transmitted infections in polygamous mating systems. *Philosophical Transactions of the Royal Society B*, **368**, e20120048.

Augustine, D.J. (1998) Modelling *Chlamydia*–koala interactions: coexistence, population dynamics and conservation implications. *Journal of Applied Ecology*, **35**, 261–272.

Bateman, A.J. (1948) Intra-sexual selection in *Drosophila*. *Heredity*, **2**, 349–368.

Bauch, C.T. & McElreath, R. (2016) Disease dynamics and costly punishment can foster socially imposed monogamy. *Nature Communications*, **7**, 11219.

Baverud, V., Nystrom, C. & Johansson, K.E. (2006) Isolation and identification of *Taylorella asinigenitalis* from the genital tract of a stallion, first case of a natural infection. *Veterinary Microbiology*, **116**, 294–300.

Boots, M. & Knell, R.J. (2002) The evolution of risky behaviour in the presence of a sexually transmitted disease. *Proceedings of the Royal Society of London B*, **269**, 585–589.

Brown, A. & Grice, R. (1984) Isolation of *Chlamydia psiltaci* from koalas (*Phascolarctos cinereus*). *Australian Veterinary Journal*, **61**, 413–413.

Chahroudi, A., Permar, S. & Pandrea, I. (2014) Chapter 13 – SIV transmission in natural hosts A2 – Ansari, Aftab A. In: Silvestri, G. (ed.), *Natural Hosts of SIV*. Amsterdam: Elsevier.

Cockram, F. & Jackson, A. (1974) Isolation of a *Chlamydia* from cases of keratoconjunctivitis in koalas. *Australian Veterinary Journal*, **50**, 82–83.

Cohen, M.S. (1998) Sexually transmitted diseases enhance HIV transmission: no longer a hypothesis. *Lancet*, **351**, 5–7.

Eames, K.T.D. & Keeling, M.J. (2002) Modeling dynamic and network heterogeneities in the spread of sexually transmitted diseases. *Proceedings of the National Academy of Sciences of the United States of America*, **99**, 13,330–13,335.

Escallón, C., Becker, M.H., Walke, J.B., et al. (2017) Testosterone levels are positively correlated with cloacal bacterial diversity and the relative abundance of Chlamydiae in breeding male rufous-collared sparrows. *Functional Ecology*, **31**, 192–203.

Ezenwa, V.O., Etienne, R.S., Luikart, G., Beja-Pereira, A. & Jolles, A.E. (2010) Hidden consequences of living in a wormy world: nematode-induced immune suppression facilitates tuberculosis invasion in African buffalo. *American Naturalist*, **176**, 613–624.

Fauvergue, X. (2013) A review of mate-finding Allee effects in insects: from individual behavior to population management. *Entomologia Experimentalis et Applicata*, **146**, 79–92.

Gascoigne, J., Berec, L., Gregory, S. & Courchamp, F. (2009) Dangerously few liaisons: a review of mate-finding Allee effects. *Population Ecology*, **51**, 355–372.

Getz, W.M. & Pickering, J. (1983) Epidemic models: thresholds and population regulation. *American Naturalist*, **121**, 892–898.

Grassl, J., Peng, Y., Baer-Imhoof, B., et al. (2017) Infections with the sexually transmitted pathogen *Nosema apis* trigger an immune response in the seminal fluid of honey bees (*Apis mellifera*). *Journal of Proteome Research*, **16**, 319–334.

Grassly, N.C., Fraser, C. & Garnett, G.P. (2005) Host immunity and synchronized epidemics of syphilis across the United States. *Nature*, **433**, 417–421.

Gupta, S., Anderson, R.M. & May, R.M. (1989) Networks of sexual contacts – implications for the pattern of spread of HIV. *AIDS*, **3**, 807–817.

Haddrill, P.R., Majerus, M.E.N. & Shuker, D.M. (2013) Variation in male and female mating behaviour among different populations of the two-spot ladybird, *Adalia bipunctata* (Coleoptera: Coccinellidae). *European Journal of Entomology*, **110**, 87–93.

Haddrill, P.R., Shuker, D.M., Amos, W., Majerus, M.E.N. & Mayes, S. (2008) Female multiple mating in wild and laboratory populations of the two-spot ladybird, *Adalia bipunctata*. *Molecular Ecology*, **17**, 3189–3197.

Hagos, A., Abebe, G., Buscher, P., Goddeeris, B. M. & Claes, F. (2010) Serological and parasitological survey of dourine in the Arsi-Bale highlands of Ethiopia. *Tropical Animal Health and Production*, **42**, 769–776.

Hamilton, W.D. (1990) Mate choice near or far? *American Zoologist*, **30**, 341–352.

Handasyde, K.A. (1986) Factors affecting reproduction in the female koala "Phascolarctos cinereus". PhD thesis, Monash University.

Handsfield, H.H., Lipman, T.O., Harnisch, J.P., Tronca, E. & Holmes, K.K. (1974) Asymptomatic gonorrhea in men. *New England Journal of Medicine*, **290**, 117–123.

Hart, B.L., Korinek, E. & Brennan, P. (1987) Postcopulatory genital grooming in male-rats – prevention of sexually-transmitted infections. *Physiology & Behavior*, **41**, 321–325.

Hethcote, H. & Yorke, J.A. (1984) *Gonorrhea Transmission Dynamics and Control*. Berlin: Springer-Verlag.

Hurst, G.D.D., Jiggins, F.M., Schulenburg, J.H.G. V.D., et al. (1999a) Male-killing *Wolbachia* in two species of insect. *Proceedings of the Royal Society of London B*, **266**, 735–740.

Hurst, G.D.D., Sharpe, R.G., Broomfield, A.H., et al. (1995) Sexually transmitted disease in a promiscuous insect, *Adalia bipunctata*. *Ecological Entomology*, **20**, 230–236.

Hurst, G.D.D., Von Der Schulenburg, J.H.G., Majerus, T.M.O., et al. (1999b) Invasion of one insect species, *Adalia bipunctata*, by two different male-killing bacteria. *Insect Molecular Biology*, **8**, 133–139.

Jackson, M., White, N., Giffard, P. & Timms, P. (1999) Epizootiology of *Chlamydia* infections in two free-range koala populations. *Veterinary Microbiology*, **65**, 225–234.

Ji, W., White, P.C.L. & CLout, M.N. (2005) Contact rates between possums revealed by proximity data loggers. *Journal of Applied Ecology*, **42**, 595–604.

Jones, S.L., Pastok, D. & Hurst, G.D.D. (2015) No evidence that presence of sexually transmitted infection selects for reduced mating rate in the two spot ladybird, *Adalia bipunctata*. *Peer J*, **3**, e1148.

Keeling, M. (2005) The implications of network structure for epidemic dynamics. *Theoretical Population Biology*, **67**, 1–8.

Keeling, M.J. (1999) The effects of local spatial structure on epidemiological invasions. *Proceedings of the Royal Society of London B*, **266**, 859–867.

Knell, R.J. (1999) Sexually transmitted disease and parasite mediated sexual selection. *Evolution*, **53**, 957–961.

Knell, R.J. & Webberley, K.M. (2004) Sexually transmitted diseases of insects: distribution, ecology, evolution and host behaviour. *Biological Reviews*, **79**, 557–581.

Kokko, H. & Rankin, D.J. (2006) Lonely hearts or sex in the city? Density-dependent effects in mating systems. *Philosophical Transactions of the Royal Society of London B*, **361**, 319–334.

Kokko, H., Ranta, E., Ruxton, G. & Lundberg, P. (2002) Sexually transmitted disease and the evolution of mating systems. *Evolution*, **56**, 1091–1100.

Kulkarni, S. & Heeb, P. 2007. Social and sexual behaviours aid transmission of bacteria in birds. *Behavioural Processes*, **74**, 88–92.

Lockhart, A.B., Thrall, P.H. & Antonovics, J. (1996) Sexually transmitted diseases in animals: ecological and evolutionary implications. *Biological Reviews*, **71**, 415–471.

Loehle, C. (1995) Social barriers to pathogen transmission in wild animal populations. *Ecology*, **76**, 326–335.

Lombardo, M.P., Thorpe, P.A. & Power, H.W. (1999) The beneficial sexually transmitted microbe hypothesis of avian copulation. *Behavioral Ecology*, **10**, 333–337.

Lunney, D., Crowther, M.S., Wallis, I., et al. (2012) Koalas and climate change: a case study on the Liverpool Plains, north-west New South Wales. In: Lunney, D. & Hutchings, P. (eds.), *Wildlife and Climate*

Change: Towards Robust Conservation Strategies for Australian Fauna (pp. 150–168). Mosman, NSW: Royal Zoological Society of New South Wales.

Luong, L.T., Platzer, E.G., Zuk, M. & Giblin-Davis, R.M. (2000) Venereal worms: sexually transmitted nematodes in the decorated cricket. *Journal of Parasitology*, **86**, 471–477.

May, R.M. & Anderson, R.M. (1979) Population biology of infectious diseases: Part II. *Nature*, **280**, 455–461.

May, R.M. & Anderson, R.M. (1987) Transmission dynamics of HIV infection. *Nature*, **326**, 137–142.

May, R.M., Gupta, S. & McLean, A.R. (2001) Infectious disease dynamics: what characterizes a successful invader? *Philosophical Transactions of the Royal Society of London B*, **356**, 901–910.

McColl, K., Martin, R., Gleeson, L., Handasyde, K. & Lee, A. (1984) *Chlamydia* infection and infertility in the female koala (*Phascolarctos cinereus*). *Veterinary Record*, **115**, 655–655.

Mitchell, P., Bilney, R. & Martin, R. (1988) Population-structure and reproductive status of koalas on Raymond Island, Victoria. *Wildlife Research*, **15**, 511–514.

Moore, S.L. & Wilson, K. (2002) Parasites as a viability cost of sexual selection in natural populations of mammals. *Science*, **297**, 2015–2018.

Morand, S. (1993) Sexual transmission of a nematode: study of a model. *Oikos*, **66**, 48–54.

Morand, S. & Faliex, E. (1994) Study on the life cycle of a sexually transmitted nematode parasite of a terrestrial snail. *Journal of Parasitology*, **80**, 1049–1052.

Nahrung, H.F. & Allen, G.R. (2004) Sexual selection under scramble competition: mate location and mate choice in the eucalypt leaf beetle *Chrysophtharta agricola* (Chapuis) in the field. *Journal of Insect Behavior*, **17**, 353–366.

Nahrung, H.F. & Clarke, A.R. (2007) Sexually-transmitted disease in a sub-tropical eucalypt beetle: infection of the fittest? *Evolutionary Ecology*, **21**, 143–156.

Nunn, C.L. (2003) Behavioural defenses against sexually transmitted diseases in primates. *Animal Behaviour*, **66**, 37–48.

Nunn, C.L. & Altizer, S. (2004) Sexual selection, behaviour and sexually transmitted diseases. In: Kappeler, P.M. & van Schaik, C.P. (eds.), *Sexual Selection in Primates: New and Comparative Perspectives* (pp. 117–130). Cambridge: Cambridge University Press.

Nunn, C.L., Scully, E.J., Kutsukake, N., et al. (2014) Mating competition, promiscuity, and life history traits as predictors of sexually transmitted disease risk in primates. *International Journal of Primatology*, **35**, 764–786.

Otti, O., McTighe, A.P. & Reinhardt, K. (2013) In vitro antimicrobial sperm protection by an ejaculate-like substance. *Functional Ecology*, **27**, 219–226.

Pastok, D., Hoare, M.J., Ryder, J.J., et al. (2016) The role of host phenology in determining the incidence of an insect sexually transmitted infection. *Oikos*, **125**, 636–643.

Peng, Y., Grassl, J., Millar, A.H. & Baer, B. (2016) Seminal fluid of honeybees contains multiple mechanisms to combat infections of the sexually transmitted pathogen *Nosema apis*. *Proceedings of the Royal Society of London B*, **283**, 2015.1785.

Perry, J.C., Sharpe, D.M.T. & Rowe, L. (2009) Condition-dependent female remating resistance generates sexual selection on male size in a ladybird beetle. *Animal Behaviour*, **77**, 743–748.

Poiani, A. & Wilks, C. (2000) Sexually transmitted diseases: a possible cost of promiscuity in birds? *The Auk*, **117**, 1061–1065.

Poinar, G.O.J. (1970) *Orycetonema genitalis* gen. et sp. nov. (Rhabditidae: Nematoda) from the genital system of *Orycetes monoceros* L. (Scarabaeidae: Coleoptera) in West Africa. *Journal of Helminthology*, **44**, 1–10.

Riddick, E.W. (2010) Ectoparasitic mite and fungus on an invasive lady beetle: parasite coexistence and influence on host survival. *Bulletin of Insectology*, **63**, 13–20.

Rowe, L. (1992) Convenience polyandry in a water strider – foraging conflicts and female control of copulation frequency and guarding duration. *Animal Behaviour*, **44**, 189–202.

Rushmore, J., Caillaud, D., Hall, R.J., et al. (2014) Network-based vaccination improves prospects for disease control in wild chimpanzees. *Journal of the Royal Society Interface*, **11**(97), 20140349.

Rushmore, J., Caillaud, D., Matamba, L., et al. (2013) Social network analysis of wild chimpanzees provides insights for predicting infectious disease risk. *Journal of Animal Ecology*, **82**, 976–986.

Ryder, J.J., Hoare, M.-J., Pastok, D., et al. (2014) Disease epidemiology in arthropods is altered by the presence of nonprotective symbionts. *American Naturalist*, **183**, E89–E104.

Ryder, J.J., Miller, M.R., White, A., Knell, R.J. & Boots, M. (2007) Host–parasite population dynamics under combined frequency- and density-dependent transmission. *Oikos*, **116**, 2017–2026.

Ryder, J.J., Pastok, D., Hoare, M.-J., et al. (2013) Spatial variation in food supply, mating behavior, and sexually transmitted disease epidemics. *Behavioral Ecology*, **24**, 723–729.

Ryder, J.J., Webberley, K.M., Boots, M. & Knell, R.J. (2005) Measuring the transmission dynamics of a sexually transmitted disease. *Proceedings of the National Academy of Sciences of the United States Of America*, **102**, 15,140–15,143.

Samakovlis, C., Kylsten, P., Kimbrell, D.A., Engström, A. & Hultmark, D. (1991) The *Andropin* gene and its product, a male-specific antibacterial peptide in *Drosophila melanogaster*. *EMBO J*, **10**, 163–169.

Schmid-Hempel, P. (1998) *Parasites of Social Insects*, Princeton, NJ: Princeton University Press.

Seeman, O.D. & Nahrung, H.F. (2004) Female biased parasitism and the importance of host generation overlap in a sexually transmitted parasite of beetles. *Journal of Parasitology*, **90**, 114–118.

Simmons, A.M. & Rogers, C.E. (1990) Distribution and prevalence of an ectoparasitic nematode, *Noctuidonema guyanese*, on moths of the fall armyworm (Lepidoptera: Noctuidae) in the tropical Americas. *Journal of Entomological Science*, **25**, 510–518.

Simmons, A.M. & Rogers, C.E. (1994) Effects of an ectoparasitic nematode, *Noctuidonema guyanese* on adult longevity and egg fertility in *Spodoptera frugiperda* (Lepidoptera: Noctuidae). *Biological Control*, **4**, 285–289.

Smith, C.C. & Mueller, U.G. (2015) Sexual transmission of beneficial microbes. *Trends in Ecology & Evolution*, **30**, 438–440.

Stalder, K., Vaz, P.K., Gilkerson, J.R., et al. (2015) Prevalence and clinical significance of Herpesvirus infection in populations of Australian marsupials. *PLoS ONE*, **10**.

Suganuma, K., Narantsatsral, S., Battur, B., et al. (2016) Isolation, cultivation and molecular characterization of a new *Trypanosoma equiperdum* strain in Mongolia. *Parasites & Vectors*, **9**, 481.

Sugimoto, C., Isayama, Y., Sakazaki, R. & Kuramochi, S. (1983) Transfer of *Hemophilus equigenitalis* Taylor et al. 1978 to the genus *Taylorella* gen-nov as *Taylorella equigenitalis* comb. nov. *Current Microbiology*, **9**, 155–162.

Telfer, S., Lambin, X., Birtles, R., et al. (2010) Species interactions in a parasite community drive infection risk in a wildlife population. *Science*, **330**, 243–246.

Waterman, J.M. (2010) The adaptive function of masturbation in a promiscuous African ground squirrel. *PLoS ONE*, **5**, e13060.

Webberley, K.M., Buszko, J., Isham, V. & Hurst, G.D.D. (2006a) Sexually transmitted disease epidemics in a natural insect population. *Journal of Animal Ecology*, **75**, 33–43.

Webberley, K.M. & Hurst, G.D.D. (2002) The effect of aggregative overwintering on an insect sexually transmitted parasite system. *Journal of Parasitology*, **88**, 707–712.

Webberley, K.M., Hurst, G.D.D., Buszko, J. & Majerus, M.E.N. (2002) Lack of parasite-mediated sexual selection in a ladybird/sexually transmitted disease system. *Animal Behaviour*, **63**, 131–141.

Webberley, K.M., Hurst, G.D.D., Husband, R.W., et al. (2004) Host reproduction and a sexually transmitted disease: causes and consequences of *Coccipolipus hippodamiae* distribution on coccinellid beetles. *Journal of Animal Ecology*, **73**, 1–10.

Webberley, K.M., Tinsley, M.C., Sloggett, J.J., Majerus, M.E.N. & Hurst, G.D.D.

(2006b) Spatial variation in the incidence of a sexually transmitted parasite of the ladybird beetle *Adalia bipunctata* (Coleoptera: Coccinellidae). *European Journal of Entomology*, **103**, 793–797.

Weigler, B.J., Girjes, A.A., White, N.A., et al. (1988) Aspects of the epidemiology of *Chlamydia psittaci* infection in a population of koalas (*Phascolarctos cinereus*) in southeastern Queensland, Australia. *Journal of Wildlife Diseases*, **24**, 282–291.

Welch, V.L., Sloggett, J.J., Webberley, K.M. & Hurst, G.D.D. (2001) Short-range clinal variation in the prevalence of a sexually transmitted fungus associated with urbanisation. *Ecological Entomology*, **26**, 547–550.

Werren, J.H., Hurst, G.D.D., Zhang, W., et al. (1994) Rickettsial relative associated with male killing in the ladybird beetle (*Adalia bipunctata*). *Journal of Bacteriology*, **176**, 388–394.

White, J., Richard, M., Massot, M. & Meylan, S. (2011) Cloacal bacterial diversity increases with multiple mates: evidence of sexual transmission in female common lizards. *PLoS ONE*, **6**, e22339.

White, N. & Timms, P. (1994) *Chlamydia psittaci* in a koala (*Phascolarctos cinereus*) population in south-east Queensland. *Wildlife Research*, **21**, 41–47.

Xiang, J., Wünschmann, S., Diekema, D.J., et al. (2001) Effect of coinfection with GB virus C on survival among patients with HIV infection. *New England Journal of Medicine*, **345**, 707–714.

Yorke, J.A., Hethcote, H.W. & Nold, A. (1978) Dynamics and control of the transmission of gonnorhea. *Sexually Transmitted Diseases*, **5**, 51–56.

PART II

Understanding between-host processes

Using insect baculoviruses to understand how population structure affects disease spread

BRET D. ELDERD AND GREG DWYER

8.1 Introduction

In the late 1970s, Anderson and May published a series of ground-breaking papers arguing that parasites and pathogens could, on their own, determine the population sizes of their animal hosts (Anderson & May, 1978; May & Anderson, 1979). As part of their argument, they championed the use of epidemiological models that include host reproduction in descriptions of animal host–pathogen interactions (Hethcote, 1976). This work helped drive a nearly exponential increase in the number of studies that use mechanistic mathematical models to study disease spread, whether in humans (e.g. Keeling & Rohani, 2008) or in wildlife (e.g. Hudson et al., 2002).

A central plank in Anderson and May's argument was that regulation of the host by the pathogen in host–pathogen models occurs for realistic values of the model parameters. They used informal methods of parameter estimation, but more recent work has shown that statistically robust methods can provide deeper insights into mechanisms of disease spread (e.g. King et al., 2008). Robust methods of fitting models to data therefore represent a key tool for understanding the mechanisms that drive the dynamics of host–pathogen interactions.

A key issue, however, is that robust parameter estimation is typically used to estimate all of a model's parameter sets from a single data set (Ionides et al., 2006), an approach that requires extensive data sets. Such data sets are often available for human diseases (Keeling & Rohani, 2008), but are rare for the vertebrate diseases that have dominated much of the modelling literature (McCallum, 2016). Moreover, for many vertebrate diseases, experiments are logistically impractical, which is problematic because an overreliance on observational data can make it difficult to identify model mechanisms (King et al., 2008), increasing the risk that the wrong model will fit the data.

These problems are particularly severe when models are used to identify the mechanisms that drive host-pathogen population cycles. In models of interspecific interactions, including host–pathogen interactions, modest changes in model structure often have a dramatic effect on whether or not cycles occur. In Anderson and May's original models, for example, the addition of high variation in parasite burden across hosts, a phenomenon often observed in macroparasitic infections, can turn the stable, point equilibrium of simpler models into sustained oscillations (May & Anderson, 1978). The long-lived infectious stages typical of many insect pathogens can similarly turn a stable, point equilibrium into cycles (Anderson & May, 1981). In both cases, additional research has provided significant support for conclusions based on the population-cycle models (Woods & Elkinton, 1987; Hudson et al., 1998), but additional empirical research has shown that the original models substantially oversimplified the types of population structure that actually occur in nature (Wilson et al., 2002; New et al., 2009; Elderd et al., 2013). This modification of the original hypotheses is arguably a normal part of scientific progress, but the question of whether the models include the right kind of population structure, and thus whether they accurately represent nature, is clearly crucial to the success of the overall approach. More broadly, the importance of population structure for host–pathogen population cycles poses difficult challenges, because while it is sometimes the case that data are available that document the cycles themselves, it is very rarely true that the cycle data are accompanied by data on population structure, or by data on changes in population structure.

In what follows, we discuss what we have learned from insect–baculovirus interactions about how population structure affects the ability of pathogens to regulate populations of their hosts, how population structure modulates the severity of host–pathogen population cycles, and how population structure will likely interact with climate change to alter baculovirus transmission. We focus on the population structure caused by heterogeneities in the host's infection risk, but we also consider structure that is due to spatial patchiness, pathogen polymorphism, and host variation in size. Baculoviruses provide experimentally tractable systems for studying pathogen transmission, but experiments can usually only be carried out at shorter temporal scales and smaller spatial scales than the scales at which population cycles are observed. We therefore argue for the use of models to extrapolate from experiments to scales involving population cycles.

In championing this approach, we are motivated by Simon Levin's argument that success in extrapolating across scales is a key measure of the usefulness of ecological theory (Levin, 1992). In applying Levin's perspective to host–pathogen interactions, we hope to emphasise the key importance of population structure in modulating host–pathogen interactions. In disease ecology, it is currently fashionable to argue for the importance of multi-host and multi-pathogen interactions, an approach that has arisen from community ecology. While it is unquestionably true that multi-host and multi-pathogen interactions play an important role in many host–pathogen systems (Johnson et al., 2015), part of our argument is that, in many host–pathogen interactions, an understanding of population structure is more useful than more phenomenological approaches based on enumerations of the identity of the main players.

8.1.1 Baculoviruses

Interactions between insects and their baculoviruses represent easily manipulated systems in which to experimentally investigate how biotic and abiotic factors affect disease transmission (Elderd, 2013). Insects can be reared in large numbers, and they often have short generation times, making it easy to obtain the multiple replicates needed to estimate model parameters (e.g. Elderd et al., 2008). Moreover, baculoviruses terminate outbreaks of many forest-defoliating insects (Moreau & Lucarotti, 2007), and there are extensive data sets documenting population cycles in forest defoliators (Myers, 1988), making it possible to test the predictions of models of insect–baculovirus population cycles (Dwyer et al., 2004). Crop-defoliating pest populations experience similar collapses following outbreaks (Mitchell et al., 1991; Wang et al., 2015), again because of baculovirus-caused mortality (Fuxa, 1982). Finally, baculoviruses are often species-specific, or at least affect vastly fewer insect species than conventional insecticides, and so they are often used as environmentally benign insecticides (Hunter-Fujita et al., 1998). Studies of insect baculoviruses thus have implications both for basic questions in host–pathogen ecology and for biological pest control (Grzywacz et al., 2008).

Baculoviruses are ubiquitous in nature, causing fatal infections via horizontal transmission of the virus from an infected host to a susceptible host (Figure 8.1, Elderd, 2013). Virus-killed hosts release large numbers (10^6–10^9) of infectious particles known as 'occlusion bodies', each of which contains 30–50 infectious virions, which in turn contain the double-stranded DNA of the virus (Rohrmann, 2014). In Lepidopteran insects, infections generally occur when the pH-sensitive occlusion bodies dissolve in the alkaline conditions of the insect midgut, allowing the virions to bind to the midgut cells, from which the virus proceeds to infect the entire insect (Miller, 2013). Baculoviruses must kill for horizontal transmission to occur, with the proviso that mortality risk is dose-dependent, and so infection is more likely if the host consumes more occlusion bodies (Kennedy et al., 2014).

Although non-lethal 'covert' infections may lead to vertical transmission, there is only limited evidence that such infections have strong effects on epizootics, or on insect–baculovirus population cycles (Fuller et al., 2012). Covert infections may nevertheless play a key role in long-term pathogen survival in some cases (Burden et al., 2003; Myers & Cory, 2016), notably in the African armyworm (*Spodoptera exempta*) system, in which covert infections may ensure that the virus is able to persist during the dry season, or at other times of low host densities (Vilaplana et al., 2010). In insect host–pathogen models, covert infections that serve as this kind of pathogen reservoir (Burden et al., 2003) can have important effects on long-term dynamics (Boots et al., 2003; Bonsall et al., 2005), but models can often reproduce data on insect–baculovirus cycles without invoking covert infections (Fuller et al., 2012).

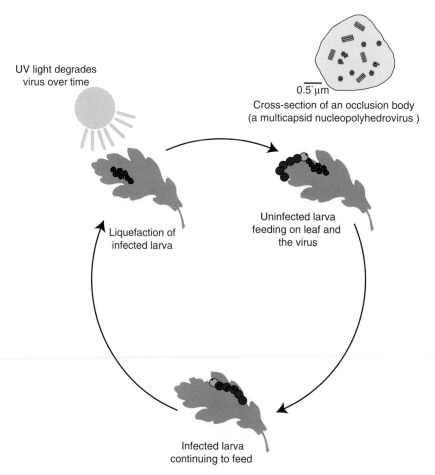

Figure 8.1 Baculovirus transmission cycle in herbivorous insects. When an uninfected larva consumes a sufficiently large number of infectious occlusion bodies, the larva becomes infected. The virus then replicates in the mid-gut, ultimately spreading throughout the host's body. Eventually, the host liquefies, releasing large numbers of occlusion bodies onto the leaf tissue on which the larva was feeding, where the occlusion bodies are available to infect additional insects. Over time, the occlusion bodies degrade due to exposure to UV light exposure. Reprinted from Elderd (2013).

The time it takes for a baculovirus to reproduce and spread within its host leads to substantial delays between infection and death (Kennedy et al., 2014), typically from 4 to 10 days (Miller, 2013). During this process, the virus may interfere with larval hormones to prevent moulting to later instars (= larval stages), even as uninfected larvae continue to moult (Hoover et al., 2011). Shortly after death, viral enzymes usually break down the insect integument, allowing occlusion bodies to ooze out onto foliage, where they are available to be consumed by other larvae (Cory & Hoover, 2006). The intensity of the resulting epizootic depends strongly on the density of both the pathogen and the host (Moreau & Lucarotti, 2007).

Because occlusion bodies are large enough to be easily visible at 400 × magnification, diagnosis can be confirmed using a light microscope (Fleming-Davies & Dwyer, 2015). Meanwhile, the existence of artificial diet for economically important species makes it possible to rear large numbers of larvae in the laboratory (Hunter-Fujita et al., 1998). In previous research, we therefore developed a protocol for estimating baculovirus transmission in the field (Dwyer, 1991; Dwyer et al., 1997), as follows. First, larvae infected at hatching are placed on foliage, and the foliage is enclosed in a mesh bag. The mesh allows for roughly natural conditions, while preventing the escape of infected larvae and the breakdown of the virus due to UV exposure (Fuller et al., 2012). The infected larvae die within 4–7 days, after which uninfected larvae are added to the foliage for a period long enough to ensure reasonably high infection rates, but short enough to prevent the death of secondarily infected larvae (Dwyer et al., 1997). Because transmission in nature generally occurs when early instars infect later instars, uninfected larvae are typically in the third or fourth instar (Elderd, 2013). Throughout this chapter, we will refer to experiments using this protocol as 'field transmission experiments'.

Data from these experiments can be fit to mechanistic models based on the well-known 'SEIR' (i.e. Susceptible–Exposed–Infected–Recovered) model, a general model of a single epizootic (Keeling & Rohani, 2008). Moreover, inserting parameters estimated from field transmission experiments into the SEIR model produces predicted infection rates that are quite close to infection rates observed in nature (Dwyer et al., 2002), while long-term models that use the experimental estimates produce realistic outbreak cycles (Dwyer et al., 2004). Long-term models can then be extended to ask applied questions, such as how best to dampen the boom and bust cycles often associated with insect pests and their pathogens (Reilly & Elderd, 2014).

These successes suggest that transmission as measured in our experiments provides a reasonable description of transmission in nature. Our experiments can thus be used to study the effects of a range of biological factors that may affect disease transmission. In what follows, we will summarise what we have learned from experiments on baculoviruses of two Lepidopteran

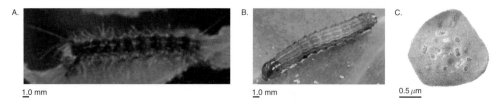

A.

1.0 mm

B.

1.0 mm

C.

0.5 μm

Figure 8.2 Larva of the (A) gypsy moth and (B) fall armyworm, each of which can be infected by a species-specific baculovirus. The (C) electron microscopic (EM) image shows a cross-section of a single occlusion body of the gypsy moth virus, which is a multicapsid nucleopolyhedrovirus. The dark objects within the grey protein coat are virions that contain the double-stranded DNA virus. (A) by Alison Hunter. (A black and white version of this figure will appear in some formats. For the colour version, please refer to the plate section.)

pests (Figure 8.2), the gypsy moth (*Lymantria dispar*) and the fall armyworm (*Spodoptera frugiperda*). The life histories of these two species differ dramatically in terms of overall life cycle, generation times, and the number of generations per year, yet our protocol has revealed important similarities in the dynamics of the baculovirus of each species.

In North America, the gypsy moth is an introduced pest of hardwood forests, and it has undergone repeated outbreaks since the 1920s (Elkinton & Liebhold, 1990). When outbreaks occur, densities rise over several orders of magnitude, leading to widespread and severe defoliation, and sometimes tree deaths. Outbreaks were historically terminated by high mortality arising from baculovirus epizootics (Woods & Elkinton, 1987), but since the introduction of the fungal pathogen *Entomophaga maimaiga* in 1989, outbreaks have been terminated by a combination of the two diseases. Recent work has suggested that competition with *E. maimaiga* may drive the baculovirus to low levels (Hajek et al., 2015), but because *E. maimaiga* prefers cool, moist weather (Hajek, 1999), and because climate-change models predict warm, dry conditions for the range of the gypsy moth, the competitive balance is likely to favour the baculovirus more strongly in the future. Meanwhile, gypsy moth dynamics at low densities are strongly affected by mortality due to generalist predators (Elkinton et al., 1996), leading to a low-density equilibrium that interacts in complex ways with the cycles driven by the baculovirus (Dwyer et al., 2004).

Like the gypsy moth, the fall armyworm is a polyphagous pest that undergoes boom and bust cycles in North America, with outbreaks that can be widespread (Fuxa, 1982) and that can economically devastate crops (Hinds & Dew, 1915). The fall armyworm's species-specific baculovirus also represents an important mortality source (Richter et al., 1987), with epizootics that begin from a viral reservoir in the soil (Fuxa & Geaghan, 1983). Unlike the gypsy moth, however, the fall armyworm has multiple generations per year, following a 'multi-voltine' life cycle, and it overwinters in Florida and Texas, USA

(Pitre & Hogg, 1983), reinvading in the spring by migrating northward until it reaches a northern limit in Ontario, Canada. The fall armyworm recently became an invasive pest in Africa (Wild, 2017), and the use of its baculovirus as a bioinsecticide may reduce crop damage there. In spite of these differences, the dynamics of the fall armyworm's baculovirus are similar to the dynamics of the baculovirus of the gypsy moth and other insects.

8.2 Models, data, and modifications

8.2.1 Epizootics, transmission, and experiments

As we described, a key feature of Anderson and May's original work was the application of models that added host reproduction (Hethcote, 1976) into single-epizootic models best known from Kermack and McKendrick's work. Because insect baculoviruses infect only larvae, however, Kermack and McKendrick's models are again relevant, serving as epizootic submodels that can be nested inside discrete-generation models of host reproduction and population cycles. The modelling framework (Figure 8.3A) for a single epizootic therefore consists of a series of ordinary differential equations describing the transmission process (Figure 8.1):

$$\frac{dS}{dt} = -\beta SP - bS, \tag{8.1}$$

$$\frac{dE_1}{dt} = \beta SP - m\xi E_1 - bE_1, \tag{8.2}$$

$$\frac{dE_i}{dt} = m\xi E_{i-1} - m\xi E_i - bE_i (i = 2, \ldots, m), \tag{8.3}$$

$$\frac{dP}{dt} = m\xi E_m - \mu P. \tag{8.4}$$

Here, the model structure differs from standard SEIR models first in that exposed hosts E_i proceed not to an infected-host class I, but to a pathogen class P that represents infectious cadavers. Because successful infections are necessarily lethal, there is no need to include a recovered class in the model. The parameter b is the background larval mortality rate, while β describes the rate at which encounters between uninfected, 'susceptible' larvae S and infectious cadavers P occur and lead to infection. The model thus subsumes several ecological and behavioural processes into the single parameter β (Anderson & May, 1991), including the rate at which susceptible hosts contact infectious cadavers, and the probability of infection given contact (Dwyer et al., 1997; McCallum et al., 2017).

To allow for a delay between infection and death, we include multiple exposed classes E_i, representing hosts that have consumed enough occlusion bodies to become infected but that have not yet died of the infection. The time

A.

B.

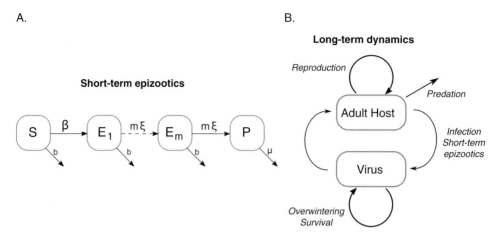

Figure 8.3 (A) Schematic of a single baculovirus epizootic, as in Equations 8.1–8.4 with symbols that are defined in the text. (B) Schematic of the long-term population dynamics of insect-baculovirus interactions as outlined in Equations 8.15–8.16. For the long-term dynamic model, covert infections can be considered to be part of the overwintering or between-epizootic survival of the virus.

in a single exposed class is exponential with mean $1/m\xi$. So the distribution of times to death for multiple exposed classes follows a sum of exponential distributions or a gamma distribution with mean $1/\xi$, where ξ is the average speed of kill, and $1/m\xi$ is the variance (Keeling & Rohani, 2008). Infected cadavers break down at a rate μ, due largely to UV inactivation.

In field transmission experiments with baculoviruses, non-virus mortality is low enough that we can set $b = 0$, while the mesh bags surrounding the foliage reduce ultraviolet radiation enough that the virus density is a constant, $P(0)$, and the decay rate $\mu = 0$ (Fuller et al., 2012). Equation 8.1 for the change in susceptible hosts is then sufficient to describe the dynamics of the disease, with initial host density $S(0)$, and it can be integrated to give:

$$-\ln\left[\frac{S(T)}{S(0)}\right] = \beta P(0)T. \tag{8.5}$$

Because we observe the density of hosts uninfected at the end of the experiment $S(T)$, β is the only unknown in Equation 8.5. We can then estimate the transmission rate β (Elderd et al., 2008) as the slope of the regression line (Figure 8.4, dashed line) of the cadaver density versus the negative log of the fraction uninfected ($-\ln[S(T)/S(0)]$).

In practice, however, the data from our experiments have shown that the relationship between pathogen density and the negative log of the fraction uninfected is strongly non-linear (e.g. Dwyer et al., 1997). An obvious way to

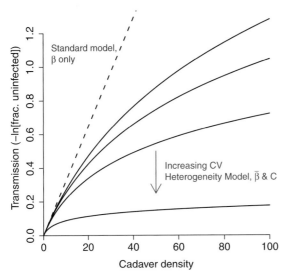

Figure 8.4 The best-fitting linear (dashed line) and non-linear (solid lines) model predictions in a field transmission experiment, due to one round of transmission. The linear dashed line assumes that all individuals are equally susceptible and that transmission therefore increases with a constant rate with increases in the density of infectious cadavers as in Equation 8.5. The curved lines show the prediction of Equation 8.14, which assumes that individuals vary in their infection risk, such that there is a mean transmission rate β and a coefficient of variation of transmission C. At low levels of heterogeneity, the non-linear transmission model converges on the linear model. As heterogeneity increases, infection rates increase more slowly with increasing pathogen density.

account for this non-linearity is to raise the density of infectious cadavers to some power, so that the transmission term becomes βSP^a, where the value of a depends on the degree of non-linearity in the data. Such a model would describe the pattern associated with the data, providing an improved fit to the data, but it would provide no understanding of the biological mechanisms driving this pattern.

A more mechanistic approach is to consider ways in which the model over-simplifies the biology of disease transmission. Indeed, transmission non-linearities may be driven by processes (McCallum et al., 2017) at the individual host level, such as host behavioural changes that may occur during encounters with cadavers (Parker et al., 2010; Eakin et al., 2015), or at the population level, such as polymorphism in the host or the pathogen. In particular, an under-lying assumption of Equations 8.1–8.4 is that all individuals are equally likely to contract the disease, so that every individual has the same risk of becoming infected. If we instead modify the model so that transmission β follows a distribution with some mean and variance (Dwyer et al., 1997), then we instead assume that hosts vary in their susceptibility, thus adding population structure to the model. The susceptible host population would then be a function of both time t and transmission β, allowing for variation in infection risk across individuals. If we additionally assume that hosts of different levels of susceptibility are equally infectious, then the model becomes (Dwyer et al., 1997):

$$\frac{\partial S}{\partial t} = -\beta S(\beta,t)P - bS(\beta,t) \tag{8.6}$$

$$\frac{dE_1}{dt} = P\int_0^\infty \beta S(\beta,t)d\beta - m\xi E_1 - bE_1, \tag{8.7}$$

$$\frac{dE_i}{dt} = m\xi E_{i-1} - m\xi E_i - bE_i (i = 2, \ldots, m) \tag{8.8}$$

$$\frac{dP}{dt} = m\xi E_m - \mu P. \tag{8.9}$$

In practice, this system of integro-partial differential equations is so computationally unwieldy that we use an approximate model, in which we assume that the distribution of transmission rates can be described in terms of a time-varying mean and a constant coefficient of variation, with the higher-order moments of the distribution assumed constant (Dwyer et al., 2000):

$$\frac{dS}{dt} = -\bar{\beta}SP\left[\frac{S(t)}{S(0)}\right]^{C^2} - bS \tag{8.10}$$

$$\frac{dE_1}{dt} = \bar{\beta}\left[\frac{S(t)}{S(0)}\right]^{C^2} SP - m\xi E_1 - bE_1, \tag{8.11}$$

$$\frac{dE_i}{dt} = m\xi E_{i-1} - m\xi E_i - bE_i (i = 2, \ldots, m), \tag{8.12}$$

$$\frac{dP}{dt} = m\xi E_m - \mu P. \tag{8.13}$$

In this model, the mean transmission rate at time t is $\bar{\beta}\left[\frac{S(t)}{S(0)}\right]^{C^2}$, where C is the coefficient of variation of the distribution of transmission rates, and $\bar{\beta}$ is the average transmission rate at the beginning of the epizootic. When transmission rates follow a gamma distribution, the model is a close approximation to Equations 8.6–8.9, but the approximation is still fairly accurate when the distribution is instead log normal, and therefore has a longer tail of high transmission rates.

Because the uninfected host population $S(t)$ always falls with time, the expression for the mean transmission rate $\bar{\beta}\left[\frac{S(t)}{S(0)}\right]^{C^2}$ makes clear that the mean also falls over time (Dwyer et al., 2000). This happens because, at the beginning of the epizootic, the most susceptible individuals become infected, and so later in the epizootic, only the less-susceptible individuals remain. Because of this effect, in our experiments, instead of Equation 8.5, we have:

$$-\ln\left[\frac{S(T)}{S(0)}\right] = \frac{1}{C^2}\ln(1 + \bar{\beta}C^2 P(0)T). \tag{8.14}$$

Even though we added variation in the host and not the pathogen, a plot of Equation 8.14 makes clear that host variation leads to a non-linear relationship between our transmission measure $-\ln\left[\frac{S(T)}{S(0)}\right]$ and pathogen density $P(0)$ (Figure 8.4). The explanation for this shape is that, at low pathogen density, only the most susceptible individuals become infected, and so transmission at first increases rapidly with increasing pathogen density (Figure 8.4, solid lines). As pathogen density increases, however, the rate of increase in transmission slows, because only highly resistant individuals remain. Moreover, as the expression for transmission $\bar{\beta}\left[\frac{S(t)}{S(0)}\right]^{C^2}$ again makes clear, increases in the coefficient of variation C lead to reductions in the infection rate, irrespective of pathogen density. As a result, when C is higher, representing higher levels of population-level heterogeneity, and thus greater population structure, our measure of transmission increases more slowly with increased pathogen density. The effect is that, at any pathogen density, higher variability in the host population leads to fewer hosts becoming infected. If instead $C \to 0$, so that hosts are effectively identical, the model converges on the linear model (Equation 8.5). These effects have been confirmed by two decades of experiments (Dwyer et al., 1997, 2005; Elderd et al., 2008, 2013; Fuller et al., 2012; Elderd & Reilly, 2014; Pa'ez et al., 2017).

By showing that host variation can strongly alter baculovirus transmission, our experiments revealed an important effect of population structure on disease spread. Other experiments have shown that spatial structure can similarly modulate baculovirus transmission (D'Amico et al., 2005), partly because gypsy moth larvae can sometimes detect and avoid virus-killed cadavers (Eakin et al., 2015). Understanding the consequences of these effects for host population dynamics, however, requires more complex models that describe long-term dynamics.

8.2.2 Long-term dynamics

Anderson and May (1981)'s models of the dynamics of invertebrate pathogens assume continuous, overlapping generations, but for many temperate-zone insects, reproduction is strongly seasonal (Altizer et al., 2006). Seasonality can seriously complicate the construction of long-term models, but for many insect pathogens, there is no disease transmission during host reproduction, and generations are often non-overlapping. In such cases, we can use difference equations to describe population change during the adult phase of the life cycle (Figure 8.3B) as follows:

$$N_{n+1} = \lambda N_n(1 - i(N_n,Z_n)),$$
(8.15)

$$Z_{n+1} = \phi N_n i(N_n,Z_n) + \gamma Z_n.$$
(8.16)

Here, N_n and Z_n are the densities of hosts and pathogens, in the form of infectious cadavers, before the epizootic in generation n and $i(N_n,Z_n)$ is the fraction of the infected larvae that are killed by the pathogen, as calculated by Equations 8.10–8.13. The reproductive rate for the adult population is λ, so that the right-hand side of Equation 8.15 describes the density of offspring of individuals that survived the epizootic and then reproduced. In this model, baculovirus density Z_{n+1} in generation $n + 1$ depends on two pathogen pools, in the form of cadavers derived from the current generation, which have between-host generation survival ϕ, and cadavers from previous generations, which survive at rate γ.

As we described, we have never needed to invoke sublethal or covert infections to explain long-term baculovirus dynamics, but the model also implicitly allows for such infections. That is, the model assumes that some fraction of the infectious cadavers survive across generations, and these cadavers could be assumed to be due to cadavers derived from covert infections. This approximation to the effects of covert infections holds as long as the number of covert infections is independent of host population size (Elderd et al., 2013), but it would not be difficult to modify the model so that it instead assumes that covert infections are due to density-dependent transmission processes.

We thus use Equations 8.10–8.13 to describe the fraction of hosts infected and the density of infectious cadavers produced in the epizootic, and then we use Equations 8.15 and 8.16 to describe host reproduction and pathogen survival between epizootics. The resulting model output can reproduce the average period and amplitude of gypsy moth outbreaks (Dwyer et al., 2004; Elderd et al., 2008, 2013; Bjørnstad et al., 2010). We note, however, that the model output is not species-specific, and that it can also be modified to describe seasonal host–pathogen interactions more generally.

As an example of such a generalisation, we note that, in many outbreaking insects, population densities are kept at low levels during inter-outbreak periods by generalist predators or parasitoids (Dwyer et al., 2004). This effect can be described by a Type III functional response that quantifies the fraction of the insect population lost to predators, according to the term $\left(1 - \frac{2abN_n}{b^2 + N_n^2}\right)$, where a is the maximum predation rate and b is the saturation constant. Allowing for this effect gives highly variable cycles that match the dynamics of real outbreaks quite closely, especially if we allow for stochastic effects of weather, which are often seen in outbreaking insects (Williams & Liebhold, 1995). Cycles produced by Equations 8.15 and 8.16 are in contrast far more regular than real cycles, either in the gypsy moth or other outbreaking insects for which sufficient data have been collected to test the models (Dwyer et al., 2004). To focus on key conceptual issues, however, in what follows we do not include either effect in the models that we present.

8.2.3 Fitting models to data

A key feature of our work is that we test mechanistic models of disease spread using a combination of experimental and observational data. The best method for determining whether the data fit a particular model remains a central question not just for disease ecology but also for ecology in general. Formal statistical model selection has become an increasingly popular method to accomplish this (Burnham & Anderson, 2002). In our case, however, the details of model selection differ substantially depending on whether we use small-scale, short-term experimental data, or large-scale observational data. Here we briefly outline the approaches that we have taken, along with the motivation for each technique.

8.2.3.1 Short-term epizootics

In model selection, there are multiple models that we want to assess, and the best-fit model is determined by comparing the ability of each model to fit the data. In the case of our non-linear models, as heterogeneity $C \to 0$, the non-linear model collapses into the linear transmission model. The classic approach to such cases is to calculate twice the ratio of the log-likelihoods of the two models, which approximates a chi-square statistic with one degree of freedom, allowing a test of statistical significance (Hilborn & Mangel, 1997). The likelihood ratio test, however, requires that we compare nested models only in pairs, whereas in many cases we would prefer to compare the ability of multiple models to describe the data.

For more than a century, individual scientists have advocated moving beyond the simple null-alternative two-model framework represented by the likelihood ratio test (Chamberlin, 1897) studies. Recently, this movement has led to the widespread adoption of methods that allow for the comparison of multiple models (e.g. Burnham & Anderson, 2002; Spiegelhalter et al., 2002; Watanabe, 2013). Burnham and Anderson (2002) in particular championed the use of the Akaike Information Criterion (AIC) and its associated metrics such as AIC weights. AIC balances model fit, calculated using the likelihood of the data, with model complexity, calculated using the number of parameters in a model. More complicated models always fit the current data set better, and are thus more likely than less complicated models. More complicated models, however, may do a poor job of predicting the next set of data collected. That is, the parameter estimates of more complicated models may rely too strongly on the data set being currently analysed, leading to model failures when additional data are collected. This effect can be measured in terms of the variance in model predictions. AIC is based on an approximation to this variance, according to which the variance is equal to the number of model parameters (Konishi & Kitagawa, 2008):

$$\text{AIC} = -2L(\Theta|\text{Data}) + 2K, \tag{8.17}$$

where $L(\Theta|\text{Data})$ is the log likelihood of the model parameters Θ given the data and K is the number of model parameters (Burnham & Anderson, 2002).

Multi-model inference can also be carried out using a Bayesian framework (Hobbs & Hooten, 2015), by using the Watanabe–Akaike Information Criterion (WAIC; Watanabe, 2013) widely, the Deviance Information Criterion (DIC; Spiegelhalter et al., 2002), or an assortment of cross-validation metrics (Hooten & Hobbs, 2015), with the method chosen depending on the model structure (see review in Hooten & Hobbs, 2015). Regardless of the details of different metrics, all take into consideration model fit and complexity. Bayesian approaches are become increasingly popular thanks to the availability of high-performance computing, but Bayesian model selection has been developed only recently (but see Hobbs et al., 2015), and thus has only recently been accessible to many researchers. In our research, Bayesian approaches have become more and more important in analysing field transmission experiments.

8.2.3.2 Long-term dynamics

So far, we have described how we confront models with data from field transmission experiments, which allow for only a single round of disease transmission. Because baculoviruses often drive insect population cycles, long-term models are typically tested with data from insect outbreaks. From an analytical perspective, the use of insect outbreak data to make inferences about models of host–pathogen population cycles is an example of an 'inverse problem' (Kendall et al., 1999), meaning that the data could arise from a variety of different processes that may or may not be related to disease transmission. Meanwhile, data on insect outbreaks typically describe only changes in the host population (Anderson & May, 1981). This is a problem because insect outbreak cycles could be driven by intraspecific density-dependent regulation, predator–prey interactions, by the host–pathogen interactions that we focus on here (Kot, 2001), or by some combination of these mechanisms. Abundant data have nevertheless shown that baculovirus mortality rates are high in outbreaks of many insects (Moreau & Lucarotti, 2007), and so there is little doubt that baculoviruses play a key role. Data on infection rates, however, are typically unavailable for the five years or more that often elapse between outbreaks. Estimating some model parameters from experimental data thus makes it much easier to compare long-term insect host–pathogen models to data (Dwyer et al., 2000).

An additional problem, however, is that, in models of population cycles, the densities of the interacting species are always at least modestly sensitive to their initial densities, and may be extremely sensitive if the model dynamics are chaotic (Dwyer et al., 2004). Kendall et al. (1999) therefore suggested that models be fit to summary statistics, such as the period or amplitude of the data, thereby combining time-series approaches with mechanistic population models. Classical time-series analyses in contrast rely on non-mechanistic models that do not account for the biology of the organism of interest. Meanwhile, theoretical ecologists have long constructed biologically explicit models, which may qualitatively reproduce patterns in the data, but often do not carry out quantitative comparisons to data. Fitting mechanistic models to time-series summary statistics therefore allows for a mixture of the two approaches.

Because we are able to carry out experiments, in our previous research we have instead first used our experimental data to estimate parameters, second we have inserted the parameter estimates into the models to make predictions, and third we have compared the model predictions to summary statistics from time-series data. Typically, we focused on the average period, the variation in the period, the average amplitude, or spectral density functions based on the data. If the model fits these data as determined by the summary statistics, the drivers of the cyclic dynamics included in the model during its formulation are worth investigating further. The usefulness of this approach for host–pathogen models has been demonstrated several times, both in our work, and in the work of others (e.g. Dwyer et al., 2004; Johnson et al., 2006; Abbott & Dwyer, 2008; Elderd et al., 2008, 2013; Bjørnstad et al., 2010). A disadvantage of the approach, however, is that it does not allow for uncertainty in the parameter values. In future research, we therefore hope to use experimental data to construct priors, to use time-series data to calculate posteriors, and then to choose between models using an appropriate metric (Gelman et al., 2014; Hooten & Hobbs, 2015).

8.2.4 Abiotic factors, population structure, and disease transmission

Although changes in the environment may influence infection rates simply by adding stochasticity, both abiotic and biotic changes can affect the host–pathogen interaction more directly. As we have described, a key feature of our model Equations 8.10–8.13 and 8.15 and 8.16 is that they allow for population structure, mostly in the form of variability in infection risk across individuals. This is important partly because changes in the environment, due for example to climate change, are often assumed to affect mean transmission, but our models allow for the possibility that environmental change may also affect variability across individuals and, thus, population structure. Environmental change may therefore alter host–pathogen interactions so that the role of heterogeneity across individuals is greatly reduced, changing transmission dynamics from non-linear to linear.

More concretely, as the climate continues to change due to anthropogenic inputs to the atmosphere, we are experiencing changes in both temperature and precipitation. A pressing question is therefore, how will disease transmission be altered by these changes? Because field transmission experiments with baculoviruses are logistically straightforward, it is possible to use insect baculoviruses to directly address this question. The answer emphasises the importance of population structure in driving the host–pathogen transmission process (Elderd & Reilly, 2014).

To illustrate this point, we used the fall armyworm system to carry out a series of short-term epizootic experiments in which we warmed experimental plots with open-top chambers (Godfree et al., 2011). In these experiments, as temperatures increased, transmission dynamics became increasingly linear (Figure 8.5). The best-fit models for these data, as chosen using AIC, showed that changes in the heterogeneity in transmission

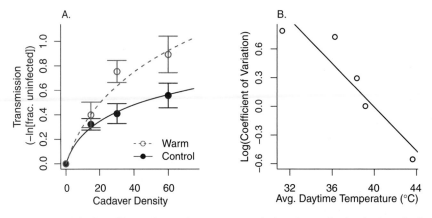

Figure 8.5 (A) The effects of warming on transmission dynamics in the baculovirus of the fall armyworm in a single experiment. The best-fit model for these data, chosen using AIC scores, includes differences in the coefficient of variation C between experimental and control treatments. (B) Over the course of three separate trials, we estimated C for the best-fit models, and we regressed average temperature against these estimates, to show that log of C fell as temperatures rose. The coefficient of variation thus declined exponentially with increasing temperature. The figure is adapted from Elderd and Reilly (2014).

parameter C are much more important than changes in the mean transmission parameter, $\bar{\beta}$ (Elderd & Reilly, 2014).

Increased temperature thus drives increased epizootic intensity, but this change is due to a decrease in the coefficient of variation associated with heterogeneity rather than to changes in the mean transmission rate. In other words, as temperatures rose in our experimental plots, hosts became increasingly similar in their risk of being infected with the disease. This change may have been driven by increases in the larval feeding rate as temperatures rose (Elderd & Reilly, 2014), because as the rate at which larvae consume leaves increases, the probability that a larva consumes a lethal dose of the virus approaches one.

It is important to note, however, that increases in temperature also increased both pathogen production and pathogen speed of kill. A faster speed of kill reduced the number of occlusion bodies per cadaver, but the boost in the number of occlusion bodies due to warming outweighed the effects of increased average speed of kill (Elderd, unpub. data). The net effects of these changes on subsequent epizootics and the long-term dynamics of the armyworm, however, are unknown. These results are important because concerns about the effects of global warming on disease dynamics typically focus on whether or not transmission rates will increase with temperature (Harvell et al., 2002; Pascual & Bouma, 2009). Our experiments in contrast have shown that warming-induced changes in heterogeneity, and thus in host population structure, may play a more important role in determining disease dynamics.

8.2.5 Biotic factors, population structure, and disease transmission

Resource quality can play an important direct role in a consumer's survival and fecundity (Lee et al., 2006; de Roode et al., 2008; Hall et al., 2009; Duffy et al., 2012,), as well as in trait-mediated indirect effects (Werner & Peacor, 2003), by altering the host's infection risk (Cory & Hoover, 2006). In many insects, baculovirus infection occurs when a larva consumes both viral occlusion bodies and the leaf tissue on which the occlusion bodies are found. The quality of the leaf tissue could therefore alter the larva's risk of infection. The insect–baculovirus interaction thus becomes trait-mediated due to changes in plant chemical defences, in turn altering both epizootic severity and host population cycles (Elderd et al., 2013).

In particular, herbivore defoliation causes some plants to increase production of secondary metabolites that are designed to deter further defoliation (Karban & Baldwin, 1997; Nykänen & Koricheva, 2004; Hunter, 2016). If these secondary metabolites are continually produced by the plant, they are considered constitutive defences. If the threat of being consumed by a herbivore varies over time, however, the cost of constitutive defences may not be worth it, because the plant is using its limited energy to produce compounds to deter herbivores that are not always a constant threat to the plant. An alternative strategy is therefore to upregulate anti-herbivore metabolites only in response to defoliation.

These 'induced defences' may then alter the insect's risk of becoming infected, because the virus and the leaf tissue containing the anti-herbivore compounds are consumed at the same time. Induced plant defences may therefore alter the infection process in the insect's mid-gut. From a population perspective, the intensity of the epizootic may therefore change as a result of the induction of plant defences. At the landscape level, the host and the pathogen may interact within a complex phytochemical landscape (Hunter, 2016), depending upon the species composition of the forest or the field, and on the strength of induction. From the host's perspective, this landscape consists of areas in which infection risk is high, and areas in which infection risk is low. The plant species composition of the landscape could therefore alter the magnitude and the periodicity of host outbreak cycles.

An illustration of these points comes from our work on the gypsy moth baculovirus (Elderd et al., 2013). Gypsy moths feed preferentially on oaks (*Quercus* spp.) (Barbosa & Krischik, 1987), which often respond to defoliation by increasing the levels of hydrolysable tannins in their foliage (Schultz & Baldwin, 1982; Wold & Marquis, 1997). Laboratory dose–response experiments showed that increases in tannin levels may affect a gypsy moth's risk of infection given exposure (Hunter & Schultz, 1993), but in dose–response experiments, larvae that do not consume the entire dose are discarded, eliminating the effects of variation in feeding behaviour (Parker et al., 2010), and altering infection risk (Eakin et al., 2015).

To test for effects of induced tannins on the gypsy moth baculovirus, we therefore instead used a field transmission experiment. In these experiments, we raised tannin levels in foliage of red oak (*Quercus rubra*) by applying a solution of jasmonic acid, a plant secondary-signalling compound that induces defensive compound production (Baldwin, 1998). These experiments showed that increased tannin levels reduce average transmission slightly, but reduce heterogeneity in transmission to undetectably low levels (Elderd et al., 2013). We therefore modified Equations 8.15 and 8.16 to allow induced defences to modulate transmission. The model is then:

$$N_{n+1} = \lambda N_n \left(1 - i(N_n, Z_n, D_n)\right) \tag{8.18}$$

$$Z_{n+1} = \phi N_n i(N_n, Z_n, D_n) + \gamma Z_n, \tag{8.19}$$

$$D_{n+1} = \alpha N_n \frac{D_n}{v + D_n}. \tag{8.20}$$

As in Equations 8.15 and 8.16, N_n and Z_n are host and pathogen densities in generation n, but now D_n is the induced defence. The fraction infected by the pathogen $i(N_n,Z_n,D_n)$ is again calculated using the SEIR model, Equations 8.10–8.13, except that now the heterogeneity parameter C is determined by the level of the induced defence D_n. To allow for effects of the induced defence D_n on virus transmission in generation n, we set the heterogeneity parameter in the epizootic Equations 8.10–8.13 to $C = C_0 e^{(-\psi(D_n+D_0))}$, where C_0 is the baseline heterogeneity and D_0 is the constitutive level of induced defences, meaning the level reached in the absence of defoliation. The density of hosts N_{n+1} in generation $n+1$ then again depends on the average number of offspring produced per host λ and the fraction killed by the pathogen $i(N_n,Z_n,D_n)$.

In the model, the induced hydrolysable tannin concentration D_{n+1} increases linearly with increasing insect density N_n, due to defoliation. The tannin concentration is also a saturating function of the previous generation's value D_n, to allow for the carry-over effect that we observed in experiments from one year to the next (Elderd et al., 2013), and with half-saturation constant v to reflect the constraints of plant physiology (Karban & Baldwin, 1997).

Allowing for induced oak defences reduces the stabilising effects of heterogeneity in transmission, so that models that include induced tannin levels are much more likely to show population cycles than are standard models. Moreover, this effect of induced defences provides a possible explanation for one of the unsolved puzzles of gypsy moth dynamics in North America. In four gypsy moth outbreaks between the mid-1970s and the mid-1990s, a mild outbreak was followed by a severe outbreak (Johnson et al., 2006; Figure 8.6). By extending our host–pathogen-induced defence model to include spatial structure, we allowed for the possibility that some parts of the forest would consist of trees that gypsy moths were capable of developing on, but that did not have hydrolysable tannins. This model can then reproduce the pattern of alternating mild and severe outbreaks seen in the data. Moreover, the pattern occurs in the data in oak-hickory forests (Johnson et al., 2006), which are roughly 43% oaks, but not in oak-pine forests, which are only 15% oaks, and the alternating pattern similarly occurs in our model when 43% of the forest is inducible, but not when the forest is 15% inducible (Elderd et al., 2013; Figure 8.7). This effect occurs because the reduced heterogeneity resulting from induced defences causes outbreaks to have a larger amplitude and a longer period on oaks.

Induced defences have similarly complex effects on the transmission of the fall armyworm baculovirus, with soybean (*Glycine max*) serving as the host's resource. Soybean self-pollinates and therefore produces genetically similar offspring, making it possible for us to disentangle the effects of induced defences from the effects of genetic differences between host

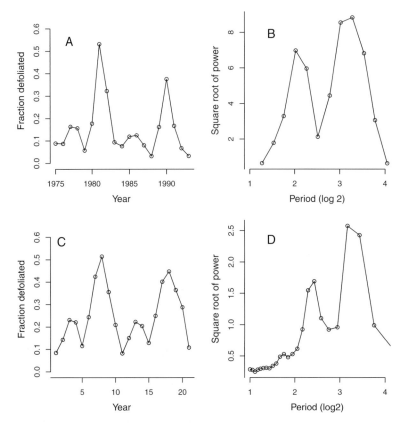

Figure 8.6 Outbreak dynamics in oak-hickory forests, in data (Johnson et al., 2005) and in a spatial version of a host–pathogen-induced defence model (Elderd et al., 2013). (A) and (C) show defoliation time series in the data and in the model, respectively. (B) and (D) are the associated power spectra, respectively, showing the strong subharmonic peak (smaller peak at shorter period) in both the data and the model. For the model we show a time series based on a single realisation, but the pattern holds up over multiple realisations, so that the spectrum for the model is an average over 100 realisations. Reprinted from Elderd et al. (2013).

plants. In our experiment, we therefore used a single genotype known as 'Stonewall', which is known to be readily inducible (Underwood et al., 2002), and we again induced defences using a jasmonic acid solution. The data and models derived from the experiment, which were analysed using a Bayesian framework, show a trend that is the mirror opposite of what we observed in the gypsy moth system (Elderd, 2019), in that induction changed the best model from linear to non-linear. This difference likely occurred because jasmonic acid induces hydrolysable tannins in oaks (Hunter & Schultz, 1993), but induces protease inhibitors and peroxidases in soybean (Underwood et al., 2002).

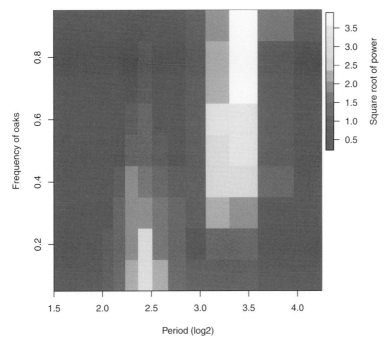

Figure 8.7 Effects of oak frequency on the power spectrum of the defoliation time series in the spatial model. The colours show the square root of the power of each period, such that dark red indicates the lowest power and white indicates the highest power. The figure thus shows that, at a low frequency of oaks, only short-period cycles occur, whereas at a high frequency of oaks, only long-period cycles occur. The relative importance of short- and long-period cycles then gradually shifts as the frequency of oaks increases, so that both short- and long-period cycles are represented in the power spectrum at intermediate frequencies of oaks. Reprinted from Elderd et al. (2013). (A black and white version of this figure will appear in some formats. For the colour version, please refer to the plate section.)

In the gypsy moth, increases in tannins increased leaf consumption and altered the probability of infection given consumption of the virus (Elderd et al., 2013), thus altering both the probability that a host contacted the pathogen and the probability of infection given contact. In contrast, for the fall armyworm, induced soybean defences decreased consumption and interfered with larval weight gain (Shikano et al., 2017). The increase in consumption that we observed in the gypsy moth may have ensured that all individuals contracted the virus, thereby reducing or eliminating the inter-individual differences that drive transmission non-linearities. The reduction in consumption that we observed in the fall armyworm in contrast may have increased differences among individuals, thereby strengthening transmission non-linearities. The question of how the effects of these induced defences on the baculovirus alter long-term fall armyworm dynamics will be the focus of future research.

8.2.6 Eco-evolutionary dynamics, population structure, and disease transmission

So far, we have focused on ecological effects, without considering how evolutionary change may alter host–pathogen dynamics. Heritable disease resistance has been documented in the hosts of many pathogens (Altizer et al., 2003), suggesting that selection for disease resistance could in theory alter host–pathogen dynamics (Dieckmann, 2002). Although there is similarly strong evidence for pathogen polymorphism, most studies of pathogen evolution consider whether selection will lead to higher virulence, but pathogen variation could also alter host–pathogen dynamics. Long-term studies of host–pathogen evolution are in general very difficult, but the ease with which insect baculovirus experiments can be carried out means that we can easily ask how genetic variation in the host or the pathogen affects the transmission process.

Evolutionary dynamics may be key to understanding baculovirus-driven insect population cycles, because the non-evolutionary model, Equations 8.15 and 8.16, predicts that host populations with a heterogeneity coefficient greater than one, $C > 1$, exhibit stable dynamics (Elderd et al., 2008), following the well-known 'CV squared greater than 1' rule (Hassell et al., 1991). Gypsy moth populations in North America, in contrast, exhibit boom and bust cycles, in which populations fluctuate over an order of magnitude from the peak of the cycle to the trough (Elkinton & Liebhold, 1990).

We therefore expected that, in field transmission experiments on the gypsy moth, estimates of heterogeneity in transmission should be less than one. However, Elderd et al. (2008) showed that, for egg masses collected from 22 different populations, median heterogeneity values were greater than one in 16 cases, and had confidence bounds overlapping one in all but one of the remaining six. According to the non-evolutionary model, gypsy moth populations should therefore exhibit stable dynamics, which is completely at odds with the data (Figure 8.8A). Additionally, for populations in which egg masses could be collected before and after outbreaks, both average transmission $\bar{\beta}$ and gypsy moth egg mass sizes were significantly smaller following outbreaks, consistent with selection for increased resistance, and a trade-off between resistance and fecundity. Additional experiments with half-sibling groups further showed that transmission $\bar{\beta}$ can be affected by a host's sire (Elderd et al., 2008), suggesting that infection risk is heritable. The data thus suggested that a key missing element in the model is natural selection for increased resistance.

We therefore modified the non-evolutionary model to allow for fluctuating selection. In the modified model, hosts with higher reproductive output have a higher transmission coefficient, reflecting their higher risk. During the

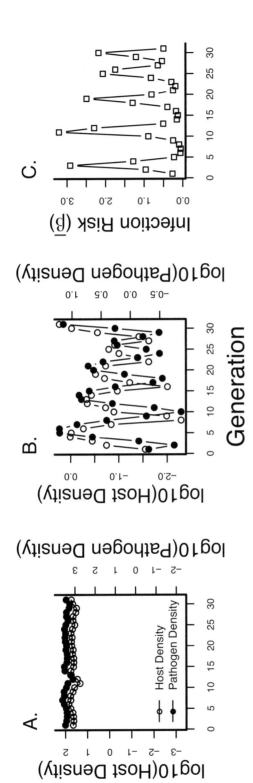

Figure 8.8 Effects of natural selection on host infection risk on insect host–pathogen population cycles. (A) Dynamics of insect host–pathogen model in the absence of natural selection on infection risk. Here the reproductive rate $\lambda = 74.6$, the effective pathogen overwintering parameter $\phi = 60$, the maximum predation rate $a = 0.96$, and the density at which maximum predation occurs $b = 0.4$. Note that variation in transmission $C = 1.12$, which produces stable dynamics, unlike the boom and bust cycles seen in defoliation data from nature. (B) Dynamics of model in which natural selection drives infection risk, such that high infection rates during outbreaks lead to increased resistance, and a cost of resistance between outbreaks leads to reduced resistance but an increased reproductive rate. Here the baseline reproductive rate $r = 0.2$, the rate of increase of reproduction with increasing susceptibility $\lambda = 9$, pathogen long-term survival $\gamma = 0.2$, and the pathogen between-generation impact $\phi = 14$. Variation in transmission $C = 2$, which when accounting for evolution produces cyclic dynamics. Here we assume that heritability is perfect, but allowing for imperfect heritability gives similar results Páez et al. (2017). (C) Corresponding changes in infection risk $\bar{\beta}$. Figure adapted from Elderd et al. (2008), © 2008 University of Chicago Press.

troughs of the population cycle when the pathogen population density is lower, there is selection for higher-fecundity/higher-risk hosts, but when the pathogen density increases, higher-risk individuals die of the disease, and the average transmission rate drops. The resulting model produces boom and bust cycles even when heterogeneity $C > 1$ (Figure 8.8B), reconciling the experimental data with the long-term observation studies showing cycles. The model also predicts sharp drops in transmission rates following a peak in the cycle (Figure 8.8C), matching observed drops in experimental transmission rate estimates from post-outbreak hosts (Elderd et al., 2008).

In the absence of a robust estimate of heritability, in the initial model we assumed that heritability was perfect, as though the host is clonal. In more recent work (Páez et al., 2017), we carried out experiments showing that heritability $h^2 \approx 0.13$, and showing that there is a substantial fecundity cost of reduced transmission. We therefore extended the model to allow for imperfect heritability, as follows:

$$N_{n+1} = rN_n[1 - i(N_n, Z_n, \bar{\beta}_n)]\left\{1 + s\bar{\beta}_n[1 - i(N_n, Z_n, \bar{\beta}_n)]^{C^2}\right\}, \qquad (8.21)$$

$$Z_{n+1} = \phi N_n i(N_n, Z_n, \bar{\beta}_n) + \gamma Z_n, \qquad (8.22)$$

$$\bar{\beta}_{n+1} = \bar{\beta}_n[1 - i(N_n, Z_n, \bar{\beta}_n)]^{h^2 C^2} \frac{\left\{1 + s\bar{\beta}_n(dC^2 + 1)[1 - i(N_n, Z_n, \bar{\beta}_n)]^{h^2 C^2}\right\}}{1 + s\bar{\beta}_n[1 - i(N_n, Z_n, \bar{\beta}_n)]^{h^2 C^2}}. \qquad (8.23)$$

Here, host density N_{n+1} is the product of baseline fecundity r, host density in the preceding generation N_n, and the fraction surviving the epizootic $[1 - i(N_n, Z_n, \bar{\beta}_n)]$. To allow for a cost of resistance, we assume that fecundity at low host and pathogen densities increases linearly with increasing infection risk $\bar{\beta}_n$, according to $1 + s\bar{\beta}_n[1 - i(N_n, Z_n, \bar{\beta}_n)]$, where s is a cost-scaling parameter. Changes in host density are thus partly driven by balancing selection, such that higher average infection risk $\bar{\beta}_n$ leads to increased mortality but also to increased fecundity. The fecundity cost of resistance is reduced, however, when the infection rate $i(N_n, Z_n, \bar{\beta}_n)$ is high, which is more likely when average infection risk is high, or when host and pathogen densities are high. Increases in average infection risk or in host and pathogen densities thus reduce the fecundity cost, but also increase host mortality. The equation for pathogen density Z_{n+1} is the same as it was in earlier models.

A key difference from Equations 8.15 and 8.16 is that here infection risk is a dynamic variable, such that $\bar{\beta}_{n+1}$ is equal to the preceding generation's infection risk $\bar{\beta}_n$ times the fraction infected $i(N_n, Z_n, \bar{\beta}_n)$, so that higher virus mortality selects for reduced risk. The cost of resistance in contrast selects for higher risk, because fecundity at low densities increases linearly with increases in previous-generation risk, $1 + s\bar{\beta}_n(h^2 C^2 + 1)[1 - i(N_n, Z_n, \bar{\beta}_n)]^{h^2 C^2}$, an effect that is again reduced by high infection rates. The symbol h^2 represents the heritability of risk, so that $h^2 C^2$ is the fraction of overall variation in risk that is due to additive genetic factors, and high values of h^2 strengthen the effects of selection. Changes in infection risk are thus determined by balancing selection, as in the case of host density, except that in contrast to host density, the change in infection risk does not depend on the baseline fecundity r.

We have also shown that there is variation in the gypsy moth baculovirus, and that this variation also follows evolutionary trade-offs, again in a way that depends on host variability (Fleming-Davies & Dwyer, 2015; Fleming-Davies et al., 2015). Field transmission experiments with 16 virus isolates showed that, across isolates, the viral breakdown rate μ, which describes viral decay on foliage, increases linearly with average transmission $\bar{\beta}$, a trade-off that is often assumed in models of the evolution of virulence (Dieckmann, 2002).

A more consequential trade-off, however, is that variation C increases with increasing average transmission. All else being equal, increased host variation is equivalent to an increase in variation in transmission, which in turn means that more resistant and more susceptible hosts have been added to the population in a way that leaves the mean unchanged. Because the addition of more resistant individuals has a bigger effect on the infection rate than does the addition of more susceptible individuals, increases in host variation reduce the infection rate. Increased host variation is therefore bad for the pathogen, and so increases in host variation with increases in the transmission rate lead to a trade-off between average transmission and variation in transmission (Fleming-Davies et al., 2015).

To allow for competition between virus strains in the SEIR model, Equations 8.10–8.13, we must track dynamic changes in the average transmission rate of each pathogen strain. The resulting model is:

$$\frac{dS}{dt} = -\beta_1 P_1 S - \beta_2 P_2 S \tag{8.24}$$

$$\frac{d\beta_1}{dt} = -P_1 \beta_1^2 C^2 - P_2 \rho C_1 C_2 \beta_1 \beta_2 \tag{8.25}$$

$$\frac{dE_{1,1}}{dt} = P_1 \beta_1 S - m_1 \xi_1 E_{1,1} \tag{8.26}$$

$$\frac{dE_{i,1}}{dt} = m_1 \xi_1 E_{i-1,1} - m_1 \xi_1 E_{i,1}, \text{for } m_1 = 2,\dots,m_1 \tag{8.27}$$

$$\frac{dP_1}{dt} = m_1 \xi_1 E_{i,1} - \mu_1 P_1 \tag{8.28}$$

Here, β_1 and β_2 are the transmission rates of the two pathogen strains, but for simplicity we include only the equations for strain 1. Also, ρ is the correlation in transmission rate between strains 1 and 2, which in this system is generally positive (Hudson et al., 2016), reducing the chances of coexistence of pathogen strains. The average transmission rate of strain 1 thus declines because of the loss of hosts infected with that strain, but it also declines because of the loss of hosts infected with strain 2 that have high susceptibility to strain 1, and likewise for strain 2.

By extending this model to allow for long-term dynamics, as in Equations 8.15 and 8.16, we showed that the trade-off between variation C and average transmission $\bar{\beta}$ can allow for coexistence, whereas the trade-off between decay μ and average transmission cannot allow for coexistence (Fleming-Davies et al., 2015). Notably, coexistence is not possible in standard models. Meanwhile, a trade-off between transmission on foliage and transmission on egg masses prevents the evolution of ever-increasing transmission (Fleming-Davies & Dwyer, 2015).

8.2.7 Future directions

Our results on induced defences and natural selection relied on improvements in experimental protocols that allowed us to reduce the uncertainty of our estimates of the heterogeneity parameter C (Dwyer et al., 2005), and this reduction illustrates how experimental data and mechanistic models iteratively interact to improve our understanding of host–pathogen dynamics. Initial estimates of uncertainty in the value of C were quite large. Improved protocols caused the confidence intervals around these estimates to be narrowed to the point where the data and the model disagreed. Modifying the models to account for eco-evolutionary processes then resulted in a reconciliation between the experimental data and the mechanistic models. This reconciliation was only possible as a result of the extensive studies needed to estimate the heterogeneity parameter C with sufficient accuracy.

More broadly, both plant defences and eco-evolutionary processes play an important role in the long-term dynamics of the gypsy moth. Induced plant defences alter the heterogeneity in infection risk (Elderd et al., 2013,) while evolutionary dynamics drive changes in the transmission rate (Elderd et al., 2008; Páz et al., 2017). Pathogen polymorphism also apparently plays an important role in determining heterogeneity in infection risk (Fleming-Davies & Dwyer, 2015; Fleming-Davies et al., 2015). Teasing out the relative contributions of defences and natural selection would require experimental manipulations that alter the above factors at the same time, an important future direction.

8.2.7.1 *Advancing analytical methods*
Most ecological research uses linear models to test whether a pattern of association exists between independent and dependent variables. While this approach will continue to be useful for many research questions, it places limits on the types of research that can be conducted. This is especially true

given that epizootic models continue to increase in complexity, and given that the population processes invoked by these models are strongly non-linear. To rigorously test non-linear epizootic models, we need statistical techniques that go beyond standard null-hypothesis tests, for example by using the model-selection techniques that we have used here (Burnham & Anderson, 2002). Bayesian methods also hold great promise, because Bayesian software continues to be developed (e.g. JAGS, STAN), as do how-to guides (e.g. Clark, 2007; Kéry, 2010; Hobbs & Hooten, 2015). While Bayesian methods have been used to address questions regarding epidemics in human populations (e.g. O'Neill, 2002; Elderd et al., 2008; Ferrari et al., 2008), such methods are just beginning to be used to confront models with epizootic data (Kennedy et al., 2014; Páez et al., 2017). We therefore argue that the best method of moving disease ecology forward is by developing mechanistic models and fitting them to data using a Bayesian analytical approach.

This is especially true when priors are highly informative. First, the use of informed priors enables researchers to integrate information across multiple studies and scales (LaDeau et al., 2011; Pepin et al., 2017). For instance, the within-host infection process at the scale of the individual provides information about epizootic spread at the scale of the population via changes in either the mean transmission rate, or in variability in the transmission rate. Traditionally, data sets collected at different scales have in contrast been analysed separately.

Second, informative priors become more useful as the number of parameters in a model continue to grow, because an increase in parameters increases the dimensionality of the fitting problem. Fitting high-dimensional models to data often leads to problems of parameter identifiability, but informative priors constrain the parameter space, thereby resolving identifiability problems (Elderd et al., 2013; Hobbs & Hooten, 2015). For historical outbreaks of smallpox, for example, using informed priors to constrain parameter space reduced collinearity in the model parameters, making it easier to estimate differences in transmission processes across multiple populations (Elderd, Dwyer & Dukic, 2013). Similarly, for a Bayesian state-space model of brucellosis transmission in the Yellowstone bison population, informed priors ensured that the Bayesian models fit to the data converged on the posterior. Convergence would not have been possible with the use of vague priors (Hobbs et al., 2015). Informative priors can thus be essential when fitting complex hierarchical models in a Bayesian context.

As we have described, we have often used small-scale experiments to make model predictions, and then we tested the model predictions with large-scale observational data, on the grounds that the models are designed to extrapolate from small-scale mechanisms to large-scale patterns. This approach can be made more rigorous using a Bayesian framework. That is, field experiments can be used to estimate the full posterior distributions associated with disease transmission parameters, such as the mean transmission rate and the heterogeneity in transmission that we have emphasised here. These posterior distributions can then be integrated into long-term dynamic models to assess whether the long-term model does a good job of reproducing large-scale data.

More broadly, however, in testing models with large-scale, long-term observational data, problems may arise due to a mis-match between the state variables in the model and the data that have been collected. For instance, long-term data sets often provide only area defoliated, a proxy for insect pest density (Doane & McManus, 1981), whereas host density is the state variable in the models. In such cases, there are latent or unobserved states that we are interested in quantifying, namely the density of insects within a forest or field. Estimating latent states is therefore a major challenge in studies of insect–pathogen interactions, as it is throughout the infectious disease literature (LaDeau et al., 2011). Additional problems with the long-term data sets may stem from observer error in defoliation estimates, which essentially makes the parameters associated with the mechanistic process model into latent variables.

Bayesian hierarchical models make it possible to disentangle observation error from process error, where process error arises from the inherent stochasticity in the process model associated with the system. Accounting for latent states and observation error in a Bayesian framework has been common in the mark–recapture literature, in which the impossibility of perfectly observing an entire population is a well-known problem (Link & Barker, 2010). The same analytical framework can be useful for problems that arise in the analysis of epizootic data. For example, the Bayesian state-space model for Yellowstone bison (Hobbs et al., 2015) used multiple data sets that contained imperfect observations to make inferences about a mechanistic process model to answer key questions about bison management. In general, Bayesian hierarchical methods allow for rigorous quantification of unobserved or latent states involved in epizootic data.

A related issue is that epizootics and long-term host–pathogen dynamics may be affected by many different mechanisms, due to either abiotic or biotic effects. Data such as the number of infected individuals therefore reflect the effects of a mixture of multiple processes, which in turn represents an additional latent variable (Elderd & Miller, 2016). Bayesian mixture models can make it possible to use the data to separately estimate the relative strength or contribution of each process. For example, Verity et al. (2014) developed a Bayesian mixture model that allows for epizootics to start from either single or multiple spatial sources, using a Dirichlet process mixture model. This approach may similarly be successful when the infection process is driven by multiple pathogen strains or multiple pathogen sources, such as the combined fungal and viral epizootics that currently affect gypsy moth populations (Hajek et al., 2015). Indeed, Hobbs et al. (2015) used a mixture model approach to tease apart the relative contribution of frequency and density-dependent transmission in brucellosis epidemics in Yellowstone bison.

8.2.7.2 *Modifying the model*

Our previous work has allowed us to understand how population structure modulates host–pathogen interactions, an insight that we would not have reached without challenging mechanistic models with data. The experimental tractability of insect–baculovirus systems suggests that, as we modify the models to include other mechanisms, we will again be able to test the model predictions. Future baculovirus experiments may thus allow us to continue to explore fundamental aspects of the ecological and evolutionary processes that govern disease transmission.

One such future ecological direction is to allow for cannibalism, a common intraspecific interaction in the animal kingdom (Fox, 1975; Polis, 1981). The benefits of cannibalism include easy access to resources and reductions in competition, but cannibalism also has costs (Polis, 1981; Rudolf et al., 2010). One such cost arises from the consumption of infected conspecifics (Pfennig, 2000), which may lead to the infection of the cannibal, but individual cannibalism may not be as disadvantageous as initially believed. In terms of disease transmission, cannibalism removes an infected or exposed individual from the population before the pathogen has a chance to spread to multiple hosts rather than just the cannibal.

Of the many Lepidopteran insects that are affected by baculoviruses, at least a modest number are cannibalistic (Richardson et al., 2010), including the fall armyworm (Williams & Hernández, 2006; Valicente et al., 2013). Baculoviruses prevent infected larvae from moulting to later instars, even as healthy individuals continue to grow (Elderd, 2013), and so an insect population with a low or moderate baculovirus infection rate will consist of healthy later instars of much larger size, and infected early instars of much smaller size. Baculovirus infections thus create size structure in host populations. Moreover, if a healthy later instar consumes an infected early instar before the virus population in the early instar has reached a high density, the larger later instar may have removed an infected host from the population, reducing epizootic severity, while experiencing only a small increase in infection risk due to cannibalism (Van Allen et al., 2017). Cannibalism may therefore reduce an insect's lifetime infection risk. Baculovirus-driven variation in size can thus lead to stage-structured cannibalism that has important consequences for epizootics (Rudolf, 2007).

To illustrate these effects, we modified an SEIR model to allow for cannibalism:

$$\frac{dS}{dt} = -\beta SP - bS - fkS\sum_{i-1}^{m}E_i, \tag{8.29}$$

$$\frac{dE_1}{dt} = \beta SP + fk\sum_{i-1}^{m}E_i - m\xi E_1 - bE_1 - kSE_1, \tag{8.30}$$

$$\frac{dE_i}{dt} = m\xi E_{i-1} - m\xi E_i - bE_i - kSE_i (i = 2, \ldots, m), \tag{8.31}$$

$$\frac{dP}{dt} = m\xi E_m - \mu P. \tag{8.32}$$

Here, f is the fraction of attacks that result in infection and k is the cannibalism-based attack rate. Using the above model, Van Allen et al. (2017) show that at high host densities the cumulative fraction infected at the end of the epizootic is less than the corresponding fraction infected in a model that does not include cannibalism. The predictions of the two models only converge when f is close to 1, at which point effectively all cannibalistic individuals become infected. Preliminary data (Elderd, unpubl. data) suggest that, in fall armyworms, cannibalism of infected first instars by uninfected fourth instars may indeed reduce infection rates. Further experiments are needed to understand the effects of this process on long-term host–pathogen dynamics.

Given that hosts and pathogens exert strong selective pressures on each other (Elderd et al., 2008; Fleming-Davies & Dwyer, 2015; Fleming-Davies et al., 2015; Páez et al., 2017), a second important area of future research is to consider the broader implications of eco-evolutionary dynamics. Within the genus *Spodoptera* in particular, environmentally driven phenotypic plasticity is widespread, including for example density-dependent prophylaxis (Reeson et al., 1998, 2000; Altizer et al., 2006), suggesting that genotypic expression may control infection risk. There are also clear indications that diversity in the host or the pathogen affects transmission dynamics in armyworms (Fuxa, 1987; Fuxa et al., 1988; Redman et al., 2016).

Similarly, if covert infections via vertical transmission play a key role in disease transmission, natural selection may again affect disease dynamics. For instance, covert infections may decrease pathogen virulence and could even result in a system in which only covertly infected hosts and the avirulent pathogen interact, with much lower infection rates (Bonsall et al., 2005). We emphasise, however, that the necessity of killing the host suggests that avirulence is unlikely to appear in baculoviruses. Meanwhile, in the gypsy moth–baculovirus interaction, there are at least modest genotype-by-genotype (G × G) effects (Fleming-Davies et al., 2015; Hudson et al., 2016).

Understanding the full effects of coevolution in these systems is therefore another future direction.

Natural selection may also be affected by genotype by genotype by environment $(G \times G \times E)$ interactions, which could allow for abiotic factors to influence the direction and the strength of selection on the host and the pathogen. Abiotic factors that are of increasing relevance of course include the effects of global warming. Given that temperatures are changing at different rates across the landscape, coevolutionary dynamics may also vary across the landscape due to local adaptation. At a landscape level, this will create a geographic mosaic, with coevolutionary hot spots where the strength of selection is high, and cold spots where the strength of selection is low (Thompson, 2005). Biotic factors may also produce a geographical mosaic of coevolution, for example because a heterogeneous phytochemical landscape may lead to spatial differences in the effects of host plant chemistry on infection risk (Hunter, 2016), an effect that may in turn be determined by plant genotypic variation (Shikano et al., 2017). Whether a coevolutionary mosaic emerges will depend upon the dispersal ability of the host and pathogen, because high dispersal rates generally reduce spatial heterogeneity. The effects of environmental factors on genotype-by-genotype interactions thus represent another future avenue of research, and may lend insight into how coevolutionary mosaics emerge in host–pathogen interactions.

8.3 Conclusions

Few host–pathogen interactions are as experimentally tractable as insect–baculovirus interactions. Baculoviruses are ubiquitous in nature and affect many insects, not just the gypsy moth and the fall armyworm that we have focused on here. In insects, baculovirus transmission is affected by both biotic and abiotic factors, which can be easily manipulated in the field. This has allowed for the development of a suite of mechanistic models that show how population structure affects epizootics and long-term host–pathogen population dynamics, and that have survived extensive testing with both experimental and observational data. These tests have used techniques from several areas of statistics, including information theory, Bayesian hierarchical models, and time-series probes. Confronting models with data has provided insights into the mechanisms determining baculovirus spread, and has suggested ways in which transmission dynamics may be similarly affected by biotic and abiotic factors in other less easily manipulated interactions. This generality arises because the data can often be described by models that have been used to describe disease transmission in many other species. As we use baculoviruses to better understand the ecological and eco-evolutionary dynamics of disease transmission, new challenges will require further model development and more advanced statistical approaches.

8.4 Acknowledgements

We acknowledge our co-authors, people who served as sounding boards, and the field assistants that helped us along the way. Our research would not have been possible without funding from the National Science Foundation, the National Institutes of Health, and the United States Department of Agriculture. BDE was funded by NSF grant 1316334 as part of the joint NSF-NIH-USDA Ecology and Evolution of Infectious Diseases programme.

References

Abbott, K.C. & Dwyer, G. (2008) Using mechanistic models to understand synchrony in forest insect populations: the North American Gypsy Moth as a case study. *American Naturalist*, **172**, 613–624.

Altizer, S., Dobson, A., Hosseini, P., et al. (2006) Seasonality and the dynamics of infectious diseases. *Ecology Letters*, **9**, 467–484.

Altizer, S., Harvell, D. & Friedle, E. (2003) Rapid evolutionary dynamics and disease threats to biodiversity. *Trends in Ecology & Evolution*, **18**, 589–596.

Anderson, R.M. & May, R.M. (1978) Regulation and stability of host-parasite population interactions: I. Regulatory processes. *The Journal of Animal Ecology*, **47**, 219–247.

Anderson, R.M. & May, R.M. (1981) The population dynamics of microparasites and their invertebrate hosts. *Philosophical Transactions of the Royal Society of London B*, **291**, 451–524.

Anderson, R.M. & May, R.M. (1991) *Infectious Disease of Humans: Dynamics and Control*. Oxford: Oxford University Press.

Baldwin, I.T. (1998) Jasmonate-induced responses are costly but benefit plants under attack in native populations. *Proceedings of the National Academy of Sciences of the United States of America*, **95**, 8113–8118.

Barbosa, P. & Krischik, V.A. (1987) Influence of alkaloids on feeding preference of eastern deciduous forest trees by the gypsy moth *Lymantria dispar*. *American Naturalist*, **130**, 53–69.

Bjørnstad, O.N., Robinet, C. & Liebhold, A.M. (2010) Geographic variation in North American gypsy moth cycles: subharmonics, generalist predators, and spatial coupling. *Ecology*, **91**, 106–118.

Bonsall, M.B., Sait, S.M. & Hails, R.S. (2005) Invasion and dynamics of covert infection strategies in structured insect–pathogen populations. *Journal of Animal Ecology*, **74**, 464–474.

Boots, M., Greenman, J., Ross, D., et al. (2003) The population dynamical implications of covert infections in host–microparasite interactions. *Journal of Animal Ecology*, **72**, 1064–1072.

Burden, J.P., Nixon, C.P., Hodgkinson, A.E., et al. (2003) Covert infections as a mechanism for long-term persistence of baculoviruses. *Ecology Letters*, **6**, 524–531.

Burnham, K. & Anderson, D. (2002) *Model Selection and Multimodal Inference: A Practical Information-theoretic Approach*. New York, NY: Springer.

Chamberlin, T.C. (1897) Studies for students: the method of multiple working hypotheses. *The Journal of Geology*, **5**, 837–848.

Clark, J.S. (2007) *Models for Ecological Data: An Introduction*. Princeton, NJ: Princeton University Press.

Cory, J.S. & Hoover, K. (2006) Plant-mediated effects in insect–pathogen interactions. *Trends in Ecology & Evolution*, **21**, 278–286.

D'Amico, V., Elkinton, J.S., Podgwaite, J.D., Buonaccorsi, J. & Dwyer, G. (2005) Pathogen clumping: an explanation for non-linear transmission of an insect virus. *Ecological Entomology*, **30**, 383–390.

Dieckmann, U. (2002) Adaptive dynamics of pathogen-host interactions. In: Dieckmann, U., Sigmund, K. & Metz, H. (eds.), *Adaptive Dynamics of Infectious Diseases: In Pursuit of Virulence Management* (pp. 39–59). Cambridge: Cambridge University Press.

Doane, C.C. & McManus, M.L. (eds.). (1981) *The Gypsy Moth: Research Toward Integrated Pest Management.* Washington, DC: USDA.

Duffy, M.A., Ochs, J.H., Penczykowski, R.M., et al. (2012) Ecological context influences epidemic size and parasite-driven evolution. *Science*, **335**, 1636–1638.

Dwyer, G. (1991) The roles of density, stage, and patchiness in the transmission of an insect virus. *Ecology*, **72**, 559–574.

Dwyer, G., Dushoff, J., Elkinton, J.S., Burand, J.P. & Levin, S.A. (2002) Variation in susceptibility: lessons from an insect virus. In: Dieckmann, U., Sigmund, K. & Metz, H. (eds.), *Adaptive Dynamics of Infectious Diseases: In Pursuit of Virulence Management* (pp. 74–84). Cambridge: Cambridge University Press.

Dwyer, G., Dushoff, J., Elkinton, J.S. & Levin, S.A. (2000) Pathogen-driven outbreaks in forest defoliators revisited: building models from experimental data. *American Naturalist*, **156**, 105–120.

Dwyer, G., Dushoff, J. & Yee, S.H. (2004) The combined effects of pathogens and predators on insect outbreaks. *Nature*, **430**, 341–345.

Dwyer, G., Elkinton, J.S. & Buonaccorsi, J.P. (1997) Host heterogeneity in susceptibility and disease dynamics: tests of a mathematical model. *American Naturalist*, **150**, 685–707.

Dwyer, G., Firestone, J. & Stevens, T.E. (2005) Should models of disease dynamics in herbivorous insects include the effects of variability in host-plant foliage quality? *American Naturalist*, **165**, 16–31.

Eakin, L., Wang, M. & Dwyer, G. (2015) The effects of the avoidance of infectious hosts on infection risk in an insect–pathogen interaction. *American Naturalist*, **185**, 100–112.

Elderd, B.D. (2013) Developing models of disease transmission: insights from ecological studies of insects and their baculoviruses. *PLoS Pathogens*, **9**, e1003372.

Elderd, B.D. (2019) Bottom-up trait-mediated indirect effects decrease pathogen transmission in a tritrophic system. *Ecology*, **100**, e02551.

Elderd, B.D., Dushoff, J. & Dwyer, G. (2008) Host–pathogen interactions, insect outbreaks, and natural selection for disease resistance. *American Naturalist*, **172**, 829–842.

Elderd, B.D., Dwyer, G. & Dukic, V. (2013) Population-level differences in disease transmission: a Bayesian analysis of multiple smallpox epidemics. *Epidemics*, **5**, 146–156.

Elderd, B.D. & Miller, T.E.X. (2016) Quantifying uncertainty in demographic models: Bayesian methods for Integral Projection Models (IPMs). *Ecological Monographs*, **86**, 125–144.

Elderd, B.D., Rehill, B.J., Haynes, K.J. & Dwyer, G. (2013) Induced plant defenses, host–pathogen interactions, and forest insect outbreaks. *Proceedings of the National Academy of Sciences of the United States of America*, **110**, 14,978–14,983.

Elderd, B.D. & Reilly, J. (2014) Warmer temperatures increase disease transmission and outbreak intensity in a host–pathogen system. *Journal of Animal Ecology*, **83**, 838–849.

Elkinton, J.S., Healy, W.M., Buonaccorsi, J.P., et al. (1996) Interactions among gypsy moths, white-footed mice, and acorns. *Ecology*, **77**, 2332–2342.

Elkinton, J. & Liebhold, A. (1990) Population dynamics of gypsy moth in North America. *Annual Review of Entomology*, **35**, 571–596.

Ferrari, M.J., Grais, R.F., Bharti, N., et al. (2008) The dynamics of measles in sub-Saharan Africa. *Nature*, **451**, 679–684.

Fleming-Davies, A.E., Dukic, V., Andreasen, V. & Dwyer, G. (2015) Effects of host heterogeneity on pathogen diversity and evolution. *Ecology Letters*, **18**, 1252–1261.

Fleming-Davies, A.E. & Dwyer, G. (2015) Phenotypic variation in overwinter environmental transmission of a baculovirus and the cost of virulence. *American Naturalist*, **186**, 797–806.

Fox, L.R. (1975) Cannibalism in natural-populations. *Annual Review of Ecology and Systematics*, **6**, 87–106.

Fuller, E., Elderd, B.D. & Dwyer, G. (2012) Pathogen persistence in the environment and insect–baculovirus interactions: disease-density thresholds, epidemic burnout, and insect outbreaks. *American Naturalist*, **179**, E70–E96.

Fuxa, J.R. (1982) Prevalence of viral infections in populations of fall armyworm, *Spodoptera frugiperda*, in Southeastern Louisiana. *Environmental Entomology*, **11**, 239–242.

Fuxa, J.R. (1987) *Spodoptera frugiperda* susceptibility to nuclear polyhedrosis-virus isolates with reference to insect migration. *Environmental Entomology*, **16**, 218–223.

Fuxa, J.R. & Geaghan, J.P. (1983) Multiple-regression analysis of factors affecting prevalence of nuclear polyhedrosis virus in *Spodoptera frugiperda* (Lepidoptera, Noctuidae) populations. *Environmental Entomology*, **12**, 311–316.

Fuxa, J., Mitchell, F. & Richter, A. (1988) Resistance of *Spodoptera frugiperda* (Lepidoptera: Noctuidae) to a nuclear polyhedrosis virus in the field and laboratory. *BioControl*, **33**, 55–63.

Gelman, A., Carlin, J.B., Stern, H.S. & Rubin, D.B. (2014) *Bayesian Data Analysis*. Boca Raton, FL: Taylor & Francis.

Godfree, R., Robertson, B., Bolger, T., Carnegie, M. & Young, A. (2011) An improved hexagon open-top chamber system for stable diurnal and nocturnal warming and atmospheric carbon dioxide enrichment. *Global Change Biology*, **17**, 439–451.

Grzywacz, D., Mushobozi, W.L., Parnell, M., Jolliffe, F. & Wilson, K. (2008) Evaluation of *Spodoptera exempta* nucleopolyhedrovirus (SpexNPV) for the field control of African armyworm (*Spodoptera exempta*) in Tanzania. *Crop Protection*, **27**, 17–24.

Hajek, A.E. (1999) Pathology and epizootiology of *Entomophaga maimaiga* infections in forest Lepidoptera. *Microbiology and Molecular Biology Reviews*, **63**, 814–835.

Hajek, A.E., Tobin, P.C. & Haynes, K.J. (2015) Replacement of a dominant viral pathogen by a fungal pathogen does not alter the collapse of a regional forest insect outbreak. *Oecologia*, **177**, 785–797.

Hall, S.R., Simonis, J.L., Nisbet, R.M., Tessier, A.J. & Caceres, C.E. (2009) Resource ecology of virulence in a planktonic host–parasite system: an explanation using dynamic energy budgets. *American Naturalist*, **174**, 149–162.

Harvell, C.D., Mitchell, C.E., Ward, J.R., et al. (2002) Ecology – Climate warming and disease risks for terrestrial and marine biota. *Science*, **296**, 2158–2162.

Hassell, M.P., May, R.M., Pacala, S.W. & Chesson, P.L. (1991) The persistence of host–parasitoid associations in patchy environments. I. A general criterion. *The American Naturalist*, **138**, 568–583.

Hethcote, H.W. (1976) Qualitative analyses of communicable disease models. *Mathematical Biosciences*, **28**, 335–356.

Hilborn, R. & Mangel, M. (1997) *The Ecological Detective: Confronting Models with Data*. Princeton, NJ: Princeton University Press.

Hinds, W. & Dew, J. (1915) The grass worm or fall army worm. Bulletin no. 186, Alabama Agricultural Experiment Station.

Hobbs, N.T., Geremia, C., Treanor, J., et al. (2015) State-space modeling to support management of brucellosis in the Yellowstone bison population. *Ecological Monographs*, **85**, 525–556.

Hobbs, N.T. & Hooten, M.B. (2015) *Bayesian Models: A Statistical Primer for Ecologists*. Princeton, NJ: Princeton University Press.

Hooten, M.B. & Hobbs, N.T. (2015) A guide to Bayesian model selection for ecologists. *Ecological Monographs*, **85**, 3–28.

Hoover, K., Grove, M., Gardner, M., et al. (2011) A gene for an extended phenotype. *Science*, **333**, 1401–1401.

Hudson, A.I., Fleming-Davies, A.E., Páez, D.J. & Dwyer, G. (2016) Genotype-by-genotype interactions between an insect and its pathogen. *Journal of Evolutionary Biology*, **29**, 2480–2490.

Hudson, P.J., Dobson, A.P. & Newborn, D. (1998) Prevention of population cycles by parasite removal. *Science*, **282**, 2256–2258.

Hudson, P.J., Rizzoli, A., Grenfell, B.T., Heesterbeek, H. & Dobson, A.P. (2002) *The Ecology of Wildlife Diseases*. Oxford: Oxford University Press.

Hunter, M.D. & Schultz, J.C. (1993) Induced plant defenses breached? Phytochemical induction protects an herbivore from disease. *Oecologia*, **94**, 195–203.

Hunter, M. (2016) *The Phytochemical Landscape: Linking Trophic Interactions and Nutrient Dynamics*. Princeton, NJ:: Princeton University Press.

Hunter-Fujita, F.R., Entwistle, P., Evans, H., et al. (1998) *Insect Viruses and Pest Management*. Chichester: John Wiley & Sons Ltd.

Ionides, E., Bretó, C. & King, A. (2006) Inference for nonlinear dynamical systems. *Proceedings of the National Academy of Sciences of the United States of America*, **103**, 18,438–18,443.

Johnson, D.M., Liebhold, A.M. & Bjørnstad, O.N. (2006) Geographical variation in the periodicity of gypsy moth outbreaks. *Ecography*, **29**, 367–374.

Johnson, D.M., Liebhold, A.M., Bjørnstad, O.N. & McManus, M.L. (2005) Circumpolar variation in periodicity and synchrony among gypsy moth populations. *Journal of Animal Ecology*, **74**, 882–892.

Johnson, P.T., De Roode, J.C. & Fenton, A. (2015) Why infectious disease research needs community ecology. *Science*, **349**, 1259504.

Karban, R. & Baldwin, I.T. (1997) *Induced Responses to Herbivory*. Chicago, IL: University of Chicago Press.

Keeling, M.J. & Rohani, P. (2008) *Modeling Infectious Diseases in Humans and Animals*. Princeton, NJ: Princeton University Press.

Kendall, B.E., Briggs, C.J., Murdoch, W.W., et al. (1999) Why do populations cycle? A synthesis of statistical and mechanistic modeling approaches. *Ecology*, **80**, 1789–1805.

Kennedy, D.A., Dukic, V. & Dwyer, G. (2014) Pathogen growth in insect hosts: inferring the importance of different mechanisms using stochastic models and response-time data. *American Naturalist*, **184**, 407–423.

Kéry, M. (2010) *Introduction to WinBUGS for Ecologists*. Boston, MA: Academic Press.

King, A.A., Ionides, E.L., Pascual, M. & Bouma, M.J. (2008) Inapparent infections and cholera dynamics. *Nature*, **454**, 877–880.

Konishi, S. & Kitagawa, G. (2008) *Information Criteria and Statistical Modeling*. New York, NY: Springer Science & Business Media.

Kot, M. (2001) *Elements of Mathematical Ecology*. Cambridge: Cambridge University Press.

LaDeau, S.L., Glass, G.E., Hobbs, N.T., Latimer, A. & Ostfeld, R.S. (2011) Data–model fusion to better understand emerging pathogens and improve infectious disease forecasting. *Ecological Applications*, **21**, 1443–1460.

Lee, K.P., Cory, J.S., Wilson, K., Raubenheimer, D. & Simpson, S.J. (2006) Flexible diet choice offsets protein costs of pathogen resistance in a caterpillar. *Proceedings of the Royal Society of London B*, **273**, 823–829.

Levin, S.A. (1992) The problem of pattern and scale in ecology: the Robert H. MacArthur award lecture. *Ecology*, **73**, 1943–1967.

Link, W.A. & Barker, R.J. (2010) *Bayesian Inference with Ecological Applications*. London: Academic Press.

May, R.M. & Anderson, R.M. (1978) Regulation and stability of host–parasite population interactions: II. Destabilizing processes. *Journal of Animal Ecology*, **47**, 249–267.

May, R.M. & Anderson, R.M. (1979) Population biology of infectious diseases: Part II. *Nature*, **280**, 455–461.

McCallum, H. (2016) Models for managing wildlife disease. *Parasitology*, **143**, 805–820.

McCallum, H., Fenton, A., Hudson, P., et al. (2017) Breaking beta: deconstructing the parasite transmission function. *Philosophical Transactions of the Royal Society of London B*, **372**, 20160084.

Miller, L.K. (2013) *The Baculoviruses*. New York, NY: Springer Science & Business Media.

Mitchell, E., McNeil, J., Westbrook, J., et al. (1991) Seasonal periodicity of fall armyworm (Lepidoptera: Noctuidae) in the Caribbean basin and northward to Canada. *Journal of Entomological Science*, **26**, 39–50.

Moreau, G. & Lucarotti, C.J. (2007) A brief review of the past use of baculoviruses for the management of eruptive forest defoliators and recent developments on a sawfly virus in Canada. *The Forestry Chronicle*, **83**, 105–112.

Myers, J.H. (1988) Can a general hypothesis explain population cycles of forest Lepidoptera? *Advances in Ecological Research*, **18**, 179–242.

Myers, J.H. & Cory, J.S. (2016) Ecology and evolution of pathogens in natural populations of Lepidoptera. *Evolutionary Applications*, **9**, 231–247.

New, L.F., Matthiopoulos, J., Redpath, S. & Buckland, S.T. (2009) Fitting models of multiple hypotheses to partial population data: investigating the causes of cycles in red grouse. *American Naturalist*, **174**, 399–412.

Nykänen, H. & Koricheva, J. (2004) Damage-induced changes in woody plants and their effects on insect herbivore performance: a meta-analysis. *Oikos*, **104**, 247–268.

O'Neill, P.D. (2002) A tutorial introduction to Bayesian inference for stochastic epidemic models using Markov chain Monte Carlo method. *Mathematical Biosciences*, **180**, 103–114.

Páez, D.J., Dukic, V., Dushoff, J., Fleming-Davies, A.E. & Dwyer, G. (2017) Eco-evolutionary theory and insect outbreaks. *American Naturalist*, **189**, 616–629.

Parker, B.J., Elderd, B.D. & Dwyer, G. (2010) Host behaviour and exposure risk in an insect–pathogen interaction. *Journal of Animal Ecology*, **79**, 863–870.

Pascual, M. & Bouma, M.J. (2009) Do rising temperatures matter? *Ecology*, **90**, 906–912.

Pepin, K.M., Kay, S.L., Golas, B.D., et al. (2017) Inferring infection hazard in wildlife populations by linking data across individual and population scales. *Ecology Letters*, **20**, 275–292.

Pfennig, D.W. (2000) Effect of predator–prey phylogenetic similarity on the fitness consequences of predation: a trade-off between nutrition and disease? *American Naturalist*, **155**, 335–345.

Pitre, H.N. & Hogg, D.B. (1983) Development of the fall armyworm (Lepidoptera, Noctuidae) on cotton, soybean and corn. *Journal of the Georgia Entomological Society*, **18**, 182–187.

Polis, G.A. (1981) The evolution and dynamics of intraspecific predation. *Annual Review of Ecology and Systematics*, **12**, 225–251.

Redman, E.M., Wilson, K. & Cory, J.S. (2016) Trade-offs and mixed infections in an obligate-killing insect pathogen. *Journal of Animal Ecology*, **85**, 1200–1209.

Reeson, A.F., Wilson, K., Cory, J.S., et al. (2000) Effects of phenotypic plasticity on

pathogen transmission in the field in a Lepidoptera–NPV system. *Oecologia*, **124**, 373–380.

Reeson, A.F., Wilson, K., Gunn, A., Hails, R.S. & Goulson, D. (1998) Baculovirus resistance in the noctuid *Spodoptera exempta* is phenotypically plastic and responds to population density. *Proceedings of the Royal Society of London B*, **265**, 1787–1791.

Reilly, J.R. & Elderd, B.D. (2014) Effects of biological control on long-term population dynamics: identifying unexpected outcomes. *Journal of Applied Ecology*, **51**, 90–101.

Richardson, M.L., Mitchell, R.F., Reagel, P.F. & Hanks, L.M. (2010) Causes and consequences of cannibalism in noncarnivorous insects. *Annual Review of Entomology*, **55**, 39–53.

Richter, A.R., Fuxa, J.R. & Abdelfattah, M. (1987) Effect of host plant on the susceptibility of *Spodoptera frugiperda* (Lepidoptera, Noctuidae) to a nuclear polyhedrosis virus. *Environmental Entomology*, **16**, 1004–1006.

Rohrmann, G.F. (2014) Baculovirus nucleocapsid aggregation (MNPV vs SNPV): an evolutionary strategy, or a product of replication conditions? *Virus Genes*, **49**, 351–357.

de Roode, J.C., Pedersen, A.B., Hunter, M.D. & Altizer, S. (2008) Host plant species affects virulence in monarch butterfly parasites. *Journal of Animal Ecology*, **77**, 120–126.

Rudolf, V.H. (2007) Consequences of stage-structured predators: cannibalism, behavioral effects, and trophic cascades. *Ecology*, **88**, 2991–3003.

Rudolf, V.H.W., Kamo, M. & Boots, M. (2010) Cannibals in space: the coevolution of cannibalism and dispersal in spatially structured populations. *American Naturalist*, **175**, 513–524.

Schultz, J.C. & Baldwin, I.T. (1982) Oak leaf quality declines in response to defoliation by gypsy moth larvae. *Science*, **217**, 149–151.

Shikano, I., Shumaker, K.L., Peiffer, M., Felton, G.W. & Hoover, K. (2017) Plant-mediated effects on an insect–pathogen interaction vary with intraspecific genetic variation in plant defences. *Oecologia*, **183**, 1121–1134.

Spiegelhalter, D.J., Best, N.G., Carlin, B.R. & van der Linde, A. (2002) Bayesian measures of model complexity and fit. *Journal of the Royal Statistical Society Series B Statistical Methodology*, **64**, 583–616.

Thompson, J. (2005) *The Geographic Mosaic of Coevolution*. Chicago, IL: University of Chicago Press.

Underwood, N., Rausher, M. & Cook, W. (2002) Bioassay versus chemical assay: measuring the impact of induced and constitutive resistance on herbivores in the field. *Oecologia*, **131**, 211–219.

Valicente, F.H., Tuelher, E.S., Pena, R.C., Andreazza, R. & Guimaraes, M.R.F. (2013) Cannibalism and virus production in *Spodoptera frugiperda* (JE Smith) (Lepidoptera: Noctuidae) larvae fed with two leaf substrates inoculated with *Baculovirus spodoptera*. *Neotropical Entomology*, **42**, 191–199.

Van Allen, B.G., Dillemuth, F.P., Flick, A.J., et al. (2017) Cannibalism and infectious disease: friend or foe? *American Naturalist*, **120**, 299–312.

Verity, R., Stevenson, M.D., Rossmo, D.K., Nichols, R.A. & Le Comber, S.C. (2014) Spatial targeting of infectious disease control: identifying multiple, unknown sources. *Methods in Ecology and Evolution*, **5**, 647–655.

Vilaplana, L., Wilson, K., Redman, E.M. & Cory, J.S. (2010) Pathogen persistence in migratory insects: high levels of vertically-transmitted virus infection in field populations of the African armyworm. *Evolutionary Ecology*, **24**, 147–160.

Wang, L., Hui, C., Sandhu, H.S., Li, Z. & Zhao, Z. (2015) Population dynamics and associated factors of cereal aphids and armyworms under global change. *Scientific Reports*, **5**, 18801.

Watanabe, S. (2013) A widely applicable Bayesian information criterion. *Journal of Machine Learning Research*, **14**, 867–897.

Werner, E. & Peacor, S. (2003) A review of trait-mediated indirect interactions in ecological communities. *Ecology*, **84**, 1083–1100.

Wild, S. (2017) African countries mobilize to battle invasive caterpillar. *Nature*, **543**, 13.

Williams, D.W. & Liebhold, A.M. (1995) Herbivorous insects and global change: potential changes in the spatial distribution of forest defoliator outbreaks. *Journal of Biogeography*, **22**, 665–671.

Williams, T. & Hernádez, O. (2006) Costs of cannibalism in the presence of an iridovirus pathogen of *Spodoptera frugiperda*. *Ecological Entomology*, **31**, 106–113.

Wilson, K., Bjørnstad, O., Dobson, A., et al. (2002) Heterogeneities in macroparasite infections: Patterns and processes. In: Hudson,P., Rizzoli, A., Grenfell,B., Heesterbeek,H. & Dobson,A.P. (eds.), *The Ecology of Wildlife Diseases* (pp. 6–44). Oxford: Oxford University Press.

Wold, E.N. & Marquis, R.J. (1997) Induced defense in white oak: effects on herbivores and consequences for the plant. *Ecology*, **78**, 1356–1369.

Woods, S. & Elkinton, J. (1987) Biomodal patterns of mortality from nuclear polyhedrosis virus in gypsy moth (*Lymantria dispar*) populations. *Journal of Invertebrate Pathology*, **50**, 151–157.

CHAPTER NINE

Infection and invasion: study cases from aquatic communities

MELANIE J. HATCHER, JAIMIE T.A. DICK,
JAMIE BOJKO, GRANT D. STENTIFORD,
PAUL STEBBING AND ALISON M. DUNN

9.1 Introduction

Invasive alien species (IAS), those that have been introduced and established outside of their native range as a result of human activities, impose a gamut of negative ecological, economic, and social impacts in their new range (from EU, 2014; GBNNSS, 2015). Such biological invasions are major drivers of biodiversity loss globally and have significant social and economic costs (£1.7 bn pa in the UK; GBNNSS, 2015) and up to $120 bn pa in the USA (Pimentel et al., 2005), with freshwater ecosystems disproportionately affected (Dudgeon et al., 2006; Ricciardi & MacIsaac, 2011). Impacts on native biological communities occur through trophic interactions (e.g. competition, parasitism, predation) and ecosystem engineering (Kumschick et al., 2015). Many of these effects are promulgated via parasites (macro- and microparasites), directly or indirectly, that are often brought in with IAS, left behind in the native habitat ('enemy release'), or are acquired in the new location (Hatcher et al., 2012b). Furthermore, parasites can themselves be invasive species (Roy et al., 2016). It is increasingly clear that more resources need to be focused on invasions as a major factor in wildlife disease: not only are parasites a major factor in IAS impacts on native communities, parallels between invasion and disease emergence call for similar approaches to prediction and control (Hatcher et al., 2012b; Dunn & Hatcher, 2015).

Perusal of the IUCN list of 100 of the World's Worst Alien Invasive Species (IUCN, 2017) illustrates the importance of parasitic disease in invasions across diverse taxa and ecosystems. Wildlife disease is cited as a driver behind the impact of many species on this list (Dunn & Hatcher, 2015). For example, the mosquito fish *Gambusia affinis*, native to America and introduced worldwide as a biocontrol agent for mosquito larvae, causes declines in macroinvertebrates through predation, and may also act as a reservoir for helminth parasites of native fish (Smith et al., 2006). In Europe, the endangered native white clawed crayfish *Austropotamobius pallipes* is being extirpated by the invasive American signal crayfish *Pacifastacus leniusculus* as a result of competition and spillover of *Aphanomyces astaci*, which causes crayfish plague, from the invasive species (Roy et al., 2016). *Batrachochytrium dendrobatidis* is the fungal parasite responsible for chytrid disease. A key driver of global amphibian declines, its spread is attributed to factors including climate change and spillover from the invasive American bullfrog (Fisher et al., 2012). The importance of spillover and emergence of disease in novel species is illustrated in several chapters in this book.

An invasion can be considered to involve four stages (Blackburn et al., 2011; Dunn & Hatcher, 2015): translocation, introduction, establishment, and wider geographic invasive spread, with associated impacts on native biota. Parasitic disease can be involved in all stages of this process (Figure 9.1; Dunn & Hatcher, 2015). Parasites may be lost in the process of invasion, releasing the host from the regulatory effects of infection. Alternatively, parasites may be cointroduced with an invasive host, sometimes going on to infect new host species in the novel range (Hatcher et al., 2012a). Such introduced parasites can have regulatory effects on (native or invasive) hosts, and can also modify competitive and trophic interactions between native and invasive species (Figure 9.1). Finally, introduced host species may act as reservoirs that amplify endemic disease, which in turn can have density- and trait-mediated effects on (native and invasive) hosts. Horizon-scanning for potential invasive threats to the UK reveals parasites to be major players as mediators of invasion, or as IAS themselves (Roy et al., 2016). Hence, biological invasions can lead to novel combinations of parasites and hosts. These changes in parasite–host associations affect not only the host species, but, through altering host interactions with other species, may have ramifications throughout the community (Hatcher et al., 2012b).

Invasive species can exert impacts on recipient ecosystems through a range of trophic interactions. Classic studies of the density effects of parasites have focused predominantly on how parasites affect competitive interactions between species (Holt & Pickering, 1985). However, parasites can also modify cannibalistic, predatory, and intraguild predatory interactions. Our group has pioneered the use of predatory functional responses to compare and predict the impact of invasive versus native predators (Dick et al., 2014, 2016) and to explore how parasites modify invasive impact through their effects on host traits (Dick et al., 2010; Paterson et al., 2015; Laverty et al., 2017). Intraguild predation (IGP), which is predation between potential competitor species, is a widespread and important structuring interaction in ecological communities including native/invader interactions (Dick et al., 1999). We have explored empirically and theoretically how the density- and trait-mediated effects of parasites can alter IGP, thus influencing the coexistence or exclusion of native/invasive species.

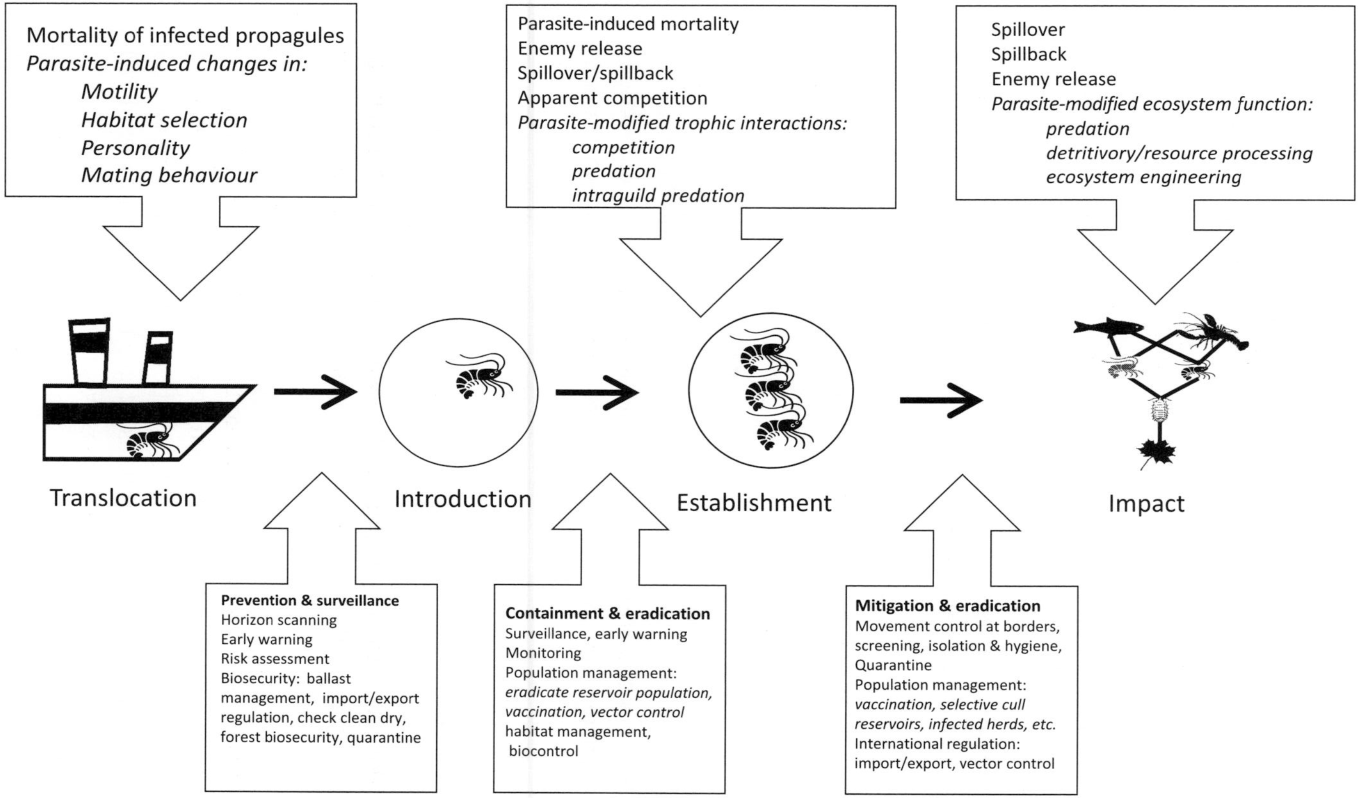
Mortality of infected propagules
Parasite-induced changes in:
Motility
Habitat selection
Personality
Mating behaviour
Parasite-induced mortality
Enemy release
Spillover/spillback
Apparent competition
Parasite-modified trophic interactions:
competition
predation
intraguild predation
Spillover
Spillback
Enemy release
Parasite-modified ecosystem function:
predation
detritivory/resource processing
ecosystem engineering
Translocation
Introduction
Establishment
Impact
Prevention & surveillance
Horizon scanning
Early warning
Risk assessment
Biosecurity: ballast management, import/export regulation, check clean dry, forest biosecurity, quarantine
Containment & eradication
Surveillance, early warning
Monitoring
Population management:
eradicate reservoir population, vaccination, vector control
habitat management,
biocontrol
Mitigation & eradication
Movement control at borders, screening, isolation & hygiene,
Quarantine
Population management:
vaccination, selective cull reservoirs, infected herds, etc.
International regulation:
import/export, vector control

Figure 9.1 Influences of parasites in biological invasions. Biological invasions can be regarded as a sequence of stages (Blackburn et al., 2011; Dunn & Hatcher, 2015); of the many potential introductions, few proceed successfully through all stages to become invasive with harmful impacts on recipient communities. Parasites enter into all stages, detailed in the top row of arrowed boxes. Biological invasions may result in changes in parasite diversity. An invasive species may introduce parasites to the recipient community, with opportunity for spillover to native hosts; it may act as a host for endemic parasites or it may lose its parasites as a result of stochastic and selective processes during invasion. Parasites may affect invasions via density (mortality) effects on host populations (standard font) or trait-mediated effects on hosts or species with which they interact (italics). Options for control are depicted in the lower arrowed boxes (options specific to parasites are in italics): few options are available at all stages, apart from biosecurity measures, which can be applicable to both invasive hosts and parasites.

In this chapter, we review our work on parasites in biological invasions in the context of wider literature on parasite–host ecology and on invasion biology. Our empirical study systems are freshwater communities, in particular amphipod crustaceans which play keystone roles in these communities. We have focused in particular on the role of trait-mediated effects of parasites, that is, the effects of infectious disease on host behaviour and life history. Parasite ecologists have classically studied the impact of parasite virulence (the direct impact of parasites on host mortality). Such parasite-induced impacts on host population density can, in turn, influence the impact of the host on other species (e.g. predators, prey, competitors). However, parasites can affect biological invasions as a result of both their density- *and* trait-mediated effects (Figure 9.1), which can potentially propagate to disparate members of ecological communities. In this chapter, we consider theoretical and empirical research in this area which has revealed that such trait effects, and the resulting changes in interactions between native and invasive species, rival the more classical density-mediated effects in magnitude (Dunn et al., 2012; Dunn & Hatcher, 2015). We begin by introducing our study systems: native and invasive amphipods, their diverse parasite assemblages, and the dominant parasites that have key impacts on biological invasions. We review laboratory and field studies that explore the importance of parasites for their individual host and for the host's trophic interactions. These studies inform development of theoretical models, applicable to a broad range of multiple host systems with shared parasites. These are reviewed in the subsequent section, which explores the implications of wildlife diseases for invasion success and impact. The novel interactions resulting from invasive species and parasites have wide-reaching implications for community structure, with tantalising evidence from our own and other studies discussed in Section 9.6. In the final sections, we look at the changes in parasite diversity as a result of the biological invasion, mapping parasite loss and introduction in ongoing amphipod invasions. We end by exploring more widely the opportunities to predict and manage wildlife diseases and highlight emerging areas for future research.

9.2 Study systems: invasive crustaceans and diseases (endemic and novel) in freshwater communities

Our study systems are freshwater invertebrate communities, in particular, the amphipod crustaceans that play keystone roles in these communities. Freshwater ecosystems are of disproportionate importance, relative to their coverage of the Earth's surface, in terms of biodiversity and extinction rates (Ledger & Milner, 2015) and for ecosystem services, including water and food provisioning for human society (Dudgeon et al., 2006). Alarmingly, freshwaters are also disproportionately affected by IAS, reflecting high anthropogenic activity and connectivity (Ricciardi & MacIsaac, 2011). From amphipod invaders that drive local species extinction to zebra mussels (*Dreissena polymorpha*) that encrust water pipes, and water hyacinth (*Eichhornia crassipes*) and floating pennywort (*Hydrocotyle ranunculoides*) clogging waterways, freshwater invaders have widespread and increasing environmental and economic impacts. Furthermore, recent reviews have also identified increases in the frequency of both endemic and novel emerging infectious diseases in these ecosystems (Okamura & Feist, 2011; Adlard et al., 2015).

Rivers and lakes in Europe, including the UK and Ireland, are affected by a suite of invasive amphipods (DAISIE, 2017) resulting from accidental introductions via transport, trade, and recreation. In Ireland, the Isle of Man and other islands, the native amphipod *Gammarus duebeni celticus* is being replaced by the invasive *Gammarus pulex* introduced deliberately from Great Britain (Dick, 1996; Dick & Platvoet, 1996). A further two species of non-native amphipods also co-occur; the North American *Gammarus tigrinus* and *Crangonyx pseudogracilis*, despite being heavily preyed upon by the other invasive and native amphipods. In mainland Europe and England, the invasive Ponto-Caspian 'killer shrimp' *Dikerogammarus villosus* is a voracious predator of macroinvertebrates (Kelly et al., 2002), with invaded regions showing a decrease in macroinvertebrate abundance and diversity (Rewicz et al., 2014). The invasive 'demon shrimp' *Dikerogammarus haemobaphes* is also spreading through Europe and may have similar ecological effects (Bovy et al., 2015).

Amphipod crustaceans are often keystone species in freshwater ecosystems. Through processing nutrients and providing prey for larger invertebrates and vertebrates, they provide important ecosystem services. They process the primary basal energy resource (leafy detritus) through shredding, with strong impacts on community structure (MacNeil et al., 1997, 2011). They also consume other invertebrate species in the food web, influencing macroinvertebrate species richness and diversity, and are key prey for commercial and recreational fish stocks, as well as for wildfowl (MacNeil et al., 1999; Kelly & Dick, 2005). A key native/invader interaction in these amphipod systems involves intraguild predation between the potentially competing native and invasive amphipod species (Dick et al., 1993): amphipod species prey on each other, particularly at vulnerable moulting periods, with differential IGP between species leading to rapid species replacements.

These amphipods are host to a diverse range of parasites (Dunn & Dick, 1998) including viruses, bacteria, protists, trematodes (Bojko et al., 2013), microsporidia (Terry et al., 2003, 2004) and acanthocephalans (MacNeil et al., 2003b) (Figure 9.2).

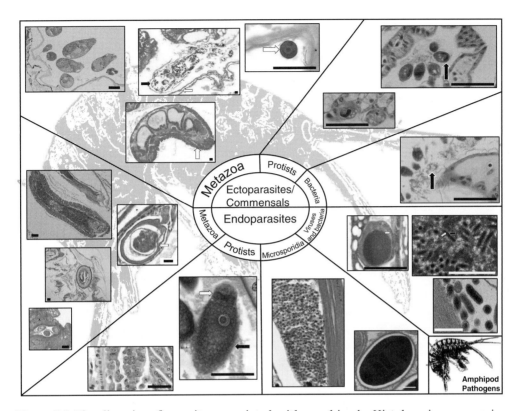

Figure 9.2 The diversity of parasites associated with amphipods. Histology images are in colour, and transmission electron micrographs are in black and white. Each section contains parasites that link with the circular labelling in the centre of the diagram. Arrows, if present, indicate the parasite. From left to right: ectoparasitic metazoa: oligochaete (from *Dikerogammarus villosus*); rotifer (from *Gammarus roeselii*); isopod (from *D. villosus*); bryozoan statoblast (from *D. villosus*). Ectoparasitic protists: ciliated gill-embedded protist (from *G. roeselii*); stalked ciliated protist (from *G. roeselii*). Ectoparasitic bacteria: filamentous bacteria (from *G. roeselii*). Endoparasitic viruses and bacteria: *Dikerogammarus villosus* bacilliform virus pathology (from *D. villosus*); DvBV (from *D. villosus*); *Aquarickettsiella gammari* (from *Gammarus fossarum*). Endoparasitic microsporidia: microsporidian pathology (from *D. haemobaphes*); *Cucumispora ornata* (from *D. haemobaphes*). Endoparasitic protists: intracellular gregarine (from *D. villosus*); extracellular gregarine (from *D. villosus*). Endoparasitic metazoa: acanthocephalan (from *D. villosus*); nematode (from *D. villosus*); *Polymorphus* sp. (from *Gammarus pulex*); digenean trematode (from *D. villosus*). In all cases, the black scale bars for histology images equate to 20 μm. In all cases the white scale bars for transmission electron micrographs equate to 500 nm. Images from Bojko et al., 2013, 2015, 2017. (A black and white version of this figure will appear in some formats. For the colour version, please refer to the plate section.)

We have focused on two prevalent parasite species and their impact on native/invader amphipod interactions in Ireland (Figure 9.3): the microsporidian *Pleistophora mulleri* and the acanthocephalan *Echinorhynchus truttae*. *Pleistophora mulleri* has a direct life cycle, infecting the musculature of its host, causing pathology and reduced host motility (Fielding et al., 2005). Laboratory experiments and field surveys demonstrate that the parasite is transmitted through cannibalism and scavenging of dead hosts and is specific to the native host *G. duebeni celticus* (MacNeil et al., 2003a). *Echinorhynchus truttae* has an indirect life cycle, using brown trout *Salmo trutta* and other fish as the definitive hosts and amphipods as the intermediate hosts. Infection of the definitive host occurs when it preys upon an infected amphipod.

Figure 9.3 Native/invasive amphipods and a subset of their parasites in Ireland, showing key trophic interactions (Hatcher et al., 2012b). N = native *Gammarus duebeni celticus*, I1 = invasive *Gammarus pulex*, I2 = invasive *Gammarus tigrinus*. E. truttae = *Echinorhynchus truttae*. Both the native *G. duebeni celticus* and the invasive *G. pulex* act as intermediate hosts for *E. truttae; Salmo trutta* and other fish act as the definitive host. *P. mulleri* = *Pleistophora mulleri*, which has a direct life cycle and is specific to the native amphipod *Gammarus duebeni celticus*. These parasites have been found to modify the trophic behaviour and interactions of their hosts, as discussed in Box 9.1. (A black and white version of this figure will appear in some formats. For the colour version, please refer to the plate section.)

9.3 Parasite-mediated indirect interactions in native/invader populations: empirical studies

Although often overlooked by ecologists, parasites are ubiquitous among plant and animal hosts; indeed, parasitism is the most widespread trophic interaction (Dobson et al., 2008). Parasites affect their hosts directly, but also exert powerful indirect effects on the species with which the host interacts. Our work has shown that parasitism can also change the outcome of other trophic interactions of the host as a result of the density and, in particular, the trait effects of the infection (Box 9.1). By modifying host behaviour, parasitism can increase or decrease the host's vulnerability to predation; alter the predatory impact of the host on lower order prey; change the propensity of the host for cannibalism; and modify intraguild predation.

Box 9.1: Parasites modify trophic interactions in aquatic communities

Intraguild predation (IGP) between native and invasive amphipods
In Ireland, the native amphipod *Gammarus duebeni celticus* is being replaced by the stronger intraguild predator *G. pulex* (Dick et al., 1999). *G. duebeni celticus* is, however, a stronger intraguild predator than the invasive *G. tigrinus* and *Crangonyx pseudogracilis* (Dick, 1996). It is surprising, then, that mixed (native and invader) populations persist in some habitats. Parasitism appears to be a key factor in modifying native–invader interactions. Both *Pleistophora mulleri* and *Echinorhynchus truttae* modify the individual fitness and the trophic interactions of the host, potentially influencing coexistence outcomes and having wider ramifications throughout the ecological community.

In field enclosure experiments, we found that parasitism affected the coexistence of native and invasive amphipods. *G. duebeni celticus* populations declined rapidly in the presence of uninfected *G. pulex* as a result of IGP (Figure B9.1.1). In contrast, when *G. pulex* were parasitised by *E. truttae*, IGP was reduced, enhancing native–invader coexistence. Importantly, this outcome did not reflect classic density-dependent effects of the infection because survival of *G. pulex* in single and mixed species populations was unaffected by *E. truttae* infection. However, parasitised *G. pulex* showed reduced IGP on the native competitor, leading to higher native survival and enhancing native–invader coexistence (MacNeil et al., 2003b).

In a parallel enclosure experiment, we found that *P. mulleri* also alters IGP between native and invasive amphipods (MacNeil et al., 2003a). Here, the parasite is specific to the native *G. duebeni celticus*, but had no direct effect on host survival; survival of infected *G. duebeni celticus* was high in both single

Box 9.1: (cont.)

and mixed species populations. However, parasitised *G. duebeni celticus* showed a weakened ability to predate competing amphipods; survival of the smaller, weaker intraguild prey *G. tigrinus* and *C. pseudogracilis* was higher in the presence of infected versus uninfected *G. duebeni celticus*. In addition to changing the predatory strength of the host, *P. mulleri* also lead to increased vulnerability of *G. duebeni celticus* to intraguild predation by *G. pulex*.

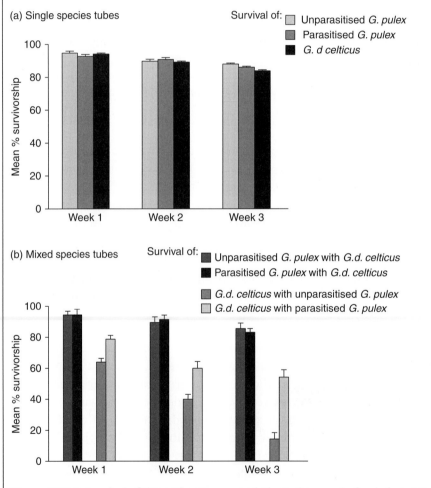

Figure B9.1.1 Survival of the native *Gammarus duebeni celticus* and of uninfected *G. pulex* and *Echinorhynchus truttae*-infected *G. pulex* in single (a) and mixed species enclosures (b). The survival of *G. pulex* was not affected by the parasite, but its strength as an intraguild predator was reduced: survival of the native *G. duebeni celticus* (which is intraguild prey for the invasive *G. pulex*) was higher in the presence of parasitised than unparasited *G. pulex*. (From MacNeil et al., 2003b.)

Box 9.1: (cont.)

Parasites and predation by higher-order predators

Echinorhynchus truttae uses amphipods as the intermediate host and is tro-phically transmitted to the definitive fish host. Following ingestion of *E. truttae* eggs, the parasite develops in the amphipod host, forming bright orange cystacanth which increases detection likelihood by predators. *E. truttae* manipulates the behaviour of its intermediate *G. pulex* host, causing increased activity and positive phototaxis. As a result, infected individuals in rivers are distributed in the water column and near the water surface where they suffer increased predation by fish, the definitive host for *E. truttae* (Figure B9.1.2; MacNeil et al., 2003c). In invaded communities in Ireland, this effect will be greater for the invasive *G. pulex*, which suffers higher parasite prevalence, than for the native *G. duebeni celticus*.

Parasites and predation on lower-order prey

Although *E. truttae* reduces the intraguild predation strength of *G. pulex*, we found that the parasite *increased* its feeding intake of lower-order prey (Dick et al., 2010). In a comparison of the predatory functional responses of infected and uninfected individuals (Dick et al., 2010) we revealed that infected indivi-duals had a 30% higher foraging rate than did uninfected individuals (Figure B9.1.3). The increased rate of prey intake by the host is likely to reflect the metabolic demands of the parasite (the cyst can be up to 24% of the mass of the

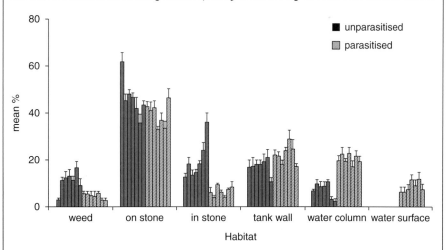

Figure B9.1.2 Distribution of uninfected (black) and *Echinorhynchus truttae*-infected (hatched) *Gammarus pulex*. The mean % of individuals located in different habitat types is shown. A higher percentage of parasitised than unparasitised individuals were found in open water (MacNeil et al., 2003c).

Box 9.1: (cont.)

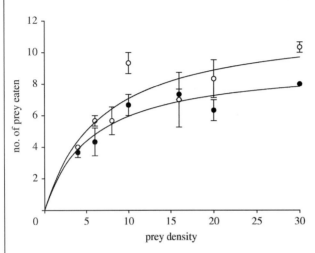

Figure B9.1.3 The predatory functional response (the relationship between the number of prey eaten and prey density) for unparasitised *Gammarus pulex* (black circles) and those parasitised with *Echinorhynchus truttae* (white circles). Prey offered were *Asellus aquaticus*. Parasitised individuals showed a higher rate of predation than did those unparasitised (Dick et al., 2010).

amphipod) as well as behavioural manipulation by the parasite which causes increased host activity. Parasitism thus has the potential to exacerbate the impact of this invasive amphipod on prey populations.

Further, there may be synergistic effects of climate change on such interactions (Figure B9.1.4), because the predatory functional response (= impact) of *G. pulex* with this parasite showed disproportionate increases at water temperatures typical of future warming scenarios (Laverty et al., 2017).

Parasitism and cannibalism

Cannibalism is a rather neglected trophic interaction, yet is reported for >3000 species and is common in stage-structured populations where generations overlap and is often associated with IGP (Rudolf, 2007). Cannibalism is very common in amphipods, where larger adults/juveniles consume smaller individuals. In addition to the direct benefits in resources, cannibalism can also reduce both intra- and interspecific competition (Claessen et al., 2004). We found that *P. mulleri* infection leads to increased cannibalism by adult *G. duebeni celticus*, with parasitised individuals consuming twice as many conspecific juveniles as uninfected individuals, likely reflecting

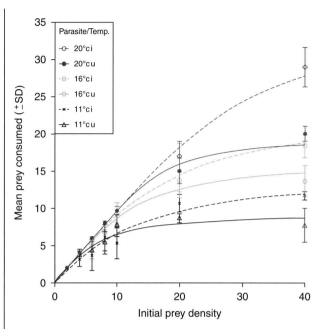

Figure B9.1.4 Predatory functional responses of *Echinorhynchus truttae*-infected (i, dashed lines) and uninfected (u, solid lines) *Gammarus pulex* at low (11°C), medium (16°C) and high (20°C) temperatures. Means are ± SD. Temperature and infection interact to increase the predatory impact of this invasive amphipod (Laverty et al., 2017).

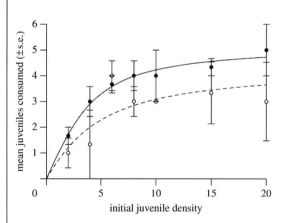

Figure B9.1.5 Parasitic infection leads to an increase in cannibalism. Functional responses of *Pleistophora mulleri*-infected (filled circles, solid line) and -uninfected (open circles, dashed line) native *Gammarus duebeni celticus* adults towards juvenile conspecific prey (Bunke et al., 2015).

Box 9.1: (cont.)

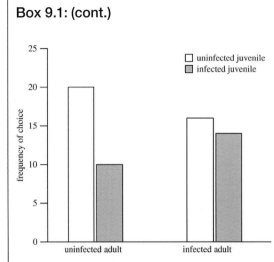

Figure B9.1.6 The frequency of consumption of uninfected versus *Pleistophora mulleri*-infected juveniles by uninfected and infected adult *Gammarus duebeni celticus*. Uninfected adults avoided cannibalising parasitised juveniles, whereas this avoidance was not observed for parasitised adults (Bunke et al., 2015).

the metabolic demand of the parasite (Figure B9.1.5). Interestingly, when given the choice, uninfected adults were less likely to cannibalise infected juveniles than uninfected ones (Figure B9.1.6), an adaptive behaviour which will gain the nutritional benefit from cannibalism but also avoid the costs of infection. In contrast, infected shrimps did not avoid parasitised conspecifics, possibly reflecting the metabolic demands of infection (Bunke et al., 2015), or an inability of infected individuals to detect infected prey.

The invasive *G. pulex* and the native *G. duebeni celticus* can both act as intermediate hosts for the acanthocephalan parasite *E. truttae*, although parasite prevalence is higher in the invasive species (MacNeil et al., 2003b). This parasite mediates several of its hosts' trophic interactions (Box 9.1). Infected hosts suffer increased vulnerability to predation by the definitive fish host (MacNeil et al., 2003c) while themselves becoming more voracious predators on smaller lower-order prey (Dick et al., 2010). In contrast, intra-guild predation strength towards other native amphipods is decreased (MacNeil et al., 2003b). The microsporidian parasite *P. mulleri* is specific to the native host *G. duebeni celticus* and leads to reduced motility and lower intraguild predation strength, as well as to increased vulnerability to becoming intraguild prey (MacNeil et al., 2003a).

These changes in the functional role of the host can mediate invasion success as well as the impact of the invader on native biota. Because native and invasive amphipods differ in their propensity for predation and detritus processing (MacNeil et al., 2011; Kenna et al., 2017), they are not functionally equivalent and thus any impact of parasitism on amphipod population dynamics or invasion outcomes potentially impacts ecosystem-level processes as well as the species composition of aquatic communities.

9.4 Parasite-mediated indirect interactions in native/invader populations: developing theoretical models

We have used mathematical models to explore and predict the impact of infections on invasions, exploring how parasites influence invasion success and community structure as a consequence of both their density and trait-mediated effects on host populations (Dunn et al., 2012). The potential for parasites to influence community composition as a result of their effects on host density, mediated via parasite-induced mortality, have been recognised for some time (Price et al., 1986; Hudson & Greenman, 1998). Our analyses take this one stage further and suggest that population dynamics and community outcomes can be equally strongly influenced by the effects of infection on host traits (e.g. behaviour), as we discuss below.

9.4.1 Density-mediated models

Pioneering models of wildlife disease revealed fundamental principles as to how parasites influence interactions between species, in terms of competitive release, trophic cascades, apparent competition (Holt & Pickering, 1985) and parasite-mediated competition (Hudson & Greenman, 1998). By reducing host population density, parasites have the potential to release non-host species from competition with the host species, release prey from predation by the host, or reduce resource availability for predators of the host, inducing trophic cascades (Price et al., 1986). Such density-mediated effects can have indirect effects on other species in the community, influencing community composition and ecosystem function (Holt et al., 2003; Hatcher et al., 2006; Hudson et al., 2006).

While the majority of theoretical treatments have explored the role parasites play in mediating competitive interactions, the empirical evidence for trophic interactions involving native and invasive amphipods suggests that interspecific interactions are driven largely via predation and intraguild predation, as opposed to competition (Dick et al., 1993). Our initial modelling work (Box 9.2) focused on how the density-mediated effects of parasitic infection might influence native/invader interactions structured by IGP, based on our empirical evidence of its potential role in invasions (Box 9.1). Intraguild predation is a widespread and frequent interaction in marine, freshwater, and terrestrial communities (Polis et al., 1989). Our models suggest that parasites can play a keystone role in maintaining coexistence or promoting interspecific replacement of host species, depending on the relative mortality impact of the parasite in the two hosts. If the parasite is more virulent to the stronger intraguild predator, it can stabilise the interaction, leading to coexistence of predator and prey; conversely, if the weaker player experiences greater virulence, parasitism will speed up its elimination (Hatcher et al., 2008). The models also revealed that parasites might additionally enable the persistence of IGP (Box 9.2); previous theoretical models of IGP demonstrated very limited conditions for its stable long-term persistence, at odds with its common occurrence in invertebrates and vertebrates (Polis et al., 1989; Holt & Polis, 1997). These general models predict that the superior intraguild predator should replace the inferior intraguild predator unless the latter species is competitively superior. For the *Gammarus* system, this would imply that biological invasion by *G. pulex* should result in replacement of the native *G. duebeni celticus*, and the other

---

Box 9.2: A density-mediated model of parasitism in native/invasive systems with intraguild predation (IGP)

As a first step in understanding how parasitism and IGP interact, we developed a model incorporating a shared parasite of two species engaged in mutual, but asymmetric, IGP (Hatcher et al., 2008). We took a similar modelling approach to that used for parasite-mediated competition (e.g. Bowers & Turner, 1997), in which two species sharing a microparasite engage in intraspecific and interspecific competition, but with the additional complexity of predation between the hosts. This model examined purely the density-mediated effects of parasitism on IGP: infected hosts had increased mortality, but did not differ from uninfected conspecifics in their predatory or competitive abilities.

We developed a continuous time two host/one microparasite model based on the *Gammarus pulex/G. duebeni celticus* system. The equational model and the general conclusions presented are broadly applicable to other invertebrate host–microparasite systems, although for model exploration we parameterised for competition and predation from our *G. pulex/G. duebeni celticus* field and laboratory estimates, with other parameters varied to allow sensitivity analysis and maintain generality (Hatcher et al., 2008). We assume a microparasite with density-dependent parasite transmission β. The parasite can impart virulence (mortality) effects on infected hosts with per-capita rate α. Transmission was varied to examine a range of conditions from a specialist parasite of one host (the case for *P. mulleri* in *G. duebeni celticus*) within a more general model of shared parasitism with differential virulence between host species. The host species engage in mutual asymmetric IGP with competititon coefficients c and intrinsic rates of increase r (for all parameters, subscripts ij denote the effect of host species j on species i). The species with higher per-capita predation rate (g) we name the IGpredator, and the weaker predator we term IGprey. IGpredator and IGprey also engage in cannibalism (per-capita rate w), often associated with intraguild predation, and frequent in *Gammarus* (Bunke et al., 2015; Box 9.1). We take the simplified SEIR

Box 9.2: (cont.)

model format, assuming hosts are either uninfected (susceptible, S) or infected and infectious (I); hence, we assume zero exposure latency and recovery. This leads to the following model, where e is the per-capita conversion efficiency for consumed prey,

$$\frac{dH_1}{dt} = r_1 H_1 (1 - c_{11}H_1 - c_{12}H_2) - (1-e)w_1 H_1^2 - (g_{12} - eg_{21})H_1 H_2 - \alpha_1 I_1$$

$$\frac{dI_1}{dt} = \beta_{11}S_1 I_1 + \beta_{12}S_1 I_2 - (1-e)w_1 H_1 I_1 - H_2 I_1(g_{12} - eg_{21}) - \alpha_1 I_1$$

$$\frac{dH_2}{dt} = r_2 H_2 (1 - c_{22}H_2 - c_{21}H_1) - (1-e)w_2 H_2^2 - (g_{21} - eg_{12})H_1 H_2 - \alpha I_2$$

$$\frac{dI_1}{dt} = \beta_{22}S_2 I_2 + \beta_{21}S_2 I_1 - (1-e)w_2 H_2 I_2 - H_1 I_2(g_{21} - eg_{12}) - \alpha_2 I_2 \qquad .$$

$$\text{(Equations 9.1 – 9.4)}$$

Parasitism operating in this way increased the range of conditions leading to host coexistence, provided the stronger intraguild player (determined by the balance between competitive and predatory effects; usually the superior predator) was more adversely affected by the parasite (Figure

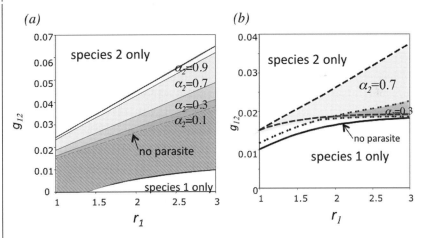

Figure B9.2.1. Impact of parasitism on coexistence under intraguild predation: a parasite with higher virulence in the stronger intraguild predator increases the parameter range for persistence (shaded); (plotted over predation by host species 2 (g_{12}) against intrinsic reproductive rate (r_1) of host species 1. (a) When IGpredator and prey engage in cannibalism ($w_1 = w_2 = 0.01$), higher virulence (higher α_2) has a greater impact enhancing coexistence; (b) without cannibalism ($w_1 = w_2 = 0$), the two species cannot coexist without the parasite. Other parameters based on data for the *Gammarus* systems: $\beta_{11} = \beta_{22} = 0.01$, $\beta_{12} = \beta_{21} = 0.001$, $e = 0.3$, $\beta_{21} = 0.01$, $\alpha_1 = 0.1$, $c_{11} = c_{22} = 0.005$, $c_{12} = c_{21} = 0.0005$. Redrawn from Hatcher, Dick & Dunn (2008).

Box 9.2: (cont.)

B9.2.1). Conversely, parasitism enhanced the rate of decline and extinction of the inferior species (usually the less-predatory species) if it suffered greater parasite-induced mortality. The keystone effects of parasitism in this model resemble those described for parasite-mediated competition, where the deleterious effects of parasitism on the superior competitor prevent exclusion of the inferior competitor (Hudson & Greenman, 1998). In competition models, the parasite reduces the population density of the superior species, thereby freeing up resources that can be exploited by the inferior species (Holt & Dobson, 2006). However, in systems with IGP, the parasite's influence can be even stronger because it also reduces predation pressure on the weaker participant, similar to top predator-induced trophic cascades in food webs (Hatcher & Dunn, 2011).

---

invasive species should fail to establish. However, apparently stable single and mixed species communities persist many decades after invasion (Dick, 1996; MacNeil et al., 2003a, 2003b), possibly as a result of the influence of parasite mediation of the powerful IGP influence.

9.4.2 Trait-mediated models

The effects of parasitism on native/invader interactions in the above model (Box 9.2) were entirely the result of numerical effects on population density. However, many of the most striking effects of parasitism we have measured empirically in our invasive systems are trait-mediated, with infection affecting the trophic interactions of hosts because it modifies propensity for, or vulnerability to, predation (Box 9.1). To examine the potential of trait-mediated effects to influence these native/invader interactions, we developed further models to include trait-modification as a result of infection. Mirroring our field and laboratory studies (Box 9.1), we allowed for two traits associated with IGP – vulnerability to predation and predatory appetite – to depend on infection status, thus allowing these traits to be modified by parasitism (Box 9.3).

These models demonstrate that the trait-mediated effects of parasitism can indeed influence population and community outcomes, in a similar and equally strong manner as can density-mediated effects. Even apparently benign parasites, those that have little or no direct impact on host mortality, can nevertheless have clear keystone effects on community structure via their trait-mediated effects on hosts (Box 9.3).

Box 9.3: A trait-mediated model of parasitism in native/invasive systems with intraguild predation (IGP)

We developed the Hatcher et al. (2008) model (Box 9.2) to include two parasite-induced trait effects, using symbolic constants to scale predation by or on the infected class, with ρ modifying the instantaneous rate of attack by intraguild predators (appetite), and ϕ modifying the consumption of intraguild prey (vulnerability). Following the previous model's structure (Box 9.2), the population dynamics for susceptibles (S) and infecteds (I) for host species 1 then become:

$$\frac{dS_1}{dt} = r_1 H_1 (1 - c_{11}H_1 - c_{12}H_2) - (1-e)wH_1^2$$
$$- [(g_{12} - eg_{21})S_1 S_2 + (\rho_2 g_{12} - e\phi_2 g_{21})S_1 I_2 - e\rho_1 g_{21} I_1 H_2] - \beta_{11} S_1 I_1 - \beta_{12} S_1 I_2$$

$$\frac{dI_1}{dt} = \beta_{11} S_1 I_1 + \beta_{12} S_1 I_2 - wI_1 H_1 - [\phi_1 g_{12} I_1 S_2 + \rho_2 g_{12} I_1 I_2] - \alpha_1 I_1,$$

(Equations 9.5 and 9.6)

with symmetrically equivalent equations for species 2 (other parameters as above, Box 9.2). The terms in Equation 9.5 for uninfected (susceptible, S) hosts reflect three components of IGP: (i) competition, using a standard representation based on Lotka–Volterra assumptions (Bowers & Turner, 1997); (ii) cannibalism (proportional to population density, weighted by coefficient of attack); and (iii) predation (linear function of IGpredator and prey densities weighted by coefficients of attack). To model trait-mediated effects, we further decomposed predation (square brackets) into interactions between infected/susceptible host classes with attack rates scaled to reflect changes in appetite (ρ) and vulnerability (ϕ) due to infection. The infected class (I) suffers loss through parasite-induced mortality, cannibalism and IGP (Equation 9.6). Parasite transmission also causes loss of susceptibles (Equation 9.5; terms with β) and gain of infecteds (Equation 9.6). Because we assumed pure horizontal parasite transmission, reproduction by infected individuals yields susceptible offspring, so energetic gains from predation/cannibalism by infecteds accrue to the susceptible class (final term within square brackets, Equation 9.5). As with the case for density-mediated effects (Box 9.2), we found that parasites with trait-mediated effects can have a strong impact on coexistence in these native/invader systems (Hatcher et al. 2014). Parasites that enhance vulnerability to predation, or decrease predatory appetite, of the stronger interguild predator can greatly enhance the conditions for coexistence of the two host species. This supports our experimental evidence that parasite-induced effects on traits acts in a similar manner to classical virulence in the population dynamics of hosts (Box 9.1). Indeed, parasites with no classical virulence (mortality), but cryptic

Box 9.3: (cont.)

virulence in the form of altered vulnerability to or propensity for predation, could have as pronounced an impact as density in promoting or inhibiting coexistence (Figure B9.3.1).

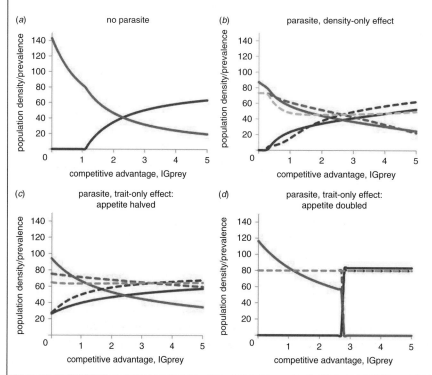

Figure B9.3.1 Trait-mediated effects of parasitism on IGP systems. Equilibrium population densities (solid lines) and parasite prevalence (dashed lines) in the more predatory species (intraguild predator; red) and the weaker predator (intraguild prey, blue) plotted against the relative competitive advantage of the intraguild prey: (a) in the absence of parasitism, a strong intraguild predator excludes competitively weak intraguild prey; (b) virulent parasites (inducing 10% and 30% mortality in the prey and predator, respectively) enable coexistence of predator and prey over a broader parameter range; (c) parasites with no mortality effect but which reduce predatory ability (appetite) strongly enhance coexistence, whereas (d) parasites that increase predation strongly reduce coexistence (Hatcher et al., 2014). (A black and white version of this figure will appear in some formats. For the colour version, please refer to the plate section.)

This combined approach to empirical tests and modelling has helped clarify the role of parasitism in mediating amphipod native/invader interactions and has highlighted the importance of both density- and trait-mediated indirect effects. Parasitism may enhance or inhibit coexistence, depending on the relative strength and direction of density and trait effects. Furthermore, parasitism may alter the *impact* of invasion, by influencing the strength of interactions between native and invasive species. In order to fully understand impact, however, we must widen our focus beyond a select group of closely interacting species, to examine community and ecosystem consequences generally.

9.5 Indirect interactions: consequences for community structure

Evidence is growing that many parasites of wildlife have effects on host traits, without necessarily causing significant mortality (e.g. Lefevre et al., 2009; Selakovic et al., 2014). In our native/invader crustacean systems, we have documented parasite-induced changes not only in vulnerability to and propensity for IGP, but in vulnerability to top predators, predation on lower trophic levels, cannibalism, detritivory, mating and mate choice (Box 9.1). The well-documented occurrence of parasite-induced behavioural manipulation by trophically transmitted parasites in a range of aquatic and terrestrial systems provides many additional cases (Lefevre et al., 2009). Our models of trait-mediated effects of parasites, together with work on free-living systems (Ohgushi et al., 2012), demonstrate the potential of these interactions to alter community structure. This could be particularly relevant in an invasion context. Trait changes may be especially common where ecological novelty, such as that generated by biological invasion, results in new species combinations and the introduced species experience novel environmental conditions and cues. Thus, the impact of parasite-induced trait effects is likely to be particularly relevant in a world dominated by invasion-related ecological novelty (Dunn & Hatcher, 2015). Evidence is also mounting for the effects of parasitism on community and ecosystem properties including energy flow and ecological stability (reviewed in Hudson et al., 2006; Poulin, 2010; Hatcher et al., 2012b). Parasites act as ecosystem engineers, altering the physical properties of ecosystems by direct effects on the environment, or via their effects on hosts (Mouritsen & Poulin, 2010). An exciting area now is to extend these ecosystem-level impact studies to predict impacts in ongoing or potential invasions. In our gammarid study systems, there is growing evidence that invaders and parasites influence energy flow in ecosystems. In many cases, invaders are not trophic analogues of the native species they replace. For instance, in the *Gammarus* system (Box 9.1), native and invasive species differ in predation, IGP, cannibalism, and propensity towards detrital processing (Dick et al., 2010; MacNeil et al., 2011; Kenna et al., 2017). In addition, parasitic infection influences resource processing, altering rates of cannibalism, predation, and IGP (Box 9.1).

Such case studies from our study systems and from the wider literature provide tantalising evidence of the potential impact of parasitism on ecosystem properties in communities undergoing invasion. More hard evidence for these effects in other systems is needed, but distinguishing cause and effect can be difficult because of interdependence between parasitism and host community structure (Hatcher et al., 2015). For instance, parasitism can potentially influence biodiversity, for example via host mortality or indirect effects propagated through species interactions. Equally, biodiversity has been demonstrated to influence infection in a number of theoretical and empirical systems (Keesing et al., 2010). This bidirectional interdependence has resulted in acute difficulties interpreting data, and lies at the heart of current controversy in the debate over disease risk and biodiversity (reviewed in Dunn & Hatcher, 2015). A full review of this complex subject is beyond the scope of this paper, but theoretical arguments suggest parasite transmission strategy is key to understanding how parasite prevalence is related to biodiversity (Holt et al., 2003). The effect of parasitism on biodiversity has received less theoretical attention, but parasitism has been implicated in extinction processes (reviewed in Hatcher et al., 2012b) as well as the many studies illustrating the impact of parasites on host population densities. Impacts on biodiversity may be particularly pronounced when parasites are themselves invasive, or associated (directly or indirectly) with keystone species involved or impacted by invasion, and this aspect forms a key consideration within current approaches to impact prediction and management (Section 9.7).

9.6 Enemy release and enemy introduction

Our empirical and theoretical studies reviewed above highlight the roles that parasites may play in mediating invasion success and impact. Biological invasions lead to interactions between novel species (natives and invaders) and can also result in changes in parasite–host relationships as a result of parasite co-introduction and loss. Key to this is the relationship between propagule pressure (numbers of individuals released and number of release events; Blackburn et al., 2011) of hosts and the introduction of their parasites (Figure 9.1). An invasive species may introduce parasites to the recipient community, with opportunity for spillover to native hosts; it may act as a host for endemic parasites (potentially acting as a sink or a reservoir) or it may lose its parasites during invasion (the process of enemy release). Invaders tend to be larger and more abundant in the invasive range than in their original ranges (Parker et al., 2013). This can be explained by the enemy release hypothesis, which posits that invasive species are successful in the new range because they benefit from escaping their natural enemies (including herbivores, predators or parasites; Keane & Crawley, 2002; Torchin et al., 2002). Loss of parasites may be driven by sampling effects (MacLeod et al., 2010). A propagule of an invasive species (which represents a subsample of the source population) may experience a loss of parasites, particularly if parasite prevalence is low in the source population. Parasites may also be lost through selective effects. Infected individuals may have lower survival, leading to a reduction in susceptible genotypes; in addition, low host density of invasive propagules may be insufficient to sustain a parasite population (Torchin et al., 2003; Colautti et al., 2004). There are two approaches to investigating possible enemy release: biogeographical studies compare parasite diversity and prevalence in the native versus the invasive range of a host, while community studies compare parasitism in invasive and endemic species in an invaded community (Hatcher & Dunn, 2011). We have used both approaches to investigate enemy release in invasive amphipods; across large-scale geographical ranges, some systems show strong evidence for enemy release whereas others show the inverse (Box 9.4).

Box 9.4: Enemy release in amphipod invasions at large geographical scales

Community study

A comparison of parasitism of native and invasive amphipods in Ireland revealed that the invasive species may benefit from enemy release. The native amphipod *Gammarus duebeni celticus* suffers a higher parasite diversity than do the invasive species *G. pulex* and *G. tigrinus*. Five parasite species were detected in the native species, but only three of these were detected in the invaders

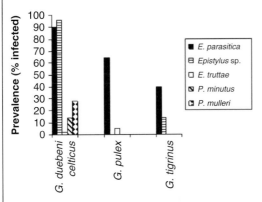

Figure B9.4.1. Parasite diversity and prevalence in three species of amphipod in Northern Ireland, the native *Gammarus duebeni celticus* and the invaders *G. pulex* and *G. tigrinus*. A higher parasite diversity was observed in the native species. Where prevalence was measured in several field sites, the average prevalence is plotted. Ectoparasites include *Embata parasitica* and *Epistylus* sp. Endoparasites were *Echinorhynchus truttae*, *Polymorphous minutus* and *Pleistophora mulleri*. From Hatcher and Dunn (2011).

Box 9.4: (cont.)

(Dunn & Dick, 1998). Parasite prevalence and burden of two of these shared parasites was higher in the native, while prevalence of the acanthocephalan *Echinorhynchus truttae* was higher in the invasive *G. pulex* (Figure B9.4.1).

Biogeographical studies

Biogeographical studies of *Dikerogammarus villosus* reveal changes in genetic diversity and parasite–host associations that are in accord with patterns of introduction and spread (Figure B9.4.2). *Dikerogammarus villosus* is native to the Ponto-Caspian region and has spread westerly throughout continental Europe over the past 20 years, with multiple introductions following a range of 'invasion corridors' (Rewicz et al., 2015). In accord with this pattern of recurrent introductions, Wattier et al. (2007) found no evidence of enemy release from microsporidian parasites or of host genetic bottlenecks in these populations.

In contrast, *D. villosus* was first reported in the UK in 2010 (MacNeil et al., 2010) and only four populations have been identified to date. Arundell et al. (2015) found a reduction in host genetic diversity in comparison to reference populations from the west coast of continental Europe and detected no microsporidian parasites. This pattern reflects the small number of colonisation events of the island, likely from source populations in the invasive range in continental Europe, resulting in genetic founder effects and enemy release. Further evidence of enemy release comes from histological screening of UK populations of *D. villosus* which revealed a high prevalence of commensal microbes, including: ciliated protists, gregarines, bryozoans and helminths, but did not detect the presence of viral, microsporidian and acanthocephalan parasites, which are present in continental populations sampled from France and Poland (Bojko et al., 2013). A microsporidian detected in a single UK individual appears to have been acquired in the invaded range (Bojko et al., 2013).

A second Ponto-Caspian invader, *D. haemobaphes*, has also been found in multiple sites in the UK. A comparison of parasite–host studies across its range suggests that several parasite species have been lost (Figure B9.4.2), although this invader appears to have cointroduced a highly prevalent, microsporidian parasite *Cucumispora ornata* (Bojko et al., 2015), which originated from German and Polish populations of *D. haemobaphes* (Grabner et al., 2015).

Crangonyx pseudogracilis is a North American amphipod introduced to Europe through shipping and the ornamental trade. Although invasive populations of *C. pseudogracilis* have undergone a genetic bottleneck, Slothouber Galbreath et al. (2010) found no evidence for enemy release in populations in the UK, France and the Netherlands, but found that two vertically transmitted parasites had been cointroduced (Figure B9.4.3).

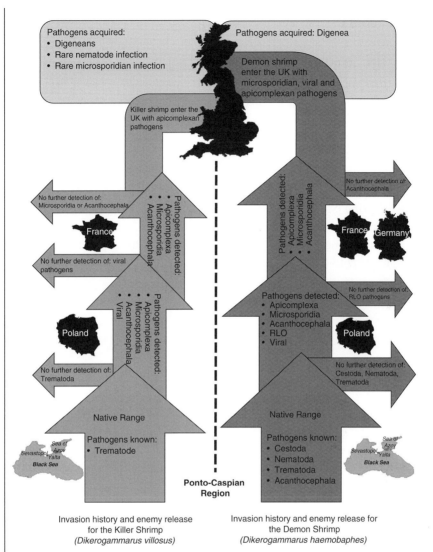

Figure B9.4.2 Invasion history of the killer shrimp (*Dikerogammarus villosus*) and the demon shrimp (*Dikerogammarus haemobaphes*) from the perspective of their parasites and enemy release, as they move from the Black Sea, through multiple corridors in Europe, to enter the UK (Bojko, 2017). Only macro- and microparasites are accounted for in the diagram, not commensal or symbiotic species. The horizontal arrows indicate where parasitic species have been lost and the vertical arrows indicate the movement of the invader. The history of each host and their parasitic profile along their invasion pathway is detailed on the left for *D. villosus* and right for *D. haemobaphes*. Parasites that appear to be acquired from the UK are detailed in the boxes at the top of the diagram. Based on current parasite profiling efforts it appears that the killer shrimp has undergone strong enemy release, leaving behind almost all known parasites during its invasion of the UK (Wattier et al., 2007; Ovcharenko et al., 2010; Wilkinson et al., 2011; Bojko et al., 2013; Arundell et al., 2015). On the other hand, it appears that the demon shrimp has carried its viral and microsporidian parasites into the UK (Bojko, 2017).

Box 9.4: (cont.)

Vertically transmitted parasites infect the host gametes and are passed from mother to offspring at reproduction. These parasites do not experience the same selective pressures as their transmission is not density-dependent, and they typically cause little virulence (Bandi et al., 2001). Hence, they are less likely to be lost during the invasion process (Mitchell & Power, 2003; Slothouber Galbreath et al., 2004). Vertically transmitted parasites which distort host sex ratios have in fact been predicted to enhance the invasion success as they may increase population growth through overproduction of female offspring (Slothouber Galbreath et al., 2004). High prevalence of the microsporidian *Fibrillanosema crangonycis* in invasive *C. pseudogracilis* populations in Europe suggests that this feminising parasite may factilitate host population growth (Slothouber Galbreath et al., 2010).

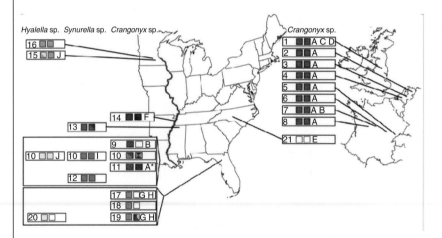

Figure B9.4.3 Distribution of *Crangonyx pseudogracilis* host genotypes and microsporidian parasites across North America (native range) and Europe (the invasive range). Boxes show sample sites (1–21); host genotype according to SSU rDNA sequence (left box) and COI mtDNA sequence (right box). Parasite species are coded A–J. Although a higher parasite diversity was found in the native range, comparison of parasite diversity conducted between invasive populations and native source populations (matched by host molecular sequence data) did not provide any evidence for a reduction in prevalence or diversity of microsporidia; two microsporidia were isolated from *C. pseudogracilis* in the source population and these were both detected in the invasive range. The feminiser *Fibrillanosema crangonycis* (parasite A) was found in all invasive populations (Slothouber Galbreath et al., 2010). (A black and white version of this figure will appear in some formats. For the colour version, please refer to the plate section.)

Our large-scale studies of parasite diversity reveal the importance of biological invasions in driving changes in parasite–host relationships (Figures B9.4.2 and B9.4.3). Invasive species may benefit from enemy release, but can also be influenced by parasite introduction and acquisition. As illustrated earlier, novel (and endemic) parasite–host associations mediate invasion success and impact on recipient communities.

9.7 Horizon scanning, predicting and managing impacts

Predicting biodiversity–parasitism relationships can be especially problematic in communities undergoing change, inevitably the case for ongoing invasion (Dunn & Hatcher, 2015). We have recently examined this problem for the *Gammarus* system, using functional responses (relationship between resource uptake and resource availability) to examine the role of parasites in influencing resource consumption and hence ecological impacts. This work reveals that the effects of parasitism are often context-dependent (Paterson et al., 2015). In particular, while parasites can both increase and decrease host feeding rates (Dick et al., 2010), this can depend on parasite type, prey type, conspecific/heterospecific presence, higher-order predators, and abiotic factors such as temperature (Paterson et al., 2015; Laverty et al., 2017). Furthermore, per-capita effects measured by functional responses need to be scaled up to take account of measures of consumer abundance. Recent development of functional response/abundance biplots and the 'Relative Impact Potential' metric (Dick et al., 2017) could be powerful new methods to understand and predict the community effects of parasites in a changing world.

In a recent horizon scanning exercise (Roy, 2016), we highlighted that the difficulty of predicting likelihood and impact of IAS is particularly pronounced for invasive parasites where novel host–parasite associations come into play. Current risk assessment models, such as those developed by the GB Non-Native Species Secretariat, rely heavily on evidence from previous examples of impact. However, in many cases, especially in relation to novel parasitism, there are few historical cases to base assessments on. Impact prediction for parasites requires we have information on parasite taxa in the source range with the potential to be pathogenic in the novel range, and on host–parasite specificity. The discovery of previously unknown invasive parasites highlights this difficulty. For example, the origin of *B. dendrobatidis*, a key driver of worldwide amphibian declines, is unknown (Fisher et al., 2012), and evidence suggests that it may be endemic to some regions, with a new virulent lineage spread by the amphibian trade (Farrer et al., 2011).

Opportunities to eliminate or control invasive species including parasites decrease as they progress through the invasion process (Figure 9.1). Thus, for new or predicted IAS, screening for parasites represents a route to detect the potential for emerging diseases that may affect native species. As little is known about the parasite profile of IAS, this may require the use of generalist molecular and microscopic diagnostics alongside targeted diagnostics for known parasites (e.g. Bojko et al., 2013d; Bass et al., 2015).

We must also consider the potential for host shifts to novel host species, and the potential for ecological and evolutionary host–parasite adaptation in the invaded range. Furthermore, we need to know about transmission dynamics and host population dynamics in the invaded range. A key issue for IAS scenarios is that that the impact of an endemic or novel parasite may differ in the new range/new host species. For example, the oomycete *Aphanomyces astaci* causes crayfish plague, which has driven local extinctions of native crayfish in Europe. This parasite was introduced to Europe over 150 years ago, but its more recent spread and impact was faciliated by spread of the invasive signal crayfish, a reservoir host in which the infection is avirulent (Filipova et al., 2013). Similarly, the trait effects of parasites may be difficult to predict. For example, the cestode *Flamingolepis liguloides* castrates the native brine shrimp *Artemia parthenogenetica*, but not the invasive *A. franciscana,* contributing to the competitive advantage of the invasive (Sanchez et al., 2012).

A further challenge to managing the threat of wildlife diseases is that they tend to fall in the gaps between regulatory bodies (Dunn & Hatcher, 2015; Roy et al., 2016). The World Organization for Animal Health (OIE) requires member countries to report and manage listed animal diseases. However, the focus of the OIE is on managed and farmed terrestrial and aquatic animals. Yet, because diseases are covered by the OIE, alien parasites are specifically excluded under the 2015 EU Regulation on Invasive Alien Species. We argue that international policy and management should take into account the strong links between biological invasions and wildlife diseases (Dunn & Hatcher, 2015) and should pay greater attention to the threats imposed by alien parasites (Roy et al., 2016).

The management framework for invasions/emerging diseases depends upon the stage of the invasion process and consists of prevention (of translocation and introduction), containment or eradication (prevent establishment), and mitigation (to limit further invasive spread (Hatcher et al., 2012b); Figure 9.1). It is recognised that preventing the introduction of an IAS is more cost-effective than attempting to eradicate or even mitigate the effect of established invaders. Key to reducing the likelihood of establishment of a putative invasive is to manage propagule pressure, and common to both disease and invasive species policy is the importance of biosecurity precautions to prevent their introduction or spread (Figure 9.1). Disease emergence bears many similarities with the process of invasion (Hatcher et al., 2012b), but interdependence between parasitism and propagule pressure (for example, enemy release), like that between parasitism and biodiversity, may complicate predictions. Ecologists may therefore need to be mindful of the potential for interplay between parasitism and propagule pressure when considering wild-life disease invasion.

Robust biosecurity reduces opportunities for accidental movement of IAS and associated parasites, therefore directly limiting propagule pressure, reducing translocation and introduction, and diminishing the subsequent likelihood of establishment (Figure 9.1). Legislation around IAS highlights the importance of preventing species introduction (EU1143, 2014; GBNNSS, 2015; IMO, 2017). Recreational water users are a high-risk group for the potential spread of aquatic IAS (Anderson et al., 2014). Campaigns such as 'Check Clean Dry' in the UK and 'Check Drain Dry' in the USA encourage good biosecurity practice among water users. Developing effective biosecurity measures is imperative in reducing further introductions. Ideally, biosecurity for both IAS and parasites should be combined, where a single measure can be used to combat both. While some measures, such as the use of hot water, have been demonstrated to be effective against a range of freshwater invasive species (Anderson et al., 2015), how effective it is as a measure for disinfecting parasite-contaminated fomites has yet to be established.

Also key to preventing the spread of IAS and parasites is the uptake and application of biosecurity by stakeholders. A study of attitudes to and uptake of biosecurity practices across a range of environmental organisations found that, while participants generally agreed on the need for biosecurity, critical barriers to biosecurity included difficulties in changing attitudes and implementing collective responsibility (Sutcliffe et al., 2018). As researchers working in the natural environment, we recognise that our own activities (from eco-tourism at an international conference, through to field sampling and manipulation) pose a risk of inadvertent movement of IAS and parasites. However, a recent survey revealed low perception of the risk of IAS and parasite spread among researchers (Shannon et al., 2019). Raising awareness and embedding good biosecurity practices into our day-to-day research activities is key to reducing the risk of spreading invasive species and parasites. Furthermore, in training ourselves, our colleagues and the next generation of students, we have an opportunity to embed biosecurity into day-to-day activities both now and as they pursue future careers in research, education, and policy. To facilitate this, we have developed a short (1 h) e-learning module (https://openeducation.black board.com/mooc-catalog/courseDetails/view?course_id=_1189_1), which we encourage readers to incorporate into their training and field work.

9.8 Conclusions

Parasites are inextricably linked to invasions; they can mediate invasion success and outcomes for recipient communities. The trait-mediated effects of parasites can be as powerful as classical density effects and merit wider consideration in terms of their impact on the host's trophic interactions.

We report on tantalising evidence of wider cascading effects that warrant deeper study.

The process of biological invasion can lead to altered parasite–host associations. We find patterns of parasite loss that mirror host invasion pathways, but also highlight the risks of introduction of invasive parasites. Horizon scanning and impact predictions are vital in identifying future risks, potential pathways of introduction and suitable management measures that can be implemented as mitigation. Predicting and managing invasive parasites is particularly challenging and it is vital that such actions consider invasive parasites as well as free-living species.

Biosecurity is a key element in reducing further introduction and spread, but further work is required, not only in developing easily applied, cost-effective and efficacious measures to combat both IAS and parasites, but in increasing awareness and good biosecurity practice among diverse stakeholders.

9.9 Acknowledgements

Thanks to the Dunn lab group, the Dick lab group and Chris Tofts for stimulating discussion and to NERC and CEFAS and BBSRC for funding.

References

Adlard, R.D., Miller, T.L. & Smit, N.J. (2015) The butterfly effect: parasite diversity, environment, and emerging disease in aquatic wildlife. *Trends in Parasitology*, **31**, 160–166.

Anderson, L.G., Dunn, A.M., Rosewarne, P.J. & Stebbing, P.D. (2015) Invaders in hot water: a simple decontamination method to prevent the accidental spread of aquatic invasive non-native species. *Biological Invasions*, **17**, 2287–2297.

Anderson, L.G., White, P.C.L., Stebbing, P.D., Stentiford, G.D. & Dunn, A.M. (2014) Biosecurity and vector behaviour: evaluating the potential threat posed by anglers and canoeists as pathways for the spread of invasive non-native species and pathogens. *PLoS ONE*, **9**, e92788.

Arundell, K., Dunn, A., Alexander, J., et al. (2015) Enemy release and genetic founder effects in invasive killer shrimp populations of Great Britain. *Biological Invasions*, **17**, 1439–1451.

Bandi, C., Dunn, A.M., Hurst, G.D.D. & Rigaud, T. (2001) Inherited microorganisms, sex-specific virulence and reproductive parasitism. *Trends in Parasitology*, **17**, 88–94.

Bass, D., Stentiford, G.D., Littlewood, D.T.J. & Hartikainen, H. (2015) Diverse applications of environmental DNA methods in parasitology. *Trends in Parasitology*, **31**, 499–513.

Blackburn, T.M., Pysek, P., Bacher, S., et al. (2011) A proposed unified framework for biological invasions. *Trends in Ecology & Evolution*, **26**, 333–339.

Bojko, J. (2017) Parasites of invasive crustacea: risks and opportunities for control. PhD thesis, University of Leeds, UK.

Bojko, J., Bacela-Spychalska, K., Stebbing, P.D., et al. (2017) Parasites, pathogens and commensals in the 'low-impact' non-native amphipod host *Gammarus roeselii*. *Parasites & Vectors*, **10**, 193.

Bojko, J., Dunn, A.M., Stebbing, P.D., et al. (2015) *Cucumispora ornata* n. sp (Fungi: Microsporidia) infecting invasive 'demon shrimp' (*Dikerogammarus haemobaphes*) in the United Kingdom. *Journal of Invertebrate Pathology*, **128**, 22–30.

Bojko, J., Stebbing, P.D., Bateman, K.S., et al. (2013) Baseline histopathological survey of a recently invading island population of 'killer shrimp', *Dikerogammarus villosus*. *Diseases of Aquatic Organisms*, **106**, 241–253.

Bovy, H.C., Barrios-O'Neill, D., Emmerson, M.C., Aldridge, D.C. & Dick, J.T.A. (2015) Predicting the predatory impacts of the 'demon shrimp' *Dikerogammarus haemobaphes*, on native and previously introduced species. *Biological Invasions*, **17**, 597–607.

Bowers, R.G. & Turner, J. (1997) Community structure and the interplay between interspecific infection and competition. *Journal of Theoretical Biology*, **187**, 95–109.

Bunke, M., Alexander, M.E., Dick, J.T.A., et al. (2015) Eaten alive: cannibalism is enhanced by parasites. *Royal Society Open Science*, **2**, 140369.

Claessen, D., de Roos, A.M. & Persson, L. (2004) Population dynamic theory of size-dependent cannibalism. *Proceedings of the Royal Society B-Biological Sciences*, **271**, 333–340.

Colautti, R.I., Ricciardi, A., Grigorovich, I.A. & MacIsaac, H.J. (2004) Is invasion success explained by the enemy release hypothesis? *Ecology Letters*, **7**, 721–733.

DAISIE (2017) DAISIE European Invasive Alien Species Gateway, accessed 2017.

Dick, J.T.A. (1996) Post-invasion amphipod communities of Lough Neagh, Northern Ireland: influences of habitat selection and mutual predation. *Journal of Animal Ecology*, **65**, 756–767.

Dick, J.T.A., Alexander, M.E., Jeschke, J.M., et al. (2014) Advancing impact prediction and hypothesis testing in invasion ecology using a comparative functional response approach. *Biological Invasions*, **16**, 735–753.

Dick, J.T.A., Armstrong, M., Clarke, H.C., et al. (2010) Parasitism may enhance rather than reduce the predatory impact of an invader. *Biology Letters*, **6**, 636–638.

Dick, J.T.A., Laverty, C., Lennon, J.J., et al. (2017) Invader Relative Impact Potential: a new metric to understand and predict the ecological impacts of existing, emerging and future invasive alien species. *Journal of Applied Ecology*, **54**, 1259–1267.

Dick, J.T.A., Montgomery, I. & Elwood, R.W. (1993) Replacement of the indigenous amphipod *Gammarus duebeni celticus* by the introduced *Gammarus pulex* – differential cannibalism and mutual predation. *Journal of Animal Ecology*, **62**, 79–88.

Dick, J.T.A., Montgomery, W.I. & Elwood, R.W. (1999) Intraguild predation may explain an amphipod replacement: evidence from laboratory populations. *Journal of Zoology*, **249**, 463–468.

Dick, J.T.A. & Platvoet, D. (1996) Intraguild predation and species exclusions in amphipods: the interaction of behaviour, physiology and environment. *Freshwater Biology*, **36**, 375–383.

Dobson, A., Lafferty, K.D., Kuris, A.M., Hechinger, R.F. & Jetz, W. (2008) Homage to Linnaeus: how many parasites? How many hosts? *Proceedings of the National Academy of Sciences of the United States of America*, **105**, 11,482–11,489.

Dudgeon, D., Arthington, A.H., Gessner, M.O., et al. (2006) Freshwater biodiversity: importance, threats, status and conservation challenges. *Biological Reviews*, **81**, 163–182.

Dunn, A.M. & Dick, J.T.A. (1998) Parasitism and epibiosis in native and non-native gammarids in freshwater in Ireland. *Ecography*, **21**, 593–598.

Dunn, A.M. & Hatcher, M.J. (2015) Parasites and biological invasions: parallels, interactions, and control. *Trends in Parasitology*, **31**, 189–199.

Dunn, A.M., Torchin, M.E., Hatcher, M.J., et al. (2012) Indirect effects of parasites in invasions. *Functional Ecology*, **26**, 1262–1274.

EU. (2014). Regulation (EU) No. 1143/2014 of the European Parliament and of the Council of 22 October 2014 on the prevention and management of the introduction and spread of invasive alien species. https://eur-lex.europa.eu/legal-content/EN/TXT/?uri=celex%3A32014R1143

Farrer, R.A., Weinert, L.A., Bielby, J., et al. (2011) Multiple emergences of genetically diverse amphibian-infecting chytrids include a globalized hypervirulent recombinant lineage. *Proceedings of the National Academy of Sciences of the United States of America*, **108**, 18,732–18,736.

Fielding, N.J., MacNeil, C., Robinson, N., et al. (2005) Ecological impacts of the microsporidian parasite *Pleistophora mulleri* on its freshwater amphipod host *Gammarus duebeni celticus*. *Parasitology*, **131**, 331–336.

Filipova, L., Petrusek, A., Matasova, K., Delaunay, C. & Grandjean, F. (2013) Prevalence of the crayfish plague pathogen *Aphanomyces astaci* in populations of the signal crayfish *Pacifastacus leniusculus* in France: evaluating the threat to native crayfish. *PLoS ONE*, **8**, e70157.

Fisher, M.C., Henk, D.A., Briggs, C.J., et al. (2012) Emerging fungal threats to animal, plant and ecosystem health. *Nature*, **484**, 186–194.

GBNNSS (2015) The Great Britain Invasive Non Native Species Strategy.

Grabner, D.S., Weigand, A.M., Leese, F., et al. (2015) Invaders, natives and their enemies: distribution patterns of amphipods and their microsporidian parasites in the Ruhr Metropolis, Germany. *Parasites & Vectors*, **8**, 419.

Hatcher, M.J., Dick, J.T.A. & Dunn, A.M. (2006) How parasites affect interactions between competitors and predators. *Ecology Letters*, **9**, 1253–1271.

Hatcher, M.J., Dick, J.T.A. & Dunn, A.M. (2008) A keystone effect for parasites in intraguild predation? *Biology Letters*, **4**, 534–537.

Hatcher, M.J., Dick, J.T.A. & Dunn, A.M. (2012a) Disease emergence and invasions. *Functional Ecology*, **26**, 1275–1287.

Hatcher, M.J., Dick, J.T.A. & Dunn, A.M. (2012b) Diverse effects of parasites in ecosystems: linking interdependent processes. *Frontiers in Ecology and the Environment*, **10**, 186–194.

Hatcher, M.J., Dick, J.T.A. & Dunn, A.M. (2014) Parasites that change predator or prey behaviour can have keystone effects on community composition. *Biology Letters*, **10**.

Hatcher, M.J., Dick, J.T.A., Paterson, R.A., et al. (2015) Trait-mediated effects of parasites on invader–native interactions. In: Mehlhorn, H. (ed.), *Host Manipulations by Parasites and Viruses* (pp. 29–47). Cham: Springer.

Hatcher, M.J. & Dunn, A.M. (2011) *Parasites in Ecological Communities; From Interactions to Ecosystems*. Cambridge: Cambridge University Press.

Holt, R.D. & Dobson, A.P. (2006) Extending the principles of community ecology to address the epidemiology of host–pathogen systems. In: Collinge, S.K.R. (ed.), *Disease Ecology: Community Structure and Pathogen Dynamics* (pp. 6–27). Oxford: Oxford University Press.

Holt, R.D., Dobson, A.P., Begon, M., Bowers, R.G. & Schauber, E.M. (2003) Parasite establishment in host communities. *Ecology Letters*, **6**, 837–842.

Holt, R.D. & Pickering, J. (1985) Infectious-disease and species coexistence – a model of Lotka–Volterra form. *American Naturalist*, **126**, 196–211.

Holt, R.D. & Polis, G.A. (1997) A theoretical framework for intraguild predation. *American Naturalist*, **149**, 745–764.

Hudson, P. & Greenman, J. (1998) Competition mediated by parasites: biological and theoretical progress. *Trends in Ecology & Evolution*, **13**, 387–390.

Hudson, P.J., Dobson, A.P. & Lafferty, K.D. (2006) Is a healthy ecosystem one that is rich in parasites? *Trends in Ecology & Evolution*, **21**, 381–385.

IMO (2017) www.imo.org/en/About/Conventions/ListOfConventions/Pages/International-Convention-for-the-Control-and-Management-of-Ships'-Ballast-Water-and-Sediments-(BWM).aspx.

IUCN (2017) Global invasive species database. www.iucngisd.org/gisd/, accessed November 2017.

Keane, R.M. & Crawley, M.J. (2002) Exotic plant invasions and the enemy release hypothesis. *Trends in Ecology & Evolution*, **17**, 164–170.

Keesing, F., Belden, L.K., Daszak, P., et al. (2010) Impacts of biodiversity on the emergence and transmission of infectious diseases. *Nature*, **468**, 647–652.

Kelly, D.W. & Dick, J.T.A. (2005) Introduction of the non-indigenous amphipod *Gammarus pulex* alters population dynamics and diet of juvenile trout *Salmo trutta*. *Freshwater Biology*, **50**, 127–140.

Kelly, D.W., Dick, J.T.A. & Montgomery, W.I. (2002) The functional role of *Gammarus* (Crustacea, Amphipoda): shredders, predators, or both? *Hydrobiologia*, **485**, 199–203.

Kenna, D., Fincham, W.N., Dunn, A.M., Brown, L.E. & Hassall, C. (2017) Antagonistic effects of biological invasion and environmental warming on detritus processing in freshwater ecosystems. *Oecologia*, **183**, 875–886.

Kumschick, S., Gaertner, M., Vila, M., et al. (2015) Ecological impacts of alien species: quantification, scope, caveats, and recommendations. *Bioscience*, **65**, 55–63.

Laverty, C., Brenner, D., McIlwaine, C., et al. (2017) Temperature rise and parasitic infection interact to increase the impact of an invasive species. *International Journal for Parasitology*, **47**, 291–296.

Ledger, M.E. & Milner, A.M. (2015) Extreme events in running waters. *Freshwater Biology*, **60**, 2455–2460.

Lefevre, T., Lebarbenchon, C., Gauthier-Clerc, M., et al. (2009) The ecological significance of manipulative parasites. *Trends in Ecology & Evolution*, **24**, 41–48.

MacLeod, C.J., Paterson, A.M., Tompkins, D.M. & Duncan, R.P. (2010) Parasites lost – do invaders miss the boat or drown on arrival? *Ecology Letters*, **13**, 516–527.

MacNeil, C., Dick, J.T. & Elwood, R.W. (1997) The trophic ecology of freshwater *Gammarus* spp. (Crustacea: Amphipoda): problems and perspectives concerning the functional feeding group concept. *Biological Reviews of the Cambridge Philosophical Society*, **72**, 349–364.

MacNeil, C., Dick, J.T.A., Hatcher, M.J., et al. (2003a) Parasite-mediated predation between native and invasive amphipods. *Proceedings of the Royal Society of London Series B*, **270**, 1309–1314.

MacNeil, C., Dick, J.T.A., Platvoet, D. & Briffa, M. (2011) Direct and indirect effects of species displacements: an invading freshwater amphipod can disrupt leaf-litter processing and shredder efficiency. *Journal of the North American Benthological Society*, **30**, 38–48.

MacNeil, C., Elwood, R.W. & Dick, J.T.A. (1999) Predator–prey interactions between brown trout *Salmo trutta* and native and introduced amphipods; their implications for fish diets. *Ecography*, **22**, 686–696.

MacNeil, C., Fielding, N.J., Dick, J.T.A., et al. (2003b) An acanthocephalan parasite mediates intraguild predation between invasive and native freshwater amphipods (Crustacea). *Freshwater Biology*, **48**, 2085–2093.

MacNeil, C., Fielding, N.J., Hume, K.D., et al. (2003c) Parasite altered micro-distribution of *Gammarus pulex* (Crustacea: Amphipoda). *International Journal for Parasitology*, **33**, 57–64.

MacNeil, C., Platvoet, D., Dick, J.T.A., et al. (2010) The Ponto-Caspian 'killer shrimp', *Dikerogammarus villosus* (Sowinsky, 1894), invades the British Isles. *Aquatic Invasions*, **5**, 441–445.

Mitchell, C.E. & Power, A.G. (2003) Release of invasive plants from fungal and viral pathogens. *Nature*, **421**, 625–627.

Mouritsen, K.N. & Poulin, R. (2010) Parasitism as a determinant of community structure on intertidal flats. *Marine Biology*, **157**, 201–213.

Ohgushi, T., Schmitz, O. & Holt, R.D. (2012) *Trait-mediated Indirect Interactions: Ecological and Evolutionary Perspectives*. Cambridge: Cambridge University Press.

Okamura, B. & Feist, S.W. (2011) Emerging diseases in freshwater systems. *Freshwater Biology*, **56**, 627–637.

Ovcharenko, M.O., Bacela, K., Wilkinson, T., et al. (2010) *Cucumispora dikerogammarz* n. gen. (Fungi: Microsporidia) infecting the invasive amphipod *Dikerogammarus villosus*: a potential emerging disease in European rivers. *Parasitology*, **137**, 191–204.

Parker, J.D., Torchin, M.E., Hufbauer, R.A., et al. (2013) Do invasive species perform better in their new ranges? *Ecology*, **94**, 985–994.

Paterson, R.A., Dick, J.T.A., Pritchard, D.W., et al. (2015) Predicting invasive species impacts: a community module functional response approach reveals context dependencies. *Journal of Animal Ecology*, **84**, 453–463.

Pimentel, D., Zuniga, R. & Morrison, D. (2005) Update on the environmental and economic costs associated with alien-invasive species in the United States. *Ecological Economics*, **52**, 273–288.

Polis, G.A., Myers, C.A. & Holt, R.D. (1989) The ecology and evolution of intraguild predation – potential competitors that eat each other. *Annual Review of Ecology and Systematics*, **20**, 297–330.

Poulin, R. (2010) Network analysis shining light on parasite ecology and diversity. *Trends in Parasitology*, **26**, 492–498.

Price, P.W., Westoby, M., Rice, B., et al. (1986) Parasite mediation in ecological interactions. *Annual Review of Ecology and Systematics*, **17**, 487–505.

Rewicz, T., Grabowski, M., MacNeil, C. & Bacela-Spychalska, K. (2014) The profile of a 'perfect' invader – the case of killer shrimp, *Dikerogammarus villosus*. *Aquatic Invasions*, **9**, 267–288.

Rewicz, T., Wattier, R., Grabowski, M., Rigaud, T. & Bacela-Spychalska, K. (2015) Out of the Black Sea: phylogeography of the invasive killer shrimp *Dikerogammarus villosus* across Europe. *PLoS ONE*, **10**, e0118121.

Ricciardi, A. & MacIsaac, H.J. (2011) *Impacts of Biological Invasions on Freshwater Ecosystems*. Malden, MA: Wiley-Blackwell.

Roy, H. (2016) Invasive species: control wildlife pathogens too. *Nature*, **530**, 281–281.

Roy, H.E., Hesketh, H., Purse, B.V., et al. (2016) Alien pathogens on the horizon: opportunities for predicting their threat to wildlife. *Conservation Letters*, **10**, 477–484.

Rudolf, V.H.W. (2007) The interaction of cannibalism and omnivory: consequences for community dynamics. *Ecology*, **88**, 2697–2705.

Sanchez, M.I., Rode, N.O., Flaven, E., et al. (2012) Differential susceptibility to parasites of invasive and native species of *Artemia* living in sympatry: consequences for the invasion of *A. franciscana* in the Mediterranean region. *Biological Invasions*, **14**, 1819–1829.

Selakovic, S., de Ruiter, P.C. & Heesterbeek, H. (2014) Infectious disease agents mediate interaction in food webs and ecosystems. *Proceedings of the Royal Society of London B*, **281**, 20132709.

Shannon, C., Quinn, C.H., Sutcliffe, C., et al. (2019) Exploring knowledge, perception of risk and biosecurity practices among researchers in the UK: a quantitative survey. *Biological Invasions*, **21**, 303–314.

Slothouber Galbreath, J.G.M., Smith, J.E., Becnel, J.J., Butlin, R.K. & Dunn, A.M. (2010) Reduction in post-invasion genetic diversity in *Crangonyx pseudogracilis* (Amphipoda: Crustacea): a genetic bottleneck or the work of hitchhiking vertically transmitted microparasites? *Biological Invasions*, **12**, 191–209.

Slothouber Galbreath, J.G.M., Smith, J.E., Terry, R.S., Becnel, J.J & Dunn, A.M. (2004) Invasion success of *Fibrillanosema crangonycis*, n.sp., n.g.: a novel vertically transmitted microsporidian parasite from the invasive amphipod host *Crangonyx pseudogracilis*. *International Journal for Parasitology*, **34**, 235–244.

Smith, K.F., Sax, D.F. & Lafferty, K.D. (2006) Evidence for the role of infectious disease in species extinction and endangerment. *Conservation Biology*, **20**, 1349–1357.

Sutcliffe, C., Quinn, C.H., Shannon, C., Glover, A. & Dunn, A.M. (2018) Exploring the attitudes to and uptake of biosecurity practices for invasive non-native species: views amongst stakeholder organisations working in UK natural environments. *Biological Invasions*, **20**, 399–411.

Terry, R.S., MacNeil, C., Dick, J.T.A., Smith, J.E. & Dunn, A.M. (2003) Resolution of a taxonomic conundrum: an ultrastructural and molecular description of the life cycle of *Pleistophora mulleri* (Pfeiffer 1895; Georgevitch 1929). *Journal of Eukaryotic Microbiology*, **50**, 266–273.

Terry, R.S., Smith, J.E., Sharpe, R.G., et al. (2004) Widespread vertical transmission and associated host sex-ratio distortion within the eukaryotic phylum Microspora. *Proceedings of the Royal Society of London Series B*, **271**, 1783–1789.

Torchin, M.E., Lafferty, K.D., Dobson, A.P., McKenzie, V.J. & Kuris, A.M. (2003) Introduced species and their missing parasites. *Nature*, **421**, 628–630.

Torchin, M.E., Lafferty, K.D. & Kuris, A.M. (2002) Parasites and marine invasions. *Parasitology*, **124**, S137–S151.

Wattier, R.A., Haine, E.R., Beguet, J., et al. (2007) No genetic bottleneck or associated microparasite loss in invasive populations of a freshwater amphipod. *Oikos*, **116**, 1941–1953.

Wilkinson, T.J., Rock, J., Whiteley, N.M., Ovcharenko, M.O. & Ironside, J.E. (2011) Genetic diversity of the feminising microsporidian parasite *Dictyocoela*: new insights into host-specificity, sex and phylogeography. *International Journal for Parasitology*, **41**, 959–966.

CHAPTER TEN

Parasite-mediated selection in red grouse – consequences for population dynamics and mate choice

JESÚS MARTÍNEZ-PADILLA, MARIUS
WENZEL, FRANÇOIS MOUGEOT,
LORENZO PÉREZ-RODRÍGUEZ, STUART
PIERTNEY AND STEPHEN M. REDPATH

10.1 Introduction

The dynamic relationship between hosts and parasites has been maintained in evolutionary time for diverse reasons (Quigley et al., 2012; Gómez et al., 2015). On the one hand, directional selection can favour genotypes of host resistance and parasite infectivity. On the other, fluctuating selection may lead to variation in the pattern of these genotypes. Both perspectives are based on the idea that parasites impose costs on hosts. However, the nature of these costs is multi-faceted. First, there is the direct drain of energetic resources that undermine the reproductive budget and survival of individuals. This energetic constraint has an impact on the physiology of hosts, which may involve activating their immune defences or creating an imbalance between oxidation and antioxidant defences, resulting in oxidative stress and damage (Mougeot et al., 2009). Second, at a behavioural level, parasites may reduce resources that hosts can invest in social and sexual displays, which can indirectly affect mate choice and intrasexual competition (Mougeot et al., 2005a). The resolution of this trade-off between two energy-demanding functions (e.g. ornament expression and homeostasis) is postulated to ensure the reliability of social and sexual signals.

Physiological and behavioural costs may influence life-history traits and the resolution of life-history trade-offs can determine individual fitness. Hosts resistant to parasite infection are expected to be positively selected because they can allocate resources to produce more offspring or survive better. Translated into a population context, hosts resistant to parasites can have a greater individual contribution to population growth or, alternatively, a reduced one after prolonged infection. There is a large body of evidence that shows how parasites influence population dynamics in several taxa, including birds (Hudson, 1986a; Hudson et al., 1998), mammals, and fish (Turchin, 2003), through their impact on the fecundity (Watson, 2013) of females and males (Ferrari et al., 2004) and survival. However, an issue central to understanding the effect of parasites on host fitness is determining the genetic bases that explain why some hosts are more resistant to parasite infection. This is particularly relevant not just for population dynamics, but also from an evolutionary context, because parasite-resistant hosts are expected to be favoured by selection transferring their genes to the next generation (Hamilton & Zuk, 1982). Therefore, a deep understanding of the consequences of parasite infection for population dynamics and sexual selection requires a detailed comprehension of the physiological, behavioural, and genomic mechanisms involved.

A remarkable difficulty in exploring the effects of parasites on hosts is that hosts are commonly parasitised by multiple parasites, where each parasite species influences different aspects of the host (Schmid-Hempel & Ebert, 2003; Schmid-Hempel, 2011). Thus, research on the effect of a particular parasite relies on the capacity to experimentally manipulate an individual's parasite abundance and to investigate its individual- and population-level effects. In addition, such manipulations carried out in natural settings will provide the most realistic picture of the complex and diverse host responses at both individual and population levels. However, studies that experimentally change parasite abundance in wild settings are rare. Here we describe how the study of the association between a nematode parasite (*Trichostrongylus tenuis*) and the red grouse (*Lagopus lagopus scoticus*; Figure 10.1) has led to a long-lasting and fruitful research programme focused on understanding the individual- and population-level causes and consequences of chronic parasite infection in a wild bird. In this chapter, we summarise the short- and long-term effects of nematode parasites on red grouse from behavioural, physiological, and genomic perspectives and their consequences for sexual selection and population dynamics. We also highlight potential avenues for future research on this particular host–parasite system.

Figure 10.1 Adult male red grouse (*Lagopus lagopus scoticus*) with pronounced red comb (a secondary sexual characteristic influenced by parasitism). Photo credit: Julian Renet. (A black and white version of this figure will appear in some formats. For the colour version, please refer to the plate section.)

10.2 The red grouse–*T. tenuis* host–parasite system

The red grouse is a tetraonid bird that inhabits heather (*Calluna vulgaris*)-dominated moorlands of upland Britain. Males are territorial, mainly monogamous, and pairs produce one brood a year (Watson et al., 1998; Hudson et al., 2002), although some males can pair with two females in the same breeding season (Redpath et al., 2006a). Both male and female red grouse display conspicuous bright red combs during social interactions, such as territorial contests and courtship (Watson & Moss, 2008), and males with bigger combs had a higher probability of mating with two females (Redpath et al., 2006a). In addition, males with bigger and redder combs (Mougeot et al., 2007b) tend to be in better body condition (see Section 10.4). Males establish their territories in autumn and defend them throughout the winter (Watson & Moss, 1988, 2008; Moss et al., 1996; Moss & Watson, 2001). Successful territorial males tend to be those in better condition and displaying bigger combs (Figure 10.2; Redpath et al., 2006a). Once the territory is established, males and females vigorously defend it against male and female intruders, respectively. Females generally start laying eggs in late April, and lay on average about seven eggs (Jenkins et al.,

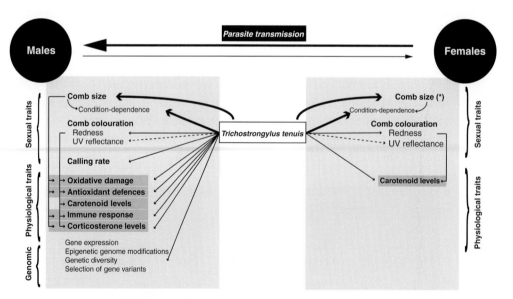

Figure 10.2 Graphical summary of the range of effects that *T. tenuis* parasites have on their red grouse host at the genomic, physiological and sexual trait levels. All lines indicate studies exploring the association between *T. tenuis* and traits related to sexual selection, physiology, or genomics. Thicker lines highlight relationships explored both at the population and individual levels. Experimental or correlational associations are denoted as solid or dashed lines, respectively. The thickness and direction of the arrows above the graph represent the risk of parasite transmission between males and females.

1963; Hudson et al., 1992; Haines, 2010). Females produce one brood per year, averaging 3.5 offspring (Jenkins et al., 1963; Hudson, 1986a; Thirgood et al., 2000; Redpath et al., 2006a; Martínez-Padilla et al., 2014b). Grouse chicks leave the nest soon after hatching and the territory structure breaks down as broods and their parents move more widely in search of food (Watson & Moss, 2008). At the beginning of autumn, young reach independence, and young males establish territories; survival prospects of non-territory holders over winter dramatically decreases (Watson, 1985; Watson & Moss, 2008).

Most red grouse older than 2 months are parasitised by *T. tenuis* (Hudson, 1986a, 1986b; Hudson et al., 1992), with infection intensities of up to 30,000 worms per host (Hudson, 1986b). This nematode has a direct life cycle with no alternative hosts. Adult worms inhabit the caeca – i.e. *blind guts* – and their eggs are voided in caecal droppings. After approximately two weeks, depending on weather conditions (Moss et al., 1993), they develop into infective larvae that migrate onto terminal heather shoots, ready to infect new grouse when feeding. However, in certain conditions, infective larvae can arrest their development for periods ranging from weeks to months. Adult grouse feed nearly exclusively on heather (Watson & Moss, 2008), particularly on heather shoots, thus increasing the probability of ingestion of infective larvae. Once ingested, larvae migrate to the caeca, where they develop into adult worms (Watson & Moss, 2008). After ingestion, mature female worms produce eggs that have to be excreted to develop into new infective larvae (Shaw & Moss, 1989; Shaw et al., 1989).

10.3 Parasites and population dynamics

Red grouse population dynamics are characterised by cyclic, although erratic (Haydon et al., 2002), population fluctuations (Martínez-Padilla et al., 2014c). The red grouse–*T. tenuis* system has provided an iconic example of the influence of parasites on population dynamics and on cycles in particular. Since Cobbold (1873) and Lovat (1911) around the turn of the twentieth century, diseases in general, and parasites in particular, have been considered important in explaining population crashes observed in red grouse populations. Many years later, a negative relationship between worm burdens and red grouse reproduction was highlighted (Potts et al., 1984), and an experimental manipulation demonstrated the effect of nematodes on grouse reproduction (Wilson & Wilson, 1978). This led to the idea that nematodes could cause red grouse population cycles. Empirical studies supported the three theoretical predictions inferred from mathematical models: low levels of aggregation of parasites (Hudson et al., 1992), negative impact on red grouse fecundity (Hudson, 1986a, 1986b; Hudson et al., 1998; Newborn & Foster, 2002; Redpath et al., 2006a), and a time-lag between host density and parasite abundance due to arrested development (Shaw, 1988; Shaw & Moss, 1989).

The hypothesis that parasites can cause population cycles in red grouse was initially tested by Hudson and collaborators (1998), where between 15% and 50% of the breeding adults were purged of parasites in some populations while others were left as controls. The populations were then monitored for 10 years and grouse abundance estimated using bag records (numbers of grouse shot by hunters in autumn). This large-scale study found that the amplitude of the cycles of red grouse was reduced in those populations where parasites had been removed, and the authors suggested that parasites were sufficient to explain the cyclic fluctuations in red grouse abundance (Hudson et al., 1998). However, despite this result, the effect of parasites on population cycles is still under debate for different reasons. First, some issues challenge the main conclusions of the study, because population density was estimated just by the number of harvested birds, and cycles still occurred (Lambin et al., 1999). Second, a similar experiment focusing on 1 km^2 areas, and on counts of live birds, produced different results. In this case, purged grouse showed higher productivity and post-breeding densities, but the treatment did not prevent the populations from declining from spring to spring (Redpath et al., 2006b). Third, parasites might not act alone but interactively with other factors. Lochmiller's model of population regulation (Lochmiller, 1996; Lochmiller & Deerenberg, 2000) posits that stress-induced immunosuppression occurs at high population density, which causes increased mortality through enhanced susceptibility to parasitism (Lochmiller, 1996). Although Lochmiller's model is not explicitly centred on testosterone, this hormone can have immunosuppressive effects in red grouse (Mougeot et al., 2004, 2006). As such, an increase in testosterone should lead to both increased aggression and physiological stress (Mougeot et al., 2005d, 2006), which in turn would cause immunosuppression (see Section 10.4). Thus, delayed density-dependent changes in aggressiveness, along with concomitant changes in testosterone levels, could be an alternative mechanism explaining the unstable population dynamics of red grouse (Mougeot et al., 2003a). Both parasites and aggressiveness could work in parallel influencing population dynamics (Piertney et al., 2008; Martínez-Padilla et al., 2014c), but triggering different physiological mechanisms at the individual level involving different trade-offs and influencing sexual selection.

Although testosterone and parasites can act together to influence population dynamics, there is a lack of experimental studies that address the joint effect of these two factors at the same time on reproduction and survival at the individual level but under different population contexts. In stressful situations, such as in high-density populations with heightened levels of aggression, individuals are expected to be physiologically challenged and both testosterone and parasites then can have a stronger impact on survival and reproduction. The relative effects of testosterone and parasites may change depending on the environmental context (e.g. intrasexual competition level), and only individually based experiments will allow their relative effects on life-history and physiological trade-offs to be teased apart. The only attempt to do so was an experiment replicated in five populations where nearly 200 young red grouse were purged of parasites and assigned to a combination of parasite and testosterone treatments at the same time. After following all individuals throughout their lives, the study suggested that testosterone had a greater influence on the individual contribution to population growth over parasites (Martínez-Padilla et al., 2014b), but this did not consider a potential mediating effect of population density. In addition, this result needs to be considered with caution because parasite challenges only moderately increased worm burdens in treated red grouse.

10.4 Physiological effects of *T. tenuis* infection and implications for honest sexual signalling and sexual selection

Since Darwin, it has been assumed that sexual selection emerges when there are differences in reproductive success caused by female choice or males competing for more mates (Darwin, 1871). Theoretical models of sexual selection suggest that the expression of extravagant ornaments reflects the phenotypic or genotypic quality of males. The 'Handicap Principle' verbally proposed by Zahavi (1975) and mathematically formulated by Grafen (1990) suggests that the 'honesty' of the signals relies on the costs inherent to produce or maintain sexual displays, where only high-quality individuals can show the most extravagant ornaments. Hamilton and Zuk (1982) set parasites as the functional link between genetic quality and ornament expression. This influential hypothesis suggests that parasite-free individuals are of superior genetic quality and that their 'good genes' improve additive genetic immunity to parasites, and thus convey a fitness benefit. Embracing Zahavian models of sexual selection and Hamilton and Zuk's ideas, Folstad and Karter suggested the Immunocompetence Handicap Hypothesis (ICHH; Folstad & Karter, 1992). According to the ICHH, testosterone plays a crucial role in sexual selection because it enhances sexual behaviours and the expression of many secondary sexual traits, but it also has immunosuppressive effects and impairs parasite resistance (Folstad & Karter, 1992). The red grouse–*T. tenuis* system has provided important contributions to our understanding of testosterone–parasite interactions in general, and to the ICHH in particular. Using the ICHH as a general framework, we describe first the effects of parasites on red grouse physiology, and then their interaction with testosterone and the resulting effects on the expression of sexually selected traits in males and females. We further show how environmental conditions may modulate these effects.

10.4.1 Effects of parasites on red grouse physiology and the expression of sexual traits

Hosts rely on a range of physiological means to prevent, cope with or reduce parasite infections. One of the most efficient ways of fighting off parasites is the immune system, designed to protect the host against a wide variety of pathogens. There is little evidence of acquired immunity to *T. tenuis* infection in red grouse (Shaw & Moss, 1989; Shaw et al., 1989; Richardson et al., 1997). However, innate immunity appears to be important, as experiments have shown that the same individuals tend to end up with similar number of *T. tenuis* parasites after purging and challenging with parasite larvae (Seivwright et al., 2004; Mougeot et al., 2005a).

Empirical and experimental studies have highlighted some of the effects that *T. tenuis* nematodes have on red grouse immune responses. Greater parasite loads have been consistently associated with a reduced body condition (Mougeot et al., 2004, 2007b; Mougeot & Redpath, 2004), with an enlarged spleen (as a proxy of immune capacity) and a reduced T-cell–mediated immune responsiveness (Mougeot & Redpath, 2004). According to the ICHH, an individual's parasite intensity and capacity to resist parasite infection could be inferred through the expression of sexual traits. Increasing nematode parasites, by means of parasite challenges with infective larvae, reduced the size of combs, particularly in adult males (Mougeot et al., 2005a).

Both male and female red grouse display supraorbital and conspicuous red combs (Mougeot et al., 2007a; Pérez-Rodríguez et al., 2016). The redness colouration of the combs is due to the deposition of carotenoid pigments in the integument (Martínez-Padilla et al., 2007; Mougeot et al., 2007b). This colour production mechanism is widespread in the animal kingdom, resulting in striking yellow, orange, or red visual displays that are used as social or sexual signals (McGraw, 2006). Animals cannot synthesise carotenoids, but obtain them from their diet (Goodwin, 1984). However, they can metabolise and transform carotenoids acquired with their food (McGraw, 2006). The diet of red grouse, nearly exclusively heather shoots (Watson & Moss, 2008), is rich in two yellow carotenoids (lutein and zeaxanthin) that are converted into red carotenoids (astaxanthin and papilioerythrinone) at the comb integument (Pérez-Rodríguez et al., 2016). Grouse diet is very rich in the yellow precursors of ornamental red carotenoids. However, intestinal parasites can exert a strong negative effect on carotenoid availability. For example, red grouse purged from or infected with *T. tenuis* experience increases or decreases in circulating carotenoids, respectively, which are mirrored by changes in comb redness (Martínez-Padilla et al., 2007; Mougeot et al., 2007b). The exact mechanism by which *T. tenuis* infection impairs carotenoid levels is unknown, but several potential and non-exclusive mechanisms are possible. First, the damage inflicted by *T. tenuis* to host intestinal mucosa during infection likely limits individual capacity to absorb ingested carotenoids. In addition, nematode infection elicits an immune response that increases oxidative stress of the host. Oxidative stress is a physiological condition whereby the production of reactive oxygen and nitrogen species (ROS/RNS) overwhelms the capacity of antioxidant defences (see below). Carotenoids are particularly sensitive to oxidative stress, either because they can act as antioxidant compounds, or because they are particularly sensitive to the action of radicals (Pérez-Rodríguez, 2009). In any event, parasite infection may lead to a depletion of circulating carotenoids during *T. tenuis* infection –as observed for other intestinal parasite infections, such as coccidiosis (Allen, 1987, 1997) – ultimately reducing the pigments available for maximising comb redness.

10.4.2 The interactive effect of parasites and testosterone on red grouse physiology

According to the ICHH, elevated testosterone enhances ornament expression, but simultaneously impairs the ability of males to cope with parasites and diseases. This dual action of testosterone would ensure reliable sexual signalling (Folstad & Karter, 1992), as only high-quality individuals would be able to afford the immunosuppressive costs of testosterone while showing the most elaborate sexual displays (Folstad & Karter, 1992). The evidence for testosterone to be immunosuppressive remains equivocal in birds (Roberts et al., 2004), although there is experimental evidence that elevated testosterone can lead to increased parasite abundance (Saino et al., 1995). In red grouse, experiments have also shown that elevated testosterone depresses cell-mediated immune responsiveness (Mougeot et al., 2004), reduces the concentration of circulating immunoglobulins (relative to albumin; Mougeot et al., 2006), and increases the ratio of heterophils to lymphocytes in the blood (Mougeot et al., 2005d). The latter findings might be indicative of increased stress and immunosuppression. Moreover, experiments have shown that males implanted with testosterone and challenged with infective *T. tenuis* larvae ended up with two times more parasites than controls a year (Seivwright et al., 2005) or six months after parasite challenge (Mougeot et al., 2006).

Experimental increases of testosterone levels by means of implants cannot distinguish between susceptibility (physiological effects) or exposure (behaviour) mechanisms to explain how testosterone increases parasite infection, because both are simultaneously enhanced. In the red grouse–*T. tenuis* system, however, another combination of implants (flutamide and ATD) was used to manipulate aggression by blocking testosterone receptors. These implants reduced in male aggressive behaviour, even though testosterone levels were higher. At the same time, the implants, like testoterone implants, increased parasite abundance after challenge (Mougeot et al., 2005b, 2005d), providing support for a physiological mechanism rather than a behavioural mechanism linking elevated testosterone to increased parasite abundance.

The response of individuals to perturbations is modulated by stress hormones (corticosterone in birds), which can act as mediators of sexual signal expression (Husak & Moore, 2008). The interaction between testosterone and parasite infection likely involves cascading effects implicating hormones other than testosterone alone, in particular corticosterone (Poiani et al., 2000; Owen-Ashley et al., 2004; Bortolotti et al., 2009b). Free-living animals experience many environmental stressors (e.g. weather, predators, parasites, social conflicts) that challenge their homeostasis (Romero, 2004). A major adaptation is the hypothalamic–pituitary–adrenal axis, which releases glucocorticoids (mainly corticosterone in the case of birds, reptiles, amphibians, and rodents) in response to stressors, allowing individuals to recover homeostasis in the best condition. However, chronic or inappropriate stress responses can exert deleterious effects, such as immunosuppression (Romero, 2004). How individuals respond to or cope with stressors is likely a major determinant of their fitness, and ornaments could reveal how individuals cope with environmental factors that may increase physiological stress. A link between stress hormones and sexual ornaments may be mediated by their effects on immunity and parasite resistance (Romero, 2004; Costantini, 2008). In that respect, parasite manipulations in red grouse were found to have no apparent effect on corticosterone levels, as measured through the amount of this hormone deposited in growing feathers (Bortolotti et al., 2009a; Mougeot, 2016). However, corticosterone levels in feathers explained the relative effectiveness of parasite challenges, or the relative impacts that testosterone implants had on sexual ornamentation (Bortolotti et al., 2009b): male red grouse that experienced more stressful events or more prolonged stress responses ended up with more parasites after a standardised challenge with infective *T. tenuis* larvae, and increased their comb size less after testosterone implant (Bortolotti et al., 2009b).

The red grouse–*T. tenuis* system has also provided relevant insights for a refinement of the ICHH, namely the Oxidation Handicap Hypothesis (OHH; von Schantz et al., 1999; Alonso-Alvarez et al., 2007). According to this hypothesis a main cost of elevated testosterone, required for a maximum expression of testosterone-dependent ornaments, is increased oxidative stress. Only individuals with a prime antioxidant system could afford this cost (increased oxidative stress) associated with maintaining the high testosterone levels required for enhanced ornamentation and territorial displays (von Schantz et al., 1999). Elevated testosterone has indeed been shown to increase ROS/RNS production and oxidative stress (Alonso-Alvarez et al., 2007), which may, in turn, impair lymphocyte proliferation and signalling pathways involved in an immune response (Larbi et al., 2007). Furthermore, immune system activation produces ROS/RNS to help counter invading pathogens or control parasite infections (Romero et al., 1998; Horak et al., 2007), but their overproduction can lead to oxidative damage when individuals lack sufficient antioxidant protection (von Schantz et al., 1999; Splettstoesser & Schuff-Werner, 2002; Halliwell & Gutteridge, 2007). During a parasite infection, the immune system cells generate ROS to combat invading pathogens, which may cause oxidative damage to the host organism, increasing the cost of immune response (Halliwell & Gutteridge, 2007). In red grouse, *T. tenuis* parasite challenges have been shown to increase oxidative damage to lipids (Mougeot et al., 2009). Parasite purging exerts the opposite effect, reducing lipid peroxidation, while increasing levels of antioxidant defences proportionally to the amount of parasite reduction (Mougeot et al., 2010). Elevated testosterone also caused increased oxidative damage and increased circulating antioxidant defences when males were simultaneously challenged with *T. tenuis* parasites. As predicted by the OHH, the ability of males to upregulate antioxidant defences explained the impacts that testosterone and parasites had on sexual ornamentation (Mougeot et al., 2009).

10.4.3 Female ornamentation and male mate choice

The theory of sexual selection has been focused mainly on the direct or indirect benefits that choosy females can get by mating with males showing more elaborated sexual displays. However, this directionality of mate choice has been questioned mainly because evolution has also maintained ornamentation in females in multiple species (Andersson & Simmons, 2006). Several hypotheses have been put forward to explain the evolution of female traits. On the one hand, some hypothesise that female ornamentation is just a non-functional, genetic by-product of male ornamentation (Lande, 1980). On the other hand, some authors hypothesise a functionality to female ornaments (Amundsen, 2000; Amundsen & Pärn, 2006; Kraaijeveld et al., 2007), providing information about individual quality to potential mates or competitors. Several tests suggest that *T. tenuis* parasites limit the expression of red supra-orbital combs in female red grouse (Martínez-Padilla et al., 2011; Vergara et al., 2011), consistent with a functionality of this trait in sexual selection contexts.

Female red grouse have similar parasite burdens to males, and high parasite infestation reduces their reproductive output (Hudson, 1986a). Because parasites detract resources from their hosts and impose a cost on females, it would be expected that evolution should favour those females that can advertise low parasite loads or capacity to resist parasite infestation. Female combs are smaller than those of males, but increase in size from autumn to spring, and from young to adult, suggesting a potential function linked with reproduction (Martínez-Padilla et al., 2011). In addition, the comb size of female red grouse increased proportionally to the number of parasites removed following an experimental purging (Martínez-Padilla et al., 2011). This suggests that comb size in females is constrained by parasites and could be a reliable proxy of individual condition (Haines, 2010). Regarding comb colouration, females displaying duller combs laid heavier eggs than those displaying redder combs, whereas no such association was found in parasite-purged females (Haines, 2010). This suggests a trade-off between attractiveness and fecundity, supporting the idea that only intermediate levels of female ornamentation, comb colouration in this case, are positively selected for (Chenoweth et al., 2006). However, the individual association between ornament size and parasite burdens is not evident at the population level, as there was no association between average comb size and mean parasite burdens in different populations (Vergara et al., 2012c). However, parasite levels in the population mediates the condition-dependence of comb size (Vergara et al., 2011). Similar to males, the strength of the positive association between body mass and the size of the ornament increases as average levels of parasites in the population increases. This suggests that the reliability of the comb signal is higher when environmental conditions worsen (i.e. when average parasite levels are higher), as only high-quality individuals are able to express the biggest combs. Thus, these results suggest that female comb size and colouration are functional traits that can be proxies of individual capacity to resist parasite infection. Like males, however, the association between ornament size and colouration in females remains to be explored at individual and population levels, along with its covariation in relation to changing environmental conditions.

Female mate choice has been the predominant explanation for the evolution of ornamental traits in males because of the direct or indirect genetic benefits females might obtain (Fisher, 1930; Kodric-Brown & Brown, 1984; Andersson, 1994; Kotiaho & Puurtinen, 2007; Cornwallis & Uller, 2009). However, several hypotheses defend the idea that male mate choice also can occur in natural populations (Amundsen, 2000), increasing direct or indirect benefits for choosy males. When pair members remain together throughout the reproductive season, avoiding choosing a heavily parasitised mate may case a relative decrease in male own parasite load, which can be considered a direct benefit because reducing the risk of being parasitised by the mate can increase reproductive output (Hudson, 1986a; Gustafsson et al., 1994) and survival (Martínez-de la Puente et al., 2010) of the choosy mate. Red grouse pairs share their time and territory during reproduction. Unsurprisingly, *T. tenuis* loads are positively correlated within pairs (Martínez-Padilla et al., 2012). Experiments manipulating parasite loads within the pair at the beginning of the breeding season in red grouse showed that individual's parasite abundance was reduced when its mate was purged of parasites (Martínez-Padilla et al., 2012). Further, this was particularly noticeable in males but was less noticeable in females. Specifically, parasite-free males suffered an increased risk of parasite infection when mated with a naturally infected female, but the opposite pattern was not apparent. The asymmetrical risk of parasitism within pairs suggests that red grouse pay a cost (increased risk of parasitism) when mated with a more parasitised individual, and that such a cost was greater for males. In a sexual selection context, these results support the idea that mate choice is not just a female issue as traditionally thought, but rather a reciprocal process (Thrall et al., 1997; Prudic et al., 2011), leaving room for potential male-mate choice by red grouse.

10.4.4 Modulating effect of environmental variation on the physiological effects of parasite infection

All these experiments support the idea that both comb size and colouration are reliable proxies of male quality and that females could benefit from choosing males displaying the most elaborated sexual displays. However, the possible indirect additive genetic resistance to nematodes (see Section 10.5), and direct benefits that females can get by choosing nematode-free males could be diluted depending on the environmental context.

Harsh environmental conditions, like increased levels of intrasexual competition, influence the expression of secondary sexual traits (Martínez-Padilla et al., 2014a) and may determine condition-dependence in male red grouse. Average population levels of parasite abundance also can be considered as another source of environmental variation. Accordingly, the average size of sexual traits in populations decreases as the average levels of parasites in the population increases (Vergara et al., 2012c). According to the condition-dependence hypothesis of secondary sexual traits detailed above, a positive correlation between the expression of a sexual trait and individual condition is expected. In a non-experimental study, the slope of the relationship between comb size and body mass (condition) increased as average parasite burden increased in the study population. Thus, regardless of the source of environmental variation (levels of aggressiveness or parasites in the population), comb size seems to be a more reliable proxy of individual condition when environmental conditions are harsh. Considering the handicap principle, this suggests that the cost of producing a signal is affordable for all individuals in the population when there are plenty of resources. However, when resources are scarce, only high-quality individuals can afford the cost of producing or maintaining this signal. This supports the idea that the handicap principle can at least work with more intensity on individuals that are experiencing harsher environmental conditions, increasing the cost of producing or maintaining the signal. However, it is unknown yet, particularly in the red grouse–parasite system, whether alive individuals in low density population (with low parasite burdens) are only those of prime quality, explaining the lack of the association between comb size and body mass (Vergara et al., 2012b). If so, positive selection on parasite-free individuals would be expected. However, genomic analyses (see Section 10.5) in red grouse suggest that there are no population allele-frequency differences between low- and high-density populations, and therefore suggest a lack of parasite-driven selection (Wenzel & Piertney, 2015; Wenzel et al., 2016), although alternative ideas need to be tested. In a supposed scenario where there is no clear suggestion of parasite-driven selection, what maintains the signal honesty of male combs? This honesty can be mediated through the effects of testosterone and associated physiological stress, not just affecting immune function as posited by Zahavian-derived handicap models, but through broadscale downscaling of investment under optimal resource allocation. Thus, these results suggest that the influence of parasites on the evolutionary dynamics of comb size in red grouse can be better understood by direct models of sexual selection. However, further analyses are still needed to reject that there are no additive genetic benefits from choosing parasite-free individuals displaying bigger supraorbital combs. For example, the genetic covariation between ornament expression and parasite burdens is as yet unknown, and could be mediated by temporal environmental heterogeneity. Quantitative genetic models can be a good statistical tool to explore this question particularly in individual-based monitored populations fluctuating in density and parasite burdens.

Population dynamics have implications for sexual selection in red grouse, particularly for the expression of sexual traits. Within a demographic perspective, competition for resources increases as population density rises. At high density, individuals are more physiologically constrained and the trade-off between deriving resources for self-maintenance and ornament expression potentially more pronounced. For example, testosterone-implanted individuals living in populations with low intrasexual competition levels (low density) increased comb redness by depleting carotenoid levels. However, when competition was greater, testosterone challenges did not affect redness of the comb, possibly because male red grouse then prioritised using carotenoids for immune purposes to fight against parasite infection (Martínez-Padilla et al., 2010). If sexual signals reliably indicate individual quality, the mean expression of a sexual trait within a population should be lower in harsher environmental conditions (Cotton et al., 2004). Red grouse is a particular case because they show a delayed density-dependence pattern, where comb size in the current year is inversely associated with population density the following year (Piertney et al., 2008). Other studies support the negative effects of population density in male red grouse, where comb size decreases as intrasexual competition increases in different populations (Vergara et al., 2012c), or when it is experimentally increased in a given area (Vergara & Martínez-Padilla, 2012), in spring and autumn, respectively. However, to further confirm negative density dependence on the expression of comb size, there is need for further exploration of the changes of comb size from one year to the next in relation to a demographic change, and not just relating the comb size in the current year to population density.

The most robust example that showed how population context influenced not just ornament size, as previously described, but its condition dependence was provided by Vergara et al. (2012a). In this study, condition dependence of sexual traits was understood as the positive association between comb size and body mass. Using data sets obtained from previous experiments on the effect of aggressiveness on population dynamics and kin structure in red grouse (Mougeot et al., 2003b, 2005c), they explored how experimentally increased aggressiveness in a population influenced the condition dependence of sexual traits in males. Results suggested that signals are reliable proxies of individual quality only when intrasexual competition is high. Finally, associations of body condition with comb size and calling behaviour were positive only for male red grouse that had their territories in control areas, with no relationship between these traits for males with territories where intrasexual competition was increased experimentally (Tarjuelo et al., 2016).

10.5 Genomics of host–parasite interactions in red grouse

Modern genomics can provide novel insight into multiple facets of host–parasite interaction and coevolution (Paterson & Piertney, 2011). For example, comparing genome-wide levels of gene expression among individuals can identify which genes in which tissues are switched on or off at particular stages of parasite infection (Lenz et al., 2013). Similarly, identifying DNA sequence variation among individuals that vary in their level of parasite burden can help to identify the genetic underpinning of parasite resistance or susceptibility and pinpoint individual genes that are subject to parasite-driven selection (Wilfert & Schmid-Hempel, 2008). Finally, characterising genome-wide variation in chemical DNA modifications such as nucleotide methylation can identify epigenetic patterns that might represent parasite-induced 'memory effects' on long-term gene regulation and physiological condition (Poulin & Thomas, 2008; Biron & Loxdale, 2012).

10.5.1 Short-term gene-expression responses to *T. tenuis* infection

The transcriptomic response of grouse caecum, liver and spleen to both acute and chronic *T. tenuis* infection has been examined following two independent field trials (Webster, 2011; Webster et al., 2011). The aims of these experiments were twofold. First, to identify the number and physiological functions of the genes that change activity in response to acute *T. tenuis* infection. This allows for assessment of whether the response is focused on immune genes or involves a broader suite of genes that may indicate alternative physiological trade-offs (Sheldon & Verhulst, 1996; Lochmiller & Deerenberg, 2000). Second, to examine how this response is modulated by high testosterone titre, assuming that both parasite load and aggression are density dependent in grouse populations (see Section 10.4) and that testosterone-induced immunosuppression in particular has broad eco-evolutionary implications (Lochmiller, 1996; Zuk & Stochr, 2002).

To identify differentially expressed genes, genome-wide transcript abundance was compared using suppression subtractive hybridisation (SSH) between RNA extracted from red grouse that were either experimentally inoculated with infective L3 larvae or given broad-spectrum anthelmintic medication (Webster et al., 2011). A large and diverse set of genes were upregulated across all three tissues in infected birds (3716 unique sequences), but less than 2% of these were associated with immune system processes. In a subsequent, more extensive, two-factor field experiment, red grouse were manipulated for *T. tenuis* burden (infected, medicated, and untreated control) and testosterone titre (testosterone administration and sham control) before differences in gene expression were compared between all groups using microarrays (Webster, 2011). This design allowed for a quantitative assay of gene expression differences, and for testing two types of eco-evolutionary models that centre on testosterone-mediated effects on individual fitness and population dynamics, that is Lochmiller's immunosuppression model of population regulation (Lochmiller, 1996), and handicap effects in sexual selection (Folstad & Karter, 1992).

According to Lochmiller's model, an increase in testosterone should lead to increased aggression and stress, which in turn causes immunosuppression. The microarray experiment identified a suite of 52 genes that were significantly upregulated in caecal tissue in response to parasite infection (Webster, 2011). Of these, 51 were subsequently downregulated under conditions of high testosterone titre. This inability of grouse to mount the necessary transcriptomic response to parasite infection under conditions of high testosterone is entirely consistent with Lochmiller's model for population regulation. That said, most of these genes were not associated with immune function, but instead represented broader metabolic functions that could reflect tolerance responses or compensatory mechanisms rather than parasite defence.

Testosterone-induced suppression of vital metabolic processes is also central to Zahavian handicap models in sexual selection theory. As described in detail earlier, these models posit that testosterone enhances the expression of sexual signals in males and at the same time depresses immune system function (ICHH) or promotes oxidative stress (OHH). To test these models on a transcriptomic level, gene expression was compared between birds with elevated testosterone and control birds, focusing on 282 genes involved in immune system processes and 65 genes involved in antioxidant activity or responses to oxidative stress (Wenzel et al., 2013). Although only up to 7% of these genes were significantly differentially expressed, the response in the caecum was entirely consistent with immunosuppression, particularly under acute infection. No evidence was discovered for an effect on antioxidant gene expression, but there was some weak evidence for a depression of oxidative damage responses under acute infection. Interestingly, testosterone had little effect on gene expression in liver or spleen, which suggests that the handicap mechanisms are effected locally at the site of infection rather than systemically. Notwithstanding, testosterone did affect caecal gene expression across the whole microarray beyond the focal genes, consistent with broad suppression of metabolic processes. This makes a case for a central role of infection-induced physiological stress in mediating handicaps, but in a more multidimensional fashion than classic models based on single physiological categories would suggest (Hill, 2011).

10.5.2 The genomic basis of chronic T. tenuis burden

In spite of the well-described physiological responses of grouse to T. tenuis, the inability to purge the infection leads to chronic worm burdens that are likely to impose energetic costs throughout life. As a consequence, an important question to ask is whether the resistance or susceptibility of grouse to chronic T. tenuis infection has any heritable genetic basis, and if so, what particular genes explain variance in T. tenuis burden among birds and are targeted by parasite-driven selection.

To estimate heritability and examine the genomic basis of T. tenuis burden, 695 red grouse were genotyped at 384 single nucleotide polymorphisms (SNPs) that were spread evenly across the chicken genome (Wenzel et al., 2015a). Genome-wide heritability was estimated as 29%, which is consistent with estimates from chicken and sheep breeds (Stear et al., 2007; Wongrak et al., 2015). Genome-wide association (GWA) modelling identified five SNPs that individually explained variance in nematode burden. A parallel study on different individuals identified associations between genotype and nematode burden in a set of 12 novel candidate genes whose expression changed in response to T. tenuis infection (Wenzel & Piertney, 2015; Wenzel et al., 2015b). Together, these studies have identified a catalogue of genes that account for differences in T. tenuis burden of up to 666 worms per bird, and are involved in a broad range of immune-system, oxidative-stress, detoxification and energy-metabolism processes.

Given these genotypic differences among individuals, it may be expected that population-level variation in parasite load drives differences in population allele frequencies as a consequence of parasite-driven selection. However, this does not appear to be the case. In a landscape system of 21 sampling sites in north-east Scotland with spatially heterogeneous parasite burdens, there was no evidence of parasite-driven population structure and directional or balancing selection for any of the genotypic variants that explain individual parasite burden (Wenzel & Piertney, 2015; Wenzel et al., 2016). One reason for these discrepancies might be that selection pressures are too low for beneficial alleles to outcompete the diversifying effects of gene flow and genetic drift, particularly given anthelmintic medication. However, this is somewhat diff-cult to reconcile with genome-wide patterns of epigenetic DNA methylation patterns across the same 21 sites. Numerous individual cytosine methylation states explained variance in *T. tenuis* burden among individual grouse, and many of these also showed evidence of directional selection at the population level (Wenzel & Piertney, 2014). Although it was not possible to establish whether these epigenetic patterns are causes or consequences of *T. tenuis* infection, these provided first evidence for an epigenetic component of chronic parasite burden, which may well reflect the physiological 'memory' of prevailing *T. tenuis* infection (Poulin & Thomas, 2008; Biron & Loxdale, 2012).

10.5.3 Towards a genetic eco-epidemiological framework of host–parasite interactions in red grouse

Several key conclusions can be distilled from the suite of studies that have examined patterns of transcriptomic, genomic, and epigenomic variation in grouse in relation to *T. tenuis* infection. Crucially, the genes that are associated with *T. tenuis* infection in grouse are not necessarily associated with immune function, but instead represent a broader range of physiological processes involving homeostasis and maintenance of condition. This challenges the traditional immune-centric perspective of parasitology, but reinforces the idea that parasite defence involves energetic trade-offs with other costly fitness components such as reproduction or competitive ability (Sheldon & Verhulst, 1996; Lochmiller & Deerenberg, 2000; Hill, 2011).

If the resolution of these trade-offs changes dynamically with prevailing environmental conditions, then it becomes relatively straightforward to envisage how cyclic population dynamics can develop. Birds at low population density with low prevailing testosterone titres, low aggression, and reduced parasite transmission are phenotypically at an advantage over birds at high density, where parasite transmission is higher and ability to cope with parasite insult is compromised by high testosterone and stress levels (Lochmiller, 1996). In this case, fecundity can be depressed and survival reduced to the point that the population can go into decline.

Another important lesson is that, while certain (epi-)genotypes do explain differences in *T. tenuis*, the lack of evidence of genomic selection suggests that the overall genomic basis of parasite susceptibility may be more complex, comprising potentially large numbers of small-effect genes that our studies were unable to detect. This is perhaps intuitive given that grouse cannot purge parasites and must cope with chronic burdens, but is counter to the focus of ecological immunogenetics where the effects of individual large-effect genes are emphasised (Wilfert & Schmid-Hempel, 2008).

These novel insights demonstrate how genomics technologies can open new windows into dynamic ecological processes such as host–parasite interactions, as well as highlighting the complex genetic basis of ecologically important phenotypes such as parasite susceptibility.

10.6 Conclusions

The grouse–*T. tenuis* system has proved to be an outstanding vehicle to explore the effect of parasites on host sexual selection and population dynamics. These nematode parasites constrain the expression of colouration and size of combs for both males and females, and also affect other sexually selected traits such as calling rate. Remarkably, the physiological cost that it imposes ensures the reliability of these sexual traits. However, individual red grouse can experience different environmental context, such as different levels of intrasexual competition, which may constrain individuals physiologically. We know little about the relative effect of parasites on individual physiology under different environmental circumstances, and therefore how the trade-off between homeostasis and investing in sexual traits might change.

Despite some uncertainty, it is clear that the parasite reduces red grouse reproduction and survival, although their role on population cycles is not yet clear. Parasite-resistant red grouse are thus expected to be selected for, because they will be able to produce more offspring or survive better (i.e. have higher fitness). The first step to exploring this was to evaluate how genomic variation captures variation in parasite burdens in populations and understand the heritable genetic bases of parasite resistance. Genes associated with parasite resistance were heritable at approximately 29%, but interestingly, there were no differences in the frequency of alleles among populations differing in parasite burdens. Thus, it is possible that the beneficial alleles for parasite resistance cannot outcompete the diversifying effects of gene flow and genetic drift. However, what is currently unknown is whether alleles for parasite resistance are also those associated with enhanced expression of sexual traits. The red grouse–*T. tenuis* system will be an excellent model to explore whether evolution has favoured selection on the covariation between parasite-resistant individuals and their ornament expression, a test of the core of Hamilton and Zuk's idea.

10.7 Acknowledgements

We acknowledge funding from multiple funding bodies to carry out different research sections described in the chapter. Only the inestimable help and support from multiple people allowed us to successfully advance in our knowledge of red grouse biology in general and sexual selection in particular. We thank the owners and gamekeepers of study sites, the British Army (Bellerby moor), RSPB (Geltsdale moor), English Natural Heritage (Moorhouse); Chris McCarthy, David Craithness, and Derek Calder for allowing us to work in Invermark and Edinglassie, respectively. The contribution of other researchers has been crucial to the successful development of red grouse research. Among the countless people that have contributed on red grouse research over the last few years, we want to thank Lucy Webster, Marianne James, Alex Douglas, Pablo Vergara, Robert Moss, Jessica Haines, and Sonja Ludwig for their invaluable help.

References

Allen, P.C. (1987) Physiological response of chicken gut tissue to coccidial infection: comparative effects of *Eimeria acervulina* and *Eimeria mitis* on mucosal mass, carotenoid content, and brush border enzyme activity. *Poultry Science*, **66**, 1306–1315.

Allen, P.C. (1997) Production of free radical species during *Eimeria maxima* infections in chickens. *Poultry Science*, **76**, 814–821.

Alonso-Alvarez, C., Bertrand, S., Faivre, B., Chastel, O. & Sorci, G. (2007) Testosterone and oxidative stress: the oxidation handicap hypothesis. *Proceedings of the Royal Society of London B*, **274**, 819.

Amundsen, T. (2000) Why are female birds ornamented? *Trends in Ecology & Evolution*, **15**, 149–155.

Amundsen, T.P.H. & Pärn, H. (2006) Female coloration: review of functional and non functional hypotheses. In Hill,G.E. & McGraw,K.J. (eds.), *Bird Coloration. Volume 2. Function and Evolution* (pp. 280–345). Cambridge, MA: Harvard University Press.

Andersson, M. (1994) *Sexual Selection*. Princeton, NJ: Princeton University Press.

Andersson, M. & Simmons, L.W. (2006) Sexual selection and mate choice. *Trends in Ecology & Evolution*, **21**, 296–302.

Biron, D.G. & Loxdale, H.D. (2012) Host–parasite molecular cross-talk during the manipulative process of a host by its parasite. *The Journal of Experimental Biology*, **216**, 148.

Bortolotti, G.R., Marchant, T., Blas, J. & Cabezas, S. (2009a) Tracking stress: localisation, deposition and stability of corticosterone in feathers. *Journal of Experimental Biology*, **212**, 1477–1482.

Bortolotti, G.R., Mougeot, F., Martínez-Padilla, J., Webster, L.M.I. & Piertney, S.B. (2009b) Physiological stress mediates the honesty of social signals. *PLoS ONE*, **4**, e4983.

Chenoweth, S.F., Doughty, P. & Kokko, H. (2006) Can non-directional male mating preferences facilitate honest female ornamentation? *Ecology Letters*, **9**, 179–184.

Cobbold, T.S. (1873) Contributions to our knowledge of grouse disease, including the description of a new species of entozoon, with remarks on a case of rot in the hare. *Veterinarian*, **46**, 163–172.

Cornwallis, C.K. & Uller, T. (2009) Towards an evolutionary ecology of sexual traits. *Trends in Ecology & Evolution*, **25**, 145–152.

Costantini, D. (2008) Oxidative stress in ecology and evolution: lessons from avian studies. *Ecology Letters*, **11**, 1238–1251.

Cotton, S., Fowler, K. & Pomiankowski, A. (2004) Do sexual ornaments demonstrate heightened condition-dependent expression as predicted by the handicap hypothesis? *Proceedings of the Royal Society of London B*, **271**, 771–783.

Darwin, C.R. (1871) *Descent of Man, and Selection in Relation to Sex*. London: John Murray.

Ferrari, N., Cattadori, I.M., Nespereira, J., Rizzoli, A. & Hudson, P.J. (2004) The role of host sex in parasite dynamics: field experiments on the yellow-necked mouse *Apodemus flavicollis. Ecology Letters*, **7**, 88–94.

Fisher, R.A. (1930) *The Genetical Theory of Natural Selection*. Oxford: Clarendon Press.

Folstad, I. & Karter, A.J. (1992) Parasites, bright males, and the immunocompetence handicap. *The American Naturalist*, **139**, 603–622.

Gómez, P., Ashby, B. & Buckling, A. (2015) Population mixing promotes arms race host–parasite coevolution. *Proceedings of the Royal Society of London B*, **282**, 20142297.

Goodwin, T.W. (1984) *The Biochemistry of Carotenoids*. London: Springer.

Grafen, A. (1990) Biological signals as handicaps. *Journal of Theoretical Biology*, **144**, 517–546.

Gustafsson, L., Nordling, D., Andersson, M.S., Sheldon, B.C. & Qvarnström, A. (1994) Infectious diseases, reproductive effort and the cost of reproduction in birds. *Philosophical Transactions of the Royal Society of London B: Biological Sciences*, **346**, 323–331.

Haines, J.A. (2010) Female ornamentation in red grouse and its potential role in sexual selection. MPhil, University of Aberdeen.

Halliwell, B. & Gutteridge, J. (2007) *Free Radicals in Biology and Medicine*. New York, NY: Oxford University Press.

Hamilton, W.D. & Zuk, M. (1982) Heritable true fitness and bright birds: a role for parasites? *Science*, **218**, 384–387.

Haydon, D.T., Shaw, D.J., Cattadori, I.M., Hudson, P.J. & Thirgood, S.J. (2002) Analysing noisy time-series: describing regional variation in the cyclic dynamics of red grouse. *Proceedings of the Royal Society of London B*, **269**, 1609–1617.

Hill, G.E. (2011) Condition-dependent traits as signals of the functionality of vital cellular processes. *Ecology Letters*, **14**, 625–634.

Horak, P., Saks, L., Zilmer, M., Karu, U. & Zilmer, K. (2007) Do dietary antioxidants alleviate the cost of immune activation? An experiment with greenfinches. *The American Naturalist*, **170**, 625–635.

Hudson, P.J. (1986a) The effect of a parasitic nematode on the breeding production of red grouse. *Journal of Animal Ecology*, **55**, 85–92.

Hudson, P.J. (1986b) *The Red Grouse: The Biology and Management of a Wild Gamebird*. Fordingbridge: The Game Conservancy Trust.

Hudson, P.J., Dobson, A.P., Cattadori, I.M., et al. (2002) Trophic interactions and population growth rates: describing patterns and identifying mechanisms. *Philosophical Transactions of the Royal Society of London B: Biological Sciences*, **357**, 1259–1271.

Hudson, P.J., Dobson, A.P. & Newborn, D. (1998) Prevention of population cycles by parasite removal. *Science*, **282**, 1–4.

Hudson, P.J., Newborn, D. & Dobson, A.P. (1992) Regulation and stability of a free-living host–parasite system: *Trichostrongylus tenuis* in red grouse. I. Monitoring and parasite reduction experiments. *Journal of Animal Ecology*, **61**, 477–486.

Husak, J.F. & Moore, I.T. (2008) Stress hormones and mate choice. *Trends in Ecology & Evolution*, **23**, 532–534.

Jenkins, D., Watson, A. & Miller, G.R. (1963) Population studies on red grouse, *Lagopus lagopus scoticus* (Lath.) in north-east Scotland. *Journal of Animal Ecology*, **32**, 317–376.

Kodric-Brown, A. & Brown, J.H. (1984) Truth in advertising: the kinds of traits favored by sexual selection. *The American Naturalist*, **124**, 305–322.

Kotiaho, J.S. & Puurtinen, M. (2007) Mate choice for indirect genetic benefits: scrutiny of the current paradigm. *Functional Ecology*, **21**, 638–644.

Kraaijeveld, K., Kraaijeveld-Smit, F.J.L. & Komdeur, J. (2007) The evolution of mutual ornamentation. *Animal Behaviour*, **74**, 657–677.

Lambin, X., Krebs, C.J., Moss, R., Stenseth, N.C. & Yoccoz, N.G. (1999) Population cycles and parasitism. *Science*, **286**, 2425–2425.

Lande, R. (1980) Sexual dimorphism, sexual selection, and adaptation in polygenic characters. *Evolution*, **34**, 292–305.

Larbi, A., Kempf, J. & Pawelec, G. (2007) Oxidative stress modulation and T cell activation. *Experimental Gerontology*, **42**, 852–858.

Lenz, T.L., Eizaguirre, C., Rotter, B., Kalbe, M. & Milinski, M. (2013) Exploring local immunological adaptation of two stickleback ecotypes by experimental infection and transcriptome-wide digital gene expression analysis. *Molecular Ecology*, **22**, 774–786.

Lochmiller, R.L. (1996) Immunocompetence and animal population regulation. *Oikos*, **76**, 594–602.

Lochmiller, R.L. & Deerenberg, C. (2000) Trade-offs in evolutionary immunology: just what is the cost of immunity? *Oikos*, **88**, 87–98.

Lovat, L. (1911) *The Grouse in Health and in Disease*. London: Smith & Elder.

Martínez-de la Puente, J., Merino, S., Tomás, G., et al. (2010) The blood parasite *Haemoproteus* reduces survival in a wild bird: a medication experiment. *Biology Letters*, **6**, 663–665.

Martínez-Padilla, J., Mougeot, F., Perez-Rodriguez, L. & Bortolotti, G.R. (2007) Nematode parasites reduce carotenoid-based signalling in male red grouse. *Biology Letters*, **3**, 161–164.

Martínez-Padilla, J., Mougeot, F., Webster, L.M.I., Perez-Rodriguez, L. & Piertney, S.B.B. (2010) Testing the interactive effects of testosterone and parasites on carotenoid-based ornamentation in a wild bird. *Journal of Evolutionary Biology*, **23**, 902–913.

Martínez-Padilla, J., Pérez-Rodríguez, L., Mougeot, F., Ludwig, S. & Redpath, S.M. (2014a) Intra-sexual competition alters the relationship between testosterone and ornament expression in a wild territorial bird. *Hormones and Behavior*, **65**, 435–444.

Martínez-Padilla, J., Pérez-Rodríguez, L., Mougeot, F., Ludwig, S.C. & Redpath, S.M. (2014b) Experimentally elevated levels of testosterone at independence reduce fitness in a territorial bird. *Ecology*, **95**, 1033–1044.

Martínez-Padilla, J., Redpath, S.M., Zeineddine, M. & Mougeot, F. (2014c) Insights into population ecology from long-term studies of red grouse *Lagopus lagopus scoticus*. *Journal of Animal Ecology*, **83**, 85–98.

Martínez-Padilla, J., Vergara, P., Mougeot, F. & Redpath, S.M. (2012) Parasitized mates increase infection risk for partners. *The American Naturalist*, **179**, 811–820.

Martínez-Padilla, J., Vergara, P., Perez-Rodriguez, L., et al. (2011) Condition- and parasite-dependent expression of a male-like trait in a female bird. *Biology Letters*, **7**, 364–367.

McGraw, K.J. (2006) Mechanics of carotenoid-based coloration. In: Hill,G.E. & McGraw,K.

J. (eds.),*Bird Coloration* (pp. 177–242). Cambridge, MA: Harvard University Press.

Moss, R. & Watson, A. (2001) Population cycles in birds of the Grouse family (Tetranoidae). *Advances in Ecological Research*, **32**, 53–111.

Moss, R. Watson, A. & Parr, R. (1996) Experimental prevention of a population cycle in Red grouse. *Ecology*, **77**, 1512–1530.

Moss, R., Watson, A., Trenholm, I.B. & Parr, R. (1993) Cecal threadworms *Trichostrongylus tenuis* in red grouse *Lagopus lagopus scoticus* – effects of weather and host density upon estimated worm burdens. *Parasitology*, **107**, 199–209.

Mougeot, F., Dawson, A., Redpath, S.M. & Leckie, F. (2005b) Testosterone and autumn territorial behavior in male red grouse *Lagopus lagopus scoticus*. *Hormones and Behavior*, **47**, 576–584.

Mougeot, F., Evans, S.A. & Redpath, S.M. (2005a) Interactions between population processes in a cyclic species: parasites reduce autumn territorial behaviour of male red grouse. *Oecologia*, **144**, 289–298.

Mougeot, F., Irvine, J.R., Seivwright, L., Redpath, S.M. & Piertney, S. (2004) Honest sexual signaling in male red grouse. *Behavioral Ecology*, **15**, 930–937.

Mougeot, F., Martínez-Padilla, J., Blount, J.D., et al. (2010) Oxidative stress and the effect of parasites on a carotenoid-based ornament. *Journal of Experimental Biology*, **213**, 400–407.

Mougeot, F., Martínez-Padilla, J., Perez-Rodriguez, L. & Bortolotti, G.R. (2007a) Carotenoid-based colouration and ultraviolet reflectance of the sexual ornaments of grouse. *Behavioral Ecology and Sociobiology*, **61**, 741–751.

Mougeot, F., Martínez-Padilla, J., Webster, L.M.I., et al. (2009) Honest sexual signalling mediated by parasite and testosterone effects on oxidative balance. *Proceedings of the Royal Society of London B*, **276**, 1093–1100.

Mougeot, F., Perez-Rodriguez, L., Martínez-Padilla, J., Leckie, F. & Redpath, S.M. (2007b) Parasites, testosterone and honest

Figure 1.1 (a) Worker of *Bombus terrestris* visiting flowers of *Ajuga reptans* (photo: P. Schmid-Hempel). (b) SEM micrograph of *Crithidia bombi*. The length is around 10 μm (photo: Boris Baer, ETH Zürich). (A black and white version of this figure will appear in some formats.)

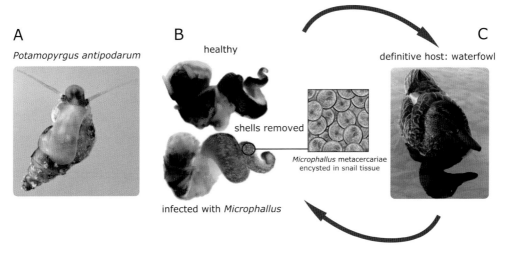

Figure 2.3 Life cycle of *Microphallus*. (A) The snail *Potamopyrgus antipodarum* dominates invertebrate communities of sub-alpine lakes of New Zealand, where it is native. Image courtesy of Bart Zijlstra, © Bart Zijlstra, www.bartzijlstra.com. (B) At least 20 species of trematode parasite infect *P. antipodarum*. The trematode species *Microphallus* is particularly prevalent in some lake populations of *P. antipodarum*. Here, two snails are shown without their shells. The upper snail is healthy. The lower snail is infected with *Microphallus* and hence sterilised: host tissues have been replaced by metacercarial cysts, magnified to the right. Image courtesy of Gabriel Harp, used under Creative Commons BY-SA 4.0. Modified from originals: images combined, line and text elements added. (C) *Microphallus* is transmitted from snail to snail by waterfowl, including this dabbling duck of the genus *Anas*. Photo taken by A.K. Gibson. (A black and white version of this figure will appear in some formats.)

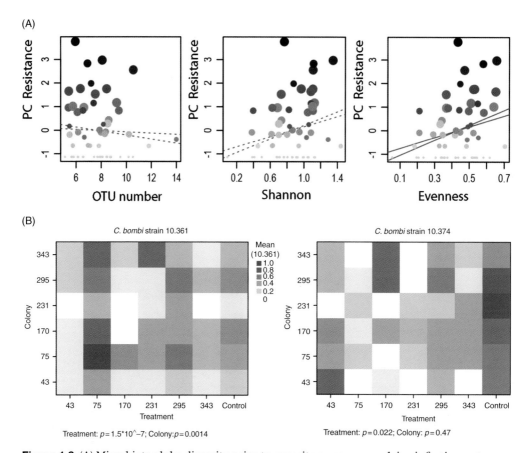

(A)

(B)

C. bombi strain 10.361

C. bombi strain 10.374

Mean
(10.361)
■ 1.0
■ 0.8
■ 0.6
■ 0.4
0.2
0

Treatment: $p = 1.5*10^{-7}$; Colony: $p = 0.0014$

Treatment: $p = 0.022$; Colony: $p = 0.47$

Figure 1.8 (A) Microbiota alpha-diversity prior to parasite exposure explains infection outcome. The panels show the relationship between variation in infection outcome (y-axis: a PC1-score combining infection intensity with diversity of parasite strains residing in the host; explaining 80.5 % of variance) with alpha-diversity measures (based on operational taxonomic units, OTUs) prior to parasite exposure (x-axis: OTU number in microbiota; Shannon = Shannon–Wiener Index of OTU diversity; Evenness of OTUs). Lines are fitted linear regression lines (general linear mixed model accounting for colony identity as a random factor). Solid lines represent statistically significant relationships ($p < 0.05$). Circle size is proportional to infection intensity, and darker fill colour indicates a higher number of resident parasite strains. Reprinted from Näpflin and Schmid-Hempel (2018). (B) Specific protection by microbiota. The heat maps for the average infection load (*C. bombi* cells in host faeces after 7 days; cells/µl faeces, see scale) are shown as a function of host background (y-axis, 'Colony') and the origin of the microbiota (x-axis, 'Treatment') that was transplanted into sterile workers from a given background. 'Controls' are bees with no transplants. The two panels refer to infection by different strains of *C. bombi*. Per panel, total $n = 356$ individuals tested (on average, 8.5 individuals per square). Reprinted from Koch and Schmid-Hempel (2012), with permission from Elsevier. (A black and white version of this figure will appear in some formats.)

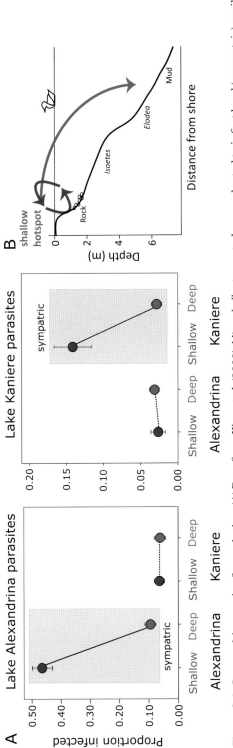

Figure 2.4 Geographic mosaic of coevolution. (A) Data from King et al. (2009). *Microphallus* trematodes are adapted to infect local (sympatric) snail hosts: Lake Alexandrina parasites are far more successful at infecting sympatric hosts, collected from the shallows of Lake Alexandrina, than they are at infecting allopatric hosts, from the shallows of Lake Kaniere (left panel). The same pattern is repeated in the right panel, showing adaptation of Lake Kaniere parasites to specifically infect local, shallow-water Lake Kaniere hosts. The *y*-axes reflect susceptibility, the proportion of hosts infected following controlled exposures to parasites. We also see that parasites are unsuccessful at infecting deep-water hosts from their local lakes; in fact, the parasites are no better at infecting deep-water hosts from their local lake than they are at infecting hosts from allopatric lakes. These results are consistent with the idea that host and parasite genotype frequencies covary in sympatric, shallow habitats. They also suggest that the covariance falls to zero in allopatric combinations, including in the deep. (B) These findings suggest that coevolution of hosts and parasites is restricted to the shallow margins of lakes. This hypothetical cross-section of a lake shows the proposed decline in coevolution, and the covariance of host and parasite genotype frequencies, with depth. The definitive hosts of *Microphallus*, ducks, forage in the shallow rocks and roots zone. Therefore, parasites infecting hosts here contribute offspring to the next generation, allowing them to adapt to infect common host genotypes in the shallow-water habitat. Ducks do not dive to forage in the deeper regions (e.g. *Elodea*). This behaviour reduces the potential for coevolution of parasites infecting hosts in the deep water, and deep-water hosts are accordingly less susceptible to the local parasite population (King et al., 2009). (A black and white version of this figure will appear in some formats.)

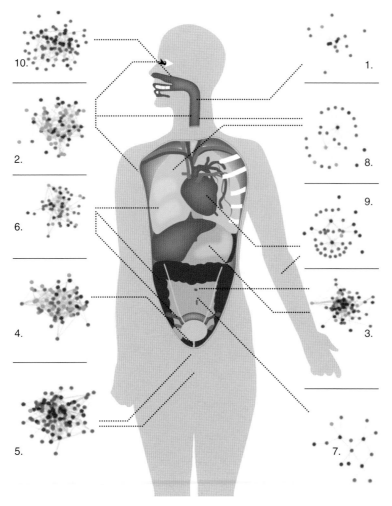

Figure 3.5 Network of reported coinfection interactions in humans, taken from a survey of 316 published articles (from Griffiths et al., 2014). The coinfection network comprises parasite (blue), immune (green), and resource (pink) nodes, forming 10 distinct modules, eight of which are associated with particular bodily sites (1, throat; 2, mixed; 3, GI; 4, genitals; 5, urinary tract or skin; 6, other mucosa; 7, bowel; 8, lower respiratory tract; 9, blood; 10, mouth). (A black and white version of this figure will appear in some formats.)

(A)

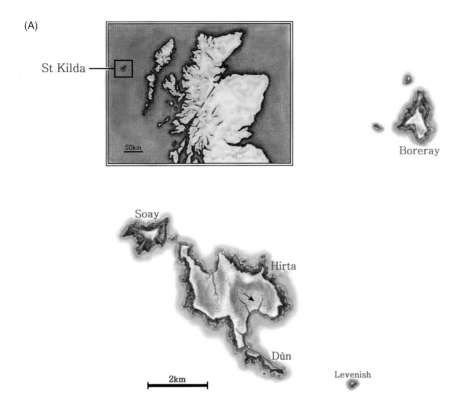

St Kilda

50km

Boreray

Soay

Hirta

Dùn

Levenish

2km

Becky Holland

(B)

Figure 4.1 The location of the isolated St Kilda archipelago and the layout of the islands (A), with the photograph of the Village Bay study area (B) taken from the approximate location and direction indicated by the black arrow. Map drawn by Becky Lister-Kaye, originally used in Graham et al. (2016) and reprinted with permission; photograph by Alexandra Sparks and used with permission. (A black and white version of this figure will appear in some formats.)

Figure 4.2 An illustration of some of the genetically determined variations in horn type and coat colour in St Kilda Soay sheep. Clockwise from top left: normal-horned light wild ewe with dark wild twins (photo by Kara Dicks); normal-horned dark wild ram (photograph by Arpat Ozgul); dark self ewe; scurred dark wild female with dark self lamb (both by Kara Dicks). All photos are used with permission. (A black and white version of this figure will appear in some formats.)

Figure 5.1 Images of a single adult African buffalo and a group of buffalo at a watering hole. (A black and white version of this figure will appear in some formats.)

Figure B6.1.1 Anther-smut disease on *Dianthus pavonius*. (A) Healthy flower (note light-coloured pollen) and (B) diseased flower with dark, smutty spores. (C) A large infected individual where every flower is diseased. (D) Surveying population size and disease prevalence along a 100-m transect in the *Parco Naturale del Marguareis* in the Western Italian Alps. (A black and white version of this figure will appear in some formats.)

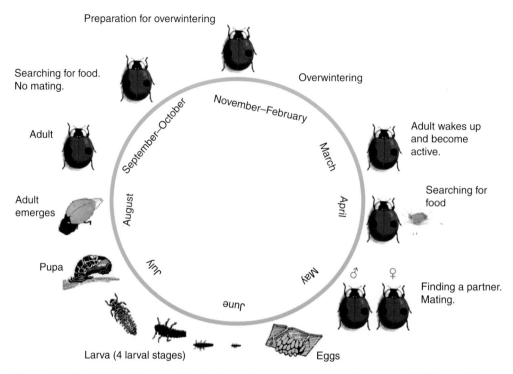

Figure 7.4 The A. bipunctata annual cycle in northern temperature regions, as typified in Stockholm, Sweden. Timings are approximate and vary between years, with new generation ladybirds emerging in July–August. Created by Dr D Pastok, with permission. (A black and white version of this figure will appear in some formats.)

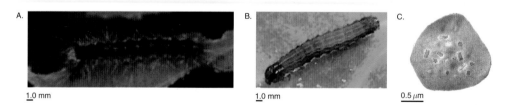

Figure 8.2 Larva of the (A) gypsy moth and (B) fall armyworm, each of which can be infected by a species-specific baculovirus. The (C) electron microscopic (EM) image shows a cross-section of a single occlusion body of the gypsy moth virus, which is a multicapsid nucleopolyhedrovirus. The dark objects within the grey protein coat are virions that contain the double-stranded DNA virus. (A) by Alison Hunter. (A black and white version of this figure will appear in some formats.)

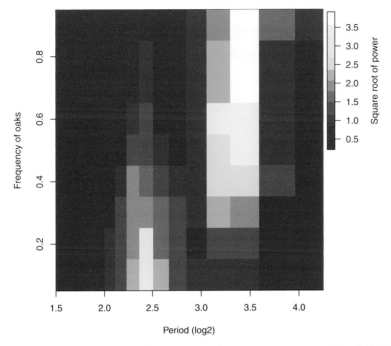

Figure 8.7 Effects of oak frequency on the power spectrum of the defoliation time series in the spatial model. The colours show the square root of the power of each period, such that dark red indicates the lowest power and white indicates the highest power. The figure thus shows that, at a low frequency of oaks, only short-period cycles occur, whereas at a high frequency of oaks, only long-period cycles occur. The relative importance of short- and long-period cycles then gradually shifts as the frequency of oaks increases, so that both short- and long-period cycles are represented in the power spectrum at intermediate frequencies of oaks. Reprinted from Elderd et al. (2013). (A black and white version of this figure will appear in some formats.)

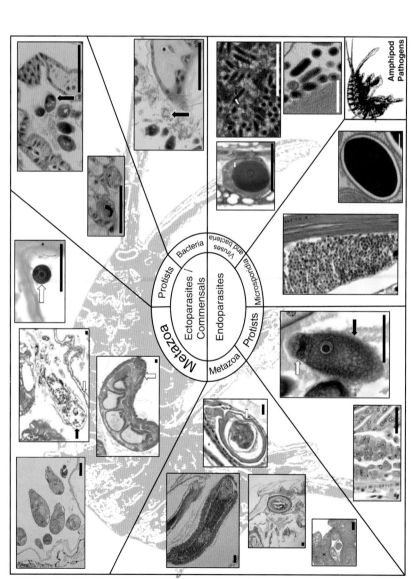

Figure 9.2 The diversity of parasites associated with amphipods. Histology images are in colour, and transmission electron micrographs are in black and white. Each section contains parasites that link with the circular labelling in the centre of the diagram. Arrows, if present, indicate the parasite. From left to right: ectoparasitic metazoa: oligochaete (from *Dikerogammarus villosus*); rotifer (from *Gammarus roeselii*); isopod (from *Gammarus roeselii*); bryozoan statoblast (from *D. villosus*). Ectoparasitic protists: ciliated gill-embedded protist (from *G. roeselii*); stalked ciliated protist (from *G. roeselii*). Ectoparasitic bacteria: filamentous bacteria (from *G. roeselii*). Endoparasitic viruses and bacteria: *Dikerogammarus villosus* bacilliform virus pathology (from *D. villosus*); DvBV (from *D. villosus*); *Aquarickettsiella gammari* (from *Gammarus fossarum*). Endoparasitic protists: microsporidian pathology (from *D. haemobaphes*); *Cucumispora ornata* (from *D. haemobaphes*). Endoparasitic protists: intracellular gregarine (from *D. villosus*); extracellular gregarine (from *D. villosus*). Endoparasitic metazoa: acanthocephalan (from *D. villosus*); nematode (from *D. villosus*); *Polymorphus* sp. (from *Gammarus pulex*); digenean trematode (from *D. villosus*). In all cases, the black scale bars for histology images equate to 20 μm. In all cases the white scale bars for transmission electron micrographs equate to 500 nm. Images from Bojko et al., 2013, 2015, 2017. (A black and white version of this figure will appear in some formats.)

Figure 9.3 Native/invasive amphipods and a subset of their parasites in Ireland, showing key trophic interactions (Hatcher et al., 2012b). N = native *Gammarus duebeni celticus*, I1 = invasive *Gammarus pulex*, I2 = invasive *Gammarus tigrinus*. *E. truttae* = *Echinorhynchus truttae*. Both the native *G. duebeni celticus* and the invasive *G. pulex* act as intermediate hosts for *E. truttae*; *Salmo trutta* and other fish act as the definitive host. *P. mulleri* = *Pleistophora mulleri*, which has a direct life cycle and is specific to the native amphipod *Gammarus duebeni celticus*. These parasites have been found to modify the trophic behaviour and interactions of their hosts, as discussed in Box 9.1. (A black and white version of this figure will appear in some formats.)

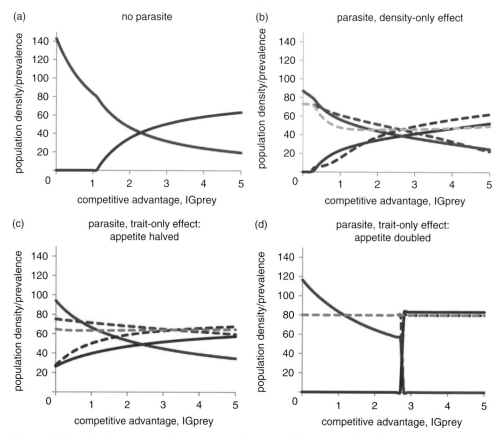

Figure B9.3.1 Trait-mediated effects of parasitism on IGP systems. Equilibrium population densities (solid lines) and parasite prevalence (dashed lines) in the more predatory species (intraguild predator; red) and the weaker predator (intraguild prey, blue) plotted against the relative competitive advantage of the intraguild prey: (a) in the absence of parasitism, a strong intraguild predator excludes competitively weak intraguild prey; (b) virulent parasites (inducing 10% and 30% mortality in the prey and predator, respectively) enable coexistence of predator and prey over a broader parameter range; (c) parasites with no mortality effect but which reduce predatory ability (appetite) strongly enhance coexistence, whereas (d) parasites that increase predation strongly reduce coexistence (Hatcher et al., 2014). (A black and white version of this figure will appear in some formats.)

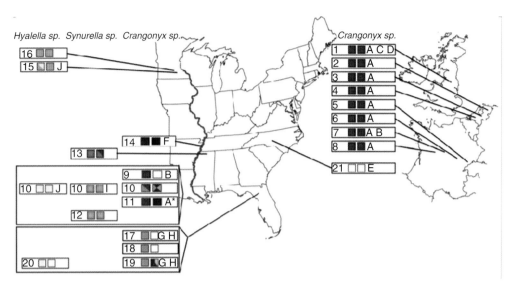

Figure B9.4.3 Distribution of *Crangonyx pseudogracilis* host genotypes and microsporidian parasites across North America (native range) and Europe (the invasive range). Boxes show sample sites (1–21); host genotype according to SSU rDNA sequence (left box) and COI mtDNA sequence (right box). Parasite species are coded A–J. Although a higher parasite diversity was found in the native range, comparison of parasite diversity conducted between invasive populations and native source populations (matched by host molecular sequence data) did not provide any evidence for a reduction in prevalence or diversity of microsporidia; two microsporidia were isolated from *C. pseudogracilis* in the source population and these were both detected in the invasive range. The feminiser *Fibrillanosema crangonycis* (parasite A) was found in all invasive populations (Slothouber Galbreath et al., 2010). (A black and white version of this figure will appear in some formats.)

Figure 10.1 Adult male red grouse (*Lagopus lagopus scoticus*) with pronounced red comb (a secondary sexual characteristic influenced by parasitism). Photo credit: Julian Renet. (A black and white version of this figure will appear in some formats.)

Figure 11.1 Images of (A,B) a healthy Tasmanian devil, and (C,D) of facial tumours. Photo credits: Menna Jones (A,C), Sarah Peck (B), Rodrigo Hamede (D). (A black and white version of this figure will appear in some formats.)

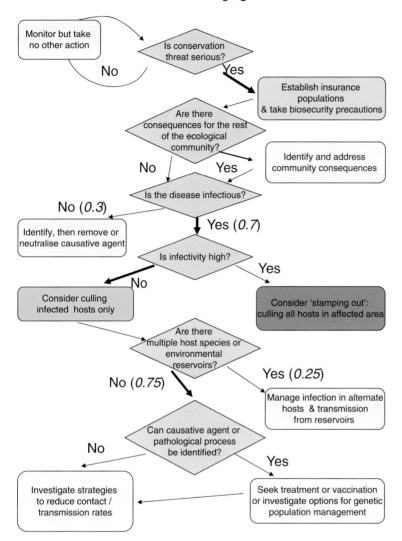

Figure 11.3 A decision tree for the management of emerging wildlife disease, with particular reference to Tasmanian devil facial tumour disease. The relative thickness of arrows indicates the current likelihood of the given path representing the true situation. Probabilities determined by consensus of expert opinion at a technical workshop on DFTD (AusVet, 2005) are shown on the arrows in italics. Colours represent the cost associated with the specified action, if it proves to be as a result of an incorrect decision: red = high, yellow/orange = medium, green = low. Reproduced from McCallum & Jones, *PLoS Biology*, 2006. (A black and white version of this figure will appear in some formats.)

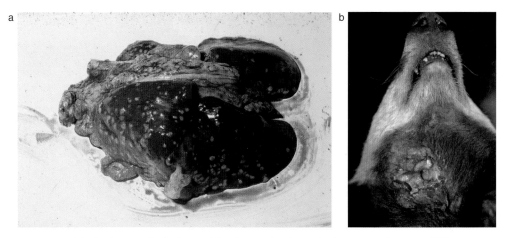

Figure 12.1 (a) The lungs of a badger with advanced tuberculosis, presenting as a diffuse distribution of lesions throughout the tissue. (b) Badger with an open suppurating submandibular abscess. *M. bovis* has been isolated from the lymph nodes and bite wounds of infected badgers. (A black and white version of this figure will appear in some formats.)

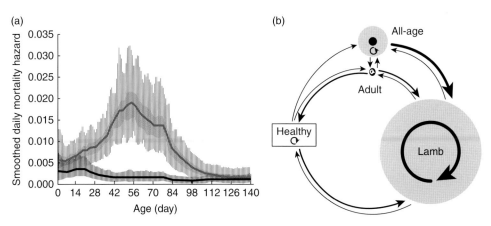

Figure 13.4 (a) 95% posterior credible intervals for daily lamb mortality hazards in diseased (grey) and healthy (black) years during summer in the Hells Canyon metapopulation. (b) Proposed state-transitions in disease status between healthy, all-age, adult-only, and lamb-only pneumonia in the Hells Canyon system. Point sizes reflect the frequency with which the system is in each state. From Cassirer et al. (2013). (A black and white version of this figure will appear in some formats.)

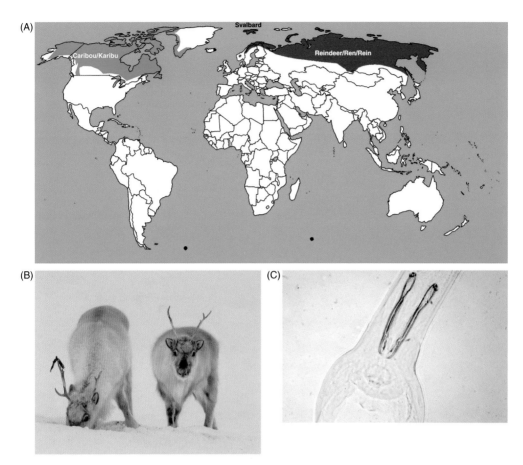

Figure 14.1 (A) The circumpolar distribution of *Rangifer tarandus*: reindeer (red shading) and caribou (green shading). Svalbard (76–81°N, 9–33°E) is shown at the centre top. Reindeer exist there with no predators or competitors. Black dots are introduced populations. © Wikipedia, TBjornstad. https://en.wikipedia.org/wiki/Reindeer#/media/File:Rangifer_tarandus_map.png (B) Adult and calf Svalbard reindeer, *Rangifer tarandus platyrhynchus*. (C) The nematode parasite *Ostertagia grühneri*. (A black and white version of this figure will appear in some formats.)

Figure 15.1 Oak powdery mildew symptoms. Clockwise from upper left corner: (1) first symptoms visible in spring, the flag shoots, corresponding to heavily infected shoots (= covered in mycelium and spores giving a white, cottony appearance) developing from buds infected in the previous season; (2) primary infections (white spots) corresponding to ascospore-derived colonies; (3) severe infection on oak seedlings; (4) infection on leaves of the first flush in a mature oak tree; (5) infection of the second flush is generally much more severe than that of the first flush; (6) severe infection leads to necrosis, distortion, early senescence of leaves and, finally, defoliation. (A black and white version of this figure will appear in some formats.)

Figure 15.4 Oak powdery mildew life cycle. Powdery mildews are obligate biotrophic parasites, i.e. they cannot live without their host and they derive their energy from living cells. Most of the fungal development is epiphyllous, the only structures within plant tissues being the intracellular haustoria which absorb nutrients from the host. Left, complete life cycle with sexual reproduction: in autumn (lower left), sexual fruiting bodies (chasmothecia) are formed on infected leaves; during winter, the chasmothecia remain dormant; in spring, the ascospores within the chasmothecia are released and airborne; primary infections result from the germination of ascospores on young susceptible leaves which produce colonies of epiphyllous mycelia bearing conidia (asexual spores); during the growing season (spring–summer), several cycles of secondary infections are produced by conidia. Right, alternative cycle without sexual reproduction: mycelium and conidia overwinter in dormant buds (under bud scales), infected buds produce 'flag shoots' and conidia produce secondary infections. (A black and white version of this figure will appear in some formats.)

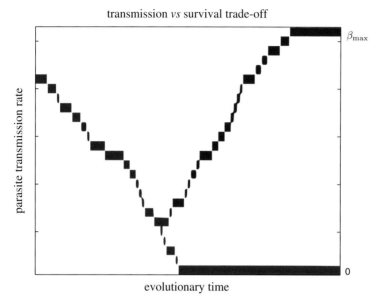

Figure B15.1.3 Evolutionary dynamics associated with model (1–2) assuming a trade-off between within-season and between-season transmission (adapted from figure 2 in Hamelin et al., 2011). There is initially one ancestral parasite type. The mutation-selection process first selects for decreasing within-season transmission (thus increasing between-season survival), and subsequently splits the parasite population into two types, one specialising in within-season transmission, and the other in between-season transmission. The ecological dynamics and the parameter values corresponding to this dimorphic evolutionary endpoint are shown in Figure B15.1.4. (A black and white version of this figure will appear in some formats.)

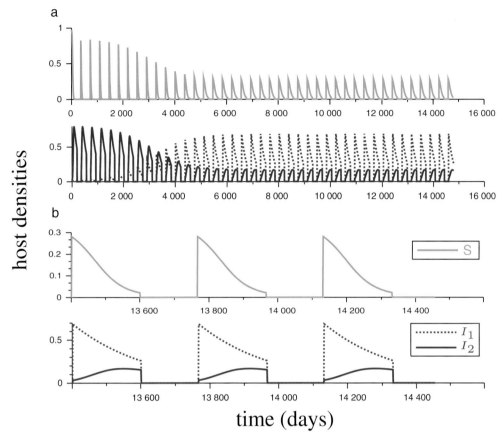

Figure B15.1.4 Long-term coexistence of two parasite species subject to periodic absence of the host plant (adapted from figure 1 in Hamelin et al., 2016). (a) Infected plant densities I_1 and I_2 as a function of time, for $k = 40$ cycles (years). (b) Zoom on the last three cycles. Parameter values: $\alpha_1 = \alpha_2 = 0.005$, $\beta_1 = 0.1$, $\beta_2 = 0.001$, $\chi_1 = 0.369$, $\chi_2 = 4.68$, $T = 365$, $\tau = 200$, and $S_0 = 1$ (without loss of generality). (A black and white version of this figure will appear in some formats.)

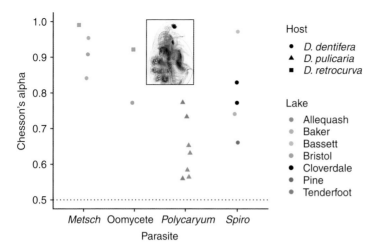

Figure 16.3 Selectivity of bluegill sunfish on *Daphnia* infected with the fungus *Metschnikowia bicuspidata*, an unnamed oomycete, the chytrid *Polycaryum laeve*, and the bacterium *Spirobacillus cienkowskii*. Data were collected by analysing the gut contents of fish collected in lakes at dawn, compared with the infection prevalence in hosts in the lake at the same time. In each case, the comparison was between infected or uninfected hosts. We used Chesson's alpha, which compares the availability of a prey type (in this case, a host infected with a particular parasite) and the selection of that prey type. Neutral selectivity is indicated by 0.5 (shown by a dotted line); the strength of selectivity for a prey type increases as alpha increases towards 1. Data on *D. dentifera* and *D. retrocurva* are from Duffy and Hall (2008) and unpublished data collected by M.A. Duffy in 2002–2003. Data on *D. pulicaria* are from Johnson et al. (2006). Points are jittered slightly along the *x*-axis. Inset figure shows the transparent body of an uninfected *D. dentifera*. (A black and white version of this figure will appear in some formats.)

Figure B18.1.1 *Rana muscosa* and *Rana sierrae* live in high-elevation lakes and streams in the Sierra Nevada mountains in California, USA. (A black and white version of this figure will appear in some formats.)

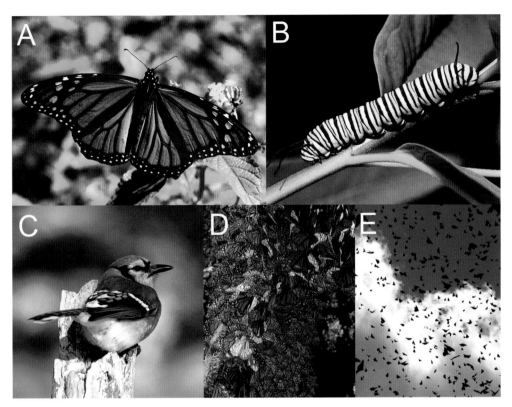

Figure 17.1 Warning colouration and long-distance migration. Monarch butterflies (*Danaus plexippus*) are well known for their bright warning colouration in both adults (A) and larvae (B). This warning colouration serves to advertise their toxicity, derived from the sequestration of milkweed chemicals called cardenolides, which make monarchs unpalatable to vertebrate predators such as blue jays (C). Monarchs are also famous for their annual autumn migration from the eastern USA and southern Canada to the oyamel fir forests in Central Mexico, where monarchs overwinter in clusters from November to March (D). When the sun breaks through, monarchs often take to the sky in the thousands (E). Photos A, B, D and E by Jaap de Roode. Photo D: Wikimedia, US Fish and Wildlife Service. (A black and white version of this figure will appear in some formats.)

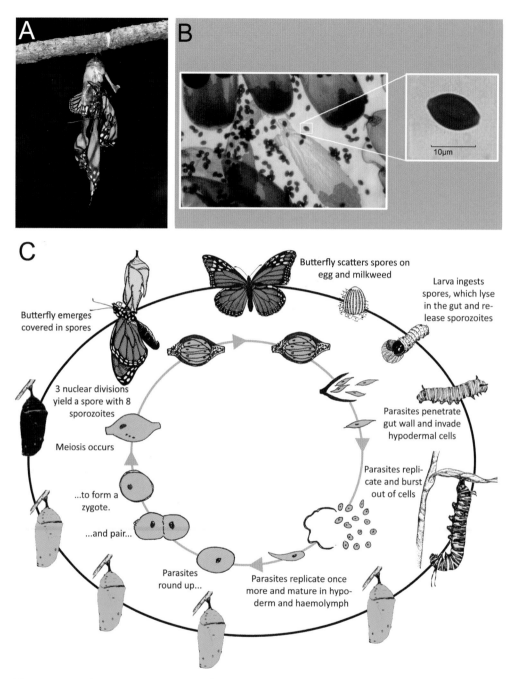

Figure 17.2 *Ophryocystis elektroscirrha* life cycle. Monarchs are commonly infected with the protozoan parasite *Ophryocystis elektroscirrha*. At high infection levels, this parasite can prevent monarchs from successfully emerging from their pupal cases (A). *O. elektroscirrha* forms hardy and dormant oocyst spores that are concentrated around the scales on the monarch's abdomen (B). Parasite infection starts with the ingestion of a spore by a larva, after which the spore releases sporozoites in the larva's midgut. The sporozoites enter the larva's tissues, after which they undergo asexual and sexual replication to form a new generation of oocyst spores in the developing integuments of the butterfly (C). Photo A by Jaap de Roode, B by Andy Davis. (A black and white version of this figure will appear in some formats.)

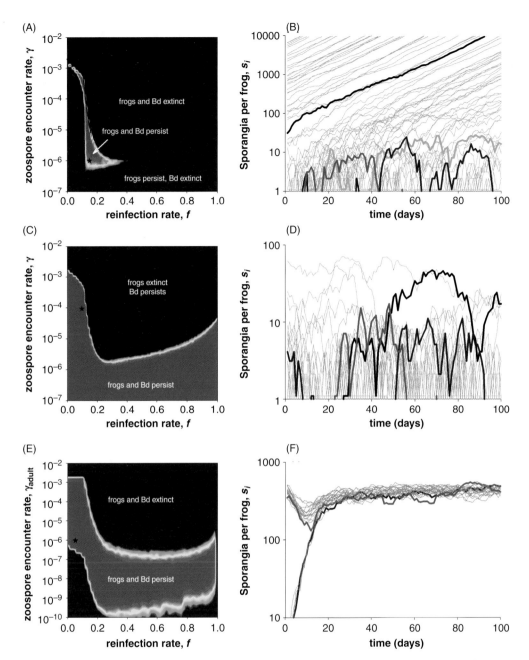

Figure B18.3.2 Results from the Briggs et al. (2010) model with: (A,B) an unstructured host population in which all individuals are equally susceptible to the pathogen, (C,D) an unstructured host population with the addition of an external source of zoospores, and (E,F) a structured host population with a long-lived tadpole stage. (A,C,E) show the probability of frogs and Bd persisting for at least 10 years as a function of reinfection rate, f, and zoospore encounter rate, $\gamma\gamma$. Shown are the fractions of 100 runs for each combination of parameters that persist for at least 10 years (colour spectrum red = 100% of runs persist, blue = 0% of runs persist). All runs are initialised with a single infected frog in an otherwise uninfected frog population at its carrying capacity, and no zoospores in the zoospore pool ($Z = 0$). (B,D,F) show examples of the within-season dynamics illustrating the dynamics of the number of sporangia on individual frogs. Coloured lines are highlighted examples of trajectories of sporangia on individual frogs. Figure reprinted from Briggs et al. (2010) (the parameter values used are given in figure 3 of that paper). (A black and white version of this figure will appear in some formats.)

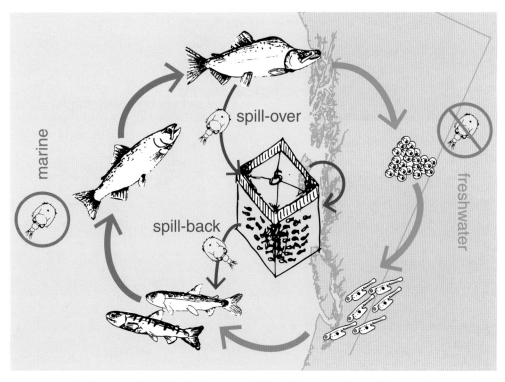

Figure 19.1 Spill-over and spill-back between wild and farmed salmon disrupts the natural separation of adults and juveniles, termed migratory allopatry, which normally minimises transmission of parasites such as sea lice to vulnerable juveniles. (A black and white version of this figure will appear in some formats.)

Figure 20.1 Male house finch exhibiting signs of conjunctivitis. (Photo reproduced with permission from Gary Mueller.) (A black and white version of this figure will appear in some formats.)

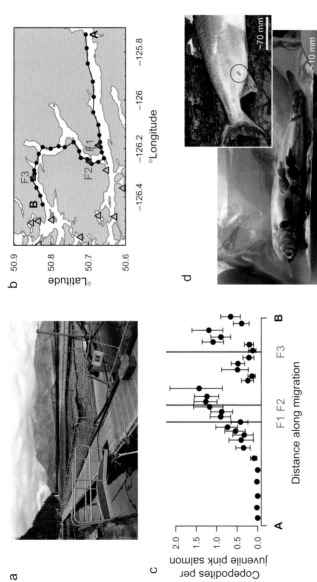

Figure 19.2 (a) An open-net salmon farm on the coast of British Columbia, Canada. (b) The migration route of juvenile salmon (black line; A to B) in the Broughton Archipelago, British Columbia, passes by several salmon farms (filled triangles). Black points are locations where juvenile pink salmon were captured and assessed for sea louse parasites (Krkošek et al., 2006). (c) The mean number of copepodid sea lice (±95% bootstrapped confidence intervals) per juvenile pink salmon sampled at black points in (b) from 18 to 28 April 2004 (Krkošek et al., 2006). (d) An infestation of motile sea lice on a juvenile pink salmon can have dramatic effects due to the large size of parasites relative to their host, while infections of adult salmon (inset) are much less pathogenic because hosts are larger and have developed protective scales. Photos: S Peacock, inset: C Miller. (A black and white version of this figure will appear in some formats.)

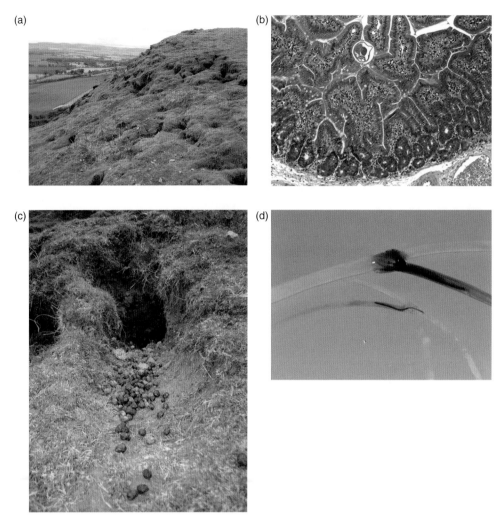

Figure 21.2 The helminth–rabbit system: the semi-natural agro-ecosystem study area (a); adults of *G. strigosum* in the stomach (b); warren entrance and rabbit faeces (c); *G. strigosum* male and female mating (d). (A black and white version of this figure will appear in some formats.)

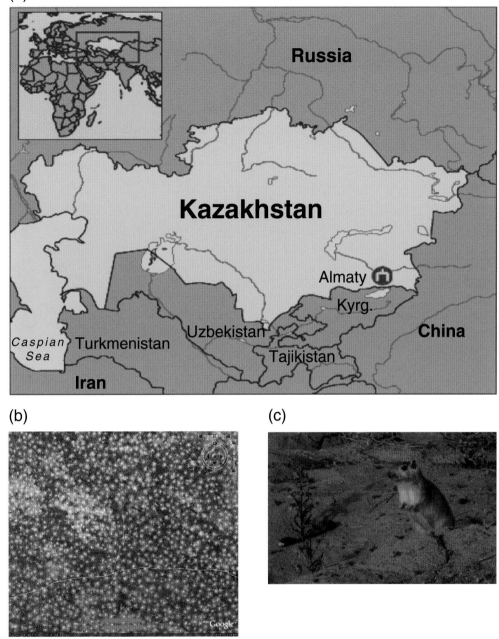

Figure 22.1 (a) The Pre-Balkhash region in Kazakhstan is located to the north-west of the city of Almaty and south of the crescent-shaped Lake Balkhash. It is part of a plague focus where the main reservoir host is the great gerbil, *Rhombomys opimus*. (b) The regular pattern created by great gerbil burrow systems, visible on satellite images. Patches of bare earth above and around the burrow systems strongly reflect the sunlight. Each bright disc represents a burrow system 10–40 m in diameter. The image (approximately 2000 m × 2000 m) was captured using the publicly available software Google Earth (http://earth.google.com/). Copyright 2008 DigitalGlobe; Europa Technologies. (After Davis et al., 2008.) (c) A great gerbil at a burrow. (A black and white version of this figure will appear in some formats.)

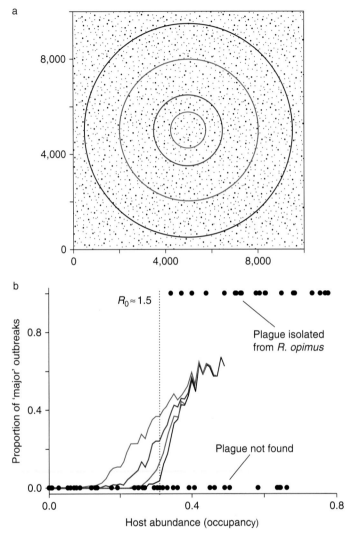

Figure 22.5 The results of a percolation model for plague epizootics in great gerbils. The landscape (a) is a 10 km × 10 km area, and the results (b) are expressed as the fraction of outbreaks that give rise to new infections at least 750 m, 1.5 km, 3 km, and 4.5 km from the site of initial infection, shown as solid lines coloured red, blue, green, and black, respectively, and corresponding to the spread of plague beyond the circles of the same colour in (a). (After Davis et al., 2008.) (A black and white version of this figure will appear in some formats.)

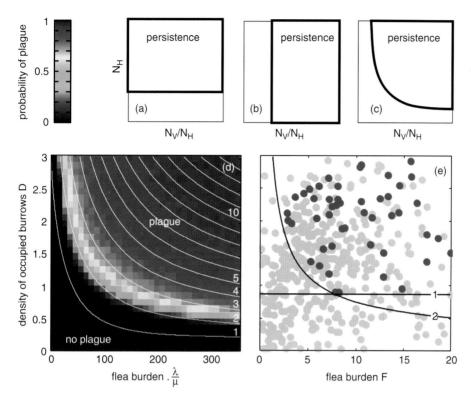

Figure 22.6 Representations of (a) a host density threshold, (b) a vector-to-host ratio threshold, and (c) a hyperbolic vector/host threshold. The vertical axis plots host abundance; the horizontal axis the ratio of vector to host abundance. (d) Simulations of a spatially explicit percolation model for plague epizootics: the fraction of simulated outbreaks that give rise to new infections at least 2 km from the site of the initial infection plotted as a function of the occupied burrow density D and the flea burden F. (e) Field data on plague presence (red dots) or absence (grey dots) as a function of F and D. Different fitting models result in different threshold shapes (curves 1 and 2 refer to models (a) and (c), respectively). (After Reijniers et al., 2012.) (A black and white version of this figure will appear in some formats.)

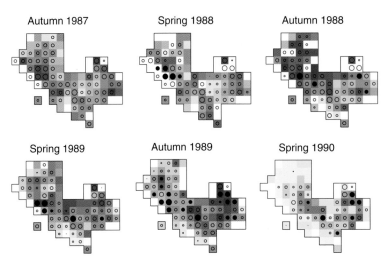

Figure 22.7 An example of a plague epizootic in the Pre-Balkhash area. Open circles, no great gerbils found positive for plague; filled circles, at least one great gerbil found positive. Circle size indicates the number of individuals tested. Light to dark shading indicates low to high great gerbil abundance. (After Heier et al., 2011.) (A black and white version of this figure will appear in some formats.)

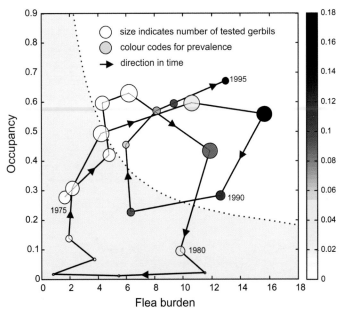

Figure 22.8 Vector–host–pathogen dynamics in the Pre-Balkhash region. Plague prevalence is plotted yearly from 1975 to 1995 in the occupancy–flea burden phase plane. The colours code the proportion of sectors that tested positive, and the size of dots is proportional to the number of gerbils tested in that year (for reference: 30,673 gerbils in 1978). Prevalence in 1981 was 0.03; in 1982 and 1983 it was zero. The dotted line corresponds to the threshold curve, derived by Reijniers et al. (2012). (After Reijniers et al., 2014.) (A black and white version of this figure will appear in some formats.)

carotenoid-based signalling of health. *Functional Ecology*, **21**, 886–898.

Mougeot, F., Piertney, S.B.B., Leckie, F., et al. (2005c) Experimentally increased aggressiveness reduces population kin structure and subsequent recruitment in red grouse *Lagopus lagopus scoticus*. *Journal of Animal Ecology*, **74**, 488–497.

Mougeot, F. & Redpath, S.M. (2004) Sexual ornamentation relates to immune function in male red grouse *Lagopus lagopus scoticus*. *Journal of Avian Biology*, **35**, 425–433.

Mougeot, F., Redpath, S.M., Leckie, F. & Hudson, P. J. (2003a) The effect of aggressiveness on the population dynamics of a territorial bird. *Nature*, **421**, 737–739.

Mougeot, F., Redpath, S.M., Moss, R., et al. (2003b) Territorial behaviour and population dynamics in red grouse *Lagopus lagopus scoticus*. I. Population experiments. *Journal of Animal Ecology*, **72**, 1073–1082.

Mougeot, F., Redpath, S.M. & Piertney, S.B. (2006) Elevated spring testosterone increases parasite intensity in male red grouse. *Behavioral Ecology*, **17**, 117–125.

Mougeot, F., Redpath, S.M., Piertney, S.B. & Hudson, P.J. (2005d) Separating behavioral and physiological mechanisms in testosterone-mediated trade-offs. *The American Naturalist*, **166**, 158–168.

Mougeot, F.L., Ádám, Z., Martínez-Padilla, J., et al. (2016) Parasites, mate attractiveness and female feather corticosterone levels in a socially monogamous bird. *Behavioral Ecology and Sociobiology*, **70**, 277–283.

Newborn, D. & Foster, R. (2002) Control of parasite burdens in wild red grouse *Lagopus lagopus scoticus* through the indirect application of anthelmintics. *Journal of Applied Ecology*, **39**, 909–914.

Owen-Ashley, N.T., Hasselquist, D. & Wingfield, J.C. (2004) Androgens and the immunocompetence handicap hypothesis: Unraveling direct and indirect pathways of immunosuppression in song sparrows. *The American Naturalist*, **164**, 490–505.

Paterson, S. & Piertney, S.B. (2011) Frontiers in host–parasite ecology and evolution. *Molecular Ecology*, **20**, 869–871.

Pérez-Rodríguez, L. (2009) Carotenoids in evolutionary ecology: re-evaluating the antioxidant role. *BioEssays*, **31**, 1116–1126.

Pérez-Rodríguez, L., de Blas, E.G., Martínez-Padilla, J., Mougeot, F. & Mateo, R. (2016) Carotenoid profile and vitamins in the combs of the red grouse (*Lagopus lagopus scoticus*): implications for the honesty of a sexual signal. *Journal of Ornithology*, **157**, 145–153.

Piertney, S.B.B., Lambin, X., MacColl, A.D.C., et al. (2008) Temporal changes in kin structure through a population cycle in a territorial bird, the red grouse *Lagopus lagopus scoticus*. *Molecular Ecology*, **17**, 2544–2551.

Poiani, A., Goldsmith, A.R. & Evans, M.R. (2000) Ectoparasites of house sparrows (*Passer domesticus*): an experimental test of the immunocompetence handicap hypothesis and a new model. *Behavioral Ecology and Sociobiology*, **47**, 230–242.

Potts, G.R., Tapper, S.C. & Hudson, P.J. (1984) Population fluctuations in Red grouse – analysis of bag records and a simulation-model. *Journal of Animal Ecology*, **53**, 21–36.

Poulin, R. & Thomas, F. (2008) Epigenetic effects of infection on the phenotype of host offspring: parasites reaching across host generations. *Oikos*, **117**, 331–335.

Prudic, K.L., Jeon, C., Cao, H. & Monteiro, A. (2011) Developmental plasticity in sexual roles of butterfly species drives mutual sexual ornamentation. *Science*, **331**, 73–75.

Quigley, B.J.Z., García López, D., Buckling, A., McKane, A.J. & Brown, S.P. (2012) The mode of host–parasite interaction shapes coevolutionary dynamics and the fate of host cooperation. *Proceedings of the Royal Society of London B*, **279**, 3742.

Redpath, S.M., Mougeot, F., Leckie, F. & Evans, A. D. (2006a) The effects of autumn testosterone on survival and productivity in red grouse *Lagopus lagopus scoticus*. *Animal Behaviour*, **71**, 1297–1305.

Redpath, S.M., Mougeot, F., Leckie, F.M., Elston, D.A. & Hudson, P.J. (2006b) Testing the role of parasites in driving the cyclic population dynamics of a gamebird. *Ecology Letters*, **9**, 410–418.

Richardson, W.S., Spivak, H., Hudson, J.E., Budacz, M.A. & Hunter, J.G. (1997) Teflon buttress inhibits recanalization of the 'uncut' Roux limb. *Gastroenterology*, **112**, A1468–A1468.

Roberts, M.L., Buchanan, K.L. & Evans, M.R. (2004) Testing the immunocompetence handicap hypothesis: a review of the evidence. *Animal Behaviour*, **68**, 227–239.

Romero, F.J., Bosch-Morell, F., Romero, M.J., et al. (1998) Lipid peroxidation products and antioxidants in human disease. *Environmental Health Perspectives*, **106**, 1229–1234.

Romero, L.M. (2004) Physiological stress in ecology: lessons from biomedical research. *Trends in Ecology & Evolution*, **19**, 249–255.

Saino, N., Møller, A.P. & Bolzern, A.M. (1995) Testosterone effects on the immune system and parasite infestations in the barn swallow (*Hirundo rustica*): an experimental test of the immunocompetence hypothesis. *Behavioral Ecology*, **6**, 397–404.

Schmid-Hempel, P. (2011) *Evolutionary Parasitology: The Integrated Study of Infections, Immunology, Ecology, and Genetics*. Oxford: Oxford University Press.

Schmid-Hempel, P.E. & Ebert, D. (2003) On the evolutionary ecology of specific immune defence. *Trends in Ecology & Evolution*, **18**, 27–32.

Seivwright, L., Redpath, S.M., Mougeot, F., Watts, L. & Hudson, P.J. (2004) Faecal egg counts provide a reliable measure of *Trichostrongylus tenuis* intensities in free-living red grouse *Lagopus lagopus scoticus*. *Journal of Helminthology*, **78**, 69–76.

Seivwright, L.J., Redpath, S.M., Mougeot, F., Leckie, F. & Hudson, P.J. (2005) Interactions between intrinsic and extrinsic mechanisms in a cyclic species: testosterone increases parasite infection in red grouse. *Proceedings of the Royal Society of London B*, **272**, 2299–2304.

Shaw, J.L. (1988) Arrested development of *Trichostrongylus tenuis* as 3rd stage larvae in red grouse. *Research in Veterinary Science*, **45**, 256–258.

Shaw, J.L. & Moss, R. (1989) The role of parasite fecundity and longevity in the success of *Trichostrongylus tenuis* in low-density red grouse populations. *Parasitology*, **99**, 253–258.

Shaw, J.L., Moss, R. & Pike, A.W. (1989) Development and survival of the free-living stages of *Trichostrongylus tenuis*, a cecal parasite of red grouse *Lagopus lagopus scoticus*. *Parasitology*, **99**, 105–113.

Sheldon, B.C. & Verhulst, S. (1996) Ecological immunology: costly parasite defences and trade-offs in evolutionary ecology. *Trends in Ecology & Evolution*, **11**, 317–321.

Splettstoesser, W.D. & Schuff-Werner, P. (2002) Oxidative stress in phagocytes – 'the enemy within'. *Microscopy Research and Technique*, **57**, 441–455.

Stear, M.J., Fitton, L., Innocent, G.T., et al. (2007) The dynamic influence of genetic variation on the susceptibility of sheep to gastrointestinal nematode infection. *Journal of the Royal Society Interface*, **4**, 767.

Tarjuelo, R., Vergara, P. & Martínez-Padilla, J. (2016) Intra-sexual competition modulates calling behavior and its association with secondary sexual traits. *Behavioral Ecology and Sociobiology*, **70**, 1633–1641.

Thirgood, S.J., Redpath, S.M., Haydon, D.T., et al. (2000) Habitat loss and raptor predation: disentangling long- and short-term causes of red grouse declines. *Proceedings of the Royal Society of London B*, **267**, 651–656.

Thrall, P.H., Antonovics, J. & Bever, J.D. (1997) Sexual transmission of disease and host mating systems: within-season reproductive success. *The American Naturalist*, **149**, 485–506.

Turchin, P. (2003) *Complex Population Dynamics: A Theoretical/Empirical Synthesis*. Princeton, NJ: Princeton University Press.

Vergara, P. & Martínez-Padilla, J. (2012) Social context decouples the relationship between a sexual ornament and testosterone levels in a male wild bird. *Hormones and Behavior*, **62**, 407–412.

Vergara, P., Martínez-Padilla, J., Mougeot, F., Leckie, F. & Redpath, S.M. (2012a) Environmental heterogeneity influences the reliability of secondary sexual traits as condition indicators. *Journal of Evolutionary Biology*, **25**, 20–28.

Vergara, P., Martínez-Padilla, J., Redpath, S.M. & Mougeot, F. (2011) The ornament–condition relationship varies with parasite abundance at population level in a female bird. *Naturwissenschaften*, **98**, 897–902.

Vergara, P., Mougeot, F., Martínez-Padilla, J., Leckie, F. & Redpath, S.M. (2012b) The condition dependence of a secondary sexual trait is stronger under high parasite infection level. *Behavioral Ecology*, **23**, 502–511.

Vergara, P., Redpath, S.M., Martínez-Padilla, J. & Mougeot, F. (2012c) Environmental conditions influence red grouse ornamentation at a population level. *Biological Journal of the Linnean Society*, **107**, 788–798.

von Schantz, T., Bensch, S., Grahn, M., Hasselquist, D. & Wittzell, H. (1999) Good genes, oxidative stress and condition-dependent sexual signals. *Proceedings of the Royal Society of London B*, **266**, 1–12.

Watson, A. (1985) Social class, socially-induced loss, recruitment and breeding of red grouse. *Oecologia*, **67**, 493–498.

Watson, A. & Moss, R. (1988) Spacing behaviour and population limitation in red grouse. *The Auk*, **105**, 207–208.

Watson, A. & Moss, R. (2008) *Grouse*. London: Collins.

Watson, A., Moss, R. & Rae, S. (1998) Population dynamics of Scottish rock ptarmigan cycles. *Ecology*, **79**, 1174–1192.

Watson, M.J. (2013) What drives population-level effects of parasites? Meta-analysis meets life-history. *International Journal for Parasitology: Parasites and Wildlife*, **2**, 190–196.

Webster, L.M.I., Mello, L.V., Mougeot, F., et al. (2011) Identification of genes responding to nematode infection in red grouse. *Molecular Ecology Resources*, **11**, 305–313.

Webster, L.M.I.P., Paterson, S., Mougeot, F., Martínez-Padilla, J. & Piertney, S.B.B. (2011) Transcriptomic response of red grouse to gastro-intestinal nematode parasites and testosterone: implications for population dynamics. *Molecular Ecology*, **20**, 920–931.

Wenzel, M.A., Douglas, A., James, M.C., Redpath, S.M. & Piertney, S.B.B. (2016) The role of parasite-driven selection in shaping landscape genomic structure in red grouse (*Lagopus lagopus scotica*). *Molecular Ecology*, **25**, 324–341.

Wenzel, M.A., James, M.C., Douglas, A. & Piertney, S.B. (2015a) Genome-wide association and genome partitioning reveal novel genomic regions underlying variation in gastrointestinal nematode burden in a wild bird. *Molecular Ecology*, **24**, 4175–4192.

Wenzel, M.A. & Piertney, S.B. (2014) Fine-scale population epigenetic structure in relation to gastro-intestinal parasite load in red grouse (*Lagopus lagopus scotica*). *Molecular Ecology*, **23**, 4256–4273.

Wenzel, M.A. & Piertney, S.B.B. (2015) Digging for gold nuggets: uncovering novel candidate genes for variation in gastrointestinal nematode burden in a wild bird species. *Journal of Evolutionary Biology*, **28**, 807–825.

Wenzel, M.A., Webster, L.M.I., Paterson, S., et al. (2013) A transcriptomic investigation of handicap models in sexual selection. *Behavioral Ecology and Sociobiology*, **67**, 221–234.

Wenzel, M.A., Webster, L.M.I., Paterson, S. & Piertney, S.B. (2015b) Identification and characterisation of 17 polymorphic candidate genes for response to parasitic nematode (*Trichostrongylus tenuis*) infection in red grouse (*Lagopus lagopus scotica*). *Conservation Genetics Resources*, **7**, 23–28.

Wilfert, L. & Schmid-Hempel, P. (2008) The genetic architecture of susceptibility to parasites. *BMC Evolutionary Biology*, **8**, 187.

Wilson, G.R. & Wilson, L.P. (1978) Haematology weight and condition of red grouse (*Lagopus lagopus scoticus*) infected with caecal threadworms (*Trichostrongylus tenuis*). *Research in Veterinary Science*, **25**, 331–336.

Wongrak, K., Daş, G., von Borstel, U.K. & Gauly, M. (2015) Genetic variation for worm burdens in laying hens naturally infected with gastro-intestinal nematodes. *British Poultry Science*, **56**, 15–21.

Zahavi, A. (1975) Mate selection – a selection for a handicap. *Journal of Theoretical Biology*, **53**, 205–214.

Zuk, M. & Stochr, A. (2002) Immune defense and host life history. *The American Naturalist*, **160**, S9–S22.

CHAPTER ELEVEN

Emergence, transmission and evolution of an uncommon enemy: Tasmanian devil facial tumour disease

MENNA E. JONES, RODRIGO HAMEDE,
ANDREW STORFER, PAUL HOHENLOHE,
ELIZABETH P. MURCHISON AND HAMISH
MCCALLUM

11.1 Introduction

Twenty years ago, the Tasmanian devil (*Sarcophilus harrisii*) was a common species. The largest extant marsupial predator (Jones, 2003), Tasmanian devils achieved notoriety locally as an 'odious scavenger' and internationally as a comical and belligerent cartoon character. In 1996, a wildlife photographer took images of a Tasmanian devil in north-east Tasmania with large tumours on its head (Hawkins et al., 2006; Figure 11.1). By 2009, the species was listed as Endangered (Hawkins et al., 2009). By 2017 the tumour disease had spread to most of the Tasmanian devil's geographic range in the island state of Tasmania (www.tassiedevil.com.au/tasdevil.nsf) (Figure 11.2), causing >90% local population decline (Lachish et al., 2007; Lazenby et al., 2018). Concern has been raised for both the extinction of the Tasmanian devil and also further extinctions that might arise as the loss of this apex predator triggers trophic cascades through Tasmanian food webs (McCallum & Jones, 2006; Jones et al., 2007; Hollings et al., 2016). As the apex predator in Tasmania (following the extinction of the larger thylacine, *Thylacinus cynocephalus*), the Tasmanian devil likely plays a useful ecological role in suppressing feral cats and thereby protecting the biodiversity of smaller vertebrate prey species (Hollings et al., 2016).

This chapter reviews Tasmanian devil facial tumour disease (DFTD), now a classic case study, to show how theory and data can be combined to manage an emerging and evolving conservation threat from a novel and unusual disease. Emerging infectious diseases (EIDs) are an increasing global threat for biodiversity, and host naivety to these novel pathogens often leads to high susceptibility and severe population impacts (Daszak et al., 2000; Tompkins et al., 2015). For most EIDs, we have poor knowledge of the ecology of the pathogen and are unable to assess the extent of conservation threat (McCallum & Jones, 2006). We describe the emergence, unfolding epidemic, and now the

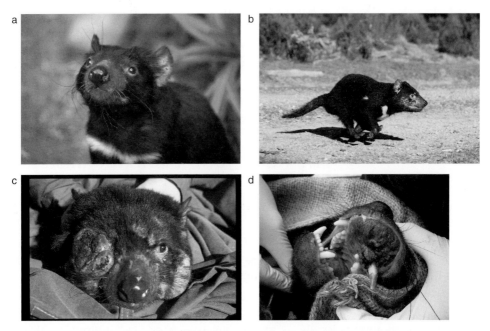

Figure 11.1 Images of (A,B) a healthy Tasmanian devil, and (C,D) of facial tumours. Photo credits: Menna Jones (A,C), Sarah Peck (B), Rodrigo Hamede (D). (A black and white version of this figure will appear in some formats. For the colour version, please refer to the plate section.)

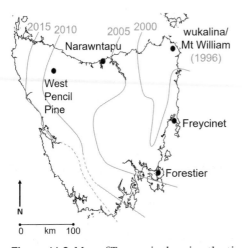

Figure 11.2 Map of Tasmania showing the timing of the spatial spread of DFTD and key research sites.

rapid evolutionary response to a transmissible cancer, a rare and different type of natural enemy (*sensu* Lafferty & Kuris, 2002) in which the infectious agent is a live cancer cell (Box 11.1). Our first step was to develop a decision tree to guide research and management of this novel transmissible cancer (McCallum &

Jones, 2006). We then quantified transmission in wild populations to identify control options and predict the epidemic outcome. Our current focus is quantifying rapid evolution in host and pathogen to understand how adaptation in the devil and potentially host–pathogen coevolution might influence transmission and epidemic outcome, and to understand how management actions can facilitate beneficial rather than detrimental adaptation. The Tasmanian devil–DFTD host–pathogen system provides a rare opportunity to study a wildlife disease in all stages of existence across the entire geographic range of a natural host species (from pre-emergence to emergence, to post-emergence decline, and potentially even endemism and host recovery).

11.2 Prioritising conservation actions and research for an emerging disease

By the time it was established that DFTD posed a conservation threat, it was too late to stamp out the disease through a culling approach. Sporadic detections of DFTD between 1996 and 2001 (Hawkins et al., 2006), and reaction-diffusion modelling (Beeton, 2011), suggest that the index case occurred somewhere in the north-east of Tasmania, probably in the early 1990s as there are no prior records of a similar disease (Pyecroft et al., 2007). In 2001–2002, the disease entered and spread 10 km along the Freycinet Peninsula, a long-term study site on the East Coast of Tasmania (Figure 11.2), causing significant localised population decline. This triggered a snap-shot trapping survey in 2003 which revealed unexpectedly low numbers of devils across the north-eastern quarter of Tasmania (Mooney, 2004).

The first detection of the disease was in 1996 at wukalina/Mt William National Park in the far north-east of Tasmania (Figure 11.2). DFTD has spread steadily westwards and southwards, currently covering most of the island-wide distribution of the devil and predicted to reach the north-west coast within a few years. A long-term study commenced on the Freycinet Peninsula in 1999, two years prior to local disease outbreak in 2001. The Forestier Peninsula was the site of a culling trial, commencing with disease outbreak in 2004. A second long-term study site was established at West Pencil Pine in 2006. Research and genetic samples collection was established in 1999 at Narawntapu.

How should you proceed when an emerging disease presents a serious conservation threat but you have little information? DFTD was used as a case study to develop a decision tree to address this wider issue of prioritising management and research for emerging diseases (Figure 11.3; McCallum & Jones, 2006). Needing to take action in the face of uncertainty is common to many ecological problems (Burgman, 2005). Delaying action until better information is available can result in greater costs and even foreclosure on the option of control, particularly when dealing with emerging diseases (Sakai et al., 2001).

Box 11.1: The nature of transmissible cancers and Tasmanian devil facial tumour disease

There are just eight known cases of transmissible cancers in nature: in dogs, in several species of marine bivalve molluscs (Metzger et al., 2015, 2016), and two in Tasmanian devils. The canine transmissible venereal tumour (CTVT) evolved ~11,000 years ago and is an evolutionarily stable cell line (Murgia et al., 2006; Murchison, 2008). Tasmanian devil facial tumour disease emerged about 20 years ago (discovered in 1996; Hawkins et al., 2006) and a second transmissible cancer (DFT2) emerged as a distinct evolutionary event more recently (Pye et al., 2016b).

Transmissible cancers are an uncommon type of natural enemy (*sensu* Lafferty & Kuris, 2002). They have some of the characteristics of a macroparasite (they grow as a macro-organism deriving nutrients from their host), but have a reproductive rate (defined by rates of cancer cell division) more typical of a microparasite. Cancers usually arise and die with their host. This is the case even for cancers associated with infectious agents: in such cancers the infectious agent such as a virus increases the probability that a host cell becomes cancerous; thus, although the virus might survive and transmit beyond its host the cancer itself will not (McCallum & Jones, 2012). In transmissible cancers, live tumour cells are the infectious agents. Transmissible cancers have taken the unusual evolutionary step to metastasise outside their host to become immortal cell lines. As tumour cells are 'rogue' host somatic cells, they do not live long outside the body of the animal. The evolution and transmission of transmissible cancers thus requires intimate and injurious contact between live tumour cells on the infected host and a break in the epidermis or mucosa of the susceptible host.

A second condition for their emergence is a mechanism for host immune system evasion. Both CTVT and DFTD downregulate expression of the Major Histocompatibility Complex (MHC) molecules which enable immune recognition of cancer cells (Siddle et al., 2013). The intimate injurious contact required for transmission of DFTD is most common in the mating season (Hamede et al., 2008), and CTVT is a venereal cancer with lesions on the genitals (Murchison, 2008). Both of these cancers would have strongly frequency-dependent transmission, as mating occurs irrespective of population density, bringing infected and susceptible individuals together.

The aetiology of the disease was not initially known. However, aetiological agent identification is not essential for more urgent conservation actions; it thus occurs relatively late in the decision tree (Figure 11.3). Indeed, transmissibility of the devil cancer was not confirmed until five years after disease

Decision tree for an emerging wildlife disease

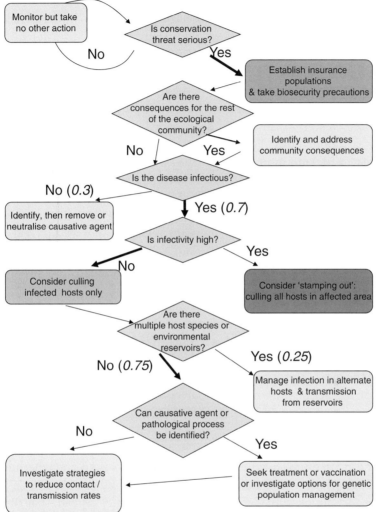

Figure 11.3 A decision tree for the management of emerging wildlife disease, with particular reference to Tasmanian devil facial tumour disease. The relative thickness of arrows indicates the current likelihood of the given path representing the true situation. Probabilities determined by consensus of expert opinion at a technical workshop on DFTD (AusVet, 2005) are shown on the arrows in italics. Colours represent the cost associated with the specified action, if it proves to be as a result of an incorrect decision: red = high, yellow/orange = medium, green = low. Reproduced from McCallum & Jones, *PLoS Biology*, 2006. (A black and white version of this figure will appear in some formats. For the colour version, please refer to the plate section.)

emergence was recognised in 2001 (Pearse & Swift, 2006). The first management actions taken by the Tasmanian government Save the Tasmanian Devil Program (STDP) were to establish an insurance metapopulation isolated from the disease (Jones et al., 2007) and apply biosecurity protocols to limit the risk of disease spread during the handling of wild devils and their transfer into captive populations (www.tassiedevil.com.au/tasdevil.nsf). The insurance metapopulation was designed to capture and retain the standing genetic diversity in devils, through the intake of founders from the wild (Jones et al., 2007; Huxtable et al., 2015). Founders included independent juveniles from then disease-free western Tasmania and orphaned pouch young from the diseased eastern populations. From 2004 to 2015, insurance populations were expanded to include intensive and free-range captive enclosures and free-living populations on an island and a fenced peninsula (Huxtable et al., 2015). Generally, larger and more natural holding facilities reduce the likelihood of genetic adaptation to captivity (Frankham, 2008), with the animals held in such facilities more suitable for wild release (Jones et al., 2007; McCallum & Jones, 2010). However, one study found that captive-management style did not influence survival, body mass change, or diet of devils one year after release (Rogers et al., 2016).

The potential for trophic cascades (Jones et al., 2007) following the decline and probable functional extinction (Hollings et al., 2015) of the Tasmanian devil over much of its range was raised as a concern right from the start of the investigation (McCallum & Jones, 2006). The extinction of the devil might be a tragedy, but the loss of the apex predator from Tasmanian ecosystems could trigger further extinctions in smaller biodiversity. This concern has been realised (Hollings et al., 2014, 2016) and will be discussed in Section 11.6.

Once urgent conservation actions have been taken to prevent extinction, early decisions that could immediately influence management of the epidemic outcome are to establish whether the disease is infectious and whether infectivity is high (Figure 11.3). Conducting experiments to establish Koch's postulates (see McCallum, 2005) would cost too much time. Instead, that the disease was infectious was established with a high level of certainty through expert opinion consensus (AusVet, 2005). This decision took into account the likely nature of the disease (possible transmissible cancer) and documented geographic spread (AusVet, 2005).

Crucially, allowing highly infectious diseases to establish may have extreme consequences including foreclosure of future control. If the basic reproductive rate R_0 is high, and the epizootic is in its very early stages, it is worth considering the feasibility of an immediate effort to 'stamp out' the disease. Stamping out, by removing all potentially infected cases, is a standard approach used with highly infectious diseases in livestock, such as foot-and-mouth disease (Scudamore & Harris, 2002). It is even possible with human diseases, by using contact tracing to find and treat or quarantine all cases, such as occurred with SARS (Donnelly et al., 2003). Stamping out is logistically much more difficult with wild animals, and has ethical considerations for endangered species. In the case of DFTD, which spread through a wild population living in a variably dense and rugged landscape, the threat was recognised far too late to use this option.

One further decision point that needs to be addressed early is whether there are multiple host species or environmental reservoirs. If this is the case, then infection in these sources needs to be managed for infection control in the focal host to be effective. Transmissible cancers such as DFTD are likely to be restricted to the species of origin, or at the least very closely related species. DFTD is known only in Tasmanian devils, although the other naturally occurring transmissible cancer in vertebrates, CTVT, that affects dogs (Murgia et al., 2006; Murchison, 2008) can infect other canids under experimental settings (Murchison, 2008), probably because of the close phylogenetic relatedness within the Family Canidae (Wayne et al., 1997).

Based on the above reasoning, most of the research on DFTD lies at the bottom of the decision tree, including strategies to reduce transmission rates in wild populations, a potential vaccine and treatment, and genetic management (Figure 11.3).

11.3 Quantifying transmission to identify control options

In established infections, disease control rests on manipulating the transmission rate. Control options for DFTD that reduce transmission rates include chemical or immune therapies, culling, and reducing contacts between infected and susceptible individuals (McCallum & Jones, 2006). Treatment with a range of standard cytotoxic drugs, and surgical excision, were found to be ineffective against DFTD (Phalen et al., 2013, 2015), even though these are effective against CTVT (Nak et al., 2005). However, some success has been met with a potential immunotherapy treatment that uses cytokines to activate MHC upregulation on the tumour cell surface, potentially revealing the tumour to the immune system of the devil (Brown et al., 2016). Without this treatment, DFTD essentially remains hidden to the devil immune system due to down-regulation of its MHC expression (Siddle et al., 2013) (Box 11.1). Another possible treatment involves immunisation with killed tumour cells, which can induce humoral and cytotoxic immune responses against DFTD cells (Kreiss et al., 2015). This response combined with the clonal nature of DFTD lends hope that developing a vaccine may be possible (Woods et al., 2015).

Two other approaches for disrupting transmission were investigated in the DFTD epidemic: selective culling of infected individuals (mid-way in the decision tree; Figure 11.3) and elucidating contact networks to identify superspreaders that could be targeted for removal. Selective culling is a more acceptable option for an endangered species than wholesale culling (stamping out). Selective culling can be effective, particularly if the population is relatively closed, if transmission is not high, and infected individuals can be identified before they become highly infectious. The removal of infected devils was trialled on the Forestier Peninsula in south-east Tasmania (Figure 11.2; Lachish et al., 2010). Favourable conditions for culling at this site include: very little movement of devils between the peninsula and the Tasmanian mainland on a road bridge across a canal; commencement of the culling almost from the outbreak of DFTD (Lachish et al., 2010); and a relatively high and uniform recapture probability for devils of about 80% (Lachish et al., 2007). Four years of trap-and-removal, during 10-day efforts every 3 months over the entire 160 km^2 area, during which nearly 200 diseased devils were removed from the population, neither reduced the force of infection nor reduced population-level impacts relative to an unmanaged but otherwise comparable devil population on Freycinet Peninsula (Lachish et al., 2010). Population models of the culling and control sites indicated that mortality from culling appeared to simply replace mortality from disease. Deterministic susceptible–exposed–infected (SEI) time-delayed models of this system indicated that unfeasibly high levels of removal would be necessary to be effective, with almost continual trapping at very high effort required. Selective culling is probably not a feasible control option for this particular disease (Beeton & McCallum, 2011). The chance of success might be improved if a pre-clinical diagnostic test were available that enabled removal of infected individuals prior to their becoming infectious. Devils are unlikely to be infectious prior to the appearance of tumours and so a blood test to detect tumour metabolites or DNA is needed. Some progress has been made towards this goal (Tovar et al., 2011; Karu et al., 2016).

Social structure and contact networks have profound influence on disease transmission (Altizer et al., 2003). Transmission rarely occurs evenly among individuals within a population. Frequently, a small number of individuals, termed 'superspreaders', will account for a disproportionately high amount of transmission (Galvani & May, 2005; Lloyd-Smith et al., 2005). If superspreaders can be identified in wild populations, they could be targeted for culling. Devils and DFTD were among the first wildlife disease systems for which host contact networks were elucidated using the then new technology, proximity-sensing loggers on radio-collars (Hamede et al., 2009). Unlike the highly aggregated social networks for many human diseases, all devils in the population appear to be well connected. Some individuals were better connected across the population than others, but the pairs of interacting devils changed between mating and non-mating seasons. Particular male–female pairs were identified in the mating season, and specific female–female associations outside the mating season. These results suggest that there is limited potential to control DFTD by targeting specific age, size or sex classes (Hamede et al., 2009).

From this point, disease investigations moved beyond the decision tree which had guided the early and critical stages of response to this emerging and devastating disease. The next phase was to gain a better understanding of transmission (Section 11.4), and how this is influenced by evolution in the devil and the tumour (Section 11.5), to predict the epidemic outcome.

11.4 Quantifying transmission to predict the epidemic outcome

Understanding the transmission dynamics of infectious diseases is crucial for predicting spread within host populations and the eventual outcome of epidemics (Anderson & May, 1979; May & Anderson, 1979). Diseases in which transmission depends more on the frequency of contacts, rather than the density of individuals, are more likely to cause extinction because they lack a host population threshold for persistence (De Castro & Bolker, 2005). Frequency-dependent transmission is more typical of diseases where transmission occurs during breeding activity or sexual contact and infection depends on the proportion of infected individuals in populations (De Castro & Bolker, 2005).

A genuine risk of extinction of the Tasmanian devil from the facial epidemic was predicted by both a deterministic mean-field model and a stochastic individually based model based on contact networks (Hamede et al., 2009), the latter predicting faster extinction and higher extinction probabilities (McCallum et al., 2009; Hamede et al., 2012). A simple age-structured deterministic model showed that transmission of DFTD is not proportional to the density of infected hosts, which suggests a strong element of frequency-dependence in the transmission dynamics (McCallum et al., 2009). This conclusion is strengthened by transmission being dependent on injurious contact when Tasmanian devils bite each other (Box 11.1), a concentration of biting injuries in the mating season (Hamede et al., 2008), and a high force of infection sustained even when population densities reach very low levels (McCallum et al., 2009).

Despite predictions of extinction from simple deterministic models (McCallum et al., 2009), devils persist at the two longest infected field sites, Freycinet and wukalina/Mt William (Figure 11.2). This was surprising given >90% population declines and infection prevalences of 50% being sustained for at least five years at both sites. A limitation of these models is that they were developed within the SEI framework, which considers all infected individuals to be equivalent, both in terms of the disease-induced death rate and their ability to transmit infection to susceptible hosts. However, evidence suggests that both the death rate from DFTD and transmissibility depend on the size of the tumours carried by an individual host (Wells et al., 2017). Integral projection models, in which demographic parameters depend on some continuous trait of the organisms in the population (Easterling et al., 2000; Coulson, 2012) are therefore a potential improvement on the standard SEI approach for modelling DFTD dynamics.

The potential for using such models for host–parasite dynamics has recently been recognised (Metcalf et al., 2016; Wilber et al., 2016). To apply these models, it is necessary to estimate the growth function of infection on hosts that survive, and also to estimate survival, fecundity, and transmission rate as functions of disease burden. State–space models were used to estimate the first three of these functions from a 10-year time series of devil and DFTD data from West Pencil Pine (Wells et al., 2017).

This analysis produced the rather startling result that devils which become infected with tumours have otherwise higher fitness, both in terms of increased survival and increased fecundity, than devils that do not become infected (Figure 11.4A,B). The most likely explanation for this result is that transmission probably occurs by an uninfected devil biting into the tumour of an infected devil (Hamede et al., 2013), and that socially dominant devils do most of the biting. The model also suggested that the force of infection at West Pencil Pine has declined in the last 3–5 years (Wells et al., 2017). Whether this is evidence of evolution of resistance or simply a consequence of fewer susceptible devils being present in the population is unclear at present.

One important result of using tumour burden-dependent demographic functions is that time delays additional to those introduced by devil age structure and the latent period between exposure and infectiousness are introduced into the system. This means that DFTD epidemics operate on a much slower timescale than those of viral or bacterial wildlife diseases. It is possible that the dramatic increases in prevalence and declines in population size observed in the first five years following disease introduction (McCallum et al., 2009a) represent the initial peak of a classic epidemic curve (see Figure 11.5). Following an initial epidemic peak, the consequences for a general epidemic may be coexistence, usually after a series of diminishing subsequent epidemic peaks, fadeout of the infection, or (in a finite population or with frequency-dependent transmission) host extinction. These outcomes can occur in the absence of evolutionary changes in either host or the pathogen. It is too early to determine the likelihood of these outcomes in the case of Tasmanian devil facial tumour disease.

11.5 Evolution

In 2017, more than 20 years since the emergence of facial tumour disease, DFTD has spread across 95% of the distributional range of the devil (Figure 11.2) and caused more than 80% population decline (Lazenby et al. 2018), with local declines of more than 94% (Lachish et al., 2007). Yet, devils still persist at low density at the longest diseased sites, Freycinet and wukalina/Mt William, and there has been no further population decline since 2008 (Figure 11.2). This raises the possibility of evolutionary adaptation to the disease.

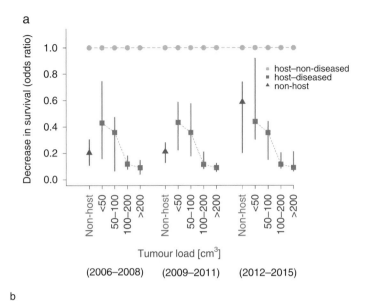

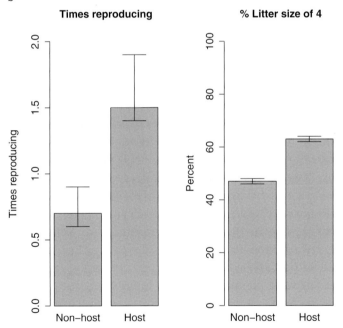

Figure 11.4 (A) Survival of Tasmanian devils at West Pencil Pine as a function of tumour load, for three time periods since disease arrival. Survival is shown as an odds ratio relative to that of non-diseased 'host' devils (from Wells et al., 2017). (B) Fecundity of Tasmanian devils at West Pencil Pine, for 'host' and non-host individuals, times reproducing and the percentage of litters of the maximum size of four (redrawn from Wells et al., 2017).

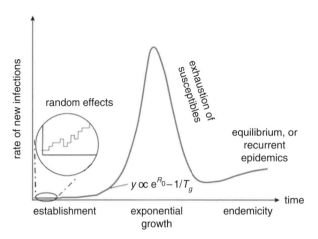

Figure 11.5 Idealised epidemic curve (Anderson et al., 2004). The early growth rate of the epidemic and the time until the epidemic peak are proportional to $(R_0 - 1)/T_g$ where R_0 is the basic reproductive rate and T_g is the generation time of the infection.

High mortality, typically associated with host naivety to emerging diseases (Roelke-Parker et al., 1996; Daszak et al., 2000; Robinson et al., 2010), places strong selective pressure on both host and pathogen. Evolution favours intermediate optimal virulence in pathogens to maximise transmission because pathogens that kill their host too fast can die out when virulence and transmission are inversely correlated (Ebert & Bull, 2003). Hosts can increase fitness by their individual abilities to avoid becoming infected (through, in the case of the Tasmanian devil, reduced aggression and biting behaviour), to resist or tolerate infection (Raberg et al., 2009), or to breed earlier to increase lifetime reproductive success (Jones et al., 2008). A dramatic reduction in aggressive behaviour towards handlers who measure and sample trapped devils suggests possible reduction in natural biting behaviour necessary for transmission (Dewar, 2013) that warrants further investigation. Plasticity in age at first breeding is within the devil's biology and is probably a response to better nutrition and faster juvenile growth rates following population decline in diseased areas (Lachish et al., 2009). In disease-free populations, most females first breed at age two and rarely at age one. Following disease-induced population decline, there has been a 16-fold increase in females that breed as one-year-old subadults (Jones et al., 2008). That only 50% of female devils can breed in their first year of independent life suggests that maternal effects, associated with the disease or precocial breeding status of the mother, and genetics may play a role (Lachish et al., 2009).

Multiple lines of evidence have shown that Tasmanian devils are evolving in response to DFTD. Using a time series of genome scan analyses across three populations (Freycinet, West Pencil Pine, Narawntapu; Figure 11.2) before and after disease emergence, rapid evolution in a small number of candidate genes associated with cancer and immune function mapped to two genomic regions has been identified (Epstein et al., 2016). In addition, complete tumour regression has been documented in some individuals in the wild, along with antibody production (Pye et al., 2016a). Some of the individuals whose tumours regress survive to a healthy old age (six years). Other devils never become infected. Tumour regressions have been recorded across more than half of the devil's range in Tasmania (from a site to the west of West Pencil Pine to wukalina/Mt William in the north-east; Ruiz-Aravena, 2019). At a population level, the recent decline in the force of infection and transmission rate (Wells et al., 2017) is consistent with evolution of resistance, but may simply be a consequence of change in the number of susceptible devils in the population.

Disease tolerance might manifest as greater ability to withstand a given pathogen or tumour burden. If this led to longer survival, lifetime reproductive success and fitness may be increased. The detailed devil–DFTD epidemiological data from West Pencil Pine does not indicate that the relationship between tumour size and mortality has changed over 10 years (Figure 11.4A), although these results are confounded with unknown effects on mortality of a change in the dominant tumour karyotype from a tetraploid to diploid karyotype (Hamede et al., 2015). Variation in the ability of individual devils to maintain body condition in the face of increasing tumour burden does suggest the potential for natural selection to operate in wild devils in favour of tolerance to DFTD (Ruiz-Aravena et al., 2018).

The tumour is also evolving, with multiple lineages emerging and changing through space and time, evident in karyotypes (Pearse et al., 2012) and in the genome (Murchison et al., 2012). Tumour ploidy is associated with different epidemic and demographic effects, with tetraploid tumours having a slower impact on devils than diploid tumours, which grow to a larger final size (Hamede et al., 2015, 2017). The CTVT emerged about 11,000 years ago and is now an evolutionary stable cell line (Murgia et al., 2006; Murchison, 2008) (Box 11.1). The possibility that the tumour and the devil will interact in a coevolutionary selection environment is yet to be explored.

The next step in the data analysis is to determine whether the putative resistance alleles identified by Epstein et al. (2016) are associated with either reduced propensity to become infected, slower tumour growth rate, or increased survival with a given tumour burden, parameters that might indicate resistance. Using the integral projection model framework, implemented through an individual-based stochastic model, long-term evolutionary trajectories for the tumour–devil interaction can be projected. An unsolved challenge is that, while behavioural characteristics such as aggressiveness and dominance appeared to be strongly associated with propensity to become infected, there is little information on the heritability of such characteristics.

11.6 Future directions

Host extinction was predicted as a real possibility in the first decade of the epidemic when population growth rate was halving annually (McCallum et al., 2009), but now appears an unlikely outcome for the Tasmanian devil–facial tumour interaction. The research detailed here is directly responsible for a shift in conservation policy from managing for extinction to managing for persistence. Unanswered questions concern the nature of evolution and potentially coevolution, and whether and how rapidly population recovery in the wild might occur. The transmissible cancer in dogs, CTVT, remains a stable cell line after about 11,000 years of evolution (Murchison et al., 2014). The rapidity of the evolutionary response in devils is remarkable, particularly given the low genetic diversity in Tasmanian devil populations (Jones et al., 2004). Significant shifts in allele frequency at functional genes associated with immune function and cancer regulation have been documented in just 4–6 generations (8–12 years). This is much faster than the 20 generations over which evolutionary responses in the European rabbit (*Oryctolagus cuniculus*) occurred in response to the myxoma virus that was introduced as a biocontrol agent (Kerr et al., 2015).

The rapidity of the evolutionary response of the devil to DFTD suggests that selection is operating on standing genetic variation, genetic diversity that was present at the time of disease emergence (Epstein et al., 2016). Despite significant loss of genetic diversity correlating with environmental changes around the last glacial maximum, and following unstable climate related to increased 'El Nino–Southern Oscillation' activity approximately 2000–4000 years ago (Brüniche-Olsen et al., 2014), it appears that devils have sufficient adaptive capacity to survive this novel disease challenge. Genetic rescue (Frankham et al., 2017) via mixing genetic subpopulations may increase the overall genetic diversity of the species and possibly increase resilience to future disease challenges, as it has done in the Florida panther (Pimm et al., 2006). However, releasing animals from the insurance populations into long-infected areas where evolution has been an ongoing process may also dilute the evolutionary response to the disease and cause outbreeding depression (Frankham et al., 2011). In addition, there is a welfare issue, as these animals will be susceptible to DFTD. The inclusion of orphaned devils from the diseased eastern parts of Tasmania into the insurance population is helpful in capturing genetic variation that has evolved in response to the disease epidemic, but knowledge of the evolutionary changes at the genome level are preliminary. In addition, genetic rescue needs to be done in an adaptive management framework, with a monitoring programme sufficient to measure the outcome of the releases for disease and population dynamics.

A burning question is how evolution could be facilitated towards desirable outcomes, such as population recovery of devils and endemism of DFTD, using the knowledge being generated about the host and pathogen evolutionary response. There are two potentially conflicting approaches here: managing for higher overall genetic diversity in the host, which may confer resilience to future diseases, and managing for locally adapted host resistance. While selective breeding for pathogen resistance has its place (le Roex et al., 2015), it can result in reduced genetic diversity and is not part of genetic rescue programmes which are frequently implemented for species with critically low genetic diversity (Frankham et al., 2017).

An important recent development in the Tasmanian devil–DFTD host–pathogen system is the emergence of a second transmissible cancer in this species (Pye et al., 2016b) (Box 11.1). This second cancer, named devil facial tumour 2 (DFT2), is a transmissible cancer which is grossly indistinguishable from DFTD (which has now been renamed DFT1). However, DFT2 tumours are histologically, cytogenetically, and genetically distinct from those caused by DFT1, indicating that DFT2 emerged independently. First observed in 2014, to date DFT2 has only been observed in a peninsula in south-east Tasmania. The emergence of DFT2 suggests that, although rare in nature, transmissible cancers may arise relatively frequently in Tasmanian devils. Thus, transmissible cancer epidemics such as that caused by DFT1 may have occurred in the past. It will be important to further address the nature of transmissible cancers in Tasmanian devils via comparative studies of DFT1 and DFT2.

Transmissible cancers are unusual pathogens (Box 11.1). Only eight naturally occurring transmissible cancers have been observed in nature: outside of DFT1 and DFT2 in Tasmanian devils, the only other naturally occurring transmissible cancer known in mammals is the 11,000-year-old CTVT (Murgia et al., 2006). The remaining five known transmissible cancers all cause leukaemia-like diseases in various species of marine bivalve molluscs (Metzger et al., 2015, 2016). Given that cancers which remain in a single host are relatively common – both in humans and in other species – the rarity of transmissible cancers suggests that cancers are unlikely to spread between hosts. This may be due to lack of transmission opportunities, or failure of incipient cancer clones to adapt to growth in allogeneic hosts. Indeed, it has been suggested that the genetic diversity of the MHC, the molecular system responsible for allograft detection, may have emerged in part due to selective pressures imposed by transmissible cancers (Murgia et al., 2006).

A big question is the future of transmissible cancers. Are we likely to see a burgeoning of new transmissible cancers in wildlife, livestock, or even humans? Are there environmental links to the emergence of new transmissible cancers, or are we just detecting more cases? Tasmanian devils have produced two different transmissible cancers in a 20-year period (Pye et al., 2016b) and three new cases were reported recently in invertebrates (Metzger et al., 2016). What is the prognosis for DFT2 and how will it interact or compete with DFT1?

Future benefits of research on the Tasmanian devil–facial tumour system will be theoretical advances in knowledge of the ecology and evolution of emerging infectious diseases in wildlife and their application to conservation. Integrating field data with genomics and mathematical models promises greater understanding of transmissible cancers and emerging infectious diseases in general, and of the epidemic and evolutionary outcomes of infectious diseases in wildlife. Specifically, integrating research on rapid evolution and potentially coevolution of host and tumour with epidemiological models will allow prediction of the potential persistence, recovery or extinction of the devil and this knowledge should guide conservation programmes such as translocations.

The potential for trophic cascades (Jones et al., 2007) following the decline and probable functional extinction (Hollings et al., 2015) of the devil over much of its range has been realised (Hollings et al., 2014, 2016). Until recently, the island of Tasmania had escaped the widespread declines and extinctions of mammals that occurred over most of the Australian mainland in the 150 years following European settlement (Woinarski et al., 2014). This can be attributed in large part to the failure of red foxes (*Vulpes vulpes*) to establish in Tasmania at that time, which is itself attributed to suppression by abundant devil populations. Tasmania's mammal community is now shifting towards domination by invasive species, with competitive release of feral cats (*Felis catus*) and expanding black rat (*Rattus rattus*) populations (Hollings et al., 2016) causing ecological changes mirroring those that occurred on the Australian mainland. Feral cats (*Felis catus*) are now considered to be the greatest threat to wildlife in Australia (Woinarski et al., 2014, 2015). At least 16 species of Tasmanian wildlife are at risk from increased cat predation; one of these, the Tasmanian subspecies of the New Holland mouse (*Pseudomys novaehollandiae*), may be on the brink of extinction (Lazenby, 2009). Direct control of feral cat populations, which relies on traditional lethal methods, is ineffective at large spatial scales (Doherty et al., 2017). Reversing the ecological damage by feral cats may be dependent on the eventual recovery of the devil.

11.7 Conclusions

Tasmanian devils, the world's largest marsupial carnivore and apex predator in Tasmania's ecosystems, have spawned two unusual pathogens – transmissible cancers – in a 20-year period. Despite their reasonably low genetic diversity, devils have responded with rapid evolution in resistance and potentially tolerance to this highly lethal epidemic disease. Proximity-sensing loggers on radio-collars to construct contact histories is useful in understanding transmission. Combining genomic analysis of evolution of both host and pathogen with state space and integral projection models, facilitated by large collections of field data and host and tumour genetic samples from multiple sites that span disease outbreak, may allow prediction of the likely epidemic outcome.

11.8 Acknowledgements

Research was funded by grants from the Australian Research Council (ARC Large Grant A00000162 to MJ, Linkage LP0561120 to MJ and HM, Linkage LP0989613 to MJ and EM, Discovery DP110102656 to MJ and HM), the US National Science Foundation (NSF DEB 1316549 to AS, PAH, MJ and HM), Eric Guiler grants from the Save the Tasmanian Devil Appeal – University of Tasmania Foundation, the Ian Potter Foundation, the Australian Academy of Science (Margaret Middleton Fund), Estate of WV Scott, the National Geographic Society, the Mohammed bin Zayed Conservation Fund, and the Holsworth Wildlife Trust. MJ received support from an ARC Future Fellowship (FT100100250) and a Fulbright Tasmania Senior Scholarship, RH from an ARC DECRA, AS as a Fulbright Senior Scholarship and Hamish McCallum as the Senior Scientist of the Save the Tasmanian Devil Program. MJ and HM were awarded an Australian Museum Eureka Prize – Sherman Prize for Environmental Science in 2011 for their contributions. MJ received the Australian Geographic Conservation Award in 2005 for contributions to the conservation of the Tasmanian devil. We acknowledge the many students who carried out different parts of this work, in particular Shelly Lachish, Nick Beeton, Sebastien Comte, David Hamilton, and Manuel Ruiz. We thank the Public Library of Science, Biology for permission to reproduce Figure 11.3 under their CC-BY copyright licence. The research was carried out under Animal Ethics approvals from the University of Tasmania and Scientific Permits from the Tasmanian Department of Primary Industry, Parks, Water and Environment.

References

Altizer, S., Nunn, C.L., Thrall, P.H., et al. (2003) Social organization and parasite risk in mammals: integrating theory and empirical studies. *Annual Review of Ecology Evolution and Systematics*, **34**, 517–547.

Anderson, R.M., Fraser, C., Ghani, A.C., et al. (2004). Epidemiology, transmission dynamics and control of SARS: the 2002–2003 epidemic. *Philosophical Transactions of the Royal Society of London Series B: Biological Sciences*, **359**, 1091–1105.

Anderson, R.M. & May, R.M. (1979) Population biology of infectious diseases. Part I. *Nature*, **280**, 361–367.

AusVet. (2005) Tasmanian devil facial tumour disease response. Technical Workshop: 29–31 August 2005. Hobart (Tasmania): Department of Primary Industries, Water, and Environment.

Beeton, N. (2011) Population and disease modelling in the Tasmanian devil. PhD thesis, University of Tasmania.

Beeton, N. & McCallum, H. (2011) Models predict that culling is not a feasible strategy to prevent extinction of Tasmanian devils from facial tumour disease. *Journal of Applied Ecology*, **48**, 1315–1323.

Brown, G.K., Tovar, C., Cooray, A.A., et al. (2016) Mitogen-activated Tasmanian devil blood mononuclear cells kill devil facial tumour disease cells. *Immunology and Cell Biology*, **94**, 673–679.

Bruniche-Olsen, A., Jones, M.E., Austin, J.J., Burridge, C.P. & Holland, B.R. (2014) Extensive population decline in the Tasmanian devil predates European settlement and Devil Facial Tumor Disease. *Biology Letters*, **10**, 20140619.

Burgman, M.A. (2005) *Risks and Decisions for Conservation and Environmental Management*. New York, NY: Cambridge University Press.

Coulson, T. (2012) Integral projections models, their construction and use in posing hypotheses in ecology. *Oikos*, **121**, 1337–1350.

Daszak, P., Cunningham, A.A. & Hyatt, A.D. (2000) Emerging infectious diseases of wildlife – threats to biodiversity and human health. *Science*, **287**, 443–449.

De Castro, F. & Bolker, B. (2005) Mechanisms of disease-induced extinction. *Ecology Letters*, **8**, 117–126.

Dewar, E. (2013) Understanding behaviour, stress and disease in Tasmanian devils: implications for selective adaptations. Honours thesis, University of Tasmania.

Doherty, T.S., Dickman, C.R., Johnson, C.N., et al. (2017) Impacts and management of feral cats *Felis catus* in Australia. *Mammal Review*, **47**(2), 83–97. https://doi.org/10.1111/mam.12080

Donnelly, C.A., Ghani, A.C., Leung, G.M., et al. (2003) Epidemiological determinants of spread of causal agent of severe acute respiratory syndrome in Hong Kong. *The Lancet*, **361**, 1761–1766.

Easterling, M.R., Ellner, S.P. & Dixon, P.M. (2000) Size-specific sensitivity: applying a new structured population model. *Ecology*, **81**, 694–708.

Ebert, D. & Bull, J.J. (2003) Challenging the trade-off model for the evolution of virulence: is virulence management feasible? *Trends in Microbiology*, **11**, 15–20.

Epstein, B., Jones, M., Hamede, R., et al. (2016) Rapid evolutionary response to a transmissible cancer in Tasmanian devils. *Nature Communications*, **7**, 12684.

Frankham, R. (2008) Genetic adaptation to captivity in species conservation programs. *Molecular Ecology*, **17**, 325–333.

Frankham, R., Ballou, J.D., Eldridge, M.D.B., et al. (2011) Predicting the probability of outbreeding depression. *Conservation Biology*, **25**, 465–475.

Frankham, R., Ballou, J.D., Ralls, K., et al. (2017) *Genetic Management of Fragmented Animal and Plant Populations*. Oxford: Oxford University Press.

Galvani, A.P. & May, R.M. (2005) Dimensions of superspreading. *Nature*, **438**, 293.

Hamede, R., Bashford, J., Jones, M. & McCallum, H. (2012) Simulating devil facial tumour disease outbreaks across empirically derived contact networks. *Journal of Applied Ecology*, **49**, 447–456.

Hamede, R.K., Bashford, J., McCallum, H. & Jones, M. (2009) Contact networks in a wild Tasmanian devil (*Sarcophilus harrisii*) population: using social network analysis to reveal seasonal variability in social behaviour and its implications for transmission of devil facial tumour disease. *Ecology Letters*, **12**, 1147–1157.

Hamede, R.K., Beeton, N.J., Carver, S. & Jones, M.E. (2017) Untangling the model muddle: empirical tumour growth in Tasmanian devil facial tumour disease. *Scientific Reports*, **7**(1), 6217.

Hamede, R.K., McCallum, H. & Jones, M. (2008) Seasonal, demographic and density-related patterns of contact between Tasmanian devils (*Sarcophilus harrisii*): implications for transmission of devil facial tumour disease. *Austral Ecology*, **33**, 614–614.

Hamede, R.K., McCallum, H. & Jones, M. (2013) Biting injuries and transmission of Tasmanian devil facial tumour disease. *Journal of Animal Ecology*, **82**, 182–190.

Hamede, R.K., Pearse, A.M., Swift, K., Barmuta, L.A., Murchison, E.P. & Jones, M.E. (2015) Transmissible cancer in Tasmanian devils: localized lineage replacement and host population response. *Proceedings of the Royal Society of London B*, **282**, 20151468.

Hawkins, C.E., Baars, C., Hesterman, H., et al. (2006) Emerging disease and population decline of an island endemic, the Tasmanian devil *Sarcophilus harrisii*. *Biological Conservation*, **131**, 307–324.

Hawkins, C.E., McCallum, H., Mooney, N., Jones, M. & Holdsworth, M. (2009) *Sarcophilus harrisii*. IUCN Red List of threatened species. Version **2009**. 1.

Hollings, T., Jones, M., Mooney, N. & McCallum, H. (2014) Trophic cascades following the disease-induced decline of an apex predator, the Tasmanian devil. *Conservation Biology*, **28**, 36–75.

Hollings, T., Jones, M., Mooney, N. & McCallum, H. (2016) Disease-induced decline of an apex predator drives invasive dominated states and threatens biodiversity. *Ecology*, **97**, 394–405.

Hollings, T., McCallum, H., Kreger, K., Mooney, N. & Jones, M. (2015) Relaxation of risk-sensitive behaviour of prey following disease-induced decline of an apex predator, the Tasmanian devil. *Proceedings of the Royal Society of London B*, **282**, 20150124.

Huxtable, S.J., Lee, D.V., Wise, P. & Save the Tasmanian Devil Program. (2015) Metapopulation management of an extreme disease scenario. In: Armstrong, D. P., Hayward, M.W., Moro, D. & Seddon, B.P. (eds.), *Advances in Reintroduction Biology of Australian and New Zealand Fauna*. Clayton, Victoria, Australia: CSIRO.

Jones, M.E. (2003) Convergence in ecomorphology and guild structure among marsupial and placental carnivores. In: Jones, M.E., Dickman, C.R. & Archer, M. (eds.), *Predators With Pouches: The Biology of Carnivorous Marsupials*. Melbourne, Australia: CSIRO Publishing.

Jones, M.E., Cockburn, A., Hamede, R., et al. (2008) Life-history change in disease-ravaged Tasmanian devil populations. *Proceedings of the National Academy of Sciences of the United States of America*, **105**, 10,023–10,027.

Jones, M.E., Jarman, P.J., Lees, C.M., et al. (2007) Conservation management of Tasmanian devils in the context of an emerging, extinction-threatening disease: devil facial tumor disease. *EcoHealth*, **4**, 326–337.

Jones, M.E., Paetkau, D., Geffen, E.L.I. & Moritz, C. (2004) Genetic diversity and population structure of Tasmanian devils, the largest marsupial carnivore. *Molecular Ecology*, **13**, 2197–2209.

Karu, N., Wilson, R., Hamede, R., et al. (2016) Discovery of biomarkers for Tasmanian devil cancer (DFTD) by metabolic profiling of serum. *Journal of Proteome Research*, **15**, 3827–3840.

Kerr, P. J., Liu, J., Cattadori, I., et al. (2015) Myxoma virus and the leporipoxviruses: an evolutionary paradigm. *Viruses*, **7**, 1020–1061.

Kreiss, A., Brown, G.K., Tovara, C., Lyons, A. B. & Woods, G.M. (2015). Evidence for induction of humoral and cytotoxic immune responses against devil facial tumor disease cells in Tasmanian devils *Sarcophilus harrisii* immunized with killed cell preparations. *Vaccine*, **33**, 3016–3025.

Lachish, S., Jones, M. & McCallum, H. (2007) The impact of disease on the survival and population growth rate of the Tasmanian devil. *Journal of Animal Ecology*, **76**, 926–936.

Lachish, S., McCallum, H. & Jones, M. (2009) Demography, disease and the devil: life-history changes in a disease-affected population of Tasmanian devils (*Sarcophilus harrisii*). *Journal of Animal Ecology*, **78**, 427–436.

Lachish, S., McCallum, H., Mann, D., Pukk, C. & Jones, M.E. (2010) Evaluation of selective culling of infected individuals to control Tasmanian devil facial tumor disease. *Conservation Biology*, **24**, 841–851.

Lafferty, K.D. & Kuris, A.M. (2002) Trophic strategies, animal diversity and body size. *Trends in Ecology & Evolution*, **17**, 507–513.

Lazenby, B. (2009) Habitat identification and hair tube surveys for the Endangered New Holland Mouse in Tasmania with a focus on the St Helens area. www .northeastbioregionalnetwork.org.au/docs/ NEBN%20final%20report.pdf (downloaded 08/06/2017): North East Bioregional Network.

Lazenby, B.T., Tobler, M.W., Brown, W.E., et al. (2018) Density trends and demographic signals uncover the long-term impact of transmissible cancer in Tasmanian devils. *Journal of Applied Ecology*, **55**, 1368–1379. https://doi.org/10.1111/1365-2664.13088

Le Roex, N., Berrington, C.M., Hoal, E.G. & Van Helden, P.D. (2015) Selective breeding: the future of TB management in African buffalo? *Acta Tropica*, **149**, 38–44.

Lloyd-Smith, J.O., Schreiber, S.J., Kopp, P.E. & Getz, W.M. (2005) Superspreading and the effect of individual variation on disease emergence. *Nature*, **438**, 355–359.

May, R.M. & Anderson, R. M. (1979) Population biology of infectious diseases. Part II. *Nature*, **280**, 455–461.

McCallum, H. (2005) Inconclusiveness of chytridiomycosis as the agent in widespread frog declines. *Conservation Biology*, **19**, 1421–1430.

McCallum, H. & Jones, M. (2006) To lose both would look like carelessness: Tasmanian devil facial tumour disease. *PLoS Biology*, **4**, e342–1674.

McCallum, H. & Jones, M. (2010) Sins of omission and sins of commission: St Thomas Aquinas and the devil. *Australian Zoologist*, **35**, 307–314.

McCallum, H. & Jones, M. (2012) Infectious cancer in wildlife. In: Aguirre, A., Daszak, P. & Ostfeld, R. (eds.), *Conservation Medicine: Applied Cases of Ecological Health* (pp. 270–283). Oxford: Oxford University Press.

McCallum, H., Jones, M., Hawkins, C., et al. (2009) Transmission dynamics of Tasmanian devil facial tumor disease may lead to disease-induced extinction. *Ecology*, **90**, 3379–3392.

Metcalf, C.J.E., Graham, A.L., Martinez-Bakker, M. & Childs, D.Z. (2016) Opportunities and challenges of Integral Projection Models for modelling host–parasite dynamics. *Journal of Animal Ecology*, **85**, 343–355.

Metzger, M.J., Reinisch, C., Sherry, J. & Goff, S.P. (2015) Horizontal transmission of clonal cancer cells causes leukemia in soft-shell clams. *Cell*, **161**, 255–263.

Metzger, M.J., Villalba, A., Carballal, M.J., et al. (2016) Widespread transmission of independent cancer lineages within multiple bivalve species. *Nature*, **534**, 705–709.

Mooney, N. (2004) The devil's new hell. *Nature Australia*, **28**, 34.

Murchison, E.P. (2008) Clonally transmissible cancers in dogs and Tasmanian devils. *Oncogene*, **27**, S19–S30.

Murchison, E.P., Schulz-Trieglaff, O.B., Ning, Z., et al. (2012) Genome sequencing and analysis of the Tasmanian devil and its transmissible cancer. *Cell*, **148**, 780–791.

Murchison, E.P., Wedge, D.C., Alexandrov, L.B., et al. (2014) Transmissable dog cancer genome reveals the origin and history of an ancient cell lineage. *Science*, **343**, 437–440.

Murgia, C., Pritchard, J.K., Kim, S.Y., Fassati, A. & Weiss, R.A. (2006) Clonal origin and evolution of a transmissible cancer. *Cell*, **126**, 477–487.

Nak, D., Nak, Y., Cangul, I.T. & Tuna, B. (2005) A clinico-pathological study on the effect of vincristine on transmissible venereal tumour in dogs. *Journal of Veterinary Medicine Series A*, **52**, 366–370.

Pearse, A.M. & Swift, K. (2006) Transmission of devil facial-tumour disease – an uncanny similarity in the karyotype of these malignant tumours means that they could be infective. *Nature*, **439**, 549–549.

Pearse, A.M., Swift, K., Hodson, P., et al. (2012) Evolution in a transmissible cancer: a study of the chromosomal changes in devil facial tumor (DFT) as it spreads through the wild Tasmanian devil population. *Cancer Genetics*, **205**, 101–112.

Phalen, D.N., Frimberger, A., Pyecroft, S., et al. (2013) Vincristine chemotherapy trials and pharmacokinetics in Tasmanian devils with Tasmanian devil facial tumor disease. *PLoS ONE*, **8**, e65133.

Phalen, D.N., Frimberger, A.E., Peck, S., et al. (2015) Doxorubicin and carboplatin trials in Tasmanian devils (*Sarcophilus harrisii*) with Tasmanian devil facial tumor disease. *The Veterinary Journal*, **206**, 312–316.

Pimm, S.L., Dollar, L. & Bass Jr, O.L. (2006) The genetic rescue of the Florida panther. *Animal Conservation*, **9**, 115–122.

Pye, R., Hamede, R., Siddle, H., et al. (2016a) Demonstration of immune responses against devil facial tumour disease in wild Tasmanian devils. *Biology Letters*, **12**, 20160553.

Pye, R.J., Pemberton, D., Tovar, C., et al. (2016b) A second transmissible cancer in Tasmanian devils. *Proceedings of the National Academy of Sciences of the United States of America*, **113**, 374–379.

Pyecroft, S.B., Pearse, A.M., Loh, R., et al. (2007) Towards a case definition for devil facial tumour disease: what is it? *EcoHealth*, **4**, 346–351.

Raberg, L., Graham, A.L. & Read, A.F. (2009) Decomposing health: tolerance and resistance to parasites in animals. *Philosophical Transactions of the Royal Society of London B*, **364**, 37–49.

Robinson, A.C., Lawson, B., Toms, M.P., et al. (2010) Emerging infectious disease leads to rapid population declines of common British birds. *PLoS ONE*, **5**, e12215.

Roelke-Parker, M.E., Munson, L., Packer, C., et al. (1996) A canine distemper virus epidemic in Serengeti lions (*Panthera leo*). *Nature*, **379**, 441–445.

Rogers, T., Fox, S., Pemberton, D. & Wise, P. (2016) Sympathy for the devil: captive-management style did not influence survival, body-mass change or diet of Tasmanian devils 1 year after wild release. *Wildlife Research*, **43**, 544–552.

Ruiz-Aravena, M. (2019). The Tasmanian devil and its transmissible cancer: physiology of the devil-DFTD interaction. PhD thesis, University of Tasmania.

Ruiz-Aravena, M., Jones, M.E., Carver, S., et al. (2018). Sex bias in ability to cope with cancer: Tasmanian devils and facial tumour disease. *Proceedings of the Royal Society of London B*, **285**, 20182239.

Sakai, A.K., Allendorf, F.W., Holt, J.S., et al. (2001) The population biology of invasive species. *Annual Review of Ecology and Systematics*, **32**, 305–332.

Scudamore, J.M. & Harris, D.M. (2002) Control of foot and mouth disease: lessons from the experience of the outbreak in Great Britain in 2001. *Revue scientifique et technique (International Office of Epizootics)*, **21**, 699–710.

Siddle, H.V., Kreiss, A., Tovar, C., et al. (2013) Reversible epigenetic down-regulation of MHC molecules by devil facial tumour disease illustrates immune escape by a contagious cancer. *Proceedings of the National Academy of Sciences of the United States of America*, **110**, 5103–5108.

Tompkins, D.M., Carver, S., Jones, M.E., Krkosek, M. & Skerratt, L.F. (2015) Emerging infectious diseases of wildlife: a critical perspective. *Trends in Parasitology*, **31**, 149–159.

Tovar, C., Obendorf, D., Murchison, E.P., et al. (2011) Tumor-specific diagnostic marker for transmissible facial tumors of Tasmanian devils: immunohistochemistry studies. *Veterinary Pathology*, **48**, 1195–1203.

Wayne, R.K., Geffen, E., Girman, D.J., et al. (1997) Molecular systematics of the Canidae. *Systematic Biology*, **46**, 622–653.

Wells, K., Hamede, R.K., Kerlin, D.H., et al. (2017a) Infection of the fittest: devil facial tumour disease has greatest effect on individuals with highest reproductive output. *Ecology Letters*, **20**, 770–778.

Wilber, M.Q., Langwig, K.E., Kilpatrick, A.M., McCallum, H.I. & Briggs, C.J. (2016) Integral Projection Models for host–parasite systems with an application to amphibian chytrid fungus. *Methods in Ecology and Evolution*, **7**, 1182–1194.

Woinarski, J.C., Burbidge, A.A. & Harrison, P.L. (2015) Ongoing unraveling of a continental fauna: decline and extinction of Australian mammals since European settlement. *Proceedings of the National Academy of Sciences of the United States of America*, **112**, 4531–4540.

Woinarski, J.C.Z., Burbidge, A.A. & Harrison, P.L. (2014) *The Action Plan for Australian Mammals 2012*. Melbourne, Australia: CSIRO Publishing.

Woods, G.M., Howson, L.J., Brown, G.K., et al. (2015) Immunology of a transmissible cancer spreading among Tasmanian devils. *The Journal of Immunology*, **195**, 23–29.

CHAPTER TWELVE

Bovine tuberculosis in badgers: sociality, infection and demography in a social mammal

JENNI L. MCDONALD, RICHARD J.
DELAHAY AND ROBBIE A. MCDONALD

12.1 Introduction

It is hard to imagine that, in the early 1970s, we knew very little about bovine tuberculosis (bTB) in the European badger (*Meles meles*). Yet now we have amassed a considerable amount of information on this significant wildlife host, and its role in the challenges of control and elimination of bTB in cattle. Since the 1970s, research has been extensive; long-term studies that allow researchers to follow individuals through time have provided a wealth of new information on the disease process in badgers. This work has revealed a substantial body of ecological and epidemiological information, making this wildlife host–pathogen system one of the best described in the world.

As this chapter will reveal, explaining ecological and epidemiological processes is far too complex to conduct from observation alone, with mechanistic understanding only reached through employing statistical and recently developed computationally intensive approaches. In this chapter we discuss some of the findings of the long-term study of a naturally infected badger population and the statistical models that have been applied. We provide an overview of the following three key concepts: (1) heterogeneity in infection states; (2) spatial structuring and host–host interactions; and (3) how demography may feed into disease ecology.

12.2 Theoretical context

A fundamental concept in disease ecology is the idea of the superspreader, an individual that contributes disproportionately to disease spread. The superspreader phenotype can arise as a result of multiple interacting factors that determine susceptibility, infectiousness, and connectivity to other hosts. Consequently, an individual's superspreading capability depends on both a physiological component, determining the degree of infectiousness of the host, and a behavioural component influencing opportunities for pathogen transmission (Lloyd-Smith et al., 2005). Our first two key concepts look at these different, but not mutually exclusive, characteristics of disease spread. First, we consider the results of studies to describe variation in infected states and identify potential classes of individuals at high risk of becoming infected and of becoming infectious. Second, we explore how the spatial structure of a population and the connectedness of individuals influence behavioural opportunities for disease spread.

12.2.1 Individual-level variation in infected state

Individual variation in infectiousness can explain disease persistence in wild populations (Shirley et al., 2003; Kramer-Schadt et al., 2009). Mathematical models accounting for heterogeneity in infectivity predict very different population outcomes compared to those that assume an average infection level (Lloyd-Smith et al., 2005). Within-host dynamics are especially important for chronic infections, which can foster a broad spectrum of infected status. Predictions of the spread and incidence of infection from mathematical models are highly sensitive to parameterisation of variability in infection status and infectiousness (Shirley et al., 2003; Keeling & Danon, 2009; Smith et al., 2012). Hosts that are highly infectious because they yield a higher output of infectious organisms are sometimes described as supershedders. Additionally, long-term chronically infectious individuals can also output large numbers of organisms over time and hence contribute to disease persistence (Kramer-Schadt et al., 2009). Therefore, both the infected state and the duration of infection are key epidemiological parameters. This chapter (Section 12.4) describes work that identifies individuals at high infection risk and those more likely to present symptoms of advanced disease. We discuss how modelling approaches and individual-based diagnostic data can help explain the underlying physiological and/or behavioural mechanisms driving these patterns.

12.2.2 Spread of disease in spatially structured hosts

Across many animal systems, social behaviours have been linked to pathogen transmission (Wendland et al., 2010; Rushmore et al., 2013), with spatial aggregations of infection being commonly observed (Joly et al., 2006; Blanchong et al., 2007). Wild animal populations commonly exhibit spatial structure, in many cases characterised by social groups of some kind. Consequently, interactions between individuals are non-random with high within-group contacts and lower between-group contact rates. This contact heterogeneity among individuals is fundamental to understanding what drives (or restricts) the spatial spread of disease through a population.

With recent technological advancements, social network analysis is now becoming more widespread, providing a means of quantifying individual variation in interactions and contacts in wild animal populations (Silk et al.,

2017a, 2017b). This approach provides a powerful means of accounting for individual heterogeneity, moving away from traditional approaches which have often assumed that individuals of similar functional groups are epidemiologically homogeneous. Here (Section 12.5) we move away from the traditional view of randomly mixing homogeneous populations and explore heterogeneous host association patterns, at the level of the group, class, and individual.

12.2.3 Host population demography

Our final key concept considers how demographic mechanisms could support the persistence of host populations that serve as reservoirs of chronic disease. The slow–fast continuum is a mainstay of mammalian life-history theory (Stearns, 1983; Gaillard et al., 2016). Investment in demographic traits (such as reproduction) is costly, resulting in a plethora of different life-history strategies across wild populations. At one end of the spectrum, 'fast' species mature quickly, have high reproductive rates and die young, and at the other end, 'slow' species mature slowly, have low reproductive rates and high life expectancy. This raises the interesting question of whether host pace of life determines the impacts of infection on host populations. Previous studies have found links between host life history and pathogen dynamics; slow-lived species invest more in pathogen defences and fast-lived species have higher reservoir competence (Johnson et al., 2012; Ostfeld et al., 2014). However, it is less clear whether the species life-history strategies may provide mechanisms to compensate for the demographic impact of pathogens on host populations.

Pathogens can cause increased host mortality and/or decreased reproductive success, often having a significant effect on host demographic variables. Demographic attributes of a host's life history may temper these negative effects and determine the potential of infected populations to persist in the environment. In Section 12.6 we elaborate on the idea that host demographic mechanisms may compensate for negative effects of disease on their survival, thus contributing to the persistence of infected populations and hence reservoir persistence.

12.3 The system

Bovine tuberculosis (bTB) is the most pressing livestock health problem in the UK. Routine herd surveillance, slaughter of positive reactors, and movement restrictions of breakdown herds (when one or more reactors are found in a herd) place a significant financial burden on the taxpayer, along with substantial emotional and monetary cost to farmers. Despite intensive testing protocols, bTB in cattle has become endemic in parts of the UK, with increasing incidence and geographic spread in some areas. This is in part driven by cattle movements and an undisclosed reservoir of infection in the cattle population, but is also linked to transmission between badgers and cattle. Consequently, disease management efforts have also focused on badgers, which are the most significant wild reservoir of bTB in the UK and thrive in the pastoral landscapes which characterise the affected areas.

Management of bTB in badgers is, however, a contentious issue. Since infection was first identified in badgers in 1971 (Murhead & Burns, 1974), various culling approaches have been implemented. A large-scale field trial explored the epidemiological consequences for cattle of culling badgers. The Randomised Badger Culling Trial (RBCT) compared the effect of reactive, proactive, and no-culling strategies. Some interesting and counter-intuitive results emerged. The first key result was that reactive culling resulted in increased herd breakdowns (Donnelly et al., 2003), and so this experimental treatment was terminated early. In contrast, when proactive culling was undertaken, the number of herd breakdowns decreased within the trial area while increased breakdowns occurred in the surrounding adjacent herds (Donnelly et al., 2006, 2007). Both these results have been explained by a process called social perturbation, whereby the typically stable social structure of badger populations is disrupted by culling, causing increased immigration and the wider ranging of remaining individuals (see McDonald et al., 2008). This leads to increased social mixing of previously territorial groups, increased bTB prevalence in badgers, and ultimately enhanced transmission to cattle.

The Bacillus Calmette–Guerin (BCG) vaccine, which has been a mainstay of tuberculosis control in humans, has been trialled in badgers. Experimental trials showed positive effects of the injectable vaccine on susceptibility and progression of bTB in captive animals (Chambers et al., 2011; Lesellier et al., 2011). In field studies using injectable vaccine, a reduction in individual risk of seroconversion was observed in vaccinated animals (Chambers et al., 2011) and in unvaccinated cubs in groups that had been vaccinated (Carter et al., 2012), but these studies did not differentiate between effects on susceptibility and infectivity. A more recent study using an oral vaccine points to a reduction in susceptibility, not infectivity, as the key process reducing *Mycobacterium bovis* incidence (Aznar et al., 2018). To date, administration of BCG to badgers has been achieved through capture–release regimes, which is labour-intensive and thus limits the potential for widespread application. A potentially more efficient and cheaper alternative is deployment of the vaccine in an edible bait (Palphramand et al., 2017), which is currently under development (Chambers et al., 2017).

In 1975, a study began on wild badgers on a site at Woodchester Park, in an area of Gloucestershire where bTB was a re-emerging problem in cattle. This high-density population exhibits a social structure that is typical of the moderate- to high-density badger populations observed across bTB-affected parts of Great Britain (Roper, 2010). The objective of the Woodchester Park study was to collect basic ecological and epidemiological data to enhance our understanding of *M. bovis*, the causative agent of bTB infection in badgers. The study involves an intensive long-term programme of regular trapping and sampling. Badgers are caught using steel mesh traps baited with peanuts. They are then taken back to a sampling facility where they are anaesthetised and examined. Each badger is given a unique identifying tattoo on the abdomen at their first sampling occasion. At every capture event, data are recorded including age-class, sex, weight, body condition, body length, reproductive status, and tooth wear. The infection status of an individual at every capture event is determined by different diagnostic tests. Samples of sputum, faeces, urine, and swabs of any abscesses or bite wounds are taken for bacterial culture of *M. bovis*. Blood samples are also collected, with various diagnostic tests having been used over the years. The Brock ELISA, which detects *M. bovis* antibodies in the blood serum, was initially applied from 1982 to 2006. This was superseded by the BrockTB StatPak antibody test (used from 2006 to 2015), which in turn was replaced by the Dual Path Platform antibody test (DPP) (from 2016 to present). In 2006, the interferon gamma test (IFN-γ) was also introduced, which detects a cell-mediated response to *M. bovis*. To date, over 3000 badgers have been captured, and with high annual recapture probabilities (estimates ~80%; Weber et al., 2013b) this relates to over 15,000 capture events. The resulting data set represents the longest time series of data on life histories and bTB infection in wild badgers.

Badgers in the Woodchester Park population provide an ideal test bed to explore variation in infection status, as routine diagnostic testing reveals a range of disease outcomes. This provides an improved understanding of the degree of individual variation in disease severity, and opportunities to explore the factors that may drive these different outcomes. The testing regime has allowed the identification of potentially highly infectious badgers, termed superexcretors, for which bacilli excretion is more frequently detected.

This longitudinal data set allows researchers to understand mechanisms underlying individual-, group-, and population-scale processes. In the rest of this chapter we study how the combination of individual epidemiological data and modelling frameworks has enabled work from Woodchester to explore host–pathogen theories in relation to badger life history and disease ecology.

12.4 Concept one: variation in disease severity and progression
12.4.1 Historical background
Wildlife reservoirs have traditionally been viewed as homogeneous populations, with limited appreciation of variation in survival, infection risk, and disease progression. Early theoretical work on the invasion and spread of

disease assumed that populations were uniform and well-mixed, with infected individuals occupying a singular category (Anderson & May, 1978; May & Anderson, 1979). However, this simplifying assumption is of limited value for understanding pathogen dynamics in populations that experience heterogeneities in the host, environment, and parasite. Here, we focus specifically on heterogeneity in host susceptibility and infectiousness, which is one component of the superspreader phenotype.

Mean-field models are often used to replicate disease dynamics. These models commonly categorise populations into subgroups such as susceptible (S), exposed (E), infectious (I), and recovered (R), resulting in a range of potential modelling frameworks (e.g. SI, SEI, SEIR). However, few models of wildlife epidemiology consider disease states beyond the standard categories that these classical frameworks provide, thus failing to acknowledge the wider variation in stages of infection.

12.4.2 Importance for predictive models

Individual-based spatial models of badgers, cattle, and bTB have been routinely used to explore and provide cost–benefit analyses for different control options (e.g. White & Harris, 1995; Shirley et al., 2003; Wilkinson et al., 2004; Smith et al., 2016). These models simulate the behaviour and infection status of individual badgers, with larger-scale measures of disease prevalence at a population level emerging. Transmission, disease progression, and disease-induced mortality are prerequisites for these models, and full sensitivity analyses show that the incidence of disease in both badgers and cattle is sensitive to these epidemiological parameters (e.g. Smith et al., 2012). Consequently, increased uncertainty surrounding epidemiological parameters will impact on the predicted outcomes of simulated control strategies. Reducing uncertainty in model parameterisation is therefore crucial to provide both robust quantitative predictions and a greater understanding of the mechanisms underlying the demographic consequences of disease.

The detailed individual-level data on the diagnostic status of badgers collected at Woodchester Park has allowed a move away from using 'out of the box' categories of infection status. Instead, these data have permitted identification of more biologically relevant categories of disease state for the badger–TB system.

12.4.3 Pathology of disease in badgers

M. bovis infection can manifest itself differently among individuals, and an infected badger may experience (and progress through) a range of infection states. Following initial infection, badgers can live with contained disease for a prolonged period (Corner et al., 2012). This containment phase is thought to result in a lengthy period of latency in a high proportion of badgers (Gallagher & Clifton-Hadley, 2000; Corner et al., 2012), with some never experiencing any clinical symptoms or becoming infectious. However, failure to control infection can result in formation of gross lesions (Figure 12.1), mycobacterial multiplication and active excretion of bacilli (Figure 12.1). In common with other host species, and mycobacterial infections, inhalation appears to be the main route of *M. bovis* infection in badgers. Consequently, infectious individuals commonly show signs of pulmonary disease, whereby open lesions in the lungs (Figure 12.1a) lead to bacilli released in aerosol form. Additionally, bite wounding is thought to be a potential route of infection by direct inoculation of bacteria into the tissues (Figure 12.1b; Gallagher et al., 1976; Jenkins et al., 2008; Jenkins, Cox & Delahay, 2012). Finally, the disease is slowly progressive, resulting in disease dissemination increasing the number of sites with gross and histopathological lesions. Badgers in this state are considered highly infectious. The distribution of these disease stages is pyramid-like; most infections are contained (Corner et al., 2012), with only a small proportion of the population showing signs of active contagious disease (~5%; Wilkinson et al., 2000; Graham et al., 2013).

The broad spectrum of epidemiological outcomes revealed from post-mortem studies of badgers indicates that, in terms of disease transmission, all infections are not equal. Badgers with high bacterial loads and severe pathology have been suggested to be particularly important for disease transmission (Gallagher & Clifton-Hadley, 2000). Although post-mortem examination and tissue culture can provide the gold standard in terms of diagnostic sensitivity, routine sequential diagnostic testing of live individuals also offers

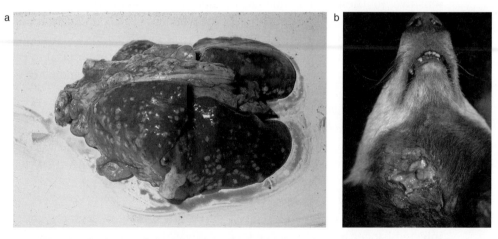

Figure 12.1 (a) The lungs of a badger with advanced tuberculosis, presenting as a diffuse distribution of lesions throughout the tissue. (b) Badger with an open suppurating submandibular abscess. *M. bovis* has been isolated from the lymph nodes and bite wounds of infected badgers. (A black and white version of this figure will appear in some formats. For the colour version, please refer to the plate section.)

unique opportunities to explore variation in infection states. Hence, badgers have been described as 'exposed' when responding positively to an antibody test, indicating that they are infected but not necessarily infectious (Delahay et al., 2000). In contrast, isolation of *M. bovis* through the culture of clinical samples clearly indicates an infectious badger. The latter have been further subdivided into 'excretor' and 'super-excretor' categories on the basis of the frequency of detection of bacteria in clinical samples (Wilkinson et al., 2000), and badgers displaying the super-excretor diagnostic pattern were found to have reduced survival (Wilkinson et al., 2000). Demographic differences across disease states highlight important individual-level variability in the effects of infection, and in the duration and transmission potential of the infectious period. Subsequent work has built on that of Wilkinson et al. (2000) to investigate the behavioural and life-history correlates of variation in disease states and progression. One question of particular interest is what the phenotype of those highly infectious badgers, termed 'super-excretors', is.

12.4.4 Multi-state CMR model

Demographic models of capture–mark–recapture (CMR) data can examine among-individual variation in vital rates (i.e. survival). Applying a multi-state model approach to live recapture data provides a means to jointly model and estimate survival and transitions between disease states, while accounting for imperfect recapture probabilities (Lebreton et al., 2009). It is a natural extension of the Cormack–Jolly–Seber model (a traditional CMR analysis); however, each time an individual is encountered it is assigned to a certain state. This state is a categorical individual covariate that can change through time. Categorisation of individuals according to their state allows estimation of state-dependent survival probabilities and transition probabilities, and hence rates of disease-induced mortality, and probabilities of infection and disease progression (Graham et al., 2013).

Under the assumption that the progression of disease is an irreversible process (i.e. that the establishment of infection, even where controlled by the host, always carries a risk of further disease progression; Corner et al., 2012), a proposed population model is shown in Figure 12.2.

Comparison of the more detailed four-stage model (Figure 12.2) with a traditional SI model revealed strong support for the inclusion of multiple infected stages (Graham et al., 2013). Applying a four-stage multi-state model (Figure 12.2) to demographic data obtained from Woodchester Park provided more detailed information on survival and progression. Males have a higher risk of infection and more rapid disease progression compared to female badgers (Graham et al., 2013). Consequently, males are more likely to become infectious and progress to the most severe disease state. Additionally, survival was strongly dependent on the disease state of the individual and the sex, with

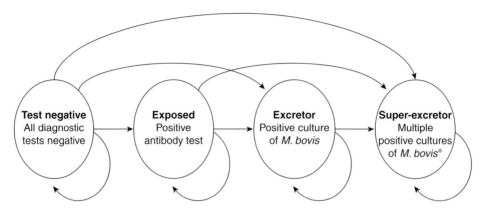

Figure 12.2 Progression of bTB in badgers through disease classes (although badgers may remain in the same infected state until death – note the presence of self-loops).*This state has multiple classifications in the literature, but all refer to multiple culture-positive results.

males having consistently lower survival than females and experiencing state-dependent increases in mortality as disease progressed (Graham et al., 2013). For example, an uninfected female badger has a 74% survival probability, compared to 67% in uninfected males. Although the survival rate of super-excretor badgers drops significantly for both sexes, the decline is more pronounced for males than females (13% and 39%, respectively). Sex differences were also observed using slightly different variations of the state-dependent classifications (Wilkinson et al., 2000; Tomlinson et al., 2013b).

12.4.5 Mechanism underlying sex differences

This line of inquiry is key to identifying the super-excretor phenotype, but to understand what drives sex-linked differences, potential underlying mechanisms need to be considered, which could be behavioural, ecological, or immunological. Work by Tomlinson et al. (2013b) found infected male badgers had both reduced survival and increased weight loss consistent with testosterone-induced immuno-suppression in males, although this study could not rule out other indirect factors that could be contributing to sex-related differences, such as behavioural differences. The fitting of individual CMR models to the Woodchester data set provided a statistical means to compare competing hypotheses using Bayesian survival trajectory analysis (BaSTA; Colchero et al., 2012). This framework allows testing of a range of mortality functions, which in this badger system can be applied to estimate time of infection as a latent variable and consequently to evaluate the effect of sex on survival post-infection. BaSTA provided the means to investigate alternative hypotheses in the absence of individual immunological traits. Comparison of the mortality curves between males and females following infection pointed to a logistic function consisting of a more rapid increase in male

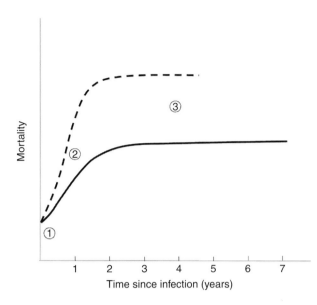

Figure 12.3 Logistic mortality trajectory of male (dashed) and female (solid) badgers following infection. At the point of infection (1) mortality rates are comparable. However, males have elevated rates of mortality increase following infection (2). Males and females show similar levels of heterogeneity in disease response as highlighted from the degree of deceleration (3). Figure adapted from McDonald et al. (2014).

mortality rates following infection driving sex differences (McDonald et al., 2014; Figure 12.3). The susceptibility of males to bTB is suggested to be due to immunological differences between the sexes. This result has been corroborated with trait-based approaches, as male badgers have been found to have weaker immune responses (as indicated by IFN-γ) than females (Tomlinson et al., 2015; Beirne et al., 2016). There is also strong support that progression of disease to an infectious stage is associated with a reduction in the IFN-γ response (Beirne et al., 2016).

12.4.6 Conclusion

Life-history data from the Woodchester Park badger population clearly demonstrate the presence of different states of bTB infection within and among individual hosts. Empirical data and theoretical models suggest the importance of distinguishing between infected and infectious (diseased) individuals, which provides a deeper understanding of individuals at high risk of developing and transmitting the disease. Being male is one key determinant of a 'super-excretor' phenotype, with increased detection of bacilli excretion. Novel modelling approaches paired with routine diagnostic testing indicate that immunological differences may explain the strong sex differences we observe. However, the possibility that physiological differences between sexes are linked to socio-spatial behaviour is an important area of future research.

Additionally, empirical demographic models provide biologically relevant disease classes, minimising uncertainty in influential parameters for mathematical models. Empirical data from the Woodchester Park population have been used to parameterise many models of bTB in badgers, and the state-dependent mortality rates described above have fed into recent models exploring the management of infection in both badgers and cattle (Smith et al., 2016).

Transmission events are not only defined by the infectiousness of the host, but also by the opportunities for disease transfer, which arise from its social interactions. The pattern of lesion development observed in infected badgers is largely consistent with direct contact via aerosol transmission or bite wounding (Jenkins et al., 2008, 2012); therefore, how individuals interact with one another will be crucial to understanding the role of super-excretors in the onward spread of infection. This brings us onto our second concept, the exploration of contact heterogeneity and opportunities for disease transfer.

12.5 Concept two: the spread of disease in spatially structured hosts – how individuals interact

12.5.1 Historical background

Transmission events require (1) an infected host and (2) meaningful contact with a susceptible individual. The first is driven by infectiousness and pathogen shedding (Section 12.4), the second by means of contact events during which transmission can occur.

Population density and social group size are metrics that have commonly been used to approximate contact likelihood, with larger populations or groups assumed to have a greater number of contact events, in accordance with the assumption of random mixing. While these metrics allow comparison of variability of contacts between populations or groups, they do not reflect individual-level variation in movement patterns. Interactions can occur between populations, between social groups, and within social groups. These interactions encompass many different behaviours such as local movement, dispersal, aggressive encounters, reproductive events, and communal living, each of which can contribute to disease spread, creating a complex mix of potential transmission routes with different weightings. Consequently, certain individuals can contribute disproportionately to disease spread by merit of their interactions with conspecifics. Recent studies of the Woodchester Park badger population have reflected a more general movement away from the traditional assumption of randomly mixing homogeneous populations, towards a recognition of heterogeneity in host association patterns at a group, class, and individual level (McDonald et al., 2018).

12.5.2 Background to social group living

A defining characteristic of badgers in the UK is their sociality. Although the social structure of badger populations varies across their geographic range, in many parts of the UK they form distinct social groups consisting of as many as 27 individuals (Rogers et al., 1997; Woodroffe et al., 2009; Roper, 2010) and defending an exclusive territory. They construct shared underground burrow systems called setts and spend up to 70% of their time below ground (Roper, 2010). Most social group territories in medium- to high-density populations contain a main sett and several smaller outlying setts. The core of the study area at Woodchester Park contains 21–23 badger social groups (Figure 12.4), a high density of badgers although similar to those studied elsewhere in the UK (Roper, 2010). A long-term pattern of clustering of bTB infection in the badger population was consistent with heterogeneity in infection risks (Delahay et al., 2000), perhaps promoted by higher rates of direct contact within social groups than among them. Consequently, social structure is likely to be a critical determinant of infection risk in badgers. This is borne out by evidence of the spatial clustering of *M. bovis* infection (Woodroffe et al., 2005) and of *M. bovis* strain types (Kelly et al., 2010) in badger populations elsewhere.

12.5.3 Within-group transmission

Previous work has found that the single most important factor in determining the infection risk of an individual is the number of infectious badgers within the social group (Vicente et al., 2007), with infectious females being of particular importance (Delahay et al., 2000; Tomlinson et al., 2013a). This is perhaps unsurprising given the sociality and shared space use of social group members. Within-group transmission is particularly important for cubs born into groups with infected adults. Cubs remain underground for 8 weeks following birth, and spend time in close contact with their mother, weaning at about 12 weeks of age. Offspring born into social groups with infectious females are at higher risk of infection (Tomlinson et al., 2013a), and this risk increases when cubs are related to the infectious females (Benton et al., 2016). Also, recent work suggests that related males may play a role in within-group transmission (Benton et al., 2016), although the exact mechanism remains largely unknown. These results highlight that the risk of infection in early life may be particularly linked to kin and sex.

12.5.4 Among-group transmission

The organisation of badger populations into social groups is suggested to mitigate disease spread, with neighbouring groups experiencing dissimilar trends in incidence (Delahay et al., 2000). However, given the chronic nature of *M. bovis* infection in badgers and the longevity of infected hosts, infection is able to persist. Consequently, despite relatively low levels of intergroup

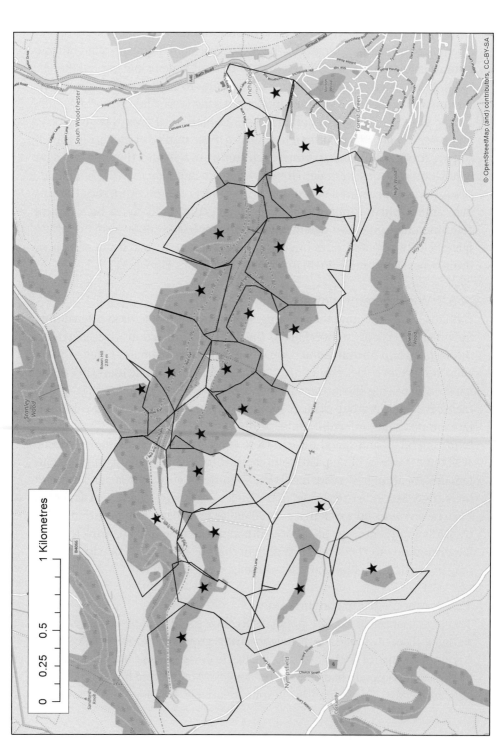

© OpenStreetMap (and) contributors, CC-BY-SA

Figure 12.4 Study area map showing the spatial distribution of badger main setts (black stars) and territory boundaries (polygons) at Woodchester Park in 1993.

movement, studies have shown that infection risk at the level of the population (Rogers et al., 1998), the social group, and the individual (Vicente et al.,
2007) are strongly related to movement patterns. Interestingly, movements
both in and out of social groups and hence fluctuating group size were found
to drive infection risks at an individual and group level (Vicente et al., 2007).
Males may be particularly important for between-group transmission as they
are more likely to move (Cheeseman et al., 1988; Rogers et al., 1998). This
behaviour may be driven by the search for breeding opportunities, with extra-
group males being responsible for approximately 50% of paternity in this
study population (Carpenter et al., 2005). Higher rates of movement in males
are likely to increase opportunities for aggressive encounters with animals
from neighbouring groups, which may be responsible for the increased bite
wounding observed in males from a range of study populations (Macdonald
et al., 2004; Delahay et al., 2006; Jenkins et al., 2008). Bite wounding has also
been implicated as a potential mode of transmission that could result in rapid
disease progression (Gallagher & Nelson, 1979; Clifton-Hadley et al., 1993;
Jenkins et al., 2008).

12.5.5 Social networks

The deployment of proximity loggers on badgers has allowed detailed
information on patterns of within- and between-group interaction to be
collected from the Woodchester Park badger population, finding clear
differences in social behaviour between bTB test-positive and test-
negative badgers. By comparing different descriptive measures, Weber
et al. (2013b) found that test-positive badgers occupied a distinct position
in the social network. These badgers had lower within-group contacts
(frequency and duration) and were more socially isolated from their resident group. However, these same individuals contributed to a greater
extent to all possible pathways of connection in the network. Radio-
tracking studies provided further evidence for differential behaviour in
relation to infection status as test-positive badgers were more likely to use
outlier setts, hence spending more time at the territorial margins (Weber
et al., 2013a). Together these studies suggest a propensity among infected
badgers to interact less frequently with their own group and more with
individuals from other groups. Overall, these results paint a picture of
test-positive badgers spending more time at territorial margins, interacting longer with neighbouring groups, and experiencing shorter within-
group contact times. The characteristics of these individuals is more
nuanced than that of the traditional super spreader; considered spread-
capacitors, infected badgers may act as transmission bridges between
groups, but they are not highly connected in all aspects of the network
(Weber et al., 2013b).

12.5.6 Implications for disease management

At the population level, stable structure mitigates the spread of disease (Delahay et al., 2000). Increased movement of badgers has been linked to increased infection risks at the level of the individual, social group, and population. Also, test-positive badgers occupy a distinctive position in the network. Consequently, when populations are stable these individuals may stabilise the flow of infection between groups; however, they also have the potential to increase spread of infection if social structure is disrupted. This work has shed light on the potential epidemiological consequences of culling-induced social perturbation (see Carter et al., 2007), and is consistent with the contention that disruption of social structure is likely to increase infection risk. The application of dynamic network models to simultaneously account for co-dynamics in the network structure and infection status will further enable researchers to reveal the underlying causation (Silk et al., 2017b). Going forward, the incorporation of empirically derived contact network models into epidemiological models would provide a robust modelling frame-work and has been highlighted as an important area of future research (Silk et al., 2017b).

12.5.7 Conclusion

Pathogens that are spread by direct contact are thought to be more prevalent in larger groups where contacts are more ubiquitous. However, empirical evidence from field studies of wildlife, including the Woodchester Park badger population, suggests an underlying contact structure that is not random. Social group living in badgers and the chronic nature of *M. bovis* infection in individual hosts allow infection to persist in clusters in badger populations. The risks of onward spread are profoundly influenced by interactions and movement within and between social groups. This intricate relationship between host social structure and pathogen dynamics can have counter-productive consequences for management interventions.

12.6 Concept three: host population demography

12.6.1 Historical background

Epidemiology and demography are interdependent population studies. The incidence and distribution of disease can have profound effects on demo-graphic parameters (births, deaths); equally, demographic mechanisms may reduce or exacerbate the impact of disease on population dynamics.

In theoretical studies, density-dependent demographic compensation can allow host populations to persist despite disease-induced mortality, with density-dependent recruitment highlighted as a key driver of population stability (Anderson & May, 1981; Thrall et al., 1993). For example, if local density is reduced due to disease-induced mortality, then competition for resources diminishes and the remaining individuals may be able to invest more in reproduction, resulting in increased recruitment of offspring into the population. The propensity for host populations to compensate in this way is thought to be linked to species-specific life-history traits. Natural selection should favour the buffering (reduction in variability) of an organism's most important vital rate (Pfister, 1998; Gaillard et al., 2000). The demographic characteristics of a slow life-history strategist (low recruitment and high adult survival) indicate survival is most influential; therefore, any density-dependent pressures are anticipated to manifest themselves through variability in recruitment rates. Long-term demographic data from the Woodchester Park badger population have been used to explore such compensatory processes.

12.6.2 Patterns of badger demography

The Woodchester Park badger population has fluctuated in size over the past 40 years of study. The prevalence and incidence of *M. bovis* infection in the population have also varied widely, but appear to bear no simple relationship with population density (Rogers et al., 1997; Delahay et al., 2013). Additionally, underlying demographic parameters (survival, reproduction) have been found to be highly variable (Rogers et al., 1997; Carpenter et al., 2005). In the absence of a comprehensive demographic analysis, however, understanding potential drivers of disease prevalence and incidence is challenging.

12.6.3 Integrated modelling framework

Many wildlife studies focus on population dynamics in terms of abundance estimates. The alternative approach is to focus on demographic drivers. However, the two are intrinsically linked; temporal changes in population abundance are a direct result of variations in demographic rates which in turn can be driven by a wide range of covariates. The complexity of population regulation is likely greater than any one individual component. The integrated population model (IPM) provides a statistical framework to explicitly link demographic rates with population dynamics, simultaneously providing more precise estimates of population size, recruitment, and survival.

The 'integrated' part of the IPM refers to the linking of two models. First, the population model, termed the state–space model, analyses count data. Accounting for observation error and demographic stochasticity, population counts are linked to demographic rates via a state equation, akin to a population model. A typical transition equation for females assuming a pre-breeding census is

$$\begin{bmatrix} N_1 \\ N_a \end{bmatrix}_{t+1} = \begin{pmatrix} \phi_j \frac{f}{2} & \phi_j \frac{f}{2} \\ \phi_a & \phi_a \end{pmatrix} \begin{bmatrix} N_1 \\ N_a \end{bmatrix}_t \tag{12.1}$$

where N_1 and N_a denote the number of one-year-old badgers and adult badgers aged ≥ 2 years old, respectively. Φ_j and Φ_a are the annual survival probabilities of juvenile and adult badgers, and f is the number of offspring produced per female (assuming there is an even sex ratio, this is divided by two). To include demographic stochasticity into the above process, an appropriate distribution is required. A Poisson distribution is appropriate to represent the number of one-year-old badgers as it yields a value between zero, assuming no births, and a large number, if reproduction is great. The binomial distribution is used to represent survival and is appropriate for modelling the number of adult badgers, generating a bounded count between zero, no adults surviving, and N_a, all adults surviving. An observation process then links the above 'true' population size to the observed population counts. Observation error (σ^2) can have different distributions; in the model discussed below a Poisson distribution was adopted, although a normal and log-normal can also be used (Kéry & Schaub, 2011).

Second, the CMR model, most commonly a Cormack–Jolly–Seber (CJS) model, analyses capture data to obtain survival estimates accounting for detection probability. This model allows both survival (Φ) and recapture probabilities (p) to vary with time.

By combining a state–space model with a CJS model, information is shared, and a powerful statistical tool is created that allows the dynamics of the population to be considered in its entirety, thus improving parameter precision and reducing any inconsistencies that might emerge from separate analyses. Covariates and potential sources of heterogeneity are easily incorporated into the framework, improving the detection of mechanisms driving age- and sex-specific survival ($\Phi_{a,s}$) and recruitment (f), such as density, disease, and environmental effects (Figure 12.5).

12.6.4 Demographic covariates

Using a Bayesian IPM to analyse the Woodchester Park badger population data provided estimates of key population processes from 1984 to 2006 (McDonald et al., 2016). Similar to previous studies, significant interannual changes in population density were detected, although the population remained relatively stable for the duration of the time period. However, incorporation of the underlying demographic rates revealed population change that was generated by low and variable recruitment rates and high and less-variable survival rates. These demographic characteristics indicate that badgers have evolved a relatively slow life-history strategy.

By incorporating disease and density as potential agents of population change into the IPM, survival rates were revealed to be susceptible to disease prevalence but resilient to density-dependent pressures. Instead, density-dependence had the greatest effect on recruitment rates, and was found to be a key driver of overall population dynamics.

$$L_{IPM}(y,m \mid N, \phi_{a,s}, f, p, \sigma^2_y) = L_{SS}(y \mid N, \phi_a, f, \sigma^2_y) \times L_{CJS}(m \mid \phi_{a,s}, p)$$

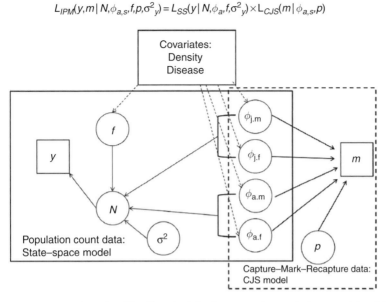

Figure 12.5 The joint likelihood of the integrated population model, which is the product of the state–space model and the Cormack–Jolly–Seber model, along with a graphical representation of an integrated population model. Small squares represent data (y: population counts, m: capture–mark–recapture data), large squares are submodels. Model fragments borrow from each other to identify parameters previously unidentifiable and improve precision of parameters, which are shown in circles, including for sex-dependent adult (Φ_a) and cub (Φ_j) survival, productivity (f) and observation error (σ^2). Temporal covariates can be naturally incorporated into this analysis to act on demographic components (dashed arrows).

Given the greater influence of survival to fitness, its insensitivity to density-dependent pressures is beneficial for population persistence (Pfister, 1998; Gaillard et al., 2000). Additionally, density-dependent recruitment provides a potential mechanism to compensate for any effect of disease-induced mortality on population dynamics. Sequential capture data from Woodchester Park show that badgers are able to reproduce successfully despite infection (Tomlinson et al., 2013b). Therefore, increased recruitment due to density reductions is likely to occur despite infection. This mechanism helps to explain how *M. bovis* infection is able to persist in badger populations.

12.6.5 Applied implications

Demographic patterns reveal that density-dependent recruitment will influence the extent and rate of recovery of badger populations that are subject to management for the control of disease. Compensatory density-dependent recruitment may result in increased births of susceptible badgers in response to population declines due to culling. Hence any reductions in the numbers of infected hosts achieved through culling could be at least in part offset by the introduction of more susceptible hosts. This could potentially compound the counter-productive impact of culling-induced perturbation of social structures, which has itself been linked to enhanced opportunities for disease transmission (Carter et al., 2007). In contrast, approaches such as vaccination would maintain population density and therefore reduce the likelihood of an increase in compensatory recruitment.

12.6.6 Conclusion

Integrated population models are a powerful recent tool in ecological studies and in this case provided simultaneous estimation of the impact of disease, density, and environment on badger survival and recruitment rates. Density-dependence impacted rates of recruitment, not survival, and was a strong determinant of badger population dynamics, while adult survival declined with increasing prevalence of diseased individuals. This improved understanding may help us better predict the likely consequences of management interventions to control bTB risks from badgers.

Additionally, broader integration of life-history theory with disease ecology can aid in identifying the drivers of host population and infection persistence. This work on bTB in badgers explored empirical links between life history and reservoir persistence, a concept previously largely confined to the theoretical literature. Although our understanding of this mechanism is at an early stage, it suggests that density-dependent recruitment may cause similar patterns of population persistence in other chronically infected slow–life-history strategists. Work is needed to explore this concept further across a range of both fast– and slow–life-history species.

Although numerous approaches are available to estimate demographic parameters from longitudinal data sets, few are capable of estimating individual and population processes simultaneously. A shortfall of this approach is that it currently fails to incorporate the intricate social structuring and variability in infectiousness. However, with computational advancement and model development the IPM provides flexibility to incorporate additional components, including multi-state models (Section 12.4), and potentially indices of network position (Section 12.5).

12.7 Unanswered questions

Many physiological and behavioural traits correlate with the acquisition of a pathogen, the progression of disease, and subsequent onwards transmission. The challenge now is to investigate these relationships for deeper causal factors. For example, increased exposure and susceptibility to infection in male badgers is intertwined with pursuit of reproductive opportunity. Males play a key role in territorial defence, with the suggestion that many enter territories of other social groups for mating opportunities (Carpenter et al., 2005; Weber et al., 2013a). Additionally, males occasionally disperse and are more likely to do so to groups with a higher proportion of female residents (Rogers et al., 1998; Macdonald et al., 2008). These behaviours secure reproductive opportunity, yet may also be associated with increased bite wounding, a transmission route that can lead to more rapid disease dissemination (Gallagher & Nelson, 1979; Clifton-Hadley et al., 1993), and potentially physiological stress, which could reduce immunocompetence and influence disease susceptibility. Indeed, physiological stress is correlated with bTB infection in another badger population (George et al., 2014). Therefore, although we know socio-spatial behaviour and physiology influence disease characteristics, understanding the relative roles of these intertwined processes requires further work.

A major theme of this chapter has been exploring correlates of increased infection risk, susceptibility, and disease progression. A key area for future work is the role that genetic inheritance may play in these processes. Studies to date have used microsatellite markers to show that the disease status of kin influences the probability that a cub may become infected (Benton et al., 2016) and immune function has been linked to genetic variation in a separate badger population (Sin et al., 2014). However, to tease apart the potential for kin-biased behaviour and heritability in disease outcome requires knowledge of the relationships and/or relatedness among individuals in a population, also known as a pedigree. Badgers give birth and care for young below ground, making it impossible to determine relationships among individuals from behavioural observation alone. Instead, molecular data must be used to determine a pedigree. This approach requires a large amount of data, which has limited its scope in wild populations to date (Clutton-Brock & Sheldon, 2010), with even fewer studies exploring causal quantitative genetic components for pathogen susceptibility (but see Graham et al., 2010). The imminent reconstruction of a 'molecular' pedigree for the Woodchester Park badger population will open up many new avenues of research. Combining health information with the pedigree will identify genetic variants involved in the susceptibility to bTB, and the potential for resistance to be heritable. Specifically, by statistically quantifying the relationship between the relatedness (genetic similarity) of individuals and similarity of a trait, such as disease acquisition and/or progression, heritability in disease outcome can be estimated. These types of 'animal models' developed in quantitative genetics can account for the confounding effects of environmental factors, partitioning the components of variance that occur in natural populations (Kruuk, 2004). This research can link with previous work on telomere length (Beirne et al., 2014, 2016) and immunocompetence (Tomlinson et al., 2012, 2015) to look at the mechanisms that promote heritable immunocompetence. Also, estimating genetic covariances with other life-history traits provides a further means to study individual-level trade-offs and life histories; for example, trade-offs between immune system and maturation time or reproductive output.

Finally, field studies of disease in wildlife populations suffer from the problem of imperfect diagnostic tests. This requires empirical analyses to make assumptions regarding the disease state of an individual based on its test result. Consequently, infection state misclassification can occur, potentially resulting in bias. Models that account for uncertainty and determine the probability of infection have been used to explore the badger–bTB system (Drewe et al., 2010; Buzdugan et al., 2017). However, the solutions to date are not perfect, being unable to account for the potentially dynamic nature of specificity (false-positives) and sensitivity (false-negatives). Integrating a dynamic multi-event model that takes account of uncertainty in state (Pradel, 2005) into demographic models, such as those discussed in this chapter, would be a valuable next step.

12.8 Overall conclusions

Since being identified as a reservoir for *M. bovis* infection in the 1970s, badgers have been the subject of much field research. The current knowledge of badger ecology and epidemiology has highlighted many complexities, some of which are discussed in this chapter. For instance, work at Woodchester Park identified disease states of varying severity beyond the traditional classifications often incorporated in empirical and theoretical studies. Badgers can experience a variety of disease states, each with differing levels of infectiousness and mortality rates. They also live in highly structured social groups, creating clusters of disease across the population. Consequently, social stability may help mitigate disease spread. Some interesting nuances arise when exploring the socio-spatial behaviour of infected badgers. Test-positive badgers are more likely to occupy distinct network positions, with high among-group contacts and low within-group contacts. This result indicates that in badger populations, there is more to being a superspreader than high contacts. This may in due course be shown to be the case in other disease systems. Furthermore, demographic intricacies including compensatory recruitment rates provide further understanding of the mechanisms underpinning the persistence of infection in badger populations. The understanding gained from long-term host–pathogen field systems with individual-based data across generations plays an important role in the development of ecological and evolutionary theory and usefully informs the development of evidence-based disease control strategies.

12.9 Acknowledgements

We thank the APHA team at Woodchester Park (past and present) for conducting the research. The study has been supported by the UK Department for Environment, Food & Rural Affairs. We thank NERC for funding; NE/M004546/1 awarded to RD and RAM, JLM research was motivated by NE/M010260/1 and is currently supported by NE/L007770/1.

References

Anderson, R.M. & May, R.M. (1978) Regulation and stability of host–parasite population interactions: I. Regulatory processes. *Journal of Animal Ecology*, **47**, 219–247.

Anderson, R.M. & May, R.M. (1981) The population dynamics of microparasites and their invertebrate hosts. *Philosophical Transactions of the Royal Society of London B: Biological Sciences*, **291**, 451–524.

Aznar, I., Frankena, K., More, S. J., et al. (2018). Quantification of *Mycobacterium bovis* transmission in a badger vaccine field trial. *Preventive Veterinary Medicine*, **149**, 29–37.

Beirne, C., Delahay, R., Hares, M. & Young, A. (2014) Age-related declines and disease-associated variation in immune cell telomere length in a wild mammal. *PLoS ONE*, **9**, e108964.

Beirne, C., Waring, L., McDonald, R.A., Delahay, R. & Young, A. (2016) Age-related declines in immune response in a wild mammal are unrelated to immune cell telomere length. *Proceedings of the Royal Society of London B*, **283**, 20152949.

Benton, C.H., Delahay, R.J., Robertson, A., et al. (2016) Blood thicker than water: kinship, disease prevalence and group size drive divergent patterns of infection risk in a social mammal. *Proceedings of the Royal Society of London B*, **283**, 20160798.

Blanchong, J.A., Scribner, K.T., Kravchenko, A.N. & Winterstein, S.R. (2007) TB-infected deer are more closely related than non-infected deer. *Biology Letters*, **3**, 104–106.

Buzdugan, S.N., Vergne, T., Grosbois, V., Delahay, R.J. & Drewe, J.A. (2017) Inference of the infection status of individuals using longitudinal testing data from cryptic populations: towards a probabilistic approach to diagnosis. *Scientific Reports*, **7**, 1111.

Carpenter, P.J., Pope, L.C., Greig, C., et al. (2005) Mating system of the Eurasian badger, *Meles meles*, in a high density population. *Molecular Ecology*, **14**, 273–284.

Carter, S.P., Chambers, M.A., Rushton, S.P., et al. (2012) BCG vaccination reduces risk of tuberculosis infection in vaccinated badgers and unvaccinated badger cubs. *PLoS ONE*, **7**, e49833.

Carter, S.P., Delahay, R.J., Smith, G.C., et al. (2007) Culling-induced social perturbation in Eurasian badgers *Meles meles* and the management of TB in cattle: an analysis of a critical problem in applied ecology. *Proceedings of the Royal Society of London B*, **274**, 2769–2777.

Chambers, M.A., Aldwell, F., Williams, G.A., et al. (2017) The effect of oral vaccination with *Mycobacterium bovis* BCG on the development of tuberculosis in captive European badgers (*Meles meles*). *Frontiers in Cellular and Infection Microbiology*, **7**(6).

Chambers, M.A., Rogers, F., Delahay, R.J., et al. (2011) Bacillus Calmette–Guérin vaccination reduces the severity and progression of tuberculosis in badgers. *Proceedings of the Royal Society of London B*, **278**, 1913–1920.

Cheeseman, C., Wilesmith, J., Stuart, F. & Mallinson, P. (1988) Dynamics of tuberculosis in a naturally infected badger population. *Mammal Review*, **18**, 61–72.

Clifton-Hadley, R., Wilesmith, J. & Stuart, F. (1993) *Mycobacterium bovis* in the European badger (*Meles meles*): epidemiological findings in tuberculous badgers from a naturally infected population. *Epidemiology and Infection*, **111**, 9–19.

Clutton-Brock, T. & Sheldon, B.C. (2010) Individuals and populations: the role of long-term, individual-based studies of animals in ecology and evolutionary biology. *Trends in Ecology & Evolution*, **25**, 562–573.

Colchero, F., Jones, O.R. & Rebke, M. (2012) BaSTA: an R package for Bayesian estimation of age-specific survival from incomplete mark–recapture/recovery data with covariates. *Methods in Ecology and Evolution*, **3**, 466–470.

Corner, L.A., O'Meara, D., Costello, E., Lesellier, S. & Gormley, E. (2012) The distribution of *Mycobacterium bovis* infection in naturally infected badgers. *The Veterinary Journal*, **194**, 166–172.

Delahay, R., Langton, S., Smith, G., Clifton-Hadley, R. & Cheeseman, C. (2000) The spatio-temporal distribution of *Mycobacterium bovis* (bovine tuberculosis) infection in a high-density badger population. *Journal of Animal Ecology*, **69**, 428–441.

Delahay, R., Walker, N., Forrester, G., et al. (2006) Demographic correlates of bite wounding in Eurasian badgers, *Meles meles* L., in stable and perturbed populations. *Animal Behaviour*, **71**, 1047–1055.

Delahay, R., Walker, N., Smith, G., et al. (2013) Long-term temporal trends and estimated transmission rates for *Mycobacterium bovis* infection in an undisturbed high-density badger (*Meles meles*) population. *Epidemiology and Infection*, **141**, 1445–1456.

Donnelly, C.A., Wei, G., Johnston, W.T., et al. (2007) Impacts of widespread badger culling on cattle tuberculosis: concluding analyses from a large-scale field trial. *International Journal of Infectious Diseases*, **11**, 300–308.

Donnelly, C.A., Woodroffe, R., Cox, D., et al. (2003) Impact of localized badger culling on tuberculosis incidence in British cattle. *Nature*, **426**, 834–837.

Donnelly, C.A., Woodroffe, R., Cox, D., et al. (2006) Positive and negative effects of widespread badger culling on tuberculosis in cattle. *Nature*, **439**, 843–846.

Drewe, J.A., Tomlinson, A.J., Walker, N.J. & Delahay, R.J. (2010) Diagnostic accuracy and optimal use of three tests for tuberculosis in live badgers. *PLoS ONE*, **5**, e11196.

Gaillard, J.-M., Festa-Bianchet, M., Yoccoz, N., Loison, A. & Toigo, C. (2000) Temporal variation in fitness components and population dynamics of large herbivores. *Annual Review of Ecology and Systematics*, **31**, 367–393.

Gaillard, J., Lemaître, J., Berger, V., et al. (2016) Life history axes of variation. In: *The Encyclopedia of Evolutionary Biology* (pp. 312–323). Oxford: Academic Press.

Gallagher, J. & Clifton-Hadley, R. (2000) Tuberculosis in badgers; a review of the disease and its significance for other animals. *Research in Veterinary Science*, **69**, 203–217.

Gallagher, J., Muirhead, R. & Burn, K. (1976) Tuberculosis in wild badgers (*Meles meles*) in Gloucestershire: pathology. *Veterinary Record*, **98**, 9–14.

Gallagher, J. & Nelson, J. (1979) Cause of ill health and natural death in badgers in Gloucestershire. *Tuberculosis*, **10**, 14–16.

George, S.C., Smith, T.E., Mac Cana, P.S., Coleman, R. & Montgomery, W.I. (2014) Physiological stress in the Eurasian badger (*Meles meles*): effects of host, disease and environment. *General and Comparative Endocrinology*, **200**, 54–60.

Graham, A.L., Hayward, A.D., Watt, K.A., et al. (2010) Fitness correlates of heritable variation in antibody responsiveness in a wild mammal. *Science*, **330**, 662–665.

Graham, J., Smith, G., Delahay, R., et al. (2013) Multi-state modelling reveals sex-dependent transmission, progression and severity of tuberculosis in wild badgers. *Epidemiology and Infection*, **141**, 1429–1436.

Jenkins, H.E., Cox, D. & Delahay, R.J. (2012) Direction of association between bite wounds and *Mycobacterium bovis* infection in badgers: implications for transmission. *PLoS ONE*, **7**, e45584.

Jenkins, H.E., Morrison, W., Cox, D., et al. (2008) The prevalence, distribution and severity of detectable pathological lesions in badgers naturally infected with *Mycobacterium bovis*. *Epidemiology and Infection*, **136**, 1350–1361.

Johnson, P.T., Rohr, J.R., Hoverman, J.T., et al. (2012) Living fast and dying of infection: host life history drives interspecific variation in infection and disease risk. *Ecology Letters*, **15**, 235–242.

Joly, D.O., Samuel, M.D., Langenberg, J.A., et al. (2006) Spatial epidemiology of chronic wasting disease in Wisconsin white-tailed deer. *Journal of Wildlife Diseases*, **42**, 578–588.

Keeling, M.J. & Danon, L. (2009) Mathematical modelling of infectious diseases. *British Medical Bulletin*, **92**, 33–42.

Kelly, G.E., McGrath, G. & More, S.J. (2010) Estimating the extent of spatial association of *Mycobacterium bovis* infection in badgers in Ireland. *Epidemiology and Infection*, **138**, 270–279.

Kéry, M. & Schaub, M. (2011) *Bayesian Population Analysis Using WinBUGS: A Hierarchical Perspective*. New York, NY: Academic Press.

Kramer-Schadt, S., Fernández, N., Eisinger, D., Grimm, V. & Thulke, H.H. (2009) Individual variations in infectiousness explain long-term disease persistence in wildlife populations. *Oikos*, **118**, 199–208.

Kruuk, L.E. (2004) Estimating genetic parameters in natural populations using the 'animal model'. *Philosophical Transactions of the Royal Society of London B: Biological Sciences*, **359**, 873–890.

Lebreton, J.D., Nichols, J.D., Barker, R.J., Pradel, R. & Spendelow, J.A. (2009) Modeling individual animal histories with multistate capture–recapture models. *Advances in Ecological Research*, **41**, 87–173.

Lesellier, S., Palmer, S., Gowtage-Sequiera, S., et al. (2011) Protection of Eurasian badgers (*Meles meles*) from tuberculosis after intra-muscular vaccination with different doses of BCG. *Vaccine*, **29**, 3782–3790.

Lloyd-Smith, J.O., Schreiber, S.J., Kopp, P.E. & Getz, W.M. (2005) Superspreading and the effect of individual variation on disease emergence. *Nature*, **438**, 355–359.

Macdonald, D., Harmsen, B., Johnson, P. & Newman, C. (2004) Increasing frequency of bite wounds with increasing population density in Eurasian badgers, *Meles meles*. *Animal Behaviour*, **67**, 745–751.

Macdonald, D.W., Newman, C., Buesching, C.D. & Johnson, P.J. (2008) Male-biased movement in a high-density population of the Eurasian badger (*Meles meles*). *Journal of Mammalogy*, **89**, 1077–1086.

May, R.M. & Anderson, R.M. (1979) Population biology of infectious diseases: Part II. *Nature*, **280**, 455–461.

McDonald, J.L., Bailey, T., Delahay, R.J., et al. (2016) Demographic buffering and compensatory recruitment promotes the persistence of disease in a wildlife population. *Ecology Letters*, **19**, 443–449.

McDonald, J.L., Robertson, A. & Silk, M.J. (2018) Wildlife disease ecology from the individual to the population: Insights from a long-term study of a naturally infected European badger population. *Journal of Animal Ecology*, **87**, 101–112.

McDonald, J.L., Smith, G.C., McDonald, R.A., Delahay, R.J. & Hodgson, D. (2014) Mortality trajectory analysis reveals the drivers of sex-specific epidemiology in natural wildlife–disease interactions. *Proceedings of the Royal Society of London B*, **281**, 20140526.

McDonald, R.A., Delahay, R.J., Carter, S.P., Smith, G.C. & Cheeseman, C.L. (2008) Perturbing implications of wildlife ecology for disease control. *Trends in Ecology & Evolution*, **23**, 53–56.

Murhead, R.M. & Burns, K.J. (1974) Tuberculosis in wild badgers in Gloucestershire: epidemiology. *Veterinary Record*, **95**, 552–555.

Ostfeld, R.S., Levi, T., Jolles, A.E., et al. (2014) Life history and demographic drivers of reservoir competence for three tick-borne zoonotic pathogens. *PLoS ONE*, **9**, e107387.

Palphramand, K., Delahay, R., Robertson, A., et al. (2017) Field evaluation of candidate baits for oral delivery of BCG vaccine to European badgers, *Meles meles*. *Vaccine*, **35**, 4402–4407.

Pfister, C.A. (1998) Patterns of variance in stage-structured populations: evolutionary predictions and ecological implications. *Proceedings of the National Academy of Sciences of the United States of America*, **95**, 213–218.

Pradel, R. (2005) Multievent: an extension of multistate capture–recapture models to uncertain states. *Biometrics*, **61**, 442–447.

Rogers, L., Cheeseman, C., Mallinson, P. & Clifton-Hadley, R. (1997) The demography of a high-density badger (*Meles meles*) population in the west of England. *Journal of Zoology*, **242**, 705–728.

Rogers, L., Delahay, R., Cheeseman, C., et al. (1998) Movement of badgers (*Meles meles*) in a high–density population: individual, population and disease effects. *Proceedings of the Royal Society of London B*, **265**, 1269–1276.

Roper, T. (2010) *Badger (Collins New Naturalist Library, Book 114)*. London: HarperCollins UK.

Rushmore, J., Caillaud, D., Matamba, L., et al. (2013) Social network analysis of wild chimpanzees provides insights for predicting infectious disease risk. *Journal of Animal Ecology*, **82**, 976–986.

Shirley, M.D., Rushton, S.P., Smith, G.C., South, A.B. & Lurz, P.W. (2003) Investigating the spatial dynamics of bovine tuberculosis in badger populations: evaluating an individual-based simulation model. *Ecological Modelling*, **167**, 139–157.

Silk, M.J., Croft, D.P., Delahay, R.J., et al. (2017a) Using social network measures in wildlife disease ecology, epidemiology, and management. *BioScience*, **67**, 245–257.

Silk, M.J., Croft, D.P., Delahay, R.J., et al. (2017b) The application of statistical network models in disease research. *Methods in Ecology and Evolution*, **8**, 1026–1041.

Sin, Y.W., Annavi, G., Dugdale, H.L., et al. (2014) Pathogen burden, co-infection and major histocompatibility complex variability in the European badger (*Meles meles*). *Molecular Ecology*, **23**, 5072–5088.

Smith, G.C., Delahay, R.J., McDonald, R.A. & Budgey, R. (2016) Model of selective and non-selective management of badgers (*Meles meles*) to control bovine tuberculosis in badgers and cattle. *PLoS ONE*, **11**, e0167206.

Smith, G.C., McDonald, R.A. & Wilkinson, D. (2012) Comparing badger (*Meles meles*) management strategies for reducing tuberculosis incidence in cattle. *PLoS ONE*, **7**, e39250.

Stearns, S.C. (1983) The influence of size and phylogeny on patterns of covariation among life-history traits in the mammals. *Oikos*, **41**, 173–187.

Thrall, P.H., Antonovics, J. & Hall, D.W. (1993) Host and pathogen coexistence in sexually transmitted and vector-borne diseases characterized by frequency-dependent disease transmission. *American Naturalist*, **142**, 543–552.

Tomlinson, A., Chambers, M., Carter, S., et al. (2013a) Heterogeneity in the risk of *Mycobacterium bovis* infection in European badger (*Meles meles*) cubs. *Epidemiology and Infection*, **141**, 1458–1466.

Tomlinson, A., Chambers, M. & Delahay, R. (2012) *Mycobacterium bovis* infection in badger cubs: re-assessing the evidence for maternally derived immunological protection from advanced disease. *Veterinary Immunology and Immunopathology*, **148**, 326–330.

Tomlinson, A., Chambers, M., Wilson, G., McDonald, R.A. & Delahay, R. (2013b) Sex-related heterogeneity in the life-history correlates of *Mycobacterium bovis* infection in European badgers (*Meles meles*). *Transboundary and Emerging Diseases*, **60**, 37–45.

Tomlinson, A.J., Chambers, M.A., McDonald, R.A. & Delahay, R.J. (2015) Association of quantitative interferon-γ responses with the progression of naturally acquired *Mycobacterium bovis* infection in wild European badgers (*Meles meles*). *Immunology*, **144**, 263–270.

Vicente, J., Delahay, R., Walker, N. & Cheeseman, C. (2007) Social organization and movement influence the incidence of bovine tuberculosis in an undisturbed high-density badger *Meles meles* population. *Journal of Animal Ecology*, **76**, 348–360.

Weber, N., Bearhop, S., Dall, S.R., et al. (2013a) Denning behaviour of the European badger (*Meles meles*) correlates with bovine tuberculosis infection status. *Behavioral Ecology and Sociobiology*, **67**, 471–479.

Weber, N., Carter, S.P., Dall, S.R., et al. (2013b) Badger social networks correlate with tuberculosis infection. *Current Biology*, **23**, R915–R916.

Wendland, L.D., Wooding, J., White, C.L., et al. (2010) Social behavior drives the dynamics of respiratory disease in threatened tortoises. *Ecology*, **91**, 1257–1262.

White, P.C. & Harris, S. (1995) Bovine tuberculosis in badger (*Meles meles*) populations in southwest England: the use of a spatial stochastic simulation model to understand the dynamics of the disease. *Philosophical Transactions of the Royal Society of London B: Biological Sciences*, **349**, 391–413.

Wilkinson, D., Smith, G., Delahay, R. & Cheeseman, C. (2004) A model of bovine tuberculosis in the badger *Meles meles*: an evaluation of different vaccination strategies. *Journal of Applied Ecology*, **41**, 492–501.

Wilkinson, D., Smith, G., Delahay, R., et al. (2000) The effects of bovine tuberculosis (*Mycobacterium bovis*) on mortality in a badger (*Meles meles*) population in England. *Journal of Zoology*, **250**, 389–395.

Woodroffe, R., Donnelly, C., Johnston, W., et al. (2005) Spatial association of *Mycobacterium bovis* infection in cattle and badgers *Meles meles*. *Journal of Applied Ecology*, **42**, 852–862.

Woodroffe, R., Donnelly, C.A., Wei, G., et al. (2009) Social group size affects *Mycobacterium bovis* infection in European badgers (*Meles meles*). *Journal of Animal Ecology*, **78**, 818–827.

CHAPTER THIRTEEN

Mycoplasma ovipneumoniae in bighorn sheep: from exploration to action

KEZIA MANLOVE, EMILY S. ALMBERG,
PAULINE L. KAMATH, RAINA K.
PLOWRIGHT, THOMAS E. BESSER AND
PETER J. HUDSON

13.1 Introduction

Bighorn sheep (*Ovis canadensis*) in the North American West have suffered an extended period of disease-related population decline since the arrival of European settlers. Domestic sheep and goats acted as reservoirs of infectious agents that spilled over into healthy bighorn sheep populations, often producing highly visible mass mortalities across all age groups. These die-offs were extensively – albeit opportunistically – documented throughout the twentieth century. The usual expectation is that host populations should rebound after epidemics, a pattern seen in wildlife diseases like phocine distemper (Klepac et al., 2009) and canine distemper (Almberg et al., 2012). However, pneumonia in bighorn sheep populations does not reliably comply with this expectation. Instead, all-age die-off events are often followed by years to decades of poor recruitment (Cassirer et al., 2013), largely due to persistent juvenile disease. Population growth rates during the many years of disease persistence are highly variable: in some years, nearly all juveniles die with disease symptoms, whereas in others most juveniles survive. The underlying factors leading to these differential outcomes remain uncertain, impeding agency response and policy development alike.

The bighorn sheep–pneumonia system highlights several crucial deficits in our ability to translate existing wildlife disease theory into effective management: the scarcity yet value of long-term studies; the limited framework linking within- and between-host disease dynamics; and the logistical challenges of managing wildlife disease. These shortcomings are compounded by crucial knowledge gaps in our understanding of the disease process itself, particularly the long-term carriage status and immune response in the bighorn host.

Pathogen spillover – the process by which infectious agents originating in one host species go on to infect individuals of a second, recipient host species – has been extensively studied in wildlife (e.g. Swinton et al., 1998;

Almberg et al., 2012). However, research has focused on acute impacts of the spillover, with much less attention on long-term epidemiology. This is despite the fact that growing numbers of wildlife systems are plagued by persistent yet highly lethal emerging diseases, such as white nose syndrome in bats (Langwig et al., 2012), chytridiomycosis in amphibians (Briggs et al., 2005), and *Mycoplasma conjunctivae* in bighorn sheep (Jansen et al., 2007). As a whole, wildlife disease ecology suffers from a deficit of long-term population-level studies documenting how pathogens transition from the transient dynamics surrounding pathogen introduction to endemism (Lloyd-Smith et al., 2009). One consequence of this knowledge gap is that we do not know how the relative importance of key parameters like infectious period, waning immunity rate, or probability of recrudescence changes through this transition. Weak data on longer-term parameters likely constrain our ability to forecast and manage newly endemic pathogens.

At this time, there is no generally accepted framework linking mechanisms that drive variation in within-host infectious period and infectiousness to population-level epidemiology. Understanding within-host mechanisms is critical in systems where the same agent can produce markedly different infections in different hosts. For example, in *Batrachochytrius dendrobatidis* (Bd) infections in amphibians, some species like the common eastern froglet (*Crinia signifera*) exhibit relatively minimal deleterious disease effects, whereas others like the northern corroboree frog (*Pseudophryne pengilleyi*) exhibit cataclysmic declines (Scheele et al., 2017). Similar diversity in host competence and importance for transmission has been observed for West Nile Virus, where the American robin (*Turdus migratorius*) plays a transmission role disproportionate to its representation in local communities, whereas the house sparrow (*Passer domesticus*) is significantly avoided by the *Culex* mosquito vectors and plays little role in transmission (Kilpatrick et al., 2006). For management of these pathogens, identifying and targeting superspreaders (individual hosts who create many secondary infections due to abnormally high sociality) or supershedders (individual hosts who create many secondary infections due to abnormally high probability of infection given contact) is crucial. Research on agents producing heterogeneous infections must be highly transdisciplinary, drawing extensively from veterinary, microbiological, genetics, and ecological research (Manlove et al., 2016b). Indeed, many pathogen–host projects that produced key insights and methodological developments for disease transmission processes – for example, phocine distemper virus in harbour seals (Swinton et al., 1998) and canine distemper virus among Serengeti carnivores (Craft et al., 2008) – included long-term studies of individually identifiable animals with a consortium of experts from many domains. By working as cross-disciplinary teams, these collaborative groups revealed important insights, several of which are state-dependent and particularly pertinent in fluctuating wildlife populations.

Wildlife disease management actions must account for biological efficacy and logistic and economic constraints, yet management limitations due to socioeconomic and spatial context are rarely discussed in the wildlife disease literature (but see Joseph et al., 2013). In the bighorn sheep–pneumonia system, economic and logistic constraints are major determinants of management actions. Access and animal handling potential vary across herds, with some animals defying capture from both ground and air. Furthermore, North American bighorn sheep populations are now embedded in a matrix of domestic sheep and goat flocks on both public and private lands (e.g. Sells et al., 2015; Heinse et al., 2016) that represent risk for future pathogen introductions regardless of a population's previous disease history. When making their decisions, managers must weigh the benefits of management action to the local bighorn herd against costs, in both dollars and local social capital, which may limit future management opportunities for bighorn sheep and other local wildlife.

Together, these issues make finding appropriate management strategies for bighorn sheep pneumonia a modern balancing act. While bighorn pneumonia remains among the most intractably challenging systems in wildlife disease ecology, at the same time it is a useful system for recognising gaps in existing theory and practice. In this chapter, we tell the remarkable story of bighorn sheep, the cryptic agent that has brought their once-robust populations to heel, and the ongoing scientific quest to spark their recovery.

13.2 Bighorn sheep life history

Bighorn sheep (*Ovis canadensis*) are one of two sheep species native to North America and are probably close relatives of the Siberian sheep that colonised North America by crossing the Bering Strait land bridge during the Pleistocene (Bunch et al., 2006; Rezaei et al., 2010). Bighorn sheep are distributed along the Rocky and Sierra Nevada mountains across the Great Basin, and throughout the south-western deserts, and occur latitudinally from southern Canada to Mexico. They are currently partitioned into three subspecies: Rocky Mountain bighorn sheep, *O. c. canadensis*; Sierra Nevada bighorn sheep, *O. c. sierrae*; and Desert Bighorn sheep, *O. c. nelsoni*, which are found at the north-eastern, western, and southern extents of the current bighorn distribution, respectively. While our research focuses primarily on the Rocky Mountain subspecies, we draw from literature on all subspecies here. Bighorn sheep are foraging generalists (Mincher et al., 2008), typically inhabiting alpine meadows and mountains, often on the drier slopes in proximity to steep and precarious escape terrain, although their habitat choices vary substantially from herd to herd (DeCesare & Pletscher, 2006).

Bighorns ewes typically survive 8–15 years (Berube et al., 1999), with year-ling rams living to a median age of six years (Festa-Bianchet, 2012). Bighorn population dynamics are density-dependent, with ewes increasing their age of primiparity (birth of the first lamb) as densities approach carrying capacity (Jorgenson et al., 1993). Gestation is roughly 174 days for the Rocky Mountain subspecies (Hogg et al., 1992), and births are pulsed in concentrations that vary according to habitat and latitude (Hass, 1997; Whiting et al., 2012), with the more southerly desert bighorn sheep exhibiting a more dispersed birth pulse than their northern conspecifics. Most ewes give birth to a single lamb and maintain close contact with that lamb until weaning, which occurs at approxi-mately 4–5 months of age (Festa-Bianchet, 1988).

Bighorn sheep are sexually dimorphic. Adult Rocky Mountain bighorn rams weigh an average of 100–105 kg (Loison et al., 1999), approximately 1.4 times the weight of adult females (Loison et al., 1999). Mating is sequentially poly-gynous and promiscuous, with rams competing for access to individual oes-trus ewes (Geist, 1971). Males engage in one or several of three reproductive strategies: tending (males consort with a single ewe in oestrus, and physically prevent other males' access); coursing (a less-dominant male challenges a tending male for access to his female); and blocking (males intercept ewes attempting to travel along particular routes) (Hogg, 1984). The preponderance of paternities are attributable to older, heavier males with larger horns, with approximately 35% of lambs sired by the single best performing ram in several studies (Coltman et al., 2002).

Outside of the fall rut, bighorns reside in sexually segregated groups (Ruckstuhl, 1998) of typically 5–25 animals (Meldrum & Ruckstuhl, 2009), with one- and two-year-old rams sometimes splitting time between ewe–lamb nursery groups and bachelor groups (Ruckstuhl & Festa-Bianchet, 2001). Most populations mix extensively during fall rut (Cassirer et al., 2013), which peaks between October and December. Bighorn home ranges are typi-cally tens of square miles, and some populations undertake regular seasonal migrations, but usually of distances less than 20 miles (Epps et al., 2007). Both males and females occasionally go on forays (DeCesare & Pletscher, 2006) of varying distance, and these also vary in destination from consistent trips to previously visited sites, to 'walk-about' trips beyond the periphery of the animals' home ranges.

13.3 A biological framework for pneumonia in bighorn sheep

Pneumonia has likely been a problem for bighorn sheep since the arrival of Old World domestic sheep (*Ovis aries*) and goats (*Capra hircus*). North American wild sheep and domestic sheep diverged approximately 5.3 million years ago (Hiendleder et al., 2002), and bighorn and domestic sheep produce viable and fertile offspring (Subramaniam et al., 2014). Bighorn sheep are known to consort with domestic sheep when given the opportunity, especially if other bighorn sheep are not present. Natural commingling of the two species is regularly documented and often followed by die-off events in local bighorns (George et al., 2008; Shannon et al., 2014); as a consequence, limiting inter-specific contact is viewed as important for protecting currently healthy herds.

Identifying the agent responsible for bighorn sheep pneumonia has been the subject of extensive laboratory research. Confusion about the causal agent was fuelled by the fact that bighorn sheep pneumonia manifests with a diverse ensemble of lesions accompanied by polymicrobial infections, making it difficult to identify the agent that initiated the infection. For decades, biologists reported spatiotemporal clusters of pneumonia in bighorn sheep where the lungs of affected sheep exhibited diverse pathologic lesions and diverse bacterial cultures, clouding the identity of the underlying driver. Conventional aerobic bacteriologic cultures of pneumonic bighorn sheep lung tissues frequently detected long-recognised respiratory pathogens such as *Mannheimia haemolytica*, *Bibersteinia trehalosi*, and *Pasteurella multocida*, but missed the numerically predominant obligate anaerobic bacterial species such as *Fusobacterium necrophorum*. *Mycoplasma ovipneumoniae*, the agent most consistently present in epizootic bighorn sheep pneumonia, was rarely identified even if mycoplasma culture media were inoculated because of its slow and inconsistent growth and its atypical colony morphology (Besser et al., 2008, 2013). Although additional work is needed to understand the roles of various secondary coinfecting agents, here we follow current within-host research which tends to focus on *M. ovipneumoniae* infection.

13.3.1 System aetiology

Theoretical disease ecologists rarely emphasise the identity of causal agents, yet identifying the key pathogens is crucial for designing data collection and documenting patterns of transmission and immunity. Use of classical criteria such as Koch's postulates was unsatisfactory, because multiple agents (or no agents) appear to pass the tests, and this was historically the case for bighorn sheep pneumonia. While lungworm (*Protostrongylus* spp), *Pasteurella* spp., and selenium deficiencies were all regarded as important in different contexts over the past 30 years (Miller et al., 2012 and references therein), a growing body of work points to *M. ovipneumoniae* as the primary underlying driver (Dassanyake et al., 2010; Besser et al., 2013). A different agent, *M. haemolytica*, was long regarded as the key epidemic agent of bighorn sheep pneumonia despite its frequently low prevalence in pneumonic bighorn sheep lungs, especially during the disease persistence phase (Besser et al., 2008). Only through intensive study of a wild system, involving close collaboration between field biologists, diagnosticians, and veterinary microbiologists, was the actual causal agent identified, and longer-term, multi-jurisdictional collaborations were required to build a body of evidence supporting *M. ovipneumoniae*'s role across the bighorn sheep range. Koch's postulates, as well as *M. ovipneumoniae*'s initial reason for failing, and eventual means of fulfilling each, are summarised in Table 13.1.

M. ovipneumoniae colonises the host's ciliated respiratory epithelium from the nose through the bronchioles, and in doing so impedes the efficacy of the ciliary escalator through unknown mechanisms that may include a combination of adhesion, ciliary cross-linking, induced production of auto-antibodies to ciliary antigens, and hydrogen peroxide host cell cytotoxicity leading to ciliary sloughing (Figure 13.1; Jones et al., 1985; Rifatbegović et al., 2011). Impeded ciliary function provides many resident microflora of the oropharynx access to the lungs. The newly arriving bacteria grow rapidly in the lower respiratory tract (LRT), and this is what usually leads to host fatality (Figure 13.1; Besser et al., 2013).

Pathogen diversity in the LRT infections of bighorn sheep dying from pneumonia led to a great deal of confusion about the aetiological agent causing the disease. A 16S rRNA analysis of lung samples from adults that died of disease failed to reveal any consistent pattern in pathogen presence, even within a single epidemic event (Besser et al., 2008). Operating under the assumption that the infection early on would likely be dominated by a single agent, wildlife and microbiologists worked together to lethally sample clinically affected lambs. When even the earliest symptomatic lambs were found to have severely affected lungs, asymptomatic lambs during the first month of life were sampled. Their efforts revealed a clear pattern: in the earliest affected lambs, 16S rRNA analyses consistently returned evidence of a nearly pure population of *M. ovipneumoniae*, but not of other agents. Armed with this new knowledge, researchers began strain typing *M. ovipneumoniae* – as well as other agents – within particular outbreak events. They observed that *M. ovipneumoniae* strain types (identified through DNA sequence polymorphisms) were conserved within outbreaks (Besser et al., 2012a), while *M. haemolytica* and other *Pasteurella* spp. strain types were not (Weiser et al., 2003; Besser et al., 2012a), supporting the early appearance of *M. ovipneumoniae* in affected lambs as consistent with a primary role for this agent in the disease.

Following clearance of the LRT infection, some hosts also clear *M. ovipneumoniae* from the upper respiratory tract. However, like other closely related *Mycoplasma* species, *M. ovipneumoniae* can sometimes produce long-term nasal infections in otherwise asymptomatic 'carrier' hosts. Longitudinal sampling suggests that chronic *M. ovipneumoniae* may last in some carriers for many years (Plowright et al., 2017). The mechanisms allowing for this chronic upper respiratory tract carriage are the subject of ongoing study. One possible mechanism, pathogen formation of biofilms (Simmons

Table 13.1 *Koch's postulates, along with impediment to fulfilment, and eventual means of circumvention in the bighorn pneumonia system.*

Postulate	Impediment to fulfilment	Eventual means of circumvention in sheep pneumonia system	Conclusion
The microorganism must be found in abundance in all hosts suffering from disease, but should not be found in healthy hosts	*M. ovipneumoniae* was difficult to detect by classical mycoplasma culture methods due to its fastidious nature	Implementation of molecular detection through polymerase chain reaction testing. Besser et al. (2013) documented *M. ovipneumoniae* in all bighorn sheep populations affected by disease, whereas 91% of populations unaffected by disease showed no history of exposure (Cassirer et al., 2018)	Postulate supported
The microorganism must be isolated from a diseased host and grown in culture	*M. ovipneumoniae* is predominant only in pneumonic lungs very early in the disease progression, but greatly overgrown by other bacteria by the time severe or fatal disease occurs. *M. ovipneumoniae* is thought to trigger those secondary bacterial infections through interference with the mucociliary escalator	Sampling progressively younger animals revealed a role for *M. ovipneumoniae* in the early phase of the lower respiratory tract infection of bighorn lambs (Besser et al., 2008). Clarifying that role justified placing attention on *M. ovipneumoniae* when revealed in the upper respiratory tract sampling protocol	Postulate supported

The microorganism should cause disease when introduced into a healthy host	*M. ovipneumoniae* likely undergoes selection for reduced virulence during colony growth (Niang et al., 1998) and early attempts to reproduce bighorn lamb pneumonia with cultured *M. ovipneumoniae* failed (Besser et al., 2008)	Non-cultured *M. ovipneumoniae*, harvested directly from nasal secretions of naturally colonised sheep after killing other bacterial flora by cell–wall–active antimicrobial drugs, reproduced the disease as well as onward transmission from those animals to other previously unexposed animals (Besser et al., 2014)	Postulate supported
The microorganism must be re-isolated from the inoculated, diseased host and identified as being identical to the original specific causal agent	This stage was not problematic, once *M. ovipneumoniae* sampling methods were developed	Culture-independent detection helped clarify pathogen presence, and strain-typing methods added evidence of onward transmission from naturally exposed hosts (Besser et al., 2012b, Cassirer et al., 2017)	Postulate supported

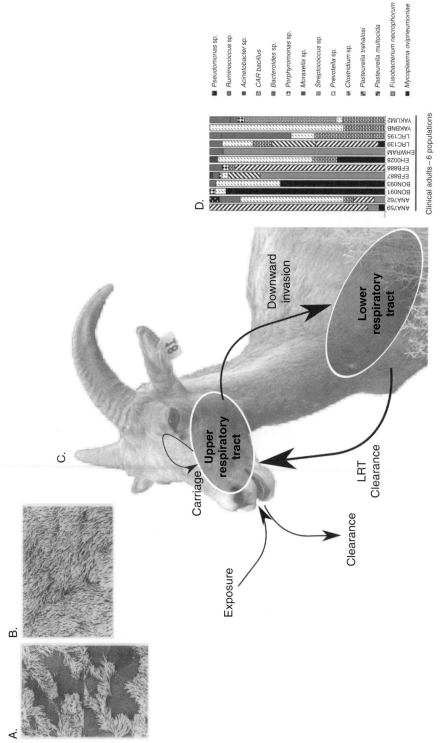

Figure 13.1 Proposed progression of *Mycoplasma ovipneumoniae*-initiated pneumonia. (A) Cilia 10 days post-*M. ovipneumoniae* infection, and (B) healthy cilia in domestic sheep (from Jones et al., 1985). (C) Schematic of disease progression in bighorn sheep. (D) Lower respiratory tract (LRT) microbial diversity in adult bighorn sheep mortalities with clinical pneumonia (from Besser et al., 2013).

et al., 2013), seems unlikely to hold here. The more than 100 known species of mycoplasmas vary dramatically in their ability to form biofilms, but consistently generate chronic infections, suggesting biofilm formation alone may not explain chronicity. Exploring alternative pathways, such as immune suppression mitigating acute immunopathology, or some form of intracellular persistence, may provide new insights.

13.3.2 Trade-offs between transmission and virulence

Preliminary evidence from captive studies suggest that LRT symptoms (coughing) are associated with a much higher exerted force of infection than asymptomatic infections (Besser et al., 2014), but may have a higher likelihood of producing disease-induced mortalities (e.g. Cassirer et al., 2013). *M. ovipneumoniae* is thus likely subject to a life-history trade-off between transmission and virulence: more virulent strains have a higher potential to transmit widely, but they must do so rapidly before killing their hosts. Because longer host survival has some positive effects on pathogen fitness, pathogen strains should not undergo run-away evolution toward higher virulence (e.g. Keeling & Rohani, 2008). Following initial exposure, *M. ovipneumoniae* appears to induce a more modulated immune response in chronically infected adult hosts, where it can cause chronic but relatively or completely asymptomatic infections. One or more chronically infected ewes likely infect the first naïve lambs within a ewe group, but intense lamb-to-lamb epidemic transmission likely predominates thereafter. The precise structure of this trade-off likely varies between bighorn and domestic sheep. Because *M. ovipneumoniae* transmission is likely facilitated by symptoms, *M. ovipneumoniae* residing in the adapted domestic sheep hosts could be subject to selection toward increased virulence (and increased transmission), whereas in bighorn sheep high virulence imposes higher costs by limiting host survival.

If pathogen evolution is rapid relative to the disease process, some host populations may benefit from evolution towards avirulence, wherein the pathogen locally evolves to lower virulence before driving the host entirely extinct. In bighorn sheep pneumonia this selective process would likely operate at a relatively long temporal lag becaue the pathogen would only face host limitations after ewes who survived the initial spillover event began to die of old age. Hopes of 'evolutionary rescue', where alleles associated with resistant phenotypes might increase in frequency in one population that could then serve as a source for reseeding other diseased herds, are commonly cited in the bighorn system. However, there is little evidence that appropriately robust resistance currently exists in any bighorn sheep population. Additionally, bighorn sheep exhibit limited cross-strain immunity (Cassirer et al., 2017): animals infected with and immune to one strain still experience acute disease when exposed to novel *M. ovipneumoniae* strains. This suggests that even

if pathogen evolution was a relevant force driving dynamics of a single
M. ovipneumoniae strain, recurrent introductions of novel strains would dampen evolutionary rescue's broad demographic benefits.

13.3.3 Spillover and multi-host disease dynamics

The host range of *M. ovipneumoniae* appears to extend to all Caprinae (Nicholas
et al., 2008). It can cause disease and induce chronic carriage in both domestic
sheep and, perhaps less frequently, domestic goats (Ayling et al., 2004; USDA,
2015). Phylogenetic studies show distinct clades of *M. ovipneumoniae* strains
detected in domestic sheep and goats, whereas strains in bighorn sheep are
found throughout the entire *M. ovipneumoniae* tree, clustering with both
domestic sheep and goat strains (Kamath et al., 2016; Maksimović et al.,
2016; Cassirer et al., 2018). Variation in host species pathology may be partially
due to differences in host susceptibility and immune response. To date, however, evidence of the precise mechanisms differentiating infection and
immune dynamics in bighorn and domestic sheep is still emerging, and this
remains an area of active investigation.

The risk posed by local domestic flocks remains relevant even in chronically
infected bighorn herds, as bighorns apparently have limited cross-strain
immunity to other *M. ovipneumoniae* strains and domestic flocks are thought
to frequently harbour more than one strain (Felts et al., 2016; Justice-Allen
et al., 2016; Cassirer et al., 2017, 2018). In one well-documented scenario, a
novel *M. ovipneumoniae* strain produced an all-age bighorn sheep die-off in an
already infected herd. Even though adults in that herd had lived with
one *M. ovipneumoniae* strain for many years, and adults were apparently
immune, the introduction of the novel strain produced respiratory disease
symptoms and mortality in all age classes. This is consistent with
M. ovipneumoniae introduction events into uninfected herds (Figure 13.2).
Apparently, resistance to the existing strain provided limited effective protection against disease derived from the novel strain. Similar scenarios have
been documented in two other wild and captive contexts (Felts et al., 2016;
Justice-Allen et al., 2016).

The high risk of disease transmission following interspecific commingling
events motivated managers to go to great lengths to isolate bighorn sheep
herds from domestic sheep and goat reservoirs (Western Association of Fish
and Wildlife Agencies Wild Sheep Working Group, 2012; Bureau of Land
Management, 2016). Research identifies locations in which bighorn sheep
and domestic sheep could overlap on the landscape (Carpenter et al., 2014;
O'Brien et al., 2014), public grazing allotments near bighorn sheep herds are
closed, land historically used by domestic sheep ranchers is purchased, and
bighorn sheep that are thought to have interacted with domestic sheep are
culled. These efforts likely reduced spillover risk to bighorn herds

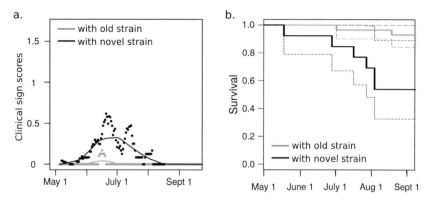

Figure 13.2 Adult ewe symptom data (a) and survival data (b) in infected but not invasion years ('with old strain'), and in the presence of novel invading *M. ovipneumoniae* strain ('with new strain'). Adapted from Cassirer et al. (2017).

substantially, but spillovers continue to occur across the range. The clear risk associated with domestic sheep and goat presence has led to an increased interest in understanding *M. ovipneumoniae* dynamics in domestic sheep flocks (e.g. USDA, 2015; Heinse et al., 2016), knowledge that will likely strengthen future capacity for managing *M. ovipneumoniae* in both bighorn and domestic sheep.

13.3.4 Pathogen control of bighorn herds

Captive studies and field observations both indicate rapid transmission throughout bighorn herds once the index bighorn case exhibits symptoms (Besser et al., 2014; Cassirer et al., 2017). Epidemic transmission, high mortality, and nearly complete exposure of all members in the herd usually follows (Figure 13.3a), usually accompanying the signature 'die-off' event.

More insidious but even more damaging than the pulse of acute mortality associated with pathogen introduction, however, are the recurrent epidemics of lamb pneumonia that occur in the die-off's wake (persistence-phase lamb and ewe survivals for Hells Canyon are shown in Figure 13.3b). Understanding the dynamics of pathogen persistence in the bighorn sheep system particularly benefited from individual-level monitoring efforts that allowed determination of cause-specific mortalities in lambs, and showed that most lamb mortalities after die-off events were attributable to pneumonia (Cassirer et al., 2013; Smith et al., 2014). Intensive lamb observations allowed researchers to describe temporal patterns in lamb mortality hazards in the wake of all-age die-offs (Figure 13.4a). These studies showed a trend in long-term population status toward annual lamb disease, with occasional years with adult or all-age mortality (Figure 13.4b).

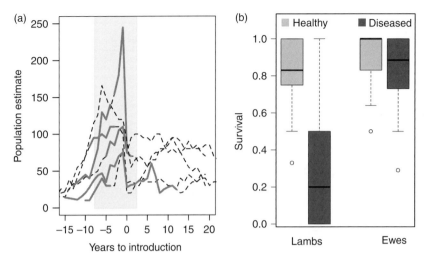

Figure 13.3 Dynamics of infected bighorn sheep populations. (a) Dynamics of nine populations that showed classic persistent disease dynamics from the Hells Canyon system of Idaho, Washington, and Oregon. Trajectories are aligned so that all populations experienced their die-off events at year '0'. The shaded region indicates the 95% posterior credible interval on the timing of trajectory changes as estimated across all the trajectories shown; solid portions of each line show 95% credible regions for the changepoint in each population's trajectory when estimated in isolation. (b) Survival of lambs (to 1 October) and ewes in the Hells Canyon system under years with no disease transmission (light grey) and with disease transmission (dark grey). At least two field studies verify that observed reductions in summer lamb survival following all-age pneumonia die-offs are directly attributable to pneumonia (Cassirer et al., 2013; Smith et al., 2014). Adapted from Manlove et al. (2016a).

Asymptomatically infected 'chronic carrier' ewes (e.g. Plowright et al., 2017) form a putative link between all-age die-offs and persistent lamb disease. Early work from the Pacific Northwest showed that adult ewes exhibit near-normal survival probabilities during subsequent years of pneumonia transmission events if they survive their first exposure event, even as more exposure events are simultaneously associated with decreased lamb survival (Plowright et al., 2013). Based on these findings, current work is focused on determining whether a subset of adults become persistently infected and serve as local reservoirs for pathogen transmission, or if disease persistence at the population level is instead due to stuttering chains of transmission (e.g. Plowright et al., 2017). Ongoing research at Oregon's well-studied Lostine population suggests some age structure to *M. ovipneumoniae* carriage, with the odds of carrying being higher among older ewes (Plowright et al., 2017).

At this point, however, it is not obvious how readily individual carriage patterns will map to management activity, as there is currently no good test to

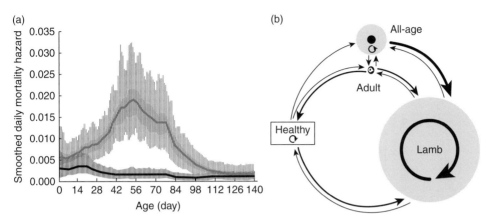

Figure 13.4 (a) 95% posterior credible intervals for daily lamb mortality hazards in diseased (grey) and healthy (black) years during summer in the Hells Canyon metapopulation. (b) Proposed state-transitions in disease status between healthy, all-age, adult-only, and lamb-only pneumonia in the Hells Canyon system. Point sizes reflect the frequency with which the system is in each state. From Cassirer et al. (2013). (A black and white version of this figure will appear in some formats. For the colour version, please refer to the plate section.)

differentiate between prime-aged and senescent adult bighorns (especially females) in the field, nor is there an animal-side test for diagnosing *M. ovipneumoniae* infection status. Instead, animals must be captured multiple times, first to determine if they are consistently infected, and eventually for their removal. This is logistically problematic, because some animals reliably evade capture after initial handling. An alternative option is to capture animals and hold them overnight while their samples are analysed using expedited testing measures, which some states have tried in recent years. This option requires appropriate overnight housing for animals, and relies on a single diagnostic testing event, precluding the possibility of differentiating between chronically and ephemerally infected animals. If current test-removal studies show promising results, or if the relation between age and infection status holds across many herds, then developing animal-side methods for ageing or diagnosing bighorns will be a crucial next step.

13.3.5 Seasonality

During its persistence phase, bighorn sheep pneumonia is highly seasonal, with dynamics largely forced by the spring birth pulse. Lamb pneumonia mortalities are concentrated approximately 8–12 weeks after the birth pulse (Cassirer & Sinclair, 2007; Cassirer et al., 2013), usually following a brief surge of symptoms and a long subclinical pneumonic phase (Besser et al., 2008).

The mechanisms underlying seasonality in this system remain somewhat cryptic. Much of our knowledge of transmission is gleaned from susceptible

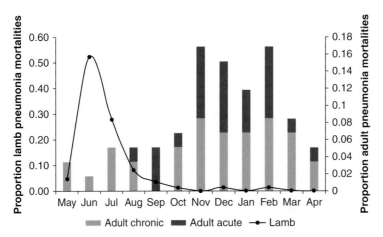

Figure 13.5 Seasonal patterns of adult and lamb pneumonia mortality. Acute and chronic pneumonia classifications are based on biopsies of pneumonic lesions, as opposed to timing within the context of an epidemic. From Cassirer et al. (2013).

lambs who act as sentinels for chronic carrier shedding. However, the presence of susceptible lambs is confounded with the period immediately following pregnancy, which is likely also a time of immunosuppression in ewes. As a consequence, current data do not allow us to differentiate between a constant rate of background shedding from chronic carriers, coupled with a seasonally pulsed presence of sentinels; and seasonally pulsed shedding. Likewise, testosterone levels during rut probably increase ram susceptibility, and may facilitate shedding from chronically infected rams, yet testosterone rises are temporally confounded with major shifts in population mixing patterns. Currently, researchers are working to couple empirically derived contact network data with information on infection and immune status to generate individual-specific metrics on force of infection under several hypothesised transmission drivers (individual antibody levels, infected host demographic group, infected host load), and linking these hypothesised drivers to realised transmission events through carefully structured logistic regression models to isolate the effects of pathogen load, host immune status, and social behaviour in driving disease dynamics (Manlove et al., 2017).

While little is known about within-host dynamics or infection intensity, a working hypothesis is that symptom burden scales with *M. ovipneumoniae* population size within individual hosts. If symptoms are in fact a proxy for pathogen load (or force of infection), then we would expect a much higher force of infection on adults during summer during the pulse of symptomatic lamb infections than during the remainder of the year when symptomatic animals are rare. Field observations, however, fail to match this expectation. Instead, the preponderance of acute pneumonia mortalities in adults during the disease persistence phase occurs during winter and this is particularly true of deaths from acute pneumonia (Figure 13.5). Consequently, although adults are likely exposed during summer, they are apparently able to successfully combat the infection in that season, and it is only during the nutritionally stressed winter season when acute disease manifests.

13.3.6 Spatial structuring and disease transmission

All-age outbreaks and persistent lamb disease operate on substantially different social structures in bighorn sheep herds, which may help explain variation in disease severity during both die-off and persistence events. All-age die-offs often occur during the fall rut when populations are relatively well-mixed, whereas summer lamb mortalities occur when populations are split into relatively discrete ewe–lamb nursery groups and groups of bachelor males (e.g. Manlove et al., 2014; Borg et al., 2017). If pathogen prevalence coming into the summer is very low and group structuring is sufficiently strong, transmission may be sequestered into a subset of groups, providing an opportunity for lambs born in groups without transmission to survive. Some evidence suggests that summer connections among nursery groups may be rare enough for this protection to kick in. One study found that the proportion of lambs dying in summers with documented disease transmission varied substantially between nursery groups, but less between populations, years, or particular ewes (Manlove et al., 2014). Lamb survival did not vary dramatically between ewe-groups in years without disease, suggesting pathogen transmission was the mechanism generating the observed variation. Furthermore, bighorn sheep retain relatively consistent group sizes even as populations decline in the aftermath of all-age die-off events and sustained poor recruitment, providing a behavioural mechanism for transmission to follow frequency-dependent–like patterns, and thus a means by which pneumonia could produce local bighorn sheep extirpations (Manlove et al., 2014).

Some managers are trying to leverage population-level sequestering of pathogen transmission by attempting to construct population structure in bighorn herds. This involves translocation of a group of animals to an area several miles from the capture site, in the hopes that they will establish locally yet retain some loose connectivity with their natal group. Although this approach has conceptual promise, these projects are in their infancy and their eventual success remains unclear.

Alternatively, several states manage bighorn sheep herds for density (or rather, population size), under the assumption that larger populations occupy more space and are therefore more likely to encounter domestic sheep and goats; or that animals living at near carrying capacity are more likely to experience nutritional stress and correspondingly increased susceptibility to disease. Several studies (Monello et al., 2001; Sells et al., 2015) report that population size is associated with increased pathogen introduction risk. This could occur if larger higher-density herds occupy larger areas or exhibit more dispersal than smaller lower-density herds. However, population sizes prior to die-off events are often small, and do not differ significantly in size from populations that remained healthy (Monello et al., 2001; Shannon et al., 2014; Cassirer et al., 2018). Additionally, there is little empirical evidence to suggest that ungulate population space use or dispersal patterns relate consistently to population size (Loison et al., 1999; Long et al., 2008). Stronger descriptions of that relation may provide valuable insights in the future.

13.3.7 Transmission and prevalence

Regardless of their aetiology, the role chronically infected bighorn sheep ewes play in disease dynamics is relatively clear: carriers spark frequent but somewhat unpredictable summer disease events in lambs. While carrier prevalence is not well-understood, and may vary from herd to herd, longitudinal data indicate that infections may concentrate in a few consistently positive animals (Plowright et al., 2017). In one well-studied set of populations, approximately 25% of years following all-age die-offs show no apparent lamb pneumonia (Cassirer et al., 2013; Manlove et al., 2016a). We hypothesise that these sporadic 'healthy' years are due to *M. ovipneumoniae* failing to transmit from chronically infected adults to young lambs, as opposed to local fade-out and recolonisation by *M. ovipneumoniae*.

Some carriers may have a higher likelihood of sparking lamb disease than others, simply due to patterns of animal behaviour. For example, preliminary evidence suggests that lambs may disproportionately carry *M. ovipneumoniae* (Manlove et al., 2017; Plowright et al., 2017). However, while yearlings are often present in nursery groups during summer, they rarely contact lambs directly (Figure 13.6), nor do they show strong symptoms of disease.

Analyses that accounted for different contact patterns found that infected yearlings posed a much lower transmission risk to lambs than did infected ewes with lambs (Manlove et al., 2017), although this finding remains to be verified in other herds. Furthermore, relatively little is known about *M. ovipneumoniae* dynamics in rams that may nevertheless play a crucial role in long-term *M. ovipneumoniae* persistence, and will undoubtedly be the subject of future investigation.

Chronic infection has long been recognised as a critical element driving persistent pneumonia in bighorn sheep (e.g. Hobbs & Miller, 1992). Managers have explored three methods for limiting infection prevalence during both

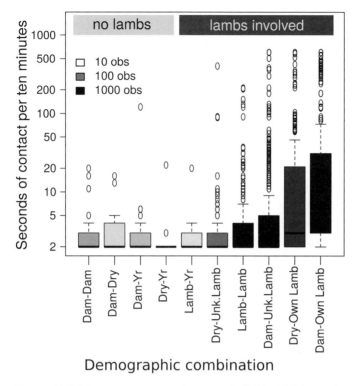

Figure 13.6 Direct contact rates between individual bighorn sheep of different demographic groups. Dam = dam with a lamb; Dry = dry ewe (ewe was never observed with a lamb, or lost her lamb prior to 1 June); Yr = yearling; Unk Lamb = lamb of unknown identity; Own Lamb = dam's own lamb. Dry ewes that birthed lambs and lost their lambs prior to 1 June could interact with their own lambs prior to 1 June. From Manlove et al. (2017).

the epidemic and persistence disease phase of pneumonia: treatment with antibiotics (McAdoo et al., 2010), anthelmintics (Miller et al., 2000), or nutritional supplements (Coggins, 2006); vaccination (Cassirer et al., 2001); and culls of test-positive animals. Treatment, supplementation, and vaccination have all had limited and inconsistent efficacy in reducing disease burden, although no trials to date have targeted *M. ovipneumoniae*, the agent best supported as the primary infectious agent initiating outbreaks. For example, most of the vaccination efforts targeted Pasteurellaceae bacteria, and thus may not have dealt with the most important driver. Several test-and-cull efforts are currently underway, targeting animals that are consistently test-positive for *M. ovipneumoniae* for removal. While these efforts appear promising, they are still in their infancy. Even if they prove successful, test-and-cull projects are effort-intensive, and may not be operationally feasible in some settings.

13.4 Mathematical models

Two classes of mathematical models have been used in the bighorn pneumonia system. The first are population viability analyses (PVAs) that forecast the long-term implications of pathogen invasion (under prespecified pathogen persistence periods). The second are disease transmission (SIR-like) models, intended to predict the pathogen persistence period itself on the basis of underlying mechanisms. Both types of models provide insights into bighorn sheep pneumonia management, and we treat each in turn below.

13.4.1 Population viability analyses

Population viability analyses (PVAs) are commonly used in wildlife conservation and management to project populations forward and allow for *in silico* management experiments (e.g. Boyce, 1992). PVAs can address two questions about bighorn sheep herds facing *M. ovipneumoniae* spillover risk. What long-term risks does a pneumonia event impose on population viability? What vital rates drive the population response to pneumonia and how would changing them impact population dynamics? PVAs addressing the consequences of bighorn sheep pneumonia should fulfil three basic requirements: capture large but variably sized all-age outbreaks; include a pathogen-persistence phase dominated by lamb disease; allow a subset of populations to recover rapidly (and apparently stochastically) whereas others are subject to long-term persistence.

Population viability models incorporating disease usually treat disease as a form of structured environment, and project population growth without modelling the disease transmission process per se. The key challenge for applying PVAs to the bighorn system therefore rests in determining how to weight the disease introduction and persistence periods; while both phases of disease stymie population growth, they do so on different timescales. If pathogen persistence is very short-lived, its impacts are low relative to the costs of die-off events. Eventually, though, persistence overcomes the costs of even the largest die-offs. Decisions about the persistence period, therefore, have strong implications on model predictions.

There are several published PVA-like models for bighorn sheep pneumonia (e.g. Clifford et al., 2009; Cahn et al., 2011; Carpenter et al., 2014; Manlove et al., 2016a), which all make different assumptions about the relative costs of invasion and persistence on population growth. The first two models appropriately separate the outbreak and persistence phases, but may underestimate the actual duration of persistence in the wild, instead capturing dynamics more consistent with the roughly 30% of herds that experience relatively rapid pathogen fade-out. In order to reproduce the long-term suppression of population growth observed in many wild herds, models with shorter persistence periods require regular pathogen reintroduction events. Common introductions, however, produce different demographic structures than persistent disease in the wild: all-age mortalities during die-offs do not fundamentally alter population age structures, whereas the juvenile-skewed mortality structure during persistence leads to a hollowing-out of populations and introduction of extinction debt (Kuussaari et al., 2009). When vital rates from die-off years are applied to persistence years, population growth is dramatically underestimated (Figure 13.7), underscoring how important it is that models differentiate between persistence and all-age die-off events, and accurately capture the persistence period.

While PVAs are useful for projecting future dynamics under discrete environmental conditions, they do not shed light on the underlying mechanisms controlling variation through time, and they provide no insights into the particular mechanisms that allow for varying population-level outcomes. Such mechanistic explorations are instead the purview of SIR-like compartmental models of pathogen transmission.

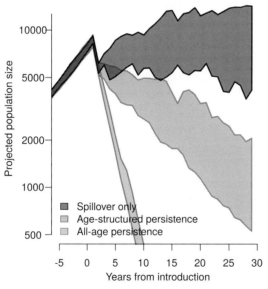

Figure 13.7 Population projections (middle 50% of simulated population sizes at each timestep). Disease was introduced at year 10 (prior to year 10, simulated populations showed robust growth, consistent with field observations of reintroduced herds, e.g. Figure 13.4a). All-age die-offs were set to kill 30% of animals, and the expected time between introduction events was 5 years. Top trajectory = die-offs only without persistence; middle trajectory = die-offs followed by persistent juvenile disease; bottom trajectory = die-offs followed by persistent all-age disease. From Manlove et al. (2016a).

13.4.2 Compartmental (SIR-like) disease transmission models

Compartmental disease transmission models offer a more detailed description of the epidemic process by capturing the mechanics of transmission and tracking the proportion of the population falling into different disease states, or 'compartments'. Individuals transition among compartments as a function of a variety of factors, which are characterised to mimic particular aspects of system biology.

The specifics of compartmental model construction depend to some extent on model objectives, and balancing biological realism against model complexity is an ongoing challenge in wildlife disease modelling efforts. That fact notwithstanding, most models of pathogen transmission in free-ranging bighorn sheep herds should probably replicate the following features: (1) acute, all-age die-off events following pathogen introduction; (2) long-term persistence with limited disease burden in a subset of bighorn adults and severe lamb die-offs in approximately three of every four summers for up to 20 years post-introduction in approximately 60–70% of herds; (3) pathogen fade-outs 2–4 years following introduction in approximately 30% of herds; and (4) widespread exposure (antibody titres in excess of 50), but relatively limited infection (~15–30%) in adults following die-off events. These features, and their implications on model construction, are summarised in Table 13.2.

Host ecology imposes a few additional structural considerations on disease models for bighorn sheep. First, the birth pulse produces an influx of susceptible hosts in the spring, and these pulses may be crucial for driving summer epidemics (Peel et al., 2014). Second, bighorn spatial ecology in the summer imposes a modular, sexually segregated population structure commensurate with peak transmission (Section 13.3.6; Manlove et al., 2014), which may slow epidemic spread in that season (Cross et al., 2005). In order to capture these features, compartmental models should likely include separate acute and chronic infection states, as well as a recovered state. Recent findings regarding age-structured prevalence suggest some animals might move between the chronic and recovered class, and some chronic animals may recrudesce to acute infections (Plowright et al., 2017), although these additional details may not be necessary for all model objectives. A schematic of important disease compartments and probable state transitions emerging from these contributing factors is shown in Figure 13.8.

To date, researchers have used compartmental transmission models for bighorn sheep pneumonia to pursue two separate questions. The first question is which management actions are likely to facilitate pathogen clearance in this system? One on-going modelling effort aims to forecast how effectively different management actions might drive *M. ovipneumoniae* fade-out in bighorn herds (Almberg et al., 2016). The critical features for testing management efficacy captured the proportion of individuals falling into each state at

Table 13.2 *Empirically observed disease features, and implications on model structure.*

Observed feature	Implication for model structure
Acute, all-age die-off events following pathogen introduction, exposing nearly all members of the population (as indicated by uniformly high antibody titres in adults; Cassirer et al., 2017; Plowright et al., 2017)	High force of infection from acutely infected individuals; high disease-induced mortality rate upon initial infection; well-mixed population structure for some of the year
Long-term persistence with limited disease burden in a subset of adults, commensurate with sporadic lamb die-offs (Cassirer & Sinclair, 2007, Cassirer et al., 2013; Plowright et al., 2017).	This pattern is consistent with a pathogen persisting in a chronic carrier class that can transmit to lambs; furthermore, the acutely infected class may be similar for all naïve animals, regardless of age
Moderate to severe lamb die-offs approximately 75% of summers for up to 20 years post-introduction (Cassirer et al., 2013; Manlove et al., 2016a)	Because lamb disease events are severe but sporadic, we suspect that chronic carriers shed at a low load relative to acutely infected individuals. Years without transmission are thought to be years in which no chronic shedder successfully transmitted pathogens to a naïve lamb. In years when a shedder does transmit to a lamb, most subsequent transmission is probably produced by the acutely infected lamb, leading to widespread outbreak events within nursery groups
Pathogen fade-outs 2–4 years following introduction in approximately 30% of herds; relatively low prevalence among adults (Manlove et al., 2016a; Plowright et al., 2017; Cassirer et al., 2017, 2018)	Only a subset of acutely infected individuals becomes chronically infected. The rest recover

different points in time following introduction, and halting transmission. Because management in this analysis operates at a temporal cross-section, waning immunity (e.g. recovered individuals becoming vulnerable to reinfection) was not deemed particularly important for determining system dynamics, and both chronic and recovered states were treated as absorbing (that is, once an individual entered either of those states, it could not be removed except by death). This limited the number of state-transitions that had to be empirically estimated. A full model sensitivity analysis was used to evaluate which rates needed to be well-estimated, and which rates had strong

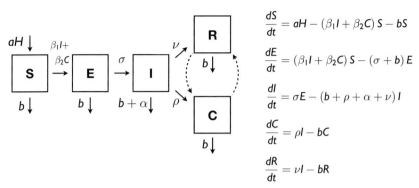

$$\frac{dS}{dt} = aH - (\beta_1 I + \beta_2 C)\,S - bS$$

$$\frac{dE}{dt} = (\beta_1 I + \beta_2 C)\,S - (\sigma + b)\,E$$

$$\frac{dI}{dt} = \sigma E - (b + \rho + \alpha + \nu)\,I$$

$$\frac{dC}{dt} = \rho I - bC$$

$$\frac{dR}{dt} = \nu I - bR$$

Figure 13.8 Model structures. While the model states are relatively clear (S = susceptible, E = exposed, I = acutely infected, C = chronically infected, R = recovered), several transitions remain ambiguous. For example, existing data do not provide a clear insight into whether recovered individuals transition directly into a chronic infection as some function of population-level force of infection; neither is it clear whether chronically infected individuals reliably recover. It is also possible that chronically infected animals may occasionally recrudesce into active acute infections, although if this process occurs, it is likely rare.

implications on system dynamics. The sensitivity analysis was followed up with a simulation study in which management was applied 20 years after pathogen introduction, and probabilities of *M. ovipneumoniae* fade-out were recorded at future cross-sections in time.

The second question is what the disease transition rates operating within this system are. The key issues in this investigation are whether the probability of becoming chronically infected varies with age (or other covariates, such as time since pathogen invasion), and whether experiencing an initial die-off event fundamentally alters an individual's future disease progression. Due to the nature of these questions, this investigation requires a somewhat more elaborate model construction that allows for variation in recovery rate, and direct exploration of whether R and C should be absorbing, or β should be constant.

13.4.3 Managing bighorn sheep pneumonia in the wild

State and federal agencies currently attempt to manage pneumonia by the following strategies (and others): removing domestic and wild sheep from areas where they may contact each other, constructing barriers to avoid contact between bighorn and domestic sheep (fences), population augmentation, population reduction (random or strategic), test and remove, and depopulation. Several states have tried a number of different management actions, but a direct comparison of results is complicated by inconsistent demographic data collection (e.g. we cannot directly compare responses from one case to another at this time). A multi-state cooperative effort to build a broad-scale experiment for adaptive management purposes is currently underway.

13.5 Open questions

Key remaining questions about carriage are whether particular environmental, pathogen, coinfection (including sinus tumours), or individual-specific conditions such as age allow for carriage or variation in disease-associated morbidity and mortality rates, and whether those conditions are amenable to management. However, these same questions are the subject of intensive study in important human bacterial systems like *Staphylococcus aureus*, and even in those well-studied cases, the causative mechanisms remain elusive. Therefore, in the bighorn system it may prove more productive in the immediate term to develop methods to identify carriers quickly, and explore population-level responses to carrier removal. Further work on disease dynamics and demographic consequences in domestic Caprinae would greatly facilitate our ability to generate consensus around disease management activities that may be of benefit to both the domestic and wild hosts.

Additionally, a rigorous cost–benefit analysis comparing the value of different data sets might help target future investigations toward the most crucial data gaps (which are likely related to the duration and stability of the chronic carriage state). It will be very important to understand whether the resistant state is absorbing. If resistant individuals remain so throughout their entire lives, management can be concentrated on carriers. However, if resistant animals eventually senesce into a susceptible state and transition to become carriers, then the rates of those transitions must be mapped to the timescale of management.

Another critical need is to be able to project population mixing patterns based on more readily available home-range data. This would provide managers insights into whether it is appropriate to manage a location of consistent disease incidence without the specific knowledge of the individuals present. This might work for highly spatially structured herds, but at this time there is no reliable means of determining spatial structure without extensive (and expensive) collaring of many animals.

13.6 Conclusions

Bighorn sheep pneumonia remains a major conservation concern. This system is somewhat unique from other wildlife disease systems in that the pathogen produces chronic infections in a subset of adult hosts, yet continues to produce acute and fatal disease in juveniles. Bighorn sheep behaviour suggests that persistent disease may follow frequency-dependent transmission patterns, yet unlike other frequency-dependent diseases of conservation concern (e.g. white nose syndrome), there is little evidence that the host is likely to benefit from evolutionary escape. Nonetheless, long-term, individual-level monitoring data from several states continue to provide new opportunities and prompt new questions about the mechanisms of pathogen persistence in bighorn sheep herds, as well as the long-term consequences of persistence on population viability. Modelling in this system draws from both the population viability analyses of conservation biology and the mechanistic models of disease ecology, with the former underscoring the long-term consequences of disease persistence, and the latter addressing means to optimise herd sizes in the face of that persistence. As agencies continue to amass more detailed and comparable data on bighorn pneumonia, we anticipate major advances in our understanding of this system over the next several years.

13.7 Acknowledgements

We thank the numerous field technicians and state biologists who have contributed to bighorn disease research, especially Frances Cassirer and her collaborators who have worked in the Hells Canyon system. This would not be possible without the sustained support of the local state agencies and forests, as well as the Morris Animal Foundation, the Wild Sheep Foundation, and the Safari Club.

References

Almberg, E.S., Cross, P.C., Dobson, A.P., et al. (2012) Parasite invasion following host reintroduction: a case study of Yellowstone's wolves. *Philosophical Transactions of the Royal Society of London B*, **367**, 2840–2851.

Almberg, E.S., Manlove, K.R., Cassirer, E.F., et al. (2016) Modeling management strategies for the control of bighorn sheep respiratory disease. *Biennial Symposium of the Northern Wild Sheep and Goat Council*, **20**, 18.

Ayling, R.D., Bashiruddin, S.E. & Nicholas, R.A.J. (2004) *Mycoplasma* species and related organisms isolated from ruminants in Britain between 1990 and 2000. *Veterinary Record*, **155**, 413–416.

Berube, C.H., Festa-Bianchet, M. & Jorgenson, J.T. (1999) Individual differences, longevity, and reproductive senescence in bighorn ewes. *Ecology*, **80**(8), 2555–2565.

Besser, T.E., Cassirer, E.F., Highland, M.A., et al. (2013) Bighorn sheep pneumonia: sorting out the cause of a polymicrobial disease. *Preventive Veterinary Medicine*, **108**(2), 85–93.

Besser, T.E., Cassirer, E.F., Potter, K.A., et al. (2008) Association of *Mycoplasma ovipneumoniae* infection with population-limiting respiratory disease in free-ranging Rocky Mountain bighorn sheep (*Ovis canadensis canadensis*). *Journal of Clinical Microbiology*, **46**(2), 423–430.

Besser, T.E., Cassirer, E.F., Potter, K.A., et al. (2014) Epizootic pneumonia of bighorn sheep following experimental exposure to *Mycoplasma ovipneumoniae*. *PLoS ONE*, **9**(10), e110039.

Besser, T.E., Cassirer, E.F., Yamada, C., et al. (2012) Survival of bighorn sheep (*Ovis canadensis*) commingled with domestic sheep (*Ovis aries*) in the absence of *Mycoplasma ovipneumoniae*. *Journal of Wildlife Diseases*, **48**(1), 168–172.

Besser, T.E., Highland, M.A., Baker, K., et al. (2012) Causes of pneumonia epizootics among bighorn sheep, western United

States, 2008–2010. *Emerging Infectious Diseases*, **18**(3), 406–414.

Borg, N.J., Mitchell, M.S., Lukacs, P.M., et al. (2017) Behavioral connectivity among bighorn sheep suggests potential for disease spread. *The Journal of Wildlife Management*, **81**(1), 38–45.

Boyce, W.M. (1992). Population viability analysis. *Annual Review of Ecology and Systematics*, **23**, 481–506.

Briggs, C.J., Vredenburg, V.T., Knapp, R.A., et al. (2005) Investigating the population-level effects of chytridiomycosis: an emerging infectious disease of amphibians. *Ecology*, **86**(12), 3149–3159.

Bunch T., Wu, C., Zhang, Y.-P., et al. (2006) Phylogenetic analysis of snow sheep (*Ovis nivicola*) and closely related taxa. *Journal of Heredity*, **97**, 21–30.

Bureau of Land Management. (2016) Management of domestic sheep and goats to sustain wild sheep. Release No. 1–1771, 2 March 2016.

Cahn, M.L., Conner, M.M., Schmitz, O.J., et al. (2011) Disease, population viability, and recovery of endangered Sierra Nevada bighorn sheep. *The Journal of Wildlife Management*, **75**(8), 1753–1766.

Carpenter, T.E., Coggins, V.L., McCarthy, C., et al. (2014) A spatial risk assessment of bighorn sheep extirpation by grazing domestic sheep on public lands. *Preventive Veterinary Medicine*, **114**(1), 3–10.

Cassirer, E.F., Manlove, K.R., Almberg, E.S., et al. (2018) Pneumonia in bighorn sheep: risk and resilience. *Journal of Wildlife Management*, **82**(1), 32–45.

Cassirer, E.F., Manlove, K.R., Plowright, R.K., et al. (2017) Evidence for strain-specific immunity to pneumonia in bighorn sheep. *The Journal of Wildlife Management*, **81**(1), 133–143.

Cassirer, E.F., Plowright, R.K., Manlove, K.R., et al. (2013) Spatio-temporal dynamics of pneumonia in bighorn sheep. *Journal of Animal Ecology*, **82**(3), 518–528.

Cassirer, E.F., Rudolph, K.M., Fowler,P., et al. (2001) Evaluation of ewe vaccination as a tool for increasing bighorn lamb survival following pasteurellosis epizootics. *Journal of Wildlife Diseases*, **37**, 49–57.

Cassirer, E. & Sinclair, A.R.E. (2007) Dynamics of pneumonia in a bighorn sheep metapopulation. *The Journal of Wildlife Management*, **71**(4), 1080–1088.

Clifford, D.L., Schumaker, B.A., Stephenson, T. R., et al. (2009) Assessing disease risk at the wildlife–livestock interface: a study of Sierra Nevada bighorn sheep. *Biological Conservation*, **142**(11), 2559–2568.

Coggins, V.L. (2006) Selenium supplementation, parasite treatment, and management of bighorn sheep at Lostine River, Oregon. *Biennial Symposium of the Northern Wild Sheep and Goat Council*, **15**, 98–106.

Coltman, D.W., Festa-Bianchet, M., Jorgenson, J. T., et al. (2002) Age-dependent sexual selection in bighorn rams. *Proceedings of the Royal Society of London B*, **269**(1487), 165–172.

Craft, M.E., Hawthorne, P.L., Packer, C., et al. (2008) Dynamics of a multihost pathogen in a carnivore community. *Journal of Animal Ecology*, **77**(6), 1257–1264.

Cross, P.C., Lloyd-Smith, J.O., Johnson, P.L., et al. (2005) Duelling timescales of host movement and disease recovery determine invasion of disease in structured populations. *Ecology Letters*, **8**(6), 587–595.

Dassanayake, R.P., Shanthalingam, S., Herndon, C.N., et al. (2010) *Mycoplasma ovipneumoniae* can predispose bighorn sheep to fatal *Mannheimia haemolytica* pneumonia. *Veterinary Microbiology*, **145**(3), 354–359.

DeCesare, N.J. & Pletscher, D.H. (2006) Movements, connectivity, and resource selection of Rocky Mountain bighorn sheep. *Journal of Mammalogy*, **87**(3), 531–538.

Epps, C.W., Wehausen, J.D., Bleich, V.C., et al. (2007) Optimizing dispersal and corridor models using landscape genetics. *Journal of Applied Ecology*, **44**(4), 714–724.

Felts, B.L., Walsh, D.P., Cassirer, E.F., Besser, T.E. & Jenks, J. (2016) *Mycoplasma ovipneumoniae* cross-strain transmissions in captive bighorn sheep. *Biennial Symposium of the Northern Wild Sheep and Goat Council*, **20**, 77–78.

Festa-Bianchet, M. (1988) Nursing behaviour of bighorn sheep: correlates of ewe age, parasitism, lamb age, birthdate and sex. *Animal Behaviour*, **36**(5), 1445–1454.

Festa-Bianchet, M. (2012) The cost of trying: weak interspecific correlations among life-history components in male ungulates. *Canadian Journal of Zoology*, **90**(9), 1072–1085.

Geist, V. (1971) *Mountain Sheep. A Study in Behaviour and Evolution*. Chicago, IL: University of Chicago Press.

George, J.L., Martin, D.J., Lukacs, P.M., et al. (2008) Epidemic pasteurellosis in a bighorn sheep population coinciding with the appearance of a domestic sheep. *Journal of Wildlife Diseases*, **44**(2), 388–403.

Hass, C.C. (1997). Seasonality of births in bighorn sheep. *Journal of Mammalogy*, **78**(4), 1251–1260.

Heinse, L.M., Hardesty, L.M. & Harris, R.B. (2016) Risk of pathogen spillover from domestic sheep and goat flocks on private land. *Wildlife Society Bulletin*, **40**(4), 625–633.

Hiendleder, S., Kaupe, B., Wassmuth, R., et al. (2002) Molecular analysis of wild and domestic sheep questions current nomenclature and provides evidence for domestication from two different subspecies. *Proceedings of the Royal Society of London B*, **269**(1494), 893–904.

Hobbs, N.T. & Miller, M.W. (1992) Interactions between pathogens and hosts: simulation of pasteurellosis epizootics in bighorn sheep populations. In: *Wildlife 2001: Populations* (pp.997–1007). Dordrecht: Springer.

Hogg, J.T. (1984) Mating in bighorn sheep: multiple creative male strategies. *Science*, **225**, 526–530.

Hogg, J.T., Hass, C.C. & Jenni, D.A. (1992) Sex-biased maternal expenditure in Rocky Mountain bighorn sheep. *Behavioral Ecology and Sociobiology*, **31**(4), 243–251.

Jansen, B.D., Krausman, P.R., Heffelfinger, J.R., et al. (2007) Population dynamics and behavior of bighorn sheep with infectious keratoconjunctivitis. *Journal of Wildlife Management*, **71**(2), 571–575.

Jones, G.E., Keir, W.A. & Gilmour, J.S. (1985). The pathogenicity of *Mycoplasma ovipneumoniae* and *Mycoplasma arginini* in ovine and caprine tracheal organ cultures. *Journal of Comparative Pathology*, **95**(4), 477–487.

Jorgenson, J.T., Festa-Bianchet, M., Lucherini, M., et al. (1993) Effects of body size, population density, and maternal characteristics on age at first reproduction in bighorn ewes. *Canadian Journal of Zoology*, **71**(12), 2509–2517.

Joseph, M.B., Mihaljevic, J.R., Arellano, A.L., et al. (2013) Taming wildlife disease: bridging the gap between science and management. *Journal of Applied Ecology*, **50**(3), 702–712.

Justice-Allen, A.E., Butler, E., Pebworth, J., et al. (2016) Investigation of pneumonia mortalities in a *Mycoplasma*-positive desert bighorn sheep population and detection of a different strain of *Mycoplasma ovipneumoniae*. *Biennial Symposium of the Northern Wild Sheep and Goat Council*, **20**, 68–72.

Kamath, P.L., Cross, P.C., Cassirer, E.F., et al. (2016) Genetic linkages among *Mycoplasma ovipneumoniae* outbreaks in wild and domestic sheep and goats. *Biennial Symposium of the Northern Wild Sheep and Goat Council*, **20**, 113.

Keeling, M.J. & Rohani, P. (2008) *Modeling Infectious Diseases in Humans and Animals*. Princeton, NJ: Princeton University Press.

Kilpatrick, A.M., Daszak, P., Jones, M.J., et al. (2006) Host heterogeneity dominates West Nile virus transmission. *Proceedings of the Royal Society of London B*, **273**, 2327–2333.

Klepac, P., Pomeroy, L.W., Bjørnstad, O.N., et al. (2009) Stage-structured transmission of phocine distemper virus in the Dutch 2002 outbreak. *Proceedings of the Royal Society of London B*, **276**(1666), 2469–2476.

Kuussaari, M., Bommarco, R., Heikkinen, R.K., et al. (2009) Extinction debt: a challenge for biodiversity conservation. *Trends in Ecology & Evolution*, **24**(10), 564–571.

Langwig, K.E., Frick, W.F., Bried, J.T., et al. (2012) Sociality, density-dependence and microclimates determine the persistence of populations suffering from a novel fungal disease, white-nose syndrome. *Ecology Letters*, **15**(9), 1050–1057.

Lloyd-Smith, J.O., George, D., Pepin, K.M., et al. (2009) Epidemic dynamics at the human-animal interface. *Science*, **326**, 1362–1367.

Loison, A., Festa-Bianchet, M., Gaillard, J.M., et al. (1999) Age-specific survival in five populations of ungulates: evidence of senescence. *Ecology*, **80**(8), 2539–2554.

Long, R.A., Rachlow, J.L. & Kie, J.G. (2008) Effects of season and scale on response of elk and mule deer to habitat manipulation. *Journal of Wildlife Management*, **72**(5), 1133–1142.

Maksimović, Z., De la Fe, C., Amores, J., et al. (2016) Comparison of phenotypic and genotypic profiles among caprine and ovine *Mycoplasma ovipneumoniae* strains. *Veterinary Record*, **180**(7), 180.

Manlove, K.R., Cassirer, E.F., Cross, P.C., et al. (2014) Costs and benefits of group living with disease: a case study of pneumonia in bighorn lambs (*Ovis canadensis*). *Proceedings of the Royal Society of London B*, **281**(1797), 20142331.

Manlove, K., Cassirer, E.F., Cross, P.C., et al. (2016a) Disease introduction is associated with a phase transition in bighorn sheep demographics. *Ecology*, **97**(10), 2593–2602.

Manlove, K.R., Cassirer, E.F., Plowright, R.K., et al. (2017) Contact and contagion: probability of transmission given contact varies with demographic state in bighorn sheep. *Journal of Animal Ecology*, **86**(4), 908–920.

Manlove, K.R., Walker, J.G., Craft, M.E., et al. (2016b) 'One Health' or three? Publication silos among the One Health disciplines. *PLoS Biology*, **14**(4), e1002448.

McAdoo, C., Wolff, P. & Cox, M. (2010) Investigation of Nevada's 2009–2010 East Humboldt Range and Ruby Mountain bighorn dieoff. *Biennial Symposium of the Northern Wild Sheep and Goat Council*, **17**, 51–52.

Meldrum, G.E. & Ruckstuhl, K.E. (2009) Mixed-sex group formation by bighorn sheep in winter: trading costs of synchrony for benefits of group living. *Animal Behaviour*, **77**(4), 919–929.

Miller, D.S., Hoberg, E., Weiser, G., et al. (2012) A review of hypothesized determinants associated with bighorn sheep (*Ovis canadensis*) die-offs. *Veterinary Medicine International*, **2012**, 796527.

Miller, M.W., Vayhinger, J.E., Bowden, D.C., et al. (2000) Drug treatment for lungworm in bighorn sheep: reevaluation of a 20-year-old management prescription. *Journal of Wildlife Management*, **64**(2), 505–512.

Mincher, B.J., Ball, R.D., Houghton, T.P., et al. (2008) Some aspects of geophagia in Wyoming bighorn sheep (*Ovis canadensis*). *European Journal of Wildlife Research*, **54**(2), 193–198.

Monello, R.J., Murray, D.L. & Cassirer, E.F. (2001) Ecological correlates of pneumonia epizootics in bighorn sheep herds. *Canadian Journal of Zoology*, **79**(8), 1423–1432.

Niang, M., Rosenbusch, R.F., Andrews, J.J., et al. (1998) Demonstration of a capsule on *Mycoplasma ovipneumoniae*. *American Journal of Veterinary Research*, **59**(5), 557–562.

Nicholas, R., Ayling, R. & McAuliffe, L. (2008) *Mycoplasma Diseases of Ruminants: Disease, Diagnosis and Control*. Cambridge, MA: CABI.

O'Brien, J.M., O'Brien, C.S., McCarthy, C., et al. (2014) Incorporating foray behavior into models estimating contact risk between bighorn sheep and areas occupied by domestic sheep. *Wildlife Society Bulletin*, **38**(2), 321–331.

Peel, A.J., Pulliam, J.R.C., Luis, A.D., et al. (2014) The effect of seasonal birth pulses on pathogen persistence in wild mammal populations. *Proceedings of the Royal Society of London B*, **281**(1786), 20132962.

Plowright, R.K., Manlove, K.R., Besser, T.E., et al. (2017) Persistent carriers explain epidemiological features of pneumonia in bighorn sheep (*Ovis canadensis*). *Ecology Letters*, **20**(10), 1325–1336.

Plowright, R.K., Manlove, K., Cassirer, E.F., et al. (2013) Use of exposure history to identify patterns of immunity to pneumonia in bighorn sheep (*Ovis canadensis*). *PLoS ONE*, **8**(4), e61919.

Rezaei, H.R., Naderi, S., Chintauan-Marquier, I.C., et al. (2010) Evolution and taxonomy of the wild species of the genus *Ovis* (Mammalia, Artiodactyla, Bovidae). *Molecular Phylogenetics and Evolution*, **54**, 315–326.

Rifatbegović, M., Maksimović, Z. & Hulaj, B. (2011) *Mycoplasma ovipneumoniae* associated with severe respiratory disease in goats. *Veterinary Record*, **168**, 565a.

Ruckstuhl, K.E. (1998) Foraging behaviour and sexual segregation in bighorn sheep. *Animal Behaviour*, **56**(1), 99–106.

Ruckstuhl, K.E. & Festa-Bianchet, M. (2001) Group choice by subadult bighorn rams: trade-offs between foraging efficiency and predator avoidance. *Ethology*, **107**(2), 161–172.

Scheele, B.C., Hunter, D.A., Brannelly, L.A., et al. (2017) Reservoir-host amplification of disease impact in an endangered amphibian. *Conservation Biology*, **31**(3), 592–600.

Sells, S.N., Mitchell, M.S., Nowak, J.J., et al. (2015) Modeling risk of pneumonia epizootics in bighorn sheep. *The Journal of Wildlife Management*, **79**(2), 195–210.

Shannon, J.M., Whiting, J.C., Larsen, R.T., et al. (2014) Population response of reintroduced bighorn sheep after observed commingling with domestic sheep. *European Journal of Wildlife Research*, **60**(5), 737–748.

Simmons, W.L., Daubenspeck, J.M., Osborne, J.D., et al. (2013) Type 1 and Type 2 strains of *Mycoplasma pneumoniae* form different biofilms. *Microbiology*, **159**, 737–747.

Smith, J.B., Jenks, J.A., Grovenburg, T.W., et al. (2014) Disease and predation: sorting out causes of a bighorn sheep (*Ovis canadensis*) decline. *PLoS ONE*, **9**(2), e88271.

Subramaniam, R., Shanthalingam, S., Bavananthasivam, J., et al. (2014) Bighorn sheep × domestic sheep hybrids survive *Mannheimia haemolytica* challenge in the absence of vaccination. *Veterinary Microbiology*, **170**, 278–283.

Swinton, J., Harwood, J., Grenfell, B.T., et al. (1998) Persistence thresholds for phocine distemper virus infection in harbour seal *Phoca vitulina* metapopulations. *Journal of Animal Ecology*, **67**, 54–68.

USDA. (2015) *Mycoplasma ovipneumoniae* on US sheep operations. USDA-APHIS-VS-CEAH. Fort Collins, CO: USDA. 708.0615

Weiser, G.C., DeLong, W.J., Paz, J.L., et al. (2003) Characterization of *Pasteurella multocida* associated with pneumonia in bighorn sheep. *Journal of Wildlife Diseases*, **39**(3), 536–544.

Western Association of Fish and Wildlife Agencies Wild Sheep Working Group. (2012) Recommendations for domestic sheep and goat management in wild sheep habitat. Available from: www.wildsheepworkinggroup.com/resources/publications/, Western Association of Fish and Wildife Agencies Wild Sheep Working Group.

Whiting, J.C., Olson, D.D., Shannon, J.M., et al. (2012) Timing and synchrony of births in bighorn sheep: implications for reintroduction and conservation. *Wildlife Research*, **39**(7), 565–572.

CHAPTER FOURTEEN

Manipulating parasites in an Arctic herbivore: gastrointestinal nematodes and the population regulation of Svalbard reindeer

R. JUSTIN IRVINE, STEVE D. ALBON,
AUDUN STIEN, ODD HALVORSEN AND
ANJA M. CARLSSON

14.1 Introduction

Variation in food availability, predation, and disease, as well as the direct effects of weather, can all potentially influence reproduction and survival, and hence the dynamics of natural populations (Begon et al., 2005). However, despite a strong theoretical framework that predicts that parasite-mediated density-dependent mortality stabilises host populations (Anderson & May, 1978), and parasite-mediated fecundity destabilises populations (May & Anderson, 1978), there is still little empirical evidence for a widespread role of parasites in driving population dynamics (Tompkins et al., 2011). This paucity of evidence may be a function of the short duration of many studies, which mitigates against quantifying the confounding effects of stochastic variation in the natural environment (Albon et al., 2002), and also because host population dynamics are often complex, making it difficult to tease out the effects of parasitism from other factors (but see Martínez-Padilla et al. and references, Chapter 10, this volume). Executing carefully designed field experiments to manipulate parasites at the scale relevant to the population size can be challenging, especially at the same time as controlling for other potential drivers of population change, such as behaviour (Redpath et al., 2006), or food (Pedersen & Grieves, 2008).

In this chapter we synthesise our long-term work on the population ecology of both Svalbard reindeer (*Rangifer tarandus platyrhynchus* Vrolik) and their gastrointestinal (abomasal) nematodes in the High Arctic. The study was motivated by the fact that the population dynamics of non-migratory Svalbard reindeer (Tyler & Øritsland, 1989) are unstable (Solberg et al., 2001; Tyler et al., 2008) and the burden of abomasal nematodes is high compared to migratory reindeer populations on the Norwegian mainland (Bye & Halvorsen, 1983; Bye, 1987). While these attributes are consistent with the theory that macroparasites can regulate host populations, theory required us to demonstrate the extent to which parasites not only depress host fecundity and/or survival, but also have a greater impact on hosts as the intensity of infection increased (*sensu* May & Anderson, 1978). In addition, there is an expectation that the intensity of infection increases with increasing host density, and therefore, a positive relationship should exist between parasite abundance and host density (Arneberg et al., 1998). Furthermore, if the parasites are highly prevalent then the impact of parasites on host fitness may have greater consequences for population growth rates than in situations where there is low prevalence, even if the low proportion of hosts infected suffer greater impact at the individual level.

Wild herbivores in general, and ruminants in particular, are good candidate model systems to further the understanding of host–parasite interactions (Jolles & Ezenwa, 2015; Ezenwa et al., Chapter 5, this volume), which can have wider consequences for the dynamics of ungulate grazing systems (Grenfell, 1988, 1992; Hutchings et al., 2000). Not only can gastrointestinal nematodes be abundant in wild ruminants (Hoberg et al., 2001) and highly prevalent as in Svalbard reindeer (Bye & Halvorsen, 1983), but also from domestic studies there is a wider appreciation of their subclinical effects, i.e. the parasites often have low pathogenicity and infected individuals show no obvious symptoms of infection (Fox, 1997). The effects of such subclinical infections are typically difficult to detect without controlled experiments, but often include reduced appetite, food assimilation and growth (Arneberg et al., 1996; Forbes et al., 2000). Furthermore, in principle, anti-parasite drugs developed for livestock can facilitate manipulative field experiments to test the costs of parasites in wild ruminant hosts (Gulland, 1992).

Here we describe how we addressed many of the issues described above to quantify the interaction between the Svalbard reindeer and its abomasal nematodes: we have used a combination of longitudinal experimental data on individual reindeer (repeated observations of uniquely marked reindeer), cross-sectional data from culled animals, and observational data on the intensity of parasite life stages. Our study over many years demonstrates (a) the importance of knowledge about parasite life histories, including species differences in the seasonality of their transmission dynamics; (b) the value of long-term experimental manipulations to estimate host impacts at varying host densities and parasite transmission rates; and (c) the need for appropriate models to evaluate the significance of findings for parasite–host population dynamics.

14.2 The Svalbard reindeer–parasite system

Rangifer tarandus (caribou and reindeer) have a circumpolar distribution (Figure 14.1a), as do many of the species of nematodes found in their gastrointestinal tract (Kutz et al., 2012).

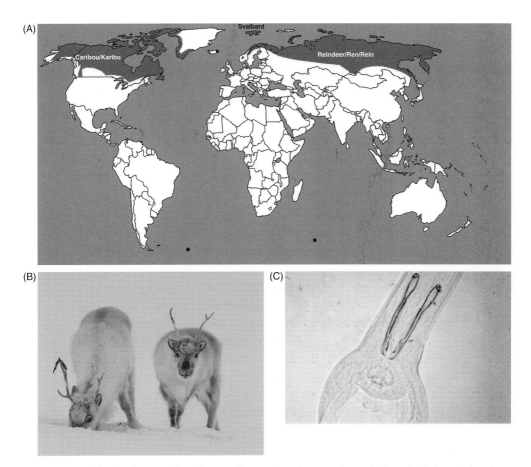

Figure 14.1 (A) The circumpolar distribution of *Rangifer tarandus*: reindeer (red shading) and caribou (green shading). Svalbard (76–81°N, 9–33°E) is shown at the centre top. Reindeer exist there with no predators or competitors. Black dots are introduced populations. © Wikipedia, TBjornstad. https://en.wikipedia.org/wiki/Reindeer#/media/File:Rangifer_tarandus_map.png (B) Adult and calf Svalbard reindeer, *Rangifer tarandus platyrhynchus*. (C) The nematode parasite *Ostertagia grühneri*. (A black and white version of this figure will appear in some formats. For the colour version, please refer to the plate section.)

Our study is based on a subpopulation of reindeer in the Colesdalen-Semeldalen–Reindalen valley system in the Nordenskiöldland peninsula, on the west of the archipelago (77°50′–78°20′N, 15°00′–17°30′E) (Figure 14.1b). The North Atlantic Current along the west coast of Spitsbergen makes the winter weather relatively mild compared to most other places at similar latitudes: the mean daily temperature in January is –16°C and in July +6°C. Over recent decades, temperatures have shown an increasing trend, in particular in winter (Gjelten et al., 2016; Albon et al., 2017), and are expected to continue to increase substantially through the twenty-first century (Førland et al., 2011). Snow persists from October to early June. However, the warming is also associated with a trend for more 'rain-on-snow' in winter, which can lead to extensive ice formation, restricting access to vegetation by the reindeer (Hansen et al., 2014) and affecting reindeer distribution (Stien et al., 2010, 2012). The growing season for plants is short and primary productivity low, typically 40–60g m^{-2}, even on the valley bottoms and vegetated lower slopes (Wegener & Odasz-Albrigtsen, 1998; Van der Wal & Stien, 2014).

Svalbard reindeer are a relatively sedentary subspecies and do not undertake long-distance seasonal migrations (Tyler & Øritsland, 1989). We follow the lives of 400–500 marked, known-aged individual females alive at any one time in a population estimated at nearly 1800 in 2015 (Bjørkvoll et al., 2016). Each April, a sample of up to 45 female and 15 male calves are marked for the first time, and previously marked females are recaptured to provide information on age-specific growth, condition, and pregnancy (Milner et al., 2003; Omsjoe et al., 2009). Summer censuses provide additional information on females with a calf at foot – the outcome of those earlier pregnancies.

Svalbard reindeer are in peak body condition in the autumn and lose body mass and fat from then until the following spring (June), when they start building up their reserves again (Reimers & Ringberg, 1983). As in many mammals, pregnancy rates depend on body mass in the autumn breeding season. Therefore, factors that affect body mass gain, in particular summer temperature and the resulting plant growth, influence fertility rates (Albon et al., 2017). However, the probability of retaining pregnancy and producing a viable calf depends on the prevailing winter weather, in particular, body mass loss due to starvation associated with the 'rain-on-snow' events (Hansen et al., 2010, 2011; Albon et al., 2017). Thus, it was important to undertake our manipulative parasite experiments over multiple years, to account for the stochastic environmental variation.

Since the late 1970s, monitoring of three subpopulations of Svalbard reindeer has revealed a twofold fluctuation in numbers (Solberg et al., 2001; Tyler et al., 2008) which reflects variation in late-winter (April) body mass (Albon et al., 2017) with covariation in birth and death rates (Tyler, 1987; Solberg et al., 2001; Bjørkvoll et al., 2016). However, during the last decade there has been a significant increase in all subpopulations, as illustrated in our study area (Figure 14.2), probably associated with the higher plant productivity in warmer summers and heavier reindeer at the onset of winter (Albon et al., 2017).

In the mid-1990s, when we started the study, the only wild vertebrate in which population regulation by macroparasites had been demonstrated was the red grouse in northern England (see Martínez-Padilla et al., Chapter 10, this volume). The paucity of examples was largely due to the fact that in most

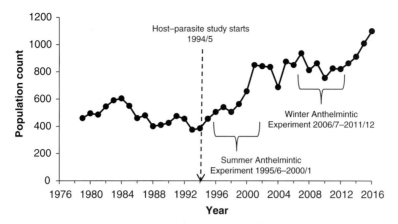

Figure 14.2 The number of Svalbard reindeer counted in the Colesdalen–Semmeldalen–Reindalen study area between 1979 and 2016 (data from Norwegian Institute for Nature Research). Also shown are the start of the host–parasite study and the periods of major experimental manipulations of abomasal nematodes using slow-release anthelmintic drugs.

wildlife systems the necessary manipulative experiments have not been designed or implemented to test the theory (Tompkins et al., 2002). Even with the benefit of the robust theoretical framework (Anderson & May, 1978; May & Anderson, 1978), our study of the role of parasites in the regulation of Svalbard reindeer would never have started if it had not been for four pieces of otherwise coincidental evidence. First, the apparent instability of Svalbard reindeer population numbers (Reimers, 1977, 1982; Tyler, 1987; and see Figure 14.2). Second, the high intensity of abomasal nematode infection in Svalbard reindeer compared to Norwegian mainland reindeer populations. Third, a positive correlation between parasite intensity and reindeer density, expressed simply as numbers per km^2, across three Norwegian Mainland populations and Svalbard (based on data in Bye & Halvorsen, 1983; Bye, 1987). Fourth, an apparent negative relationship between measures of host fat stores and the intensity of abomasal nematode infection (Halvorsen & Bye, 1986, 1999). In addition, there are no competing mammalian herbivores to co-host the nematodes (Bye et al., 1987) and no large predators to influence recruitment and survival rates compared to many herbivore host–parasite systems. Finally, the reindeer–helminth parasite system on Svalbard has the advantage of being relatively simple, and therefore potentially tractable. Three species have been recorded from the abomasum: mainly *Ostertagia grühneri* (Figure 14.1c), *Marshallagia marshalli*, and the less abundant *Teladorsagia circumcincta* (Bye & Halvorsen, 1983; Halvorsen & Bye, 1986), and no nematodes were found in a parasitological examination of 24 intestines (Halvorsen & Bye, 1986). However, eggs from Nematodirinae intestinal nematodes have been found in Svalbard reindeer faeces, indicating that other nematode species may be present. This contrasts with domestic sheep, where Crofton (1957) listed 17 gastrointestinal nematode species – 13 found in the intestine, and four from the abomasum.

Despite the advantageous features of the Svalbard reindeer case study, it is still necessary to be able to perturb the hosts or the parasites, between populations or repeatedly over many years, in order to demonstrate regulation. This was possible due to the availability of anthelmintic drugs developed for domestic livestock. These were used in the design of multi-year experiments to compare reproduction and survival in 'treated' and untreated 'control' groups and control for stochastic environmental variation in this individually marked Svalbard reindeer population.

In summary, this host–parasite system was ideally suited to test the potential role of parasites in regulating a wild host population, because intensity of infection is relatively high, the parasite community is simple, the population fluctuates in relation to changes in fecundity, and apart from stochastic weather-related effects of rain-on-snow, there are few other factors to tease out.

14.3 Contrasting parasite life histories and quantifying their impact on reindeer hosts

We focus on the two dominant species of abomasal nematodes. These have a directly transmitted life cycle, with adult worms shedding eggs which pass out of the host with the faeces. Eggs develop to infective larvae on the vegetation, where they are ingested as hosts graze and develop to adults on reaching the abomasum. In this section we describe our parallel field investigations, first, revealing the contrasting parasite life histories from a cross-sectional study of culled reindeer and second, experimentally manipulating these parasites using anthelmintics to quantify their impact on body mass, reproduction, and survival in a longitudinal study of individually marked animals. These epidemiological studies provided the parameter estimates to model the effect of the parasites species on reindeer population dynamics (see Section 14.4).

14.3.1 Parasite life-history differences – seasonal changes in the species-specific intensities

Our early work based on the total trichostrongyle population in abomasum from reindeer culled in late summer/autumn (August–October) and late winter (February–May) provided the somewhat surprising evidence of continued transmission of nematodes throughout the winter, despite low temperatures and snow-covered pastures (Halvorsen et al., 1999). The intensity of infection increased between October and April due to an increase in numbers of both adult worms and larvae in the mucosa. Thus, it appeared that larvae were ingested from the winter pastures, and while there was some degree of arrested development, others matured (Halvorsen & Bye, 1999).

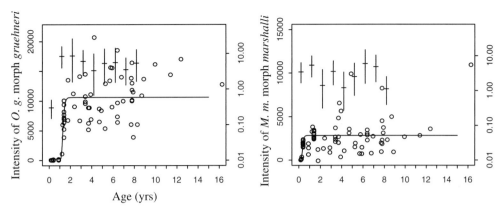

Figure 14.3 Gompertz age-intensity with 95% confidence intervals for adult *M. marshalli* and *O. gruehneri* sampled from the calves and adult female reindeer. Observed values for the nematode taxa corrected for seasonal and between-year variation in nematode abundances are plotted around the curves. For *M. marshalli* there was no significant between-year variation in the asymptotic abundance of infection. The fitted curves and adjusted residuals for *O. gruehneri* are standardised for the 1997±98 winter. Re-drawn from data in figure 2A and C in Irvine et al. (2000). © 2000 Cambridge University Press.

Coexisting species, however, may have different dynamics, leading to successional changes in intensities of species that have different developmental rates (Crofton, 1957, 1963; Boag & Thomas, 1977), and therefore detecting the impacts on hosts is likely to be difficult if the analysis is carried out at the community level (Irvine et al., 2000). In the Svalbard reindeer, we estimated the intensity of infection of the two dominant species – *O. gruehneri* and *M. marshalli* – using morphological and molecular techniques, and document how their life histories differed.

14.3.1.1 Observational studies of differences in parasite life histories
Species-specific patterns in the intensity of infection based on morphological identification of adult males (Drózdz, 1965; Bye & Halvorsen, 1983) revealed clear differences between the two main species. First, the intensity of infection with *O. gruehneri* increases slowly, reaching an asymptote only in the animal's third year of life, and does not seem to decline with age. Likewise, for *M. marshalli*, there is no decline in the intensity of infection with age, although the hosts rapidly pick up infections reaching an asymptote within the animal's first year of life (Figure 14.3; Irvine et al., 2000). Second, over-winter intensity of *M. marshalli* in the reindeer population increased threefold between October and April, while *O. gruehneri* was much less variable (Irvine et al., 2000). Faecal egg count data collected between April and October

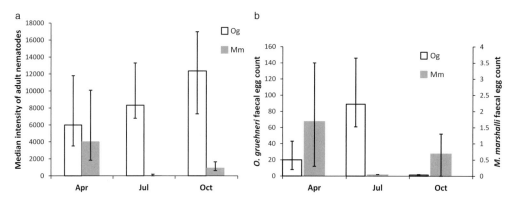

Figure 14.4 (a) Comparison of the median intensity of infection ± interquartile range (adult nematodes) of *O. gruehneri* and *M. marshalli* in adult female reindeer, and (b) comparison of the median egg output (per gram faeces) of *O. gruehneri* and *M. marshalli*. Untreated controls sampled in 1999: April ($N = 5$), July ($N = 7$) and October ($N = 7$). Redrawn from data in figure 2C and D in Irvine et al. (2001). © 2001 Cambridge University Press.

reinforced these life-history differences in Irvine et al. (2000): *M. marshalli* egg output was minimal in midsummer and higher in late winter and early autumn, whereas *O. gruehneri* egg output increased from April peaking in late July/early August, and then declined through September (Irvine et al., 2000).

These marked differences in life history between the two species were confirmed with molecular tools that make an unbiased distinction between species of adult nematodes in the abomasum and then comparing these to the patterns of faecal egg output from the same culled animals (Irvine et al., 2001). Again, this showed the striking pattern of *M. marshalli* transmission over the winter, with very low numbers of adult worms in summer and commensurate low egg output in July (Figure 14.4a). In contrast, *O. gruehneri* adult worm intensities were less variable but tended to increase over summer, with maximal egg output in summer (Figure 14.4b).

14.3.1.2 Experimental studies of differences in parasite life histories
The contrasting life histories were further explored using anthelmintics to remove parasites from a 'treated' group and quantify the reinfection rates in these hosts compared to 'untreated' control individuals. The apparent seasonal differences in life histories and transmission of the two species required two experiments, one in summer and one in winter.

14.3.1.2.1 Reinfection during summer.   Based on the life-history differences, we predicted that animals treated with an anthelmintic in late winter (April/May) would become more quickly reinfected by *O. gruehneri* during the

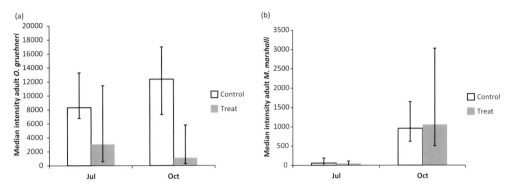

Figure 14.5 The median intensity of infection ± interquartile range (adult nematodes) of female reindeer treated with anthelmintics in late winter 1999 compared to untreated controls for (a) *O. gruehneri* and (b) *M. marshalli*. Sample sizes: July (*N* = 7 controls, 8 treated) and October (*N* = 7 controls, 7 treated). Redrawn from Stien et al. (2002a). © 2002 British Ecological Society.

following summer than by *M. marshalli*, which would only increase in the autumn. To quantify the effect of treatment on the parasites, we measured reinfection in adult reindeer injected with the anthelmintic moxidectin (Cydectin; Wyeth, Madison, NJ, USA) and compared them with untreated controls (Irvine, 2000). Samples of each group were culled three and six months post-treatment (late July and October, respectively) in 1999. Treatment significantly reduced the intensity of infection compared to untreated controls. Although all the treated animals had become reinfected to some extent with *O. gruehneri* by July, there was no further increase in the intensity of this parasite from July to October in either experimental group (Figure 14.5a). In contrast, *M. marshalli* adult intensities remained low and did not differ between treated animals and controls, although they were higher in October in both treatment groups than the negligible levels found in July (Figure 14.5b; Stien et al., 2002a).

The reduction in the number of adult *O. gruehneri* following treatment is likely to be due to both the direct removal of the adults and the larvae (both mucosa and lumen dwelling), which are predominantly *O. gruehneri* (Irvine et al., 2001), that would otherwise have developed into adults. Conversely, there was no treatment effect on the intensity of infection with adult *M. marshalli* or the intensity of the larval nematode stages three months after treatment. Indeed, there were negligible levels of *M. marshalli* in control animals culled in July (Figure 14.4a), compared to the levels found in April (Figure 14.4a), indicating that in the summer, when there is little evidence for transmission, the adult *M. marshalli* disappear from the hosts, presumably through mortality. This provides further support for the contrasting life history of this species and implies that *M. marshalli* adults were not present in the host when the anthelmintic was acting, but were transmitted after the efficacy period for the anthelmintic and then developed to adults. The strong seasonal fluctuations of *M. marshalli* suggests *M. marshalli* has a high turnover rate and short life expectancy (El-Azazy, 1995; Irvine et al., 2000), which is not dissimilar to a range of gastrointestinal nematodes found in sheep (Crofton, 1957). In contrast, the population dynamics of *O. gruehneri* shows a less pronounced seasonal fluctuation, suggesting a longer life expectancy (Irvine et al., 2000). Thus, *M. marshalli* reinfects the host every year, whereas *O. gruehneri* is likely to have a longer lifespan.

14.3.1.2.2 Reinfection during winter.   To experimentally confirm the winter transmission of *M. marshalli* we needed to study reinfection after removing parasites in the autumn. We did this by using a novel delayed-release anthelmintic bolus (Carlsson et al., 2012a), and estimating reinfection rates in reindeer culled in October, February, and April (Carlsson et al., 2012b). A subsample of reindeer treated with the delayed anthelmintic bolus that were recaught in February the following year were treated with a single dose of moxidectin in order to remove any nematodes acquired because the effect of the delayed bolus would have dissipated by mid-November. From the culled animals, the larval stages of nematodes in the abomasum were identified using molecular tools (Dallas et al., 2000), whereas adult stages were identified using conventional morphological taxonomy. The intensity of *M. marshalli* adult worms and fourth-stage larvae (L4) increased significantly from October to April (Figure 14.6d,f), indicating that reindeer were being infected with third-stage larvae (L3) from the pasture throughout the winter (Carlsson et al., 2012b). Furthermore, the proportion of L5 larvae that were *M. marshalli* larvae was high, consistent with rapid development from infective stage to adult (Figure 14.6e). In the same experiment, we showed that *O. gruehneri* exhibited no over-winter transmission, as its intensity remained stable (Figure 14.6a–c).

14.3.1.2.3 Life on the pasture: experimental insights into the free-living stages of *M. marshalli*.   While *M. marshalli* egg output to pasture occurs only in winter and transmission of infective larvae also only occurs in winter, it remains implausible that eggs can develop to infective larvae in the subzero temperatures within the same arctic winter. Thus, we hypothesised that there is a one-year time lag in the transmission of *M. marshalli*, where the parasite remains as an egg on the vegetation when deposited in winter on wind-blown ridges, and develops into the infective stage (L3) during the following summer, when conditions are more favourable (Halvorsen et al., 1999; Irvine et al., 2000). The *M. marshalli* infective larvae are then ingested the following winter

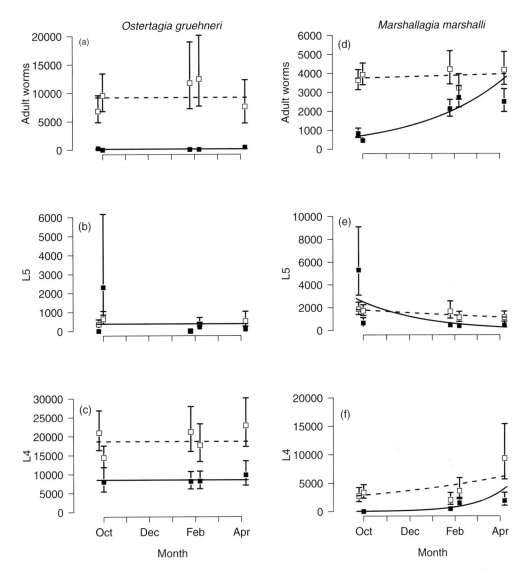

Figure 14.6 Estimated and predicted intensity of adult worms (a,d); fifth-stage larvae, L5s (b,e); and fourth-stage larvae, L4s (c,f) for *O. gruehneri* (a–c) and *M. marshalli* (d–f) in adult female reindeer not treated (open symbols, broken lines) and treated with anthelmintics (filled symbols, solid lines). Treated animals were culled and sampled in October shortly after effective release of the drug, and in February and April, 5 and 7 months later, respectively. Symbols show the estimates and standard errors for the intensity of each worm fraction for each treatment for animals culled. Lines represent the predicted intensity of nematodes over time from the minimal model. Time and host population size in year t – 1 were fitted as continuous variables and treatment was included as a two-level factor. From figure 1, Carlsson et al. (2012b). © 2012 Australian Society for Parasitology Inc).

when reindeer return to forage on the same 'ridge' plant communities used in the previous winter.

To understand the mechanisms of winter transmission of *M. marshalli* we carried out experiments in the laboratory to explore the potential for development and survival of eggs and infective third-stage larvae (L3) in simulated winter conditions (Carlsson et al., 2013). The results confirmed that while eggs can develop to the L3 stage at temperatures down to 2°C, they do not do so below freezing. In addition, we found eggs can remain viable and develop after being exposed to subzero temperatures for up to 28 months. Furthermore, L3 larvae can survive for up to 80 days at 5°C, as well as surviving rapid and short duration freezing events to temperatures below –30°C (Carlsson et al., 2013). These experiments indicate that *M. marshalli* eggs deposited during the winter are highly tolerant of the environmental conditions prevailing on Svalbard and have the potential for rapid development with the onset of spring. These results are consistent with the hypothesised one-year time delay resulting from egg deposition in winter, development during the subsequent summer, and ingestion over the next winter. They are also consistent with the observation that the intensity of infection with *M. marshalli* is related to the density of reindeer in the previous rather than current winter (Carlsson et al., 2012b).

Our discoveries of the unusual life history of *M. marshalli*, in particular its winter transmission, is supported by results from a cross-sectional and modelling study that indicated a similar pattern in the Saiga antelope (*Saiga tatarica*) of Kazakhstan, although here the infection may be reinforced from sheep grazing on pastures before Saiga migrate south to their wintering grounds (Morgan et al., 2007). In the Saiga there is a significant increase in the mean intensity of infection with *M. marshalli* during the Saiga calf's first winter, not dissimilar to what we see in Svalbard reindeer in their first winter, when infection levels reach the same as in adults (Figure 14.3b; Irvine et al., 2000).

In summary, *M. marshalli* is rapidly acquired, reaching an asymptote in the host's first year of life, and shows little annual variation. It is strongly seasonal, being virtually absent in summer and showing a significant increase over winter, which is also when egg output occurs. There are negligible numbers of L4 larvae at any time of year, suggesting that this species does not use arrested development for survival (Hoar et al., 2012a). However, there are significant numbers of L5 larvae in the winter, supporting the hypothesis that *M. marshalli* focuses transmission on the winter months, building up infection from the very low levels found in summer (Irvine et al., 2000, 2001; Irvine, 2001).

In contrast, *O. gruehneri* increases in intensity in the hosts over summer when egg production peaks (Figure 14.4b) and, at least in some years, may decline over winter, suggesting that any transmission at this time of year is insufficient to compensate for adult worm mortality (Irvine et al., 2001). It appears to be a long-lived species, with infection intensity increasing slowly until the reindeers' third year of life, which is late compared to the rate at which abomasal nematode infections typically develop in sheep and cattle (Armour, 1989). There is some evidence for arrested development, particularly in calves (Irvine et al., unpublished), with high intensities of larvae in the abomasal mucosa (L4s) in winter, presumably as a mechanism to cope when environmental conditions for the survival of free-living eggs and larvae are poor. Furthermore, developing larvae in the abomasal lumen (L5s) peak in summer: consistent with the acquisition of infective larvae and their subsequent development to adults in this period. Intensity of infection varies annually and is generally higher than *M. marshalli*.

The life-history differences revealed in our reindeer study rely on identifying the species using molecular and conventional taxonomic techniques and illustrate the importance of experimentally manipulating parasite loads, which effectively remove the parasites when the parasite effect is likely to be strong. In addition, measuring the response of the animals at the appropriate time can reveal important insights into the transmission dynamics of parasites in the wild, despite comparatively small sample sizes.

14.3.2 Parasite-specific impacts on Svalbard reindeer performance

Having established the life-history differences between the two main parasitic nematodes (summarised in Table 14.1) using the approaches described above, we used the same experimental procedures to explore the specific impact of *O. gruehneri* and *M. marshalli* on Svalbard reindeer. First, a cross-sectional observational study determined relationships between parasite intensity and reindeer performance. Second, a longitudinal study used anthelmintic treatment to remove parasites in summer and quantify the effect of treatment on the performance of individually marked reindeer. Third, a longitudinal study used anthelmintic treatment to remove parasites in winter, to quantify the effect of treatment on the performance of individually marked reindeer. Ultimately, the two experimental approaches provide parameter estimates for the impact of each parasite species on fecundity for inclusion in a model of reindeer population dynamics (see Section 14.4).

14.3.2.1 *Parasitism reduces body condition and therefore reproductive rates in Svalbard reindeer*

Cross-sectional data from a six-year study of culled animals was used to determine the impact of parasites on reindeer body mass, condition (back fat), and reproduction. Female reindeer two years and older were culled in the

Table 14.1 *A summary of the life-history differences between* O. gruehneri *and* M. marshalli.

Ostertagia gruehneri	Marshallagia marshalli
Intensity peaks in summer and declines over winter	Adult intensity peaks in winter and is virtually absent in summer
Intensity varies between years and linked to reindeer population density 2 years before	Intensity tends not to vary between years
Intensity of adults worms increases slowly as animals grow and asymptotes in the third year of life, indicating slow development and long lifespan	Intensity of adult worms reaches an asymptote by the end of animals' first winter, indicating rapid development and relatively short lifespan
Species is present in winter but mainly as arrested fourth-stage larvae. L5 larvae peak in summer	Almost absent in summer. Negligible numbers of L4s in winter but higher proportion of L5 larvae, indicating rapid development to adults
Egg output occurs in summer and not in winter and is under density-dependent control	Egg output occurs in winter and not in summer
Infective larvae on the pasture in summer are probably derived from eggs deposited the previous summer	Infective larvae are ingested in winter and derived from eggs deposited the previous winter which develop in the intervening summer

autumn (October) and in winter (February to May). After controlling for year, month, site, age, and lactation status, there was no significant relationship between the intensity of parasites in individual reindeer and either body mass or back fat depth (Stien et al., 2002a). However, while females in better condition were more likely to be pregnant, those with higher adult *O. gruehneri* infections had lower pregnancy rates (Figure 14.7).

The prediction based on the life-history differences of the two main aboma-sal nematodes was that reindeer treated with a slow-release anthelmintic would benefit from lower parasite burdens over summer, because the reinfection rate of *O. gruehneri* is not sufficient to bring the intensity of infection to the same levels as in untreated controls (see Figure 14.4a). Between 1995 and 2000 every other female caught in our main study area in late April/early May was treated with anthelmintic. Many of these individuals, together with the untreated controls, were resampled the following winter, weighed and, also from 1998, the back fat depth was estimated by ultrasound (Albon et al., 2002; Milner et al., 2003). Pregnancy status was determined using the progesterone (P4) concentration in blood samples and ultrasound diagnosis (Ropstad et al.,

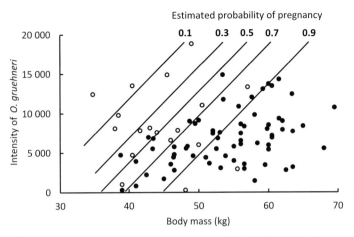

Figure 14.7 The distribution of pregnant (closed circles) and non-pregnant (open circles) adult female Svalbard reindeer culled in February–May 1995–2000 in relation to their body mass and intensity of *O. gruehneri* infection. The logistic regression estimates of a probability of pregnancy of 0.1, 0.3, 0.5, 0.7, and 0.9 are given using contour lines. From Stien et al. (2002a). © 2002 British Ecological Society, *Journal of Animal Ecology.*

1999). In addition, calf production was recorded in an annual census of the population based on the presence of a calf in late summer (end July/beginning of August). The results showed a positive effect of treatment on average body mass and back fat thickness, with treated animals being about 1.9 kg heavier (about 4% of average body mass) and with around 3.3 mm more back fat than controls (Stien et al., 2002a). In addition, the treated group had on average 11% (range 6–23%) higher pregnancy rates in April. By summer, calf production was on average still 6% higher (range 2–13%) in treated females (Figure 14.8a). Furthermore, at the population level, the benefit of treatment increased significantly as the *O. gruehneri* burden increased (Figure 14.8b). The effect of treatment on pregnancy/calf production disappeared if back fat or body mass were included in the model, implying that the effect of treatment on fecundity was acting through body condition (Albon et al., 2002; Stien et al., 2002a).

The design of this experiment did not allow detection of the potential negative effects of *M. marshalli* on the host because it is absent in the summer and therefore the anthelmintic would not affect this species. Therefore, we conducted a second experiment specifically to manipulate the winter transmission of *M. marshalli*, by delivering the anthelmintic in the autumn using the delayed-mechanism described in Carlsson et al. (2012a).

The prediction based on the life-history differences of the two abomasal nematodes was that animals treated with an anthelmintic in the autumn would benefit from lower parasite burdens of *M. marshalli* over much of the

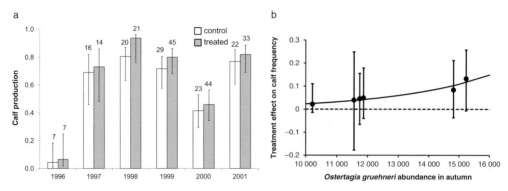

Figure 14.8 (a) The mean calf production (calves at foot per adult female) in early August each year 1996–2001. Untreated controls (open bars), and treated with anthelmintics (shaded bars) the previous winter. (b) The treatment effect on calf production plotted against the average burden of *O. gruehneri* in October. Error bars give 95% confidence limits. Redrawn from figure 1 of Albon et al. (2002). © 2002 The Royal Society.

winter (see Figure 14.6d). While treatment does also reduce levels of *O. gruehneri*, there is no transmission or development in this species over the winter, and therefore unlikely to be any pathogenic effects (Figure 14.6a–c). Thus, the treatment is mainly acting on reducing the transmission of *M. marshalli*. Reindeer body mass, back fat depth, and pregnancy were recorded at recapture in February and April, approximately 5 and 7 months, respectively, after the anthelmintic was released from the bolus. Surprisingly, the analysis showed little effect of removing parasites over winter on adult and yearling body mass or pregnancy rates (Carlsson et al., 2018). This experimental result contrasts with studies from central Asia, where *M. marshalli* infection has been observed to have negative impacts on domestic sheep, causing a reduction of meat and wool production (Igrashev, 1973), as well as poor body condition in juvenile female Saiga antelope (Morgan et al., 2005). Despite Svalbard reindeer losing body mass over the winter (Albon et al., 2017), there was little additional impact of the autumn anthelmintic treatment on body mass loss by April (on average 0.6 kg; Carlsson et al., 2018), even when taking into account the annual variation in back fat depth at this time of year. The lack of an effect of *M. marshalli* in winter may be because the treatment was not sufficient to reduce nematode burdens for the whole winter and animals did become reinfected, although not to the same extent as controls (Figure 14.6d). However, even in the group that had a further treatment (injectable moxidectin) in February, there was still little or no effect of removing parasites on host performance.

These results suggest that the impact of the abomasal nematodes of Svalbard reindeer is highest in summer when food is plentiful, and is low when environmental conditions are poor and animals are losing weight. The taxonomy and systematics of *Marshallagia* across its reported range have not been well defined (Drózdz, 1965, 1995) and it may, in fact, consist of a species complex (Hoberg et al., 2012). One could therefore speculate that the geno-species of *M. marshalli* on Svalbard is relatively benign or has evolved lower virulence on the archipelago. In contrast, the impact of *O. gruehneri* detected by our experiment may be because it removed parasites from the period leading up to and after calving (three months from April) when animals are in poorest condition. Parasites of medium virulence are candidates for having a role in population regulation (Pederson & Fenton, 2015). In support of the relatively low levels of virulence is the apparent lack of evidence of an immune response. If there was acquired immunity then the worm burdens should peak in young animals and decline on older animals as immunity develops (Colditz et al., 1996). However, worm burdens remained high throughout the animals' lives (Figure 14.3; Irvine et al., 2000). In addition, unpublished data show that plasma-circulating pepsinogen and gastrin levels are at low levels, and are not positively related to the intensity of infection or numbers of abomasal mucosa-dwelling larvae (L4s). Histology also indicated little patholo-gical change in the abomasal mucosa of infected animals, and low levels of mast cells and eosinophils are also indicative of no immune response (Irvine, unpublished).

14.4 Modelling parasite population dynamics and their influence on reindeer host population dynamics

The series of experiments we conducted in different seasons and over multiple years demonstrate that *O. gruehneri* can significantly depress reindeer body condition (body mass and body fat) and consequently depress fecundity. In contrast, *M. marshalli* appears to be non-pathogenic. However, as a precursor to modelling how this host–parasite interaction influences the population dynamics of Svalbard reindeer (Section 14.4.2), we developed a model for the fecundity of the parasite itself.

14.4.1 Modelling parasite fecundity and intensity of infection

Transmission rate depends on egg output onto the pasture, which will influ-ence the availability of infective larvae (L3) that can subsequently be ingested by reindeer (Figure 14.9). We wanted to understand how parasite fecundity is affected by the density of adult worms in the host and how the intensity of infection is related to reindeer density.

O. gruehneri egg production is focused on the summer months (Figures 14.4b and 14.10a) and depends on the density of adult worms at this time of year (Irvine et al., 2001). Stien et al. (2002b) developed a mathematical model that describes both the observed intensity dependence of fecundity of the worms, that is, how worm density in a host depresses egg production, and seasonality

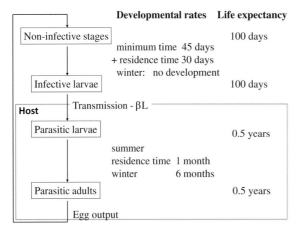

Figure 14.9 Schematic model of *O. gruehneri* life cycle dynamics. Adult parasite egg output to the pasture leads to infective third-stage larvae (L3), whose intensity depends on development and survival rates (determined from unpublished results of field trials). Transmission of infective larvae from the pasture is dependent on β, which represents the contact rate between the transmission stage and hosts and depends on host density (May & Anderson, 1978; McCallum et al., 2017). The ingested larvae develop to adults depending on development rates: larvae ingested after summer ends are arrested until the following spring (L4) and therefore have longer residence times.

of the average egg output of *O. gruehneri*. The model was parameterised using data obtained from reindeer culled throughout the year, with the exception of the Polar Night: November–January. The seasonal pattern predicted by the model was also evaluated using an independent data set of faecal egg counts derived from the faeces of live animals sampled between April and September 1997 (Figure 14.10a). In addition, a simple model of the reindeer rate of faeces production based on available quantitative and qualitative information was used to change the scale of the model from eggs per gram faeces per nematode to eggs per day per nematode.

First, the expected egg output per gram of faeces from a reindeer with a given intensity of *O. gruehneri* infection was assumed to follow the model

$$E(epg|i) = \lambda i^{(1+\beta)} \tag{14.1}$$

where λ and β are parameters estimated from the data, i is the intensity of infection of *O. gruehneri* and the egg output per gram faeces per nematode is λi^{β}. The best model for investigating seasonality was a bell-shaped curve for $\lambda(t)$, because it gave a good description of the low levels of eggs per gram faeces in the early and late months of the year and allowed for the long period of low egg output throughout the arctic winter with a minimum of parameters. Despite the lack of data from November to January, the model predicted that

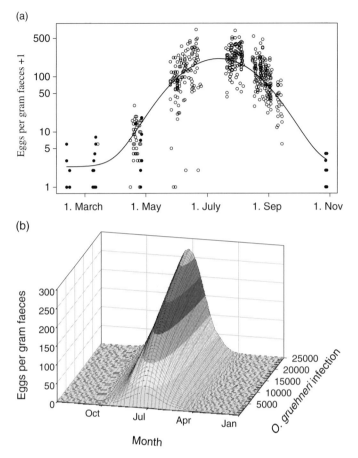

Figure 14.10 (a) Observed eggs per gram faeces +1 from Svalbard reindeer in 1997 (circles) and the predicted number of eggs per gram faeces using the same model as above and assuming a constant intensity of infection over the season equivalent to the observed average intensity (15,200) of *O. gruehneri* per reindeer (line). Data from live reindeer (open circles) and culled reindeer that were also used to estimate the parameters of model (closed circles). (b) Predicted values of *O. gruehneri* eggs per gram faeces in relation to time of year and intensity of *O. gruehneri* infection using the statistically most parsimonious model and parameter estimates. From Stien et al. (2002). © 2002 Australian Society for Parasitology Inc.

egg output during this period was at the same low level as observed in October and February (Figure 14.10b). The model was fitted to egg count data assuming a negative binomial error distribution (Wilson & Grenfell, 1997), with the variance parameter k being a linear function of the predicted eggs per gram faeces (Irvine et al., 2000).

The model describes the egg output from the nematode population in individual reindeer well. Overall this model was successful at accounting for both the variation in eggs per gram faeces with increasing intensities of infection and the seasonal trend showing a peak in the middle of the summer and corresponds well with the observed seasonal pattern (Figure 14.10b).

The model fit was explored assuming different levels of adult *O. gruehneri*, which showed that there was little difference in the ability of the model to predict egg output at low or high intensities of adult worms. This implies that the power to predict differences in intensities of infection from egg counts is poor, probably due to the large variance in egg counts and sampling error.

The next step was to estimate faeces production rate. The only estimates available from the literature were for the summer. We estimated winter rates based on dry matter intake and digestibility values from the literature and used these to parameterise a bell-shaped seasonal pattern similar to the egg output function above. Egg production rate was therefore the product of egg production per gram of faeces and faecal production rate. The model estimates that egg output increases from 0.2 to 120 eggs per nematode per day over the season in a reindeer with an intensity of infection of 5000 adult *O. gruehneri* and is consistent with the observed egg output that is closely focused on the summer season. This indicates that the intensity-dependent (intraspecific competition) egg output (Irvine et al., 2001) causes a decrease in nematode egg output of 29% with a doubling of infection rate so that egg output per host per day only increases by 42% with a doubling of intensity of infection. This model provides insights into the implications of the annual variation in intensity of infection, which typically varies between 5000 and 17,000 *O. gruehneri* per host. A fourfold increase in adult nematode intensity is required to double the egg output onto pasture. However, reindeer populations also vary and are increasing. Therefore, it is likely that annual variation in reindeer population density is more important for pasture contamination than infection intensity per se.

14.4.2 Modelling reindeer population dynamics and the consequences of including the effect of parasites on fitness

The understanding of the drivers of egg output, and therefore pasture contamination in relation to intensity of infection and host density, are key factors in developing a model for how parasites may regulate the population of Svalbard reindeer at densities around those observed in the field. Regulation of the host population by a parasite can occur when the parasite transmission stage production rate (λ) > (host birth rate (a)+ parasite death rate (μ) + parasite-induced host mortality rate(α)) (Anderson & May, 1978).

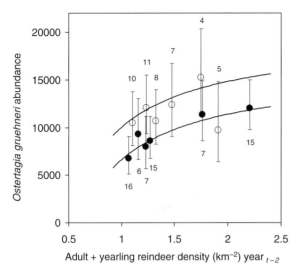

Figure 14.11 The estimated *O. gruehneri* intensity in October in relation to adult and yearling reindeer summer density two years earlier in Colesdalen (filled circles) and Sassendalen (open circles). (Estimates for regression lines: $M^* = \beta 1,i\, Ht\text{-}2/(0.56 + Ht\text{-}2) - 1$ 779 726, β 1, Colesdalen = 1 800 412, β 1, Sassendalen = 1 795 008). The valley-specific annual estimates of the intensity of *O. gruehneri* were estimated as the asymptotic intensity of infection with age using the linear model $M^* = $ valley + year + valley: year. Error bars give 95% confidence limits for the estimates and the sample sizes on which the estimates are based are given above (Colesdalen) or below (Sassendalen) the error bars. From Albon et al. (2002). © 2002 The Royal Society.

From the results outlined above, although the distribution of parasites is aggregated, we know that in Svalbard reindeer, prevalence is high with all animals infected. From culled reindeer we showed that annual variation in the degree to which parasites depressed fecundity was positively related to the intensity of *O. gruehneri* infection the previous October, which in turn was related to host density two years earlier, consistent with the multi-year lifespan of *O. gruehneri* (Figure 14.11).

Also, we know from the six-year experimental manipulation of the *O. gruehneri* parasite burdens in the reindeer that the anthelmintic treatment in April–May increased the probability of a female having a calf in the next year, compared with untreated controls (Figure 14.8a) and that the depressive effect of parasites increased with the intensity of infection (Figure 14.8b). However, treatment did not influence reindeer over-winter survival. In addition to the treatment effect, there was a strong negative effect of winter precipitation on the probability of female reindeer having a calf (Albon et al., 2002, 2017; Stien et al., 2012). These experimental and observational data were used to parameterise a simple matrix model.

Our models were based on Anderson and May (1978) and in their simplest form have two parts:

Host dynamics:

$$dH/dt = (a - b)H - \alpha P \qquad (14.2)$$

Parasite dynamics:

$$dP/dt = P\left(\lambda H/(H0 + H) - (b + \mu + \alpha) - \alpha P/H\right) \qquad (14.3)$$

First, a multinomial logit model was used to estimate the probability of an adult female reindeer being pregnant ($p1$) and the probability of having a calf in summer given that it was pregnant ($p2$). The size and confidence limits of the effect of parasite treatment, year and winter precipitation on these two probabilities were estimated using a simulation approach where 5000 random samples were drawn from the probability distribution of $p1$ and $p2$. Pairs of the independent random samples of $p1$ and $p2$ were then multiplied to generate the probability of having a calf (p(calf)) (Albon et al., 2002). The probability of having a calf was related to the intensity of *O. gruehneri* the previous October using a generalised linear model. Survival estimates were calculated from summer sightings of reindeer using the standard Cormack–Jolly–Seber survival model (Lebreton et al., 1992) in the program MARK (White & Burnham, 1999). These estimates were used to see if there was any evidence for a difference in survival between control animals and those treated with an anthelmintic, as well as those that were not part of the experiment. Animals were categorised into calves, yearlings, prime-aged adults (2–7 years old), and unknown age adults. Mortality of calves over the first summer is low, around 1% (Reimers, 1983; Tyler, 1987). Variation in the parasite intensity of infection followed a negative binomial distribution and was modelled to account for year, reproductive and individual variation (Irvine et al., 2000; Heinzmann et al., 2009). The effect of host density on the between-year variation in the intensity of *O. gruehneri* was investigated using analysis of deviance.

The dynamics of the reindeer population were analysed using a Leslie matrix model with nine age classes (calves, yearlings, 2-, 3-, 4-, 5-, 6-, 7- and >7-year-olds) as well as unknown age animals caught as adults (at this stage of the project the oldest known age females were born in 1993, hence the need for grouping older animals). The fecundity of calves and yearlings was assumed to be zero. The effect of winter precipitation was included stochastically by randomly drawing observations from the previous 21 years of winter precipitation values (Albon et al., 2002). Calf production was negatively related to winter precipitation. Prime-aged animals had a higher survival rate than other age classes and there was no evidence that their survival varied between years. Unknown aged animals had a lower survival rate, which like calf recruitment varied between

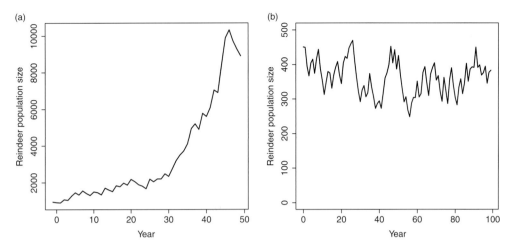

Figure 14.12 Output from the matrix model of the Svalbard reindeer population using annual survival estimates within the observed range for calves and predicted range for prime-aged animals (age one to seven years) and old animals (equal to or greater than 8 years old). (a) Running the model with just the survival estimates produces a low (due to the stochastic weather effects on calving) but exponential growth rate of 2.5% per year. (b) Adding the small parasite-mediated impact on fecundity effect (6–13%) is enough to constrain the population growth rate that is already small. Based on outputs from the models used in Albon et al. (2002).

years in relation to winter precipitation. The annual variation in the intensity of infection in adults was not related to host density in the same year or year$_{t-1}$, but was related to host density in year$_{t-2}$ (Figure 14.11).

The model predicted that the reindeer would become extinct if both calf and old-aged survival was low, and would go into unbounded growth if these age classes had high probabilities of survival. If we used the range of estimates for annual calf survival between 0.66 and 0.82 (derived from our own observations and Tyler & Øritsland, 1999), together with the estimate for the survival of old animals of 0.62, the model predicts densities of the host of between 1.1 and 3.1 reindeer km^{-2} – within the observed range from census counts. Importantly, if the effect of parasites on fecundity is not included, the model does not predict regulation implying that in this data-based model, the effect of parasites is sufficient to regulate the population (Albon et al., 2002), although other drivers that have not been included, such as density-dependence in food supply, may also have a role.

Our study provides what is still comparatively rare evidence supporting the theory that a macroparasite can regulate a wild host population. This has only been possible by working in a relatively simple system and through a combination of experimentation over an extended period of time, cross-sectional investigation of culled animals to estimate parasite life histories, and using the results to parameterise mathematical models to explore the impact of parasites on population dynamics. The extent to which macroparasites, such as gastrointestinal nematodes, can regulate their host populations has been the subject of studies in other systems that are more complex, where other factors such as nutritional limitation, predation, behaviour, and competitors may also be important. What is common to all these examples is the use of manipulative experiments to tease apart the impact of parasites. For example, experiments to manipulate food supply and parasites in white-footed mice, *Peromyscus leucopus*, demonstrated the importance of parasites rather than food supply on breeding success (Vandergrift et al., 2008). In a similar study of snowshoe hares, the effect of parasite removal on hare survival depended on the nutritional status of the host (Murray et al., 1997). In the case of the cyclical mountain hare populations in Scotland, experimental removal of parasites did reduce fecundity, but the effect was not strong enough to drive the cycles but was implicated in their amplitude and interacted with other factors affecting hare demography (Townsend et al., 2009). In the feral Soay sheep population in Scotland, survival was enhanced when gastrointestinal nematodes are removed particularly in young animals and males where immunity to parasites is less effective (Gulland, 1992). The impact of parasites on the sheep may increase in years of high density when food supply becomes limiting and energy requirements are higher and therefore contribute to reducing survival in these years (Grenfell et al., 1998; Coulson et al., 2001). However, scaling up the impact of parasites on individual fitness to demonstrate their role in Soay sheep dynamics would require experimental designs that would not be logistically feasible.

14.5 Future challenges: reindeer–nematode interactions in a warming Arctic

It is generally recognised that the Arctic is particularly sensitive to the effects of climate warming, with models projecting an increase of up to 5°C in mean annual surface air temperatures by the end of the twenty-first century (Kattsov & Källén, 2005). There is much speculation about the impact of this warming and is likely to vary with the nature of the host–parasite interaction (Kutz et al., 2009). To date, we do not know the upper temperature thresholds for development of free-living nematodes. If, as expected, snow melt continues to occur earlier, and summer temperatures continue to increase, egg developmental rates and/or larval survival rates may increase with consequences for transmission rates (Hoar et al., 2012b). While an increase in winter temperatures may lead to higher infection levels of *M. marshalli* due to increased development rates and survival of free-living stages (Kutz et al., 2005; Hudson et al., 2006). These changes could also increase competition between

O. gruehneri and *M. marshalli*, with unknown consequences for the fitness of the reindeer host.

   The summer warming on Svalbard is associated with significantly greater plant productivity (Van der Val & Stien, 2014) and heavier reindeer in the autumn (Albon et al., 2017), which may be able to tolerate higher parasite burdens. However, reindeer numbers have doubled over the last two decades and are much more numerous than when we experimentally tested the effects of *O. gruehneri*. Consequently, we might predict that as reindeer density increases, the intensity of infection will increase and as a result, reindeer reproduction will be depressed more than witnessed in our studies 20 years ago. Only by building on our experience of the system, and undertaking a new series of experiments repeated over several years, will we be able to obtain the parameters to model the current, and future, dynamics of the parasite–reindeer interaction.

14.6 Conclusions

The widespread occurrence of gastrointestinal nematodes in ruminants suggests that they may be of importance in the population dynamics of many species (Arneberg et al., 1996). Our study shows that it may be difficult to detect the negative effect of this group of parasites from observational studies alone. Even when these parasites appear to depress host condition and performance, causation may be difficult to demonstrate, with, for example, uncertainty as to whether animals are in poor condition because of the impact of parasites, or whether the high parasite loads are due to the reduced resistance to infection for animals that are in poor condition. The power of cross-sectional or observational-based information may also be compromised by small sample sizes, restricted because of the ethical consideration – culling large numbers of reindeer in our study area would have impacted the population dynamics. Also, small samples sizes are more likely to have a large variance due to one or more confounding factors, such as age or body condition, or the vagaries of particular years. On the other hand, experimental manipulations of parasite loads have several potential advantages, maximising the parasite differences between treatment and control groups and timing this for when the effect of the parasite is likely to be greatest, and also balancing the groups in terms of age and/or body condition (McCallum, 2000; Pedersen & Fenton, 2015). Combining the observational data with insights and using the results to inform the modelling of the host population dynamics allows us to scale up from individual impacts to explore population regulation. These design features, together with the opportunity of repeating them over several years, offer a greater likelihood of determining the significance of this group of parasites in natural systems and their role in population dynamics (Tompkins & Begon, 1999; Tompkins et al., 2011).

14.7 Acknowledgements

We thank the Governor of Svalbard for permission to undertake the research and for the support of the Environment Department. We are especially grateful to Rolf Langvatn and Steve Coulson in the department of Arctic Terrestrial Biology at the University Centre in Svalbard (UNIS) and Fred Skankke Hansen and Jørn Dybdal of the UNIS logistical and technical staff for supporting the field campaigns. The data collection relied on numerous field assistants, including veterinary students from the Norwegian School of Veterinary Science. Statistical advice was provided by Mark Brewer and David Elston, BioSS.

The work was funded by the Research Council of Norway (TERRØK programme 1994–1996, Arktik Lys programme 1996–1999 and REINCLIM 2012–16); the Natural Environment Research Council, UK (1997–2000: GR3/10811); the Amundsen Foundation; Centre for Ecology and Hydrology; The Macaulay Institute; the Macaulay Development Trust; NINA, UNIS, and the Norwegian School of Veterinary Science.

References

Albon, S.D., Irvine, R.J., Halvorsen, O., et al. (2017) Contrasting effects of summer and winter warming on body mass explain population dynamics in a food-limited Arctic herbivore. *Global Change Biology*, **23**, 1374–1389. doi:10.1111/gcb.13435

Albon, S.D., Stien, A., Irvine, R.J., et al. (2002) The role of parasites in the dynamics of a reindeer population. *Proceedings of the Royal Society of London B*, **269**, 1625–1632.

Anderson, R.M. & May, R. M. (1978) Regulation and stability of host-parasite population interactions. I. Regulatory processes. *Journal of Animal Ecology*, **47**, 219–247.

Armour, J. (1989) The influence of host immunity on the epidemiology of trichostrongyle infections in cattle. *Veterinary Parasitology*, **32**, 5–19.

Arneberg, P., Folstad, I. & Karter, A.J. (1996) Gastrointestinal nematodes depress food intake in naturally infected reindeer. *Parasitology*, **112**, 213–219.

Arneberg, P., Skorping, A., Grenfell, B. & Read, A.F. (1998) Host densities as determinants of abundance in parasite communities. *Proceedings of the Royal Society of London B*, **265**, 1283–1289. DOI 10.1098/rspb.1998.0431

Begon, M., Townsend, C.R. & Harper, J. (2005) *Ecology: From Individuals to Ecosystems*, 4th edition. Oxford: Wiley-Blackwell.

Bjørkvoll, E., Lee, A.M., Grøtan, V., et al. (2016) Demographic buffering of life histories? Implications of the choice of measurement scale. *Ecology*, **97**, 40–47.

Boag, B. & Thomas, R.J. (1977) Epidemiological studies on gastro-intestinal nematode parasites of sheep: the seasonal number of generations and succession of species. *Research in Veterinary Science*, **22**, 62–77.

Bye, K. (1987). Abomasal nematodes from three Norwegian wild reindeer populations. *Canadian Journal of Zoology*, **65**, 677–680.

Bye, K. & Halvorsen, O. (1983). Abomasal nematodes of the Svalbard reindeer (*Rangifer tarandus platyrhynchus* Vrolik). *Journal of Wildlife Diseases*, **19**, 101–103.

Bye, K., Halvorsen, O. & Nilssen, K. (1987) Immigration and regional distribution of abomasal nematodes of Svalbard reindeer. *Journal of Biogeography*, **14**, 451–458.

Carlsson, A.M., Albon, S.D., Coulson, S.J., et al. (2018) Little impact of over-winter parasitism on a free-ranging ungulate in the high Arctic. *Functional Ecology*; **32**, 1046–1056. https://doi.org/10.1111/1365-2435.13037

Carlsson, A.M., Irvine, R.J., Wilson, K., et al. (2012) Disease transmission in an extreme environment: nematode parasites infect reindeer during the Arctic winter. *International Journal of Parasitology*, **42**,786–795. doi:10.1016/j. ijpara.2012.05.007.

Carlsson, A.M., Irvine, R.J., Wilson, K. & Coulson, S.J. (2013) Adaptations to the Arctic: low-temperature development and cold tolerance in the free-living stages of a parasitic nematode from Svalbard. *Polar Biology*, **36**, 997–1005. doi:10.1007/s00300-013-1323-7.

Carlsson, A.M., Wilson, K. & Irvine, R.J. (2012) Development and application of a delayed-release anthelmintic intra-ruminal bolus system for experimental manipulation of nematode worm burdens. *Parasitology*, **139**, 1086–1092.

Colditz, I.G., Watson, D.L., Gray, G.D. & Eady, S.J. (1996) Some relationships between age, immune responsiveness and resistance to parasites in ruminants. *International Journal for Parasitology*, **26**, 869–877. doi:10.1016/S0020-7519(96)80058-0.

Coulson, T., Catchpole, E.A., Albon, S.D., et al. (2001) Age, sex, density, winter weather, and population crashes in Soay sheep. *Science*, **292**, 1528–1531.

Crofton, H.D. (1957) Nematode parasite populations in sheep on lowland farms. III. The seasonal incidence of species. *Parasitology*, **47**, 304–318.

Crofton, H.D. (1963) Nematode parasite populations in sheep and on pasture. Technical Communication No. 35 of the Commonwealth Bureau of Helminthology. St Albans, UK.

Dallas, J.F., Irvine, R.J., Halvorsen, O. & Albon, S. D. (2000) Identification by polymerase chain reaction (PCR) of *Marshallagia marshalli* and *Ostertagia gruehneri* from Svalbard reindeer. *International Journal of Parasitology*, **30**, 863–866.

Drózdz, J. (1965) Studies on helminths and helminthiases in Cervidae. I. Revision of the subfamily Ostertagiinae Sarwar, 1956 and an attempt to explain the phylogenesis of its representatives. *Acta Parasitologica Polonica*, **13**, 445–481.

Drózdz, J. (1995) Polymorphism in the Ostertagiinae Lopez-Neyra, 1947 and comments on the systematics of these nematodes. *Systematic Parasitology*, **32**, 91–99.

El-Azazy, O.M.E. (1995) Seasonal changes and inhibited development of the abomasal nematodes of sheep and goats in Saudi Arabia. *Veterinary Parasitology*, **58**, 91–98.

Forbes, A.B., Huckle, C.A., Gibb, M.J., Rook, A.J. & Nuthall, R. (2000) Evaluation of the effects of nematode parasitism on grazing behaviour, herbage intake and growth in young grazing cattle. *Veterinary Parasitology*, **90**, 111–118.

Fox, M.T. (1997) Pathophysiology of infection with gastrointestinal nematodes in domestic ruminants: recent developments. *Veterinary Parasitology*, **72**, 285–308.

Førland, E.J., Benestad, B., Hanssen-Bauer, I., Haugen, J.E. & Skaugen, T.E. (2011) Temperature and precipitation development at Svalbard 1900–2100. *Advances in Meteorology*, **2011**, 893790. doi:10.1155/2012/893790.

Gjelten, H.J., Nordli, O., Isaksen, K., et al. (2016) Air temperature variations and gradients along the coast and fjords of western Spitsbergen. *Polar Biology*, **35**, 29878. doi.org/10.3402/polar.v35.29878

Grenfell, B.T. (1988) Gastrointestinal nematode parasites and the stability and productivity of intensive ruminant grazing systems. *Philosophical Transactions of the Royal Society of London B*, **321**, 541–563.

Grenfell, B.T. (1992) Parasitism and the dynamics of ungulate grazing systems. *American Naturalist*, **139**, 907–929.

Grenfell, B.T., Wilson, K., Finkenstädt, B.F., et al. (1998) Noise and determinism in synchronized sheep dynamics. *Nature*, **394**, 674–677.

Gulland, F.M.D. (1992) The role of nematode parasites in Soay sheep (*Ovis aries* L.) mortality during a population crash. *Parasitology*, **105**, 493–503.

Halvorsen, O. & Bye K. (1986). Parasitter i svalbardrein 1. Rundmark i lùpen [in Norwegian]. In: Øritsland, N.A. (ed.), *Svalbardreinen og dens livsgrunnlag* (pp. 120–133). Oslo: Universitetsforlaget.

Halvorsen, O. & Bye, K. (1999) Parasites, biodiversity, and population dynamics in an ecosystem in the High Arctic. *Veterinary Parasitology*, **84**, 205–227.

Halvorsen, O., Stien, A., Irvine, J., Langvatn, R. & Albon, S. (1999) Evidence for continued transmission of parasitic nematodes in reindeer during the Arctic winter. *International Journal of Parasitology*, **29**, 567–579.

Hansen, B.B., Aanes, R., Herfindal, I., Kohler, J. & Sæther, B-E. (2011) Climate, icing, and wild arctic reindeer: past relationships and future prospects. *Ecology*, **92**, 1917–1923.

Hansen, B.B., Aanes, R. & Sæther, B-E. (2010) Feeding-crater selection by High-arctic reindeer facing ice-blocked pastures. *Canadian Journal of Zoology*, **88**, 170–177.

Hansen, B.B., Isaksen, K., Benestad, R.E., et al. (2014) Warmer and wetter winters: characteristics and implications of an extreme event in the High Arctic. *Environmental Research Letters*, **9**, 114021. doi:10.1088/1748-9326/9/11/114021

Heinzmann, D., Barbour, A.D. & Torgerson, P.R. (2009) Compound processes as models for clumped parasite data. *Mathematical Biosciences*, **222**(1), 27–35. DOI:10.1016/j.mbs.2009.08.007.

Hoar, B., Eberhardt, A. & Kutz, S. (2012a) Obligate larval inhibition of *Ostertagia gruehneri* in *Rangifer tarandus*? Causes and consequences in an Arctic system. *Parasitology*, **139**, 1339–1345. doi:10.1017/S0031182012000601

Hoar, B.M., Ruckstuhl, K. & Kutz, S. (2012b) Development and availability of the free-living stages of *Ostertagia gruehneri*, an abomasal parasite of barrenground caribou (*Rangifer tarandus groenlandicus*) on the Canadian tundra. *Parasitology*, **139**, 1093–1100.

Hoberg, E.P., Galbreath, K.E., Cook, J.A., Kutz, S. J. & Polley, L. (2012) Northern host–parasite assemblages: history and biogeography on the borderlands of episodic climate and environmental transition. *Advances in Parasitology*, **79**, 1–97.

Hoberg, E.P., Kocan, A.A. & Richard, L.G. (2001) Gastrointestinal strongyles in wild ruminants. In: Samuel,W.M., Pybus,M.J. & Kocan,A.A. (eds.), *Parasitic Diseases of Wild Mammals* (pp. 193–227). London: Manson Publishing/Veterinary Press.

Hudson, P.J., Cattadori, I.M., Boag, B. & Dobson, A.P. (2006) Climate disruption and parasite–host dynamics: patterns and processes associated with warming and the frequency of extreme climatic events. *Journal of Helminthology*, **80**, 175–182.

Hutchings, M.R., Kyriazakis, I., Papachristou, T. G., Gordon, I.J. & Jackson, F. (2000) The herbivores' dilemma: trade-offs between nutrition and parasitism in foraging decisions. *Oecologia*, **124**, 242–251.

Igrashev, I.K. (1973) *Helminths and Helminthoses of the Karakul Sheep*. Tashkent, Uzbekistan: National Academy of Sciences of the Uzbekistan Soviet Socialist Republic, Institute of Zoology and Parasitology.

Irvine, R.J. (2000) Use of moxidectin treatment in the investigation of abomasal nematodiasis in wild reindeer (*Rangifer tarandus platyrhynchus*). *Veterinary Record*, **147**, 570–573.

Irvine, R.J. (2001) Contrasting life-history traits and population dynamics in two co-existing gastrointestinal nematodes of Svalbard reindeer. PhD Thesis. University of Stirling, Stirling.

Irvine, R.J., Stien, A., Dallas, J.F., et al. (2001) Contrasting regulation of fecundity in two abomasal nematodes of Svalbard reindeer (*Rangifer tarandus platyrhynchus*). *Parasitology*, **122**, 673–681.

Irvine, R.J., Stien, A., Halvorsen, O., Langvatn, R. & Albon, S.D. (2000) Life-history strategies and population dynamics of abomasal nematodes in Svalbard reindeer (*Rangifer tarandus platyrhynchus*). *Parasitology*, **120**, 297–311.

Jolles, A.E. & Ezenwa, V.O. (2015) Ungulates as model systems for the study of disease processes in natural populations. *Journal of Mammalogy*, **96**, 4–15.

Kattsov, V.M., Källén, E., Symon, C., Arris, L. & Hill, B. (2005) Future climate change: modeling and scenarios for the Arctic. In: Arctic Climate Impact Assessment (pp. 100–150). www.acia.uaf.edu

Kutz, S.J., Ducrocq, J., Verocai, G.G., et al. (2012) Parasites in ungulates of Arctic North

America and Greenland: a view of contemporary diversity, ecology, and impact in a world under change. *Advances in Parasitology*, **79**, 99–252.

Kutz, S.J., Hoberg, E.P., Polley, L. & Jenkins, E.J. (2005) Global warming is changing the dynamics of Arctic host–parasite systems. *Proceedings of the Royal Society of London B*, **272**, 2571–2576. doi:10.1098/rspb.2005.3285

Kutz, S.J., Jenkins, E.J., Veitch, A.M., et al. (2009) The Arctic as a model for anticipating, preventing, and mitigating climate change impacts on host–parasite interactions. *Veterinary Parasitology*, **3**, 217–228.

Lebreton, J.-D., Burnham, K. P., Clobert, J. & Anderson, D. R. (1992) Modeling survival and testing biological hypotheses using marked animals: a unified approach with case studies. *Ecological Monographs*, **62**, 67–118.

May, R.M. & Anderson, R.M. (1978) Regulation and stability of host–parasite population interactions. II. Destabilising processes. *Journal of Animal Ecology*, **47**, 249–267.

McCallum, H. (2000) *Population Parameters*. Oxford: Blackwell Science Ltd.

McCallum, H., Fenton, A., Hudson, P.J., et al. (2017) Breaking beta: deconstructing the parasite transmission function. *Philosophical Transactions of the Royal Society of London Series B*, **372**, 20160084. doi:10.1098/rstb.2016.0084

Milner, J.M., Stien, A., Irvine, R.J., et al. (2003) Body condition in Svalbard reindeer and the use of blood parameters as indicators of condition and fitness. *Canadian Journal of Zoology*, **81**, 1566–1578.

Morgan, E.R., Medley, G.F., Torgerson, P.R., Shaikenov, B.S. & Milner-Gulland, E.J. (2007) Parasite transmission in a migratory multiple host system. *Ecological Modelling*, **200**, 511–520. doi:10.1016/j.ecolmodel.2006.09.002.

Morgan, E.R., Shaikenov, B., Torgerson, P.R., Medley, G.F. & Milner-Gulland, E.J. (2005) Helminths of Saiga antelope in Kazakhstan: implications for conservation and livestock production. *Journal of Wildlife Diseases*, **41**, 149–162. https://doi.org/10.7589/0090-3558-41.1.149.

Murray, D.L., Cary, J.R. & Keith, L.B. (1997) Interactive effects of sublethal nematodes and nutritional status on snowshoe hare vulnerability to predation. *Journal of Animal Ecology*, **66**, 250–264.

Omsjoe, E.H., Stien, A., Irvine, R.J., et al. (2009) Evaluating capture stress and its effect on reproductive success of Svalbard reindeer. *Canadian Journal Zoology*, **87**, 73–85.

Pedersen, A.B. & Fenton, A. (2015) The role of antiparasite treatment experiments in assessing the impact of parasites on wildlife. *Trends in Parasitology*, **31**, 200–211. 10.1016/j.pt.2015.02.004.

Pedersen, A.B. & Grieves, T. J. (2008) The interaction of parasites and resource cause crashes in a wild mouse population. *Journal of Animal Ecology*, **77**, 370–377.

Redpath, S.M., Mougeot, F., Leckie, F.M., Elston, D.A. & Hudson, P. J. (2006) Testing the role of parasites in driving the cyclic population dynamics of a gamebird. *Ecology Letters*, **9**, 410–418.

Reimers, E. (1977) Population dynamics of two subpopulations of reindeer in Svalbard. *Arctic and Alpine Research*, **9**, 369–381.

Reimers, E. (1982) Winter mortality and population trends of reindeer on Svalbard, Norway. *Arctic and Alpine Research*, **14**, 295–300. doi:10.2307/1550792.

Reimers, E. & Ringberg, T. (1983) Seasonal changes in body weights of Svalbard reindeer from birth to maturity. *Acta Zoologica Fennica*, **175**, 69–72.

Ropstad, E., Johansen, O., King, C., et al. (1999) Comparison of plasma progesterone, transrectal ultrasound and pregnancy specific proteins (PSPB) used for pregnancy diagnosis in reindeer. *Acta Veterinaria Scandinavia*, **40**, 151–162.

Solberg, E.J., Jordhøy, P., Strand, O., et al. (2001) Effects of density-dependence and climate on the dynamics of a Svalbard reindeer population. *Ecography*, **24**, 441–451.

Stien, A., Ims, R.A., Albon, S.D., et al. (2012) Congruent responses to weather variability in high arctic herbivores. *Biology Letters*, **8**, 1002–1005.

Stien, A., Irvine, R.J., Langvatn, R., et al. (2002a) The impact of gastrointestinal nematodes on wild reindeer: experimental and cross-sectional studies. *Journal of Animal Ecology*, **71**, 937–945.

Stien, A., Irvine, R.J., Langvatn, R., Albon, S.D. & Halvorsen, O. (2002b) The population dynamics of *Ostertagia gruehneri* in reindeer: a model for the seasonal and intensity dependent variation in nematode fecundity. *International Journal of Parasitology*, **32**, 991–996.

Stien, A., Loe, L.E., Mysterud, A., et al. (2010) Icing events trigger range displacement in a high-arctic ungulate. *Ecology*, **91**, 915–920.

Tompkins, D.M. & Begon, M. (1999) Parasites can regulate wildlife populations. *Parasitology Today*, **15**, 311–313.

Tompkins, D.M., Dobson, A.P., Arneberg, P., et al. (2002) Parasites and host population dynamics. In: Hudson, P., Rizzoli, A., Grenfell, B., Heesterbeek, H. & Dobson, A. (eds.), *The Ecology of Wildlife Diseases* (pp. 45–62). New York, NY: Oxford University Press.

Tompkins, D.M., Dunn, A. M., Smith, M. J. & Telfer, S. (2011) Wildlife diseases: from individuals to ecosystems. *Journal of Animal Ecology*, **80**, 19–38.

Townsend, S.E., Newey, S., Thirgood, S.J., Matthews, L. & Haydon, D.T. (2009) Can parasites drive population cycles in mountain hares? *Proceedings of the Royal Society of London B*, **276**, 1611–1617. doi:10.1098/rspb.2008.1669.

Tyler, N.J.C. (1987) Natural limitation of the abundance of the high Arctic Svalbard reindeer. PhD thesis, University of Cambridge.

Tyler, N.J.C., Forchhammer, M.C. & Øritsland, N. A. (2008) Nonlinear effects of climate and density in the dynamics of a fluctuating population of reindeer. *Ecology*, **98**, 1675–1686.

Tyler, N. & Øritsland, N.A. (1989) Why don't Svalbard reindeer migrate? *Holarctic Ecology*, **12**, 369–376.

Tyler, N. & Øritsland, N.A. (1999) Varig ustabilitet og bestandsregulering hos Svalbardrein (in Norwegian). In: Bengtson, S.A., Mehlum, F. & Severinsen, T. (eds.), *Svalbardtundraens økologi* (pp. 139–147). Tromsø: Norsk Polarinstituttmdelelser nr. 150.

Vandergrift, K.J., Raffel, T.R. & Hudson, P.J. (2008) Parasites prevent summer breeding in white-footed mice, *Peromyscus leucopus*. *Ecology*, **89**, 2251–2258.

Van der Wal, R. & Stien, A. (2014) High-arctic plants like it hot: a long-term investigation of between-year variability in plant biomass. *Ecology*, **95**, 3414–3427.

Wegener, C. & Odasz-Albrigtsen, A.M. (1998) Do Svalbard reindeer regulate standing crop in the absence of predators? A test of the "exploitation ecosystems" model. *Oecologia*, **116**, 202–206.

White, G.C. & Burnham, K.P. (1999) Program Mark: survival estimation from populations of marked animals. *Bird Study*, **46**, S120–S139.

Wilson, K. & Grenfell, B.T. (1997) Generalised linear modelling for parasitologists. *Parasitology Today*, **13**, 33–38.

PART III

Understanding wildlife disease ecology at the community and landscape level

CHAPTER FIFTEEN

The ecological and evolutionary trajectory of oak powdery mildew in Europe

MARIE-LAURE DESPREZ-LOUSTAU,
FRÉDÉRIC M. HAMELIN AND BENOIT
MARÇAIS

15.1 Introduction

All plants interact with a diversity of pathogens, increasingly recognised as playing major roles in population and community ecology and evolutionary dynamics (e.g. Mordecai, 2011; Bever et al., 2015). Although by definition pathogens inflict fitness costs to the individuals they infect, their effects in natural plant communities may be subtle, often passing unnoticed. Indeed, disease impact is rarely catastrophic over large spatial scales in coevolved systems. Disease prevalence may be high at the meta-population level, but epidemics in wild plant–pathogen systems ('pathosystems', *sensu* Robinson, 1976), are often limited in time and space and have a low to moderate impact (Burdon et al., 2013; Jousimo et al., 2014). By contrast, plant diseases may have catastrophic effects in agricultural ecosystems or when new (non-native) pathogens are introduced into plant communities (Pautasso et al., 2005). Agricultural ecosystems are characterised by high environmental and genetic uniformity, favouring pathogen transmission and leading to the emergence of highly virulent host-specialised plant pathogens (Stukenbrock & McDonald, 2008). Conversely, wild plant communities are much more diverse but can be severely affected by introduced non-coevolved pathogens (Pautasso et al., 2005; Desprez-Loustau et al., 2007).

Despite the contrasting features of different plant–pathogen associations (i.e. wild versus cultivated ecosystems, coevolved versus non-coevolved interactions), Burdon et al. (2013) suggested they could be placed on the same continuum. Trajectories along this continuum are driven by ecological and genetic changes which contribute to the dynamic stability/instability of host–pathogen associations at different times. Oak powdery mildew in Europe illustrates this concept well. This foliar disease (Figure 15.1) is now one of the most common in European forests. It generally has moderate impact with highly variable prevalence over space and time, as typical of native plant–pathogen associations (Marçais & Desprez-Loustau, 2014).

Figure 15.1 Oak powdery mildew symptoms. Clockwise from upper left corner: (1) first symptoms visible in spring, the flag shoots, corresponding to heavily infected shoots (= covered in mycelium and spores giving a white, cottony appearance) developing from buds infected in the previous season; (2) primary infections (white spots) corresponding to ascospore-derived colonies; (3) severe infection on oak seedlings; (4) infection on leaves of the first flush in a mature oak tree; (5) infection of the second flush is generally much more severe than that of the first flush; (6) severe infection leads to necrosis, distortion, early senescence of leaves and, finally, defoliation. (A black and white version of this figure will appear in some formats. For the colour version, please refer to the plate section.)

However, very severe damage including high local mortality rates was reported when the disease suddenly appeared and spread throughout Europe at the start of the twentieth century (Mougou et al., 2008; Figure 15.2). This raised fears that European oaks might disappear, just as current pathogen invasions are considered a threat to indigenous forest species (e.g. ash dieback caused by *Hymenoscyphus fraxineus*; Pautasso et al., 2013). The invasion of Europe by oak powdery mildew thus provides a case study for

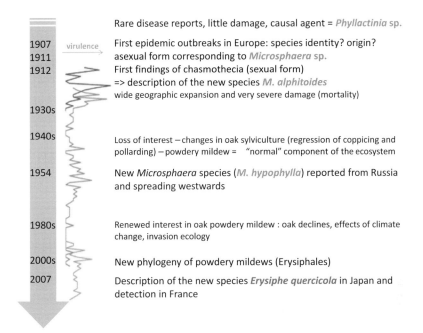

Rare disease reports, little damage, causal agent = *Phyllactinia* sp.

1907   virulence   First epidemic outbreaks in Europe: species identity? origin?
1911   asexual form corresponding to *Microsphaera* sp.
1912   First findings of chasmothecia (sexual form)
=> description of the new species *M. alphitoides*
wide geographic expansion and very severe damage (mortality)

1930s

1940s   Loss of interest – changes in oak sylviculture (regression of coppicing and pollarding) – powdery mildew =   "normal" component of the ecosystem

1954   New *Microsphaera* species (*M. hypophylla*) reported from Russia and spreading westwards

1980s   Renewed interest in oak powdery mildew : oak declines, effects of climate change, invasion ecology

2000s   New phylogeny of powdery mildews (Erysiphales)

2007   Description of the new species *Erysiphe quercicola* in Japan and detection in France

Figure 15.2 Short history of oak powdery mildew disease in Europe, showing the successive invasions (and descriptions) of several fungal pathogen species. Temporal trends of virulence, defined as the damage caused by disease in oak stands, were reconstructed from an analysis of the literature (represented as lines on the left). Three proxies for virulence (represented with different shades) were extracted from: (1) 1912–1931, *Annales des Epiphyties (France)* – number of expressions related to oak powdery mildew damage in 'Annual phytopathological reports'; (2) *Review of Applied Mycology* (1922–1970) and *WoS* (1970–2000) – number of publications dedicated to oak powdery mildew; (3) 1989–2015, French National Health Service (DSF) – index of disease severity.

investigating the mechanisms underlying the epidemiological and evolutionary trajectory from a typical invasion pattern, towards the establishment of a new pathosystem in which the pathogen is integrated into its new environment.

Several non–mutually exclusive hypotheses may explain the observed trajectory of the oak powdery mildew pathosystem. Evolution of the pathogen towards lower virulence might be expected (Sacristan & Garcia-Arenal, 2008). Models predict evolution of virulence to intermediate levels when very high virulence is associated with lower pathogen fitness due to host death, i.e. when the positive relationship between transmission and virulence saturates and becomes a trade-off (Bull, 1994; Lenski & May, 1994). Furthermore, theory predicts that, early in emergence before an evolutionary equilibrium is reached, epidemic conditions (particularly the availability of large populations of susceptible hosts) can impose a transient selection pressure leading to high virulence. This pressure subsequently decreases as the epidemic depletes the pool of susceptible hosts (Bull & Ebert, 2008; Berngruber et al., 2013). There are very few examples of plant pathosystems supporting these theoretical predictions (Jarosz & Davelos, 1995; but see Escriu et al., 2003). However, what is known of the history of oak powdery mildew in Europe (Mougou et al., 2008) suggests that this system may follow this pattern (Figure 15.2). Unfortunately, experimental support through comparative inoculation studies is not possible in the absence of a historical strain collection.

Jarosz and Davelos (1995) suggested that important characteristics of many plant pathosystems challenge the pivotal assumptions of simple adaptive models of virulence. First, although classical epidemiological models developed for animal and human populations assume that host availability ultimately limits pathogen populations, the suitability of environmental conditions may also be a critical factor for plant pathogens, as illustrated by the disease triangle (i.e. plant, pathogen, and environment) widely used by plant pathologists (Francl, 2001). In particular, for a biotrophic foliar pathogen of a broadleaf tree like oak powdery mildew, climate-driven seasonality is expected to have very strong direct and indirect effects (Tack & Laine, 2014; Penczykowski et al., 2015). Second, multiple infections of one or several pathogens on the same host is the rule rather than the exception in plants, even if a single disease is considered. The use of advanced molecular techniques has revealed a huge, previously undescribed fungal diversity (e.g. Tedersoo et al., 2014), leading to the suggestion that many plant pathogens represent several closely related sibling or cryptic species (Crous & Groenewald, 2005; Feau et al., 2011). Many plant diseases are therefore caused by a complex of different pathogens, as was recently shown for oak powdery mildew (Takamatsu et al., 2007).

In this chapter, we provide an overview of the available empirical data for the oak powdery mildew pathosystem, showing how these data support and call into question evolutionary epidemiology theory, in the context of a novel interaction following the introduction of the pathogen. We first explore the potential effects of seasonality and the occurrence of a pathogen complex on theoretical predictions of the evolution of virulence, and more generally the eco-evolutionary dynamics of the pathosystem. We then consider the evolution of oak resistance, including the evolutionary potential of oak populations under powdery mildew pressure and the possible role of the biotic environment of the pathogen in the phyllosphere.

15.2 Climate-driven seasonality: interannual disease transmission

Evolution of virulence has classically been explored through SIR epidemic models in which the host population is continuously present (Anderson & May, 1982; Alizon et al., 2009). Models of epidemic disease in animals generally take seasonality into account through fluctuations in the disease transmission rate (Keeling & Rohani, 2008). In contrast, for many plant diseases (e.g. of annual plants, or foliar diseases of deciduous trees), the host is present during only a fraction of the year (referred to hereafter as the 'season'). At the end of the season, infected material is removed (e.g. dead plants or leaves) and the parasite switches to survival forms (e.g. overwintering in leaf debris in the soil litter, or in dormant buds of perennial hosts). At the beginning of the next growth period, the survival forms of the parasite generate primary infections in the host population, initiating a new epidemic cycle. Secondary host-to-host infections then take over from primary infections.

Plant disease dynamics over several seasons have therefore been explored through models combining discrete-time events (including periodic demographic crashes in the host and pathogen populations) with continuous-time epidemiological dynamics over the season (Madden et al., 2007; van den Berg et al., 2011). Models combining continuous- and discrete-time dynamics are widely used in biomathematics and are sometimes termed semi-discrete models (Mailleret & Lemesle, 2009). Such a model accounting for effects of seasonality on the evolution of pathogen virulence is presented in Box 15.1. In this context, the duration of host absence becomes a key parameter. Exploring the effects of seasonality, van den Berg et al. (2011) suggested that in addition to the virulence–transmission trade-off, a second trade-off may occur between pathogen transmission during the season and pathogen survival outside it. The virulence outcome depends on which trade-off is most relevant. If the virulence–transmission trade-off prevails, pathogen transmission and virulence are predicted to decrease with decreasing off-season duration. In contrast, if the transmission–survival trade-off prevails, pathogen transmission (and possibly virulence) is predicted to increase with decreasing off-season duration. Relevant to oak powdery mildew, records of winter temperature in Europe show a long-term warming trend. Tree phenology has already changed significantly during the last century, with both earlier budburst in spring and later leaf fall in autumn (Sparks & Carey, 1995; Menzel 2000). For oak, this earlier budburst may account for a 10% increase in the duration of leaf presence since the 1950s (Sparks et al., 1997).

It remains difficult to attribute changes in oak powdery mildew virulence to past effects of climate, as it is unclear which of the two trade-offs (virulence–transmission or transmission–survival) prevails in this system. Decreasing virulence during the twentieth century implies that the

Box 15.1: Seasonality, semi-discrete epidemic models, and the evolution of virulence in plant parasites

We introduce a simple semi-discrete model accounting for seasonality with two types of infected individuals which we then use in two different but related contexts. (i) The two types correspond to different strains of the same species. Under certain conditions, evolution tends to select the strain with the largest reproductive number, and we discuss the implications of climate change (e.g. increasing season length) for the evolution of virulence in plant parasites. Under broader conditions, evolutionary branching may occur, leading to dimorphism in the parasite population. (ii) The two types are then assumed to correspond to different parasite species. We show that the two species can coexist in the long run while exploiting the same resource, contradicting the competitive exclusion principle (Armstrong & McGehee, 1980).

Model

For simplicity, we assume that total host density is constant throughout the season. Let S, I, and R be the densities of susceptible, infected, and removed (e.g. defoliated) hosts, respectively. In addition, let $I = I_1 + I_2$ with I_1 and I_2 representing hosts infected with type 1 and by type 2 parasites, respectively (for simplicity, we ignore multiple infections at the host scale chosen, e.g. the leaf). Let T be the duration of an annual cycle (one year), and k be a cycle index. Also, let τ be the length of the season. Let β_1 and β_2 be the secondary infection rates associated with type 1 and type 2 parasites, respectively. Similarly, let α_1 and α_2 be the disease-induced removal rate (virulence) associated with type 1 and type 2 parasites, respectively.

During the season, i.e. for all t between kT and $kT + \tau$, the epidemiological dynamics are described by an SIR model (Kermack & McKendrick, 1927; Segarra et al., 2001). For $i = 1, 2$, the model reads

$$\frac{dS}{dt} = -S(\beta_1 I_1 + \beta_2 I_2),$$
$$\frac{dI_i}{dt} = I_i(\beta_i S - \alpha_i). \tag{15.1}$$

From season to season, i.e. from $kT + \tau$ to $(k + 1)T$, the dynamics are described by a discrete-time model. Let S_0 be the initial susceptible host density (which is assumed to be renewed each year regardless of disease incidence) and χ be a composite parameter aggregating survival forms production per infected leaf, survival probability, and primary infection rate (Mailleret et al., 2012). This parameter is specific to each type of parasite, and χ_i will be referred to as the between-season transmission

Box 15.1: (cont.)

parameter associated with type i. Assuming that primary infections occur over a shorter timescale than secondary infections, we consider: for $i = 1, 2,$

$$S((k+1)T) = S_0 \exp\left(-\sum_{j=1}^{2} \chi_j I_j(kT + \tau)\right),$$

$$I_i((k+1)T) = S_0\left(1 - \exp\left(-\sum_{j=1}^{2} \chi_j I_j(kT + \tau)\right)\right) \times \frac{\chi_i I_i(kT + \tau)}{\sum_{j=1}^{2} \chi_j I_j(kT + \tau)}.$$

$$(15.2)$$

The exponential term represents the probability of a susceptible leaf escaping primary infection. The fraction represents the probability of infection with species i given that infection occurred (Hamelin et al., 2011). The annual cycle repeats. Figure B15.1.1 illustrates the model. Table B.15.1.1 provides a list of the parameters and variables for equations (15.1) and (15.2).

Evolutionary invasion analysis

Let I_1 be a resident monomorphic population challenged by a small mutant subpopulation I_2. Assuming that the resident population is at ecological

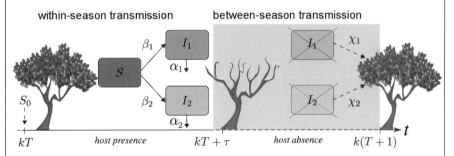

Figure B15.1.1 Flow-chart of the model associated with equations (15.1) and (15.2). At the beginning of the season ($t = kT$), a density S_0 of susceptible hosts (e.g. green leaves) is made available to the parasites. Susceptible hosts can be infected by type 1 or type 2 parasites. The within-season transmission rates of type 1 and type 2 parasites are β_1 and β_2, respectively. The hosts infected by type 1 and type 2 are continuously removed (e.g. defoliated) from the system at rates α_1 and α_2, respectively. At the end of the season (time $t = kT + \tau$), both susceptible and infected hosts are removed (e.g. leaves fall to the ground) and the parasites switch to survival forms (e.g. free-living spores). At the beginning of the next season (time $t = k(T+1)$), survival forms generate new infections. The between-season transmission rates of type 1 and type 2 parasites are χ_1 and χ_2, respectively. Solid and dashed lines correspond to discrete- and continuous-time processes in the model, respectively.

Box 15.1: (cont.)

Table B15.1.1 *Model parameters and variables*

Parameter	Variable	Units
Length of the season	τ	[time] ($\leq$ 1a)
Length of the off-season	$T - \tau$	[time] ($\leq$ 1a)
Within-season transmission rates	β_1, β_2	[space/time]
Between-season transmission parameters	χ_1, χ_2	[space]
Infected leaf removal rate	α_1, α_2	[1/time]
Initial and maximum host density	S_0	[1/space]

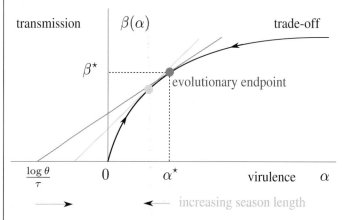

Figure B15.1.2 Classical graphical solution of the optimal virulence strategy, maximising the basic reproductive number, for a possible trade-off between transmission and virulence (black solid curve). The differentiation of R_0 with respect to alpha indicates that the optimum is the point at which the dark grey tangent line passes through the point $(\log(\theta)/\tau,0)$ (Alizon et al., 2009; van den Berg et al., 2011). The originality here is that $\theta = \chi S_0 \ll 1$ is a season-to-season transmission parameter, and τ is the length of the season. Hence, increasing the length of the season decreases the evolutionarily stable level of virulence (light grey tangent line).

equilibrium when the mutant is introduced, it can be shown (Hamelin et al., 2011) that the mutant can invade if

$$\chi_2 \exp\left(\left[\beta_2 \overline{S_1} - \alpha_2\right]\tau\right) > \chi_1 \exp\left(\left[\beta_1 \overline{S_1} - 1\right]\tau\right), \tag{15.3}$$

where $\overline{S_1}$ is the mean healthy host density at the equilibrium corresponding to the resident parasite population. This quantity depends on $(\alpha_1, \beta_1, \chi_1)$, but no explicit expression of $\overline{S_1}$ is known.

Box 15.1: (cont.)

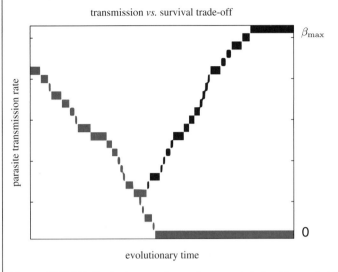

transmission *vs.* survival trade-off

Figure B15.1.3 Evolutionary dynamics associated with model (1–2) assuming a trade-off between within-season and between-season transmission (adapted from figure 2 in Hamelin et al., 2011). There is initially one ancestral parasite type. The mutation-selection process first selects for decreasing within-season transmission (thus increasing between-season survival), and subsequently splits the parasite population into two types, one specialising in within-season transmission, and the other in between-season transmission. The ecological dynamics and the parameter values corresponding to this dimorphic evolutionary endpoint are shown in Figure B15.1.4. (A black and white version of this figure will appear in some formats. For the colour version, please refer to the plate section.)

Considering a trade-off between transmission and virulence (β versus α), a simplification occurs for small χ values. Let $\beta(\alpha)$ represent the trade-off function, which is increasing and concave (Figure B15.1.2). In this case, it can be shown (van den Berg et al., 2011; Mailleret et al., 2012) that evolution selects the value of α maximising the basic reproduction number of the parasite:

$$R_0 = \frac{\beta(\alpha)S_0}{\alpha - \frac{\log(\theta)}{\tau}},$$

(15.4)

where $= \chi\, S_0 << 1$. Interestingly, increasing the length of the growing season τ decreases the evolutionarily stable virulence, maximising R_0 (Figure B15.1.2). This is because increasing the season length increases the possible gain of parasite fitness associated with host longevity.

Box 15.1: (cont.)

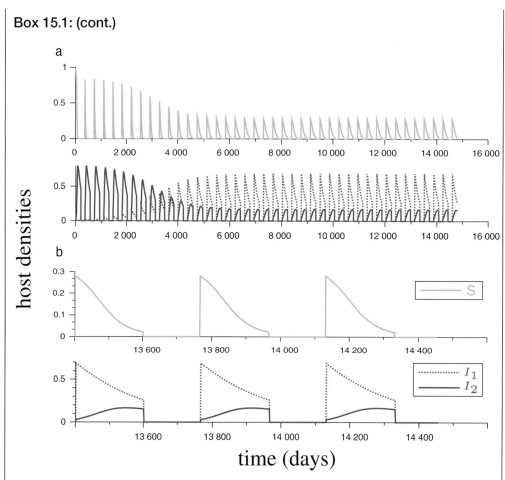

Figure B15.1.4 Long-term coexistence of two parasite species subject to periodic absence of the host plant (adapted from figure 1 in Hamelin et al., 2016). (a) Infected plant densities I_1 and I_2 as a function of time, for $k = 40$ cycles (years). (b) Zoom on the last three cycles. Parameter values: $a_1 = a_2 = 0.005$, $\beta_1 = 0.1$, $\beta_2 = 0.001$, $\chi_1 = 0.369$, $\chi_2 = 4.68$, $T = 365$, $\tau = 200$, and $S_0 = 1$ (without loss of generality). (A black and white version of this figure will appear in some formats. For the colour version, please refer to the plate section.)

Considering a trade-off between in-season and between-season transmission (β versus χ) yields different evolutionary outcomes. Starting from a monomorphic population, evolutionary branching may lead to a stable dimorphism in the population: one type specialises on within-season transmission whereas the other type specialises on between-season transmission (Hamelin et al., 2011; Figure B15.1.3).

Long-term coexistence of two parasites exploiting the same plant host
A trade-off between within-season and between-season transmission can thus lead to long-term coexistence of two parasite species. Moreover, the two species may significantly overlap in time without compromising their coexistence

Box 15.1: (cont.)

(Kisdi, 2012). For instance, Figure B15.1.4 shows model dynamics for a parameter set enabling the two species to coexist (Mailleret et al., 2012; Hamelin et al., 2016). A fast outbreak of type 1 at the beginning of the season leaves enough susceptible hosts for a second outbreak of type 2 because type 2 has a greater within-season transmission rate than type 1. However, type 2 has a lower between-season transmission rate than type 1, which is at an advantage during the primary infection phase at the beginning of the next season. Thus, type 2 does not interfere with the early outbreak of type 1, and both parasite species succeed and coexist on a single host plant.

virulence–transmission trade-off prevails. However, aerially dispersed plant pathogens are potentially subject to both trade-offs (van den Berg et al., 2011). In oak powdery mildew, premature leaf shedding observed in response to high levels of infection (Hajji et al., 2009) may underlie both trade-offs by immediately decreasing the pool of spores available for secondary infections (i.e. within-season transmission) and preventing the fungus from forming its resting structures (for overwintering) in autumn on senescent leaves (see below).

Environmental conditions during the off-season are very important for oak powdery mildew epidemiology, as highlighted for another powdery mildew disease on a wild herbaceous plant (Tack et al., 2014; Penczykowski et al., 2015) and other tree diseases (e.g. Aguayo et al., 2014). The analysis of climatic variables related to between-year variation in oak powdery mildew severity showed unexpectedly that off-season variables (such as winter temperature in particular) rather than climatic variables during the season had significant effects, with severe epidemics occurring only after mild winters (Marçais & Desprez-Loustau, 2014; Figure 15.3A). Interestingly, the role of warm winters in the severity of epidemics in the early twentieth century was emphasized by some authors (Vuillemin, 1910a; Figure 15.3B). Colder winters in the following decades (www .meteofrance.fr/documents/10192/35608/25066–43.gif/) may partly account for the reported decrease in disease severity after the 1920s (Figure 15.2).

Off-season environmental conditions may affect between-season disease transmission through different mechanisms. Cold winters may decrease pathogen survival. Powdery mildews overwinter in two forms (Figure 15.4), mycelia and spores persisting on leaf primordia within dormant buds protected by bud scales, and specialised resting structures called chasmothecia (the sexual fruiting bodies

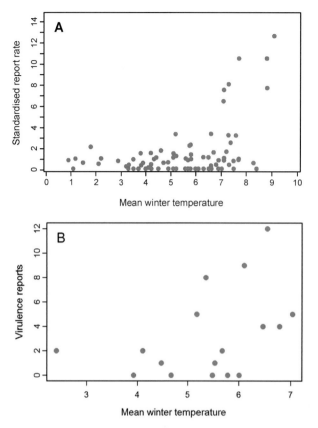

Figure 15.3 Winter temperature and oak powdery mildew disease in France. Disease data from two periods: (A) 1912–1931 (annual phytopathological reports of *Annales des Epiphyties*) and (B) 1989–2006 (disease reports in the DSF database; see Marçais & Desprez-Loustau, 2014) – meteorological data from Meteo France.

of the fungus, with thick melanised walls) which form on infected leaves in the autumn (Glawe, 2008). Chasmothecia may remain on dead leaves in the litter or may detach from the leaves and come to rest in bark crevices and leaf scars on the trunk, which may provide the best sites for overwintering (Pearson & Gadoury, 1987). For overwintering in dormant buds, primary inoculum consists of the highly infected shoots emerging from infected buds at budburst, called 'flag shoots'. For overwintering as chasmothecia, the primary inoculum consists of ascospores, generated in these fruiting bodies once dormancy has been released. Several cycles of secondary infections occur over the season in both cases, mediated by conidia (asexually produced spores; Figure 15.4).

Winter climatic conditions may be a major factor determining which over-wintering mode prevails, as observed for other plant parasites (Halkett et al., 2004). Most tropical powdery mildew species lack chasmothecia (Piepenbring

Figure 15.4 Oak powdery mildew life cycle. Powdery mildews are obligate biotrophic parasites, i.e. they cannot live without their host and they derive their energy from living cells. Most of the fungal development is epiphyllous, the only structures within plant tissues being the intracellular haustoria which absorb nutrients from the host. Left, complete life cycle with sexual reproduction: in autumn (lower left), sexual fruiting bodies (chasmothecia) are formed on infected leaves; during winter, the chasmothecia remain dormant; in spring, the ascospores within the chasmothecia are released and airborne; primary infections result from the germination of ascospores on young susceptible leaves which produce colonies of epiphyllous mycelia bearing conidia (asexual spores); during the growing season (spring–summer), several cycles of secondary infections are produced by conidia. Right, alternative cycle without sexual reproduction: mycelium and conidia overwinter in dormant buds (under bud scales), infected buds produce 'flag shoots' and conidia produce secondary infections. (A black and white version of this figure will appear in some formats. For the colour version, please refer to the plate section.)

et al., 2011). Conversely, for hop and apple powdery mildews, very low temperatures have been shown to have a deleterious effect on fungal survival in buds (Liyanage & Royle, 1976; Spotts & Chen, 1984), and there is also evidence of better oak powdery mildew survival in buds during mild winters (Marçais et al., 2017). Despite this sensitivity, pathogen hibernation in buds has the advantage of providing a 'green bridge' between two growing seasons in temperate climates; the pathogen experiences no discontinuity in host availability and can resume its development in perfect synchrony with that of the host as soon as weather conditions are favourable for leaf development.

Between-season transmission may also be affected by off-season temperature through effects on synchrony between bud burst and ascospore release from chasmothecia. Oak leaves display ontogenic resistance, i.e. they are susceptible to powdery mildew only a short period after their emergence (Edwards & Ayres, 1982). The temporal coincidence of ascospore primary inoculum production and susceptible leaf tissue emergence in spring is thus critical in this pathosystem, conditioning the initiation of epidemics each year. Oak–fungus phenological synchrony clearly illustrates the 'encounter filter' of host–parasite interactions (*sensu* Combes, 2001; Figure 15.4). By using an altitudinal temperature gradient, we have shown that (1) both fungus (ascospore release) and oak (budburst) phenologies respond to temperature; (2) their responses are different, leading to differences in the phenological match between budburst and the presence of ascospores across altitudes; (3) oak phenology is a potential determinant of disease severity at the end of the growing season, in particular with early flushing trees at low altitudes likely to escape infections whereas late trees had a significantly higher percentage of their leaf area infected (Desprez-Loustau et al., 2010; Dantec et al., 2015).

Unlike oaks, which display local adaptation for phenology within Europe (Ducousso et al., 1996), no differentiation between European populations of *Erysiphe alphitoides* was detected in terms of the phenology of ascospore production (Marçais et al., 2009). It is possible that the fungus has not had time to adapt to the local climate as it has only been present in Europe for a century. However, the pathogen was found to show patterns of local adaptation at individual host tree level in terms of infection success over the same period (Roslin et al., 2007; Desprez-Loustau et al., 2011). The plasticity in powdery mildew phenology and the high local diversity of oak phenology may account for a relatively weak selection pressure on fungus phenology.

15.3 Epidemiological implications of a pathogen complex

The oak powdery mildew pathosystem has an additional layer of complexity, in that the disease is not caused by a single pathogen species but by a complex of closely related species (Figure 15.2).

Using the nuclear ribosomal DNA sequence (a region used as barcode for fungi; Schoch et al., 2012), Takamatsu (2013) and Takamatsu et al. (2015) thoroughly revised the phylogeny of powdery mildews. They showed that at least seven closely related species in the *Erysiphe* genus, with a common ancestor probably of Asian origin, affect Asian oaks (Limkaisang et al., 2006; Takamatsu et al., 2007). At the time of oak powdery mildew invasion in Europe, these species were unknown and mycologists initially thought that the pathogen had been introduced from North America, as for grapevine powdery mildew a few decades earlier. However, the morphology of the invasive pathogen differentiated it from all described species known to infect oak, and the fungus was therefore described as the new species *E. alphitoides*. One of the other species in the clade described by Takamatsu et al. (2007), *E. hypophylla*, was later shown to have spread westwards in Europe in the 1950s–1960s (Viennot-Bourgin, 1968; Figure 15.2).

The recently described *E. quercicola* has been shown to occur together with *E. alphitoides* and *E. hypophylla* in France, in addition to *Phyllactinia* spp., which may be an endemic powdery mildew species (Mougou et al., 2008; Mougou-Hamdane et al., 2010; Figure 15.2). A recent survey showed that *E. alphitoides* predominates in most of Europe, with *E. quercicola* and *E. hypophylla* having much lower frequencies and more restricted distributions, towards the south for *E. quercicola* and the north-east for *E. hypophylla*. However, the different species can co-occur in a single region, stand, tree, leaf and even lesion (Mougou-Hamdane et al., 2010; Marçais et al., 2017).

The existence of pathogen complexes in both the putative region of origin and the invaded area raises several questions. The co-occurrence of closely related pathogen species exploiting the same host plant apparently challenges the competitive-exclusion principle (Amarasekare, 2003). Can time partitioning account for this coexistence (Loreau, 1992; Chesson, 2000)? From an epidemiological perspective, could temporal differences between the pathogens result in greater host damage due to more complete resource exploitation? Such a complementarity effect between species has rarely been considered for pathogens, but is one of the mechanisms underlying the well-established positive relationship between plant species richness and ecosystem productivity (Loreau & Hector, 2001).

From mathematical analysis and numerical simulation of semi-discrete models including seasonality, van den Berg et al. (2011) concluded that a trade-off between pathogen transmission rate and survival between cropping seasons could not account for the evolutionary branching observed in many plant pathogens. However, Hamelin et al. (2011) and Mailleret et al. (2012), revisiting this issue with the same type of model and further analysis, showed that evolutionary branching and coexistence through temporal niche partitioning might be biologically possible. Moreover, Hamelin et al. (2016) showed that coexistence may not only be possible but also plausible, as it can occur in a significant part of the parameter space of the model. Models also predict that the most frequent species at the beginning of the season may become the least frequent by the end without compromising the long-term coexistence of the two species. Hence, the existence of a trade-off between in-season and off-season transmission may allow sibling plant pathogens to coexist, with some species performing mainly as primary infectors (with high levels of interseason transmission) and others mainly as secondary infectors (with a large capacity to generate secondary cycles of infection within a season).

This generic model fits nicely with several plant pathosystems in which pathogens belong to a complex of cryptic species (or lineages) with various modes of overwintering and differing in temporal dynamics (Fitt et al., 2006; Montarry et al., 2008). A similar situation applies to oak powdery mildew, for which the two most frequent species in France, *E. alphitoides* and *E. quercicola*, produce similar symptoms on leaves but overwinter in different ways. Up to now, chasmothecia have been strictly associated with *E. alphitoides*. Conversely, recent collections of

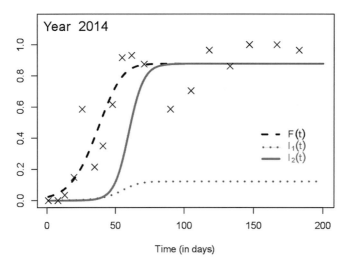

Figure 15.5 Fitting of a semi-discrete epidemiological model with seasonality to empirical data for *Erysiphe alphitoides* and *E. quercicola* temporal dynamics, through a maximum-likelihood method (see Hamelin et al., 2016). The dashed curve represents the frequency of species 2 (*E. alphitoides*) relative to that of species 1 (*E. quercicola*), i.e. F = I2/(I1 + I2), as fitted to the data (represented by crosses). The dotted and solid curves represent the associated (inferred) densities of species 1 (*E. quercicola*) and species 2 (*E. alphitoides*), respectively.

flag shoots (presumably associated with hibernating colonies of oak powdery mildew in buds) yielded only *E. quercicola* (Feau et al., 2012), although flag shoots were commonly reported in the years following invasion by *E. alphitoides* (Woodward et al., 1929; Kerling, 1966). Similar differences in the mode of over-wintering have been reported in the putative native area in Asia, with *E. alphitoides* often forming chasmothecia whereas *E. quercicola* seems to over-winter preferentially in buds, although this species has occasionally been reported to form chasmothecia in this region (Takamatsu et al., 2007). The difference in the mode of winter survival between *E. alphitoides* and *E. quercicola* results in different temporal dynamics in spring at a given site: *E. quercicola* appears first in the season (in the form of flag shoots just after budburst), but its relative frequency decreases over time, and *E. alphitoides* is dominant at most sites by the end of the season (Feau et al., 2012). The generic seasonal model of Hamelin et al. (2011) provides a satisfactory fit to the joint dynamics of the two oak powdery mildew cryptic species (Figure 15.5); parameter estimation suggests that *E. alphitoides* has a higher secondary infection rate and lower between-season transmission rate than *E. quercicola* (Hamelin et al., 2016).

The possible effects of coinfection on disease dynamics and impact, and on pathogen evolution, have recently attracted attention (e.g. Alizon et al., 2013), including for plant pathosystems. However, the effects of multiple infections on disease severity outcome and pathogen transmission are difficult to predict because mechanisms of interaction between pathogenic strains may be direct or indirect (acting through the host), and may act in opposite directions: synergistic or antagonistic interactions, complementarity effects, cross-protection, etc. (Susi et al., 2015; Tollenaere et al., 2016). Moreover, the severity and impact of coinfections may be context-dependent, varying with the effects of environmental conditions on each pathogen (Bearchell et al., 2005; Fitt et al., 2006). In a large survey across France, we tested the hypothesis that *E. alphitoides* and *E. quercicola* occurrence in the same plot would cause greater disease severity, due to temporal complementarity with *E. quercicola* principally affecting the first flush of oak leaves and *E. alphitoides* the second. However, no such effect was shown at the host population scale, with disease severity being primarily explained by the prevalence of the most virulent species *E. alphitoides* (Marçais et al., 2017).

15.4 Intrinsic resistance and phyllosphere microbial interactions

In the dynamic interplay between hosts and parasites, not only virulence levels change, but resistance would be expected to evolve in the host population. However, genetic changes in long-lived species such as trees are expected to be slow, extending over long evolutionary timescales incompatible with responses to invading pathogens. Nevertheless, large populations of forest trees often display considerable variation in disease susceptibility, even to pathogens that they have not coevolved with. For most epidemics, a small percentage of trees display significant levels of resistance (Ennos, 2015; Budde et al., 2016). In the current epidemic of ash dieback in Europe, 1–5% of trees in all populations studied display high levels of genetic resistance, indicating that natural (or artificial) selection for much higher levels of resistance should be possible (Budde et al., 2016). Such pre-existing or 'serendipitous resistance' (Burdon et al., 2013) may result from evolution under the influence of other selective pressures, i.e. exapted resistance. For example, disease resistance may be related to phenological traits selected under abiotic pressure or may have evolved in response to native pathogens resembling the introduced one (Newcombe, 1998; Budde et al., 2016).

The oak powdery mildew pathosystem has several characteristics that might favour evolution of resistance in oak populations, particularly during the period following the introduction of this pathogen into Europe. First, like many forest trees, oaks produce a large number of offspring (at least in mast years), and disease impact is highest at the seedling stage. Disease resistance is thus expected to be an important determinant of fitness at a stage when competition among individuals is strong. Several authors in the early twentieth century reported very high seedling mortality rates in areas invaded by the pathogen (Marçais & Desprez-Loustau, 2014). Recent studies based on exclusion experiments (using fungicides) and dendrochronological approaches demonstrated fitness costs of infection in the form of growth loss or mortality (Desprez-Loustau et al., 2014; Marcais & Desprez-Loustau, 2014; Bert et al., 2016). Second, pathogen pressure acts on populations displaying high levels of individual variation in disease-related traits (Desprez-Loustau et al., 2014; Bert et al., 2016). Moreover, this variation is genetically determined (Desprez-Loustau et al., 2014) with moderate to high heritability estimates (ranging from 0.38 to 0.66) when comparing descendants in a single pedigree (Bartholomé et al., unpublished). Quantitative trait loci (QTL) analyses have identified several candidate disease resistance loci in *Q. robur* (Bartholomé et al., unpublished).

The evolution of disease resistance is also dependent on phenotypic and genetic correlations between traits which will ultimately determine the resistance–fitness relationship. For example, Dantec et al. (2015) showed that the phenology–fitness relationship was opposite under exposure to powdery mildew or frost. Furthermore, the evolution of disease resistance may interact with disease tolerance, i.e. mechanisms that do not limit infection, but reduce its negative consequences on host fitness (Roy & Kirchner, 2000). Tolerance to damage is related to plant vigour (Weis et al., 2000) and may play a key role in the outcome of infections, as long recognised for plant–herbivore interactions (Baucom & de Roode, 2011). Our results suggest that tolerance, positively correlated with growth potential, might overcome resistance effects on fitness, assessed by oak seedling survival under natural infection (Desprez-Loustau et al., 2014). Testing for an increase in resistance in oak populations since the introduction of powdery mildew would require comparing levels in pre- and post-invasion oak populations. Very old trees that are still alive and were already mature when invasion occurred in the early twentieth century (i.e. older than 150 years) may be considered representative of pre-epidemic populations, because mortality at the time of invasion was mostly reported for seedlings and young trees, and not for mature trees in high forests (Viney, 1970). Comparisons of the susceptibility to disease of the offspring of these trees to that of trees from younger cohorts (subject to pathogen selection pressure as juveniles) may provide an indication of the selective forces at work.

The microbial community living in association with trees, particularly in the phyllosphere, may also influence the potential of tree populations to cope with emerging diseases (Budde et al., 2016); there is increasing evidence for its potential role in mediating susceptibility or resistance to disease (e.g. Berendsen et al., 2012; Busby et al., 2016). Moreover, as microbial communities are highly dynamic over time, they may supply the plant with a defence arsenal evolving at the same pace as pathogens. This could play a critical role in long-lived species such as trees, which are exposed to a great diversity of pathogens during their lifetime (Lively et al., 2014; Budde et al., 2016). Jakuschkin et al. (2016) have shown that *E. alphitoides* is involved in a complex network of interactions in the phyllosphere. Their study, combining metabarcoding and network inference methods, demonstrated that infection with *E. alphitoides* was accompanied by significant changes in the composition of the foliar fungal and bacterial communities. Several potential bacterial and fungal antagonists to *E. alphitoides* were identified.

Interestingly, the involvement of an antagonist in the decline of the disease was first suggested early in the years following the oak powdery mildew invasion in Europe. Vuillemin (1910b) observed that the powdery mildew fungus was itself parasitised by another fungus, from the genus *Cicinnobolus*, and he suggested that this hyperparasite might be acting as a natural regulatory agent of the disease. These observations are consistent with the 'pathogen accumulation hypothesis' proposed for long-term decline in the density and distribution of some invasive species (generally plants; Flory & Clay, 2013). *Ampelomyces quisqualis*, previously known as *Cicinnobolus cesatii*, was described from infected grapevine leaves a few years after the appearance of grapevine powdery mildew in Europe in the 1850s (Emmons, 1930; Kiss et al., 2004). We have detected *A. quisqualis* in oak powdery mildew lesions all over Europe, but its impact on disease epidemiology remains to be investigated.

15.5 Future prospects

Several developments are likely to increase our understanding of the pathosystem and help predict its future trajectory, involving the combination of various modelling approaches and the acquisition of empirical data guided by theory.

15.5.1 Disease modelling over multiple growing seasons, including climate effects

The development of models capturing the long-term behaviour of pathosystems over multiple growing seasons, including temporal changes in host availability and pathogen overwintering (particularly for perennial hosts), has been identified as a key challenge in plant epidemiology (Cunniffe et al., 2015). Our semi-discrete model provides a generic approach to this issue. Its application to oak powdery mildew highlights the need to explore transmission–virulence and transmission–survival trade-offs to improve predictions of the effects of climate change, through increases in growing season duration, on the pathosystem.

Virulence–transmission trade-offs have rarely been estimated for plant pathogens (Doumayrou et al., 2013; Pasco et al., 2016); an alternative could be to study fitness as a function of virulence (Alizon & Michalakis, 2015). Assessing pathogen fitness and virulence is not straightforward (Gilchrist et al., 2006; Alizon et al., 2009), but they could be measured at leaf level for oak powdery mildew. We may consider fitness as the total production of spores (i.e. the product of leaf lifespan and spore production per day), and virulence as the decrease in leaf lifespan. Several isolates should then be compared to determine whether the fitness–virulence function peaks at an intermediate virulence level. Furthermore, a possible partial virulence–overwintering trade-off could be investigated by quantifying the production of chasmothecia by isolates from different climates. However, assessing the between-season transmission parameter (χ in Box 15.1) would also require the quantification of pathogen winter survival, primary inoculum production in spring, and the success of primary infections.

As described above, primary infection success is governed by good phenological synchrony between host and pathogen, determined largely by the plastic response of both pathogen and host to environmental cues (especially temperature; Desprez-Loustau et al., 2010; Altizer et al., 2013). Available data for fungal ascospore and oak budburst timings (Marcais et al., 2009; Vitasse et al., 2011) should make it possible to adjust semi-mechanistic models of phenology, based on chilling and forcing phases driven by temperature (Chuine et al., 2013), to simulate phenological synchrony over space and time (including for climate change scenarios). Disease data from the Forest Health Service database (Marçais & Desprez-Loustau, 2014) could be used to validate this synchrony index as a predictor of disease severity. Climate change is also likely to affect disease dynamics within the growing season, through effects on parasite performance and host immunity. Linking epidemiological models with the metabolic theory of ecology (Brown et al., 2004) is a promising approach to addressing this question (Altizer et al., 2013); applying this theory to the oak powdery mildew system provides an exciting framework for empirical studies.

15.5.2 Integrating tree population dynamics through age-structured modelling

Our semi-discrete model (Box 15.1) includes the default assumption of constant host population size within and between seasons. An obvious improvement would be to incorporate host growth dynamics (van den Berg et al., 2011; Cunniffe et al., 2015). In oaks, which display polycyclic shoot growth, within-season growth dynamics are characterised by the occurrence of successive flushes of new shoots separated by resting phases within the same vegetative period (Verdú & Climent, 2007). The continuous phase of our model could, therefore, be split into several phases. However, most mature trees have only two flushes. The first flush is mostly infected by the primary inoculum, whereas subsequent cycles of secondary inoculum infect the second flush. Thus, our model with two different transmission parameters for primary and secondary inoculum captures the within-season dynamics to some extent.

Future models could include oak demography by distinguishing between juvenile and mature stages. Indeed, seedlings and trees differ in many traits likely to affect disease dynamics, such as phenology (Vitasse, 2013); polycyclism, which is more marked in seedlings, with up to four or five flushes (Desprez-Loustau et al., 2014); height, which has been shown to have a strong influence over the likelihood of flag shoots being produced, and thus between-season transmission (Marçais et al., 2017); and possibly leaf traits that could affect within-season transmission. Spatial structure also differs considerably between the juvenile and mature stages (with very high densities at the seedling stage) and this will likely affect dispersal–transmission. In particular, autoinfection (i.e. caused by inoculum produced on the same plant) would be expected to increase strongly between the seedling and mature stages, with increasing host genotype area and decreasing host density. This prediction is consistent with observed patterns of oak powdery mildew adaptation at tree level (Roslin et al., 2007), and similar observations for oak insect herbivores supporting the adaptive deme formation hypothesis (Zandt & Mopper, 1998).

15.5.3 From a simple binary interaction to a network of interacting species

The questions of evolutionary branching and the coexistence of cryptic pathogen species could also be explored with this new seasonal model including oak population dynamics (juvenile and mature oaks) and transmission–survival trade-off, and also with the virulence–transmission trade-off which was not considered previously (Hamelin et al., 2011). Available data strongly suggest differences in the distribution patterns of *E. alphitoides* and *E. quercicola* between seedlings and trees in the same stand (unpublished data). Differences between seedlings and trees may also influence the infection of oak powdery mildew fungi with the mycoparasite *A. quisqualis* (e.g. through dispersal and microclimate), to which *E. alphitoides* and *E. quercicola* may not be equally susceptible. Incorporating the tritrophic interaction into the host structured semi-discrete model could be easily tested with observational data.

Our model can currently simulate several pathogen species, but it includes only one host species. However, like many plant pathogens, *E. alphitoides* and *E. quercicola* can infect several species (including *Q. petraea* and *Q. robur*, the most common oaks in Europe). Potential differences in virulence and transmission according to host and pathogen species, as well as relative host densities, are critical for eco-evolutionary disease dynamics (Cunniffe et al., 2015). Species diversity in both hosts and pathogens is likely to affect competition relationships at both levels and the evolution of pathogen virulence and host resistance. Plant pathologists have shown great interest in these questions at the infraspecific level, focusing on the evolution of pathogen populations in host cultivar mixtures, mostly with a gene-for-gene model underlying strict host specificity (Jeger, 2000). Much less attention has been paid to this issue in diverse wild plant communities (Bever et al., 2015). Differences in susceptibility to powdery mildew between oak species have been reported. In particular, *Q. pyrenaica* has been reported to suffer the highest mortality in early epidemics, and *Q. robur* appears to be slightly more susceptible than *Q. petraea* (Marçais & Desprez-Loustau, 2014). Reciprocally, *E. alphitoides* and *E. quercicola* seem to display some differences in *Quercus* host species preference (Takamatsu et al., 2007), including in Europe (Marçais et al., 2017 and unpublished data). Oak powdery mildew may therefore be an important driver of the joint dynamics of the different oak species occurring together in mixed stands in many areas across Europe, and may affect the many ecosystem services they provide.

15.5.4 Evolution of oak resistance and tolerance: growth–defence relationships

A key concept in plant defence theory, based on considerations of the cost of resistance, is the growth–defence trade-off hypothesis (Brown, 2003; Huot et al., 2014). However, its generality still requires empirical support. An immuno-ecological approach, with experiments using oak genotypes under various levels of resource supply and pathogen pressure, could inform on phenotypic plasticity of defence investments and on relationships between defence and growth in the oak powdery mildew pathosystem. However, no oak material is yet available for direct estimation of the cost of single genes, as was done in *Arabidopsis* using isogenic lines (Tian et al., 2003). Modelling the evolution of host resistance through a growth–defence trade-off, either in the short term (same temporal scale as the pathogen cycle, with resistance mediated by the microbiota) or in the longer term (adaptive evolution of the host through an increase in intrinsic resistance), would be novel in the framework of semi-discrete models.

An alternative or complementary approach would be to use a stochastic individual-based, genetically explicit simulation framework such as Nemo (Guillaume & Rougemont, 2006) or Metapop (Soularue & Kremer, 2012). For example, disease and resistance evolution could be simulated on landscapes heterogeneous for climate (temperature) and resource availability. Environmental factors would condition tree fitness through a survival-defence trade-off associated with phenology (Dantec et al., 2015) and a growth–defence trade-off. In contrast to defence, growth rate can be positively related to tolerance, with very different epidemiological and evolutionary outcomes (Roy & Kirchner, 2000; Best et al., 2014; Cronin et al., 2014).

Exploring how these two strategies have evolved in the oak powdery mildew pathosystem, both from observations and modelling, is a very interesting avenue of research.

Rapid progress in the acquisition of genomic resources for both oaks (Plomion et al., 2018) and powdery mildew should soon facilitate investigations of coevolutionary and coadaptation dynamics in this pathosystem. In particular, the recent release of a draft genome sequence of *E. alphitoides* (Dutech et al., unpublished) provides valuable genomic resources to identify molecular markers for population genetic and phylogeographic studies. Studies based on living and herbarium specimens and Bayesian analyses will make it possible to reconstruct the invasion history of the three *Erysiphe* species, in particular to give further support or not to the hypothesis of an introduction from Asia. Whole-genome approaches in both powdery mildew and oak will also make it possible to study selection patterns at gene level and to disentangle adaptation processes in the host–pathogen interaction. Population genomic studies of powdery mildew on different hosts and at different geographic locations, and reciprocally of oaks in different regions or at different times (historical samples) likely to be subject to different disease pressures, may lead to the identification of 'hot' spots and 'cold' spots of coevolution in the native and introduced areas.

15.6 Conclusions

The oak powdery mildew pathosystem has displayed dramatic changes over the last century in Europe, from being an emerging disease with pathogen invasion dynamics, causing high damage, towards a new equilibrium with lower levels of damage. Several non–mutually exclusive hypotheses potentially account for the trajectory followed, including a decrease in the virulence of introduced pathogens, a reciprocal increase in the resistance of oak populations, and also effects of biotic (phyllosphere microbes) and abiotic (climate) environmental factors. Understanding the pathosystem requires two important characteristics to be accounted for: seasonality and the occurrence of a pathogen complex with several cryptic species. Observational data strongly suggest that the severity of annual epidemics is linked to between-season transmission of the pathogen, including off-season survival and primary inoculum success in spring. Climate-driven phenological synchrony between host and pathogen thus appears to be crucial. A semi-discrete model accounting for seasonality in the pathosystem can explain the coexistence of cryptic pathogen species with differing within-season and between-season transmission rates.

While emerging diseases caused by invasive pathogens are increasingly frequent in wild populations (e.g. Fisher et al., 2012), mobilising much research on the outbreak phase, understanding mechanisms explaining long-term dynamics of such diseases is also critical. Oak powdery mildew is a powerful case study for exploring many questions in theoretical and applied plant epidemiology (Jeger, 2000; Cunniffe et al., 2015) in the wider context of the evolutionary ecology of invasion and disease (Lively et al., 2014).

15.7 Acknowledgements

The authors gratefully acknowledge the special contribution of Cyril Dutech, Dominique Piou, Corinne Vacher, Xavier Capdevielle, Gilles Saint-Jean, Olivier Caël, Olivier Fabreguette, and Martine Martin to the research on oak powdery mildew. Funding and cooperation with the French Forest Health Service (Département Santé des Forêts) provided great help. The modelling study benefitted from a grant of the French National Research Agency (ANR) as part of the 'Programme blanc 2013' (ANR-13-BSV7-0011, Funfit project) and the 2013 BiodivERsA call on 'Invasive species and biological invasions' (ANR-13-EBID-0005-01). We thank Andrin Gross for constructive comments on the manuscript and Julie Sappa for English editing.

References

Aguayo, J., Elegbede, F., Husson, C., Saintonge, F.X. & Marçais, B. (2014) Modeling climate impact on an emerging disease, the *Phytophthora alni* induced alder decline. *Global Change Biology*, **20**, 3209–3221.

Alizon, S., de Roode, J. C. & Michalakis, Y. (2013) Multiple infections and the evolution of virulence. *Ecology Letters*, **16**, 556–567.

Alizon, S., Hurford, A., Mideo, N. & Van Baalen, M. (2009) Virulence evolution and the trade-off hypothesis: history, current state of affairs and the future. *Journal of Evolutionary Biology*, **22**, 245–259.

Alizon, S. & Michalakis, Y. (2015) Adaptive virulence evolution: the good old fitness-based approach. *Trends in Ecology & Evolution*, **30**, 248–254.

Altizer, S., Ostfeld, R.S., Johnson, P.T., Kutz, S. & Harvell, C.D. (2013) Climate change and infectious diseases: from evidence to a predictive framework. *Science*, **341**(6145), 514–519.

Amarasekare, P. (2003) Competitive coexistence in spatially structured environments: a synthesis. *Ecology Letters*, **6**, 1109–1122.

Anderson, R.M. & May, R.M. (1982) Coevolution of hosts and parasites. *Parasitology*, **85**, 411–426.

Armstrong, R.A. & McGhee, R. (1980) Competitive exclusion. *The American Naturalist*, **115**, 151–170.

Baucom, R.S. & de Roode, J.C. (2011) Ecological immunology and tolerance in plants and animals. *Functional Ecology*, **25**, 18–28.

Bearchell, S.J., Fraaije, B.A., Shaw, M.W. & Fitt, B. D. (2005) Wheat archive links long-term fungal pathogen population dynamics to air pollution. *Proceedings of the National Academy of Sciences of the United States of America*, **102**, 5438–5442.

Berendsen, R.L., Pieterse, C.M. & Bakker, P.A. (2012) The rhizosphere microbiome and plant health. *Trends in Plant Science*, **17**, 478–486.

Berngruber, T.W., Froissart, R., Choisy, M. & Gandon, S. (2013) Evolution of virulence in emerging epidemics. *PLoS Pathogens*, **9**(3), e1003209.

Bert, D., Lasnier, J.-B., Capdevielle, X., Dugravot, A. & Desprez-Loustau, M.L. (2016) Powdery mildew decreases the radial growth of oak trees with cumulative and delayed effects over years. *PLoS ONE*, **11** (5), e0155344.

Best, A., White, A. & Boots, M. (2014) The coevolutionary implications of host tolerance. *Evolution*, **68**, 1426–1435.

Bever, J.D., Mangan, S.A. & Alexander, H.M. (2015) Maintenance of plant species diversity by pathogens. *Annual Review of Ecology, Evolution, and Systematics*, **46**, 305–325.

Brown, J.H., Gillooly, J.F., Allen, A.P., Savage, V. M. & West, G.B. (2004) Toward a metabolic theory of ecology. *Ecology*, **85**, 1771–1789.

Brown, J.K. (2003) A cost of disease resistance: paradigm or peculiarity? *Trends in Genetics*, **19**, 667–671.

Budde, K.B., Nielsen, L.R., Ravn, H.P. & Kjær, E.D. (2016) The natural evolutionary potential of tree populations to cope with newly introduced pests and pathogens – lessons learned from forest health catastrophes in recent decades. *Current Forestry Reports*, **2**, 18–29.

Bull, J.J. (1994) Perspective: virulence. *Evolution*, **48**, 1423–1437.

Bull, J.J. & Ebert, D. (2008) Invasion thresholds and the evolution of nonequilibrium virulence. *Evolutionary Applications*, **1**, 172–182.

Burdon, J.J., Thrall, P.H. & Ericson, L. (2013) Genes, communities & invasive species: understanding the ecological and evolutionary dynamics of host–pathogen interactions. *Current Opinion in Plant Biology*, **16**(4), 400–405.

Busby, P.E., Ridout, M. & Newcombe, G. (2016) Fungal endophytes: modifiers of plant disease. *Plant Molecular Biology*, **90**, 645–655.

Chesson, P. (2000) Mechanisms of maintenance of species diversity. *Annual Review of Ecology and Systematics*, **31**, 343–366.

Chuine, I., de Cortazar-Atauri, I.G., Kramer, K. & Hänninen, H. (2013) Plant development models. In: Schwarz, M.D. (ed.), *Phenology: An Integrative Environmental Science* (pp. 275–293). Dordrecht: Springer.

Combes, C. (2001) *Parasitism: The Ecology and Evolution of Intimate Interactions*. Chicago, IL: University of Chicago Press.

Cronin, J.P., Rúa, M.A. & Mitchell, C.E. (2014) Why is living fast dangerous?

Disentangling the roles of resistance and tolerance of disease. *The American Naturalist*, **184**, 172–187.

Crous, P.W. & Groenewald, J.Z. (2005) Hosts, species and genotypes: opinions versus data. *Australasian Plant Pathology*, **34**, 463–470.

Cunniffe, N.J., Koskella, B., Metcalf, C.J.E., et al. (2015) Thirteen challenges in modelling plant diseases. *Epidemics*, **10**, 6–10.

Dantec, C.F., Ducasse, H., Capdevielle, X., et al. (2015) Escape of spring frost and disease through phenological variations in oak populations along elevation gradients. *Journal of Ecology*, **103**, 1044–1056.

Desprez-Loustau, M.L., Feau, N., Mougou-Hamdane, A. & Dutech, C.C. (2011) Interspecific and intraspecific diversity in oak powdery mildews in Europe: coevolution history and adaptation to their hosts. *Mycoscience*, **52**, 165–173.

Desprez-Loustau, M.L., Robin, C., Buee, M., et al. (2007) The fungal dimension of biological invasions. *Trends in Ecology & Evolution*, **22**, 472–480.

Desprez-Loustau, M.L., Saint-Jean, G., Barres, B., Dantec, C. & Dutech, C.C. (2014) Oak powdery mildew changes growth patterns in its host tree: host tolerance response and potential manipulation of host physiology by the parasite. *Annals of Forest Science*, **71**, 563–573.

Desprez-Loustau, M.L., Vitasse, Y., Delzon, S., et al. (2010) Are plant pathogen populations adapted for encounter with their host? A case study of phenological synchrony between oak and an obligate fungal parasite along an altitudinal gradient. *Journal of Evolutionary Biology*, **23**, 87–97.

Doumayrou, J., Avellan, A., Froissart, R. & Michalakis, Y. (2013) An experimental test of the transmission–virulence trade-off hypothesis in a plant virus. *Evolution*, **67**, 477–486.

Ducousso, A., Guyon, J.P. & Kremer, A. (1996) Latitudinal and altitudinal variation of bud burst in western populations of sessile oak (*Quercus petraea* (Matt) Liebl). *Annals of Forest Science*, **53**, 775–782.

Edwards, M.C. & Ayres, P.G. (1982) Seasonal changes in resistance of *Quercus petraea* (sessile oak) leaves to *Microsphaera alphitoides*. *Transactions of the British Mycological Society*, **78**, 569–571.

Emmons, C.W. (1930) *Cicinnobolus cesatii*, a study in host-parasite relationships. *Bulletin of the Torrey Botanical Club*, **57**, 421–441.

Ennos, R.A. (2015) Resilience of forests to pathogens: an evolutionary ecology perspective. *Forestry*, **88**, 41–52.

Escriu, F., Fraile, A. & García-Arenal, F. (2003) The evolution of virulence in a plant virus. *Evolution*, **57**, 755–765.

Feau, N., Decourcelle, T., Husson, C., Desprez Loustau, M.L. & Dutech, C.C. (2011) Finding single copy genes out of sequenced genomes for multilocus phylogenetics in non-model fungi. *PLoS ONE*, **6**(4), e18803.

Feau, N., Lauron-Moreau, A., Piou, D., et al. (2012) Niche partitioning of the genetic lineages of the oak powdery mildew complex. *Fungal Ecology*, **5**, 154–162.

Fisher, M.C., Henk, D.A., Briggs, C.J., et al. (2012) Emerging fungal threats to animal, plant and ecosystem health. *Nature*, **484**(7393), 186–194.

Fitt, B.D., Huang, Y., van den Bosch, F. & West, J. S. (2006) Coexistence of related pathogen species on arable crops in space and time. *Annual Review of Phytopathology*, **44**, 163–82.

Flory, S.L. & Clay, K. (2013) Pathogen accumulation and long-term dynamics of plant invasions. *Journal of Ecology*, **101**, 607–613.

Francl, L.J. (2001) The disease triangle: a plant pathological paradigm revisited. Plant Health Instructor, DOI:10.1094/PHI-T-2001-0517-01

Gilchrist, M.A., Sulsky, D.L. & Pringle, A. (2006). Identifying fitness and optimal life-history strategies for an asexual filamentous fungus. *Evolution*, **60**, 970–979.

Glawe, D.A. (2008) The powdery mildews: a review of the world's most familiar (yet poorly known) plant pathogens. *Annual Review of Phytopathology*, **46**, 27–51.

Guillaume, F. & Rougemont, J. (2006) Nemo: an evolutionary and population genetics programming framework. *Bioinformatics*, **22**, 2556–2557.

Hajji, M., Dreyer, E. & Marçais, B. (2009) Impact of *Erysiphe alphitoides* on transpiration and photosynthesis in *Quercus robur* leaves. *European Journal of Plant Pathology*, **125**, 63–72.

Halkett, F., Harrington, R., Hullé, M., et al. (2004) Dynamics of production of sexual forms in aphids: theoretical and experimental evidence for adaptive 'coin-flipping' plasticity. *The American Naturalist*, **163**, E112–E125.

Hamelin, F.M., Bisson A., Desprez-Loustau M. L., Fabre F. & Mailleret L. (2016) Temporal niche differentiation of parasites sharing the same plant host: oak powdery mildew as a case study. *Ecosphere*, **7**, e01517.

Hamelin, F.M., Castel, M., Poggi, S., Andrivon, D. & Mailleret, L. (2011) Seasonality and the evolutionary divergence of plant parasites. *Ecology*, **92**, 2159–2166.

Huot, B., Yao, J., Montgomery, B.L. & He, S.Y. (2014) Growth–defense tradeoffs in plants: a balancing act to optimize fitness. *Molecular Plant*, **7**, 1267–1287.

Jakuschkin, B., Fievet, V., Schwaller, L., et al. (2016) Deciphering the pathobiome: intra- and interkingdom interactions involving the pathogen *Erysiphe alphitoides*. *Microbial Ecology*, **72**, 870–880.

Jarosz, A.M. & Davelos, A.L. (1995) Effects of disease in wild plant populations and the evolution of pathogen aggressiveness. *New Phytologist*, **129**, 371–387.

Jeger, M.J. (2000) Theory and plant epidemiology. *Plant Pathology*, **49**, 651–658.

Jousimo, J., Tack, A.J., Ovaskainen, O., et al. (2014) Ecological and evolutionary effects of fragmentation on infectious disease dynamics. *Science*, **344**(6189), 1289–1293.

Keeling, M.J. & Rohani, P. (2008) *Modeling Infectious Diseases in Humans and Animals*. Princeton, NJ: Princeton University Press.

Kerling, L.C.P. (1966) The hibernation of the oak mildew. *Plant Biology*, **15**, 76–83.

Kermack, W.O. & McKendrick, A.G. (1927) A contribution to the mathematical theory of epidemics. *Proceedings of the Royal Society of London A*, **115**, 700–721.

Kisdi, E. (2012) F1000 Prime Recommendation of Hamelin FM et al., Ecology 2011, 92(12),2159–66. F1000 Prime.

Kiss, L., Russell, J.C., Szentivány, O., Xu, X. & Jeffries, P. (2004) Biology and biocontrol potential of *Ampelomyces* mycoparasites, natural antagonists of powdery mildew fungi. *Biocontrol Science and Technology*, **14**, 635–651.

Lenski, R.E. & May, R.M. (1994) The evolution of virulence in parasites and pathogens: reconciliation between two competing hypotheses. *Journal of Theoretical Biology*, **169**, 253–265.

Limkaisang, S., Cunnington, J.H, Wui, L.K., et al. (2006) Molecular phylogenetic analyses reveal a close relationship between powdery mildew fungi on some tropical trees and *Erysiphe alphitoides*, an oak powdery mildew. *Mycoscience*, **47**, 327–335.

Lively, C.M., de Roode, J.C., Duffy, M.A., Graham, A.L. & Koskella, B. (2014) Interesting open questions in disease ecology and evolution. *The American Naturalist*, **184**(S1), S1–S8.

Liyanage, A.D.S. & Royle, D.J. (1976) Overwintering of *Sphaerotheca humuli*, the cause of hop powdery mildew. *Annals of Applied Biology*, **83**, 381–394.

Loreau, M. (1992) Time scale of resource dynamics and coexistence through time partitioning. *Theoretical Population Biology*, **41**, 401–412.

Loreau, M. & Hector, A. (2001) Partitioning selection and complementarity in biodiversity experiments. *Nature*, **412** (6842), 72–76.

Madden, L.V., Hughes, G. & Bosch, F. (2007) *The Study of Plant Disease Epidemics*. St Paul, MN: American Phytopathological Society (APS Press).

Mailleret, L., Castel, M., Montarry, J. & Hamelin, F.M. (2012) From elaborate to compact seasonal plant epidemic models and back: is competitive exclusion in the details? *Theoretical Ecology*, **5**, 311–324.

Mailleret, L. & Lemesle, V. (2009) A note on semi-discrete modelling in the life sciences. *Philosophical Transactions of the Royal Society of London A*, **367**, 4779–4799.

Marcais, B. & Desprez-Loustau, M.L. (2014) European oak powdery mildew: impact on trees, effects of environmental factors, and potential effects of climate change. *Annals of Forest Science*, **71**, 633–642.

Marcais, B., Kavkova, M. & Desprez-Loustau, M. L. (2009) Phenotypic variation in the phenology of ascospore production between European populations of oak powdery mildew. *Annals of Forest Science*, **66**, 814.

Marçais, B., Piou, D., Dezette, D. & Desprez-Loustau, M.L. (2017) Can oak powdery mildew severity be explained by indirect effects of climate on the composition of the *Erysiphe* pathogenic complex? *Phytopathology*, **107**, 570–579.

Menzel, A. (2000). Trends in phenological phases in Europe between 1951 and 1996. *International Journal of Biometeorology*, **44**(2), 76–81.

Montarry, J., Cartolaro, P., Delmotte, F., Jolivet, J. & Willocquet, L. (2008) Genetic structure and aggressiveness of *Erysiphe necator* populations during grapevine powdery mildew epidemics. *Applied and Environmental Microbiology*, **74**, 6327–6332.

Mordecai, E.A. (2011) Pathogen impacts on plant communities: unifying theory, concepts, and empirical work. *Ecological Monographs*, **81**, 429–441.

Mougou, A., Dutech, C.C. & Desprez-Loustau, M. L. (2008) New insights into the identity and origin of the causal agent of oak powdery mildew in Europe. *Forest Pathology*, **38**, 275–287.

Mougou-Hamdane, A., Giresse, X., Dutech, C.C. & Desprez Loustau, M.L. (2010) Spatial distribution of lineages of oak powdery mildew fungi in France, using quick molecular detection methods. *Annals of Forest Science*, **67**, 212.

Newcombe, G. (1998) A review of exapted resistance to diseases of *Populus*. *European Journal of Forest Pathology*, **28**, 209–216.

Pasco, C., Montarry, J., Marquer, B. & Andrivon, D. (2016) And the nasty ones lose in the end: foliar pathogenicity trades off with asexual transmission in the Irish famine pathogen *Phytophthora infestans*. *New Phytologist*, **209**, 334–342.

Pautasso, M., Aas, G., Queloz, V. & Holdenrieder, O. (2013) European ash (*Fraxinus excelsior*) dieback – a conservation biology challenge. *Biological Conservation*, **158**, 37–49.

Pautasso, M., Holdenrieder, O. & Stenlid, J. (2005) Susceptibility to fungal pathogens of forests differing in tree diversity. In: Scherer-Lorenzen, M., Körner, C. & Schulze, E.-D. (eds.), *Forest Diversity and Function* (pp. 263–289). Berlin: Springer.

Pearson, R.C. & Gadoury, D.M. (1987) Cleistothecia, the source of primary inoculum for grape powdery mildew in New York. *Phytopathology*, **77**, 1509–1514.

Penczykowski, R.M., Walker, E., Soubeyrand, S. & Laine, A.L. (2015) Linking winter conditions to regional disease dynamics in a wild plant–pathogen metapopulation. *New Phytologist*, **205**, 1142–1152.

Piepenbring, M., Hofmann, T.A., Kirschner, R., et al. (2011) Diversity patterns of Neotropical plant parasitic microfungi. *Ecotropica*, **17**, 27–40.

Plomion, C., Aury, J.M., Amselem, J., et al. (2018) Oak genome reveals facets of long lifespan. *Nature Plants*, **4**, 440.

Robinson, R.A. (1976) *Plant Pathosystems*. Berlin: Springer.

Roslin, T., Laine, A.-L. & Gripenberg, S. (2007) Spatial population structure in an obligate plant pathogen colonizing oak *Quercus robur*. *Functional Ecology*, **21**, 1168–1177.

Roy, B.A. & Kirchner, J.W. (2000) Evolutionary dynamics of pathogen resistance and tolerance. *Evolution*, **54**, 51–63.

Sacristan, S. & Garcia-Arenal F. (2008) The evolution of virulence and pathogenicity in plant pathogen populations. *Molecular Plant Pathology*, **9**, 369–384.

Schoch, C.L., Seifert, K.A., Huhndorf, S., et al. (2012) Nuclear ribosomal internal transcribed spacer (ITS) region as a universal DNA barcode marker for Fungi. *Proceedings of the National Academy of Sciences of the United States of America*, **109**, 6241–6246.

Segarra, J., Jeger, M.J. & Van den Bosch, F. (2001) Epidemic dynamics and patterns of plant diseases. *Phytopathology*, **91**, 1001–1010.

Soularue, J.P. & Kremer, A. (2012) Assortative mating and gene flow generate clinal phenological variation in trees. *BMC Evolutionary Biology*, **12**, 79.

Sparks, T.H. & Carey, P.D. (1995) The responses of species to climate over two centuries: an analysis of the Marsham phenological record, 1736–1947. *Journal of Ecology*, **83**, 321.

Sparks, T.H., Carey, P.D. & Combes, J. (1997) First leafing dates of trees in Surrey between 1947 and 1996. *The London Naturalist*, **76**, 15–20.

Spotts, R.A. & Chen, P.M. (1984) Cold hardiness and temperature responses of healthy and mildew-infected terminal buds of apple during dormancy. *Phytopathology*, **74**, 542–544.

Stukenbrock, E.H. & McDonald, B.A. (2008) The origins of plant pathogens in agro-ecosystems. *Annual Review of Phytopathology*, **46**, 75–100.

Susi, H., Barrès, B., Vale, P.F. & Laine, A.L. (2015) Co-infection alters population dynamics of infectious disease. *Nature Communications*, **6**, 5975.

Tack, A.J. & Laine, A.L. (2014) Ecological and evolutionary implications of spatial heterogeneity during the off-season for a wild plant pathogen. *New Phytologist*, **202**, 297–308.

Takamatsu, S. (2013) Origin and evolution of the powdery mildews (Ascomycota, Erysiphales). *Mycoscience*, **54**, 75–86.

Takamatsu, S., Braun, U., Limkaisang, S., et al. (2007) Phylogeny and taxonomy of the oak powdery mildew *Erysiphe alphitoides sensu lato*. *Mycological Research*, **111**, 809–826.

Takamatsu, S., Ito, H., Shiroya, Y., Kiss, L. & Heluta, V. (2015) First comprehensive phylogenetic analysis of the genus *Erysiphe* (Erysiphales, Erysiphaceae) I. The *Microsphaera* lineage. *Mycologia*, **107**, 475–489.

Tedersoo, L., Bahram, M., Põlme, S., *et al.* (2014) Global diversity and geography of soil fungi. *Science*, **346**(6213), 1256688.

Tian, D., Traw, M.B., Chen, J. Q., Kreitman, M. & Bergelson, J. (2003) Fitness costs of R-gene-mediated resistance in *Arabidopsis thaliana*. *Nature*, **423**(6935), 74–77.

Tollenaere, C., Susi, H. & Laine, A.-L. (2016) Evolutionary and epidemiological implications of multiple infection in plants. *Trends in Plant Science*, **21**, 80–90.

van den Berg, F., Bacaer, N., Metz, J.A.J., Lannou, C. & van den Bosch, F. (2011) Periodic host absence can select for both higher or lower parasite transmission rates. *Evolutionary Ecology*, **25**, 121–137.

Verdú, M. & Climent, J. (2007) Evolutionary correlations of polycyclic shoot growth in *Acer* (Sapindaceae). *American Journal of Botany*, **94**, 1316–1320.

Viennot-Bourgin, G. (1968) Note sur des Erysiphacees. *Bulletin Trimestriel de la Societe Mycologique de France*, **84**, 117–118.

Viney, R. (1970) L'oïdium du Chêne: incident léger ou désastre. *Revue Forestière Française*, **22**, 365–369.

Vitasse, Y. (2013) Ontogenic changes rather than difference in temperature cause understory trees to leaf out earlier. *New Phytologist*, **198**, 149–155.

Vitasse, Y., François, C., Delpierre, N., et al. (2011) Assessing the effects of climate change on the phenology of European temperate trees. *Agricultural and Forest Meteorology*, **151**, 969–980.

Vuillemin, P. (1910a) Le déclin de la maladie du blanc du chêne. Bulletin de l'Office forestier du Centre et de l'Ouest, 347–350.

Vuillemin, P. (1910b) Un ennemi naturel de l'Oïdium du Chêne. *Bulletin de la Société Mycologique de France*, **26**.

Weis, A.E., Simms, E.L. & Hochberg, M.E. (2000) Will plant vigor and tolerance be genetically correlated? Effects of intrinsic growth rate and self-limitation on regrowth. *Evolutionary Ecology*, **14**, 331–352.

Woodward, R.C., Waldie, J.S.L. & Steven, H.M. (1929) Oak mildew and its control in forest nurseries. *Forestry*, **3**, 38–56.

Zandt, P.A.V. & Mopper, S. (1998) A meta-analysis of adaptive deme formation in phytophagous insect populations. *The American Naturalist*, **152**, 595–604.

CHAPTER SIXTEEN

Healthy herds or predator spreaders? Insights from the plankton into how predators suppress and spread disease

MEGHAN A. DUFFY, CARLA E. CÁCERES
AND SPENCER R. HALL

16.1 Introduction

Predators may strongly shape disease in wildlife populations (Packer et al., 2003; Ostfeld & Holt, 2004). Typically, most theory envisions that predators suppress disease, especially in cases where predators prey selectively on infected hosts (Packer et al., 2003; Hall et al., 2005). This has led to the prominent idea that predators 'keep the herds healthy' – an idea that is so prominent that it has made its way into cartoons and candy bar wrappers. However, empirically, we know that predation is not always associated with reduced disease. Indeed, sometimes we see exactly the opposite pattern: a strong *positive* relationship between predation and disease. One of the most striking patterns in the host–parasite system that our work focuses on is that host populations in lakes that have more invertebrate predators are more likely to have outbreaks of a virulent fungus (Figure 16.1) (Cáceres et al., 2009; Strauss et al., 2016). A key question that emerges, then, is what determines whether predators promote or prevent disease?

Rates of parasitism in a single host can vary substantially across space and over time; understanding when predators would be predicted to control disease and when they would be predicted to fuel it might help explain this spatiotemporal variation. One well-studied example of spatiotemporal variation in parasitism comes from red grouse and the parasitic nematode, *Trichostrongylus tenuis* (Hudson, 1986; Hudson et al., 1992) (see also Chapter 10, this volume). Between 1979 and 1983, the number of worms per bird varied between 1000 (in 1982) and 9000 (in 1983) (Hudson, 1986). Looking across space, some estates had < 1000 worms per bird on average, while others had an average of > 10,000 worms per bird (Hudson et al., 1992). As will be discussed more below, some of this variation is likely explained by variation in predation pressure. Another example is provided by Lyme disease, which is a vector-borne disease that has emerged as a problematic infection of humans; Lyme cases in humans vary greatly spatially as well as temporally (Li et al.,

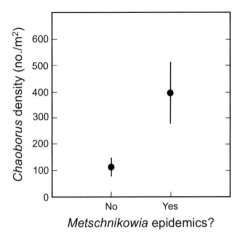

Figure 16.1 Densities of *Chaoborus* midge larvae in lakes that do and do not have epidemics of the fungus *Metschnikowia bicuspidata*. Figure reproduced from Cáceres et al. (2009), with permission.

2014). Just within the state of Virginia in the USA, counts of human Lyme cases ranged from 66 to 1233 between 1998 and 2011 (Li et al., 2014). There was also substantial variation across space, with much higher rates in some counties. Perhaps most interestingly, while there was a general trend over time towards more counties with Lyme and more Lyme within counties, some counties that had high rates of Lyme in one year had very low rates in a subsequent year (Li et al., 2014). Most of the research on ecological drivers of variation in Lyme disease risk to humans has focused on variation in host community composition (Ostfeld & Keesing, 2000; Salkeld et al., 2013; Wood & Lafferty, 2013; Turney et al., 2014). However, as discussed below, predators can also explain some of the spatiotemporal variation (Levi et al., 2012).

Understanding the different mechanisms by which predators can influence disease is also important because it can inform disease control measures. One recent paper argued that 'managing assemblages of predators represents an underused tool for the management of human and wildlife diseases' (Rohr et al., 2015), and another recent paper raised the potential of reducing Lyme disease risk in humans via predator manipulation (Levi et al., 2012). Perhaps most notably, the UK continues to cull badgers – where culling is a particularly efficient form of predation by humans – in an effort to reduce disease in livestock from bovine tuberculosis (Department for Environment Food and Rural Affairs, 2016) (see also Chapter 12, this volume). The assumption of culling campaigns is that higher predation will drive 'healthy herds'. However, past culling campaigns have actually *increased* bovine tuberculosis (Donnelly et al., 2003). Unless we develop a more comprehensive

---

Box 16.1: Introduction to the *Daphnia*–parasite–predator system

Our work has centred around a system with one host, one pathogen, and two predators with contrasting effects on disease transmission. The focal host is *Daphnia dentifera*, which is one of the dominant grazers in stratified lakes in the Midwestern USA (Tessier & Woodruff, 2002), as well as a main food resource for planktivorous fish such as the bluegill sunfish (Mittelbach, 1981). The focal parasite is the fungus *Metschnikowia bicuspidata*, which is the dominant pathogen in many of our Midwestern study lakes (Duffy et al., 2010; Hall et al., 2010; Auld et al., 2014; Penczykowski et al., 2014). The fungus is highly virulent, reducing fecundity and lifespan and increasing fish predation risk (Duffy & Hall, 2008). The dominant vertebrate predator is the bluegill sunfish (*Lepomis macrochirus*), which is a visual predator. Bluegill are highly selective predators on infected hosts, presumably due to their increased opacity (Duffy et al., 2005; Duffy & Hall, 2008) and serve as a healthy herds predator. The dominant invertebrate predator in our system are larvae of the phantom midge, *Chaoborus* spp. (Tessier & Woodruff, 2002; Strauss et al., 2016). Midge larvae are gape-limited, tactile predators (Pastorok, 1981). They do not feed selectively on infected hosts, but are 'sloppy feeders', regurgitating infectious spores along with the corpses of infected hosts (Cáceres et al., 2009). As a result, they serve as predator spreaders. The effects of fish and midge larvae on disease arise from a variety of different mechanisms, as reviewed in the main text.

The main other species of hosts in our study lakes are *Daphnia pulicaria*, *D. retrocurva*, and *Ceriodaphnia dubia* (Tessier & Woodruff, 2002; Strauss et al., 2016). Importantly, all three of these hosts are much less susceptible to infection than *D. dentifera* and, as a result, serve as 'friendly competitors', competing for algal food but also diluting disease (Hall et al., 2009, 2010; Cáceres et al., 2014; Strauss et al., 2015, 2016). In addition to the fungus *Metschnikowia*, daphniids in our study lakes also sometimes host other parasites, including bacteria, fungi, microsporidia, and oomycetes (Rodrigues et al., 2008; Duffy et al., 2010, 2015).

---

understanding of when and how predators influence disease, management strategies that propose to reintroduce or augment predator populations could backfire (Choisy & Rohani, 2006).

In this chapter, we review eight different mechanisms by which predators can influence disease in their prey populations. We give general examples of each mechanism, but also focus in particular on the *Daphnia*–parasite system that has been the focus of our research over the past 15 years (Box 16.1).

Table 16.1 *Summary of the different mechanisms by which predators can influence disease in their prey populations and whether (and when) that mechanism should increase or decrease disease.*

Mechanism	Effect on disease
1. Predator-driven reduction in host density	Can increase or decrease disease
2. Selective predation	Usually decreases disease, but can increase in specific scenarios
3. Predator-driven shifts in host demography or class structure	Can increase or decrease disease
4. Predator-driven shifts in competitor community composition	Can increase or decrease disease
5. Shifts in predator community composition	Can increase or decrease disease
6. Trait-mediated indirect effects of predators and trade-offs associated with predation	Can increase or decrease disease
7. Predator consumption of carcasses and/or spore spreading	Decreases disease if spores cannot survive predator consumption; can increase and spread disease if spores can survive consumption
8. Fuelling of spore production by predator-driven trophic cascades	Increases disease if higher resources increase spore production; however, can decrease disease if resources stimulate immune responses in hosts

16.2 What are the mechanisms via which predators can suppress or promote disease?

We lay out eight different mechanisms by which predators can influence disease in their prey populations (Table 16.1), describing the theory underlying the mechanism, providing empirical examples from diverse study systems, and then providing evidence from our focal *Daphnia*–parasite system (Box 16.1; Figure 16.2).

1. Predator-driven reduction in host density

Theoretically, if predators reduce the density of their prey (i.e. the host) populations, this should reduce disease in systems with density-dependent transmission (Packer et al., 2003; Keeling & Rohani, 2008). However, empirical evidence of predators reducing host density and that, in turn, reducing disease has been mixed. Some correlative studies show a negative relationship between predators and disease, as predicted by the general theory; for

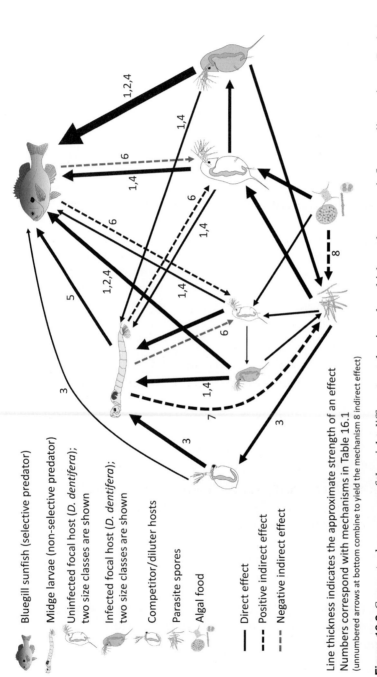

Bluegill sunfish (selective predator)

Midge larvae (non-selective predator)

Uninfected focal host (*D. dentifera*);
two size classes are shown

Infected focal host (*D. dentifera*);
two size classes are shown

Competitor/diluter hosts

Parasite spores

Algal food

——— Direct effect

– – – Positive indirect effect

– – – Negative indirect effect

Line thickness indicates the approximate strength of an effect
Numbers correspond with mechanisms in Table 16.1
(unnumbered arrows at bottom combine to yield the mechanism 8 indirect effect)

Figure 16.2 Conceptual summary of the eight different mechanisms by which predators can influence disease in our *Daphnia*–parasite system. Numbers on arrows correspond to the mechanisms in Table 16.1 and given in the text. Arrows showing infected hosts taking up spores and competitors eating algae were omitted for simplicity as they do not directly relate to any of the mechanisms discussed here.

example, lobsters reduced densities of sea urchins, reducing the likelihood that a population experienced an outbreak of a bacterial disease (Lafferty, 2004). Experimental studies have also revealed a negative relationship between predators and disease mediated by prey/host density: for example, in an aphid–parasitoid system, treatments that contained a predator had reductions in both host density and parasitism (Snyder & Ives, 2001). However, in other cases, empirical studies have shown that density reduction is ineffective at controlling disease or even counter-productive. Widespread non-selective culling of hosts has not been effective at reducing rabies in dogs and wildlife (Morters et al., 2013). Culling of badgers in small areas where there have been bovine tuberculosis outbreaks (reactive culling) not only failed to reduce disease, but actually increased tuberculosis incidence in cattle, perhaps due to increased long-distance movements (Donnelly *et al.*, 2003) (see also Chapter 12, this volume). Thus, while predators sometimes reduce disease via prey/host density reduction, this pattern is not universal.

Theory points us to specific scenarios where we would predict to see predator-driven reductions in host density drive increased disease in hosts (that is, predators promoting disease). First, if parasites actively seek and attack hosts, reducing host density might increase disease. Empirical support for this mechanism comes from an experiment that manipulated predator density and monitored the densities of their tadpole prey and the abundance of parasites that attacked the tadpoles (Rohr et al., 2015). In high-predator diversity treatments, higher predator density was associated with lower tadpole host density and higher abundances of parasite metacercariae per tadpole; however, in low-predator diversity treatments, higher predator density was associated with fewer metacercariae per tadpole (Rohr et al., 2015). Second, even in cases where parasites do not actively seek and attack hosts, increased host density can sometimes decrease encounter rates. In our *Daphnia*–parasite system, high host densities depress host feeding rate, reducing spore uptake; in these cases, there can be a unimodal relationship between host density and disease risk, with disease highest at intermediate densities (Civitello et al., 2013). Third, if hosts invest more in defence at high densities – a phenomenon known as density-dependent prophylaxis (DDP) (Wilson & Cotter, 2009) – decreased host density might increase disease. While we do not know of empirical examples where predator-driven changes in host density and DDP combined to alter disease levels, DDP on its own has empirical support from a variety of invertebrate systems (reviewed in Wilson & Cotter, 2009).

Predators can only reduce disease via reductions in prey/host density if there is a clear relationship between host density and disease. Evidence for such a relationship in our *Daphnia*–parasite system is equivocal. Looking across populations, there is no significant relationship between density of our focal host, *Daphnia dentifera*, and prevalence of the fungal parasite *Metschnikowia* in lakes in Southwestern Michigan (Cáceres et al., 2006; Hall et al., 2010) or Indiana (Penczykowski et al., 2014; Strauss et al., 2016). Looking within populations, a study of fine-scale dynamics of fungal epidemics in five Michigan lakes revealed that the density of infected individuals at a given time was actually slightly *negatively* related to the density of susceptible individuals at the time of infection (Duffy et al., 2009); it is not possible to say at this time what underlies this pattern, although it is consistent with density-dependent prophylaxis. Moreover, in our *Daphnia*–parasite system, the relationship between host density and disease can depend on the metric used: Indiana lakes did not show a significant relationship between overall host density and infection prevalence, but did show a significant positive relationship between overall host density and the density of infected hosts (Strauss et al., 2016). Finally, as discussed in the previous paragraph, we sometimes see a unimodal relationship between host density and infection prevalence. This occurs as a result of impacts of host density on feeding rate, because hosts ingest spores while feeding (Civitello et al., 2013). Overall, it seems unlikely that predators reduce disease in our *Daphnia* system simply due to reductions in host density.

2. Selective culling

If predators prey selectively on infected hosts (perhaps because they are easier to detect or catch), they should be particularly effective at reducing disease in their host populations (Packer et al., 2003; Hall et al., 2005). In most cases, we predict a reduction in disease when predators prey selectively on infected hosts. However, in certain specific scenarios, it is possible for selective predation to increase disease in prey populations (Holt & Roy, 2007).

There is some empirical support for a 'healthy herds' effect of selective predation. Red grouse that are infected with a caecal nematode are more easily detected by dogs that have been trained to locate birds by scent; if predators also locate grouse by scent, this argues that predators should prey selectively on infected grouse (Hudson et al., 1992) (see also Chapter 10, this volume). Moreover, estates that had higher predator control (and, therefore, lower predation rates) had birds that were more heavily infected, suggesting that predators reduce infection burdens in their host populations (Hudson et al., 1992). In Section 16.1, we noted that some estates averaged < 1000 worms per bird, while others had > 10,000 on average; this variation correlated with the number of (human) keepers on the estate, with estates with the most keepers having the highest disease burdens (Hudson et al., 1992). Keepers control predators of grouse, so estates with more keepers should have fewer predators. Thus, this pattern is consistent with healthy herds predation reducing disease burden in grouse.

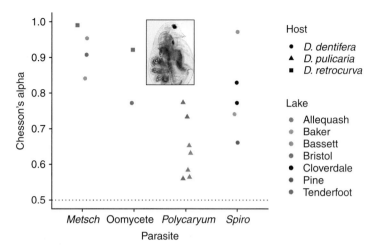

Figure 16.3 Selectivity of bluegill sunfish on *Daphnia* infected with the fungus *Metschnikowia bicuspidata*, an unnamed oomycete, the chytrid *Polycaryum laeve*, and the bacterium *Spirobacillus cienkowskii*. Data were collected by analysing the gut contents of fish collected in lakes at dawn, compared with the infection prevalence in hosts in the lake at the same time. In each case, the comparison was between infected or uninfected hosts. We used Chesson's alpha, which compares the availability of a prey type (in this case, a host infected with a particular parasite) and the selection of that prey type. Neutral selectivity is indicated by 0.5 (shown by a dotted line); the strength of selectivity for a prey type increases as alpha increases towards 1. Data on *D. dentifera* and *D. retrocurva* are from Duffy and Hall (2008) and unpublished data collected by M.A. Duffy in 2002–2003. Data on *D. pulicaria* are from Johnson et al. (2006). Points are jittered slightly along the *x*-axis. Inset figure shows the transparent body of an uninfected *D. dentifera*. (A black and white version of this figure will appear in some formats. For the colour version, please refer to the plate section.)

There is strong evidence for selective culling in fish–*Daphnia*–parasite systems, with visual fish predators feeding highly selectively on *Daphnia* infected with a diverse suite of pathogens, including the yeast *Metschnikowia*, the bacterium *Spirobacillus cienkowskii*, the chytrid *Polycaryum laeve*, and an undescribed oomycete that fills the body cavity with hyphae (Figure 16.3; Duffy et al., 2005; Johnson et al., 2006; Duffy & Hall, 2008). Corixids have also been found to prey selectively on *Daphnia magna* infected with the bacterium *Pasteuria ramosa* (Goren & Ben-Ami, 2017).

Does this selective culling by fish reduce disease in *Daphnia*? Modelling, time-series data, and across-lake comparisons all suggest yes (Duffy et al., 2005, 2012; Hall et al., 2005; Johnson et al., 2006; Duffy & Hall, 2008; Rapti & Cáceres, 2016). For example, lakes with smaller-bodied individuals (indicating high fish predation) have less disease (Duffy et al., 2012), and, within lakes, disease outbreaks occur in autumn as lakes cool and fish predation rates decrease (Duffy et al., 2005). However, one experimental test did not find an effect of fish predation on disease, perhaps due to very high transmission rates in the experimental mesocosms (Duffy, 2007).

3. Shifts in host demography or class structure

If predators prey selectively on particular host stages (or ages), and if those stages (ages) are differentially susceptible to parasites, this can lead to predator-driven shifts in host demography altering disease in prey/host populations. If predators shift demography towards ages or stages that are less susceptible to disease (or that harbour lower disease burdens), that should reduce disease; however, if the shift is towards ages or stages that are more susceptible or harbour higher disease burdens, then predators will promote disease. A special case of a shift in host class structure can occur in systems with acquired immunity. If there are costs associated with having been infected in the past or with being immune, increased predation can drive increased disease under certain conditions (Holt & Roy, 2007). While we are not aware of a direct example of predators reducing disease via shifts in host demography, predators that prey primarily on larval insects should reduce parasitism in cases where the parasitoids attack developing larvae (e.g. Kistler, 1985). An empirical example of a predator-driven shift in host demography driving an increase in disease comes from a system where large snails are more likely to be infected by a trematode parasite, but also less vulnerable to predation by birds (Byers et al., 2015). As a result, habitats with high predation pressure also have high disease (Byers et al., 2015).

In our system, fish shift *Daphnia* populations towards smaller body sizes, both due to feeding preferentially on larger *Daphnia* (Brooks & Dodson, 1965) and by inducing plastic changes in body size (e.g. Hesse *et al.*, 2012). Smaller-bodied animals are less susceptible to the fungal parasite (Hall et al., 2007), so we would predict fish should shift the population towards a size structure that is more disease-resistant. Conversely, midge larvae prey heavily on small-bodied *Daphnia* (Spitze, 1985; Elser et al., 1987). In addition to finding experimentally that midge larvae prey more on juveniles than adults, our field surveys have revealed that lakes with more midge larvae have a lower proportion of juveniles at the start of the epidemic season (S.R. Hall, unpublished data). These findings support a role of predators in shifting host demography towards more vulnerable stages. In addition, if predators drive trophic cascades (as discussed in mechanism no. 8), the increase in resources should speed development of the remaining juveniles into adults (de Roos & Persson, 2013). Together, in our system, it seems likely that visual predators (fish) shift the host population towards smaller, more-resistant animals and that gape-limited predators such as midge larvae shift the host population towards larger, more-susceptible individuals. However, we have not yet tested this experimentally.

4. Shifts in competitor community composition

Species often differ in their competence as hosts, with low-competence hosts potentially 'diluting' disease for high-competence hosts (Keesing et al., 2010). Host species that are highly competent hosts might also be more vulnerable to predation; for example, hosts with a 'weedier' life history that invests little in defences against natural enemies might be more vulnerable to predation and disease. In these cases, increased predation could decrease disease. Conversely, if there are trade-offs in resistance to different natural enemies (as discussed more below), predators may spread disease by selecting for prey/ host communities that are defended against predators but not parasites – that is, predators may thwart a dilution effect by eating the diluters. Overall, predators can change community composition in ways that strengthen or weaken the dilution effect.

One potential example of predators strengthening a dilution effect comes from the Lyme disease system for which the dilution effect was originally proposed (Ostfeld & Keesing, 2000). Lyme cases in humans are higher when red fox density is lower, perhaps as a result of foxes preying on small mammals such as mice, which are highly competent hosts for the bacterium that causes Lyme disease (Levi et al., 2012).

In our *Daphnia*–parasite system, fish feed preferentially on larger *Daphnia* (Brooks & Dodson, 1965) while midge larvae feed selectively on smaller-bodied hosts (as discussed in mechanism no. 3). Increased fish predation can drive shifts towards communities with higher frequencies of *Ceriodaphnia*, while increased predation by midge larvae should result in fewer *Ceriodaphnia*. Given that *Ceriodaphnia* are an important diluter host in our *Daphnia*–fungus system (Strauss et al., 2015, 2016), changes in community composition mediated by predators alter disease in our focal host (Strauss et al., 2016). (Note: by 'diluter host', we mean other potential hosts that generally reduce disease in our focal host.)

5. Shifts in predator community composition

Predators might also reduce disease in a focal host by altering the density of other predators. Returning to the Lyme disease example: as discussed above, more foxes drive lower abundance of small mammals such as mice, reducing disease risk in humans (Levi et al., 2012). Fox density, in turn, is driven by coyote density, with coyotes suppressing fox density; this leads to a positive relationship between the abundance of coyotes and disease in humans (Levi et al., 2012).

Changing the density of other predators is a very important way in which fish influence disease in *Daphnia*. Bluegill sunfish prey upon midge larvae (González & Tessier, 1997); midge larvae spread disease, so this predation by fish on midge larvae can indirectly reduce disease in *Daphnia* (Strauss et al., 2016). In our lake systems, in theory, increases in the densities of piscivorous fish could increase disease by reducing densities of healthy herds predators. Unfortunately, we do not have data on piscivorous fish in our study lakes, and so are unable to explore this hypothesis at present.

6. Trait-mediated indirect effects (TMIEs)

Predators might have indirect effects on disease in hosts by impacting host traits relevant to infection (such as immune function, body size, behaviour, and habitat use). In some cases, the TMIEs might increase disease, but in others they can reduce disease. A study on wood frog tadpoles found that exposure to predator chemical cues reduced the intensity of infections by the chytrid fungus *Batrachochytrium dendrobatidis* (Bd), possibly due to stress-induced immune system enhancement (Groner & Relyea, 2015). Conversely, beetles move belowground in response to aboveground predators, increasing their exposure to pathogenic nematodes and fungi (Ramirez & Snyder, 2009). Moreover, exposure to predators weakens the immune response of the beetles, rendering them even more susceptible to pathogens (Ramirez & Snyder, 2009). An influence of predators on immune function has been shown in a variety of systems. For example, a study on house sparrows found that exposure to a predator reduced their T-cell-mediated immune response and drove higher prevalence and intensity of malaria infections (Navarro et al., 2004). Because organisms have finite resources, investment in traits that protect against predators can mean that there will be fewer resources available to invest in defences against parasites (including immune function). This means that there will often be trade-offs that constrain an individual's ability to respond effectively to multiple natural enemies.

In our *Daphnia*–parasite system, we predicted TMIEs of fish predators would reduce disease, based on effects on host body size. While chemical cues from fish did indeed reduce host body size in an experimental study, they also increased the per-spore susceptibility of hosts, cancelling out the decreased susceptibility associated with smaller body size (Bertram et al., 2013). In an earlier study, we found that exposure to chemical signals from midge larvae induced larger body size and higher susceptibility (Duffy et al., 2011); however, the Bertram et al. (2013) study did not find an effect of midge chemical cues on host body size or disease-related traits. Studies on other *Daphnia*–microparasite systems have found that TMIEs of fish did not influence *Daphnia*'s ability to induce life-history changes in response to parasites (Lass & Bittner, 2002) and did not change parasite virulence but decreased parasite spore yield (Coors & De Meester, 2011). Combined with the results of the Bertram et al. study, these results suggest that the net impact of TMIEs of fish on parasitism in *Daphnia* might be modest.

In our system, larger-bodied individuals are more susceptible to infection but less susceptible to predation by midge larvae. Given these strong links between body size, predation risk, and disease risk, we would predict a trade-off among genotypes between susceptibility to these two natural enemies, mediated by body size. A trade-off in resistance to fish predation and parasitism was found in a different *Daphnia*–parasite system. In that system, the trade-off was mediated by habitat use: genotypes that resided near the bottom of a pond avoided fish predation but encountered more parasite spores, increasing disease risk (Decaestecker et al., 2002).

If there is a trade-off between susceptibility to midge larvae and the fungus in our system, we might predict there would be evolutionary cycles driven by selection from predators and parasites. For example, high intensity of predation by midge larvae would select for larger- and/or faster-growing genotypes, increasing infection risk in the population and fuelling a large disease outbreak. That would then select for higher resistance, smaller bodies, and slower growth, which would then render the population more susceptible to predation by midge larvae. We have previously found evidence that fish predation rate influences epidemic size which, in turn, influences evolution of resistance to disease (Duffy et al., 2012). We plan to explore eco-evolutionary dynamics in midge–*Daphnia*–parasite systems in the future.

7. Predator consumption of carcasses and/or spore spreading

Predators commonly consume free-living stages of parasites (i.e. spores) or carcasses of infected individuals. If the parasite is digested by the predator, this should decrease infection in the focal host population (Johnson et al., 2010; Bidegain et al., 2016). However, in many cases, the parasite is not fully digested by the predator, leading the predator to spread spores in the environment, increasing host exposure to disease. In an example of predators reducing disease by consuming free-living parasites, damselfly nymphs prey upon infectious stages of the trematode *Ribeiroia ondatrae*, reducing infection prevalence in a focal amphibian host by approximately 50% (Orlofske et al., 2012). Conversely, faecal samples collected from scavengers (including jackals, hyenas, and vultures) that preyed on the carcasses of anthrax-infected ungulates were found to frequently contain high numbers of anthrax spores, suggesting that they could generate new foci of infection (Lindeque & Turnbull, 1994).

Spore spreading might be particularly important in certain habitat types. For example, in stratified lakes, hosts that die from virulent effects of a parasite are likely to settle out of the water column before they release their spores. However, if a predator consumes infected hosts and releases

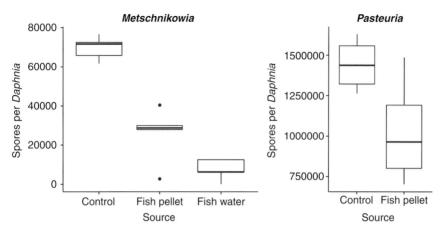

Figure 16.4 Recovery of parasite spores after passage through a fish gut. Data are shown for control infected *Daphnia* that were not fed to a fish and for *Daphnia* that were fed to a fish. In the experiment done on the fungus *Metschnikowia* (reported in Duffy 2009), spores were retrieved from fish faecal pellets and from the water in the beaker where the fish had been feeding. In the experiment done on the bacterium *Pasteuria* (collected by S.K.J.R. Auld and M.A. Duffy), we only collected the fish faecal pellet and did not attempt to quantify spores released into the water. In the *Metschnikowia* study, the median for control *Daphnia* was ~72,000 spores/*Daphnia*, whereas, after combining the data from the fish faecal pellets and water, it was 35,000 spores/*Daphnia* for those fed to fish. For *Pasteuria*, the median was ~1,438,000 for control *Daphnia* and ~964,000 for those fed to fish. At present, we don't know how many spores are in the water column during epidemics or how much of an impact on disease these reductions in spore yield would be predicted to have. However, for the bacterium *Spirobacillus cienkowskii*, we know that spore concentrations in the water column can exceed 4000 cells/ml; moreover, there was a linear relationship between spore density at the sediment–water interface on one sampling day and the prevalence of infection in *Daphnia* one week later (Thomas et al., 2011).

the spores in the water column, those spores are then in close proximity to new hosts. Settling of dead hosts is likely to be common in many aquatic habitats (including lakes, oceans, rivers, and estuaries); standard disease models need to be extended to consider these habitats, especially given the potential economic and ecological importance of their parasites (Harvell et al., 2004; Lafferty et al., 2015; Bidegain et al., 2016).

We are not aware of evidence of predators of *Daphnia* directly consuming spores from the water column or of them eating infected carcasses. However, we do know that they consume infected hosts. Fish only partially digest the spores contained in infected hosts: somewhat fewer spores are retrieved from *Daphnia* that have been fed to fish (vs. infected *Daphnia* that were not fed to fish), but there is no significant effect of fish gut passage on the infectivity of those spores (Duffy, 2009; Figures 16.4 and 16.5). However, it is likely that the

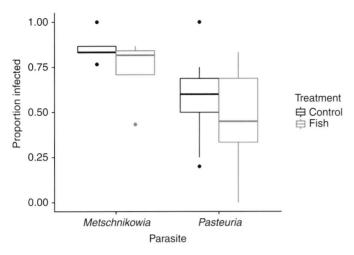

Figure 16.5 Spores of both the fungus *Metschnikowia* and the bacterium *Pasteuria* remain viable after passage through bluegill sunfish guts. Data are shown for spores from control *Daphnia* that were not fed to fish (black bars) and for spores retrieved from fish faecal pellets (grey bars). These spores were used in infection assays, where individuals were exposed to a set spore dose for 24 hours. 'Control' and 'fish' treatments received the same spore dose. In the *Metschnikowia* experiment, both treatments were exposed to 500 spores/ml; for *Pasteuria,* both treatments were exposed to 2000 spores/ml. *Metschnikowia* data are from Duffy (2009). *Pasteuria* data are unpublished data collected by S.K.J.R. Auld and M.A. Duffy.

effects of fish gut passage differ between different parasites (e.g. species that produce spores with thinner cell walls are likely to be impacted more strongly).

There is strong evidence for midge larvae spreading parasite spores in our system and for this increasing disease in our focal host. Midge larvae release spores when they regurgitate infected corpses, driving higher disease in experimental microcosms (Cáceres et al., 2009). Moreover, lakes with more midge larvae have more disease (Cáceres et al., 2009; Penczykowski et al., 2014; Strauss et al., 2016). Theory shows that the release of spores in the water column by this sloppy feeding is crucial for allowing disease outbreaks to occur in stratified lakes (Cáceres et al., 2009; Auld et al., 2014).

While we do not know of *Daphnia* predators that consume free-living stages of parasites from the water column, we do know that daphniids can consume free-living stages of parasites of other organisms. Daphniids feed on zoospores of fungi that infect diatoms (Kagami et al., 2004), the chytrid fungus *Bd* that attacks amphibians (Buck et al., 2011; Searle et al., 2013; Hite et al., 2016), viral parasites of frogs (Johnson & Brunner, 2014), and oomycete brood parasites of copepods (Valois & Burns, 2016). Thus, *Daphnia* might promote 'healthy herds' in other host–parasite systems in their role as a key grazer in lake and pond food webs.

8. Fuelling of spore production by predator-driven trophic cascades

Predators might fuel disease via trophic cascades. Trophic cascades occur when predators reduce the density of their prey populations, leading to increases in density at the next lower trophic level (Pace et al., 1999). If a trophic cascade increases resource levels, it could increase parasite production in infected prey/hosts. At present, we do not know of any evidence showing the full link of increased predation driving increased resources driving increased parasitism. However, we know that, in some systems, higher resource levels increase parasite production (Smith, 2007). For example, increasing fructose in the diet of rats increased the number of eggs produced by a macroparasite, and, five weeks after infection, mature parasite eggs were only found in rats that were fed high fructose levels (Keymer et al., 1983). However, sometimes higher resource levels stimulate the host immune system, leading to reduced parasite production (Cressler et al., 2014); sticking with examples from rodent–macroparasite systems, feeding mice high-protein diets decreased worm burdens 20–30 days post-infection (Michael & Bundy, 1992).

In the *Daphnia*–parasite system, we know that increasing resource levels increase epidemic size, in part by increasing spore yield from infected hosts (Civitello et al., 2015). This argues that, if predators drive trophic cascades, this should fuel epidemics. Lakes with more midge larvae have more algal resources for hosts (S.R. Hall, unpublished data), which is consistent with a trophic cascade. However, we do not yet know whether this reflects a cascade or an underlying productivity gradient. Thus, further work is needed to see if increased predators increase resources and, as a result, increase disease.

16.3 Summary of impacts of predation on our *Daphnia*–parasite system

Fish reduce disease in *Daphnia*, whereas midge larvae spread disease. In both cases, the predators influence disease via several mechanisms that operate simultaneously. Fish prey highly selectively on infected hosts. Fish also drive shifts in the community composition of competitors and predators in a way that decreases disease risk for *Daphnia*. Thus, fish are healthy herds predators in our system. On the other hand, midge larvae promote disease. One of the strongest, most consistent field patterns in our system is a positive relationship between invertebrate predator density and disease (Figure 16.1) (Cáceres et al., 2009; Penczykowski et al., 2014; Strauss et al., 2016). Midge larvae spread disease via sloppy predation on infected hosts (Cáceres et al., 2009), and can increase disease risk to our focal host by reducing the density of a key diluter host.

Future work is required to determine the relative strengths of the different mechanisms and whether there are eco-evolutionary dynamics in the predator–*Daphnia*–parasite system. One thing that is particularly needed is experiments that allow us to assess the impacts of multiple mechanisms simultaneously. For example, our understanding of the net effects of predation on disease in our system would benefit greatly from experiments that are done in stratified systems (e.g. whole-water column bag enclosures) that contain fish, midge larvae, and *Ceriodaphnia*. Ideally, these studies would manipulate not only fish predation rate, but also density of midge larvae and small-bodied diluter hosts. Such an experiment would allow us to directly test the direct and indirect effects of fish predators on disease in *Daphnia* and might help explain why the one prior experimental test of the role of fish predation on fungal disease in *Daphnia* did not find an effect (Duffy, 2007).

An interesting open question is whether and how global change will alter the influence of predators on disease in our system. One study has already considered direct impacts of temperature, finding that predators might be more effective at suppressing disease in a warmer world (Hall et al., 2006). However, this temperature-driven increase in predation rate might be thwarted by changes in water clarity. Inland waters in much of north-eastern North America and Europe are becoming browner due to increased precipitation, land-use change, and recovery from anthropogenic acidification (Williamson et al., 2015). Selective predation can disappear in systems with high dissolved organic carbon, likely because infected hosts are less visible in darker water (Johnson et al., 2006). Thus, at present, it is not clear whether fish will be more or less effective as healthy herds predators as lakes simultaneously become warmer and browner.

We have often used models to try to understand the different mechanisms by which predators can influence disease in their prey populations (e.g. Duffy et al., 2005; Hall et al., 2005, 2006; Duffy & Hall, 2008; Cáceres et al., 2009; Auld et al., 2014). We have created models that study one or a few specific mechanisms, but have not yet developed a model that synthesises across all eight of these mechanisms. Our long-term goal is to take the models we have developed for different mechanisms and to use these as modules to create a more synthetic model. Among other things, having a synthetic model would allow us to better predict how global climate change will alter the influence of predation on diseases in our system.

16.4 Conclusions

Predators have the potential to suppress disease or to spread it, via a variety of mechanisms. At present, there is stronger evidence for some mechanisms than for others, although some of this likely reflects different amounts of research effort. Our hope is that the framework we lay out in this chapter for thinking about how predators influence disease via different mechanisms will motivate additional research on some of the mechanisms that have not been as well studied. Such research is likely to help explain spatiotemporal variation in disease as well as inform management strategies.

Importantly, a single predator can have conflicting impacts on disease. For example, damselfly larvae had conflicting density- and trait-mediated indirect effects on a tadpole–trematode system, leading to no significant relationship between predator density and disease in tadpoles (Rohr et al., 2015). Predators can also interact. In our system, fish are intraguild predators, preying on both midge larvae and *Daphnia*. This has meant that it sometimes has been difficult to disentangle healthy herds and predator spreader phenomena from field data collected on natural populations, given that the two predators tend to be negatively correlated and are predicted to have opposite effects on disease. Fortunately, path analysis can help us tease things apart in these situations (although there can still be issues when potential drivers strongly covary). Our recent synthetic analysis revealed that, in our system, a key way in which fish predation influences disease in *Daphnia* is by increasing the abundance of the diluter species *Ceriodaphnia* (Strauss et al., 2016). We also know that fish predation decreases density of midge larvae (González & Tessier, 1997) and that midge larvae spread disease (Cáceres et al., 2009); thus, a second way in which fish predation might influence disease is via effects on midge density (Strauss et al., 2016). The potential for a single predator to have multiple, opposing effects on disease, and for healthy herds predators and predator spreaders to interact, might help explain spatiotemporal variation in the impacts of predators on disease. Further research into the specific mechanisms by which predators influence disease – and the relative importance of those mechanisms in different ecosystems – should help us develop a better predictive understanding of how predators should influence disease in their prey.

16.5 Acknowledgements

Our work on this topic over the past 15 years has been supported by the National Science Foundation (0235119, 0235039, 0328516, 0508270, 0532728, 0613510, 0614316, 0827396, 0841679, 0841817, 1053525, 1069157, 1120316, 1120804, 1129198, 1305836, 1353749, 1353806, 1354407, 1406846,

1655656, 1655665, and 1655856). Alan Tessier was instrumental in the development of this system and in developing the early work on the influence of predation on host–parasite interactions. We are grateful to our laboratory members and collaborators for their help in uncovering the roles of predators in the *Daphnia*–parasite system. This chapter was improved by feedback from Alex Strauss. Unpublished data shown in Figures 16.4 and 16.5 were collected by Stuart Auld and Meghan Duffy. This is Kellogg Biological Station contribution #2003.

References

Auld, S.K., Hall, S.R., Ochs, J.H., Sebastian, M. & Duffy, M.A. (2014) Predators and patterns of within-host growth can mediate both among-host competition and evolution of transmission potential of parasites. *American Naturalist*, **18**, S77–S90.

Bertram, C.R., Pinkowski, M., Hall, S.R., Duffy, M.A. & Cáceres, C.E. (2013) Trait-mediated indirect effects, predators, and disease: test of a size-based model. *Oecologia*, **173**, 1023–1032.

Bidegain, G., Powell, E.N., Klinck, J.M., Ben-Horin, T. & Hofmann, E.E. (2016) Marine infectious disease dynamics and outbreak thresholds: contact transmission, pandemic infection, and the potential role of filter feeders. *Ecosphere*, **7**, e01286.

Brooks, J.L. & Dodson, S.I. (1965) Predation, body size, and composition of plankton. *Science*, **150**, 28–35.

Buck, J., Truong, L. & Blaustein, A. (2011) Predation by zooplankton on *Batrachochytrium dendrobatidis*: biological control of the deadly amphibian chytrid fungus? *Biodiversity and Conservation*, **20**, 3549–3553.

Byers, J.E., Malek, A.J., Quevillon, L.E., Altman, I. & Keogh, C.L. (2015) Opposing selective pressures decouple pattern and process of parasitic infection over small spatial scale. *Oikos*, **124**, 1511–1519.

Cáceres, C.E., Hall, S.R., Duffy, M.A., Tessier, A.J., Helmle, C. & MacIntyre, S. (2006) Physical structure of lakes constrains epidemics in *Daphnia* populations. *Ecology*, **87**, 1438–1444.

Cáceres, C.E., Knight, C.J. & Hall, S.R. (2009) Predator spreaders: predation can enhance parasite success in a planktonic host–parasite system. *Ecology*, **90**, 2850–2858.

Cáceres, C.E., Tessier, A.J., Duffy, M.A. & Hall, S. R. (2014) Disease in freshwater zooplankton: what have we learned and where are we going? *Journal of Plankton Research*, **36**, 326–333.

Choisy, M. & Rohani, P. (2006) Harvesting can increase severity of wildlife disease epidemics. *Proceedings of the Royal Society of London Series B*, **273**, 2025–2034.

Civitello, D.J., Pearsall, S., Duffy, M.A. & Hall, S. R. (2013) Parasite consumption and host interference can inhibit disease spread in dense populations. *Ecology Letters*, **16**, 626–634.

Civitello, D.J., Penczykowski, R.M., Smith, A.N., et al. (2015) Resources, key traits, and the size of fungal epidemics in *Daphnia* populations. *Journal of Animal Ecology*, **84**, 1010–1017.

Coors, A. & De Meester, L. (2011) Fitness and virulence of a bacterial endoparasite in an environmentally stressed crustacean host. *Parasitology*, **138**, 122–131.

Cressler, C.E., Nelson, W.A., Day, T. & McCauley, E. (2014) Disentangling the interaction among host resources, the immune system and pathogens. *Ecology Letters*, **17**, 284–293.

de Roos, A.M. & Persson, L. (2013) *Population and Community Ecology of Ontogenetic Development*. Princeton, NJ: Princeton University Press.

Decaestecker, E., De Meester, L. & Ebert, D. (2002) In deep trouble: habitat selection constrained by multiple enemies in zooplankton. *Proceedings of the National Academy of Science of the United States of America*, **99**, 5481–5485.

Department for Environment Food and Rural
    Affairs (2016) Summary of badger control
    monitoring during 2016. www.gov.uk/gov
    ernment/uploads/system/uploads/attach
    ment_data/file/578436/summary-badger-
    control-monitoring-2016.pdf
Donnelly, C.A., Woodroffe, R., Cox, D.R., et al.
    (2003) Impact of localized badger culling
    on tuberculosis incidence in British cattle.
    Nature, **426**, 834–837.
Duffy, M.A. (2007) Selective predation,
    parasitism, and trophic cascades in
    a bluegill–*Daphnia*–parasite system.
    Oecologia, **153**, 453–460.
Duffy, M.A. (2009) Staying alive: the
    post-consumption fate of parasite spores
    and its implications for disease dynamics.
    Limnology and Oceanography, **54**, 770–773.
Duffy, M.A., Cáceres, C.E., Hall, S.R., Tessier, A.J.
    & Ives, A.R. (2010) Temporal, spatial, and
    between-host comparisons of patterns of
    parasitism in lake zooplankton. *Ecology*, **91**,
    3322–3331.
Duffy, M.A. & Hall, S.R. (2008) Selective
    predation and rapid evolution can jointly
    dampen effects of virulent parasites on
    Daphnia populations. *American Naturalist*,
    171, 499–510.
Duffy, M.A., Hall, S.R., Cáceres, C.E. & Ives, A.R.
    (2009) Rapid evolution, seasonality and the
    termination of parasite epidemics. *Ecology*,
    90, 1441–1448.
Duffy, M.A., Hall, S.R., Tessier, A.J. &
    Huebner, M. (2005) Selective predators
    and their parasitized prey: are epidemics
    in zooplankton under top-down
    control? *Limnology and Oceanography*, **50**,
    412–420.
Duffy, M.A., Housley, J.M., Penczykowski, R.M.,
    Cáceres, C.E. & Hall, S.R. (2011) Unhealthy
    herds: indirect effects of predators
    enhance two drivers of disease spread.
    Functional Ecology, **25**, 945–953.
Duffy, M.A., James, T.Y. & Longworth, A. (2015)
    Ecology, virulence, and phylogeny of
    Blastulidium paedophthorum, a widespread
    brood parasite of *Daphnia* spp. *Applied &
    Environmental Microbiology*, **81**, 5486–5496.
Duffy, M.A., Ochs, J.H., Penczykowski, R.M.,
    et al. (2012) Ecological context influences

epidemic size and parasite-mediated
    selection. *Science*, **335**, 1636–1638.
Elser, M.M., Vonende, C.N., Sorrano, P. &
    Carpenter, S.R. (1987) *Chaoborus*
    populations: response to food web
    manipulation and potential effects on
    zooplankton communities. *Canadian
    Journal of Zoology*, **65**, 2846–2852.
González, M.J. & Tessier, A.J. (1997) Habitat
    segregation and interactive effects of
    multiple predators on a prey assemblage.
    Freshwater Biology, **38**, 179–191.
Goren, L. & Ben-Ami, F. (2017) To eat or not to eat
    infected food: a bug's dilemma.
    Hydrobiologia, **798**, 25–32.
Groner, M.L. & Relyea, R.A. (2015) Predators
    reduce *Batrachochytrium dendrobatidis*
    infection loads in their prey. *Freshwater
    Biology*, **60**, 1699–1704.
Hall, S.R., Becker, C.R., Simonis, J.L., et al. (2009)
    Friendly competition: evidence for
    a dilution effect among competitors in
    a planktonic host–parasite system. *Ecology*,
    90, 791–801.
Hall, S.R., Duffy, M.A. & Cáceres, C.E. (2005)
    Selective predation and productivity
    jointly drive complex behavior in host-
    parasite systems. *American Naturalist*, **165**,
    70–81.
Hall, S.R., Sivars-Becker, L., Becker, C., et al.
    (2007) Eating yourself sick: transmission of
    disease as a function of feeding biology of
    hosts. *Ecology Letters*, **10**, 207–218.
Hall, S.R., Smyth, R., Becker, C.R., et al. (2010)
    Why are *Daphnia* in some lakes sicker?
    Disease ecology, habitat structure, and the
    plankton. *BioScience*, **60**, 363–375.
Hall, S.R., Tessier, A.J., Duffy, M.A., Huebner, M.
    & Cáceres, C.E. (2006) Warmer does not
    have to mean sicker: temperature and
    predators can jointly drive timing of
    epidemics. *Ecology*, **87**, 1684–1695.
Harvell, D., Aronson, R., Baron, N., et al. (2004)
    The rising tide of ocean diseases: unsolved
    problems and research priorities. *Frontiers
    in Ecology and the Environment*, **2**, 375–382.
Hesse, O., Engelbrecht, W., Laforsch, C. &
    Wolinska, J. (2012) Fighting parasites and
    predators: how to deal with multiple
    threats? *BMC Ecology*, **12**, 12.

Hite, J.L., Bosch, J., Fernández-Beaskoetxea, S., Medina, D. & Hall, S.R. (2016) Joint effects of habitat, zooplankton, host stage structure and diversity on amphibian chytrid. *Proceedings of the Royal Society of London B*, **283**, 20160832.

Holt, R.D. & Roy, M. (2007) Predation can increase the prevalence of infectious disease. *American Naturalist*, **169**, 690–699.

Hudson, P.J. (1986) The effect of a parasitic nematode on the breeding production of red grouse. *Journal of Animal Ecology*, **55**, 85–92.

Hudson, P.J., Dobson, A.P. & Newborn, D. (1992) Do parasites make prey vulnerable to predation? Red grouse and parasites. *Journal of Animal Ecology*, **61**, 681–692.

Johnson, A. & Brunner, J. (2014) Persistence of an amphibian ranavirus in aquatic communities. *Diseases of Aquatic Organisms*, **111**, 129–138.

Johnson, P.T.J., Dobson, A., Lafferty, K.D., et al. (2010) When parasites become prey: ecological and epidemiological significance of eating parasites. *Trends in Ecology & Evolution*, **25**, 362–371.

Johnson, P.T.J., Stanton, D.E., Preu, E.R., Forshay, K.J. & Carpenter, S.R. (2006) Dining on disease: how interactions between parasite infection and environmental conditions affect host predation risk. *Ecology*, **87**, 1973–1980.

Kagami, M., Van Donk, E., de Bruin, A., Rijkeboer, M. & Ibelings, B.W. (2004) *Daphnia* can protect diatoms from fungal parasitism. *Limnology and Oceanography*, **49**, 680–685.

Keeling, M.J. & Rohani, P. (2008) *Modeling Infectious Diseases in Humans and Animals.* Princeton, NJ: Princeton University Press.

Keesing, F., Belden, L.K., Daszak, P., et al. (2010) Impacts of biodiversity on the emergence and transmission of infectious diseases. *Nature*, **468**, 647–652.

Keymer, A., Crompton, D.W.T. & Walters, D.E. (1983) Parasite population biology and host nutrition – dietary fructose and *Moniliformis* (Acanthocephala). *Parasitology*, **87**, 265–278.

Kistler, R.A. (1985) Host-age structure and parasitism in a laboratory system of two

hymenopterous parasitoids and larvae of *Zabrotes subfasciatus* (Coleoptera, Bruchidae). *Environmental Entomology*, **14**, 507–511.

Lafferty, K.D. (2004) Fishing for lobsters indirectly increases epidemics in sea urchins. *Ecological Applications*, **14**, 1566–1573.

Lafferty, K.D., Harvell, C.D., Conrad, J.M., et al. (2015) Infectious diseases affect marine fisheries and aquaculture economics. *Annual Review of Marine Science*, **7**, 471–496.

Lass, S. & Bittner, K. (2002) Facing multiple enemies: parasitised hosts respond to predator kairomones. *Oecologia*, **132**, 344–349.

Levi, T., Kilpatrick, A.M., Mangel, M. & Wilmers, C.C. (2012) Deer, predators, and the emergence of Lyme disease. *Proceedings of the National Academy of Sciences of the United States of America*, **109**, 10,942–10,947.

Li, J., Kolivras, K.N., Hong, Y., et al. (2014) Spatial and temporal emergence pattern of Lyme disease in Virginia. *The American Journal of Tropical Medicine and Hygiene*, **91**, 1166–1172.

Lindeque, P.M. & Turnbull, P.C.B. (1994) Ecology and epidemiology of anthrax in the Etosha National Park, Namibia. *Onderstepoort Journal of Veterinary Research*, **61**, 71–83.

Michael, E. & Bundy, D.A.P. (1992) Nutrition, immunity and helminth infection: effect of dietary protein on the dynamics of the primary antibody response to *Trichuris muris* (Nematoda) in CBA/Ca mice. *Parasite Immunology*, **14**, 169–183.

Mittelbach, G.G. (1981) Patterns of invertebrate size and abundance in aquatic habitats. *Canadian Journal of Fisheries and Aquatic Sciences*, **38**, 896–904.

Morters, M.K., Restif, O., Hampson, K., et al. (2013) Evidence-based control of canine rabies: a critical review of population density reduction. *Journal of Animal Ecology*, **82**, 6–14.

Navarro, C., de Lope, F., Marzal, A. & Møller, A.P. (2004) Predation risk, host immune response, and parasitism. *Behavioral Ecology*, **15**, 629–635.

Orlofske, S.A., Jadin, R.C., Preston, D.L. & Johnson, P.T.J. (2012) Parasite transmission in complex communities: predators and alternative hosts alter pathogenic infections in amphibians. *Ecology*, **93**, 1247–1253.

Ostfeld, R.S. & Holt, R.D. (2004) Are predators good for your health? Evaluating evidence for top-down regulation of zoonotic disease reservoirs. *Frontiers in Ecology and the Environment*, **2**, 13–20.

Ostfeld, R.S. & Keesing, F. (2000) Biodiversity and disease risk: the case of Lyme disease [Biodiversidad y Riesgo de Enfermedades: El Caso de la Enfermedad de Lyme]. *Conservation Biology*, **14**, 722–728.

Pace, M.L., Cole, J.J., Carpenter, S.R. & Kitchell, J. F. (1999) Trophic cascades revealed in diverse ecosystems. *Trends in Ecology and Evolution*, **14**, 483–488.

Packer, C., Holt, R.D., Hudson, P.J., Lafferty, K.D. & Dobson, A.P. (2003) Keeping the herds healthy and alert: implications of predator control for infectious disease. *Ecology Letters*, **6**, 797–802.

Pastorok, R.A. (1981) Prey vulnerability and size selection by *Chaoborus* larvae. *Ecology*, **62**, 1311–1324.

Penczykowski, R.M., Hall, S.R., Civitello, D.J. & Duffy, M.A. (2014) Habitat structure and ecological drivers of disease. *Limnology and Oceanography*, **59**, 340–348.

Ramirez, R.A. & Snyder, W.E. (2009) Scared sick? Predator–pathogen facilitation enhances exploitation of a shared resource. *Ecology*, **90**, 2832–2839.

Rapti, Z. & Cáceres, C.E. (2016) Effects of intrinsic and extrinsic host mortality on disease spread. *Bulletin of Mathematical Biology*, **78**, 235–253.

Rohr, J.R., Civitello, D.J., Crumrine, P.W., et al. (2015) Predator diversity, intraguild predation, and indirect effects drive parasite transmission. *Proceedings of the National Academy of Sciences of the United States of America*, **112**, 3008–3013.

Salkeld, D.J., Padgett, K.A. & Jones, J.H. (2013) A meta-analysis suggesting that the relationship between biodiversity and risk of zoonotic pathogen transmission

is idiosyncratic. *Ecology Letters*, **16**, 679–686.

Searle, C.L., Mendelson, J.R., Green, L.E. & Duffy, M.A. (2013) *Daphnia* predation on the amphibian chytrid fungus and its impacts on disease risk in tadpoles. *Ecology and Evolution*, **3**, 4129–4138.

Smith, V. (2007) Host resource supplies influence the dynamics and outcome of infectious disease. *Integrative and Comparative Biology*, **47**, 310–316.

Snyder, W.E. & Ives, A.R. (2001) Generalist predators disrupt biological control by a specialist parasitoid. *Ecology*, **82**, 705–716.

Spitze, K. (1985) Functional response of an ambush predator: *Chaoborus americanus* predation on *Daphnia pulex*. *Ecology*, **66**, 938–949.

Strauss, A.T., Civitello, D.J., Cáceres, C.E. & Hall, S.R. (2015) Success, failure and ambiguity of the dilution effect among competitors. *Ecology Letters*, **18**, 916–926.

Strauss, A.T., Shocket, M.S., Civitello, D.J., et al. (2016) Habitat, predators, and hosts regulate disease in *Daphnia* through direct and indirect pathways. *Ecological Monographs*, **86**, 393–411.

Tessier, A.J. & Woodruff, P. (2002) Cryptic trophic cascade along a gradient of lake size. *Ecology*, **83**, 1263–1270.

Thomas, S.H., Bertram, C., van Rensburg, K., Caceres, C.E. & Duffy, M.A. (2011) Spatiotemporal dynamics of free-living stages of a bacterial parasite of zooplankton. *Aquatic Microbial Ecology*, **63**, 265–272.

Turney, S., Gonzalez, A. & Millien, V. (2014) The negative relationship between mammal host diversity and Lyme disease incidence strengthens through time. *Ecology*, **95**, 3244–3250.

Valois, A.E. & Burns, C.W. (2016) Parasites as prey: *Daphnia* reduce transmission success of an oomycete brood parasite in the calanoid copepod *Boeckella*. *Journal of Plankton Research*, **38**, 1281–1288.

Williamson, C.E., Overholt, E.P., Pilla, R.M., et al. (2015) Ecological consequences of long-term browning in lakes. *Scientific Reports*, **5**, 18666.

Wilson, K. & Cotter, S.C. (2009) Density-dependent prophylaxis in insects. In: Whitman,D.W. & Ananthakrishnan,T.N. (eds.), *Phenotypic Plasticity of Insects: Mechanisms and Consequences* (pp. 137–176). Boca Raton, FL: CRC Press.

Wood, C.L. & Lafferty, K.D. (2013) Biodiversity and disease: a synthesis of ecological perspectives on Lyme disease transmission. *Trends in Ecology & Evolution*, **28**, 239–247.

CHAPTER SEVENTEEN

Multi-trophic interactions and migration behaviour determine the ecology and evolution of parasite infection in monarch butterflies

JACOBUS C. DE ROODE, SONIA ALTIZER
AND MARK D. HUNTER

17.1 Introduction

The monarch butterfly (*Danaus plexippus*) is an iconic species famous for two biological concepts that continue to motivate scientific research (Zhan et al., 2014; Gustafsson et al., 2015). First, monarchs are a textbook example of warning colouration and plant-derived toxicity to predators (Brower & Fink, 1985). Monarch larvae have highly visible black, white, and yellow stripes, and adults are bright orange, with black and white accents (Figure 17.1A,B). Monarch larvae feed on milkweeds (mostly in the genus *Asclepias*), and sequester a particular group of toxic secondary chemicals, called cardenolides, from these host plants (Malcolm & Brower, 1989). This sequestration makes monarchs distasteful and toxic, and their bright colouration warns vertebrate predators of their toxicity (Malcolm, 1994). Classical studies carried out by Brower and colleagues demonstrated that avian predators, such as blue jays (Figure 17.1C), quickly learn to associate the bright colours with bitter taste and emesis, leading to avoidance of these unsuitable prey (Brower et al., 1968; Brower & Fink, 1985). Second, monarchs are famous for their spectacular annual migration in eastern North America, during which hundreds of millions of monarchs travel thousands of kilometres from as far north as Canada to overwinter in the oyamel forests of Central Mexico (Figure 17.1D,E) (Urquhart, 1976; Brower, 1995). A shorter migration persists in the western USA, where monarchs overwinter along the California coast (Nagano et al., 1993). Monarch migration has long captured the interest of the public; establishing the monarch autumn migration routes was one of the first large-scale examples of citizen science, with members of the public gluing tags on monarch wings to help elucidate the monarch's migratory pathways (Urquhart & Urquhart, 1978).

While the use of toxic host plants and seasonal migration have profoundly shaped monarch ecology and evolution, recent work shows that an obligate

Figure 17.1 Warning colouration and long-distance migration. Monarch butterflies (*Danaus plexippus*) are well known for their bright warning colouration in both adults (A) and larvae (B). This warning colouration serves to advertise their toxicity, derived from the sequestration of milkweed chemicals called cardenolides, which make monarchs unpalatable to vertebrate predators such as blue jays (C). Monarchs are also famous for their annual autumn migration from the eastern USA and southern Canada to the oyamel fir forests in Central Mexico, where monarchs overwinter in clusters from November to March (D). When the sun breaks through, monarchs often take to the sky in the thousands (E). Photos A, B, D and E by Jaap de Roode. Photo D: Wikimedia, US Fish and Wildlife Service. (A black and white version of this figure will appear in some formats. For the colour version, please refer to the plate section.)

protozoan parasite plays an integral role in these classic phenomena (Altizer & de Roode, 2015). Studies during the past decade have illustrated that monarchs are a model system to understand the effects of multi-trophic interactions (including medicinal plant use) and long-distance animal migration on the ecology and evolution of infectious disease. In this chapter, we review what monarchs have taught us about interactions among plants, insects, and parasites, and the mechanisms by which animal migration alters infection outcomes. In considering key outcomes of infection, we consider not only infection status and load, but also host investment in resistance and tolerance, and effects on parasite transmission and virulence evolution. We examine conceptual underpinnings, results of empirical work, and modelling approaches that bridge data and theory. We outline open questions and priorities for future work, including recommendations for integrating animal migration and multi-trophic interactions in the context of ongoing environmental change to better understand the consequences for host–parasite interactions in a changing world.

17.2 The monarch–parasite system

Monarch butterflies are best known for their migratory population in North America, but they also occur in non-migratory populations in many locations around the world, including Central America, Australia, Spain, and multiple Caribbean and Pacific Islands (Zalucki & Clarke, 2004; Pierce et al., 2014; Zhan et al., 2014). In migratory populations, monarchs undergo 3–4 generations of breeding before embarking on their seasonal migration, while in non-migratory populations, monarchs breed year-round. Monarchs are commonly infected with a debilitating protozoan parasite, *Ophryocystis elektroscirrha* (McLaughlin & Myers, 1970). This sporozoan (syn. Apicomplexan) is a specialist on monarch butterflies (Barriga et al., 2016), and forms hardy oocyst spores on the exterior integument of adult monarchs (Figure 17.2A, B). Spores are clustered among the butterfly scales and concentrated mostly on the abdomen (Leong et al., 1992). When infected female butterflies lay eggs on milkweed leaves, parasite spores are passively transferred to the eggs and milkweed, after which they are consumed by early instar caterpillars. The spores then lyse in the midgut, and emerging sporozoites penetrate the gut wall, enter the haemolymph and hypodermal tissues, and undergo asexual and sexual replication during the late larval and pupal stages (McLaughlin & Myers, 1970). Sexual reproduction is followed by spore formation, and adult butterflies emerge from their pupal cases with a new generation of parasite spores on the outsides of their bodies (Figure 17.2C). Although most parasite transmission occurs vertically, from mothers to their offspring, horizontal transmission also occurs when male or female butterflies deposit spores on milkweeds, which are then consumed by unrelated caterpillars (referred to as environmental transmission; Altizer et al., 2004). In addition, infected males can transfer spores to females during mating (de Roode et al., 2009), after which the females can transfer them to their offspring (Altizer et al., 2004).

O. elektroscirrha causes considerable harm to monarchs, reducing pre-adult survival, adult body mass, mating ability, fecundity, flight ability, and adult lifespan (Altizer & Oberhauser, 1999; Bradley & Altizer, 2005; de Roode et al., 2007, 2009; de Roode, Yates & Altizer, 2008). Caterpillars that are infected with a single parasite spore can metamorphose into adults carrying over one million spores (de Roode et al., 2007). This high level of replication is essential for the parasite's transmission to new hosts. Higher numbers of

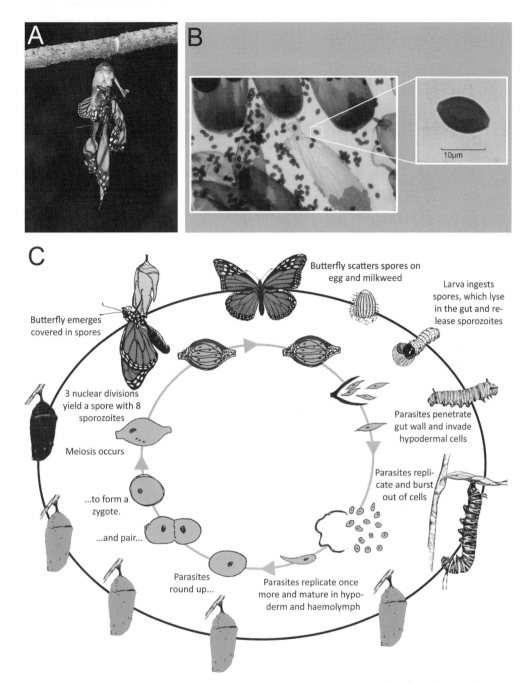

Figure 17.2 *Ophryocystis elektroscirrha* life cycle. Monarchs are commonly infected with the protozoan parasite *Ophryocystis elektroscirrha*. At high infection levels, this parasite can prevent monarchs from successfully emerging from their pupal cases (A). *O. elektroscirrha* forms hardy and dormant oocyst spores that are concentrated around the scales on the monarch's abdomen (B). Parasite infection starts with the ingestion of a spore by a larva, after which the spore releases sporozoites in the larva's midgut. The sporozoites enter the larva's tissues, after which they undergo asexual and sexual replication to form a new generation of oocyst spores in the developing integuments of the butterfly (C). Photo A by Jaap de Roode, B by Andy Davis. (A black and white version of this figure will appear in some formats. For the colour version, please refer to the plate section.)

spores on adult butterflies increase the probability of transmission between hosts, but also cause greater harm to hosts (de Roode, Yates & Altizer, 2008). Thus, while high parasite replication provides benefits in terms of increased transmission rate, it also reduces transmission opportunities by reducing the probability that monarchs become adults, mate, lay eggs, and migrate successfully. As a consequence, natural selection has favoured parasites with intermediate replication rates and hence intermediate virulence (de Roode, Yates & Altizer, 2008; de Roode & Altizer, 2010). The monarch–parasite system therefore provides a key empirical demonstration of the often assumed virulence–transmission trade-off model that is used to explain the evolution of virulence (Alizon et al., 2009; Alizon & Michalakis, 2015). As has been demonstrated for many other host–parasite systems, there is genetic variation among monarch genotypes and populations in host resistance and tolerance to infection (de Roode & Altizer, 2010; Lefèvre et al., 2011; Sternberg et al., 2013), and genetic variation among parasite genotypes in infectivity, host exploitation rate, and virulence (de Roode, Yates & Altizer, 2008; de Roode & Altizer, 2010; Sternberg et al., 2013). Against this backdrop of rich natural history and foundational knowledge, we have found that the chemistry of milkweeds and their associated herbivores and symbionts can determine key epidemiological traits, which interact with the monarchs' annual migratory cycle to drive parasite transmission dynamics and evolution.

17.3 Multi-trophic interactions as determinants of infection

17.3.1 Trait-mediated indirect effects

By definition, herbivores rely on plant material for their nutritional needs. However, for insect herbivores like monarchs, plants also provide a place to live, protection from natural enemies, a modified microclimate, and a source of pharmaceuticals (Speight et al., 2008). In other words, plant physical and chemical traits define how insect herbivores interact with their abiotic and biotic environment (Hunter, 2016). Monarch caterpillars are specialist feeders of milkweeds, and the nutritional and defensive chemicals of these plants affect monarch performance as well as the efficacy of their parasites.

When plant traits influence interactions between herbivores and other members of their ecological communities, we call such interactions trait-mediated indirect effects (TMIEs) (Abrams, 1995; Werner & Peacor, 2003; Figure 17.3). They are indirect because the plant (milkweed) mediates the effect of one community member (parasite) on another (monarch). They are trait-mediated because they rely on variation in the quality, rather than in the quantity or density, of the plant (Forbey & Hunter, 2012). In monarchs, the pharmaceutical and nutritional quality of milkweed plants alter parasite virulence, monarch resistance, and monarch tolerance to infection.

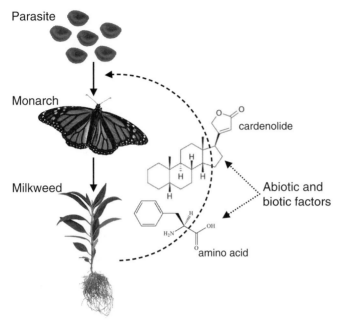

Figure 17.3 Trait-mediated indirect effects. Plant chemical and physical traits influence indirectly the interaction between herbivores and their natural enemies. Solid arrows represent direct effects and the dashed arrow is a trait-mediated indirect effect (TMIE). Molecules are a cardenolide and an amino acid, to represent the pharmaceutical and nutritional properties of milkweed, respectively. Milkweed pharmaceutical and nutritional traits are also the product of biotic and abiotic factors, adding cascading indirect effects (dotted arrow) to the interaction between monarchs and their parasites. Photos by Jaap de Roode.

17.3.2 Milkweed toxins, TMIEs, and host–parasite interactions in monarchs

As specialists of milkweed, monarchs have evolved resistance to cardenolides, the toxic steroids synthesised by a majority of milkweed species (Agrawal et al., 2012; Petschenka et al., 2013; Pierce et al., 2016). There are over 100 species of milkweed in North America alone, and these vary markedly in the diversity and concentration of cardenolides that they express (Woodson, 1954; Malcolm & Brower, 1989; Zehnder & Hunter, 2007). Cardenolides inactivate sodium–potassium ion channels that cross the membranes of eukaryotic cells (Malcolm & Brower, 1989). Monarchs have evolved sodium–potassium channels with reduced sensitivity to cardenolides (Zhu et al., 2008; Dobler et al., 2012; Zhen et al., 2012) and can sequester cardenolides in their own tissues, thus conferring protection against vertebrate predators (Brower et al., 1968; Brower & Fink, 1985). The use of plant chemistry by herbivores to reduce the impacts of natural enemies is a classic form of a TMIE (Price et al., 1980).

Although formulated originally to describe plant-mediated effects on predators and parasitoids of insects, the concept of TMIEs applies equally well to
agents of disease (Felton et al., 1987; Keating & Yendol, 1987; Hunter & Schultz,
1993; Cory & Hoover, 2006).

Our first experiments on the effects of milkweeds on monarch–parasite
interactions implicated cardenolides as medicinal compounds for monarchs.
We demonstrated that *O. elektroscirrha*-infected larvae feeding on the high-
cardenolide milkweed *Asclepias curassavica* (indicated with symbol *cur* in
Figure 17.4A) experienced lower parasite growth and lived longer as adults
than did infected larvae feeding on the low-cardenolide *A. incarnata* (indicated
with symbol *inc* in Figure 17.4A) (de Roode et al., 2008). In other words, milkweed chemistry influenced monarch resistance to *O. elektroscirrha* and the
realised virulence of the parasite, with effects larger than those typically
observed among parasite strains. In subsequent work with many additional
milkweed species, we confirmed that high-cardenolide milkweeds are more
pharmaceutically active against *O. elektroscirrha* than are low-cardenolide milkweeds, reducing parasite growth and increasing monarch lifespan (Figure
17.4A,B; Sternberg et al., 2012a). Moreover, by manipulating toxin dose during
the infection process, we showed that cardenolides are the primary chemical
trait affecting the outcome of *O. elektroscirrha* infection (Gowler et al., 2015).
Follow-up experiments have also shown that it is not just the overall concentration of cardenolides that correlates with parasite resistance, but also their
toxicity, as measured by their polarity (Tao et al., 2016).

Whereas resistance against parasites depends on the probability of infection
and subsequent parasite replication, tolerance to parasites represents the
ability of infected hosts to maintain fitness as parasite burden increases;
tolerant hosts suffer smaller declines in fitness per additional parasite than
do intolerant hosts (Råberg et al., 2007, 2009; Baucom & de Roode, 2011;
Clough et al., 2016). In addition to their effects on monarch resistance, we
discovered that some milkweed species confer greater tolerance to the parasite (Sternberg et al., 2012). Specifically, high foliar concentrations of cardenolides and nutrients combine to increase the tolerance of monarchs to
infection (Sternberg et al., 2012; Tao et al., 2015), potentially as a result of
smaller per-capita parasite spore size (Hoang et al., 2017). In short, some
milkweed species help monarchs to mitigate the deleterious impacts of parasite infection, so that butterflies maintain fitness as parasite load increases.
However, when overall cardenolide concentrations, or their relative toxicity,
become too high, the benefits to monarchs diminish, likely as a result of
negative effects of cardenolides on monarch health (Figure 17.4B; Sternberg
et al., 2012; Tao et al., 2016). Thus, although monarchs are largely resistant to
cardenolides, very high concentrations and highly toxic forms of cardenolides
can be detrimental to their health (Zalucki et al., 1990, 2001).

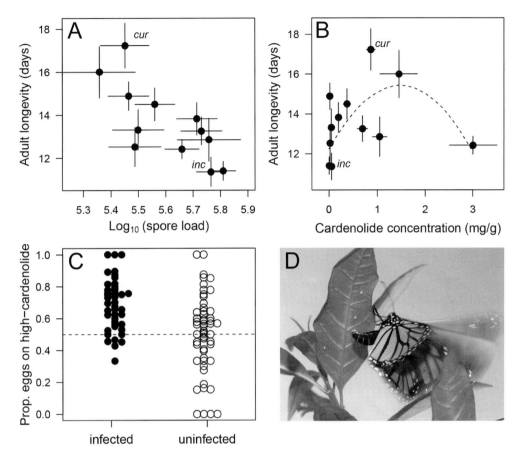

Figure 17.4 Medicinal effects of milkweeds and monarch medication. Milkweed species are important drivers of parasite growth (as indicated by spore load on adult butterflies) and virulence (as measured by the inverse of monarch adult lifespan), as shown for an experiment involving 12 different milkweed species (A). Increasing concentrations of cardenolides are associated with greater alleviation of parasite virulence, up to a point where the concentration is so high that it is also detrimental to monarchs (B). The data point in B with the highest concentration of cardenolides is *Asclepias physocarpa*. When given a choice between the medicinal *Asclepias curassavica* and the non-medicinal *A. incarnata*, infected monarchs from the western USA preferentially lay their eggs on *A. curassavica*, while uninfected monarchs have no preference (C). A monarch ovipositing on *A. curassavica* is shown in panel D. Error bars in panels A and B are ±1 s.e. m., and *A. curassavica* (*cur*) and *A. incarnata* (*inc*) are annotated. Data from Sternberg et al. (2012b) and Lefèvre et al. (2010). Photo in D by Jaap de Roode.

Given that milkweeds mediate the resistance and tolerance of monarchs to *O. elektroscirrha*, we asked whether monarchs might exhibit medication behaviours and actively choose plants that reduce the fitness costs of infection. Medication behaviours are now recognised as common across diverse taxa of animals, including insects (de Roode et al., 2013). We discovered that infected female monarchs choose to lay their eggs more frequently on the medicinal *A. curassavica* than on the non-medicinal *A. incarnata* in laboratory dual-choice experiments (Figure 17.4C,D). In contrast, uninfected females show no oviposition preference between milkweeds (Lefèvre et al., 2010). Moreover, the females make adaptive choices; when we reared the offspring of infected monarchs on the plants that their mothers had chosen, larvae reared on the medicinal milkweeds suffered lower spore loads and lived longer as adults than did larvae reared on non-medicinal plants (Lefèvre et al., 2010, 2012). Our results demonstrate that monarchs engage in a form of trans-generational medication, in which infected mothers choose pharmaceutically active milkweeds with which to protect their offspring from parasite infection.

We discovered a second form of trans-generational medication in monarchs, in which females deposit cardenolides in their eggs. We reared monarchs on high- or low-cardenolide milkweeds and mated them in all possible combinations of parental diet. We then measured the concentration of cardenolides in their eggs and the resistance of their offspring to *O. elektroscirrha* infection. We found that both maternal and paternal diets contributed to the cardenolide concentration of eggs; when both males and females were reared on medicinal milkweeds, eggs contained higher cardenolide concentrations than when one or both parents were reared on non-medicinal milkweeds (Sternberg et al., 2015). Critically, monarchs reared from the highest cardenolide eggs exhibited the greatest resistance to experimental infection with *O. elektroscirrha*. Together, the medicinal choices of females during oviposition, and the transfer of cardenolides to offspring in eggs, provide a powerful combination of trans-generational medication in monarchs (Lefèvre et al., 2010, 2012; Sternberg et al., 2015).

17.3.3 Cascading TMIEs: multiple indirect effects determine how plant toxicity and nutritional quality influence monarch infection with *O. elektroscirrha*

The pharmaceutical and nutritional traits of milkweeds that influence *O. elektroscirrha* are themselves subject to diverse impacts from additional abiotic and biotic interactions (Figure 17.3). For example, the nutritional and defensive traits of milkweed vary with soil nutrient availability (Zehnder & Hunter, 2008, 2009), temperature (Couture et al., 2015), water availability (Andrews, 2015), association with fungal mutualists (Vannette & Hunter, 2011; Tao et al., 2015), previous herbivory (Van Zandt & Agrawal, 2004; Zehnder & Hunter, 2007), and latitude (Rasmann & Agrawal, 2011; Woods et al., 2012). Whenever multiple biotic agents act to change key plant traits, we should observe TMIE cascades, whereby linked TMIEs generate complex interactions among organisms (Liere & Larsen, 2010; Hsieh et al., 2012). This is of fundamental importance in disease ecology, wherein environmental context has powerful and pervasive impacts on supposedly pairwise interactions between parasites and their hosts (Altizer et al., 2013; Civitello et al., 2013; Johnson et al., 2015). For example, low-quality diet results in stunted growth of waterfleas and reduced transmission of their fungal parasites (Penczykowski et al., 2014). In addition, the presence of non-competent amphibian species can reduce the transmission of trematode parasites in freshwater ponds (Johnson et al., 2013).

In the monarch system, TMIE cascades influence the effects of *O. elektroscirrha* on butterfly fitness. As one example of this, milkweed–oleander aphids, *Aphis nerii*, reduce the foliar cardenolide concentrations of some toxic milkweeds (Zehnder & Hunter, 2007). We therefore hypothesised that aphids would reduce the pharmaceutical value of milkweeds for infected monarchs. As predicted, a typical medicinal milkweed, *A. curassavica*, was rendered non-medicinal by the feeding activity of *A. nerii*, thereby increasing both disease symptoms and transmission potential of *O. elektroscirrha* (de Roode et al., 2011b). The loss of pharmaceutical activity against *O. elektroscirrha* was associated with aphid-mediated reduction in the foliar concentrations of two lipophilic cardenolides, supporting the hypothesis that lipophilic cardenolides are the most biologically active (Malcolm & Zalucki, 1996). More recently, we also found that association of milkweed roots with arbuscular mycorrhizal fungi altered the tolerance of monarchs to *O. elektroscirrha*, through changes in nutritional (phosphorus) and secondary (cardenolide) chemistry (Tao et al., 2015). These examples illustrate that interactions among monarchs, milkweeds, and *O. elektroscirrha* depend critically on the ecological community within which the parasite–host–resource interaction takes place.

17.3.4 Theoretical approaches to multi-trophic interactions

So far, our theoretical work on multi-trophic interactions has focused on two questions: (1) how do medicinal milkweeds affect parasite virulence evolution; and (2) given geographic variation in parasite risk, what type of medication behaviour can we expect monarchs to evolve? To address the first question, we developed a mechanistic model based on existing theory of vaccination. Imperfect vaccines, which reduce parasite growth but do not prevent infection, can select for parasites with greater intrinsic growth and virulence (Gandon & Michalakis, 2000; Gandon et al., 2001; de Roode et al., 2011a; Cousineau & Alizon, 2014). Under this definition, milkweed cardenolides represent imperfect vaccines for monarchs.

Our model assumed that (a) virulence follows the trade-off hypothesis noted earlier, and (b) natural selection on parasites acts to maximise their lifetime transmission (Anderson & May, 1982, 1991; May & Anderson, 1983; Bremermann & Thieme, 1989). For parasites causing acute and chronic infections, lifetime transmission increases with transmission rate but decreases with increasing clearance by the host and with host death (Levin & Pimentel, 1981; Anderson & May, 1982; Bremermann & Pickering, 1983; Sasaki & Iwasa, 1991; Antia et al., 1994; Van Baalen & Sabelis, 1995; Frank, 1996). In the absence of constraints, parasites are expected to evolve an infinite transmission rate and minimum virulence. However, under the trade-off hypothesis, increasing parasite transmission rate comes at the cost of higher virulence and premature host death, which reduces the infectious period (Alizon et al., 2009). Therefore, highly virulent parasites are selected against because they kill their host before transmitting to new hosts. However, imperfect vaccines reduce the expressed growth of parasites, and thereby reduce the growth of highly virulent parasites to below the level at which they cause excessive mortality in treated individuals. As such, imperfect vaccines remove the cost of high virulence, and select for parasites with higher levels of intrinsic growth and virulence (Gandon & Michalakis, 2000; Gandon et al., 2001; Mackinnon et al., 2008; de Roode et al., 2011a; Cousineau & Alizon, 2014; Read et al., 2015). These parasites would overcome treatment within treated hosts, and express elevated virulence in untreated individuals, thus putting untreated individuals at higher risk.

As noted earlier, the monarch–parasite system is a key exemplar in support of the trade-off hypothesis. Cross-infection studies have also shown an association between host resistance and parasite virulence, demonstrating that incomplete parasite resistance can select for increased parasite virulence in this system (Sternberg et al., 2013). In addition, medicinal milkweeds act like imperfect vaccines, in that they reduce parasite growth, but do not block infection completely. Using an optimality model, we demonstrated that medicinal milkweeds therefore act in the same way that imperfect vaccines do, selecting for parasites with higher levels of intrinsic virulence (Figure 17.5; de Roode et al., 2011a). Because monarchs are globally distributed (Pierce et al., 2014; Zhan et al., 2014) and inhabit locations that vary in their milkweed communities (Ackery & Vane-Wright, 1984), we should be able to associate the medicinal properties of milkweeds with the intrinsic levels of virulence across natural populations; this will form the basis of future work and will provide an empirical test of vaccination theory.

Our second modelling study addressed specifically the levels of parasite risk (measured as population-level parasite prevalence) under which monarchs are likely to evolve plastic versus fixed medication strategies. Plastic medication is a form of phenotypic plasticity by which infected, but not

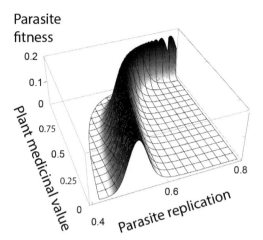

Figure 17.5 Consequences of medication for virulence evolution. The use of medicinal milkweeds can select for increased virulence, as indicated by the results of an optimality model. Parasite fitness (*y*-axis) is a function of parasite replication (*x*-axis), with highest fitness obtained at an intermediate level of replication. With increasing medicinal values (*z*-axis), parasite fitness is maximised at increasing levels of parasite replication. Thus, medicinal milkweeds are expected to select for parasites with higher replication, and hence higher virulence. Reproduced from de Roode et al. (2011a).

uninfected, monarchs preferentially lay their eggs on medicinal milkweed (Lefèvre et al., 2010). Fixed medication, on the other hand, is a form of medication whereby all monarchs, whether infected or not, preferentially oviposit on medicinal milkweed. We created a game theory model (Choisy & de Roode, 2014), and found that plastic medication was favoured under low and moderate parasite prevalence. However, when parasite prevalence reached very high levels, exceeding 90% of hosts, fixed medication was favoured instead. This occurred because at high parasite prevalence, the benefit of medication always outweighs the cost. This theoretical framework is relevant, because monarch populations vary greatly in their parasite prevalence, ranging from less than 10% in western and eastern North America to close to 100% in South Florida (Altizer et al., 2000; Altizer & de Roode, 2015). Carrying out medication studies with monarchs collected from wild populations, we have so far found evidence for plastic medication in western (Lefèvre et al., 2010) and eastern (Lefèvre et al., 2012) North America, where prevalence is low, and evidence for fixed medication in South Florida, where prevalence is high (unpublished results). However, more studies are necessary to conclude unequivocally that parasite risk drives the evolution of medication strategies across natural monarch populations.

17.4 Animal migration as a driver of host–parasite ecology and evolution

17.4.1 Mechanisms by which long-distance migration alters parasite dynamics

Animal migrations are widespread and have profound ecological consequences, including for host–parasite dynamics (Dingle, 1996; Bowlin et al., 2010; Bauer & Hoye, 2014). On the one hand, animal migration can facilitate parasite dispersal as hosts move over long distances, and could increase host exposure to a variety of natural enemies, including agents of disease, as migrants encounter diverse habitats across a broad geographic range (Dwyer & Elkinton, 1995; Rappole et al., 2000; Owen et al., 2006). On the other hand, growing evidence from migratory animals indicates that long-distance movements often have the opposite effect, lowering the risks of attack by natural enemies, including predators and infectious diseases (Lank et al., 2003; McKinnon et al., 2010; Altizer et al., 2011, 2015).

Decreased infection risk in response to long-distance migration can arise from several mechanisms, including consequences of migration for (i) parasite transmission opportunities, (ii) the survival of infected hosts, and (iii) spatial separation between susceptible juveniles and infectious adults (reviewed in Altizer et al., 2011). First, prolonged use of habitats allows parasite infectious stages that can persist outside of hosts to accumulate over time. Consequently, migration might allow animals to escape from contaminated habitats (i.e. 'migratory escape'; Bartel et al., 2011). Between intervals of habitat use, harsh winters and a lack of hosts could eliminate most parasites, allowing animals to return to largely disease-free conditions (as has been observed for reindeer affected by warble flies; Folstad et al., 1991). Similar effects can occur with harsh dry periods: for example, in the African armyworm, viral loads build up gradually during the wet season, but start at low levels each year following the dry season (Graham et al., 2012). Second, long-distance migration can lower parasite prevalence by removing infected animals from the population (i.e. 'migratory culling'). This happens when diseased animals are less likely to migrate long distances owing to the combined energetic costs of migration and infection. Observations consistent with reduced movement ability or propensity for infected animals have been reported for fall armyworm moths affected by parasitic nematodes (Simmons & Rogers, 1991) and for Bewick's swans affected by low-parasitic avian influenza viruses (Van Gils et al., 2007). Third, some migratory animals travel to spawning grounds where adults die or leave after depositing eggs or juveniles. This strategy results in a spatial separation between juveniles that are vulnerable to infection and adults that harbour disease-causing agents ('migratory allopatry'). Evidence that this process lowers infection risk comes from long-term studies of sea lice in Pacific salmon (Krkošek et al., 2007b; Costello, 2009) (Chapter 19, this volume).

17.4.2 Migration and parasite infection in monarchs

During the past two decades, we have examined the consequences of seasonal migration for interactions between monarchs and *O. elektroscirrha*. Monarchs in eastern North America migrate up to 4500 km each autumn from as far north as Canada to overwinter in the neovolcanic mountains of Central Mexico (Urquhart & Urquhart, 1978; Brower, 1995). By comparison, monarchs in western North America occupy a smaller breeding range and migrate shorter distances to winter along the coast of California (Nagano et al., 1993). Monarchs also form populations that breed year-round (and do not migrate long distances) in tropical and subtropical locations, as noted earlier (Ackery & Vane-Wright, 1984; Vane-Wright, 1993; Zalucki & Clarke, 2004). This naturally occurring variation in migration behaviour makes monarchs well-suited for studying the effects of migration on host–parasite ecology and evolution.

Large-scale comparisons of average infection prevalence across migratory and non-migratory monarch populations both within North America and worldwide indicate that, in general, *O. elektroscirrha* prevalence is lowest (less than 10%) in regions where monarchs migrate long distances seasonally, reaches intermediate values (10–50%) in areas where monarchs migrate shorter distances (or undergo annual range contractions and expansions), and infection prevalence is highest (50–100%), in areas where monarchs breed year-round and do not migrate (Altizer et al., 2000; Altizer & de Roode, 2015). This dramatic variation in infection prevalence is especially evident across North American monarch populations (Figure 17.6), and signals that long-distance migration is likely limiting parasite transmission in wild monarchs.

A series of observational field studies have provided support for migratory escape in causing low infection prevalence in migratory monarch populations. For example, analyses of temporal changes in *O. elektroscirrha* prevalence within eastern North American monarchs show that, during the monarch's summer breeding season, parasite prevalence increases over time and peaks at the end of the breeding season (just prior to the monarch's autumn migration), consistent with expectations for migratory escape (Bartel et al., 2011; Figure 17.7A). In comparing monarchs breeding seasonally in temperate habitats with those breeding year-round in tropical or subtropical habitats, differences in climate drive differences in the timing of milkweed availability, which in turn drive differences in the seasonality of monarch reproduction. In areas where monarchs breed year-round, *O. elektroscirrha* spores accumulate on milkweed leaves, causing higher rates of new infection than in temperate sites with highly seasonal monarch reproduction, where milkweed plants die

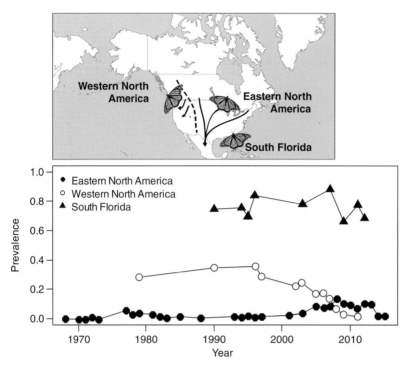

Figure 17.6 Associations between migration distance and parasite prevalence. Geographic variation in *O. elektroscirrha* prevalence in North America. In eastern North America, monarchs migrate the longest distance to wintering sites in Central Mexico. In western North America, monarchs occupy a smaller breeding range and migrate shorter distances to wintering sites along the coast of California. In South Florida monarchs breed year-round and do not migrate. Data from Altizer et al. (2000) and S. Altizer and J.C. de Roode (unpublished).

back during the autumn, and emerge in the spring without parasite spores present (Altizer et al., 2004).

Evidence for migratory culling has come from a comparison of infection prevalence along the US east coast during the autumn migration. As monarchs move southwards towards their overwintering sites in Mexico, *O. elektroscirrha* infections are less common at more southerly migratory stopover sites, consistent with the hypothesis that infected monarchs are dropping out of the autumn migration (Bartel et al., 2011; Figure 17.7B). Other support for migratory culling comes from work using stable isotopes to identify the natal origins of monarchs sampled at overwintering sites in Mexico. Isotope data suggest that uninfected monarchs originate from more northerly latitudes, and have travelled farther distances to Mexico, than have infected butterflies. Moreover,

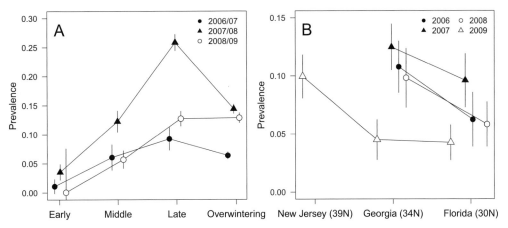

Figure 17.7 Migratory escape and culling. (A) Parasite prevalence (proportion of monarchs heavily infected) during the early, middle and late breeding season and overwintering phase in eastern North America and Mexico over three annual migratory cycles. (B) Parasite prevalence for wild-caught eastern North American migrating adults from three different locations (New Jersey, Georgia, and Florida, USA), arranged from north (left) to south (right) along the eastern autumn migratory flyway from 2006 to 2009. Approximate latitudes are shown. Bars show ±1 s.e.m. Data reproduced from Bartel et al. (2011).

within the infected group, monarchs with higher quantitative spore loads originate from more southerly latitudes, indicating that heavily infected monarchs originating from farther north are less likely to reach Mexico (Altizer et al., 2015). Additionally, experiments using captive-reared healthy and infected monarchs flown in a tethered flight mill demonstrate that monarchs infected with *O. elektroscirrha* fly shorter distances and with reduced flight speeds, relative to uninfected monarchs, again supporting the mechanism of migratory culling (Bradley & Altizer, 2005). In combination, this work indicates that both migratory culling and migratory escape can cause variation in *O. elektroscirrha* prevalence within and among wild monarch populations.

17.4.3 Migration, immunity, and host and parasite evolution

Migration can also affect host–parasite interactions by influencing immune defences and host resistance to infection (Møller & Erritzøe, 1998; Hegemann et al., 2012). Energetically expensive movements, physiological stress, and the need for fat accumulation to fuel migration can reduce investment in costly immunity (Owen et al., 2006; Owen & Moore, 2008a, 2008b; Buehler et al., 2010), as has been shown in crickets (Adamo & Parsons, 2006), European starlings (Nebel et al., 2013), pigeons (Matson et al., 2012), and other birds

(Owen & Moore, 2006). Negative relationships between long-distance migration and immune defence can result from immunosuppression, or from immunomodulation, whereby animals adjust components of their immune response to a desired level to increase migration success.

So far, our understanding of the effects of migration on monarch immunity remains limited, but recent studies indicate that migration is more likely to result in immunosuppression than in modulation. Food restriction lowers monarch innate defences, and some immune defences are associated with smaller body sizes in uninfected monarchs (McKay et al., 2016a). Thus, migrating monarchs that must accumulate lipid reserves and expend energy to undertake long journeys might show lower immunity relative to non-migratory individuals. In support of this idea, monarchs that undertook long experimental flights on sequential days had lower haemocyte concentrations than less-active butterflies (McKay et al., 2016b). Moreover, among wild autumn-migrating monarchs, lipid concentration was associated negatively with one measure of immune defence (phenoloxidase activity) in both healthy and infected monarchs (Satterfield et al., 2013), suggesting that migrating monarchs might face trade-offs between immune defence and energy for flight. Such trade-offs have been found in other systems, such as crickets, where stress-induced lipid transport can result in immune suppression (Adamo & Parsons, 2006; Adamo et al., 2008).

Over longer timescales, migration could serve as a selective force operating on host resistance and tolerance evolution, and on the evolution of parasite virulence. If migrating animals encounter more diverse parasite assemblages, or if migratory culling imposes a strong selective force against susceptibility to infection, greater levels of parasite resistance might arise in migratory species or populations (Piersma, 1997; Møller & Erritzøe, 1998; Altizer, 2001). Parasites might also respond to migration-mediated selection, with less-virulent parasites being favoured by long-distance migrations, assuming that animals harbouring infections must survive the rigours of migratory journeys.

Cross-infection experiments have not found population-level differences in resistance between eastern and western North American monarchs (de Roode, Yates & Altizer, 2008; de Roode & Altizer, 2010), but have shown that non-migratory monarchs from Hawaii and South Florida are more resistant and tolerant than are migratory monarchs from eastern North America (Sternberg et al., 2013). These studies suggest that migration per se is not a strong selective force for increased genetic resistance and tolerance in monarchs, potentially as a result of complicating factors such as variation in the medicinal properties of the milkweeds that monarchs use in their local populations (Sternberg et al., 2012). These same studies also detected genetic variation in parasite virulence, but not consistently lower virulence in parasites from longer-distance migrants. Thus, although parasites in western North

America (short migration distance) were more virulent than those in eastern North America (long migration distance) (de Roode, Yates & Altizer, 2008; de Roode & Altizer, 2010), parasites from South Florida (no migration) had similar virulence to those from eastern North America (Sternberg et al., 2013). As outlined above, it is possible that other factors, such as host genetic resistance (Sternberg et al., 2013) and medicinal milkweed, could be stronger drivers of parasite virulence instead.

17.4.4 Theoretical approaches to studying migration and infection dynamics

Mathematical modelling approaches to investigating animal migration and infection have included both general frameworks and more specific models focused on the dynamics of monarch–parasite interactions. Using a general framework, Hall et al. (2014) modelled a population of animals that migrate annually between breeding and wintering areas as driven by seasonal changes in habitat suitability (Figure 17.8A). Running the deterministic model with and without a directly transmitted parasite (for which transmission was limited to the breeding range) showed that the most effective migration strategy in the presence of a virulent parasite – based on maximising host population size – was for animals to spend less time at their breeding habitat each year (Figure 17.8B). Results also showed a modest increase in migration distance in the presence of infection. Thus, the model provided support for migration as a way of reducing the harmful effects of parasites through both migratory escape (spending less time in habitats where transmission occurs) and migratory culling (travelling slightly longer distances). Using a similar modelling framework, Johns and Shaw (2016) varied the time spent migrating, disease-related migration mortality, and overall migration mortality. Results showed that migration generally lowered infection prevalence, and that populations that spent more time migrating (i.e. escape), and that had costlier migrations (i.e. culling, with greater mortality either for diseased hosts only or overall) had lower prevalence of infection. Shaw et al. (2016) extended this work to provide theoretical support for a third mechanism that they termed migratory recovery, whereby infected animals recover from infection, or otherwise lose their parasites, during migratory journeys.

In modelling work focused on monarch–*O. elektroscirrha* interactions (Altizer et al., 2004), infection dynamics in the absence of migration showed that combined vertical (infected females to offspring) and horizontal (from infected males to females to offspring) transmission could lead to extremely high infection prevalence in sedentary populations, even in the presence of substantial parasite virulence. More recent monarch-specific infection models have examined within-patch dynamics and the roles of different transmission modes (especially environmental transmission from parasites accumulating

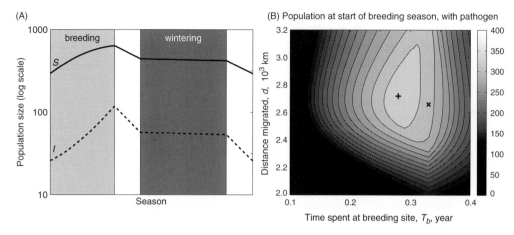

Figure 17.8 Population dynamics and migration strategy. (A) Example population dynamics of susceptible (*S*) and infected (*I*) individuals moving annually between breeding and wintering habitat. Parasite transmission occurs only at the breeding site and most mortality occurs during two migratory intervals (unshaded areas). Specific migratory strategy shown is for time spent on breeding grounds $T_b = 0.33$ year, and migratory distance $d = 2.66 \times 10^3$ km. Details of model structure and other parameter values used for simulation are provided in Hall et al. (2014). (B) Effect of migratory strategy on host population size after introduction of parasite. The migratory strategy is characterised by the time spent at the breeding site (T_b) and distance migrated (*d*), and the magnitude of each response variable is depicted by contour lines and the grey scale bar. The equilibrium population size, *N*, is measured at the start of the breeding season (*t* = 0). The 'x' marks the migratory strategy that maximises the population size prior to parasite introduction; the '+' marks the strategy that maximises population size following parasite introduction. In both plots, results are illustrated for a parasite with transmission rate $\beta = 0.01$, and which induces a moderate cost to migratory survival (*cm* = 0.5). Figures reproduced from Hall et al. (2014).

on contaminated milkweed) on parasite invasion and persistence during the summer breeding period (Satterfield et al., 2017). Together, these findings underscore the importance of different transmission modes for the spread of parasite infection, and these transmission modes will likely vary depending on whether monarchs adopt migratory or sedentary strategies. In particular, opportunities for environmental transmission should be highest in sedentary populations where spores can accumulate on host plant leaves, whereas transmission in migratory populations might be dominated by vertical transmission (Altizer et al., 2004; Satterfield et al., 2017). Future work is needed to explicitly model parasite transmission in the context of monarch migration, perhaps by adopting a migratory network approach (Taylor & Norris, 2010; Taylor et al., 2016) to explore how *O. elektroscirrha* parasites respond to monarch migratory movements between habitat nodes across the breeding and wintering ranges.

17.5 Integrating multi-trophic interactions and migration

Our studies of TMIEs and migration make it clear that variation in the pharmaceutical and nutritional chemistry of milkweed contributes in a fundamental way to the interactions between monarchs and *O. elektroscirrha*. Because phytochemistry varies enormously at landscape, regional, and continental scales (Hunter, 2016), we should expect migratory animals like monarchs to encounter substantial variation in the medicinal quality of their host plants as they undertake their seasonal migrations. Indeed, seasonal measurements of the cardenolides sequestered in monarch wings illustrate that monarchs vary widely in the pharmaceutical quality of the plants that they encounter over the course of a typical year (Malcolm & Brower, 1989; Hunter et al., 1996). Milkweed species from southern latitudes express higher constitutive cardenolide concentrations, and greater cardenolide induction, than do species from northern latitudes (Rasmann & Agrawal, 2011). As a consequence, during recolonisation of northern breeding sites from overwintering sites in Mexico, successive generations of northward migrants feed on milkweeds of decreasing cardenolide concentration (Hunter et al., 1996) and therefore pharmaceutical activity (Sternberg et al., 2012). In addition, in the most southern parts of the USA, subtropical climates allow tropical milkweed, *A. curassavica*, to persist year-round, resulting in the loss of migratory behaviour from some southern populations (Satterfield et al., 2015, 2016). Furthermore, permanent populations of tropical milkweed in the southern USA also host permanent populations of *Aphis nerii*; aphid feeding can eliminate the medicinal qualities of milkweed for monarchs infected with *O. elektroscirrha* by reducing the concentrations of two potent cardenolides (de Roode et al., 2011b). How these co-occurring processes ultimately affect host–parasite dynamics remains an open question, and integrative models will be required to determine the relevance of each of these factors in driving parasite transmission and prevalence.

   Anthropogenic forces are changing the timing and extent of animal migrations (Wilcove, 2008; Visser et al., 2009; Evans et al., 2012). In multiple animal species, there are shifts towards shorter migration distances or sedentary behaviour in response to milder winter climates and year-round food availability (Van der Ree et al., 2006). For example, many Spanish white storks, which normally migrate to Africa each winter, forego migration and subsist on city landfills in Spain year-round (Flack et al., 2016; Gilbert et al., 2016). Monarchs are no exception. The numbers of migratory monarchs observed at wintering sites in Mexico have declined sharply in recent years, in part due to deforestation of overwintering sites in Mexico and the loss of native larval host plants in the northern breeding range (Brower et al., 2012; Pleasants & Oberhauser, 2013; Vidal & Rendón-Salinas, 2014). Simultaneously, the number of sedentary monarchs inhabiting areas along the Atlantic and Mexican coast is increasing. As milkweed habitat declines, nature enthusiasts are eager to plant nectar flowers and milkweed resources that support monarch populations. The most commonly planted milkweed in gardens is the non-native tropical milkweed (*A. curassavica*), which is attractive and easy to grow. Unlike most native milkweeds that enter dormancy in the autumn, tropical milkweed grows year-round in mild climates protected from hard freeze events (Batalden & Oberhauser, 2015). As noted earlier, tropical milkweed also has high concentrations of cardenolides, is attractive to monarchs, and can lower the severity and virulence of parasite infection (de Roode et al., 2008; Lefèvre et al., 2010). In the southern USA, reports of monarchs breeding throughout the year have increased during the past two decades, likely in response to year-round milkweed availability (Howard et al., 2010).

Two recent studies have shown that these newly sedentary monarch populations in both the south-eastern USA and in coastal California harbour high prevalence of *O. elektroscirrha* infection. Analysis of two consecutive years of citizen science data illustrate that *O. elektroscirrha* prevalence at sedentary sites in the south-eastern USA is five times higher than prevalence in migratory monarchs sampled at their summer breeding range or overwintering sites in Mexico (Satterfield et al., 2015; Figure 17.9A,B). A similar analysis for western monarchs illustrates that butterflies sampled in tropical milkweed gardens with year-round breeding are nine times more likely to be infected with *O. elektroscirrha* than are monarchs sampled at seasonal breeding sites or coastal overwintering locations (Satterfield et al., 2016; Figure 17.9C,D). Thus, the altered migration landscape, combined with the increased planting of non-native high-cardenolide milkweed, is stripping a subset of North American monarchs of the population-level anti-prevalence benefits of migration, while providing imperfect individual resistance to parasite growth.

These altered dynamics could have major consequences for the ecology and evolution of monarchs and their parasites. As we noted above, sedentary monarchs, which do not accrue the benefits of migratory escape or migratory culling, support higher parasite prevalence than do non-migratory monarchs (Satterfield et al., 2015, 2016). Based on a modelling study (Choisy & de Roode, 2014), we would expect these newly non-migratory monarchs to exhibit a fixed medication strategy, preferring to lay eggs on the most medicinal milkweeds available to them because the risk of infection is so high. As a consequence of their fixed behaviour, we would also expect to see rapid evolution of increased parasite virulence in non-migratory monarchs. Prophylactic use of medicinal milkweed will select for increased parasite virulence under the conditions imposed by imperfect vaccines (de Roode et al., 2011a). Low costs of transmission among sedentary conspecifics, loss of migratory culling, and the evolutionary effects of imperfect medication could provide a 'perfect storm' of virulence evolution in non-migratory

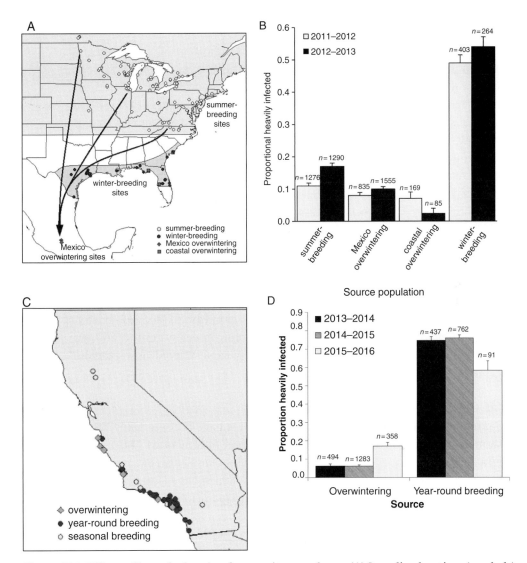

Figure 17.9 Effects of loss of migration for parasite prevalence. (A) Sampling locations (symbols) and major autumn migratory routes (arrows) in eastern North America. Symbols show sampling locations used to compare infection prevalence for summer-breeding sites and Mexico overwintering sites of migratory monarchs. Also shown are winter-breeding sites (solid circles) for non-migratory monarchs breeding year-round on tropical milkweed. (B) Proportions of eastern North American monarchs heavily infected with *O. elektroscirrha* across sources and years of sampling. (C) Sampling locations for western North American monarchs indicating wintering sites, seasonal breeding only on native milkweeds, and year-round breeding on tropical milkweed. (D) Proportions of western North American monarchs heavily infected across sources and years of sampling. Data and maps reproduced from Satterfield et al. (2015, 2016).

monarchs. If this happens, the greatest impacts of increased virulence evolution will likely be felt by migratory monarchs that encounter non-migratory populations during their travels. Our recent work indicates that migratory and non-migratory populations interact in the southern USA, and that there is spillover of parasites from non-migratory to migratory individuals (Satterfield et al., 2018). Such spillover would represent the transmission of *O. elektroscirrha* strains of particularly high virulence to a population of monarchs that is especially susceptible to infection due to the energetic demands of their long and strenuous migration.

As increasing numbers of migratory species are currently undergoing similar shifts from migratory to sedentary behaviour, we will see increasing risks of parasite spillover between migratory and sedentary populations (Krkošek et al., 2005, 2007a; Epstein et al., 2006; Plowright et al., 2011). It is imperative that future work considers the extent to which sedentary populations increase disease risk for migratory populations of the same species, and pose spillover risks for other species. We should investigate the degree to which sedentary populations influence migratory behaviour and interact with migrants that pass through sedentary sites during their seasonal journeys. Monarch butterflies and their parasites will remain an important model system to address how these changes in migration will ultimately drive altered host–parasite dynamics, both within monarchs and beyond.

17.6 Conclusions

Monarch butterflies and their protozoan parasites have become a key model system to investigate the effects of multi-trophic interactions and animal migration on disease ecology and evolution. The chemicals that monarchs sequester from their milkweed host plants and which they advertise to predators with bright warning colouration also reduce parasite infection. Infected monarchs can preferentially use toxic milkweeds as a form of medication for their offspring. While this provides individual-level benefits, theory shows that such medication can also select for high parasite virulence. The seasonal migration that monarchs undergo from the USA and Canada to Mexico has proven to be a potent mechanism to reduce parasite prevalence, with monarchs escaping parasite-contaminated habitats and infected monarchs being culled during strenuous migratory flight. Current trends show a loss of migration of some North American monarchs and the increasing formation of sedentary populations in southern regions of the USA. Moreover, naïve conservation efforts are increasing the planting of non-native milkweeds. These developments are stripping a subset of monarchs of their ability to reduce population-level prevalence, while potentially providing more monarchs with the ability to select medicinal plants. Future work is needed to determine the consequences of these developments for changes in parasite prevalence and the evolution of parasite virulence.

17.7 Acknowledgements

We would like to thank the many undergraduate and graduate students, postdocs, technicians, and collaborators who carried out experiments, fed larvae, grew plants, derived equations, facilitated fieldwork, and stimulated discussion and ideas, including Aamina Ahmad, Samuel Alizon, Paola Barriga, Becky Bartel, Lincoln Brower, Allen Chiang, Marc Choisy, Tyler Faits, Laura Gold, Camden Gowler, Kevin Hoang, Maggie Kelavkar, Thierry Lefèvre, Kristoffer Leon, Hui Li, James Li, Yiwen Li, Carlos Lopez, Michael Maudsley, Andrew Mongue, Karen Oberhauser, Lindsey Oliver, Amanda Pierce, Yamini Potini, Rachel Rarick, Eduardo Rendón, Eleanore Sternberg, Hillary Streit, Leiling Tao, Michelle Tsai, Andy Yates, Rebecca Wang, Jo Williams, and Myron Zalucki. This work was supported by Emory University, the University of Georgia, the University of Michigan, and by the National Science Foundation, grants DEB-1019746, DEB-1257160, and DEB-1256115.

References

Abrams, P.A. (1995) Implications of dynamically variable traits for identifying, classifying, and measuring direct and indirect effects in ecological communities. *American Naturalist*, **146**, 112–134.

Ackery, P.R. & Vane-Wright, R.I. (1984) *Milkweed Butterflies: Their Cladistics and Biology*. Ithaca, NY: Cornell University Press.

Adamo, S. & Parsons, N. (2006) The emergency life-history stage and immunity in the cricket, *Gryllus texensis*. *Animal Behaviour*, **72**, 235–244.

Adamo, S., Roberts, J., Easy, R. & Ross, N. (2008) Competition between immune function and lipid transport for the protein apolipophorin III leads to stress-induced immunosuppression in crickets. *Journal of Experimental Biology*, **211**, 531–538.

Agrawal, A.A., Petschenka, G., Bingham, R.A., Weber, M.G. & Rasmann, S. (2012) Toxic cardenolides: chemical ecology and coevolution of specialized plant–herbivore interactions. *New Phytologist*, **194**, 28–45.

Alizon, S., Hurford, A., Mideo, N. & Van Baalen, M. (2009) Virulence evolution and the trade-off hypothesis: history, current state of affairs and the future. *Journal of Evolutionary Biology*, **22**, 245–259.

Alizon, S. & Michalakis, Y. (2015) Adaptive virulence evolution: the good old fitness-based approach. *Trends in Ecology & Evolution*, **30**, 248–254.

Altizer, S., Bartel, R. & Han, B.A. (2011) Animal migration and infectious disease risk. *Science*, **331**, 296–302.

Altizer, S. & de Roode, J.C. (2015) Monarchs and their debilitating parasites: immunity, migration, and medicinal plant use. In: Oberhauser, K.O., Altizer, S. & Nail, K. (eds.), *Monarchs in a Changing World: Biology and Conservation of an Iconic Insect* (pp. 83–93). Ithaca, NY:Cornell University Press.

Altizer, S., Hobson, K., Davis, A., de Roode, J. & Wassenaar, L. (2015) Do healthy monarchs migrate farther? Tracking natal origins of parasitized vs. uninfected monarch butterflies overwintering in Mexico. *PLoS ONE*, **10**, e0141371.

Altizer, S., Ostfeld, R.S., Johnson, P.T.J., Kutz, S. & Harvell, C.D. (2013) Climate change and infectious diseases: from evidence to a predictive framework. *Science*, **341**, 514–519.

Altizer, S.M. (2001) Migratory behaviour and host–parasite co-evolution in natural populations of monarch butterflies infected with a protozoan parasite. *Evolutionary Ecology Research*, **3**, 611–632.

Altizer, S.M. & Oberhauser, K.S. (1999) Effects of the protozoan parasite *Ophryocystis elektroscirrha* on the fitness of monarch butterflies (*Danaus plexippus*). *Journal of Invertebrate Pathology*, **74**, 76–88.

Altizer, S.M., Oberhauser, K.S. & Brower, L.P. (2000) Associations between host migration and the prevalence of a protozoan parasite in natural populations of adult monarch butterflies. *Ecological Entomology*, **25**, 125–139.

Altizer, S.M., Oberhauser, K.S. & Geurts, K.A. (2004) Transmission of the protozoan parasite, *Ophryocystis elektroscirrha*, in monarch butterfly populations: implications for prevalence and population-level impacts. In: Oberhauser, K.S. & Solensky, M. (eds.), *The Monarch Butterfly: Biology and Conservation* (pp. 203–218). Ithaca, NY: Cornell University Press.

Anderson, R.M. & May, R.M. (1982) Coevolution of hosts and parasites. *Parasitology*, **85**, 411–426.

Anderson, R.M. & May, R.M. (1991) *Infectious Diseases of Humans – Dynamics and Control*. Oxford: Oxford University Press.

Andrews, H. (2015) Changes in water availability and variability affect plant defenses and herbivore responses in grassland forbs. Master's thesis, University of Michigan.

Antia, R., Levin, B.R. & May, R.M. (1994) Within-host population dynamics and the evolution and maintenance of microparasite virulence. *American Naturalist*, **144**, 457–472.

Barriga, P.A., Sternberg, E.D., Lefèvre, T., de Roode, J.C. & Altizer, S. (2016) Occurrence and host specificity of a neogregarine protozoan in four milkweed butterfly hosts (*Danaus* spp.). *Journal of Invertebrate Pathology*, **140**, 75–82.

Bartel, R.A., Oberhauser, K.S., de Roode, J.C. & Altizer, S. (2011) Monarch butterfly migration and parasite transmission in eastern North America. *Ecology*, **92**, 342–351.

Batalden, R.V. & Oberhauser, K.S. (2015) Potential changes in eastern North American monarch migration in response to an introduced milkweed, *Asclepias curassavica*. In: Oberhauser, K.S., Nail, K.R. & Altizer, S. (eds.), *Monarchs in a Changing World: Biology and Conservation of an Iconic Butterfly*. Ithaca, NY: Cornell University Press.

Baucom, R.S. & de Roode, J.C. (2011) Ecological immunology and tolerance in plants and animals. *Functional Ecology*, **25**, 18–28.

Bauer, S. & Hoye, B.J. (2014) Migratory animals couple biodiversity and ecosystem functioning worldwide. *Science*, **344**, 1242552.

Bowlin, M.S., Bisson, I.A., Shamoun-Baranes, J., et al. (2010) Grand challenges in migration biology. *Integrative and Comparative Biology*, **50**, 261–279.

Bradley, C.A. & Altizer, S. (2005) Parasites hinder monarch butterfly flight: implications for disease spread in migratory hosts. *Ecology Letters*, **8**, 290–300.

Bremermann, H.J. & Pickering, J. (1983) A game-theoretical model of parasite virulence. *Journal of Theoretical Biology*, **100**, 411–426.

Bremermann, H.J. & Thieme, H.R. (1989) A competitive exclusion principle for pathogen virulence. *Journal of Mathematical Biology*, **27**, 179–190.

Brower, L.P. (1995) Understanding and misunderstanding the migration of the monarch butterfly (Nymphalidae) in North America: 1857–1995. *Journal of the Lepidopterists' Society*, **49**, 304–385.

Brower, L.P. & Fink, L.S. (1985) A natural toxic defense system – cardenolides in butterflies versus birds. *Annals of the New York Academy of Sciences*, **443**, 171–188.

Brower, L.P., Ryerson, W.N., Coppinger, L. & Glazier, S.C. (1968) Ecological chemistry and the palatability spectrum. *Science*, **161**, 1349–1351.

Brower, L.P., Taylor, O.R., Williams, E.H., et al. (2012) Decline of monarch butterflies overwintering in Mexico: is the migratory phenomenon at risk? *Insect Conservation and Diversity*, **5**, 95–100.

Buehler, D.M., Tieleman, B.I. & Piersma, T. (2010) How do migratory species stay healthy over the annual cycle? A conceptual model for immune function and for resistance to disease. *Integrative and Comparative Biology*, **50**, 346–357.

Choisy, M. & de Roode, J.C. (2014) The ecology and evolution of animal medication: genetically fixed response versus phenotypic plasticity. *American Naturalist*, **184**, S31–S46.

Civitello, D.J., Penczykowski, R.M., Hite, J.L., Duffy, M.A. & Hall, S.R. (2013) Potassium stimulates fungal epidemics in *Daphnia* by increasing host and parasite reproduction. *Ecology*, **94**, 380–388.

Clough, D., Prykhodko, O. & Råberg, L. (2016) Effects of protein malnutrition on tolerance to helminth infection. *Biology Letters*, **12**.

Cory, J.S. & Hoover, K. (2006) Plant-mediated effects in insect–pathogen interactions. *Trends in Ecology and Evolution*, **21**, 278–286.

Costello, M.J. (2009) How sea lice from salmon farms may cause wild salmonid declines in Europe and North America and be a threat to fishes elsewhere. *Proceedings of the Royal Society of London B*, **276**, 3385–3394.

Cousineau, S.V. & Alizon, S. (2014) Parasite evolution in response to sex-based host heterogeneity in resistance and tolerance. *Journal of Evolutionary Biology*, **27**, 2753–2766.

Couture, J.J., Serbin, S.P. & Townsend, P.A. (2015) Elevated temperature and periodic water stress alter growth and quality of common milkweed (*Asclepias syriaca*) and monarch (*Danaus plexippus*) larval performance. *Arthropod–Plant Interactions*, **9**, 149–161.

de Roode, J.C. & Altizer, S. (2010) Host–parasite genetic interactions and virulence–transmission relationships in natural populations of monarch butterflies. *Evolution*, **64**, 502–514.

de Roode, J.C., Chi, J., Rarick, R.M. & Altizer, S. (2009) Strength in numbers: high parasite burdens increase transmission of a protozoan parasite of monarch butterflies (*Danaus plexippus*). *Oecologia*, **161**, 67–75.

de Roode, J.C., Gold, L.R. & Altizer, S. (2007) Virulence determinants in a natural butterfly–parasite system. *Parasitology*, **134**, 657–668.

de Roode, J.C., Lefèvre, T. & Hunter, M.D. (2013) Self-medication in animals. *Science*, **340**, 150–151.

de Roode, J.C., Lopez Fernandez de Castillejo, C., Faits, T. & Alizon, S. (2011a) Virulence evolution in response to anti-infection resistance: toxic food plants can select for virulent parasites of monarch butterflies. *Journal of Evolutionary Biology*, **24**, 712–722.

de Roode, J.C., Pedersen, A.B., Hunter, M.D. & Altizer, S. (2008) Host plant species affects virulence in monarch butterfly parasites. *Journal of Animal Ecology*, **77**, 120–126.

de Roode, J.C., Rarick, R.M., Mongue, A.J., Gerardo, N.M. & Hunter, M.D. (2011b) Aphids indirectly increase virulence and transmission potential of a monarch butterfly parasite by reducing defensive chemistry of a shared food plant. *Ecology Letters*, **14**, 453–461.

de Roode, J.C., Yates, A.J. & Altizer, S. (2008) Virulence–transmission trade-offs and population divergence in virulence in a naturally occurring butterfly parasite. *Proceedings of the National Academy of Sciences of the United States of America*, **105**, 7489–7494.

Dingle, H. (1996) *Migration: The Biology of Life on the Move*. Oxford: Oxford University Press.

Dobler, S., Dalla, S., Wagschal, V. & Agrawal, A. A. (2012) Community-wide convergent evolution in insect adaptation to toxic cardenolides by substitutions in the Na, K-ATPase. *Proceedings of the National Academy of Sciences of the United States of America*, **109**, 13,040–13,045.

Dwyer, G. & Elkinton, J.S. (1995) Host dispersal and the spatial spread of insect pathogens. *Ecology*, **76**, 1262–1275.

Epstein, J.H., McKee, J., Shaw, P., et al. (2006) The Australian white ibis (*Threskiornis molucca*) as a reservoir of zoonotic and livestock pathogens. *EcoHealth*, **3**, 290–298.

Evans, K.L., Newton, J., Gaston, K.J., et al. (2012) Colonisation of urban environments is associated with reduced migratory behaviour, facilitating divergence from ancestral populations. *Oikos*, **121**, 634–640.

Felton, G.W., Duffey, S.S., Vail, P.V., Kaya, H.K. & Manning, J. (1987) Interaction of nuclear polyhedrosis virus with catechols: potential incompatability for host-plant resistence against noctuid larvae. *Journal of Chemical Ecology*, **13**, 947–957.

Flack, A., Fiedler, W., Blas, J., et al. (2016) Costs of migratory decisions: a comparison across eight white stork populations. *Science Advances*, **2**, e1500931.

Folstad, I., Nilssen, A.C., Halvorsen, O. & Andersen, J. (1991) Parasite avoidance: the cause of post-calving migrations in *Rangifer? Canadian Journal of Zoology*, **69**, 2423–2429.

Forbey, J.S. & Hunter, M.D. (2012) The herbivore's prescription: a pharm-ecological perspective on host plant use by vertebrate and invertebrate herbivores. In: Iason, G.R., Dicke,M. & Hartley,S.E. (eds.), *The Ecology of Plant Secondary Matabolites: From Genes to Global Processes* (pp. 78–100). Cambridge: Cambridge University Press.

Frank, S.A. (1996) Models of parasite virulence. *Quarterly Review of Biology*, **71**, 37–78.

Gandon, S., Mackinnon, M.J., Nee, S. & Read, A.F. (2001) Imperfect vaccines and the evolution of pathogen virulence. *Nature*, **414**, 751–756.

Gandon, S. & Michalakis, Y. (2000) Evolution of parasite virulence against qualitative or quantitative host resistance. *Proceedings of the Royal Society of London B*, **267**, 985–990.

Gilbert, N.I., Correia, R.A., Silva, J.P., et al. (2016) Are white storks addicted to junk food? Impacts of landfill use on the movement and behaviour of resident white storks (*Ciconia ciconia*) from a partially migratory population. *Movement Ecology*, **4**, 7.

Gowler, C.D., Leon, K.E., Hunter, M.D. & de Roode, J.C. (2015) Secondary defense chemicals in milkweed reduce parasite infection in monarch butterflies, *Danaus plexippus*. *Journal of Chemical Ecology*, **41**, 520–523.

Graham, R.I., Grzywacz, D., Mushobozi, W.L. & Wilson, K. (2012) *Wolbachia* in a major African crop pest increases susceptibility to viral disease rather than protects. *Ecology Letters*, **15**, 993–1000.

Gustafsson, K.M., Agrawal, A.A., Lewenstein, B.V. & Wolf, S.A. (2015) The monarch butterfly through time and space: the social construction of an icon. *Bioscience*, **65**, 612–622.

Hall, R.J., Altizer, S. & Bartel, R.A. (2014) Greater migratory propensity in hosts lowers pathogen transmission and impacts. *Journal of Animal Ecology*, **83**, 1068–1077.

Hegemann, A., Matson, K.D., Both, C. & Tieleman, B.I. (2012) Immune function in a free-living bird varies over the annual cycle, but seasonal patterns differ between years. *Oecologia*, **170**, 605–618.

Hoang, K.M., Tao, L., Hunter, M.D. & de Roode, J.C. (2017) Host diet affects the morphology of a butterfly parasite. *Journal of Parasitology*, **103**, 228–236.

Howard, E., Aschen, H. & Davis, A.K. (2010) Citizen science observations of monarch butterfly overwintering in the southern United States. *Psyche: A Journal of Entomology*, **2010**, 689301.

Hsieh, H.Y., Liere, H., Soto, E.J. & Perfecto, I. (2012) Cascading trait-mediated interactions induced by ant pheromones. *Ecology and Evolution*, **2**, 2181–2191.

Hunter, M.D. (2016) *The Phytochemical Landscape. Linking Trophic Interactions and Nutrient Dynamics*. Princeton, NJ: Princeton University Press.

Hunter, M.D., Malcolm, S.B. & Hartley, S.E. (1996) Population-level variation in plant secondary chemistry and the population biology of herbivores. *Chemoecology*, **7**, 45–56.

Hunter, M.D. & Schultz, J.C. (1993) Induced plant defenses breached? Phytochemical induction protects an herbivore from disease. *Oecologia*, **94**, 195–203.

Johns, S. & Shaw, A.K. (2016) Theoretical insight into three disease-related benefits of migration. *Population Ecology*, **58**, 213–221.

Johnson, P.T.J., de Roode, J.C. & Fenton, A. (2015) Why infectious disease research needs community ecology. *Science*, **349**, 1259504.

Johnson, P.T.J., Preston, D.L., Hoverman, J.T. & Richgels, K.L.D. (2013) Biodiversity decreases disease through predictable changes in host community competence. *Nature*, **494**, 230–233.

Keating, S.T. & Yendol, W.G. (1987) Influence of selected host plants on gypsy moth (Lepidoptera, Lymantriidae) larval mortality caused by a baculovirus. *Environmental Entomology*, **16**, 459–462.

Krkošek, M., Ford, J.S., Morton, A., et al. (2007a) Declining wild salmon populations in relation to parasites from farm salmon. *Science*, **318**, 1772–1775.

Krkošek, M., Gottesfeld, A., Proctor, B., et al. (2007b) Effects of host migration, diversity and aquaculture on sea lice threats to Pacific salmon populations. *Proceedings of the Royal Society of London B*, **274**, 3141–3149.

Krkošek, M., Lewis, M.A. & Volpe, J.P. (2005) Transmission dynamics of parasitic sea lice from farm to wild salmon. *Proceedings of the Royal Society of London B*, **272**, 689–696.

Lank, D.B., Butler, R.W., Ireland, J. & Ydenberg, R.C. (2003) Effects of predation danger on migration strategies of sandpipers. *Oikos*, **103**, 303–319.

Lefèvre, T., Chiang, A., Kelavkar, M., et al. (2012) Behavioural resistance against a protozoan parasite in the monarch butterfly. *Journal of Animal Ecology*, **81**, 70–79.

Lefèvre, T., Oliver, L., Hunter, M.D. & de Roode, J.C. (2010) Evidence for trans-generational medication in nature. *Ecology Letters*, **13**, 1485–1493.

Lefèvre, T., Williams, A.J. & de Roode, J.C. (2011) Genetic variation for resistance, but not tolerance, to a protozoan parasite in the monarch butterfly. *Proceedings of the Royal Society of London B*, **278**, 751–759.

Leong, K.L.H., Kaya, H.K., Yoshimura, M.A. & Frey, D.F. (1992) The occurrence and effect of a protozoan parasite, *Ophryocystis elektroscirrha* (Neogregarinida, Ophryocystidae) on overwintering monarch butterflies, *Danaus plexippus* (Lepidoptera, Danaidae) from two California winter sites. *Ecological Entomology*, **17**, 338–342.

Levin, S. & Pimentel, D. (1981) Selection of intermediate rates of increase in parasite-host systems. *American Naturalist*, **117**, 308–315.

Liere, H. & Larsen, A. (2010) Cascading trait-mediation: disruption of a trait-mediated mutualism by parasite-induced behavioral modification. *Oikos*, **119**, 1394–1400.

Mackinnon, M.J., Gandon, S. & Read, A.F. (2008) Virulence evolution in response to vaccination: the case of malaria. *Vaccine*, **26**, C42–C52.

Malcolm, S.B. (1994) Milkweeds, monarch butterflies and the ecological significance of cardenolides. *Chemoecology*, **5**, 101–117.

Malcolm, S.B. & Brower, L.P. (1989) Evolutionary and ecological implications of cardenolide sequestration in the monarch butterfly. *Experientia*, **45**, 284–295.

Malcolm, S.B. & Zalucki, M.P. (1996) Milkweed latex and cardenolide induction may resolve the lethal plant defence paradox. *Entomologia Experimentalis et Applicata*, **80**, 193–196.

Matson, K.D., Horrocks, N.P., Tieleman, B.I. & Haase, E. (2012) Intense flight and endotoxin injection elicit similar effects on leukocyte distributions but dissimilar effects on plasma-based immunological indices in pigeons. *Journal of Experimental Biology*, **215**, 3734–3741.

May, R.M. & Anderson, R.M. (1983) Epidemiology and genetics in the coevolution of parasites and hosts. *Proceedings of the Royal Society of London B*, **219**, 281–313.

McKay, A.F., Ezenwa, V.O. & Altizer, S. (2016a) Consequences of food restriction for immune defense, parasite infection, and fitness in monarch butterflies. *Physiological and Biochemical Zoology*, **89**, 389–401.

McKay, A.F., Ezenwa, V.O. & Altizer, S. (2016b) Unravelling the costs of flight for immune defenses in the migratory monarch butterfly. *Integrative and Comparative Biology*, **56**, 278–289.

McKinnon, L., Smith, P.A., Nol, E., et al. (2010) Lower predation risk for migratory birds at high latitudes. *Science*, **327**, 326–327.

McLaughlin, R.E. & Myers, J. (1970) *Ophryocystis elektroscirrha* sp. n., a neogregarine pathogen of monarch butterfly *Danaus plexippus* (L.) and the Florida queen butterfly *D. gilippus berenice* Cramer. *Journal of Protozoology*, **17**, 300–305.

Møller, A.P. & Erritzøe, J. (1998) Host immune defence and migration in birds. *Evolutionary Ecology*, **12**, 945–953.

Nagano, C.D., Sakai, W.H., Malcolm, S.B., et al. (1993) Spring migration of monarch butterflies in California. In: Zalucki,M.P. (ed.), *Biology and Conservation of the Monarch Butterfly* (pp. 217–232). Los Angeles, CA: Natural History Museum of Los Angeles County.

Nebel, S., Buehler, D.M., MacMillan, A. & Guglielmo, C.G. (2013) Flight performance of western sandpipers, *Calidris mauri*, remains uncompromised when mounting an acute phase immune response. *Journal of Experimental Biology*, **216**, 2752–2759.

Owen, J., Moore, F., Panella, N., et al. (2006) Migrating birds as dispersal vehicles for West Nile virus. *EcoHealth*, **3**, 79.

Owen, J. & Moore, F.R. (2008a) Relationship between energetic condition and indicators of immune function in thrushes during spring migration. *Canadian Journal of Zoology*, **86**, 638–647.

Owen, J.C. & Moore, F.R. (2006) Seasonal differences in immunological condition of three species of thrushes. *The Condor*, **108**, 389–398.

Owen, J.C. & Moore, F.R. (2008b) Swainson's thrushes in migratory disposition exhibit reduced immune function. *Journal of Ethology*, **26**, 383–388.

Penczykowski, R.M., Lemanski, B.C., Sieg, R.D., et al. (2014) Poor resource quality lowers transmission potential by changing foraging behaviour. *Functional Ecology*, **28**, 1245–1255.

Petschenka, G., Fandrich, S., Sander, N., et al. (2013) Stepwise evolution of resistance to toxic cardenolides via genetic substitutions in the NA$^+$/K$^+$-ATPase of milkweed butterflies (Lepidoptera, Danaini). *Evolution*, **67**, 2753–2761.

Pierce, A.A., de Roode, J.C. & Tao, L. (2016) Comparative genetics of Na$^+$/K$^+$-ATPase in monarch butterfly populations with varying host plant toxicity. *Biological Journal of the Linnean Society*, **119**, 194–200.

Pierce, A.A., Zalucki, M.P., Bangura, M., et al. (2014) Serial founder effects and genetic differentiation during worldwide range expansion of monarch butterflies. *Proceedings of the Royal Society of London B*, **281**, 20142230.

Piersma, T. (1997) Do global patterns of habitat use and migration strategies co-evolve with relative investments in immunocompetence due to spatial variation in parasite pressure? *Oikos*, **80**, 623–631.

Pleasants, J.M. & Oberhauser, K.S. (2013) Milkweed loss in agricultural fields because of herbicide use: effect on the monarch butterfly population. *Insect Conservation and Diversity*, **6**, 135–144.

Plowright, R.K., Foley, P., Field, H.E., et al. (2011) Urban habituation, ecological connectivity and epidemic dampening: the emergence of Hendra virus from flying foxes (*Pteropus* spp.). *Proceedings of the Royal Society of London B*, **278**, 3703–3712.

Price, P.W., Bouton, C.E., Gross, P., et al. (1980) Interactions among three tropic levels: influence of plants on interactions between insect herbivores and natural enemies. *Annual Review of Ecology and Systematics*, **11**, 41–65.

Råberg, L., Graham, A.L. & Read, A.F. (2009) Decomposing health: tolerance and resistance to parasites in animals. *Philosophical Transactions of the Royal Society of London, Series B: Biological Sciences*, **364**, 37–49.

Råberg, L., Sim, D. & Read, A.F. (2007) Disentangling genetic variation for resistance and tolerance to infectious disease in animals. *Science*, **318**, 318–320.

Rappole, J.H., Derrickson, S.R. & Hubálek, Z. (2000) Migratory birds and spread of West Nile virus in the Western Hemisphere. *Emerging Infectious Diseases*, **6**, 319.

Rasmann, S. & Agrawal, A.A. (2011) Latitudinal patterns in plant defense: evolution of cardenolides, their toxicity and induction following herbivory. *Ecology Letters*, **14**, 476–483.

Read, A.F., Baigent, S.J., Powers, C., et al. (2015) Imperfect vaccination can enhance the transmission of highly virulent pathogens. *PLoS Biology*, **13**, e1002198.

Sasaki, A. & Iwasa, Y. (1991) Optimal growth schedule of pathogens within a host: switching between lytic and latent cycles. *Theoretical Population Biology*, **39**, 201–239.

Satterfield, D.A., Altizer, S., Williams, M.-K. & Hall, R.J. (2017) Environmental persistence influences infection dynamics for a butterfly pathogen. *PLoS ONE*, **12**, e0169982.

Satterfield, D.A., Maerz, J.C. & Altizer, S. (2015) Loss of migratory behaviour increases infection risk for a butterfly host. *Proceedings of the Royal Society of London B*, **282**, 20141734.

Satterfield, D.A., Maerz, J.C., Hunter, M.D., et al. (2018) Migratory monarchs that encounter resident monarchs show life-history differences and higher rates of parasite infection. *Ecology Letters*, **21**, 1670–1680.

Satterfield, D.A., Villablanca, F.X., Maerz, J.C. & Altizer, S. (2016) Migratory monarchs wintering in California experience low infection risk compared to monarchs breeding year-round on non-native milkweed. *Integrative and Comparative Biology*, **56**, 343–352.

Satterfield, D.A., Wright, A.E. & Altizer, S. (2013) Lipid reserves and immune defense in healthy and diseased migrating monarchs *Danaus plexippus*. *Current Zoology*, **59**, 393–402.

Shaw, A.K., Binning, S.A., Hall, S.R. & Michalakis, Y. (2016) Migratory recovery from infection as a selective pressure for the evolution of migration. *The American Naturalist*, **187**, 491–501.

Simmons, A.M. & Rogers, C.E. (1991) Dispersal and seasonal occurrence of *Noctuidonema guyanense*, an ectoparasitic nematode of adult fall armyworm (Lepidoptera: Noctuidae), in the United States 2. *Journal of Entomological Science*, **26**, 136–148.

Speight, M.R., Hunter, M.D. & Watt, A.D. (2008) *The Ecology of Insects: Concepts and Applications*, 2nd edn. Oxford: Wiley-Blackwell.

Sternberg, E.D., Lefèvre, T., Li, J., et al. (2012) Food plant derived disease tolerance and resistance in a natural butterfly–plant–parasite interaction. *Evolution*, **66**, 3367–3376.

Sternberg, E.D., Li, H., Wang, R., Gowler, C. & de Roode, J.C. (2013) Patterns of host-parasite adaptation in three populations of monarch butterflies infected with a naturally occurring protozoan disease: virulence, resistance, and tolerance. *American Naturalist*, **182**, E235–E248.

Sternberg, E.D., de Roode, J.C. & Hunter, M.D. (2015) Trans-generational parasite protection associated with paternal diet. *Journal of Animal Ecology*, **84**, 310–321.

Tao, L., Gowler, C.D., Ahmad, A., Hunter, M.D. & de Roode, J.C. (2015) Disease ecology across soil boundaries: effects of below-ground fungi on above-ground host–parasite interactions. *Proceedings of the Royal Society of London B*, **282**, 20151993.

Tao, L., Hoang, K.M., Hunter, M.D. & de Roode, J.C. (2016) Fitness costs of animal medication: anti-parasitic plant chemicals reduce fitness of monarch butterfly hosts. *Journal of Animal Ecology*, **85**, 1246–1254.

Taylor, C.M., Laughlin, A.J. & Hall, R.J. (2016) The response of migratory populations to phenological change: a migratory flow network modelling approach. *Journal of Animal Ecology*, **85**, 648–659.

Taylor, C.M. & Norris, D.R. (2010) Population dynamics in migratory networks. *Theoretical Ecology*, **3**, 65–73.

Urquhart, F.A. (1976) Found at last: the monarch's winter home. National Geographic, 161–173.

Urquhart, F.A. & Urquhart, N.R. (1978) Autumnal migration routes of the eastern population of the monarch butterfly (*Danaus p. plexippus* L.; Danaidae; Lepidoptera) in North America to the overwintering site in the Neovolcanic Plateau of Mexico. *Canadian Journal of Zoology*, **56**, 1759–1764.

Van Baalen, M. & Sabelis, M.W. (1995) The dynamics of multiple infection and the evolution of virulence. *American Naturalist*, **146**, 881–910.

Van der Ree, R., McDonnell, M., Temby, I., Nelson, J. & Whittingham, E. (2006) The establishment and dynamics of a recently established urban camp of flying foxes

(*Pteropus poliocephalus*) outside their geographic range. *Journal of Zoology*, **268**, 177–185.

Van Gils, J.A., Munster, V.J., Radersma, R., et al. (2007) Hampered foraging and migratory performance in swans infected with low-pathogenic avian influenza A virus. *PLoS ONE*, **2**, e184.

Van Zandt, P.A. & Agrawal, A.A. (2004) Specificity of induced plant responses to specialist herbivores of the common milkweed *Asclepias syriaca*. *Oikos*, **104**, 401–409.

Vane-Wright, R.I. (1993) The Columbus hypothesis: an explanation for the dramatic 19th century range expansion of the monarch butterfly. In: Malcolm,S.B. & Zalucki,M.P. (eds.), *Biology and Conservation of the Monarch Butterfly* (pp. 179–187). Los Angeles, CA: Natural History Museum of Los Angeles County.

Vannette, R.L. & Hunter, M.D. (2011) Plant defence theory re-examined: nonlinear expectations based on the costs and benefits of resource mutualisms. *Journal of Ecology*, **99**, 66–76.

Vidal, O. & Rendón-Salinas, E. (2014) Dynamics and trends of overwintering colonies of the monarch butterfly in Mexico. *Biological Conservation*, **180**, 165–175.

Visser, M.E., Perdeck, A.C., van Balen, J. & Both, C. (2009) Climate change leads to decreasing bird migration distances. *Global Change Biology*, **15**, 1859–1865.

Werner, E.E. & Peacor, S.D. (2003) A review of trait-mediated indirect interactions in ecological communities. *Ecology*, **84**, 1083–1100.

Wilcove, D.S. (2008) *No Way Home: The Decline of the World's Great Animal Migrations.* Washington, DC: Island Press.

Woods, E.C., Hastings, A.P., Turley, N.E., Heard, S.B. & Agrawal, A.A. (2012) Adaptive geographical clines in the growth and defense of a native plant. *Ecological Monographs*, **82**, 149–168.

Woodson, R.E. (1954) The North American species of *Asclepias* L. *Annals of the Missouri Botanical Garden*, **41**, 1–211.

Zalucki, M.P., Brower, L.P. & Malcolm, S.B. (1990) Oviposition by *Danaus plexippus* in relation to cardenolide content of 3 *Asclepias* species in the southeastern USA. *Ecological Entomology*, **15**, 231–240.

Zalucki, M.P. & Clarke, A.R. (2004) Monarchs across the Pacific: the Columbus hypothesis revisited. *Biological Journal of the Linnean Society*, **82**, 111–121.

Zalucki, M.P., Malcolm, S.B., Paine, T.D., et al. (2001) It's the first bites that count: survival of first-instar monarchs on milkweeds. *Austral Ecology*, **26**, 547–555.

Zehnder, C.B. & Hunter, M.D. (2007) Interspecific variation within the genus *Asclepias* in response to herbivory by a phloem-feeding insect herbivore. *Journal of Chemical Ecology*, **33**, 2044–2053.

Zehnder, C.B. & Hunter, M.D. (2008) Effects of nitrogen deposition on the interaction between an aphid and its host plant. *Ecological Entomology*, **33**, 24–30.

Zehnder, C.B. & Hunter, M.D. (2009) More is not necessarily better: the impact of limiting and excessive nutrients on herbivore population growth rates. *Ecological Entomology*, **34**, 535–543.

Zhan, S., Zhang, W., Niitepõld, K., et al. (2014) The genetics of monarch butterfly migration and warning colouration. *Nature*, **514**, 317–321.

Zhen, Y., Aardema, M.L., Medina, E.M., Schumer, M. & Andolfatto, P. (2012) Parallel molecular evolution in a herbivore community. *Science*, **337**, 1634–1637.

Zhu, H., Casselman, A. & Reppert, S.M. (2008) Chasing migration genes: a brain expressed sequence tag resource for summer and migratory monarch butterflies (*Danaus plexippus*). *PLoS ONE*, **3**, e1345.

CHAPTER EIGHTEEN

When chytrid fungus invades: integrating theory and data to understand disease-induced amphibian declines

MARK Q. WILBER, PIETER T.J. JOHNSON
AND CHERYL J. BRIGGS

18.1 Introduction

Globally, amphibian populations are experiencing unprecedented declines (Stuart et al., 2004; Skerratt et al., 2007). While there are many contributing factors including habitat loss and environmental contamination, emerging infectious disease is a major cause of these declines (Daszak et al., 2003; Stuart et al., 2004; Skerratt et al., 2007). Of particular concern is the pathogen *Batrachochytrium dendrobatidis* (Bd), an aquatic fungus that infects the skin of amphibians and leads to the disease chytridiomycosis (Box 18.1; Longcore et al., 1999; Voyles et al., 2009). Chytridiomycosis can lead to drastic population declines and, in some cases, species extinction (Daszak et al., 2003). Bd has been identified in over 500 species of amphibians across six continents (Fisher et al., 2012), making it one of the most widespread and devastating vertebrate pathogens in documented history (Skerratt et al., 2007).

Despite the general severity of chytridiomycosis, the outcome of Bd invasion into an amphibian population can be highly variable. Different species of amphibians, and even divergent populations of the same species of amphibian, have shown population-level outcomes ranging from extirpation to little or no impact following Bd invasion (Briggs et al., 2005; Skerratt et al., 2007; Kilpatrick et al., 2010; Doddington et al., 2013; Savage & Zamudio, 2016). In parts of the world, Bd is still invading and leading to epizootics of chytridiomycosis (Bletz et al., 2015; Clare et al., 2016; Jani et al., 2017), while in other areas Bd has been present for decades and is currently persisting with amphibian hosts in an enzootic state (Briggs et al., 2010; Knapp et al., 2016; Scheele et al., 2017). Understanding when the invasion of Bd into an amphibian population will lead to extirpation and when it will have negligible effects is an important conservation question for mitigating Bd-induced amphibian declines (Woodhams et al., 2011).

Identifying the characteristics of host–parasite systems that allow for parasite invasion and host regulation is a central goal in epidemiology (Anderson &

Box 18.1: Chytrid fungus and amphibian declines

Natural history of *Batrachochytrium dendrobatidis*
Batrachochytrium dendrobatidis (Bd) is an aquatic fungus with a life cycle consisting of two stages: a free-living, motile zoospore and a reproductive zoosporangium (Longcore et al., 1999). Motile Bd zoospores encyst in the keratinised tissue of amphibian skin and form zoosporangia (Kilpatrick et al., 2010). Additional zoospores then form within this zoosporangium and are released back into the aquatic environment where they can immediately reinfect the same host or become part of the environmental pool of zoospores (Kilpatrick et al., 2010).

Amphibians infected with Bd can suffer from the disease known as chytridiomycosis. The symptoms of chytridiomycosis can include lethargy, increased skin sloughing, lack of appetite, and mortality (Voyles et al., 2007). Chytridiomycosis causes amphibian death by disrupting the ability of amphibian skin to osmoregulate, which leads to severe osmotic imbalance and cardiac arrest (Voyles et al., 2007, 2009). Chytridiomycosis can also have sublethal, negative effects on amphibians including reduced foraging in tadpoles (Hanlon et al., 2015), reduction in body size (Hanlon et al., 2015), and, potentially, a decrease in reproduction ability (Bielby et al., 2015).

Bd and the mountain yellow-legged frog
Many of our examples throughout the text focus on Bd dynamics in populations of the mountain yellow-legged frog complex (*Rana muscosa* and *Rana sierrae*; Figure B18.1.1). Mountain yellow-legged frogs live in high-elevation lakes and streams in the Sierra Nevada mountains in California, USA. While once abundant throughout the Sierra Nevada, the introduction of trout for recreational fishing between 1900 and 1960 led to large declines in mountain yellow-legged frog populations (Knapp & Matthews, 2000; Knapp et al., 2016). After the introduction of trout, Bd likely invaded Yosemite National Park in the Sierra Nevada in the 1970s and the remaining *R. sierrae* populations suffered severe Bd-induced declines (Knapp et al., 2016). Currently, *R. sierrae* are actually showing large-scale population recoveries in the presence of Bd (Knapp et al., 2016). In contrast, populations of *R. muscosa* in more southern regions of the Sierra Nevada are currently experiencing Bd-induced declines and extinctions (Briggs et al., 2005; Vredenburg et al., 2010; Jani et al., 2017). Conservation efforts such as translocations of persistent populations, fungicide treatments, and captive breeding are all currently being implemented to attempt to mitigate these Bd-induced population declines (R.A. Knapp et al., unpublished).

Box 18.1: (cont.)

Figure B18.1.1 *Rana muscosa* and *Rana sierrae* live in high-elevation lakes and streams in the Sierra Nevada mountains in California, USA. (A black and white version of this figure will appear in some formats. For the colour version, please refer to the plate section.)

References

Bielby, J., Fisher, M.C., Clare, F.C., Rosa, G.M. & Garner, T.W.J. (2015) Host species vary in infection probability, sub-lethal effects, and costs of immune response when exposed to an amphibian parasite. *Scientific Reports*, **5**, 1–8.

Briggs, C.J., Vredenburg, V.T.,Knapp, R.A. & Rachowicz, L.J. (2005) Investigating the population-level effects of chytridiomycosis: an emerging infectious disease of amphibians. *Ecology*, **86**, 3149–3159.

Hanlon, S.M., Lynch, K.J., Kerby, J. & Parris, M.J. (2015) *Batrachochytrium dendrobatidis* exposure effects on foraging efficiencies and body size in anuran tadpoles. *Diseases of Aquatic Organisms*, **112**, 237–242.

Jani, A.J., Knapp, R.A. & Briggs, C.J. (2017) Epidemic and endemic pathogen dynamics correspond to distinct host population microbiomes at a landscape scale. *Proceedings of the Royal Society of London B*, **284**, 20170944.

Kilpatrick, A.M., Briggs, C.J. & Daszak, P. (2010) The ecology and impact of chytridiomycosis: an emerging disease of amphibians. *Trends in Ecology and Evolution*, **25**, 109–118.

Knapp, R.A. & Matthews, K.R. (2000) Non-native mountain fish introductions and the decline of the mountain yellow-legged frog from within protected areas. *Conservation Biology*, **14**, 428–438.

Knapp, R.A., Fellers, G.M., Kleeman, P.M., et al. (2016) Large-scale recovery of an endangered amphibian despite ongoing exposure to multiple stressors. *Proceedings of the National Academy of Sciences of the United States of America*, **113**, 11,889–11,894.

Longcore, J.E., Pessier, A.P. &Nichols, D.K. (1999) *Batrachochytrium dendrobatidis* gen. et sp. nov., a chytrid pathogenic to amphibians. *Mycologia*, **91**, 219–227.

Voyles, J., Berger, L., Young, S., et al. (2007) Electrolyte depletion and osmotic imbalance in amphibians with chytridiomycosis. *Diseases of Aquatic Organisms*, **77**, 113–118.

Voyles, J., Young, S., Berger, L., et al. (2009) Pathogenesis of chytridiomycosis, a cause of catastrophic amphibian declines. *Science*, **326**, 5–8.

Vredenburg, V.T., Knapp, R.A., Tunstall, T.S. & Briggs, C.J. (2010) Dynamics of an emerging disease drive large-scale amphibian population extinctions. *Proceedings of the National Academy of Sciences of the United States of America*, **107**, 9689–9694.

May, 1991; Diekmann & Heesterbeek, 2000). Much of this work has focused on microparasites, pathogens such as bacteria and viruses that reproduce within their host and often invoke a strong immune response (Anderson & May, 1979), for which identifying properties such as pathogen transmission, pathogen pathogenicity, and host growth rate generally allows one to characterise different population-level disease trajectories (Anderson & May, 1991; Diekmann & Heesterbeek, 2000). However, Bd and other fungal pathogens typically categorised as microparasites also exhibit characteristics of macroparasites, e.g. helminths and ectoparasites that do not directly reproduce within/on a host (Anderson & May, 1979). This is because many critical epidemiological parameters, such as pathogen-induced mortality rate, are highly dependent on the amount of Bd on a given host (Vredenburg et al., 2010; Woodhams et al., 2011). This is similar to macroparasite systems where the number of parasites within a host needs to be explicitly modelled to capture load-dependent pathology (Diekmann & Heesterbeek, 2000). In general, host–microparasite models tend to focus on how transmission dynamics affect population-level outcomes, but rarely focus on pathogen load. Because of the nature of Bd infections (see Box 18.1), both transmission dynamics and load dynamics must be considered, and thus, one also needs to elucidate the factors that affect fungal load on individual hosts (Briggs et al., 2010; Fisher et al., 2012). This makes amphibian–Bd systems an ideal case study for building a framework that synthesises how both transmission and load dynamics affect different host population-level outcomes upon pathogen invasion.

In this chapter we address three questions. First, what are the potential trajectories of amphibian host populations following Bd invasion? Second, how are each of these trajectories influenced by both the transmission dynamics and load dynamics governing an amphibian–Bd system? Third, how do ecological, evolutionary, and environmental factors affect both transmission and load dynamics, which in turn influence the population-level outcome of an amphibian–Bd system? We define transmission dynamics as the processes by which an amphibian acquires a Bd infection, while Bd-load dynamics are the processes that affect the growth of Bd on an individual host, conditional on infection. To answer these questions, we build a general framework that simplifies the different population-level trajectories of amphibian–Bd systems into a series of branch points (Figure 18.1). Each of these branch points is affected by either the transmission dynamics or the load dynamics underlying an amphibian–Bd system. By integrating relevant disease ecology theory and empirical data, this framework provides a unified approach to consider variable population-level trajectories across amphibian–Bd systems. Ultimately, knowledge of the factors that determine which trajectory an amphibian population takes at each branch point may help guide the development of effective mitigation strategies to positively change the

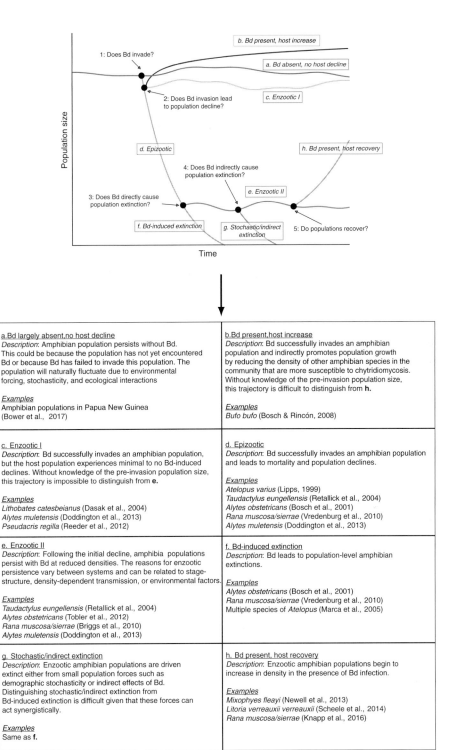

a. Bd absent, no host decline

b. Bd present, host increase

c. Enzootic I

d. Epizootic

h. Bd present, host recovery

e. Enzootic II

f. Bd-induced extinction

g. Stochastic/indirect extinction

1: Does Bd invade?

2: Does Bd invasion lead to population decline?

3: Does Bd directly cause population extinction?

4: Does Bd indirectly cause population extinction?

5: Do populations recover?

Population size

Time

a.Bd largely absent, no host decline	b.Bd present, host increase
Description: Amphibian population persists without Bd. This could be because the population has not yet encountered Bd or because Bd has failed to invade this population. The population will naturally fluctuate due to environmental forcing, stochasticity, and ecological interactions *Examples* Amphibian populations in Papua New Guinea (Bower et al., 2017)	*Description*: Bd successfully invades an amphibian population and indirectly promotes population growth by reducing the density of other amphibian species in the community that are more susceptible to chytridiomycosis. Without knowledge of the pre-invasion population size, this trajectory is difficult to distinguish from **h**. *Examples* *Bufo bufo* (Bosch & Rincón, 2008)
c. Enzootic I	d. Epizootic
Description: Bd successfully invades an amphibian population, but the host population experiences minimal to no Bd-induced declines. Without knowledge of the pre-invasion population size, this trajectory is impossible to distinguish from **e**. *Examples* *Lithobates catesbeianus* (Dasak et al., 2004) *Alytes muletensis* (Doddington et al., 2013) *Pseudacris regilla* (Reeder et al., 2012)	*Description*: Bd successfully invades an amphibian population and leads to mortality and population declines. *Examples* *Atelopus varius* (Lipps, 1999) *Taudactylus eungellensis* (Retallick et al., 2004) *Alytes obstetricans* (Bosch et al., 2001) *Rana muscosa/sierrae* (Vredenburg et al., 2010) *Alytes muletensis* (Doddington et al., 2013)
e. Enzootic II	f. Bd-induced extinction
Description: Following the initial decline, amphibia populations persist with Bd at reduced densities. The reasons for enzootic persistence vary between systems and can be related to stage-structure, density-dependent transmission, or environmental factors. *Examples* *Taudactylus eungellensis* (Retallick et al., 2004) *Alytes obstetricans* (Tobler et al., 2012) *Rana muscosa/sierrae* (Briggs et al., 2010) *Alytes muletensis* (Doddington et al., 2013)	*Description*: Bd leads to population-level amphibian extinctions. *Examples* *Alytes obstetricans* (Bosch et al., 2001) *Rana muscosa/sierrae* (Vredenburg et al., 2010) Multiple species of *Atelopus* (Marca et al., 2005)
g. Stochastic/indirect extinction	h. Bd present, host recovery
Description: Enzootic amphibian populations are driven extinct either from small population forces such as demographic stochasticity or indirect effects of Bd. Distinguishing stochastic/indirect extinction from Bd-induced extinction is difficult given that these forces can act synergistically. *Examples* Same as **f**.	*Description*: Enzootic amphibian populations begin to increase in density in the presence of Bd infection. *Examples* *Mixophyes fleayi* (Newell et al., 2013) *Litoria verreauxii verreauxii* (Scheele et al., 2014) *Rana muscosa/sierrae* (Knapp et al., 2016)

Figure 18.1 Framework for contextualizing different population trajectories in amphibian–Bd systems. The black points give the five branch points at which the trajectories of amphibian–Bd systems can diverge. The boxes refer to the different population-level trajectories observed in amphibian–Bd systems.

outcome of Bd invasion and protect threatened amphibians from population declines and disease-induced extinction.

18.2 A framework for different population-level outcomes in amphibian–Bd systems

We begin our discussion of this framework by considering a naïve amphibian population (i.e. not yet exposed to Bd) that is persisting at a stable density (Figure 18.1). From this starting point, an amphibian population is then exposed to Bd and the resulting population-level trajectory is determined by a series of branch points (Figure 18.1). The trajectory taken at any branch point is dictated by either the transmission dynamics, the Bd-load dynamics, or both. Multiple ecological, evolutionary, and environmental factors affect the transmission and load dynamics at a given branch point, such that they in turn influence the trajectory taken by the amphibian–Bd system.

In the following sections, we discuss each of these branch points and give empirical examples of when amphibian populations have taken different trajectories at these branch points. We highlight general epidemiological theory that describes when a host–pathogen system will follow a given trajectory and explore how this theory has been used to understand the different population-level outcomes in amphibian–Bd systems.

18.2.1 Branch point 1: does Bd invade an amphibian host population?

The first branch determines whether Bd successfully invades an amphibian population. While there are thousands of examples of Bd successfully invading amphibian populations (Skerratt et al., 2007), there are far fewer documented examples of Bd failing to invade. This is often the case for wildlife disease as monitoring usually occurs after a pathogen has already invaded and impacted a host population (Lloyd-Smith et al., 2005). An example of both failed and successful Bd invasions is seen in populations of the mountain yellow-legged frog complex (*Rana muscosa* and *R. sierrae*, Box 18.1). As Bd has invaded the thousands of lakes and streams supporting *R. muscosa/sierrae* populations (Vredenburg et al., 2010), monitoring efforts have detected populations that transitioned from Bd-negative to Bd-positive and back to Bd-negative, all without a Bd epizootic occurring (R.A. Knapp et al., unpublished). While often undetected, it is likely that failed Bd invasions occur in other amphibian species. Here we discuss how *transmission dynamics* affect the ability of Bd, and pathogens in general, to invade a naïve host population.

18.2.1.1 *Transmission dynamics and R_0*

The probability of a pathogen invading a host population is a function of the basic reproduction number R_0 (Allen, 2015). R_0 is the average number of secondary cases a single infected host produces in an entirely susceptible population (Anderson & May, 1991). Particularly, for a population with a single infected host, the probability b that a pathogen invades is approximately given by (Allen, 2015)

$$b = \begin{cases} 1 - \dfrac{1}{R_0} & R_0 > 1 \\ 0 & R_0 \leq 1 \end{cases}. \tag{18.1}$$

This equation indicates that even if $R_0 > 1$, pathogen invasion may fail due to chance alone (Figure 18.2). However, quantifying this uncertainty requires calculating R_0.

R_0 is inherently tied to the transmission dynamics within a system (Diekmann & Heesterbeek, 2000; Lloyd-Smith et al., 2005). Transmission dynamics describe the per-capita rate at which susceptible hosts become infected (i.e. the force of infection, $f(I)$). While many factors such as host behaviour, host susceptibility, host–pathogen compatibility, pathogen infectivity, and community composition affect the force of infection (Combes, 2000; Diekmann & Heesterbeek, 2000; McCallum, 2012), the rate of contact between infected and uninfected hosts is a fundamental component of transmission in directly transmitted diseases (Diekmann & Heesterbeek, 2000; McCallum et al., 2001; Begon et al., 2002).

A common assumption in wildlife disease models is that the rate of contacts per host increases linearly with increasing host density (McCallum et al., 2001; Begon et al., 2002; Lloyd-Smith et al., 2005). This is known as density-dependent transmission and could emerge if individuals move and contact each other randomly in an area (McCallum et al., 2001; Begon et al., 2002). In contrast, another assumption is that the rate of contacts per host is constant as host density increases. This is known as frequency-dependent transmission and could emerge if contacts only occur within a social group and group size does not change with density (McCallum et al., 2001; Begon et al., 2002). While more complex relationships between contact rate and host density are often considered (McCallum et al., 2001), these two transmission functions are commonly used and effectively illustrate the influence of transmission dynamics on R_0.

For example, a Susceptible–Infected–Susceptible (SIS) model (Figure 18.2A) with density-dependent transmission leads to $R_0 = \frac{\beta H}{\alpha + \gamma}$. In contrast, an SIS model with frequency-dependent transmission leads to $R_0 = \frac{\beta'}{\alpha + \gamma}$. The crucial difference is that for density-dependent transmission R_0 scales with total population density H and for frequency-dependent transmission it does not. This suggests that if, for example, the management goal was to try and reduce the probability of Bd invading a naïve amphibian population (i.e. decrease R_0), reducing population density via culling would be a theoretically effective strategy given density-dependent transmission, but would be completely

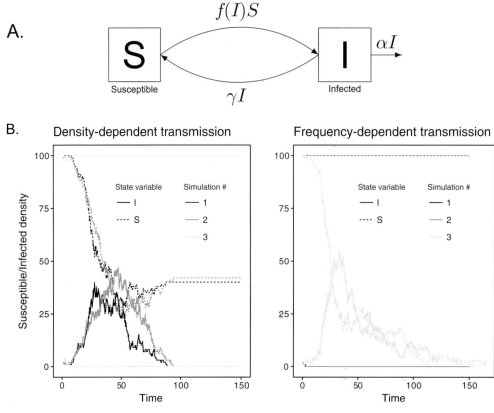

Figure 18.2 (A) Susceptible–Infected–Susceptible (SIS) model where γ is the rate of host recovery, α is the rate of pathogen-induced host mortality, and $f(I)$ is the force of infection describing the per-capita rate at which susceptible individuals transition to infected individuals. Under density-dependent transmission $f(I) = \beta I$ and under frequency-dependent transmission $f(I) = \beta' I / H$, where H is the total population size and β and β' are transmission parameters. (B) Trajectories from three stochastic simulations of the SIS model given density- and frequency-dependent transmission. Given that Bd invades, frequency-dependent transmission can directly lead to disease-induced host extinction, while density-dependent transmission cannot. Each model starts with one infected host and 100 susceptible hosts. The parameters values are $\gamma = 0.1$ time^{-1}, $\alpha = 0.04$ time^{-1}, and $f(I = 1) = 0.003$ time^{-1}. $R_0 = 2.14$ for both models. Notice that even though $R_0 = 2.14 > 1$ for both models, the pathogen can still fail to invade (e.g. simulation 3 for density-dependent transmission and simulations 1 and 2 for frequency-dependent transmission).

ineffective given frequency-dependent transmission. Thus, characterising the transmission function has important implications for managing Bd invasions (Woodhams et al., 2011).

To this end, Wilber et al. (2017) sought to characterise the transmission function for the mountain yellow-legged frog–Bd system (see also Rachowicz & Briggs, 2007). They set up replicated mesocosms with different densities of uninfected adult frogs, placed infected tadpoles into the mesocosms, and monitored the transmission dynamics by repeatedly measuring the Bd load of all animals in a mesocosm. They then fit both frequency- and density-dependent models to the transmission data and found that the experimental data were best described by a density-dependent transmission function. Moreover, Wilber et al. (2017) also found that accounting for an environmental Bd reservoir, along with density-dependent host contact, led to an even better description of the transmission dynamics. Incorporating this transmission function into a dynamic model (Box 18.2), they found that the presence of an environmental zoospore pool almost guaranteed successful Bd invasion for realistic host densities (Figure B18.2.2; Wilber et al., 2017). While we discuss the importance of the environmental zoospore pool more thoroughly in the following sections, future mesocosm and laboratory studies attempting to quantify Bd transmission should also measure the dynamics of the zoospore pool and potential factors affecting these dynamics (detailed below). This will help amphibian ecologists better quantify the transmission function and improve our understanding of the conditions under which Bd will successfully invade a host population.

18.2.2 Branch point 2: does an infected amphibian population decline?
Once Bd has successfully invaded an amphibian host population (branch point 1), the next branch point determines whether or not Bd invasion leads to population decline (Figure 18.1). For example, Savage and Zamudio (2016) examined different populations of the lowland leopard frog *Lithobates yavapaiensis* and found that while all populations were infected with Bd (i.e. Bd had successfully invaded), some populations were experiencing greater Bd-induced mortality than others. Savage et al. (2015) hypothesised that innate genetic differences in the hosts led to different trajectories of these amphibian populations upon Bd invasion. In another example, Bd successfully invaded populations of the Mallorcan midwife toad *Alytes muletensis*, but these populations did not suffer severe Bd-induced declines (Doddington et al., 2013). In this case, the lack of severe Bd-induced declines was partially because these populations were infected with a hypovirulent Bd strain (Farrer et al., 2011; Doddington et al., 2013). These examples illustrate that properties of both the host and the pathogen dictate whether Bd invasion results in amphibian population declines.

The population trajectory at this branch point depends on the *load dynamics* of Bd. This is because Bd-induced host mortality is highly load-dependent (Voyles et al., 2009; Vredenburg et al., 2010). For many

---

Box 18.2: Load-dependent model of amphibian–Bd dynamics and extensions

An amphibian–Bd integral projection model
Understanding the load dynamics of Bd is important for predicting the population-level trajectory of an amphibian–Bd system (Briggs et al., 2010; Jani et al., 2017). To this end, Wilber et al. (2016) developed a discrete-time variant of an SIS model (Figure 18.2A) in which Bd load was modelled as a continuous host attribute. Bd load is considered continuous because in practice it is measured via molecular analyses from standardised amphibian skin swabs (Boyle et al., 2004).

This discrete-time, continuous-load model takes the form of an integral projection model (IPM) (Easterling et al., 2000) and is useful because it can be directly parameterised from host-level data. Specifically, the number of susceptible hosts in a population at time $t + 1$, $S(t + 1)$, is given by

$$S(t + 1) = S(t)s_0\left[1 - \phi(I(x, t))\right] + \int_x I(x, t)s(x)l(x)dx, \tag{18.2}$$

where the length of a time step is on the scale of the generation time of Bd (4–10 days; Woodhams et al., 2008). The first term in this equation gives the number of susceptible hosts who survive $S_{(t)}s_0$ and remain uninfected $(1 - \phi(I(x, t)))$ in a time step. $\phi(I(x, t))$ is the transmission function, which is defined below. The second term gives the number of infected hosts who survive with a Bd load x ($s(x)$), lose an infection ($l(x)$) and enter the susceptible class in a time step.

The number of infected hosts with Bd load x' at time $t + 1$ ($I(x', t + 1)$) is given by

$$I(x', t + 1) = \int_x I(x, t)s(x)(1 - l(x))G(x', x)dx + S(t)s_0\phi(I(x, t))G_0(x'). \tag{18.3}$$

The first term in this equation gives the number of infected individuals that survive with load x ($s(x)$), do not lose their infection $(1 - l(x))$ and transition to load x' in a time step ($G(x', x)$). The second term gives the number of uninfected individuals that transition to an infected individual $(\phi(I(x, t)))$ with load x' ($G_0(x')$) in a time step.

Finally, the number of zoospores in the zoospore pool at time $t + 1$ ($Z(t + 1)$) is given by

$$Z(t + 1) = Z(t)\nu + \mu_A \int_x xI_A(x, t)dx - \psi(S_A(t), Z(t)), \tag{18.4}$$

Box 18.2: (cont.)

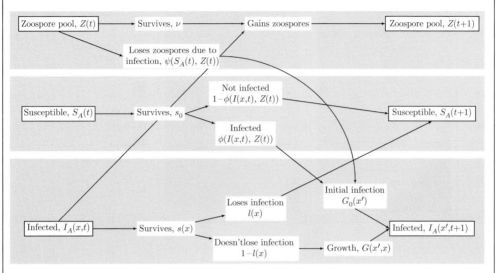

Figure B18.2.1 Flow chart for the host–parasite IPM model described in Box 18.2. Reproduced from Wilber et al. (2017).

where v is the survival probability of zoospores in a time step, μ_A is the proportion of total zoospores on adults that are contributed to the zoospore pool in a time step, and $\psi(S_A(t), Z(t))$ is the removal of zoospores from the zoospore pool by frogs transitioning from uninfected to infected.

$\phi(I(x,t))$ describes the transmission function of the amphibian–Bd system under consideration. For example, in the *R. muscosa*–Bd system, a mesocosm experiment demonstrated that the best-fit transmission function had the form

$$\phi\Big(Z(t), I(x,t)\Big) = 1 - \exp\left(-\left[\beta_0 Z(t) + \beta_1 \int_x I(x,t)dx\right]\right), \tag{18.5}$$

where β_0 and β_1 are both transmission parameters with units time^{-1}. This function shows that transmission depends on both contacts with the zoospore pool and contacts with infected hosts (Wilber et al., 2017).

The above equations are composed of five load-dependent vital rate functions ($s(x)$, $l(x)$, $G(x', x)$, $G_0(x')$, ($\phi(I(x,t))$, all of which can be estimated from individual-level trajectories of Bd loads and Bd transmission experiments (Wilber et al., 2016). These estimated functions can then be used to parameterise the load-dependent IPM.

Box 18.2: (cont.)

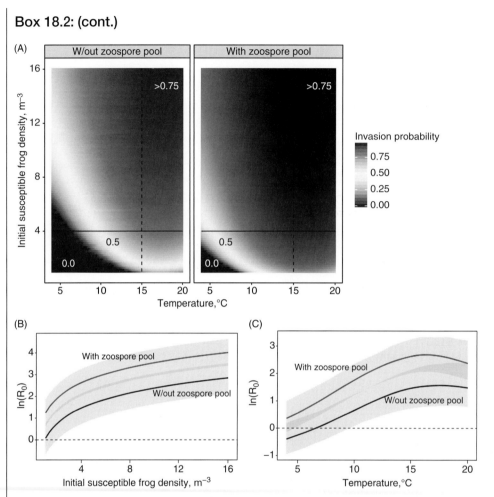

Figure B18.2.2 (A) R_0 and the invasion probability of Bd $(1 - \frac{1}{R_0})$ for different temperatures and host densities with and without an environmental zoospore pool. The numbers in (A) give the invasion probability for a given region of the plot. This calculation of R_0 uses the experimentally estimated transmission function from Wilber et al. (2017) that includes transmission via density-dependent host contact and contact with zoospores in the zoospore pool. The dashed, vertical lines in (A) correspond to the curves shown in (B), where $\ln(R_0)$ is plotted against initial adult density when temperature is $15°C$. The solid, horizontal lines in (A) correspond to the curves shown in (C), where $\ln(R_0)$ is plotted against temperature when initial adult density is four adults per m^3. The grey regions give the 95% credible intervals. The dashed lines in (B) and (C) correspond to $R_0 = 1$ $(\ln(R_0) = 0)$, below which Bd cannot invade. Figure reprinted in black and white from Wilber et al. (2017).

Box 18.2: (cont.)

Including temperature-dependence in the host–parasite IPM
Temperature-dependence can be included in this IPM framework by allowing the various vital rate functions to depend on temperature. For example, Wilber et al. (2016) used a laboratory experiment in which *Rana muscosa* were exposed to Bd at different temperatures to parameterise a temperature-dependent loss of infection function $(l(x))$, Bd growth function $(G(x', x))$, and the initial infection function $(G_0(x'))$ for an IPM. Using this temperature-dependent IPM as well as an experimentally parameterised transmission function, Wilber et al. (2017) computed the ability of Bd to invade a fully susceptible *R. musocsa* population under different temperatures and densities (Figure B18.2.2). They found that while there was a slight protective effect of low temperatures on the ability of Bd to invade a *R. muscosa* population, this protective effect was largely removed when transmission from the zoospore pool was included (Figure B18.2.2).

References

Boyle, D.G., Boyle, D.B., Olsen, V., Morgan, J.A.T. & Hyatt, A.D. (2004) Rapid quantitative detection of chytridiomycosis (*Batrachochytrium dendrobatidis*) in amphibian samples using real-time Taqman PCR assay. *Diseases of Aquatic Organisms*, **60**, 141–148.

Briggs, C.J., Knapp, R.A. & Vredenburg, V.T. (2010) Enzootic and epizootic dynamics of the chytrid fungal pathogen of amphibians. *Proceedings of the National Academy of Sciences of the United States of America*, **107**, 9695–9700.

Easterling, M.R., Ellner, S.P. & Dixon, P.M. (2000) Size-specific sensitivity: applying a new structured population model. *Ecology*, **81**, 694–708.

Jani, A.J., Knapp, R.A. & Briggs, C.J. (2017) Epidemic and endemic pathogen dynamics correspond to distinct host population microbiomes at a landscape scale. *Proceedings of the Royal Society of London B*, **284**, 20170944.

Wilber, M.Q., Knapp, R.A., Toothman, M. & Briggs, C.J. (2017) Resistance, tolerance and environmental transmission dynamics determine host extinction risk in a load-dependent amphibian disease. *Ecology Letters*, **30**, 1169–1181.

Wilber, M.Q., Langwig, K.E., Kilpatrick, A.M., McCallum, H.I. & Briggs, C.J. (2016) Integral projection models for host–parasite systems with an application to amphibian chytrid fungus. *Methods in Ecology and Evolution*, **7**, 1182–1194.

Woodhams, D.C., Alford, R.A., Briggs, C.J., Johnson, M. & Rollins-Smith, L.A. (2008) Life-history trade-offs influence disease in changing climates: strategies of an amphibian pathogen. *Ecology*, **89**, 1627–1639.

susceptible amphibian species, when the Bd load on a host exceeds some approximate species-specific threshold, the probability of host survival declines rapidly (Stockwell et al., 2010; Vredenburg et al., 2010; DiRenzo et al., 2014; Wilber et al., 2016). Some amphibian species are able to prevent Bd from reaching this threshold and are thus able to persist with high Bd prevalence, but lower mean loads (Stockwell et al., 2010). Similarly, particular strains of Bd are less virulent, which can correlate with reduced Bd loads (e.g. Doddington et al., 2013). Determining why different species and/or populations of amphibians show different load dynamics is important for predicting both whether an amphibian population will experience a Bd-induced decline and the magnitude of that decline.

We discuss the load dynamics of Bd through the lens of resistance and tolerance – two distinct mechanisms that can affect Bd load dynamics and the population-level trajectory at branch point 2. Resistance is the ability of a host to reduce or eliminate pathogen load, conditional on pathogen exposure (Figure 18.3; Medzhitov et al., 2012). In contrast, tolerance does not affect pathogen load, but rather reduces the effect of a given load on host fitness (Råberg et al., 2009; Medzhitov et al., 2012). Resistance is often defined as the inverse of maximum infection load and tolerance as the slope of the relationship between infection load and some measure of host fitness (Figure 18.3; Råberg et al., 2009). Pathogen virulence is implicit in the definitions of resistance and tolerance and is defined as the effect of a pathogen at some load on the fitness of a host (Råberg et al., 2009). Many mechanisms underly both resistance and tolerance (e.g. host innate and acquired immunity, behaviour, tissue repair, etc.; Medzhitov et al., 2012), but it is often easier to experimentally measure resistance and tolerance as defined above and relate them to population-level outcomes.

Both increased resistance and tolerance can reduce or eliminate population declines. For example, increasing resistance decreases mean Bd load on an amphibian host and thus increases survival probability (Figure 18.3). Changes in host resistance can be genetically based (e.g. Savage et al., 2015), but can also be driven by a host's behaviour (Adams et al., 2017), a host's environment (Raffel et al., 2012), and/or the strain of Bd infecting a host (Farrer et al., 2011). In the following sections we focus on how two particular factors, variability in Bd virulence and changes in temperature, affect host resistance and can thus affect Bd-induced population declines.

18.2.2.1 *Variability in Bd virulence*

Experimental infection studies have shown that Bd exhibits a large amount of variation in virulence across different strains (Farrer et al., 2011; Doddington et al., 2013; Becker et al., 2017). In these studies, Bd strains that kill amphibian hosts more quickly are considered more virulent. Note that this definition of virulence does not explicitly consider Bd load. In addition to examining the time of death, studies should also measure Bd load over the time course of

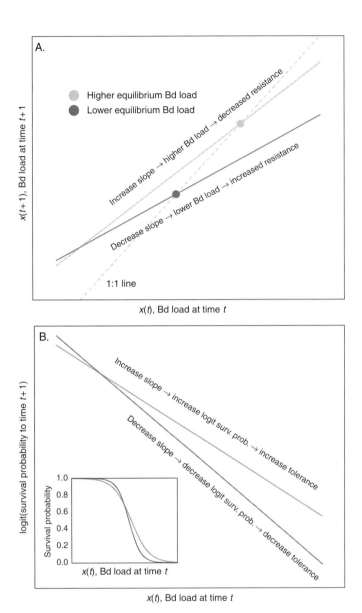

Figure 18.3 (A) The growth function of Bd on an amphibian host (e.g. $x_{t+1} = b_0 + b_1 x_t$) showing how Bd load x at time t (x_t) relates to Bd load at time $t+1$ (x_{t+1}) and its relation to host resistance. (B) The survival function (e.g. $\text{logit}\left(s(x_t)\right) = a_0 - a_1 x_t$) and its relation to host tolerance. "logit" indicates a logit transform on $s(x_t)$: the probability of a host surviving from time t to $t+1$ with a load of x_t. The inset plot shows how logit host survival probability translates into survival probability. Note that pathogen virulence could be defined as the effect of the pathogen on host survival at the equilibrium level of Bd load (i.e. $a_1 \frac{b_0}{1-b_1}$) and is thus a product of the Bd growth function determining host resistance and the survival function determining host tolerance.

these infection experiments (e.g. Doddington et al., 2013). This would provide a straightforward way to place Bd virulence in the context of how a given Bd load affects the probability of survival, which is consistent with defining virulence as a product of host tolerance and host resistance (Figure 18.3; Råberg et al., 2009). Moreover, this would help highlight that Bd load per se is not necessarily a consistent predictor of virulence across different strains of Bd (Fisher et al., 2009). This is because morphological characteristics of Bd, such as zoosporangium size, can interact with Bd load such that amphibians infected with similar loads do not experience the same fitness consequences (Fisher et al., 2009).

Variability in Bd virulence has a strong genetic component (Fisher et al., 2009; Farrer et al., 2011; Rosenblum et al., 2013; Refsnider et al., 2015). Of the five currently identified Bd lineages, the Global Panzootic Lineage (BdGPL) is consistently more virulent in experimental infection studies (Farrer et al., 2011; Doddington et al., 2013; Becker et al., 2017) and has been implicated in Bd-induced amphibian declines around the world (Farrer et al., 2011; Rosenblum et al., 2013). However, within the BdGPL, particular strains are not consistently virulent to all amphibian species and particular amphibian species are not consistently affected by all strains (Rosenblum et al., 2013; Becker et al., 2017). It is important to understand variable virulence in Bd strains because amphibian populations that are able to persist in the presence of one Bd strain can still be highly susceptible to closely related strains (Becker et al., 2017).

To explore the importance of variable strain virulence on population-level trajectories of amphibians, Doddington et al. (2013) built a dynamic model of Mallorcan midwife toad populations. Using experimental infections, they estimated the virulence of two different Bd strains, one within the virulent BdGPL lineage and the other within the less-virulent BdCape lineage. They then incorporated these estimates into a dynamic model parameterised from additional laboratory experiments and field observations. Doddington et al. (2013) found that upon the invasion of the more-virulent BdGPL strain, an epizootic ensued and amphibian populations declined. However, in their model Bd tended to go extinct before driving the toad populations to extinction. In contrast, when the populations were invaded with the less-virulent BdCape strain that was actually infecting the populations in the field, the model predicted that subsequent population declines were less severe and toads and Bd could often coexist. This was consistent with their observations that Mallorcan toad populations were generally persisting with BdCape in the field.

18.2.2.2 *Temperature and Bd load*
There are a number of different environmental variables that can affect the load dynamics of Bd, such as moisture, hydrological dynamics, and

temperature (Woodhams et al., 2011; Raffel et al., 2012, 2015; Adams et al., 2017). Temperature is the most frequently studied of these abiotic variables, due to its potential to influence amphibian population trajectories following Bd invasion (e.g. Piotrowski et al., 2004; Woodhams et al., 2008; Kilpatrick et al., 2010; Doddington et al., 2013; Cohen et al., 2017). To understand the role of temperature on Bd load dynamics, it is critical to study how processes underlying infection, such as the activation of the host immune response and the growth of the pathogen, respond to changes in temperature.

Important immunological processes of amphibians, such as the production of lymphocytes, neutrophils, and antibody synthesis, can either increase or decrease, depending on the direction and magnitude of the temperature change (Maniero & Carey, 1997; Raffel et al., 2006, 2012). Similarly, Bd survival, growth, and reproduction are highly temperature-dependent (Woodhams et al., 2008). In vitro, Bd growth rates are highest between 17 and 25°C, with a marked decrease in growth above and below these temperatures (Piotrowski et al., 2004). In vivo, the effect of temperature on Bd infection is highly host-dependent (Kilpatrick et al., 2010) and is a result of the interaction between host and Bd temperature-dependent infection processes (Raffel et al., 2012). For example, while Bd shows increasing growth rates between 4 and 20°C on *R. muscosa* (Wilber et al., 2016), Bd shows decreased growth rates on red-spotted newts (*Notophthalmus viridescens*) and Cuban tree frogs (*Osteopilus septentrionalis*) when temperatures are increased from 15 to 25°C (Raffel et al., 2012, 2015).

Given that Bd load dynamics are highly temperature-dependent, how might this temperature dependence affect whether Bd infection leads to population-level declines? Using the same model for Mallorcan midwife toad populations described in the previous section, Doddington et al. (2013) sought to understand why a single invaded toad population was experiencing a population-level decline, while all other invaded toad populations were either stable or increasing. Doddington et al. (2013) showed that the different population-level trajectories could be largely explained by an empirically estimated, temperature-dependent increase in the rate of a toad losing a Bd infection. This study illustrates that temperature-dependent changes in Bd load dynamics can have significant implications on amphibian population trajectories. Future work should try to link both absolute changes in temperature as well as temperature variability to population-level models of amphibian–Bd dynamics (Raffel et al., 2012; Cohen et al., 2017).

18.2.3 Branch point 3: does Bd directly drive the amphibian population extinct?

Once an amphibian population has experienced Bd-induced population declines, branch point 3 determines whether Bd directly drives an amphibian population extinct or whether an amphibian population can persist with Bd in an enzootic state (Figure 18.1). While we distinguish this branch point from branch point 4 in which Bd indirectly results in host extinction (see next section), in practice these two branch points are difficult to distinguish. Some canonical examples of Bd-induced population-level extinctions include *Rana muscosa/sierrae* in North America (Vredenburg et al., 2010), multiple species in the genus *Atepolus* in Central and South America (Marca et al., 2005), species in the genus *Litoria* in eastern Australia (Laurance et al., 1996; Skerratt et al., 2007), and the common midwife toad *Alytes obstetricans* in Spain (Bosch et al., 2001). Populations of these same species have also avoided extinction and now persist at reduced densities in an enzootic state (Retallick et al., 2004; Briggs et al., 2005; Perez et al., 2014).

Theory highlights that *transmission dynamics* ultimately determine whether a pathogen can drive a host population extinct (De Castro & Bolker, 2005; McCallum, 2012). The general criterion for disease-induced extinction is that the force of infection does not decrease to zero with decreasing density of infected hosts (De Castro & Bolker, 2005). This criterion can be met via a number of transmission mechanisms including frequency-dependent transmission and/or environmental reservoirs for the pathogens (McCallum, 2012). Because we have discussed frequency-dependent transmission above, we focus on how abiotic and biotic reservoirs can affect whether an amphibian population experiences Bd-induced extinction.

18.2.3.1 *Abiotic reservoirs*

To account for the effect of an environmental reservoir on extinction dynamics, it is important to characterise the average lifetime of a pathogen in the environment, the rate at which infected hosts contribute pathogens to the environment, the reproductive rate of the pathogen in the environment, and the contact between hosts and the environmental pathogen pool (Godfray et al., 1999). Numerous studies have sought to quantify these four characteristics in amphibian–Bd systems.

Regarding environmental persistence, laboratory studies have shown that Bd zoospores can persist for up to 7–12 weeks in sterilised lake water and moist sand (Johnson & Speare, 2003, 2005). In the field, Bd has been detected in water samples from aquatic habitats and in moist terrestrial environments (Chestnut et al., 2014; Kolby et al., 2015). While these studies indicate that Bd can persist in the abiotic environment, understanding the details of Bd persistence in the field is still an important area of research. For example, aquatic filter feeders such as *Daphnia* or tadpoles may reduce Bd persistence time in the environment by ingesting Bd zoospores during feeding (Venesky et al., 2013). Similarly, other microorganisms in the environment may compete with or consume Bd (Schmeller et al., 2014), reducing its persistence time in the environment and subsequently the risk of Bd-induced extinction (Godfray et al., 1999).

Infected amphibian hosts can also potentially produce large number of infective zoospores that contribute to the environmental pool (Briggs et al., 2010; DiRenzo et al., 2014). The number of zoospores produced per zoosporangium varies with temperature and one study found it to be between 161 at lower temperatures (10°C) and 65 at higher temperatures (23°C) (Woodhams et al., 2008). However, linking this single zoosporangium production to the production of zoospores by an infected amphibian in the field is still a work in progress. Similarly, while saprophytic growth of Bd is possible (i.e. growth on decaying organic material), there is not yet any evidence that this is occurring.

Finally, the environmental zoospore pool is only important if amphibian hosts actually come in contact with it. Experiments by Courtois et al. (2017) and Hagman and Alford (2015) showed that the environmental zoospore pool plays an important role in Bd infection dynamics for the lake-dwelling common midwife toad *Alytes obstetricans* and the stream-dwelling green-eyed tree frog *Litoria serrata*, respectively. While these experiments demonstrate that contact with the zoospore pool is occurring, contact will vary with the life history and behaviour of amphibian species. For example, if adult amphibians are primarily terrestrial or actively avoid zoospores (e.g. McMahon et al., 2014), then this will limit contact with the zoospore pool and transmission will have to be driven by other mechanisms.

Including these characteristics of the zoospore pool into population-level models has helped identify when amphibian–Bd populations will show Bd-induced extinction versus enzootic dynamics. Briggs et al. (2010) developed an individual-based model to explore when *R. muscosa*–Bd systems exhibited Bd-induced extinction versus enzootic persistence (Box 18.3). Importantly, the model explicitly tracked the Bd load on each individual frog so that infected frogs with more zoosporangia contributed proportionally more zoospores to the environmental pool. This model produced results consistent with previous theory on environmental reservoirs and highlighted additional complexities in amphibian–Bd systems. For example, Drawert et al. (2017) used the model to show that reducing amphibian density (e.g. via culling) had little net positive effect on mitigating Bd-induced amphibian extinction, consistent with theory showing that pathogens with long-lived environmental stages and a high rate of production of pathogens via hosts will be able to persist in a host population even when host density is quite low (Anderson & May, 1981). In place of the importance of host density in determining population-level outcomes, Briggs

Box 18.3: Exploring epizootic and enzootic dynamics in amphibian–Bd systems

Briggs et al. (2010) used a stochastic individual-based model to explore whether the two types of dynamics observed in the mountain yellow-legged frog/Bd system in the California Sierra Nevada (i.e. epizootic and enzootic dynamics) could simply represent different time points in the same stochastic dynamical system. That is, does the observation of epizootic dynamics with a high probability of disease-induced extinction in some lakes, but enzootic dynamics with sublethal Bd infection in other lakes, actually require any differences between the lakes, e.g. in frog susceptibility, Bd virulence, and/or environmental conditions?

To explore this question, Briggs et al. (2010) developed a model (Figure B18.3.1) that follows the number of zoosporangia on each frog i at time t ($S_i(t)$, 'zoosporangia', i.e. the Bd load on the frog), and the number of zoospores in the lake at time tt($Z(t)$, the 'zoospore pool'). The model assumes that uninfected frogs become infected only through encountering zoospores in the zoospore pool (that is, unlike in the Wilber et al., 2017, model in Box 18.2, there is no direct host-to-host transmission). Transmission from the zoospore pool occurs at rate $\beta = \gamma v$, where γ is the encounter rate, and v is the fraction of zoospores that successfully encyst on the frog skin following encounter. Each zoospore that successfully encysts on the frog becomes a zoosporangium. Zoosporangia release zoospores at rate η. The model assumes that a fraction f of these zoospores immediately re-encounter the same frog, and the remaining $(1-f)$ enter the zoospore pool. Zoosporangia die at rate σ, and zoospores in the pool die at rate μ. A frog dies when its Bd load exceeds a lethal threshold, S_{max}. The model assumes that when a frog dies, all of the zoosporangia on a frog also die. If $N(t)$ is the total number of (living) frogs in the population at time t, then the deterministic version of this model can be expressed as a system of $N(t)+1$ ordinary differential equations (however, stochasticity plays an important role in the dynamics, so Briggs et al., 2010, instead used a stochastic version of this model):

$$S_i(t) = \beta Z(t) + \eta v f S_i(t) \text{ for } S_i(t) \leq S_{max}$$

$$Z(t) = \sum_{i=1}^{N(t)} \eta(1-f)S_i(t) - \gamma N(t)Z(t) - \mu Z(t). \tag{18.6}$$

For a given set of parameters, and at given $N(t)$, this model assumes that the Bd load on a frog will either increase exponentially until it reaches S_{max} and the frog dies, or decreases exponentially, and the frog loses the infection.

This load-dependent model describes only the short-term dynamics of Bd transmission and disease-induced mortality. To explore the long-term

Box 18.3: (cont.)

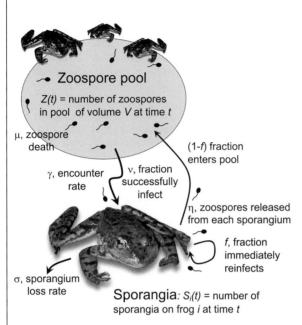

Figure B18.3.1 Diagram of Bd load–dependent model describing Bd transmission and disease-induced mortality. The model follows $S_i(t)$, the number of sporangia on each frog i, and $Z(t)$, the number of zoospores in a body of water (the zoospore pool), at time t. Figure reprinted from Briggs et al. (2010).

impact of Bd on the frog population, the demographic processes of birth, death, and maturation must be added to the model. To approximate the highly seasonal system in the California Sierra Nevada, in which the lakes are covered in ice for up to eight months per year, Briggs et al. (2010) assumed that frog reproduction occurred in a discrete pulse as soon as the lake thaws out in the spring, while Bd transmission and disease-induced mortality occurs continuously. Briggs et al. (2010) explored three alternative frog life histories: (1) an unstructured model approximating an amphibian system with a very short tadpole stage, which assumes that all host individuals are equally susceptible to the pathogen; (2) a stage-structured model with a tadpole and an adult stage; and (3) a model that included the realistic stage-structure of the mountain yellow-legged frog system (including a tadpole stage that lasts up to 3 years, a 2-year subadult stage, and a long-lived adult stage). In all of the models, density-dependence was included in the frog population in the recruitment to the adult stage (the model assumed that the lake could sustain a maximum of K adult frogs, and any additional recruits died or dispersed away from the lake).

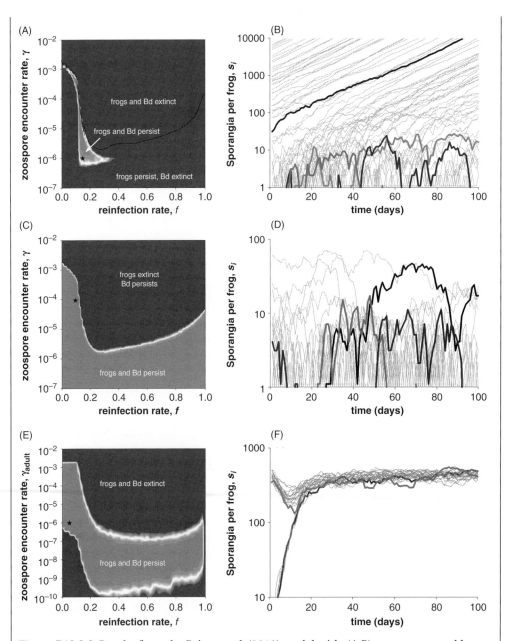

Figure B18.3.2 Results from the Briggs et al. (2010) model with: (A,B) an unstructured host population in which all individuals are equally susceptible to the pathogen, (C,D) an unstructured host population with the addition of an external source of zoospores, and (E,F) a structured host population with a long-lived tadpole stage. (A,C,E) show the probability of frogs and Bd persisting for at least 10 years as a function of reinfection rate, f, and zoospore encounter rate, γ. Shown are the fractions of 100 runs for each combination of parameters that persist for at least 10 years (colour spectrum red = 100% of runs persist, blue = 0% of runs

Box 18.3: (cont.)

persist). All runs are initialised with a single infected frog in an otherwise uninfected frog population at its carrying capacity, and no zoospores in the zoospore pool ($Z = 0$). (B,D,F) show examples of the within-season dynamics illustrating the dynamics of the number of sporangia on individual frogs. Coloured lines are highlighted examples of trajectories of sporangia on individual frogs. Figure reprinted from Briggs et al. (2010) (the parameter values used are given in figure 3 of that paper). (A black and white version of this figure will appear in some formats. For the colour version, please refer to the plate section.)

For the unstructured model, Briggs et al. (2010) found that either extinction of the frogs, or extinction of the pathogen, occurred for most realistic ranges of parameters. Coexistence of the frog and the fungus could occur in only a narrow region of parameter space (Figure B18.3.2). However, the presence of a tadpole stage that could become infected and carry high Bd loads, but not die until after metamorphosis, could make coexistence of the frog and fungus possible over a wide range of parameters (Figure B18.3.2). Coexistence was especially likely if the adult frogs tended to lose the infection, but get continually reinfected from the pool of zoospores released from the tadpoles. Similarly, an external source of zoospores (as might come from an environmental reservoir for Bd, or the presence a more Bd-tolerant host species in the lakes) can allow for coexistence of the frogs and fungus through continually reinfecting a host that would otherwise lose the infection (Figure B18.3.2).

The model with the realistic stage structure of the mountain yellow-legged frog system illustrated that the same model could produce both the enzootic and epizootic dynamics observed in the field. This suggests that alternative mechanisms, such as selection for reduced frog susceptibility and/or reduced Bd virulence are not necessary to explain the different disease dynamics observed simultaneously in different parts of the California Sierra Nevada.

References
Briggs, C.J., Knapp, R.A. & Vredenburg, V.T. (2010) Enzootic and epizootic dynamics of the chytrid fungal pathogen of amphibians. *Proceedings of the National Academy of Sciences of the United States of America*, **107**, 9695–9700.

Wilber, M.Q., Knapp, R.A., Toothman, M. & Briggs, C.J. (2017) Resistance, tolerance and environmental transmission dynamics determine host extinction risk in a load-dependent amphibian disease. *Ecology Letters*, **30**, 1169–1181.

et al. (2010) found that density-independent characteristics of zoospores, such as the rate at which zoospores reinfected the same amphibians after being released from the zoosporangia, could determine whether an amphibian population experienced Bd-induced extinction or persisted enzootically with Bd. This model illustrates that differences in zoospore pool dynamics can determine whether one population experiences Bd-induced extinction or enzootic persistence following disease-induced population declines.

18.2.3.2 *Biotic reservoirs*

Biotic reservoirs also play an important role in determining whether or not disease can drive a host population extinct (McCallum, 2012). We loosely define a biotic reservoir as an alternative host for the pathogen that is generally more tolerant than the focal host. The simplest way that a biotic reservoir can increase the risk of disease-induced extinction is by providing an alternative host on which a pathogen can reproduce and persist, independent of the density of the focal host. Similar to pathogen reproduction in the environment, a biotic reservoir would allow the density of a focal host to decrease without decreasing the force of infection.

Intraspecific and interspecific biotic reservoirs have been identified in amphibian–Bd systems. In some frog species, long-lived tadpoles do not suffer from chytridiomycosis and can provide biotic reservoirs in which Bd can persist and replicate (Briggs et al., 2010). The aforementioned model by Briggs et al. (2010) (Box 18.3) showed that the presence of a tadpole reservoir could help maintain Bd in *R. muscosa* populations. Considering interspecific reservoirs, both amphibian and non-amphibian reservoirs of Bd have been identified. Bd has been detected on water fowl (Garmyn et al., 2012), crayfish (McMahon et al., 2013), zebrafish (Liew et al., 2017), and reptiles (Kilburn et al., 2011). Of these, only crayfish and zebrafish have been shown to maintain Bd infections (McMahon et al., 2013; Liew et al., 2017) and only crayfish have been shown to transmit this infection to amphibian hosts (McMahon et al., 2013). Within a community of amphibians, it is not uncommon for some species to be at high risk of Bd-induced declines and others to be relatively tolerant of Bd (Stockwell et al., 2016; Scheele et al., 2017). In this case, Bd can replicate on tolerant host species, enter the environmental pool, infect susceptible host species, and drive them to extinction (McCallum, 2012). For example, Pacific chorus frogs (*Pseudacris regilla*) are relatively tolerant of Bd and may contribute to Bd-induced declines of mountain yellow-legged frogs by functioning as a reservoir for Bd (Reeder et al., 2012). Moreover, it is possible that some species of amphibians within a community could be 'supershedders' that release a disproportionately large number of zoospores into the environment over the course of Bd infection (DiRenzo et al., 2014). 'Supershedders' could significantly increase the severity of epizootics and the Bd-induced extinction risk for other amphibian species in the community by increasing both the force of infection as well as the zoospore dose upon initial infection.

18.2.4 Branch point 4: does Bd indirectly drive the amphibian population extinct?

Branch point 3 illustrates that direct Bd-induced extinction is a result of both the transmission dynamics driving the system as well as Bd-induced mortality. However, Bd can also indirectly hasten the extinction of amphibian populations through two distinct mechanisms: sublethal effects of Bd on amphibian fitness and forces that hasten the extinction of small populations (Figure 18.1; Lande et al., 2003; Garner et al., 2009). Many of the empirical examples of Bd-induced population extinction mentioned in the previous section were likely augmented by these indirect effects of Bd on amphibian populations.

18.2.4.1 *The extinction of small populations*

As population size decreases, the probabilistic nature of births and deaths of individuals in the population known as demographic stochasticity can lead to population-level extinction – this can occur even if the small population is not expected to decline (Lande et al., 2003). The probability of extinction due to demographic stochasticity is directly related to population size, such that its effects are largest in smaller populations (Lande et al., 2003). In the context of host–pathogen systems, this implies that a severe initial epizootic in which the host population is substantially reduced will increase the probability of population extinction, even if a pathogen does not directly drive a host population extinct. Therefore, understanding the factors determining the size of an initial Bd epizootic are critical for determining extinction risk due to small population forces.

One simple factor that augments the size of a Bd epizootic is the initial density of susceptible hosts. To illustrate this, consider a simple SIS model (Figure 18.2A) with density-dependent transmission in which amphibians do not recover from infection (i.e. $\gamma = 0$). Given this model, the proportion of hosts that remain uninfected after the epizootic ($s(\infty)$) is given by the root of the equation $\ln(s(\infty)) = R_0(s(\infty) - 1) + \ln(s(0))$, where $s(0)$ is the proportion of susceptible hosts at the start of the epizootic (Diekmann & Heesterbeek, 2000). Figure 18.4 shows that populations with larger initial population density actually experience much larger disease-induced population declines and are thus more susceptible to extinction due to demographic stochasticity following an epizootic than populations with small initial densities. This result highlights that even without transmission from an environmental reservoir and/or frequency-dependent transmission, large amphibian

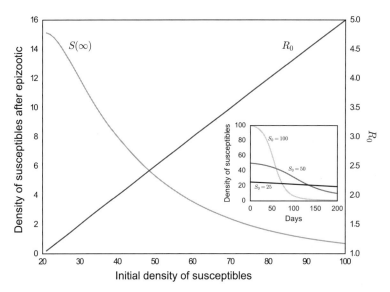

Figure 18.4 The relationship between the final size of an epizootic $S(\infty)$, initial density of susceptibles in a population (S_0) and R_0. $R_0 = \beta S_0/\alpha$ (for an SIS model with $\gamma = 0$, Figure 18.2A) where S_0 is the initial density of susceptibles, $\beta = 0.001$ day^{-1}, and $\alpha = 0.02$ day^{-1}. The inset figure shows the epizootic trajectories for the SI model with $S_0 = 100, 50,$ and 25.

populations can still be at substantial risk of extinction. This might be a very real risk for amphibian species where there is little probability of recovery after initial infection and initial population densities are high (Fisher et al., 2012).

18.2.4.2 *Sublethal effects of Bd on amphibian hosts*
While Bd-induced mortality due to chytridiomycosis is the most obvious way that Bd can affect amphibian hosts, there are a number of sublethal effects of chytridiomycosis that have important implications for host fitness. For example, Garner et al. (2009) exposed tadpoles of the common midwife toad *Alytes obstetricans* to different doses of Bd and found that, while tadpoles were able to clear Bd infections, tadpole survival probability through metamorphosis and the body size at metamorphosis were significantly reduced with increasing Bd exposure. Moreover, studies have also shown that Bd infection can reduce body mass of tadpoles, metamorphs, and adults (Retallick & Miera, 2007; Hanlon et al., 2015). This could be a result of the energetic cost of clearing Bd infection or the effect of Bd infection on foraging (Garner et al., 2009; Hanlon et al., 2015).

The sublethal effects of Bd on amphibian body size can have important implications on amphibian reproduction. Increased amphibian body mass at metamorphosis has been shown to increase post-metamorphic survival and decrease the time until reproductive body size is obtained (Smith, 1987; Altwegg & Reyer, 2003). Similarly, it is speculated that decreased female body condition can lead to reduced egg size (Garner et al., 2009), which results in reduced tadpole growth rate and body size at metamorphosis and, subsequently, reduced tadpole survival (e.g. Semlitsch, 1990). If the sublethal effects of Bd act to reduce amphibian body size, which in turn impacts reproduction and the survival of the next generation of tadpoles, population-level declines and extinctions can occur even if Bd is no longer present in the population. In terms of the framework presented here, this means that in some cases both the current load dynamics and the past load dynamics (e.g. the initial Bd exposure) must be accounted for to understand the current population-level trajectory.

18.2.5 Branch point 5: does the amphibian population recover from Bd-induced population declines?

The final branch point we consider is if, after persisting in an enzootic state with reduced population density, the amphibian population begins to increase (Figure 18.1). This population-level trajectory has been observed in many *R. sierrae* populations that are showing significant increases in population size in the presence of Bd (Knapp et al., 2016). The recovering populations tend to have significantly lower Bd loads than those observed during the initial epizootic (Knapp et al., 2016). Similarly, populations of the whistling tree frog *Litoria verreauxii verreauxii*, which likely experienced past Bd-induced population declines in south eastern Australia, have recently shown range expansion and population increases in the presence of Bd (Scheele et al., 2014, 2017).

Amphibian population recoveries following Bd-induced declines are only beginning to be documented and the mechanisms affecting this branch point are not yet well understood. In theory, both changes in *transmission dynamics* and *load dynamics* could promote the recovery of amphibian populations. Here we restrict our attention to potential load-dependent mechanisms of population recovery, recognising that changing transmission dynamics and/or environmental variables such as temperature may also be playing a role in population recovery.

Evolutionary changes in amphibian resistance and/or Bd virulence can have significant effects on Bd load dynamics and thus the ability of a host population to recover. For example, simply passaging Bd over multiple generations in the laboratory can lead to a reduced virulence (Langhammer et al., 2013). This reduction in Bd virulence is correlated with reduced chromosomal copy numbers, suggesting a genetic component to virulence attenuation (Refsnider et al., 2015). Given the important effects of variable Bd virulence on amphibian population trajectories (branch point 2), more studies are needed to understand the evolution of Bd virulence over the course of an epizootic and how this affects both the ability of amphibian populations to enter an enzootic state (branch point 3) and recover from disease-induced declines (branch point 5). This is will require repeated Bd samples throughout the epizootic, enzootic, and recovery trajectories.

From the host's perspective, standing variation in resistance mechanisms may rescue amphibian populations from Bd-induced extinction and promote recovery. Studies have identified individual- and population-level variation in genetic traits putatively leading to Bd resistance (Savage & Zamudio, 2011, 2016; Ellison et al., 2015). Moreover, studies have also identified signatures of directional selection on these alleles conferring Bd resistance following Bd invasion, tentatively suggesting that selection for these traits is helping rescue some vulnerable amphibian populations (Savage & Zamudio, 2016). Given that large-scale population recoveries in the presence of Bd are beginning to be documented for multiple amphibian species (Knapp et al., 2016; Scheele et al., 2017), determining the role of resistance in whether amphibian populations recover from Bd epizootics is an emerging frontier in empirical and theoretical amphibian disease ecology.

18.3 Future directions

Our framework identifies two particular characteristics of amphibian–Bd systems that need immediate attention to improve our understanding of variable population-level outcomes following Bd invasion: the nature of Bd transmission and the ability of amphibians to regulate Bd load through resistance or tolerance mechanisms. Regarding transmission, theory shows us that the ability of Bd to invade the system (branch point 1), the propensity of Bd to cause host extinction (branch point 3), and the propensity of populations to recover from Bd declines (branch point 5) are all influenced by the characteristics of Bd transmission. However, there are few published studies that have successfully identified the factors leading to Bd transmission. To fill in this important data gap, experiments are needed that simultaneously manipulate amphibian host density and track the number of zoospores in the zoospore pool. If these experiments are not possible, fitting and comparing different transmission models to time-series data of infected amphibian populations can provide an alternative way to identify the basic structure of the transmission function (e.g. McCallum et al., 2009).

Regarding resistance and tolerance, it is becoming increasingly evident that the severity of Bd-induced population declines as well as the ability of amphibians to recover from Bd epizootics depends on the ability of amphibians within the population to regulate Bd load through resistance or tolerance mechanisms (Knapp et al., 2016; Savage & Zamudio, 2016). Thus it will be important for future studies to identify the role of heterogeneity in resistance and/or tolerance as well as the mechanisms underlying these traits (Savage & Zamudio, 2011, 2016; Ellison et al., 2015). Moreover, it will be critical to determine the heritability of these resistance and tolerance traits and any trade-off that they have with host fitness (Boots et al., 2009). Ideally, some type of common-garden experiment is needed in which susceptible and non-susceptible amphibian populations are reared in the absence and presence of Bd and reproductive success (or a well-known proxy) is measured.

18.4 Conclusions

Determining why amphibian populations, and host populations in general, show variable outcomes in response to pathogen invasion is a major conservation goal (Woodhams et al., 2011; Langwig et al., 2015). Here we identify eight general population-level trajectories in response to Bd infection that have been observed in amphibian populations and five branch points at which amphibian populations can diverge along these different trajectories. By identifying how and when transmission dynamics and load dynamics affect the trajectories of amphibian populations at each branch point, this framework can be used to inform the most reasonable management strategies conditional on the current and past trajectory of an amphibian–Bd system (e.g. should one manage for transmission dynamics, load dynamics, or both?). While this framework is motivated by amphibian–Bd systems, we anticipate that it will also provide a useful lens through which to view the relative importance of transmission and load dynamics in other host–pathogen systems.

18.5 Acknowledgements

This work was supported by the National Institute of Health (NIH) Ecology and Evolution of Infectious Diseases Grant R01GM109499, the National Science Foundation (NSF) (Long Term Research in Environmental Biology grant DEB-1557190 and grant DEB-1149308) and the David and Lucile Packard Foundation. M. Wilber was supported by a NSF, USA, Graduate Research Fellowship (Grant No. DGE 1144085).

References

Adams, A.J., Kupferberg, S.J., Wilber, M.Q., et al. (2017) Extreme drought, host density, sex, and bullfrogs influence fungal pathogen infection in a declining lotic amphibian. *Ecosphere*, **8**(3), e01740.

Allen, L.J.S. (2015) *Stochastic Population and Epidemic Models: Persistence and Extinction*. London: Springer International Publishing.

Altwegg, R. & Reyer, H.-U. (2003) Patterns of natural selection on size at metamorphosis in water frogs. *Evolution*, **57**, 872–882.

Anderson, R.M. & May, R.M. (1979) Population biology of infectious diseases: Part I. *Nature*, **280**, 361–367.

Anderson, R.M. & May, R.M. (1981) The population dynamics of microparasites and their invertebrate hosts. *Philosophical Transactions of the Royal Society of London B*, **291**, 451–524.

Anderson, R.M. & May, R.M. (1991) *Infectious Diseases of Humans: Dynamics and Control*. Oxford: Oxford University Press.

Becker, C.G., Greenspan, S.E., Tracy, K.E., et al. (2017) Variation in phenotype and virulence among enzootic and panzootic amphibian chytrid lineages. *Fungal Ecology*, **26**, 45–50.

Begon, M., Bennett, M., Bowers, R.G., et al. (2002) A clarification of transmission terms in host–microparasite models: numbers, densities and areas. *Epidemiology and Infection*, **129**, 147–153.

Bletz, M.C., Rosa, G.M., Andreone, F., et al. (2015) Widespread presence of the pathogenic fungus *Batrachochytrium dendrobatidis* in wild amphibian communities in Madagascar. *Scientific Reports*, **5**, 1–10.

Boots, M., Best, A., Miller, M.R. & White, A. (2009) The role of ecological feedbacks in the evolution of host defence: what does theory tell us? *Philosophical Transactions of the Royal Society of London. Series B, Biological Sciences*, **364**, 27–36.

Bosch, J., Martínez-Solano, I. & García-París, M. (2001) Evidence of a chytrid fungus infection involved in the decline of the common midwife toad (*Alytes obstetricans*) in protected areas of central Spain. *Biological Conservation*, **97**, 331–337.

Briggs, C.J., Knapp, R.A. & Vredenburg, V.T. (2010) Enzootic and epizootic dynamics of the chytrid fungal pathogen of amphibians. *Proceedings of the National Academy of Sciences of the United States of America*, **107**, 9695–9700.

Briggs, C.J., Vredenburg, V.T., Knapp, R.A. & Rachowicz, L.J. (2005) Investigating the population-level effects of chytridiomycosis: an emerging infectious disease of amphibians. *Ecology*, **86**, 3149–3159.

Chestnut, T., Anderson, C., Popa, R., et al. (2014) Heterogeneous occupancy and density estimates of the pathogenic fungus *Batrachochytrium dendrobatidis* in waters of North America. *PLoS ONE*, **9**, e106790.

Clare, F.C., Halder, J.B., Daniel, O., et al. (2016) Climate forcing of an emerging pathogenic fungus across a montane multi-host community. *Philosophical Transactions of the Royal Society of London B: Biological Sciences*, **371**, 20150454.

Cohen, J.M., Venesky, M.D., Sauer, E.L., et al. (2017) The thermal mismatch hypothesis explains host susceptibility to an emerging infectious disease. *Ecology Letters*, **20**, 184–193.

Combes, C. (2000) *Parasitism: The Ecology and Evolution of Intimate Interactions*. Chicago, IL: The University of Chicago Press.

Courtois, E.A., Loyau, A., Bourgoin, M. & Schmeller, D.S. (2017) Initiation of *Batrachochytrium dendrobatidis* infection in the absence of physical contact with infected hosts – a field study in a high altitude lake. *Oikos*, **126**, 843–851.

Daszak, P., Cunningham, A.A. & Hyatt, A.D. (2003) Infectious disease and amphibian population declines. *Diversity and Distributions*, **9**, 141–150.

De Castro, F. & Bolker, B. (2005) Mechanisms of disease-induced extinction. *Ecology Letters*, **8**, 117–126.

Diekmann, O. & Heesterbeek, J.A.P. (2000) *Mathematical Epidemiology of Infectious Disease: Model Building, Interpretation, and Analysis*. New York, NY: John Wiley & Sons.

DiRenzo, G.V., Langhammer, P.F., Zamudio, K.R. & Lips, K.R. (2014) Fungal infection intensity and zoospore output of *Atelopus zeteki*, a potential acute chytrid supershedder. *PLoS ONE*, **9**, e93356.

Doddington, B.J., Bosch, J., Oliver, J.A., et al. (2013) Context-dependent amphibian host population response to an invading pathogen. *Ecology*, **94**, 1795–1804.

Drawert, B., Griesemer, M., Petzold, L.R. & Briggs, C.J. (2017) Using stochastic epidemiological models to evaluate conservation strategies for endangered amphibians. *Journal of The Royal Society Interface*, **14**, 20170480.

Ellison, A.R., Tunstall, T., Direnzo, G.V., et al. (2015) More than skin deep: functional genomic basis for resistance to amphibian chytridiomycosis. *Genome Biology and Evolution*, **7**, 286–298.

Farrer, R.A., Weinert, L.A., Bielby, J., et al. (2011) Multiple emergences of genetically diverse amphibian-infecting chytrids include a globalized hypervirulent recombinant lineage. *Proceedings of the National Academy of Sciences of the United States of America*, **108**, 18,732–18,736.

Fisher, M.C., Bosch, J., Yin, Z., et al. (2009) Proteomic and phenotypic profiling of the amphibian pathogen *Batrachochytrium dendrobatidis* shows that genotype is linked to virulence. *Molecular Ecology*, **18**, 415–429.

Fisher, M.C., Henk, D.A., Briggs, C.J., et al. (2012) Emerging fungal threats to animal, plant and ecosystem health. *Nature*, **484**, 186–194.

Garmyn, A.,Rooij, P. van, Pasmans, F., et al. (2012) Waterfowl: potential environmental reservoirs of the chytrid fungus *Batrachochytrium dendrobatidis. PLoS ONE*, **7**, e35038.

Garner, T.W.J., Walker, S., Bosch, J., et al. (2009) Life history tradeoffs influence mortality associated with the amphibian pathogen *Batrachochytrium dendrobatidis. Oikos*, **118**, 783–791.

Godfray, H.C.J., Briggs, C.J., Barlow, N.D., et al. (1999) A model of insect–pathogen dynamics in which a pathogenic bacterium can also reproduce saprophytically. *Proceedings of the Royal Society of London B*, **266**, 233–240.

Hagman, M. & Alford, R.A. (2015) Patterns of *Batrachochytrium dendrobatidis* transmission between tadpoles in a high-elevation rainforest stream in tropical Australia. *Diseases of Aquatic Organisms*, **115**, 213–221.

Hanlon, S.M., Lynch, K.J., Kerby, J. & Parris, M.J. (2015) *Batrachochytrium dendrobatidis* exposure effects on foraging efficiencies and body size in anuran tadpoles. *Diseases of Aquatic Organisms*, **112**, 237–242.

Jani, A.J., Knapp, R.A. & Briggs, C.J. (2017) Epidemic and endemic pathogen dynamics correspond to distinct host population microbiomes at a landscape scale. *Proceedings of the Royal Society of London B*, **284**, 20170944.

Johnson, M.L. & Speare, R. (2003) Survival of *Batrachochytrium dendrobatidis* in water: quarantine and disease control implications. *Emerging Infectious Diseases*, **9**, 922–925.

Johnson, M.L. & Speare, R. (2005) Possible modes of dissemination of the amphibian chytrid *Batrachochytrium dendrobatidis* in the environment. *Diseases of Aquatic Organisms*, **65**, 181–186.

Kilburn, V., Ibáñez, R. & Green, D. (2011) Reptiles as potential vectors and hosts of the amphibian pathogen *Batrachochytrium dendrobatidis* in Panama. *Diseases of Aquatic Organisms*, **97**, 127–134.

Kilpatrick, A.M., Briggs, C.J. & Daszak, P. (2010) The ecology and impact of chytridiomycosis: an emerging disease of amphibians. *Trends in Ecology and Evolution*, **25**, 109–118.

Knapp, R.A., Fellers, G.M., Kleeman, P.M., et al. (2016) Large-scale recovery of an endangered amphibian despite ongoing exposure to multiple stressors. *Proceedings of the National Academy of Sciences of the United States of America*, **113**, 11,889–11,894.

Kolby, J.E., Ramirez, S.D., Berger, L., et al. (2015) Terrestrial dispersal and potential environmental transmission of the amphibian chytrid fungus (*Batrachochytrium dendrobatidis*). *PLoS ONE*, **10**, e0125386.

Lande, R., Engen, S. & Saether, B.-E. (2003) *Stochastic Population Dynamics in Ecology and Conservation*. Oxford: Oxford University Press.

Langhammer, P.F., Lips, K.R., Burrowes, P.A., et al. (2013) A fungal pathogen of amphibians, *Batrachochytrium dendrobatidis*, attenuates in pathogenicity with in vitro passages. *PLoS ONE*, **8**, e77630.

Langwig, K.E., Voyles, J., Wilber, M.Q., et al. (2015) Context-dependent conservation responses to emerging wildlife diseases. *Frontiers in Ecology and the Environment*, **13**, 195–202.

Laurance, W.F., McDonald, K.R. & Speare, R. (1996) Epidemic disease and the catastrophic decline of Australian rain forest frogs. *Conservation Biology*, **10**, 406–413.

Liew, N., Mazon Moya, M.J., Wierzbicki, C.J., et al. (2017) Chytrid fungus infection in zebrafish demonstrates that the pathogen can parasitize non-amphibian vertebrate hosts. *Nature Communications*, **8**, 15048.

Lloyd-Smith, J.O., Cross, P.C., Briggs, C.J., et al. (2005) Should we expect population thresholds for wildlife disease? *Trends in Ecology and Evolution*, **20**, 511–519.

Longcore, J.E., Pessier, A.P. & Nichols, D.K. (1999) *Batrachochytrium dendrobatidis* gen. et sp. nov., a chytrid pathogenic to amphibians. *Mycologia*, **91**, 219–227.

Maniero, G.D. & Carey, C. (1997) Changes in selected aspects of immune function in the leopard frog, *Rana pipiens*, associated with exposure to cold. *Journal of Comparative Physiology B*, **167**, 256–263.

Marca, E.L., Lips, K.R., Lötters, S., et al. (2005) Catastrophic population declines and extinctions in neotropical harlequin frogs (Bufonidae: *Atelopus*). *Biotropica*, **37**, 190–201.

McCallum, H. (2012) Disease and the dynamics of extinction. *Philosophical Transactions of the Royal Society of London B: Biological Sciences*, **367**, 2828–2839.

McCallum, H., Barlow, N. & Hone, J. (2001) How should pathogen transmission be modelled? *Trends in Ecology and Evolution*, **16**, 295–300.

McCallum, H., Jones, M., Hawkins, C., et al. (2009) Transmission dynamics of Tasmanian devil facial tumor disease may lead to disease-induced extinction. *Ecology*, **90**, 3379–3392.

McMahon, T.A., Brannelly, L.A., Chatfield, M.W. H., et al. (2013) Chytrid fungus *Batrachochytrium dendrobatidis* has nonamphibian hosts and releases chemicals that cause pathology in the absence of infection. *Proceedings of the National Academy of Sciences of the United States of America*, **110**, 210–215.

McMahon, T.A., Sears, B.F., Venesky, M.D., et al. (2014) Amphibians acquire resistance to live and dead fungus overcoming fungal immunosuppression. *Nature*, **511**, 224–227.

Medzhitov, R., Schneider, D.S. & Soares, M.P. (2012) Disease tolerance as a defense strategy. *Science*, **335**, 936–941.

Perez, R., Richards-Zawacki, C.L., Krohn, A.R., et al. (2014) Field surveys in Western Panama indicate populations of *Atelopus varius* frogs are persisting in regions where *Batrachochytrium dendrobatidis* is now enzootic. *Amphibian and Reptile Conservation*, **8**, 30–35.

Piotrowski, J.S., Annis, S.L. & Longcore, J.E. (2004) Physiology of *Batrachochytrium dendrobatidis*, a chytrid pathogen of amphibians. *Mycologia*, **96**, 9–15.

Rachowicz, L.J. & Briggs, C.J. (2007) Quantifying the disease transmission function: effects of density on *Batrachochytrium dendrobatidis* transmission in the mountain yellow-legged frog *Rana muscosa*. *The Journal of Animal Ecology*, **76**, 711–721.

Raffel, T.R., Halstead, N.T., McMahon, T.A., Davis, A.K. & Rohr, J.R. (2015) Temperature variability and moisture synergistically interact to exacerbate an epizootic disease. *Proceedings of the Royal Society of London B*, **282**, 20142039.

Raffel, T.R., Rohr, J.R., Kiesecker, J.M. & Hudson, P.J. (2006) Negative effects of changing temperature on amphibian immunity under field conditions. *Functional Ecology*, **20**, 819–828.

Raffel, T.R., Romansic, J.M., Halstead, N.T., et al. (2012) Disease and thermal acclimation in a more variable and unpredictable climate. *Nature Climate Change*, **3**, 146–151.

Råberg, L., Graham, A.L. & Read, A.F. (2009) Decomposing health: tolerance and resistance to parasites in animals. *Philosophical Transactions of the Royal Society of London B: Biological Sciences*, **364**, 37–49.

Reeder, N.M.M., Pessier, A.P. & Vredenburg, V.T. (2012) A reservoir species for the emerging amphibian pathogen *Batrachochytrium dendrobatidis* thrives in a landscape decimated by disease. *PLoS ONE*, **7**, e33567.

Refsnider, J.M., Poorten, T.J., Langhammer, P.F., Burrowes, P.A. & Rosenblum, E.B. (2015) Genomic correlates of virulence attenuation in the deadly amphibian chytrid fungus, *Batrachochytrium dendrobatidis*. *G3: Genes| Genomes|Genetics*, **5**, 2291–2298.

Retallick, R.W.R., McCallum, H. & Speare, R. (2004) Endemic infection of the amphibian chytrid fungus in a frog community post-decline. *PLoS Biology*, **2**, e351.

Retallick, R.W.R. & Miera, V. (2007) Strain differences in the amphibian chytrid *Batrachochytrium dendrobatidis* and non-permanent, sub-lethal effects of infection. *Diseases of Aquatic Organisms*, **75**, 201–207.

Rosenblum, E.B., James, T.Y., Zamudio, K.R., et al. (2013) Complex history of the amphibian-killing chytrid fungus revealed with genome resequencing data. *Proceedings of the National Academy of Sciences of the United States of America*, **110**, 9385–9390.

Savage, A.E., Becker, C.G. & Zamudio, K.R. (2015) Linking genetic and environmental factors in amphibian disease risk. *Evolutionary Applications*, **8**, 560–572.

Savage, A.E. & Zamudio, K.R. (2011) MHC genotypes associate with resistance to a frog-killing fungus. *Proceedings of the National Academy of Sciences of the United States of America*, **108**, 16,705–16,710.

Savage, A.E. & Zamudio, K.R. (2016) Adaptive tolerance to a pathogenic fungus drives major histocompatibility complex evolution in natural amphibian populations. *Proceedings of the Royal Society of London B*, **283**, 20153115.

Scheele, B.C., Guarino, F., Osborne, W., et al. (2014) Decline and re-expansion of an amphibian with high prevalence of chytrid fungus. *Biological Conservation*, **170**, 86–91.

Scheele, B.C., Skerratt, L.F., Grogan, L.F., et al. (2017) After the epidemic: ongoing declines, stabilizations and recoveries in amphibians afflicted by chytridiomycosis. *Biological Conservation*, **206**, 37–46.

Schmeller, D.S., Blooi, M., Martel, A., et al. (2014) Microscopic aquatic predators strongly affect infection dynamics of a globally emerged pathogen. *Current Biology*, **24**, 176–180.

Semlitsch, R.D. (1990) Effects of body size, sibship, and tail injury on the susceptibility of tadpoles to dragonfly predation. *Canadian Journal of Zoology*, **68**, 1027–1030.

Skerratt, L.F., Berger, L., Speare, R., et al. (2007) Spread of chytridiomycosis has caused the rapid global decline and extinction of frogs. *EcoHealth*, **4**, 125–134.

Smith, D.C. (1987) Adult recruitment in chorus frogs: effects of size and date at metamorphosis. *Ecology*, **68**, 344–350.

Stockwell, M.P., Bower, D.S., Clulow, J. & Mahony, M.J. (2016) The role of non-declining amphibian species as alternative hosts for *Batrachochytrium dendrobatidis* in an amphibian community. *Wildlife Research*, **43**, 341–347.

Stockwell, M.P., Clulow, J. & Mahony, M.J. (2010) Host species determines whether infection load increases beyond disease-causing thresholds following exposure to the amphibian chytrid fungus. *Animal Conservation*, **13**, 62–71.

Stuart, S.N., Chanson, J.S., Cox, N.A., et al. (2004) Status and trends of amphibian declines and extinctions worldwide. *Science*, **306**, 1783–1786.

Venesky, M.D., Liu, X., Sauer, E.L. & Rohr, J.R. (2013) Linking manipulative experiments to field data to test the dilution effect. *Journal of Animal Ecology*, **83**, 557–565.

Voyles, J., Young, S., Berger, L., et al. (2009) Pathogenesis of chytridiomycosis, a cause of catastrophic amphibian declines. *Science*, **326**, 5–8.

Vredenburg, V.T., Knapp, R.A., Tunstall, T.S. & Briggs, C.J. (2010) Dynamics of an emerging disease drive large-scale amphibian population extinctions. *Proceedings of the National Academy of Sciences of the United States of America*, **107**, 9689–9694.

Wilber, M.Q., Knapp, R.A., Toothman, M. & Briggs, C.J. (2017) Resistance, tolerance and environmental transmission dynamics determine host extinction risk in a load-dependent amphibian disease. *Ecology Letters*, **30**, 1169–1181.

Wilber, M.Q., Langwig, K.E., Kilpatrick, A.M., McCallum, H.I. & Briggs, C.J. (2016) Integral projection models for host–parasite systems with an application to amphibian chytrid fungus. *Methods in Ecology and Evolution*, **7**, 1182–1194.

Woodhams, D.C., Alford, R.A., Briggs, C.J., Johnson, M. & Rollins-Smith, L.A. (2008) Life-history trade-offs influence disease in changing climates: strategies of an amphibian pathogen. *Ecology*, **89**, 1627–1639.

Woodhams, D.C., Bosch, J., Briggs, C.J., et al. (2011) Mitigating amphibian disease: strategies to maintain wild populations and control chytridiomycosis. *Frontiers in Zoology*, **8**, 8.

CHAPTER NINETEEN

Ecology of a marine ectoparasite in farmed and wild salmon

STEPHANIE J. PEACOCK, ANDREW W.
BATEMAN, BRENDAN CONNORS, SEAN
GODWIN, MARK A. LEWIS AND MARTIN
KRKOŠEK

19.1 Introduction

The global demand for seafood has outpaced wild fisheries and led to a dramatic increase in aquaculture over the last 30 years (FAO, 2016). Fish that are farmed in open-net pens can exchange parasites and pathogens with wild fish populations (Bjørn et al., 2001; Krkošek et al., 2006), which can change the structure of host populations in coastal seas (Krkošek, 2016). The potential implications of this change for the health and conservation of wild fish populations has spurred research into the causes (Revie et al., 2003; Bateman et al., 2016) and consequences (Krkošek et al., 2011b; Thorstad et al., 2015; Vollset et al., 2015) of parasite transmission between farmed and wild fish, contributing to the general understanding of host–parasite ecology in wild and domesticated animals. This chapter describes the new theoretical insights that have been gleaned from the study of the factors influencing sea louse parasites shared by farmed and wild salmon. We focus on research in Pacific Canada, where wild salmon still outnumber their domesticated counterparts and are an important ecological, economic, and cultural resource.

Host migration and species diversity jointly influence sea louse dynamics on wild salmon. A natural separation of juvenile and adult wild salmon that results from extensive host migration reduces transmission of parasites to small, vulnerable juveniles (Krkošek et al., 2007b). However, the recent introduction of a domestic reservoir host – farmed salmon – has undermined the parasite-related benefits of migration for wild salmon (Krkošek et al., 2006). In Section 19.2 we discuss the roles of host diversity, migration, and reservoir hosts in parasite transmission, and how these factors have affected parasite abundances – and survival – of wild Pacific salmon.

The impact of sea lice differs between farmed and wild salmon, and this has fuelled controversy over how significant these parasites are to host survival (Marty et al., 2010; Krkošek et al., 2011b; Vollset et al., 2015). For wild salmon, ecological processes of the host – namely predation and competition –

combine to influence parasite and host survival, sometimes in unexpected ways. In Section 19.3 we describe how inter- and intraspecific competition and predation mediate the effects of sea lice on wild salmon. Model analyses suggest that the impact of parasites on host populations may be more or less than previously thought, depending on the details of host ecology.

The impact of sea louse parasites on hosts has been the focus of the salmon-farming controversy, but in the last section of this chapter we consider how conditions in aquaculture and wild environments affect parasites. Farming practices generally promote the evolution of pathogen virulence, with high density, accelerated generation time, and low genetic variability in the host population – and aquaculture is no exception (Kennedy et al., 2016). Sea lice have also evolved resistance to chemotherapeutants in many regions, threatening the sustainability the industry (Aaen et al., 2015). The selection pressures for both virulence and drug resistance are influenced by the exchange of parasites between farmed and wild salmon, providing a case study of potential evolutionary ecosystem services that wild hosts may provide (Kreitzman et al., 2018).

Finally, we conclude the chapter with some lousy lessons that have been learned about the management of parasites for wildlife conservation. The potential for sea lice to affect wild salmon ecology and survival seems clear, but the relative importance of sea lice versus other environmental and human factors continues to be debated (Vollset et al., 2018). Theory suggests that the long-term coexistence of wild and farmed salmon hinges on our ability to manage parasites proactively and limit transmission to wild salmon (Orobko, 2016), and a precautionary approach is required to ensure the sustainability of wild salmon in perpetuity.

19.2 Anthropogenic changes to a host–parasite system

Pacific salmon (*Oncorhynchus* spp.) are anadromous fishes that hatch in freshwater rivers or lakes, migrate to spend most of their lives in the ocean, and return to spawn in their natal freshwaters. While in the ocean, Pacific salmon are susceptible to infection by sea lice (*Lepeophtheirus salmonis* and *Caligus clemensi*), which are native marine ectoparasitic crustaceans that are unable to survive in freshwater (Box 19.1). Nearly all Pacific salmon are semelparous and die soon after spawning, long before juveniles hatch and migrate to the open ocean. These life-history characteristics result in a natural separation between adult and juvenile subpopulations, termed migratory allopatry (Krkošek et al., 2007b), that limits transmission of sea lice from adults to vulnerable juveniles during their period of sympatry in the nearshore marine environment (Figure 19.1).

The parasite-avoidance benefits of migratory allopatry can be disrupted by the year-round presence of hosts in nearshore environments (Figure 19.1).

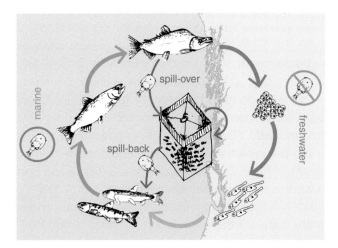

Figure 19.1 Spill-over and spill-back between wild and farmed salmon disrupts the natural separation of adults and juveniles, termed migratory allopatry, which normally minimises transmission of parasites such as sea lice to vulnerable juveniles. (A black and white version of this figure will appear in some formats. For the colour version, please refer to the plate section.)

Box 19.1: Natural history of sea louse parasites

Sea lice are naturally occurring marine ectoparasitic copepods that feed on the epidermis, musculature, and blood of host fish (Pike & Wadsworth, 2000). Two species of sea lice are common on Pacific salmon: *Caligus clemensi* is a generalist parasite of many fish species, including salmon, herring, and stickleback (Table 19.1). *Lepeophtheirus salmonis* (Figure 19.2d) is a salmon specialist and tends to be larger and more pathogenic to hosts (Costello, 2006).

Adult wild salmon often have a low infection intensity but high prevalence of sea lice, with low pathogenicity for adult hosts at endemic levels (Costello, 2006). High burdens of sea lice can cause host morbidity, and the control of sea lice is costly for salmon farms (Costello, 2009). Pathogenicity is highly dependent on the relative sizes of host and parasite, and even low burdens of *L. salmonis* can cause morbidity and mortality of juvenile salmon (Krkošek et al., 2006; Brauner et al., 2012).

As adults, sea lice are polygynous and mobile on the surface of their hosts and move among hosts to find mating opportunities or evade predation (Connors et al., 2011). Sea lice reproduce sexually, and male and female adult sea lice are easily distinguished (Johnson & Albright, 1991a). Males will also form pre-copulatory pairs with pre-adult females, waiting until they reach sexual maturity and are able to mate (Ritchie et al., 1996). These mate-searching and mate-guarding behaviours may increase the probability

Box 19.1: (cont.)

of finding a suitable mate at low parasite densities, and potentially offset Allee effects in the parasite population (Krkošek et al., 2012).

Once mated, gravid females extrude eggstrings from which free-living nauplii hatch. Nauplii have the potential to disperse tens of kilometres with ocean currents before moulting into infectious copepodites. The development time is highly temperature-dependent (Johnson & Albright, 1991b), and thus the dispersal potential of nauplii may vary (Groner et al., 2014). Copepodites must attach to a host before moulting through two chalimus stages that are attached to the host by a central filament (Hamre et al., 2013), and two pre-adult stages that are mobile on the host. The generation time is highly temperapture-dependent, ranging from 16 weeks at 7°C to < 8 weeks at 12°C (Heuch et al., 2000).

Because *L. salmonis* are a salmon-specific parasite and the majority of salmonids in Pacific Canada are semelparous, there are few alternate hosts for *L. salmonis* over winter near river mouths (although cutthroat trout and winter-run Chinook may be present, their densities are typically very low; Krkošek et al., 2007b; Table 19.1). The generalist sea louse *C. clemensi* can have higher prevalence on young juvenile salmon than *L. salmonis* because *C. clemensi* has a broader range of hosts, including herring and stickleback (Table 19.1), which can be abundant in nearshore environments over winter and when juvenile salmon emerge from rivers in early spring (Jones et al., 2006; Krkošek et al., 2007a). However, *C. clemensi* tends to be less pathogenic than *L. salmonis* (Costello, 2006), and thus juvenile salmon mortality due to *C. clemensi* is generally low in natural systems (Krkošek et al., 2007b, 2011b).

In recent decades, reductions in the growth of fisheries coupled with aquaculture expansion (FAO, 2016) have led to large numbers of domesticated salmonids now inhabiting some coastal ecosystems, altering the dynamics of sea lice on wild salmonids (Thorstad *et al.*, 2015; Krkošek, 2016). Farmed Atlantic salmon (*Salmo salar*) raised in open-net pens (Figure 19.2a,b) can act as reservoir hosts that acquire sea lice from returning adult salmon in the fall (spill-over), harbour and amplify sea louse populations over the winter, and then transmit sea lice to out-migrating juvenile salmon in the spring (spill-back, Figure 19.1; Daszak et al., 2000). The presence of farmed salmon thereby disrupts migratory allopatry and can lead to *L. salmonis* infestations of vulnerable juvenile salmon (Krkošek et al., 2007b). Indeed, sea louse infestations of wild juvenile salmon along their migration tend to intensify once these salmon have passed salmon farms (Figure 19.2c,d; Krkošek et al., 2006), suggesting that farms can act as infestation hotspots. Fewer sea lice have been

Table 19.1 *Host species for sea lice.* *

Hosts of *Caligus clemensi* and *Lepeophtheirus salmonis*	
Chum salmon *Oncorhynchus keta*	Migrate to sea immediately after hatching Generation time of 3–6 years Direct mortality due to sea lice[1,2] No evidence of population-level declines correlated with sea louse infestations[3]
Pink salmon *O. gorbuscha*	Migrate to sea immediately after hatching Generation time of 2 years Direct mortality[1,2] and increased predation[4] due to sea lice Population-level declines correlated with sea louse infestations[5,6,7]
Coho salmon *O. kisutch*	Spend 1 year in freshwater before migrating to sea Generation time of 3–5 years Major predators of juvenile pink and chum salmon in freshwater and near-shore marine Show selective predation on pink salmon[8,9] and parasitised prey[4,9] Incur trophic amplification of sea lice[10] Population-level declines correlated with sea louse infestations[6,11]
Sockeye salmon *O. nerka*	Spend 1–2 years in freshwater before migrating to sea Generation time of 3–5 years Mainly infested with *C. clemensi* Impact of *C. clemensi* on competitive foraging[12] and growth Negative population-level impact of aquaculture production, mediated by competition with pink salmon[13]
Chinook salmon *O. tshawytscha*	Ocean-type may migrate to sea immediately; stream-type spend one year in freshwater Most spend 3–4 years in the ocean, but as few as one year and as many as 8 years Return to spawn relatively early, in June-July (hence the term 'spring salmon'), and may be the first adult salmon to transmit lice to juveniles in the absence of farms
Cutthroat trout *O. clarkii clarkii*	Do not migrate to the open ocean but reside in streams and brackish bays year-round Periodic forays into freshwater likely regulate infestations Predators of juvenile pink and chum salmon
Farmed Atlantic salmon *Salmo salar*	Non-native species in Pacific Canada Housed in open-net pens over an 18-month production cycle Can acquire sea lice from returning adult salmon, and transmit back to out-migrating juveniles in the spring Sea lice are managed above a threshold parasite burden by harvest and treatment with chemotherapeutants[7,14]
Hosts of *Caligus clemensi* only	
Pacific herring *Clupea pallasii pallasii*	Predominant forage fish in Pacific Northwest Aggregate nearshore for mass spawning in late winter/early spring, but migration patterns are not well described

Table 19.1 (*cont.*)

	Large source population for *C. clemensi* during initial period of juvenile pink and chum out-migration
Three-spined	Year-round residents of nearshore and brackish waters
stickleback	Low abundance relative to herring and salmon
Gasterosteus	Suitable hosts for *C. clemensi*
aculeatus	Reported to have infestations of *L. salmonis*[15] but no evidence that the latter can complete its life cycle on stickleback[16]

* Not an exhaustive list of all host species, but covers the most common hosts mentioned in the chapter. Literature cited: (1) Morton and Routledge, 2005, (2) Krkošek et al., 2006, (3) Peacock et al., 2014, (4) Krkošek et al., 2011a, (5) Krkošek et al., 2007a, (6) Krkošek et al., 2011b, (7) Peacock et al., 2013, (8) Hargreaves and LeBrasseur, 1985, (9) Peacock et al., 2015, (10) Connors et al., 2010a, (11) Connors et al., 2010b, (12) Godwin et al., 2015, (13) Connors et al., 2012, (14) Saksida et al., 2010, (15) Jones et al., 2006, (16) Losos et al., 2010.

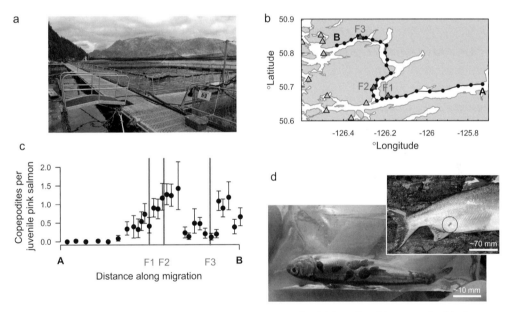

Figure 19.2 (a) An open-net salmon farm on the coast of British Columbia, Canada. (b) The migration route of juvenile salmon (black line; A to B) in the Broughton Archipelago, British Columbia, passes by several salmon farms (filled triangles). Black points are locations where juvenile pink salmon were captured and assessed for sea louse parasites (Krkošek et al., 2006). (c) The mean number of copepodid sea lice (±95% bootstrapped confidence intervals) per juvenile pink salmon sampled at black points in (b) from 18 to 28 April 2004 (Krkošek et al., 2006). (d) An infestation of motile sea lice on a juvenile pink salmon can have dramatic effects due to the large size of parasites relative to their host, while infections of adult salmon (inset) are much less pathogenic because hosts are larger and have developed protective scales. Photos: S Peacock, inset: C Miller. (A black and white version of this figure will appear in some formats. For the colour version, please refer to the plate section.)

observed on out-migrating wild salmon in regions without salmon farming (Krkošek et al., 2007b) and in years when farms are fallow (Morton et al., 2005). Similarly, in Europe, sea louse numbers on wild trout are higher in regions of intensive salmon aquaculture than in areas without farms (reviewed by Thorstad et al., 2015).

The population-level impacts of parasites on wildlife can be exacerbated by the presence of reservoir hosts, such as domestic animal populations, because the usual density-dependent mechanisms that regulate epizootics do not apply (De Castro & Bolker, 2005). There is empirical evidence from other host–parasite systems that, in the absence of reservoir hosts, parasites may be at least as important as predation in regulating wild population dynamics (Watson, 2013). Theory predicts that this control of wild populations will cause the parasite populations to self-regulate: high parasite burdens result in parasite-induced host mortality, and for parasites with density-dependent transmission like sea lice (Frazer et al., 2012; Jansen et al., 2012), lower host population density leads to less transmission (De Castro & Bolker, 2005). However, in the presence of reservoir hosts, infestation pressure can remain high, even at low densities of wildlife hosts, potentially leading to host extinction (De Castro & Bolker, 2005; Krkošek et al., 2013a). Evolutionary similarity to domesticated animals has also been identified as an important factor increasing the potential risk of parasites to wildlife (Pedersen et al., 2007). Together, these factors highlight the potential for parasite-mediated declines of exposed wild salmon populations and heighten the conservation concern about sea louse transmission from farmed salmon to migrating wild juvenile salmon (Krkošek et al., 2007a).

The impact of farm-origin sea lice on wild Pacific salmon differs among host species, in part due to interspecific variation in life-history traits (Table 19.1). While some salmon species, including coho salmon and sockeye salmon, spend a year or two in freshwater before migrating to sea, pink salmon and chum salmon enter the marine environment immediately after hatching (Groot & Margolis, 1991). Pink and chum salmon are small and lack protective scales when entering the marine environment and are therefore expected to be the Pacific salmon species most vulnerable to farm-origin sea lice. Indeed, field-based experiments with wild-caught pink and chum salmon have demonstrated significant direct louse-induced individual mortality for both species (Krkošek et al., 2009; Figure 19.3a). Other salmonids, such as cutthroat trout and Dolly Varden, migrate in and out of coastal seas and estuaries on an annual basis and may moderate the impact of sea lice by periodically returning to freshwater, thereby reducing their louse loads. In Europe, where there is a longer history of sea louse transmission from salmon farms, heavily infested Atlantic sea trout (*Salmo trutta*) have been found to return early to freshwater

a) Individual per-louse effect   b) Population-level effect

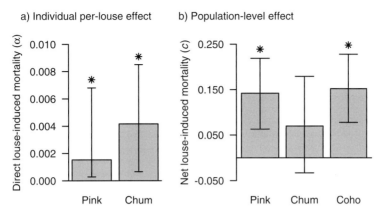

Figure 19.3 (a) The individual parasite-induced mortality (per sea louse per day) of captive pink and chum salmon estimated from field-based experiments (coho salmon estimate was not available) (Krkošek et al., 2009). (b) The population-level effect of farm-origin sea lice on wild salmon survival for pink and coho salmon (Krkošek et al., 2011a) and chum salmon (Peacock et al., 2014), shown as the parameter for louse-induced mortality (c) in an adapted Ricker population model for spawner–recruit data (Krkošek et al., 2011b). In both panels, bars are 95% confidence intervals on the estimates and stars indicate effects that are significantly different from zero.

(Thorstad et al., 2015), suggesting that life history and behaviour not only moderate the effects of sea lice, but may also be adaptive in response to them.

In Pacific Canada, much research has focused on whether direct parasite-induced mortality of host individuals results in reduced overall survival and recruitment for host populations. Studies in Europe have used an experimental approach to answering this question by tracking the oceanic survival of individual smolts that have been treated with anti-louse chemotherapeutants to that of untreated conspecifics. These studies have shown a significant decline in survival due to sea louse infection (Krkošek et al., 2013b; Vollset et al., 2015), but such an approach is more challenging for Pacific salmon due to their small size as juveniles (limiting marking options), variable age at maturity, and high natural mortality at sea. However, long-term data on spawner abundance in coastal British Columbia, Canada, allow for spatial and temporal comparisons of survival for populations exposed and unexposed to salmon farming, thus providing the opportunity for correlative examinations of the effect of sea lice from farmed salmon on wild salmon population dynamics. These comparisons have revealed a negative correlation between sea louse outbreaks on farmed salmon and survival of pink and coho salmon (Krkošek et al., 2007a, 2011b; Connors et al., 2010b). Similar analyses have identified aquaculture production, together with ocean climate and interspecific competition at sea, as factors associated with decline of sockeye salmon populations (Connors et al., 2012). Chum salmon populations, however, show no correlation between their survival rates and the magnitude of sea louse outbreaks on sympatric farmed salmon (Peacock et al., 2014; Figure 19.3b), despite estimates of direct parasite-induced mortality that are similar to pink salmon at the individual level. The data for chum salmon suggest that direct parasite-induced mortality (Figure 19.3a) is not the only factor determining the population-level impacts of parasites (Figure 19.3b). The discrepancy between individual- and population-level effects of sea lice has spurred further research into the ecological interactions of hosts that might mediate population-level effects.

19.3 Ecological factors mediating the impact of parasites

The true impact of parasites on wildlife populations can be difficult to estimate because animals rarely die from parasites alone. Before parasite burdens reach intensities that result in parasite-induced mortality, the *ecological* effects of parasites – that is, the ways in which parasites affect a host's ability to compete for food or avoid predators – become apparent. Thus, indirect ecological effects of parasites may determine how parasitism affects wildlife populations more than direct parasite-induced mortality (Ives & Murray, 1997; Hatcher et al., 2012).

19.3.1 Competition

Competition for resources is a fundamental challenge for all wildlife. Chief among these resources is food, as feeding determines the nutrients and energy an individual can put towards movement, growth, reproduction, and immune responses. For Pacific salmon, which migrate in large aggregations through variable prey densities, competition for food likely plays a large role in determining growth and survival (Groot & Margolis, 1991).

19.3.1.1 *Intraspecific competition*

Parasites can change the outcome of competitive interactions between individuals within a group, and these changes can have implications for host survival. Juvenile salmon may be particularly susceptible to parasite effects on competition, as they migrate in large schools to swamp and evade predators (Eggers, 1978; Furey et al., 2016). In environments with limited resources, parasitism can shift the competitive balance between individuals over food.

The influence of sea louse parasites on foraging in salmon has been best-studied in sockeye salmon (Table 19.1). Juvenile sockeye salmon feed primarily on zooplankton, which are spatially and temporally patchy (Chittenden et al., 2010; McKinnell et al., 2014). Some populations of juvenile sockeye salmon experience over 99% prevalence of *C. clemensi* sea lice while migrating through these patchy and food-limited environments (Price et al., 2011; Godwin et al.,

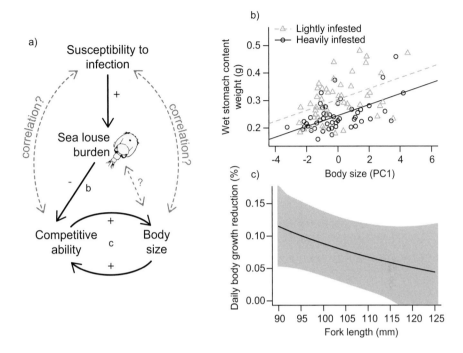

Figure 19.4 (a) The relationship between sea louse parasites, competitive ability, and body size for juvenile sockeye salmon has been investigated in field-based experiments, but the net impact on the host population may depend on whether susceptibility to infestation is biased towards individuals of a certain body size or competitive ability. (b) Comparison of body size and wet stomach content weigh between heavily infested (top ~10% of sample infection intensity) and lightly infested (bottom ~10% of sample infection intensity) juvenile sockeye salmon. Heavy infestation has been related to reduced competitive ability, but the competitive ability is also strongly related to body size. (c) Examination of growth increments for heavily infested and uninfested fish suggest that the percent daily reduction in body growth per sea louse (i.e. heavily infested – uninfested / uninfested) is a decreasing function of body size (line = mean, shaded region = ±95% CI). See Godwin et al. (2015, 2017) for details.

2015). *Caligus clemensi* tend to be less pathogenic than *L. salmonis* to juvenile fish because *C. clemensi* are smaller and more mobile and hence spend less time on individual hosts (Table 19.1; Costello, 2006), but high parasite burdens may nonetheless have ecological effects on host fitness (Figure 19.4a).

Field experiments suggest that heavily infested juvenile sockeye salmon have lower competitive foraging abilities than lightly infested or uninfested individuals (Figure 19.4b; Godwin et al., 2015), leading to reduced foraging success (Godwin et al., 2017) and body growth (Figure 19.4c; Godwin et al., 2017). Studies in Europe corroborate this finding, with scale analyses of sea trout showing reduced growth associated with intensive salmon farming and sea louse infestations (Thorstad et al., 2015). Furthermore, larger juvenile sockeye salmon also have higher rates of feeding (as measured by stomach content weight) than smaller conspecifics (Figure 19.4b), and daily growth increments on otoliths (ear bones) indicate larger fish have faster growth rates that are less-affected by parasites, thereby potentially amplifying divergent growth between infested and uninfested fish. Growth is a key component of fitness for many organisms, especially salmon, whose early marine growth is a determinant of overall survival (Beamish et al., 2004; Moss et al., 2005). Over time, these louse-associated growth effects may therefore ultimately affect survival.

While competitive outcomes can be understood at the level of individuals, ecologists are typically interested in population-level impacts. The net effect of parasite-modified competition on host populations may depend on whether the susceptibility to infestation is independent of both body size and competitive foraging ability of individuals (Figure 19.4a). If infestation is non-random such that individuals that are either smaller or less competitive are also more susceptible to infestation, then the impact of parasite-modified competition will reinforce existing differences in growth potential. In this case, population-level effects of reduced growth and survival due to sea lice may be compensatory, as those individuals would have been 'lost' from the population even in the absence of sea lice. However, if infestation is independent of body size or competitive ability, then 'healthier' individuals may also suffer infestations and a reduction in competitive ability, resulting in fewer highly competitive individuals. This may result in less equal resource allocation within the host population, and overall lower population health.

19.3.1.2 *Interspecific competition*

The previous section indicates that parasite-modified intraspecific resource competition occurs for juvenile sockeye salmon, but the influence of parasites can also include interspecific competition for resources (Hatcher et al., 2006). How parasite-modified competition affects communities depends on whether the parasite is shared among competitors, and whether the stronger or the weaker competitor is more affected by the parasite (Hudson & Greenman, 1998). If the stronger competitor is affected, then parasite-modified competition can promote coexistence, whereas if the weaker competitor is affected, then parasites may result in exclusion of the weaker competitor.

For Pacific salmon, interspecific competition can influence the growth, age-at-maturity, and survival of individuals as well as recruitment (Ruggerone & Connors, 2015). The number of recruits per spawner in sockeye salmon from the Fraser River, for instance, is negatively correlated with pink salmon abundance at oceanic scales due to competitive interactions between sockeye and pink salmon as adults in the Pacific Ocean (Figure 19.5; Connors et al.,

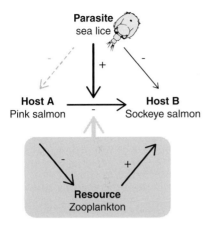

Figure 19.5 The impact of resource competition with pink salmon in the open Pacific Ocean on sockeye salmon survival may be amplified when farmed salmon (and their associated sea lice and other pathogens) are abundant (Connors et al., 2012). This indirect effect of parasite-modified competition is stronger than the direct effect of parasites alone. Sea lice also affect pink salmon survival at local scales (dashed light arrow), but competitive interactions with adult sockeye salmon occur at oceanic scales and thus the pink salmon competitors do not share the same infestation pressure as their sockeye salmon competitors.

2012). Aquaculture production occurring on wild juvenile sockeye migration routes, which is correlated with increased transmission of sea lice to juvenile salmon (Price et al., 2010, 2011), appears to amplify the negative impact of competition with pink salmon later in marine life (Connors et al., 2012). Thus, the reduced competitive foraging ability observed in small-scale, individual-level experiments (Figure 19.4b) may translate to lower survival of sockeye salmon populations. The interactive effect of pink salmon competition and aquaculture production is stronger than the effect of aquaculture production alone suggesting that in this case, the indirect effect of parasites via parasite-modified competition is more important than direct effects on sockeye salmon survival (Figure 19.5).

19.3.2 Predation

For most wildlife, predation affects individual survival and shapes the characteristics, including parasite loads, of surviving populations. For juvenile salmon, predation is the primary source of mortality, causing up to 90% mortality of pink salmon populations during the first three months of marine life (Parker, 1968). Mounting theory and evidence suggest that sea louse effects on predation may be a key determinant of the population-level impacts of epizootics.

19.3.2.1 *Parasite-mediated predation with a single prey species*

The effect of predation on host–parasite dynamics depends on whether parasites make prey more or less susceptible to predation (Packer et al., 2003). In many species, infected prey are easier for predators to identify and catch, making those prey more susceptible to predation than uninfected conspecifics (Hudson et al., 1992; Johnson et al., 2006). However, if predators incur a cost for consuming infested prey, as is the case with trophically transmitted parasites (Lafferty, 1992), they may avoid parasitised prey.

Yearling coho salmon are one of the main predators of juvenile pink and chum salmon during their early marine life (Hargreaves & LeBrasseur, 1986). Experiments have shown that predators, including coho salmon smolts and cutthroat trout, preferentially target juvenile pink and chum salmon that are infested with sea lice (Krkošek et al., 2011a). Whether this selective predation results in increased mortality in the prey population depends on whether predation on parasitised prey is compensatory or additive to predation that would occur in the absence of parasites. If predators preferentially target parasitised prey but do not increase overall consumption, predation is compensatory and also leads to lower average parasite burdens among prey as heavily infested individuals are consumed.

Theory that merges host–macroparasite models with predator–prey models has helped to shed light on the conditions under which compensatory parasite-mediated predation occurs. Classical host–macroparasite models track the abundance of hosts (H) and the mean parasite burden (M; Box 19.2). These models have been adapted for juvenile salmon and sea lice to track a cohort of juvenile salmon that becomes infected and whose survival declines due to direct parasite-induced mortality *and* predation following a type II functional response (Figure 19.6a; Krkošek et al., 2011a).

The type II functional response describes a predation rate that increases with prey density until predators are limited by the time it takes to handle and digest prey. The predation rate is described by two parameters: a capture rate and a handling time (Holling, 1959). For juvenile salmon, experiments suggest that the capture rate increases with the prey's parasite burden (Krkošek et al., 2011a; Peacock et al., 2014). The type II functional response often applied to fish predation can be adapted to incorporate an increase in the capture rate with increasing mean parasite burden, M, such that the average predation rate within the prey population is:

$$f_{(H,M)} = \frac{\overbrace{(\theta + \sigma M)}^{\text{capture rate}} H}{1 + T_h(\theta + \sigma M)H} \qquad (19.1)$$

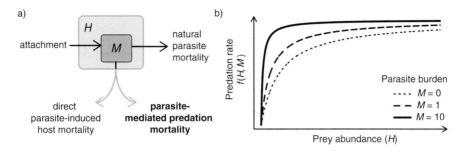

Figure 19.6 (a) Graphical description of a host–macroparasite model adapted to juvenile salmon and sea lice to include predation. The parasite load M increases due to attachment of free-living larvae and decreases due to natural parasite mortality. Juvenile salmon hosts H suffer mortality during their first few months of marine life due to parasites and parasite-mediated predation. (b) The rate of parasite-mediated predation is assumed to follow a type II functional response, with capture rates increasing with the mean parasite burden, M. As prey abundance increases, predators are limited by the time it takes to handle and digest prey, and the three lines eventually converge.

Box 19.2: Modelling host–parasite population dynamics

Mathematical models describing the growth and spread of infectious pathogens through a host population have been integral to the understanding of disease dynamics in both human and wildlife populations (May & Anderson, 1991; Hudson et al., 2002). In contrast to SIR models (Anderson & May, 1979), macroparasite models track the intensity of infection and the degree of parasite aggregation among hosts. Parasite aggregation is common (Shaw et al., 1998) and can fundamentally change how parasites influence host populations because mortality of heavily infected hosts will result in disproportionate mortality in the parasite population (Anderson & May, 1978). Explicitly considering the parasite burden and distribution among hosts is therefore important when the impact on hosts is proportional to parasite burden, as is the case of sea louse infestations of salmon.

Anderson and May (1978) developed a mathematical model for understanding host–macroparasite dynamics that consisted of two equations. The first equation describes the change in the host population, H:

$$\frac{dH}{dt} = \left(\underbrace{a}_{\text{birth}} - \underbrace{b}_{\substack{\text{natural} \\ \text{mortality}}} - \overbrace{\underbrace{\alpha \sum_{i=0}^{\infty} i\, q(i)}_{\substack{\text{parasite-induced} \\ \text{mortality}}}}^{\text{host mortality}} \right) H \qquad (19.2)$$

where a is the rate of host birth and b is the rate of natural (background) host mortality. The rate of parasite-induced host mortality depends on the number of parasites per host, and is equal to αi for a host infected with

Box 19.2: (cont.)

i parasites. The parasite-induced mortality of the host population is derived by considering the mortality of hosts with i parasites multiplied by the proportion of hosts that harbour i parasites, $q(i)$ and summed over all possible numbers of parasites. This term can be simplified to the expected parasite-induced mortality from the mean parasite burden, $M = P/H$:

$$\frac{dH}{dt} = (a - b - \alpha M)H \tag{19.3}$$

The total parasite population changes according to:

$$\frac{dP}{dt} = \underbrace{\beta LH}_{\text{transmission}} - \underbrace{\mu P}_{\substack{\text{natural} \\ \text{mortality}}} - \underbrace{\sum_{i=0}^{\infty} (b + \alpha i)\, i\, q(i)}_{\substack{\text{mortality due to} \\ \text{host mortality}}} \tag{19.4}$$

where β is the transmission coefficient, $L(t)$ is the density of infectious parasite larvae in the environment, μ is the mortality rate of parasites. The model assumes that parasites die when their host dies due to (1) natural mortality at rate b, and (2) parasite-induced host mortality at per-parasite rate α. The second component of this term depends on the aggregation of parasites among hosts; when parasites are highly aggregated, host mortality due to parasites will tend to result in higher rates of parasite death as many parasites die along with their heavily infested hosts. A negative binomial distribution, which is common for macroparasites (Shaw et al., 1998) is assumed.

Finally, to complete the parasite life cycle, the pool of infectious parasite larvae in the environment changes according to:

$$\frac{dL}{dt} = \kappa P - \gamma L - \beta LH \tag{19.5}$$

where κ is the rate of shedding of parasite larvae by attached parasites and γ is the per-capita mortality of parasite larvae in the environment. Often, the larval stage is short relative to the host and parasite dynamics, and a common assumption is that parasite larvae are at equilibrium ($dL/dt = 0$). This assumption simplifies the model to just two equations: one for the host population and one for the attached parasite population. In other cases, the density of infectious larvae is influenced by external forces and may be modelled separately. For example, the densities of larvae produced by sea lice on farmed salmon are much greater than the reproduction of lice on juvenile salmon themselves (Krkošek et al., 2005). Thus, models of sea louse dynamics on juvenile salmon have either included salmon farms as external sources of parasite larvae (e.g. Krkošek et al., 2005, 2006) or assumed that the density of larvae is constant (e.g. Krkošek et al., 2011a; Peacock et al., 2014).

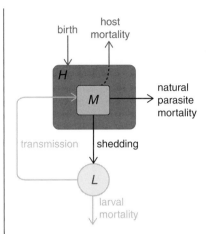

Figure B19.2.1 Model diagram for a host–macroparasite population model with three dynamic variables: the host population H, mean parasite burden M, and density of infectious larvae in the environment L. The model assumes that parasites die when their host dies (dashed line).

where H is the abundance of prey (i.e. hosts), θ is the baseline capture rate in the absence of parasites, σ is the per-parasite increase in the capture rate, and T_h is the handling time (Krkošek et al., 2011a, Peacock et al., 2014). The predation rate increases with the number of parasites at low prey abundance but not at high prey densities, where predators are limited by their handling time (Figure 19.6b). When predators are limited by prey handling time parasites alter *who* gets eaten, but not the overall *number* of prey consumed, and parasite-mediated predation is said to be compensatory. Analysis of the host–parasite population model (Figure 19.6a) also indicates that predation can amplify host mortality due to parasitism while simultaneously decreasing parasite burdens, creating a paradox that parasite-induced mortality may be high when observed parasite burdens are low (Krkošek et al., 2011a).

19.3.2.2 *Multi-host food webs*

Additional complexity may arise in multi-host systems if generalist parasites alter food web dynamics, for example by shifting predator pressure among prey species. Juvenile pink and chum salmon have similar early life histories (Table 19.1) and both are susceptible to sea louse infestations (Figure 19.3a) and experience high levels of predation during early marine life (Parker, 1969); however, coho predators seem to selectively consume pink salmon over chum salmon (Hargreaves & LeBrasseur, 1985; Peacock et al., 2015). The reasons for this prey preference are unknown, but it may be that preference increases when prey are infested and easier to catch (Peacock et al., 2014). This shift in predation would not only affect mortality

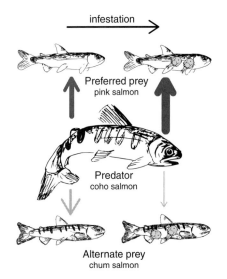

Figure 19.7 Sea lice make juvenile pink and chum salmon more vulnerable to predation by coho salmon, resulting in selective predation on infested prey. However, in this multi-prey system, predators preferentially consume pink salmon over chum salmon. Thus, when prey are infested and easier to catch, predation may focus on preferred prey (pink), which can result in a parasite-mediated release from predation for alternate prey (chum). Here, the thickness of the arrows represents the relative predation rates in this conceptual model.

of pink salmon, but could relieve mortality of the less-desirable prey, chum salmon (Figure 19.7).

Once again, formalising these ideas in a mathematical model helps to clarify assumptions and mechanisms, and allows for an exploration of the possible outcomes in the multi-prey scenario. The type II functional response in equation (19.1) can be adapted to allow for predation on multiple species with both selective predation on parasitised prey and preferential capture of one prey species over another (Figure 19.8a). The average predation rate on prey of species 1 with M_1 parasites, in the presence of an alternate prey, type 2, can be written:

$$f_1(H_1, H_2, M_1, M_2) = \frac{(\theta_1 + \sigma_1 M_1)H_1}{1 + T_h[(\theta_1 + \sigma_1 M_1)H_1 + (\theta_2 + \sigma_2 M_2)H_2]} \tag{19.6}$$

The definitions of parameters are as given for equation (19.1), but with subscripts 1 and 2 referring to the species-specific parameters and variables. The key difference from equation (19.1) is that the denominator in the multi-prey functional response considers the total time that each predator spends catching and consuming prey of both species.

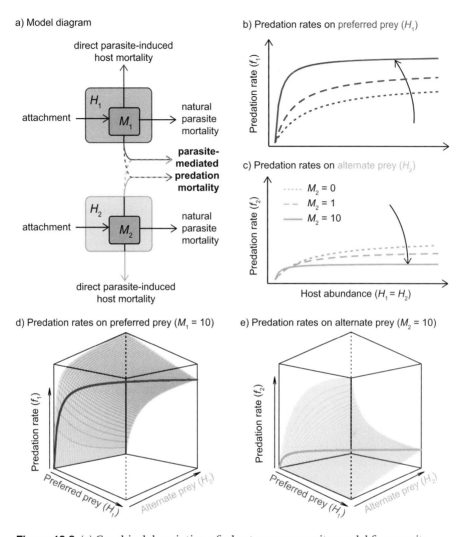

a) Model diagram

b) Predation rates on preferred prey (H_1)

c) Predation rates on alternate prey (H_2)

- - - - $M_2 = 0$
- - $M_2 = 1$
—— $M_2 = 10$

d) Predation rates on preferred prey ($M_1 = 10$)

e) Predation rates on alternate prey ($M_2 = 10$)

Figure 19.8 (a) Graphical description of a host–macroparasite model for parasite-mediated predation on two host species, H_1 and H_2, that interact via a shared predator (dashed lines; equation (19.5)). Predation rates on the two hosts may differ due to a predator preference. (b) Predation rates on preferred prey will tend to increase with parasite burden (Figure 19.6). (c) Predation rates on alternate prey will decline with parasite burden, but this decline depends on the abundance of prey (d,e; shown here for $M_1 = M_2 = 10$). Notably, if the abundance of preferred prey is low, predation rates on alternate prey will remain high (d). The lines in (d) and (e) correspond to the solid curves in (b) and (c), respectively, where $H_1 = H_2$.

In the case of juvenile salmon, the two prey species of interest are pink salmon (denoted by subscript 1) and chum salmon (denoted by subscript 2). Because coho salmon preferentially consume pink salmon over chum salmon, it can be assumed that $\theta_1 > \theta_2$. If predators not only show a base preference for pink salmon, but also increase that preference when prey is parasitised (Figure 19.8b,c), then $\sigma_1 > \sigma_2$. In this case, the capture rate of pink salmon increases with parasites more quickly than the capture rate of chum salmon increases with parasites. This model reveals that chum salmon may experience a 'parasite-mediated release' from predation (Peacock et al., 2014), whereas predation rates on preferred pink salmon increase with parasites regardless of prey density (Figure 19.8b,c). If the shift in predation pressure towards preferred prey is extreme and pink salmon are abundant enough to satiate predators (Figure 19.8d,e), then reduced predation on chum salmon may offset the direct effects of sea lice, or even result in a predation-mediated benefit of infestation. This may explain why there is no evidence of a population-level effect of sea lice on chum salmon, despite the significant declines in pink salmon correlated with the same sealouse epizootics (Figure 19.3b).

19.3.2.3 *Parasites that escape predation*

Although some parasites with complex life cycles rely on their hosts being eaten in order to complete their life cycle (Lafferty, 1999), other parasites – including sea lice – find the gut of a predator to be an inhospitable place. Sea lice have been observed to abandon their hosts during predation events (Connors et al., 2008); a substantial proportion of those that escape end up on predators (Connors et al., 2008). Trophic transmission of sea lice from prey to predators can amplify parasites on predators that are suitable hosts, such as coho salmon (Connors et al., 2010a). This trophic transmission may explain why coho salmon, although older, larger, and therefore less-vulnerable to the effects of sea lice when they enter the marine environment, seem to show reduced survival associated with sea louse epizootics (Figure 19.3b; Connors et al., 2010b).

19.4 Evolution of virulence and drug resistance

Host–parasite dynamics in wildlife are complicated by the ecological effects that parasites can have, but parasites of domesticated animals are subject to very different conditions. Domesticated hosts are often held in relatively high densities, and normally do not need to evade predators or compete for food to the same extent as their wild counterparts. They are often treated with drugs to reduce or eliminate parasite burdens (Van Boeckel et al., 2015). These conditions change the potential impact of parasites on hosts, but also affect the parasite traits – particularly virulence and drug resistance – selected for in agriculture and aquaculture (Mennerat et al., 2010).

19.4.1 Virulence

When hosts are abundant and at high density, parasites may invest in reproduction rather than survival, heavily exploiting individual hosts with little
consequence for parasite fitness since the chance of infecting other hosts is
high (Mennerat et al., 2010). Infestation with multiple species or strains of
parasite can also lead to competition among parasites and select for virulent
parasite strains (May & Nowak, 1995; van Baalen & Sabelis, 1995). Further, low
genetic diversity typical of domesticated hosts may facilitate the spread and
rapid evolution of parasites (Altizer et al., 2003). As described earlier in this
chapter, farming practices serve to free parasites from natural regulation,
a feature of natural systems that would normally reduce virulence (Lenski &
May, 1994). Finally, a number of disease-management practices employed in
aquaculture may themselves select for increased virulence (Kennedy et al.,
2016).

Evidence from salmon farming indicates that predictions of increased virulence have been borne out, at least in part. For example, salmon aquaculture
has been implicated in selecting for more virulent *Flavobacterium columnare*
bacteria (Pulkkinen et al., 2010; Sundberg et al., 2016). Also, sea lice associated
with salmon farms in Norway produce eggs faster than wild-type sea lice
(Mennerat et al., 2010). Little work has been carried out in general on virulence
evolution in macroparasites, however, and salmon farming may present
a good test case. Unfortunately, the potential for pathogen transmission to
wild fish species carries grave implications for populations unequipped to deal
with pathogens that evolved in a domestic environment (Daszak et al., 2000).

19.4.2 Drug resistance

Salmon farmers have relied heavily on chemical treatments to manage sea lice
at substantial annual cost (Costello, 2009), for example up to 23% of total
production costs in Norway (Nilsen et al., 2017). A number of chemotherapeutants are used, the most common of which is emamectin benzoate (EB, trade
name SLICE; Burridge et al., 2010). In most salmon farming regions of the
world, sea lice have evolved resistance to EB due to strong selection pressure
for mutations that confer resistance to chemotherapeutants and the relatively
short generation time of sea lice that allows these mutations to spread quickly
in the parasite population (Aaen et al., 2015). However, resistance has failed to
emerge in the Pacific despite a similar duration of chemotherapeutant use
(Saksida et al., 2010). Recent theory suggests this is because the large abundance of wild Pacific salmon provides a refuge from selection for drug resistance (Kreitzman et al., 2018).

Pest resistance to chemical treatment is a problem in agriculture generally, and avoiding its evolution has been the subject of much study. Theory
suggests that the maintenance of an untreated 'refuge' pest population,

connected to a treated population via migration, can serve as a source of wild-type susceptible genes and avoid or delay treatment resistance (Comins, 1977). With aggressive treatment to ensure remaining resistance alleles are recessive, wild-type resistant hybrids that result from mating with immigrants are removed (the 'high-dose/refuge' strategy; Gould, 1998; Tabashnik et al., 2013).

Several models have explored how sea lice exchange between wild and farmed salmon may affect EB resistance (Ashander, 2010; Murray, 2011; McEwan et al., 2015; Kreitzman et al., 2018). Consistent with agricultural theory, these models indicate that a large untreated refuge population, connectivity between wild and domesticated hosts, and aggressive treatment oppose the evolution of resistance. A small refuge (e.g. North Atlantic salmon farming regions) appears to produce resistance in sea lice, whereas a large wild-host refuge (e.g. British Columbia) can preclude resistance (McEwan et al., 2015). Wild- and farmed-host populations of sea lice in British Columbia appear to be genetically connected (Messmer et al., 2011), and wild salmon spawning in the vicinity of salmon farms likely serve as an important link between these populations (Ashander, 2010). Thus, wild salmon may provide an ecosystem service by helping to maintain treatment susceptibility in sea lice on salmon farms (Ashander, 2010; Kreitzman et al., 2018).

19.5 Implications for conservation and management

The potential impact of parasites on wildlife species may be most pronounced in systems where wildlife are sympatric with domestic reservoir hosts (Tompkins et al., 2015). Evolution in domesticated species and the indirect ecological effects of parasites on host predation and competition may be the primary mode by which parasites affect wildlife populations in these situations (Hatcher et al., 2006; Krkošek et al., 2011a; Godwin et al., 2015). Further, indirect effects of parasites in multi-host communities may result in unexpected outcomes that are not obvious from pairwise interactions (Connors et al., 2012; Peacock et al., 2014).

Advice for conservation management can arise from host ecology such as migration timing (Krkošek et al., 2007b). Delousing can be effective for conserving wild salmon when treatment is coordinated to reduce parasite numbers during the migration of wild juvenile salmon (Peacock et al., 2013; Bateman et al., 2016). Not only has this strategy proven effective, it does not necessarily require additional treatment during a production cycle (Peacock et al., 2013), and so it does not lead to additional financial costs or elevated selection for drug resistance. However, environmental variability, such as anomalous ocean temperatures, can alter both the timing of wild salmon migrations and parasite development, leading to failure to control parasites (Bateman et al., 2016). These lessons may be increasingly applicable in other systems as environmental change results in species range shifts, changes in parasite and host phenology (Kutz et al., 2014), and emerging infectious disease (Jones et al., 2008; Tompkins et al., 2015).

The timing of delousing treatments not only affects transmission of sea lice to juvenile wild salmon, but also transmission among farms. Coordinated area management involves the synchronised timing of treatments among farms at a regional scale, which may require cooperation of multiple aquaculture companies. Coordinated area management reduces reinfection from nearby farms (Murray & Salama, 2016; Peacock et al., 2016) and may also slow the evolution of drug resistance by reducing the chance that surviving lice can find mates (Krkošek et al., 2012; Groner et al., 2014). Other measures to minimise transmission among farms include stocking single age classes and fallowing to avoid perpetuating infection (Costello, 2004).

Global trends in salmon production from wild and farmed fish populations indicate fisheries stagnation and rapid expansion of domesticated fish will likely intensify sea louse spill-over and spill-back dynamics (Krkošek, 2016). Host density thresholds that arise due to density-dependent transmission occur at regional scales (Frazer et al., 2012; Jansen et al., 2012), and maintaining regional salmon aquaculture production below such thresholds may provide a means for avoiding costs of sea louse outbreaks. Alternatively, closed containment production of farmed fish is one way to eliminate the spill-over and spill-back dynamics of sea lice between wild and farmed salmon. The economic viability of such production systems is not clear (Liu et al., 2016), but trends are towards affordability as losses due to sea louse infestation of both wild and farmed fish continue to escalate and consideration of the external costs of open-net pen aquaculture are more fully deliberated.

Bioeconomic models that include the costs (e.g. parasite transmission) and benefits (reduced commercial harvest) of aquaculture for wild fish populations suggest stable coexistence of productive wild fisheries and aquaculture only if negative ecological feedbacks of domesticated animals on wildlife are kept below a threshold (Orobko, 2016). The definition of the threshold itself must include the reciprocal economic interactions between domesticated animals and wildlife, as well as the ecological effects of parasites on wildlife. The case study of sea louse parasites on farmed and wild salmon illustrates that the sustainability of both domesticated animals and wildlife depends on the broader anthropogenic and biological context of host–parasite interactions.

19.6 Conclusions

The ecological processes by which parasites affect domesticated versus wild animals differ, and the ecological context of host–parasite interactions can yield unexpected outcomes for wildlife health. For example, parasites can mediate food web dynamics of hosts, resulting in host resilience to epidemics

Table 19.2 *Conclusions (references:* [1]*Schumaker 2013;* [2]*Viana et al., 2015;* [3]*Pruvot et al., 2014, 2016;* [4]*Tian et al., 2015;* [5]*Dhondt et al., 2013;* [6]*Lafferty & Ben-Horin, 2013).*

Pathogen	Location(s)	Wild host	Domestic host	Spill-over/spill-back	Ecological effects	Ref
Brucellosis (*Brucella abortus*)	Greater Yellowstone Area, USA	Bison (*Bison bison*), elk (*Cervus elaphus*)	Cattle (*Bos taurus*)	Spill-over/-back has hindered the eradication of bovine brucellosis	*Migration* – Food supplementation in the park aims to reduce natural winter migration of bison and elk to outside areas; *Competition* – Competition among ungulate species reduces habitat overlap and transmission	1
Canine distemper virus (morbillivirus)	USA, Africa	Wild canines, felids (e.g. lions (*Panthera leo*))	Dogs (*Canis lupus familiaris*)	Transmission among multiple domestic and wild species yields complex host community	*Evolution* – Host switching facilitates spread to new species	2
Giant liver fluke (*Fascioloides magna*)	Alberta, Canada	Elk (*Cervus elaphus*)	Cattle (*Bos taurus*)	Cattle are dead-end hosts, reducing prevalence in sympatric elk through a 'dilution' effect	*Migration* – Evidence of migratory escape by elk; non-migratory herds are significantly more likely to be infected	3
Avian influenza virus	Asia	Wild waterbirds	Poultry	Domestic waterbirds often grazed on rice paddy fields in contact with wild waterbirds	*Migration* – Migratory birds may be responsible for the spread of H5N1 in Asia; *Evolution* – Mutation into highly pathogenic H5N1 strain	4
Mycoplasma gallisepticum	North America	House finch (*Haemorhous mexicanus*)	Poultry (Galliformes)	Spill-over to finches followed by spread to other Passerines, resulting in multi-host community	*Migration* – Spread from eastern to western North America via wild bird dispersal; *Evolution* – increasing virulence in eastern North America, substantial spatial and temporal genetic variation in bacterium	5
Withering-Syndrome Rickettsia-Like Organism (WS-RLO)	California, USA	Black abalone (*Haliotis cracherodii*)	Red abalone (*Haliotis rufescens*)	Domestic abalone more resistant to the bacterium, acting as reservoir hosts		6

or high parasite-induced host mortality at low measured parasite burden. Untangling these indirect effects of parasites in ecosystems is critical to the conservation and sustainable management of wildlife, where parasites are a growing threat.

The spill-over and spill-back of parasites and pathogens between wild and domestic hosts is not limited to salmon aquaculture, nor is it a new phenomenon. There are other examples of pathogen transmission between domesticated hosts and wildlife that touch on the themes discussed in this chapter (Table 19.2). Studying these systems requires integrating information on both direct and indirect effects from multiple sources. Controlled laboratory experiments are well suited to determining the direct physiological effects of parasitism on individuals in an isolated and stable environment. Field-based behavioural studies can look at how parasites mediate isolated interactions such as predation or competition. Together, these sources can identify the range of possible effects, and inform broader analysis, but the specifics of any interaction can be heavily influenced by the black box of ecology. Which pathway is most important? As the case study of salmon and sea lice has exemplified, it depends: the highly contingent nature of the interactions means that it's important to assess net effects through large-scale manipulative experiments, if possible, or data on long-term population dynamics and health (e.g. parasite loads) in correlative analysis. Long-term ecological data are critical for untangling how and why parasites are maintained in cases where multiple domesticated and wild host species interact, such as with canine distemper in Tanzania's Serengeti ecosystem (Viana et al., 2015).

As the global human population grows, and with it the demand for protein, disease transmission between domesticated animals and wildlife is likely to increase. Emerging infectious diseases are limiting production in agriculture and aquaculture, threatening pollinator communities and the crops that depend on them, and bringing into question the sustainability of wildlife populations (Table 19.2; Tompkins et al., 2015). Finding solutions that minimise disease transmission and allow for sustainable coexistence of wildlife and domesticated animals is necessary both for the conservation of imperilled wildlife (such as Pacific salmon) and for feeding a growing human population. The theory and models inspired by the case of sea louse parasites on farmed and wild salmon may help understand and predict threats in other systems.

19.7 Acknowledgements

Much of the research described in this chapter was made possible by the hard work and dedication of those at the Salmon Coast Field Station, most notably Alexandra Morton, Scott Rogers, Coady Webb, Zephyr Polk, and Lauren Portner, and by the support of the Echo Bay community including Eric Nelson, Billy Proctor, Chris and Hannah Bennett, Yvonne and Al Maximchuck, and Pierre

Landry. We acknowledge research contributions from Larry Dill (Simon Fraser University), John Reynolds (Simon Fraser University), John Volpe (University of Victoria), Craig Orr (Watershed Watch Salmon Society), the Hakai Institute, and Fisheries and Oceans Canada. Funding was provided by the Natural Sciences and Engineering Research Council of Canada (NSERC), MITACS, ESSA Technologies Ltd, and the Killam Foundation.

References

Aaen, S.M., Helgesen, K.O., Bakke, M.J., Kaur, K. & Horsberg, T.E. (2015) Drug resistance in sea lice: a threat to salmonid aquaculture. *Trends in Parasitology*, **31**, 72–81.

Altizer, S., Harvell, D. & Friedle, E. (2003) Rapid evolutionary dynamics and disease threats to biodiversity. *Trends in Ecology and Evolution*, **18**, 589–596.

Anderson, R. M. & May, R. M. (1978) Regulation and stability of host–parasite population interactions: I. Regulatory processes. *Journal of Animal Ecology*, **47**, 219–247.

Anderson, R. M. & May, R. M. (1979) Population biology of infectious diseases: Part I. *Nature*, **280**, 361–367.

Ashander, J. (2010) Effects of parasite exchange between wild and farmed salmon. MSc thesis, University of Alberta. DOI:10.6084/M9.FIGSHARE.1584651

Bateman, A.W., Peacock S.J., Connors, B.M., et al. (2016) Recent failure in control of sea louse outbreaks on salmon in the Broughton Archipelago, British Columbia. *Canadian Journal of Fisheries & Aquatic Sciences*, **73**, 1164–1172.

Beamish, R.J., Mahnken, C. & Neville C.M. (2004) Evidence that reduced early marine growth is associated with lower marine survival of coho salmon. *Transactions of the American Fisheries Society*, **133**, 26–33.

Bjørn, P.A., Finstad, B. & Kristoffersen, R. (2001) Salmon lice infection of wild sea trout and Arctic char in marine and freshwaters: the effects of salmon farms. *Aquaculture Research*, **32**, 947–962.

Brauner, C.J., Sackville, M., Gallagher, Z., et al. (2012) Physiological consequences of the salmon louse (*Lepeophtheirus salmonis*) on juvenile pink salmon (*Oncorhynchus gorbuscha*): implications for wild salmon ecology and management, and for salmon aquaculture. *Philosophical Transactions of the Royal Society of London: Series B, Biological Sciences*, **367**, 1770–1779.

Burridge, L., Weis, J.S., Cabello, F., Pizarro, J. & Bostick K. (2010) Chemical use in salmon aquaculture: a review of current practices and possible environmental effects. *Aquaculture*, **306**, 7–23.

Chittenden, C.M., Jensen, J.L.A., Ewart, D., et al. (2010) Recent salmon declines: a result of lost feeding opportunities due to bad timing? *PLoS ONE*, **5**, e12423.

Comins, H.N. (1977) The development of insecticide resistance in the presence of migration. *Journal of Theoretical Biology*, **64**, 177–197.

Connors, B.M., Braun, D.C., Peterman, R.M.M., et al. (2012) Migration links ocean-scale competition and local ocean conditions with exposure to farmed salmon to shape wild salmon dynamics. *Conservation Letters*, **5**, 304–312.

Connors, B.M., Hargreaves, N.B., Jones, S.R.M. & Dill, L.M. (2010a) Predation intensifies parasite exposure in a salmonid food chain. *Journal of Applied Ecology*, **47**, 1365–1371.

Connors, B.M., Krkošek, M. & Dill, L.M. (2008) Sea lice escape predation on their host. *Biology Letters*, **4**, 455–457.

Connors, B.M., Krkošek, M., Ford, J. & Dill, L.M. (2010b) Coho salmon productivity in relation to salmon lice from infected prey and salmon farms. *Journal of Applied Ecology*, **47**, 1372–1377.

Connors, B.M., Lagasse, C. & Dill, L.M. (2011) What's love got to do with it? Ontogenetic changes in drivers of dispersal in a marine ectoparasite. *Behavioral Ecology*, **22**, 588–593.

Costello, M.J. (2004) A checklist of best practice for sea lice control on salmon farms. *Caligus*, **8**, 18.

Costello, M.J. (2006) Ecology of sea lice parasitic on farmed and wild fish. *Trends in Parasitology*, **22**, 475–483.

Costello, M.J. (2009) The global economic cost of sea lice to the salmonid farming industry. *Journal of Fish Diseases*, **32**, 115.

Daszak, P., Cunningham, A. & Hyatt, A. (2000) Emerging infectious diseases of wildlife–threats to biodiversity and human health. *Science*, **287**, 443.

De Castro, F. & Bolker, B. (2005) Mechanisms of disease-induced extinction. *Ecology Letters*, **8**, 117–126.

Dhondt, A., Dobson, A., Hochachka, W.M., et al. (2013) Multiple host transfers, but only one successful lineage in a continent-spanning emergent pathogen. *Proceedings of the Royal Society of London B*, **280**, 20131068.

Eggers, D.M. (1978) Limnetic feeding behavior of juvenile sockeye salmon in Lake Washington and predator avoidance. *Limnology and Oceanography*, **23**, 1114–1125.

FAO (2016) *The State of the World Fisheries and Aquaculture (SOFIA) 2016*. Rome: FAO.

Frazer, L.N., Morton, A. & Krkošek, M. (2012) Critical thresholds in sea lice epidemics: evidence, sensitivity and subcritical estimation. *Proceedings of the Royal Society of London B*, **279**, 1950–1958.

Furey, N.B., Hinch, S.G., Bass, A.L., et al. (2016) Predator swamping reduces predation risk during nocturnal migration of juvenile salmon in a high-mortality landscape. *Journal of Animal Ecology*, **85**, 948–959.

Godwin, S.C., Dill, L.M., Krkošek, M. & Price, M. H.H. (2017) Reduced growth in wild juvenile sockeye salmon *Oncorhynchus nerka* infected with sea lice. *Journal of Fish Biology*, **91**, 41–57.

Godwin, S.C., Dill, L.M., Reynolds, J.D. & Krkošek, M. (2015) Sea lice, sockeye salmon, and foraging competition: lousy fish are lousy competitors. *Canadian Journal of Fisheries & Aquatic Sciences*, **72**, 1113–1120.

Godwin, S.C., Krkošek, M., Reynolds, J.D., Rogers, L.A. & Dill, L.M. (2017) Heavy sea louse infection is associated with decreased stomach fullness in wild juvenile sockeye salmon. *Canadian Journal of Fisheries and Aquatic Sciences*, **75**, 1587–1595.

Gould, F. (1998) Sustainability of transgenic insecticidal cultivars: integrating pest genetics and ecology. *Annual Review of Entomology*, **43**, 701–726.

Groner, M.L., Gettinby, G., Stormoen, M., Revie, C.W. & Cox, R. (2014) Modelling the impact of temperature-induced life history plasticity and mate limitation on the epidemic potential of a marine ectoparasite. *PLoS ONE*, **9**, e88465.

Groot, C. & Margolis, L. (1991) *Pacific Salmon Life Histories*. Vancouver, B.C.: UBC Press.

Hamre, L.A., Eichner, C., Caipang, C.M.A., et al. (2013) The salmon louse *Lepeophtheirus salmonis* (Copepoda: Caligidae) life cycle has only two chalimus stages. *PLoS ONE*, **8**, e73539.

Hargreaves, N. B. & LeBrasseur, R. J. (1985) Species selective predation on juvenile pink (*Oncorhynchus gorbuscha*) and chum salmon (*O. keta*) by coho salmon (*O. kisutch*). *Canadian Journal of Fisheries and Aquatic Sciences*, **42**, 659–668.

Hargreaves, N.B. & LeBrasseur, R.J. (1986) Size selectivity of coho (*Oncorhynchus kisutch*) preying on juvenile chum salmon (*O. keta*). *Canadian Journal of Fisheries and Aquatic Sciences*, **43**, 581–586.

Hatcher, M.J., Dick, J.T.A. & Dunn, A.M. (2006) How parasites affect interactions between competitors and predators. *Ecology Letters*, **9**, 1253–1271.

Hatcher, M.J., Dick, J.T.A. & Dunn, A.M. (2012) Diverse effects of parasites in ecosystems: linking interdependent processes. *Frontiers in Ecology and the Environment*, **10**, 186–194.

Heuch, P.A., Nordhagen, J.R. & Schram, T.A. (2000) Egg production in the salmon louse [*Lepeophtheirus salmonis* (Krøyer)] in relation to origin and water temperature. *Aquaculture Research*, **31**, 805–814.

Holling, C.S. (1959) Some characteristics of simple types of predation and parasitism. *The Canadian Entomologist*, **91**, 385–398.

Hudson, P.J., Dobson, A.P. & Newborn, D. (1992) Do parasites make prey vulnerable to predation? Red grouse and parasites. *Journal of Animal Ecology*, **61**, 681–692.

Hudson, P. & Greenman, J. (1998) Competition mediated by parasites: biological and theoretical progress. *Trends in Ecology and Evolution*, **13**, 387–390.

Hudson, P.J., Rizzoli, A.P., Grenfell, B.T., Heesterbeek, J.A.P. & Dobson, A.P. (2002) *Ecology of Wildlife Diseases*. Oxford: Oxford University Press.

Ives, A.R. & Murray, D.L. (1997) Can sublethal parasitism destabilize predator–prey population dynamics? A model of snowshoe hares, predators and parasites. *Journal of Animal Ecology*, **66**, 265–278.

Jansen, P.A., Kristoffersen, A.B., Viljugrein, H., et al. (2012) Sea lice as a density-dependent constraint to salmonid farming. *Proceedings of the Royal Society of London B*, **279**, 2330–2338.

Johnson, P.T.J., Stanton, D.E., Preu, E.R., Forshay, K.J. & Carpenter, S.R. (2006) Dining on disease: how interactions between infection and environment affect predation risk. *Ecology*, **87**, 1973–1980.

Johnson, S.C. & Albright, L.J. (1991a) The developmental stages of *Lepeophtheirus salmonis* (Krøyer, 1837) (Copepoda: Caligidae). *Canadian Journal of Zoology*, **69**, 929–950.

Johnson, S.C. & Albright, L. J. (1991b) Development, growth, and survival of *Lepeophtheirus salmonis* (Copepoda: Caligidae) under laboratory conditions. *Journal of the Marine Biological Association of the United Kingdom*, **71**, 425–436.

Jones, K.E., Patel, N.G., Levy, M.A., et al. (2008) Global trends in emerging infectious diseases. *Nature*, **451**, 990–993.

Jones, S.R.M., Prosperi-Porta, G., Kim, E., Callow, P. & Hargreaves, N.B. (2006) The occurrence of *Lepeophtheirus salmonis* and *Caligus clemensi* (Copepoda: Caligidae) on three-spine stickleback *Gasterosteus aculeatus* in coastal British Columbia. *The Journal of Parasitology*, **92**, 473–480.

Kennedy, D.A., Kurath, G., Brito, I.L., et al. (2016) Potential drivers of virulence evolution in aquaculture. *Evolutionary Applications*, **9**, 344–354.

Kreitzman, M., Ashander, J., Driscoll, J., et al. (2018) An evolutionary ecosystem service: wild salmon sustain the effectiveness of parasite control on salmon farms. *Conservation Letters*, **11**, e12395.

Krkošek, M. (2016) Population biology of infectious diseases shared by wild and farmed fish. *Canadian Journal of Fisheries & Aquatic Sciences*, **74**, 620–628.

Krkošek, M., Ashander, J., Frazer, L.N., & Lewis, M.A. (2013a) Allee effect from parasite spill-back. *American Naturalist*, **182**, 640–652.

Krkošek, M., Connors, B.M., Ford, H., et al. (2011a) Fish farms, parasites, and predators: implications for salmon population dynamics. *Ecological Applications*, **21**, 897–914.

Krkošek, M., Connors B.M., Lewis M.A. & Poulin, R. (2012) Allee effects may slow the spread of parasites in a coastal marine ecosystem. *The American Naturalist*, **179**, 401–412.

Krkošek, M., Connors B.M., Morton A., et al. (2011b) Effects of parasites from salmon farms on productivity of wild salmon. *Proceedings of the National Academy of Sciences of the United States of America*, **108**, 14,700–14,704.

Krkošek, M., Ford, J.S., Morton, A., *et al.* (2007a) Declining wild salmon populations in relation to parasites from farm salmon. *Science*, **318**, 1772.

Krkošek, M., Gottesfeld, A., Proctor, B., et al. (2007b) Effects of host migration, diversity and aquaculture on sea lice threats to Pacific salmon populations. *Proceedings of the Royal Society of London B*, **274**, 3141–3149.

Krkošek, M., Lewis, M.A., Morton, A., Frazer, L.N. & Volpe, J.P. (2006) Epizootics of wild fish induced by farm fish. *Proceedings of the National Academy of Sciences of the United States of America*, **103**, 15,506–15,510.

Krkošek, M., Lewis, M.A., Volpe, J.P. & Krkošek, M. (2005) Transmission dynamics of parasitic sea lice from farm to wild salmon. *Proceedings of the Royal Society of London B*, **272**, 689–696.

Krkošek, M., Morton, A., Volpe, J.P. & Lewis, M.A. (2009) Sea lice and salmon population dynamics: effects of exposure time for migratory fish. *Proceedings of the Royal Society of London B*, **276**, 2819–2828.

Krkošek, M., Revie, C.W., Gargan, P.G., et al. (2013b) Impact of parasites on salmon recruitment in the Northeast Atlantic

Ocean. *Proceedings of the Royal Society of London B*, **280**, 20122359.

Kutz, S.J., Hoberg, E.P., Molnár, P.K., Dobson A. & Verocai, G.G. (2014) A walk on the tundra: host–parasite interactions in an extreme environment. *International Journal for Parasitology: Parasites and Wildlife*, **3**, 198–208.

Lafferty, K.D. (1992) Foraging on prey that are modified by parasites. *The American Naturalist*, **140**, 854–867.

Lafferty, K.D. (1999) The evolution of trophic transmission. *Parasitology Today*, **15**, 111–115.

Lafferty, K.D. & Ben-Horin, T. (2013) Abalone farm discharges the withering syndrome pathogen into the wild. *Frontiers in Microbiology*, **4**, 1–5.

Lenski, R. & May, R. (1994) The evolution of virulence in parasites and pathogens: reconciliation between two competing hypotheses. *Journal of Theoretical Biology*, **169**, 253–265.

Liu, Y., Rosten, T.W., Henriksen, K., et al. (2016) Comparative economic performance and carbon footprint of two farming models for producing Atlantic salmon (*Salmo salar*): land-based closed containment system in freshwater and open net pen in seawater. *Aquacultural Engineering*, **71**, 1–12.

Losos, C.J.C., Reynolds, J.D. & Dill,L.M. (2010) Sex-selective predation by three spine sticklebacks on sea lice: a novel cleaning behaviour. *Ethology*, **116**, 981–989.

Marty, G.D., Saksida, S.M. & Quinn, T.J. (2010) Relationship of farm salmon, sea lice, and wild salmon populations. *Proceedings of the National Academy of Sciences of the United States of America*, **107**, 22,599–22,604.

May, R.M. & Anderson, R.M. (1991) *Infectious Diseases of Humans*. Oxford: Oxford University Press.

May, R.M. & Nowak, M.A. (1995) Coinfection and the evolution of parasite virulence. *Proceedings of the Royal Society of London B*, **261**, 209–215.

McEwan, G.F., Groner, M.L., Fast, M.D., Gettinby, G. & Revie, C.W. (2015) Using agent-based modelling to predict the role of wild refugia in the evolution of

resistance of sea lice to chemotherapeutants. *PLoS ONE*, **10**, 1–23.

McKinnell, S., Curchitser, E., Groot, K., Kaeriyama, M. & Trudel, M. (2014) Oceanic and atmospheric extremes motivate a new hypothesis for variable marine survival of Fraser River sockeye salmon. *Fisheries Oceanography*, **23**, 322–341.

Mennerat, A., Nilsen, F., Ebert, D., & Skorping, A. (2010) Intensive farming: evolutionary implications for parasites and pathogens. *Evolutionary Biology*, **37**, 59–67.

Messmer, A.M., Rondeau, E.B., Jantzen, S.G., et al. (2011) Assessment of population structure in Pacific *Lepeophtheirus salmonis* (Krøyer) using single nucleotide polymorphism and microsatellite genetic markers. *Aquaculture*, **320**, 183–192.

Morton, A. & Routledge, R. (2005) Mortality rates for juvenile pink (*Oncorhynchus gorbuscha*) and chum (*O. keta*) salmon infested with sea lice (*Lepeophtheirus salmonis*) in the Broughton Archipelago. *Alaska Fishery Research Bulletin*, **11**, 146–152.

Morton, A., Routledge, R.D. & Williams, R. (2005) Temporal patterns of sea louse infestation on wild Pacific salmon in relation to the fallowing of Atlantic salmon farms. *North American Journal of Fisheries Management*, **25**, 811–821.

Moss, J.H., Beauchamp, D.A., Cross, A.D., et al. (2005) Evidence for size-selective mortality after the first summer of ocean growth by pink salmon. *Transactions of the American Fisheries Society*, **134**, 1313–1322.

Murray, A. (2011) A simple model to assess selection for treatment-resistant sea lice. *Ecological Modelling*, **222**, 1854–1862.

Murray, A.G. & Salama, N.K.G. (2016) A simple model of the role of area management in the control of sea lice. *Ecological Modelling*, **337**, 39–47.

Nilsen, A., Nielsen, K.V., Biering, E. & Bergheim, A. (2017) Effective protection against sea lice during the production of Atlantic salmon in floating enclosures. *Aquaculture*, **466**, 41–50.

Orobko, M. (2016) Alternate stable states in coupled fishery–aquaculture systems. MSc thesis, University of Toronto. ProQuest Number: 10130697.

Packer, C., Holt, R.D., Hudson, P.J., Lafferty, K.D. & Dobson, A.P. (2003) Keeping the herds healthy and alert: implications of predator control for infectious disease. *Ecology Letters*, **6**, 797–802.

Parker, R.R. (1968) Marine mortality schedules of pink salmon of the Bella Coola River, central British Columbia. *Journal of the Fisheries Research Board of Canada*, **25**, 757–794.

Parker, R.R. (1969) Predator–prey relationship among pink and chum salmon fry and coho smolts in a central British Columbia inlet. *Fisheries Research Board of Canada Manuscript Report Series*, **1019**.

Peacock, S.J., Bateman, A.W., Krkošek, M. & Lewis, M.A. (2016) The dynamics of coupled populations subject to control. *Theoretical Ecology*, **9**, 365–380.

Peacock, S.J., Connors, B.M., Krkošek, M., Irvine, J.R. & Lewis, M.A. (2014) Can reduced predation offset negative effects of sea louse parasites on chum salmon? *Proceedings of the Royal Society of London B*, **281**, 20132913.

Peacock, S.J., Krkošek, M., Bateman, A. W. &. Lewis, M.A. (2015) Parasitism and food web dynamics of juvenile Pacific salmon. *Ecosphere*, **6**, 1–16.

Peacock, S.J., Krkošek, M., Proboszcz, S., Orr, C. & Lewis, M.A. (2013) Cessation of a salmon decline with control of parasites. *Ecological Applications*, **23**, 606–620.

Pedersen, A.B., Jones, K.E., Nunn, C.L. & Altizer, S. (2007) Infectious diseases and extinction risk in wild mammals. *Conservation Biology*, **21**, 1269–1279.

Pike, A.W. & Wadsworth, S.L. (2000), Sealice on salmonids: their biology and control. *Advances in Parasitology*, **44**, 233–337.

Price, M.H.H., Morton, A. & Reynolds, J. D. (2010) Evidence of farm-induced parasite infestations on wild juvenile salmon in multiple regions of coastal British Columbia, Canada. *Canadian Journal of Fisheries and Aquatic Sciences*, **67**, 1925–1932.

Price, M.H.H., Proboszcz, S.L., Routledge, R.D., et al. (2011) Sea louse infection of juvenile sockeye salmon in relation to marine salmon farms on Canada's west coast. *PLoS ONE*, **6**, e16851.

Pruvot, M., Lejeune, M., Kutz, S., et al. (2016) Better alone or in ill company? the effect of migration and inter-species comingling on *Fascioloides magna* infection in elk. *PLoS ONE*, **11**, e0159319.

Pruvot, M., Seidel, D., Boyce, M.S., et al. (2014) What attracts elk onto cattle pasture ? Implications for inter-species disease transmission. *Preventive Veterinary Medicine*, **117**, 326–339.

Pulkkinen, K., Suomalainen, L.-R., Read, A.F., et al. (2010) Intensive fish farming and the evolution of pathogen virulence: the case of columnaris disease in Finland. *Proceedings of the Royal Society of London B*, **277**, 593–600.

Revie, C.W., Gettinby, G., Treasurer, J.W. & Wallace, C. (2003) Identifying epidemiological factors affecting sea lice *Lepeophtheirus salmonis* abundance on Scottish salmon farms using general linear models. *Diseases of Aquatic Organisms*, **57**, 85–95.

Ritchie, G., Mordue (Luntz), A.J., Pike, A.W. & Rae, G.H. (1996) Observations on mating and reproductive behaviour of *Lepeophtheirus salmonis*, Krøyer (Copepoda: Caligidae). *Journal of Experimental Marine Biology and Ecology*, **201**, 285–298.

Ruggerone, G.T. & Connors, B.M. (2015) Productivity and life history of sockeye salmon in relation to competition with pink and sockeye salmon in the North Pacific Ocean. *Canadian Journal of Fisheries & Aquatic Sciences*, **72**, 818–833.

Saksida, S. M., Morrison, D. & Revie, C.W. (2010) The efficacy of emamectin benzoate against infestations of sea lice, *Lepeophtheirus salmonis*, on farmed Atlantic salmon, *Salmo salar* L., in British Columbia. *Journal of Fish Diseases*, **33**, 913–917.

Schumaker, B. (2013) Risks of *Brucella abortus* spillover in the Greater Yellowstone Area. *Revue scientifique et technique (International Office of Epizootics)*, **32**, 71–77.

Shaw, D.J., Grenfell, B.T. & Dobson, A.P. (1998) Patterns of macroparasite aggregation in wildlife host populations. *Parasitology*, **117**, 597–610.

Sundberg, L.-R., Ketola, T., Laanto, E., et al. (2016) Intensive aquaculture selects for increased virulence and interference competition in bacteria. *Proceedings of the Royal Society of London B*, **283**, 20153069.

Tabashnik, B., Brévault, T. & Carrière, Y. (2013) Insect resistance to Bt crops: lessons from the first billion acres. *Nature Biotechnology*, **31**, 510–521.

Thorstad, E.B., Todd, C.D., Uglem, I., et al. (2015) Effects of salmon lice *Lepeophtheirus salmonis* on wild sea trout *Salmo trutta* – a literature review. *Aquaculture Environment Interactions*, **7**, 91–113.

Tian, H., Zhou, S., Dong, L., et al. (2015) Avian influenza H5N1 viral and bird migration networks in Asia. *Proceedings of the National Academy of Sciences of the United States of America*, **112**, 172–177.

Tompkins, D.M., Carver, S., Jones M.E., Krkošek, M. & Skerratt, L.F. (2015) Emerging infectious diseases of wildlife: a critical perspective. *Trends in Parasitology*, **31**, 149–159.

van Baalen, M. & Sabelis, M. (1995) The dynamics of multiple infection and the evolution of virulence. *The American Naturalist*, **146**, 881.

Van Boeckel, T.P., Brower, C., Gilbert, M., et al. (2015) Global trends in antimicrobial use in food animals. *Proceedings of the National Academy of Sciences of the United States of America*, **112**, 5649–5654.

Viana, M., Cleaveland, S., Matthiopoulos, J., et al. (2015) Dynamics of a morbillivirus at the domestic–wildlife interface: canine distemper virus in domestic dogs and lions. *Proceedings of the National Academy of Sciences of the United States of America*, **112**, 1464–1469.

Vollset, K.W., Dohoo, I., Karlsen, Ø., et al. (2018) Disentangling the role of sea lice on the marine survival of Atlantic salmon. *ICES Journal of Marine Science*, **75**, 50–60.

Vollset, K.W., Krontveit, R.I., Jansen, P.A., et al. (2015) Impacts of parasites on marine survival of Atlantic salmon: a meta-analysis. *Fish and Fisheries*, **17**, 714–730.

Watson, M.J. (2013) What drives population-level effects of parasites? Meta-analysis meets life-history. *International Journal for Parasitology: Parasites and Wildlife*, **2**, 190–196.

CHAPTER TWENTY

Mycoplasmal conjunctivitis in house finches: the study of an emerging disease

ANDRÉ A. DHONDT, ANDREW P. DOBSON
AND WESLEY M. HOCHACHKA

20.1 Introduction

Relatively few opportunities exist to study the early stages of interaction between a parasite and a host species in which it had just emerged, causing a major epidemic. Even rarer is the opportunity to study this emergence in a system in which a great deal was known about both parasite and host prior to the emergence, especially in a system that is also tractable for experimental studies. In this chapter we describe one such system in which *Mycoplasma gallisepticum*, a bacterial pathogen in poultry that is transmitted directly or through fomites, expanded its host range to a wild songbird species, the house finch (*Haemorhous mexicanus*) (Figure 20.1). We have studied this system for over 20 years with a large group of colleagues, using a combination of field studies, controlled experiments, and mathematical models. This has allowed us to gain a better understanding of this host–pathogen system and to provide a template to study the 'systems biology' of the ecological and evolutionary dynamics of emerging pathogens. Rather than presenting a single, detailed example of the interplay between empirical studies and theory from our work, we will present a series of briefer examples of the ways in which we have been able to tie together field research with controlled experiments and models over the course of our studies on this system.

Our work started early in 1994, shortly after the initial reports of house finches with severe conjunctivitis in Maryland, USA. Clinical signs and gross lesions ranged from mild to severe unilateral or bilateral conjunctival swelling with serous to mucopurulent drainage and nasal exudate. The poultry pathogen *M. gallisepticum* was soon identified as the cause of the observed disease outbreak, satisfying all of the criteria of Koch's postulates (Ley et al., 1996). The epidemic spread rapidly across North America (Fischer et al., 1997; Duckworth et al., 2003; Dhondt et al., 2006; Ley et al., 2006). Because the severe eye lesions of diseased birds could be identified at a distance, and because house finches regularly visit bird feeders near people's houses, we

Figure 20.1 Male house finch exhibiting signs of conjunctivitis. (Photo reproduced with permission from Gary Mueller.) (A black and white version of this figure will appear in some formats. For the colour version, please refer to the plate section and the cover.)

were able to harness the power of Citizen Science to follow in detail the spread of the epidemic and its impact on host numbers (Dhondt et al., 1998; Hochachka & Dhondt, 2000).

20.2 Epidemic spread of the emerging disease

It is unusual to have detailed data on the spread of a naturally emerging wildlife disease in a system in which host abundance was monitored for several decades before and after the disease emerged. Three such longitudinal data sets provide information on variation in house finch abundance: the Christmas Bird Count since about 1900 (Butcher et al., 1990), the Breeding Bird Survey since 1966 (Sauer et al., 2003) and Project FeederWatch since 1986 (Bonter & Cooper, 2012). The House Finch Disease Survey built on Project FeederWatch and provided site-specific data on the presence and absence of symptomatic house finches within months of the first discovery of clinical disease in house finches. This made it possible to analyse the expansion rate of the epidemic in the context of diffusive spread theory (Hengeveld, 1989; Murray, 1993). As predicted by theory, the radial expansion of the epidemic progressed in a linear fashion during the first 6 months (Dhondt et al., 1998). A later analysis confirmed that the diffusion approximation works well to predict the spread of the disease for much of the early spread, but showed that the rate of epidemic spread decreased about 24 months after disease emergence (Figure 20.2) (Hosseini et al., 2006). Various factors influenced the rate of

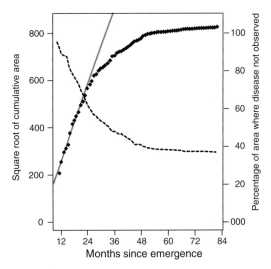

Figure 20.2 Geographic expansion of the epidemic caused by *Mycoplasma gallisepticum* in house finches. The square root of the cumulative area where symptomatic finches have been observed (black diamonds) plotted against months since the disease initially emerged. The solid grey line is the linear regression of the square root of area against the months since emergence for the second year of disease spread. If the disease had spread according to diffusion theory, this linear relationship should have continued over the course of disease spread. The black dashed line represents the percentage of cumulative area where observers had not yet reported symptomatic finches. (From Hosseini et al., 2006; with permission.)

spread: spread was significantly slower during the breeding season (when house finches are more sedentary); faster spread occurred with greater host density, which tends to increase with human density; and it was influenced by local geography with slower spread at higher elevation (where house finches are less abundant). Because house finches frequently use bird feeders provided by humans in the eastern (introduced) part of their range they are more abundant in more urbanised regions. The data also made it possible to compare the rate of disease spread to that of the introduced host (Elliott & Arbib Jr, 1953; Hill et al., 2012); the host dispersal was an order of magnitude slower than the pathogen's. This led us to conclude that 'emerging diseases can spread much faster than their hosts, given higher reproductive rates and a lack of non-linear limitations on growth rates at low levels of disease prevalence, even when underlying movement processes are similar' (Hosseini et al., 2006).

20.3 Seasonal variation in prevalence

Many host–pathogen systems show regular oscillations that resonate with, or are compounded by, seasonal variations in transmission rates. The precise mechanisms that drive these vary between different systems and can only rarely be examined using experimental studies (Altizer et al., 2006). Early on we observed that disease prevalence was strongly seasonal both in local populations (Hartup et al., 2001a; Altizer et al., 2004a; Dhondt et al., 2005), and at the continental scale (Altizer et al., 2004b; Dhondt et al., 2006). We therefore used our data to model this seasonal variation and identify factors driving it using three approaches. First, we used 77 months of the House Finch Disease Survey data across eastern North America to characterise seasonal patterns relative to long-term trends using the X-11 Census Method for classical seasonal decomposition as refined by the US Census Bureau to decompose time-series data into (1) a seasonal component, (2) a longer-term trend–cycle component, and (3) noise or random error. As we had data from across most of eastern North America we were able to compare these trends in three climatic regions that differed in January minimum temperature (Altizer et al., 2004b). Second, we modelled the impact on parasite–host dynamics of host seasonal breeding, host seasonal social aggregation and partial immunity in those birds that recover from infection (Hosseini et al., 2004). Finally, we performed a long-term aviary experiment to test the role of the introduction of disease-naïve juveniles in a group of recovered, asymptomatic carriers, and the role of reintroduction of the pathogen in a recovered population at a time when disease prevalence in the wild is minimal (Dhondt et al., 2012).

20.3.1 Decomposition of variation in disease prevalence

Using 25,000 individual observations collected between November 1994 and March 2001 with reports from observers in eastern North America (east of –95° longitude and south of 50° latitude), Altizer et al. (2004b) demonstrated that following initial establishment *M. gallisepticum* exhibited marked fluctuations in prevalence at a continent-wide scale. Monthly prevalence averaged between 3.5% and 22.5%. Changes in prevalence not only occurred over long (year) and short (months) time periods, but also differed between regions (Figure 20.3). In general, annual prevalence cycles occurred in all three regions with a peak in autumn and a second in late winter, separated by an early winter (December) minimum. Prevalence was at its lowest during the breeding season, a result also observed in detailed local population studies (Hartup & Kollias, 1999; Roberts et al., 2001). Differences in annual minima and maxima were more extreme in the south. Furthermore, the timing of the peaks differed between regions. In the southern regions the autumn peak was earlier and the late-winter peak later than in the other regions. The analysis also documented multi-year fluctuations in disease prevalence that were much more pronounced in the southern region.

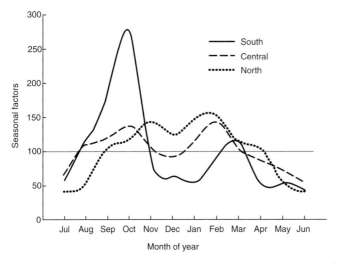

Figure 20.3 Seasonal variation in disease prevalence in house finches based on observations from the House Finch Disease Survey (east of −95° longitude and south of 50° latitude) in three climatic regions that differed in minimum January temperature. The dotted line represents the northern region (minimum January temperature ≤ −9° C), the long dash represents the central region (minimum January temperature between −8.9°C and −3°C), and the solid line represents the southern region (minimum January temperature > −3°C). The seasonal variation in disease prevalence is similar in all regions: a late-autumn peak, followed by a December minimum, followed by a late-winter peak, and by a breeding season minimum. Further south, the autumn peak is earlier and higher, and the late winter peak later and lower. (From Altizer et al., 2004; with permission.)

20.3.2 Seasonal birth, social aggregation, and variation in immunity following recovery as factors driving seasonal variation of disease prevalence

As described above, regular seasonal variation in prevalence of mycoplasmal conjunctivitis occurs in wild populations. In this section we evaluate the possible effect of three mechanisms that could cause this seasonality, in particular we examine the mechanisms that cause the observed double peak (autumn and late winter), and what causes the regional differences in the timing of these maxima. Note that we found that in natural populations a substantial proportion of diseased birds do recover (Faustino et al., 2004) and that house finches that recovered from an infection remain partially immune against reinfection for at least 14 months (Sydenstricker et al., 2005).

Two life-history traits are sufficient to cause seasonal variation in disease prevalence. Seasonal reproduction introduces a cohort of *Mycoplasma*-naïve juveniles into the population, which significantly amplifies the pool of susceptible hosts and creates a recurrent seasonal autumn outbreak. House finches are multi-brooded, but clutch size and number of clutches varies along a latitudinal gradient. In the south, birds start breeding earlier and the breeding season lasts longer (Hill et al., 2012). A higher number of susceptible juveniles, therefore, join southern populations over a longer period of time than in the north. This change in annual resources available to the pathogen leads to an earlier late-summer/early-autumn peak in the south, and higher levels of prevalence.

In house finches, as in most seed eaters (Newton, 1972), social organisation changes with season: birds live in pairs or in small groups in the breeding season, but aggregate in flocks in autumn and winter. Again, this change in behaviour contributes to seasonal variation in disease prevalence, as transmission will increase with flock size. One of the strongest effects we see when *M. gallisepticum* appeared in the east was a significant reduction in observed flock size in the eastern United States (Hochachka & Dhondt, 2006). This reflects both a net reduction in overall abundance and a response to levels of within-group transmission.

While house finches remain partially immune to reinfection for an extended period, resistance to reinfection varies among individuals (Sydenstricker et al., 2005). For that reason we modelled the system not just as a susceptible–infected–recovered model, but divided the infected class into novel infections and reinfections (birds that become infected from the recovered stage). This generates a gamma-distributed loss of immunity with time that provides a simple model of both heterogeneity and non-exponentially distributed immunity (Hosseini et al., 2004).

In order to model seasonal and latitudinal effects we quantified the patterns of seasonal breeding, and social aggregation across a latitudinal gradient in the eastern range of the house finch, supplemented with known field and laboratory information on immunity to *M. gallisepticum* in finches. Our model captured the major features of the seasonal and latitudinal variation in dynamics of the house finch–*M. gallisepticum* system. Three main features of house finch biology drive these sustained fluctuations in prevalence: seasonality of breeding, annual changes in social aggregation, and the partial immunity of finches to *M. gallisepticum*. The two seasonal processes can each cause a single annual peak, but only together can they create the semi-annual peaks because the two processes are out of phase. Sustained immunity to *M. gallisepticum* would dampen these cycles too much to allow both seasonal processes to affect the disease dynamics sufficiently to cause the empirically observed semi-annual pattern.

20.3.3 Experiments to test the origin of seasonal epidemics

The observation that in this natural system a new epidemic occurs each autumn, while disease prevalence during the breeding season is very low or even zero, begs the question as to the reservoir of the pathogen that starts the new outbreak. To test whether asymptomatic but apparently fully recovered individuals are the source of the new epidemic, we performed an experiment with a small number of house finches at low density (Dhondt et al., 2012). We kept groups of 11 juvenile house finches that were *M. gallisepticum*-free in an aviary with a total volume of about 40 m^3. We introduced *M. gallisepticum* in each of three groups in February 2008 by instilling *M. gallisepticum* inoculum in both eyes of one of the birds in each group. By analysing conjunctival swabs from the birds' eyes (from which *M. gallisepticum* DNA can be detected if present), or by testing blood samples (in which *M. gallisepticum*-specific anti-bodies can be found), we found that in the subsequent weeks 28 of the 30 birds showed evidence of having been exposed through horizontal transmission from the source bird. By early June, 14 weeks after the introduction of the pathogen in the groups, no birds remained with evidence of *M. gallisepticum* infection, a condition very similar to that observed in the wild. The birds were allowed to breed, but the young removed. In mid-September we mimicked the addition of a cohort of juveniles by placing eight wild-caught, *M. gallisepticum*-free juvenile house finches in each group. At that time all adults were still asymptomatic and *M. gallisepticum*-free. Nevertheless, in each of the three groups about half of the individuals (both adults and juveniles) developed signs of *M. gallisepticum* infection through transmission from adults to juveniles. In each of the three groups, *M. gallisepticum* DNA was first detected in the conjunctival swab of an adult which must, therefore, have been at the origin of the autumn 'epidemic'. This result shows that *M. gallisepticum* does not need to be introduced in a population through a carrier immigrant, but that an outbreak can be caused by a relapsing bird. By March 2009, when again all birds had fully recovered, we reintroduced *M. gallisepticum* by inoculating one adult and one juvenile. This reintroduction of *M. gallisepticum* at a time of the year when disease prevalence is usually very low and decreasing was sufficient to cause a further outbreak in each of the groups. This result indicates that the introduction of *M. gallisepticum* in an age-structured group that has previously been exposed is sufficient to cause a disease outbreak even at a time of the year when in the wild the disease is barely present.

This experiment confirms both hypotheses as to the origin of autumn outbreaks in age-structured populations: an increase in mycoplasmal conjunctivitis can be caused by the relapse of a recovered adult when naïve juveniles join the population, and/or it can be caused by the introduction of the pathogen in a population through an infected immigrant. Note that the immigrant does not necessarily have to be a house finch because American goldfinches (*Spinus tristis*) are also competent reservoir species and can transmit *M. gallisepticum* (Dhondt et al., 2013, 2014). Even mostly asymptomatic species can contribute to disease in house finches, as shown by the observation that mycoplasmal conjunctivitis in house finches not only increases with house finch abundance, but also with the numbers of northern cardinals (*Cardinalis cardinalis*) (States et al., 2009), a species occasionally reported with conjunctivitis (Hartup et al., 2001b).

20.4 Long-term changes in disease prevalence and host population size

Because bird abundance across North America has been monitored since about 1900, the impact of any event that may affect bird numbers can be evaluated through a before and after comparison. Data from the Christmas Bird Count, Project FeederWatch and the Breeding Bird Survey demonstrated, for example, that the introduction and expansion of house finches in eastern North America was followed by a decrease in house sparrow *Passer domesticus* abundance, an effect that was reversed when house finch numbers started to decline following the epidemic of mycoplasmal conjunctivitis that reduced house finch numbers again (Cooper et al., 2007). By combining data of the Christmas Bird Count (winter bird abundance) with those of the House Finch Disease Survey (disease prevalence in house finches), and by taking advantage of the gradual spread of the epidemic, we were able to show that within each 2×2 km block (an area of about 40,000 km^2) about 2.5 years after the new disease had become established house finch numbers declined by around 50% (Hochachka & Dhondt, 2000). This effect is qualitatively similar to that predicted by a simple SEI model of the dynamics of conjunctivitis. This model divides the host population into susceptible (S), exposed (E), and infectious (I) birds in which we assume that exposed birds may transmit the pathogen, but at a higher rate ($\varepsilon\beta$) than infectious birds. This is crucially different from the classical SEI model in that significant amount of transmission occurs from the E class, before overt visible signs of clinical disease caused by the presence of the pathogen are visible in the I class. Infected birds remain in the exposed, asymptomatic stage for a time period, $1/\gamma$, and experience an elevated mortality rate, $\rho\alpha$, but this is proportionately less than that experienced by visibly infectious birds, α; we also assume that infectious birds may lose their infection and return to the susceptible pool after a time period, $1/\theta$. Alternatively, they may develop immunity which eventually wanes before returning them to the susceptible pool. The dynamics may be described by three coupled differential equations for S, E, and I. The finch population is assumed to be regulated and will settle to some steady equilibrium at (b – d)K/b in the absence of the pathogen; we assume this equilibrium is determined by the birth, b, and death, d, rates of the host,

Table 20.1 *Definitions of symbols used in the model*

Parameter	Symbol
Birth rate of finch host	b
Death rate of host	d
Density at which birth rate declines to zero	K
Rate of pathogen transmission	β
Rate of loss of infection	θ
Relative rate of transmission from Exposed hosts, with respect to Infected hosts	ε
Rate of transition from Exposed to Infectious State	γ
Relative increase in pathogen-induced mortality in Exposed host with respect to Infected	ρ
Pathogen induced increase in mortality for Infected hosts	α

and the availability of resources such as food or roosting sites, designated, K. All parameters are defined in Table 20.1.

$$\frac{dS}{dt} = b(S + E + I)\left(\frac{K - (S + E + I)}{K}\right) + \theta I - dS - \beta S(I + \varepsilon E) \tag{20.1}$$

$$\frac{dE}{dt} = \beta S(I + \varepsilon E) - (d + \gamma + \rho \alpha)E \tag{20.2}$$

$$\frac{dI}{dt} = \gamma E - (d + \alpha + \theta)I \tag{20.3}$$

When rates of transmission are relatively low and the pathogen has low levels of virulence ($\beta < 1$, $\alpha < d$) the model has relatively stable dynamics and settles to a steady equilibrium, N*, E*, I* (note S* = N* – E* – I*), at a significantly lower density than in the absence of the pathogen, this reduction is driven by deaths of exposed and infected hosts. While the expressions for equilibrium numbers of infected, I, and exposed, E, hosts are relatively straightforward, they both include a term in N, the total population size (S + E + I), this has quite a complex formulation.

$$I^* = \frac{\gamma E^*}{(d + \alpha)} \tag{20.4}$$

$$E^* = \frac{N^*\left(b\left(\frac{K - N^*}{K}\right) - d\right)}{(d + \delta + \rho \alpha)} \tag{20.5}$$

$$N^* = \frac{K\left((b - d) - \frac{c_1}{c_2}\right) \pm \sqrt{\beta^2 K^2 c_2^2 c_3^2 \left(2\left((d - b)\frac{c_1}{c_2} - bd\right) + 1 + b^2 + d^2 + \frac{4c_1^2}{\beta c_2 c_3 bK}\right)}}{2b} \tag{20.6}$$

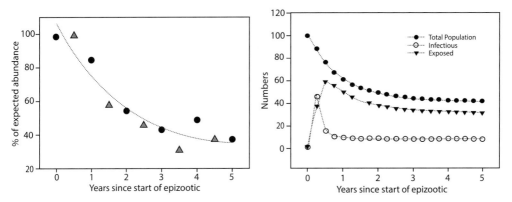

Figure 20.4 Decline of house finch abundance following the epidemic of mycoplasmal conjunctivitis in eastern North America. The left panel illustrates the observed monotonic decline of house finch abundance in eastern North America following the epidemic. The right panel illustrates the dynamics of the model described in this section illustrating the response of a house finch population to the arrival of a single infectious individual. The total bird population is illustrated by the solid black dots, the numbers of exposed and visibly infectious birds by the open and solid circles. The relative decline in host abundance is largely determined by the magnitude of α (mortality) and β (transmission), changes in the parameters determining relative pathology and transmission from exposed birds have little impact neither does the recovery rate of infectious individuals. (From Dhondt et al., 2005; with permission.)

where $c_1 = (d + \delta + \rho\alpha)$, $c_2 = \left(1 + \frac{\gamma}{(d+\alpha)}\right)$, and $c_3 = \left(\varepsilon + \frac{\gamma}{(d+\alpha)}\right)$.

Larger rates of transmission and significant levels of mortality produce sustained epidemic cycles; these are not observed in the house finch–*M. gallisepticum* system. Instead, we observe a significant reduction in house finch abundance with no dramatic fluctuations in host abundance and pathogen prevalence (Figure 20.4). The *M. gallisepticum*–house finch system provides a striking example of how a relatively benign pathogen may have a significant impact on the abundance of its host.

20.5 Evolution of virulence of *M. gallisepticum* in house finches

Unlike many emerging pathogens, *M. gallisepticum* was well known and studied prior to its emergence in house finches in the mid-1990s because of its global impact on commercial poultry (Levisohn & Kleven, 2000). Routine monitoring for this bacterium was therefore carried out in commercial poultry-raising facilities in the USA. This resulted in the collection and archiving of *M. gallisepticum* isolates, one of which was located at North Carolina State University and curated by David Ley, who joined the team studying *M. gallisepticum* after it emerged in house finches. This work on the bacterium in domestic poultry provided us with expertise in the handling of *M. gallisepticum* and provided a home for the reference collection of isolates from wild songbirds built throughout our study (Ley et al., 2016). David Ley's archive of poultry isolates also provided the reference genetic material from the bacterium's original hosts. As a result, it was possible to study both the changes associated with the host transfer from domestic poultry to house finches, and with the subsequent evolution of the bacterium in house finches.

In the next section we will describe the processes of host transfer and subsequent bacterial evolution, and their roles in motivating a better theoretical understanding of the short-term evolutionary dynamics of pathogens during emergence in a new host and the subsequent spatial spread of the pathogens in novel host species.

20.5.1 A single evolutionary lineage of *M. gallisepticum* in house finches

While novel pathogens continue to emerge, the dynamics of biological invasions remain poorly understood (Woolhouse et al., 2005) and are a major threat to biodiversity. Our data show that *M. gallisepticum* moves back and forth between poultry and house finches, but that the successful invasion of a novel host is a rare event (Hochachka et al., 2013). Thus, *M. gallisepticum* from house finches represents a distinct clade separate from *M. gallisepticum* in domestic poultry, indicating that the 'house finch' clade resulted from a single successful host transfer after which it rapidly evolved. Studies using more complete sequencing confirmed independently that all isolates from house finches belong to a single clade and estimated that clade diverged from typical poultry lineages less than 20 years ago (Delaney et al., 2012), and possibly as little as 5 years prior to the first detection of the bacterium in house finches in the winter of 1993–94 (Tulman et al., 2012). This estimated period between divergence of the 'house finch' clade and the emergence of the pathogen as the cause of epidemic conjunctivitis in house finches may have represented the time needed for the bacterium to evolve to survive in a novel species of host. Note that molecular studies indicate that *M. gallisepticum* is continuing to evolve in house finches (Delaney et al., 2012; Backstroem et al., 2013a, 2013b; Pflaum et al., 2016;).

The single successful clade of *M. gallisepticum* is spatially segregated into eastern North American and western North American subclades (Hochachka et al., 2013). Even though the initial spread of *M. gallisepticum* throughout eastern North America was a broad-front diffusion process (Hosseini et al., 2006), the Great Plains (the grassland area in the middle of North America and south of the boreal forest zone) represented a challenge to the dispersal of the bacteria. These had to be carried by infected hosts (presumably house finches or American goldfinches, see Section 20.3.3), because the bacteria have a very limited lifespan outside of a host (Dhondt et al., 2007a). Because severe disease caused by *M. gallisepticum* lowers the activity of house finches (e.g. Dhondt et al., 2007c; Bouwman & Hawley, 2010), in addition to lowering survival rates of the finches (Faustino et al., 2004), we believe that the Great Plains represents a barrier to dispersal for house finches, and thus to the dispersal of *M. gallisepticum* as it dispersed westward across North America.

While our data indicate that we are examining the evolution of a single lineage of *M. gallisepticum* in house finches, we have multiple lines of evidence that the bacteria regularly are transferred between species of potential hosts. In addition to the initial successful transfer from poultry to house finches, at least one other transfer has occurred between these two groups of hosts. Hochachka et al. (2013) reported both a case in which a 'poultry' *M. gallisepticum* isolate was found in a single house finch in New York, and one or more instances of 'house finch' clade *M. gallisepticum* in a set of turkey farms. Another such case was described by Ferguson et al. (2003). These cases were found without a deliberate effort to identify host jumps by *M. gallisepticum*, which we believe indicates that regular transfers between domestic poultry and house finches have, and likely continue, to occur albeit with limited success.

We have also shown that other wild passerine bird species are regularly exposed to *M. gallisepticum*. We have detected *M. gallisepticum* using polymerase chain reaction (PCR) on conjunctival swab samples from over 25 species of wild passerine (Dhondt et al., 2014); however, we have detected antibodies to *Mycoplasma* at far higher rates than the actual *M. gallisepticum* DNA, which suggests that the success of the bacteria in non-house finch hosts is limited. Experiments on potential alternative songbird hosts reinforce our belief that house finches are by far the most important hosts for the bacterium. We have experimentally examined the impact of *M. gallisepticum* on American goldfinches, house sparrows (*Passer domesticus*) and black-capped chickadees (*Poecile atricapillus*) as these are common visitors to bird feeders in the eastern USA and thus most likely to act as potential additional host species. Although house sparrows can be experimentally infected with *M. gallisepticum* in individually caged birds, they neither develop eye lesions, nor sufficient levels of infection to infect naïve hosts (Dhondt et al., 2008). Black-capped chickadees maintain a low-level infection for a month or more, but do not develop eye lesions (Dhondt et al., 2015). In contrast, American goldfinches can transmit *M. gallisepticum*, although they only develop very limited eye lesions (Dhondt et al., 2008, 2013). Additional evidence for the role of more reservoir species comes from the combined analysis of results from the House Finch Disease Survey (providing data on variation in disease prevalence in house finches) and of Project FeederWatch (providing data on variation in the abundance of various feeder birds). This analysis showed that disease prevalence in house finches increases with increasing number of house finches, but also with increasing numbers of northern cardinal (States et al., 2009) and possibly with increasing numbers of American goldfinch (unpublished).

In combination, our work on host transfer suggests that the process of transfer per se has not limited the range of hosts in which the bacterium is thriving, but rather the need for *M. gallisepticum* to adapt to a host species limits the range of hosts in which this bacterium successfully persists.

20.5.2 Observed patterns of change virulence

We have been able to assay the virulence of multiple isolates of the bacterium (Hawley et al., 2013) because of our ability to keep house finches in captivity, because we systematically collected, identified, cultured, and archived isolates (Ley et al., 2016), and because it is possible to conduct controlled experimental infections with *M. gallisepticum*. These experiments showed that within eastern North America, and separately within western North America, the severity of clinical disease caused by *M. gallisepticum* – which we have used as an empirical measure of bacterial virulence – has been higher for bacterial isolates collected later in time after the establishment of the bacterium on each side of North America. The only decline in virulence that we found was between the first isolate of *M. gallisepticum* that we obtained from western North America and isolates circulating in eastern North America at the same time (Figure 20.5).

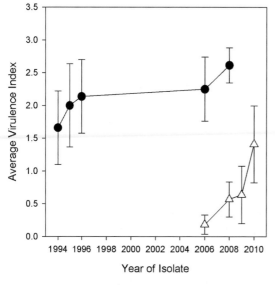

Figure 20.5 Changes in virulence (severity of disease) of *M. gallisepticum* isolates in house finches in relation to the date they were collected in the wild. Both in eastern (filled circles) and western (open triangles) North America virulence gradually increased once the disease had become endemic. While the virulence of the 2006 California strain, which successfully made it across from the eastern house finch range, was much lower than a contemporary eastern strain, western isolates rapidly increased in virulence following establishment of the pathogen in the region. (After Hawley et al., 2013; with permission.)

Models created to understand the mechanisms behind evolutionary changes in virulence, such as those described above, rely on trade-offs between epidemiological parameters, most commonly transmission and virulence (Ebert & Herre, 1996). Relatively unique to our system is the presence of empirical results that show that such trade-offs exist. We found that pathogen load correlates with virulence (Hawley et al., 2013), and subsequently that high-virulence isolates were also transmitted more efficiently (Figure 20.5; Williams et al., 2014).

Models of virulence evolution also need to make assumptions about variation in the hosts in which the pathogens are living, as systematic changes in hosts through time can affect the course of evolution. This is relevant for our understanding of the variation in virulence between eastern and western subclades of M. gallisepticum, where these differences among bacterial isolates were demonstrated in 'common garden' experiments, whereby we exposed eastern and western house finches in Ithaca, NY to an eastern and a western strain of M. gallisepticum (Hawley et al., 2010). The severity of the disease that the bacterium causes could also depend on genetic differences between eastern and western North American house finches. The house finches in eastern North America have originated from a small, founder population introduced into the New York City area in the early 1940s (Elliott & Arbib Jr, 1953); due to the genetic bottleneck at introduction, eastern North America's house finches have a lower genetic diversity than finches from the native, western range of the species (Hawley et al., 2006, 2008). However, we found that while differences among bacterial isolates caused substantial variation in severity of disease, there were no detectable differences in the response to infection by house finches from eastern and western populations (Hawley et al., 2010). So, our theoretical work has been built on the assumption that we are largely trying to explain the evolution of the bacterium against a background of hosts that are not changing genetically in any substantial ways through time and space. Here we note that the bacterium has a generation time that is measured in hours, while the avian hosts only pass through five to eight generations a decade; there are thus differences of three to five orders of magnitude in the evolutionary rate at which host and parasite can respond to selection for virulence and resistance.

20.5.3 Virulence evolution in non-equilibrium conditions

Our finding that virulence has increased through time, and reversed this trend when the bacterium was travelling from eastern to western North America (Figure 20.5; Hawley et al., 2013), suggests the potential for different evolutionary dynamics to occur when a pathogen is dispersing and entering a naïve host population than under endemic conditions once established in a local population. This observation was the motivation for the development and exploration of a model that examines the selective pressures that affect virulence during the spread of a pathogen through the spatial range of its host (Osnas et al., 2015), which may differ from the selective pressures experienced under the equilibrium conditions that have already been well studied. Osnas et al. (2015) based their model on the following assumptions.

(1) The dispersal of a pathogen requires that it is carried by its host from one location to another over any distance that is not trivially short.
(2) Hosts infected by a pathogen have reduced mobility, therefore travelling less and for shorter distances, than non-diseased hosts (Dhondt et al., 2007b).
(3) Infected hosts have a lower probability of survival than non-infected hosts.
(4) More infectious strains of a pathogen will produce infections in hosts that render the host less mobile and more likely to die than strains of a pathogen that are less infectious. Here we define 'more infectious' as strains that can spread more rapidly from one individual host to another, these strains will have a higher R_0 when they first appear in the population.

All of these conditions apply to *M. gallisepticum* within house finches, and are likely to also apply more widely. Adapting a model of the temporal dynamics to a model of susceptible and infected hosts, Osnas et al. (2015) found that less-virulent pathogen strains will dominate the leading edge of a spatially expanding epidemic, while more virulent strains will increase in frequency at later stages after invasion when the disease is endemic and levels of herd immunity potentially select for strains with different immunological properties (Figure 20.4).

20.5.4 Virulence evolution in endemic populations

We have also used empirical results from our studies to motivate models that explore the evolution of virulence of pathogens under the endemic conditions that have led to increasing virulence of isolates of *M. gallisepticum* in regions where the bacterium has become established (Figure 20.6).

Diseased house finches are highly efficient at transmitting *M. gallisepticum* to new hosts shortly after the finches become infected, even though conjunctival disease increases in severity and infection continues for 2 or more weeks (Figure 20.7; Dhondt et al., 2008). Transmission before the appearance of clinical disease is found for other pathogens including human immunodeficiency virus (HIV; Shubber et al., 2014) and the prions causing chronic wasting disease (Potapov et al., 2013). Osnas and Dobson (2010) explored the consequences of this decoupling of the time of infectiousness and disease during the course of infection. If transmission occurs before pathology is expressed it creates the potential for the pathogen to exhibit much higher levels of virulence than when the two occur simultaneously, as is assumed in the classic models for coevolution of the myxoma virus in rabbits. In the extreme case,

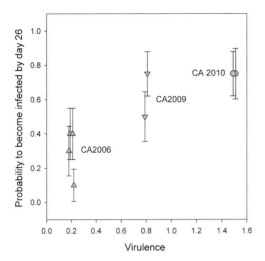

Figure 20.6 Virulence and transmission rate. The transmission rate in groups of 12 house finches kept in large aviaries increased in parallel with the observed increase in virulence shown in Figure 20.4. Transmission rate was measured as the probability of a bird becoming infected by day 26 after experimental introduction of *M. gallisepticum* in the group. Each symbol (± 1 SE) represents the results from one aviary. All isolates in this graphs were collected in California, USA. The number indicates the year in which the isolate was collected. (See also Figure 20.4.) (Unpublished.)

when all transmission occurs before pathology appears, then there are essentially no constraints on virulence and selection will allow it to run away to very high levels. In the house finch–*M. gallisepticum* system, transmission continues once clinical disease appears (as measured by eye scores) but at reduced levels; this creates a trade-off that reduces levels of virulence, although they are still significantly higher than if pathology were expressed earlier in the infection. Effectively R_0, the basic reproduction number of the pathogen, is now the sum of transmission during the early and late stages of infection

$$R_0 = \frac{\beta}{(d + \rho\alpha + \gamma)} + \frac{\gamma}{(d + \rho\alpha + \gamma)} \frac{\phi\beta}{(d + \alpha + \gamma)}. \tag{20.7}$$

As ρ (relative virulence in early stage of infection) and Φ (relative transmission when pathology is expressed) are low in the house finch system, there is considerable potential for selection for virulence to much higher levels than when pathology occurs soon after infection (Osnas & Dobson, 2010).

Expanding on this initial model (Osnas & Dobson, 2010), we looked at the consequences of additionally allowing a pathogen to successfully live in more than one host species (Osnas & Dobson, 2012). This model suggests that the potential for strains with different levels of virulence to coexist is now dependent upon the relative rate of within- versus between-species transmission. This echoes

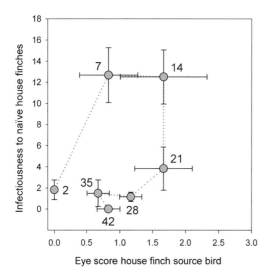

Figure 20.7 Changes in clinical signs and infectiousness of house finches over the course of an infection. Conjunctival swabs of house finches inoculated with the VA1994 *M. gallisepticum* isolate were taken at different time points after inoculation and used to infect a naïve house finch. The response of the latter was used as a measure of infectiousness. The numbers by each point represents the number of days post-inoculation. Severity of the eye lesions lag behind the degree to which source birds are infectious. Thus, on day 2 post-inoculation (PI), when house finches show no clinical signs yet, successful pathogen transmission already happens. Infectiousness is maximal on days 7 and 14 PI, although clinical signs on day 7 are much less severe than on day 14. On days 14 and 21 PI clinical signs are the same, although infectiousness on day 21 is much less than on day 14. On day 42 post-inoculation, clinical signs are still visible, but transmission no longer occurs. (After Dhondt et al., 2008; with permission.)

some earlier results obtained by Hochberg and Holt (1990) and Holt et al. (2003) regarding coexistence of competing parasites that share a host species. In this case multiple strains of the pathogen which exhibit different levels of virulence can coexist when rates of transmission between species are less than rates within host species. However, under the conditions of the house finch–*M. gallisepticum* system, where there appears to be tight adaptation of a pathogen to a single host, a single, dominant strain of the pathogen will evolve, and selection will favour relatively high virulence, especially when transmission of this pathogen can occur before the pathology associated with infection.

20.6 The role of capture–mark–recapture analyses to estimate disease prevalence without bias

Throughout the course of the study we have wrestled with finding viable ways of extrapolating between controlled laboratory experiments on individually infected birds, experiments with groups of caged birds, or theoretical models and examining data from birds in the field. House finches have proved curiously idiosyncratic to work with in the field. Our initial assumption that most Eastern American towns had mostly resident populations that undertake short-term migrations in autumn and winter was soon falsified when we tried to set up a colour-banded population on the Cornell campus at Ithaca; house finches are highly ephemeral, constantly moving across the landscape, forming, dissolving, and reforming new social groups. These insights stem from our intense three-year, capture–mark–release–recapture (CMRR) study of individually colour-banded birds at several locations in and around Ithaca, NY. The objective of that study was to measure the possible effect of disease on apparent survival and transition rates between diseased and non-diseased individuals, while accounting for any possible differences in the rates at which diseased and non-diseased birds are encountered (trapped or observed). Any differences in encounter rates with the presence of disease would mean that biased estimates of disease prevalence would be produced by estimating disease prevalence as the simple proportion of individuals trapped or observed with clinical disease. At each of two sites we trapped birds on the same day each week. At four sites we re-observed birds at weekly intervals. By keeping the interval between captures and between observations constant it was possible to reduce the number of parameters that needed to be estimated in our multi-state CMRR models. For our model calculations we split the data into seven time periods, each being a different year and season within year.

Unsurprisingly we found that symptomatic birds had a lower apparent survival rate, although only in six of the seven time periods; perhaps more surprisingly, the likelihood of encountering an individual bird depended on whether the bird had clinical disease and this dependency was at times complex (Faustino et al., 2004). On average, birds with clinical disease were less likely to be encountered than non-symptomatic individuals in six of the seven time periods. However, in two of the time periods examined this difference in encounter rates with disease state of a bird was further modified by temperature on the trapping/observation date (a disease × temperature statistical interaction), and in three other time periods the effect of disease state on encounter rate varied among the weekly trapping/observation periods (a disease × time statistical interaction): in three of four time periods in two periods the effect of disease on encounter rate was additive with time (disease + time), in three periods it was interactive with time (disease × time), and in two periods the best model for encounter rate was interactive with temperature (disease × temperature).

The general relevance of these results is that accurate measurements of disease prevalence in wild populations may only be possible through analysis of data using CMRR models. While it would be relatively easy to estimate and correct for fixed effect of disease state on encounter rate (i.e. statistical additive effects), only careful CMRR model calculations allow the exact calculation of encounter rate when disease state interacts with another parameter. The magnitudes of potential biases caused by failure to correct for differences in encounter rates was nicely illustrated by Chris Jennelle and colleagues (Jennelle et al., 2007). Using state-specific detection probabilities they compared apparent prevalence observed from actual counts of infected and uninfected finches to prevalence corrected for health-state-specific detection probabilities. Detection probabilities for uninfected finches were generally higher than those for infected birds, but in some periods the corrected prevalence was more than double the apparent one. This result is to some extent surprising, as behavioural observations indicate that when individuals are infected with *M. gallisepticum* they spend more time at a feeder and are more frequently alone compared to the same individuals when healthy (Hawley et al., 2007).

Because many of the birds in this study were re-observed but not recaptured, and because house finches infected with *M. gallisepticum* frequently develop conjunctivitis in one eye only, we were confronted with the problem that for some birds of which we were only able to see one of the eyes we were uncertain about its disease state. Rather than exclude such observations from the analyses, Conn and Cooch (2009) developed a model extension to relax this assumption by using a hidden Markov (or multi-event) modelling framework. Such a model can incorporate data from encounters of unknown state. This increased the richness of ecological data sets available for estimating life-history and state-transition parameters with multi-state models. This approach of treating state as a hidden Markov process allows records with uncertain state to be used, increasing the precision of survival and state-transition parameters in multi-state mark–recapture studies.

20.7 Conclusions

Mycoplasmal conjunctivitis is an unusually well-studied, naturally emerging wildlife disease. Because the pathogen is economically important in poultry around the world, its genetics and virulence have been well studied in its original host. Even before the bacteria successfully jumped to wild house finches in North America in the early 1990s, these had also been well studied. *M. gallisepticum* causes clinical disease in the house finches that is visible at a distance, and because finches visit bird feeders readily the participation of thousands of citizen scientists made it possible to track the epidemic in amazing detail. Our work – the close collaboration among veterinarians, avian ecologists, microbiologists, immunologists, and statistical and mathematical modellers – allowed us to explore and understand this system from a number of perspectives, leading to the following conclusions.

(1) While the initial epidemic was able to cause a monotonic decline of host abundance to half of that expected had the disease not emerged, the magnitude of the decline was tied to pre-disease density with areas of highest pre-disease density of finches showing the greatest declines.

(2) The initial epidemic of this emerging disease exhibited simple diffusive spread although the habitats selected by the bird hosts constrained this to relatively low-lying areas along valley floors rather than directly over mountain ranges.

(3) Geographically varying seasonal differences in prevalence of disease existed, with the observed seasonal bimodal peaks in disease prevalence explicable only as the result of different seasonal processes (reproduction, social aggregation) that are out of phase with each other, as well as partial immunity of recovered birds.

(4) Estimates of disease prevalence calculated directly from field observations can be biased, because diseased and non-diseased birds are encountered at different rates, for which corrections can be calculated by employing statistical methods such as capture–mark–release–recapture analyses.

(5) The epidemic of this emerging disease is the result of a single successful host jump of the poultry pathogen *M. gallisepticum*, although our data show repeated and reciprocal exchange between poultry and house finches.

(6) After its initial emergence in house finches, *M. gallisepticum* virulence evolved rapidly, either increasing or decreasing depending on the selection pressures encountered, including changes in selection pressure between initial epidemic outbreak in a naïve population and endemic infection.

Our work to date has pointed to several diverse avenues for continuing work, including the identification of the genetic basis for changes in virulence, and the roles of coinfection with multiple pathogens in affecting host immune systems and subsequently altering pathogen evolution and the potential for disease emergence. As with the work described in this chapter, any future work will require collaboration among researchers with diverse interests and skills.

20.8 Acknowledgements

The research was supported by NSF grants DEB 0094456 and EF 0622705, and by NIH grant R01GM085232, all part of the Ecology and Evolution of Infectious Diseases programme. We thank Erik Osnas, Evan Cooch, Keila Dhondt and two anonymous reviewers for constructive comments on the manuscript. We are grateful to all our colleagues who collaborated in this research project: Jim Adelman, Sonia Altizer, Paul Conn, Véronique Connolly, Evan Cooch, Andy Davis, Jonathan DeCoste, Keila Dhondt, Melanie Driscoll, Cristina Faustino, Steven Geary, Jessica Grodio, Barry Hartup, Dana Hawley, Parviez Hosseini, Paul Hurtado, Chris Jennelle, Mari Kimura, George Kollias, Heidi Kollias, David

Ley, Priscilla O'Connell, Erik Osnas, Ton Schat, Simon Starkey, Sarah States, Elliot Swarthout, Edan Tulman, and the late Paul Williams, to whose memory we dedicate this chapter.

References

Altizer, S., Davis, A.K., Cook, K.C. & Cherry, J.J. (2004a) Age, sex, and season affect the risk of mycoplasmal conjunctivitis in a southeastern house finch population. *Canadian Journal of Zoology - Revue Canadienne De Zoologie*, **82**, 755–763.

Altizer, S., Dobson, A., Hosseini, P., et al. (2006) Seasonality and the dynamics of infectious diseases. *Ecology Letters*, **9**, 467–484.

Altizer, S., Hochachka, W.M. & Dhondt, A.A. (2004b) Seasonal dynamics of mycoplasmal conjunctivitis in eastern North American house finches. *Journal of Animal Ecology*, **73**, 309–322.

Backstroem, N., Shipilina, D., Blom, M.P.K. & Edwards, S.V. (2013a) *Cis*-regulatory sequence variation and association with *Mycoplasma* load in natural populations of the house finch (*Carpodacus mexicanus*). *Ecology and Evolution*, **3**, 655–666.

Backstroem, N., Zhang, Q. & Edwards, S.V. (2013b) Evidence from a house finch (*Haemorhous mexicanus*) spleen transcriptome for adaptive evolution and biased gene conversion in passerine birds. *Molecular Biology and Evolution*, **30**, 1046–1050.

Bonter, D.N. & Cooper, C.B. (2012) Data validation in citizen science: a case study from Project FeederWatch. *Frontiers in Ecology and the Environment*, **10**, 305–309.

Bouwman, K.M. & Hawley, D.M. (2010) Sickness behaviour acting as an evolutionary trap? Male house finches preferentially feed near diseased conspecifics. *Biology Letters*, **6**, 462–465.

Butcher, G.S., Fuller, M.R., Mcallister, L.S. & Geissler, P.H. (1990) An evaluation of the Christmas bird count for monitoring population trends of selected species. *Wildlife Society Bulletin*, **18**, 129–134.

Conn, P.B. & Cooch, E.G. (2009) Multistate capture–recapture analysis under imperfect state observation: an application to disease models. *Journal of Applied Ecology*, **46**, 486–492.

Cooper, C.B., Hochachka, W.M. & Dhondt, A.A. (2007) Contrasting natural experiments confirm competition between house finches and house sparrows. *Ecology*, **88**, 864–870.

Delaney, N.F., Balenger, S., Bonneaud, C., et al. (2012) Ultrafast evolution and loss of CRISPRs following a host shift in a novel wildlife pathogen, *Mycoplasma gallisepticum*. *PLoS Genetics*, **8**(2), e1002511.

Dhondt, A.A., Altizer, S., Cooch, E.G., et al. (2005) Dynamics of a novel pathogen in an avian host: mycoplasmal conjunctivitis in house finches. *Acta Tropica*, **94**, 77–93.

Dhondt, A.A., Badyaev, A.V., Dobson, A.P., et al. (2006) Dynamics of mycoplasmal conjunctivitis in the native and introduced range of the host. *Ecohealth*, **3**, 95–102.

Dhondt, A.A., Decoste, J.C., Ley, D.H. & Hochachka, W.M. (2014) Diverse wild bird host range of *Mycoplasma gallisepticum* in eastern North America. *PLoS ONE*, **9**(7), e103553.

Dhondt, A.A., Dhondt, K.V., Hawley, D.M. & Jennelle, C.S. (2007a) Experimental evidence for transmission of *Mycoplasma gallisepticum* in house finches by fomites. *Avian Pathology*, **36**, 205–208.

Dhondt, A.A., Dhondt, K.V. & Hochachka, W.M. (2015) Response of black-capped chickadees to house finch *Mycoplasma gallisepticum*. *PLoS ONE*, **10**(4), e0124820.

Dhondt, A.A., Dhondt, K.V., Hochachka, W.M. & Schat, K.A. (2013) Can American goldfinches function as reservoirs for *Mycoplasma gallisepticum*? *Journal of Wildlife Disease*, **49**, 49–54.

Dhondt, A.A., Dhondt, K.V. & McCleery, B.V. (2008) Comparative infectiousness of three passerine bird species after experimental inoculation with *Mycoplasma gallisepticum*. *Avian Pathology*, **37**, 635–640.

Dhondt, A.A., Driscoll, M.J.L. & Swarthout, E.C.
H. (2007b) House finch *Carpodacus
mexicanus* roosting behaviour during the
non-breeding season and possible effects of
mycoplasmal conjunctivitis. *Ibis*, **149**, 1–9.

Dhondt, A.A., States, S.L., Dhondt, K. . & Schat, K.
A. (2012) Understanding the origin of
seasonal epidemics of mycoplasmal
conjunctivitis. *Journal of Animal Ecology*, **81**,
996–1003.

Dhondt, A.A., Tessaglia, D.L. & Slothower, R.L.
(1998) Epidemic mycoplasmal
conjunctivitis in house finches from
Eastern North America. *Journal of Wildlife
Disease*, **34**, 265–280.

Dhondt, K.V., Dhondt, A.A. & Ley, D.H. (2007c)
Effects of route of inoculation on
Mycoplasma gallisepticum infection in
captive house finches. *Avian Pathology*, **36**,
475–479.

Duckworth, R.A., Badyaev, A.V., Farmer, K.L.,
Hill, G.E. & Roberts, S.R. (2003) First case of
Mycoplasma gallisepticum infection in the
western range of the house finch
(*Carpodacus mexicanus*). *Auk*, **120**, 528–530.

Ebert, D. & Herre, E.A. (1996) The evolution of
parasitic diseases. *Parasitology Today*, **12**,
96–101.

Elliott, J. & Arbib Jr, R. (1953) Origin and status of
the house finch in the eastern United
States. *Auk*, **70**, 31–37.

Faustino, C.R., Jennelle, C.S., Connolly, V., et al.
(2004) *Mycoplasma gallisepticum* infection
dynamics in a house finch population:
seasonal variation in survival, encounter
and transmission rate. *Journal of Animal
Ecology*, **73**, 651–669.

Ferguson, N.A., Hermes, D., Leiting, V.A. &
Kleven, S.H. (2003) Characterization of
a naturally occurring infection of
a *Mycoplasma gallisepticum* house finch-like
strain in turkey breeders. *Avian Diseases*, **47**,
523–530.

Fischer, J.R., Stallknecht, D.E., Luttrell, M.P.,
Dhondt, A.A. & Converse, K.A. (1997)
Mycoplasmal conjunctivitis in wild
songbirds: the spread of a new contagious
disease in a mobile host population.
Emerging Infectious Diseases, **3**, 69–72.

Hartup, B.K., Bickal, J.M., Dhondt, A.A., Ley, D.H.
& Kollias, G.V. (2001a) Dynamics of

conjunctivitis and *Mycoplasma gallisepticum*
infections in house finches. *Auk*, **118**,
327–333.

Hartup, B.K., Dhondt, A.A., Sydenstricker, K.V.,
Hochachka, W.M. & Kollias, G.V. (2001b)
Host range and dynamics of mycoplasmal
conjunctivitis among birds in North
America. *Journal of Wildlife Disease*, **37**, 72–81.

Hartup, B.K. & Kollias, G.V. (1999) Field
investigation of *Mycoplasma gallisepticum*
infections in house finch (*Carpodacus
mexicanus*) eggs and nestlings. *Avian
Diseases*, **43**, 572–576.

Hawley, D.M., Briggs, J., Dhondt, A.A. &
Lovette, I.J. (2008) Reconciling molecular
signatures across markers: mitochondrial
DNA confirms founder effect in invasive
North American house finches (*Carpodacus
mexicanus*). *Conservation Genetics*, **9**, 637–643.

Hawley, D.M., Davis, A.K. & Dhondt, A.A. (2007)
Transmission-relevant behaviours shift
with pathogen infection in wild house
finches (*Carpodacus mexicanus*). *Canadian
Journal of Zoology – Revue Canadienne De
Zoologie*, **85**, 752–757.

Hawley, D.M., Dhondt, K.V., Dobson, A.P., et al.
(2010) Common garden experiment
reveals pathogen isolate but no host
genetic diversity effect on the dynamics of
an emerging wildlife disease. *Journal of
Evolutionary Biology*, **23**, 1680–1688.

Hawley, D.M., Hanley, D., Dhondt, A.A. &
Lovette, I.J. (2006) Molecular evidence for
a founder effect in invasive house finch
(*Carpodacus mexicanus*) populations
experiencing an emergent disease
epidemic. *Molecular Ecology*, **15**, 263–275.

Hawley, D.M., Osnas, E.E., Dobson, A.P., et al.
(2013) Parallel patterns of increased
virulence in a recently emerged wildlife
pathogen. *PLoS Biology*, **11**(5), e1001570.

Hengeveld, H. 1989. *Dynamics of Biological
Invasions.*, London: Chapman and Hall.

Hill, G.E., Badyaev, A.V. & Belloni, V. (2012)
House finch (*Haemorhous mexicanus*). In
Rodewald, P.G. (ed.), *The Birds of North
America*. Ithaca, NY:Cornell Laboratory of
Ornithology.

Hochachka, W.M. & Dhondt, A.A. (2000)
Density-dependent decline of host
abundance resulting from a new infectious

disease. *Proceedings of the National Academy of Sciences of the United States of America*, **97**, 5303–5306.

Hochachka, W.M. & Dhondt, A.A. (2006) House finch (*Carpodacus mexicanus*) population- and group-level responses to a bacterial disease. *Ornithological Monographs*, **60**(1), 30–43.

Hochachka, W.M., Dhondt, A.A., Dobson, A., et al. (2013) Multiple host transfers, but only one successful lineage in a continent-spanning emergent pathogen. *Proceedings of the Royal Society of London B*, **280**(1766).

Hochberg, M.E. & Holt, R.D. (1990) The coexistence of competing parasites. 1. The role of cross-species infection. *American Naturalist*, **136**, 517–541.

Holt, R.D., Dobson, A.P., Begon, M., Bowers, R.G. & Schauber, E.M. (2003) Parasite establishment in host communities. *Ecology Letters*, **6**, 837–842.

Hosseini, P.R., Dhondt, A.A. & Dobson, A. (2004) Seasonality and wildlife disease: how seasonal birth, aggregation and variation in immunity affect the dynamics of *Mycoplasma gallisepticum* in house finches. *Proceedings of the Royal Society of London B*, **271**, 2569–2577.

Hosseini, P.R., Dhondt, A.A. & Dobson, A.P. (2006) Spatial spread of an emerging infectious disease: conjunctivitis in house finches. *Ecology*, **87**, 3037–3046.

Jennelle, C.S., Cooch, E.G., Conroy, M.J. & Senar, J.C. (2007) State-specific detection probabilities and disease prevalence. *Ecological Applications*, **17**, 154–167.

Levisohn, S. & Kleven, S.H. (2000) Avian mycoplasmosis (*Mycoplasma gallisepticum*). *Revue Scientifique et Technique de l'Office International des Epizooties*, **19**, 425–442.

Ley, D.H., Berkhoff, J.E. & Mclaren, J.M. (1996) *Mycoplasma gallisepticum* isolated from house finches (*Carpodacus mexicanus*) with conjunctivitis. *Avian Diseases*, **40**, 480–483.

Ley, D.H., Hawley, D.M., Geary, S.J. & Dhondt, A. A. (2016) House finch (*Haemorhous mexicanus*) conjunctivitis, and *Mycoplasma* spp. isolated from North American wild birds, 1994–2015. *Journal of Wildlife Diseases*, **52**, 669–673.

Ley, D.H., Sheaffer, D.S. & Dhondt, A.A. 2006. Further western spread of *Mycoplasma gallisepticum* infection of house finches. *Journal of Wildlife Diseases*, **42**, 429–431.

Murray, J.D. (1993) *Mathematical Biology*. Second corrected edition. Berlin: Springer-Verlag.

Newton, I. (1972). *Finches*. London: Collins.

Osnas, E.E. & Dobson, A.P. (2010) Evolution of virulence when transmission occurs before disease. *Biology Letters*, **6**, 505–508.

Osnas, E.E. & Dobson, A.P. (2012) Evolution of virulence in heterogeneous host communities under multiple trade-offs. *Evolution*, **66**, 391–401.

Osnas, E.E., Hurtado, P.J. & Dobson, A.P. (2015) Evolution of pathogen virulence across space during an epidemic. *American Naturalist*, **185**, 332–342.

Pflaum, K., Tulman, E.R., Beaudet, J., Liao, X. & Geary, S.J. (2016) Global changes in *Mycoplasma gallisepticum* phase-variable lipoprotein gene *vlhA* expression during in vivo infection of the natural chicken host. *Infection and Immunity*, **84**, 351–355.

Potapov, A., Merrill, E., Pybus, M., Coltman, D. & Lewis, M.A. (2013) Chronic wasting disease: possible transmission mechanisms in deer. *Ecological Modelling*, **250**, 244–257.

Roberts, S.R., Nolan, P.M., Lauerman, L.H., Li, L. Q. & Hill, G.E. (2001) Characterization of the mycoplasmal conjunctivitis epizootic in a house finch population in the southeastern USA. *Journal of Wildlife Diseases*, **37**, 82–88.

Sauer, J.R., Fallon, J.E. & Johnson, R. (2003) Use of North American Breeding Bird Survey data to estimate population change for bird conservation regions. *Journal of Wildlife Management*, **67**, 372–389.

Shubber, Z., Mishra, S., Vesga, J.F. & Boily, M.C. (2014) The HIV Modes of Transmission model: a systematic review of its findings and adherence to guidelines. *Journal of the International Aids Society*, **17**(1), 18928.

States, S.L., Hochachka, W.M. & Dhondt, A.A. (2009) Spatial variation in an avian host community: implications for disease dynamics. *Ecohealth*, **6**, 540–545.

Sydenstricker, K.V., Dhondt, A.A., Ley, D.H. & Kollias, G.V. (2005) Re-exposure of captive house finches that recovered from

Mycoplasma gallisepticum infection. *Journal of Wildlife Diseases*, **41**, 326–333.

Tulman, E.R., Liao, X., Szczepanek, S.M., et al. (2012) Extensive variation in surface lipoprotein gene content and genomic changes associated with virulence during evolution of a novel North American house finch epizootic strain of *Mycoplasma gallisepticum*. *Microbiology*, **158**, 2073–2088.

Williams, P.D., Dobson, A.P., Dhondt, K.V., Hawley, D.M. & Dhondt, A.A. (2014) Evidence of trade-offs shaping virulence evolution in an emerging wildlife pathogen. *Journal of Evolutionary Biology*, **27**, 1271–1278.

Woolhouse, M.E.J., Haydon, D.T. & Antia, R. (2005) Emerging pathogens: the epidemiology and evolution of species jumps. *Trends in Ecology & Evolution*, **20**, 238–244.

CHAPTER TWENTY-ONE

Processes generating heterogeneities in infection and transmission in a parasite–rabbit system

ISABELLA M. CATTADORI, ASHUTOSH
PATHAK AND BRIAN BOAG

21.1 Introduction

Understanding how host heterogeneities to infection are generated and how they influence the dynamics and spread of infectious diseases remains a challenging issue in disease ecology and evolution. Host–parasite interactions play an essential role in shaping host variation to infections. On one hand, the degree of susceptibility and immunocompetence determines how good a host is in preventing or controlling an infection; on the other hand, the level of virulence and ability to transmit describes how accomplished a parasite is in avoiding the host constraints. All else being equal, we should expect some variation in the host population as part of these inherent, often genetically driven, properties of the two parties. However, individual hosts do age, reproduce, adjust their behaviour or microbiota with time and, in so doing, generate additional sources of variation that can affect host–parasite interactions. A large body of work has examined the contribution of these hosts' characteristics and the general conclusion is that they often modulate host responses and disease outcome in a non-linear manner, adding a further level of complexity to the system (Anderson & Gordon, 1982; Hayes et al., 2010; Cizauskas et al., 2015; Izhar & Ben-Ami, 2015). In natural settings host populations are also exposed to external perturbations, such as changes in climate, infections with other parasite species, or anthropogenic disturbance (Figure 21.1). These perturbations can exacerbate or mitigate the way the host's characteristics affect the parasite as well as directly altering parasite dynamics and traits, such as fecundity, and lead to further variation in infection and transmission among hosts.

A challenge in the ecology of infectious diseases is to disentangle the contribution of these sources of variation, specifically, to understand how external perturbations interact with the hosts' properties to affect parasite dynamics and life history, and the consequences over time and space. A powerful approach is to integrate long-term field studies of natural

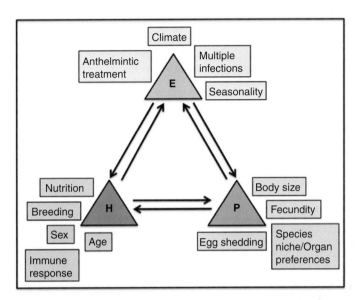

Figure 21.1 Diagram showing the interactions among hosts (H), parasites (P), and environment (E). For each of the three variables we have reported the components that have been considered in the rabbit system and that can contribute to generate host heterogeneity to infection and transmission in this system. Only the impact of external disturbance (e.g. climate changes, drug treatment, and multiple infections) has been addressed in this chapter, although other components have been implicitly included (e.g. host age, immune response, seasonality).

populations with detailed laboratory manipulations; the latter allowing insights into within-host processes while controlling for confounding effects of inherent variation in host exposure or susceptibility commonly found in the field. The rabbit–helminth system (Figure 21.2) has proved to be particularly suitable in that we have detailed historical data on the parasites and the host from wild populations, and have performed laboratory experiments to characterise the fundamental components and responses over the course of the infection.

We take an ecological approach to the study of the rabbit–parasite system and explore how external perturbations alter the trophic relationship between the host and its parasites and contribute to heterogeneity in infection and transmission. We synthesise findings on the role of three disturbances: (i) seasonality and climate changes, (ii) coinfection with a second parasite species, and (iii) anthelmintic treatments. We then outline parsimonious mechanisms, based on mathematical models and analytical approaches, which explain the patterns observed. Findings from this system have far-reaching repercussions for a wide range of ecological and health issues, and inform a variety of host–parasite systems of wildlife, agricultural animals and humans, where experiments and long-term

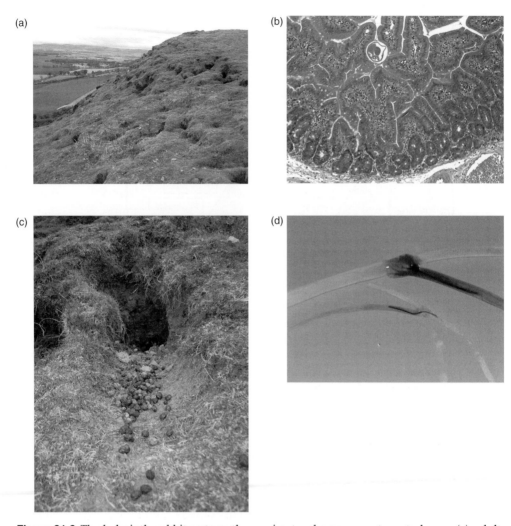

Figure 21.2 The helminth–rabbit system: the semi-natural agro-ecosystem study area (a); adults of *G. strigosum* in the stomach (b); warren entrance and rabbit faeces (c); *G. strigosum* male and female mating (d). (A black and white version of this figure will appear in some formats. For the colour version, please refer to the plate section.)

data are often difficult to conduct or obtain. In this context, we provide future directions, such as how an integrated knowledge of the mechanisms of infection and spread is necessary if we are to understand processes and patterns of parasite dynamics in natural settings.

21.2 The system

The European rabbit (*Oryctolagus cuniculus*) is native to south-west Europe and north-west Africa, but over the centuries has been widely introduced in many other countries worldwide. Animals construct interconnected burrows where they live in families; dominant males are polygamous, females can also be dominant and, like males, defend their territory. Juvenile males disperse in spring while juvenile females tend to stay with the family. Based on the location and population density, reproduction can be restricted to a few months or occur for most of the year (Thompson & King, 1994; Hoffman & Smith, 2005). Because of the damage caused to biodiversity and farming, the European rabbit is often considered a pest that needs to be controlled.

We have detailed monthly data on hosts and parasites from two rabbit populations sampled in a semi-natural ecosystem at the interface with arable land in Scotland (UK): the first population was monitored from 1977 to 2002 and the second from 2000 to 2014. Both populations were sampled using standar-dised protocols and details are available on the host (e.g. age, sex, breeding status) and its common infections (e.g. parasite species, prevalence and/or intensity). For the second population we also collected host blood sera and helminth biometrics (e.g. body length and eggs in utero). Details on daily climatic variables were also recorded. The laboratory experiments were per-formed using the New Zealand white rabbit, a common breed of the European rabbit, commercially available from research suppliers. Parasites for the labora-tory work were isolated from our study sites (*Graphidium strigosum*) or kindly provided by Dr Kerboeuf (INRA, France, *Trichostrongylus retortaeformis*) and Dr Harvill (University of Georgia–Athens, USA, *Bordetella bronchiseptica*).

Our work primarily focused on three main parasites, two helminths and one bacterium. *Trichostrongylus retortaeformis* and *Graphidium strigosum* are gastro-intestinal helminths that commonly infect the European rabbit. *T. retortaeformis* has a relatively small body size and lower per-capita fecundity than *G. strigosum* (Audebert et al., 2000; Massoni et al., 2011). Infections occur via ingestion of herbage contaminated with third-stage infective larvae; *T. retortaeformis* colonises the small intestine with a preference for the duode-num while *G. strigosum* inhabits the stomach, primarily the fundic region (Murphy et al., 2011). Sexual maturation is much faster for *T. retortaeformis* than *G. strigosum* and after reproduction eggs are shed into the environment with the rabbit's faeces (pre-patency: ~11 and 40 days, respectively). Free-living stages are exposed to the same environmental drivers such as climate and biotic factors. Both helminths have a long history of coevolution with the rabbit (Audebert & Durette-Desset, 2007) and although causing chronic and recurring infections, they exhibit distinct ecological properties (details provided in the next section) that make them an excellent model for exploring trophic interac-tions both within and between hosts. Moreover, the system has many simila-rities (e.g. mode of transmission, life cycle, or type of immune reaction) with communities of gastrointestinal helminths of agricultural animals, wildlife, and humans, and provides fundamental insights on disease ecology across taxa.

The respiratory bacterium *Bordetella bronchiseptica* has been isolated from the respiratory tract of many wild mammal species including rabbits and causes regular outbreaks and chronic infections in domesticated animals kept in crowded conditions (Pathak et al., 2011). By 90 days post initial infection, *B. bronchiseptica* is cleared from the lungs and trachea of laboratory rabbits by an effective immune response but persists in the nasal cavity (Pathak et al., 2010; Thakar et al., 2012). *B. bronchiseptica* is closely related to the human subspecies *B. pertussis* and *B. parapertussis*, responsible for whooping cough outbreaks and notably re-emergent in the USA (Jackson & Rohani, 2014). Given the similar properties and mode of transmission, *B. bronchiseptica* is an invaluable model for studying the dynamics and transmission of whooping cough and, more generally, respiratory bacterial infections of livestock concern (Brogden et al., 1998; Kao et al., 2007).

21.3 Fundamental host–parasite processes

Given that host responses to infections and parasite reactions to host constraints are often highly heterogeneous, it is not surprising that within any host population there is large variation in the intensity of infection among individuals. This intrinsic variation of the host is determined by changes in susceptibility and resistance, namely the ability to control the infection and reinfections, alongside differences in exposure to infective stages (Anderson & May, 1978). For parasitic helminths, resistance commonly engages a 'type 2' immune reaction by the host, with functions and factors that can take weeks or years to reach full effectiveness (Jackson et al., 2009; Yazdanbakhsh & Sacks, 2010). This partly explains the persistence of parasitic infections and the lack or weak life-long protection against reinfections often observed. Parasite immunology has been well described theoretically and experimentally (e.g. Stear et al., 1999; Anthony et al., 2007; Allen & Maizels, 2011), including the defensive properties from hosts with different genotypes or immunocompetence (e.g. Raberg et al., 2007; Stear et al., 2009; McRae et al., 2015), the consequences to the epidemiology of infection and the evolution of resistance (e.g. Bowers, 1999; Restif & Koella, 2004; James et al., 2009), and more recently the molecular and evolutionary outcomes of tolerance to infections (Roy & Kirchner, 2000; Miller et al., 2005; Allen & Sutherland, 2014). From an epidemiological perspective, the extent of the protective immune response to helminths is proportional to the accumulated exposure to infective stages, in addition to the immune status of the host at the time of the infection and the properties of the parasite.

We have characterised the immune response of the rabbit to *T. retortaeformis* and *G. strigosum* from laboratory trials and a wild rabbit population, and below provide some general insights that can guide understanding of the dynamics of infection of our system under perturbations. Laboratory experiments were based on rabbits challenged with a single dose or trickle-dosed every week (the total amount of infective stages delivered was the same in the two types of trials); animals were sampled at fixed time points and samples from the small intestine, duodenum, and the stomach fundus (tissue and mucus), as well as blood sera, were used for the analyses. The wild rabbit population was randomly sampled every month and the gastrointestinal tract and blood were collected from every individual for parasitological and immunological work. Three branches of the immune response and associated factors were examined: (i) the type 2 anti-inflammatory response, commonly involved in the removal/control of parasitic helminths; (ii) the type 1 inflammatory reaction, a critical player in protecting against microparasites (viruses, bacteria); and (iii) the regulatory response implicated in tissue repair/regeneration and tolerance to infection (Allen & Sutherland, 2014; McRae et al., 2015). It is important to remember that the same factor might have different functions, including activities specific to different branches of the immune system, depending on the local polarisation of the immune response and the macro-/microparasite involved. Likewise, it has been proposed that the protective type 2 response to macro parasites is also involved in tissue repair and regeneration (Allen & Sutherland, 2014).

For the rabbit–helminth system, we found that *T. retortaeformis* is reduced during the course of the infection, and the pattern is consistent in field and laboratory settings. *T. retortaeformis* stimulates a type 1–type 2 immune response (i.e. inflammatory and anti-inflammatory activities) in that an initially high IFNγ gene expression wanes during the course of the infection to values that are comparable to IL4 and IL10 (Murphy et al., 2011; Thakar et al., 2012). The initial IFNγ inflammatory response is probably caused by local bacterial infiltration into the small intestinal mucosa damaged by the parasites moving into the tissue during colonisation and development (Murphy et al., 2011; Van Kuren et al., 2013). The anti-inflammatory IL4 plays an important role in the clearance of this helminth (Thakar et al., 2012), while IL10 is an anti-inflammatory cytokine that downregulates the IFNγ expression while also contributing to regulatory functions and tolerance (Redpath et al., 2014). We have also quantified the expression of other cytokines and transcription factors and while they were clearly upregulated, values were relatively low except for the anti-inflammatory IL13, which is also important for parasite clearance (Cattadori et al., 2019). The modelling of the immuno-dynamic network of infection, using a discrete Boolean framework, showed that the activation of an anti-inflammatory type 2 response, namely, the relatively rapid recruitment of antibodies (IgA and IgG) together with eosinophils, was responsible for the control but not the complete removal of *T. retortaeformis* from the small intestine (Thakar et al., 2012). The IgA and IgG trends recoded in the laboratory were also observed in the wild rabbits (Cattadori et al., 2014).

Similar studies were performed for *G. strigosum* infections. We found that parasites persist in the stomach with no strong evidence of immune control despite a clear 'type 2' response (Murphy et al., 2011, 2013; Pathak et al., 2012). IL4 and IL13 remain proportionally high through the course of infection, with lower expression of the inflammatory IFNγ and Tbet, and the anti-inflammatory GATA3 and IL10; the remaining immune factors exhibited relatively low values (Cattadori et al., 2019). The movements of *G. strigosum* into the stomach mucosa, both by the establishing larvae and adult worms (Van Kuren et al., 2013), caused tissue damage and local recruitment of immune cells (Murphy et al., 2011). However, and contrary to *T. retortaeformis*, the inflammatory response (i.e. IFNγ and Tbet) did not exceed the defensive anti-inflammatory reaction (i.e. IL4, IL13, and GATA3), probably to prevent immuno-pathology in an environment that is chemically and physiologically relatively extreme. Despite the defensive profile by cytokines and transcription factors, we found consistently low levels of species-specific and total IgA antibody in the stomach mucus (Murphy et al., 2011; Cattadori et al., 2018), supporting the hypothesis that some of the cell-mediated defences against the parasite are relatively weak. However, it should be noted that given the properties of the stomach, it is possible that the protective effectors are down-regulated by the host while it also attempts to repair/regenerate the tissue damaged by the infection (Cattadori et al., 2019). Another possibility is that *G. strigosum* contributes to its own persistence by manipulating or circumventing host immunity. As noted for *T. retortaeformis*, the IgA and IgG responses of wild rabbits against *G. strigosum* were similar to laboratory animals. Overall, whether these studies were from experimental trials or field observations, there was always heterogeneity in the immune response to the infection among rabbits.

At the host population level, a convex relationship between host age and parasite intensity where intensity increases, peaks and then decreases in older individuals, should be indicative of a defensive immune response, which develops proportionately to the force of infection (i.e. rate of accumulated parasite acquisition) and controls the parasite in older hosts (Anderson & May, 1978; Woolhouse, 1992). A convex profile can also be generated by changes in the host and/or parasite properties for instance, differences in the intensity of infection among host of diverse age- or parasite-induced host mortality (Cattadori et al., 2005). On the contrary, the regular accumulation of parasites with host age should be indicative of a weak or no immune control, including parasite manipulation of host defences. Here, parasite dynamics should be driven by ecological processes, such as competition for resources that builds proportionally to parasite intensity. The age–intensity relationship has been widely used in epidemiology to provide fundamental understanding to the processes affecting disease dynamics (Hudson & Dobson, 1989; Woolhouse,

1992; Duerr et al., 2003), including the emergence of host heterogeneity to infection (Lloyd-Smith et al., 2005), and the identification of the individual hosts responsible for the majority of the infection and transmission (Grenfell & Anderson, 1989).

The contrasting immuno-dynamics described for *T. retortaeformis* and *G. strigosum* were confirmed when we applied the age–intensity relationship to rabbit populations. We showed that *T. retortaeformis* infection follows a convex age–intensity profile while *G. strigosum* exponentially accumulates with host age (Cattadori et al., 2005, 2008, 2014; Pathak et al., 2012). To explain these patterns mechanistically, we developed epidemiological models based on an age-structured rabbit population that included the relative contribution of host immune defences and intensity-dependent parasite constraints. Simulations were consistent with these general trends, specifically, *T. retortaeformis* is regulated by an immune response that develops proportionately to the accumulated force of infection, as well as the degree of host immunocompetence (i.e. the ability to develop a successful immune reaction), and is controlled in older rabbits (Cornell et al., 2008; Mignatti et al., 2016). In contrast, *G. strigosum* is mainly regulated by direct intensity-dependent processes, most likely parasite competition for space and food, which build with the accumulated intensity of infection (Mignatti et al., 2016).

In summary, distinctive organ properties and immune functions, combined with the specificity of parasite attributes and host characteristics, create well-defined host–parasite relationships that generate heterogeneities in the responses of both parties and ultimately affect the dynamics of infection. However, external perturbations are expected to alter these relationships, raising the question of whether disturbances enhance or suppress individual variation to infection, and whether the impact affects more heavily some hosts than others. In the following sections we shall examine and discuss the contribution of three different types of perturbations on parasite dynamics: (i) the impact of seasonality and long-term climate changes; (ii) the role of co-infection with a second parasite (either a helminth or a bacterium); and (iii) the effect of anthelmintic treatments.

21.3.1 Climate and seasonality

Most of the predictive models and experimental manipulations investigating climate changes and infectious diseases have overlooked the modulatory contribution of the host on climate impact. Studies have primarily focused on how climate changes can affect host exposure, the risk of infection or disease spread, and the emergence of novel infectious agents (e.g. Molnár et al., 2013; Raffel et al., 2013; Paull & Johnson, 2014). However, as highlighted by our work (Cattadori et al., 2005, 2014, 2018; Murphy et al., 2011, 2013; Thakar et al., 2012) and others (Maizels, 2009; Bourke et al., 2011; Girgis et al., 2013), host immunity to infections is an important source of variation among individuals; hence how immunity alters the way climate affects host–parasite interactions needs to be accounted for. Indeed, we might expect different outcomes driven by both the type of interaction and the scale at which these processes are examined. Here we investigate (i) whether an increase in exposure to parasites, caused by climate warming, is associated with a proportional increase in the intensity of infection in hosts with protective immunity, and (ii) how this pattern contrasts if hosts fail to show an effective immune response. In other words, we explore if heterogeneities in the immune response to a parasite exacerbate or suppress the effect that climate changes have on the dynamics of infection.

If parasites are modulated by host immunity then we should expect weak or no long-term changes in the intensity of infection with warming because immunity controls the parasite burden in the host population (Figure 21.3a). At the seasonal scale, however, climate warming is expected to shift the peak of infection towards the younger, less-competent hosts, and increase the variation in infection between individuals (Figure 21.4a). This seasonal change in the host age–parasite intensity relationship caused by climate warming is based on the 'peak shift' concept (Anderson & May, 1978; Woolhouse, 1998). Briefly, this concept assesses the interaction between the force of infection (i.e. parasite acquisition) and the host immune response, and suggests that a high force of infection stimulates a faster immune response that leads to parasite intensities peaking at earlier host age compared to a lower force of infection that results in a lower parasite burden that peaks in older hosts because of an immune response that develops more slowly. The 'peak shift' concept has been empirically described by us and others (Woolhouse, 1998; Cattadori et al., 2005; Blackwell et al., 2011). Here we suggest that this pattern can be exacerbated by the interaction between climate warming and host immunity, specifically, by increasing the force of infection warming can further shift the peak of infection toward the even younger hosts (Figure 21.4a). In contrast, if the parasite is weakly controlled by immunity then it should accumulate with host age and constrained by its own density (Figures 21.2b and 21.3b).

We tested the long-term and seasonal impact of climate warming on our soil-transmitted gastrointestinal helminths, *T. retortaeformis* and *G. strigosum*, from the rabbit population sampled monthly between 1977 and 2002 in Scotland. At this latitude, seasonality regulates the life cycle of the host and the parasites (Cattadori et al., 2005, 2008); more recently, the system has also been under the influence of temperature warming (Harvell et al., 2009; Hernandez et al., 2013) and increasing air relative humidity (Mignatti et al., 2016). As previously described, we also know that the two parasites exhibit contrasting dynamics of infection and distinctive response to host immunity. We developed an age-structured epidemiological model that explicitly

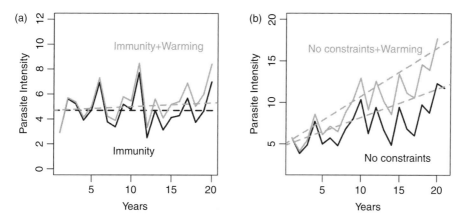

Figure 21.3 Hypothetical scenarios of mean parasite infection in a host population over years with (upper line) and without (lower line) climate warming, and (a) in the presence and (b) absence of immune control.

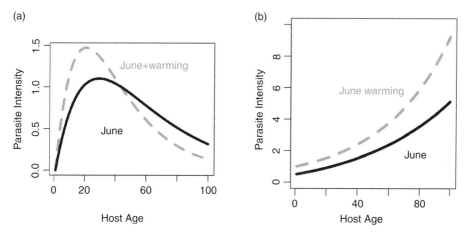

Figure 21.4 Hypothetical scenarios of mean parasite infection by host age in a host population from a month with (dotted line) and without (solid line) climate warming, and in the presence (a) and absence (b) of immune control.

accounted for the daily temperature and humidity available from the study site, and included the regulatory effects of host immunity and parasite density-dependence. Model simulations indicate that *T. retortaeformis* dynamics are affected by host immunity and the linear positive effect of mean air temperature on free-living stages, consistent with our experimental manipulations (Murphy et al., 2011; Hernandez et al., 2013). In the long term, the mean intensity of infection remains relatively constant in the rabbit population as immunity controls the annual accumulation of parasites (Mignatti et al., 2016). In contrast, *G. strigosum* dynamics are constrained mainly by intensity-dependent ecological forces (i.e. competition for resources) and the linear positive impact of relative humidity on free-living stages. Over the years, *G. strigosum* mean intensity accumulates in the host population proportionately to the force of infection, although within-host parasite regulation and mortality of free-living stages prevent the parasite population from growing exponentially (Mignatti et al., 2016). Overall, these trends are consistent with a scenario where immunity suppresses the long-term positive effect of climate warming on the parasite population (the example of *T. retortaeformis*) (Figure 21.3a), which is observed if immunity has a weak impact on parasite regulation (the example of *G. strigosum*; Figure 21.3b). In other words, over the years, while climate warming increases the survival of free-living stages of both parasites on the pasture and thus, the force of infection, immunity, and to a significantly lesser extent parasite density-dependence, keeps the mean parasite burden and the associated shedding rate under control in the rabbit population.

We also investigated these patterns seasonally, by examining how changes in the host age–parasite intensity relationship were influenced by monthly changes in climate. Simulations were combined and compared between the 'cold' (1980–1989) and the most recent 'warm' (1993–2002) decade recorded in the study site (Hernandez et al., 2013). We showed that for *T. retortaeformis* an increase in the monthly temperature, from the cold to the warm decade, significantly shifted the peak of infection towards the younger hosts for the June and July rabbit cohorts (Mignatti et al., 2016). In other words, in the warmer decade rabbits born in July and June were exposed to a higher force of infection, and parasite accumulated even faster in the younger animals than rabbits of the same age-cohort from the colder period (Figure 21.4a). This faster accumulation means that the peak of infection was reached at younger age in the warmer than colder decade and supports the postulated effect of climate warming on the monthly shift in infection and transmission of *T. retortaeformis*. For *G. strigosum* we found no support for immune-driven changes in the age–intensity relationship among months, consistent with the lack or weak immune regulation of this parasite. *G. strigosum* accumulates with host age and adults consistently carry most of the infection; moreover, higher infections were observed in the summer months and hosts became infected at a faster rate in the warmer and more humid decade (Mignatti et al., 2016). These findings indicate that climate warming increases *G. strigosum* transmission and infection both within and between years, with adults carrying most of the burden (Figures 21.2b and 21.3b).

This work highlighted three main outcomes of the role of climate on the study system. First, intensity-dependence generated through host immunity is more effective in buffering the impact of climate warming on *T. retortaeformis* than is the intensity-dependence in population processes to *G. strigosum*. Indeed, although not fully effective and life-long protecting, immunity keeps *T. retortaeformis* mean infection relatively constant over the years, while the ecological processes of regulation of *G. strigosum* do not. Second, under climate warming monthly changes in the relationship between climate and host immune response to the infection increase parasite burden in younger rabbits, and amplify the variation in infection among individuals. Specifically, warmer conditions increase the survival of free-living stages, which then infect younger and less-immune-protected hosts with higher numbers. This is particularly important because it suggests that younger hosts with lower immunocompetence are at higher risk of infection with climate warming. Third, parasite species that stimulate a weak or no host immune reaction are more greatly influenced by climate changes and, as a result, hosts suffer higher infections across all age groups as conditions get warmer.

These general conclusions can be extended to other host–parasite systems, particularly involving soil-transmitted parasites, where host immunity can mitigate the impact of climate on infection and transmission. This also warrants attention when designing and predicting the success of anthelmintic treatments. Indeed, under climate warming and some level of host resistance, even more consideration should be given to reducing the infection of younger hosts.

21.3.2 Coinfection

The presence of one parasite can increase host susceptibility to a second parasite species, but can also trigger the pathogenicity of a parasite already present that would otherwise cause minor or no disease (Brady et al., 1999; Hudson et al., 2008). Moreover, by impairing the immuno-physiological functions of the host, coinfections can augment among-host variation in infection and shedding, and increase the likelihood of super shedding and/or super-spreading individuals (i.e. hosts that disproportionately shed a large number of parasites or infect secondary hosts) (Lloyd-Smith et al., 2005; Garske & Rhodes, 2008). Hence, the biology of infection is determined both by the nature and status of the primary infection, and the history of current and past coinfections.

Using a theoretical approach where we simulated changes in transmission (or invasion) of parasite species A, by varying the prevalence of parasite species B as well as host susceptibility, we showed that one parasite could potentially facilitate the transmission of a second parasite species, or the invasion by a novel agent, if there is a positive covariation between infectiousness (i.e. ability of an infectious host to infect naïve individuals) and susceptibility (Graham et al., 2007). The extreme of this scenario is where highly coinfected individuals can lead to super shedding and/or super spreading events. These 'super-cases' have been identified in a growing number of studies of single infections, and are proposed to influence epidemic outbreaks and transmission (Lloyd-Smith et al., 2005; Chase-Topping et al., 2008). However, whether 'super-cases' generated from single or coinfections are responsible for the majority of disease spread remains contentious (e.g. Kao et al., 2007; Pathak et al., 2010; Lass et al., 2013). This is particularly problematic for parasitic helminths because fecundity and shedding could be negatively related to, or exhibit non-linear relationships with, the intensity of infection (Keymer, 1982; Quinnell et al., 1990; Tompkins & Hudson, 1999; Figure 21.5). Coinfections can modify these relationships by altering host responses and parasite traits to the point that we cannot predict the infection–transmission relationship based on the intensity of infection, or by examining these associations in single-infected individuals (Thakar et al., 2012). Tentatively, we suggest that coinfections are expected to modify the infection–fecundity–shedding relationship in parasites that are immune-regulated or in direct competition for resources.

We investigated patterns of infection and shedding in single and dual infections with our two gastrointestinal helminths, *T. retortaeformis* and *G. strigosum*, from our rabbit population sampled monthly from 2000 to 2014 in Scotland (Cattadori et al., 2014). We also report on patterns of infections from laboratory experiments (Murphy et al., 2011, 2013). Our general prediction is that coinfection with the second parasite can increase host heterogeneity in the burden of the focal parasite but can also generate non-linearities between infection and shedding such that the degree of variation in infection

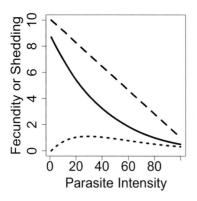

Figure 21.5 Examples of three potential relationships between parasite fecundity (or parasite egg shedding) and intensity of infection in helminths.

might not match the degree of variation in shedding. Field studies showed that compared to single-infected rabbits, coinfected hosts carried higher *T. retortaeformis* intensities, but those worms were shorter and females had fewer eggs in utero (Cattadori et al., 2014). Further investigations showed that the number of eggs in utero increased with parasite intensity in dual-infected but not in single-infected animals, and this was not caused by longer females but eggs that appeared to be produced at a faster rate by females of similar length. We also showed that for every rabbit both potential shedding (the total number of eggs in utero by the population of infecting females) and real shedding (the number of eggs in host's faeces) were comparable between single- and coinfected hosts. Therefore, for *T. retortaeformis*, single- and co-infected rabbits carried different parasite loads but shed a similar amount of eggs. This indicates that the intensity of infection cannot be considered a robust predictor of shedding for helminth coinfections, and that we cannot rely on single infections to predict patterns of infection and shedding in coinfections (Cattadori et al., 2014). Moreover, given the relatively lower para-site fecundity, and despite a positive fecundity–infection relationship, the probability that coinfected rabbits could become supershedders for this hel-minth appears relatively weak. This general trend is also highlighted when examining the host age–parasite intensity (or shedding) relationship. Indeed, while there are heterogeneities both in the intensity of infection and shedding among rabbits of different age classes, only intensity of infection was signifi-cantly different between single and coinfections, once host age was taken into account. This further supports the mismatch between infection and shedding, where the rabbits that carry the majority of the infection are not necessarily the ones that shed the most or can lead to supershedding events.

In the laboratory, rabbits were infected with a single dose of one or both helminths, and then sampled at fixed time. Findings showed that *T. retortaeformis* intensities decreased through the course of the trial and were comparable between single and dual infection (Murphy et al., 2013). The lack of a significant difference in the parasite burden between trials was partly caused by variation in the intensity of infection among rabbits both within and between sampling points. Compared to the natural settings and considering that the laboratory doses were estimated from natural infections, it is highly possible that host and environmental dissimilarities (i.e. age, sex, month of sampling, breeding status), besides differences in exposure, might have contributed to the disparities between laboratory and natural findings.

A similar exercise was performed for *G. strigosum*. In the field and compared to single-infected hosts, dual-infected rabbits harboured fewer *G. strigosum* but parasites were longer and females carried more eggs. Both the number of eggs in utero and female parasite body length were negatively related to intensity of infection and this trend was consistent in single- and coinfected animals

(Cattadori et al., 2014). Potential shedding (eggs in utero) and actual shedding (eggs in faeces) increased with the intensity of infection, and this was more pronounced in dual- than single-infected rabbits. Overall, we found that higher numbers of eggs shed in faeces were associated with lower intensities of infection in dual-infected rabbits. This is consistent with our previous observation that there is a discrepancy between intensity of infection and egg shedding, indicating that this pattern holds true also for helminths that are under a weak or no immune control, like *G. strigosum*. This trend was further confirmed when host age was taken into account; specifically, shedding, but not intensity of infection, was comparable among rabbits of the same age from single and dual infection (Cattadori et al., 2014). Therefore, and consistent with *T. retortaeformis*, these results support the hypothesis that we cannot predict shedding based on parasite burden and, as a corollary of this, there is a low probability that rabbits can become supershedders of *G. strigosum*.

In the laboratory, we found that dual-infected rabbits carried higher *G. strigosum* infections than single-infected hosts (Murphy et al., 2013), which is in contrast with field observations (Cattadori et al., 2014). As suggested for *T. retortaeformis*, the discrepancies between laboratory and field results are probably associated with confounding effects caused by variation in susceptibility and exposure of the wild hosts, as well as the impact of environmental factors.

Using two gastrointestinal parasites with contrasting dynamics of infection and host immune responses, we showed that the presence of the second species can increase host heterogeneity to infection. However, while we do see variation in shedding, this does not necessarily reflect the same degree of variation in infection. Previous work has suggested that the presence of a second parasite species can affect parasite sexual maturity, body size, or fecundity (Poulin, 2007). Our work is in line with these studies by showing that coinfections can alter host–parasite and parasite–parasite interactions, and contribute to host heterogeneity in infection and transmission. However, our work also suggests that the risk of supershedding events arising from coinfection by helminths is probably low. This is partly because of the intrinsic properties of helminths (e.g. sexual reproduction, different life stages) and their life-history strategies, and partly because of the complexities in host–parasite regulation.

As part of our work on coinfection, we also examined the role of these two gastrointestinal helminths on the dynamics of *Bordetella bronchiseptica* infection in the respiratory tract of laboratory rabbits. Parasites were dispensed in a single dose at the same time and rabbits were sampled at fixed times during 4-month-long trials. Dual infections with either *T. retortaeformis* or *G. strigosum* did not change the dynamics of *Bordetella* in the lower respiratory tract:

bacteria were removed from the lungs and trachea with no significant delay induced by the helminth (Pathak et al., 2012; Thakar et al., 2012). However, a higher bacterial load was found in the nose of rabbits dual-infected with *G. strigosum*. Modelling of the immuno-dynamics of *Bordetella–T. retortaeformis* infection in the lungs suggested that T helper cell–mediated antibodies and neutrophils led to phagocytosis and clearance of *B. bronchiseptica* (Thakar et al., 2012). This pattern should be also expected in the coinfection with *G. strigosum* (Pathak et al., 2012). The bacterium also affected the dynamics of the two helminths. Compared to single infections, *T. retortaeformis* was removed more quickly from the small intestine while *G. strigosum* persisted with similar high intensities (Pathak et al., 2012; Thakar et al., 2012). These findings reiterate our general conclusions that coinfection with a second species can increase host heterogeneity to infection, and also highlight the overlooked role of bacteria on helminth dynamics and the fact that the same parasite colonising different organs can exhibit different reactions during coinfections, namely, *Bordetella* in the lungs versus the nose.

In summary, in the epidemiology of multi-species infections there are many aspects of the infection–transmission process that remain poorly understood. Efforts should be directed to quantify the relationship between host infectivity and degree of shedding, including the conditions that can lead to supershedders and how immunity influences the duration of infection and, from here, the rate of shedding. The influence of host attributes on coinfection produces additional conflicting results that require resolution. For instance, parasite interactions can vary with host sex (Curtale et al., 2007; Allotey & Gyapong, 2008; Gao et al., 2010) and age (Brooker et al., 2007). However, these effects are likely confounded by group-specific risk factors or differences in exposure, in addition to changes in susceptibility due to the interplay between coinfection and host factors. Finally, there is a fundamental shortage of data on multi-species infections and, more crucially, data on the intensity of infection from specific organs if parasites colonise different parts of the host. Lastly, we need to be able to quantify the intensity of these infections; prevalence tells us how common a coinfection is in a host population but does not provide any insight on the within-host processes of parasite interaction that affect their intensity of infection, virulence, shedding, or disease severity.

21.3.3 Anthelmintic treatment

In areas endemic to helminth infections, anthelmintic drugs can only remove the parasites for a relatively short period of time. By stopping the treatment, parasite intensities can bounce back to pre-treatment levels (Sabatelli et al., 2008; Keiser & Utzinger, 2008; Jia, 2012), because protection is not complete or life-long and hosts can be reinfected if exposed to infective stages. However, while treatments can alleviate the severity of infection for a limited time, they can also affect parasite traits, like fecundity and growth, during the recolonisation and expansion of the parasite population between treatments. By disrupting the host–parasite interactions in the pre-treatment, and by impacting the parasite dynamics and life strategy during reinfections, anthelmintic therapies can influence transmission and risk of infection. For example, multiple reinfections following treatments of hosts with some level of resistance can lead to fast expulsion or slow accumulation of parasites but can also cause stunted growth and low fecundity because of a more reactive host immune response developed from previous infections (Stear & Bishop, 1999; Bleay et al., 2007; Luong et al., 2011). Yet, parasites can accumulate at the same rate and grow to the same size between treatments if there are no immune limitations and competition for resources is minimal, especially during the initial phase of recolonisation. Parasites can also develop resistance to drugs and experience minor changes in density (e.g. Geerts & Gryseels, 2000; James et al., 2009; Reynolds et al., 2016), or even adapt growth and fecundity to overcome the drug effects. Ultimately, by affecting parasite intensity and their traits, anthelmintic treatments can contribute to heterogeneities in host infection and parasite dynamics, including evolution.

How parasite traits relate to the intensity of infection, and how these relationships change before and after anthelmintic treatment, is still not completely clear. Two possible scenarios can be predicted (Figure 21.6). If parasites are controlled by the host immune response then we should expect differences in the dynamics of infection before and after treatment because of differences in the development and intensity of the immune reaction (Figure 21.6b). In other words, an immune response already stimulated in the pre-treatment should react faster (due to immune memory) and constrain the parasites more vigorously in the post-treatment. Alternatively, if parasites are regulated by within-host ecological processes, such as intensity-dependent competition for resources, then, all else being equal, the dynamics of infection should follow similar trajectories before and after treatment (Figure 21.6a).

We looked for evidence of these scenarios in laboratory experiments where rabbits were trickle-dosed every week with 400 T. retortaeformis infective stages, and treated with an anthelmintic halfway through the experiment before resuming the infection under the same regime a month later. Animals were sampled at fixed points to quantify parasitological and immunological data. We then used these results to develop a within-host state–space mathematical framework of the dynamics of infection that linked an observation model with a dynamical model (Ghosh et al., 2018). The observation model combines cross-sectional data on parasite intensity, body length, and fecundity (i.e. eggs in utero), with longitudinal data on egg shedding in hosts' faeces. The dynamic model describes the unobservable time progression of the

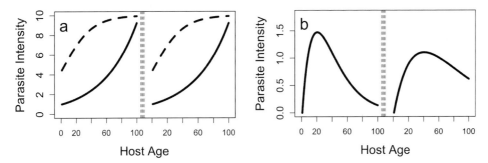

Figure 21.6 Relationship between host age and parasite intensity before and after anthelmintic treatment (shaded grey area), in (a) parasites that are not regulated (continuous line) or are controlled (dotted line) by intensity-dependent parasite constraints, and (b) parasites that are regulated by host immunity. Only the parasites that are immune-constrained show differences in the age-intensity profile before and after anthelmintic treatment.

parasite states. Our goal was to explain how host heterogeneities in the intensity of infection and shedding are generated before and after drug treatment and to identify the parsimonious processes driving parasite dynamics, namely, establishment and expulsion (Ghosh et al., 2018).

Simulations well reflected the empirical data. *T. retortaeformis* mean intensity of infection was comparable before and after treatment, but parasite accumulation was delayed by one sampling point and fecundity was lower in the post-treatment due to shorter worms that carried fewer eggs in utero (Ghosh et al., 2018). Before and after treatment, parasite dynamics were driven by the establishment of infective larvae and the relatively low clearance of adult stages, with both processes affected by accumulated exposure and adult intensities. Importantly, the extent of these processes was very rabbit-specific, to the point that we did not find significant differences between pre- and post-treatment when averages among rabbits were used. This confirmed the high variation in host–parasite interactions and outcomes among rabbits both within and between treatments. The evidence of a convex host age–parasite intensity relationship and slower accumulation of parasites post-treatment, combined with stunted worms and reduced shedding, supported our previous finding that *T. retortaeformis* is controlled by the rabbit immune response (Ghosh et al., 2018). This was confirmed by finding a significant negative effect of antibodies (IgA and IgG) on parasite length. Together, these findings are in agreement with our previous work (Cattadori et al., 2005; Murphy et al., 2011; Thakar et al., 2012; Mignatti et al., 2016). Overall, while it did not affect the mean parasite burden, the anthelmintic treatment modified the dynamics of parasite accumulation and individual growth, which then affected fecundity and shedding. The effect of this perturbation was in addition to the intrinsic variation among individual rabbits observed. Furthermore, the anthelmintic treatment contributed to generate non-linearities in parasite dynamics, where similar mean intensities of infection before and after treatment were associated with lower shedding in the post-treatment. This mismatch suggests caution when using observations of shedding to predict intensities of infection between treatments, or vice versa. Importantly, while the dynamics of infection can be fundamentally similar between treatments, parasite life history can vary and contribute to heterogeneities in shedding and, thus, risk of infection.

Our work is consistent with previous studies that only reported on specific components of the parasite life cycle and dynamics (Audebert et al., 2000, 2003; Massoni et al., 2011). By combining experimental manipulations and detailed parasitological observations with a modelling approach, we provided a holistic view of the within-host dynamics of *T. retortaeformis* infection and how perturbation with an anthelmintic drug can influence specific components of the parasite life history (Ghosh et al., 2018). The general conclusion from our work is that parasitic reinfection in resistant hosts usually leads to delayed parasite accumulation and stunted parasite growth. Specifically, our modelling approach provides a mechanistic overview of these interactions, and highlights where heterogeneities in parasite dynamics emerge and how the counting on a restricted number of parasite variables (e.g. egg shedding only) might generate inaccurate conclusions on the dynamics of infection and related life-history traits.

Given the growing concern about the development of resistance to drug treatments, understanding the impact of these treatments on the ecology of infection, and how parasite traits adjust to perturbations, is important for providing alternative and possibly long-term approaches to the control of parasites while reducing the risk of infection. The evidence that treatments can have greater consequences on parasite development and/or fecundity than those on parasite numbers could be a possible avenue to explore, particularly given recent progress in molecular biology and diagnostic techniques.

21.4 Future directions

The mechanistic understanding of host–parasite interactions, and the recognition of the critical processes and factors within the host that drive dynamics of infection and transmission between hosts, continue to be the focus of much work on the ecology and evolution of infectious diseases. The challenge is to identify common features that can be captured by a few fundamental host responses and associated dynamics of infection. For example, it is apparent from the rabbit–helminth system that the relationship between intensity of infection and degree of shedding is often non-linear. Although this could be expected, for practical reasons this relationship is frequently assumed to be linear, and we need to identify general rules that can relate infection to transmission more precisely. One approach would be to use an allometric correction that takes into account parasite size to quantify fecundity and shedding, and then to calculate the degree of host shedding based on the intensity of infection and the parasite sex ratio. Another possibility is to use an empirical approach that estimates the infection–shedding relationship under a range of scenarios, and then apply this information to similar systems. This knowledge is critical when estimating the risk of infection and also when managing helminth infections (e.g. informing on the selection of individuals to treat, or the treatment frequency, based on the degree of shedding).

Our work also emphasises that there are many sources of disturbance that can alter the intrinsic properties of the hosts and their parasites, and the way they interact. The challenge is to understand at what point they should be taken into account and how. For instance, given the widespread prevalence of multi-parasite infections, how parasite species interact with each other and influence their long-term persistence at the host population level remains an underdeveloped topic. Progress has been made in understanding the molecular processes of parasite interaction, particularly the modulatory role of host immunity. However, more work needs to be done to clarify how a second parasite species influences a parasite epidemiology. We showed that during a coinfection we cannot predict the dynamics of infection and shedding based on our understanding of single infection processes; likewise, we cannot predict how coinfections could affect the degree of variation among hosts. To address this, one possibility is to develop theoretical models on the epidemiology of multi-species infection based on parameter ranges that cover a variety of scenarios. More fruitfully, we need long-term data on parasite intensity and degree of shedding, rather than prevalence. These data are not always easy to obtain, especially if the coinfecting parasites are not causing disease or are difficult to quantify. To overcome this issue, one possibility is to base the priority of data collection on the endemicity and prevalence of the parasite, besides its level of disease severity. Laboratory experiments can complement population-level studies by informing on critical parameters and fundamental relationships, such as temporal changes in infection–shedding during the course of coinfection. Ultimately, we need more epidemiological models of coinfections that while describing specific systems can also embrace aspects and mechanisms of broader relevance to other settings and taxa.

Environmental disturbance, such as climate change and habitat disruption, influences host exposure. A large body of work has focused on disentangling how these drivers alter parasite dynamics and risk of infection. However, under the same environmental threats, some individuals are at higher risk than others because of differences in their susceptibility. Therefore, understanding how within-host processes affect host susceptibility and, in turn, how this interacts with environmental changes is another important topic that needs further attention. The recent rapid advancement and low cost of many molecular techniques have made it possible to quantify many physiological and immunological components of the host, allowing exploration of how susceptibility (and related resistance and tolerance to infections) changes under environmental perturbations or extreme conditions. For systems where host and parasite populations can be experimentally manipulated over multiple generations, many of these interactions can be examined in the laboratory to provide accurate measurements over time and under controlled conditions. In the field, knowing critical molecular properties of the host, and how they vary under environmental perturbations, can inform on infection risk, identify individuals at higher risk, and inform how environmental changes can alter these patterns. In this respect there is no doubt that parasite treatments, like anthelmintic drugs, can be affected by environmental changes but also by the presence of a second infection or an individual's microbiome (Elias et al., 2006; Hayes et al., 2010; Blackwell et al., 2013; Pedersen & Antonovics, 2013). This suggests that many host–parasite processes could be addressed more broadly by embracing a more holistic approach to identifying major sources of variability and from here, better ways to control them. New tools are constantly becoming available to quantify host and parasite data; the general agreement is that we need a stronger combination of empirical and theoretical work to explain processes of infection from within to between hosts.

21.5 Conclusions

We used a rabbit–parasite system and a combination of field observations, laboratory manipulations, and analytical and modelling methodologies to examine how host heterogeneities to infection are generated (specifically, the contributions of climate change, multi-species parasitic infections, and anthelmintic treatments). We showed that the impact of these forces can generate unexpected outcomes, or relationships that tend to be ignored while actually being important sources of variation among hosts. More attention should be paid to these drivers and how they affect the dynamics of infection and persistence at the host population level while not dismissing the contribution of host susceptibility.

21.6 Acknowledgements

The authors would like to thank all the undergraduate students that provided technical assistance with the parasitological and immunological work, the James Hutton Institute (UK) for supplying the meteorological data, and the farmers in Scotland for allowing the sampling of the rabbit populations.

References

Allen, J.E. & Maizels, R.M. (2011) Diversity and dialogue in immunity to helminths. *Nature Reviews Immunology*, **11**, 375–388.

Allen, J.E. & Sutherland, T.E. (2014) Host protective roles of type 2 immunity: parasite killing and tissue repair, flip sides of the same coin, *Seminars in Immunology*, **26**, 329–340.

Allotey, P. & Gyapong, M. (2008) Gender in tuberculosis research. *International Journal of Tuberculosis and Lung Disease*, **12**, 831–836.

Anderson, R.M. & Gordon, D.M. (1982) Processes influencing the distribution of parasite numbers within host populations with special emphasis on parasite-induced host mortalities. *Parasitology*, **85**, 373–398.

Anderson, R.M. & May, R.M. (1978) Regulation and stability of host–parasite population interactions I: regulatory processes. *Journal of Animal Ecology*, **47**, 219–247.

Anthony, R.M., Rutitzky, L.I., Urban, J.F., Stadecker, M.J. & Gause, W.C. (2007) Protective immune mechanisms in helminth infection. *Nature Reviews Immunology*, **7**, 975–987.

Audebert, F., Cassone, J., Hoste, H. & Durette-Desset, M.C. (2000) Morphogenesis and distribution of *Trichostrongylus retortaeformis* in the intestine of the rabbit. *Journal of Helminthology*, **74**, 95–107.

Audebert, F. & Durette-Desset, M.C. (2007) Do lagomorphs play a relay role in the evolution of the Trichostrongylina nematodes? *Parasite*, **14**, 183–197.

Audebert, F., Vuong, P.N. & Durette-Desset, M.C. (2003) Intestinal migrations of *Trichostrongylus retortaeformis* (Trichostrongylina, Trichostrongylidae) in the rabbit. *Veterinary Parasitology*, **112**, 131–146.

Blackwell, A.D., Gurven, M.D., Sugiyama, L.S., et al. (2011) Evidence for a peak shift in a humoral response to helminths: age profiles of IgE in the Shuar of Ecuador, the Tsimane of Bolivia, and the US NHANES. *PLoS Neglected Tropical Diseases*, **5**, e1218.

Blackwell, A.D., Martin, M., Kaplan, H. & Gurven, M. (2013) Antagonism between two intestinal parasites in humans: the importance of co-infection for infection risk and recovery dynamics. *Proceedings of the Royal Society of London B*, **280**, 20131671.

Bleay, C., Wilkes, C.P., Paterson, S. & Viney, M.E. (2007) Density-dependent immune responses against the gastrointestinal nematode *Strongyloides ratti*. *International Journal for Parasitology*, **37**, 1501–1509.

Bowers, R.G. (1999) A baseline model for the apparent competition between many host strains: the evolution of host resistance. *Journal of Theoretical Biology*, **200**, 65–75.

Bourke, C.D., Maizels, R.M. & Mutapi, F. (2011) Acquired immune heterogeneity and its sources in human helminth infection. *Parasitology*, **138**, 139–159.

Brady, M.T., O'Neill, S.M., Dalton, J.P. & Mills, K. H. (1999) *Fasciola hepatica* suppresses a protective Th1 response against *Bordetella pertussis*. *Infection and Immunity*, **67**, 5372–5378.

Brogden, K.A., Lehmkuhl, H.D. & Cutlip, R.C. (1998) *Pasteurella haemolytica* complicated respiratory infections in sheep and goats. *Veterinary Research*, **29**, 233–254.

Brooker, S., Akhwale, W., Pullan, R., et al. (2007) Epidemiology of *Plasmodium*–helminth co-infection in Africa: populations at risk, potential impact on anemia, and prospects for combining control. *The American Journal of Tropical Medicine and Hygiene*, **77**(S6), 88–98.

Cattadori, I.M., Boag, B., Bjørnstad, O.N., Cornell, S. & Hudson, P.J. (2005) Immuno-epidemiology and peak shift in a seasonal host-nematode system. *Proceedings of the Royal Society of London B*, **272**, 1163–1169.

Cattadori, I.M., Boag, B. & Hudson P.J. (2008) Parasite co-infection and interaction as drivers of host heterogeneity. *International Journal for Parasitology*, **38**, 371–380.

Cattadori, I.M., Pathak, A.K. & Ferrari, M.J. (2019) Changes in helminth–host interactions under external disturbances: dynamics of infection, parasite traits and host immune responses. Under review.

Cattadori, I.M., Wagner, B.R., Wodzinski, L.A., et al. (2014) Infections do not predict shedding in co-infections with two helminths from a natural system. *Ecology*, **95**, 1684–1692.

Chase-Topping, M., Gally, D., Low, C., Matthews, L. & Woolhouse, M. (2008) Super-shedding and the link between human infection and livestock carriage of *Escherichia coli* O157. *Nature Reviews Microbiology*, **6**, 904–912.

Cizauskas, C.A., Turner, W.C., Pitts, N. & Getz, W.M. (2015) Seasonal patterns of hormones, macroparasites, and microparasites in wild African ungulates: the interplay among stress, reproduction, and disease. *PLoS ONE*, **10**, 0120800.

Cornell, S., Bjørnstad, O.N., Cattadori, I.M., Boag B. & Hudson P.J. (2008) Seasonality, cohort-dependence and the development of immunity in a natural host-nematode system. *Proceedings of the Royal Society of London B*, **275**, 473–591.

Curtale, F., Wahab Hassanein, Y.A., Barduagni, P., et al. (2007) Human fascioliasis infection: gender differences within school-age children from endemic areas of the Nile Delta, Egypt. *Transactions of the Royal Society of Tropical Medicine and Hygiene*, **101**, 155–160.

Duerr, H.P., Dietz, K. & Eichner, M. (2003) On the interpretation of age–intensity profiles and dispersion patterns in parasitological surveys. *Parasitology*, **126**, 87–101.

Elias, D., Akuffo, H. & Britton, S. (2006) Helminths could influence the outcome of vaccines against TB in the tropics. *Parasite Immunology*, **28**, 507–513.

Gao, L., Zhou, F., Li, X. & Jin, Q. (2010) HIV/TB co-infection in mainland China: a meta-analysis. *PLoS ONE*, **5**, e10736.

Garske, T. & Rhodes, C.J. (2008) The effect of superspreading on epidemic outbreak size distributions. *Journal of Theoretical Biology*, **253**, 228–237.

Geerts, S. & Gryseels, S. (2000) Drug resistance in human helminths: current situation and lessons from livestock. *Clinical Microbiology Reviews*, **13**, 207–222.

Ghosh, S., Ferrari, M.J., Pathak, A.K. & Cattadori, I.M. (2018). Changes in parasite traits, rather than intensity, affect the dynamics of infection under external perturbation. *PLoS Computational Biology*, **14**(6), e1006167.

Girgis, N.M., Gundra, U.M. & Loke, P. (2013) immune regulation during helminth infections. *PLoS Pathogens*, **9**, e1003250.

Graham, A., Cattadori, I.M., Lloyd-Smith, J., Ferrari, M. & Bjornstad, O.N. (2007) Transmission consequences of co-infection: cytokines writ large? *Trends in Parasitology*, **6**, 284–291.

Grenfell, B. T. & Anderson, R. M. (1989) Pertussis in England and Wales: an investigation of transmission dynamics and control by mass vaccination. *Proceedings of the Royal Society of London B*, **236**, 213–252.

Harvell, D., Altizer, S., Cattadori, I.M., Harrington, L. & Weil, E. (2009) Climate change and wildlife diseases: when does the host matter the most? *Ecology*, **90**, 912–920.

Hayes, K.S., Bancroft, A.J., Goldrick, M., et al. (2010) Exploitation of the intestinal microflora by the parasitic nematode *Trichuris muris*. *Science*, **328**, 1391–1394.

Hernandez, A.D., Poole, A. & Cattadori, I.M. (2013) Climate changes influence free-living stages of soil-transmitted parasites of European rabbits. *Global Change Biology*, **19**, 1028–1042.

Hoffman, R.S. & Smith, A.T. (2005) "Order Lagomorpha". In: Wilson, D.E. & Reeder, D. M. (eds.), *Mammal Species of the World: A Taxonomic and Geographic Reference* (3rd ed.). Baltimore, MD: Johns Hopkins University Press.

Hudson, P.J. & Dobson, A.P. (1989) Population biology of *Trichostrongylus tenuis*, a parasite of economic importance for red grouse management. *Parasitology Today*, **5**, 283–291.

Hudson, P.J., Perkins, S.E. & Cattadori, I.M. (2008) The emergence of wildlife disease and the application of ecology. In: Ostfeld, R. (ed.), *Infectious Disease Ecology: Effects of Ecosystems on Disease and of Disease on Ecosystems*, (1st edn, pp. 347–367). Princeton, NJ: Princeton University Press.

Izhar, R. & Ben-Ami, F. (2015) Host age modulates parasite infectivity, virulence and reproduction. *Journal of Animal Ecology*, **84**, 1018–1028.

Jackson, D.W. & Rohani, P. (2014) Perplexities of pertussis: recent global epidemiological trends and their potential causes. *Epidemiology and Infection*, **142**, 672–684.

Jackson, J.A., Friberg, I.M., Little, S. & Bradley, J.E. (2009) Review series on helminths, immune modulation and the hygiene hypothesis: immunity against helminths and immunological phenomena in modern human populations: coevolutionary legacies? *Immunology*, **126**, 18–27.

James, C.E., Hudson, A.L. & Davey, M.W. (2009) Drug resistance mechanisms in helminths: is it survival of the fittest? *Trends in Parasitology*, **25**, 328–335.

Jia, T.W., Melville, S., Utzinger, J., King, C.H. & Zhou, X.N. (2012) Soil-transmitted helminth reinfection after drug treatment: a systematic review and meta-analysis. *PLoS Neglected Tropical Diseases*, **6**, e1621.

Kao, R.R., Gravenor, M.B., Charleston, B., et al. (2007) *Mycobacterium bovis* shedding patterns from experimentally infected calves and the effect of concurrent infection with bovine viral diarrhoea virus. *Journal of The Royal Society Interface*, **4**, 545–551.

Keiser, J. & Utzinger, J. (2008) Efficacy of current drugs against soil-transmitted helminth infections: systematic review and meta-analysis. *Journal of the American Medical Association*, **299**, 1937–1948.

Keymer, A. (1982) Density-dependent mechanisms in the regulation of intestinal helminth populations. *Parasitology*, **84**, 573–587.

Lass, S., Hudson, P.J., Thakar, J., et al. (2013) Generating super-shedders: co-infection increases bacterial load and egg production of a gastrointestinal helminth. *Journal of the Royal Society Interface*, **10**, 20120588.

Lloyd-Smith, J.O., Schreiber, S.J., Kopp, P.E. & Getz, W.M. (2005) Superspreading and the effect of individual variation on disease emergence. *Nature*, **438**, 355–359.

Luong, L.T., Vigliotti, B.A. & Hudson, P.J. (2011) Strong density-dependent competition and acquired immunity constrain parasite establishment: implications for parasite aggregation. *International Journal for Parasitology*, **41**, 505–511.

Maizels, R.M. (2009) Parasite immunomodulation and polymorphisms of the immune system. *Journal of Biology*, **8**, 62.

Massoni, J., Cassone, J., Durette-Desset, M.C. & Audebert, F. (2011) Development of *Graphidium strigosum* (Nematoda, Haemonchidae) in its natural host, the rabbit (*Oryctolagus cuniculus*) and comparison with several Haemonchidae parasites of ruminants. *Parasitology Research*, **109**, 25–36.

McRae, K.M., Stear, M.J., Good, B. & Keane, O.M. (2015) The host immune response to gastrointestinal nematode infection in sheep. *Parasite Immunology*, **37**, 605–613.

Mignatti, A., Boag, B. & Cattadori, I.M. (2016) Host immunity shapes the impact of climate changes on the dynamics of parasite infections. *Proceedings of the National Academy of Sciences of the United States of America*, **113**, 2970–2975.

Miller, M. R., White, A. & Boots, M. (2005) The evolution of host resistance: tolerance and control as distinct strategies. *Journal of Theoretical Biology*, **236**, 198–207.

Molnár, P.K., Kutz, S.J., Hoar, B.M. & Dobson, A.P. (2013) Metabolic approaches to understanding climate change impacts on seasonal host–macroparasite dynamics. *Ecology Letters*, **16**, 9–21.

Murphy, L., Nalpas, N., Stear, M. & Cattadori I.M. (2011) The role of immunity on the dynamics of chronic gastrointestinal nematode infections of rabbits. *Parasite Immunology*, **33**, 287–302.

Murphy, L., Pathak, A.K. & Cattadori, I.M. (2013) A co-infection with two gastrointestinal nematodes alters host immune responses and only partially parasite dynamics. *Parasite Immunology*, **35**, 421–432.

Pathak, A.K., Boag, B., Poss, M., Harvill, E. & Cattadori, I.M. (2011) Seasonal incidence of *Bordetella bronchiseptica* in an age-structured free-living rabbit population. *Epidemiology and Infection*, **14**, 1–10.

Pathak, A.K., Creppage, K.E., Werner, J.R. & Cattadori, I.M. (2010) Immune regulation of a chronic bacteria infection and consequences for pathogen transmission. *BMC Microbiology*, **10**, 226.

Pathak, A.K., Pelensky, C., Boag, B. & Cattadori, I.M. (2012) Immuno-epidemiology of chronic bacterial and helminth co-infections: observations from the field and evidence from the laboratory. *International Journal for Parasitology*, **42**, 647–655.

Paull, S.H. & Johnson, P.T.J. (2014) Experimental warming drives a seasonal shift in the timing of host–parasite dynamics with consequences for disease risk. *Ecology Letters*, **4**, 445–453.

Pedersen, A.B. & Antonovics, J. (2013) Anthelmintic treatment alters the parasite community in a wild mouse host. *Biology Letters*, **9**, 20130205.

Poulin, R. (2007) *Evolutionary Ecology of Parasites* (2nd edn). Princeton, NJ: Princeton University Press.

Quinnell, R.J., Medley, G.F. & Keymer, A.E. (1990) The regulation of gastrointestinal helminth populations. *Philosophical Transactions of the Royal Society of London B: Biological Sciences*, **330**, 191–201.

Raberg, L., Sim, D. & Read, A.F. (2007) Disentangling genetic variation for resistance and tolerance to infectious diseases in animals. *Science*, **318**, 812–814.

Raffel, T.R., Romansic, J.M., Halstead, N.T., et al. (2013) Disease and thermal acclimation in a more variable and unpredictable climate. *Nature Climate Change*, **3**, 146–151.

Redpath, S.A., Fonseca, N.M. & Perona-Wright, G. (2014) Protection and pathology during parasite infection: IL-10 strikes the balance. *Parasite Immunology*, **36**, 233–252.

Restif, O. & Koella, J.C. (2004) Concurrent evolution of resistance and tolerance to pathogens. *The American Naturalist*, **164**, 90–102.

Reynolds, A., Lindström, J., Johnson, P.C. & Mable, B.K. (2016) Evolution of drug-tolerant nematode populations in response to density reduction. *Evolutionary Applications*, **9**, 726–738.

Roy, B.A. & Kirchner, J.W. (2000) Evolutionary dynamics of pathogen resistance and tolerance. *Evolution*, **54**, 51–63.

Sabatelli, L., Ghani, A.C., Rodrigues, L.C., Hotez, P.J. & Brooker, S. (2008) Modelling heterogeneity and the impact of chemotherapy and vaccination against human hookworm parasite. *Journal of the Royal Society Interface*, **5**, 1329–1341.

Stear M.J. & Bishop, S.C. (1999) The curvilinear relationship between worm length and fecundity of *Teladorsagia circumcincta*. *International Journal for Parasitology*, **29**, 777–780.

Stear M.J., Boag, B., Cattadori, I.M. & Murphy, L. (2009) Genetic variation in resistance to mixed, predominantly *Teladorsagia circumcincta* nematode infections of sheep: from heritabilities to gene identification. *Parasite Immunology*, **31**, 274–282.

Stear, M.J., Strain, S. & Bishop, S.C. (1999) Mechanisms underlying resistance to nematode infection. *International Journal for Parasitology*, **29**, 51–56.

Thakar, J., Pathak, A.K., Murphy, L., Albert, R. & Cattadori, I.M. (2012) Network model of immune responses reveals key effectors to single and co-infection kinetics by a respiratory bacterium and a gastrointestinal helminth. *PLoS Computational Biology*, **8**, e1002345.

Thompson, H.V. & King, C.M. (1994) *The European Rabbit*. Oxford: Oxford University Press.

Tompkins, D.M. & Hudson, P.J. (1999) Regulation of nematode fecundity in the ring-necked pheasant (*Phasianus colchicus*): not just density dependence. *Parasitology*, **118**, 417–423.

Van Kuren, A., Boag, B., Hrubar, E. & Cattadori, I. M. (2013) Variability in the intensity of nematode larvae from gastrointestinal tissues of a natural herbivore. *Parasitology*, **140**, 632–640.

Woolhouse, M.E.J. (1992) A theoretical framework for the immunoepidemiology of helminth infection. *Parasite Immunology*, **14**, 563–578.

Woolhouse, M.E. (1998) Patterns in parasite epidemiology: the peak shift. *Parasitology Today*, **14**, 428–434.

Yazdanbakhsh, M. & Sacks, D.L. (2010) Why does immunity to parasites take so long to develop? *Nature Reviews Immunology*, **10**, 80–81.

CHAPTER TWENTY-TWO

Sylvatic plague in Central Asia: a case study of abundance thresholds

MIKE BEGON, STEPHEN DAVIS, ANNE LAUDISOIT, HERWIG LEIRS AND JONAS REIJNIERS

22.1 Introduction

22.1.1 Abundance thresholds

In their authoritative review of abundance threshold theory for wildlife disease, Lloyd-Smith et al. (2005) stress its central importance in infectious disease epidemiology, but also the rarity with which it has been applied in wildlife systems and the uncertainty regarding its utility in that context. We will not attempt to repeat that review here, but some fundamental points must be established. The basic idea behind abundance thresholds is a simple one, going back at least to Bartlett's (1957) investigation of a 'critical community size' for the persistence of human measles: for an infection to sustain itself, each infected individual must give rise to at least one further infected individual over the course of its lifetime, and this will only occur if susceptible hosts are sufficiently available as targets for new infection. For directly transmitted infections, this in turn will only be the case if there are enough susceptible hosts in the population, or if they are at a high enough density, for infectious hosts to contact a sufficient number of them for a successful transmission event to occur. Infection, like a fire, will only spread if there is sufficient fuel.

Although clearly related to one another, a distinction should be made between abundance thresholds for invasion and persistence. For invasion, the threshold is the minimum host population size allowing a single infectious individual to successfully introduce an infection into a wholly susceptible host population. The number of secondary infections that the invading infectious host gives rise to is the basic reproduction number of the infection, R_0, and as is well known, infections will only invade if $R_0 > 1$. For persistence, the focus switches to the number or density of susceptible hosts in a population required to prevent an established infection from fading out and ultimately disappearing from a population.

This distinction is arguably of particular importance for wildlife as opposed to, say, human infections, because marked fluctuations in overall host abundance are more likely, over and above any fluctuations in the numbers of susceptible hosts within a population of fixed overall size, generated by the waxing and waning of the infection itself. Hence, wildlife populations might be expected to repeatedly rise above invasion thresholds and then fall below persistence thresholds giving rise to an appearance–disappearance–reappearance cycle for wildlife infections.

Abundance thresholds are thus of fundamental importance in our attempts to understand the dynamics of infection in wildlife. In addition, attempts to control infections through culling, vaccination, or sterilisation, or even to time interventions so as to coincide with the periods of greatest disease risk, are all likely to be based either on reducing host abundance to below a threshold or anticipating its rise above one. Identifying and manipulating these thresholds may also therefore have substantial applied significance.

22.1.2 The plague system

Plague (*Yersinia pestis* infection) is now largely confined to foci in wildlife populations, but historical events such as the Black Death across medieval Europe demonstrate the disease's devastating potential (Stenseth et al., 2008), and persistent contemporary human outbreaks in Africa, Asia and the Americas have led to its being characterised as a (re)emerging infection (Morse, 1995). The plague system in the Pre-Balkhash region of Kazakhstan (Figure 22.1a) has been subject to particularly extensive study. The desert and semi-desert belt extending across central Asia, of which the Pre-Balkhash is a part, consists of a vast area of mixed vegetation and shrubs that extends from the Caspian Sea in the west to the Chinese border in the south-east of Kazakhstan where the Pre-Balkhash region is situated. Since around 1950, the national (previously USSR) anti-plague service established to prevent the occurrence of human cases has been largely successful (Onishchenko & Kutyrev, 2004). In the Pre-Balkhash region, great gerbils (*Rhombomys opimus*) are the main reservoir host, and only very rarely show signs of disease, with plague transmitted between them by a variety of flea species, of which *Xenopsylla* spp. are the most important. Great gerbils inhabit complex burrow systems as extended family groups. Indeed, these burrow systems are visible on satellite images (Figure 22.1b) due to the depletion of vegetation in the central and the surrounding areas of the system, where gerbil foraging is most intense (Addink et al., 2010). The number, position, and size of the burrow systems generally change very little over time, but the proportion of burrow systems occupied by family groups may fluctuate dramatically, making that proportion ('occupancy') an effective proxy for great gerbil abundance (Davis et al., 2004).

Surveillance by the anti-plague services, since their inception to the present day, consists of sampling the wild rodent and flea populations, and then attempting to isolate *Y. pestis* bacteria from rodent blood and organs and their fleas. When plague is found in areas close to human habitation, the risk of transmission to humans is reduced by treating rodent burrows with insecticide. Ecological (mainly abundance) data on flea and rodent (especially great gerbil) populations have also been recorded since monitoring began. Fleas are sampled biannually both from the captured gerbils and from burrow entrances (to which they are attracted by the presence of field workers as potential hosts), while the burrow occupancy by the gerbils is also monitored biannually, and the density of burrows across the landscape rechecked around every five years, as it changes relatively little. In addition, serological data on the presence of plague antibody in rodents are available from the early 1970s. The Pre-Balkhash plague focus is divided into 'large squares', each divided into four 20 km × 20 km primary squares, each of which is in turn divided into four 10 km × 10 km 'sectors'. There are data for more than 350 sectors, although the intensity and regularity of sampling varies considerably, essentially reflecting differences in accessibility and proximity to human settlements (Figure 22.2). The resulting archive is therefore unique for a wildlife infection system in terms of the number of years sampled, the spatial extent of the sampling, and the level of detail available.

22.2 A threshold abundance from time-series data

The resulting time series for gerbil abundance, measured as occupancy, show marked fluctuations, from effectively zero occupancy (no gerbils detected) to values in excess of 90%, with extended periods of high and low occupancy, but no consistent periodicity or regular cycles (Figure 22.3). The prevalence of plague bacteria in the rodent and flea samples also varies, with extended periods during which it apparently disappears, at least at the 'large square' scale (Figure 22.2). In the first attempt to examine the system from an abundance threshold perspective, therefore, Davis et al. (2004) sought to determine whether the appearance and disappearance of plague was associated with gerbil abundance rising above or falling below a particular level of occupancy.

Focusing on two large squares for which the data set was especially rich, data were combined on an annual basis. Detectable infection cannot be expected to appear or disappear instantaneously as a threshold is crossed. Hence, plague presence in a particular year was related to gerbil occupancy in the present year, and to occupancy in each of the five previous years, and also to combinations of consecutive years, taken in pairs and triplets. Following some model exploration, a threshold autoregressive model with a cumulative Weibull distribution was chosen, and where combination of years were examined, the weightings of their respective contributions were

(a)

(b)   (c)
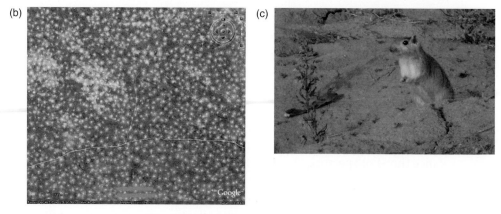

Figure 22.1 (a) The Pre-Balkhash region in Kazakhstan is located to the north-west of the city of Almaty and south of the crescent-shaped Lake Balkhash. It is part of a plague focus where the main reservoir host is the great gerbil, *Rhombomys opimus*. (b) The regular pattern created by great gerbil burrow systems, visible on satellite images. Patches of bare earth above and around the burrow systems strongly reflect the sunlight. Each bright disc represents a burrow system 10–40 m in diameter. The image (approximately 2000 m × 2000 m) was captured using the publicly available software Google Earth (http://earth.google.com/). Copyright 2008 DigitalGlobe; Europa Technologies. (After Davis et al., 2008.) (c) A great gerbil at a burrow. (A black and white version of this figure will appear in some formats. For the colour version, please refer to the plate section.)

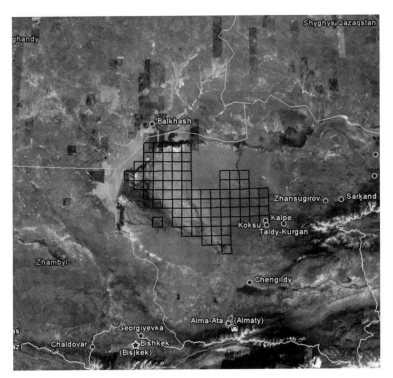

Figure 22.2 Satellite image of the Pre-Balkhash region with the locations marked of the most intensively sampled Primary Squares (20 km × 20 km). (Source: Google Earth). (After Heier et al., 2011.)

varied in order to find the model of best fit. The results are shown in Figure 22.4. The best model (based on AIC values) included occupancies from both 1 and 2 years previously, although AIC was less than 2 for the models with only a 2-year delay (0.71) and years 1, 2 and 3 previously (1.41). For the best model, the weightings for 1 and 2 years previously were 0.59 and 0.87, respectively. The occupancies themselves were in the region of 50%.

The results are therefore notable in providing a rare demonstration that abundance thresholds may have a reality that extends from epidemiological models to field data. The results are also notable in being predictive. There was little support for models that included contemporary occupancy, but armed with data on occupancy in the present year, the models can estimate the likelihood of plague's presence two years hence. With additional data from one year ago, the prediction for the following year should be more reliable still. This raises the question, of course, of the biological basis for these particular time lags, to which we return later.

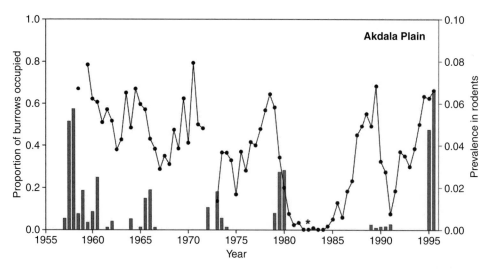

Figure 22.3 Spring and autumn estimates of the proportion of burrows occupied (filled circles connected by solid lines, left axis) and prevalence of plague (vertical bars, right axis) in great gerbil populations from a large square in the Akdala Plain region of the Pre-Balkhash plague focus of Kazakhstan. In autumn 1982 (marked by an asterisk) no great gerbils were tested for plague. (After Davis et al., 2004.)

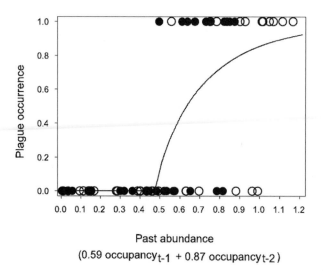

Past abundance

$(0.59 \text{ occupancy}_{t-1} + 0.87 \text{ occupancy}_{t-2})$

Figure 22.4 The relationship between the likelihood of detecting plague (solid line) and past burrow occupancy rates, plus data on presence/absence of plague in two Large Square sites (open circles and filled circles). The likelihood of detecting *Y. pestis* is 0 below a threshold value of 0.476 [95% confidence interval (0.355, 0.572)], but rises rapidly once the threshold is attained and continues to increase for larger values. The functional form of the relation is the cumulative Weibull distribution function. (After Davis et al., 2004.)

On the other hand, the results also suggest that such predictions will be uncertain. In particular, whereas the model indicates that below the threshold plague was never found, above the threshold plague might or might not be found. There were numerous false-positive observations, where plague was expected (on the basis of the threshold criterion) but not detected. A threshold abundance appeared, therefore, to be a necessary but not a sufficient condition for plague to be detectable in the system. To some degree, this simply reflects the model being probabilistic rather than 'wrong'. It does suggest, though, that there is more to the presence and absence of plague than a sufficiency of hosts.

Davis et al. (2007b), therefore, subjected the model's predictive ability to more rigorous, out-of-sample testing, and investigated possible reasons for the false-positive observations. They first applied the model selected in Davis et al. (2004) to a further 421 observations at the large square scale from squares other than the two from which the model was derived (for which there were 65 observations). They also applied this model to 537 additional observations at the primary square scale (that is, one quarter of a large square), as well as 110 observations at this scale from the two original large squares. The model continued to perform well below the threshold: plague was found in only around 4% of the new observations where it was not expected. Above the threshold, for the original large squares, the model performed as well at the primary square scale as at the (original) large square scale. However, for the new large squares the proportion of false-positives (observations above the threshold but without plague) more than doubled at both scales. The probabilistic nature of the model (the probability of plague above the threshold was finite but not 1) means that some false-positives are to be expected. Nonetheless, outside the original large squares, the numbers of false-positives were around 17% above expectations. Clearly, there is a need to account for the false-positive explanations both within and outside the expectations of the model.

Davis et al. (2007b) examined six possible causes. Of these, and without going into details of the methods used, a build-up of resistance to infection in the gerbils (and hence insufficient susceptible gerbils) received no support. Neither did any direct effect of climate (as opposed to climate affecting host or flea abundance, as it undoubtedly does; Kausrud et al., 2007; Samia et al. 2011). There was some support for effects from two further factors that are taken up below, although in neither case did these appear to account for large numbers of the false-positives. The first was that a sufficient abundance of fleas might also be necessary for effective onward transmission of infection. The second was that the processes of invasion and fade out might require separate thresholds, and including gerbil occupancies immediately prior to fade-out might erroneously lower the threshold estimate for invasion and thus generate false-positives around the beginnings of outbreaks. Two final possible causes also appeared to be important. First, inclusion of serological data where these were available, through which it is much easier to detect plague, suggested that plague may often have been missed simply as a result of sample sizes being too small. Second, the absence of plague despite there being sufficient gerbils often seemed to occur when plague was also not detected in surrounding areas. That is, plague failed to invade a population with sufficient susceptible hosts because it had become locally extinct.

22.3 The threshold as a percolation phenomenon

The concept of an abundance threshold in epidemiological theory is normally associated with the idea of there being a sufficient density of susceptible hosts for an infectious host, mixing with that population, to make at least one contact leading to a new infection during its period of infectiousness. Indeed, the most common derivations of an abundance threshold assume that hosts mix freely within the whole population in a manner analogous to 'mass action' processes in physics. It is well understood that spatial and social structures in real populations make this idealised view of transmission only an approximation of the truth (Lloyd-Smith et al., 2005). However, the demonstration of an abundance threshold for plague in great gerbils, where their fixed burrow systems dictate that most of their contact is with near neighbours in the landscape, led Davis et al. (2008) to question altogether the applicability of a conventional R_0-based foundation in this case. They sought evidence, rather, for the abundance threshold being a critical percolation phenomenon.

Percolation theory is most commonly associated with the flow of liquid through a porous medium. Epidemiological analogies had been anticipated (e.g. Grassberger, 1983), with infection flowing through space from one permissive (susceptible) location to another, but Davis et al. (2008) were the first to demonstrate the applicability of percolation thresholds in a natural infectious disease system. It was possible to do so, in particular, because it had previously been demonstrated that infection moves sufficiently rapidly through family groups (the occupants on one burrow system) for the burrow systems themselves to be considered either susceptible to plague infection, infected, or recovered (Davis et al., 2007a). Plague infection can then be thought of as passing from burrow to burrow when a gerbil moves from its home burrow to visit another burrow (as they often do), and is either susceptible but is bitten there by an infected flea which passes on the infection, or is itself infected and deposits an infected flea at the burrow it visits that goes on to transmit plague to a susceptible host.

Thus, in the same way as water percolates through soil from air space to air space, plague may percolate across the landscape from burrow to burrow. What is critical here, though, is that percolation, intrinsically, has threshold properties. When soils are too compact (not enough air space) water will not percolate, whereas when there are sufficient air spaces percolation will occur. However, the transition between the two is not gradual. There is a critical fraction of permissive air space below which percolation beyond a limited cluster of air spaces is impossible and above which it is inevitable. Davis et al. (2008) therefore sought to discover whether a similar phenomenon might be applicable to the plague system, given the known disposition of burrows across the landscape, the scale over which fleas move, carried by their gerbil hosts, and the scale at which plague monitoring had been carried out.

A set of burrow locations was reconstructed from satellite images taken within the study area of the Pre-Balkhash, and occupied burrows assigned at random among these for a range of occupancy levels. Infection was then introduced at the occupied burrow closest to the centre of the set, and an epidemic, or failed epidemic, initiated. Such epidemics were simulated using data on flea dispersal distances and burrow recovery rates to set the pace of the subsequent spread of infection. At each time step, an infected burrow was chosen at random, which could either lose its infected status (that is, recover) or pass infection on to a susceptible burrow, which it would do if an appropriate flea movement occurred during the time step and reached a susceptible rather than an infected or recovered burrow. A simulation ended when there were either no more infected burrows or infection had spread more than 4.5 km from the initiation point. The outcome for each occupancy level was then determined as the proportion of 200 simulations in which the epidemic 'succeeded' in spreading. Results are shown in Figure 22.5.

The pattern of outcomes depended upon how the 'success' of an epidemic was defined. Even the most abortive epidemics may succeed, by chance, in progressing to one or two secondarily-infected burrows, but Davis et al. (2008) required the infection to spread at least 750 m from the initiation point to constitute minimal success, with further annuli at 1.5 km, 3 km, and 4.5 km representing progressively more established successful invasions. At 750 m, the rise in success rate as occupancy increased was gradual, but as the annuli increased in size, the switch from non-invasion to invasion took on an increasingly threshold appearance. (A 'perfect' threshold is only to be expected for an annulus of infinite size.) Hence, the percolation model, parameterised from field data, suggests a threshold occupancy of around 31%. This compares with the estimate from field data of 33% for the best single-year model in Davis et al. (2004) with a AIC of only 0.71 compared to the best model, as described above. Interestingly, the calculation of an equivalent of R_0 at this threshold – the number of burrows, averaged over the simulations, infected by the initiating infectious burrow – was approximately

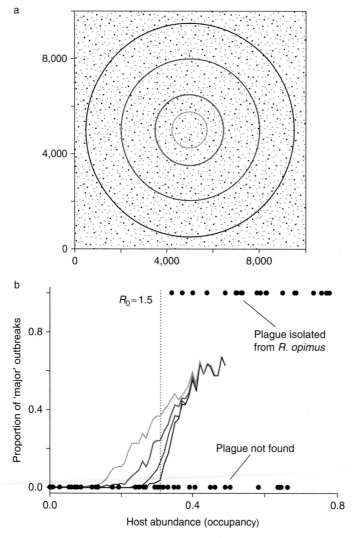

Figure 22.5 The results of a percolation model for plague epizootics in great gerbils. The landscape (a) is a 10 km × 10 km area, and the results (b) are expressed as the fraction of outbreaks that give rise to new infections at least 750 m, 1.5 km, 3 km, and 4.5 km from the site of initial infection, shown as solid lines coloured red, blue, green, and black, respectively, and corresponding to the spread of plague beyond the circles of the same colour in (a). (After Davis et al., 2008.) (A black and white version of this figure will appear in some formats. For the colour version, please refer to the plate section.)

1.5. There is a threshold abundance for the plague system, but the spatial structure dictates that this is neither a mass action threshold, nor one at which $R_0 = 1$.

22.4 A gerbil and a spillover threshold?

There is interest in the maintenance of plague in great gerbils as a wildlife infection system in its own right, but the system has only been studied, and takes on additional interest, because plague is zoonotic. Samia et al. (2011) therefore explored whether the system overall could be shown to have two separate thresholds: the one relating to plague in the great gerbils, but also a second, describing the spillover of plague from the gerbils into the human population. Their approach included no spatially explicit elements and differed in technical (statistical) details from the approach of Davis et al. (2004), utilising a generalised threshold mixed model, the development of which was motivated by the gerbil–plague system (Samia et al., 2007). They also included flea burden (the estimated average number of fleas per gerbil) and flea infectious force (the product of flea abundance and the prevalence of plague) as potential explanatory variables, as well as a number of climatic measures as explanatory variables themselves of the various biotic metrics. For the gerbil threshold, their conclusions showed an encouraging correspondence with those of Davis et al. (2004): that gerbil abundance 1.5–2 years earlier needs to be sufficiently high for a plague outbreak to occur in the rodents.

Abundance thresholds generally, whether mass action or percolation-based, arise out of the need for there to be sufficient appropriate contacts within a host population for onward transmission to occur. Thus, any threshold linking plague infection in great gerbil populations to spillover of plague into humans would be analogous rather than conventional, because it is likely to reflect a sufficiency of contacts of humans with fleas infected by gerbils, rather than between infectious and susceptible humans, or of humans with fleas infected by humans. (Outbreaks in humans are only ever episodic, and the abundance of susceptible humans varies little, even over extended time series.) Nonetheless, using human plague data for the whole of Kazakhstan, Samia et al. (2011) were able to support such a threshold: a generalised threshold model applied to the time series of human cases was a far superior fit to the data than models without a threshold. The threshold quantity was the abundance (burden) of fleas around one year earlier. This is consistent with the idea that plague is most likely to spill over into humans when there are not only sufficient infected fleas for transmission to occur, but also a high ratio of fleas to rodents, increasing the tendency of fleas to bite humans having failed to find their more usual, gerbil host.

22.5 A hyperbolic joint host–vector threshold

Davis et al.'s (2007b) reconsideration of the original threshold analysis, and the examination by Samia et al. (2011) of a possible human spillover threshold, both argued for further consideration of a potential role for fleas in the threshold dynamics of plague in great gerbils. Indeed, fundamental considerations themselves indicate that a vector-borne infection (or any infection requiring more than one host) can only invade and persist if there are sufficient numbers of both host species. General models for vector-borne infections suggest that when a fixed (host density-independent) biting rate of the vector is assumed, as it often is, for example with mosquitoes, then the invasion threshold is a ratio of vector to host abundance: in the case of the gerbil–plague system, the flea burden (Figure 22.6b; see Keeling & Rohani, 2008). Alternatively, if the contact rate increases with the density of both host and vector, then the threshold

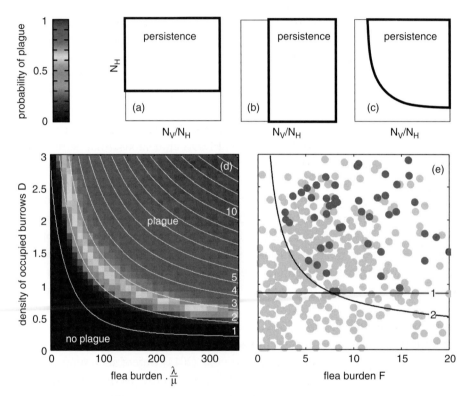

Figure 22.6 Representations of (a) a host density threshold, (b) a vector-to-host ratio threshold, and (c) a hyperbolic vector/host threshold. The vertical axis plots host abundance; the horizontal axis the ratio of vector to host abundance. (d) Simulations of a spatially explicit percolation model for plague epizootics: the fraction of simulated outbreaks that give rise to new infections at least 2 km from the site of the initial infection plotted as a function of the occupied burrow density D and the flea burden F. (e) Field data on plague presence (red dots) or absence (grey dots) as a function of F and D. Different fitting models result in different threshold shapes (curves 1 and 2 refer to models (a) and (c), respectively). (After Reijniers et al., 2012.) (A black and white version of this figure will appear in some formats. For the colour version, please refer to the plate section.)

should depend on the product of host and vector abundances, as is also conventionally assumed for macroparasites, like worms, with obligatory passage between, for example, both a vertebrate and an invertebrate host. The threshold then appears as a hyperbolic curve with limbs for each separate host or vector species (Figure 22.6c; see Holt et al., 2003).

Therefore, Reijniers et al. (2012) incorporated flea burden both into a revision of Davis et al.'s (2008) percolation model and into a reanalysis of field data. In particular, they incorporated into the model the assumption that the rate at which infected fleas leave one burrow and infect other, susceptible burrows on arrival is proportional to the flea burden. In a more general context, this is an assumption that the force of infection transforming susceptible into infected hosts in one 'species' (in this case, burrow systems) is proportional to the abundance of a second species. This is certainly reasonable for the gerbil–plague system (a visit of a gerbil from one burrow to another is more likely to result in transmission, the more fleas it is carrying), and is supported by field data (see below), but it is not inevitable. For example, the spread of plague within prairie dog (*Cynomys* spp.) towns in the USA appears not to depend on flea burden (Brinkerhoff et al., 2010), although this in turn is reasonable given the more limited role of fleas in that system (Webb et al., 2006). The results from this revised percolation model – in this case, the proportion of 1000 simulations in which infection travelled more than 2 km – are shown in Figure 22.6d.

These results confirm that the model shows an invasion threshold that is a hyperbolic-like curve in burrow density/flea burden–space. As the flea burden decreases, the occupied burrow density threshold compensates by shifting to larger values. Equally, greater numbers of fleas being transported can compensate for lower occupancy levels that imply larger distances between neighbouring burrows. From a percolation perspective, the probability contours in Figure 22.6d join combinations of flea burden and the density of occupied burrows with the same network connectivity.

Reijniers et al. (2012) then went on to test the validity of such a hyperbolic threshold model with field data. Again, they used retrospective data on abundances – in this case combining data from the present year with data from one and two years previously. However, they did not limit themselves to sectors with long time series, but included data from throughout the Pre-Balkhash focus whenever there were such 'triplets' of observations (for three consecutive years) for plague presence, flea burden, and the density of occupied burrows. Density of occupied burrows was used as a proxy for gerbil abundance in this case, rather than occupancy (proportion of burrows that are occupied), because over the whole Pre-Balkhash, burrow density can vary considerably between locations. Hence, burrow density can be assumed to be constant at the large-square scale (as in earlier studies) but not at the whole-focus scale. Results are shown in Figure 22.6e. Model comparisons, using AIC values, confirmed that a hyperbolic curve constructed from the percolation model performed far better than the original model (Davis et al., 2004) excluding fleas (AIC = 13.5), and better still than a model based only on flea burden (AIC = 40.0), although similarly to a product-of-abundances model lacking any spatially explicit element (AIC = −1.9).

Model and data analyses agree, therefore, that the hyperbolic curve generated by the inclusion of fleas captures the threshold properties of the system better than the simple threshold based on gerbil abundance alone. Indeed, a large number of observations that would have been classified as false-positives because they lie above the gerbil threshold can now be seen to be, in fact, true negatives because they lie below (to the left of) the flea-burden arm of the joint threshold (Figure 22.6e). This raises the prospect of improved predictive models, if flea burdens can be consistently monitored and included, although, as the figure makes clear, a large number of false-positives are likely to remain.

22.6 Distinguishing invasion and persistence in space

Another issue raised by Davis et al. (2007b), namely the potential importance of distinguishing invasion and persistence thresholds, was taken up by Heier et al. (2011). Their approach was spatially explicit in that the invasion or persistence of plague in a given primary square (20 km × 20 km) was related to (i) the presence or absence of plague in that square in the previous season (spring and autumn data were treated separately rather than combined), (ii) the presence or absence of plague in the eight neighbouring squares in the previous season, and (iii) gerbil occupancy averaged over the current season and the three preceding seasons. No threshold abundance, as such, was sought, but distinguishing the effects of abundance on invasion and persistence nonetheless sheds light on how their respective thresholds may differ. Specimen data are shown in Figure 22.7.

Analyses showed that while the effect of gerbil abundance of plague invasion was strongly significant, there was no significant effect on persistence. They also showed significant effects of plague in neighbouring squares on both persistence and invasion. However, while the effect on invasion was significant for spring but not for autumn, the effect on persistence was significant for autumn but not for spring. Nonetheless, in the context of abundance thresholds, the results support the idea that invasion and persistence may be different. They also confirm that a sufficiency of hosts may be necessary for an infection to invade a population from outside but, once established, any dependence of fade-out on host abundance may be less easy to establish because even when an infection is declining in a population it may take time to disappear. This is because infected animals

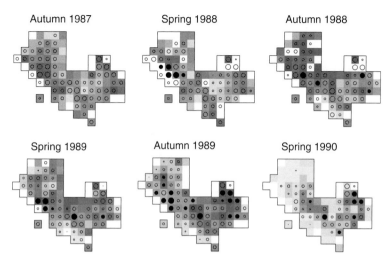

Figure 22.7 An example of a plague epizootic in the Pre-Balkhash area. Open circles, no great gerbils found positive for plague; filled circles, at least one great gerbil found positive. Circle size indicates the number of individuals tested. Light to dark shading indicates low to high great gerbil abundance. (After Heier et al., 2011.) (A black and white version of this figure will appear in some formats. For the colour version, please refer to the plate section.)

may remain infectious for some time after conditions are no longer conducive to transmission and, even when $R_0 < 1$ and infected individuals give rise to fewer than one new infection, some new cases of infection will be generated. The process of declining prevalence of infections may be further protracted by the immigration of infected individuals from populations nearby.

22.7 Cyclic time series around the threshold

The distinction between invasion and persistence thresholds was also taken up by Reijniers et al. (2014), although in a different context. In doing so, they also returned to the question of the length of the time delays between a sufficient abundance and the appearance of plague, first raised by Davis et al. (2004). The hyperbolic threshold model was used, but in this case data were combined across the whole Pre-Balkhash focus so that the focus could shift to the annual dynamics of the system. This was justified by patterns of both occupancy and flea burden having previously been shown to vary synchronously (although separately) over large areas (Reijniers et al., 2012). Plague dynamics were studied as a prevalence: the proportion of monitored sectors for which plague was reported. The results, from 1975 to 1995, are shown in Figure 22.8.

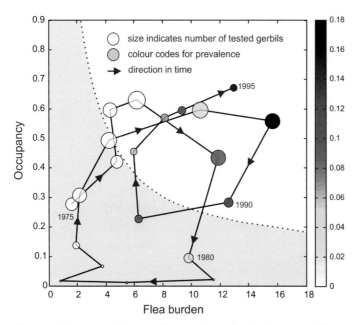

Figure 22.8 Vector–host–pathogen dynamics in the Pre-Balkhash region. Plague prevalence is plotted yearly from 1975 to 1995 in the occupancy–flea burden phase plane. The colours code the proportion of sectors that tested positive, and the size of dots is proportional to the number of gerbils tested in that year (for reference: 30,673 gerbils in 1978). Prevalence in 1981 was 0.03; in 1982 and 1983 it was zero. The dotted line corresponds to the threshold curve, derived by Reijniers et al. (2012). (After Reijniers et al., 2014.) (A black and white version of this figure will appear in some formats. For the colour version, please refer to the plate section.)

The prevalence time series moved in a clockwise circular motion in occupancy–flea burden space. Over the 20 years, there were 2.5 of these cycles. Thus, flea burden appeared to 'follow' occupancy with a lag of approximately 2 years, which was confirmed by cross-correlation analyses. These dynamics were in turn associated with the plague dynamics. Plague prevalence followed occupancy with a lag of approximately 2 years and flea burden with a lag of roughly 1 year. Plague itself had no detectable effect on gerbil abundance. The general disposition of these cycles clearly fits the position of the threshold curve: most positive prevalences were above it and most absences of plague below it. Indeed, there was some tendency for the very highest prevalences to be furthest above the curve.

However, the time lags in the system are also apparent. Retrospective abundance exceeded the threshold in 1977, but it was not until two years later (when abundance had fallen, although flea burden had increased) that plague was detected. Conversely, abundance fell below the threshold in 1980 but it was one year later that plague disappeared, and fell below again in 1991, but never disappeared during that cycle because it rose above the threshold again in 1992. These results therefore support the idea that persistence thresholds are likely, in practice, to be lower than invasion thresholds, but are also consistent with Davis et al.'s (2007b) suggestion that on first exceeding a threshold, infection prevalences may be too low to be detected.

22.8 Towards an automated threshold determination

To repeat a point made initially, the interest of wildlife epidemiologists in abundance thresholds is partly driven by the insights it may provide into infection dynamics, but also by the potential utility of identifying and responding to these thresholds in disease control. In the case of plague in the Pre-Balkhash, this would mean predicting when the joint abundance of gerbils and fleas looks set to exceed the threshold, so as to intervene and prevent this from happening. In practice, although the anti-plague agencies there have not acted on the basis of threshold abundances, their response to the more immediate threat posed by plague being detected in the gerbils has been to kill fleas (not the gerbils themselves) in areas at the greatest risk of human contact. These practical considerations, however, also emphasise the importance of having cost-effective means of monitoring abundance at an appropriate temporal resolution and over a sufficiently wide spatial scale.

Monitoring procedures, going back to the inception of the programme in 1949, have involved teams of trappers travelling from a limited number of permanent stations to a variable number of field sites accessible by the rough roads through the desert, and then returning those samples for testing within days of their being collected. Hence, sampling, designed for monitoring rather than scientific purposes, has been limited by cost, manpower, and accessibility. Davis et al. (2008) had noted that individual burrow systems were visible in satellite images of the region, as the gerbils removed vegetation from close to the burrow entrances, and brought soil to the surface, creating (relatively) vegetation-free areas around each burrow (Figure 22.1).

This raised the possibility that the abundance of gerbils (although not fleas), in relation to thresholds, might be monitored remotely from such images, decreasing the manpower required, increasing accessibility to areas distant from roads, although with costs determined by the ways in which those images would be provided. There are two challenges involved in this. The first is to develop automated means of detecting burrow systems from the images and hence determining the overall density and disposition of burrows in particular regions. This sets an upper limit for gerbil abundance and provides a measure of the potential for plague spread. However, the second and greater challenge would then be to distinguish occupied and unoccupied burrows from the image, and hence estimate occupancy (abundance) itself.

Following a pilot study by Addink et al. (2010), Wilschut et al. (2013a) first used medium-resolution satellite images to classify areas in the region into landscape types based on brightness, greenness, and topography, recognising that the accuracy with which burrows could be identified might itself vary with landscape. This turned out to be the case. Software was developed from training data sets to identify putative burrows in high-resolution images from their image characteristics. These were then compared with the distributions of burrow systems observed in nature. Overall accuracies were encouraging, with medians of 86% for producer's accuracy (the percentage of actual burrows identified) and 82% for user's accuracy (the percentage of predicted burrows that were actually burrows), but while these accuracies remained high in most landscape types, user's accuracy fell to 58% in landscapes dominated by shrub vegetation.

Nonetheless, Wilschut et al. (2013b) were able to apply this method to larger areas of the landscape, unobserved directly, with a view to mapping the larger-scale distribution of the burrow systems. In particular, they asked whether there were identifiable potential 'barriers' to plague spread (areas of low burrow density) and conversely potential 'corridors' (areas of high density), setting these as areas with burrow densities one standard deviation less or more than the means for areas as a whole. These were indeed apparent, and tended to occur predominantly with a north-west–south-east orientation. This is shown for one of the three areas studied in Figure 22.9.

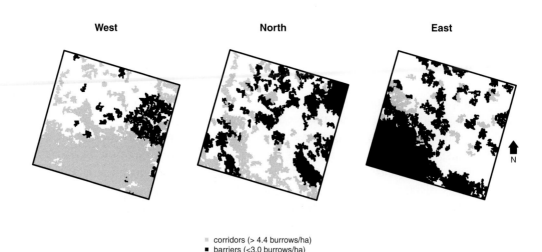

West　　　**North**　　　**East**

N

▪ corridors (> 4.4 burrows/ha)
▪ barriers (<3.0 burrows/ha)

Figure 22.9 Burrow density in a 20 km × 20 km study area in the Pre-Balkhash region, estimated remotely from satellite images, using image analysis software trained by the analysis of images of known density. Areas with densities less than one standard deviation or more than one standard deviation from the mean, as indicated, were designated 'barriers' and 'corridors' for plague spread, respectively. (After Wilschut et al., 2013b.)

More generally, this analysis makes the important point that all threshold values are inevitably abstractions – applicable overall or at large spatial scales, but likely, often, to be overridden by local variations. For example, invasion may occur along a corridor even though the overall occupancy in the area, or density of occupied burrows, is below a notional threshold; or invasion may fail despite occupancy in an area being above the threshold, because the potential source of the invasion is located in or next to a barrier. Wilschut et al. (2015) demonstrated that the distribution of occupied burrows was also clustered; and Levick et al. (2015) provided functional underpinning for this by relating occupancy status to physical and biological factors at a burrow's location. It remains an open question, though, whether it will prove possible to detect occupancy status from satellite images with sufficient accuracy.

22.9 Conclusions

Demonstrable abundance thresholds for disease in wildlife systems remain a rarity, but the plague–great gerbil system of Central Asia provides grounds for believing that these are more than mere theoretical constructs. For example, in seeking to understand the effects of climate on gerbil and plague dynamics, Kausrud et al. (2007) incorporated Davis et al.'s (2004) threshold in their model of the system. Lloyd-Smith et al. (2005) have also noted the fundamental importance of abundance thresholds, and their rarity, but they went on to question their utility in a wildlife context. It is true that detailed study of a natural system, such as ours, calls into question the simplest of views of what an abundance threshold might be – a threshold relevant to both invasion and persistence referring to the contemporary abundance of a single host, above which contacts between randomly mixing hosts occur at a high enough rate. The realities are that invasion and persistence should be distinguished, and can be; that abundances may need to be integrated over time and combined, appropriately, for all agents in the system; and that there is more than one way of generating a threshold, but all have their roots in a sufficiency of contacts. However, more positively than Lloyd-Smith et al., we see all this as an enrichment of the concept and ultimately a reaffirmation of its importance. We should always judge our theoretical concepts by setting them against the realties of natural systems, but in doing so, we cannot expect them to be so perfect and general as to escape reconsideration. We simply require them to be useful. For us, studies of sylvatic plague in Central Asia confirm, clearly, the utility of abundance thresholds.

22.10 Acknowledgements

We are grateful to the European Union (STEPICA: ICA2-CT2000-10048) and the Wellcome Trust (063576/Z/01/Z and 090213/Z/09/Z) for funding. As to the identity of the fieldworkers and scientists in Kazakhstan who collected the data that has been so valuable to us, the identities of many of them are unknown to us, and even those we know are too numerous to mention by name. It would be wrong, though, despite the risk of its being invidious, not to express our thanks to those who have been particularly helpful and supportive of our work: Vladimir Ageyev, Vladimir Dubyanskiy, and the late Nikolay Klassovskiy.

References

Addink, E.A., De Jong S.M., Davis, S.A., et al. (2010) The use of high-resolution remote sensing for plague surveillance in Kazakhstan. *Remote Sensing of Environment*, **114**, 674–681.

Bartlett, M.S. (1957) Measles periodicity and community size. *Journal of the Royal Statistical Society, Series A*, **120**, 48–71.

Brinkerhoff, R.J., Collinge, S.K., Ray, C. & Gage, K.L. (2010) Rodent and flea abundance fail to predict a plague epizootic in black-tailed prairie dogs. *Vector-Borne and Zoonotic Diseases*, **10**, 47–52.

Davis, S., Begon, M., De Bruyn, L., et al. (2004) Predictive thresholds for plague in Kazakhstan. *Science*, **304**, 736–738.

Davis, S., Klassovskiy, N., Ageyev, V., et al. (2007a) Plague metapopulation dynamics in a natural reservoir: the burrow system as the unit of study. *Epidemiology and Infection*, **135**, 740–748.

Davis, S., Leirs, H., Viljugrein, H., et al. (2007b) Empirical assessment of a threshold model for sylvatic plague. *Journal of the Royal Society Interface*, **4**, 649–657.

Davis, S., Trapman, P., Leirs, H., Begon, M. & Heesterbeek, J.A.P. (2008) The abundance threshold for plague as a critical percolation phenomenon. *Nature*, **454**, 634–637.

Grassberger, P. (1983) On the critical behaviour of the general epidemic process and dynamical percolation. *Mathematical Biosciences*, **63**, 157–172.

Heier, L., Storvik, G.O., Davis, S.A., et al. (2011) Emergence, spread, persistence and fade-out of sylvatic plague in Kazakhstan. *Proceedings of the Royal Society of London B*, **278**, 2915–2923.

Holt, R.D., Dobson, A.P., Begon, M., Bowers, R.G. & Schauber, E.M. (2003) Parasite establishment in host communities. *Ecology Letters*, **6**, 837–842.

Kausrud, K.L., Viljugrein, H., Frigessi, A., et al. (2007) Climatically-driven synchrony of gerbil populations allows large-scale plague outbreaks. *Proceedings of the Royal Society of London B*, **274**, 1963–1969.

Keeling, M.J. & Rohani, P.R. (2008) *Modeling Infectious Diseases in Humans and Animals*. Princeton, NJ: Princeton University Press.

Levick, B., Laudisoit, A., Wilschut, L., et al. (2015) The perfect burrow, but for what? Identifying local habitat conditions promoting the presence of the hosts and vectors of the Kazakh plague system. *PLoS ONE*, **10**, e0136962.

Lloyd-Smith, J.O., Cross, P.C., Briggs, C.J., et al. (2005) Should we expect population thresholds for wildlife disease? *Trends in Ecology and Evolution*, **20**, 511–519.

Morse SS. (1995) Factors in the emergence of infectious diseases. *Emerging Infectious Diseases*, **1**, 7–15.

Onishchenko, G.G. & Kutyrev, V.V. (2004) *Natural Plague Foci in the Caucasus, Caspian Sea Region, Middle Asia and Siberia*. Moscow: Meditsina [in Russian].

Reijniers, J., Begon, M., Ageyev, V. & Leirs, H. (2014) Plague epizootic cycles in Central Asia. *Biology Letters*, **10**, 20140302.

Reijniers, J., Davis, S., Begon, M., et al. (2012) A curve of thresholds governs plague epizootics in Central Asia. *Ecology Letters*, **15**, 554–560.

Samia, N.I., Chan K.S. & Stenseth N.C. (2007) A generalized threshold mixed model for analyzing nonnormal nonlinear time series, with application to plague in Kazakhstan. *Biometrika*, **94**, 101–118.

Samia, N.I., Kausrud, K.L., Heesterbeek, H., et al. (2011) Dynamics of the plague–wildlife–human system in Central Asia are controlled by two epidemiological thresholds. *Proceedings of the National Academy of Sciences of the United States of America*, **108**, 14,527–14,532.

Stenseth, N.C., Atshabar, B.B., Begon, M., et al. (2008) Plague: past, present and future. *PLoS Medicine*, **5**, 9–13.

Webb, C.T., Brooks, C.P., Gage, K.L. & Antolin, M.F. (2006) Classic flea borne transmission does not drive plague epizootics in prairie dogs. *Proceedings of the National Academy of Sciences of the United States of America*, **103**, 6236–6241.

Wilschut, L.I., Addink, E.A. Heesterbeek, J.A.P., et al. (2013a) Mapping the distribution of the main host for plague in a complex landscape in Kazakhstan: an object-based approach using SPOT-5 XS, Landsat 7 ETM +, SRTM and multiple Random Forests. *International Journal of Applied Earth Observation and Geoinformation*, **23**, 81–94.

Wilschut L.I., Addink, E.A., Heesterbeek, H., et al. (2013b) Potential corridors and barriers for plague spread in central Asia. *International Journal of Health Geographics*, **12**, 49.

Wilschut, L.I., Laudisoit, A., Hughes, N.K., et al. (2015) Spatial distribution patterns of plague hosts: point pattern analysis of the burrows of great gerbils in Kazakhstan. *Journal of Biogeography*, **42**, 1281–1292.

Index